Mastering

Microsoft® Visual Basic® 2010

Mastering

Microsoft® Visual Basic® 2010

Evangelos Petroutsos

WILEY

Wiley Publishing, Inc.

Acquisitions Editor: Agatha Kim
Development Editor: Mary Ellen Schutz
Technical Editor: Kirstin Juhl
Production Editor: Rachel McConlogue
Copy Editors: Judy Flynn and Kim Wimpsett
Editorial Manager: Pete Gaughan
Production Manager: Tim Tate
Vice President and Executive Group Publisher: Richard Swadley
Vice President and Publisher: Neil Edde
Book Designers: Maureen Forys and Judy Fung
Proofreader: Rebecca Rider
Indexer: Jack Lewis
Project Coordinator, Cover: Lynsey Stanford
Cover Designer: Ryan Sneed
Cover Image: © Pete Gardner/DigitalVision/Getty Images

Copyright © 2010 by Wiley Publishing, Inc., Indianapolis, Indiana

Published simultaneously in Canada

ISBN: 978-0-470-53287-4

For general information on our other products and services or to obtain technical support, please contact our Customer Care Department within the U.S. at (877) 762-2974, outside the U.S. at (317) 572-3993 or fax (317) 572-4002.

Wiley also publishes its books in a variety of electronic formats. Some content that appears in print may not be available in electronic books.

Library of Congress Cataloging-in-Publication Data

Petroutsos, Evangelos.
  Mastering Microsoft Visual Basic 2010 / Evangelos Petroutsos. -- 1st ed.
     p. cm.
  ISBN 978-0-470-53287-4 (paper/website)
  1. Microsoft Visual BASIC. 2. BASIC (Computer program language) I. Title.
QA76.73.B3P487 2010
005.2'768--dc22

                                    2010000339

10 9 8 7 6 5 4 3 2 1

Dear Reader,

Thank you for choosing *Mastering Microsoft Visual Basic 2010*. This book is part of a family of premium-quality Sybex books, all of which are written by outstanding authors who combine practical experience with a gift for teaching.

Sybex was founded in 1976. More than 30 years later, we're still committed to producing consistently exceptional books. With each of our titles, we're working hard to set a new standard for the industry. From the paper we print on to the authors we work with, our goal is to bring you the best books available.

I hope you see all that reflected in these pages. I'd be very interested to hear your comments and get your feedback on how we're doing. Feel free to let me know what you think about this or any other Sybex book by sending me an email at nedde@wiley.com. If you think you've found a technical error in this book, please visit http://sybex.custhelp.com. Customer feedback is critical to our efforts at Sybex.

Best regards,

Neil Edde
Vice President and Publisher
Sybex, an Imprint of Wiley

To my dearest and most precious ones, Nepheli and Eleni-Myrsini

Acknowledgments

Many people contributed to this book, and I would like to thank them all. I first want to express my deep appreciation to Danijel Arsenovski for contributing and revising several chapters, and especially for his work on Chapter 17, "Using the Entity Data Model." Many thanks to the book's technical editor, Kirstin Juhl, who has read this book with great care and a particular attention to detail. Thank you, Kirstin. I also want to thank the folks at Microsoft for their commitment to Visual Basic. Visual Basic remains my absolute favorite language.

Special thanks to the talented people at Sybex — to all of them and to each one individually — starting with my "Gentle Editor," Mary Ellen Schutz, who has taken this book under her wing and improved it in numerous ways. To acquisitions editor Agatha Kim, who has followed the progress of this book from its conception through its completion. (She will keep working on this book long after I'm done with this page). To Pete Gaughan, editorial manager; Rachel McConlogue, production editor; Judy Flynn and Kim Wimpsett, copyeditors; Rebecca Rider, proofreader; Jack Lewis, indexer; the compositors at Laserwords; and everyone else who added their expertise and talent to this book.

About the Author

Evangelos Petroutsos is a computer engineer by education, but he has spent most of his professional life developing applications and digging through databases. He has a degree in computer engineering from the University of California, Santa Barbara, and several years of professional experience at the California Institute of Technology. He has worked as a consultant for many companies, large and small, and has taught courses on Visual Basic and databases. He especially enjoys writing and teaching. With over 25 years of experience in this industry, he makes his living by optimizing code and databases.

When he's not obsessed with a new technology, he spends time with his family and friends, reads science books, and finds excuses to visit every state in the country.

Contents at a Glance

Contents

Introduction

Welcome to Microsoft's Visual Basic 2010, another milestone version of the most popular programming language for building Windows and web applications. In modern software development, however, the language is only one of the components we use to build applications. The most important component is the .NET Framework, which is an indispensable component of every application; it's actually more important than the language itself. You can think of the Framework as an enormous collection of functions for just about any programming task. All drawing methods, for example, are part of the System.Drawing class. To draw a rectangle, you call the `DrawRectangle` method of the System.Drawing class, passing the appropriate arguments. To create a new folder, you call the `CreateDirectory` method of the Directory class, and to retrieve the files in a folder, you call the `GetFiles` method of the same class.

The Framework contains all the functionality of the operating system and makes it available to your application through methods. Methods are very similar to functions, which extend the basic capabilities of a language. The Framework is a huge collection of such methods, organized in units according to their role and in a way that makes it fairly easy to locate the methods for the task at hand. The language and the Framework are the two "programming" components absolutely necessary to build Windows applications. It's possible to develop applications with these two components alone, but the process would be awfully slow.

The software development process relies on numerous tools that streamline the coding experience. The third component is an integrated environment that hosts those tools, enabling you to perform many common tasks with point-and-click operations. It's basically an environment in which you can design your forms with visual tools and write code as well. This environment, provided by Visual Studio, is known as an integrated development environment, or IDE. You'll be amazed by the functionality provided by the tools of Visual Studio: you can actually design a functional data-driven application without writing a single line of code. You can use similar tools in the same environment to design a fancy data-driven web page without a single line of code. Visual Studio even provides tools for manipulating databases and allows you to switch between tasks, all in the same, streamlined environment. You realize, of course, that Visual Studio isn't about writing applications without code; it just simplifies certain tasks through wizards, and more often than not, we step in and provide custom code to write a functional application. Even so, Visual Studio provides numerous tools, from debugging tools that help you track and fix all kinds of bugs in your code to database-manipulation tools and deployment wizards that streamline the process of deploying applications.

This book shows you how to use Visual Studio 2010 and Visual Basic 2010 to design rich Windows and web applications. We'll start with the visual tools and then we'll explore Visual Basic and the Framework. A Windows application consists of a visual interface and code behind the elements of the interface. (The code handles the user actions on the visual interface, such as the click of a button, the selection of a menu item, and so on.) You'll use the tools of Visual Studio to build the visual interface, and then you'll program the elements of the application with Visual Basic. For any nontrivial processing, such as file and folder manipulation, data storage, and so on, you'll use the appropriate classes of the .NET Framework. A substantial segment of this book deals with the most useful components of the Framework. We will also explore databases and data-driven applications, which are the most common type of business applications. Finally, we'll go through the basics of web programming. You'll learn how to build web applications with Visual Basic and how to write web services.

The Mastering Series

The Mastering series from Sybex provides outstanding instruction for readers with intermediate and advanced skills in the form of top-notch training and development for those already working in their field and clear, serious education for those aspiring to become pros. Every Mastering book includes the following:

◆ Real-World Scenarios, ranging from case studies to interviews, that show how the tool, technique, or knowledge presented is applied in actual practice

◆ Skill-based instruction, with chapters organized around real tasks rather than abstract concepts or subjects

◆ Self-review test questions, so you can be certain you're equipped to do the job right

Who Should Read This Book?

You don't need a solid knowledge of Visual Basic to read this book, but you do need a basic understanding of programming. You need to know the meaning of variables and functions and how an If…Then structure works. This book is aimed at the typical programmer who wants to get the most out of Visual Basic. It covers the topics I felt are of use to most VB programmers, and it does so in depth. Visual Basic 2010 and the .NET Framework 4.0 are two extremely rich programming tools, and I had to choose between a superficial coverage of many topics and an in-depth coverage of fewer topics. To make room for more topics, I have avoided including a lot of reference material and lengthy listings. For example, you won't find complete project listings or form descriptions. I assume that you can draw a few controls on a form and set their properties and that you don't need long descriptions of the control properties (even if you don't know how to design a form, you'll learn how in the first two chapters). I'm also assuming that you don't want to read the trivial segments of each application. Instead, the listings concentrate on the "meaty" part of the code: the procedures that explain the topic at hand.

The topics covered in this book were chosen to provide a solid understanding of the principles and techniques for developing applications with Visual Basic. Programming isn't about new keywords and functions. I chose the topics I felt every programmer should learn in order to master the language. I was also motivated by my desire to present useful, practical examples. You will not find all topics equally interesting or important. My hope is that everyone will find something interesting and something of value for their daily work — whether it's an application that maps the folders and files of a drive to a TreeView control, an application that prints tabular data, a data-driven application for editing customers or products, or an application that saves a collection of objects to a file.

Many books offer their readers long, numbered sequences of steps to accomplish a task. Following instructions simplifies certain tasks, but programming isn't about following instructions.

It's about being creative; it's about understanding principles and being able to apply the same techniques in several practical situations. And the way to creatively exploit the power of a language such as Visual Basic 2010 is to understand its principles and its programming model.

In many cases, I provide a detailed, step-by-step procedure that will help you accomplish a task, such as designing a menu, for example. But not all tasks are as simple as designing menus. I explain why things must be done in a certain way, and I present alternatives and try to connect new topics to those explained earlier in the book. In several chapters, I expand on applications developed in earlier chapters. Associating new knowledge with something you have mastered already provides positive feedback and a deeper understanding of the language.

This book isn't about the hottest features of the language either; it's about solid programming techniques and practical examples. After you master the basics of programming Windows applications with Visual Basic 2010 and you feel comfortable with the more advanced examples of the book, you will find it easy to catch up with the topics not discussed in this book.

How about the Advanced Topics?

Some of the topics discussed in this book are nontrivial, and quite a few topics can be considered advanced. Creating collections of custom objects and querying them and exposing some functionality in the form of web services are not trivial topics, but these are the tools that will allow you to make the most of Visual Studio.

You may also find some examples to be more difficult than you expected. I have tried to make the text and the examples easy to read and understand, but not unrealistically simple. Understanding the basic functions for manipulating files and folders isn't difficult. To make the most of these functions, however, you need to understand how to scan a folder's files, including the files in its subfolders and the files in their subfolders, with a technique known as recursion. To make each chapter as useful as possible, I've included nontrivial examples, which will provide a better understanding of the topics. In addition, many of these examples can be easily incorporated into your applications.

You can do a lot with the TreeView control with very little programming, but to make the most out of this control, you must be ready for some advanced programming — nothing terribly complicated, but some things just aren't trivial. Programming most of the operations of the TreeView control, for instance, is not complicated, but if your application calls for populating a TreeView control with an arbitrary number of branches (such as mapping a directory structure to a TreeView control), the code can get complex. The same goes for printing; it's fairly straightforward to write a program that prints some text, but printing tabular reports takes substantial coding effort.

The reason I've included the more advanced examples is that the corresponding chapters would be incomplete without them. If you find some material to be over your head at first reading, you can skip it and come back to it after you have mastered other aspects of the language. But don't let a few advanced examples intimidate you. Most of the techniques are well within the reach of an average VB programmer. The few advanced topics were included for the readers who are willing to take that extra step and build elaborate interfaces by using the latest tools and techniques.

There's another good reason for including advanced topics. Explaining a simple topic, such as how to populate a collection with items, is very simple. But what good is it to populate a collection if you don't know how to save it to disk and read back its items in a later session? Likewise, what good is it to learn how to print simple text files? In a business environment, you will most likely be asked to print a tabular report, which is substantially more complicated than printing text. One of my goals in writing this book was to exhaust the topics I've chosen to discuss and present all the information you need to do something practical: not just how to create collections, but also how to save them in disk files; not just how to write to a file, but also how to prompt users for a filename with the same dialog box all Windows applications use; not just how to print something, but also how to create a preview of the printout. In short, I've tried to include everything you need to know in order to incorporate in your applications the features everybody has come to expect from a Windows application.

The Structure of the Book

This book isn't meant to be read from cover to cover, and I know that most people don't read computer books this way. Each chapter is independent of the others, although all chapters contain references to other chapters. Each topic is covered in depth; however, I make no assumptions about the reader's knowledge of the topic. As a result, you may find the introductory sections of a chapter too simple. The topics become progressively more advanced, and even experienced programmers will find some new information in most chapters. Even if you are familiar with the topics in a chapter, take a look at the examples. I have tried to simplify many of the advanced topics and to demonstrate them with clear, practical examples.

This book tries to teach through examples. Isolated topics are demonstrated with short examples, and at the end of many chapters you'll build a large, practical application (a real-world application) that "puts together" the topics and techniques discussed throughout the chapter. You may find some of the more advanced applications a bit more difficult to understand, but you shouldn't give up. Simpler applications would have made my job easier, but the book wouldn't deserve the Mastering title, and your knowledge of Visual Basic wouldn't be as complete.

The book starts with the fundamentals of Visual Basic, even though very little of it is specific to version 2010. You'll learn how to design visual interfaces with point-and-click operations and how to program a few simple events, such as the click of the mouse on a button. After reading the first two chapters, you'll understand the structure of a Windows application. Then you'll explore the elements of the visual interface (the basic Windows controls) and how to program them. You'll also learn about the My object and code snippets, two features that make Visual Basic so simple and fun to use (again). These two objects will also ease the learning process and make it much simpler to learn the features of the language.

In Part 2, I discuss in detail the basic components of Windows applications. I explain the most common controls you'll use in building Windows forms as well as how to work with forms: how to design forms, how to design menus for your forms, how to create applications with multiple forms, and so on. You will find detailed discussions of many Windows controls as well as how to take advantage of the built-in dialog boxes, such as the Font and Color dialog boxes, in your applications.

Visual Basic 2010 is a truly object-oriented language, and objects are the recurring theme in every chapter. Part 3 of the book (Chapter 8, Chapter 9, and Chapter 10) contains a formal and more systematic treatment of objects. You will learn how to build custom classes and controls, which will help you understand object-oriented programming a little better. You will also learn about inheritance and will see how easy it is to add custom functionality to existing classes through inheritance.

Part 4 deals with some of the most common classes of the .NET Framework. The Framework is at the very heart of Windows programming; it's your gateway to the functionality of the operating system itself. The first chapter in this part of the book is an introduction to the

Framework at large, and it shows you how to use the basic classes for manipulating files and folders, how to manipulate data and time, how to work with time spans, how to create graphics and printouts, and other interesting aspects of the Framework. In the next chapter you'll learn how to use collections in your code and then you'll find a chapter on XML and a chapter on LINQ. You will see how easy it is to create and use XML in your VB code as well as how to query collections, XML, and databases with a new language that's embedded into VB: Language Integrated Query (LINQ). LINQ is the hottest new technology that allows you to query data with widely different structures, and data from different sources, in a uniform way.

The first 14 chapters deal with the fundamentals of the language and Windows applications. Following these chapters, you will find an overview of the data-access tools. I'm assuming that the majority of you will eventually build a data-driven application. The emphasis in Part 5 is on the visual tools, and you will learn how to query databases and present data to the user. You will also find information on programming the basic objects of ADO.NET and write simple data-driven Windows applications.

In the last few chapters of this book you will learn about web applications, the basics of ASP.NET 4, how to develop data-bound web applications, and how to write web services. Since I could not discuss both Windows and web applications in the same detail, I've decided to focus on Windows applications, and in the last few chapters (Part 6) show you how to apply your knowledge to the Web. While the interface is totally different, the essential code is the same.

Don't Miss the Tutorials

In addition to the printed material, this book is accompanied by a number of tutorials, which you can download from www.sybex.com/go/masteringvb2010. These tutorials are actual chapters (some of them quite lengthy); we couldn't include them in the printed version of the book, so we included them as PDF files. They are as follows:

- Accessing Files and Folders

- Creating Graphics with VB 2010

- Printing with VB 2010

- Making the Most of the ListView and TreeView Controls

This book is a revision of *Mastering Visual Basic 2008*. As the book couldn't keep growing — and we had to make room for new topics — we decided to remove some chapters that were included in the previous edition of the book from the printed version. These chapters have been revised and edited and you will find them in PDF format at this book's website. Throughout this book, I'll be referring to them as tutorials; they're complete chapters with sample projects and the same structure as the book's chapters. You can download the tutorials from the same site as the book's projects and read them on your computer screen.

Downloading This Book's Code

The code for the examples and projects can be downloaded from the Sybex website (www.sybex.com). At the main page, you can find the book's page by searching for the author, the title, or the ISBN (9780470187425) and then clicking the book's link listed in the search results. On the book's page, click the Download link and it will take you to the download page. Or, you can go directly to the book's page at www.sybex.com/go/masteringvb2010. The downloaded source code is a ZIP file, which you can unzip with the WinZip utility.

HOW TO REACH THE AUTHOR

Despite our best efforts, a book of this size is bound to contain errors. Although a printed medium isn't as easy to update as a website, I will spare no effort to fix every problem you report (or I discover). The revised applications, along with any other material I think will be of use to the readers of this book, will be posted on the Sybex website. If you have any problems with the text or the applications in this book, you can contact me directly at pevangelos@yahoo.com.

Although I can't promise a response to every question, I will fix any problems in the examples and provide updated versions. I would also like to hear any comments you may have on the book, about the topics you liked or did not like and how useful the examples are. Your comments will be carefully considered for future editions.

Mastering
Microsoft® Visual Basic® 2010

Part 1

Visual Basic: The Language

- ◆ Chapter 1: Getting Started with Visual Basic 2010
- ◆ Chapter 2: Handling Data
- ◆ Chapter 3: Visual Basic Programming Essentials

Chapter 1

Getting Started with
Visual Basic 2010

I'm assuming that you have installed one of the several versions of Visual Studio 2010. For this book, I used the Professional edition of Visual Studio, but just about everything discussed in this book applies to the Standard edition as well. Some of the Professional edition features that are not supported by the Standard edition include the database tools, which are discussed in Chapter 15 through Chapter 18 of this book.

You may have already explored the new environment on your own, but I'm going to start with an overview of Visual Studio and its basic tools for the benefit of readers who aren't familiar with them. I will not assume any prior knowledge of Visual Basic 6 or Visual Basic .NET, just some familiarity with programming at large.

As you already know, Visual Basic 2010 is just one of the languages you can use to build applications with Visual Studio 2010. I happen to be convinced that it is also the simplest, most convenient language, but this isn't really the issue; I'm assuming you have your reasons to code in VB or you wouldn't be reading this book. What you should keep in mind is that Visual Studio 2010 is an integrated environment for building, testing, debugging, and deploying a variety of applications: Windows applications, web applications, classes and custom controls, and even console applications. It provides numerous tools for automating the development process, visual tools for performing many common design and programming tasks, and more features than any author could hope to cover.

In this chapter, you'll learn how to do the following:

◆ Navigate the integrated development environment of Visual Studio

◆ Understand the basics of a Windows application

Exploring the Integrated Development Environment

Visual Basic 2010 is just one of the languages you can use to program your applications. The language is only one aspect of a Windows application. The visual interface of the application isn't tied to a specific language, and the same tools you'll use to develop your application's interface will also be used by all programmers, regardless of the language they'll use to code the application.

To simplify the process of application development, Visual Studio provides an environment that's common to all languages, known as an *integrated development environment (IDE)*. The purpose of the IDE is to enable the developer to do as much as possible with visual tools before writing code. Even as you write code, the IDE will help you in many ways. For example, it underlines errors, it suggests the keywords that may appear at the current place in your code in a list, and it even provides tools for locating and fixing errors (a process known as *debugging*).

The IDE provides tools for designing, executing, and debugging your applications. It will be a while before you explore all the elements of the IDE, and I will explain the various items as needed in the course of the book. In the following sections, you'll look at the basic components of the IDE you'll be using to build simple Windows applications. You'll learn how its tools allow you to quickly design the user interface of your application as well as how to program the application.

The IDE is your second desktop, and you'll be spending most of your productive hours in this environment.

The Start Page

When you run Visual Studio 2010 for the first time, you will be prompted to select the type of projects you plan to build so that the environment can be optimized for that specific type of development. I'm assuming that you have initially selected the Visual Basic Development settings, which will optimize your copy of Visual Studio for building Windows and web applications with Visual Basic 2010. You can always change these settings, as explained at the end of this section.

After the initial configuration, you will see a window similar to the one shown in Figure 1.1. The Recent Projects tab will be empty, of course, unless you have already created some test projects. Visual Studio 2010 will detect the settings of a previous installation, so if you're upgrading from an earlier version of Visual Studio, the initial screen will not be identical to the one shown in Figure 1.1.

FIGURE 1.1
This is what you'll see when you start Visual Studio for the first time.

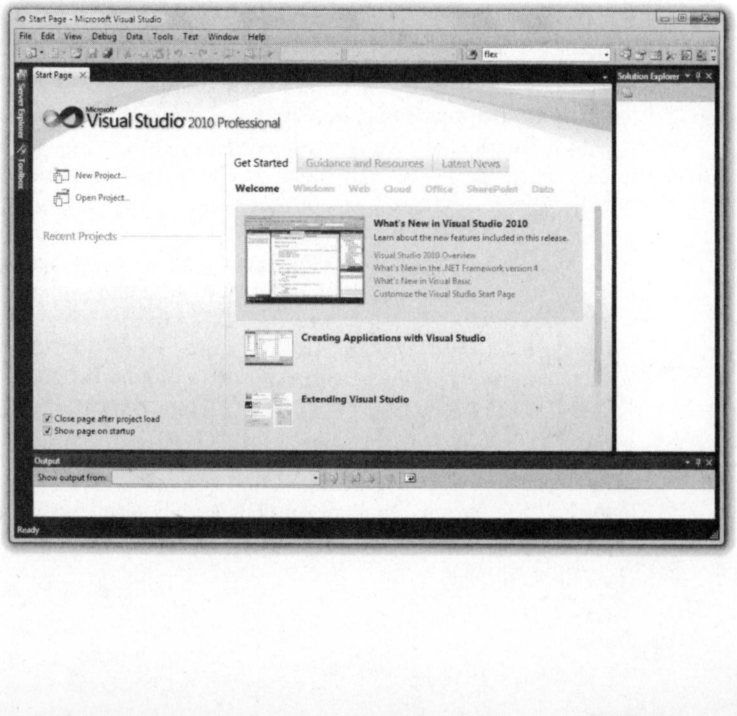

On the Start Page window of Visual Studio, you will see the following panes under the Get Started heading:

Welcome   Click the Welcome tab to see a series of links that provide developer assistance for using Visual Studio. These links include What's New In Visual Studio 2010, Creating Applications With Visual Studio, and Extending Visual Studio, among others. Other related links may be added as this book goes to the printer.

Windows   Here you'll find a list of topics related to Windows application development. Windows applications, frequently referred to as desktop applications, are the applications you install on a local computer and execute locally.

Web   Here you'll find a list of topics related to web application development. Web applications are executed on a remote computer, the web server, and you interact with them through a browser.

Cloud, Office, SharePoint   In addition to Windows and web applications, Visual Studio can be used to develop applications for Office and SharePoint as well as applications that use a new Microsoft platform for building distributed applications, the Azure platform. These three types of projects aren't discussed in this book.

Data   Here you'll find a list of topics related to data-driven programming. All applications that interact with a database are data driven; they can be Windows or web applications. The principles of interacting with a database (retrieve, display, and update database data) are the same regardless of whether you use them to build Windows or web applications.

Recent Projects   Here you see a list of the projects you opened most recently with Visual Studio, and you can select the one you want to open again — chances are you will continue working on the same project as the last time. Each project name is a hyperlink, and you can open a project by clicking its name. Above the list of recent projects there are two hyperlinks — one for creating a new project and another one for opening a new solution. You will find more information on solutions and projects later in this chapter.

Most developers will skip the Start Page. To do so, open the Tools menu and choose the Import And Export Settings command to start a configuration wizard. In the first dialog box of the wizard, select the Reset All Settings check box and then click the Next button. The next screen of the wizard prompts you for a location in which to save the new settings so that Visual Studio can read them every time it starts. Leave the default location as is and click Next again to see the last screen of the wizard, in which you're prompted to select a default collection of settings. This collection depends on the options you've installed on your system. I installed Visual Studio 2010 with Visual Basic only on my system, and I was offered the following options (among others): General Development Settings, Visual Basic Development Settings, and Web Development. For the default configuration of my copy of Visual Studio, and for the purpose of this book, I chose Visual Basic Development Settings so that Visual Studio could optimize the environment for a typical VB developer. Click the Finish button to see a summary of the process and then close the wizard.

Starting a New Project

At this point, you can create a new project and start working with Visual Studio. To best explain the various items of the IDE, let's build a simple form. The form is the window of your application — it's what users will see on their Desktop when they run your application.

The basic work item with Visual Studio is the solution, which is a container for one or more projects. When you create a set of related projects, they should belong to the same solution. (In this book, you'll learn how to build individual, unrelated projects.) Even when you create an individual new project, though, Visual Studio automatically creates a solution for it. You can add a new or existing project to the solution at any time.

Open the File menu and choose New Project, or click the New Project link on the Start Page. In the New Project dialog box that pops up (see Figure 1.2), you'll see a list of project types you can create with Visual Studio. The most important ones are Windows Forms Applications, which are typical Windows applications with one or more forms (windows); Console Applications, which are simple applications that interact with the user through a text window (the console); Windows Forms Control Libraries, which are collections of custom controls; and Class Libraries, which are collections of classes. These are the project types I'll cover in depth in this book.

FIGURE 1.2

The New Project dialog box

If you have Visual Basic 2010 Express edition installed, you will see fewer project types in the New Project dialog box, but all of the projects discussed in this book are included.

Notice the Create Directory For Solution check box in the dialog box shown in Figure 1.2. If this box is checked, Visual Studio will create a new folder for the solution under the folder you specify in the Location box. You also have the option to create a new solution or add the project to the current solution, if you have one open at the time. While following along with the projects of this book, you should create a new solution for each project and store it in its own folder.

You may discover at some point that you have created too many projects and you don't really need all of them. You can remove unwanted projects from your system by deleting the corresponding folders — no special action is required. You'll know it's time to remove unneeded project folders when Visual Studio suggests project names such as WindowsApplication9 or WindowsApplication49.

For this project, select the Windows Forms Application template; Visual Studio suggests the name WindowsApplication1 as the project name. Change it to **MyTestApplication**, select the Create Directory For Solution check box, and then click the OK button to create the new project.

What you see now is the Visual Studio IDE displaying the Form Designer for a new project, as shown in Figure 1.3. The main window of your copy of Visual Studio may be slightly different, but don't worry about it. I'll go through all the components you need to access in the process of designing, coding, and testing a Windows application.

FIGURE 1.3
The integrated development environment of Visual Studio 2010 for a new project

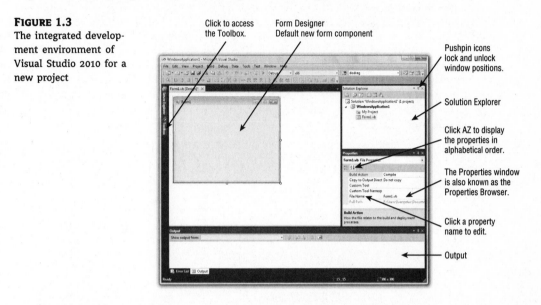

Click to access the Toolbox.

Form Designer
Default new form component

Pushpin icons lock and unlock window positions.

Solution Explorer

Click AZ to display the properties in alphabetical order.

The Properties window is also known as the Properties Browser.

Click a property name to edit.

Output

The new project contains a form already: the *Form1* component in the Solution Explorer. The main window of the IDE is the Form Designer, and the gray surface on it is the window of your new application in design mode. Using the Form Designer, you'll be able to design the visible interface of the application (place various components of the Windows interface on the form and set their properties) and then program the application.

The default environment is rather crowded, so let's hide a few of the toolbars that we won't use in the projects of the first few chapters. You can always show any of the toolbars at any time. Open the View menu and choose Toolbars. You'll see a submenu with 28 commands that are toggles. Each command corresponds to a toolbar, and you can turn the corresponding toolbar on or off by clicking one of the commands in the Toolbars submenu. For now, turn off all the toolbars except the Layout and Standard toolbars. These are the toolbars shown by default and you shouldn't hide them; if you do (perhaps to make more room for the designer), this is the place where you go to make them visible again.

The last item in the Toolbars submenu is the Customize command; Customize leads to a dialog box in which you can specify which of the toolbars and which of the commands you want to see. After you have established a work pattern, use this menu to customize the environment for the way you work with Visual Studio. You can hide just about any component of the IDE, except for the main menu — after all, you have to be able to undo the changes!

Using the Windows Form Designer

To design the form, you must place on it all the controls you want to display to the user at runtime. The controls are the components of the Windows interface (buttons, text boxes, radio buttons, lists, and so on). Open the Toolbox by moving the pointer over the Toolbox tab at the far left; the Toolbox, shown in Figure 1.4, pulls out. This Toolbox contains an icon for each control you can use on your form.

FIGURE 1.4
Windows Forms Toolbox
of the Visual Studio IDE

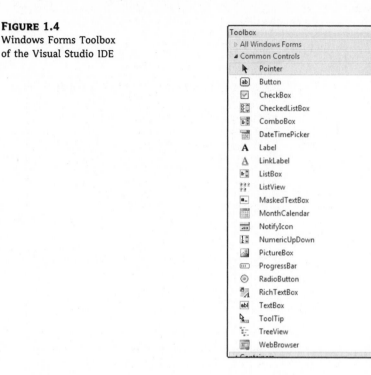

The controls are organized into groups according to function on the interface. In the first part of the book, you'll create simple Windows applications and you'll use the controls on the Common Controls tab. When you develop web applications, you will see a different set of icons in the Toolbox.

To place a control on the form, you can double-click the icon for the control. A new instance with a default size will be placed on the form. Then you can position and resize it with the mouse. Or you can select the control from the Toolbox with the mouse and then click and drag the mouse over the form and draw the outline of the control. A new instance of the control will be placed on the form, and it will fill the rectangle you specified with the mouse. Start by placing a TextBox control on the form.

The control properties will be displayed in the Properties window. Figure 1.5 shows the properties of a TextBox control. This window, at the far right edge of the IDE and below the Solution Explorer, displays the properties of the selected control on the form. If the Properties window is not visible, open the View menu and choose Properties Window, or press F4. If no control is selected, the properties of the selected item in the Solution Explorer are displayed.

In the Properties window, also known as the Properties Browser, you see the properties that determine the appearance of the control and (in some cases) its function. The properties are organized in categories according to their role. The properties that determine the appearance of the control are listed alphabetically under the header Appearance, the properties that determine the control's behavior are listed alphabetically under the header Behavior, and so on.

You can click the AZ button on the window's title bar to display all properties in alphabetical order. After you familiarize yourself with the basic properties, you will most likely switch to the alphabetical list.

FIGURE 1.5
Properties of a TextBox control

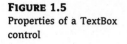

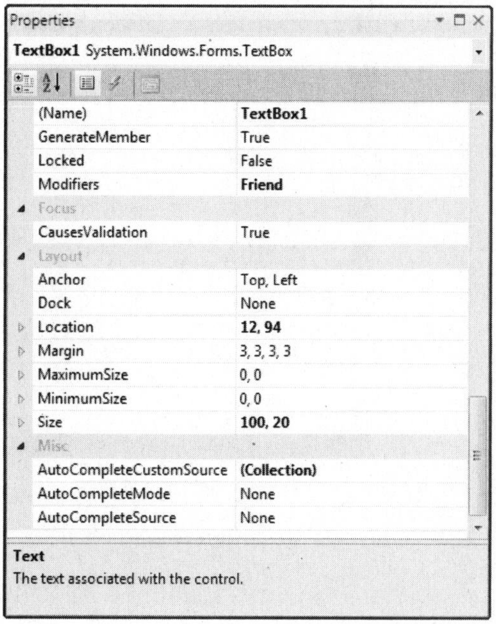

Properties	▾ □ ×
TextBox1 System.Windows.Forms.TextBox	▾

(Name)	**TextBox1**
GenerateMember	True
Locked	False
Modifiers	**Friend**
▴ Focus	
CausesValidation	True
▴ Layout	
Anchor	Top, Left
Dock	None
▹ Location	**12, 94**
▹ Margin	**3, 3, 3, 3**
▹ MaximumSize	**0, 0**
▹ MinimumSize	**0, 0**
▹ Size	**100, 20**
▴ Misc	
AutoCompleteCustomSource	**(Collection)**
AutoCompleteMode	None
AutoCompleteSource	None

Text
The text associated with the control.

REARRANGING THE IDE WINDOWS

As soon as you place a control on the form, the Toolbox retracts to the left edge of the Designer. You can fix this window on the screen by clicking the pushpin icon on the Toolbox's toolbar. (It's the icon next to the Close icon at the upper-right corner of the Toolbox window, and it appears when the Toolbox window is docked but not while it's floating.)

You can easily rearrange the various windows that make up the IDE by moving them around with the mouse. Move the pointer to a window's title bar, press the left mouse button, and drag the window around. If you can't move a window with the mouse, it's because the window's position is locked. In this case, click the pushpin icon to unlock the window's position and then move it around with the mouse.

As you move the window, eight semitransparent buttons with arrows appear on the screen, indicating the areas where the window can be docked, as shown in the following screen shot. Keep moving the window until the pointer hovers over one of these buttons and the docking area appears in semitransparent blue color. Find a position you like and release the mouse button to dock it. If you release the mouse button while the pointer is not on top of an arrow, the window is not docked. Instead, it remains where you dropped it as a floating window, and you can move it around with your mouse at will.

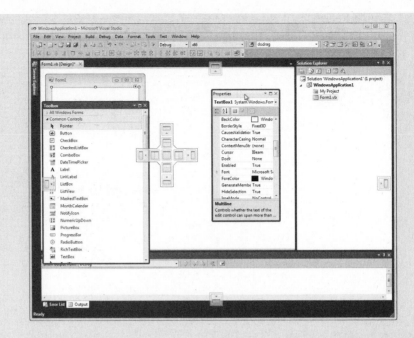

Most developers would rather work with docked windows, and the default positions of the IDE windows are quite convenient. If you want to open even more windows and arrange them differently on the screen, use the docking feature of the IDE to dock the additional windows.

Locate the TextBox control's Text property and set it to **My TextBox Control** by entering the string into the box next to the property name. The control's Text property is the string that appears in the control (the caption), and most controls have a Text property.

Next locate its BackColor property and select it with the mouse. A button with an arrow appears next to the current setting of the property. Click this button and you'll see a dialog box with three tabs (Custom, Web, and System), as shown in Figure 1.6. In this dialog box, you can select the color that will fill the control's background. Set the control's background color to yellow and notice that the control's appearance changes on the form.

One of the settings you'll want to change is the font of the various controls. While the TextBox control is still selected on the form, locate the Font property in the Properties window. You can click the plus sign in front of the property name and set the individual properties of the font, or you can click the ellipsis button to invoke the Font dialog box. Here you can set the control's font and its attributes and then click OK to close the dialog box. Set the TextBox control's Font property to Verdana, 14 points, bold. As soon as you close the Font dialog box, the control on the form is adjusted to the new setting.

There's a good chance that the string you assigned to the control's Text property won't fit in the control's width when rendered in the new font. Select the control on the form with the mouse and you will see eight handles along its perimeter. Rest the pointer over any of these handles and it will assume a shape indicating the direction in which you can resize the control.

Make the control long enough to fit the entire string. If you have to, resize the form as well. Click somewhere on the form, and when the handles appear along its perimeter, resize it with the mouse.

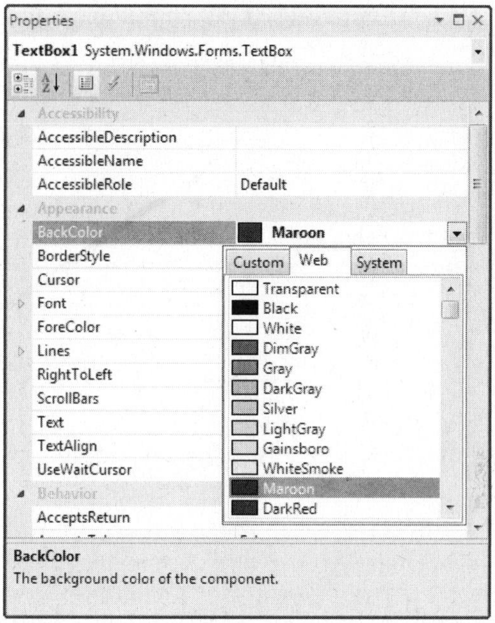

FIGURE 1.6
Setting a color property in the Properties window

Some controls, such as the Label, Button, and CheckBox controls, support the AutoSize property; AutoSize determines whether the control is resized automatically to accommodate the caption. The TextBox control, as well as many others, doesn't support the AutoSize property. If you attempt to make the control tall enough to accommodate a few lines of text, you'll realize that you can't change the control's height. By default, the TextBox control accepts a single line of text, and you must set its MultiLine property to True before you can resize the TextBox control vertically.

THE FONT IS A DESIGN ELEMENT

Like documents, forms should be designed carefully and follow the rules of a printed page design. At the very least, you shouldn't use multiple fonts on your forms, just as you shouldn't mix different fonts on a printed page. You could use two font families on rare occasions, but you shouldn't overload your form. You also shouldn't use the bold style in excess.

To avoid adjusting the Font property for multiple controls on the form, set the font for the form first because each control you place on a form inherits the form's font. If you change the form's font, the controls will be adjusted accordingly, but this may throw off the alignment of the controls on the form. Experiment with a few Label controls, select a font that you like that's appropriate for your interface (you shouldn't use a handwritten style with a business application, for example), and then set the form's Font property to the desired font. Every time you add a new form to the application, you should start by setting its Font property to that same font so that the entire application will have a consistent look.

The font is the most basic design element, whether you're designing forms or a document. Various components of the form may have a different font size, even a different style (like bold or italics), but there must be a dominant font family that determines the look of the form. The Verdana family was designed for viewing documents on computer monitors and is a popular choice. Another great choice is Segoe UI, a new font family introduced with Windows Vista. The Segoe Print font has a distinguished handwritten style, and you can use it with graphics applications.

The second most important design element is color, but don't get too creative with colors unless you're a designer. I recommend that you stay with the default colors and use similar shades to differentiate a few elements of the interface.

The design of a modern interface has become a new discipline in application development, and there are tools for designing interfaces. One of them is Microsoft's Expression Blend, which enables designers to design the interface and developers to write code without breaking each other's work. You can download a trial version of Expression Blend from www.microsoft.com/expression.

So far, you've manipulated properties that determine the appearance of the control. Now you'll change a property that determines not only the appearance, but also the function of the control. Locate the Multiline property. Its current setting is False. Expand the list of available settings and change it to True. (You can also change it by double-clicking the name of the property. This action toggles the True/False settings.) Switch to the form, select the TextBox control, and make it as tall as you wish.

The Multiline property determines whether the TextBox control can accept one (if Multiline = False) or more (if Multiline = True) lines of text. Set this property to True, go back to the Text property, set it to a long string, and press Enter. The control breaks the long text into multiple lines. If you resize the control, the lines will change, but the entire string will fit in the control because the control's WordWrap property is True. Set it to False to see how the string will be rendered on the control.

Multiline TextBox controls usually have a vertical scroll bar so users can quickly locate the section of text that they're interested in. Locate the control's ScrollBars property and expand the list of possible settings by clicking the button with the arrow. This property's settings are *None, Vertical, Horizontal,* and *Both*. Set it to *Vertical*, assign a very long string to its Text property, and watch how the control handles the text. At design time, you can't scroll the text on the control; if you attempt to move the scroll bar, the entire control will be scrolled. The scroll bar will work as expected at runtime. (It will scroll the text vertically.)

You can also make the control fill the entire form. Start by deleting any other controls you may have placed on the form and then select the multiline TextBox. Locate the Dock property in the Properties window and keep double-clicking the name of the property until its setting changes to *Fill*. (You'll learn a lot more about docking controls in Chapter 6, "Working with Forms.") The TextBox control fills the form and is resized as you resize the form, both at design time and runtime.

To examine the control's behavior at runtime, press F5. The application will be compiled, and a few moments later, a window filled with a TextBox control (like the one shown in

Figure 1.7) will appear on the Desktop. This is what the users of your application would see (if this were an application worth distributing, of course).

FIGURE 1.7
A TextBox control displaying multiple text lines

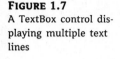

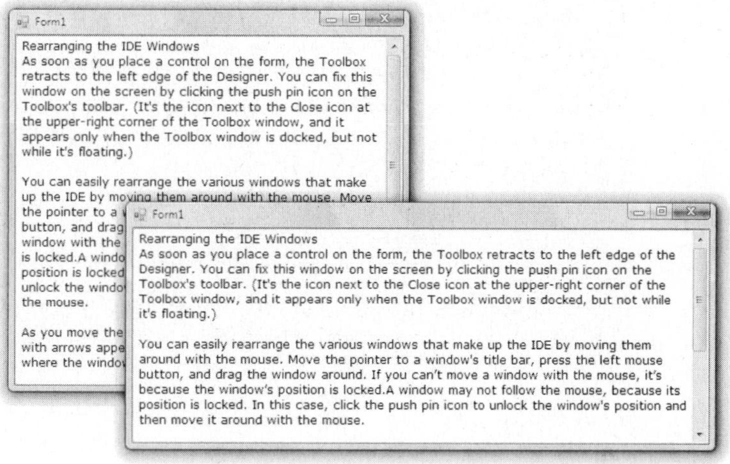

Enter some text on the control, select part of the text, and copy it to the Clipboard by pressing Ctrl+C. You can also copy text from any other Windows application and paste it on the TextBox control. Right-click the text on the control and you will see the same context menu you get with Notepad; you can even change the reading order of the text — not that you'd want to do that with a Western language. When you're finished, open the Debug menu and choose Stop Debugging. This will terminate your application's execution, and you'll be returned to the IDE. The Stop Debugging command is also available as a button with a blue square icon on the toolbar. Finally, you can stop the running application by clicking the Close button in the application's window.

The design of a new application starts with the design of the application's form, which is the application's user interface, or UI. The design of the form determines to a large extent the functionality of the application. In effect, the controls on the form determine how the application will interact with the user. The form itself could serve as a prototype, and you could demonstrate it to a customer before even adding a single line of code. By placing controls on the form and setting their properties, you're implementing a lot of functionality before coding the application. The TextBox control with the settings discussed in this section is a functional text editor.

Creating Your First VB Application

In this section, I will walk you through the development of a simple application to demonstrate not only the design of the interface, but also the code behind the interface. You'll build an application that allows users to enter the name of their favorite programming language, and the application will evaluate the choice. Objectively, VB is a step ahead of all other languages, and it will receive the best evaluation. All other languages get the same grade — good — but not VB.

The project is called WindowsApplication1. You can download the project from www.sybex.com/go/masteringvb2010 and examine it, but I suggest you follow the steps outlined in this section to build the project from scratch. Start a new project, use the default name, **WindowsApplication1**, and place a TextBox and a Button control on the form. Use the mouse to position and resize the controls on the form, as shown in Figure 1.8.

FIGURE 1.8
A simple applica-
tion that processes a
user-supplied string

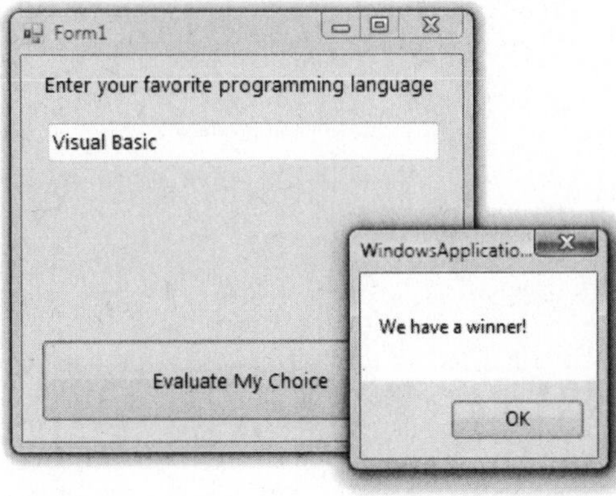

Start by setting the form's Font property to Segoe UI, 9 pt. Arrange and size the controls as shown in Figure 1.8. Then, place a Label control on the form and set its Text property to **Enter your favorite programming language**. The Label will be resized according to its caption because the control's AutoSize property is True by default. To be sure that a Label control will not grow too long and cover other controls on the form, set its AutoSize property to False and size it manually. As you move the controls around on the form, you'll see some blue lines connecting the edges of the controls when they're aligned. These lines are called *snap lines*, and they allow you to align controls on the form.

Now you must insert some code to evaluate the user's favorite language. Windows applications are made up of small code segments, called event handlers, which react to specific actions such as the click of a button, the selection of a menu command, the click of a check box, and so on. For this example, you want to program the action of clicking the button. When the user clicks the button, you want to execute some code that will display a message.

The Windows programming model is known as event-driven programming, as it's based on programming events. A Windows form contains controls, such as Buttons, CheckBoxes, TextBoxes, and so on. These controls react to certain events, which are usually initiated by the user. A button click, checking or clearing a check box, a drag and a drop operation — all are examples of user-initiated events. You decide the events to which your application should react and then program the desired actions by inserting some code into the event's handler. Event handlers are independent of one another, and you can focus on one event at a time.

To insert some code behind the Button control, double-click the control. You'll see the form's code window, which is shown in Figure 1.9. You will see only the definition of the procedure, not the code that is shown between the two statements in the figure. The statement beginning with Private... is too long to fit on the printed page, so I had to break it into two lines. When a line is too long, you can break it into two (or more) lines by pressing Enter. In previous versions, you had to insert a space followed by an underscore to indicate that the statement continues on the following line. Alternatively, you can turn on the word wrap feature of the editor (you'll see shortly how to adjust the editor's properties). Notice that I also inserted quite a bit of space before the second half of the first code line. It's customary to indent continued lines so they can be easily distinguished from the other lines.

FIGURE 1.9
Outline of a subroutine that handles the Click event of a Button control

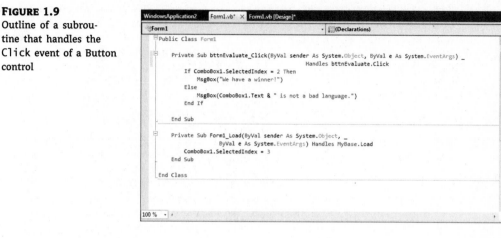

```
WindowsApplication2    Form1.vb*  ×  Form1.vb [Design]*
Form1                                              ▼  (Declarations)
Public Class Form1

    Private Sub bttnEvaluate_Click(ByVal sender As System.Object, ByVal e As System.EventArgs) _
                                   Handles bttnEvaluate.Click
        If ComboBox1.SelectedIndex = 2 Then
            MsgBox("We have a winner!")
        Else
            MsgBox(ComboBox1.Text & " is not a bad language.")
        End If

    End Sub

    Private Sub Form1_Load(ByVal sender As System.Object, _
                           ByVal e As System.EventArgs) Handles MyBase.Load
        ComboBox1.SelectedIndex = 3
    End Sub

End Class

100 %  ▼
```

The editor opens a subroutine, which is delimited by the following statements:

```
Private Sub Button1_Click(ByVal sender As System.Object,
            ByVal e As System.EventArgs) Handles Button1.Click

End Sub
```

At the top of the main pane of the Designer, you will see two tabs named after the form: the Form1.vb [Design] tab and the Form1.vb tab. The first tab is the Windows Form Designer (in which you build the interface of the application with visual tools), and the second is the code editor (in which you insert the code behind the interface). At the top of the code editor, which is what you see in Figure 1.9, are two ComboBoxes. The one on the left contains the names of the controls on the form. The one on the right contains the names of events each control recognizes. When you select a control (or an object, in general) in the left list, the other list's contents are adjusted accordingly. To program a specific event of a specific control, select the name of the control in the left list (the Objects list) and the name of the event in the right list (the Events list). While *Button1* is selected in the Objects list, open the Events list to see the events to which the button can react.

The Click event happens to be the default event of the Button control. To program the Button's Click event, double-click the Button on the form and the editor will open a window with the Button1_Click subroutine. This subroutine is an event handler, which is invoked automatically every time an event takes place. The event of interest in our example is the Click event of the *Button1* control. Every time the *Button1* control on the form is clicked, the Button1_Click subroutine is activated. To react to the Click event of the button, you must insert the appropriate code in this subroutine.

There are more than two dozen events for the Button control, and it is among the simpler controls. (After all, what can you do to a button besides click it?) Most of the controls recognize a very large number of events, which we rarely code. I've never seen a button that reacts to a double-click, even though you can program this event, or coding for the KeyPress event, which is fired when the user presses a key when the button has the focus. When programming a TextBox control, however, the KeyPress event is one of the most common events to code.

The definition of the event handler can't be modified; this is the event handler's signature (the arguments it passes to the application). All event handlers in VB 2010 pass two arguments to the application: the *sender* argument, which is an object that represents the control that fired the event, and the *e* argument, which provides additional information about the event.

The name of the subroutine is made up of the name of the control, followed by an underscore and the name of the event (Button1_Click). This is just the default name, and you can change it to anything you like (such as EvaluateLanguage, for this example, or StartCalculations). What makes this subroutine an event handler is the keyword Handles at the end of the statement. The Handles keyword tells the compiler which event this subroutine is supposed to handle. Button1.Click is the Click event of the *Button1* control. If there were another button on the form, the *Button2* control, you'd have to write code for a subroutine that would handle the Button2.Click event. Each control recognizes many events, and you can provide a different event handler for each control and event combination. Of course, we never program every possible event for every control.

The controls have a default behavior and handle the basic events on their own. The TextBox control knows how to handle keystrokes. The CheckBox control (a small square with a check mark) changes state by hiding or displaying the check mark every time it's clicked. The Scroll-Bar control moves its indicator (the button in the middle of the control) every time you click one of the arrows at the two ends. Because of this default behavior of the controls, you need not supply any code for the events of most controls on the form.

If you change the name of the control after you have inserted some code in an event handler, the name of the event handled by the subroutine will be automatically changed. The name of the subroutine, however, won't change. If you change the name of the *Button1* control to *bttnEvaluate*, the subroutine's header will become

```
Private Sub Button1_Click(ByVal sender As System.Object,
             ByVal e As System.EventArgs) Handles bttnEvaluate.Click


End Sub
```

Rename the Button1_Click subroutine to **EvaluateLanguage**. You must edit the code to change the name of the event handler. I try to name the controls before adding any code to the application so that their event handlers will be named correctly. Alternatively, you can use your own name for each event handler. The default names of the controls you place on a form are quite generic, and you should change them to something more meaningful. I usually prefix the control names with a few characters that indicate the control's type (such as txt, lbl, bttn, and so on), followed by a name that reflects the function of the control on the form. Names such as *txtLanguage* and *bttnEvaluate* make your code far more readable. It's a good practice to change the default names of the controls as soon as you add the controls to the form. Names such as *Button1, Button2, Button3,* and so on, don't promote the readability of your code. With the exception of this first sample project, I'm using descriptive names for the controls used in this book's projects.

Let's add some code to the Click event handler of the *Button1* control. When this button is clicked, I want to examine the text the user entered in the text box. If it's *Visual Basic,*

I want to display one message; if not, I want to display a different message. Insert the lines of Listing 1.1 between the `Private Sub` and `End Sub` statements. (I'm showing the entire listing here, but there's no reason to retype the first and last statements.)

LISTING 1.1:   Processing a user-supplied string

```
Private Sub EvaluateLanguage(ByVal sender As System.Object,
             ByVal e As System.EventArgs) Handles Button1.Click
   Dim language As String
   language = TextBox1.Text
   If language = "Visual Basic" Then
      MsgBox("We have a winner!")
   Else
      MsgBox(language & " is not a bad language.")
   End If
End Sub
```

Here's what this code does. First, it assigns the text of the TextBox control to the variable *language*. A variable is a named location in memory where a value is stored. Variables are where you store the intermediate results of your calculations when you write code. All variables are declared with a `Dim` statement and have a name and a type. The first statement declares a new variable, the *language* variable, with the `Dim` statement and sets its type to String (it's a variable that will store text).

You could also declare and assign a value to the *language* variable in a single step:

```
Dim language = TextBox1.Text
```

The compiler will create a String variable, because the statement assigns a string to the variable. We'll come back to the topic of declaring and initializing variables in Chapter 2, "Handling Data."

Then the program compares the value of the *language* variable to the string **Visual Basic**, and depending on the outcome of the comparison, it displays one of two messages. The `MsgBox()` function displays the message that you passed as an argument by placing it between the parentheses in a small window with an OK button, as shown in Figure 1.8. The argument for a `MsgBox()` function must be a string. Users can view the message and then click the OK button to close the message box.

Even if you're not familiar with the syntax of the language, you should be able to understand what this code does. Visual Basic is the simplest of the languages supported by Visual Studio 2010, and I will discuss the various aspects of the language in detail in the following chapters. In the meantime, focus on understanding the process of developing a Windows application: how to build the visible interface of the application and how to program the events to which you want your application to react.

The code of this first application isn't very robust. If the user doesn't enter the string with the exact spelling shown in the listing, the comparison will fail. You can convert the string to uppercase and then compare it with VISUAL BASIC to eliminate differences in case. To convert a string to uppercase, use the ToUpper method of the String class. The following expression returns the string stored in the *language* variable, converted to uppercase:

```
language.ToUpper
```

You should also take into consideration the fact that the user might enter *VB* or *VB2010*, or something similar. You never know what users may throw at your application, so whenever possible you should try to limit their responses to the number of available choices. In this case, you could display the names of certain languages (the ones you're interested in) and force the user to select one of them.

One way to display a limited number of choices is to use a ComboBox control. In the next section, you'll revise your sample application so that users won't have to enter the name of the language. You'll force them to select their favorite language from a list so that you won't have to validate the string supplied by the user.

Making the Application More User Friendly

Start a new project: the WindowsApplication2 project. Do not select the Create Directory For Solution check box; save the project from within the IDE. As soon as the project is created, open the File menu and choose Save All to save the project. When the Save Project dialog box appears, click the Browse button to select the folder where the project will be saved. In the Project Location dialog box that appears, select an existing folder or create a new folder such as **MyProjects** or **VB.NET Samples**.

Open the Toolbox and double-click the ComboBox tool icon. A ComboBox control will be placed on your form. Now, place a Button control on the form and position it so that your form looks like the one shown in Figure 1.10. Then set the Text property for the button to **Evaluate My Choice**.

FIGURE 1.10
Displaying options in a
ComboBox control

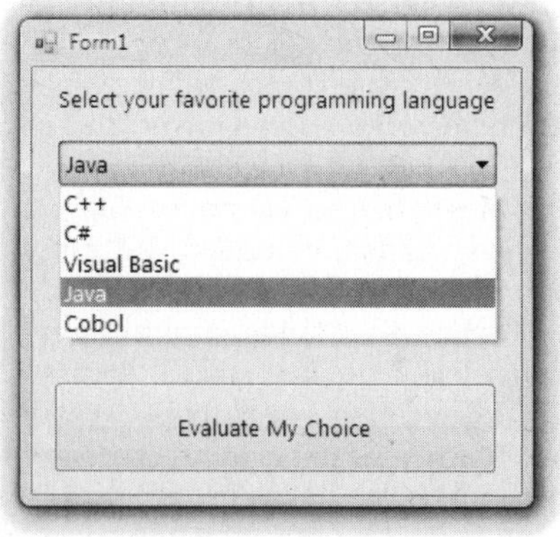

You must now populate the ComboBox control with the valid choices. Select the ComboBox control on the form by clicking it with the mouse and locate its Items property in the Properties window. The setting of this property is Collection, which means that the Items property doesn't have a single value; it's a collection of items (strings, in this case). Click the ellipsis button and you'll see the String Collection Editor dialog box, as shown in Figure 1.11.

FIGURE 1.11
Click the ellipsis button next to the Items property of a ComboBox to see the String Collection Editor dialog box.

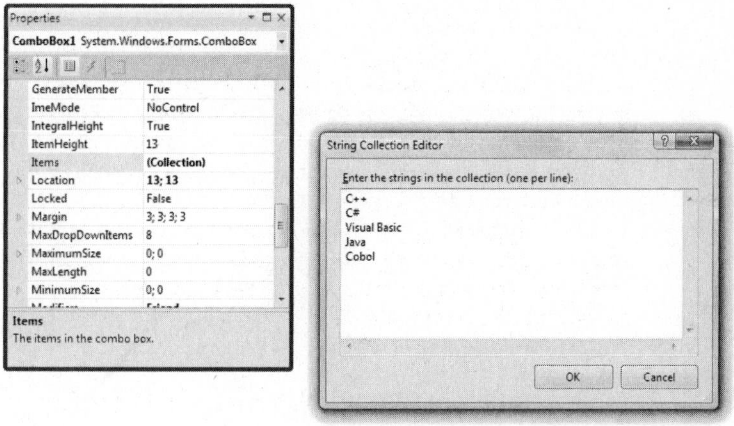

The main pane in the String Collection Editor dialog box is a TextBox, in which you can enter the items you want to appear in the ComboBox control at runtime. Enter the following strings, one per row and in the order shown here:

C++

C#

Visual Basic

Java

Cobol

Click the OK button to close the dialog box. The items you just entered will not appear on the control at design time, but you will see them when you run the project. Before running the project, set one more property. Locate the ComboBox control's Text property and set it to **Select your favorite programming language**. This is not an item of the list; it's the string that will initially appear on the control.

You can run the project now and see how the ComboBox control behaves. Press F5 and wait a few seconds. The project will be compiled, and you'll see the form displayed on your Desktop, on top of the Visual Studio window. I'm sure you know how the ComboBox control behaves in a typical Windows application, and your sample application is no exception. You can select an item on the control, either with the mouse or with the keyboard. Click the button with the arrow to expand the list and then select an item with the mouse. Or press the down or up arrow keys to scroll through the list of items. The control isn't expanded, but each time you click an arrow button, the next or previous item in the list appears on the control. Press the Tab key to move the focus to the Button control and press the spacebar to emulate a Click event (or simply click the Button control).

You haven't told the application what to do when the button is clicked yet, so let's go back and add some code to the project. Stop the application by clicking the Stop button on the toolbar (the solid black square) or by choosing Debug ➤ Stop Debugging from the main menu. When the form appears in design mode, double-click the button and the code window will open, displaying an empty `Click` event handler. Insert the statements shown in Listing 1.2 between the `Private Sub` and `End Sub` statements.

LISTING 1.2:   The revised `Click` event handler

```
Private Sub Button1_Click(ByVal sender As System.Object,
            ByVal e As System.EventArgs) Handles Button1.Click
    Dim language As String
    language = ComboBox1.Text
    If language = "Visual Basic" Then
        MsgBox("We have a winner!")
    Else
        MsgBox(language & "is not a bad language.")
    End If
End Sub
```

When the form is first displayed, a string that doesn't correspond to a language is displayed in the ComboBox control. This is the string that prompts the user to select a language; it isn't a valid selection because it's not included in the list of items.

You can also preselect one of the items from within your code when the form is first loaded. When a form is loaded, the Load event of the Form object is raised. Double-click somewhere on the form and the editor will open the form's Load event handler:

```
Private Sub Form1_Load(ByVal sender As System.Object,
            ByVal e As System.EventArgs) Handles MyBase.Load
End Sub
```

Enter the following code to select the `Visual Basic` item when the form is loaded:

```
Private Sub Form1_Load(ByVal sender As System.Object,
            ByVal e As System.EventArgs) Handles MyBase.Load
    ComboBox1.SelectedIndex = 2
End Sub
```

`SelectedIndex` is a property of the ComboBox control that returns the index of the selected item in the Items collection. You can set it to an integer value from within your code to select an item on the control, and you can also use it to retrieve the index of the selected item in the list. Instead of comparing strings, you can compare the `SelectedIndex` property to the value that corresponds to the index of the item Visual Basic, with a statement such as the following:

```
If ComboBox1.SelectedIndex = 2 Then
    MsgBox("We have a winner!")
Else
    MsgBox(ComboBox1.Text & " is not a bad language.")
End If
```

The Text property of the ComboBox control returns the text on the control, and it's used to print the selected language's name. The & symbol is an operator, similar to the arithmetic operators, that concatenates two strings. The first string is the Text property of the ComboBox control and the second string is a literal enclosed in double quotes. To combine the two, use the concatenation operator.

Of course, if you insert or remove items from the list, you must edit the code accordingly. If you run the application and test it thoroughly, you'll realize that there's a problem with the ComboBox control. Users can type in the control a new string, which will be interpreted as a language. By default, the ComboBox control allows users to type in something in addition to selecting an item from the list. To change the control's behavior, select it on the form and locate its DisplayStyle property in the Properties window. Expand the list of possible settings for the control and change the property's value from *DropDown* to *DropDownList*. Run the application again and test it; your sample application has become bulletproof. It's a simple application, but you'll see more techniques for building robust applications in Chapter 4, "GUI Design and Event-Driven Programming."

The controls on the Toolbox are more than nice pictures you can place on your forms. They encapsulate a lot of functionality and expose properties that allow you to adjust their appearance and their functionality. Most properties are usually set at design time, but quite frequently you change the properties of various controls from within your code. And it should be obvious by now that the changes take place from within the code that resides in the handlers for the events to which the application should react.

Now that you're somewhat familiar with the process of building Windows applications, and before you look into any additional examples, I will quickly present the components of the Visual Studio IDE.

Understanding the IDE Components

The IDE of Visual Studio 2010 contains numerous components, and it will take you a while to explore them. It's practically impossible to explain in a single chapter what each tool, window, and menu command does. I'll discuss specific tools as we go along and as the topics become more and more advanced. In the following sections, I will go through the basic items of the IDE — the ones you'll use in the following few chapters to build simple Windows applications.

The IDE Menus

The IDE menus provide access to a variety of commands; some lead to submenus. Notice that most menus can be displayed as toolbars. Also, not all options are available at all times. The options that cannot possibly apply to the current state of the IDE are either invisible or disabled. The Edit menu is a typical example. It's quite short when you're designing the form and quite lengthy when you edit code. The Data menu disappears altogether when you switch to the code editor — you can't use these menu options while editing code. If you open an XML document in the IDE, the XML item will be added to the menu bar of Visual Studio. Yes, Visual Studio can handle XML files too. Not only that, but Visual Basic provides built-in support for XML files, which I'll help you explore in Chapter 13, "XML in Modern Programming."

FILE MENU

The File menu contains commands for opening and saving projects or project items as well as commands for adding new or existing items to the current project. For the time being, use the

New ➤ Project command to create a new project, Open ➤ Project/Solution to open an existing project or solution, Save All to save all components of the current project, and the Recent Projects submenu to open one of the recent projects.

EDIT MENU

The Edit menu contains the usual editing commands. Among these commands are the Advanced command and the IntelliSense command. Both commands lead to submenus, which are discussed next. Note that these two items are visible only when you're editing your code and are invisible while you're designing a form.

Edit ➤ Advanced Submenu

The following options are the more-interesting ones available through the Edit ➤ Advanced submenu:

View White Space   Space characters (necessary to indent lines of code and make it easy to read) are replaced by periods.

Word Wrap   When a code line's length exceeds the length of the code window, the line is automatically wrapped.

Comment Selection/Uncomment Selection   Comments are lines you insert between your code statements to document your application. Every line that begins with a single quote is a comment; it is part of the code, but the compiler ignores it. Sometimes, you want to disable a few lines from your code but not delete them (because you want to be able to restore them later, should you change your mind). A simple technique to disable a line of code is to comment it out (insert the comment symbol in front of the line). The Comment Selection/Uncomment Selection command allows you to comment (or uncomment) large segments of code in a single move.

Edit ➤ IntelliSense Submenu

Edit ➤ IntelliSense leads to a submenu with five options, which are described next. IntelliSense is a feature of the editor (and other Microsoft applications) that displays as much information as possible, whenever possible. When you type the name of a control and the following period, IntelliSense displays a list of the control's properties and methods so that you can select the desired one — no more guessing at names. When you type the name of a function and an opening parenthesis, IntelliSense will display the syntax of the function — its arguments. The IntelliSense submenu includes the following options:

List Members   When this option is on, the editor lists all the members (properties, methods, events, and argument list) in a drop-down list. This list appears when you enter the name of an object or control followed by a period. Then, you can select the desired member from the list using either the mouse or the keyboard. Let's say your form contains a control named *TextBox1* and you're writing code for this form. When you enter the name of the control followed by a period (**TextBox1.**), a list with the members of the TextBox control will appear (as shown in Figure 1.12).

In addition, a description of the selected member is displayed in a ToolTip box, as you can see in the same figure. Select the Text property and then enter the equal sign, followed by a string in quotes, as follows:

```
TextBox1.Text = "Your User Name"
```

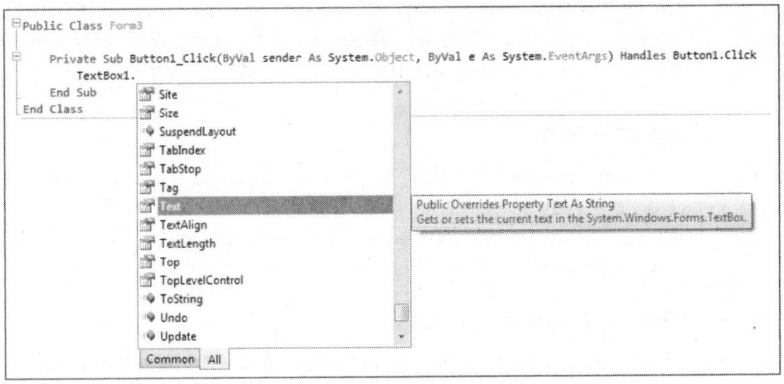

FIGURE 1.12
Viewing the members of
a control in the Intelli-
Sense drop-down list

If you select a property that can accept a limited number of settings, you will see the names of the appropriate constants in a drop-down list. If you enter the following statement, you will see the constants you can assign to the property (see Figure 1.13):

```
TextBox1.TextAlign =
```

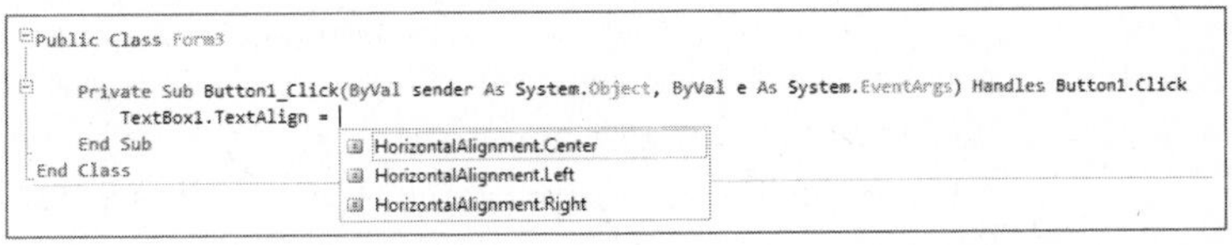

FIGURE 1.13
Viewing the possible
settings of a prop-
erty in the IntelliSense
drop-down list

Again, you can use your mouse to select the desired value. The drop-down list with the members of a control or object (the Members list) remains open until you type a terminator key (the Esc or End key) or select a member by pressing the spacebar or the Enter key.

Parameter Info While editing code, you can move the pointer over a variable, method, or property and see its declaration in a pop-up box. You can also jump to the variable's definition or the body of a procedure by choosing Go To Definition from the context menu that appears if you right-click the variable or method name in the code window.

Quick Info Quick Info is another IntelliSense feature that displays information about commands and functions. When you type an opening parenthesis following the name of a function, for example, the function's arguments will be displayed in a ToolTip box. The first argument appears in bold font; after a value for this argument is entered, the next one is shown in bold. If an argument accepts a fixed number of settings, these values will appear in a drop-down list, as explained previously.

Complete Word The Complete Word feature enables you to complete the current word by pressing Ctrl+spacebar. For example, if you type **TextB** and then press Ctrl+spacebar, you will see a list of words that you're most likely to type (TextBox, TextBox1, and so on).

Insert Snippet This command opens the Insert Snippet window at the current location in the code editor window. Code snippets, which are an interesting feature of Visual Studio 2010, are discussed in the section "Using Code Snippets" later in this chapter.

Edit ➤ *Outlining Submenu*

A practical application contains a substantial amount of code in a large number of event handlers and custom procedures (subroutines and functions). To simplify the management of the code window, the Outlining submenu contains commands that collapse and expand the various procedures.

Let's say you're finished editing the Click event handlers of several buttons on the form. You can reduce these event handlers to a single line that shows the names of the procedures with a plus sign in front of them. You can expand a procedure's listing at any time by clicking the plus sign. When you do so, a minus sign appears in front of the procedure's name, and you can click it to collapse the body of the procedure again. The Outlining submenu contains commands to handle the outlining of the various procedures or to turn off outlining and view the complete listings of all procedures. You will use these commands as you write applications with substantial amounts of code:

Hide Selection This option lets you hide the selected code segment. You can select part of a routine or multiple routines, which are hidden as a whole with this command. To display the hidden code, click the plus icon on the left margin, or use the Stop Hiding Selection command.

Toggle Outlining Expansion This option lets you change the outline mode of the current procedure. If the procedure's definition is collapsed, the code is expanded, and vice versa.

Toggle All Outlining This option is similar to the Toggle Outlining Expansion option, but it toggles the outline mode of the current document. A form is reduced to a single statement. A file with multiple classes is reduced to one line per class.

Stop Outlining This option turns off outlining and adds a new command to the Outlining submenu, Start Automatic Outlining, which you can select to turn on automatic outlining again.

Stop Hiding Current This option stops hiding the currently hidden selection.

Collapse To Definitions This option reduces the listing to a list of procedure headers.

VIEW MENU

This menu contains commands that allow you to display any toolbar or window of the IDE. The Other Windows command leads to a submenu with the names of some standard windows, including the Output and Command windows. The Output window is the console of the application. The compiler's messages, for example, are displayed in the Output window. The Command window allows you to enter and execute statements. When you debug an application, you can stop it and enter VB statements in the Command window. Another related window is the Immediate window, which is very similar to the Command window, and it has the advantage of displaying the IntelliSense box as you type. You'll see how to use these windows later in this book (they're used mostly for debugging).

PROJECT MENU

This menu contains commands for adding items to the current solution (an item can be a form, a file, a component, or another project). The last option in this menu is the Project Properties command, which opens the project's properties pages. The Add Reference and Add Web Reference commands allow you to add references to .NET components and web components, respectively. These two commands are also available in the project's shortcut menu (to open this menu, right-click the name of the project in the Solution Explorer).

BUILD MENU

The Build menu contains commands for building (compiling) your project. The two basic commands in this menu are Build and Rebuild All. The Build command compiles (builds the executable for) the entire solution, but it doesn't compile any components of the project that haven't changed since the last build. The Rebuild All command clears any existing files and builds the solution from scratch. Every time you start your application, Visual Studio recompiles it as needed so you don't usually have to build your application to execute it. There are situations (when you add custom classes and controls to your application) when you must build the project. These topics are discussed later in this book.

DEBUG MENU

This menu contains commands to start or end an application as well as the basic debugging tools. The basic commands of this menu are discussed briefly in Chapter 4.

DATA MENU

This menu contains commands you will use with projects that access data. You'll see how to use this short menu's commands in the discussion of the visual database tools in Chapter 16 through Chapter 18.

FORMAT MENU

The Format menu, which is visible only while you design a Windows or web form, contains commands for aligning the controls on the form. The commands accessible from this menu are discussed in Chapter 4. The Format menu is invisible when you work in the code editor — the commands apply to the visible elements of the interface.

TOOLS MENU

This menu contains a list of useful tools, such as the Macros command, which leads to a sub-menu with commands for creating macros. Just as you can create macros in a Microsoft Office application to simplify many tasks, you can create macros to automate many of the repetitive tasks you perform in the IDE. The last command in this menu, the Options command, leads to the Options dialog box, in which you can fully customize the environment. The Choose Tool-box Items command opens a dialog box that enables you to add more controls to the Toolbox. In Chapter 9, "Building Custom Windows Controls," you'll learn how to design custom controls and add them to the Toolbox.

WINDOW MENU

This is the typical Window menu of any Windows application. In addition to the list of open windows, it contains the Hide command, which hides all toolboxes, leaving the entire window of the IDE devoted to the code editor or the Form Designer. The toolboxes don't disappear completely; they're all retracted, and you'll be able see the tabs on the left and right edges of the IDE window. To expand a toolbox, just hover the mouse pointer over the corresponding tab.

HELP MENU

This menu contains the various help options. The Dynamic Help command opens the Dynamic Help window, which is populated with topics that apply to the current operation. The Index command opens the Index window, in which you can enter and get help on a specific topic.

The Toolbox Window

The Toolbox window contains all the controls you can use to build your application interface. This window is usually retracted, and you must move the pointer over it to view the Toolbox. The controls in the Toolbox are organized in various tabs, so take a look at them to become familiar with their functions.

In the first few chapters, we'll work with the controls in the Common Controls and Menus & Toolbars tabs. The Common Controls tab contains the icons for the most common Windows controls, while the All Windows Controls tab contains all the controls you can place on your form. The Data tab contains the icons for the objects you will use to build data-driven applications (they're explored later in this book). The Menus & Toolbars tab contains the Menu and ContextMenu controls (they're discussed in Chapter 4) among others. On the Printing tab you will find all the controls you'll need to create printouts, and they're discussed briefly in Chapter 11 and in more detail in the tutorial "Printing with Visual Basic." The Dialogs tab contains controls for implementing the common dialog controls, which are so common in Windows interfaces; they're discussed in Chapter 7, "More Windows Controls."

The Solution Explorer Window

The Solution Explorer window contains a list of the items in the current solution. A solution can contain multiple projects, and each project can contain multiple items. The Solution Explorer displays a hierarchical list of all the components, organized by project. You can right-click any component of the project and choose Properties in the context menu to see the selected component's properties in the Properties window. If you select a project, you will see the Project Properties dialog box. You will find more information on project properties in the following chapter.

If the solution contains multiple projects, you can right-click the project you want to become the startup form and select Set As StartUp Project. (The Startup project is the one that starts executing when you press F5 in the IDE.) You can also add items to a project with the Add Item command from the context menu or remove a component from the project with the Exclude From Project command. This command removes the selected component from the project but doesn't affect the component's file on the disk. The Delete command removes the selected component from the project and also deletes the component's file from the disk.

If a project contains many items, you can organize them into folders. Right-click the project name and select Add from the context menu. From the shortcut menu that appears, select New Folder. To move an existing item into a folder, just drag it and drop it on one of the project folders.

The Properties Window

This window (also known as the Properties Browser) displays all the properties of the selected component and their settings. Every time you place a control on a form, you switch to this window to adjust the appearance of the control. You have already seen how to manipulate the basic properties of a control through the Properties window, and you will find many more examples in this and the following chapter.

Many properties are set to a single value, such as a number or a string. If the possible settings of a property are relatively few, they're displayed as meaningful constants in a drop-down list. Other properties are set through a more elaborate interface. Color properties, for example, are set on a Color dialog box that's displayed right in the Properties window. Font properties are set through the usual Font dialog box. Collections are set in a Collection Editor dialog box, in which you can enter one string for each item of the collection, as you did for the items of the ComboBox control earlier in this chapter.

If the Properties window is hidden, or if you have closed it, you can choose View ➢ Properties Window or right-click a control on the form and choose Properties, or you can simply press F4 to bring up this window. There will be times when one control might totally overlap another control, and you won't be able to select the hidden control and view its properties. In this case, you can select the desired control in the ComboBox at the top of the Properties window. This box contains the names of all the controls on the form, and you can select a control on the form by selecting its name from this box.

The Output Window

The Output window is where many of the tools, including the compiler, send their output. Every time you start an application, a series of messages is displayed in the Output window. These messages are generated by the compiler, and you need not understand them at this point. If the Output window is not visible, choose View ➢ Other Windows ➢ Output from the menu.

The Command and Immediate Windows

While testing a program, you can interrupt its execution by inserting a breakpoint. When the breakpoint is reached, the program's execution is suspended and you can execute a statement in the Immediate window. Any statement that can appear in your VB code can also be executed in the Immediate window. To evaluate an expression, enter a question mark followed by the expression you want to evaluate, as in the following samples, where *result* is a variable in the program you interrupted:

```
? Math.Log(35)
? "The answer is " & result.ToString
```

You can also send output to this window from within your code with the `Debug.Write` and `Debug.WriteLine` methods. Actually, this is a widely used debugging technique — to print the values of certain variables before entering a problematic area of the code. There are more elaborate tools to help you debug your application, but printing a few values to the Immediate window is a time-honored practice in programming with VB.

In many of the examples of this book, especially in the first few chapters, I use the `Debug.WriteLine` statement to print something to the Immediate window. To demonstrate the use of the `DateDiff()` function, for example, I'll use a statement like the following:

```
Debug.WriteLine(DateDiff(DateInterval.Day, #3/9/2007#, #5/15/2008#))
```

When this statement is executed, the value 433 (which is the number of days between the two dates) will appear in the Immediate window. This statement demonstrates the syntax of the `DateDiff()` function, which returns the difference between the two dates in days. Sending some output to the Immediate window to test a function or display the results of intermediate calculations is a common practice.

To get an idea of the functionality of the Immediate window, switch back to your first sample application and insert the `Stop` statement after the `End If` statement in the button's `Click` event handler. Run the application, select a language, and click the button on the form. After displaying a message box, the application will reach the `Stop` statement and its execution will be suspended. You'll see the Immediate window at the bottom of the IDE. If it's not visible, open the Debug menu and choose Windows ➢ Immediate. In the Immediate window, enter the following statement:

```
? ComboBox1.Items.Count
```

Then, press Enter to execute it. Notice that IntelliSense is present while you're typing in the Immediate window. The expression prints the number of items in the ComboBox control. (Don't worry about the numerous properties of the control and the way I present them here; they're discussed in detail in Chapter 5, "Basic Windows Controls.") As soon as you press Enter, the value 5 will be printed on the following line.

You can also manipulate the controls on the form from within the Immediate window. Enter the following statement and press Enter to execute it:

```
ComboBox1.SelectedIndex = 4
```

The fifth item on the control will be selected (the indexing of the items begins with 0). However, you can't see the effects of your changes because the application isn't running. Press F5 to resume the execution of the application and you will see that the item Cobol is now selected in the ComboBox control.

The Immediate window is available only while the application's execution is suspended. To continue experimenting with it, click the button on the form to evaluate your choice. When the `Stop` statement is executed again, you'll be switched to the Immediate window.

Unlike the Immediate window, the Command window is available at design time. The Command window allows you to access all the commands of Visual Studio by typing their names in this window. If you enter the string **Edit** followed by a period, you will see a list of all commands of the Edit menu, including the ones that are not visible at the time, and you can invoke any of these commands and pass arguments to them. For example, if you enter **Edit.Find "Margin"** in the Command window and then press Enter, the first instance of the string Margin will be located in the open code window. To start the application, you can type **Debug.Start**. You can add a new project to the current solution with the `AddProj` command, and so on. Most developers hardly ever use this window in designing or debugging applications.

The Error List Window

This window is populated by the compiler with error messages if the code can't be successfully compiled. You can double-click an error message in this window and the IDE will take you to the line with the statement in error — which you should fix. Change the `MsgBox()` function name to **MssgBox()**. As soon as you leave the line with the error, the name of the function will be underlined with a wiggly red line and the following error description will appear in the Error List window:

```
Name 'MssgBox' is not declared
```

Correct the function name (it should be MsgBox with one *s*) and the error number will disappear from the Error List window. The Error List window has two more tabs, the Warnings tab and the Messages tab, which display various warnings.

Setting Environment Options

The Visual Studio IDE is highly customizable. I will not discuss all the customization options here, but I will show you how to change the default settings of the IDE. Open the Tools menu and select Options (the last item in the menu). The Options dialog box appears, in which you can set all the options regarding the environment. Figure 1.14 shows the options for the fonts of the various items of the IDE. Here you can set the font for the Text Editor, dialog boxes, toolboxes, and so on. Select an item in the tree in the left pane list and then set the font for this item in the box below.

FIGURE 1.14
The Fonts And Colors options

Figure 1.15 shows the Projects And Solutions options. The top box indicates the default location for new projects. The Save New Projects When Created check box determines whether the editor will create a new folder for the project when it's created. If you uncheck this box, then Visual Studio will create a folder in the Temp folder. Projects in the Temp folder will be removed when you run the Disk Cleanup utility to claim more space on your hard drives.

By default, Visual Studio saves the changes to the current project every time you press F5. You can change this behavior by setting the Before Building option in the Build And Run page, under the Project And Solutions branch. If you change this setting, you must save your project from time to time with the File ➢ Save All command.

Most of the tabs in the Options dialog box are straightforward, and you should take a look at them. If you don't like some of the default aspects of the IDE, this is the place to change them. If you switch to the Basic item under the Text Editor branch of the tree in the left pane of the Options dialog box, you will find the Line Numbers option. Select this check box to display numbers in front of each line in the code window. The Options dialog box contains a lot of options for customizing your work environment, and it's worth exploring on your own. Before you make any changes in the Visual Studio options, make sure you save the current settings with the Import And Exporting Settings command accessible from the Tools menu.

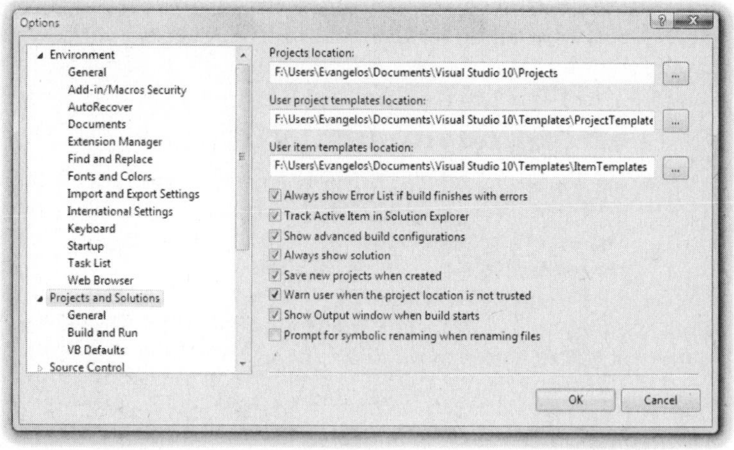

FIGURE 1.15
The Projects And Solutions options

Building a Console Application

Apart from Windows applications, you can use Visual Studio 2010 to build applications that run in a command prompt window. The command prompt window isn't really a DOS window, even though it looks like one. It's a text window, and the only way to interact with an application is to enter lines of text and read the output generated by the application, which is displayed in this text window, one line at a time. This type of application is called a console application, and I'm going to demonstrate console applications with a single example. We will not return to this type of application later in the book because it's not what you're supposed to do as a Windows developer.

The console application you'll build in this section, ConsoleApplication1, prompts users to enter the name of their favorite language. It then prints the appropriate message on a new line, as shown in Figure 1.16.

FIGURE 1.16
A console application uses the command prompt window to interact with the user.

Start a new project. In the New Project dialog box, select the template Console Application. You can also change its default name from ConsoleApplication1 to a more descriptive name. For this example, don't change the application's name.

A console application doesn't have a user interface, so the first thing you'll see is the code editor's window with the following statements:

```
Module Module1

    Sub Main()

    End Sub

End Module
```

Unlike a Windows application, which is a class, a console application is a module. `Main()` is the name of a subroutine that's executed automatically when you run a console application. The code you want to execute must be placed between the statements `Sub Main()` and `End Sub`. Insert the statements shown in Listing 1.3 in the application's `Main()` subroutine.

LISTING 1.3:   Console application

```
Module Module1
    Sub Main()
        Console.WriteLine("Enter your favorite language")
        Dim language As String
        language = Console.ReadLine()
        language = language.ToUpper
        If language = "VISUAL BASIC" Or
                language = "VB" Or
                language = "VB.NET" Or
                language = "VISUAL BASIC 2010" Then
            Console.WriteLine("We have a winner!")
        Else
            Console.WriteLine(language & " is not a bad language.")
        End If
        Console.WriteLine()
        Console.WriteLine()
        Console.WriteLine("PRESS ENTER TO EXIT")
        Console.ReadLine()
    End Sub
End Module
```

This code is quite similar to the code of the equivalent Windows applications we developed earlier, except that it uses the `Console.WriteLine` statement to send its output to the command prompt window instead of a message box.

A console application doesn't react to events because it has no visible interface. However, it's easy to add some basic elements of the Windows interface to a console application. If you change the `Console.WriteLine` method call into the `MsgBox()` function, the message will be displayed in a message box.

One reason to build a console application is to test a specific feature of the language without having to build a user interface. Many of the examples in the documentation are console applications; they demonstrate the topic at hand and nothing more. If you want to test the `DateDiff()` function, for example, you can create a new console application and enter the lines from Listing 1.4 in its `Main()` subroutine.

LISTING 1.4:   Testing the `DateDiff()` function with a console application

```
Sub Main()
    Console.WriteLine(DateDiff(DateInterval.Day, #3/9/2000#, #5/15/2008#))
    Console.WriteLine("PRESS ENTER TO EXIT")
    Console.ReadLine()
End Sub
```

The last two lines will be the same in every console application you write. Without them, the command prompt window will close as soon as the `End Sub` statement is reached, and you won't have a chance to see the result. The `Console.ReadLine` method waits until the user presses the Enter key.

Console applications are convenient for testing short code segments, but Windows programming is synonymous with designing graphical user interfaces, so you won't find any more console applications in this book.

Using Code Snippets

Visual Basic 2010 comes with a lot of predefined code snippets for selected actions, and you can insert these snippets into your code as needed. Let's say you want to insert the statements for writing some text to a file, but you have no idea how to access files. Create an empty line in the listing (press the Enter key a couple of times at the end of a code line). Then open the Edit menu and choose IntelliSense ➢ Insert Snippet (or right-click somewhere in the code window and choose Insert Snippet from the context menu).

When Insert Snippet opens, you will see a list of the snippets, organized in folders according to their function, as shown in Figure 1.17. Double-click any folder name to see the subfolders or actual snippets available for that function. Try it out. Double-click the Fundamentals folder and take a look at the options available to you: Collections, Data Types, File System, and Math. Double-click the filesystem item to see a list of common file-related tasks, as shown in Figure 1.18. Scroll down and locate the item Write Text To A File in the list. Now, double-click it to insert that snippet at the current location in the code window.

The following snippet will be inserted in your code:

```
My.Computer.FileSystem.WriteAllText("C:\test.txt", "Text", True)
```

To write some text to a file, you need to call the `WriteAllText` method of the `My.Computer.FileSystem` object. You can replace the strings shown in the snippet with actual values. The first string is the filename, the second string is the text to be written to the file, and the last argument of the method determines whether the text will be appended to the file (if False) or will overwrite any existing text (if True).

Each snippet shows you the basic statements for performing a common task, and you can edit the code inserted by Visual Studio as needed. A real-world application would probably prompt the user for a filename via the File common dialog box and then use the filename specified by the user in the dialog box instead of a hard-coded filename.

FIGURE 1.17
The code snippets are organized according to function.

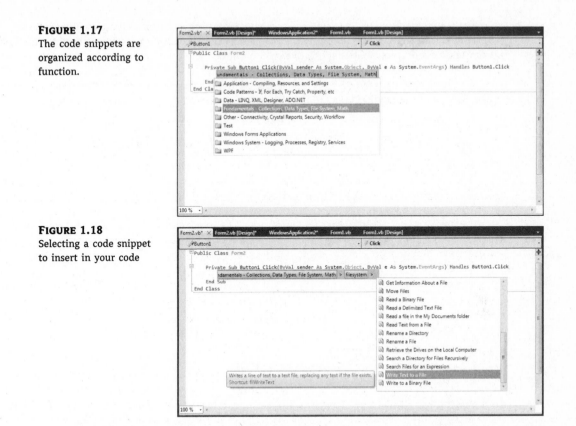

FIGURE 1.18
Selecting a code snippet to insert in your code

As you program, you should always try to find out whether there's a snippet for the task at hand. Sometimes you can use a snippet without even knowing how it works. Although snippets can simplify your life, they won't help you understand the Framework, which is discussed in detail throughout this book.

Using the My Component

You have probably noticed that the code snippets available through Visual Studio use an entity called My — a peculiar object that was introduced with VB 2005 to simplify many programming tasks. As you saw in the preceding code snippet, the My component allowed you to write some text to a file with a single statement, the WriteAllText method. If you're familiar with earlier versions of Visual Basic, you know that to actually write text to a file you must first open a file, then write some text to it, and finally close the file. The My component allows you to perform all these operations with a single statement.

Another example is the Play method, which you can use to play back a WAV file from within your code:

```
My.Computer.Audio.Play ("C:\Sounds\CountDown.wav")
```

Or you can use it to play back a system sound:

```
My.Computer.Audio.PlaySystemSound(System.Media.SystemSounds.Exclamation)
```

The method that plays back the sound is the `Play` method, and the method that writes text to a file is the `WriteAllText` method. However, you can't call them directly through the `My` component; they're not methods of the `My` component. If they were, you'd have to dig hard to find out the method you need. The `My` component exposes six components, which contain their own components. Here's a description of the basic components of the `My` component and the functionality you should expect to find in each component:

My.Application   The Application component provides information about the current application. The `CommandLineArgs` property of My.Application returns a collection of strings, which are the arguments passed to the application when it was started. Typical Windows applications aren't called with command-line arguments, but it's possible to start an application and pass a filename as an argument to the application (the document to be opened by the application, for example). The `Info` property is an object that exposes properties such as `DirectoryPath` (the application's default folder), `ProductName`, `Version`, and so on.

My.Computer   This component exposes a lot of functionality via a number of properties, many of which are objects. The My.Computer.Audio component lets you play back sounds. The My.Computer.Clipboard component lets you access the Clipboard. To find out whether the Clipboard contains a specific type of data, use the `ContainsText`, `ContainsImage`, `ContainsData`, and `ContainsAudio` methods. To retrieve the contents of the Clipboard, use the `GetText`, `GetImage`, `GetData`, and `GetAudioStream` methods. Assuming that you have a form with a TextBox control and a PictureBox control, you can retrieve text or image data from the Clipboard and display it on the appropriate control with the following statements:

```
If My.Computer.Clipboard.ContainsImage Then
    PictureBox1.Image = My.Computer.Clipboard.GetImage
End If
If My.Computer.Clipboard.ContainsText Then
    TextBox2.Text = My.Computer.Clipboard.GetText
End If
```

You may have noticed that using the `My` component in your code requires that you write long statements. You can shorten them substantially via the `With` statement, as shown next:

```
With My.Computer.Clipboard
    If .ContainsImage Then
        PictureBox1.Image = .GetImage
    End If
    If .ContainsText Then
        TextBox2.Text = .GetText
    End If
End With
```

When you're executing multiple statements on the same object, you can specify the object in a `With` statement and call its methods in the block of the `With` statement by specifying the method name prefixed with a dot. The `With` statement is followed by the name of the object to which all following methods apply and is terminated with the `End With` statement.

Another property of the `My.Computer` component is the `FileSystem` object that exposes all the methods you need to access files and folders. If you enter the expression

`My.Computer.FileSystem` followed by a dot, you will see all the methods exposed by the `FileSystem` component. Among them, you will find `DeleteFile`, `DeleteDirectory`, `RenameFile`, `RenameDirectory`, `WriteAllText`, `ReadAllText`, and many more. Select a method and then type the opening parenthesis. You will see the syntax of the method in a ToolTip. The syntax of the `CopyFile` method is as follows:

```
My.Computer.FileSystem.CopyFile(
        sourceFileName As String, destinationFileName As String)
```

Just specify the path of the file you want to copy and the new file's name, and you're finished. This statement will copy the specified file to the specified location.

You will notice that the ToolTip box with the syntax of the `CopyFile` method has multiple versions, which are listed at the left side of the box along with arrow up and arrow down icons. Click these two buttons to see the next and previous versions of the method. The second version of the `CopyFile` method is as follows:

```
My.Computer.FileSystem.CopyFile(
        sourceFileName As String, destinationFileName As String,
        overwrite As Boolean)
```

The *overwrite* argument specifies whether the method should overwrite the destination file if it exists.

The third version of the method accepts a different third argument that determines whether the usual copy animation will be displayed as the file is being copied.

The various versions of the same method differ in the number and/or type of their arguments, and they're called overloaded forms of the method. Instead of using multiple method names for the same basic operation, the overloaded forms of a method allow you to call the same method name and adjust its behavior by specifying different arguments.

My.Forms   This component lets you access the forms of the current application. You can also access the application's forms by name, so the Forms component isn't the most useful one.

My.Settings   This component lets you access the application settings. These settings apply to the entire application and are stored in an XML configuration file. The settings are created from within Visual Studio, and you use the Settings component to read them.

My.User   This component returns information about the current user. The most important property of the User component is the `CurrentPrincipal` property, which is an object that represents the credentials of the current user.

My.WebServices   The WebServices component represents the web services referenced by the current application.

The My component gives beginners unprecedented programming power and allows you to perform tasks that would require substantial code if implemented with earlier versions of the language, not to mention the research it would take to locate the appropriate methods in the Framework. You can explore the My component on your own and use it as needed. My is not a substitute for learning the language and the Framework. It can help you initially, but you can't go far without learning the methods of the Framework for handling files or any other feature.

Let's say you want to locate all the files of a specific type in a folder, including its sub-folders. Scanning a folder and its subfolders to any depth is quite a task (you'll find the code in the tutorial "Accessing Folders and Files," which you can download from www.sybex.com/go/masteringvb2010). You can do the same with a single statement by using the My component:

```
Dim files As ReadOnlyCollection(Of String)
files = My.Computer.FileSystem.GetFiles("D:\Data", True, "*.txt")
```

The GetFiles method populates the *files* collection with the pathnames of the text files in the folder D:\Data and its subfolders. However, it won't help you if you want to process each file in place. Moreover, this GetFiles method is synchronous: If the folder contains many sub-folders with many files, it will block the interface until it retrieves all the files. In the tutorial "Accessing Folders and Files," you'll see the code that retrieves filenames and adds them to a control as it goes along.

If you're already familiar with VB, you may think that the My component is an aid for the abso-lute beginner or the nonprogrammer. This isn't true. VB is about productivity, and the My com-ponent can help you be more productive with your daily tasks, regardless of your knowledge of the language or programming skills. If you can use My to save a few (or a few dozen) state-ments, do it. There's no penalty for using the My component because the compiler replaces the methods of the My component with the equivalent method calls to the Framework.

The Bottom Line

Navigate the integrated development environment of Visual Studio.   To simplify the pro-cess of application development, Visual Studio provides an environment that's common to all languages, known as an integrated development environment (IDE). The purpose of the IDE is to enable the developer to do as much as possible with visual tools before writing code. The IDE provides tools for designing, executing, and debugging your applications. It's your second desktop, and you'll be spending most of your productive hours in this environment.

Master It   Describe the basic components of the Visual Studio IDE.

Understand the basics of a Windows application.   A Windows application consists of a visual interface and code. The visual interface is what users see at runtime: a form with controls with which the user can interact — by entering strings, checking or clearing check boxes, clicking buttons, and so on. The visual interface of the application is designed with visual tools. The visual elements incorporate a lot of functionality, but you need to write some code to react to user actions.

Master It   Describe the process of building a simple Windows application.

Chapter 2

Handling Data

This chapter and the next discuss the fundamentals of any programming language: variables and data types. A variable stores data, which is processed with statements. A program is a list of statements that manipulate variables. To write even simple applications, you need a basic understanding of some fundamental topics, such as the data types (the kind of data you can store in a variable), the scope and lifetime of variables, and how to write procedures and pass arguments to them. In this chapter, we'll explore the basic data types of Visual Basic, and in the following one, you'll learn about procedures and flow-control statements.

If you're new to Visual Basic, you may find some material in this chapter less than exciting. It covers basic concepts and definitions — in general, tedious, but necessary, material. Think of this chapter as a prerequisite for the following ones. If you need information on core features of the language as you go through the examples in the rest of the book, you'll probably find it here.

In this chapter, you'll learn how to do the following:

◆ Declare and use variables

◆ Use the native data types

◆ Create custom data types

◆ Use arrays

Variables

In Visual Basic, as in any other programming language, variables store values during a program's execution. A variable has a name and a value. The variable *UserName*, for example, might have the value Joe, and the variable *Discount* might have the value 0.35. *UserName* and *Discount* are variable names, and Joe and 0.35 are their values. Joe is a string (that is, text), and 0.35 is a numeric value. When a variable's value is a string, it must be enclosed in double quotes. In your code, you can refer to the value of a variable by the variable's name.

In addition to a name and a value, variables have a data type, which determines what kind of values you can store to a variable. VB 2010 supports several data types (and they're discussed in detail later in this chapter). It's actually the Common Language Runtime (CLR) that supports the data types, and the data types are common to all languages, not just to Visual Basic. The data type of a variable is specified when the variable is declared, and you should always declare variables before using them. (I'll tell you more about declaring variables in the next section.)

The various data types are discussed in detail later in this chapter, but let me start with some simple examples to demonstrate the concepts of using variables in an application. One of the available numeric data types is the Decimal data type; it can store both integer and non-integer values. For example, the following statements calculate and display the discount for the amount of $24,500:

```
Dim Amount As Decimal
Dim Discount As Decimal
Dim DiscountedAmount As Decimal
Amount = 24500
Discount = 0.35
DiscountedAmount = Amount * (1 - Discount)
MsgBox("Your price is $" & DiscountedAmount.ToString)
```

If you enter these statements in a button's Click event handler to test them, the compiler may underline the statement that assigns the value 0.35 to the *Discount* variable and generate an error message. To view the error message, hover the pointer over the underlined segment of the statement in error. This will happen if the Strict option is on. (I discuss the Strict option, along with two more options of the compiler, later in this chapter.) By default, the Strict option is off and the statement won't generate an error.

The compiler treats any numeric value with a fractional part as a Double value and detects that you're attempting to assign a Double value to a Decimal variable. To specify that a numeric value should be treated as a Decimal type, use the following notation:

```
Discount = 0.35D
```

As you will see later, the *D* character at the end of a numeric value indicates that the value should be treated as a Decimal value, and there are a few more type characters (see Table 2.2 later in this chapter). I've used the Decimal data type here because it's commonly used in financial calculations.

The amount displayed on the message box by the last line of code depends on the values of the *Discount* and *Amount* variables. If you decide to offer a better discount, all you have to do is change the value of the *Discount* variable. If you didn't use the *Discount* variable, you'd have to make many changes throughout your code. In other words, if you coded the line that calculated the discounted amount as follows, you'd have to look for every line in your code that calculates discounts and change the discount from 0.35 to another value:

```
DiscountedAmount = 24500 * (1 - 0.35)
```

When you change the value of the *Discount* variable in a single place in your code, the entire program is up-to-date and it will evaluate the proper discount on any amount.

Declaring Variables

In most programming languages, variables must be declared in advance. Historically, the reason for doing this has been to help the compiler generate the most efficient code. If the compiler knows all the variables and their types ahead of time, it can produce the most compact and efficient, or optimized, code. For example, when you tell the compiler that the variable *Discount* will hold a number, the compiler sets aside a certain number of bytes for the *Discount* variable to use.

When programming in VB 2010, you should declare your variables because this is the default mode, and Microsoft recommends this practice strongly. If you attempt to use an undeclared variable in your code, VB 2010 will throw an exception. It will actually catch the error as soon as you type in the line that uses the undeclared variable, underlining it with a wiggly line. It is possible to change the default behavior and use undeclared variables the way most people did with earlier versions of VB, but all the examples in this book use explicitly declared variables. In any case, you're strongly encouraged to declare your variables.

You already know how to declare variables with the Dim statement and the As keyword, which introduces their type:

```
Dim meters As Integer
Dim greetings As String
```

The first variable, *meters*, will store integers, such as 3 or 1,002; the second variable, *greetings*, will store text. You can declare multiple variables of the same or different type in the same line, as follows:

```
Dim Qty As Integer, Amount As Decimal, CardNum As String
```

If you want to declare multiple variables of the same type, you need not repeat the type. Just separate all the variables of the same type with commas and set the type of the last variable:

```
Dim Length, Width, Height As Integer, Volume, Area As Double
```

This statement declares three Integer variables and two Double variables. Double variables hold fractional values (or floating-point values, as they're usually called) that are similar to the Single data type except that they can represent non-integer values with greater accuracy.

An important aspect of variables is their *scope*, a topic that's discussed in more detail later in this chapter. In the meantime, bear in mind that all variables declared with the Dim statement exist in the module in which they were declared. If the variable *Count* is declared in a subroutine (an event handler, for example), it exists only in that subroutine. You can't access it from outside the subroutine. Actually, you can have a *Count* variable in multiple procedures. Each variable is stored locally, and they don't interfere with one another.

VARIABLE-NAMING CONVENTIONS

When declaring variables, you should be aware of a few naming conventions:

◆ A variable's name must begin with a letter or an underscore character, followed by more letters or digits.

◆ It can't contain embedded periods or other special punctuation symbols. The only special character that can appear in a variable's name is the underscore character.

- ◆ It mustn't exceed 1,024 characters.

- ◆ It must be unique within its scope. This means that you can't have two identically named variables in the same subroutine, but you can have a variable named *counter* in many different subroutines.

Variable names are not case sensitive: *myAge*, *myage*, and *MYAGE* all refer to the same variable in your code. Actually, as you enter variable names in your code, the editor converts their casing so that they match their declaration.

VARIABLE INITIALIZATION

Visual Basic allows you to initialize variables in the same line that declares them. The following statement declares an Integer variable and immediately places the value 3,045 in it:

```
Dim distance As Integer = 3045
```

This statement is equivalent to the following two:

```
Dim distance As Integer
distance = 3045
```

It is also possible to declare and initialize multiple variables (of the same or different type) on the same line:

```
Dim quantity As Integer = 1, discount As Single = 0.25
```

Types of Variables

You've learned how to declare variables and that all variables should have a type. But what data types are available? Visual Basic recognizes the following five categories of variables:

- ◆ Numeric
- ◆ String
- ◆ Boolean
- ◆ Date
- ◆ Object

The two major variable categories are numeric and string. Numeric variables store numbers, and string variables store text. Object variables can store any type of data. Why bother to specify the type if one type suits all? On the surface, using object variables might seem like a good idea, but they have their disadvantages. Integer variables are optimized for storing integers, and date variables are optimized for storing dates. Before VB can use an object variable, it must determine its type and perform the necessary conversions. If the variable is declared with a specific type, these conversions are not necessary.

Text is stored in string variables, but numbers can be stored in many formats, depending on the size of the number and its precision. That's why there are many types of numeric variables. The String and Date data types are much richer in terms of the functionality they expose and are discussed in more detail in Chapter 11, "The Framework at Large."

NUMERIC VARIABLES

You'd expect that programming languages would use the same data type for numbers. After all, a number is a number. But this couldn't be further from the truth. All programming languages provide a variety of numeric data types, including the following:

- ◆ Integer (there are several Integer data types)
- ◆ Decimal
- ◆ Single (floating-point numbers with limited precision)
- ◆ Double (floating-point numbers with extreme precision)

Decimal, Single, and Double are the three basic data types for storing floating-point numbers (numbers with a fractional part). The Double data type can represent these numbers more accurately than the Single type and is used almost exclusively in scientific calculations. The Integer data types store whole numbers. The data type of your variable can make a difference in the results of the calculations. The proper variable types are determined by the nature of the values they represent, and the choice of data type is frequently a trade-off between precision and speed of execution (less-precise data types are manipulated faster). Visual Basic supports the numeric data types shown in Table 2.1. In the Data Type column, I show the name of each data type and the corresponding keyword in parentheses.

Integer Variables

There are three types of variables for storing integers, and they differ only in the range of numbers each can represent. As you understand, the more bytes a type takes, the larger values it can hold. The type of Integer variable you'll use depends on the task at hand. You should choose the type that can represent the largest values you anticipate will come up in your calculations. You can go for the Long type, to be safe, but Long variables take up four times as much space as Short variables and it takes the computer longer to process them.

Single- and Double-Precision Numbers

The Single and Double data type names come from single-precision and double-precision numbers. Double-precision numbers are stored internally with greater accuracy than single-precision numbers. In scientific calculations, you need all the precision you can get; in those cases, you should use the Double data type.

The Single and Double data types are approximate; you can't represent any numeric value accurately and precisely with these two data types. The problem stems from the fact that computers must store values in a fixed number of bytes, so some accuracy will be lost. Instead of discussing how computers store numeric values, I will demonstrate the side effects of using the wrong data type with a few examples.

The result of the operation $1 \div 3$ is 0.333333... (an infinite number of the digit 3). You could fill 256 MB of RAM with *3s,* and the result would still be truncated. Here's a simple example that demonstrates the effects of truncation.

In a button's Click event handler, declare two variables as follows:

```
Dim a As Single, b As Double
```

TABLE 2.1:   Visual Basic numeric data types

DATA TYPE	MEMORY REPRESENTATION	STORES
Byte (Byte)	1 byte	Integers in the range 0 to 255.
Signed Byte (SByte)	1 byte	Integers in the range −128 to 127.
Short (Int16)	2 bytes	Integer values in the range −32,768 to 32,767.
Integer (Int32)	4 bytes	Integer values in the range −2,147,483,648 to 2,147,483,647.
Long (Int64)	8 bytes	Integer values in the range −9,223,372,036,854,755,808 to 9,223,372,036,854,755,807.
Unsigned Short (UShort)	2 bytes	Positive integer values in the range 0 to 65,535.
Unsigned Integer (UInteger)	4 bytes	Positive integers in the range 0 to 4,294,967,295.
Unsigned Long (ULong)	8 bytes	Positive integers in the range 0 to 18,446,744,073,709,551,615.
Single Precision (Single)	4 bytes	Single-precision floating-point numbers. A single precision variable can represent negative numbers in the range −3.402823E38 to −1.401298E−45 and positive numbers in the range 1.401298E−45 to 3.402823E38. The value 0 can't be represented precisely (it's a very, very small number, but not exactly 0).
Double Precision (Double)	8 bytes	Double-precision floating-point numbers. A double precision variable can represent negative numbers in the range −1.79769313486232E308 to −4.94065645841247E−324 and positive numbers in the range 4.94065645841247E−324 to 1.79769313486232E308.
Decimal (Decimal)	16 bytes	Integer and floating-point numbers scaled by a factor in the range from 0 to 28. See the description of the Decimal data type for the range of values you can store in it.

Then enter the following statements:

```
a = 1 / 3
Debug.WriteLine(a)
```

Run the application, and you should get the following result in the Output window:

```
.3333333
```

There are seven digits to the right of the decimal point. Break the application by pressing Ctrl+Break and append the following lines to the end of the previous code segment:

```
a = a * 100000
Debug.WriteLine(a)
```

This time, the following value will be printed in the Output window:

```
33333.34
```

The result is not as accurate as you might have expected initially — it isn't even rounded properly. If you divide *a* by 100,000, the result will be as follows:

```
0.3333334
```

This number is different from the number we started with (0.3333333). The initial value was rounded when we multiplied it by 100,000 and stored it in a Single variable. This is an important point in numeric calculations, and it's called *error propagation*. In long sequences of numeric calculations, errors propagate. Even if you can tolerate the error introduced by the Single data type in a single operation, the cumulative errors might be significant.

Let's perform the same operations with double-precision numbers, this time using the variable *b*. Add these lines to the button's Click event handler:

```
b = 1 / 3
Debug.WriteLine(b)
b = b * 100000
Debug.WriteLine(b)
```

This time, the following numbers are displayed in the Output window:

```
0.333333333333333
33333.3333333333
```

The results produced by the double-precision variables are more accurate.

Why are such errors introduced in our calculations? The reason is that computers store numbers internally with two digits: zero and one. This is very convenient for computers because electronics understand two states: on and off. As a matter of fact, all the statements are translated into bits (zeros and ones) before the computer can understand and execute them. The binary numbering system used by computers is not much different from the decimal system we humans use; computers just use fewer digits. We humans use 10 different digits to represent any number, whole or fractional, because we have 10 fingers (in effect, computers count with just two fingers). Just as with the decimal numbering system, in which some numbers can't be precisely represented, there are numbers that can't be represented precisely in the binary system.

Let me give you a more illuminating example. Create a single-precision variable, *a*, and a double-precision variable, *b*, and assign the same value to them:

```
Dim a As Single, b As Double
```

```
a = 0.03007
b = 0.03007
```

Then print their difference:

```
Debug.WriteLine(a-b)
```

If you execute these lines, the result won't be zero! It will be −6.03199004634014E−10. This is a very small number that can also be written as 0.000000000603199004634014. Because different numeric types are stored differently in memory, they don't quite match. What this means to you is that all variables in a calculation should be of the same type.

Eventually, computers will understand mathematical notation and will not convert all numeric expressions into values as they do today. If you multiply the expression 1/3 by 3, the result should be 1. Computers, however, must convert the expression 1/3 into a value before they can multiply it by 3. Because 1/3 can't be represented precisely, the result of the (1/3) × 3 will not be exactly 1. If the variables a and b are declared as Single or Double, the following statements will print 1:

```
a = 3
b = 1 / a
Debug.WriteLine(a * b)
```

If the two variables are declared as Decimal, however, the result will be a number very close to 1 but not exactly 1 (it will be 0.9999999999999999999999999999 — there will be 28 digits after the decimal point). Fortunately, these errors do not surface with typical business-line applications, but you should be aware of truncation errors and how they may affect your calculations. In business applications, we always round our results to two decimal digits and the value 0.999999 of the preceding example will be rounded to 1.00.

The Decimal Data Type

Variables of the Decimal type are stored internally as integers in 16 bytes and are scaled by a power of 10. The scaling power determines the number of decimal digits to the right of the floating point, and it's an integer value from 0 to 28. When the scaling power is 0, the value is multiplied by 10^0, or 1, and it's represented without decimal digits. When the scaling power is 28, the value is divided by 10^{28}(which is 1 followed by 28 zeros — an enormous value), and it's represented with 28 decimal digits.

The largest possible value you can represent with a Decimal value is an integer: 79,228, 162,514,264,337,593,543,950,335. The smallest number you can represent with a Decimal variable is the negative of the same value. These values use a scaling factor of 0. When the scaling factor is 28, the largest value you can represent with a Decimal variable is quite small, actually. It's 7.9228162514264337593543950335 (and the smallest value is the same with a minus sign). This is a very small numeric value (not quite 8), but it's represented with extreme accuracy. The number zero can't be represented precisely with a Decimal variable scaled by a factor of 28. The smallest positive value you can represent with the same scaling factor is 0.00...01 (there are 27 zeros between the decimal period and the digit 1) — an extremely small value, but still not quite zero. The more accuracy you want to achieve with a Decimal variable, the smaller the range of available values you have at your disposal — just as with everything else in life.

When using decimal numbers, the compiler keeps track of the decimal digits (the digits following the decimal point) and treats all values as integers. The value 235.85 is represented as the integer 23585, but the compiler knows that it must scale down the value by 100 when it finishes using it. Scaling down by 100 (that is, 10^2) corresponds to shifting the decimal point by two places. First, the compiler multiplies this value by 100 to make it an integer. Then, it divides it by 100 to restore the original value. Let's say that you want to multiply the following values:

```
328.558 * 12.4051
```

First, the compiler turns them into integers. The compiler remembers that the first number has three decimal digits and the second number has four decimal digits. The result of the multiplication will have seven decimal digits. So the compiler can multiply the following integer values:

```
328558 * 124051
```

It then treats the last seven digits of the result as decimals. The result of the multiplication is 40,757,948,458. The actual value after taking into consideration the decimal digits is 4,075.7948458. This is how the compiler manipulates the Decimal data type.

TYPE CHARACTERS

As I mentioned earlier, the *D* character at the end of a numeric value specifies that the number should be converted into a Decimal value. By default, every value with a fractional part is treated as a Double value because this type can accommodate fractional values with the greatest possible accuracy. Assigning a Double value to a Decimal variable will produce an error if the Strict option is on, so you must specify explicitly that the two values should be converted to the Decimal type. The *D* character at the end of the value is called a type character. Table 2.2 lists all of the type characters that are available in Visual Basic.

TABLE 2.2:   Type characters

TYPE CHARACTER	DESCRIPTION	EXAMPLE
C	Converts value to a Char type	Dim ch As String = "A"c
D or @	Converts value to a Decimal type	Dim price As Decimal = 12.99D
R or #	Converts value to a Double type	Dim pi As Double = 3.14R
I or %	Converts value to an Integer type	Dim count As Integer = 99I
L or &	Converts value to a Long type	Dim distance As Long = 1999L
S	Converts value to a Short type	Dim age As Short = 1S
F or !	Converts value to a Single type	Dim velocity As Single = 74.99F

If you perform the same calculations with Single variables, the result will be truncated (and rounded) to three decimal digits: 4,075.795. Notice that the Decimal data type didn't introduce any rounding errors. It's capable of representing the result with the exact number of decimal digits provided the Decimal type can accommodate both operands and their result. This is the real advantage of Decimals, which makes them ideal for financial applications. For scientific calculations, you must still use Doubles. Decimal numbers are the best choice for calculations that require a specific precision (such as four or eight decimal digits).

INFINITY AND OTHER ODDITIES

The Framework can represent two very special values, which may not be numeric values themselves but are produced by numeric calculations: NaN (not a number) and Infinity. If your calculations produce NaN or Infinity, you should give users a chance to verify their data, or even recode your routines as necessary. For all practical purposes, neither NaN nor Infinity can be used in everyday business calculations.

NOT A NUMBER (NaN)

NaN is not new. Packages such as Wolfram Mathematica and Microsoft Excel have been using it for years. The value NaN indicates that the result of an operation can't be defined: It's not a regular number, not zero, and not infinity. NaN is more of a mathematical concept rather than a value you can use in your calculations. The Log() function, for example, calculates the logarithm of positive values. By definition, you can't calculate the logarithm of a negative value. If the argument you pass to the Log() function is a negative value, the function will return the value NaN to indicate that the calculations produced an invalid result. You may find it annoying that a numeric function returns a non-numeric value, but it's better than if it throws an exception. Even if you don't detect this condition immediately, your calculations will continue and they will all produce NaN values.

Some calculations produce undefined results, such as infinity. Mathematically, the result of dividing any number by zero is infinity. Unfortunately, computers can't represent infinity, so they produce an error when you request a division by zero. Visual Basic will report a special value, which isn't a number: the Infinity value. If you call the ToString method of this value, however, it will return the string Infinity. Let's generate an Infinity value. Start by declaring a Double variable, *dblVar*:

```
Dim dblVar As Double = 999
```

Then divide this value by zero:

```
Dim infVar as Double
infVar = dblVar / 0
```

And display the variable's value:

```
MsgBox(infVar)
```

The string Infinity will appear in a message box. This string is just a description; it tells you that the result is not a valid number (it's a very large number that exceeds the range of numeric values that can be represented with any data type), but it *shouldn't* be used in other calculations. However, you *can* use the Infinity value in arithmetic operations. Certain operations with infinity make sense; others don't. If you add a number to infinity, the result is still infinity (any number, even an arbitrarily large one, can still be increased). If you divide a value by infinity, you'll get the zero value, which also makes sense. If you divide one Infinity value by another Infinity value, you'll get the second odd value, NaN.

Another calculation that will yield a non-number is the division of a very large number by a very small number (a value that's practically zero, but not quite). If the result exceeds the largest value that can be represented with the Double data type, the result is Infinity. Declare three variables as follows:

```
Dim largeVar As Double = 1E299
Dim smallVar As Double = 1E-299
Dim result As Double
```

The notation 1E299 means 10 raised to the power of 299, which is an extremely large number. Likewise, 1E-299 means 10 raised to the power of –299, which is equivalent to dividing 10 by a number as large as 1E299.

Then divide the large variable by the small variable and display the result:

```
result = largeVar / smallVar
MsgBox(result)
```

The result will be Infinity. If you reverse the operands (that is, you divide the very small by the very large variable), the result will be zero. It's not exactly zero, but the Double data type can't accurately represent numeric values that are very, very close (but not equal) to zero.

You can also produce an Infinity value by multiplying a very large (or very small) number by itself many times. But clearly, the most absurd method of generating an Infinity value is to assign the Double.PositiveInfinity or Double.NegativeInfinity value to a variable!

The result of the division 0 / 0, for example, is not a numeric value. If you attempt to enter the statement 0 / 0 in your code, however, VB will catch it even as you type, and you'll get the error message *Division by zero occurs in evaluating this expression.*

To divide zero by zero, set up two variables as follows:

```
Dim var1, var2 As Double
Dim result As Double
var1 = 0
var2 = 0
result = var1 / var2
MsgBox(result)
```

If you execute these statements, the result will be NaN. Any calculations that involve the *result* variable will also yield NaN. The following statements will produce a NaN value:

```
result = result + result
result = 10 / result
```

```
result = result + 1E299
MsgBox(result)
```

If you make *var2* a very small number, such as 1E-299, the result will be zero. If you make *var1* a very small number, the result will be Infinity.

For most practical purposes, Infinity is handled just like NaN. They're both numbers that shouldn't occur in business applications (unless you're projecting the national deficit in the next 50 years), and when they do, it means that you must double-check your code or your data. They are much more likely to surface in scientific calculations, and they must be handled with the statements described in the next section.

Testing for Infinity and NaN

To find out whether the result of an operation is a NaN or Infinity, use the IsNaN and IsInfinity methods of the Single and Double data types. The Integer data type doesn't support these methods, even if it's possible to generate Infinity and NaN results with integers. If the IsInfinity method returns True, you can further examine the sign of the Infinity value with the IsNegativeInfinity and IsPositiveInfinity methods.

In most situations, you'll display a warning and terminate the calculations. The statements of Listing 2.1 do just that. Place these statements in a button's Click event handler and run the application.

LISTING 2.1:   Handling NaN and Infinity values

```
Dim var1, var2 As Double
Dim result As Double
var1 = 0
var2 = 0
result = var1 / var2
If Double.IsInfinity(result) Then
    If Double.IsPositiveInfinity(result) Then
        MsgBox("Encountered a very large number. Can't continue")
    Else
        MsgBox("Encountered a very small number. Can't continue")
    End If
Else
    If Double.IsNaN(result) Then
        MsgBox("Unexpected error in calculations")
    Else
        MsgBox("The result is : " & result.ToString)
    End If
End If
```

This listing will generate a NaN value. Set the value of the *var1* variable to 1 to generate a positive Infinity value or to –1 to generate a negative Infinity value. As you can see, the IsInfinity, IsPositiveInfinity, IsNegativeInfinity, and IsNaN methods require that the variable be passed as an argument.

If you change the values of the *var1* and *var2* variables to the following values and execute the application, you'll get the message *Encountered a very large number*:

```
var1 = 1E+299
var2 = 1E-299
```

If you reverse the values, you'll get the message *Encountered a very small number*. In either case, the program will terminate gracefully and let the user know the type of problem that prevents the completion of the calculations.

BYTE VARIABLES

None of the previous numeric types is stored in a single byte. In some situations, however, data are stored as bytes, and you must be able to access individual bytes. The Byte data type holds an integer in the range of 0 to 255. Bytes are frequently used to access binary files, image and sound files, and so on. To declare a variable as a Byte, use the following statement:

```
Dim n As Byte
```

The variable *n* can be used in numeric calculations too, but you must be careful not to assign the result to another Byte variable if its value might exceed the range of the Byte type. If the variables *A* and *B* are initialized as:

```
Dim A As Byte, B As Byte
A = 233
B = 50
```

the following statement will produce an overflow exception:

```
Debug.WriteLine(A + B)
```

The result (283) can't be stored in a single byte. Visual Basic generates the correct answer, but it can't store it into a Byte variable.

BOOLEAN OPERATIONS WITH BYTES

The operators that won't cause overflows are the Boolean operators And, Or, Not, and Xor, which are frequently used with Byte variables. These aren't logical operators that return True or False; they combine the matching bits in the two operands and return another byte. If you combine the numbers 199 and 200 with the AND operator, the result is 192. The two values in binary format are 11000111 and 11001000. If you perform a bitwise AND operation on these two values, the result is 11000000, which is the decimal value 192.

In addition to the Byte data type, VB 2010 provides a Signed Byte data type, SByte, which can represent signed values in the range from −128 to 127. The bytes starting with the 1 bit represent negative values. The range of positive values is less by one than the range of negative values because the value 0 is considered a positive value (its first bit is 0).

BOOLEAN VARIABLES

The Boolean data type stores True/False values. Boolean variables are, in essence, integers that take the value −1 (for True) and 0 (for False). Actually, any nonzero value is considered True. Boolean variables are declared as

```
Dim failure As Boolean
```

and they are initialized to False. Even so, it's a good practice to initialize your variables explicitly, as in the following code segment. Boolean variables are used in testing conditions, such as the following:

```
Dim failure As Boolean = False
' other statements …
If failure Then MsgBox("Couldn't complete the operation")
```

They are also combined with the logical operators And, Or, Not, and Xor. The Not operator toggles the value of a Boolean variable. The following statement is a toggle:

```
running = Not running
```

If the variable *running* is True, it's reset to False and vice versa. This statement is a shorter way of coding the following:

```
Dim running As Boolean
If running = True Then
    running = False
Else
    running = True
End If
```

Boolean operators operate on Boolean variables and return another Boolean as their result. The following statements will display a message if one (or both) of the variables ReadOnly and Hidden are True (in the following example, the *ReadOnly* and *Hidden* variables might represent the corresponding attributes of a file):

```
If ReadOnly Or Hidden Then
    MsgBox("Couldn't open the file")
Else
    ' statements to open and process file…
End If
```

The condition of the If statement combines the two Boolean values with the Or operator. If one or both of them are True, the final expression is True.

STRING VARIABLES

The String data type stores only text, and string variables are declared as follows:

```
Dim someText As String
```

You can assign any text to the variable *someText*. You can store nearly 2 GB of text in a string variable (that's 2 billion characters, and it's much more text than you care to read on a computer screen). The following assignments are all valid:

```
Dim aString As String
aString = "Now is the time for all good men to come "
             "to the aid of their country"
aString = ""
aString = "There are approximately 25,000 words in this chapter"
aString = "25,000"
```

The second assignment creates an empty string, and the last one creates a string that just happens to contain numerals, which are also characters. The difference between these two variables is that they hold different values:

```
Dim aNumber As Integer = 25000
Dim aString As String = "25,000"
```

The *aString* variable holds the characters 2, 5, comma, 0, 0, and 0, and *aNumber* holds a single numeric value. However, you can use the variable *aString* in numeric calculations and the variable *aNumber* in string operations. VB will perform the necessary conversions as long as the Strict option is off. In general, you should turn on the Strict option because it will help you catch possible runtime errors, as discussed in the section "The Strict, Explicit, and Infer Options." The recommended practice is to convert strings to numbers and numbers to strings explicitly as needed using the methods discussed in the section "Converting Variable Types," later in this chapter. Even if you prefer to work with the Strict option off, which is the default value, it's recommended that you turn it on temporarily to spot any areas in your code that might cause runtime errors.

CHARACTER VARIABLES

Character variables store a single Unicode character in two bytes. In effect, characters are Unsigned Short integers (UInt16), but the Framework provides all the tools you need to work with characters without having to resort to their numeric values (a very common practice for the older among us).

To declare a Character variable, use the Char data type:

```
Dim char1, char2 As Char
```

You can initialize a Char variable by assigning either a character or a string to it. In the latter case, only the first character of the string is assigned to the variable. The following statements will print the characters *a* and *A* to the Output window:

```
Dim char1 As Char = "a", char2 As Char = "ABC"
Debug.WriteLine(char1)
Debug.WriteLine(char2)
```

These statements will work only if the Strict option is off. If it's on, the values assigned to the *char1* and *char2* variables will be marked in error and the code will not compile. To fix the error, change the Dim statement as follows:

```
Dim char1 As Char = "a"c, char2 As Char = "A"c
```

(This tells the compiler to treat the values of the variables as characters, not strings.) When the Strict option is on, you can't assign a string to a Char variable and expect that only the first character of the string will be used.

UNICODE OR ANSI

The Integer values that correspond to the English characters are the ANSI (American National Standards Institute) codes of the equivalent characters. The following statement will print the value 65:

```
Debug.WriteLine(Convert.ToInt32("a"))
```

If you convert the Greek character alpha (α) to an integer, its value is 945. The Unicode value of the famous character π is 960. Unicode and ANSI values for English characters are the same, but all "foreign" characters have a unique Unicode value.

Character variables are used in conjunction with strings. You'll rarely save real data as characters. However, you might have to process the individual characters in a string, one at a time. Let's say the string variable password holds a user's new password, and you require that passwords contain at least one special symbol. The code segment of Listing 2.2 scans the password and rejects it if it contains letters and digits only.

LISTING 2.2:   Processing individual characters

```
Dim password As String, ch As Char
Dim i As Integer
Dim valid As Boolean = False
While Not valid
    password = InputBox("Please enter your password")
    For i = 0 To password.Length - 1
        ch = password.Chars(i)
        If Not Char.IsLetterOrDigit(ch) Then
            valid = True
            Exit For
        End If
    Next
    If valid Then
        MsgBox("You new password will be activated immediately! ")
    Else
        MsgBox("Your password must contain at least one special symbol! ")
    End If
End While
```

If you are not familiar with the If...Then, For...Next, or While...End While structures, you can read their descriptions in the following chapter.

The code prompts the user with an input box to enter a password. The *valid* variable is Boolean and it's initialized to False. (You don't have to initialize a Boolean variable to False because this is its default initial value, but it does make the code easier to read.) It's set to True from within the body of the loop only if the password contains a character that is not a letter or a digit. We set it to False initially, so the While...End While loop will be executed at least once. This loop will keep prompting the user until a valid password is entered.

The For...Next loop scans the string variable *password*, one letter at a time. At each iteration, the next letter is copied into the *ch* variable. The Chars property of the String data type is an array that holds the individual characters in the string (another example of the functionality built into the data types).

Then the program examines the current character. The IsLetterOrDigit method of the Char data type returns True if a character is either a letter or a digit. If the current character is a symbol, the program sets the *valid* variable to True so that the outer loop won't be executed again, and it exits the For...Next loop. Finally, it prints the appropriate message and either prompts for another password or quits.

DATE VARIABLES

Date variables store date values that may include a time part (or not), and they are declared with the Date data type:

```
Dim expiration As Date
```

The following are all valid assignments:

```
expiration = #01/01/2010#
expiration = #8/27/1998 6:29:11 PM#
expiration = "July 2, 2011"
expiration = Today()
```

NOW AND TODAY

By the way, the Today() function returns the current date and time, while the Now() function returns the current date. You can also retrieve the current date by calling the Today property of the Date data type: Date.Today.

The pound sign tells Visual Basic to store a date value to the *expiration* variable, just as the quotes tell Visual Basic that the value is a string. You can store a date as a string to a Date variable, but it will be converted to the appropriate format.

The format of the date inside the pound characters is determined by the regional settings (found in Control Panel). In the United States, the format is *mm/dd/yy*. (In other countries, the format is *dd/mm/yy*.) If you assign an invalid date to a Date variable, such as 23/04/2012, the statement will be underlined and an error message will appear in the Task List window. The description of the error is *Date constant is not valid*.

You can also perform arithmetic operations with date values. VB recognizes your intention to subtract dates and it properly evaluates their difference. The result is a TimeSpan object, which represents a time interval. If you execute the following statements, the value 638.08:49:51.4970000 will appear in the Output window:

```
Dim d1, d2 As Date
d1 = Now
d2 = #1/1/2004#Debug.WriteLine(d1 - d2)
```

The value of the TimeSpan object represents an interval of 638 days, 8 hours, 49 minutes, and 51.497 seconds.

CONVERTING BETWEEN LOCALES

In a global environment like ours, handling dates has gotten a bit complicated. If you live in the United States and you receive a data file that includes dates from a company in the United Kingdom, you should take into consideration the locale of the computer that generated the file. To specify the locale of a date value, use the Parse method of the DateTime class, which accepts two arguments: the date to be parsed and a CultureInfo object that represents the date's locale. (If you find this tip too advanced on first reading, please make a note and look it up when you have to deal with dates in different cultures).

The date 25/12/2011 is a valid UK date, but if you attempt to assign this value to a Date variable (assuming that your computer's locale is English-US), the statement will generate an error. To convert the date to US format, create a CultureInfo that represents the locale of the original date:

```
Dim UK As New CultureInfo("en-GB")
```

Then call the DateTime.Parse method, as follows, to convert the date value to a valid date:

```
Dim D1 As Date
D1 = DateTime.Parse("25/12/2011", UK)
```

The following code segment compares two dates with different locales to one another and prints an appropriate message that indicates whether the two dates are equal (in this example, they are):

```
Dim D1, D2 As Date
Dim UK As New CultureInfo("en-GB")
Dim US As New CultureInfo("en-US")
D1 = DateTime.Parse("27/8/2010", UK)
D2 = DateTime.Parse("8/27/2010", US)
If D1 = D2 Then
    MsgBox("Same date")
Else
    MsgBox("Different dates")
End If
```

Dates like 3/4/2025 or 4/3/2025 are valid in any culture, but they may not be correct unless you interpret them with the proper locale, so be careful when importing dates. You can look up the locales of other countries in the documentation. For example, fr-FR is France's French locale, fr-BE is Belgium's French locale, and fr-CH is Switzerland's French locale. For Switzerland, a culturally diverse place, there's also a German locale, the de-CH locale. The problem of locales is also addressed by XML, which is the definitive standard for data exchange, and it's discussed later in this book in Chapter 13, "XML in Modern Programming," and Chapter 14, "Introduction to LINQ."

You'll face a similar issue with formatted numeric values because some locales use the period as the decimal separator while others use it as a separator for thousands. The two formatted values 19,000.99 and 19.000,99 are valid in different cultures, but they're not the same at once. To properly convert these formatted numbers, use the Parse method of the Decimal or Double class, passing as argument the string to be parsed and the locale of the original value (the US locale for 19,999.99 and the UK locale for 19,999.99). Again, examine the following statements that convert these two formatted numeric strings into numeric values, taking into consideration the proper locale. The statements are equivalent to the ones I showed you earlier for handling dates. For this example, I'll use the Italian language locale; that locale uses the period as the thousands separator and the coma as the decimal separator.

```
Dim val1, val2 As Decimal
Dim IT As New CultureInfo("it-IT")
Dim US As New CultureInfo("en-US")
val1 = System.Decimal.Parse("19,999.99", IT)
val2 = System.Decimal.Parse("19,999.99", US)
If val1 = val2 Then
    MsgBox("Same values")
Else
    MsgBox("Different values")
End If
```

Many developers try to remove the thousands separator(s) from the formatted number and then replace the period with a coma (or vice versa). Use the technique shown here; it will work regardless of the current locale and it's so much easier to read and so much safer.

The Strict, Explicit, and Infer Options

The Visual Basic compiler provides three options that determine how it handles variables:

◆ The Explicit option indicates whether you will declare all variables.

◆ The Strict option indicates whether all variables will be of a specific type.

◆ The Infer option indicates whether the compiler should determine the type of a variable from its value.

These options have a profound effect on the way you declare and use variables, and you should understand what they do. By exploring these settings, you will also understand a little better how the compiler handles variables. It's recommended that you turn on all three, but old VB developers may not want to follow this advice.

VB 2010 doesn't *require* that you declare your variables, but the default behavior is to throw an exception if you attempt to use a variable that hasn't been previously declared. If an undeclared variable's name appears in your code, the editor will underline the variable's name with a wiggly line, indicating that it caught an error. The description of the error will appear in the Task List window below the code window. If you rest the cursor over the segment in question, you will see the description of the error in a ToolTip box.

To change the default behavior, you must insert the following statement at the beginning of the file:

```
Option Explicit Off
```

The `Option Explicit` statement must appear at the very beginning of the file. This setting affects the code in the current module, not in all files of your project or solution. You can turn on the Strict (as well as the Explicit) option for an entire solution. Open the project's properties page (right-click the project's name in Solution Explorer and select Properties), select the Compile tab, and set the Strict and Explicit options accordingly, as shown in Figure 2.1.

FIGURE 2.1
Setting the variable-related options on the project's properties pages

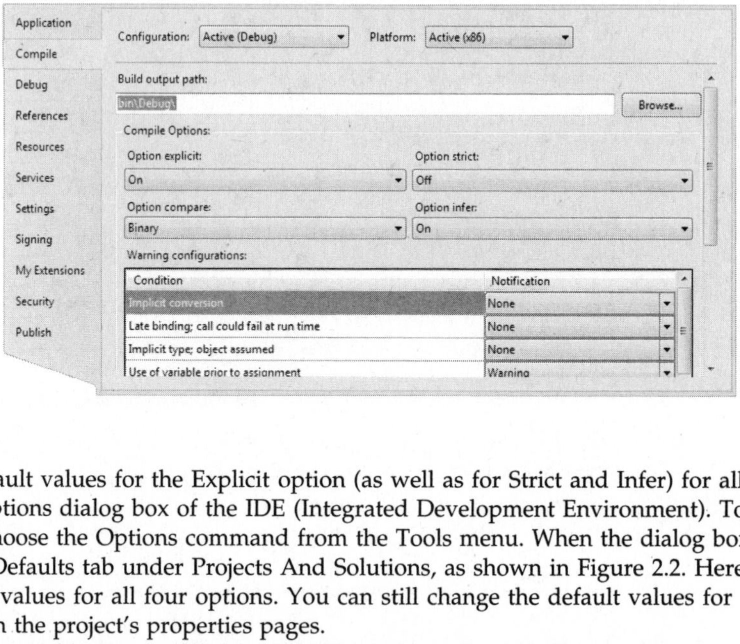

You can also set default values for the Explicit option (as well as for Strict and Infer) for all projects through the Options dialog box of the IDE (Integrated Development Environment). To open this dialog box, choose the Options command from the Tools menu. When the dialog box appears, select the VB Defaults tab under Projects And Solutions, as shown in Figure 2.2. Here you can set the default values for all four options. You can still change the default values for specific projects through the project's properties pages.

The way undeclared variables are handled by VB 2010 is determined by the Explicit and Strict options, which can be either on or off. The Explicit option requires that all variables used in the code are declared before they're used. The Strict option requires that variables are declared with a specific type. In other words, the Strict option disallows the use of generic variables that can store any data type.

The default value of the Explicit statement is On. This is also the recommended value, and you should not make a habit of changing this setting. By setting the Explicit option to Off, you're telling VB that you intend to use variables without declaring them. As a consequence, VB can't make any assumption about the variable's type, so it uses a generic type of variable that can hold any type of information. These variables are called Object variables, and they're equivalent to the old variants.

FIGURE 2.2
Setting the
variable-related options
in the Visual Studio
Options dialog box

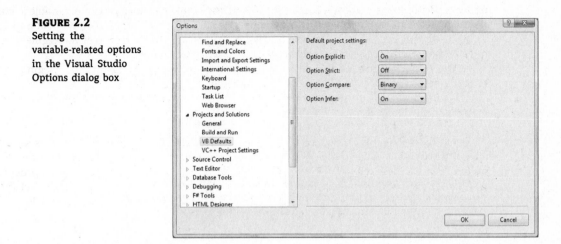

While the option Explicit is set to Off, every time Visual Basic runs into an undeclared variable name, it creates new variable on the spot and uses it. Visual Basic adjusts the variable's type according to the value you assign to it. With Explicit turned off, create two variables, *var1* and *var2*, by referencing them in your code with statements like the following ones:

```
var1 = "Thank you for using Fabulous Software"
var2 = 49.99
```

The *var1* variable is a string variable, and *var2* is a numeric one. You can verify this with the GetType method, which returns a variable's type. The following statements print the highlighted types shown below each statement:

```
Debug.WriteLine "Variable var1 is " & var1.GetType().ToString
```
Variable var1 is System.String
```
Debug.WriteLine "Variable var2 is " & var2.GetType().ToString
```
Variable var2 is System.Double

Later in the same program, you can reverse the assignments:

```
var1 = 49.99
var2 = "Thank you for using Fabulous Software"
```

If you execute the preceding type-checking statements again, you'll see that the types of the variables have changed. The *var1* variable is now a Double, and *var2* is a String. The type of a generic variable is determined by the variable's contents, and it can change in the course of the application. Of course, changing a variable's type at runtime doesn't come without a performance penalty (a small one, but nevertheless some additional statements must be executed).

Another related option is the Strict option, which is off by default. The Strict option tells the compiler whether the variables should be *strictly typed*. A strictly typed (or strongly typed) variable must be declared with a specific type and it can accept values of the same type only.

With the Strict option set to Off, you can use a string variable that holds a number in a numeric calculation:

```
Dim a As String = "25000"
Debug.WriteLine a / 2
```

The last statement will print the value 12500 in the Immediate window. Likewise, you can use numeric variables in string calculations:

```
Dim a As Double = 31.03
a = a + "1"
```

After the execution of the preceding statements, the a variable will still be a Double and will have the value 32.03. If you turn the Strict option on by inserting the following statement at the beginning of the file, you won't be able to mix and match variable types:

```
Option Strict On
```

If you attempt to execute any of the last two code segments while the Strict option is on, the editor will underline a segment of the statement to indicate an error. If you rest the cursor over the underlined segment of the code, the following error message will appear in a tip box:

```
Option strict disallows implicit conversions from String to Double
```

or any type conversion is implied by your code.

When the Strict option is set to On, the compiler will allow some implicit conversions between data types, but not always. For example, it will allow you to assign the value of an integer to a Long, but not the opposite. The Long value might exceed the range of values that can be represented by an Integer variable.

TYPE INFERENCE

One of the trademark features of BASIC, including earlier versions of Visual Basic, was the ability to use variables without declaring them. It has never been a recommended practice, yet VB developers loved it. This feature is coming back to the language, only in a safer manner. VB 2010 allows you to declare variables by assigning values to them. The compiler will infer the type of the variable from its value and will create a variable of the specific type behind the scenes. The following statement creates an Integer variable:

```
Dim count = 2999
```

Behind the scenes, the compiler will create a typed variable with the following statement:

```
Dim count As Integer = 2999
```

To request the variable's type, use the GetType method. This method returns a Type object, which represents the variable's type. The name of the type is given by the ToString property. The following statement will print the highlighted string in the Immediate window:

```
Debug.WriteLine(count.GetType.ToString)
System.Int32
```

The *count* variable is of the Integer type (the 32-bit integer variety, to be precise). If you attempt to assign a value of a different type, such as a date, to this variable later in your code, the editor will underline the value and generate a warning like this: *Value of type 'Date' cannot be converted to Integer*. The compiler has inferred the type of the value assigned initially to the variable and created a variable of the same type. That's why subsequent statements can't change the variable's type. Behind the scenes, the compiler will actually insert a Dim statement, as if you had declared the variable explicitly.

If the Infer option is off, the compiler will handle variables declared without a specific type depending on the Strict option. If the Strict option is off, the compiler will create an Object variable, which can store any value, even values of different types in the course of the application. If the Strict option is on, the compiler will reject the declaration; it will underline the variable's name with a wiggly line and generate the following warning: *Option Strict On requires all variable declarations to have an As clause*.

Object Variables

Variants — variables without a fixed data type — were the bread and butter of VB programmers up to version 6. Variants are the opposite of strictly typed variables: They can store all types of values, such as integers, strings, characters, you name it. If you're starting with VB 2010, you should use strongly typed variables. However, variants are a major part of the history of VB, and most applications out there (the ones you may be called to maintain) use them. I will discuss variants briefly in this section and show you what was so good (and bad) about them.

Variants, or object variables, are the most flexible data type because they can accommodate all other types. A variable declared as Object (or a variable that hasn't been declared at all) is handled by Visual Basic according to the variable's current contents. If you assign an integer value to an object variable, Visual Basic treats it as an integer. If you assign a string to an object variable, Visual Basic treats it as a string. Variants can also hold different data types in the course of the same program. Visual Basic performs the necessary conversions for you.

To declare a variant, you can turn off the Strict option and use the `Dim` statement without specifying a type, as follows:

```
Dim myVar
```

You can use object variables in both numeric and string calculations. Suppose that the variable *modemSpeed* has been declared as Object with one of the following statements:

```
Dim modemSpeed            ' with Option Strict = Off
Dim modemSpeed As Object  ' with Option Strict = On
```

Later in your code, you assign the following value to it:

```
modemSpeed = "28.8"
```
You can treat the *modemSpeed* variable as a string and use it in statements such as the following:

```
MsgBox "We suggest a " & modemSpeed & " modem."
```

This statement displays the following message:

```
"We suggest a 28.8 modem."
```

You can also treat the *modemSpeed* variable as a numeric value, as in the following statement:

```
Debug.WriteLine "A " & modemSpeed & " modem can transfer " &
                 modemSpeed * 1024 / 8 & " bytes per second."
```

This statement displays the following message:

```
"A 28.8 modem can transfer 3686.4 bytes per second."
```

The first instance of the *modemSpeed* variable in the preceding statement is treated as a string because this is the variant's type according to the assignment statement (we assigned a string to it). The second instance, however, is treated as a number (a single-precision number). The compiler sees that it's used in a numeric calculation and converts it to a double value before using it.

Another example of this behavior of variants can be seen in the following statements:

```
Dim I, S
I = 10
S = "11"
Debug.WriteLine(I + S)
Debug.WriteLine(I & S)
```

The first `WriteLine` statement will display the numeric value **21**, whereas the second statement will print the string **1011**. The plus operator (+) tells VB to add two values. In doing so, VB must convert the two strings into numeric values and then add them. The concatenation operator (&) tells VB to concatenate the two strings.

Visual Basic knows how to handle object variables in a way that makes sense. The result may not be what you had in mind, but it certainly is dictated by common sense. If you really want to concatenate the strings 10 and 11, you should use the concatenation operator (&), which tells Visual Basic exactly what to do. Quite impressive, but for many programmers, this is a strange behavior that can lead to subtle errors — and they avoid it. Keep in mind that if the value of the S variable were the string A1, then the code would compile fine but would crash at runtime. And this is what we want to avoid at all costs: an application that compiles without warnings but crashes at runtime. Using strongly typed variables is one of the precautions you can take to avoid runtime errors. Keep in mind that a program that prompts users for data, or reads it from a file, may work for quite a while, just because it's reading valid data, and crash when it encounters invalid data. It's up to you to decide whether to use variants and how far you will go with them. Sure, you can perform tricks with variants, but you shouldn't overuse them to the point that others can't read your code.

Variables as Objects

Variables in Visual Basic are more than just names or placeholders for values. They're intelligent entities that can not only store but also process their values. I don't mean to scare you, but I think you should be told: VB variables are objects. And here's why: A variable that holds dates is declared as such with the following statement:

```
Dim expiration As Date
```

To assign a date value to the *expiration* variable, use a statement like this:

```
expiration = #1/1/2003#
```

So far, nothing out of the ordinary; this is how we always used variables, in most languages. In addition to holding a date, however, the *expiration* variable can manipulate dates. The following expression will return a new date that's three years ahead of the date stored in the expiration variable:

```
expiration.AddYears(3)
```

The AddYears method returns a new date, which you can assign to another date variable:

```
Dim newExpiration As Date
newExpiration = expiration.AddYears(3)
```

AddYears is a method that knows how to add a number of years to a Date variable. By adding a number of years (or months, or days) to a date, we get back another date. The method will take into consideration the number of days in each month and the leap years, which is a totally nontrivial task if we had to code it ourselves. There are similarly named methods for adding months, days, and so on. In addition to methods, the Date type exposes properties, such as the Month and Day properties, which return the date's month and day number, respectively. The keywords following the period after the variable's name are called *methods* and *properties*, just like the properties and methods of the controls you place on a form to create your application's visual interface. The methods and properties (or the *members*) of a variable expose the functionality that's built into the class representing the variable itself. Without this built-in functionality, you'd have to write some serious code to extract the month from a date variable, to add a number of days to a given date, to figure out whether a character is a letter or a digit or a punctuation symbol, and so on. Much of the functionality that you'll need in an application that manipulates dates, numbers, or text has already been built into the variables themselves.

Don't let the terminology scare you. Think of variables as placeholders for values and access their functionality with expressions like the ones shown earlier. Start using variables to store values, and if you need to process them, enter a variable's name followed by a period to see a list of the members it exposes. In most cases, you'll be able to figure out what these members do by just reading their names. I'll come back to the concept of variables as objects, but I wanted to hit it right off the bat. A more detailed discussion of the notion of variables as objects can be found in Chapter 8, "Working with Objects," which discusses objects in detail.

BASIC DATA TYPES VERSUS OBJECTS

Programming languages can treat simple variables much more efficiently than they treat objects. An integer takes two bytes in memory, and the compiler will generate very efficient code to manipulate an integer variable (add it to another numeric value, compare it to another integer, and so on). If you declare an integer variable and use it in your code as such, Visual Basic doesn't create an object to represent this value. It creates a new variable for storing integers, like good old BASIC. After you call one of the variable's methods, the compiler emits code to create the actual object. This process is called *boxing*, and it introduces a small delay, which is truly insignificant compared to the convenience of manipulating a variable through its methods.

As you've seen by now, variables are objects. This shouldn't come as a surprise, but it's an odd concept for programmers with no experience in object-oriented programming. We haven't covered objects and classes formally yet, but you have a good idea of what an object is. It's an entity that exposes some functionality by means of properties and methods. The TextBox control is an object and it exposes the Text property, which allows you to read or set the text on the control. Any name followed by a period and another name signifies an object. The name after the period is a property or method of the object.

Converting Variable Types

In many situations, you will need to convert variables from one type into another. Table 2.3 shows the methods of the Convert class that perform data-type conversions.

TABLE 2.3:   The data-type conversion methods of the Convert class

METHOD	CONVERTS ITS ARGUMENT TO
ToBoolean	Boolean
ToByte	Byte
ToChar	Unicode character
ToDateTime	Date
ToDecimal	Decimal
ToDouble	Double
ToInt16	Short Integer (2-byte integer, Int16)
ToInt32	Integer (4-byte integer, Int32)
ToInt64	Long (8-byte integer, Int64)
ToSByte	Signed Byte
CShort	Short (2-byte integer, Int16)
ToSingle	Single
ToString	String
ToUInt16	Unsigned Integer (2-byte integer, Int16)
ToUInt32	Unsigned Integer (4-byte integer, Int32)
ToUInt64	Unsigned Long (8-byte integer, Int64)

In addition to the methods of the Convert class, you can still use the data-conversion functions of VB (CInt() to convert a numeric value to an Integer, CDbl() to convert a numeric value to a Double, CSng() to convert a numeric value to a Single, and so on), which you can look up in the documentation. If you're writing new applications in VB 2010, use the new Convert class to convert between data types.

To convert the variable initialized as

```
Dim A As Integer
```

to a Double, use the ToDouble method of the Convert class:

```
Dim B As Double
B = Convert.ToDouble(A)
```

Suppose you have declared two integers, as follows:

```
Dim A As Integer, B As Integer
A = 23
B = 7
```

The result of the operation A / B will be a Double value. The statement

```
Debug.Write(A / B)
```

displays the value 3.28571428571429. The result is a Double value, which provides the greatest possible accuracy. If you attempt to assign the result to a variable that hasn't been declared as Double and the Strict option is on, the editor will generate an error message. No other data type can accept this value without loss of accuracy. To store the result to a Single variable, you must convert it explicitly with a statement like the following:

```
Dim C As Single = Convert.ToSingle(A / B)
```

You can also use the DirectCast() function to convert a variable or expression from one type to another. The DirectCast() function is identical to the CType() function. Let's say the variable *A* has been declared as String and holds the value 34.56. The following statement converts the value of the *A* variable to a Decimal value and uses it in a calculation:

```
Dim A As String = "34.56"
Dim B As Double
B = DirectCast(A, Double) / 1.14
```

The conversion is necessary only if the Strict option is on, but it's a good practice to perform your conversions explicitly. The following section explains what might happen if your code relies on implicit conversions.

WIDENING AND NARROWING CONVERSIONS

In some situations, VB 2010 will convert data types automatically, but not always. Let's say you have declared and initialized two variables, an Integer and a Double, with the following statements:

```
Dim count As Integer = 99
Dim pi As Double = 3.1415926535897931
```

If the Strict option is off and you assign the variable *pi* to the *count* variable, the *count* variable's new value will be 3. (The Double value will be rounded to an Integer value, according to the variable's type.) Although this may be what you want, in most cases it's an oversight that will lead to incorrect results.

If the Strict option is on and you attempt to perform the same assignment, the compiler will generate an error message to the effect that you can't convert a Double to an Integer. The exact message is *Option Strict disallows implicit conversions from Double to Integer*.

When the Strict option is on, VB 2010 will allow conversions that do not result in loss of accuracy (precision) or magnitude. These conversions are called *widening conversions*. When you assign an Integer value to a Double variable, no accuracy or magnitude is lost. This is a widening conversion because it goes from a narrower to a wider type and will therefore be allowed when Strict is on.

On the other hand, when you assign a Double value to an Integer variable, some accuracy could be lost (the decimal digits may be truncated). This is a *narrowing conversion* because we go from a data type that can represent a wider range of values to a data type that can represent a narrower range of values. With the Strict option on, such a conversion will not be allowed.

Because you, the programmer, are in control, you might want to give up the accuracy — presumably, it's no longer needed. Table 2.4 summarizes the widening conversions that VB 2010 will perform for you automatically.

TABLE 2.4:   VB 2010 widening conversions

ORIGINAL DATA TYPE	WIDER DATA TYPE
Any type	Object
Byte	Short, Integer, Long, Decimal, Single, Double
Short	Integer, Long, Decimal, Single, Double
Integer	Long, Decimal, Single, Double
Long	Decimal, Single, Double
Decimal	Single, Double
Single	Double
Double	None
Char	String

If the Strict option is on, the compiler will point out all the statements that may cause run-time errors and you can reevaluate your choice of variable types. Even if you're working with the Strict option off, you can turn it on momentarily to see the compiler's warnings and then turn it off again.

Formatting Numbers

So far, you've seen how to use the basic data types. Let me digress here for a moment and mention that the basic data types are no longer part of the language (Visual Basic or C#). They're actually part of the Common Language Runtime (CLR), which is a basic component of Visual Studio (actually, it's the core of Visual Studio and it's shared by all languages that can be used with Visual Studio). You can treat this note as fine print for now, but don't be surprised when you read in the documentation that the basic data types are part of the CLR. All data types expose a ToString method, which returns the variable's value (a number or date) as a string so that it can be used with other strings in your code. The ToString method formats numbers and dates in many ways, and it's probably one of the most commonly used methods. You can call the ToString method without any arguments, as we have done so far, to convert any value to a string. With many types, the ToString method, however, accepts an optional argument, which determines how the value will be formatted as a string. For example, you can format a number as currency by prefixing it with the appropriate symbol (such as the dollar symbol) and displaying it with two decimal digits, and you can display dates in many formats. Some reports require that negative amounts are enclosed in parentheses. The ToString method allows you to display numbers and dates, and any other type, in any way you wish.

Notice that ToString is a method, not a property. It returns a value that you can assign to a string variable or pass as arguments to a function such as MsgBox(), but the original value is not affected. The ToString method can also format a value if called with an optional argument:

```
ToString(formatString)
```

The *formatString* argument is a format specifier (a string that specifies the exact format to be applied to the variable). This argument can be a specific character that corresponds to a pre-determined format (a standard format string, as it's called) or a string of characters that have special meaning in formatting numeric values (a picture format string). Use standard format strings for the most common formatting options, and use picture strings to specify unusual formatting requirements. To format the value 9959.95 as a dollar amount, you can use the C format specifier, which stands for *Currency*:

```
Dim Amnt As Single = 9959.95
Dim strAmnt As String
strAmnt = Amnt.ToString("C")
```

Or use the following picture numeric format string:

```
strAmnt = Amnt.ToString("$#,###.00")
```

Both statements will format the value as $9,959.95. If you're using a non-U.S. version of Windows, the currency symbol will change accordingly. If you're in the United States, use the Regional And Language Options tool in Control Panel to temporarily change the current culture to a European one and the amount will be formatted with the Euro sign.

The picture format string is made up of literals and characters that have special meaning in formatting. The dollar sign has no special meaning and will appear as is. The # symbol is a digit placeholder; all # symbols will be replaced by numeric digits, starting from the right. If the number has fewer digits than specified in the string, the extra symbols to the left will be ignored. The comma tells the ToString method to insert a comma between thousands. The period is the decimal point, which is followed by two more digit placeholders. Unlike the # sign, the 0 is a special placeholder: If there are not enough digits in the number for all the zeros you've specified, a 0 will appear in the place of the missing decimal digits. If the original value had been 9959.9, for example, the last statement would have formatted it as $9,959.90. If you used the # placeholder instead, the string returned by the ToString method would have a single decimal digit.

STANDARD NUMERIC FORMAT STRINGS

The ToString method of the numeric data types recognizes the standard numeric format strings shown in Table 2.5.

The format character can be followed by an integer. If present, the integer value specifies the number of decimal places that are displayed. The default accuracy is two decimal digits.

TABLE 2.5:   Standard numeric format strings

FORMAT CHARACTER	DESCRIPTION	EXAMPLE
C or c	Currency	(12345.67).ToString("C") returns $12,345.67.
D or d	Decimal	(123456789).ToString("D") returns 123456789. It works with integer values only.
E or e	Scientific format	(12345.67).ToString("E") returns 1.234567E + 004.
F or f	Fixed-point format	(12345.67).ToString("F") returns 12345.67.
G or g	General format	Returns a value either in fixed-point or scientific format.
N or n	Number format	(12345.67).ToString("N") returns 12,345.67.
P or p	Percentage	(0.12345).ToString("N") returns 12.35%.
R or r	Round-trip	(1 / 3).ToString("R") returns 0.33333333333333331 (where the G specifier would return a value with fewer decimal digits: 0.333333333333333).
X or x	Hexadecimal format	250.ToString("X") returns FA.

The C format string causes the ToString method to return a string representing the number as a currency value. An integer following the C determines the number of decimal digits that are displayed. If no number is provided, two digits are shown after the decimal separator. Assuming that the variable *value* has been declared as Decimal and its value is 5596, then the expression value.ToString("C") will return the string $5,596.00. If the value of the variable were 5596.4499, then the expression value.ToString("C3") would return the string $5,596.450. Also note that the C format string formats negative amounts in a pair of parentheses, as is customary in business applications.

Notice that not all format strings apply to all data types. For example, only integer values can be converted to hexadecimal format, and the D format string works with integer values only.

PICTURE NUMERIC FORMAT STRINGS

If the format characters listed in Table 2.5 are not adequate for the control you need over the appearance of numeric values, you can provide your own picture format strings. Picture format strings contain special characters that allow you to format your values exactly as you like. Table 2.6 lists the picture formatting characters.

TABLE 2.6: Picture numeric format strings

FORMAT CHARACTER	DESCRIPTION	EFFECT
0	Display zero placeholder	Results in a nonsignificant zero if a number has fewer digits than there are zeros in the format
#	Display digit placeholder	Replaces the symbol with only significant digits
.	Decimal point	Displays a period (.) character
,	Group separator	Separates number groups — for example, 1,000
%	Percent notation	Displays a % character
E + 0, E − 0, e + 0, e − 0	Exponent notation	Formats the output of exponent notation
\	Literal character	Used with traditional formatting sequences such as \n (newline)
""	Literal string	Displays any string within single or double quotation marks literally
;	Section separator	Specifies different output if the numeric value to be formatted is positive, negative, or zero

The following statements will print the highlighted values:

```
Dim Amount As Decimal = 42492.45
Debug.WriteLine(Amount.ToString("$#,###.00"))
$42,492.45
Amount = 0.2678
Debug.WriteLine(Amount.ToString("0.000"))
0.268
Amount = -24.95
Debug.WriteLine(Amount.ToString("$#,###.00;($#,###.00)"))
($24.95)
```

User-Defined Data Types

In the previous sections, we used variables to store individual values (or scalar values, as they're called). As a matter of fact, most programs store sets of data of different types. For example, a program for balancing your checkbook must store several pieces of information for each check: the check's number, amount, date, and so on. All these pieces of information are necessary to process the checks, and ideally, they should be stored together.

What we need is a variable that can hold multiple related values of the same or different type. You can create custom data types that are made up of multiple values using Structures. A Structure allows you to combine multiple values of the basic data types and handle them as a whole. For example, each check in a checkbook-balancing application is stored in a separate Structure (or record), as shown in Figure 2.3. When you recall a given check, you need all the information stored in the Structure.

FIGURE 2.3
Pictorial representation
of a structure

Record Structure

Check Number	Check Date	Check Amount	Check Paid To

Array of Records

Check Number	Check Date	Check Amount	Check Paid To
275	11/04/2010	104.25	Gas Co.
276	11/09/2010	48.76	Books
277	11/12/2010	200.00	VISA
278	11/21/2010	631.50	Rent

To define a Structure in VB 2010, use the Structure statement, which has the following syntax:

```
Structure structureName
    Dim variable1 As varType
    Dim variable2 As varType
    ...
    Dim variablen As varType
End Structure
```

varType can be any of the data types supported by the CLR or the name of another Structure that has been defined already. The Dim statement can be replaced by the Private or Public access modifiers. For Structures, Dim is equivalent to Public.

After this declaration, you have in essence created a new data type that you can use in your application. *structureName* can be used anywhere you'd use any of the base types (Integers, Doubles, and so on). You can declare variables of this type and manipulate them as you manipulate all other variables (with a little extra typing). The declaration for the CheckRecord Structure shown in Figure 2.3 is as follows:

```
Structure CheckRecord
    Dim CheckNumber As Integer
    Dim CheckDate As Date
    Dim CheckAmount As Single
    Dim CheckPaidTo As String
End Structure
```

This declaration must appear outside any procedure; you can't declare a Structure in a subroutine or function. Once declared, the CheckRecord Structure becomes a new data type for your application.

To declare variables of this new type, use a statement such as this one:

```
Dim check1 As CheckRecord, check2 As CheckRecord
```

To assign a value to one of these variables, you must separately assign a value to each one of its components (they are called fields), which can be accessed by combining the name of the variable and the name of a field separated by a period, as follows:

```
check1.CheckNumber = 275
```

Actually, as soon as you type the period following the variable's name, a list of all members to the CheckRecord Structure will appear, as shown in Figure 2.4. Notice that the Structure supports a few members on its own. You didn't write any code for the Equals, GetType, and ToString members, but they're standard members of any Structure object, and you can use them in your code. Both the GetType and ToString methods will return a string like ProjectName.FormName + CheckRecord. You can provide your own implementation of the ToString method, which will return a more meaningful string:

```
Public Overrides Function ToString() As String
    Return "CHECK # " & CheckNumber & " FOR " & CheckAmount.ToString("C")
End Function
```

I haven't discusses the Overrides keyword yet; it tells the compiler to override the default implementation of the ToString method. For the time being, use it as shown here to create your custom ToString method. This, as well as other object-related terms, are discussed in detail in Chapter 8.

As you understand, Structures are a lot like objects that expose their fields as properties and then expose a few members of their own. The following statements initialize a variable of the CheckRecord type:

```
check2.CheckNumber = 275
check2.CheckDate = #09/12/2010#
```

```
check2.CheckAmount = 104.25
check2.CheckPaidTo = "Gas Co."
```

FIGURE 2.4
Variables of custom types expose their members as properties.

Examining Variable Types

Besides setting the types of variables and the functions for converting between types, Visual Basic provides the `GetType` method. `GetType` returns a string containing the name of the variable type (`Int32`, `Decimal`, and so on). All variables expose this method automatically, and you can call it like this:

```
Dim var As Double
Debug.WriteLine "The variable's type is " & var.GetType.ToString
```

There's also a `GetType` operator, which accepts as an argument a type and returns a Type object for the specific data type. The `GetType` method and `GetType` operator are used mostly in `If` structures, like the following one:

```
If var.GetType() Is GetType(Double) Then
    ' code to handle a Double value
End If
```

Notice that the code doesn't reference data type names directly. Instead, it uses the value returned by the `GetType` operator to retrieve the type of the class System.Double and then compares this value to the variable's type with the `Is` (or the `IsNot`) keyword. If you attempt to express this comparison with the equals operator (=), the editor will detect the error and suggest that you use the Is operator. This syntax is a bit arcane for BASIC developers; just make a note, and when you need to find out a variable's type in your application, use it as is.

IS IT A NUMBER, STRING, OR DATE?

Another set of Visual Basic functions returns variable data types, but not the exact type. They return a True/False value indicating whether a variable holds a numeric value, a date, or an array. The following functions are used to validate user input, as well as data stored in files, before you process them.

IsNumeric() Returns True if its argument is a number (Short, Integer, Long, Single, Double, Decimal). Use this function to determine whether a variable holds a numeric value before passing it to a procedure that expects a numeric value or before processing it as a number. The following statements keep prompting the user with an InputBox for a numeric value. The user must enter a numeric value or click the Cancel button to exit. As long as the user enters non-numeric values, the InputBox keeps popping up and prompting for a numeric value:

```
Dim strAge as String = ""
Dim Age As Integer
While Not IsNumeric(strAge)
    strAge = InputBox("lease enter your age")
End While
Age = Convert.ToInt16(strAge)
```

The variable *strAge* is initialized to a non-numeric value so that the While...End While loop will be executed at least once.

IsDate() Returns True if its argument is a valid date (or time). The following expressions return True because they all represent valid dates:

```
IsDate(#10/12/2010#)
IsDate("10/12/2010")
IsDate("October 12, 2010")
```

IsArray() Returns True if its argument is an array.

A Variable's Scope

In addition to a type, a variable has a scope. The scope (or visibility) of a variable is the section of the application that can see and manipulate the variable. If a variable is declared within a procedure, only the code in the specific procedure has access to that variable; the variable doesn't exist for the rest of the application. When the variable's scope is limited to a procedure, it's called local.

Suppose that you're coding the handler for the Click event of a button to calculate the sum of all even numbers in the range 0 to 100. One possible implementation is shown in Listing 2.3.

LISTING 2.3:   Summing even numbers

```
Private Sub Button1_Click(ByVal sender As Object, _
             ByVal e As System.EventArguments) _
             Handles Button1.Click
    Dim i As Integer
    Dim Sum As Integer = 0
    For i = 0 to 100 Step 2
        Sum = Sum + i
    Next
    MsgBox "The sum is " & Sum.ToString
End Sub
```

The variables *i* and *Sum* are local to the Button1_Click() procedure. If you attempt to set the value of the *Sum* variable from within another procedure, Visual Basic will complain that the variable hasn't been declared. (Or, if you have turned off the Explicit option, it will create another *Sum* variable, initialize it to zero, and then use it. But this won't affect the variable *Sum* in the Button1_Click() subroutine.) The *Sum* variable is said to have procedure-level scope; it's visible within the procedure and invisible outside the procedure.

Sometimes, however, you'll need to use a variable with a broader scope: a variable that's available to all procedures within the same file. This variable, which must be declared outside any procedure, is said to have a module-level scope. In principle, you could declare all variables outside the procedures that use them, but this would lead to problems. Every procedure in the file would have access to any variable, and you would need to be extremely careful not to change the value of a variable without good reason. Variables that are needed by a single procedure (such as loop counters) should be declared in that procedure.

Another type of scope is the block-level scope. Variables introduced in a block of code, such as an If statement or a loop, are local to the block but invisible outside the block. Let's revise the previous code segment so that it calculates the sum of squares. To carry out the calculation, we first compute the square of each value and then sum the squares. The square of each value is stored to a variable that won't be used outside the loop, so we can define the *sqrValue* variable in the loop's block and make it local to this specific loop, as shown in Listing 2.4.

LISTING 2.4:   A variable scoped in its own block

```
Private Sub Button1_Click(ByVal sender As Object, _
             ByVal e As System.EventArguments) _
             Handles Button1.Click
    Dim i, Sum As Integer
    For i = 0 to 100 Step 2
        Dim sqrValue As Integer
        sqrValue = i * i
        Sum = Sum + sqrValue
    Next
    MsgBox "The sum of the squares is " & Sum
End Sub
```

The *sqrValue* variable is not visible outside the block of the For...Next loop. If you attempt to use it before the For statement or after the Next statement, the code won't compile.

The *sqrValue* variable maintains its value between iterations. The block-level variable is not initialized at each iteration, even though there's a Dim statement in the loop.

Finally, in some situations, the entire application must access a certain variable. In this case, the variable must be declared as Public. Public variables have a global scope; they are visible from any part of the application. To declare a public variable, use a Public statement in place of a Dim statement. Moreover, you can't declare public variables in a procedure. If you have multiple forms in your application and you want the code in one form to see a certain variable in another form, you can use the Public modifier.

So, why do we need so many types of scope? You'll develop a better understanding of scope and which type of scope to use for each variable as you get involved in larger projects. In general, you should try to limit the scope of your variables as much as possible. If all variables were declared within procedures, you could use the same name for storing a temporary value in each procedure and be sure that one procedure's variables wouldn't interfere with those of another procedure, even if you use the same name.

A Variable's Lifetime

In addition to type and scope, variables have a lifetime, which is the period for which they retain their value. Variables declared as Public exist for the lifetime of the application. Local variables, declared within procedures with the Dim or Private statement, live as long as the procedure. When the procedure finishes, the local variables cease to exist, and the allocated memory is returned to the system. Of course, the same procedure can be called again, and then the local variables are re-created and initialized again. If a procedure calls another, its local variables retain their values while the called procedure is running.

You also can force a local variable to preserve its value between procedure calls by using the Static keyword. Suppose that the user of your application can enter numeric values at any time. One of the tasks performed by the application is to track the average of the numeric values. Instead of adding all the values each time the user adds a new value and dividing by the count, you can keep a running total with the function RunningAvg(), which is shown in Listing 2.5.

LISTING 2.5:   Calculations with global variables

```
Function RunningAvg(ByVal newValue As Double) As Double
    CurrentTotal = CurrentTotal + newValue
    TotalItems = TotalItems + 1
    RunningAvg = CurrentTotal / TotalItems
End Function
```

You must declare the variables *CurrentTotal* and *TotalItems* outside the function so that their values are preserved between calls. Alternatively, you can declare them in the function with the Static keyword, as shown in Listing 2.6.

LISTING 2.6:   Calculations with local Static variables

```
Function RunningAvg(ByVal newValue As Double) As Double
    Static CurrentTotal As Double
```

```
    Static TotalItems As Integer
    CurrentTotal = CurrentTotal + newValue
    TotalItems = TotalItems + 1
    RunningAvg = CurrentTotal / TotalItems
End Function
```

The advantage of using static variables is that they help you minimize the number of total variables in the application. All you need is the running average, which the RunningAvg() function provides without making its variables visible to the rest of the application. Therefore, you don't risk changing the variable values from within other procedures.

Variables declared in a form module outside any procedure take effect when the form is loaded and cease to exist when the form is unloaded. If the form is loaded again, its variables are initialized as if it's being loaded for the first time.

Variables are initialized when they're declared, according to their type. Numeric variables are initialized to zero, string variables are initialized to a blank string, and object variables are initialized to Nothing.

Constants

Some variables don't change value during the execution of a program. These variables are constants that appear many times in your code. For instance, if your program does math calculations, the value of pi (3.14159...) might appear many times. Instead of typing the value 3.14159 over and over again, you can define a constant, name it pi, and use the name of the constant in your code. The statement

```
circumference = 2 * pi * radius
```

is much easier to understand than the equivalent

```
circumference = 2 * 3.14159 * radius
```

The manner in which you declare constants is similar to the manner in which you declare variables except that you use the Const keyword, and in addition to supplying the constant's name, you must also supply a value, as follows:

```
Const constantname As type = value
```

Constants also have a scope and can be Public or Private. The constant *pi*, for instance, is usually declared in a module as Public so that every procedure can access it:

```
Public Const pi As Double = 3.14159265358979
```

The rules for naming variables also apply to naming constants. The constant's value is a literal value or a simple expression composed of numeric or string constants and operators. You can't use functions in declaring constants. By the way, the specific value I used for this example need not be stored in a constant. Use the pi member of the Math class instead (Math.pi).

Arrays

A standard structure for storing data in any programming language is the array. Whereas individual variables can hold single entities, such as one number, one date, or one string, arrays can hold sets of data of the same type (a set of numbers, a series of dates, and so on). An array has a name, as does a variable, and the values stored in it can be accessed by a number or index.

For example, you could use the variable *Salary* to store a person's salary:

```
Salary = 34000
```

But what if you wanted to store the salaries of 16 employees? You could either declare 16 variables — *Salary1*, *Salary2*, and so on up to *Salary16* — or declare an array with 16 elements. An array is similar to a variable: It has a name and multiple values. Each value is identified by an index (an integer value) that follows the array's name in parentheses. Each different value is an element of the array. If the array *Salaries* holds the salaries of 16 employees, the element *Salaries(0)* holds the salary of the first employee, the element *Salaries(1)* holds the salary of the second employee, and so on up to the element *Salaries(15)*. Yes, the default indexing of arrays starts at zero, as odd as it may be for traditional BASIC developers.

Declaring Arrays

Arrays must be declared with the Dim (or Public) statement followed by the name of the array and the index of the last element in the array in parentheses, as in this example:

```
Dim Salary(15) As Integer
```

Salary is the name of an array that holds 16 values (the salaries of the 16 employees) with indices ranging from 0 to 15. *Salary(0)* is the first person's salary, *Salary(1)* the second person's salary, and so on. All you have to do is remember who corresponds to each salary, but even this data can be handled by another array. To do this, you'd declare another array of 16 elements:

```
Dim Names(15) As String
```

Then assign values to the elements of both arrays:

```
Names(0) = "Joe Doe"
Salary(0) = 34000
Names(1) = "Beth York"
Salary(1) = 62000
...
Names(15) = "Peter Smack"
Salary(15) = 10300
```

This structure is more compact and more convenient than having to hard-code the names of employees and their salaries in variables.

All elements in an array have the same data type. Of course, when the data type is Object, the individual elements can contain different kinds of data (objects, strings, numbers, and so on).

Arrays, like variables, are not limited to the basic data types. You can declare arrays that hold any type of data, including objects. The following array holds colors, which can be used later in the code as arguments to the various functions that draw shapes:

```
Dim colors(2) As Color
colors(0) = Color.BurlyWood
colors(1) = Color.AliceBlue
colors(2) = Color.Sienna
```

The Color class represents colors, and among the properties it exposes are the names of the colors it recognizes.

A better technique for storing names and salaries is to create a structure and then declare an array of this type. The following structure holds names and salaries:

```
Structure Employee
    Dim Name As String
    Dim Salary As Decimal
End Structure
```

Insert this declaration in a form's code file, outside any procedure. Then create an array of the Employee type:

```
Dim Emps(15) As Employee
```

Each element in the *Emps* array exposes two fields, and you can assign values to them by using statements such as the following:

```
Emps(2).Name = "Beth York"
Emps(2).Salary = 62000
```

The advantage of using an array of structures instead of multiple arrays is that the related information will always be located under the same index. The code is more compact, and you need not maintain multiple arrays.

Initializing Arrays

Just as you can initialize variables in the same line in which you declare them, you can initialize arrays, too, with the following constructor (an array initializer, as it's called):

```
Dim nameArray() As type = {entry0, entry1, … entryN}
```

Here's an example that initializes an array of strings:

```
Dim Names() As String = {"Joe Doe", "Peter Smack"}
```

This statement is equivalent to the following statements, which declare an array with two elements and then set their values:

```
Dim Names(1) As String
```

```
Names(0) = "Joe Doe"
Names(1) = "Peter Smack"
```

The number of elements in the curly brackets following the array's declaration determines the dimensions of the array, and you can't add new elements to the array without resizing it. If you need to resize the array in your code dynamically, you must use the ReDim statement and supply the new size of the array in parentheses.

ARRAY LIMITS

The first element of an array has index 0. The number that appears in parentheses in the Dim statement is one fewer than the array's total capacity and is the array's upper limit (or upper bound). The index of the last element of an array (its upper bound) is given by the method GetUpperBound, which accepts as an argument the dimension of the array and returns the upper bound for this dimension. The arrays we have examined so far are one-dimensional, and the argument to be passed to the GetUpperBound method is the value 0. The total number of elements in the array is given by the method GetLength, which also accepts a dimension as an argument. The upper bound of the following array is 19, and the capacity of the array is 20 elements:

```
Dim Names(19) As Integer
```

The first element is *Names(0)*, and the last is *Names(19)*. If you execute the following statements, the highlighted values will appear in the Output window:

```
Debug.WriteLine(Names.GetLowerBound(0))
0
Debug.WriteLine(Names.GetUpperBound(0))
19
```

To assign a value to the first and last element of the *Names* array, use the following statements:

```
Names(0) = "First entry"
Names(19) = "Last entry"
```

To iterate through the array elements, use a loop like the following one:

```
Dim i As Integer, myArray(19) As Integer
For i = 0 To myArray.GetUpperBound(0)
  myArray(i) = i * 1000
Next
```

The number of elements in an array is given by the expression myArray.GetUpper Bound(0) + 1. You can also use the array's Length property to retrieve the count of elements. The following statement will print the number of elements in the array *myArray* in the Output window:

```
Debug.WriteLine(myArray.Length)
```

Still confused with the zero-indexing scheme, the count of elements, and the index of the last element in the array? You can make the array a little larger than it needs to be and ignore the first element. Just make sure that you never use the zero element in your code — don't store a value in the element Array(0), and you can then ignore this element. To get 20 elements, declare an array with 21 elements as Dim MyArray(20) As type and then ignore the first element.

Multidimensional Arrays

One-dimensional arrays, such as those presented so far, are good for storing long sequences of one-dimensional data (such as names or temperatures). But how would you store a list of cities *and* their average temperatures in an array? Or names and scores, years and profits, or data with more than two dimensions, such as products, prices, and units in stock? In some situations, you will want to store sequences of multidimensional data. You can store the same data more conveniently in an array of as many dimensions as needed.

Figure 2.5 shows two one-dimensional arrays — one of them with city names, the other with temperatures. The name of the third city would be *City(2)*, and its temperature would be *Temperature(2)*.

FIGURE 2.5

Two one-dimensional arrays and the equivalent two-dimensional array

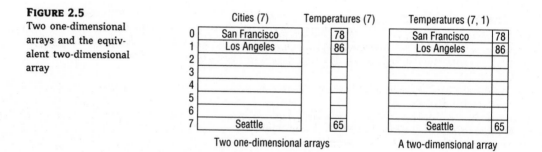

A two-dimensional array has two indices: The first identifies the row (the order of the city in the array), and the second identifies the column (city or temperature). To access the name and temperature of the third city in the two-dimensional array, use the following indices:

```
Temperatures(2, 0)    ' is the third city's name
Temperatures(2, 1)    ' is the third city's average temperature
```

The benefit of using multidimensional arrays is that they're conceptually easier to manage. Suppose you're writing a game and want to track the positions of certain pieces on a board. Each square on the board is identified by two numbers: its horizontal and vertical coordinates. The obvious structure for tracking the board's squares is a two-dimensional array, in which the first index corresponds to the row number and the second corresponds to the column number. The array could be declared as follows:

```
Dim Board(9, 9) As Integer
```

When a piece is moved from the square in the first row and first column to the square in the third row and fifth column, you assign the value 0 to the element that corresponds to the initial position:

```
Board(0, 0) = 0
```

And you assign 1 to the square to which it was moved to indicate the new state of the board:

```
Board(2, 4) = 1
```

To find out whether a piece is on the top-left square, you'd use the following statement:

```
If Board(0, 0) = 1 Then
   ' piece found
Else
   ' empty square
End If
```

This notation can be extended to more than two dimensions. The following statement creates an array with 1,000 elements (10 by 10 by 10):

```
Dim Matrix(9, 9, 9)
```

You can think of a three-dimensional array as a cube made up of overlaid two-dimensional arrays, such as the one shown in Figure 2.6.

FIGURE 2.6
Pictorial representations of one-, two-, and three-dimensional arrays

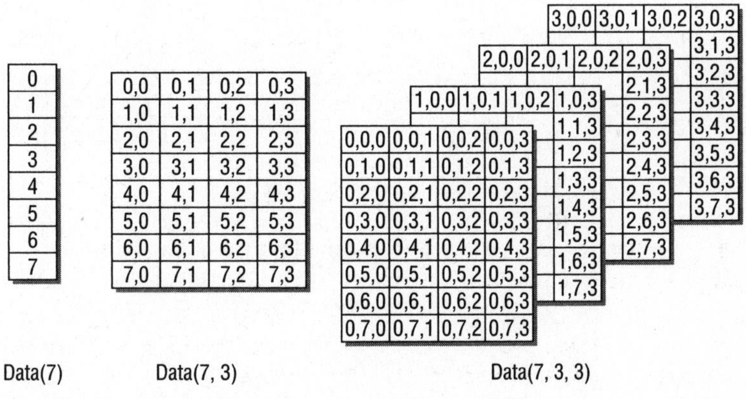

It is possible to initialize a multidimensional array with a single statement, just as you do with a one-dimensional array. You must insert enough commas in the parentheses following the array name to indicate the array's rank. The following statements initialize a two-dimensional array and then print a couple of its elements:

```
Dim a(,) As Integer = {{10, 20, 30}, {11, 21, 31}, {12, 22, 32}}
Console.WriteLine(a(0, 1))    ' will print 20
Console.WriteLine(a(2, 2))    ' will print 32
```

You should break the line that initializes the dimensions of the array into multiple lines to make your code easier to read:

```
Dim a(,) As Integer = {{10, 20, 30},
                       {11, 21, 31},
                       {12, 22, 32}}
```

If the array has more than one dimension, you can find out the number of dimensions with the `Array.Rank` property. Let's say you have declared an array for storing names and salaries by using the following statements:

```
Dim Employees(1,99) As Employee
```

To find out the number of dimensions, use the following statement:

```
Employees.Rank
```

When using the `Length` property to find out the number of elements in a multidimensional array, you will get back the total number of elements in the array (2 × 100 for our example). To find out the number of elements in a specific dimension, use the `GetLength` method, passing as an argument a specific dimension. The following expressions will return the number of elements in the two dimensions of the array:

```
Debug.WriteLine(Employees.GetLength(0))
2
Debug.WriteLine(Employees.GetLength(1))
100
```

Because the index of the first array element is zero, the index of the last element is the length of the array minus 1. Let's say you have declared an array with the following statement to store player statistics for 15 players and there are five values per player:

```
Dim Statistics(14, 4) As Integer
```

The following statements will return the highlighted values shown beneath them:

```
Debug.WriteLine(Statistics.Rank)
2                               ' dimensions in array
Debug.WriteLine(Statistics.Length)
75                              ' total elements in array
Debug.WriteLine(Statistics.GetLength(0))
15                              ' elements in first dimension
Debug.WriteLine(Statistics.GetLength(1))
5                               ' elements in second dimension
Debug.WriteLine(Statistics.GetUpperBound(0))
14                              ' last index in the first dimension
Debug.WriteLine(Statistics.GetUpperBound(1))
4                               ' last index in the second dimension
```

Multidimensional arrays are becoming obsolete because arrays (and other collections) of custom structures and objects are more flexible and convenient.

Collections

Historically, arrays are the primary structures for storing sets of data, and for years they were the primary storage mechanism for in-memory data manipulation. In this field, however, where technologies grow in and out of style overnight, arrays are being replaced by other, more flexible and more powerful structures, the collections. Collections are discussed in detail in Chapter 12, but I should mention them briefly in this chapter, not only for completeness, but also because collections are used a lot in programming and you will find many examples of collections in this book's chapters.

A collection is a dynamic data storage structure: You don't have to declare the size of a collection ahead of time. Moreover, the position of the items in a collection is not nearly as important as the position of the items in an array. New items are appended to a collection with the Add method, while existing items are removed with the Remove method. (Note that there's no simple method of removing an array element, short of copying the original array to a new one and skipping the element to be removed.) The collection I just described is the List collection, which is very similar to an array. To declare a List collection, use the New keyword:

```
Dim names As New List(Of String)
```

The New keyword is literally new to you; use it to create variables that are true objects (any variable that's not of a basic data type or structure). The New keyword tells the compiler to create a variable of the specified type and initialize it. The List collection must be declared with a specific data type, which is specified with the Of keyword in parentheses. All items stored in the example *names* list must be strings. A related collection is the ArrayList collection, which is identical to the List collection but you don't have to declare the type of variables you intend to store in it because you can add objects of any type to an ArrayList collection.

To create a collection of color values, use the following declaration:

```
Dim colors As New List(Of Color)
```

The following statements add a few items to the two collections:

```
names.Add("Richard")
names.Add("Nancy")
colors.Add(Color.Red)
colors.Add(TextBox1.BackColor)
```

Another collection is the Dictionary collection, which allows you to identify each element by a key instead of an index value. The following statement creates a new Dictionary collection for storing names and birth dates:

```
Dim BDays As New Dictionary(Of String, Date)
```

The first data type following the Of keyword is the data type of the keys, while the following argument is the data type of the values you want to store to the collection. Here's how you add data to a Dictionary collection:

```
BDays.Add("Manfred", #3/24/1972#)
BDays.Add("Alfred", #11/24/1959#)
```

To retrieve the birth date of Manfred, use the following statement:

```
BDays("Manfred")
```

Finally, you can use collections to store custom objects too. Let's say you have three variables that represent checks (they're of the CheckRecord custom type presented earlier in this chapter in the section "User-Defined Data Types"). You can add them to a List collection just as you would add integers or strings to a collection:

```
Dim Checks As New List(Of CheckRecord)
Checks.Add(check1)
Checks.Add(check2)
Checks.Add(check3)
```

A seasoned developer would store the same data to a Dictionary collection using the check number as an index value:

```
Dim Checks As New Dictionary(Of Integer, CheckRecord)
Checks.Add(check1.CheckNumber, check1)
```

An application that uses this structure can prompt the user for a specific check number, retrieve it by its index from the Checks collection and display it to the user. As you will see in Chapter 12, a big advantage of collections over arrays is that collections allow you to remove elements with the Remove method.

The Bottom Line

Declare and use variables. Programs use variables to store information during their execution, and different types of information are stored in variables of different types. Dates, for example, are stored in variables of the Date type, while text is stored in variables of the String type. The various data types expose a lot of functionality that's specific to a data type; the methods provided by each data type are listed in the IntelliSense box.

Master It How would you declare and initialize a few variables?

Master It Explain briefly the Explicit, Strict, and Infer options.

Use the native data types. The CLR recognized the following data types, which you can use in your code to declare variables: String, numeric data types (Integer, Double, and so on), Date, Char and Boolean types.

All other variables, or variables that are declared without a type, are Object variables and can store any data type or any object.

Master It   How will the compiler treat the following statement?

```
Dim amount = 32
```

Create custom data types.   Practical applications need to store and manipulate multiple data items, not just integers and strings. To maintain information about people, we need to store each person's name, date of birth, address, and so on. Products have a name, a description, a price, and other related items. To represent such entities in our code, we use structures, which hold many pieces of information about a specific entity together.

Master It   Create a structure for storing products and populate it with data.

Use arrays.   Arrays are structures for storing sets of data as opposed to single-valued variables.

Master It   How would you declare an array for storing 12 names and another one for storing 100 names and Social Security numbers?

Chapter 3

Visual Basic Programming Essentials

The one thing you should have learned about programming in Visual Basic so far is that an application is made up of small, self-contained segments. The code you write isn't a monolithic listing; it's made up of small segments called procedures, and you work on one procedure at a time.

In this chapter we'll explore the two types of procedures supported by Visual Basic: subroutines and functions — the building blocks of your applications. We'll discuss them in detail: how to call them with arguments and how to retrieve the results returned by the functions. You'll learn how to use the built-in functions that come with the language as well as how to write your own subroutines and functions.

The statements that make up the core of the language are actually very few. The flexibility of any programming language is based on its capacity to alter the sequence in which the statements are executed through a set of so-called flow-control statements. These are the statements that literally make decisions and react differently depending on the data, user actions, or external conditions. Among other topics, in this chapter you'll learn how to do the following:

- ♦ Use Visual Basic's flow-control statements

- ♦ Write subroutines and functions

- ♦ Pass arguments to subroutines and functions

Flow-Control Statements

What makes programming languages so flexible and capable of handling every situation and programming challenge with a relatively small set of commands is their capability to examine external or internal conditions and act accordingly. Programs aren't monolithic sets of commands that carry out the same calculations every time they are executed; this is what calculators (and extremely simple programs) do. Instead, they adjust their behavior depending on the data supplied; on external conditions, such as a mouse click or the existence of a peripheral; even on a coding mistake you haven't caught during your tests.

In effect, the statements discussed in the first half of this chapter are what programming is all about. Without the capability to control the flow of the program, computers would just be bulky calculators. You have seen how to use the If statement to alter the flow of execution in previous chapters, and I assume you're somewhat familiar with these kinds of statements. In this section, you'll find a formal discussion of flow-control statements, which are grouped into two major categories: decision statements and looping statements.

Decision Statements

Applications need a mechanism to test conditions, and they take a different course of action depending on the outcome of the test. Visual Basic provides three statements that allow you to alter the course of the application based on the outcome of a condition:

◆ If...Then

◆ If...Then...Else

◆ Select Case

IF...THEN STATEMENTS

The If...Then statement tests an expression, which is known as a condition. If the condition is True, the program executes the statement(s) that follow the Then keyword up to the End If statement, which terminates the conditional statement. The If...Then statement can have a single-line or a multiple-line syntax. To execute one statement conditionally, use the single-line syntax as follows:

```
If condition Then statement
```

To execute multiple statements conditionally, embed the statements within an If and End If statement, as follows:

```
If condition Then
   ' Statement
   ' Statement
End If
```

Conditions are logical expressions that evaluate to a True/False value and they usually contain comparison operators — equals (=), different (<>), less than (<), greater than (>), less than or equal to (<=), and so on — and logical operators — And, Or, Xor, and Not. Here are a few examples of valid conditions:

```
If (age1 < age2) And (age1 > 12) Then …
If score1 = score2 Then …
```

The parentheses are not really needed in the first sample expression, but they make the code a little easier to read and understand. Sometimes parentheses are mandatory, to specify the order in which the expression's parts will be evaluated, just as math formulae may require parentheses to indicate the precedence of calculations.

The expressions can get quite complicated. The following expression evaluates to True if the *date1* variable represents a date earlier than the year 2005 and either one of the *score1* and *score2* variables exceeds 90 (you could use it locate high scores in a specific year):

```
If (date1 < #1/1/2005) And (score1 > 90 Or score2 > 90) Then
    ' statements
End If
```

The parentheses around the last part of the comparison are mandatory because we want the compiler to perform the following comparison first:

```
score1 > 90 Or score2 > 90
```

If either variable exceeds 90, the preceding expression evaluates to True and the initial condition is reduced to the following:

```
If (date1 < #1/1/2008) And (True) Then
```

The compiler will evaluate the first part of the expression (it will compare two dates) and finally it will combine two Boolean values with the And operator: If both values are True, the entire condition is True; otherwise, it's False. If you didn't use parentheses, the compiler would evaluate the three parts of the expression:

```
expression1: date1 < #1/1/2008#
expression2: score1 < 90
expression3: score2 < 90
```

Then it would combine *expression1* with *expression2* using the And operator, and finally it would combine the result with *expression3* using the Or operator. If *score2* were greater than 90, the entire expression would evaluate to True, regardless of the value of the *date1* and *score1* variables.

IF...THEN...ELSE STATEMENTS

A variation of the If...Then statement is the If...Then...Else statement, which executes one block of statements if the condition is True and another block of statements if the condition is False. The syntax of the If...Then...Else statement is as follows:

```
If condition Then
    statementblock1
Else
    statementblock2
End If
```

Visual Basic evaluates the condition; if it's True, VB executes the first block of statements and then jumps to the statement following the End If statement. If the condition is False, Visual Basic ignores the first block of statements and executes the block following the Else keyword.

A third variation of the If...Then...Else statement uses several conditions, with the ElseIf keyword:

```
If condition1 Then
    statementblock1
ElseIf condition2 Then
    statementblock2
ElseIf condition3 Then
    statementblock3
```

```
Else
    statementblock4
End If
```

You can have any number of ElseIf clauses. The conditions are evaluated from the top, and if one of them is True, the corresponding block of statements is executed. The Else clause, which is optional, will be executed if none of the previous expressions is True. Listing 3.1 is an example of an If statement with ElseIf clauses.

LISTING 3.1:   Multiple ElseIf statements

```
score = InputBox("Enter score")
If score < 50 Then
    Result = "Failed"
ElseIf score < 75 Then
    Result = "Pass"
ElseIf score < 90 Then
    Result = "Very Good"
Else
    Result = "Excellent"
End If
MsgBox Result
```

MULTIPLE *IF...THEN* STRUCTURES VERSUS *ELSEIF*

Notice that after a True condition is found, Visual Basic executes the associated statements and skips the remaining clauses. It continues executing the program with the statement immediately after End If. All following ElseIf clauses are skipped, and the code runs a bit faster. That's why you should prefer the complicated structure with the ElseIf statements used in Listing 3.1 to this equivalent series of simple If statements:

```
If score < 50 Then
    Result = "Failed"
End If
If score < 75 And score >= 50 Then
    Result = "Pass"
End If
If score < 90 And score > =75 Then
    Result = "Very Good"
End If
If score >= 90 Then
    Result = "Excellent"
End If
```

With the multiple If statements, the compiler will generate code that evaluates all the conditions, even if the score is less than 50.

The order of the comparisons is vital when you're using multiple `ElseIf` statements. Had you written the previous code segment with the first two conditions switched, like the following segment, the results would be quite unexpected:

```
If score < 75 Then
    Result = "Pass"
ElseIf score < 50 Then
    Result = "Failed"
ElseIf score < 90 Then
    Result = "Very Good"
Else
    Result = "Excellent"
End If
```

Let's assume that *score* is 49. The code would compare the *score* variable to the value 75. Because 49 is less than 75, it would assign the value `Pass` to the variable *Result*, and then it would skip the remaining clauses. Thus, a student who scored 49 would have passed the test! So be extremely careful and test your code thoroughly if it uses multiple `ElseIf` clauses. You must either make sure they're listed in the proper order or use upper and lower limits, as in the sidebar "Multiple If…Then Structures versus `ElseIf`." It goes without saying that such a code segment should be tested for all possible intervals of the *score* variable.

THE IIf() FUNCTION

Not to be confused with the If…Then statement, the IIf() function is also part of the language. This built-in function accepts as an argument an expression and two values, evaluates the expression, and returns the first value if the expression is True or the second value if the expression is False. The IIf() function has the following syntax:

```
IIf(expression, TruePart, FalsePart)
```

The TruePart and FalsePart arguments are objects. (They can be integers, strings, or any built-in or custom object.) The IIf() function is a more compact notation for simple If statements, and you can use it to shorten If…Then…Else expressions. Let's say you want to display one of the strings "Close" or "Far", depending on the value of the *distance* variable. Instead of a multiline If statement, you can call the IIf() function as follows:

```
Dim result As String
Result = IIf(distance > 1000, "Far", "Close")
MsgBox(result)
```

Another typical example of the IIf() function is in formatting negative values. It's fairly common in business applications to display negative amounts in parentheses. Use the IIf() statement to write a short expression that formats negative and positive amounts differently, like the following one:

```
IIf(amount < 0, " (" & Math.Abs(amount).ToString("#.00") & ")",
    amount.ToString("#.00"))
```

The Abs method of the Math class returns the absolute value of a numeric value, and the "#.oo" argument of the ToString method specifies that the amount should be formatted as a currency amount with two decimal digits. You can insert the preceding statement anywhere you would display the *amount* variable. Assign a positive or negative value to the *amount* variable and then pass the entire expression to the MsgBox() function to display the formatted value:

```
MsgBox(
    IIf(amount < 0, "(" & Math.Abs(amount).ToString("#.00") & ")",
        amount.ToString("#.00")))
```

SELECT CASE STATEMENTS

An alternative to the efficient but difficult-to-read code of the multiple ElseIf structure is the Select Case structure, which compares the same expression to different values. The advantage of the Select Case statement over multiple If…Then…ElseIf statements is that it makes the code easier to read and maintain.

The Select Case structure evaluates a single expression at the top of the structure. The result of the expression is then compared with several values; if it matches one of them, the corresponding block of statements is executed. Here's the syntax of the Select Case statement:

```
Select Case expression
    Case value1
      ' statementblock1
    Case value2
      ' statementblock2
        .
        .
        .
    Case Else
        statementblockN
End Select
```

A practical example based on the Select Case statement is shown in Listing 3.2.

LISTING 3.2:   Using the Select Case statement

```
Dim Message As String
Select Case Now.DayOfWeek
    Case DayOfWeek.Monday
        message = "Have a nice week"
    Case DayOfWeek.Friday
        message = "Have a nice weekend"
    Case Else
        message = "Welcome back! "
End Select
MsgBox(message)
```

In the listing, the expression that's evaluated at the beginning of the statement is the Now.DayOfWeek method. This method returns a member of the DayOfWeek enumeration, and you can use the names of these members in your code to make it easier to read. The value of this expression is compared with the values that follow each Case keyword. If they match, the block of statements up to the next Case keyword is executed, and the program skips to the statement following the End Select statement. The block of the Case Else statement is optional and is executed if none of the previous cases matches the expression. The first two Case statements take care of Fridays and Mondays, and the Case Else statement takes care of the other days.

Some Case statements can be followed by multiple values, which are separated by commas. Listing 3.3 is a revised version of the previous example. The code of Listing 3.3 handles Saturdays and Sundays.

LISTING 3.3:   A Select Case statement with multiple cases per clause

```
Select Case Now.DayOfWeek
    Case DayOfWeek.Monday
        message = "Have a nice week"
    Case DayOfWeek.Tuesday, DayOfWeek.Wednesday, DayOfWeek.Thursday
        message = "Welcome back!"
    Case DayOfWeek.Friday, DayOfWeek.Saturday, DayOfWeek.Sunday
        message = "Have a nice weekend!"
End Select
MsgBox(message)
```

Monday, weekends, and weekdays are handled separately by three Case statements. The second Case statement handles multiple values (all workdays except for Monday and Friday). Monday is handled by a separate Case statement. This structure doesn't contain a Case Else statement because all possible values are examined in the Case statements; the DayOfWeek method can't return another value.

The Case statements can get a little more complex. For example, you may want to distinguish a case where the variable is larger (or smaller) than a value. To implement this logic, use the Is keyword, as in the following code segment that distinguishes between the first and second half of the month:

```
Select Now.Day
    Case Is < 15
        MsgBox("It's the first half of the month")
    Case Is >= 15
        MsgBox("It's the second half of the month")
End Select
```

SHORT-CIRCUITING EXPRESSION EVALUATION

A common pitfall of evaluating expressions with VB is to attempt to compare a Nothing value to something. An object variable that hasn't been set to a value can't be used in calculations or comparisons. Consider the following statements:

```
Dim B As SolidBrush
B = New SolidBrush(Color.Cyan)
If B.Color = Color.White Then
    MsgBox("Please select another brush color")
End If
```

These statements create a SolidBrush object variable, the *B* variable, and then examine the brush color and prohibit the user from drawing with a white brush. The second statement initializes the brush to the cyan color. (Every shape drawn with this brush will appear in cyan.) If you instead attempted to use the *B* variable without initializing it (that is, if you had not included the line that creates a new SolidBrush object), a runtime exception would be thrown: the infamous `NullReferenceException` would be thrown when the program gets to the `If` statement because the *B* variable has no value (it's Nothing), and the code attempts to compare it to something. Nothing values can't be compared to anything. Comment out the second statement by inserting a single quote in front of it and then execute the code to see what will happen. Then restore the statement by removing the comment mark.

Actually, as soon as you comment out the statement that initializes the *B* variable, the editor will underline the *B* variable and it will generate the warning *Variable B is used before it has been assigned a value. A null reference exception could result at runtime.*

Let's fix it by making sure that *B* is not Nothing:

```
If B IsNot Nothing And B.Color = Color.White Then
    MsgBox("Please select another brush color")
End If
```

The `If` statement should compare the `Color` property of the *B* object, only if the *B* object is not Nothing. But this isn't the case. The `AND` operator evaluates all terms in the expression and then combines their results (True or False values) to determine the value of the expression. If they're all True, the result is also True. However, it won't skip the evaluation of some terms as soon as it hits a False value. To avoid unnecessary comparisons, use the `AndAlso` operator. The `AndAlso` operator does what the `And` operator should have done in the first place: it evaluates the expressions from left to right, and when it encounters a False value, it stops evaluating the remaining terms because they won't affect the result. If one of its operands is False, the entire expression will evaluate to False. In other words, if *B* is Nothing, there's no reason to examine its color; the entire expression will evaluate to False, regardless of the brush color. Here's how to use the `AndAlso` operator:

```
If B IsNot Nothing AndAlso B.Color = Color.White Then
    MsgBox("Please select another brush color")
End If
```

The `AndAlso` operator is said to short-circuit the evaluation of the entire expression as soon as it runs into a False value. As soon as one of the parts in an `AndAlso` operation turns out to be False, the entire expression is False and there's no need to evaluate the remaining terms.

There's an equivalent operator for short-circuiting OR expressions: the OrElse operator. The OrElse operator can speed the evaluation of logical expressions a little by returning True when the first operand evaluates to True (the result of the OR operation will be True, regardless of the value of the second operand). Another good reason for short-circuiting expression evaluation is to help performance. If the second term of an And expression takes longer to execute (it has to access a remote database, for example), you can use the AndAlso operator to make sure that it's not executed when it's not needed.

Loop Statements

Loop statements allow you to execute one or more lines of code repetitively. Many tasks consist of operations that must be repeated over and over again, and loop statements are an important part of any programming language. Visual Basic supports the following loop statements:

◆ For...Next

◆ Do...Loop

◆ While...End While

FOR...NEXT LOOPS

Unlike the other two loops, the For...Next loop requires that you know the number of times that the statements in the loop will be executed. The For...Next loop has the following syntax:

```
For counter = start To end [Step increment]
  ' statements
Next [counter]
```

The keywords in the square brackets are optional. The arguments *counter*, *start*, *end*, and *increment* are all numeric. The loop is executed as many times as required for the *counter* variable's value to reach (or exceed) the *end* value. The variable that appears next to the For keyword is the loop's *counter*, or *control* variable.

In executing a For...Next loop, Visual Basic does the following:

1. Sets the *counter* variable equal to the *start* variable (this is the control variable's initial value).

2. Tests to see whether *counter* is greater than *end*. If so, it exits the loop without executing the statements in the loop's body, not even once. If *increment* is negative, Visual Basic tests to see whether the *counter* value is less than the *end* value. If it is, it exits the loop.

3. Executes the statements in the block.

4. Increases the *counter* variable by the amount specified with the *increment* argument following the Step keyword. If the *increment* argument isn't specified, *counter* is increased by 1. If *Step* is a negative value, *counter* is decreased accordingly.

5. Continues with step 2.

The For...Next loop in Listing 3.4 scans all the elements of the numeric array *data* and calculates their average.

LISTING 3.4:   Iterating an array with a For...Next loop

```
Dim i As Integer, total As Double
For i = 0 To data.Length
   total = total + data(i)
Next i
Debug.WriteLine (total / Data.Length)
```

The single most important thing to keep in mind when working with For...Next loops is that the loop's ending value is set at the beginning of the loop. Changing the value of the *end* variable in the loop's body won't have any effect. For example, the following loop will be executed 10 times, not 100 times:

```
Dim endValue As Integer = 10
Dim i as Integer
For i = 0 To endValue
   endValue = 100
   ' more statements
Next i
```

You can, however, adjust the value of the *counter* variable from within the loop. The following is an example of an endless (or infinite) loop:

```
For i = 0 To 10
   Debug.WriteLine(i)
   i = i - 1
Next i
```

This loop never ends because the loop's control variable, in effect, is never increased. (If you try this, press Ctrl+Break to interrupt the endless loop.)

DO NOT MANIPULATE THE LOOP COUNTER

Manipulating the control variable of a For...Next loop is strongly discouraged. This practice will most likely lead to bugs, such as infinite loops, overflows, and so on. If the number of repetitions of a loop isn't known in advance, use a Do...Loop or a While...End While structure (discussed shortly). To jump out of a For...Next loop prematurely, use the Next For statement. You can also use the Continue For statement to continue with the next iteration of the loop (in other words, jump to the beginning of the loop and start a new iteration).

The *increment* argument can be either positive or negative. If *start* is greater than *end*, the value of *increment* must be negative. If not, the loop's body won't be executed, not even once.

VB 2010 allows you to declare the counter in the For statement. The control variable ceases to exist when the program bails out of the loop:

```
For i As Integer = 1 to 10
   Debug.WriteLine(i.ToString)
```

```
Next
Debug.WriteLine(i.ToString)
```

The *i* variable is used as the loop counter and it's not visible outside the loop. The last statement won't even compile; the editor will underline it with a wiggly line and will generate the error message *Name 'i' is not declared.*

FOR EACH...NEXT LOOPS

This is a variation of the classic For loop and it's used to iterate through the items of a collection or array. Let's say you have declared an array of strings like the following:

```
Dim months() As String = _
            {"January", "February", "March", "April", "May", "June"}
```

You can iterate through the month names with a For Each loop like the one that follows:

```
For Each month As String In months
    Debug.WriteLine(month)
Next
```

The *month* control variable need not be declared if the Infer option is on. The compiler will figure out the type of the control variable based on the types of the values you're iterating over, which in our example are strings. You can easily write the equivalent For...Next loop for the same task, but the For Each loop is more elegant. It also provides a variable that represents the current item at each iteration.

Let's look at a more interesting example of the For Each loop to get an idea of the type of operations it's best suited for. The Process class of the Framework provides methods for inspecting the process running on the target computer at any time. These are the processes you see in the Processes tab of the Task Manager. Each process is represented by a Process object, which in turn exposes several useful properties (such as the name of the process, the physical memory it's using, and so on) as well as methods to manipulate the processes, including the Kill method that terminates a process.

The GetProcesses method returns an array of Process objects, one for each running process. To iterate through the current processes, you can use a For Each loop like the following:

```
Dim processes() = Process.GetProcesses
For Each Proc As Process In processes
    Debug.WriteLine(Proc.ProcessName & "    " & 
                        Proc.PrivateMemorySize64.ToString)
Next
```

This loop will display a list like the following in the Output window:

```
taskeng          10588160
svchost          11476992
YahooMessenger   20496384
sqlservr         104538112
```

```
svchost          4255744
svchost          6549504
SearchIndexer    53612544
sqlwriter        3715072
searchFilterHost 3514368
cmd              2080768
iexplore         250073088
```

As you can see, the For Each loop is much more elegant than a For...Next loop when it comes to iterating through the items of a collection. The loop's counter is not an index, but an object that represents the current entity — provided that all elements are of the same type, of course. Many developers use a For Each...Next loop whenever possible, even in situations where a trivial For...Next loop would suffice. Compare the loops in Listing 3.5 and Listing 3.6 for iterating through the elements of an array of integers.

LISTING 3.5:   Using a For...Next loop

```
Dim numbers() = {10, 11, 12, 13, 14, 15, 16, 17, 18, 19, 20}
For i As Integer = 1 to numbers.Length - 1
    `       Process value numbers(i)
Next
```

LISTING 3.6:   Using a For Each...Next loop

```
Dim numbers() = {10, 11, 12, 13, 14, 15, 16, 17, 18, 19, 20}
For Each number As Integer In numbers
    `       Process value number
Next
```

Although I declare the control variable in both of the preceding loops, this isn't mandatory as long as you have turned on type inference. The compiler will figure out the proper type from the type of the objects that make up the collection you're iterating.

Do Loops

The Do...Loop statement executes a block of statements for as long as a condition is True or until a condition becomes True. Visual Basic evaluates an expression (the loop's condition), and if it's True, the statements in the loop body are executed. The expression is evaluated either at the beginning of the loop (before any statements are executed) or at the end of the loop (after the block statements are executed at least once). If the expression is False, the program's execution continues with the statement following the loop. These two variations use the keywords While and Until to specify how long the statements will be executed. To execute a block of statements while a condition is True, use the following syntax:

```
Do While condition
    ' statement-block
Loop
```

To execute a block of statements until the condition becomes True, use the following syntax:

```
Do Until condition
   ' statement-block
Loop
```

When Visual Basic executes these loops, it first evaluates *condition*. If *condition* is False, a Do...While loop is skipped (the statements aren't even executed once) but a Do...Until loop is executed. When the Loop statement is reached, Visual Basic evaluates the expression again; it repeats the statement block of the Do...While loop if the expression is True or repeats the statements of the Do...Until loop if the expression is False. In short, the Do...While loop is executed when the condition is True (while the condition is True), and the Do...Until loop is executed when the condition is False (until the condition becomes True).

A last variation of the Do statement, the Do...Loop statement, allows you to always evaluate the condition at the end of the loop, even in a While loop. Here's the syntax of both types of loop, with the evaluation of the condition at the end of the loop:

```
Do
   ' statement-block
Loop While condition
```

```
Do
   ' statement-block
Loop Until condition
```

As you can guess, the statements in the loop's body are executed at least once, even in the case of the While loop, because no testing takes place as the loop is entered.

Here's a typical example of using a Do...Loop: Suppose that the variable *MyText* holds some text (like the Text property of a TextBox control) and you want to count the words in the text. (We'll assume that there are no multiple spaces in the text and that the space character separates successive words.) To locate an instance of a character in a string, use the IndexOf method of the String class. This method accepts two arguments: the starting location of the search and the character being searched. The following loop repeats for as long as there are spaces in the text. Each time the IndexOf method finds another space in the text, it returns the location of the space. When there are no more spaces in the text, the IndexOf method returns the value -1, which signals the end of the loop, as shown:

```
Dim MyText As String =
        "The quick brown fox jumped over the lazy dogs"
Dim position, words As Integer
position = 0
words = 0
Do While position >= 0
    position = MyText.IndexOf(" ", position + 1)
    words += 1
Loop
MsgBox("There are " & words & " words in the text")
```

The Do...Loop is executed while the IndexOf method function returns a positive number, which means that there are more spaces (and therefore words) in the text. The variable *position* holds the location of each successive space character in the text. The search for the next space starts at the location of the current space plus 1 (so the program won't keep finding the same space). For each space found, the program increases the value of the *words* variable, which holds the total number of words when the loop ends. By the way, there are simpler methods of breaking a string into its constituent words, such as the `Split` method of the String class. This is just an example of the `Do…While` loop.

You might notice a problem with the previous code segment: It assumes that the text contains at least one word. You should insert an `If` statement that detects zero-length strings and doesn't attempt to count words in them. You can also use the `IsNullOrEmpty` method of the String class, which returns True if a String variable is empty or Nothing.

You can code the same routine with the `Until` keyword. In this case, you must continue searching for spaces until *position* becomes −1. Here's the same code with a different loop:

```
Dim position As Integer = 0
Dim words As Integer = 0
Do Until position = -1
    position = MyText.IndexOf(" ", position + 1)
    words = words + 1
Loop
MsgBox("There are " & words & " words in the text")
```

WHILE LOOPS

The `While…End While` loop executes a block of statements as long as a condition is True. The loop has the following syntax:

```
While condition
  ' statement-block
End While
```

If *condition* is True, the statements in the block are executed. When the `End While` statement is reached, control is returned to the `While` statement, which evaluates *condition* again. If *condition* is still True, the process is repeated. If *condition* is False, the program resumes with the statement following `End While`.

The loop in Listing 3.7 prompts the user for numeric data. The user can type a negative value to indicate he's done entering values and terminate the loop. As long as the user enters positive numeric values, the program keeps adding them to the `total` variable.

LISTING 3.7:   Reading an unknown number of values

```
Dim number, total As Double
number = 0
While number => 0
    total = total + number
    number = InputBox("Please enter another value")
End While
```

I've assigned the value 0 to the *number* variable before the loop starts because this value isn't negative and doesn't affect the total.

Sometimes, the condition that determines when the loop will terminate can't be evaluated at the top of the loop. In these cases, we declare a Boolean value and set it to True or False from within the loop's body. Here's the outline of such a loop:

```
Dim repeatLoop As Boolean
repeatLoop = True
While repeatLoop
    ' statements
    If condition Then
        repeatLoop = True
    Else
        repeatLoop = False
    End If
End While
```

You may also see an odd loop statement like the following one:

```
While True
    ' statements
End While
```

It's also common to express the True condition in one of the following two forms:

```
While 1 = 1
```

or

```
While True
```

Now, there's no good reason to use statements like these; I guess they're leftovers from old programs. The seemingly endless loops must be terminated from within the body using an Exit While statement, which is called when a condition becomes True or False. The following loop terminates when a condition is met in the loop's body:

```
While True
    ' statements
    If condition Then Exit While
    ' more statements
End While
```

Of course, this code isn't elegant and you should avoid it, except when you're implementing some complicated logic that can't be easily coded differently.

Nested Control Structures

You can place, or nest, control structures inside other control structures (such as an If...Then block within a For...Next loop) or nest multiple If...Then blocks within one another. Control structures in Visual Basic can be nested in as many levels as you want. The editor automatically indents the bodies of nested decision and loop structures to make the program easier to read.

When you nest control structures, you must make sure that they open and close within the same structure. In other words, you can't start a For…Next loop in an If statement and close the loop after the corresponding End If. The following code segment demonstrates how to nest several flow-control statements:

```
For a = 1 To 100
    ' statements
    If a = 99 Then
        ' statements
    End If
    While b < a
        ' statements
        If total <= 0 Then
            ' statements
        End If
    End While
    For c = 1 to a
        ' statements
    Next c
Next a
```

I show the names of the control variables after the Next statements to make the code more readable to humans. To find the matching closing statement (Next, End If, or End While), move down from the opening statement until you hit a line that starts at the same column. This is the matching closing statement. Notice that you don't have to align the nested structures yourself; the editor reformats the code automatically as you type. It also inserts the matching closing statement — the End If statement is inserted automatically as soon as you enter an If statement and press Enter, for example. Not only that, but as soon as you click in a control or loop statement, the editor highlights the corresponding ending statement.

Listing 3.8 shows a typical situation with nested loops. The two nested loops scan all the elements of a two-dimensional array.

LISTING 3.8:   Iterating through a two-dimensional array

```
Dim Array2D(6, 4) As Integer
Dim iRow, iCol As Integer
For iRow = 0 To Array2D.GetUpperBound(0)
    For iCol = 0 To Array2D.GetUpperBound(1)
        Array2D(iRow, iCol) = iRow * 100 + iCol
        Debug.Write(iRow & ", " & iCol & " = " &
                    Array2D(iRow, iCol) & " ")
    Next iCol
    Debug.WriteLine()
Next iRow
```

The outer loop (with the *iRow* counter) scans each row of the array. At each iteration, the inner loop scans all the elements in the row specified by the counter of the outer loop (*iRow*). After the inner loop completes, the counter of the outer loop is increased by one, and the inner loop is executed again — this time to scan the elements of the next row. The loop's body consists of two statements that assign a value to the current array element and then print it in the Output window. The current element at each iteration is Array2D(iRow, iCol).

Another typical example of nested loops is the code that iterates through the cells of a ListView control. (This control is discussed in Chapter 7, "More Windows Controls," and also in the tutorial "The ListView and TreeView controls.") The ListView control is basically a grid — not an editable one, I'm afraid, but an excellent tool for displaying tabular data. To iterate through the control's cells, you must set up a loop that iterates through its rows and a nested loop that iterates through the current row's cells. Each row of the ListView control is a ListViewItem object, which provides information about the rows' cells through the SubItems property. The SubItems property is an array of values, one for each cell of the grid's row. The expression ListView1.Items(2).SubItems(1).Text returns the contents of the second cell in the control's third row. The following code segment iterates through the cells of any ListView control, regardless of the number of rows and columns it contains:

```
For iRow As Integer = 0 To ListView1.Items.Count - 1
    Dim LI As ListViewItem = ListView1.Items(iRow)
    For iCol As Integer = 0 To LI.SubItems.Count - 1
      ' process cell LI.SubItems(iCol)
    Next
Next
```

The two nested For...Next loops are quite old-fashioned. In modern VB, you'd write the same code as follows:

```
Dim str As String = ""
For Each LI As ListViewItem In ListView1.Items
    For Each cell In LI.SubItems
        str = str & cell.Text.ToString & vbTab
    Next
    str = str & vbCrLf
Next
MsgBox(str)
```

The preceding code segment gradually builds a string with the contents of the ListView control, separating cells in the same row with a tab (*vbTab* constant) and consecutive rows with a line feed (*vbCrLf* constant). You can also nest multiple If statements. The code in Listing 3.9 tests a user-supplied value to determine whether it's positive; if so, it determines whether the value exceeds a certain limit.

LISTING 3.9:   Simple nested If statements

```
Dim Income As Decimal
Income = Convert.ToDecimal(InputBox("Enter your income"))
If Income > 0 Then
```

```
    If Income > 12000 Then
        MsgBox "You will pay taxes this year"
    Else
        MsgBox "You won't pay any taxes this year"
    End If
Else
    MsgBox "Bummer"
End If
```

The *Income* variable is first compared with zero. If it's negative, the Else clause of the If...Then statement is executed. If it's positive, it's compared with the value 12,000, and depending on the outcome, a different message is displayed. The code segment shown here doesn't perform any extensive validations and assumes that the user won't enter a string when prompted for income.

The Exit and Continue Statements

The Exit statement allows you to prematurely exit from a block of statements in a control structure, from a loop, or even from a procedure. Suppose that you have a For...Next loop that calculates the square root of a series of numbers. Because the square root of negative numbers can't be calculated (the Math.Sqrt method will generate a runtime error), you might want to halt the operation if the array contains an invalid value. To exit the loop prematurely, use the Exit For statement as follows:

```
For i = 0 To UBound(nArray)
    If nArray(i) < 0 Then
        MsgBox("Can't complete calculations" & vbCrLf & _
                "Item " & i.ToString & " is negative! "
        Exit For
    End If
    nArray(i) = Math.Sqrt(nArray(i))
Next
```

If a negative element is found in this loop, the program exits the loop and continues with the statement following the Next statement.

There are similar Exit statements for the Do loop (Exit Do), the While loop (Exit While), the Select statement (Exit Select), and functions and subroutines (Exit Function and Exit Sub). If the previous loop was part of a function, you might want to display an error and exit not only the loop, but also the function itself by using the Exit Function statement.

Sometimes you may need to continue with the following iteration instead of exiting the loop (in other words, skip the body of the loop and continue with the following value). In these cases, you can use the Continue statement (Continue For for For... Next loops, Continue While for While loops, and so on).

Writing and Using Procedures

Now that you have seen the decision and looping structures of Visual Basic, let's move on to procedures. In traditional programming languages, procedures are the basic building blocks of every application. And what exactly is a traditional language? Well, a procedural language, of course. A procedural language is one that requires you to specify how to carry out specific tasks by writing procedures. A procedure is a series of statements that tell the computer how to carry out a specific task. The task could be the calculation of a loan's monthly payment (a task that can be coded literally with a single statement) or the retrieval of weather data from a remote server. In any case, the body of statements form a unit of code that can be invoked by name, not unlike scripts or macro commands but much more flexible and certainly more complex.

The idea of breaking a large application into smaller, more manageable sections is not new to computing. Few tasks, programming or otherwise, can be managed as a whole. Using event handlers is just one example of breaking a large application into smaller tasks.

For example, when you write code for a control's Click event, you concentrate on the event at hand — namely, how the program should react to the Click event. What happens when the control is double-clicked or when another control is clicked is something you will worry about later — in another control's event handler. This divide-and-conquer approach isn't unique to programming events. It permeates the Visual Basic language, and developers write even the longest applications by breaking them into small, well-defined, easily managed tasks. Each task is performed by a procedure that is written and tested separately from the others. As mentioned earlier, the two types of procedures supported by Visual Basic are subroutines and functions.

Subroutines perform actions and they don't return any result. Functions, on the other hand, perform some calculations and return a value. This is the only difference between subroutines and functions. Both subroutines and functions can accept arguments (values you pass to the procedure when you call it). Usually, the arguments are the values on which the procedure's code acts. Arguments and the related keywords are discussed in detail later in this chapter.

Subroutines

A subroutine is a block of statements that carries out a well-defined task. The block of statements is placed within a set of Sub...End Sub statements and can be invoked by name. The following subroutine displays the current date in a message box:

```
Sub ShowDate()
    MsgBox("Today's date is " & Now().ToShortDateString)
End Sub
```

To use it in your code, you can just enter the name of the function in a line of its own:

```
ShowDate()
```

To experiment with the procedures presented in this chapter, start a new Windows project, place a button on the main form, and then enter the definition of the ShowDate() subroutine outside any event handler. In the button's Click event handler, enter the statement **ShowDate()**. If you run the application and click the button, the current date will appear on a message box. The single statement in the event handler calls the ShowDate() subroutine, which displays the current date. Your main program calls the subroutine by name and it doesn't care how complex the subroutine is.

Normally, the task performed by a subroutine is more sophisticated than this, but even this simple subroutine is a block of code isolated from the rest of the application. The statements in a subroutine are executed, and when the End Sub statement is reached, control returns to the calling code. It's possible to exit a subroutine prematurely by using the Exit Sub statement. In effect, a subroutine is a set of statements that perform a very specific task, and you can invoke them by name. Use subroutines to break your code into smaller, more manageable units and certainly if you're coding tasks that may be used in multiple parts of the application. Note that the ShowDate() subroutine can be called from any event handler in the current form.

All variables declared within a subroutine are local to that subroutine. When the subroutine exits, all variables declared in it cease to exist.

Most procedures also accept and act upon arguments. The ShowDate() subroutine displays the current date in a message box. If you want to display any other date, you have to implement it differently and add an argument to the subroutine:

```
Sub ShowDate(ByVal aDate As Date)
    MsgBox(aDate.ToShortDateString)
End Sub
```

aDate is a variable that holds the date to be displayed; its type is Date. The ByVal keyword means that the subroutine sees a copy of the variable, not the variable itself. What this means practically is that the subroutine can't change the value of the variable passed by the calling code.

To display a specific date with the second implementation of the subroutine, use a statement like the following:

```
Dim myBirthDate = #2/9/1960#
ShowDate(myBirthDate)
```

Or, you can pass the value to be displayed directly without the use of an intermediate variable:

```
ShowDate(#2/9/1960#)
```

If you later decide to change the format of the date, there's only one place in your code you must edit — the statement that displays the date from within the ShowDate() subroutine.

Functions

A function is similar to a subroutine, but a function returns a result. Because they return values, functions — like variables — have types. The value you pass back to the calling program from a function is called the return value, and its type determines the type of the function. Functions accept arguments, just like subroutines. The statements that make up a function are placed in a set of Function…End Function statements, as shown here:

```
Function NextDay() As Date
    Dim theNextDay As Date
    theNextDay = Now.AddDays(1)
    Return theNextDay
End Function
```

Functions are called like subroutines — by name — but their return value is usually assigned to a variable. To call the NextDay() function, use a statement like this:

```
Dim tomorrow As Date = NextDay()
```

Because functions have types like variables, they can be used anywhere you'd use a variable name. You will find several examples of practical functions later in this chapter, both built-in functions that are part of the language and custom functions. Subroutines are being gradually replaced by functions, and in some languages there are no subroutines, just functions. Even if you need a procedure to perform some task without returning a value, you can implement it as a function that returns a True/False value to indicate whether the operations completed successfully or not.

The Function keyword is followed by the function name and the As keyword that specifies its type, similar to a variable declaration. Inside the preceding sample function, AddDays is a method of the Date type, and it adds a number of days to a date value. The NextDay() function returns tomorrow's date by adding one day to the current date. NextDay() is a custom function, which calls the built-in AddDays method to complete its calculations.

The result of a function is returned to the calling program with the Return statement, which is followed by the value you want to return from your function. This value, which is usually a variable, must be of the same type as the function. In our example, the Return statement happens to be the last statement in the function, but it could appear anywhere; it could even appear several times in the function's code. The first time a Return statement is executed, the function terminates and control is returned to the calling code.

You can also return a value to the calling routine by assigning the result to the name of the function. The following is an alternate method of coding the NextDay() function:

```
Function NextDay() As Date
    NextDay = Now.AddDays(1)
End Function
```

Notice that this time I've assigned the result of the calculation to the function's name directly and haven't use a Return statement. This assignment, however, doesn't terminate the function as the Return statement does. It sets up the function's return value, but the function will terminate when the End Function statement is reached or when an Exit Function statement is encountered.

Similar to the naming of variables, a custom function has a name that must be unique in its scope (which is also true for subroutines, of course). If you declare a function in a form, the function name must be unique in the form. If you declare a function as Public or Friend, its name must be unique in the project. Functions have the same scope rules as variables and can be prefixed by many of the same keywords. In effect, you can modify the default scope of a function with the keywords Public, Private, Protected, Friend, and Protected Friend. In addition, functions have types, just like variables, and they're declared with the As keyword.

Suppose that the function CountWords() counts the number of words and the function CountChars() counts the number of characters in a string. The average length of a word in the string *longString* could be calculated as follows:

```
Dim longString As String, avgLen As Double
longString = TextBox1.Text
avgLen = CountChars(longString) / CountWords(longString)
```

The first executable statement gets the text of a TextBox control and assigns it to a variable, which is then used as an argument to the two functions. When the third statement executes, Visual Basic first calls the functions CountChars() and CountWords() with the specified arguments and then divides the results they return.

The CountWords() function uses the Split method, which isolates the words in a string and returns them as an array of strings. Then the code reads the length of the array, which equals the number of words in the string. The Split method accepts as an argument a character, which is the delimiter it will use to break the string into words. The space character being passed as an argument is enclosed in double quotes, but this is a string, not a character. It's a string that contains a single character, but a string nevertheless. To convert the space string (" ") into a character value, you just append the c character to the string. The number of words in the string is the length of the array that holds the individual words, the *words* array.

```
Function CountWords(ByVal longString As String) As Integer
    Dim words = longString.Split(" "c)
    Return words.Length
End Function

Function CountChars(ByVal longString As String) As Integer
    longString = longString.Replace(" ", "")
    Return longString.Length
End Function
```

You can call functions in the same way that you call subroutines, but the result won't be stored anywhere. For example, the function Convert() might convert the text in a text box to uppercase and return the number of characters it converted. Normally, you'd call this function as follows:

```
nChars = Convert()
```

If you don't care about the return value — you only want to update the text on a TextBox control — you would call the Convert() function with the following statement:

```
Convert()
```

Most of the procedures in an application are functions, not subroutines. The reason is that a function can return (at the very least) a True/False value that indicates whether it completed successfully or not. In the remainder of this chapter, I will focus on functions, but the same principles apply to subroutines as well, except for the return value.

Arguments

Subroutines and functions aren't entirely isolated from the rest of the application. Most procedures accept arguments from the calling program. Recall that an argument is a value you pass to the procedure and on which the procedure usually acts. This is how subroutines and functions communicate with the rest of the application.

Subroutines and functions may accept any number of arguments, and you must supply a value for each argument of the procedure when you call it. Some of the arguments may be optional, which means you can omit them; you will see shortly how to handle optional arguments.

Let's implement a simple custom function to demonstrate the use of arguments. The Min() function, shown next, is a custom function that accepts two arguments and returns the smaller one. Once you write the function, you can call it from within your code just like any built-in function. The difference is that while the built-in functions are always available, the custom functions are available only to the project in which they are declared. Here's the implementation of the Min() function:

```
Function Min(ByVal a As Single, ByVal b As Single) As Single
    Min = IIf(a < b, a, b)
End Function
```

Interestingly, the Min() function calls the IIf() built-in function. IIf() is a built-in function that evaluates the first argument, which is a logical expression. If the expression is True, the IIf() function returns the second argument. If the expression is False, the function returns the third argument.

To call the Min() custom function, use a few statements like the following:

```
Dim val1 As Single = 33.001
Dim val2 As Single = 33.0011
Dim smallerVal as Single
smallerVal = Min(val1, val2)
MsgBox("The smaller value is " & smallerVal)
```

If you execute these statements (place them in a button's Click event handler), you will see the following in a message box:

```
The smaller value is 33.001
```

Or you can insert these statements in the Main subroutine of a Console application and replace the call to the MsgBox function with a call to the Console.WriteLine method to see the output on a console window. Here's what the entire Console application's code should look like:

```
Module Module1

    Sub Main()
        Dim val1 As Single = 33.001
        Dim val2 As Single = 33.0011
        Dim smallerVal As Single
        smallerVal = Min(val1, val2)
        Console.WriteLine("The smaller value is " & smallerVal)
        Console.ReadKey()
    End Sub

    Function Min(ByVal a As Single, ByVal b As Single) As Single
        Min = IIf(a < b, a, b)
    End Function

End Module
```

If you attempt to call the same function with two Double values with a statement like the following, you will see the value 3.33 in the Immediate window:

```
Debug.WriteLine(Min(3.33000000111, 3.33000000222))
```

The compiler converted the two values from Double to Single data type and returned one of them. Which one is it? It doesn't make a difference because when converted to Single, both values are the same.

Interesting things will happen if you attempt to use the Min() function with the Strict option turned on. Insert the statement Option Strict On at the very beginning of the file, or set Option Strict to On in the Compile tab of the project's properties pages. The editor will underline the statement that implements the Min() function: the IIf() function. The IIf() function accepts two Object variables as arguments and returns one of them as its result. The Strict option prevents the compiler from converting an Object to a numeric variable. To use the IIf() function with the Strict option, you must change the Min implementation as follows:

```
Function Min(ByVal a As Object, ByVal b As Object) As Object
    Min = IIf(Val(a) < Val(b), a, b)
End Function
```

It's possible to implement a Min() function that can compare arguments of all types (integers, strings, dates, and so on).

Argument-Passing Mechanisms

One of the most important topics in implementing your own procedures is the mechanism used to pass arguments. The examples so far have used the default mechanism: passing arguments by value. The other mechanism is passing them by reference. Although most programmers use the default mechanism, it's important to know the difference between the two mechanisms and when to use each.

By Value versus by Reference

When you pass an argument by value, the procedure sees only a copy of the argument. Even if the procedure changes this copy, the changes aren't reflected in the original variable passed to the procedure. The benefit of passing arguments by value is that the argument values are isolated from the procedure and only the code segment in which they are declared can change their values.

In VB 6, the default argument-passing mechanism was by reference, and this is something you should be aware of, especially if you're migrating VB 6 code to VB 2010.

To specify the arguments that will be passed by value, use the ByVal keyword in front of the argument's name. If you omit the ByVal keyword, the editor will insert it automatically because it's the default option. Suppose you're creating a function called Degrees() to convert temperatures from degrees Celsius to degrees Fahrenheit. To declare that the Degrees() function's argument is passed by value, use the ByVal keyword in the argument's declaration as follows:

```
Function Degrees(ByVal Celsius as Single) As Single
    Return((9 / 5) * Celsius + 32)
End Function
```

To see what the ByVal keyword does, add a line that changes the value of the argument in the function:

```
Function Degrees(ByVal Celsius as Single) As Single
    Dim Fahrenheit = (9 / 5) * Celsius + 32
    Celsius = 0
    Return Fahrenheit
End Function
```

Now call the function as follows:

```
Dim CTemp As Single = InputBox("Enter temperature in degrees Celsius")
Dim FTemp As Single = Degrees(CTemp)
MsgBox(CTemp.ToString & " degrees Celsius are " &
        FTemp & " degrees Fahrenheit")
```

If you enter the value *32*, the following message is displayed:

```
32 degrees Celsius are 89.6 degrees Fahrenheit
```

The value you specify in the InputBox is stored in the *CTemp* variable, which is then passed to the Degrees() function. The function's return value is then stored in the *FTemp* variable, which is then used to display the result to the user. Replace the ByVal keyword with the ByRef keyword in the function's definition and call the function with the same statements; the program will display the following message:

```
0 degrees Celsius are 89.6 degrees Fahrenheit
```

When the *CTemp* argument was passed to the Degrees() function, its value was 32. But the function changed its value, and upon return it was 0. Because the argument was passed by reference, any changes made by the procedure affected the calling code's variable that was passed into the function.

RETURNING MULTIPLE VALUES

If you want to write a function that returns more than a single result, you will most likely pass additional arguments by reference and set their values from within the function's code. The CalculateStatistics() function, shown a little later in this section, calculates the basic statistics of a data set. The values of the data set are stored in an array, which is passed to the function by reference. The CalculateStatistics() function must return two values: the average and standard deviation of the data set. Here's the declaration of the CalculateStatistics() function:

```
Function CalculateStatistics(ByRef Data() As Double,
            ByRef Avg As Double, ByRef StDev As Double) As Integer
```

The declaration of a procedure is basically its signature; it includes all the information you need in order to use the procedure in your call. Of course, you have to know what the various arguments represent, but this is where the documentation comes in. It's also possible to add a short description for each argument, which will appear in the IntelliSense box, as with the built-in procedures. You'll learn how to automate the documentation of your procedures in the last section of this chapter. The function returns an integer, which is the number of values in the data set. The two important values calculated by the function are returned in the *Avg* and *StDev* arguments:

```
Function CalculateStatistics(ByRef Data() As Double,
            ByRef Avg As Double, ByRef StDev As Double) As Integer
    Dim i As Integer, sum As Double, sumSqr As Double, points As Integer
    points = Data.Length
    For i = 0 To points - 1
        sum = sum + Data(i)
        sumSqr = sumSqr + Data(i) ^ 2
    Next
    Avg = sum / points
    StDev = System.Math.Sqrt(sumSqr / points - Avg ^ 2)
    Return(points)
End Function
```

To call the `CalculateStatistics()` function from within your code, set up an array of Doubles and declare two variables that will hold the average and standard deviation of the data set:

```
Dim Values() = {102.301, 391.200, 19.29, 179.42, 88.031, 208.01}
Dim average, deviation As Double
Dim points As Integer
points = CalculateStatistics(Values, average, deviation)
Debug.WriteLine(points & " values processed.")
Debug.WriteLine("The average is " & average.ToString & " and ")
Debug.WriteLine("the standard deviation is " & deviation.ToString)
```

The simplest method for a function to effectively return multiple values is to pass to it arguments by reference using the ByRef keyword. However, the definition of your functions might become cluttered, especially if you want to return more than a few values. Another problem with this technique is that it's not clear whether an argument must be set before calling the function. As you will see shortly, it is possible for a function to return an array or a custom structure with fields for any number of values.

A NOTE ON REFACTORING CODE

A relatively new term in computer programming, *refactoring*, refers to rewriting a piece of code using procedures. As developers, we tend to insert a lot of code in applications. We start coding a simple operation, and once we get it to work, we realize that we can improve it or add more features to it. The result is a procedure that keeps growing. It doesn't take a rocket scientist to realize that large segments of code are hard to understand and even harder to maintain. That's why there are tools that allow us to break large procedures into smaller ones. The process isn't automatic, of course. As soon as you realize that a procedure has gotten too long, you can select segments of it and implement them as procedures: You move the code into a procedure and insert a call to the procedure in the code's place. The process isn't trivial because you need to pass arguments to the procedure. Refactoring tools do just that: They remove a code segment from a routine and use it to create a new routine. I won't discuss refactoring tools in this book, but you should know that help is available when you decide to reorganize your code.

Built-in Functions

VB provides many functions that implement common or complicated tasks, and you can look them up in the documentation. (You'll find them in the Visual Studio ➤ Visual Basic ➤ Reference ➤ Functions branch of the contents tree in the Visual Studio documentation.) There are functions for the common math operations, functions to perform calculations with dates (these are truly complicated operations), financial functions, and many more. When you use the built-in functions, you don't have to know how they work internally — just how to call them and how to retrieve the return value.

The Pmt() function, for example, calculates the monthly payments on a loan. All you have to know is the arguments you must pass to the function and how to retrieve the result. The syntax of the Pmt() function is as follows, where *MPay* is the monthly payment, *Rate* is the monthly interest rate, and *NPer* is the number of payments (the duration of the loan in months). *PV* is the loan's present value (the amount you took from the bank):

```
MPay = Pmt(Rate, NPer, PV, FV, Due)
```

Due is an optional argument that specifies when the payments are due (the beginning or the end of the month), and *FV* is another optional argument that specifies the future value of an amount. This isn't needed in the case of a loan, but it can help you calculate how much money you should deposit each month to accumulate a target amount over a given time. (The amount returned by the Pmt() function is negative because it's a negative cash flow — it's money you owe — so pay attention to the sign of your values.)

To calculate the monthly payment for a $20,000 loan paid off over a period of six years at a fixed interest rate of 7.25%, you call the Pmt() function, as shown in Listing 3.10.

LISTING 3.10:   Using the Pmt() built-in function

```
Dim mPay, totalPay As Double
Dim Duration As Integer = 6 * 12
Dim Rate As Single = (7.25 / 100) / 12
Dim Amount As Single = 20000
mPay = -Pmt(Rate, Duration, Amount)
totalPay = mPay * Duration
MsgBox("Your monthly payment will be " & mPay.ToString("C") &
          vbCrLf & "You will pay back a total of " &
          totalPay.ToString("C"))
```

Notice that the interest (7.25%) is divided by 12 because the function requires the monthly interest. The value returned by the function is the monthly payment for the loan specified with the *Duration, Amount,* and *Rate* variables. If you place the preceding lines in the Click event handler of a button, run the project, and then click the button, the following message will appear in a message box:

```
Your monthly payment will be $343.39
You will pay back a total of $24,723.80
```

Let's say you want to accumulate $40,000 over the next 15 years by making monthly deposits of equal amounts. To calculate the monthly deposit amount, you must call the Pmt() function, passing 0 as the present value and the target amount as the future value. Replace the statements in the button's Click event handler with the following and run the project:

```
Dim mPay As Double
Dim Duration As Integer = 15 * 12
Dim Rate As Single = (4.0 / 100.0) / 12
Dim Amount As Single = -40000.0
mPay = Pmt(Rate, Duration, 0, Amount)
MsgBox("A monthly deposit of " & mPay.ToString("C") & vbCrLf &
        "every month will yield $40,000 in 15 years")
```

It turns out that if you want to accumulate $40,000 over the next 15 years to send your kid to college, assuming a constant interest rate of 4%, you must deposit $162.54 every month. You'll put out almost $30,000, and the rest will be the interest you earn.

Pmt() is one of the simpler financial functions provided by the Framework, but most of us would find it really difficult to write the code for this function. Because financial calculations are quite common in business programming, many of the functions you might need already exist, and all you need to know is how to call them. If you're developing financial applications, you should look up the financial functions in the documentation. You can experiment with the Pmt() function (and learn the basics of banking) by finding out the monthly payments for a loan and an investment of the same amount and same duration, using the current interest rates.

Let's look at another useful built-in function, the MonthName() function, which accepts as an argument a month number and returns the name of the month. This function is not as trivial as you might think because it returns the month name or its abbreviation in the language of the current culture. The MonthName() function accepts as arguments the month number and a True/False value that determines whether it will return the abbreviation or the full name of the month. The following statements display the name of the current month (both the abbreviation and the full name). Every time you execute these statements, you will see the current month's name in the current language:

```
Dim mName As String
mName = MonthName(Now.Month, True)
MsgBox(mName)     ' prints "Jan"
mName = MonthName(Now.Month, False)
MsgBox(mName)     ' prints "January"
```

A similar function, the WeekDayName() function, returns the name of the week for a specific weekday. This function accepts an additional argument that determines the first day of the week. (See the documentation for more information on the syntax of the WeekDayName() function.)

The primary role of functions is to extend the functionality of the language. Many functions that perform rather common practical operations have been included in the language, but they aren't nearly enough for the needs of all developers or all types of applications. Besides the built-in functions, you can write custom functions to simplify the development of your custom applications, as explained in the following section.

Custom Functions

Most of the code we write is in the form of custom functions or subroutines that are called from several places in the application. Subroutines are just like functions except that they don't return a value, so we'll focus on the implementation of custom functions. With the exception of a function's return value, everything else presented in this and the following section applies to subroutines as well.

Let's look at an example of a fairly simple (but not trivial) function that does something useful. Books are identified by a unique international standard book number (ISBN), and every application that manages books needs a function to verify the ISBN, which is made up of 12 digits followed by a check digit. To calculate the check digit, you multiply each of the 12 digits by a constant; the first digit is multiplied by 1, the second digit is multiplied by 3, the third digit by 1 again, the fourth digit by 3, and so on. The sum of these multiplications is then divided by 10, and we take the remainder. The check digit is this remainder subtracted from 10. To calculate the check digit for the ISBN 978078212283, compute the sum of the following products:

$$9 * 1 + 7 * 3 + 8 * 1 + 0 * 3 + 7 * 1 + 8 * 3 +$$
$$2 * 1 + 1 * 3 + 2 * 1 + 2 * 3 + 8 * 1 + 3 * 3 = 99$$

The sum is 99; when you divide it by 10, the remainder is 9. The check digit is 10 – 9, or 1, and the book's complete ISBN is 9780782122831. The ISBNCheckDigit() function, shown in Listing 3.11, accepts the 12 digits of the ISBN as an argument and returns the appropriate check digit.

LISTING 3.11: The ISBNCheckDigit() custom function

```
Function ISBNCheckDigit(ByVal ISBN As String) As String
    Dim i As Integer, chksum As Integer = 0
    Dim chkDigit As Integer
    Dim factor As Integer = 3
    For i = 0 To 11
        factor = 4 - factor
        chksum += factor * Convert.ToInt16(ISBN.SubString(i, 1))
    Next
    Return (10 - (chksum Mod 10)).ToString
End Function
```

The ISBNCheckDigit() function returns a string value because ISBNs are handled as strings, not numbers. (Leading zeros are important in an ISBN but are totally meaningless, and omitted, in a numeric value.) The SubString method of a String object extracts a number of characters from the string to which it's applied. The first argument is the starting location in the string, and the second is the number of characters to be extracted. The expression ISBN.SubString(i, 1) extracts one character at a time from the *ISBN* string variable. During the first iteration of the loop, it extracts the first character; during the second iteration, it extracts the second character; and so on.

The extracted character is a numeric digit stored as a character, which is converted to its numeric value and then multiplied by the *factor* variable value. The result is added to the *chkSum* variable. This variable is the checksum of the ISBN. After it has been calculated, we divide it by 10 and take its remainder (the Mod operator returns the remainder of this division), which we subtract from 10. This is the ISBN's check digit and the function's return value.

You can use this function in an application that maintains a book database to make sure all books are entered with a valid ISBN. You can also use it with a web application that allows viewers to request books by their ISBN. The same code will work with two different applications, and you can even pass it to other developers. Developers using your function don't have to know how the check digit is calculated, just how to call the function and retrieve its result. In Chapter 8, "Working with Objects," you'll learn how to package this function as a method so that other developers can use it without having access to your code. They will be able to call it to calculate an ISBN's check digit, but they won't be able to modify the function's code.

To test the ISBNCheckDigit() function, start a new project, place a button on the form, and enter the following statements in its Click event handler (or open the ISBN project in the folder with this chapter's sample projects at **www.sybex.com/go/masteringvb2010**):

```
Private Sub Button1_Click(ByVal sender As System.Object,
                ByVal e As System.EventArgs) Handles Button1.Click
    Console.WriteLine("The check Digit is " &
                ISBNCheckDigit("978078212283"))
End Sub
```

After inserting the code of the ISBNCheckDigit() function and the code that calls the function, your code editor should look like Figure 3.1. You can place a TextBox control on the form and pass the Text property of the control to the ISBNCheckDigit() function to calculate the check digit.

FIGURE 3.1
Calling the
ISBNCheckDigit()
function

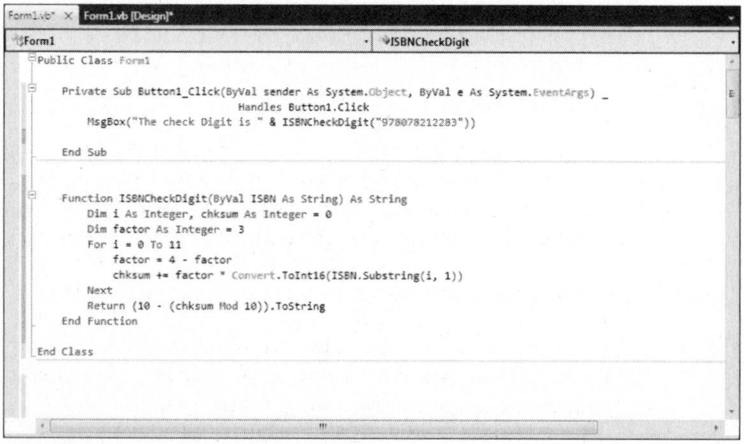

A similar algorithm is used for calculating the check digit of credit cards: the Luhns algorithm. You can look it up on the Internet and write a custom function for validating credit card numbers.

Passing Arguments and Returning Values

So far, you've learned how to write and call procedures with a few simple arguments and how to retrieve the function's return value and use it in your code. This section covers a few advanced topics on argument-passing techniques and how to write functions that return multiple values, arrays of values, and custom data types.

PASSING AN UNKNOWN NUMBER OF ARGUMENTS

Generally, all the arguments that a procedure expects are listed in the procedure's definition, and the program that calls the procedure must supply values for all arguments. On occasion, however, you might not know how many arguments will be passed to the procedure. Procedures that calculate averages or, in general, process multiple values can accept from a few to several arguments whose count is not known at design time. Visual Basic supports the ParamArray keyword, which allows you to pass a variable number of arguments to a procedure. There are situations where you might not know in advance whether a procedure will be called with two or two dozen arguments, and this is where the ParamArray comes in very handy because it allows you to pass an array with any number of arguments.

Let's look at an example. Suppose that you want to populate a ListBox control with elements. To add a single item to the ListBox control, you call the Add method of its Items collection as follows:

```
ListBox1.Items.Add("new item")
```

This statement adds the string new item to the *ListBox1* control. If you frequently add multiple items to a ListBox control from within your code, you can write a subroutine that performs this task. The following subroutine adds a variable number of arguments to the *ListBox1* control:

```
Sub AddNamesToList(ByVal ParamArray NamesArray() As Object)
    Dim x As Object
    For Each x In NamesArray
        ListBox1.Items.Add(x)
    Next x
End Sub
```

This subroutine's argument is an array prefixed with the keyword ParamArray. This array holds all the parameters passed to the subroutine. If the parameter array holds items of the same type, you can declare the array to be of the specific type (string, integer, and so on). To add items to the list, call the AddNamesToList() subroutine as follows:

```
AddNamesToList("Robert", "Manny", "Renee", "Charles", "Madonna")
```

If you want to know the number of arguments actually passed to the procedure, use the Length property of the parameter array. The number of arguments passed to the AddNamesToList() subroutine is given by the following expression:

```
NamesArray.Length
```

The following loop goes through all the elements of the *NamesArray* array and adds them to the list (this is an alternate implementation of the `AddNamesToList` subroutine):

```
Dim i As Integer
For i = 0 to NamesArray.Length
    ListBox1.Items.Add(NamesArray(i))
Next i
```

A procedure that accepts multiple arguments relies on the order of the arguments. To omit some of the arguments, you must use the corresponding comma. Let's say you want to call such a procedure and specify the first, third, and fourth arguments. The procedure must be called as follows:

```
ProcName(arg1, , arg3, arg4)
```

The arguments to similar procedures are frequently of equal stature, and their order doesn't make any difference. A function that calculates the mean or other basic statistics of a set of numbers, or a subroutine that populates a ListBox or ComboBox control, is prime candidates for this type of implementation. If the procedure accepts a variable number of arguments that aren't equal in stature, you should consider the technique described in the following section. If the function accepts a parameter array, the parameter array must be the last argument in the list, and none of the other parameters can be optional.

NAMED ARGUMENTS

You learned how to write procedures with optional arguments and how to pass a variable number of arguments to the procedure. The main limitation of the argument-passing mechanism, though, is the order of the arguments. By default, Visual Basic matches the values passed to a procedure to the declared arguments by their order (which is why the arguments you've seen so far are called positional arguments).

This limitation is lifted by Visual Basic's capability to understand named arguments. With named arguments, you can supply arguments in any order because they are recognized by name and not by their order in the list of the procedure's arguments. Suppose you've written a function that expects three arguments: a name, an address, and an email address:

```
Sub CreateContact(Name As String, Address As String, EMail As String)
```

Presumably, this subroutine creates a new contact with the specified data, but right now we're not interested in the implementation of the function, just how to call it. When calling this subroutine, you must supply three strings that correspond to the arguments *Name*, *Address*, and *EMail*, in that order. You can call this subroutine as follows:

```
CreateContact("Peter Evans", "2020 Palm Ave., Santa Barbara, CA 90000",
              "PeterEvans@example.com")
```

However, there's a safer way. You can call it by supplying the arguments in any order by their names:

```
CreateContact(Address:= "2020 Palm Ave., Santa Barbara, CA 90000",
              EMail:= "PeterEvans@example.com", Name:= "Peter Evans")
```

The := operator assigns values to the named arguments. Because the arguments are passed by name, you can supply them in any order.

To test this technique, enter the following subroutine declaration in a form's code:

```
Sub CreateContact(ByVal Name As String, ByVal Address As String,
                  ByVal EMail As String)
    Debug.WriteLine(Name)
    Debug.WriteLine(Address)
    Debug.WriteLine(EMail)
End Function
```

Then call the CreateContact() subroutine from within a button's Click event with the following statement:

```
Debug.WriteLine(
        CreateContact(Address:= "2020 Palm Ave., Santa Barbara, CA 90000",
                      Name:= "Peter Evans", EMail:= "PeterEvans@example.com"))
```

You'll see the following in the Immediate window:

```
Peter Evans
2020 Palm Ave., Santa Barbara, CA 90000
PeterEvans@example.com
```

The subroutine knows which value corresponds to which argument and can process them the same way that it processes positional arguments. Notice that the subroutine's definition is the same, whether you call it with positional or named arguments. The difference is in how you call the subroutine and not how you declare it.

Named arguments make code safer and easier to read, but because they require a lot of typing, most programmers don't use them. Besides, when IntelliSense is on, you can see the definition of the function as you enter the arguments, and this minimizes the chances of swapping two values by mistake.

FUNCTIONS RETURNING ARRAYS

In addition to returning custom data types, VB 2010 functions can return arrays. This is an interesting possibility that allows you to write functions that return not only multiple values, but also any number of values.

In this section, we'll write the Statistics() function, similar to the CalculateStatistics() function you saw a little earlier in this chapter. The Statistics() function returns the statistics in an array. Moreover, it returns not only the average and the standard deviation, but the minimum and maximum values in the data set as well. One way to declare a function that calculates all the statistics is as follows:

```
Function Statistics(ByRef DataArray() As Double) As Double()
```

This function accepts an array with the data values and returns an array of Doubles. To implement a function that returns an array, you must do the following:

1. Specify a type for the function's return value and add a pair of parentheses after the type's name. Don't specify the dimensions of the array to be returned here; the array will be declared formally in the function.

2. In the function's code, declare an array of the same type and specify its dimensions. If the function should return four values, use a declaration like this one:

```
Dim Results(3) As Double
```

The Results array, which will be used to store the results, must be of the same type as the function — its name can be anything.

3. To return the Results array, simply use it as an argument to the Return statement:

```
Return(Results)
```

4. In the calling procedure, you must declare an array of the same type without dimensions:

```
Dim Statistics() As Double
```

5. Finally, you must call the function and assign its return value to this array:

```
Stats() = Statistics(DataSet())
```

Here, *DataSet* is an array with the values whose basic statistics will be calculated by the Statistics() function. Your code can then retrieve each element of the array with an index value as usual.

Overloading Functions

There are situations in which the same function must operate on different data types or a different number of arguments. In the past, you had to write different functions, with different names and different arguments, to accommodate similar requirements. The Framework introduced the concept of function overloading, which means that you can have multiple implementations of the same function, each with a different set of arguments and possibly a different return value. Yet all overloaded functions share the same name. Let me introduce this concept by examining one of the many overloaded functions that comes with the .NET Framework.

The Next method of the System.Random class returns a random integer value from –2,147,483,648 to 2,147,483,647. (This is the range of values that can be represented by the Integer data type.) We should also be able to generate random numbers in a limited range of integer values. To emulate the throw of a die, we want a random value in the range from 1 to 6, whereas for a roulette game we want an integer random value in the range from 0 to 36. You can specify an upper limit for the random number with an optional integer argument. The following statement will return a random integer in the range from 0 to 99:

```
randomInt = rnd.Next(100)
```

You can also specify both the lower and upper limits of the random number's range. The following statement will return a random integer in the range from 1,000 to 1,999:

```
randomInt = rnd.Next(1000, 2000)
```

To use the Random class in your code, you must create a variable of this type and then call its methods:

```
Dim rnd As New Math.Random
MsgBox(rnd.Next(1, 6))
```

The same method behaves differently based on the arguments we supply. The behavior of the method depends on the type of the arguments, the number of the arguments, or both. As you will see, there's no single function that alters its behavior based on its arguments. There are as many different implementations of the same function as there are argument combinations. All the functions share the same name, so they appear to the user as a single multifaceted function. These functions are overloaded, and you'll see how they're implemented in the following section.

If you haven't turned off the IntelliSense feature of the editor, as soon as you type the opening parenthesis after a function or method name, you'll see a yellow box with the syntax of the function or method. You'll know that a function, or a method, is overloaded when this box contains a number and two arrows. Each number corresponds to a different overloaded form, and you can move to the next or previous overloaded form by clicking the two little arrows or by pressing the arrow keys.

Let's return to the Min() function we implemented earlier in this chapter. The initial implementation of the Min() function is shown next:

```
Function Min(ByVal a As Double, ByVal b As Double) As Double
    Min = IIf(a < b, a, b)
End Function
```

By accepting Double values as arguments, this function can handle all numeric types. VB 2010 performs automatic widening conversions (it can convert Integers and Decimals to Doubles), so this trick makes the function work with all numeric data types. However, what about strings? If you attempt to call the Min() function with two strings as arguments, you'll get a compiler error. The Min() function just can't handle strings.

To write a Min() function that can handle both numeric and string values, you must write two Min() functions. All Min() functions must be prefixed with the Overloads keyword. The following statements show two different implementations of the same function, one for numbers and another one for strings:

```
Overloads Function Min(ByVal a As Double, ByVal b As Double) As Double
    Min = Convert.ToDouble(IIf(a < b, a, b))
End Function

Overloads Function Min(ByVal a As String, ByVal b As String) As String
    Min = Convert.ToString(IIf(a < b, a, b))
End Function
```

You need a third overloaded form of the same function to compare dates. If you call the `Min()` function, passing as an argument two dates as in the following statement, the `Min()` function will compare them as strings and return (incorrectly) the first date:

```
Debug.WriteLine(Min(#1/1/2011#, #3/4/2010#))
```

This statement is not even valid when the Strict option is on, so you clearly need another over-loaded form of the function that accepts two dates as arguments, as shown here:

```
Overloads Function Min(ByVal a As Date, ByVal b As Date) As Date
    Min = Convert.ToDateTime(IIf(a < b, a, b))
End Function
```

If you now call the `Min()` function with the dates #1/1/2011# and #3/4/2010#, the function will return the second date, which is chronologically smaller than the first. Assuming that you have inserted the three forms of the `Min()` function in your code as shown in Figure 3.2, as soon you enter the name of the function, the IntelliSense box will display the first form of the function. Click the buttons with the arrows to see the other ones and select the appropriate form.

FIGURE 3.2
(Top) The implementation of three overloaded forms of a function.
(Bottom) The three overloaded forms of the `Min()` function in the IntelliSense list.

```
Overloads Function Min(ByVal a As Date, ByVal b As Date) As Date
    Min = Convert.ToDateTime(IIf(a < b, a, b))
End Function

Overloads Function Min(ByVal a As Double, ByVal b As Double) As Double
    Min = Convert.ToDouble(IIf(a < b, a, b))
End Function

Overloads Function Min(ByVal a As String, ByVal b As String) As String
    Min = Convert.ToString(IIf(a < b, a, b))
End Function
```

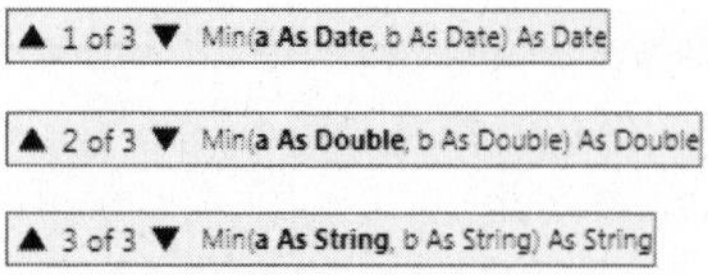

```
▲ 1 of 3 ▼  Min(a As Date, b As Date) As Date
```

```
▲ 2 of 3 ▼  Min(a As Double, b As Double) As Double
```

```
▲ 3 of 3 ▼  Min(a As String, b As String) As String
```

If you're wondering about the `Convert.ToDateTime` method, it's used because the `IIf()` function returns a value of the Object type. Each of the overloaded forms of the `Min()` function, however, has a specific type. If the Strict option is on (the recommended setting), you should make sure the function returns the appropriate type by converting the result of the `IIf()` function to the corresponding type, as shown in the preceding `Min()` examples.

VB2010 AT WORK: THE OVERLOADEDFUNCTIONS PROJECT

Let's look into a more complicated overloaded function, which makes use of some topics discussed later in this book. The `CountFiles()` function that follows counts the number of files in a folder that meet certain criteria. The criteria could be the size of the files, their type, or the date they were created. You can come up with any combination of these criteria, but the following are the most useful combinations. (These are the functions I would use, but you can create even more combinations or introduce new criteria of your own.) The names of the arguments are self-descriptive, so I won't explain what each form of the CountFiles() function does.

```
CountFiles(ByVal minSize As Integer, ByVal maxSize As Integer) As Integer
CountFiles(ByVal fromDate As Date, ByVal toDate As Date) As Integer
CountFiles(ByVal type As String) As Integer
CountFiles(ByVal minSize As Integer, ByVal maxSize As Integer,
           ByVal type As String) As Integer
CountFiles(ByVal fromDate As Date, ByVal toDate As Date,
           ByVal type As String) As Integer
```

Listing 3.12 shows an implementation of these overloaded forms of the CountFiles() function. (I'm not showing all overloaded forms of the function; you can open the Overloaded-Functions project in the IDE and examine the code.) Because we haven't discussed file operations yet, most of the code in the function's body will be new to you — but it's not hard to follow. For the benefit of readers who are totally unfamiliar with file operations, I included a statement that prints in the Immediate window the type of files counted by each function. The Debug.WriteLine statement prints the values of the arguments passed to the function along with a description of the type of search it will perform. The overloaded form that accepts two integer values as arguments prints something like this:

```
You've requested the files between 1000 and 100000 bytes
```

The overloaded form that accepts a string as an argument prints the following:

```
You've requested the .EXE files
```

LISTING 3.12: The overloaded implementations of the CountFiles() function

```
Overloads Function CountFiles(
                ByVal minSize As Integer, ByVal maxSize As Integer) As Integer
    Debug.WriteLine("You've requested the files between " &
                minSize & " and " & maxSize & " bytes")
    Dim files() As String
    files = System.IO.Directory.GetFiles("c:\windows")
    Dim i, fileCount As Integer
    For i = 0 To files.GetUpperBound(0)
       Dim FI As New System.IO.FileInfo(files(i))
       If FI.Length >= minSize And FI.Length <= maxSize Then
          fileCount = fileCount + 1
       End If
    Next
    Return(fileCount)
End Function

Overloads Function CountFiles(
```

```
                        ByVal fromDate As Date, ByVal toDate As Date) As Integer
    Debug.WriteLine("You've requested the count of files created from " &
                        fromDate & " to " & toDate)
    Dim files() As String
    files = System.IO.Directory.GetFiles("c:\windows")
    Dim i, fileCount As Integer
    For i = 0 To files.GetUpperBound(0)
        Dim FI As New System.IO.FileInfo(files(i))
        If FI.CreationTime.Date >= fromDate And
                FI.CreationTime.Date <= toDate Then
            fileCount = fileCount + 1
        End If
    Next
    Return(fileCount)
End Function

Overloads Function CountFiles(ByVal type As String) As Integer
    Debug.WriteLine("You've requested the " & type & " files")
    ' Function Implementation

End Function

Overloads Function CountFiles(
                    ByVal minSize As Integer, ByVal maxSize As Integer,
                    ByVal type As String) As Integer
    Debug.WriteLine("You've requested the " & type &
                    " files between " & minSize & " and " &
                    maxSize & " bytes")
    ' Function implementation
End Function

Overloads Function CountFiles(
                    ByVal fromDate As Date,
                    ByVal toDate As Date, ByVal type As String) As Integer
    Debug.WriteLine("You've requested the " & type &
                    " files created from " & fromDate & " to " & toDate)
    ' Function implementation
End Function
```

If you're unfamiliar with the Directory and File objects, focus on the statement that prints to the Immediate window and ignore the statements that actually count the files that meet the specified criteria. After reading the tutorial "Accessing Folders and Files," published at www.sybex.com/go/masteringvb2010, you can revisit this example and understand the statements that select the qualifying files and count them.

Start a new project and enter the definitions of the overloaded forms of the function on the form's level. Listing 3.12 is lengthy, but all the overloaded functions have the same structure and differ only in how they select the files to count. Then place a TextBox and a button on the form, as shown in Figure 3.3, and enter a few statements that exercise the various overloaded forms of the function (such as the ones shown in Listing 3.13) in the button's `Click` event handler.

LISTING 3.13:   Testing the overloaded forms of the `CountFiles()` function

```
Private Sub Button1_Click(…) Handles Button1.Click
    TextBox1.AppendText(CountFiles(1000, 100000) &
               " files with size between 1KB and 100KB" & vbCrLf)
    TextBox1.AppendText(CountFiles(#1/1/2006#, #12/31/2006#) &
               " files created in 2006" & vbCrLf)
    TextBox1.AppendText(CountFiles(".BMP") & " BMP files" & vbCrLf)
    TextBox1.AppendText(CountFiles(1000, 100000, ".EXE") &
               " EXE files between 1 and 100 KB" & vbCrLf)
    TextBox1.AppendText(CountFiles(#1/1/2006#, #12/31/2007#, ".EXE") &
               " EXE files created in 2006 and 2007")
End Sub
```

FIGURE 3.3
The OverloadedFunctions project

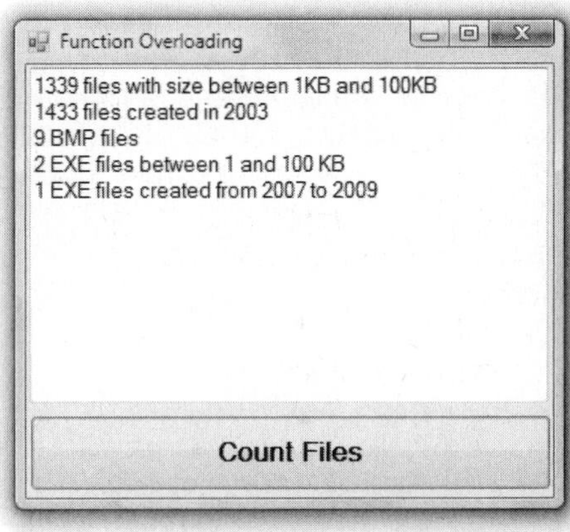

The button calls the various overloaded forms of the `CountFiles()` function one after the other and prints the results on the TextBox control. From now on, I'll be omitting the list of arguments in the most common event handlers, such as the `Click` event handler, because they're always the same and they don't add to the readability of the code. In place of the two arguments, I'll insert an ellipsis to indicate the lack of the arguments.

Function overloading is used heavily throughout the language. There are relatively few functions (or methods, for that matter) that aren't overloaded. Every time you enter the name of a function followed by an opening parenthesis, a list of its arguments appears in the drop-down list with the arguments of the function. If the function is overloaded, you'll see a number in front of the list of arguments, as shown in Figure 3.4. This number is the order of the overloaded form of the function, and it's followed by the arguments of the specific form of the function. The figure shows all the forms of the CountFiles() function.

FIGURE 3.4
The overloaded forms
of the CountFiles()
function

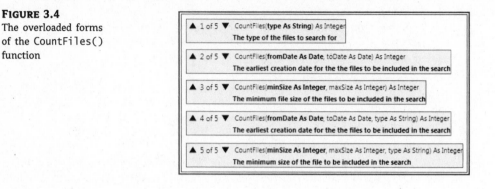

DOCUMENTING FUNCTIONS

When working with overloaded functions and methods, you need as much help from the editor as possible because there are many arguments taken in total. You can document each argument of each overloaded form with a short description that will be displayed in the IntelliSense box as the user enters the argument values for the selected form, as shown in Figure 3.4. The same techniques apply to all functions, of course, not just to overloaded functions. While you can get by without documenting functions that are not overloaded, it's almost a necessity when working with overloaded functions. To document a function, enter three single quotes in an empty line of the editor, just before the function's definition. As soon as you type the third quote, the editor will insert a boilerplate for the function as follows:

```
''' <summary>
''' 
''' </summary>
''' <param name="fromDate"></param>
''' <param name="toDate"></param>
''' <param name="type"></param>
''' <returns></returns>
''' <remarks></remarks>
```

Enter any comments about the function in the summary section, even notes to yourself about future improvements, desired but not implemented features, and so on. There's a param section for each of the arguments where you must insert a short description regarding each argument. This is the description that will appear in the IntelliSense drop-down list as the user enters each argument. Finally, in the returns section you must enter the function's description, which will be also displayed in the IntelliSense list. Here's the documentation of one of the overloaded forms of the CountFiles method:

```
''' <summary>
''' 
''' </summary>
```

```
'''    <param name="minSize">The minimum size of the file to be included
       in the search</param>
'''    <param name="maxSize">The maximum size of the file to be included
       in the search</param>
'''    <param name="type">The number of files of the specified type</param>
'''    <returns>The number of files with a size in a given range
       and of a specific type</returns>
'''    <remarks></remarks>
```

The Bottom Line

Use Visual Basic's flow-control statements Visual Basic provides several statements for controlling the flow of control in a program: decision statements, which change the course of execution based on the outcome of a comparison, and loop statements, which repeat a number of statements while a condition is true or false.

Master It Explain briefly the decision statements of Visual Basic.

Write subroutines and functions To manage large applications, break your code into small, manageable units. These units of code are the subroutines and functions. Subroutines perform actions and don't return any values. Functions, on the other hand, perform calculations and return values. Most of the language's built-in functionality is in the form of functions.

Master It How will you create multiple overloaded forms of the same function?

Pass arguments to subroutines and functions Procedures and functions communicate with one another via arguments, which are listed in a pair of parentheses following the procedure's name. Each argument has a name and a type. When you call a procedure, you must supply values for each argument, and the types of the values should match the types listed in the procedure's definition.

Master It Explain the difference between passing arguments by value and passing arguments by reference.

Part 2

Developing Windows Applications

Chapter 4

GUI Design and Event-Driven Programming

The first three chapters of this book introduced you to the basics of designing applications with Visual Studio 2010 and the components of the Visual Basic language. You know how to design graphical user interfaces (GUIs) and how to use Visual Basic statements to program events for the various controls. You also know how to write functions and subroutines and how to call the functions and subroutines that are built into Visual Basic.

In this chapter, you'll design a few more Windows applications — this time, a few practical applications with more functional interfaces and a bit of code that does something more practical. You'll put together the information presented so far in the book by building Windows applications with the visual tools of Visual Studio, and you'll see how the applications interact with users by coding the events of interest. If you are new to Visual Studio, you should design the examples on your own using the instructions in the text rather than open the projects for this chapter (available for download at www.sybex.com/go/masteringvb2010) and look at the code.

In this chapter, you will learn how to do the following:

◆ Design graphical user interfaces

◆ Program events

◆ Write robust applications with error handling

On Designing Windows Applications

As you recall from Chapter 1, "Getting Started with Visual Basic 2010," the design of a Windows application consists of two distinct phases: the design of the application's interface and the coding of the application. The design of the interface is performed with visual tools and consists of creating a form with the relevant elements. These elements are the building blocks of Windows applications and are called controls.

The available controls are shown in the Toolbox and are the same elements used by all Windows applications. You can purchase additional controls from third-party vendors or create your own custom controls. After you install third-party or custom controls, they will appear in the Toolbox alongside the built-in controls. In addition to being visually rich, the controls embed a lot of functionality. The TextBox control, for example, can handle text on its own, without any programming effort on your part. The ComboBox control expands the list with its items when users click the arrow button and displays the selected item in its edit box. In general, the basic functionality of the controls is built in by design so that all applications maintain a consistent look.

The interface dictates how users will interact with your application. To prompt users for text or numeric data, use TextBox controls. When it comes to specifying one or more of several options, you have many choices: You can use a ComboBox control from which users can select an option, or you can put a few CheckBox controls on a form that users can select or clear. If you want to display a small number of mutually exclusive options, place a few RadioButton controls on the form. Every time the user selects an option, the previously selected one is cleared. To initiate actions, place one or more Button controls on the form. You will learn more about basic Windows controls and their properties in Chapter 5, "The Basic Windows Controls."

Controls expose a large number of properties, which are displayed in the Properties window at design time. You use these properties to adjust not only the appearance of the controls on the form but their functionality as well. The process of designing the interface consists mostly of setting the properties of the various controls. By the way, you can also set the properties of controls through code. The code will take effect in runtime. You will see some examples of such code in the next chapter.

An important aspect of the design of your application's user interface is the alignment of the controls on the form. Controls that are next to one another should be aligned horizontally. Controls that are stacked should have either their left or right edges aligned vertically. You should also make sure the controls are spaced equally. The integrated development environment (IDE) provides all the tools for sizing, aligning, and spacing controls on the form, and you'll see these tools in action through examples in this chapter.

By designing the interface you have practically outlined how the application will interact with the user. The next step is to actually implement the interaction by writing some code. The programming model of Visual Basic is event driven: As the user interacts with the controls on your form, some code is executed in response to user actions. The user's actions cause events, and each control recognizes its own set of events and handles them through subroutines, which are called *event handlers*. When users click a button, the control's Click event is fired, and you must insert the relevant code in the control's Click event handler. The event-driven programming model has proven very successful because it allows developers to focus on handling specific actions. It allows you to break a large application into smaller, manageable units of code and implement each unit of code independently of any other.

Developing Windows applications is a conceptually simple process, but there's a methodology to it and it's not trivial. Fortunately, the IDE provides many tools to simplify the process; it will even catch most of the errors in your code as you type. You have seen how to use some of the tools of the IDE in the first three chapters. In this chapter, I'll present these tools through examples.

Building a Loan Calculator

One easy-to-implement, practical application is a program that calculates loan parameters. Visual Basic provides built-in functions for performing many types of financial calculations, and you need only a single line of code to calculate the monthly payment given the loan amount, its duration, and the interest rate. Designing the user interface, however, takes much more effort.

Regardless of the language you use, you must go through the following process to develop an application:

1. Decide what the application will do and how it will interact with the user.

2. Design the application's user interface according to the requirements of step 1.

3. Write the actual code behind the events you want to handle.

🌐 Real World Scenario

USING PROTOTYPES TO CAPTURE APPLICATION REQUIREMENTS

A prototype is an incomplete version of an application that simulates some aspects of application functionality. The prototype is created by using constant or hard-coded values to supplant values the program should calculate in runtime. For example, a prototype for the Loan Calculator application (see Figure 4.1) might display the form with all of the controls necessary for loan calculation. However, when the user presses the Monthly Payment button, the value that appears in the Monthly Payment text box would always be the same hard-coded value and would not vary with input from the other controls.

Most commonly, prototypes are used to simulate the user interface. The purpose of the prototype is to get the customer's approval on the appearance and functionality of an application. Instead of reading documentation or analyzing drawings of the interface, users can actually try out the application. This often facilitates user feedback in early application development stages. Some prototypes are throw-away applications while others can be evolved further into fully functional applications. Visual Basic is well known for its rapid prototyping features.

Understanding How the Loan Calculator Application Works

Following the first step of the process outlined previously, you decide that the user should be able to specify the amount of the loan, the interest rate, and the duration of the loan in months. You must, therefore, provide three text boxes in which the user can enter these values.

Another parameter affecting the monthly payment is whether payments are made at the beginning or at the end of each month, so you must also provide a way for the user to specify whether the payments will be early (first day of the month) or late (last day of the month). The most appropriate type of control for entering Yes/No or True/False type of information is the CheckBox control. This control is a toggle: If it's selected, you can clear it by clicking it; if it's cleared, you can select it by clicking again. The user doesn't enter any data in this control (which means you need not anticipate user errors with this control), and it's the simplest method for specifying values with two possible states.

Figure 4.1 shows a user interface that matches our design specifications. This is the main form of the LoanCalculator project, which you will find in this chapter's folder on the book's project download site.

The user enters all the information on the form and then clicks the Monthly Payment button to calculate the monthly payment. The program will calculate the monthly payment and display it in the lower TextBox control. All the action takes place in the Monthly Payment button's Click event handler.

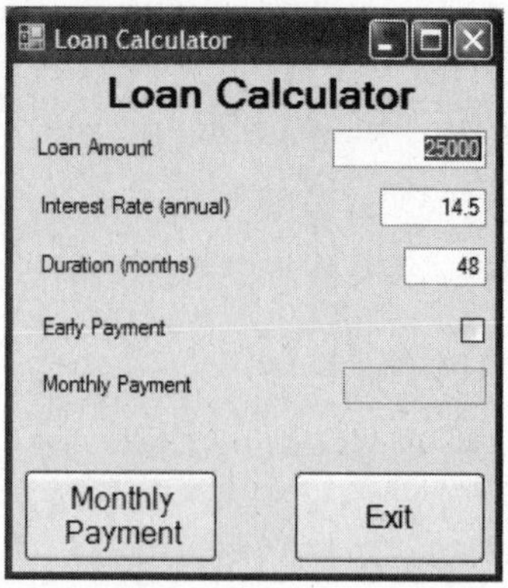

FIGURE 4.1
LoanCalculator is a simple financial application.

To calculate the monthly payments on a loan, we call the built-in Pmt () function, whose syntax is as follows:

```
MonthlyPayment = Pmt(InterestRate, Periods, Amount, FutureValue, Due)
```

THE Pmt () FUNCTION

Here's how the Pmt () function works. The interest rate, argument *InterestRate*, is specified as a monthly rate. If the annual interest rate is 14.5 percent, the value entered by the user in the Interest Rate box should be 14.5. The user will express the rate as a percentage, but the function accepts the decimal value. To convert percentage to a decimal value, you need to multiply the annual percentage rate by 0.01. Finally, since this is the annual rate and you need a monthly value, you need to divide the value by 12. The mathematical expression for converting the annual interest rate specified by the user to a monthly interest rate accepted by the Pmt() function is: `0.01 * annualInterestRate / 12`. In this example, with a 14.5 annual rate, the monthly rate will be 0.145/12. The duration of the loan, the *Periods* argument, is specified in number of months, and the *Amount* argument is the total loan amount. The *FutureValue* argument is the value of the loan at the end of the period, which should be zero (it would be a positive value for an investment), and the last argument, *Due*, specifies when payments are due. The value of *Due* can be one of the constants *DueDate.BegOfPeriod* and *DueDate.EndOfPeriod*. These two constants are built into the language, and you can use them without knowing their exact value.

The present value of the loan is the amount of the loan with a negative sign. It's negative because you don't have the money now. You're borrowing it — it is money you owe to the bank. Future value represents the value of something at a stated time — in this case, what the loan will be worth when it's paid off. This is what one side owes the other at the end of the specified period. So the future value of a loan is zero.

You don't need to know how the Pmt () function calculates the monthly payment, just how to call it and how to retrieve the results. To calculate the monthly payment on a loan of $25,000 with an interest rate of 14.5 percent, payable over 48 months and payments due the last day of the payment period (which in this case is a month), you'd call the Pmt() function as follows:

```
Pmt(0.145 / 12, 48, -25000, 0, DueDate.EndOfPeriod)
```

The Pmt() function will return the value 689.448821287218. Because it's a dollar amount, you must round it to two decimal digits on the interface. Notice the negative sign in front of the *Amount* argument in the statement. If you specify a positive amount, the result will be a negative payment. The payment and the loan's amount have different signs because they represent different cash flows. The loan's amount is money you *owe* to the bank, whereas the payment is money you *pay* to the bank.

The last two arguments of the Pmt() function are optional. The Parameter Info feature of the IntelliSense autocompletion system built into Visual Studio will indicate optional parameters by placing them inside the square brackets in the Parameter Info pop-up window, as shown here.

```
        Payment = Pmt(LoanIRate, LoanDuration, -LoanAmount, 0, payEarly)
        txtPayment Pmt(Rate As Double, NPer As Double, PV As Double, [FV As Double = 0.0], [Due As Microsoft.VisualBasic.DueDate = DueDate.EndOfPeriod]) As Double
    End Sub     Required. Double specifies the interest rate per period. For example, if you get a car loan at an annual percentage rate (APR) of 10
                percent and make monthly payments, the rate per period is 0.1/12, or 0.0083.

    Private Sub txtAmount_TextChanged(ByVal sender As System.Object,
    ByVal e As System.EventArgs) Handles txtAmount.TextChanged,
        txtDuration.TextChanged, txtRate.TextChanged
        txtPayment.Clear()
    End Sub
```

If you omit optional parameters, Visual Basic uses their default values, which are 0 for the *FutureValue* argument and *DueDate.BegOfPeriod* for the *Due* argument. You can entirely omit these arguments and call the Pmt() function like this:

```
Pmt(0.145 / 12, 48, -25000)
```

Calculating the amount of the monthly payment given the loan parameters is quite simple. For this exercise, what you need to understand are the parameters of a loan and how to pass them to the Pmt() function. You must also know how the interest rate is specified to avoid invalid values. Although the calculation of the payment is trivial, designing the interface will take a bit of effort. You need to make sure the interface is easily understood and intuitive. When the user is confronted with the application, they should be able to guess easily what the application is doing and how they can interact with it. The application should also behave according to the principle of least surprise. For example, if the user presses the Tab button, they expect that focus of the controls will move from right to left or from top to bottom. Also, the user will expect the application to perform basic data validation. If the application detects invalid data, the user will expect that the focus will be set on the control containing the invalid value so that they can immediately correct the entered value. These are just a few example characteristics of well-behaved applications.

If you wish to learn more about GUI guidelines that Microsoft recommends for applications running on Windows 7 and Windows Vista, you can download the "Windows User Experience Interaction Guidelines" PDF file from MSDN. You will find the download link at the following URL: http://msdn.microsoft.com/en-us/library/aa511258.aspx.

Designing the User Interface

Now that you know how to calculate the monthly payment and understand the basics of good interface design, you can design your own user interface. To do so, start a new Windows Forms project, name it *LoanCalculator*, and rename its form to *frmLoan*. Your first task is to decide the font and size of the text you'll use for the controls on the form. The form is the container for the controls, and they receive some of the form's properties, such as the font. You can change the font later during the design, but it's a good idea to start with the right font. At any rate, don't try to align the controls if you're planning to change their fonts. The change will, most likely, throw off your alignment efforts.

The book's sample project uses the 10-point Verdana font. To change it, select the form with the mouse, double-click the name of the Font property in the Properties window to open the Font dialog box, and select the desired font and attributes. I use the Verdana and Seago fonts a lot because they're clean and they were designed for viewing on monitors. Of course, this is a personal choice. Avoid elaborate fonts and don't mix different fonts on the same form (or in different forms of the same application).

To design the form shown in Figure 4.1, follow these steps:

1. Place four labels on the form and assign the captions (the Text property of each control) listed in Table 4.1 to them.
   You don't need to change the default names of the four Label controls on the form because their captions are all you need. You aren't going to add any code to them.

2. Place a TextBox control next to each label. Use the information in Table 4.2 to set the Name and Text property values. I used meaningful names for the TextBox controls because we'll use them in our code shortly to retrieve the values entered by the user on these controls. These initial values correspond to a loan of $25,000 with an interest rate of 14.5 percent and a payoff period of 48 months.

TABLE 4.1: LoanCalulator label captions

NAME	TEXT
Label1	Amount
Label2	Duration (months)
Label3	Interest Rate (annual)
Label4	Monthly Payment

TABLE 4.2: LoanCalulator TextBox control names and default value text

NAME	TEXT
txtAmount	25000
txtDuration	48
txtRate	14.5
txtPayment	

3. The fourth TextBox control is where the monthly payment will appear. The user isn't supposed to enter any data in this box, so set the ReadOnly property to True to lock the control and prevent users from entering data. You'll be able to change its value from within your code, but users won't be able to type anything in it. (We could have used a Label control instead, but the uniform look of TextBoxes on a form is usually preferred.) You will also notice that the TextBox controls have a 3D frame. Experiment with the control's BorderStyle property to discover the available styles for the control's frame (I've used the Fixed3D setting for the TextBox controls).

4. Next, place a CheckBox control on the form. By default, the control's caption is *CheckBox1*, and it appears to the right of the check box. Because we want the titles to be to the left of the corresponding controls, we'll change this default appearance.

5. Select the check box with the mouse, and in the Properties window locate the CheckAlign property. Its value is *MiddleLeft*. If you expand the drop-down list by clicking the arrow button, you'll see that this property has many different settings, and each setting is shown as a square. Select the button that will center the text vertically and right-align it horizontally. The string *MiddleRight* will appear in the Properties window when you click the appropriate button.

6. With the check box selected, locate the Name property in the Properties window, and set it to *chkPayEarly*.

7. Change the CheckBox's caption by entering the string *Early Payment* in its Text property field.

8. Place a Button control in the bottom-left corner of the form. Name it bttnShowPayment, and set its Text property to *Monthly Payment*.

9. Finally, place another Button control on the form, name it bttnExit, and set its Text property to *Exit*.

ALIGNING THE CONTROLS

Your next step is to align the controls on the form. The IDE provides commands to align the controls on the form, all of which can be accessed through the Format menu. To align the controls that are already on the form, follow these steps:

1. Select the four labels on the form. The handles of all selected controls will be black except for one control whose handles will be white. To specify the control that will be used as a reference for aligning the other controls, click it after making the selection. (You can select multiple controls either by using the mouse to draw a rectangle that encloses them or by clicking each control while holding down the Ctrl button.)

2. With the four text boxes selected, choose Format ≻ Align ≻ Lefts to left-align them. Don't include the check box in this selection.

3. Resize the CheckBox control. Its left edge should align with the left edges of the Label controls, and its right edge should align with the right edges of the Label controls. In case the resizing markers do not appear on the CheckBox control, set the value of its AutoSize property to False.

4. Select all the Label and the CheckBox controls and choose Format ≻ Vertical Spacing ≻ Make Equal. This action will space the controls vertically. Then align the baseline of

each TextBox control with the baseline of the matching Label control. To do so, move each TextBox control with the mouse until you see a magenta line that connects the baseline of the TextBox control you're moving and that of the matching Label control.

Your form should now look like the one shown in Figure 4.1. Take a good look at it and make sure no controls are misaligned. In the interface design process, you tend to overlook small problems such as a slightly misaligned control. The user of the application, however, instantly spots such mistakes.

Programming the Loan Application

Now you've created the interface, run the application, and seen how it behaves. Next you'll enter a few values in the text boxes, change the state of the check box, and test the functionality already built into the application. Clicking the Monthly Payment button won't have any effect because we have not yet added any code. If this were a prototype you were building for a customer, you would add a statement in the Monthly Payment button to display a random value in the Monthly Payment box.

When you double-click the control for the first time, Visual Studio will generate an empty default event handler declaration for you. Next time you double-click the control, Visual Studio will bring you to the event handler. If you're happy with the user interface, stop the application, open the form, and double-click the Monthly Payment Button control. Visual Basic opens the code window and displays the definition of the ShowPayment_Click event:

```
Private Sub bttnShowPayment_Click(...) Handles
    bttnPayment.Click
```

Because all Click event handlers have the same signature (they provide the same two arguments), I'll be omitting the list of arguments from now on. Actually, all event handlers have two arguments, and the first of them is always the control that fired the event. The type of the second argument differs depending on the type of the event. Place the pointer between the lines Private Sub and End Sub, and enter the rest of the lines of Listing 4.1. (You don't have to reenter the first and last lines that declare the event handler.)

LISTING 4.1: The Code behind the Monthly Payment button

```
Private Sub bttnShowPayment_Click(ByVal (…)
            Handles bttnShowPayment.Click
    Dim Payment As Double
    Dim LoanIRate As Double
    Dim LoanDuration As Integer
    Dim LoanAmount As Integer

    LoanAmount = Convert.ToInt32(txtAmount.Text)
    LoanIRate = 0.01 * Convert.ToDecimal(txtRate.Text) / 12
    LoanDuration = Convert.ToInt32(txtDuration.Text)
    Dim payEarly As DueDate
    If chkPayEarly.Checked Then
        payEarly = DueDate.BegOfPeriod
```

```
    Else
        payEarly = DueDate.EndOfPeriod
    End If
    Payment = Pmt(LoanIRate, LoanDuration, -LoanAmount, 0, payEarly)
    txtPayment.Text = Payment.ToString("#.00")
End Sub
```

The code window should now look like the one shown in Figure 4.2. In previous versions of Visual Basic, you would use the underscore character at the end of the first part of the long line. For the most part, this is no longer necessary; Visual Basic in Visual Studio 2010 supports implicit line continuations. I'm using implicit line continuations in this book a lot to fit long lines on the printed page. The same statement you see as multiple lines in the book may appear in a single, long line in the project.

FIGURE 4.2
The Show Payment button's `Click` event handler

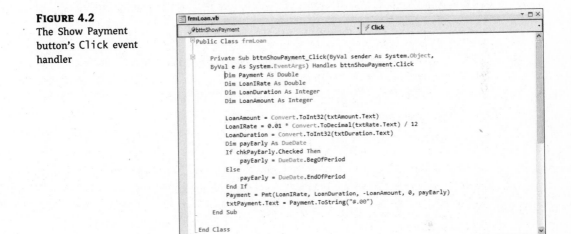

You don't have to break long lines manually as you enter code in the editor's window. Open the Edit menu and choose Advanced ➢ Word Wrap. The editor will wrap long lines automatically. While the word wrap feature is on, a check mark appears in front of the Edit ➢ Advanced ➢ Word Wrap command. To turn off word wrapping, select the same command again.

 **Real World Scenario**

ENUMERATION TYPES

Enumerations are a special kind of type in Visual Basic language used to define a set of logically related unchanging literal values. A typical example for an enumeration is DayOfWeek that contains members for each day of the week (*DayOfWeek.Monday*, *DayOfWeek.Tuesday*, and so on). Enumerations are declared with the Enum keyword, in following fashion:

```
Public Enum DayOfWeek
    Monday
    Tuesday
    Wednesday
    Thursday
    Friday
    Saturday
    Sunday
End Enum
```

By using Enum instead of simple constant literal values, you add type safety to your application. For example, if you define the function that has a day as the DayOfWeek parameter, as in TicketPrice(movie as Movie, day as DayOfWeek) as Decimal, the code that is calling the function will have to pass a value defined in the DayOfWeek enum as a parameter, as in following statement:

```
Dim price = TicketPrice(avatarMovie, DayOfWeek.Saturday)
```

Had you defined the days of the week names as constants, as in following code, you would not be able to perform type checking:

```
Const Monday As String = "Monday"
Const Tuesday As String = "Tuesday"
Const Wednesday As String = "Wednesday"
'  ...
```

Had you no Enum construct in Visual Basic, you would have to resort to constants. When you use constants, the TicketPrice function would have to declare the *day* parameter as String, meaning that when invoking the function, you could pass just any String value. Using the Enum type, however, you know that value belongs to predefined enumeration.

In Listing 4.1, the first line of code within the subroutine declares a variable. It lets the application know that *Payment* is a variable for storing a floating-point number (a number with a decimal part) — the Double data type. The line before the If statement declares a variable of the DueDate type. This is the type of argument that determines whether the payment takes place at the beginning or the end of the month. The last argument of the Pmt() function must be a variable of this type, so we declare a variable of the DueDate type. As mentioned earlier in this chapter, DueDate is an enumeration with two members: *BegOfPeriod* and *EndOfPeriod*.

The first really interesting statement in the subroutine is the If statement that examines the value of the *chkPayEarly* CheckBox control. If the control is selected, the code sets the *payEarly* variable to *DueDate.BegOfPeriod*. If not, the code sets the same variable to *DueDate.EndOfPeriod*. The ComboBox control's Checked property returns True if the control is selected at the time and False otherwise. After setting the value of the *payEarly* variable, the code calls the Pmt() function, passing the values of the controls as arguments:

♦ The first argument is the interest rate. The value entered by the user in the txtRate TextBox is multiplied by 0.01 so that the value 14.5 (which corresponds to 14.5 percent) is passed to the Pmt() function as 0.145. Although we humans prefer to specify interest rates as integers (8 percent) or floating-point numbers larger than 1 (8.24 percent), the Pmt() function expects to read a number that's less than 1. The value 1 corresponds to 100 percent. Therefore, the value 0.1 corresponds to 10 percent. This value is also divided by 12 to yield the monthly interest rate.

◆ The second argument is the duration of the loan in months (the value entered in the *txtDuration* TextBox).

◆ The third argument is the loan's amount (the value entered in the *txtAmount* TextBox).

◆ The fourth argument (the loan's future value) is 0 by definition.

◆ The last argument is the *payEarly* variable, which is set according to the status of the *chkPayEarly* control.

The last statement in Listing 4.1 converts the numeric value returned by the Pmt() function to a string and displays this string in the fourth TextBox control. The result is formatted appropriately with the following expression:

```
Payment.ToString("#.00")
```

The *Payment* variable is numeric, and all numeric variables provide the method ToString, which formats the numeric value and converts it to a string. The character # stands for the integer part of the variable. The period separates the integer from the fractional part, which is rounded to two decimal digits. The Pmt() function returns a precise number, such as 372.2235687646345, and you should round it to two decimal digits and format it nicely before displaying it. For more information on formatting numeric (and other) values, see the section "Formatting Numbers" in Chapter 2, "VB Programming Essentials." Finally, the formatted string is assigned to the Text property of the TextBox control on the form.

🌐 Real World Scenario

A CODE SNIPPET FOR CALCULATING MONTHLY LOAN PAYMENTS

If you didn't know about the Pmt() built-in function, how would you go about calculating loan payments? Code snippets to the rescue!

1. Right-click somewhere in the code window, and from the context menu, choose the Insert Snippet command.

2. Double-click the Fundamentals folder to see another list of items.

3. This time, double-click the Math folder and then select the snippet *Calculate a Monthly Payment on a Loan*.

The following code will be inserted at the location of the pointer:

```
Dim futureValue As Double = 0
Dim payment As Double
payment1 = Pmt(0.05 / 12, 36, -1000, futureValue, DueDate.EndOfPeriod)
```

> The snippet demonstrates the use of the Pmt() function. All you have to do is replace the values of the various parameters with the data from the appropriate controls on the form.
>
> If you don't know how to use the arguments of the Pmt() function, start editing the function's arguments and you will see their description in the usual tooltip box, as with all built-in functions.

The code of the LoanCalculator sample project is a bit different and considerably longer than what I have presented here. The statements discussed in the preceding text are the bare minimum for calculating a loan payment. The user can enter all kinds of unreasonable values on the form and cause the program to crash. In the next section, you'll see how you can validate the data entered by the user, catch errors, and handle them gracefully (that is, give the user a chance to correct the data and proceed) as opposed to terminating the application with a runtime error.

Validating the Data

If you enter a non-numeric value in one of the fields, the program will crash and display an error message. For example, if you enter **twenty** in the Duration text box, the program will display the error message shown in Figure 4.3. A simple typing error can crash the program. This isn't the way Windows applications should work. Your applications must be able to handle all kinds of user errors, provide helpful messages, and in general, guide the user in running the application efficiently. If a user error goes unnoticed, your application will either end abruptly or will produce incorrect results without an indication.

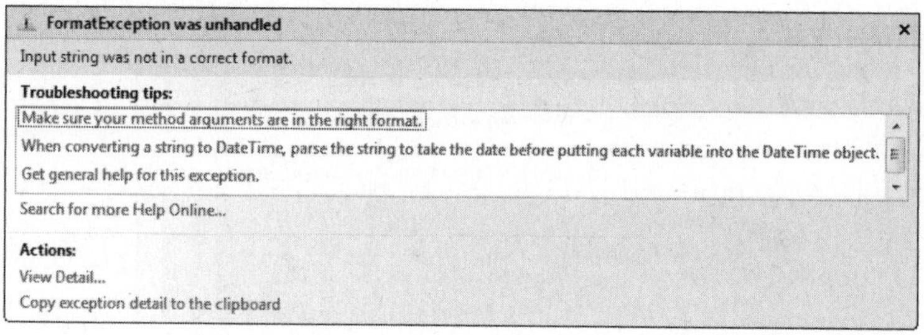

FIGURE 4.3
The FormatException error message means that you supplied a string where a numeric value was expected.

Visual Basic will take you back to the application's code window in which the statements that caused the error will be highlighted in green. Obviously, we must do something about user errors. One way to take care of typing errors is to examine each control's contents; if the controls don't contain valid numeric values, display your own descriptive message and give the user another chance. Listing 4.2 is the revised Click event handler that examines the value of each text box before attempting to use it in any calculations.

LISTING 4.2: Revised Show Payment button

```
Private Sub bttnShowPayment_Click(...) Handles bttnPayment.Click
    Dim Payment As Double
```

```
Dim LoanIRate As Double
Dim LoanDuration As Integer
Dim LoanAmount As Integer

' Validate amount
If IsNumeric(txtAmount.Text) Then
    LoanAmount = Convert.ToInt32(txtAmount.Text)
Else
    MsgBox("Invalid amount, please re-enter")
    txtAmount.Focus()
    txtAmount.SelectAll()
    Exit Sub
End If
' Validate interest rate
If IsNumeric(txtRate.Text) Then
    LoanIRate = 0.01 * Convert.ToDouble(txtRate.Text) / 12
Else
    MsgBox("Invalid interest rate, please re-enter")
    txtRate.Focus()
    txtRate.SelectAll()
    Exit Sub
End If
' Validate loan's duration
If IsNumeric(txtDuration.Text) Then
    LoanDuration = Convert.ToInt32(txtDuration.Text)
Else
    MsgBox("Please specify the loan's duration as a number of months")
    txtDuration.Focus()
    txtDuration.SelectAll()
    Exit Sub
End If
' If all data were validated, proceed with calculations
Dim payEarly As DueDate
If chkPayEarly.Checked Then
    payEarly = DueDate.BegOfPeriod
Else
    payEarly = DueDate.EndOfPeriod
End If
Payment = Pmt(LoanIRate, LoanDuration, -LoanAmount, 0, payEarly)
txtPayment.Text = Payment.ToString("#.00")
End Sub
```

First, we declare three variables in which the loan's parameters will be stored: *LoanAmount*, *LoanIRate*, and *LoanDuration*. These values will be passed to the Pmt() function as arguments. Each text box's value is examined with an If structure. If the corresponding text box holds a valid number, its value is assigned to the numeric variable. If not, the program displays a warning and exits the subroutine without attempting to calculate the monthly payment. Before exiting the subroutine, however, the code moves the focus to the text box with the invalid value and selects the text in the textbox because this is the control that the user will most likely edit. After fixing the incorrect value, the user can click the Show Payment button again. `IsNumeric()` is another built-in function that accepts a variable and returns True if the variable is a number and False otherwise.

You can run the revised application and check it out by entering invalid values in the fields. Notice that you can't specify an invalid value for the last argument; the CheckBox control won't let you enter a value. You can only select or clear it, and both options are valid. The actual calculation of the monthly payment takes a single line of Visual Basic code. Displaying it requires another line of code. Adding the code to validate the data entered by the user, however, is an entire program. And that's the way things are.

 **Real World Scenario**

WRITING WELL-BEHAVED APPLICATIONS

Well-behaved applications must contain data-validation code. If an application such as Loan-Calculator crashes because of a typing mistake, nothing really bad will happen. The user will try again or else give up on your application and look for a more professional one. However, if the user has been entering data for hours, the situation is far more serious. It's your responsibility as a programmer to make sure that only valid data are used by the application and that the application keeps working, no matter how the user misuses or abuses it.

Our sample application is not typical because it calculates the result with a single function call, but in developing typical business applications, you must write a substantial amount of code to validate user input. The reason for validating user input is to control inputs to your code so that you can ensure that it behaves correctly and that you can provide specific error messages to help the user identify the error and correct it.

You will notice that the sample applications included in this book don't contain much data-validation code, because it would obscure the "useful" code that applies to the topic at hand. Instead, they demonstrate specific techniques. You can use parts of the examples in your applications, but you should provide your own data-validation code (and error-handling code, as you'll see in a moment).

Now run the application one last time and enter an enormous loan amount. Try to find out what it would take to pay off the national debt with a reasonable interest rate in, say, 72 months. The program will crash again (as if you didn't know). This time the program will go down with a different error message, as shown in Figure 4.4. Visual Basic will complain about an overflow. The exact message is *Value was either too large or too small for an Int32*, and the program will stop at the line that assigns the contents of the *txtAmount* TextBox to the *LoanAmount* variable. Press the Break button and the offending statement in the code will be highlighted.

An overflow is a numeric value too large for the program to handle. This error is usually produced when you divide a number by a very small value. When you attempt to assign a very large value to an Integer variable, you'll also get an overflow exception.

Actually, in the LoanCalculator application, any amount greater than 2,147,483,647 will cause an overflow condition. This is the largest value you can assign to an Integer variable; it's plenty for our banking needs but not nearly adequate for handling government deficits.

As you learned in Chapter 2, Visual Basic provides other types of variables, which can store enormous values (making the national debt look really small). In the meantime, if you want the loan calculator to be truly useful, change the declaration of the *LoanAmount* variable to the following:

```
Dim LoanAmount As Double
```

FIGURE 4.4
Very large values can cause the application to crash and display this error message.

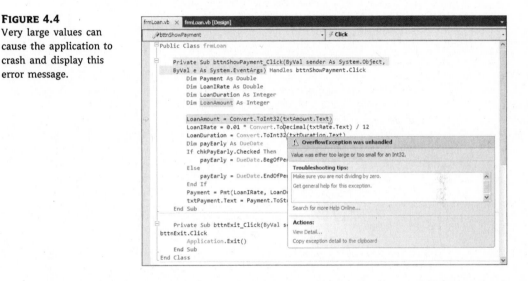

The Double data type can hold much larger values. Besides, the Double data type can also hold non-integer values. Not that anyone will ever apply for a loan of $25,000 and some cents, but if you want to calculate the precise monthly payment for a debt you have accumulated, you should be able to specify a non-integer amount. In short, I should have declared the *LoanAmount* variable with the Double data type in the first place. By the way, there's another integer type, the Long data type, which can hold much larger integer values.

An overflow error can't be caught with data-validation code. There's always a chance that your calculations will produce overflows or other types of math errors. Data validation won't help here; you just don't know the result before you carry out the calculations. You need something called *error handling*, or exception handling. This is additional code that can handle errors after they occur. In effect, you're telling VB that it shouldn't stop with an error message, which would be embarrassing for you and wouldn't help the user one bit. Instead, VB should detect the error and execute the proper statements to handle the error. Obviously, you must supply these statements. (You'll see examples of handling errors at runtime shortly.)

The sample application works as advertised, and it's fail-safe. Yet there's one last touch you can add to the application. The various values on the form are not always in synch. Let's say you've calculated the monthly payment for a specific loan and then you want to change the duration of the loan to see how it affects the monthly payment. As soon as you change the duration of the loan, and before you click the Monthly Payment button, the value in the Monthly Payment box doesn't correspond to the parameters of the loan. Ideally, the monthly payment should be cleared as soon as the user starts editing one of the loan's parameters. To do so, you must insert a statement that clears the *txtPayment* control. But what's the proper event handler for this statement? The TextBox control fires the TextChanged event every time its text is changed, and this is the proper place to execute the statement that clears the monthly payment on the form. Because there are three TextBox controls on the form, you must program the TextChanged event of all three controls or write an event handler inside the *frmLoan* class that handles all three events:

```
Private Sub txtAmount_TextChanged(ByVal (…) Handles
                txtAmount.TextChanged, txtDuration.TextChanged,
                txtRate.TextChanged
    txtPayment.Clear()
End Sub
```

Yes, you can write a common handler for multiple events, as long as the events are of the same type and they're all listed after the Handles keyword. You'll see another example of the same technique in the following sample project.

One of the sample projects for this chapter is a revised version of the LoanCalculator project, the LoanCalculator-Dates project, which uses a different interface. Instead of specifying the duration of the loan in months, this application provides two instances of the DateTimePicker control, which is used to specify dates. Delete the TextBox control and the corresponding Labels and insert two new Label controls and two DateTimePicker controls on the form. Name the DateTimePicker controls dtFrom and dtTo. Users can set the loan's starting and ending dates on these two controls and the program calculates the duration of the loan in months with the following statement:

```
LoanDuration = DateDiff(DateInterval.Month,
                dtFrom.Value, dtTo.Value) + 1
```

The DateDiff() function returns the difference between two dates in the interval supplier as the first argument to the function. The rest of the code doesn't change; as long as the *LoanDuration* variable has the correct value, the same statements will produce the correct result. If you open the project, you'll find a few more interesting statements that set the *dtFrom* control to the first date of the selected month and the *dtTo* control to the last date of the selected month.

Building a Calculator

This next application is more advanced, but it's not as advanced as it looks. It's a calculator with a typical visual interface that demonstrates how Visual Basic can simplify the programming of fairly advanced operations. If you haven't tried it, you may think that writing an application such as this one is way too complicated for a beginner, but it isn't. The MathCalculator application is shown in Figure 4.5.

The application emulates the operation of a handheld calculator and implements basic arithmetic operations. It has the look of a math calculator, and you can easily expand it by adding more features. In fact, adding features such as cosines and logarithms is actually simpler than performing the basic arithmetic operations. This interface will also give you a chance to exercise most of the tools of the IDE for aligning and spacing the controls on a form.

Designing the User Interface

The application's interface is straightforward, but it takes a bit of effort. You must align the buttons on the form and make the calculator look as much like a handheld calculator as possible. Start a new Windows Forms project, the MathCalculator project, and rename the main form from Form1.vb to frmCalculator.vb.

Designing the interface of the application isn't trivial because it's made up of many buttons, all perfectly aligned on the form. To simplify the design, follow these steps:

1. Select a font that you like for the form. All the command buttons you'll place on the form will inherit this font. The MathCalculator sample application uses 10-point Verdana font. I've used a size of 12 points for the Period button because the 10-point period was too small and very near the bottom of the control.

2. Add the Label control, which will become the calculator's display. Set its BorderStyle property to Fixed3D so that it will have a 3D look, as shown in Figure 4.5. Change its ForeColor and BackColor properties too, if you want it to look different from the rest of the form. The sample project uses colors that emulate the — now extinct — green CRT monitors. Name the Label control **lblDisplay**.

3. Draw a Button control on the form, change its Text property to **1**, and name it **bttn1**. Size the button carefully so that its caption is centered on the control. The other buttons on the form will be copies of this one, so make sure you've designed the first button as best as you can before you start making copies of it. You can also change the button's style with the FlatStyle property. (You can experiment with the Popup, Standard, and System settings for this property.)

4. Place the button in its final position on the form. At this point, you're ready to create the other buttons for the calculator's digits. Right-click the button and choose Copy from the context menu. The Button control is copied to the Clipboard, and now you can paste it on the form (which is much faster than designing an identical button).

5. Right-click somewhere on the form, choose Paste, and the button copied to the Clipboard will be pasted on the form. The copy will have the same caption as the button it was copied from, and its name will be Button1.

6. Now set the button's Name property to **bttn2** and its Text property to **2**. This button is the digit 2. Place the new button to the right of the previous button. You don't have to align the two buttons perfectly now; later we'll use the commands of the Format menu to align the buttons on the form. As you move the control around on the form, one or more lines may appear on the design surface at times. These lines are called *snap lines*, and they appear

as soon as a control is aligned (vertically or horizontally) with one or more of the existing controls on the form. The snap lines allow you to align controls with the mouse. Blue snap lines appear when the control's edge is aligned with the edge of another control. Red snap lines appear when the control's baseline is aligned with the baseline of another control. The baseline is the invisible line on which the characters of the control's caption are based.

7. Repeat steps 5 and 6 eight more times, once for each numeric digit. Each time a new Button control is pasted on the form, Visual Basic names it Button1 and sets its caption to 1; you must change the Name and Text properties. You can name the buttons anything you like, but a name that indicates their role in the application is preferred.

8. When the buttons of the numeric digits are all on the form, place two more buttons, one for the C (Clear) operation and one for the Period button. Name them **bttnClear** and **bttnDecimalPoint**, and set their captions accordingly. Use a larger font size for the Period button to make its caption easier to read.

9. When all the digit buttons of the first group are on the form and in their approximate positions, align them by using the commands of the Format menu. You can use the snap lines to align horizontally and vertically the various buttons on the form, but you must still space the controls manually, which isn't a trivial task. Here's how you can align the buttons perfectly via the Format menu:

   a. First, align the buttons of the top row. Start by aligning the 1 button with the left side of the lblDisplay Label. Then select all the buttons of the top row and make their horizontal spacing equal (choose Format ➤ Horizontal Spacing ➤ Make Equal). Then do the same with the buttons in the first column; this time, make sure their vertical distances are equal (Format ➤ Vertical Spacing ➤ Make Equal).

   b. Now you can align the buttons in each row and each column separately. Use one of the buttons you aligned in the last step as the guide for the rest of them. The buttons can be aligned in many ways, so don't worry if somewhere in the process you ruin the alignment. You can always use the Undo command in the Edit menu. Select the three buttons on the second row and align their tops by using the first button as a reference. To set the anchor control for the alignment, click it with the mouse while holding down the Ctrl key. Do the same for the third and fourth rows of buttons. Then do the same for the four columns of buttons, using the top button as a reference.

10. Now, place the buttons for the arithmetic operations on the form — addition (+), subtraction (−), multiplication (*), and division (/). Name the addition button **bttnPlus**, the subtraction button **bttnMinus**, the multiplication button **bttnMultiply**, and the division button **bttnDivide**.

11. Finally, place the Equals button on the form, name it **bttnEquals**, and make it wide enough to span the space of two operation buttons. Use the commands on the Format menu to align these buttons, as shown in Figure 4.5. The form shown in Figure 4.5 has a few more buttons, which you can align by using the same techniques you used to align the numeric buttons.

If you don't feel quite comfortable with the alignment tools of the IDE, you can still position the controls on the form through the x and y components of each control's Location property. (They're the x- and y-coordinates of the control's upper-left corner on the form.) The various alignment tools are among the first tools of the IDE you'll master, and you'll be creating forms with perfectly aligned controls in no time at all.

Programming the MathCalculator

Now you're ready to add some code to the application. Double-click one of the digit buttons on the form and you'll see the following in the code window:

```
Private Sub bttn1_Click(ByVal sender As System.Object,
        ByVal e As System.EventArgs) Handles
        bttn1.Click

End Sub
```

This is the Click event's handler for a single digit button. Your first inclination might be to program the Click event handler of each digit button, but repeating the same code 10 times isn't very productive. (Not to mention that if you decide to edit the code later, the process must be repeated 10 times.) We're going to use the same event handler for all buttons that represent digits. All you have to do is append the names of the events to be handled by the same subroutine after the Handles keyword. You should also change the name of the event handler to something that indicates its role. Because this subroutine handles the Click event for all the digit buttons, let's call it DigitClick(). Here's the revised declaration of a subroutine that can handle all the digit buttons:

```
Private Sub DigitClick(ByVal sender As System.Object,
            ByVal e As System.EventArgs)
            Handles bttn0.Click, bttn1.Click, bttn2.Click,
            bttn3.Click, bttn4.Click, bttn5.Click, bttn6.Click,
            bttn7.Click, bttn8.Click, bttn9.Click
End Sub
```

You don't have to type all the event names; as soon as you insert the first comma after bttn0.Click, a drop-down list with the names of the controls will open and you can select the name of the next button with the down arrow. Press the spacebar to select the desired control (*bttn1, bttn2*, and so on), and then type the period. This time, you'll see another list with the names of the events for the selected control. Locate the Click event and select it by pressing the spacebar. Type the next comma and repeat the process for all the buttons. This extremely convenient feature of the language is IntelliSense: The IDE presents the available and valid keywords as you type.

When you press a digit button on a handheld calculator, the corresponding digit is appended to the display. To emulate this behavior, insert the following line in the Click event handler:

```
lblDisplay.Text = lblDisplay.Text + sender.Text
```

This line appends the digit clicked to the calculator's display. The *sender* argument of the Click event represents the control that was clicked (the control that fired the event). The Text property of this control is the caption of the button that was clicked. For example, if you have already entered the value 345, clicking the digit 0 displays the value 3450 on the Label control that acts as the calculator's display.

The expression sender.Text is not the best method of accessing the Text property of the button that was clicked, but it will work as long as the Strict option is off. As discussed in

Chapter 2, we must cast the *sender* object to a specific type (the Button type) and then call its Text method:

```
CType(sender, Button).Text
```

The code behind the digit buttons needs a few more lines. After certain actions, the display should be cleared. After one of the buttons that correspond to math operations is pressed, the display should be cleared in anticipation of the second operand. Actually, the display must be cleared as soon as the first digit of the second operand is pressed and not as soon as the math operator button is pressed. Likewise, the display should also be cleared after the user clicks the Equals button. Revise the `DigitClick` event handler, as shown in Listing 4.3.

LISTING 4.3:   The `DigitClick` event

```
Private Sub DigitClick(ByVal sender As System.Object,
                    ByVal e As System.EventArgs)
                    Handles bttn1.Click, bttn2.Click, bttn3.Click,
                    bttn4.Click, bttn5.Click, bttn6.Click,
                    bttn7.Click, bttn8.Click, bttn9.Click
    If clearDisplay Then
        lblDisplay.Text = ""
        clearDisplay = False
    End If
    lblDisplay.Text = lblDisplay.Text + sender.text
End Sub
```

The *clearDisplay* variable is declared as Boolean, which means it can take a True or False value. Suppose the user has performed an operation and the result is on the calculator's display. The user now starts typing another number. Without the If clause, the program would continue to append digits to the number already on the display. This is not how calculators work. When the user starts entering a new number, the display must be cleared. Our program uses the *clearDisplay* variable to know when to clear the display.

The Equals button sets the *clearDisplay* variable to True to indicate that the display contains the result of an operation. The `DigitClick()` subroutine examines the value of this variable each time a new digit button is pressed. If the value is True, `DigitClick()` clears the display and then prints the new digit on it. The subroutine also sets *clearDisplay* to False so that when the next digit is pressed, the program won't clear the display again.

What if the user makes a mistake and wants to undo an entry? The typical handheld calculator has no Backspace key. The Clear key erases the current number on the display. Let's implement this feature. Double-click the C button and enter the code of Listing 4.4 in its Click event.

LISTING 4.4:   Programming the Clear button

```
Private Sub bttnClear_Click (ByVal sender As System.Object,
            ByVal e As System.EventArgs) Handles bttnClear.Click
    lblDisplay.Text = ""
End Sub
```

Now we can look at the Period button. A calculator, no matter how simple, should be able to handle fractional numbers. The Period button works just like the digit buttons, with one exception. A digit can appear any number of times in a numeric value, but the decimal point can appear only once. A number such as 99.991 is valid, but you must make sure the user can't enter numbers such as 23.456.55. After a decimal point is entered, this button must not insert another one. The code in Listing 4.5 accounts for this.

LISTING 4.5:   Programming the Period button

```
Private Sub bttnDecimalPointClick(…) Handles bttnDecimalPoint.Click
    If lblDisplay.Text.IndexOf(".") >= 0 Then
        Exit Sub
    Else
        lblDisplay.Text = lblDisplay.Text & "."
    End If
End Sub
```

IndexOf is a method that can be applied to any string. The expression lblDisplay.Text is a string (the text on the Label control), so we can call its IndexOf method. The expression lblDisplay.Text.IndexOf(".") returns the location of the first instance of the period in the caption of the Label control. If this number is zero or positive, the number entered contains a period already and another can't be entered. In this case, the program exits the subroutine. If the method returns –1, the period is appended to the number entered so far, just like a regular digit.

Check out the operation of the application. We have already created a functional user interface that emulates a handheld calculator with data-entry capabilities. It doesn't perform any operations yet, but we have already created a functional user interface with only a small number of statements.

CODING THE MATH OPERATIONS

Now we can move to the interesting part of the application: the coding of the math operations. Let's start by defining the three variables listed in Table 4.3.

TABLE 4.3:   Math operation variable definitions

VARIABLE	DEFINITION
Operand1	The first number in the operation
MathOperator	The desired operation
Operand2	The second number in the operation

When the user clicks one of the math symbols, the application will store the value of the operand in the variable *Operand1*. If the user then clicks the Plus button, the program must make a note to itself that the current operation is an addition and set the *clearDisplay* variable to True so that the user can enter another value (the second value to be added). The symbol of the operation is stored in the *MathOperator* variable. The user enters another value and then clicks the Equals button to see the result. At this point, your program must do the following:

1. Read the value on the display into the *Operand2* variable.

2. Perform the operation indicated by the *MathOperator* variable with the two operands.

3. Display the result and set the *clearDisplay* variable to True.

The Equals button must perform the following operation:

```
Operand1 MathOperator Operand2
```

Suppose the number on the display when the user clicks the Plus button is 3342. The user then enters the value 23 and clicks the Equals button. The program must carry out the addition: 3342 + 23.

If the user clicks the Division button, the operation is as follows: 3342 ÷ 23.

Variables are local in the subroutines in which they are declared. Other subroutines have no access to them and can't read or set their values. Sometimes, however, variables must be accessed from many places in a program. The variables *Operand1*, *Operand2*, and *Operator*, as well as the *clearDisplay* variable, must be accessed from within more than one subroutine, so they must be declared outside any subroutine; their declarations usually appear at the beginning of the class code with the following statements:

```
Dim clearDisplay As Boolean
Dim Operand1 As Double
Dim Operand2 As Double
Dim MathOperator As String
```

These variables are called *form-wide variables*, or simply *form variables*, because they are visible from within any subroutine on the form. Let's see how the program uses the *MathOperator* variable. When the user clicks the Plus button, the program must store the value + in the *MathOperator* variable. This takes place from within the Plus button's Click event.

All variables that store numeric values are declared as variables of the Double type, which can store values with the greatest possible precision. The Boolean type takes two values: True and False. You have already seen how the *clearDisplay* variable is used.

With the variable declarations out of the way, we can now implement the operator buttons. Double-click the Plus button, and in the Click event's handler, enter the lines shown in Listing 4.6.

LISTING 4.6:   The Plus button

```
Private Sub bttnPlus_Click(ByVal (…) Handles bttnPlus.Click
    Operand1 = Convert.ToDouble(lblDisplay.Text)
    MathOperator = "+"
    clearDisplay = True
End Sub
```

The variable *Operand1* is assigned the value currently on the display. The Convert.ToDouble() method converts its argument to a double value. The Text property of the Label control is a string. The actual value stored in the Text property is not a number. It's a string such as 428, which is different from the numeric value 428. That's why we use the Convert.ToDouble method to convert the value of the Label's caption to a numeric value. The remaining buttons do the same, and I won't show their listings here.

After the second operand is entered, the user can click the Equals button to calculate the result. When this happens, the code of Listing 4.7 is executed.

LISTING 4.7: The Equals button

```
Private Sub bttnEquals_Click(ByVal (…) Handles bttnEquals.Click
    Dim result As Double
    Operand2 = Convert.ToDouble(lblDisplay.Text)
    Select Case MathOperator
        Case "+"
            result = Operand1 + Operand2
        Case "-"
            result = Operand1 - Operand2
        Case "*"
            result = Operand1 * Operand2
        Case "/"
            If Operand2 <> "0" Then
                result = Operand1 / Operand2
            End If
    End Select
    lblDisplay.Text = result.ToString
    clearDisplay = True
End Sub
```

The *result* variable is declared as Double so that the result of the operation will be stored with maximum precision. The code extracts the value displayed in the Label control and stores it in the variable *Operand2*. It then performs the operation with a Select Case statement. This statement compares the value of the *MathOperator* variable to the values listed after each Case statement. If the value of the *MathOperator* variable matches one of the Case values, the following statement is executed.

Division takes into consideration the value of the second operand because if it's zero, the division can't be carried out. The last statement carries out the division only if the divisor is not zero. If *Operand2* happens to be zero, nothing happens.

Now run the application and check it out. It works just like a handheld calculator, and you can't crash it by specifying invalid data. We didn't have to use any data-validation code in this example because the user doesn't get a chance to type invalid data. The data-entry mechanism is foolproof. The user can enter only numeric values because there are only numeric digits on the calculator. The only possible error is to divide by zero, and that's handled in the Equals button.

Of course, users should be able to just type the numeric values; you shouldn't force them to click the digit buttons on the interface. To intercept keystrokes from within your code, you must first set the form's `KeyPreview` property to True. By default, each keystroke is reported to the control that has the focus at the time and fires the keystroke-related events: the `KeyDown`, `KeyPress`, and `KeyUp` events. Sometimes we need to handle certain keystrokes from a central place, and we set the form's `KeyPreview` property to True so that keystrokes are reported first to the form and then to the control that has the focus. We can intercept the keystrokes in the form's `KeyPress` event and handle them in this event handler. Insert the statements shown in Listing 4.8 in the form's `KeyPress` event handler.

LISTING 4.8: Handling keystrokes at the form's level

```
Private Sub CalculatorForm_KeyPress(ByVal sender As Object,
        ByVal e As System.Windows.Forms.KeyPressEventArgs) Handles
        Me.KeyPress
    Select Case e.KeyChar
        Case "1" : bttn1.PerformClick()
        Case "2" : bttn2.PerformClick()
        Case "3" : bttn3.PerformClick()
        Case "4" : bttn4.PerformClick()
        Case "5" : bttn5.PerformClick()
        Case "6" : bttn6.PerformClick()
        Case "7" : bttn7.PerformClick()
        Case "8" : bttn8.PerformClick()
        Case "9" : bttn9.PerformClick()
        Case "0" : bttn0.PerformClick()
        Case "." : bttnDecimalPoint.PerformClick()
        Case "C", "c" : bttnClear.PerformClick()
        Case "+" : bttnPlus.PerformClick()
        Case "-" : bttnMinus.PerformClick()
        Case "*" : bttnMultiply.PerformClick()
        Case "/" : bttnDivide.PerformClick()
        Case "=" : bttnEquals.PerformClick()
    End Select
End Sub
```

This event handler examines the key pressed by the user and invokes the `Click` event handler of the appropriate button by calling its `PerformClick` method. This method allows you to "click" a button from within your code. When the user presses the digit 3, the form's `KeyPress` event handler intercepts the keystrokes and emulates the click of the `bttn3` button. Because the large Select Case statement doesn't handle characters and punctuation symbols, there's no way for the user to enter invalid digits when a number is expected.

Using the Basic Debugging Tools

Our sample applications work nicely and are quite easy to test and fix if you discover something wrong with them (but only because they're very simple applications). As you write code, you'll soon discover that something doesn't work as expected, and you should be able to find out why and then fix it. The process of eliminating errors in logic — as opposed to errors in syntax, which are caught by the compiler — is called *debugging*. Visual Studio provides the tools to simplify the process of debugging. There are a few simple debugging techniques you should know, even as you work with simple projects.

Open the MathCalculator project in the code editor and place the pointer in the line that calculates the difference between the two operands. Let's pretend there's a problem with this line and we want to follow the execution of the program closely to find out what's going wrong with the application. Press F9 and the line will be highlighted in brown. This line has become a *breakpoint*: As soon as it is reached, the program will stop.

Another way to add a breakpoint is to use the Breakpoint option in the context menu. You can display the context menu in the editor by right-clicking the line of code where you wish the execution to stop. Finally, there is a special window in Visual Studio that displays breakpoints. You can display the Breakpoints window by navigating to the Debug ➢ Windows ➢ Breakpoints menu options in Visual Studio. In this window, you can see all the breakpoints in the solution, deactivate and activate breakpoints, attach conditions and labels to breakpoints, and even view some breakpoint-related statistics.

VISUAL STUDIO FUNCTION KEYS AND KEYBOARD SHORTCUTS

F9 is not the only useful function key or shortcut key combination available in Visual Studio. The following list includes some of the function key commands and shortcut key combinations you will find useful.

FUNCTION KEY	COMMAND
F1	Context-Sensitive Help
F5	Run Application In Debug Mode
Shift + F5	Run Application Without Debugging
F7	Toggle Design View - Code View
F9	Toggle Breakpoint
F10	Step Over (while Debugging)
F11	Step Into (while Debugging)
F12	Go To Definition
Ctrl + ,	"Navigate To" Window
Ctrl + .	Generate Code Stubs
Ctrl + Mouse Wheel	Zoom In / Zoom Out In Code Window
Ctrl + Shift	Highlight All Keyword References

Press F5 to run the application and perform a subtraction. Enter a number; click the minus button and then another number, and finally, click the Equals button. The application will stop, and the code editor will open. The breakpoint will be highlighted in yellow. You're still in runtime mode, but the execution of the application is suspended. You can even edit the code in break mode and then press F5 to continue the execution of the application. Hover the pointer over the *Operand1* and *Operand2* variables in the code editor's window. The value of the corresponding variable will appear in a small ToolTip box. Move the pointer over any variable in the current event handler to see its value. These are the values of the variables just prior to the execution of the highlighted statement.

The *result* variable is zero because the statement hasn't been executed yet. If the variables involved in this statement have their proper values (if they don't, you know that the problem is prior to this statement and perhaps in another event handler), you can execute this statement by pressing F10, which executes only the highlighted statement. The program will stop at the next line. The next statement to be executed is the End Select statement.

Find an instance of the *result* variable in the current event handler, rest the pointer over it, and you will see the value of the variable after it has been assigned a value. Now you can press F10 to execute another statement or press F5 to return to normal execution mode.

You can also evaluate expressions involving any of the variables in the current event handler by entering the appropriate statement in the Immediate window. The Immediate window appears at the bottom of the IDE. If it's not visible, open the Debug menu and choose Windows ➤ Immediate. The current line in the command window is prefixed with the greater-than symbol (reminiscent of the DOS days). Place the cursor next to it and enter the following statement:

```
? Operand1 / Operand2
```

The quotient of the two values will appear in the following line. The question mark is just a shorthand notation for the Print command.

If you want to know the current value on the calculator's display, enter the following statement:

```
? lblDisplay.Text
```

This statement requests the value of a control's property on the form. The current value of the Label control's Text property will appear in the following line.

You can also evaluate math expressions with statements such as the following:

```
? Math.Log(3/4)
```

Log() is the logarithm function and a method of the Math class. With time, you'll discover that the Immediate window is a handy tool for debugging applications. If you have a statement with a complicated expression, you can request the values of the expression's individual components and make sure they can be evaluated.

Now move the pointer over the breakpoint and press F9 again. This will toggle the breakpoint status, and the execution of the program won't halt the next time this statement is executed.

If the execution of the program doesn't stop at a breakpoint, it means that the statement is never reached. In this case, you must search for the bug in statements that are executed before the breakpoint is reached. Chances are that the statement that was not reached was in an If statement that wasn't executed, or in a subroutine that has never been called. For example, if you didn't assign the proper value to the *MathOperator* variable, the Case clause for the subtraction operation will never be reached. You should place the breakpoint at the first executable statement of the Click event handler for the Equals button to examine the values of all variables the moment this subroutine starts its execution. If all variables have the expected values, you will continue testing the code forward. If not, you'd have to test the statements that lead to this statement — the statements in the event handlers of the various buttons.

Another simple technique for debugging applications is to print the values of certain variables in the Immediate window. Although this isn't a debugging tool, it's common practice among VB programmers. Many programmers print the values of selected variables before and after the execution of some complicated statements. To do so, use the statement `Debug.WriteLine` followed by the name of the variable you want to print, or an expression:

```
Debug.WriteLine(Operand1)
```

This statement sends its output to the Immediate window. This is a simple technique, but it works. You can also use it to test a function or method call. If you're not sure about the syntax of a function, pass an expression that contains the specific function to the `Debug.WriteLine` statement as an argument. If the expected value appears in the Immediate window, you can go ahead and use it in your code.

In the project's folder, you will find the `MoreFeatures.txt` document, which describes how to add more features to the math calculator. Such features include the inversion of a number (the 1/x button), the negation of a number (the +/− button), and the usual math functions (logarithms, square roots, trigonometric functions, and so on).

Exception Handling

Crashing this application won't be as easy as crashing the LoanCalculator application. If you start multiplying very large numbers, you won't get an overflow exception. Enter a very large number by repeatedly typing the digit **9**; then multiply this value with another equally large value. When the result appears, click the multiplication symbol and enter another very large value. Keep multiplying the result with very large numbers until you exhaust the value range of the Double data type (that is, until the result is so large that it can't be stored to a variable of the Double type). When this happens, the string *infinity* will appear in the display. This is Visual Basic's way of telling you that it can't handle very large numbers. This isn't a limitation of VB; it's the way computers store numeric values: They provide a limited number of bytes for each variable. (We discussed oddities such as infinity in Chapter 2.)

You can't create an overflow exception by dividing a number by zero, either, because the code will not even attempt to carry out this calculation. In short, the MathCalculator application is pretty robust. However, we can't be sure that users won't cause the application to generate an exception, so we must provide some code to handle all types of errors.

EXCEPTIONS VERSUS ERRORS

Errors that occur during application execution are now called exceptions. They used to be called errors in pre-.NET versions of Visual Basic. You can think of them as exceptions to the normal (or intended) flow of execution. If an exception occurs, the program must execute special statements to handle it — statements that wouldn't be executed normally. I think they're called exceptions because *error* is a word nobody likes and most people can't admit they wrote code that contains errors. The term *exception* can be vague. What would you rather tell your customers: that the application you wrote has errors or that your code has raised an exception? You may not have noticed it, but the term *bug* is not used as frequently anymore; bugs are now called *known issues*. The term *debugging*, however, hasn't changed yet.

How do you prevent an exception raised by a calculation? Data validation won't help. You just can't predict the result of an operation without actually performing the operation. And if the operation causes an overflow, you can't prevent it. The answer is to add a *structured exception handler*. Most of the sample application's code is straightforward, and you can't easily generate an exception for demonstration purposes. The only place where an exception may occur is the handler of the Equals button, where the calculations take place. This is where you must add an exception handler. The outline of the structured exception handler is the following:

```
Try
   ' statements block
Catch Exception
   ' handler block
Finally
   ' cleanup statements block
End Try
```

The program will attempt to perform the calculations, which are coded in the *statements block*. If the program succeeds, it continues with the *cleanup statements* in the Finally section of the handler. These statements are mostly cleanup code used to release reserved resources, and the Finally section of the statement is optional. If it's missing, the program execution continues with the statement following the End Try statement. If an error occurs in the first block of statements, the Catch Exception section is activated and the statements in the *handler block* are executed. If present, the Finally block is executed next. As you can see, the Finally block is executed no matter the outcome of statements block execution; error or no error, you can be certain that cleanup code is executed and important resources like database connections and file handlers are released.

The Catch Exception block is where you handle the error. There's not much you can do about errors that result from calculations. All you can do is display a warning and give the user a chance to change the values. There are other types of errors, however, that can be handled much more gracefully. If your program can't read a file from a CD drive, you can give the user a chance to insert the CD and retry. In other situations, you can prompt the user for a missing value and continue. If the application attempts to write to a read-only file, for example, chances are that the user specified a file on a CD drive or a file with its read-only attribute set. You can display a warning, exit the subroutine that saves the data, and give the user a chance to either select another filename or change the read-only attribute of the selected file.

 **Real World Scenario**

EXCEPTION HANDLING

A common programming mistake is to place the cleanup code inside the statements block and to omit the Finally block altogether. Such code can result in a dreaded *memory leak* problem. This way some precious computing resources end up without being recovered. When unmanaged resources (like file handles and database connections) are accessed, they have to be released explicitly or they will stay in memory and the program might eventually stall. Unfortunately, since the cleanup code is placed inside the statements block, the program executions will jump to the Catch block immediately after the error is raised, thus omitting the cleanup statements.

What makes such memory leak problems even more sinister is the fact that they are produced only under exceptional conditions. If everything goes well, all resources are recovered. If an error is produced, however, resources are leaked. Under such circumstances a program can go on without crashing for quite some time. Usual debugging techniques are often helpless under such circumstances. You will typically have to employ some special tools like *memory profilers* to pinpoint the exact block of code responsible for producing the memory leak.

The following snippet is a simplified illustration of such a scenario. The code assumes that the SomeFile.txt file has an integer written on the first line. If this is true, the application will correctly close the writer. However, if you encounter something else — for example, the characters *abc* on the first line in the file — the error handler will prevent the application from crashing but will not close the writer.

To test the snippet, create a new Console Application project. Change the name of Module1 to ResourceLeakingModule and make sure it is marked as a startup object. Copy the following code to ResourceLeakingModule:

```
Imports System.IO

Module ResourceLeakingModule

    Sub Main()
        Dim fileReader As StreamReader
        Dim firstNumber As Integer
        Try
            fileReader = File.OpenText("C:\SomeFile.txt")
            firstNumber = fileReader.ReadLine
            Console.WriteLine("At this point execution already " &
                "jumped over to catch block")
            fileReader.Close() 'should go to Finally block
        Catch ex As Exception
            Console.WriteLine("fileReader has not been closed")
            ' Wait so that output can be read
            Console.ReadLine()
        End Try
    End Sub

End Module
```

Now create a SomeFile.txt file in the root of your C drive and write **abc** on the first line of the file. You can place the file in some other location as long as you modify the snippet so it points to the correct location of the file.

The way you can resolve the memory leak problem in this case is to place a fileReader.Close() statement inside the Finally block. Another way to release unmanaged resources correctly is to employ Visual Basic's Using statement. This statement is convenient as long as you can release the resource inside the same block of code that you used to create the resource.

In general, there's no unique method to handle all exceptions. You must consider all types of exceptions that your application may cause and handle them on an individual basis. What's important about error handlers is that your application doesn't crash; it simply doesn't perform the operation that caused the exception (this is also known as the *offending operation*, or *offending statement*) and continues.

The error handler for the MathCalculator application must inform the user that an error occurred and abort the calculations — it does not even attempt to display a result. If you open the Equals button's `Click` event handler, you will find the statements detailed in Listing 4.9.

LISTING 4.9:   Revised Equals button

```
Private Sub bttnEquals_Click(…) Handles bttnEquals.Click
    Dim result As Double
    Operand2 = Convert.ToDouble(lblDisplay.Text)
    Try
        Select Case MathOperator
            Case "+"
                result = Operand1 + Operand2
            Case "-"
                result = Operand1 - Operand2
            Case "*"
                result = Operand1 * Operand2
            Case "/"
                If Operand2 <> "0" Then result = Operand1 / Operand2
        End Select
        lblDisplay.Text = result
    Catch exc As Exception
        MsgBox(exc.Message)
        result = "ERROR"
    Finally
        clearDisplay = True
    End Try
End Sub
```

Most of the time, the error handler remains inactive and doesn't interfere with the operation of the program. If an error occurs, which most likely will be an overflow error, the error-handling section of the Try…Catch…End Try statement will be executed. This code displays a message box with the description of the error, and it also displays the string ERROR on the calculator's display. The Finally section is executed regardless of whether an exception occurred. In this example, the Finally section sets the clearDisplay variable to True so that when another digit button is clicked, a new number will appear on the display.

The Bottom Line

Design graphical user interfaces.   A Windows application consists of a graphical user interface and code. The interface of the application is designed with visual tools and consists of controls that are common to all Windows applications. You drop controls from the Toolbox window onto the form, size and align the controls on the form, and finally set their properties through the Properties window. The controls include quite a bit of functionality right out of the box, and this functionality is readily available to your application without a single line of code.

Master It   Describe the process of aligning controls on a form.

Program events.   Windows applications follow an event-driven model: We code the events to which we want our application to respond. For example, an application reacts to Click events of the various buttons. You select the actions to which you want your application to react and program these events accordingly.

When an event is fired, the appropriate event handler is automatically invoked. Event handlers are subroutines that pass two arguments to the application: the *sender* argument (which is an object that represents the control that fired the event) and the *e* argument (which carries additional information about the event).

Master It   How will you handle certain keystrokes regardless of the control that receives them?

Write robust applications with error handling.   Numerous conditions can cause an application to crash, but a well-written application should be able to detect abnormal conditions and handle them gracefully. To begin with, *you should always validate your data* before you attempt to use them in your code. A well-known computer term is "garbage in, garbage out," which means you shouldn't perform any calculations on invalid data.

Master It   How will you execute one or more statements in the context of a structured exception handler?

Chapter 5

Basic Windows Controls

In previous chapters, we explored the environment of Visual Basic and the principles of event-driven programming, which is the core of VB's programming model. In the process, we briefly explored a few basic controls through the examples. The .NET Framework provides many more controls, and all of them have a multitude of trivial properties (such as Font, BackgroundColor, and so on), which you can set either in the Properties window or from within your code.

This chapter explores in depth the basic Windows controls: the controls you'll use most often in your applications because they are the basic building blocks of typical rich client-user interfaces. Rather than look at the background and foreground color, font, and other trivial properties of all controls, we'll look at the properties unique to each control and see how these properties are used in building functional, rich user interfaces.

In this chapter, you'll learn how to do the following:

♦ Use the TextBox control as a data-entry and text-editing tool

♦ Use the ListBox, CheckedListBox, and ComboBox controls to present lists of items

♦ Use the ScrollBar and TrackBar controls to enable users to specify sizes and positions with the mouse

The TextBox Control

The TextBox control is the primary mechanism for displaying and entering text. It is a small text editor that provides all the basic text-editing facilities: inserting and selecting text, scrolling if the text doesn't fit in the control's area, and even exchanging text with other applications through the Clipboard.

The TextBox control is an extremely versatile data-entry tool that can be used for entering and editing single lines of text, such as a number or a password or an entire text file. Figure 5.1 shows a few typical examples. All the boxes in Figure 5.1 contain text—some a single line, some several lines. The scroll bars you see in some text boxes are part of the control. You can specify which scroll bars (vertical and/or horizontal) will be attached to the control, and they appear automatically whenever the control's contents exceed the visible area of the control.

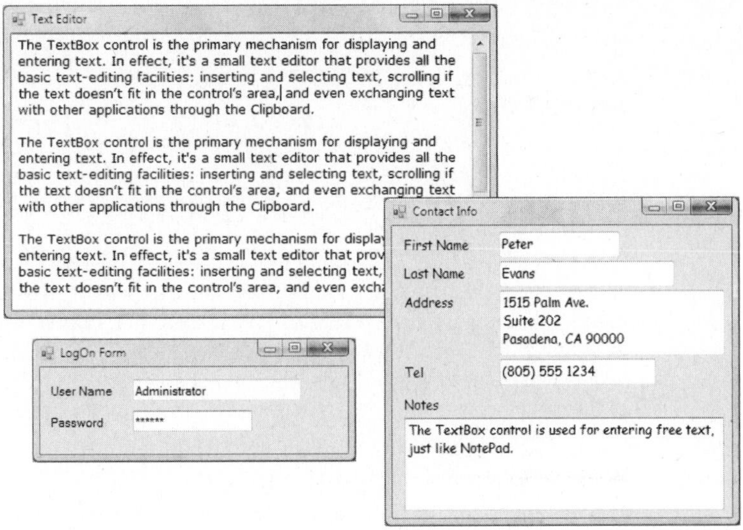

FIGURE 5.1
Typical uses of the
TextBox control

Basic Properties

Let's start with the properties that specify the appearance and, to some degree, the functionality of the TextBox control; these properties are usually set at design time through the Properties window. Then, we'll look at the properties that allow you to manipulate the control's contents and interact with users from within your code.

TEXTALIGN

This property sets (or returns) the alignment of the text on the control, and its value is a member of the HorizontalAlignment enumeration: Left, Right, or Center. The TextBox control doesn't allow you to format text (mix different fonts, attributes, or colors), but you can set the font in which the text will be displayed with the Font property as well as the control's background color with the BackColor property.

MULTILINE

This property determines whether the TextBox control will hold a single line or multiple lines of text. Every time you place a TextBox control on your form, it's sized for a single line of text and you can change its width only. To change this behavior, set the MultiLine property to True. When creating multiline TextBoxes, you will most likely have to set one or more of the MaxLength, ScrollBars, and WordWrap properties in the Properties window.

MAXLENGTH

This property determines the number of characters that the TextBox control will accept. Its default value is 32,767, which was the maximum number of characters the VB 6 version of the control could hold. Set this property to zero so that the text can have any length up to the control's capacity limit—2,147,483,647 characters, to be exact. To restrict the number of characters that the user can type, set the value of this property accordingly.

The MaxLength property of the TextBox control is often set to a specific value in data-entry applications to prevent users from entering more characters than can be stored in a database field. A TextBox control for entering international standard book numbers (ISBNs), for instance, shouldn't accept more than 13 characters.

SCROLLBARS

This property lets you specify the scroll bars you want to attach to the TextBox if the text exceeds the control's dimensions. Single-line text boxes can't have a scroll bar attached, even if the text exceeds the width of the control. Multiline text boxes can have a horizontal or a vertical scroll bar or both.

If you attach a horizontal scroll bar to the TextBox control, the text won't wrap automatically as the user types. To start a new line, the user must press Enter. This arrangement is useful for implementing code editors in which lines must break explicitly. If the horizontal scroll bar is missing, the control inserts soft line breaks when the text reaches the end of a line, and the text is wrapped automatically. You can change the default behavior by setting the WordWrap property.

WORDWRAP

This property determines whether the text is wrapped automatically when it reaches the right edge of the control. The default value of this property is True. If the control has a horizontal scroll bar, however, you can enter very long lines of text. The contents of the control will scroll to the left, so the insertion point is always visible as you type. You can turn off the horizontal scroll bar and still enter long lines of text; just use the left/right arrow keys to bring any part of the text into view. You can experiment with the WordWrap and ScrollBars properties in the TextPad sample application, which is described later in this chapter.

Notice that the WordWrap property has no effect on the actual line breaks. The lines are wrapped automatically, and there are no hard breaks (returns) at the end of each line. Open the TextPad project, enter a long paragraph, and resize the window — the text is automatically adjusted to the new width of the control.

🌐 Real World Scenario

A FUNCTIONAL TEXT EDITOR BY DESIGN

A TextBox control with its MaxLength property set to 0, its MultiLine and WordWrap properties set to True, and its ScrollBars property set to Vertical is, on its own, a functional text editor. Place a TextBox control with these settings on a form, run the application, and check out the following:

◆ Enter text and manipulate it with the usual editing keys: Delete, Insert, Home, and End.

◆ Select multiple characters with the mouse or the arrow keys while holding down the Shift key.

◆ Move segments of text around with Copy (Ctrl+C), Cut (Ctrl+X), and Paste (Ctrl+V or Shift+Insert) operations.

◆ Right-click the control to see its context menu; it contains all the usual text-editing commands (and a few Unicode-related commands you'll never use).

◆ Exchange data with other applications through the Clipboard.

You can do all this without a single line of code! If you use the My object, you can save and load files by using two lines of code. Shortly, you'll see what you can do with the TextBox control if you add some code to your application, but first let's continue our exploration of the properties that allow us to manipulate the control's functionality.

ACCEPTSRETURN, ACCEPTSTAB

These two properties specify how the TextBox control reacts to the Enter and Tab keys. The Enter key activates the default button on the form, if there is one. The default button is usually an OK button that can be activated with the Enter key, even if it doesn't have the focus. In a multiline TextBox control, however, we want to be able to use the Enter key to change lines. The default value of the AcceptsReturn property is False, so pressing Enter does not create a new line on the control. If you leave this property's value set to False, users can still create new lines in the TextBox control, but they'll have to press Ctrl+Enter. If the form contains no default button, the Enter key creates a new line regardless of the AcceptsReturn setting.

Likewise, the AcceptsTab property determines how the control reacts to the Tab key. Normally, the Tab key takes you to the next control in the Tab order, and we generally avoid changing the default setting of the AcceptsTab property. In a multiline TextBox control, however, you may want the Tab key to insert a Tab character in the text of the control instead; to do this, set the control's AcceptsTab property to True (the default value is False). If you change the default value, users can still move to the next control in the Tab order by pressing Ctrl+Tab. Notice that the AcceptsTab property affects only the TextBox controls.

CHARACTERCASING

This property tells the control to change the casing of the characters as they're entered by the user. Its default value is Normal, and characters are displayed as typed. You can set it to Upper or Lower to convert the characters to upper- or lowercase automatically.

PASSWORDCHAR

This property turns the characters typed into any character you specify. If you don't want to display the actual characters typed by the user (when entering a password, for instance), use this property to define the character to appear in place of each character the user types.

The default value of this property is an empty string, which tells the control to display the characters as entered. If you set this value to an asterisk (*), for example, the user sees an asterisk in the place of every character typed. This property doesn't affect the control's Text property, which contains the actual characters. If the PasswordChar property is set to any character, the user can't copy or cut the text on the control.

READONLY, LOCKED

If you want to display text on a TextBox control but prevent users from editing it (such as for an agreement or a contract they must read, software installation instructions, and so on), you can set the ReadOnly property to True. When ReadOnly is set to True, you can put text on the control from within your code and users can view it yet they can't edit it.

To prevent editing of the TextBox control with VB 6, you had to set the Locked property to True. Oddly, the Locked property is also supported, but now it has a very different function. The Locked property of VB 2010 locks the control at design time (so that you won't move it or change its properties by mistake as you design the form).

Text-Manipulation Properties

Most of the properties for manipulating text in a TextBox control are available at runtime only. The following sections present a breakdown of each property.

TEXT

The most important property of the TextBox control is the Text property, which holds the control's text. You can set this property at design time to display some text on the control initially and read it from within your code to obtain the user's input and process it.

Notice that there are two methods of setting the Text property at design time. For single-line TextBox controls, set the Text property to a short string, as usual. For multiline TextBox controls, open the Lines property and enter the text in the String Collection Editor window, which will appear. In this window, each paragraph is entered as a single line of text. When you're finished, click OK to close the window; the text you entered in the String Collection Editor window will be placed on the control. Depending on the width of the control and the setting of the WordWrap property, paragraphs may be broken into multiple lines.

At runtime, use the Text property to extract the text entered by the user or to replace the existing text. You can also manipulate it with the members of the String class. The following expression returns the number of characters in the TextBox1 control:

```
Dim strLen As Integer = TextBox1.Text.Length
```

The IndexOf method of the String class will locate a specific string in the control's text. The following statement returns the location of the first occurrence of the string **Visual** in the text:

```
Dim location As Integer
location = TextBox1.Text.IndexOf("Visual")
```

For more information on locating strings in a TextBox control, see the section "VB 2010 at Work: The TextPad Project" later in this chapter, where we'll build a text editor with search-and-replace capabilities.

To store the control's contents in a file, use a statement such as the following:

```
My.Computer.FileSystem.WriteAllText(
        "MyText.txt", TextBox1.Text, False, System.Text.Encoding.UTF8)
```

The first argument is the name of the file where the text will be saved and the second argument is the text to be saved. The following argument is a True/False value that indicates whether the text will be appended to the file (if True) or whether it will replace the file's contents. That holds true if the file exists, of course. If the file doesn't exist, a new one will be created.

Similarly, you can read the contents of a text file into a TextBox control by using a statement such as the following:

```
TextBox1.Text = My.Computer.FileSystem.ReadAllText("MyText.txt")
```

To locate all instances of a string in the text, use a loop like the one in Listing 5.1. This loop locates successive instances of the string **Basic** and then continues searching from the character following the previous instance of the word in the text. To locate the last instance of a string in the text, use the LastIndexOf method. You can write a loop similar to the one in Listing 5.1 that scans the text backward.

LISTING 5.1: Locating all instances of a string in a TextBox

```
Dim startIndex = -1
startIndex = TextBox1.Text.IndexOf("Basic", startIndex + 1)
While startIndex > 0
   Console.WriteLine "String found at " & startIndex
   startIndex = TextBox1.Text.IndexOf("Basic", startIndex + 1)
End While
```

To test this code segment, place a multiline TextBox and a Button control on a form; then enter the statements of the listing in the button's Click event handler. Run the application and enter some text on the TextBox control. Make sure the text contains the word *Basic* or change the code to locate another word, and click the button. Notice that the IndexOf method performs a case-sensitive search.

Use the Replace method to replace a string with another within the line, the Split method to split the line into smaller components (such as words), and any other method exposed by the String class to manipulate the control's text.

The AppendText method appends the string specified by its argument to the control as is, without any line breaks between successive calls. If you want to append individual paragraphs to the control's text, you must insert the line breaks explicitly, with a statement such as the following (vbCrLf is a constant for the carriage return/newline characters):

```
Dim newString = "enter some text here"
TextBox1.AppendText(newString & vbCrLf)
```

LINES

In addition to using the Text property, you can access the text on the control by using the Lines property. The Lines property is a string array, and each element holds a paragraph of text. You can iterate through the text lines with a loop such as the following:

```
Dim iLine As Integer
For iLine = 0 To TextBox1.Lines.Length - 1
    ' process string TextBox1.Lines(iLine)
    Debug.WriteLine TextBox1.Lines(iLine)Next
```

Because the Lines property is an array, it supports the Length property, which returns the number of items in the array. Each element of the *Lines* array is a string, and you can call any of the String class's methods to manipulate it. Just keep in mind that you can't alter the text on the control by editing the *Lines* array. However, you can set the control's text by assigning an array of strings to the Lines property at design time.

Text-Selection Properties

The TextBox control provides three properties for manipulating the text selected by the user: `SelectedText`, `SelectionStart`, and `SelectionLength`. Users can select a range of text with a click-and-drag operation and the selected text will appear in reverse color. You can access the selected text from within your code through the `SelectedText` property and its location in the control's text through the `SelectionStart` and `SelectionLength` properties.

SELECTEDTEXT

This property returns the selected text, enabling you to manipulate the current selection from within your code. For example, you can replace the selection by assigning a new value to the `SelectedText` property. To convert the selected text to uppercase, use the `ToUpper` method of the String class:

```
TextBox1.SelectedText = TextBox1.SelectedText.ToUpper
```

SELECTIONSTART, SELECTIONLENGTH

Use these two properties to read the text selected by the user on the control or to select text from within your code. The `SelectionStart` property returns or sets the position of the first character of the selected text, somewhat like placing the cursor at a specific location in the text and selecting text by dragging the mouse. The `SelectionLength` property returns or sets the length of the selected text.

Suppose the user is seeking the word *Visual* in the control's text. The `IndexOf` method locates the string but doesn't select it. The following statements select the word in the text, highlight it, and bring it into view so that users can spot it instantly:

```
Dim seekString As String = "Visual"
Dim strLocation As Long
strLocation = TextBox1.Text.IndexOf(seekString)
If strLocation > 0 Then
    TextBox1.SelectionStart = strLocation
    TextBox1.SelectionLength = seekString.Length
End If
TextBox1.ScrollToCaret()
```

These lines locate the string *Visual* (or any user-supplied string stored in the *seekString* variable) in the text and select it by setting the `SelectionStart` and `SelectionLength` properties of the TextBox control. If the located string lies outside the visible area of the control, the user must scroll the text to bring the selection into view. The TextBox control provides the `ScrollToCaret` method, which brings the section of the text with the cursor (the *caret position*) into view.

The few lines of code shown previously form the core of a text editor's Find command. Replacing the current selection with another string is as simple as assigning a new value to the `SelectedText` property, and this technique provides you with an easy implementation of a Find and Replace operation.

LOCATING THE CURSOR POSITION IN THE CONTROL

The SelectionStart and SelectionLength properties always have a value even if no text is selected on the control. In this case, SelectionLength is 0, and SelectionStart is the current position of the pointer in the text. If you want to insert some text at the pointer's location, simply assign it to the SelectedText property, even if no text is selected on the control.

In addition to using the SelectionStart and SelectionLength properties, you can select text on the control with the Select method, which accepts as arguments the starting position and the length of the selection:

```
TextBox1.Select(start, length)
```

A variation of the Select method is the SelectAll method, which selects all the text on the control. Finally, the DeselectAll method deselects any text on the control.

HIDESELECTION

The selected text in the TextBox does not remain highlighted when the user moves to another control or form; to change this default behavior, set the HideSelection property to False. Use this property to keep the selected text highlighted, even if another control, form, or a dialog box, such as a Find & Replace dialog box, has the focus. Its default value is True, which means that the text doesn't remain highlighted when the TextBox loses the focus.

Undoing Edits

An interesting feature of the TextBox control is that it can automatically undo the most recent edit operation. To undo an operation from within your code, you must first examine the value of the CanUndo property. If it's True, the control can undo the operation; then you can call the Undo method to undo the most recent edit.

An edit operation is the insertion or deletion of characters. Entering text without deleting any is considered a single operation and will be undone in a single step. Even if the user has spent an hour entering text (without making any corrections), you can make all the text disappear with a single call to the Undo method. Fortunately, the deletion of the text becomes the most recent operation, which can be undone with another call to the Undo method. In effect, the Undo method is a toggle. When you call it for the first time, it undoes the last edit operation. If you call it again, it redoes the operation it previously undid. You can disable the redo operation by calling the ClearUndo method, which clears the undo buffer of the control. You should call it from within an Undo command's event handler to prevent an operation from being redone. In most cases, you should give users the option to redo an operation, especially because the Undo method can delete an enormous amount of text from the control.

VB 2010 at Work: The TextPad Project

The TextPad application, shown in Figure 5.2, demonstrates most of the TextBox control's properties and methods described so far. TextPad is a basic text editor that you can incorporate into your programs and customize for special applications. The TextPad project's main form is covered by a TextBox control, whose size is adjusted every time the user resizes the form. This feature doesn't require any programming—just set the `Dock` property of the TextBox control to `Fill`.

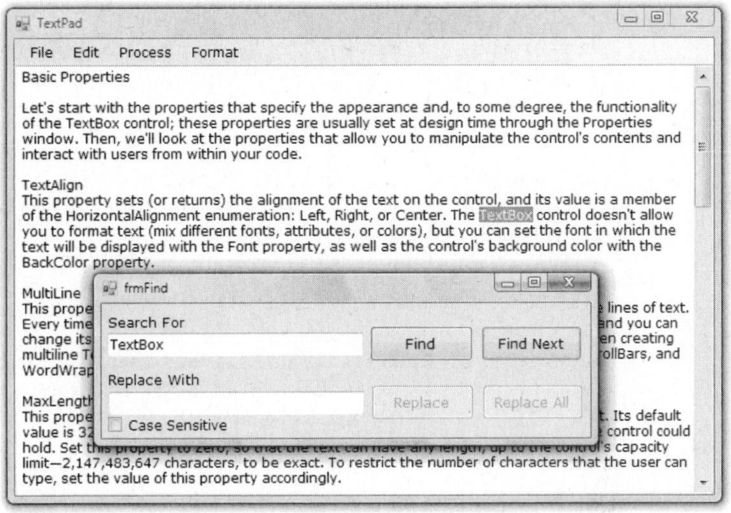

FIGURE 5.2
TextPad demonstrates the most useful properties and methods of the TextBox control.

The name of the application's main form is *frmTextPad*, and the name of the Find & Replace dialog box is *frmFind*. You can design the two forms as shown in the figures of this chapter, or you can open the TextPad project. To design the application's interface from scratch, place a MenuStrip control on the form. The control will be docked to the top of the form automatically. Then place a TextBox control on the main form, name it *txtEditor*, and set the following properties: `Multiline` to True, `MaxLength` to 0 (to edit text documents of any length), `HideSelection` to False (so that the selected text remains highlighted even when the main form doesn't have the focus), and `Dock` to Fill, so that it will fill the form.

The menu bar of the form contains all the commands you'd expect to find in any text editing application; they're listed in Table 5.1.

The File menu commands are implemented with the Open and Save As dialog boxes, the Font command with the Font dialog box, and the Color command with the Color dialog box. These dialog boxes are discussed in the following chapters, and as you'll see, you don't have to design them yourself. All you have to do is place a control on the form and set a few properties; the Framework takes it from there. The application will display the standard Open File/Save File/Font/Color dialog boxes, in which the user can select or specify a filename, or select a font or color. Of course, we'll provide a few lines of code to actually move the text into a file (or read it from a file and display it on the control), change the control's background color, and so on. I'll discuss the commands of the File menu in Chapter 7, "More Windows Controls."

THE EDITING COMMANDS

The options on the Edit menu move the selected text to and from the Clipboard. For the TextPad application, all you need to know about the Clipboard is that the `SetText` method places the currently selected text on the Clipboard and the `GetText` method retrieves information from the Clipboard (see Figure 5.3).

TABLE 5.1:   The TextPad form's menu

MENU	COMMAND	DESCRIPTION
File	New	Clears the text
	Open	Loads a new text file from disk
	Save	Saves the text to its file on disk
	Save As	Saves the text with a new filename on disk
	Print	Prints the text
	Exit	Terminates the application
Edit	Undo/Redo	Undoes/redoes the last edit operation
	Copy	Copies selected text to the Clipboard
	Cut	Cuts the selected text
	Paste	Pastes the Clipboard's contents to the editor
	Select All	Selects all text in the control
	Find & Replace	Displays a dialog box with Find and Replace options
Process	Convert To Upper	Converts selected text to uppercase
	Convert To Lower	Converts selected text to lowercase
	Number Lines	Numbers the text lines
Format	Font	Sets the text's font, size, and attributes
	Page Color	Sets the control's background color
	Text Color	Sets the color of the text
	WordWrap	Toggle menu item that turns text wrapping on and off

The Copy command, for example, is implemented with a single line of code (txtEditor is the name of the TextBox control). The Cut command does the same, and it also clears the selected text. The code for these and for the Paste command, which assigns the contents of the Clipboard to the current selection, is presented in Listing 5.2.

If no text is currently selected, the Clipboard's text is pasted at the pointer's current location. If the Clipboard contains a bitmap (placed there by another application) or any other type of data that the TextBox control can't handle, the paste operation will fail; that's why we handle the Paste operation with an If statement. You could provide some hint to the user by including an Else clause that informs them that the data on the Clipboard can't be used with a text-editing application.

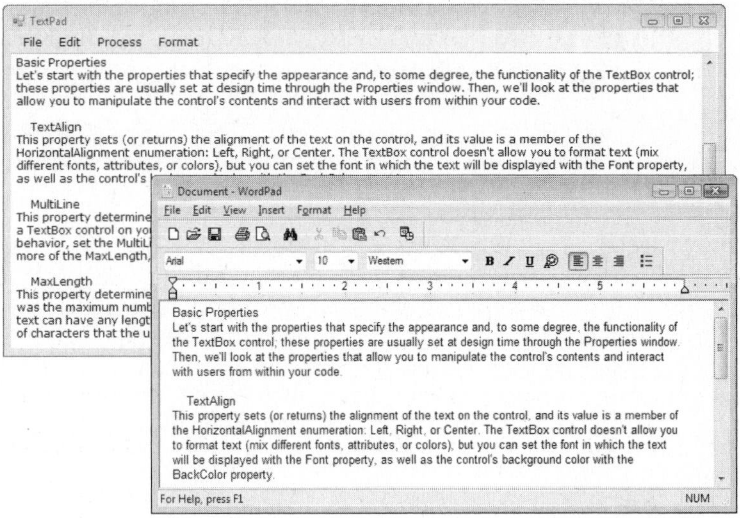

FIGURE 5.3

The Copy, Cut, and Paste operations of the TextPad application can be used to exchange text with any other application.

LISTING 5.2:   The Cut, Copy, and Paste commands

```
Private Sub EditCopyItem_Click(…)
             Handles EditCopyItem.Click
    If txtEditor.SelectionLength > 0 Then
        Clipboard.SetText(txtEditor.SelectedText)
    End If
End Sub

Private Sub EditCutItem_Click(…)
             Handles EditCutItem.Click
    Clipboard.SetText(txtEditor.SelectedText)
    txtEditor.SelectedText = ""
End Sub

Private Sub EditPasteItem_Click(…)
             Handles EditPasteItem.Click
    If Clipboard.ContainsText Then
        txtEditor.SelectedText = Clipboard.GetText
    End If
End Sub
```

THE PROCESS AND FORMAT MENUS

The commands of the Process and Format menus are straightforward. The Format menu commands open the Font or Color dialog box and change the control's Font, ForeColor, and BackColor properties. You will learn how to use these controls in the following chapter. The

Upper Case and Lower Case commands of the Process menu are also trivial: They select all the text, convert it to uppercase or lowercase, respectively, and assign the converted text to the control's `SelectedText` property with the following statements:

```
txtEditor.SelectedText = txtEditor.SelectedText.ToLower
txtEditor.SelectedText = txtEditor.SelectedText.ToUpper
```

Notice that the code uses the `SelectedText` property to convert only the selected text, not the entire document. The Number Lines command inserts a number in front of each text line and demonstrates how to process the individual lines of text on the control. However, it doesn't remove the line numbers, and there's no mechanism to prevent the user from editing the line numbers or inserting/deleting lines after they have been numbered. Use this feature to create a numbered listing or to number the lines of a file just before saving it or sharing it with another user. Listing 5.3 shows the Number Lines command's code and demonstrates how to iterate through the TextBox control's *Lines* array.

LISTING 5.3: The Number Lines command

```
Private Sub ProcessNumberLinesItem_Click(…)
            Handles ProcessNumberLines.Click
    Dim iLine As Integer
    Dim newText As New System.Text.StringBuilder()
    For iLine = 0 To txtEditor.Lines.Length - 1
        newText.Append((iLine + 1).ToString & vbTab &
                    txtEditor.Lines(iLine) & vbCrLf)
    Next
    txtEditor.SelectAll()
    Clipboard.SetText(newText.ToString)
    txtEditor.Paste()
End Sub
```

This event handler uses a StringBuilder variable. The StringBuilder class, discussed in Chapter 11, "The Framework at Large," is equivalent to the String class; it exposes similar methods and properties, but it's much faster at manipulating dynamic strings than the String class.

SEARCH AND REPLACE OPERATIONS

The last option in the Edit menu—and the most interesting—displays a Find & Replace dialog box (shown earlier in Figure 5.2). This dialog box works like the similarly named dialog box of Microsoft Word and many other Windows applications. The buttons in the Find & Replace dialog box are relatively self-explanatory:

Find The Find command locates the first instance of the specified string in the text after the cursor location. If a match is found, the Find Next, Replace, and Replace All buttons are enabled.

Find Next   This command locates the next instance of the string in the text. Initially, this button is disabled; it's enabled only after a successful Find operation.

Replace   This command replaces the current selection with the replacement string and then locates the next instance of the same string in the text. Like the Find Next button, it's disabled until a successful Find operation occurs.

Replace All   This command replaces all instances of the string specified in the Search For box with the string in the Replace With box.

To design the Find & Replace form, add a new form to the project (select Add New Item from the project's context menu) and place the following controls on it:

◆   A TextBox control and the Search for Label control.

◆   A TextBox control and the Replace with Label control.

◆   A CheckBox control with the caption Case Sensitive.

◆   The Find, Find Next, Replace, and Replace All buttons.

Set the new form's TopMost property to True; you want this form to remain on top of the main form, even when it doesn't have the focus. Whether the search is case sensitive or not depends on the status of the Case Sensitive CheckBox control. If the string is found in the control's text, the program will highlight it by selecting it. In addition, the code will call the TextBox control's ScrollToCaret method to bring the selection into view. The Find Next button takes into consideration the location of the pointer and searches for a match *after* the current location. If the user moves the pointer somewhere else and then clicks the Find Next button, the program will locate the first instance of the string after the current location of the pointer—and not necessarily after the last match. Of course, you can always keep track of the location of each match and continue the search from this location. The Find button executes the code shown in Listing 5.4.

LISTING 5.4:   The Find button

```
Private Sub bttnFind_Click(…) Handles bttnFind.Click
    Dim selStart As Integer
    If chkCase.Checked = True Then
        selStart =
            frmTextPad.txtEditor.Text.IndexOf(
            searchWord.Text, StringComparison.Ordinal)
    Else
        selStart =
            frmTextPad.txtEditor.Text.IndexOf(
            searchWord.Text,
            StringComparison.OrdinalIgnoreCase)
    End If
    If selStart = -1 Then
        MsgBox("Text not found")
        Exit Sub
    End If
```

```
        frmTextPad.txtEditor.Select(
                    selStart, searchWord.Text.Length)
        bttnFindNext.Enabled = True
        bttnReplace.Enabled = True
        bttnReplaceAll.Enabled = True
        frmTextPad.txtEditor.ScrollToCaret()
    End Sub
```

The Find button examines the value of the chkCase CheckBox control, which specifies whether the search will be case sensitive and calls the appropriate form of the IndexOf method. The first argument of this method is the string we're searching for; the second argument is the search mode, and its value is a member of the StringComparison enumeration: Ordinal for case-sensitive searches and OrdinalIgnoreCase for case-insensitive searches. If the IndexOf method locates the string, the program selects it by calling the control's Select method with the appropriate arguments. If not, it displays a message. Notice that after a successful Find operation, the Find Next, Replace, and Replace All buttons on the form are enabled.

The code of the Find Next button is the same, but it starts searching at the character following the current selection:

```
    selStart = frmTextPad.txtEditor.Text.IndexOf(
            searchWord.Text,
            frmTextPad.txtEditor.SelectionStart + 1,
            StringComparison.Ordinal)
```

The Replace button replaces the current selection with the replacement string and then locates the next instance of the find string. The Replace All button replaces all instances of the search word in the document. Listing 5.5 presents the code behind the Replace and Replace All buttons.

LISTING 5.5:   The Replace and Replace All operations

```
Private Sub bttnReplace_Click(…) Handles bttnReplace.Click
    If frmTextPad.txtEditor.SelectedText <> "" Then
        frmTextPad.txtEditor.SelectedText = replaceWord.Text
    End If
      bttnFindNext_Click(sender, e)
End Sub

Private Sub bttnReplaceAll_Click(…) Handles bttnReplaceAll.Click
    Dim curPos, curSel As Integer
    curPos = frmTextPad.txtEditor.SelectionStart
    curSel = frmTextPad.txtEditor.SelectionLength
    frmTextPad.txtEditor.Text =
        frmTextPad.txtEditor.Text.Replace(
        searchWord.Text.Trim, replaceWord.Text.Trim)
```

```
    frmTextPad.txtEditor.SelectionStart = curPos
    frmTextPad.txtEditor.SelectionLength = curSel
End Sub
```

The `Replace` method is case sensitive, which means that it replaces instances of the search argument in the text that have the exact same spelling as its first argument. For a case-insensitive replace operation, you must write the code to perform consecutive case-insensitive search-and-replace operations. Alternatively, you can use the `Replace` built-in function to perform case-insensitive searches. Here's how you'd call the `Replace` function to perform a case-insensitive replace operation:

```
Replace(frmTextPad.txtEditor.Text, searchWord.Text.Trim,
    replaceWord.Text.Trim, , , CompareMethod.Text)
```

The last, optional, argument determines whether the search will be case-sensitive (`Compare-Method.Binary`) or case-insensitive (`CompareMethod.Text`).

When you're searching for a string in the text, the active form is the `frmFind` form and any selection you make from within your code in the main form's TextBox control isn't highlighted by default. You must set the `HideSelection` property of the TextBox control to False to highlight the selected text on a control that doesn't currently have the focus. This is a common property for many controls, and you should remember to change it to False if you want the selection to remain visible even when the control loses the focus. (You will use this property most often with the TextBox, ListBox, ListView, and TreeView controls.)

THE UNDO/REDO COMMANDS

The Undo command (shown in Listing 5.6) is implemented with a call to the `Undo` method. However, because the `Undo` method works like a toggle, we must also toggle its caption from Undo to Redo (and vice versa) each time the command is activated.

LISTING 5.6: The Undo/Redo command of the Edit menu

```
Private Sub EditUndoItem_Click(…)
        Handles EditUndoItem.Click
    If EditUndoItem.Text = "Undo" Then
        If txtEditor.CanUndo Then
            txtEditor.Undo()
            EditUndoItem.Text = "Redo"
        End If
    Else
        If txtEditor.CanUndo Then
            txtEditor.Undo()
            EditUndoItem.Text = "Undo"
        End If
    End If
End Sub
```

The TextBox control doesn't provide more granular undo operations — unlike Word, which keeps track of user actions (insertions, deletions, replacements, and so on) and then undoes them in steps. If you edit the text after an undo operation, you can no longer redo the last undo operation. This means that as soon as the contents of the TextBox control change, the caption of the first command in the Edit menu must become Undo, even if it's Redo at the time. To detect the action of editing the control's contents and reset the Undo command's caption, insert the following statement in the `TextChanged` event of the TextBox control:

```
EditUndoItem.Text = "Undo"
```

If you need a more-granular undo feature, you should use the RichTextBox control, which is discussed in detail in Chapter 7. The RichTextBox control can display formatted text, but it can also be used as an enhanced TextBox control.

Capturing Keystrokes

Another event that is quite commonly used in programming the TextBox control is the `KeyPress` event, which occurs every time a key is pressed and reports the character that was pressed. You can use this event to capture certain keys and modify the program's behavior depending on the character typed.

By capturing keystrokes, you can process the data as they are entered, in real time. For example, you can make sure that a TextBox accepts only numeric or hexadecimal characters and rejects all others. To implement a binary editor, use the `KeyPress` event handler shown in Listing 5.7.

LISTING 5.7:   Handling keystrokes

```
Private Sub TextBox1_KeyPress(…) Handles TextBox1.KeyPress
    If Char.IsLetterOrDigit(e.KeyChar) Then
        Select Case UCase(e.KeyChar)
            Case "1", "2", "3", "4", "5", "6", "7", "8", "9", "0"
                TextBox1.SelectedText = e.KeyChar
            Case "A", "B", "C", "D", "E", "F"
                TextBox1.SelectedText = UCase(e.KeyChar)
        End Select
        e.Handled = True
    End If
End Sub
```

The very first executable statement in the event handler examines the key that was pressed and exits if it is a special editing key (Delete, Backspace, Ctrl+V, and so on). If so, the handler exits without taking any action. The `KeyChar` property of the `e` argument of the `KeyPress` event reports the key that was pressed. The code converts it to a string and then uses a `Case` statement to handle individual keystrokes. If the user pressed the a or the 1 key, for example, the code displays the corresponding uppercase character ("1" or "A"). If the character pressed is not among the characters that may appear in hexadecimal values, the code skips it by setting the `Handled` property to True.

You can process the characters pressed from within the KeyDown event handler, only this time you must set the SuppressKeyPress property to True:

```
Private Sub TextBox1_KeyDown(…) Handles TextBox1.KeyDown
    Dim ch As Windows.Forms.Keys
    ch = e.KeyCode
    If Char.IsLetterOrDigit(Chr(ch)) Then
        Select Case ch
            Case Keys.D1, Keys.D2, Keys.D3, Keys.D4, Keys.D5,
                Keys.D6, Keys.D7, Keys.D8, Keys.D9, Keys.D0
                TextBox1.SelectedText = Chr(ch)
            Case Keys.A, Keys.B, Keys.C, Keys.D, Keys.E, Keys.F
                TextBox1.SelectedText = UCase(Chr(ch))
            Case Else

        End Select
        e.SuppressKeyPress = True
    End If
End Sub
```

CANCELING KEYSTROKES

Before you exit the event handler, you must "kill" the original key that was pressed so it won't appear on the control. You do this by setting the Handled property to True, which tells VB that it shouldn't process the keystroke any further. If you omit this statement, the special characters will be printed twice: once in their transformed format and once as regular characters (Aa, Bb, and so on).

CAPTURING FUNCTION KEYS

Another common feature used in all types of applications is the assignment of special operations to the function keys. The Notepad application, for example, uses the F5 function key to insert the current date and time at the cursor's location. You can do the same with the TextPad application, but you can't use the KeyPress event — the KeyChar argument doesn't report function keys. The events that can capture the function keys are the KeyDown and KeyUp events. Also, unlike the KeyPress event, these two events don't report the character pressed but instead report the key's code (a special number that distinguishes each key on the keyboard, also known as the *scancode*) through the e.KeyCode property.

The keycode is unique for each key, not each character. Lower- and uppercase characters have different ASCII values but the same keycode because they are on the same key. For example, the number 4 and the $ symbol have the same keycode because the same key on the keyboard generates both characters. Along with the key's code, the KeyDown and KeyUp events also report the state of the Shift, Ctrl, and Alt keys through the e.Shift, e.Alt, and e.Control properties.

The KeyUp event handler shown in Listing 5.8 uses the F5 and F6 function keys to insert the current date and time in the document. It also uses the F7 and F8 keys to insert two predefined strings in the document.

LISTING 5.8:   KeyUp event examples

```
Private Sub txtEditor_KeyUp(ByVal sender As Object,
      ByVal e As System.Windows.Forms.KeyEventArgs)
      Handles txtEditor.KeyUp
   Select Case e.KeyCode
      Case Keys.F5 :
              txtEditor.SelectedText =
              Now().ToLongDateString
      Case Keys.F6 :
              txtEditor.SelectedText =
              Now().ToLongTimeString
      Case Keys.F7 :
              txtEditor.SelectedText =
              "MicroWeb Designs, Inc."
      Case Keys.F8 :
              txtEditor.SelectedText =
              "Another user-supplied string"
   End Select
End Sub
```

Windows already uses some of the function keys (for example, the F1 key for help), and you shouldn't modify their original functions. With a little additional effort, you can provide users with a dialog box that lets them assign their own strings to function keys. You'll probably have to take into consideration the status of the Shift, Control, and Alt properties of the event's e argument. To find out whether *two* of the modifier keys are pressed along with a key, use the AND operator with the appropriate properties of the e argument. The following If clause detects the Ctrl and Alt keys:

```
If e.Control AND e.Alt Then
   { Both Alt and Control keys were down}
End If
```

If you need to control the keystrokes from within your code (a rather common scenario in an advanced, functional user interface design), you should be aware of the order of the events fired every time a key is pressed. First, the KeyDown event is fired; this event is fired before the keystroke is passed to the control. This is the event in which you should "kill" any keystrokes that you don't want to be processed normally by the control, or replace them with a different key. Then the KeyPress event is fired, if the keystroke corresponds to a character, number, or symbol but not a control key. Finally, the KeyUp event is fired. By that time, the keystroke has already been processed by the control and it's too late to kill or replace the original keystroke. Can you guess what will happen if you insert the following statements in a TextBox control's (or Form's) KeyDown event handler?

```
If e.KeyCode = Keys.A Then
    e.SuppressKeyPress = True
End If
```

The A key will never be processed, as if the keyboard isn't working with this application.

Autocomplete Properties

One set of interesting properties of the TextBox control are the autocomplete properties. Have you noticed how Internet Explorer prompts you with possible matches as soon as you start typing an address or your username in a text box (or in the address bar of the browser)? You can easily implement such boxes with a single-line TextBox control and the autocomplete properties. Please note that these properties apply to single-line TextBoxes only.

Let me review the properties that relate to automatic completion. You may wish to open the AutoCompleteTextBoxes project (available for download from www.sybex.com/go/mastering-vb2010) to experiment with the settings of these properties while reading the text. The Auto-CompleteMode property determines whether, and how, the TextBox control will prompt users, and its setting is a member of the AutoCompleteMode enumeration: Suggest, Append, SuggestAppend, and None. In Append mode, the TextBox control selects the first matching item in the list of suggestions and completes the text. In SuggestAppend mode, the control suggests the first matching item in the list, as before, but it also expands the list. In Suggest mode, the control simply opens a list with the matching items but doesn't select any of them. Regular TextBox controls have their AutoCompleteMode property set to None.

The AutoCompleteSource property determines where the list of suggestions comes from; its value is a member of the AutoCompleteSource enumeration, which is shown in Table 5.2.

TABLE 5.2: The members of the AutoCompleteSource enumeration

MEMBER	DESCRIPTION
AllSystemSources	The suggested items are the names of system resources.
AllUrl	The suggested items are the URLs visited by the target computer. Does not work if you're deleting the recently viewed pages.
CustomSource	The suggested items come from a custom collection.
FileSystem	The suggested items are filenames.
HistoryList	The suggested items come from the computer's history list.
RecentlyUsedList	The suggested items come from the Recently Used folder.
None	The control doesn't suggest any items.

To demonstrate the basics of the autocomplete properties, I've included the AutoComplete-TextBoxes project, which you can download from www.sybex.com/go/masteringvb2010. The main form of the project is shown in Figure 5.4. This project allows you to set the autocomplete mode and source for a single-line TextBox control. The top TextBox control uses a custom list of words, while the lower one uses one of the built-in autocomplete sources (file system, URLs, and so on).

Once you set the AutoCompleteSource to CustomSource, you must also populate an AutoCompleteStringCollection object with the desired suggestions and assign it to the

AutoCompleteCustomSource property. The AutoCompleteStringCollection is just a collection of strings. Listing 5.9 shows statements in a form's Load event that prepare such a list and use it with the *TextBox1* control.

FIGURE 5.4
Suggesting words with the AutoCompleteSource property

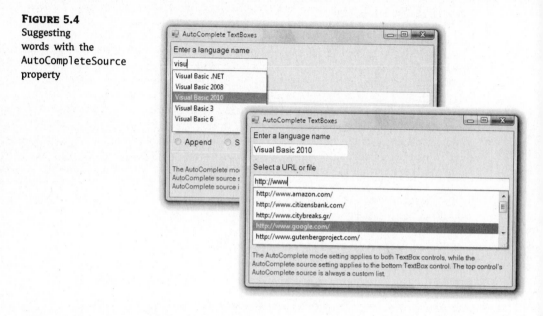

LISTING 5.9:   Populating a custom AutoCompleteSource property

```
Private Sub Form1_Load(…) Handles MyBase.Load
    Dim knownWords As New AutoCompleteStringCollection
    knownWords.Add("Visual Basic 2008")
    knownWords.Add("Visual Basic .NET")
    knownWords.Add("Visual Basic 6")
    knownWords.Add("Visual Basic")
    knownWords.Add("Framework")
    TextBox1.AutoCompleteCustomSource = knownWords
    TextBox1.AutoCompleteSource = AutoCompleteSource.CustomSource
    TextBox1.AutoCompleteMode = AutoCompleteMode.Suggest
    TextBox2.AutoCompleteSource = AutoCompleteSource.RecentlyUsedList
    TextBox2.AutoCompleteMode = AutoCompleteMode.Suggest
End Sub
```

The *TextBox1* control on the form will open a drop-down list with all possible matches in the knownWords collection as soon as the user starts typing in the control, as shown in the top part of Figure 5.4.

Real World Scenario

DATA-ENTRY APPLICATIONS

Typical business applications contain numerous forms for data entry, and the most common element on data-entry forms is the TextBox control. Data-entry operators are very efficient with the keyboard, and they should be able to use your application without reaching for the mouse.

Seasoned data-entry operators can't live without the Enter key; they reach for this key at the end of each operation. In my experience, a functional interface should add intelligence to this keystroke: the Enter key should perform the obvious or most likely operation at any time. When data is being entered, for example, it should take the user to the next control in the Tab order. Consider a data-entry screen like the one shown in the following image, which contains several TextBox controls, a DataTimePicker control for entering dates, and two CheckBox controls. This is the main form of the Simple Data Entry Form sample project, which you will find at www.sybex.com/go/masteringvb2010 along with the other projects available for use with this book.

The application demonstrates how to use the Enter key intelligently: Every time the Enter key is pressed, the focus is moved to the next control in the Tab order. Even if the current control is a CheckBox, this keystroke doesn't change the status of the CheckBox controls; it simply moves the focus forward.

You could program the KeyUp event of each control to react to the Enter key, but this approach can lead to maintenance problems if you add new controls to an existing form. The best approach is to intercept the Enter keystroke at the form level, before it reaches a control. To do so, you must set the KeyPreview property of the form to True. This setting causes the key events to be fired first at the form level and then at the control that has the focus. In essence, it allows you to handle certain keystrokes for multiple controls at once. The KeyUp event handler of the sample project's main form intercepts the Enter keystroke and reacts to it by moving the focus to the next control in the Tab order via the ProcessTabKey method. This method simulates the pressing of the Tab key, and it's called with a single argument, which is a Boolean value: True moves the focus forward, and False moves it backward. Here's the code in the KeyDown event handler of the application's form that makes the interface much more

functional and intuitive (you can open the DataEntry project, examine all of the code, and see
how it functions):

```
Private Sub frmDataEntry_KeyDown(
            ByVal sender As Object,
            ByVal e As System.Windows.Forms.KeyEventArgs)
            Handles Me.KeyUp
    If e.KeyCode = Keys.Enter And Not (e.Alt Or e.Control) Then
        If Me.ActiveControl.GetType Is GetType(TextBox) Or
            Me.ActiveControl.GetType Is GetType(CheckBox) Or
            Me.ActiveControl.GetType Is
            GetType(DateTimePicker) Then
            If e.Shift Then
                Me.ProcessTabKey(False)
            Else
                Me.ProcessTabKey(True)
            End If
        End If
    End If
End Sub
```

It's important to program the KeyDown event if you want to be able to process keystrokes
before the control captures them, or even if you want to cancel keystrokes. If you insert the
same code in the KeyUp event, the keystrokes will be processed by the control first and then
by your code. There are a couple of things you should notice about this handler. First, it
doesn't react to the Enter key if it was pressed along with the Alt or Ctrl key. The Shift key,
on the other hand, is used to control the direction in the Tab order. The focus moves forward
with the Enter keystroke and moves backward with the Shift + Enter keystroke. Also, the
focus is handled automatically only for the TextBox, CheckBox, and DataTimePicker controls.
When the user presses the Enter key when a button has the focus, the program reacts as
expected by invoking the button's Click event handler.

The ListBox, CheckedListBox, and ComboBox Controls

The ListBox, CheckedListBox, and ComboBox controls present lists of choices from which the
user can select one or more of the items. The first two are illustrated in Figure 5.5.

FIGURE 5.5
The ListBox and
CheckedListBox controls

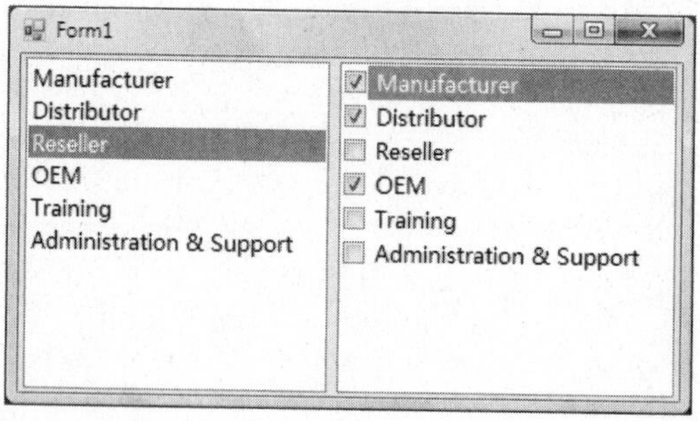

The ListBox control occupies a user-specified amount of space on the form and is populated with a list of items. If the list of items is longer than can fit on the control, a vertical scroll bar appears automatically.

The CheckedListBox control is a variation of the ListBox control. It's identical to the List-Box control, but a check box appears in front of each item. The user can select any number of items by checking or clearing the boxes. As you know, you can also select multiple items from a ListBox control by pressing the Shift or Ctrl key.

The ComboBox control also contains multiple items but typically occupies less space on the screen. The ComboBox control is an expandable ListBox control: The user can expand it to make a selection and collapse it after the selection is made. The real advantage of the Combo-Box control, however, is that the user can enter new information in the ComboBox rather than being forced to select from the items listed.

To add items to any of the three controls at design time, locate the Items property in the Properties window for the control and click the ellipsis button. When the String Collection Editor window pops up, you can add the items you want to display in the list. Each item must appear on a separate text line, and blank text lines will result in blank lines in the list. These items will appear in the list when the form is loaded, but you can add more items (or remove existing ones) from within your code at any time. They appear in the same order as entered on the String Collection Editor window unless the control has its Sorted property set to True, in which case the items are automatically sorted regardless of the order in which you've specified them.

The next sections explore the ListBox control's properties and methods. Later in the chapter, you'll see how the same properties and methods can be used with the ComboBox control.

Basic Properties

In the following sections, you'll find the properties that determine the functionality of the List-Box, CheckedListBox, and ComboBox controls. These properties are usually set at design time, but you can change the settings from within your application's code.

INTEGRALHEIGHT

This property can be set to a True/False value that indicates whether the control's height will be adjusted to avoid the partial display of the last item. When IntegralHeight is set to True, the control's actual height changes in multiples of the height of a single line, so only an integer number of rows are displayed at all times.

ITEMS

The Items property is a collection that holds the list items for the control. At design time, you can populate this list through the String Collection Editor window. At runtime, you can access and manipulate the items through the methods and properties of the Items collection, which are described in the section ''Manipulating the Items Collection'' later in this chapter.

MULTICOLUMN

A ListBox control can display its items in multiple columns if you set its MultiColumn property to True. The problem with multicolumn ListBoxes is that you can't specify the column in which each item will appear. ListBoxes (and CheckedListBoxes) with many items and the MultiColumn property set to True expand horizontally, not vertically. A horizontal scroll bar will be attached to a multicolumn ListBox so that users can bring any column into view. This property does not apply to the ComboBox control.

SELECTIONMODE

This property, which applies to the ListBox and CheckedListBox controls only, determines how the user can select the list's items. The possible values of this property—members of the SelectionMode enumeration—are shown in Table 5.3.

TABLE 5.3: The SelectionMode enumeration

VALUE	DESCRIPTION
None	No selection at all is allowed.
One	(Default) Only a single item can be selected.
MultiSimple	Simple multiple selection: A mouse click (or pressing the spacebar) selects or deselects an item in the list. You must click all the items you want to select.
MultiExtended	Extended multiple selection: Press Shift and click the mouse (or press one of the arrow keys) to select multiple contiguous items. This process highlights all the items between the previously selected item and the current selection. Press Ctrl and click the mouse to select or deselect multiple single items in the list.

SORTED

When this property is True, the items remain sorted at all times. The default is False because it takes longer to insert new items in their proper location. This property's value can be set at design time as well as runtime. The items in a sorted ListBox control are sorted in ascending and case-sensitive order, also known as phone book order. Because of this, the ListBox control won't sort numeric data. The number 10 will appear in front of the number 5 because the numeric value of the string *10* is smaller than the numeric value of the string *5*. If the numbers are formatted as *010* and *005*, they will be sorted correctly.

TEXT

The Text property returns the selected text on the control. Although you can set the Text property for the ComboBox control at design time, this property is available only at runtime for the other two controls. Notice that the items need not be strings. By default, each item is an object. For each object, however, the control displays a string, which is the same string returned by the object's ToString method.

Manipulating the Items Collection

To manipulate a ListBox control from within your application, you should be able to do the following:

◆ Add items to the list

◆ Remove items from the list

◆ Access individual items in the list

The items in the list are represented by the Items collection. You use the members of the Items collection to access the control's items and to add or remove items. The Items property exposes the standard members of a collection, which are described later in this section.

Each member of the Items collection is an object. In most cases, we use ListBox controls to store strings, but it's also common to store objects to this control. When you add an object to a ListBox control, a string is displayed on the corresponding line of the control. This is the string returned by the object's ToString method. You can display any other property of the object by setting the control's ValueMember property to the name of the property.

If you add a Font object and a Rectangle object to the Items collection with the statements

```
ListBox1.Items.Add(New Font("Verdana", 12, FontStyle.Bold))
ListBox1.Items.Add(New Rectangle(0, 0, 100, 100))
```

then the following strings appear on the first two lines of the control:

```
[Font: Name=Verdana, Size=12, Units=3, GdiCharSet=1, gdiVerticalFont=False]
{X=0, Y=0, Width=100, Height=100}
```

However, you can access the members of the two objects because the ListBox stores objects, not their descriptions. The following statement prints the width of the Rectangle object (the output produced by the statement is highlighted):

```
Debug.WriteLine(ListBox1.Items.Item(1).Width)
100
```

The expression in the preceding statement is *late-bound*, which means that the compiler doesn't know whether the first object in the Items collection is a Rectangle object and it can't verify the member Width. If you attempt to call the Width property of the first item in the collection, you'll get an exception at runtime indicating that the code has attempted to access a missing member. The missing member is the Width property of the Font object.

The proper way to read the objects stored in a ListBox control is to examine the type of the object first and then attempt to retrieve a property (or call a method) of the object, but only if it's of the appropriate type. Here's how you would read the Width property of a Rectangle object:

```
If ListBox1.Items.Item(0).GetType Is
GetType(Rectangle) Then
    Debug.WriteLine(CType(ListBox1.Items.Item(0), Rectangle).Width)
End If
```

THE *ADD* METHOD

To add items to the list, use the Items.Add or Items.Insert method. The Add method accepts as an argument the object to be added to the list. New items are appended to the end of the list, unless the Sorted property has been set to True. The following loop adds the elements of the array *words* to a ListBox control, one at a time:

```
Dim words(100) As String
{ statements to populate array }
```

```
Dim i As Integer
For i = 0 To 99
   ListBox1.Items.Add(words(i))
Next
```

Then, to iterate through all the items on the control, use a loop such as the following:

```
Dim i As Integer
For i = 0 To ListBox1.Items.Count - 1
   { statements to process item ListBox1.Items(i) }
Next
```

You can also use the For Each…Next statement to iterate through the Items collection, as shown here:

```
Dim itm As Object
For Each itm In ListBox1.Items
   { process the current item, represented by the itm variable }
Next
```

When you populate a ListBox control with a large number of items, call the BeginUpdate method before starting the loop and call the EndUpdate method when you're done. These two methods turn off the visual update of the control while you're populating it, and they speed up the process considerably. When the EndUpdate method is called, the control is redrawn with all the items.

THE *INSERT* METHOD

To insert an item at a specific location, use the Insert method, whose syntax is as follows:

```
ListBox1.Items.Insert(index, item)
```

Remember that you must declare the item prior to using it. If you don't initialize it, you will get a null ref.

The item parameter is the object to be added, and index is the location of the new item. (The first item's index in the list is zero).

THE *CLEAR* METHOD

The Clear method removes all the items from the control. Its syntax is quite simple:

```
ListBox1.Items.Clear
```

THE *COUNT* PROPERTY

This is the number of items in the list. If you want to access all the items with a For…Next loop, the loop's counter must go from 0 to ListBox.Items.Count - 1, as shown in the example of the Add method.

THE *COPYTO* METHOD

The CopyTo method of the Items collection retrieves all the items from a ListBox control and stores them in the array passed to the method as an argument. The syntax of the CopyTo method is as follows, where `destination` is the name of the array that will accept the items, and `index` is the index of an element in the array where the first item will be stored:

```
ListBox1.CopyTo(destination, index)
```

The array that will hold the items of the control must be declared explicitly and must be large enough to hold all the items.

THE *REMOVE* AND *REMOVEAT* METHODS

To remove an item from the list, you can simply call the Items collection's Remove method, passing the object to be removed as an argument. If the control contains strings, pass the string to be removed. If the same string appears multiple times on the control, only the first instance will be removed.

You can also remove an item by specifying its position in the list via the RemoveAt method, which accepts as argument the position of the item to be removed:

```
ListBox1.Items.RemoveAt(index)
```

The index parameter is the order of the item to be removed, and the first item's order is 0.

THE *CONTAINS* METHOD

The Contains method of the Items collection—not to be confused with the control's Contains method—accepts an object as an argument and returns a True/False value that indicates whether the collection contains this object. Use the Contains method to avoid the insertion of identical objects into the ListBox control. The following statements add a string to the Items collection only if the string isn't already part of the collection:

```
Dim itm As String = "Remote Computing"
If Not ListBox1.Items.Contains(itm) Then
    ListBox1.Items.Add(itm)
End If
```

Selecting Items

The ListBox control allows the user to select either one or multiple items, depending on the setting of the SelectionMode property. In a single-selection ListBox control, you can retrieve the selected item by using the SelectedItem property and its index by using the SelectedIndex property. SelectedItem returns the selected item, which is an object. The text of the selected item is reported by the Text property.

If the control allows the selection of multiple items, they're reported with the Selected-Items property. This property is a collection of objects and exposes the same members as the Items collection. Because the ComboBox does not allow the selection of multiple items, it provides only the SelectedIndex and SelectedItem properties.

To iterate through all the selected items in a multiselection ListBox control, use a loop such as the following:

```
For Each itm As Object In ListBox1.SelectedItems
    Debug.WriteLine(itm)
Next
```

The *itm* variable should be declared as Object because the items in the ListBox control are objects. If they're all of the same type, you can convert them to the specific type and then call their methods. If all the items are of the Rectangle type, you can use a loop like the following to print the area of each rectangle:

```
For Each itm As Rectangle In ListBox1.SelectedItems
    Debug.WriteLine(itm.Width * itm.Height)
Next
```

VB 2010 at Work: The ListBox Demo Project

The ListBox Demo application (shown in Figure 5.6) demonstrates the basic operations of the ListBox control. The two ListBox controls on the form operate slightly differently. The first has the default configuration: Only one item can be selected at a time, and new items are appended after the existing item. The second ListBox control has its Sorted property set to True and its MultiSelect property set according to the values of the two RadioButton controls at the bottom of the form.

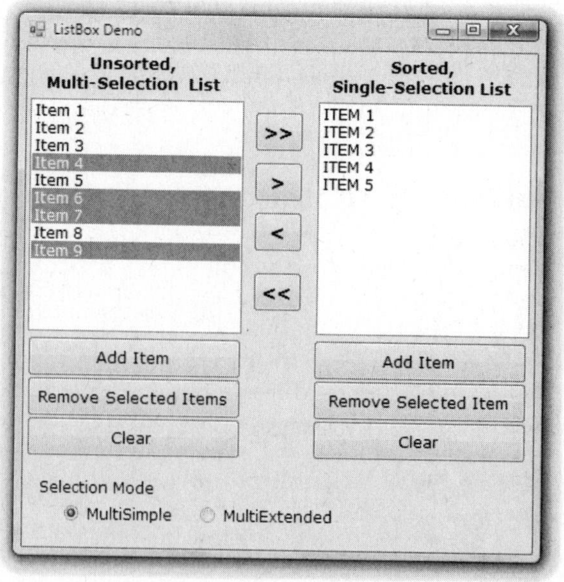

FIGURE 5.6
ListBox Demo demonstrates most of the operations you'll perform with ListBoxes.

The code for the ListBox Demo application contains much of the logic you'll need in your ListBox manipulation routines. It shows you how to do the following:

◆ Add and remove items at runtime

◆ Transfer items between lists at runtime

◆ Handle multiple selected items

◆ Maintain sorted lists

THE ADD ITEM BUTTONS

The Add Item buttons use the InputBox() function to prompt the user for input, and then they add the user-supplied string to the ListBox control. The code is identical for both buttons (see Listing 5.10).

LISTING 5.10:   The Add Item buttons

```
Private Sub bttnSourceAdd_Click(…)
          Handles bttnSourceAdd.Click
    Dim ListItem As String
    ListItem = InputBox("Enter new item's name")
    If ListItem.Trim <> "" Then
        sourceList.Items.Add(ListItem)
    End If
End Sub
```

Notice that the subroutine examines the data entered by the user to avoid adding blank strings to the list. The code for the Clear buttons is also straightforward; it simply calls the Clear method of the Items collection to remove all entries from the corresponding list.

REMOVING ITEMS FROM THE TWO LISTS

The code for the Remove Selected Item button is different from that for the Remove Selected Items button (both are presented in Listing 5.11). The code for the Remove Selected Item button removes the selected item, while the Remove Selected Items buttons must scan all the items of the left list and remove the selected one(s).

LISTING 5.11:   The Remove buttons

```
Private Sub bttnDestinationRemove_Click(…)
          Handles bttnDestinationRemove.Click
    destinationList.Items.Remove( destinationList.SelectedItem)
End Sub
```

```
Private Sub bttnSourceRemove_Click(…)
              Handles bttnSourceRemove.Click
    Dim i As Integer
    For i = 0 To sourceList.SelectedIndices.Count - 1
        sourceList.Items.RemoveAt( sourceList.SelectedIndices(0))
    Next
End Sub
```

Notice that the code of the second event handler (the one that removes multiple selected items) always removes the first item in the SelectedIndices collection. If you attempt to remove the item SelectedIndices(i), you will remove the first selected item during the first iteration. After an item is removed from the selection, the remaining items are no longer at the same locations. (In effect, you have to refresh the SelectedIndices collection.) The second selected item will take the place of the first selected item, which was just deleted, and so on. By removing the first item in the SelectedIndices collection, we make sure that all selected items, and only those items, will be eventually removed.

MOVING ITEMS BETWEEN LISTS

The two single-arrow buttons (located between the ListBox controls shown in Figure 5.6) transfer selected items from one list to another. The button with the single arrow pointing to the right transfers the items selected in the left list after it ensures that the list contains at least one selected item. Its code is presented in Listing 5.12. First, it adds the item to the second list, and then it removes the item from the original list. Notice that the code removes an item by passing it as an argument to the Remove method because it doesn't make any difference which one of two identical objects will be removed.

LISTING 5.12:   Moving the selected items

```
Private Sub bttnSourceMove_Click(…)
              Handles bttnSourceMove.Click
    While sourceList.SelectedIndices.Count > 0
        destinationList.Items.Add(sourceList.Items(
                sourceList.SelectedIndices(0)))
        sourceList.Items.Remove(sourceList.Items(
                sourceList.SelectedIndices(0)))
    End While
End Sub
```

The second single-arrow button transfers items in the opposite direction. The destination control (the one on the right) doesn't allow the selection of multiple items, so you can use the SelectedIndex and SelectedItem properties. The event handler that moves a single item from the right to the left ListBox is shown next:

```
sourceList.Items.Add(destinationList.SelectedItem)
destinationList.Items.RemoveAt(destinationList.SelectedIndex)
```

Searching the ListBox

Two of the most useful methods of the ListBox control are the FindString and FindString-Exact methods, which allow you to quickly locate any item in the list. The FindString method locates a string that partially matches the one you're searching for; FindStringExact finds an exact match. If you're searching for *Man* and the control contains a name such as *Mansfield*, FindString matches the item but FindStringExact does not.

Both the FindString and FindStringExact methods perform case-insensitive searches. If you're searching for *visual* and the list contains the item *Visual*, both methods will locate it. The syntax for both methods is the same, where *searchStr* is the string you're searching for:

```
itemIndex = ListBox1.FindString(searchStr)
```

An alternative form of both methods allows you to specify the index where the search begins:

```
itemIndex = ListBox1.FindString(searchStr,
                                startIndex)
```

The FindString and FindStringExact methods work even if the ListBox control is not sorted. You need not set the Sorted property to True before you call one of the searching methods on the control. Sorting the list will help the search operation, but it takes the control less than 100 milliseconds to find an item in a list of 100,000 items, so the time spent to sort the list isn't worth it. Before you load thousands of items in a ListBox control, however, you should probably consider a more-functional interface.

VB 2010 AT WORK: THE LISTBOXFIND APPLICATION

The application you'll build in this section (seen in Figure 5.7) populates a list with a large number of items and then locates any string you specify. Click the button Populate List to populate the ListBox control with 10,000 random strings. This process will take a few seconds and will populate the control with different random strings every time. Then, you can enter a string in the TextBox control at the bottom of the form. As you type characters (or even delete characters in the TextBox), the program will locate the closest match in the list and select (highlight) this item.

FIGURE 5.7
The ListBoxFind application

The sample application reacts to each keystroke in the TextBox control and locates the string you're searching for as you enter characters. The Find Item button does the same, but I thought I should demonstrate the efficiency of the ListBox control and the type of functionality you'd expect in a rich client application.

The code (shown in Listing 5.13) attempts to locate an exact match via the FindStringExact method. If it succeeds, it reports the index of the matching element. If not, it attempts to locate a near match with the FindString method. If it succeeds, it reports the index of the near match (which is the first item on the control that partially matches the search argument) and terminates. If it fails to find either an exact or a near match, it reports that the string wasn't found in the list.

LISTING 5.13:   Searching the list

```
Private Sub TextBox1_TextChanged(…) Handles TextBox1.TextChanged
    Dim srchWord As String = TextBox1.Text.Trim
    If srchWord.Length = 0 Then Exit Sub
    Dim wordIndex As Integer
    wordIndex = ListBox1.FindStringExact(srchWord)
    If wordIndex >= 0 Then
        ListBox1.TopIndex = wordIndex
        ListBox1.SelectedIndex = wordIndex
    Else
        wordIndex = ListBox1.FindString(srchWord)
        If wordIndex >= 0 Then
            ListBox1.TopIndex = wordIndex
            ListBox1.SelectedIndex = wordIndex
        Else
            Debug.WriteLine("Item " & srchWord &
                             " is not in the list")
        End If
    End If
End Sub
```

If you search for *SAC*, for example, and the control contains a string such as SAC or sac or sAc, the program will return the index of the item in the list and will report an exact match. If no exact match can be found, the program will return something like SACDEF, if such a string exists on the control, as a near match. If none of the strings on the control starts with the characters *SAC*, the search will fail.

The application is quite responsive even if you increase the size of the ListBox control to 100,000 items, except that the process of generating the random strings and populating the control takes considerably longer. In a practical application, however, you should never have to display that many items to the user. (Consider an overhaul of your application interface before you present the user with an enormous list.)

The Populate List button creates 10,000 random items with the help of the Random class. First, it generates a random value in the range 1 through 20, which is the length of the string (not all strings have the same length). Then the program generates as many random characters as the length of the string and builds the string by appending each character to it. These random numbers are in the range of 65 to 91 and they're the ANSI values of the uppercase characters.

By the way, this technique for generating random strings is not a contrived sample of VB code. I've used similar techniques on several occasions to populate large database tables with data and optimize my queries and data-driven applications for performance.

The ComboBox Control

The ComboBox control is similar to the ListBox control in the sense that it contains multiple items and the user may select one, but it typically occupies less space onscreen. The ComboBox is practically an expandable ListBox control, which can grow when the user wants to make a selection and retract after the selection is made. Normally, the ComboBox control displays one line with the selected item because this control doesn't allow multiple-item selection. The essential difference, however, between ComboBox and ListBox controls is that the ComboBox allows the user to specify items that don't exist in the list.

There are three types of ComboBox controls. The value of the control's DropDownStyle property determines which box is used; these values are shown in Table 5.4.

TABLE 5.4:   DropDownStyle options for the ComboBox control

VALUE	EFFECT
DropDown	(Default) The control is made up of a drop-down list, which is visible at all times, and a text box. The user can select an item from the list or type a new one in the text box.
DropDownList	This style is a drop-down list from which the user can select one of its items but can't enter a new one. The control displays a single item, and the list is expanded as needed.
Simple	The control includes a text box and a list that doesn't drop down. The user can select from the list or type in the text box.

The ComboBox Styles project, shown in Figure 5.8, demonstrates the three styles of the ComboBox control. This is another common element of the Windows interface, and its properties and methods are identical to those of the ListBox control. Load the ComboBox Styles project in the Visual Basic IDE and experiment with the three styles of the ComboBox control.

The DropDown and Simple ComboBox styles allow the user to select an item from the list or enter a new one in the edit box of the control. Moreover, they're collapsed by default and they display a single item unless the user expands the list of items to make a selection. The DropDownList style is similar to a ListBox control in the sense that it restricts the user to selecting an item (the user cannot enter a new one). However, it takes much less space on the form than a ListBox does because normally it displays a single item. When the user wants to make a selection, the DropDownList expands to display more items. After the user has made a selection, the list contracts to a single line again. Finally, the DropDownList style of the control doesn't allow the user to enter a new string in the edit area; users are restricted to selecting one of the existing items.

FIGURE 5.8

The ComboBox Styles project

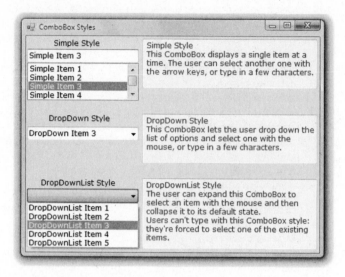

Most of the properties and methods of the ListBox control also apply to the ComboBox control, shown in Figure 5.9. The Items collection gives you access to the control's items, and the SelectedIndex and SelectedItem properties give you access to the current selection. You can also use the FindString and FindStringExact methods to locate any item in the control from within your code. Both methods return the index of the item you're searching for on the control, or the value –1 if no such item exists.

FIGURE 5.9

You can use the DropDownWidth property to save space.

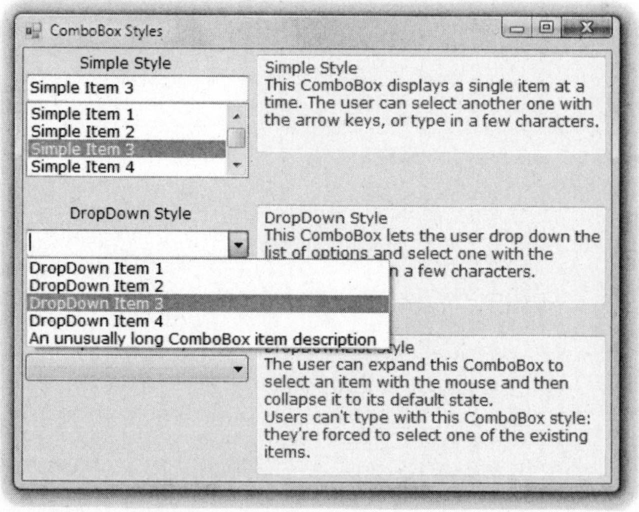

There's one aspect worth mentioning regarding the operation of the control. Although the edit box at the top allows you to enter a new string, the new string doesn't become a new item in the list. It remains there until you select another item or you clear the edit box. You can provide some code to add any string entered by the user in the control's edit box to the list of existing items.

The most common use of the ComboBox control is as a lookup table. The ComboBox control takes up very little space on the form, but it can be expanded at will. You can save even more space when the ComboBox is contracted by setting it to a width that's too small for the longest item. Use the `DropDownWidth` property, which is the width of the segment of the drop-down list. By default, this property is equal to the control's `Width` property. The second ComboBox control in Figure 5.9 contains an unusually long item. The control is wide enough to display the default selection. When the user clicks the arrow to expand the control, the drop-down section of the control is wider than the default width so that the long items can be read.

ADDING ITEMS TO A COMBOBOX AT RUNTIME

Although the ComboBox control allows users to enter text in the control's edit box, it doesn't provide a simple mechanism for adding new items at runtime. Let's say you provide a Combo-Box with city names. Users can type the first few characters and quickly locate the desired item. But what if they want to specify a new city name? You can provide this capability with two simple techniques. The simpler one is to place a button with an ellipsis (three periods) right next to the control. When users want to add a new item to the control, they can click the button and be prompted for the new item.

A more-elegant and user-friendly approach is to examine the control's `Text` property as soon as the control loses focus or the user presses the Enter key. If the string entered by the user doesn't match an item on the control, you must add a new item to the control's Items collection and select the new item from within your code. The FlexComboBox project demonstrates how to use both techniques in your code. The main form of the project, which is shown in Figure 5.10, is a simple data-entry screen. It's not the best data-entry form, but it's meant for demonstration purposes.

FIGURE 5.10
The FlexComboBox project demonstrates two techniques for adding new items to a ComboBox at runtime.

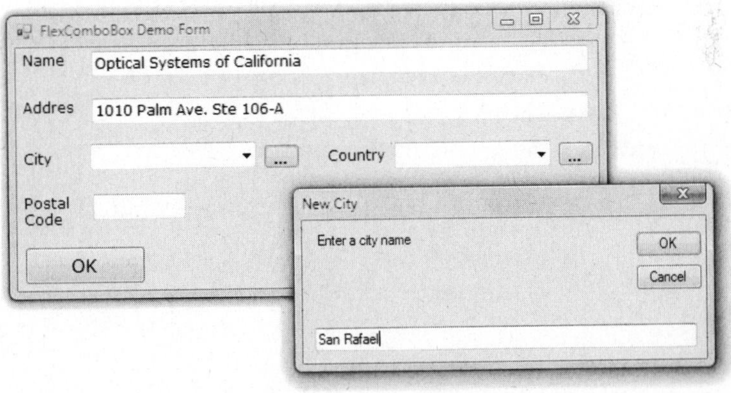

You can either enter a city name (or country name) and press the Tab key to move to another control or click the button next to the control to be prompted for a new city/country name. The application will let you enter any city/country combination. You should provide code to limit the cities within the selected country, but this is a nontrivial task. You also need to store the new city names entered on the first ComboBox control to a file (or a database table) so users will find them there the next time they run the application. I haven't made the application elaborate; I've added the code only to demonstrate how to add new items to a ComboBox control at runtime.

VB 2010 AT WORK: THE FLEXCOMBO PROJECT

The ellipsis button next to the City ComboBox control prompts the user for the new item via the InputBox() function. Then it searches the Items collection of the control via the FindString method, and if the new item isn't found, it's added to the control. Then the code selects the new item in the list. To do so, it sets the control's SelectedIndex property to the value returned by the Items.Add method or the value returned by the FindString method, depending on whether the item was located or added to the list. Listing 5.14 shows the code behind the ellipsis button.

LISTING 5.14:   Adding a new item to the ComboBox control at runtime

```
Private Sub Button1_Click(…) Button1.Click
    Dim itm As String
    itm = InputBox("Enter new item", "New Item")
    If itm.Trim <> "" Then AddElement(ComboBox1, itm)
End Sub
```

The AddElement() subroutine, which accepts the control you are adding to and a string as arguments and adds the string to the control, is shown in Listing 5.15. If the item doesn't exist in the control, it's added to the Items collection. If the item is already a member of the Items collection, it's selected. As you will see, the same subroutine will be used by the second method for adding items to the control at runtime.

LISTING 5.15:   The AddElement() subroutine

```
Sub AddElement(ByRef control As ComboBox, ByVal newItem As String)
    Dim idx As Integer
    If ComboBox1.FindString(newItem) > 0 Then
        idx = control.FindString(newItem)
    Else
        idx = control.Items.Add(newItem)
    End If
    control.SelectedIndex = idx
End Sub
```

You can also add new items at runtime by adding the same code in the control's `LostFocus` event handler:

```
Private Sub ComboBox1_LostFocus(…) Handles ComboBox1.LostFocus
    Dim newItem As String = ComboBox1.Text
    AddElement(ComboBox1, newItem)
```

For an even more functional interface, capture the Enter keystroke in the control's `KeyUp` event, add the new item to the list (if needed), and then move the focus to the next control on the form, as discussed earlier in this chapter.

The ScrollBar and TrackBar Controls

The ScrollBar and TrackBar controls let the user specify a magnitude by moving a selector between its minimum and maximum values. In some situations, the user doesn't know in advance the exact value of the quantity to specify (and in this case, a text box would suffice), so your application must provide a more-flexible mechanism for specifying a value along with some type of visual feedback.

The vertical scroll bar that lets a user move up and down a long document is a typical example of the use of the ScrollBar control. The scroll bar and visual feedback are the prime mechanisms for repositioning the view in a long document or in a large picture that won't fit entirely in a window.

The TrackBar control is similar to the ScrollBar control, but it doesn't cover a continuous range of values. The TrackBar control has a fixed number of tick marks and users can place the slider's indicator to the desired value.

In short, the ScrollBar control should be used when the exact value isn't as important as the value's effect on another object or data element. The TrackBar control should be used when the user can type a numeric value and the value your application expects is a number in a specific range — for example, integers between 0 and 100 or a value between 0 and 5 inches in steps of 0.1 inches (0.0, 0.1, 0.2 . . . 5.0). The TrackBar control is preferred to the TextBox control in similar situations because there's no need for data validation on your part. The user can specify only valid numeric values with the mouse.

The ScrollBar Control

There's no ScrollBar control per se in the Toolbox; instead, there are two versions of it: the HScrollBar and VScrollBar controls. They differ only in their orientation, but because they share the same members, I will refer to both controls collectively as ScrollBar controls. Actually, both controls inherit from the ScrollBar control, which is an abstract control: It is used to implement vertical and horizontal scroll bars, but it can't be used directly on a form. Moreover, the HScrollBar and VScrollBar controls are not displayed in the Common Controls tab of the Toolbox. You have to open the All Windows Forms tab to locate these two controls.

The ScrollBar control is a long stripe, which allows users to select a value between the two ends of the control. The left (or bottom) end of the control corresponds to its minimum value; the other end is the control's maximum value. The current value of the control is determined by the position of the indicator, which can be scrolled between the minimum and maximum values. The basic properties of the ScrollBar control, therefore, are properly named `Minimum`, `Maximum`, and `Value`.

Minimum The control's minimum value. The default value is 0, but because this is an Integer value, you can set it to negative values as well.

Maximum The control's maximum value. The default value is 100, but you can set it to any value that you can represent with the Integer data type.

Value The control's current value, specified by the indicator's position.

To cover a range of non-integers, you must supply the code to map the actual values to Integer values. For example, to cover a range from 2.5 to 8.5, set the `Minimum` property to 25, set the `Maximum` property to 85, and divide the control's value by 10. If the range you need is from −2.5 to 8.5, set the `Minimum` property to −25 and the `Maximum` value to 85, and divide the `Value` property by 10.

There are two more properties that allow you to control the movement of the indicator: the `SmallChange` and `LargeChange` properties. The first property is the amount by which the indicator changes when the user clicks one of the arrows at the two ends of the control. The `LargeChange` property is the displacement of the indicator when the user clicks somewhere in the scroll bar itself. You can manipulate a scroll bar by using the keyboard as well. Press the arrow keys to move the indicator in the corresponding direction by `SmallChange` and the Page Up/Page Down keys to move the indicator by `LargeChange`.

VB 2010 AT WORK: THE COLORS PROJECT

Figure 5.11 shows the main form of the Colors sample project, which lets the user specify a color by manipulating the value of its basic colors (red, green, and blue) through scroll bars. Each basic color is controlled by a scroll bar and has a minimum value of 0 and a maximum value of 255. By adjusting the value of each of the basic colors, you can create (almost) any color imaginable. This is what the Colors application does.

FIGURE 5.11
The Colors application demonstrates the use of the ScrollBar control.

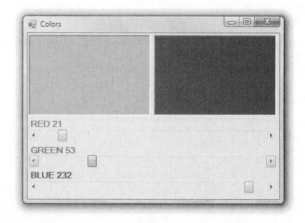

As the scroll bar is moved, the corresponding color is displayed, and the user can easily specify a color without knowing the exact values of its primary components. All the user needs to know is whether the desired color contains, for example, too much red or too little green. With the help of the scroll bars and the immediate feedback from the application, the user can easily pinpoint the desired color.

THE SCROLLBAR CONTROL'S EVENTS

You can monitor the changes of the ScrollBar's value from within your code by using two events: ValueChanged and Scroll. Both events are fired every time the indicator's position is changed. If you change the control's value from within your code, only the ValueChanged event will be fired.

The Scroll event can be fired in response to many different actions, such as the scrolling of the indicator with the mouse, a click on one of the two buttons at the ends of the scroll bars, and so on. If you want to know the action that caused this event, you can examine the Type property of the second argument of the event handler. The value of the e.Type property is a member of the ScrollEventType enumeration (LargeDecrement, SmallIncrement, Track, and so on).

HANDLING THE EVENTS IN THE COLORS APPLICATION

The two PictureBox controls display the color designed with the three scroll bars. The left PictureBox is colored from within the Scroll event, whereas the other one is colored from within the ValueChanged event. Both events are fired as the user scrolls the scroll bar's indicator, but in the Scroll event handler of the three scroll bars, the code examines the value of the e.Type property and reacts to it only if the event was fired because the scrolling of the indicator has ended. For all other actions, the event handler doesn't update the color of the left PictureBox.

If the user attempts to change the Color value by clicking the two arrows of the scroll bars or by clicking in the area to the left or to the right of the indicator, both PictureBox controls are updated. While the user slides the indicator or keeps pressing one of the end arrows, only the PictureBox to the right is updated.

The conclusion from this experiment is that you can program either event to provide continuous feedback to the user. If this feedback requires too many calculations, which would slow down the reaction of the corresponding event handler, you can postpone the reaction until the user has stopped scrolling the indicator. You can detect this condition by examining the value of the e.Type property. When it's ScrollEventType.EndScroll, you can execute the appropriate statements. Listing 5.16 shows the code behind the Scroll and ValueChanged events of the scroll bar that controls the red component of the color. The code of the corresponding events of the other two controls is identical.

LISTING 5.16:   Programming the ScrollBar control's scroll event

```
Private Sub redBar_Scroll(…) Handles redBar.Scroll
    If e.Type = ScrollEventType.EndScroll Then
        ColorBox1()
        lblRed.Text = "RED " & redBar.Value.ToString("###")
    End If
End Sub

Private Sub redBar_ValueChanged(…) Handles redBar.ValueChanged
    ColorBox2()
End Sub
```

The ColorBox1() and ColorBox2() subroutines update the color of the two PictureBox controls by setting their background colors. You can open the Colors project in Visual Studio and examine the code of these two routines.

The TrackBar Control

The TrackBar control is similar to the ScrollBar control, but it lacks the granularity of ScrollBar. Suppose that you want the user of an application to supply a value in a specific range, such as the speed of a moving object. Moreover, you don't want to allow extreme precision; you need only a few distinct settings. The user can set the control's value by sliding the indicator or by clicking on either side of an indicator like the one shown in Figure 5.12.

FIGURE 5.12
The Inches application demonstrates the use of the TrackBar control in specifying an exact value in a specific range.

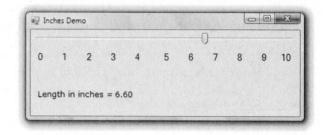

Granularity determines how specific you want to be in measuring. In measuring distances between towns, a granularity of a mile is quite adequate. In measuring (or specifying) the dimensions of a building, the granularity could be on the order of a foot or an inch. The TrackBar control lets you set the type of granularity that's necessary for your application.

Similar to the ScrollBar control, SmallChange and LargeChange properties are available. SmallChange is the smallest increment by which the Slider value can change. The user can change the slider by the SmallChange value only by sliding the indicator. (Unlike with the ScrollBar control, there are no arrows at the two ends of the Slider control.) To change the Slider's value by LargeChange, the user can click on either side of the indicator.

VB 2010 AT WORK: THE INCHES PROJECT

Figure 5.12 demonstrates a typical use of the TrackBar control. The form in the figure is an element of a program's user interface that lets the user specify a distance between 0 and 10 inches in increments of 0.2 inches. As the user slides the indicator, the current value is displayed on a Label control below the TrackBar. If you open the Inches application, you'll notice that there are more stops than there are tick marks on the control. This is made possible with the TickFrequency property, which determines the frequency of the visible tick marks.

You might specify that the control has 50 stops (divisions) but that only 10 of them will be visible. The user can, however, position the indicator on any of the 40 invisible tick marks. You can think of the visible marks as the major tick marks and the invisible ones as the minor tick marks. If the TickFrequency property is 5, only every fifth mark will be visible. The slider's indicator, however, will stop at all tick marks.

When using the TrackBar control on your interfaces, you should set the TickFrequency property to a value that helps the user select the desired setting. Too many tick marks are confusing and difficult to read. Without tick marks, the control isn't of much help. You might also consider placing a few labels to indicate the value of selected tick marks, as I have done in this example.

The properties of the TrackBar control in the Inches application are as follows:

```
Minimum = 0
Maximum = 50
SmallChange = 1
LargeChange = 5
TickFrequency = 5
```

The TrackBar needs to cover a range of 10 inches in increments of 0.2 inches. If you set the SmallChange property to 1, you have to set LargeChange to 5. Moreover, the TickFrequency is set to 5, so there will be a total of five divisions in every inch. The numbers below the tick marks were placed there with properly aligned Label controls.

The label at the bottom needs to be updated as the TrackBar's value changes. This is signaled to the application with the Change event, which occurs every time the value of the control changes, either through scrolling or from within your code. The ValueChanged event handler of the TrackBar control is shown next:

```
Private Sub TrackBar1_ValueChanged(…) Handles TrackBar1.ValueChanged
    lblInches.Text = "Length in inches = " &
                Format(TrackBar1.Value / 5, "#.00")
End Sub
```

The Label controls below the tick marks can also be used to set the value of the control. Every time you click one of the labels, the following statement sets the TrackBar control's value. Notice that all the Label controls' Click events are handled by a common handler. (There are more event handlers following the Handles keyword in the listing.)

```
Private Sub Label_Click(…) Handles Label1.Click, Label2.Click, …
    TrackBar1.Value = CInt(CType(sender, Label).text) * 5
End Sub
```

The code is a bit complicated, but it will compile with the Strict option on. The CType() function converts its argument, which is an Object variable and may represent any of the Labels on the form, to a Label object. Then it converts the Label's caption to an integer value (the string "1" to the numeric value 1, and so on) by calling the CInt() function. CInt() is a VB function; the equivalent method of the Framework is System.Convert.ToInt32. The captions of all Labels are numbers by design, so the conversion will never fail. This value is then assigned to the Value property of the TrackBar control.

The Bottom Line

Use the TextBox control as a data-entry and text-editing tool. The TextBox control is the most common element of the Windows interface, short of the Button control, and it's used to display and edit text. You can use a TextBox control to prompt users for a single line of text (such as a product name) or a small document (a product's detailed description). You can actually implement a functional text editor by placing a TextBox control on a form and setting a few of its properties.

Master It   What are the most important properties of the TextBox control? Which ones would you set in the Properties windows at design time?

Master It   How would you implement a control that suggests lists of words matching the characters entered by the user?

Use the ListBox, CheckedListBox, and ComboBox controls to present lists of items.   The ListBox control contains a list of items from which the user can select one or more, depending on the setting of the SelectionMode property.

Master It   How would you locate an item in a ListBox control?

Use the ScrollBar and TrackBar controls to enable users to specify sizes and positions with the mouse.   The ScrollBar and TrackBar controls let the user specify a magnitude by scrolling a selector between its minimum and maximum values. The ScrollBar control uses some visual feedback to display the effects of scrolling on another entity, such as the current view in a long document.

Master It   Which event of the ScrollBar control would you code to provide visual feedback to the user?

Chapter 6

Working with Forms

In Visual Basic, the form is the container for all the controls that make up the user interface. When a Visual Basic application is executing, each window it displays on the Desktop is a form. The terms *form* and *window* describe the same entity. A window is what the user sees on the Desktop when the application is running. A form is the same entity at design time. The proper term is *Windows form*, as opposed to *web form*, but I will refer to them as forms. This term includes both typical Windows forms and dialog boxes, which are simple forms you use for very specific actions, such as to prompt the user for a particular piece of data or to display critical information. A dialog box is a form with a small number of controls, no menus, and usually an OK and a Cancel button to close it.

Forms have a built-in functionality that is always available without any programming effort on your part. You can move a form around, resize it, and even cover it with other forms. You do so with the mouse or with the keyboard through the Control menu.

In previous chapters, you concentrated on placing the elements of the user interface on forms, setting their properties, and adding code behind selected events. Now you'll look at forms themselves and at a few related topics. In this chapter, you'll learn how to do the following:

- ◆ Use form properties
- ◆ Design applications with multiple forms
- ◆ Design dynamic forms
- ◆ Design menus

Forms have many trivial properties that won't be discussed here. Instead, let's jump directly to the properties that are unique to forms and then look at how to manipulate forms from within an application's code.

The Appearance of Forms

Applications are made up of one or more forms — usually more than one. You should craft your forms carefully, make them functional, and keep them simple and intuitive. You already know how to place controls on the form, but there's more to designing forms than populating them with controls. The main characteristic of a form is the title bar on which the form's caption is displayed (see Figure 6.1).

FIGURE 6.1
The elements of the
form

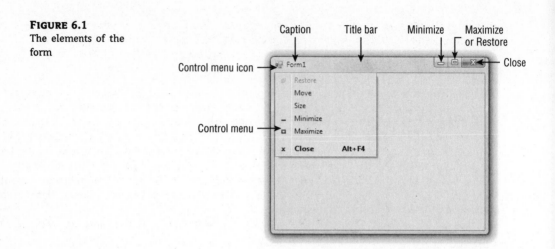

Clicking the Control menu icon opens the Control menu, which contains the commands listed in Table 6.1. On the right end of the title bar are three buttons: Minimize, Maximize, and Close. Clicking these buttons performs the associated function. When a form is maximized, the Maximize button is replaced by the Restore button. When clicked, the Restore button resets the form to its size and position before it was maximized, and it's replaced by the Maximize button. To access the Control menu from the keyboard, press Alt and then the down arrow key.

TABLE 6.1:   Commands of the Control menu

COMMAND	EFFECT
Restore	Restores a maximized form to the size it was before it was maximized; available only if the form has been maximized.
Move	Lets the user move the form around with the arrow keys.
Size	Lets the user resize the form with the arrow keys.
Minimize	Minimizes the form.
Maximize	Maximizes the form.
Close	Closes the current form. (Closing the application's main form terminates the application.)

Properties of the Form Object

You're familiar with the appearance of forms, even if you haven't programmed in the Windows environment in the past; you have seen nearly all types of windows in the applications you're using every day. The floating toolbars used by many graphics applications, for example, are actually forms with a narrow title bar. The dialog boxes that prompt for critical information or prompt you to select the file to be opened are also forms. You can duplicate the look of any window or dialog box through the following properties of the Form object.

ACCEPTBUTTON, CANCELBUTTON

These two properties let you specify the default Accept and Cancel buttons. The Accept button is the one that's automatically activated when you press Enter, no matter which control has the focus at the time; it is usually the button with the OK caption. Likewise, the Cancel button is the one that's automatically activated when you hit the Esc key; it is usually the button with the Cancel caption. To specify the Accept and Cancel buttons on a form, locate the AcceptButton and CancelButton properties of the form and select the corresponding controls from a drop-down list, which contains the names of all the buttons on the form. For more information on these two properties, see the section "Forms versus Dialog Boxes," later in this chapter.

AUTOSCALEMODE

This property determines how the control is scaled, and its value is a member of the AutoScaleMode enumeration: *None* (automatic scaling is disabled); *Font* (the controls on the form are scaled relative to the size of the font); *Dpi*, which stands for dots per inch (the controls on the form are scaled relative to the display resolution); and *Inherit* (the controls are scaled according to the AutoScaleMode property of their parent class). The default value is *Font*; if you change the form's font size, the controls on it are scaled to the new font size. As a result, the entire form is resized.

AUTOSCROLL

The AutoScroll property is a True/False value that indicates whether scroll bars (as shown in Figure 6.2) will be automatically attached to the form if the form is resized to a point that not all its controls are visible. Use this property to design large forms without having to worry about the resolution of the monitor on which they'll be displayed. Scrolling forms are not very common, but they're easy to implement. The AutoScroll property is used in conjunction with two other properties (described a little later in this section): AutoScrollMargin and AutoScrollMinSize. Note that the AutoScroll property applies to a few controls as well, including the Panel and SplitContainer controls. For example, you can create a form with a fixed and a scrolling pane by placing two Panel controls on it and setting the AutoScroll property of one of them (the Panel control you want to scroll) to True.

FIGURE 6.2
If the controls don't fit in a form's visible area, scroll bars can be attached automatically.

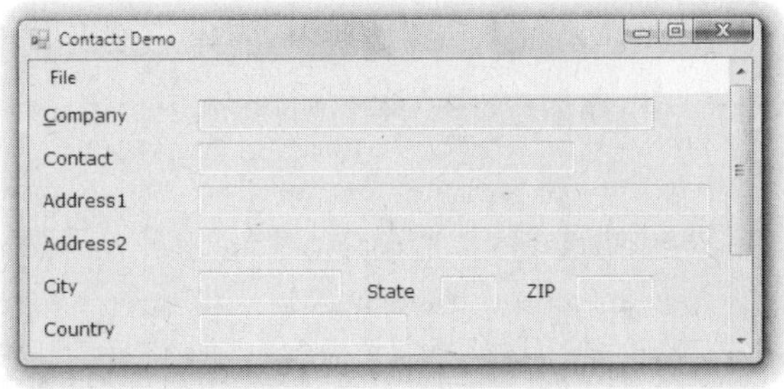

The `AutoScroll` property is rarely used with data-entry forms, but it's used routinely to display large images. You'll see how to create a scrolling form for displaying large images later in this chapter in the section on anchoring and docking controls.

AUTOSCROLLPOSITION

This property is available from within your code only (you can't set this property at design time but it can be set at runtime from within your code), and it indicates the number of pixels that the form was scrolled up or down. Its initial value is zero, and it takes on a value when the user scrolls the form (provided that the `AutoScroll` property is True). Use this property to find out the visible controls from within your code or to scroll the form from within your application's code to bring a specific control into view.

AUTOSCROLLMARGIN

This is a margin, expressed in pixels, that's added around all the controls on the form. If the form is smaller than the rectangle that encloses all the controls adjusted by the margin, the appropriate scroll bar(s) will be displayed automatically.

AUTOSCROLLMINSIZE

This property lets you specify the minimum size of the form before the scroll bars are attached. If your form contains graphics that you want to be visible at all times, set the `Width` and `Height` members of the `AutoScrollMinSize` property to the dimensions of the graphics. (Of course, the graphics won't be visible at all times, but the scroll bars indicate that there's more to the form than can fit in the current window.) Notice that this isn't the form's minimum size; users can make the form even smaller. To specify a minimum size for the form, use the `MinimumSize` property, described later in this section.

Let's say the `AutoScrollMargin` property of the form is 180×150. If the form is resized to fewer than 180 pixels horizontally or 150 pixels vertically, the appropriate scroll bars will appear automatically as long as the `AutoScroll` property is True. If you want to enable the `AutoScroll` feature when the form's width is reduced to anything fewer than 250 pixels, set the `AutoScrollMinSize` property to (250, 0). In this example, setting `AutoScrollMinSize.Width` to anything less than 180, or `AutoScrollMinSize.Height` to anything less than 150, will have no effect on the appearance of the form and its scroll bars.

BRINGING SELECTED CONTROLS INTO VIEW

In addition to the `Autoscroll` properties, the Form object provides a `Scroll` method, which allows you to scroll a form programmatically, and `ScrollControlIntoView`, which scrolls the form until the specified control comes into view. The `Scroll` method accepts as arguments the horizontal and vertical displacements for the scrolling operation, whereas `ScrollControlIntoView` accepts as an argument the control you want to bring into view. Notice that activating a control with the Tab key automatically brings the next control into view if it's not already visible on the form. Finally, the `Scroll` event is fired every time a form is scrolled.

FORMBORDERSTYLE

The FormBorderStyle property determines the style of the form's border; its value is one of the FormBorderStyle enumeration members, which are shown in Table 6.2. You can make the form's title bar disappear altogether by setting the form's FormBorderStyle property to FixedToolWindow, the ControlBox property to False, and the Text property (the form's caption) to an empty string. However, a form like this can't be moved around with the mouse and will probably frustrate users.

TABLE 6.2:   The FormBorderStyle enumeration

VALUE	EFFECT
Fixed3D	A window with a fixed visible border "raised" relative to the main area. Unlike the None setting, this setting allows users to minimize and close the window.
FixedDialog	A fixed window used to implement dialog boxes.
FixedSingle	A fixed window with a single-line border.
FixedToolWindow	A fixed window with a Close button only. It looks like a toolbar displayed by drawing and imaging applications.
None	A borderless window that can't be resized. This setting is rarely used.
Sizable	(default) A resizable window that's used for displaying regular forms.
SizableToolWindow	Same as the FixedToolWindow, but it's resizable. In addition, its caption font is smaller than the usual.

Create a simple form and try out the various settings of the FormBorderStyle property to find out how this property affects the appearance of the form.

CONTROLBOX

This property is also True by default. Set it to False to hide the control box icon and disable the Control menu. Although the Control menu is rarely used, Windows applications don't disable it. When the ControlBox property is False, the three buttons on the title bar are also disabled. If you set the Text property to an empty string, the title bar disappears altogether.

MINIMIZEBOX, MAXIMIZEBOX

These two properties, which specify whether the Minimize and Maximize buttons will appear on the form's title bar, are True by default. Set them to False to hide the corresponding buttons on a form's title bar.

MINIMUMSIZE, MAXIMUMSIZE

These two properties read or set the minimum and maximum size of a form. When users resize the form at runtime, the form won't become any smaller than the dimensions specified by the

MinimumSize property or any larger than the dimensions specified by the MaximumSize property. The MinimumSize property is a Size object, and you can set it with a statement like the following:

```
Me.MinimumSize = New Size(400, 300)
```

Or you can set the width and height separately:

```
Me.MinimumSize.Width = 400
Me.MinimumSize.Height = 300
```

The MinimumSize.Height property includes the height of the form's title bar; you should take that into consideration. If the minimum usable size of the form is 400×300, use the following statement to set the MinimumSize property:

```
Me.MinimumSize = New Size(400, 300 + SystemInformation.CaptionHeight)
```

The default value of both properties is (0, 0), which means that no minimum or maximum size is imposed on the form and the user can resize it as desired.

USE THE SYSTEMINFORMATION CLASS TO READ SYSTEM INFORMATION

The height of the caption is not a property of the Form object, even though it's used to determine the useful area of the form (the total height minus the caption bar). Keep in mind that the height of the caption bar is given by the CaptionHeight property of the System-Information object. You should look up the SystemInformation object; it exposes a lot of useful properties, such as BorderSize (the size of the form's borders), Border3DSize (the size of three-dimensional borders), CursorSize (the cursor's size), and many more.

KEYPREVIEW

This property enables the form to capture all keystrokes before they're passed to the control that has the focus. Normally, when you press a key, the KeyPress event of the control with the focus is triggered (as well as the KeyUp and KeyDown events), and you can handle the keystroke from within the control's appropriate handler. In most cases, you let the control handle the keystroke and don't write any form code for that.

Some forms perform certain actions when you hit a specific key (the F5 key for refreshing the form being a very common example), no matter which control on the form has the focus. If you want to use these keystrokes in your application, you must set the KeyPreview property to True. Doing so enables the form to intercept all keystrokes, so you can process them from within the form's keystroke event handlers. To handle a specific keystroke at the form's level, set the form's KeyPreview property to True and insert the appropriate code in the form's KeyDown or KeyUp event handler (the KeyPress event isn't fired for the function and other non-character keys).

The same keystrokes are then passed to the control with the focus, unless you kill the keystroke by setting its SuppressKeystroke property to True when you process it on the form's level. For more information on processing keystrokes at the form level and using special keystrokes throughout your application, see the Contacts project later in this chapter as well as the TextPad project discussed in Chapter 5, "The Basic Window Controls."

SIZEGRIPSTYLE

This property gets or sets the style of the sizing handle to display in the lower-right corner of the form. You can set it to a member of the SizeGripStyle enumeration: *Auto* (the size grip is displayed as needed), *Show* (the size grip is displayed at all times), or *Hide* (the size grip is not displayed, but users can still resize the form with the mouse).

STARTPOSITION, LOCATION

The StartPosition property, which determines the initial position of the form when it's first displayed, can be set to one of the members of the FormStartPosition enumeration: *CenterParent* (the form is centered in the area of its parent form), *CenterScreen* (the form is centered on the monitor), *Manual* (the position of the form is determined by the Location property), *WindowsDefaultLocation* (the form is positioned at the Windows default location), and *WindowsDefaultBounds* (the form's location and bounds are determined by Windows defaults). The Location property allows you to set the form's initial position at design time or to change the form's location at runtime.

TOPMOST

This property is a True/False setting that lets you specify whether the form will remain on top of all other forms in your application. Its default value is False, and you should change it only on rare occasions. Some dialog boxes, such as the Find & Replace dialog box of any text-processing application, are always visible, even when they don't have the focus. For more information on using the TopMost property, see the discussion of the TextPad project in Chapter 5. You can also add a professional touch to your application by providing a CheckBox control that determines whether a form should remain on top of all other forms of the application.

SIZE

Use the Size property to set the form size at design time or at runtime. Normally, the form width and height are controlled by the user at runtime. This property is usually set from within the form Resize event handler to maintain a reasonable aspect ratio when the user resizes the form. The Form object also exposes the Width and Height properties for controlling its size.

Placing Controls on Forms

The first step in designing your application interface is, of course, the analysis and careful planning of the basic operations you want to provide through your interface. The second step is to design the forms. Designing a form means placing Windows controls on it and setting the control properties (and finally, of course, writing code to handle the events of interest). Visual Studio is a rapid application development (RAD) environment. This doesn't mean that you're expected to develop applications rapidly. It has come to mean that you can rapidly prototype an application and show something to the customer. And this is made possible through the visual tools that come with Visual Studio, especially the new Form Designer.

To place controls on your form, you select them in the Toolbox and then draw, on the form, the rectangle in which the control will be enclosed. Or you can double-click the control's icon to place an instance of the control on the form. Or you can just drag the desired control from the Toolbox and drop it on the form. All controls have a default size, and you can resize the control on the form by using the mouse.

Each control's dimensions can also be set in the Properties window through the Size property. The Size property is a composite property that exposes the Width and Height fields, which are expressed in pixels. Likewise, the Location property returns (or sets) the coordinates of the top-left corner of the control. In "Building Dynamic Forms at Runtime" later in this chapter, you'll see how to create new controls at runtime and place them in a specific location on a form from within your code.

As you place controls on the form, you can align them in groups with the relevant commands from the Format menu. Select multiple controls on the form by using the mouse and the Shift (or Ctrl) key, and then align their edges or center them vertically and horizontally with the appropriate command from the Format menu. To align the left edges of a column of TextBoxes, choose the Format ➤ Align ➤ Left command. You can also use the commands from the Format ➤ Make Same Size command to adjust the dimensions of the selected controls. (To make them equal in size, make the widths or heights equal.)

As you move controls around with the mouse, a blue snap line appears when the controls become aligned with another control. Release the mouse while the snap line is visible to leave the control aligned with the one indicated by the snap lines. The blue snap lines indicate edge alignment. Most of the time, you need to align not the edges of two controls but their baselines (the baseline of the text on the control). The snap lines that indicate baseline alignment are red. Figure 6.3 shows both types of snap lines. When you're aligning a Label control with its matching TextBox control on a form, you want to align their baselines, not their frames (especially if you consider that the Label controls are always displayed without borders). If the control is aligned with other controls in both directions, two snap lines will appear — a horizontal one and a vertical one.

FIGURE 6.3
Edge alignment (vertical) and baseline alignment (horizontal)

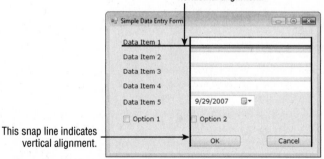

One of the most important (and most overlooked) aspects of designing forms is the alignment of the controls on the form. Whether the form contains a lot of controls or just a few, the application is more professional looking and easier for the end user to interact with when the programmer spends the time to align the controls one to another and group them functionally. Try to group controls together based on their functionality. Try to present an uncluttered interface to the end user. Once you have aligned the controls on the form as discussed in this section, you can select them all and lock them in place by setting their Locked property to True. When the Locked property is True, the designer won't allow you to move them around by mistake.

Setting the *TabIndex* Property

Another important issue in form design is the tab order of the controls on the form. As you know, by default, pressing the Tab key at runtime takes you to the next control on a form. The tab order of the controls is the order in which they were placed on the form, but this is hardly ever what we want. When you design the application, you can specify the order in which the controls receive the focus (the *tab order*, as it is known) with the help of the TabIndex property. Each control has its own TabIndex setting, which is an integer value. When the Tab key is pressed, the focus is moved to the control whose tab order immediately follows the tab order of the current control (the one with the next larger TabIndex property value).

To specify the tab order of the various controls, you can set their TabIndex property in the Properties window or you can choose the Tab Order command from the View menu. The tab order of each control will be displayed on the corresponding control, as shown in Figure 6.4. (The form shown in the figure is the Contacts application, which is discussed shortly.)

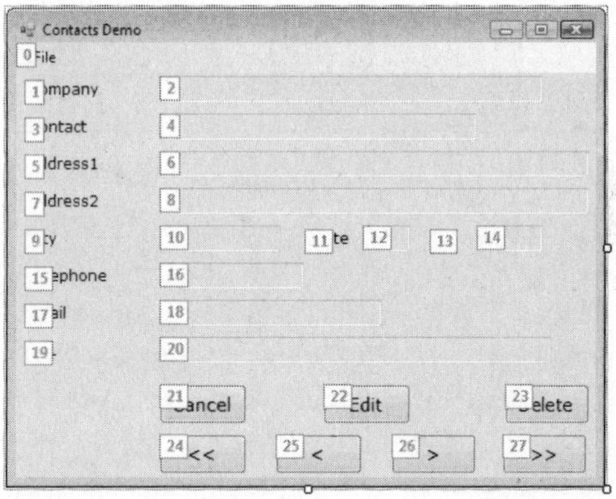

FIGURE 6.4
Setting the tab order of the controls on the main form of the Contacts project

To set the tab order of the controls, click each control in the order in which you want them to receive the focus. You must click all of them in the desired order, starting with the first control in the tab order. Each control's index in the tab order appears in the upper-left corner of the control. When you're finished, choose the Tab Order command from the View menu again to hide the numbers. Note that Label controls never receive the focus, but they have their own TabIndex value. When the next control to receive the focus is a Label control, the focus is moved automatically to the next control in the tab order until a control that can actually receive the focus is reached.

⊕ Real World Scenario

DESIGN WITH THE USER IN MIND

Designing functional forms is a crucial step in the process of developing Windows applications. Most data-entry operators don't work with the mouse, and you must make sure that all the actions (such as switching to another control, opening a menu, clicking a button, and so on) can be performed with the keyboard. This requirement doesn't apply to graphics applications, of course, but most applications developed with VB are business applications, and users should be able to perform most of the tasks with the keyboard, not with the mouse.

In my experience, the most important aspect of the user interface of a business application is the handling of the Enter keystroke. When a TextBox control has the focus, the Enter keystroke should advance the focus to the next control in the tab order; when a list control (such as the ListBox or ListView control) has the focus, the Enter keystroke should invoke the same action as double-clicking the current item. The idea is to package as much intelligence into the Enter keystroke as possible. The sample project in the following section demonstrates many of the features you'd expect from a data-entry application.

If you're developing a data-entry form, you must take into consideration the needs of the users. Make a prototype and ask the people who will use the application to test-drive it. Listen to their objections carefully, collect all the information, and then use it to refine your application's user interface. Don't defend your design — just learn from the users. They will uncover all the flaws of the application and they'll help you design the most functional interface. In addition, they will accept the finished application with fewer objections and complaints if they know what to expect.

VB 2010 at Work: The Contacts Project

I want to conclude with a simple data-entry application that demonstrates many of the topics discussed here as well as a few techniques for designing easy-to-use forms. Figure 6.5 shows a data-entry form for maintaining contact information, and I'm sure you will add your own fields to make this application more useful.

FIGURE 6.5
A simple data-entry screen

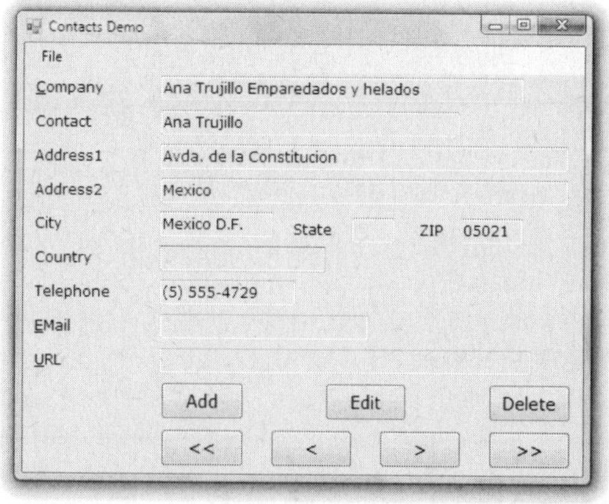

You can navigate through the contacts by clicking the arrow keys on the keyboard as well as add new contacts or delete existing ones by clicking the appropriate buttons. When you're entering a new contact, the buttons shown in Figure 6.5 are replaced by the usual OK and Cancel buttons. The action of adding a new contact, or editing an existing one, must end by clicking one of these two buttons. After a new contact is committed or the action is canceled, the usual navigation buttons appear again.

Now, it's your turn to design the Contacts project. Create a new VB project and place the controls you see in Figure 6.5 on the application's form, align them appropriately, and lock them in position. Or, if you prefer, open the Contacts sample project available for download from `www.sybex.com/go/masteringvb2010`. After the controls are on the form, the next step is to set their tab order. You must specify a value for the `TabIndex` property even for controls that never receive focus, such as the Label controls. In addition to setting the tab order of the controls, use shortcut keys to give the user quick access to the most common fields. The shortcut keys are displayed as underlined characters on the corresponding labels. Notice that the Label controls have shortcut keys, even though they don't receive the focus. When you press the shortcut key of a Label control, the focus is moved to the following control in the tab order, which (on this form) is the TextBox control next to it.

If you open the application and run it now, you'll see that the focus moves from one TextBox to the next with the Tab key and that the labels are skipped. After the last TextBox control, the focus is moved to the buttons and then back to the first TextBox control. To add a shortcut key for the most common fields, determine which fields will have shortcut keys and then which keys will be used for that purpose. Being the Internet buffs that we all are, let's assign shortcut keys to the Company, EMail, and URL fields. Locate each label's `Text` property in the Properties window and insert the & symbol in front of the character you want to act as a shortcut for each Label. The `Text` property of the three controls should be **&Company**, **&EMail**, and **&URL**.

Shortcut keys are activated at runtime by pressing the shortcut character while holding down the Alt key. The shortcut key will move the focus to the corresponding Label control, but because labels can't receive the focus, the focus is moved immediately to the next control in the tab order, which is the adjacent TextBox control.

The contacts are stored in an ArrayList object, which is similar to an array but a little more convenient. We'll discuss ArrayLists in Chapter 12, "Storing Data in Collections." For now, you can ignore the parts of the application that manipulate the contacts and focus on the design issues.

Start by loading the sample data included with the application that you downloaded from `www.sybex.com/go/masteringvb2010`. Open the File menu and choose Load. You won't be prompted for a filename; the application always opens the same file in its root folder (it's the `CONTACTS.BIN` file). After reading about the OpenFileDialog and SaveFileDialog controls, you can modify the code so that it prompts the user to choose the file to read from or write to. Then enter a new contact by clicking the Add button or edit an existing contact by clicking the Edit button. Both actions must end with the OK or Cancel button. In other words, users must explicitly end the operation and cannot switch to another contact while adding or editing a contact without committing or discarding the changes.

The code behind the various buttons is straightforward. The Add button hides all the navigational buttons at the bottom of the form and clears the TextBoxes in anticipation of a new contact record. The OK button saves the new contact to an ArrayList structure and redisplays the navigational buttons. The Cancel button ignores the data entered by the user and likewise displays the navigational buttons. In all cases, when the user switches back to the view mode, the code locks all the TextBoxes by setting their `ReadOnly` property to True.

HANDLING KEYSTROKES

Although the Tab key is the Windows method of moving to the next control on the form, most users will find it more convenient to use the Enter key for that purpose. The Enter key is the most important one on the keyboard, and applications should handle it intelligently. When the user presses Enter in a single-line TextBox, for example, the obvious action is to move the focus to the following control. I included a few statements in the KeyDown event handlers of the TextBox controls to move the focus to the following one:

```
Private Sub txtAddress1_KeyDown(…) Handles txtAddress1.KeyDown
    If e.KeyData = Keys.Enter Then
        e.SuppressKeyPress = True
        txtAddress2.Focus()
    End If
End Sub
```

If you use the KeyUp event handler instead, the result won't be any different, but an annoying beeping sound will be emitted with each keystroke. The beep occurs when the button is depressed, so you must intercept the Enter key as soon as it happens and not after the control receives the notification for the KeyDown event. The control will still catch the KeyUp event and it will beep because it's a single-line TextBox control (the beep is an audible warning that the specific key shouldn't be used in a single-line TextBox control). To avoid the beep sound, the code "kills" the keystroke by setting the SuppressKeystroke property to True.

 **Real World Scenario**

PROCESSING KEYS FROM WITHIN YOUR CODE

The code shown in the preceding KeyDown event handler will work, but you must repeat it for every TextBox control on the form. A more convenient approach is to capture the Enter keystroke in the form's KeyDown event handler and process it for all TextBox controls. First, you must figure out whether the control with the focus is a TextBox control. The property Me.ActiveControl returns a reference to the control with the focus. To find out the type of the active control and compare it to the TextBox control's type, use the following If statement:

```
If Me.ActiveControl.GetType Is GetType(TextBox) Then
' process the Enter key
End If
```

Once you can figure out the active control's type, you need a method of simulating the Tab keystroke from within your code so you don't have to code every TextBox control's KeyDown event. An interesting method of the Form object is the ProcessTabKey method, which imitates the Tab keystroke. Calling the ProcessTabKey method is equivalent to pressing the Tab key from within your code. The method accepts a True/False value as an argument, which indicates whether it will move the focus to the next control in the tab order (if True) or to the previous control in the tab order.

Start by setting the form's KeyPreview property to True and then insert the following statements in the form's KeyDown event handler:

```
If e.KeyCode = Keys.Enter Then
    If Me.ActiveControl.GetType Is GetType(TextBox) Then
```

```
            e.SuppressKeyPress = True
            If e.Shift Then
                Me.ProcessTabKey(False)
            Else
                Me.ProcessTabKey(True)
            End If
        End If
    End If
```

The last topic demonstrated in this example is how to capture certain keystrokes regardless of the control that has the focus. We'll use the F10 keystroke to display the total number of contacts entered so far. Assuming that you have already set the form's KeyPreview property to True, enter the following code in the form's KeyDown event:

```
If e.Keycode = keys.F10 Then
    MsgBox("There are " & MyContacts.Count.ToString & " contacts in the database")
    e.Handled = True
End If
```

Listing 6.1 shows the complete handler for the form's KeyDown event, which also allows you to move to the next or previous contact by using the Alt+Plus or Alt+Minus keys, respectively.

LISTING 6.1:   Handling keystrokes in the form's KeyDown event handler

```
Public Sub Form1_KeyDown(ByVal sender As Object,
          ByVal e As System.WinForms.KeyEventArgs)
                    Handles Form1.KeyUp
    If e.Keycode = Keys.F10 Then
        MsgBox("There are " & MyContacts.Count.ToString &
            " contacts in the database")
        e.Handled = True
    End If
    If e.KeyCode = Keys.Subtract And e.Modifiers = Keys.Alt Then
        bttnPrevious.PerformClick
    End If
    If e.KeyCode = Keys.Add And e.Modifiers = Keys.Alt Then
        bttnNext.PerformClick
    End If
    If e.KeyCode = Keys.Enter Then
        If Me.ActiveControl.GetType Is GetType(TextBox) Then
            e.SuppressKeyPress = True
            If e.Shift Then
                Me.ProcessTabKey(False)
            Else
                Me.ProcessTabKey(True)
```

```
            End If
        End If
    End If
End Sub
```

Anchoring and Docking

A common issue in form design is the design of forms that can be properly resized. For instance, you might design a nice form for a given size, but when it's resized at runtime, the controls are all clustered in the upper-left corner. Or a TextBox control that covers the entire width of the form at design time suddenly "cringes" on the left when the user drags out the window. If the user makes the form smaller than the default size, part of the TextBox could be invisible because it's outside the form. You can attach scroll bars to the form, but that doesn't really help — who wants to type text and have to scroll the form horizontally? It makes sense to scroll vertically because you get to see many lines at once, but if the TextBox control is wider than the form, you can't read entire lines.

Visual Studio provides several techniques for designing forms that scale nicely. The two most important of them are the Anchor and Dock properties.

ANCHORING CONTROLS

The Anchor property lets you attach one or more edges of the control to corresponding edges of the form. The anchored edges of the control maintain the same distance from the corresponding edges of the form.

Place a TextBox control on a new form, set its MultiLine property to True, and then open the control's Anchor property in the Properties window. You will see a rectangle within a larger rectangle and four pegs that connect the small control to the sides of the larger box (see Figure 6.6). The large box is the form, and the small one is the control. The four pegs are the anchors, which can be either white or gray. The gray anchors denote a fixed distance between the control and the edge of the form. By default, the control is placed at a fixed distance from the upper-left corner of the form. When the form is resized, the control retains its size and its distance from the upper-left corner of the form.

FIGURE 6.6
The settings for the
Anchor property

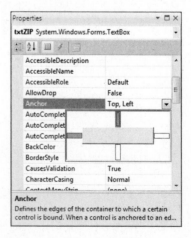

Let's say you're designing a simple form with a TextBox control that must fill the width of the form, be anchored to the top of the form, and leave some space for a few buttons at the bottom. You also want your form to maintain this arrangement regardless of its size. Make the TextBox control as wide as the form (allowing, perhaps, a margin of a few pixels on either side). Then place a couple of buttons at the bottom of the form and make the TextBox control tall enough that it stops above the buttons. This is the form of the Anchor sample project.

Now open the TextBox control's Anchor property and make all four anchors gray by clicking them. This action tells the Form Designer to resize the control accordingly, so that the distances between the sides of the control and the corresponding sides of the form remain the same as those you set at design time. Select each button on the form and set their Anchor properties in the Properties window: Anchor the left button to the left and bottom of the form and the right button to the right and bottom of the form.

Resize the form at design time without running the project and you'll see that all the controls are resized and rearranged on the form at all times. Figure 6.7 shows the Anchor project's main form in two different sizes.

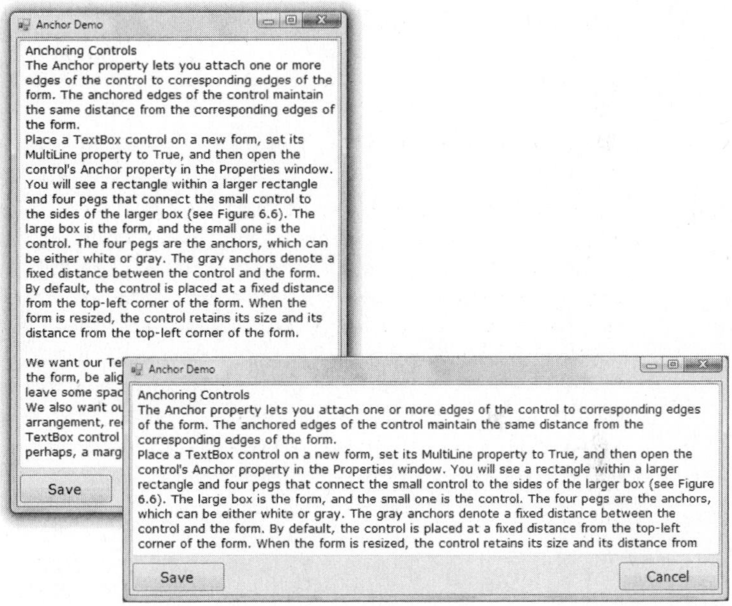

FIGURE 6.7
Use the Anchor property of the various controls to design forms that can be resized gracefully at runtime.

Yet, there's a small problem: If you make the form very narrow, there will be no room for both buttons across the form's width. The simplest way to fix this problem is to impose a minimum size for the form. To do so, you must first decide the form's minimum width and height and then set the MinimumSize property to these values. You can also use the AutoScroll properties, but it's not recommended that you add scroll bars to a small form like ours. Use the AutoScroll properties for large forms with many controls that can't be resized with the form.

DOCKING CONTROLS

In addition to the Anchor property, most controls provide a Dock property, which determines how a control will dock on the form. The default value of this property is None.

Create a new form, place a multiline TextBox control on it, and then open the Dock property for the control. The various rectangular shapes are the settings of the property. If you click the middle rectangle, the control will be docked over the entire form: It will expand and shrink both horizontally and vertically to cover the entire form. This setting is appropriate for simple forms that contain a single control, usually a TextBox, and sometimes a menu. Try it out.

Let's create a more complicated form with two controls (see the Docking sample project at www.sybex.com/go/masteringvb2010). The form shown in Figure 6.8 contains a TreeView control on the left and a ListView control on the right. The two controls display folder and file data on an interface that's very similar to that of Windows Explorer. The TreeView control displays the directory structure, and the ListView control displays the selected folder's files.

FIGURE 6.8
Filling a form with two
controls

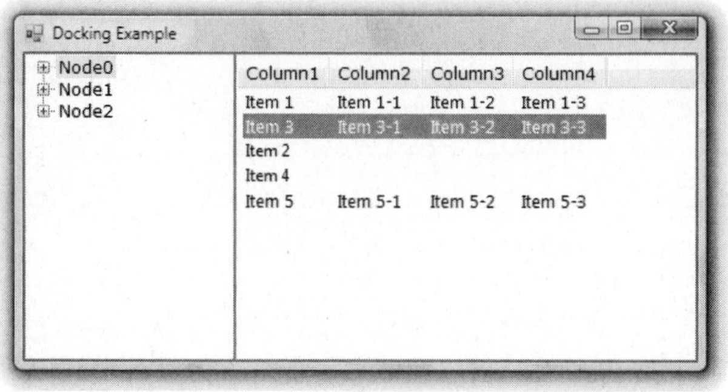

Place a TreeView control on the left side of the form and a ListView control on the right side of the form. Then dock the TreeView to the left and the ListView to the right. If you run the application now, as you resize the form, the two controls remain docked to the two sides of the form — but their sizes don't change. If you make the form wider, there will be a gap between the two controls. If you make the form narrower, one of the controls will overlap the other.

End the application, return to the Form Designer, select the ListView control, and set its Dock property to Fill. This time, the ListView will change size to take up all the space to the right of the TreeView. The ListView control will attempt to fill the form, but it won't take up the space of another control that has been docked already. The TreeView and ListView controls are discussed in the tutorial "The TreeView and ListView Controls," which you can download from www.sybex.com/go/masteringvb2010. That's why I've populated them with some fake data at design time. In the tutorial, you'll learn how to populate these two controls at runtime with folder names and filenames, respectively, and build a custom Windows Explorer.

🌐 Real World Scenario

SCROLLING PICTUREBOX

An interesting technique I should mention here is how to create a scrolling form for displaying large images. The basic requirement is that the image can't take up the entire form; you need some space for a menu, a few buttons, or other controls to interact with the form. The image must be displayed on a PictureBox control with its SizeMode property set to *AutoSize*. This setting causes the PictureBox to adjust to the size of the image it contains. Place the various controls you need for your interface on the form, as shown here, and then place a Panel on the form. Anchor the Panel to all four edges of the form so that it's resized along with the form. Then set its `AutoScroll` property to True. Finally, place a PictureBox control on the Panel and align its upper-left corner with the upper-left corner of the Panel control. Do not anchor or dock this control, because its size will be determined by the size of the image it contains, not by its container's size. Now assign a large image to the PictureBox control (you can use any of the images in the Sample Pictures folder).

If you run the application now, you will see as much of the upper-left corner of the image as can fit on the Panel control. You can resize the form to see more of the image or scroll it around with the two scroll bars to bring any segment of the image into view. This technique allows you to display an image of any size on a form of any (usually smaller) size.

Splitting Forms into Multiple Panes

So far, the form for the Docking sample project you've designed behaves better than the initial design, but it's not what you really expect from a Windows application. The problem with the form in Figure 6.8 is that users can't change the relative widths of the controls. In other words, they can't make one of the controls narrower to make room for the other, which is a fairly common concept in the Windows interface.

The narrow bar that allows users to control the relative sizes of two controls is a splitter. When the cursor hovers over a splitter, it changes to a double arrow to indicate that the bar can be moved. By moving the splitter, you can enlarge one of the two controls while shrinking the other. The Form Designer provides a special control for creating resizable panes on a form: the SplitContainer control. We'll design a new form with two TextBoxes and a splitter between them so that users can change the relative size of the two controls.

Start by placing a SplitContainer control on the form. The SplitContainer consists of two Panel controls, the *Panel1* and *Panel2* controls, and a vertical splitter between them. This is the default configuration; you can change the orientation of the splitter by using the control's `Orientation` property. Also by default, the two panels of the Splitter control are resized proportionally as you resize the form. If you want to keep one of the panels fixed and have the other one take up the remaining space of the form, set the control's `FixedPanel` property to the name of the panel you want to retain its size.

Next, place a TextBox control in the left panel of the SplitContainer control and set its `Multiline` property to True. You don't need to do anything about its size because we'll dock it in the panel to which it belongs. With the TextBox control selected, locate its `Dock` property and set it to *Fill*. The TextBox control will fill the left panel of the SplitContainer control. Do the same with another TextBox control, which will fill the right panel of the SplitContainer control. Set this control's `Multiline` property to True and its `Dock` property to *Fill*.

Now run the project and check out the functionality of the SplitContainer. Paste some text on the two controls and then change their relative sizes by sliding the splitter between them, as shown in Figure 6.9. You will find this project, called Splitter1, at www.sybex.com/go/masteringvb2010 among the sample projects for this chapter.

FIGURE 6.9
The SplitContainer control lets you change the relative size of the controls on either side.

Splitter

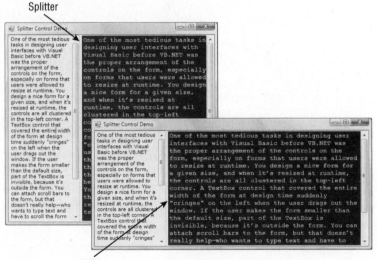

Splitter

Let's design a more elaborate form with two SplitContainer controls, such as the one shown in Figure 6.10. (It's the form in the Splitter2 sample project.) This form, which resembles the interface of Microsoft Office Outlook, consists of a TreeView control on the left (where the folders are displayed), a ListView control (where the selected folder's items are displayed), and a TextBox control (where the selected item's details are displayed). Because we haven't discussed the ListView and TreeView controls yet, I'm using three TextBox controls with different background colors; the process of designing the form is identical regardless of the controls you put on it.

Start by placing a SplitContainer control on the form. Then place a multiline TextBox control on the left panel of the SplitContainer control and set the TextBox control's `Dock` property to *Fill*. The TextBox control will fill the left panel of the SplitContainer control. Place another SplitContainer in the right panel of the first SplitContainer control. This control will be automatically docked in its panel and will fill it. Its orientation, however, is vertical, and the splitter will separate the panel into two smaller vertical panes. Select the second SplitContainer control, locate its `Orientation` property in the Properties window, and set it to *Horizontal*.

FIGURE 6.10
An elaborate form with
two splitter controls

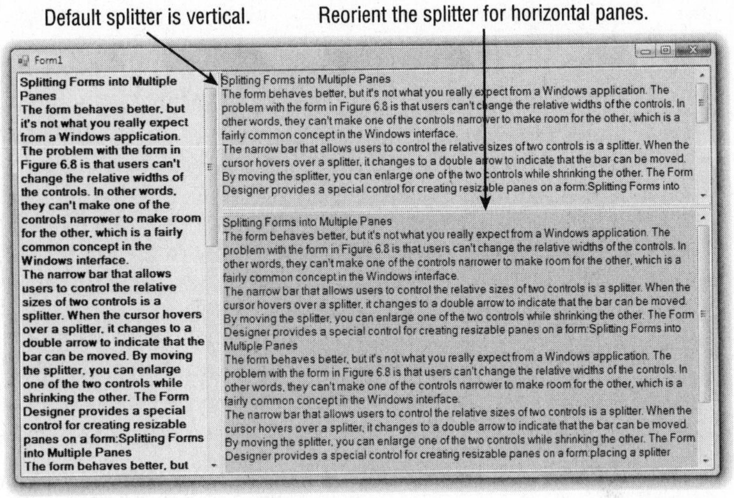

Default splitter is vertical.   Reorient the splitter for horizontal panes.

Now you can fill each of the panels with a TextBox control. Set each TextBox control's `BackgroundColor` to a different color, its `MultiLine` property to True, and its `Dock` property to *Fill*. The TextBox controls will fill their containers, which are the panels of the two SplitContainer controls, not the form. If you look up the properties of a SplitContainer control, you'll see that it's made up of two Panel controls, which are exposed as properties of the SplitContainer control, the `Panel1` and `Panel2` controls. You can set many of the properties of these two constituent controls, such as their font and color, their minimum size, and so on. They even expose an `AutoScroll` property so that users can scroll the contents of each one independently of the other. You can also set other properties of the SplitContainer control, such as the `SplitterWidth` property, which is the width of the splitter bar between the two panels in pixels, and the `SplitterIncrement` property, which is the smallest number of pixels that the splitter bar can be moved in either direction.

So far, you've seen what the Form Designer and the Form object can do for your application. Let's switch our focus to programming forms and explore the events triggered by the Form object.

Form Events

The Form object triggers several events. The most important are `Activated`, `Deactivate`, `FormClosing`, `Resize`, and `Paint`.

THE *ACTIVATED* AND *DEACTIVATE* EVENTS

When more than one form is displayed, the user can switch from one to the other by using the mouse or by pressing Alt+Tab. Each time a form is activated, the `Activated` event takes place. Likewise, when a form is activated, the previously active form receives the `Deactivate` event. Insert the code you want to execute when a form is activated (set certain control properties, for example) and when a form loses the focus or is deactivated in these two event handlers. These two events are the equivalents of the Enter and Leave events of the various controls. Notice that there's an inconsistency in the names of the two events: the Activated event takes place after the form has been activated, whereas the Deactivate event takes place right before the form is deactivated.

THE *FORMCLOSING* AND *FORMCLOSED* EVENTS

The FormClosing event is fired when the user closes the form by clicking its Close button. If the application must terminate because Windows is shutting down, the same event will be fired. Users don't always quit applications in an orderly manner, and a professional application should behave gracefully under all circumstances. The same code you execute in the application Exit command must also be executed from within the FormClosing event. For example, you might display a warning if the user has unsaved data, you might have to update a database, and so on. Place the code that performs these tasks in a subroutine and call it from within your menu's Exit command as well as from within the FormClosing event's handler.

You can cancel the closing of a form by setting the e.Cancel property to True. The event handler in Listing 6.2 displays a message box informing the user that the data hasn't been saved and gives them a chance to cancel the action and return to the application.

LISTING 6.2:   Canceling the closing of a form

```
Public Sub Form1_FormClosing (...) Handles Me.FormClosing
    Dim reply As MsgBoxResult
    reply = MsgBox("Document has been edited. " &
            "OK to terminate application, Cancel to " &
            "return to your document.", MsgBoxStyle.OKCancel)
    If reply = MsgBoxResult.Cancel Then
        e.Cancel = True
    End If
End Sub
```

The e argument of the FormClosing event provides the CloseReason property, which reports how the form is closing. Its value is one of the following members of the CloseReason enumeration: *FormOwnerClosing, MdiFormClosing, None, TaskManagerClosing, WindowsShutDown, ApplicationExitCall,* and *UserClosing.* The names of the members are self-descriptive, and you can query the CloseReason property to determine how the window is closing.

THE *RESIZE, RESIZEBEGIN,* AND *RESIZEEND* EVENTS

The Resize event is fired every time the user resizes the form by using the mouse. In the past, programmers had to insert quite a bit of code in the Resize event's handler to resize the controls and possibly rearrange them on the form. With the Anchor and Dock properties, much of this overhead can be passed to the form itself. If you want the two sides of the form to maintain a fixed ratio, however, you have to resize one of the dimensions from within the Resize event handler. Let's say the form's width-to-height ratio must be 3:4. Assuming that you're using the form's height as a guide, insert the following statement in the `Resize` event handler to make the width equal to three-fourths of the height:

```
Private Form1_Resize (…) Handles Me.Resize
    Me.Width = (0.75 * Me.Height)
End Sub
```

The `Resize` event is fired continuously while the form is being resized. If you want to keep track of the initial form's size and perform all the calculations after the user has finished resizing the form, you can use the `ResizeBegin` and `ResizeEnd` events, which are fired at the beginning and after the end of a resize operation, respectively. Store the form's width and height to two global variables in the `ResizeBegin` event and use these two variables in the `ResizeEnd` event handler to adjust the positions of the various controls on the form.

THE *SCROLL* EVENT

The `Scroll` event is fired by forms that have the `AutoScroll` property set to True when the user scrolls the form. The second argument of the `Scroll` event handler exposes the `OldValue` and `NewValue` properties, which are the displacements of the form before and after the scroll operation. This event can be used to keep a specific control in view when the form's contents are scrolled.

The `AutoScroll` property is handy for large forms, but it has a serious drawback: It scrolls the entire form. In most cases, you want to keep certain controls in view at all times. Instead of a scrollable form, you can create forms with scrollable sections by exploiting the `AutoScroll` properties of the Panel and/or the SplitContainer controls. You can also reposition certain controls from within the form's `Scroll` event handler. Let's say you have placed a few controls on a Panel container and you want to keep this panel at the top of a scrolling form. The following statements in the form's `Scroll` event handler reposition the panel at the top of the form every time the user scrolls the form:

```
Private Sub Form1_Scroll(…) Handles Me.Scroll
    Panel1.Top = Panel1.Top + (e.NewValue - e.OldValue)
End Sub
```

THE *PAINT* EVENT

This event takes place every time the form must be refreshed, and we use its handler to execute code for any custom drawing on the form. When you switch to another form that partially or totally overlaps the current one and then switch back to the first form, the `Paint` event will be fired to notify your application that it must redraw the form. The form will refresh its controls automatically, but any custom drawing on the form won't be refreshed automatically. This event is discussed in more detail in the tutorial "Drawing and Painting with Visual Basic 2008," where the Framework's drawing methods are presented. You can download the tutorial from www.sybex.com/go/masteringvb2010.

Loading and Showing Forms

Most practical applications are made up of multiple forms and dialog boxes. One of the operations you'll have to perform with multiform applications is to load and manipulate forms from within other forms' code. For example, you might want to display a second form to prompt the user for data specific to an application. You must explicitly load the second form and read the information entered by the user when the auxiliary form is closed. Or you might want to maintain two forms open at once and let the user switch between them. A text editor and its Find & Replace dialog box is a typical example.

You can access a form from within another form using its name. Let's say that your application has two forms, named *Form1* and *Form2*, and that *Form1* is the project's startup form. To show *Form2* when an action takes place on *Form1*, call the Show method of the auxiliary form:

```
Form2.Show
```

This statement brings up *Form2* and usually appears in a button's or menu item's Click event handler. To exchange information between two forms, use the techniques described in the section "Sharing Variables between Forms" later in this chapter.

The Show method opens a form in a modeless manner: The two forms are equal in stature on the desktop, and the user can switch between them. You can also display the second form in a modal manner, which means that users can't return to the form from which they invoked it without closing the second form. While a modal form is open, it remains on top of the desktop, and you can't move the focus to any other form of the same application (but you can switch to another application). To open a modal form, use the ShowDialog method:

```
Form2.ShowDialog
```

A dialog box is simply a modal form. When you display forms as dialog boxes, change the border of the forms to the setting *FixedDialog* and invoke them with the ShowDialog method. Modeless forms are more difficult to program because the user may switch among them at any time. Moreover, the two forms that are open at once must interact with one another. When the user acts on one of the forms, it might necessitate changes in the other, and you'll see shortly how this is done. If the two active forms don't need to interact, display one of them as a dialog box.

When you're finished with the second form, you can either close it by calling its Close method or hide it by calling its Hide method. The Close method closes the form, and its resources are returned to the system. The Hide method sets the form's Visible property to False; you can still access a hidden form's controls from within your code, but the user can't interact with it.

The Startup Form

A typical application has more than a single form. When an application starts, the main form is loaded. You can control which form is initially loaded by setting the startup object in the project Properties window. To open this dialog box, right-click the project's name in the Solution Explorer and select Properties. In the project's Properties pages, switch to the Application tab and select the appropriate item in the Startup Form combo box. By default, the IDE suggests the name of the first form it created, which is *Form1*. If you change the name of the form, Visual Basic will continue using the same form as the startup form with its new name.

You can also start an application by using a subroutine without loading a form. This subroutine is the MyApplication_Startup event handler, which is fired automatically when the application starts. To display the *AuxiliaryForm* object from within the Startup event handler, use the following statement:

```
Private Sub MyApplication_Startup (…) Handles Me.Startup
    System.Windows.Forms.Application.Run(New AuxiliaryForm())
End Sub
```

To view the `MyApplication_Startup` event handler, click the View Application Events button at the bottom of the Application pane in the project's Properties window. This action will take you to the MyApplication code window, where you can select the MyApplication Events item in the object list and the Startup item in the events list.

Controlling One Form from within Another

Loading and displaying a form from within another form's code is fairly trivial. In some situations, this is all the interaction you need between forms. Each form is designed to operate independently of the others, but they can communicate via public variables (see the following section). In most situations, however, you need to control one form from within another's code. Controlling the form means accessing its controls and setting or reading values from within another form's code.

SHARING VARIABLES BETWEEN FORMS

The preferred method for two forms to communicate with each other is through public variables. These variables are declared in the form's declarations section, outside any procedure, with the keyword `Public`. If the following declarations appear in `Form1`, the variable *NumPoints* and the array *DataValues* can be accessed by any procedure in Form1 as well as from within the code of any form belonging to the same project:

```
Public NumPoints As Integer
Public DataValues(100) As Double
```

To access a public variable declared in `Form1` from within another form's code, you must prefix the variable's name by the name of the form, as in the following:

```
Form1.NumPoints = 99
Form1.DataValues(0) = 0.3395022
```

In effect, the two public variables have become properties of the form in which they were declared. You can use the same notation to access the controls on another form. If *Form1* contains the *TextBox1* control, you can use the following statement to read its text:

```
Form1.TextBox1.Text
```

The controls on a form can be accessed by the code in another form because the default value of the `Modifiers` property of the controls on a form is *Friend*, which means that all components in a solution can access them. Other settings of the `Modifiers` property are *Public* (any application can access the control) and *Private* (the control is private to the form to which it belongs and cannot be accessed from code outside its own form). There are two more values, *Protected* and *Protected Friend*, which apply to inherited forms, a topic that's not covered in this book.

If a button on *Form1* opens the auxiliary form *Form2,* you can set selected controls to specific values before showing the auxiliary form. The following statements should appear in a button's or menu item's Click event handler:

```
Form2.TextBox1.Text = "some text"
Form2.DateTimePicker1.Value = Today
Form2.Show()
```

You can also create a variable to represent another form and access the auxiliary form through this variable. Let's say you want to access the resources of *Form2* from within the code of *Form1.* Declare the variable *auxForm* to represent *Form2* and then access the resources of *Form2* with the following statements:

```
Dim auxForm As Form2
auxForm.TextBox1.Text = "some text"
auxForm.DateTimePicker1.Value = Today
auxForm.Show
```

MULTIPLE INSTANCES OF A SINGLE FORM

Note that the variable that represents an auxiliary form is declared without the New keyword. The *auxForm* variable represents an existing form. If we used the New keyword, we'd create a new instance of the corresponding form. This technique is used when we want to display multiple instances of the same form, as in an application that allows users to open multiple documents of the same type.

Let's say you're designing an image-processing application or a simple text editor. Each new document should be opened in a separate window. Obviously, you can't design many identical forms and use them as needed. The solution is to design a single form and create new instances of it every time the user opens an existing document or creates a new one. These instances are independent of one another and they may interact with the main form.

The approach described here is reminiscent of Multiple Document Interface (MDI) applications. The MDI interface requires that all windows be contained within a parent window, and although once very popular, it's going slowly out of style. The new interfaces open multiple independent windows on the Desktop. Each window is an instance of a single form and it's declared with the New keyword. I've used this style of interface to redesign the TextPad application of Chapter 5, and I've included the revised application in this chapter's projects for your reference. Open the project in Visual Studio and examine its code, which contains a lot of comments.

Forms versus Dialog Boxes

Dialog boxes are special types of forms with very specific functionality that prompt the user for data. The Open and Save dialog boxes are two of the most familiar dialog boxes in Windows. They're so common that they're actually known as common dialog boxes. Technically, a dialog box is a good old form with its FormBorderStyle property set to *FixedDialog.* Like forms, dialog boxes might contain a few simple controls, such as Labels, TextBoxes, and Buttons. Don't overload a dialog box with controls and functionality; you'll end up with a regular form. Dialog boxes are supposed to present a few options and perform very simple tasks. There are exceptions, of course, like the Printer Setup dialog box, but dialog boxes are usually simple forms with a pair of OK/Cancel buttons.

Figure 6.11 shows a couple of dialog boxes you have certainly seen while working with Windows applications. The Caption dialog box of Word is a modal dialog box: You must close it before switching to your document. The Find and Replace dialog box is modeless: It allows you to switch to your document, yet it remains visible while open even if it doesn't have the focus.

FIGURE 6.11
Typical dialog boxes
used by Word

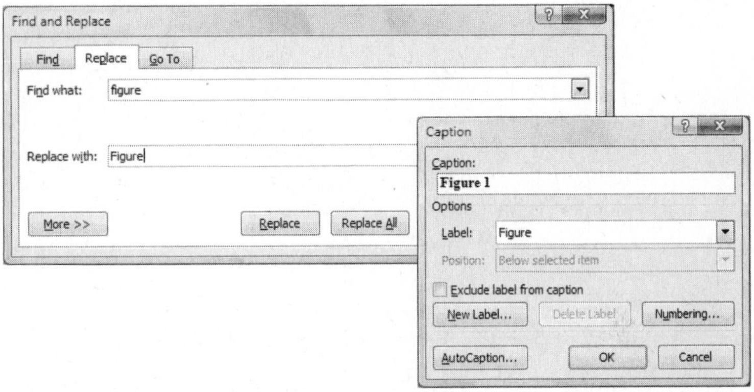

Notice that some dialog boxes, such as Open, Color, and even the humble MessageBox, come with the Framework, and you can incorporate them in your applications without having to design them.

A characteristic of dialog boxes is that they provide an OK and a Cancel button. The OK button tells the application that you're finished using the dialog box and the application can process the information in it. The Cancel button tells the application that it should ignore the information in the dialog box and cancel the current operation. As you will see, dialog boxes allow you to quickly find out which buttons were clicked to close them so that your application can take a different action in each case.

In short, the difference between forms and dialog boxes is artificial. If it were really important to distinguish between the two, they'd be implemented as two different objects — but they're the same object. So, without any further introduction, let's look at how to create and use dialog boxes.

To create a dialog box, start with a Windows form, set its `FormBorderStyle` property to `FixedDialog`, and set the `ControlBox`, `MinimizeBox`, and `MaximizeBox` properties to False. Then add the necessary controls on the form and code the appropriate events, as you would do with a regular Windows form.

Figure 6.12 shows a simple dialog box that prompts the user for an ID and a password (see the Password sample project available for download from www.sybex.com/go/masteringvb2010). The dialog box contains two TextBox controls (next to the appropriate labels) and the usual OK and Cancel buttons.

Now, to design your own Password main form, start a new project, rename the form **MainForm**, and place a button on it. This is the application main form, and we'll invoke the dialog box from within the button's `Click` event handler. Then add a new form to the project, name it **PasswordForm**, and place on it the controls shown in Figure 6.12.

FIGURE 6.12
A simple dialog box
that prompts users for a
username and password

To display a modal form, you call the ShowDialog method instead of the Show method. You already know how to read the values entered on the controls of the dialog box. You also need to know which button was clicked to close the dialog box. To convey this information from the dialog box back to the calling application, the Form object provides the DialogResult property. This property can be set to one of the values shown in Table 6.3 to indicate which button was clicked. The *DialogResult.OK* value indicates that the user has clicked the OK button on the form. There's no need to place an OK button on the form; just set the form's DialogResult property to *DialogResult.OK*.

TABLE 6.3: The DialogResult enumeration

VALUE	DESCRIPTION
Abort	The dialog box was closed with the Abort button.
Cancel	The dialog box was closed with the Cancel button.
Ignore	The dialog box was closed with the Ignore button.
No	The dialog box was closed with the No button.
None	The dialog box hasn't been closed yet. Use this option to find out whether a modeless dialog box is still open.
OK	The dialog box was closed with the OK button.
Retry	The dialog box was closed with the Retry button.
Yes	The dialog box was closed with the Yes button.

The dialog box need not contain any of the buttons mentioned here. It's your responsibility to set the value of the DialogResult property from within your code to one of the settings shown in the table. This value can be retrieved by the calling application. The code behind the two buttons in the dialog box is quite short:

```
Private Sub bttnOK_Click(…) Handles bttnOK.Click
    Me.DialogResult = DialogResult.OK
```

```
      Me.Close
    End Sub

    Private Sub bttnCancel_Click(…) Handles bttnCancel.Click
        Me.DialogResult = DialogResult.Cancel
        Me.Close
    End Sub
```

The event handler of the button that displays this dialog box should contain an `If` statement that examines the value returned by the `ShowDialog` method:

```
    If PasswordForm.ShowDialog = DialogResult.OK Then
        ' { process the user selection }
    End If
```

Depending on your application, you might allow the user to close the dialog box by clicking more than two buttons. Some of them must set the `DialogResult` property to `DialogResult.OK`, others to `DialogResult.Cancel`.

If the form contains an Accept and a Cancel button, you don't have to enter a single line of code in the modal form. The user can enter values on the various controls and then close the dialog box by pressing the Enter or Cancel key. The dialog box will close and will return the `DialogResult.OK` or `DialogResult.Cancel` value. The Accept button sets the form's `DialogResult` property to `DialogResult.OK` automatically, and the Cancel button sets the same property to `DialogResult.Cancel`. Any other button must set the `DialogResult` property explicitly. Listing 6.3 shows the code behind the Log In button on the sample project's main form.

LISTING 6.3:   Prompting the user for an ID and a password

```
Private Sub Button1_Click(…) Handles Button1.Click
    If PasswordForm.ShowDialog() = DialogResult.OK Then
        If PasswordForm.txtUserID.Text = "" Or
                PasswordForm.txtPassword.Text = "" Then
            MsgBox("Please specify a user ID and a password to connect")
            Exit Sub
        End If
        MsgBox("You were connected as " & PasswordForm.txtUserID.Text)
    Else
        MsgBox("Connection failed for user " & PasswordForm.txtPassword.Text)
    End If
End Sub
```

VB 2010 AT WORK: THE MULTIPLEFORMS PROJECT

It's time to write an application that puts together the topics discussed in this section. The MultipleForms project, available for download from www.sybex.com/go/masteringvb2010, consists of a main form, an auxiliary form, and a dialog box. All three components of the application interface are shown in Figure 6.13. The buttons on the main form display both the auxiliary form and the dialog box.

FIGURE 6.13
The MultipleForms
project interface

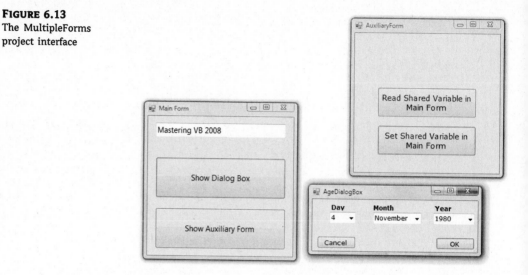

Let's review the various operations you want to perform — they're typical for many situations, not for only this application. At first, you must be able to invoke both the auxiliary form and the dialog box from within the main form; the Show Auxiliary Form and Show Dialog Box buttons do this. The main form contains a variable declaration: *strProperty*. This variable is, in effect, a property of the main form and is declared as public with the following statement:

```
Public strProperty As String = "Mastering VB 2010"
```

The main form calls the auxiliary form's Show method to display it in a modeless manner. The auxiliary form button with the caption Read Shared Variable In Main Form reads the *strProperty* variable of the main form with the following statement:

```
Private Sub bttnReadShared_Click(…) Handles bttnReadShared.Click
    MsgBox(MainForm.strProperty, MsgBoxStyle.OKOnly,
            "Public Variable Value")
End Sub
```

Using the same notation, you can set this variable from within the auxiliary form. The following event handler prompts the user for a new value and assigns it to the shared variable of the main form:

```
Private Sub bttnSetShared_Click(…) Handles bttnSetShared.Click
    Dim str As String
    str = InputBox("Enter a new value for strProperty")
    MainForm.strProperty = str
End Sub
```

The two forms communicate with each other through public properties. Let's make this communication a little more elaborate by adding an event. Every time the auxiliary form sets the value of the *strProperty* variable, it raises an event to notify the main form. The main form, in turn, uses this event to display the new value of the string on the TextBox control as soon as the code in the auxiliary form changes the value of the variable and before it's closed.

To raise an event, you must declare the event name in the form's declaration section. Insert the following statement in the auxiliary form's declarations section:

```
Event strPropertyChanged()
```

Now add a statement that fires the event. To raise an event, call the `RaiseEvent` statement and pass the name of the event as an argument. This statement must appear in the `Click` event handler of the Set Shared Variable In Main Form button, right after setting the value of the shared variable. As soon as the user clicks the button, the auxiliary form notifies the main form by raising the `strPropertyChanged` event. Listing 6.4 shows the revised event handler.

LISTING 6.4:   Raising an event

```
Private Sub bttnSetShared_Click(…) Handles bttnSetShared.Click
    Dim str As String
    str = InputBox("Enter a new value for strProperty")
    MainForm.strProperty = str
    RaiseEvent strPropertyChanged
End Sub
```

The event will be raised, but it will go unnoticed if you don't handle it from within the main form's code. To handle the event, you must create a variable that represents the auxiliary form with the `WithEvents` keyword:

```
Dim WithEvents FRM As New AuxiliaryForm()
```

The `WithEvents` keyword tells VB that the variable is capable of raising events and that VB should listen for events from the specific form. If you expand the drop-down list with the objects in the code editor, you will see the name of the *FRM* variable, along with the other controls you can program. Select *FRM* in the list and then expand the list of events for the selected item. In this list, you will see the `strPropertyChanged` event. Select it and the definition of an event handler will appear. Enter these statements in this event's handler:

```
Private Sub FRM_strPropertyChanged() Handles FRM.strPropertyChanged
    TextBox1.Text = strProperty
    Beep()
End Sub
```

It's a simple handler, but it's adequate for demonstrating how to raise and handle custom events on the form level. If you want, you can pass arguments to the event handler by including them in the declaration of the event. To pass the original and the new value through the strPropertyChanged event, use the following declaration:

```
Event strPropertyChanged(ByVal oldValue As String,
                         ByVal newValue As String)
```

If you run the application now, you'll see that the value of the TextBox control in the main form changes as soon as you change the property's value in the auxiliary form. You can actually change the value of the variable several times before closing the auxiliary form, and each time the current value will be displayed on the main form.

Of course, you can update the TextBox control on the main form directly from within the auxiliary form's code. Use the expression *MainForm.TextBox1* to access the control and then manipulate it as usual. Events are used to perform some actions on a form when an action takes place. The benefit of using events, as opposed to accessing members of another form from within your code, is that the auxiliary form need not know anything about the form that called it. The auxiliary form raises the event, and it's the calling form's responsibility to handle it. Moreover, the event handler in the main form may perform other actions in addition to setting a control's value; it may submit something to a database, log the action, and perform any other operation suited for the application at hand.

Let's see now how the main form interacts with the dialog box. What goes on between a form and a dialog box is not exactly interaction; it's a more timid type of behavior. The form displays the dialog box and waits until the user closes the dialog box. Then it looks at the value of the DialogResult property to find out whether it should even examine the values passed back by the dialog box. If the user has closed the dialog box with the Cancel (or an equivalent) button, the application ignores the dialog box settings. If the user closed the dialog box with the OK button, the application reads the values and proceeds accordingly.

Before showing the dialog box, the code of the Show Dialog Box button sets the values of certain controls on the dialog box. In the course of the application, it usually makes sense to suggest a few values in the dialog box so that the user can accept the default values by pressing the Enter key. The main form reads a date on the dialog box's controls and then displays the dialog box with the statements given in Listing 6.5.

LISTING 6.5:   Displaying a dialog box and reading its values

```
Protected Sub Button3_Click(…) Handles Button3.Click
' Preselects the date 4/11/1980
   AgeDialog.cmbMonth.Text = "4"
   AgeDialog.cmbDay.Text = "11"
   AgeDialog.CmbYear.Text = "1980"
   AgeDialog.ShowDialog()
   If AgeDialog.DialogResult = DialogResult.OK Then
      MsgBox(AgeDialog.cmbMonth.Text & " " &
             AgeDialog.cmbDay.Text & "," &
             AgeDialog.cmbYear.Text)
   Else
      MsgBox("OK, we'll protect your vital personal data")
```

```
      End If
End Sub
```

To close the dialog box, you can click the OK or Cancel button. Each button sets the `DialogResult` property to indicate the action that closed the dialog box. The code behind the two buttons is shown in Listing 6.6.

LISTING 6.6:   Setting a dialog box `DialogResult` property

```
Protected Sub bttnOK_Click(…) Handles bttnOK.Click
    Me.DialogResult = DialogResult.OK
End Sub

Protected Sub bttnCancel_Click(…) Handles bttnCancel.Click
    Me.DialogResult = DialogResult.Cancel
End Sub
```

Because the dialog box is modal, the code in the Show Dialog Box button is suspended at the line that shows the dialog box. As soon as the dialog box is closed, the code in the main form resumes with the statement following the one that called the `ShowDialog` method of the dialog box. This is the `If` statement in Listing 6.5 that examines the value of the `DialogResult` property and acts accordingly.

Building Dynamic Forms at Runtime

Sometimes you won't know in advance how many instances of a given control might be required on a form. Let's say you're designing a form for displaying the names of all tables in a database. It's practically impossible to design a form that will accommodate every database users might throw at your application. Another typical example is a form for entering family-related data, which includes the number of children in the family and their ages. As soon as the user enters (or changes) the number of children, you should display as many TextBox controls as there are children to collect their ages.

For these situations, it is possible to design dynamic forms, which are populated at runtime. The simplest approach is to create more controls than you'll ever need and set their `Visible` properties to False at design time. At runtime, you can display the controls by switching their `Visible` properties to True. As you know already, quick-and-dirty methods are not the most efficient ones. You must still rearrange the controls on the form to make it look nice at all times. The proper method to create dynamic forms at runtime is to add controls to and remove them from your form as needed from within your code using the techniques discussed in the following sections.

Just as you can create new instances of forms, you can also create new instances of any control and place them on a form. The Form object exposes the `Controls` property, which is a collection that contains all the controls on the form. This collection is created automatically as you place controls on the form at design time, and you can access the members of this collection from within your code. It is also possible to add new members to the collection, or remove existing members, with the `Add` and `Remove` methods of the Form object accordingly.

The Form's *Controls* Collection

All the controls on a form are stored in the Controls collection, which is a property of the Form object. The Controls collection exposes members for accessing and manipulating the controls at runtime, and they're the usual members of a collection:

Add Method The Add method adds a new element to the Controls collection. In effect, it adds a new control on the current form. The Add method accepts a reference to a control as an argument and adds it to the collection. Its syntax is the following, where *controlObj* is an instance of a control:

```
Controls.Add(controlObj)
```

To place a new Button control on the form, declare a variable of the Button type, set its properties, and then add it to the Controls collection:

```
Dim bttn As New  System.Windows.Forms.Button
bttn.Text = "New Button"
bttn.Left = 100
bttn.Top = 60
bttn.Width = 80
Me.Controls.Add(bttn)
```

Remove Method The Remove method removes an element from the Controls collection. It accepts as an argument either the index of the control to be removed or a reference to the control to be removed (a variable of the Control type that represents one of the controls on the form). The syntax of these two forms of the Remove method is as follows:

```
Me.Controls.Remove(index)
Me.Controls.Remove(controlObj)
```

Count Property and All Method The Count property returns the number of elements in the Controls collection. Notice that if there are container controls, such as a Panel control, the controls in the containers are not included in the count. The Panel control has its own Controls collection. The All method returns all controls on a form (or a container control) as an array of the System.WinForms.Control type.

Clear Method The Clear method removes all the elements of the Controls array and effectively clears the form.

The Controls collection is also a property of any control that can host other controls. As you recall from our discussion of the Anchor and Dock properties, it's customary to place controls on a panel and handle them collectively as a section of the form. They are moved along with the panel at design time, and they're rearranged as a group at runtime. The Panel belongs to the form's Controls collection, and it provides its own Controls collection, which lets you access the controls on the panel.

VB 2010 AT WORK: THE SHOWCONTROLS PROJECT

The ShowControls project (shown in Figure 6.14) demonstrates the basic methods of the Controls property. Download the ShowControls project from www.sybex.com/go/

masteringvb2010, open it, and add any number of controls on the main form. You can place a panel to act as a container for other controls as well. Just don't remove the button at the top of the form (the Scan Controls On This Form button); it contains the code to list all the controls.

FIGURE 6.14
Accessing the controls on a form at runtime

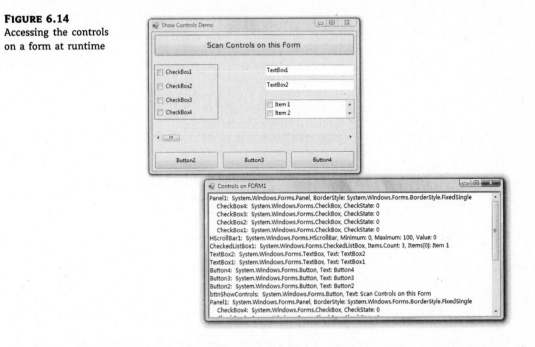

The code behind the Scan Controls On This Form button enumerates the elements of the form's `Controls` collection. The code doesn't take into consideration containers within containers. This would require a recursive routine, which would scan for controls at any depth. The code that iterates through the form's `Controls` collection and prints the names of the controls in the Output window is shown in Listing 6.7.

LISTING 6.7:   Iterating the Controls collection

```
Private Sub Button1_Click(…) Handles Button1.Click
    Dim Control As Windows.Forms.Control
    For Each Control In Me.Controls
        Debug.WriteLine(Control.ToString)
        If Control.GetType Is GetType(System.Windows.Forms.Panel) Then
            Dim nestedControl As Windows.Forms.Control
            For Each nestedControl In Control.Controls
                Debug.WriteLine("    " & nestedControl.ToString)
            Next
        End If
    Next
End Sub
```

The form shown in Figure 6.15 produced the following (partial) output (the controls on the Panel are indented to stand out in the listing):

```
Panel1:           System.Windows.Forms.Panel,
BorderStyle:      System.Windows.Forms.BorderStyle.FixedSingle
   CheckBox4:     System.Windows.Forms.CheckBox, CheckState: 0
   CheckBox3:     System.Windows.Forms.CheckBox, CheckState: 0
HScrollBar1:      System.Windows.Forms.HScrollBar,
                  Minimum: 0, Maximum: 100, Value: 0
CheckedListBox1:  System.Windows.Forms.CheckedListBox,
                  Items.Count: 3, Items[0]: Item 1
TextBox2:         System.Windows.Forms.TextBox,
                  Text: TextBox2
```

To find out the type of individual controls, call the `GetType` method. The following statement examines whether the control in the first element of the `Controls` collection is a TextBox:

```
If Me.Controls(0).GetType Is GetType( System.Windows.Forms.TextBox) Then
   MsgBox("It's a TextBox control")
End If
```

Notice the use of the `Is` operator in the preceding statement. The equals operator would cause an exception because objects can be compared only with the `Is` operator. (You're comparing instances, not values.)

To access other properties of the control represented by an element of the `Controls` collection, you must first cast it to the appropriate type. If the first control of the collection is a TextBox control, use the `CType()` function to cast it to a TextBox variable and then request its `SelectedText` property:

```
If Me.Controls(0).GetType Is GetType( System.Windows.Forms.TextBox) Then
    Debug.WriteLine(CType(Me.Controls(0), TextBox).SelectedText)
End If
```

The `If` statement is necessary, unless you can be sure that the first control is a TextBox control. If you omit the `If` statement and attempt to convert the control to a TextBox, a runtime exception will be thrown if the object `Me.Controls(0)` isn't a TextBox control.

VB 2010 AT WORK: THE DYNAMICFORM PROJECT

To demonstrate how to handle controls at runtime from within your code, I included the DynamicForm project (Figure 6.15) on www.sybex.com/go/masteringvb2010. It's a simple data-entry window for a small number of data points. The user can specify at runtime the number of data points she wants to enter, and the number of TextBoxes on the form is adjusted automatically.

The control you see at the top of the form is the NumericUpDown control. All you really need to know about this control is that it displays an integer in the range specified by its `Minimum` and `Maximum` properties and allows users to select a value. It also fires the `ValueChanged` event every time the user clicks one of the two arrows or types another value in its edit area. This event handler's code adds or removes controls on the form so that the number of text boxes (as well as the number of corresponding labels) matches the value on the control. Listing 6.8 shows the handler for the `ValueChanged` event of the *NumericUpDown1* control.

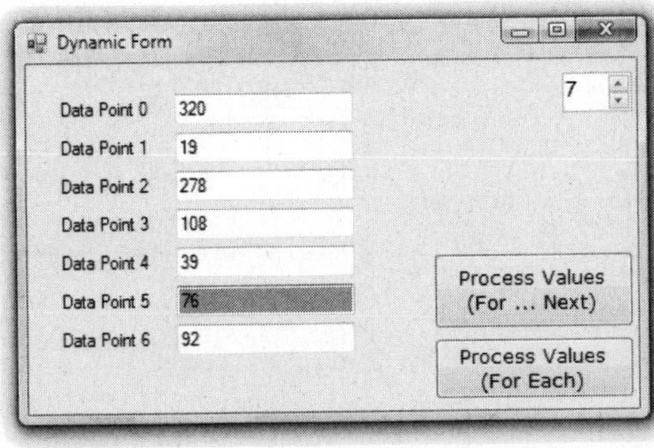

FIGURE 6.15
The DynamicForm
project

LISTING 6.8:   Adding and removing controls at runtime

```
Private Sub NumericUpDown1_ValueChanged(…)  Handles NumericUpDown1.ValueChanged
    Dim TB As New TextBox()
    Dim LBL As New Label()
    Dim i, TBoxes As Integer
    '   Count all TextBox controls on the Form
    For i = 0 To Me.Controls.Count - 1
        If Me.Controls(i).GetType Is
                    GetType(System.Windows.Forms.TextBox) Then
            TBoxes = TBoxes + 1
        End If
    Next
    ' Add new controls if number of controls on the Form is less
    ' than the number specified with the NumericUpDown control
    If TBoxes < NumericUpDown1.Value Then
        TB.Left = 100: TB.Width = 120
        TB.Text = ""
        For i = TBoxes To CInt(NumericUpDown1.Value) - 1
            TB = New TextBox()
            LBL = New Label()
            If NumericUpDown1.Value = 1 Then
                TB.Top = 20: TB.TabIndex = 0
            Else
                TB.Top = Me.Controls(Me.Controls.Count - 2).Top + 25
            End If
            ' Set the trivial properties of the new controls
            LBL.Left = 20: LBL.Width = 80
            LBL.Text = "Data Point " & i
            LBL.Top = TB.Top + 3
            TB.Left = 100: TB.Width = 120
```

```
                    TB.Text = ""
                    ' add controls to the form
                    Me.Controls.Add(TB)
                    Me.Controls.Add(LBL)
                    TB.TabIndex = Convert.ToInt32(NumericUpDown1.Value)
                    ' and finally connect their GotFocus/LostFocus events
                    ' to the appropriate handler
                    AddHandler TB.Enter,
                            New System.EventHandler(AddressOf TBox_Enter)
                    AddHandler TB.Leave,
                            New System.EventHandler(AddressOf TBox_Leave)
                Next
            Else
                For i = Me.Controls.Count - 1 To Me.Controls.Count -
                        2 * (TBoxes - CInt(NumericUpDown1.Value)) Step -2
                    Me.Controls.Remove(Controls(i))
                    Me.Controls.Remove(Controls(i - 1))
                Next
            End If
    End Sub
```

The code is lengthy but straightforward; most of the statements just set the basic properties of the Label and TextBox controls on the form. Ignore the AddHandler statements for now; they're discussed in the following section. First, the code counts the number of TextBoxes on the form; then it figures out whether it should add or remove elements from the Controls collection. To remove controls, the code iterates through the last *n* controls on the form and removes them. The number of controls to be removed is the following, where *TBoxes* is the total number of controls on the form minus the value specified in the NumericUpDown control:

```
2 * (TBoxes - NumericUpDown1.Value)
```

If the value entered in the NumericUpDown control is less than the number of TextBox controls on the form, the code removes the excess controls from within a loop. At each step, it removes two controls, one of them a TextBox and the other a Label control with the matching caption. (That's why the loop variable is decreased by two.) The code also assumes that the first two controls on the form are the Button and the NumericUpDown controls. If the value entered by the user exceeds the number of TextBox controls on the form, the code adds the necessary pairs of TextBox and Label controls to the form.

To add controls, the code initializes a TextBox (*TB*) and a Label (*LBL*) variable. Then, it sets their locations and the label's caption. The left coordinate of all labels is 20, their width is 80, and their Text property (the label's caption) is the order of the data item. The vertical coordinate is 20 pixels for the first control, and all other controls are 3 pixels below the control on the previous row. After a new control is set up, it's added to the Controls collection with one of the following statements:

```
Me.Controls.Add(TB)     ' adds a TextBox control
Me.Controls.Add(LBL)    ' adds a Label control
```

To use the values entered by the user on the dynamic form, we must iterate the Controls collection, extract the values in the TextBox controls, and read their values. Listing 6.9 shows how the Process Values button scans the TextBox controls on the form and performs some basic calculations with them (counting the number of data points and summing their values).

LISTING 6.9:   Reading the controls on the form

```
Private Sub Button1_Click(…) Handles Button1.Click
    Dim TBox As TextBox
    Dim Sum As Double = 0, points As Integer = 0
    Dim iCtrl As Integer
    For iCtrl = 0 To Me.Controls.Count - 1
        If Me.Controls(iCtrl).GetType Is
                GetType(System.Windows.Forms.TextBox) Then
            TBox = CType(Me.Controls(iCtrl), TextBox)
            If IsNumeric(TBox.Text) Then
                Sum = Sum + Val(TBox.Text)
                points = points + 1
            End If
        End If
    Next
    MsgBox("The sum of the " & points.ToString &
            " data points is " & Sum.ToString)
End Sub
```

Real World Scenario

HANDLING REPEATED DATA ITEMS

Dynamic forms are actually quite common even in business-line applications. There are situations where users are expected to enter or review multiple items of information on a single form. If each data item consists of several fields (such as names, ages, and the like), your best bet is to design a form like the following one.

This form, which is part of the DynamicDataEntry project, is a more typical example of a dynamic form, which allows users to enter an unknown number of dependant members (or any other entity, for that matter). Although you can create an auxiliary form where the user can enter each entry, the form shown here works better because it allows the user to focus on a single form.

Initially the form is populated with the appropriate controls for entering a single member. Users can click the "Add new member" link to create a new entry. On the left you see the form in its initial state and on the right you see the same form after adding four members. The "Remove member" link removes the last member from the form. Users can enter any number of dependant members on this form by adding new entries. If the number of entries exceeds the height of the form, a scroll bar appears. Notice that the scroll bar scrolls the entries for the members and not the fixed items on the form, which are the two links at the top and the Done Entering Members button at the bottom. You can change the structure of each entry to enable other types of data (such as room types in a hotel reservation system, a student's courses and grades, the statistics of various teams, and so on).

I will not present the full code for the application here; it is well documented and you can examine it on your own. The individual entries are made up of a number of controls, all on a Panel control. This allows you to use the same name for the controls. There's no naming conflict since the controls belong to a different Panel. All individual panels are placed on another larger Panel control, which is anchored to all four sides of the form and resizes nicely along with the form. The AutoScroll property on this Panel control was set to True so that the appropriate scroll bars appear automatically should the user have a large number of members to enter.

Adding and removing entries is quite straightforward. I will show you only the code that iterates through all entries and processes them:

```
For Each ctrl As Control In Me.Controls("pnlAllMembers").Controls
    If ctrl.GetType Is GetType(System.Windows.Forms.Panel) Then
        Name = ctrl.Controls("txtName").Text
        Age = CType(ctrl.Controls("cbAge"), ComboBox).SelectedItem
        If CType(ctrl.Controls("rdMale"), RadioButton).Checked
                    Then sex = "Male"
        If CType(ctrl.Controls("rdFemale"), RadioButton).Checked
                    Then sex = "Female"
        message &= "NAME: " & Name & vbCrLf &
                "AGE: " & Age & vbCrLf &
                "SEX: " & sex & vbCrLf &
```

```
                              "----------------------------" & vbCrLf
        End If
    Next
```

The outer loop goes through the controls on the *pnlAllMembers* Panel control, which is the large panel with the entries. If the current control is a Panel, we can process it. Normally, all child controls on the *pnlAllMembers* Panel will be also Panel controls; you may choose to add other control as well. Then the code accesses each individual control by name. *txtName* is the name of the TextBox control for the member's name and it's always the same regardless of the entry to which it belongs. The code gradually builds a string with the data of the dependant members and displays them. A real-world application would submit the same data to a database, convert it to XML format, and store it locally or process the data in some other meaningful way. You can open the DynamicDataEntry project and examine its code, which is actually quite short considering all the flexibility.

If you make the form wide, the various entries will still be lined up in a single column, leaving most of the form empty. How about entering some code in the form's resizing events to display the entries in multiple columns depending on the width of the form?

Creating Event Handlers at Runtime

You saw how to add controls on your forms at runtime and how to access the properties of these controls from within your code. In many situations, this is all you need: a way to access the properties of the controls (the text on a TextBox control or the status of a CheckBox or RadioButton control). What good is a Button control, however, if it can't react to the Click event? The only problem with the controls you add to the Controls collection at runtime is that they don't react to events. It's possible, though, to create event handlers at runtime, and this is what you'll learn in this section.

To create an event handler at runtime, create a subroutine that accepts two arguments — the usual *sender* and *e* arguments — and enter the code you want to execute when a specific control receives a specific event. The type of the *e* argument must match the definition of the second argument of the event for which you want to create a handler. Let's say that you want to add one or more buttons at runtime on your form and these buttons should react to the Click event. Create the ButtonClick() subroutine and enter the appropriate code in it. The name of the subroutine can be anything; you don't have to make up a name that includes the control's or the event's name.

After the subroutine is in place, you must connect it to an event of a specific control. The ButtonClick() subroutine, for example, must be connected to the Click event of a Button control. The statement that connects a control's event to a specific event handler is the AddHandler statement, whose syntax is as follows:

```
AddHandler control.event, New System.EventHandler(AddressOf ButtonClick)
```

Consider, for example, an application that performs certain calculations with an existing subroutine. To connect the ProcessNow() subroutine to the Click event of the *Calculate* button, use the following statement:

```
AddHandler Calculate.Click,
        New System.EventHandler(AddressOf ProcessNow)
```

You can use similar statements to connect the same subroutine to other control event handlers. You can also associate multiple controls' Click event handler with the `ProcessNow()` subroutine.

Let's add a little more complexity to the DynamicForm application. I'll program the `Enter` and `Leave` events of the TextBox controls added to the form at runtime. When a TextBox control receives the focus, I'll change its background color to a light yellow, and when it loses the focus, I'll restore the background to white so the user knows which box has the focus at any time. I'll use the same handlers for all TextBox controls. (The code for the two handlers is shown in Listing 6.10.)

LISTING 6.10:   Event handlers added at runtime

```
Private Sub TBox_Enter(ByVal sender As Object,
                       ByVal e As System.EventArgs)
    CType(sender, TextBox).BackColor = color.LightCoral
End Sub

Private Sub TBox_Leave(ByVal sender As Object,
                       ByVal e As System.EventArgs)
    CType(sender, TextBox).BackColor = color.White
End Sub
```

The two subroutines use the *sender* argument to find out which TextBox control received or lost the focus, and they set the appropriate control's background color. (These subroutines are not event handlers yet because they're not followed by the `Handles` keyword — at least, not before we associate them with an actual control and a specific event.) This process is done in the same segment of code that sets the properties of the controls we create dynamically at runtime. After adding the control to the `Me.Controls` collection, call the following statements to connect the new control's `Enter` and `Leave` events to the appropriate handlers:

```
AddHandler TB.Enter, New System.EventHandler(AddressOf TBox_Enter)
AddHandler TB.Leave, New System.EventHandler(AddressOf TBox_Leave)
```

Note that you don't have to raise the event from within your code; neither do you specify the arguments to the event. Since you've associated the two routines with the Click event handler, the compiler knows that they're Click event handlers and passes the appropriate arguments to them. All you have to do is make sure the signatures of the two routines match the signature of the Click event handler.

Run the DynamicForm application and see how the TextBox controls handle the focus-related events. With a few statements and a couple of subroutines, we were able to create event handlers at runtime from within our code.

DESIGNING AN APPLICATION GENERATOR

In the preceding sections of this chapter, you learned how to create new forms from within your code and how to instantiate them. In effect, you have the basic ingredients for designing applications from within your code. Designing an application from within the code is not a trivial task, but now you have a good understanding of how an application generator works. You can even design a wizard that prompts the user for information about the appearance of the form and then design the form from within your code.

Designing Menus

Menus are among the most common and most characteristic elements of the Windows user interface. Even in the old days of character-based displays, menus were used to display methodically organized choices and guide the user through an application. Despite the visually rich interfaces of Windows applications and the many alternatives, menus are still the most popular means of organizing a large number of options. Many applications duplicate some or all of their menus in the form of toolbar icons, but the menu is a standard fixture of a form. You can turn the toolbars on and off, but not the menus.

The Menu Editor

Menus can be attached only to forms, and they're implemented through the MenuStrip control. The items that make up the menu are ToolStripMenuItem objects, which belong to a MenuStrip control (they're the menu options) or to another ToolStripMenuItem (they form submenus). As you will see, the MenuStrip control and ToolStripMenuItem objects give you absolute control over the structure and appearance of the menus of your application. The MenuStrip control is a variation of the Strip control, which is the base of menus, toolbars, and status bars.

You can design menus visually and then program their Click event handlers. In principle, that's all there is to a menu: You specify its items (the menu commands) and then you program each command's actions, as if the menu items were buttons. Depending on the needs of your application, you might want to enable and disable certain commands, add context menus to some of the controls on your form, and so on. Because each item in a menu is represented by a ToolStripMenuItem object, you can control the application's menus from within your code by manipulating the properties of the ToolStripMenuItem objects. Let's start by designing a simple menu, and I'll show you how to manipulate the menu objects from within your code as we go along.

Double-click the MenuStrip icon in the Toolbox. (You'll find the MenuStrip control in the Menus & Toolbars tab of the Toolbox.) An instance of the MenuStrip control will be added to the form, and a single menu command will appear on your form. Its caption will be **Type Here**. If you don't see the first menu item on the form right away, select the MenuStrip control in the Components tray below the form. Do as the caption says: Click it and enter the first command caption, File, as shown in Figure 6.16. To add items under the File menu, press Enter. To enter another command in the main menu, press Tab. Depending on your action, another box will be added and you can type the caption of the next command in it. Press Enter to move to the next item vertically and Tab to move to the next item horizontally. To insert a separator enter a hyphen (-) as the item's caption.

When you hover the pointer over a menu item, a drop-down button appears to the right of the item. Click this button to select the type of item you'll place on the menu. This item can be a MenuItem object, a separator, a ComboBox, or a TextBox. In this chapter, I'll focus on menu items, which are by far the most common elements on a menu. The last two options, however, allow you to build elaborate menus, reminiscent of the Office menus.

FIGURE 6.16
Designing a menu on
the form

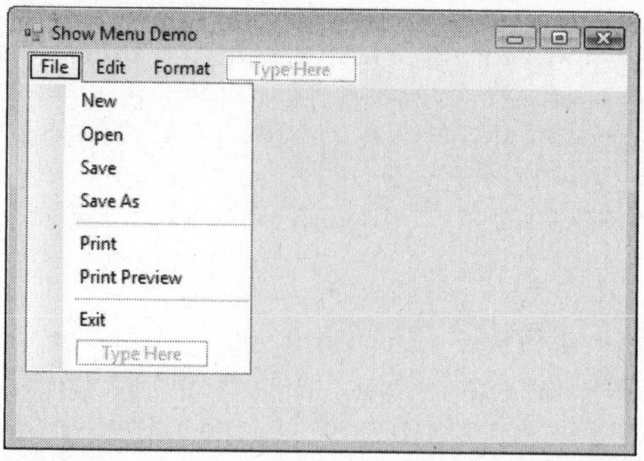

Enter the items you wish to include in the File menu — **New**, **Open**, **Save**, **SaveAs**, and **Exit** — and then click somewhere on the form. All the temporary items (the ones with the Type Here caption) will disappear, and the menu will be finalized on the form.

To add the Edit menu, select the MenuStrip icon to activate the visual menu editor and then click the File item. In the new item that appears next to the File item on the control, enter the string **Edit**. Press Enter and you'll switch to the first item of the Edit menu. Fill the Edit menu with the usual editing commands. Table 6.4 shows the captions (property Text) and names (property Name) for each menu and each command. You can also insert a standard menu with the Insert Standard Items command of the MenuStrip object's context menu.

TABLE 6.4: The captions and names of the File and Edit menus

CAPTION	NAME	CAPTION	NAME
File	FileMenu	**Tools**	ToolsMenu
New	FileNew	**Edit**	EditMenu
Open	FileOpen	Undo	EditCopy
Save	FileSave	Redo	EditRedo
Save As	FileSaveAs	Cut	EditCut
Print	FilePrint	Copy	EditCopy
Print Preview	FilePrintPreview	Paste	EditPaste
Exit	FileExit	Select All	EditSelectAll
		Help	HelpMenu

The bold items in Table 6.4 are the names of the first-level menus (File and Edit); the captions that are indented in the table are the commands on these two menus. The default names of the menu items you add visually to the application's menu are based on the item's caption followed by the suffix ToolStripMenuItem (*FileToolStripMenuItem*, *NewToolStripMenuItem*, and so on). You'll probably want to change the default names to something less redundant. To do so, change the `Name` property in the Properties window. To view the properties of a menu item, right-click it and select Properties from the context menu. One of the properties you should try out is the `LayoutStyle` property, which determines the orientation of the menu.

The most convenient method of editing a menu is to use the Items Collection Editor window, which is shown in Figure 6.17. This isn't a visual editor, but you can set all the properties of each menu item in the dialog box without having to switch to the Properties window.

FIGURE 6.17
Editing a menu with the
Items Collection Editor

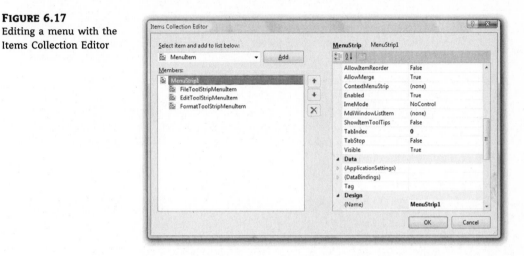

The Add button adds to the menu an item of the type specified in the combo box next to it (a menu item, combo box, or text box). To insert an item at a different location, add it to the menu and then use the arrow buttons to move it up or down. As you add new items, you can set their `Text` and `Name` properties on the right pane of the editor. You can also set their font, set the alignment and orientation of the text, and specify an image to be displayed along with the text. To add an image to a menu item, locate the `Image` property and click the ellipsis button. A dialog box in which you can select the appropriate resource will appear. Notice that all the images you use on your form are stored as resources of the project. You can add all the images and icons you might need in a project to the same resource file and reuse them at will. The `TextImageRelation` property allows you to specify the relative positions of the text and the image. You can also select to display text only, images only, or text and images for each menu item with the `DisplayStyle` property.

If the menu item leads to a submenu, you must also specify the submenu's items. Locate the `DropDownItems` property and click the ellipsis button. An identical window will appear, in which you can enter the drop-down items of the current menu item. Notice that the menu on the form is continuously updated while you edit it in the Items Collection Editor window, so you can see the effects of your changes on the form. Personally, I'm more productive with the editor than with the visual tools, mainly because all the properties are right there and I don't have to switch between the design surface and the Properties window.

Note that except for MenuItems, you can add ComboBoxes and TextBoxes to a menu. The TextBox control can be used to facilitate search operations, similar to the Search box of the browsers. You can also display a number of options in a ComboBox control on the menu. The advantage of the ComboBox menu item is that the selected option is visible at all times.

ComboBoxes are used in the menus of Office applications a lot (a typical example is the Font name and size ComboBoxes that allow you to change the current selections' font name and size).

The ToolStripMenuItem Properties

The ToolStripMenuItem class represents a menu command, at any level. If a command leads to a submenu, it's still represented by a ToolStripMenuItem object, which has its own collection of ToolStripMenuItem objects: the DropDownItems property, which is a collection and it's made up of ToolStripMenuItem objects. The ToolStripMenuItem class provides the following properties, which you can set in the Properties window at design time or manipulate from within your code:

Checked　Some menu commands act as toggles, and they are usually selected (checked) to indicate that they are on or deselected (unchecked) to indicate that they are off. To initially display a check mark next to a menu command, set its Checked property to True. You can also access this property from within your code to change the checked status of a menu command at runtime. For example, to toggle the status of a menu command called FntBold, use this statement:

```
FntBold.Checked = Not FntBold.Checked
```

Enabled　Some menu commands aren't always available. The Paste command, for example, has no meaning if the Clipboard is empty (or if it contains data that can't be pasted in the current application). To indicate that a command can't be used at the time, you set its Enabled property to False. The command then appears grayed out in the menu, and although it can be highlighted, it can't be activated.

IsOnDropDown　If the menu command represented by a ToolStripMenuItem object belongs to a submenu, its IsOnDropDown property is True; otherwise, it's False. The IsOnDropDown property is read-only and False for the items on the first level of the menu.

Visible　To remove a command temporarily from the menu, set the command's Visible property to False. The Visible property isn't used frequently in menu design. In general, you should prefer to disable a command to indicate that it can't be used at the time (some other action is required to enable it). Making a command invisible frustrates users, who might spend time trying to locate the command in another menu.

PROGRAMMING MENU COMMANDS

When a menu item is selected by the user, it triggers a Click event. To program a menu item, insert the appropriate code in the item's Click event handler. The Exit command's code would be something like the following:

```
Sub menuExit(…) Handles menuExit.Click
    End
End Sub
```

If you need to execute any cleanup code before the application ends, place it in the CleanUp() subroutine and call this subroutine from within the Exit item's Click event handler:

```
Sub menuExit(…) Handles menuExit.Click
    CleanUp()
    End
End Sub
```

The same subroutine must also be called from within the `FormClosing` event handler of the application's main form because some users might terminate the application by clicking the form's Close button.

An application's Open menu command contains the code that prompts the user to select a file and then open it. You will see many examples of programming menu commands in the following chapters. All you really need to know now is that each menu item is a ToolStrip-MenuItem object and each fires the `Click` event every time it's selected with the mouse or the keyboard. In most cases, you can treat the `Click` event handler of a ToolStripMenuItem object just like the `Click` event handler of a Button.

Another interesting event of the ToolStripMenuItem is the `DropDownOpened` event, which is fired when the user opens a menu or submenu (in effect, when the user clicks a menu item that leads to a submenu). In this event's handler, you can insert code to modify the submenu. The Edit menu of just about any application contains the ubiquitous Cut/Copy/Paste commands. These commands are not meaningful at all times. If the Clipboard doesn't contain text, the Paste command should be disabled. If no text is selected, the Copy and Cut commands should also be disabled. Here's how you could change the status of the Paste command from within the `DropDownOpened` event handler of the Edit menu:

```
If My.Computer.Clipboard.ContainsText Then
    PasteToolStripMenuItem.Enabled = True
Else
    PasteToolStripMenuItem.Enabled = True
End If
```

Likewise, to change the status of the Cut and Copy commands, use the following statements in the `DropDownOpened` event of the ToolStripMenuItem that represents the Edit menu:

```
If txtEditor.SelectedText.Trim.Length > 0 Then
    CopyToolStripMenuItem.Enabled = True
    CutToolStripMenuItem.Enabled = True
Else
    CopyToolStripMenuItem.Enabled = False
    CutToolStripMenuItem.Enabled = False
End If
```

USING ACCESS AND SHORTCUT KEYS

Menus provide a convenient way to display a large number of choices to the user. They allow you to organize commands in groups, according to their functions, and are available at all times. Opening menus and selecting commands with the mouse, however, can be an inconvenience. When using a word processor, for example, you don't want to have to take your hands off the keyboard and reach for the mouse. To simplify menu access, Windows forms support access keys and shortcut keys.

Access Keys

Access keys allow the user to open a menu by pressing the Alt key and a letter key. To open the Edit menu in all Windows applications, for example, you can press Alt+E. E is the Edit menu's access key. After the menu is open, the user can select a command with the arrow keys or by pressing another key, which is the command's access key, without holding down the Alt key.

Access keys are designated by the designer of the application and are marked with an underline character. To assign an access key to a menu item, insert the ampersand symbol (&) in front of the character you want to use as an access key in the ToolStripMenuItem's Text property.

DEFAULT ACCESS KEYS ARE BASED ON ITEM CAPTIONS

If you don't designate access keys, Visual Basic will use the first character in the caption of each top-level menu as its access key. The user won't see the underline character under the first character but can open the menu by pressing the first character of its caption while holding down the Alt key. If two or more menu captions begin with the same letter, the first (leftmost and topmost) menu will open.

Because the & symbol has a special meaning in menu design, you can't use it in a menu item's caption. To actually display the & symbol in a caption, prefix it with another & symbol. For example, the caption **&Drag** produces a command with the caption Drag (the first character is underlined because it's the access key). The caption **Drag && Drop** will create another command whose caption will be Drag & Drop. Finally, the string **&Drag && Drop** will create another command with the caption Drag & Drop (note the underline character in front of the first uppercase *D* in the string).

Shortcut Keys

Shortcut keys are similar to access keys, but instead of opening a menu, they run a command when pressed. Assign shortcut keys to frequently used menu commands so that users can reach them with a single keystroke. Shortcut keys are combinations of the Ctrl key and a function or character key. For example, the usual *access* key for the Close command (after the File menu is opened with Alt+F) is C, but the usual *shortcut* key for the Close command is Ctrl+W.

To assign a shortcut key to a menu command, drop down the ShortcutKeys list in the ToolStripMenuItem's Properties window and select a keystroke. Specify a modifier (Shift, Ctrl, or Alt) and a key. When assigning access and shortcut keys, take into consideration the well-established Windows standards. Users expect Alt+F to open the File menu, so don't use Alt+F for the Format menu. Likewise, pressing Ctrl+C universally performs the Copy command; don't use Ctrl+C as a shortcut for the Cut command.

Manipulating Menus at Runtime

Dynamic menus change at runtime to display more or fewer commands, depending on the current status of the program. The following sections explore two techniques for implementing dynamic menus:

◆ Creating short and long versions of the same menu

◆ Adding and removing menu commands at runtime

CREATING SHORT AND LONG MENUS

A common technique in menu design is to create long and short versions of a menu. If a menu contains many commands and most of the time only a few of them are needed, you can create one menu with all the commands and another with the most common ones. The first menu is the long one, and the second is the short one. The last command in the long menu should be Short Menu, and when selected, it should display the short version. The last command in the short menu should be Long Menu (or Full Menu), and it should display the long version.

Figure 6.18 shows a long and a short version of the same menu from the LongMenu project. The short version omits infrequently used commands and is easier to handle.

FIGURE 6.18
The two versions of the
Format menu of the
LongMenu application

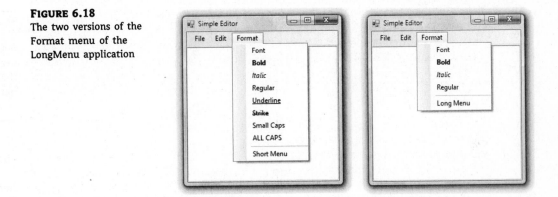

To implement the LongMenu command, start a new project and create a menu with the options shown in Figure 6.18. Listing 6.11 is the code that shows/hides the long menu in the MenuSize command's Click event.

LISTING 6.11:   The MenuSize menu item's Click event

```
Private Sub mnuSize_Click(…) Handles mnuSize.Click
    If mnuSize.Text = "Short Menu" Then
        mnuSize.Text = "Long Menu"
    Else
        mnuSize.Text = "Short Menu"
    End If
    mnuUnderline.Visible = Not mnuUnderline.Visible
    mnuStrike.Visible = Not mnuStrike.Visible
    mnuSmallCaps.Visible = Not mnuSmallCaps.Visible
    mnuAllCaps.Visible = Not mnuAllCaps.Visible
End Sub
```

The subroutine in Listing 6.11 doesn't do much. It simply toggles the Visible property of certain menu commands and changes the command's caption to Short Menu or Long Menu, depending on the menu's current status.

ADDING AND REMOVING COMMANDS AT RUNTIME

I conclude the discussion of menu design with a technique for building dynamic menus, which grow and shrink at runtime. Many applications maintain a list of the most recently opened files in the File menu. When you first start the application, this list is empty, and as you open and close files, it starts to grow.

The RunTimeMenu project, available for download from www.sybex.com/go/mastering vb2010, demonstrates how to add items to and remove items from a menu at runtime. The main menu of the application's form contains the Run Time Menu submenu, which is initially empty.

The two buttons on the form add commands to and remove commands from the Run Time Menu. Each new command is appended at the end of the menu, and the commands are removed from the bottom of the menu first (the most recently added commands are removed first). To change this order and display the most recent command at the beginning of the menu, use the Insert method instead of the Add method to insert the new item. Listing 6.12 shows the code behind the two buttons that add and remove menu items.

LISTING 6.12:   Adding and removing menu items at runtime

```
Private Sub bttnAddItem_Click(…) Handles bttnAddItem.Click
   Dim Item As New ToolStripMenuItem
   Item.Text = "Run Time Option" &
            RunTimeMenuToolStripMenuItem.DropDownItems.Count.ToString
   RunTimeMenuToolStripMenuItem.DropDownItems.Add(Item)
   AddHandler Item.Click, New System.EventHandler(AddressOf OptionClick)
End Sub

Private Sub bttnRemoveItem_Click(…) Handles bttnRemoveItem.Click
   If RunTimeMenuToolStripMenuItem.DropDownItems.Count > 0 Then
       Dim mItem As ToolStripItem
       Dim items As Integer =
                 RunTimeMenuToolStripMenuItem.DropDownItems.Count
       mItem = RunTimeMenuToolStripMenuItem.DropDownItems(items - 1)
   RunTimeMenuToolStripMenuItem.DropDownItems.Remove(mItem)
   End If
End Sub
```

The Remove button's code uses the Remove method to remove the last item in the menu by its index after making sure the menu contains at least one item. The Add button adds a new item and sets its caption to Run Time Option *n*, where *n* is the item's order in the menu. In addition, it assigns an event handler to the new item's Click event. This event handler is the same for all the items added at runtime; it's the OptionClick() subroutine. All the runtime options invoke the same event handler — it would be quite cumbersome to come up with a separate event handler for different items. In the single event handler, you can examine the name of the ToolStripMenuItem object that invoked the event handler and act accordingly. The OptionClick() subroutine used in Listing 6.13 displays the name of the menu item that invoked it. It doesn't do anything, but it shows you how to figure out which item of the Run Time Menu was clicked.

LISTING 6.13:   Programming dynamic menu items

```
Private Sub OptionClick(…)
    Dim itemClicked As New ToolStripMenuItem
    itemClicked = CType(sender, ToolStripMenuItem)
    MsgBox("You have selected the item " & itemClicked.Text)
End Sub
```

CREATING CONTEXT MENUS

Nearly every Windows application provides a context menu that the user can invoke by right-clicking a form or a control. (It's sometimes called a shortcut menu or pop-up menu.) This is a regular menu, but it's not anchored on the form. It can be displayed anywhere on the form or on specific controls. Different controls can have different context menus, depending on the operations you can perform on them at the time.

To create a context menu, place a ContextMenuStrip control on your form. The new context menu will appear on the form just like a regular menu, but it won't be displayed there at runtime. You can create as many context menus as you need by placing multiple instances of the ContextMenuStrip control on your form and adding the appropriate commands to each one. To associate a context menu with a control on your form, set the `ContextMenu` property for that control to the name of the corresponding context menu.

Designing a context menu is identical to designing a regular menu. The only difference is that the first command in the menu is always ContextMenuStrip and it's not displayed along with the menu.

The Bottom Line

Visual form design   Forms expose a lot of trivial properties for setting their appearance. In addition, they expose a few properties that simplify the task of designing forms that can be resized at runtime. The `Anchor` property causes a control to be anchored to one or more edges of the form to which it belongs. The `Dock` property allows you to place on the form controls that are docked to one of its edges. To create forms with multiple panes that the user can resize at runtime, use the SplitContainer control. If you just can't fit all the controls in a reasonably sized form, use the `AutoScroll` properties to create a scrollable form.

Master It   You've been asked to design a form with three distinct sections. You should also allow users to resize each section. How will you design this form?

Design applications with multiple forms.   Typical applications are made up of multiple forms: the main form and one or more auxiliary forms. To show an auxiliary form from within the main form's code, call the auxiliary form's Show method, or the ShowDialog method if you want to display the auxiliary form modally (as a dialog box).

Master It   How will you set the values of selected controls in a dialog box, display them, and then read the values selected by the user from the dialog box?

Design dynamic forms.   You can create dynamic forms by populating them with controls at runtime through the form's `Controls` collection. First, create instances of the appropriate controls by declaring variables of the corresponding type. Then set the properties of each of these variables that represent controls. Finally, place the control on the form by adding the corresponding variable to the form's `Controls` collection.

Master It   How will you add a TextBox control to your form at runtime and assign a handler to the control's `TextChanged` event?

Design menus.   Both form menus and context menus are implemented through the Menu-Strip control. The items that make up the menu are ToolStripMenuItem objects. The ToolStripMenuItem objects give you absolute control over the structure and appearance of the menus of your application.

Master It   What are the two basic events fired by the ToolStripMenuItem object?

Chapter 7

More Windows Controls

In this chapter, I will continue the discussion of the Windows controls. I'll start with the controls that implement the common dialog boxes and the RichTextBox control. Then I will deal with two more advanced controls, TreeView and ListView.

The .NET Framework provides a set of controls for displaying common dialog boxes, such as the Open and Color dialog boxes. Each of these controls encapsulates a large amount of functionality that would take a lot of code to duplicate. The common dialog controls are fundamental components because they enable you to design user interfaces with the look and feel of a Windows application.

You'll also explore the RichTextBox control, which is an advanced version of the TextBox control. The RichTextBox control provides all the functionality you'll need to build a word processor — WordPad is actually built around the RichTextBox control. The RichTextBox control allows you to format text by mixing fonts and attributes, aligning paragraphs differently, and so on.

The TreeView and ListView controls implement two of the more-advanced data structures. TreeView can be used to present a hierarchical list — a tree in which items that belong to other items appear under their parent with the proper indentation. For instance, a list of city and state names should be structured so that each city appears under the corresponding state. ListView can be used to present a "flat" structure where each item has a number of subitems. A typical example is a file, whose most important attributes are name, size, type, and modification date. These attributes can be presented as subitems in a list of files.

The TreeView and ListView controls were designed to hide much of the complexity of these structures, and they do this very well. They are among the more-advanced controls, and they are certainly more difficult to program than the ones discussed in the preceding chapters. These two controls, however, are the basic makings of unique user interfaces, as you'll see in this chapter's examples.

In this chapter you'll learn how to do the following:

◆ Use the OpenFileDialog and SaveFileDialog controls to prompt users for filenames.

◆ Use ColorDialog and FontDialog controls to prompt users for colors and typefaces.

◆ Use the RichTextBox control as an advanced text editor to present richly formatted text.

◆ Use the TreeView and ListView controls to present hierarchical lists and lists of structured items.

The Common Dialog Controls

A rather tedious, but quite common, task in nearly every application is to prompt the user for filenames, font names and sizes, or colors to be used by the application. Designing your own dialog boxes for these purposes would be a hassle, not to mention that your applications wouldn't conform to the basic Windows interface design principles. Truth be told, users are not fond of surprises, and all your creative effort will most likely backfire. Unexpected interface features are guaranteed to curb GUI usability and result in a number of frustrated users. In fact, all Windows applications use standard dialog boxes for common operations; two of them are shown in Figure 7.1. These dialog boxes are implemented as standard controls in the Toolbox. To use any of the common dialog controls in your interface, just place the appropriate control from the Dialogs section of the Toolbox on your form and activate it from within your code by calling the ShowDialog method.

FIGURE 7.1
The Open and Font common dialog boxes

The common dialog controls are invisible at runtime, and they're not placed on your forms because they're implemented as modal dialog boxes and they're displayed as needed. You simply add them to the project by double-clicking their icons in the Toolbox; a new icon appears in the components tray of the form, just below the Form Designer. The following common dialog controls are in the Toolbox under the Dialogs tab:

OpenFileDialog Lets users select a file to open. It also allows the selection of multiple files for applications that must process many files at once.

SaveFileDialog   Lets users select or specify the path of a file in which the current document will be saved.

FolderBrowserDialog   Lets users select a folder (an operation that can't be performed with the OpenFileDialog control).

ColorDialog   Lets users select a color from a list of predefined colors or specify custom colors.

FontDialog   Lets users select a typeface and style to be applied to the current text selection. The Font dialog box has an Apply button, which you can intercept from within your code and use to apply the currently selected font to the text without closing the dialog box.

There are three more common dialog controls: the PrintDialog, PrintPreviewDialog, and PageSetupDialog controls. These controls are discussed in detail in the tutorial "Printing with Visual Basic 2010," available for download from www.sybex.com/go/masteringvb2010, in the context of VB's printing capabilities.

Using the Common Dialog Controls

To display any of the common dialog boxes from within your application, you must first add an instance of the appropriate control to your project. Then you must set some basic properties of the control through the Properties window. Most applications set the control's properties from within the code because common dialogs interact closely with the application. When you call the Color common dialog, for example, you should preselect a color from within your application and make it the default selection on the control. When prompting the user for the color of the text, the default selection should be the current setting of the control's ForeColor property. Likewise, the Save dialog box must suggest a filename when it first pops up (or the filename's extension, at least).

To display a common dialog box from within your code, you simply call the control's ShowDialog method, which is common for all controls. Note that all common dialog controls can be displayed only modally and they don't expose a Show method. As soon as you call the ShowDialog method, the corresponding dialog box appears onscreen, and the execution of the program is suspended until the box is closed. Using the Open, Save, and FolderBrowser dialog boxes, users can traverse the entire structure of their drives and locate the desired filename or folder. When the user clicks the Open or Save button, the dialog box closes and the program's execution resumes. The code should read the name of the file selected by the user through the FileName property and use it to open the file or store the current document there. The folder selected in the FolderBrowserDialog control is returned to the application through the SelectedPath property.

Here is the sequence of statements used to invoke the Open common dialog and retrieve the selected filename:

```
If OpenFileDialog1.ShowDialog = Windows.Forms.DialogResult.OK Then
    fileName = OpenFileDialog1.FileName
    ' Statements to open the selected file
End If
```

The ShowDialog method returns a value indicating how the dialog box was closed. You should read this value from within your code and ignore the settings of the dialog box if the operation was cancelled.

The variable *fileName* in the preceding code segment is the full pathname of the file selected by the user. You can also set the FileName property to a filename, which will be displayed when the Open dialog box is first opened:

```
OpenFileDialog1.FileName =
            "C:\WorkFiles\Documents\Document1.doc"
If OpenFileDialog1.ShowDialog =
            Windows.Forms.DialogResult.OK Then
    fileName = OpenFileDialog1.FileName
    ' Statements to open the selected file
End If
```

Similarly, you can invoke the Color dialog box and read the value of the selected color by using the following statements:

```
ColorDialog1.Color = TextBox1.BackColor
If ColorDialog1.ShowDialog = DialogResult.OK Then
    TextBox1.BackColor = ColorDialog1.Color
End If
```

The ShowDialog method is common to all controls. The Title property is also common to all controls and it's the string displayed in the title bar of the dialog box. The default title is the name of the dialog box (for example, *Open, Color,* and so on), but you can adjust it from within your code with a statement such as the following:

```
ColorDialog1.Title = "Select Drawing Color"
```

The ColorDialog Control

The Color dialog box, shown in Figure 7.2, is one of the simplest dialog boxes. Its Color property returns the color selected by the user or sets the initially selected color when the user opens the dialog box.

FIGURE 7.2
The Color dialog box

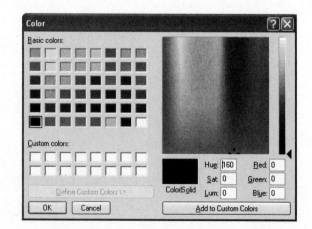

The following statements set the initial color of the ColorDialog control, display the dialog box, and then use the color selected in the control to fill the form. First, place a ColorDialog control in the form and then insert the following statements in a button's Click event handler:

```
Private Sub Button1_Click(…) Handles Button1.Click
    ColorDialog1.Color = Me.BackColor
    If ColorDialog1.ShowDialog = Windows.Forms.DialogResult.OK Then
        Me.BackColor = ColorDialog1.Color
    End If
End Sub
```

The following sections discuss the basic properties of the ColorDialog control.

ALLOWFULLOPEN

Set this property to True if you want users to be able to open the dialog box and define their own custom colors, as you can in the one shown in Figure 7.2. The AllowFullOpen property doesn't open the custom section of the dialog box; it simply enables the Define Custom Colors button in the dialog box. Otherwise, this button is disabled.

ANYCOLOR

This property is a Boolean value that determines whether the dialog box displays all available colors in the set of basic colors.

COLOR

This is the color specified on the control. You can set it to a color value before showing the dialog box to suggest a reasonable selection. On return, read the value of the same property to find out which color was picked by the user in the control:

```
ColorDialog1.Color = Me.BackColor
If ColorDialog1.ShowDialog = DialogResult.OK Then
    Me.BackColor = ColorDialog1.Color
End If
```

CUSTOMCOLORS

This property indicates the set of custom colors that will be shown in the dialog box. The Color dialog box has a section called Custom Colors, in which you can display 16 additional custom colors. The CustomColors property is an array of integers that represent colors. To display three custom colors in the lower section of the Color dialog box, use a statement such as the following:

```
Dim colors() As Integer = {222663, 35453, 7888}
ColorDialog1.CustomColors = colors
```

You'd expect that the *CustomColors* property would be an array of Color values, but it's not. You can't create the array *CustomColors* with a statement such as this one:

```
Dim colors() As Color =
            {Color.Azure, Color.Navy, Color.Teal}
```

Because it's awkward to work with numeric values, you should convert color values to integer values by using a statement such as the following:

```
Color.Navy.ToArgb
```

The preceding statement returns an integer value that represents the color navy. This value, however, is negative because the first byte in the color value represents the transparency of the color. To get the value of the color, you must take the absolute value of the integer value returned by the previous expression. To create an array of integers that represent color values, use a statement such as the following:

```
Dim colors() As Integer =
         {Math.Abs(Color.Gray.ToArgb),
          Math.Abs(Color.Navy.ToArgb),
          Math.Abs(Color.Teal.ToArgb)}
```

Now you can assign the *colors* array to the CustomColors property of the control and the colors will appear in the Custom Colors section of the Color dialog box.

SOLIDCOLORONLY

This indicates whether the dialog box will restrict users to selecting solid colors only. This setting should be used with systems that can display only 256 colors. Although today few systems can't display more than 256 colors, some interfaces are limited to this number. When you run an application through Remote Desktop, for example, only the solid colors are displayed correctly on the remote screen regardless of the remote computer's graphics card (and that's for efficiency reasons).

The FontDialog Control

The Font dialog box, shown in Figure 7.3, lets the user review and select a font and then set its size and style. Optionally, by clicking the Apply button users can also select the font's color and even apply the current settings to the selected text on a control of the form without closing the dialog box. This button isn't displayed by default; to show this button, you must set the control's ShowApply property to True. To see how the Apply button is used, see the description of the ShowApply property a little later in this section.

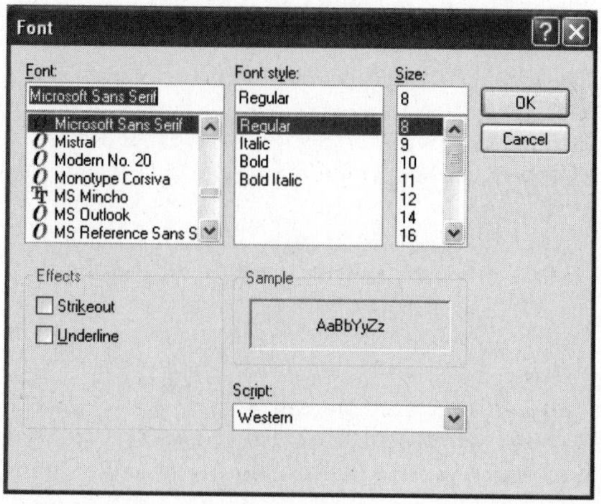

FIGURE 7.3
The Font dialog box

When the dialog is closed by clicking the OK button, you can retrieve the selected font by using the control's Font property. In addition to the OK button, the Font dialog box may contain the Apply button, which reports the current setting to your application. You can intercept the Click event of the Apply button and adjust the appearance of the text on your form while the common dialog is still visible.

The main property of this control is the Font property, which sets the initially selected font in the dialog box and retrieves the font selected by the user. The following statements display the Font dialog box after setting the initial font to the current font of the TextBox1 control. When the user closes the dialog box, the code retrieves the selected font and assigns it to the same TextBox control:

```
FontDialog1.Font = TextBox1.Font
If FontDialog1.ShowDialog = DialogResult.OK Then
    TextBox1.Font = FontDialog1.Font
End If
```

Use the following properties to customize the Font dialog box before displaying it.

ALLOWSCRIPTCHANGE

This property is a Boolean value that indicates whether the Script combo box will be displayed in the Font dialog box. This combo box allows the user to change the current character set and select a non-Western language (such as Greek, Hebrew, Cyrillic, and so on).

ALLOWVERTICALFONTS

This property is a Boolean value that indicates whether the dialog box allows the display and selection of both vertical and horizontal fonts. Its default value is False, which displays only horizontal fonts.

COLOR, SHOWCOLOR

The Color property sets or returns the selected font color. To enable users to select a color for the font, you must also set the ShowColor property to True.

FIXEDPITCHONLY

This property is a Boolean value that indicates whether the dialog box allows only the selection of fixed-pitch fonts. Its default value is False, which means that all fonts (fixed- and variable-pitch fonts) are displayed in the Font dialog box. Fixed-pitch fonts, or monospaced fonts, consist of characters of equal widths that are sometimes used to display columns of numeric values so that the digits are aligned vertically.

FONT

This property is a Font object. You can set it to the preselected font before displaying the dialog box and assign it to a Font property upon return. You've already seen how to preselect a font and how to apply the selected font to a control from within your application.

You can also create a new Font object and assign it to the control's Font property. Upon return, the TextBox control's Font property is set to the selected font:

```
Dim newFont As New Font("Verdana", 12, FontStyle.Underline)
FontDialog1.Font = newFont
If FontDialog1.ShowDialog() = DialogResult.OK Then
    TextBox1.ForeColor = FontDialog1.Color
End If
```

FONTMUSTEXIST

This property is a Boolean value that indicates whether the dialog box forces the selection of an existing font. If the user enters a font name that doesn't correspond to a name in the list of available fonts, a warning is displayed. Its default value is True, and there's no reason to change it.

MAXSIZE, MINSIZE

These two properties are integers that determine the minimum and maximum point size the user can specify in the Font dialog box. Use these two properties to prevent the selection of extremely large or extremely small font sizes because these fonts might throw off a well-balanced interface (text will overflow in labels, for example).

SHOWAPPLY

This property is a Boolean value that indicates whether the dialog box provides an Apply button. Its default value is False, so the Apply button isn't normally displayed. If you set this property to True, you must also program the control's Apply event — the changes aren't applied automatically to any of the controls in the current form.

The following statements display the Font dialog box with the Apply button:

```
Private Sub Button2_Click(...) Handles Button2.Click
    FontDialog1.Font = TextBox1.Font
    FontDialog1.ShowApply = True
    If FontDialog1.ShowDialog = DialogResult.OK Then
        TextBox1.Font = FontDialog1.Font
    End If
End Sub
```

The FontDialog control raises the Apply event every time the user clicks the Apply button. In this event's handler, you must read the currently selected font and use it in the form so that users can preview the effect of their selection:

```
Private Sub FontDialog1_Apply(...) Handles FontDialog1.Apply
    TextBox1.Font = FontDialog1.Font
End Sub
```

SHOWEFFECTS

This property is a Boolean value that indicates whether the dialog box allows the selection of special text effects, such as strikethrough and underline. The effects are returned to the application as attributes of the selected Font object, and you don't have to do anything special in your application.

The OpenDialog and SaveDialog Controls

Open and Save As, the two most widely used common dialog boxes (see Figure 7.4), are implemented by the OpenFileDialog and SaveFileDialog controls. Nearly every application prompts users for filenames, and the .NET Framework provides two controls for this purpose. The two dialog boxes are nearly identical, and most of their properties are common, so we'll start with the properties that are common to both controls.

FIGURE 7.4
The Open and Save As common dialog boxes

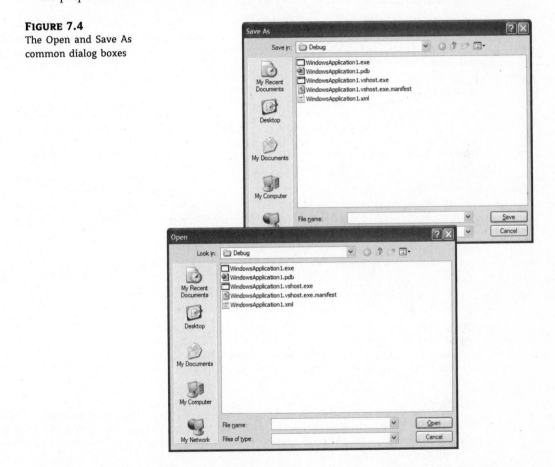

When either of the two controls is displayed, it rarely displays all the files in any given folder. Usually the files displayed are limited to the ones that the application recognizes so that users can easily spot the file they want. The Filter property limits the types of files that will appear in the Open or Save As dialog box.

It's also standard for the Windows interface not to display the extensions of filenames (although Windows distinguishes files by their filename extensions). The file type ComboBox, which appears at the bottom of the form next to the File Name box, contains the various file types recognized by the application. The various file types can be described in plain English with long descriptive names and without their filename extensions.

The extension of the default file type for the application is described by the `DefaultExtension` property, and the list of the file types displayed in the Save As Type box is determined by the `Filter` property.

To prompt the user for a file to be opened, use the following statements. The Open dialog box displays the files with the filename extension `.bin` only:

```
OpenFileDialog1.DefaultExt = ".bin"
OpenFileDialog1.AddExtension = True
OpenFileDialog1.Filter = "Binary Files|*.bin"
If OpenFileDialog1.ShowDialog() =
                Windows.Forms.DialogResult.OK Then
    Debug.WriteLine(OpenFileDialog1.FileName)
End If
```

The following sections describe the properties of the OpenFileDialog and SaveFileDialog controls.

ADDEXTENSION

This property is a Boolean value that determines whether the dialog box automatically adds an extension to a filename if the user omits it. The extension added automatically is the one specified by the `DefaultExtension` property, which you must set before calling the `ShowDialog` method. This is the default filename extension of the files recognized by your application.

CHECKFILEEXISTS

This property is a Boolean value that indicates whether the dialog box displays a warning if the user enters the name of a file that does not exist in the Open dialog box or if the user enters the name of a file that exists in the Save dialog box.

CHECKPATHEXISTS

This property is a Boolean value that indicates whether the dialog box displays a warning if the user specifies a path that does not exist as part of the user-supplied filename.

DEFAULTEXT

This property sets the default extension for the filenames specified on the control. Use this property to specify a default filename extension, such as `.txt` or `.doc`, so that when a file with no extension is specified by the user, the default extension is automatically appended to the filename. You must also set the `AddExtension` property to True. The default extension property starts with the period, and it's a string — for example, `.bin`.

DEREFERENCELINKS

This property indicates whether the dialog box returns the location of the file referenced by the shortcut or the location of the shortcut itself. If you attempt to select a shortcut on your Desktop when the `DereferenceLinks` property is set to False, the dialog box will return to your application a value such as C:\WINDOWS\SYSTEM32\lnkstub.exe, which is the name of the shortcut, not the name of the file represented by the shortcut. If you set the DereferenceLinks property to True, the dialog box will return the actual filename represented by the shortcut, which you can use in your code.

FILENAME

Use this property to retrieve the full path of the file selected by the user in the control. If you set this property to a filename before opening the dialog box, this value will be the proposed filename. The user can click OK to select this file or select another one in the control. The two controls provide another related property, the FileNames property, which returns an array of filenames. To find out how to allow the user to select multiple files, see the discussion of the MultiSelect and FileNames properties later in this chapter.

FILTER

This property is used to specify the type(s) of files displayed in the dialog box. To display text files only, set the Filter property to **Text files|*.txt**. The pipe symbol separates the description of the files (what the user sees) from the actual filename extension (how the operating system distinguishes the various file types).

If you want to display multiple extensions, such as .bmp, .gif, and .jpg, use a semicolon to separate extensions with the Filter property. Set the Filter property to the string **Images|*.bmp;*.gif;*.jpg** to display all the files of these three types when the user selects Images in the Save As Type combo box under the box with the filename.

Don't include spaces before or after the pipe symbol because these spaces will be displayed on the dialog box. In the Open dialog box of an image-processing application, you'll probably provide options for each image file type as well as an option for all images:

```
OpenFileDialog1.Filter =
    "Bitmaps|*.bmp|GIF Images|*.gif|" &
    "JPEG Images|*.jpg|All Images|*.bmp;*.gif;*.jpg"
```

FILTERINDEX

When you specify more than one file type when using the Filter property of the Open dialog box, the first file type becomes the default. If you want to use a file type other than the first one, use the FilterIndex property to determine which file type will be displayed as the default when the Open dialog box is opened. The index of the first type is 1, and there's no reason to ever set this property to 1. If you use the Filter property value of the example in the preceding section and set the FilterIndex property to 2, the Open dialog box will display GIF files by default.

INITIALDIRECTORY

This property sets the initial folder whose files are displayed the first time that the Open and Save dialog boxes are opened. Use this property to display the files of the application's folder or to specify a folder in which the application stores its files by default. If you don't specify an initial folder, the dialog box will default to the last folder where the most recent file was opened or saved. It's also customary to set the initial folder to the application's path by using the following statement:

```
OpenFileDialog1.InitialDirectory = Application.ExecutablePath
```

The expression `Application.ExecutablePath` returns the path in which the application's executable file resides.

RESTOREDIRECTORY

Every time the Open and Save As dialog boxes are displayed, the current folder is the one that was selected by the user the last time the control was displayed. The `RestoreDirectory` property is a Boolean value that indicates whether the dialog box restores the current directory before closing. Its default value is False, which means that the initial directory is not restored automatically. The `InitialDirectory` property overrides the `RestoreDirectory` property.

FILENAMES

If the Open dialog box allows the selection of multiple files (you have set the `MultiSelect` property to True), the `FileNames` property contains the pathnames of all selected files. `FileNames` is a collection, and you can iterate through the filenames with an enumerator. This property should be used only with the OpenFileDialog control, even though the SaveFileDialog control exposes a `FileNames` property.

MULTISELECT

This property is a Boolean value that indicates whether the user can select multiple files in the dialog box. Its default value is False, and users can select a single file. When the `MultiSelect` property is True, the user can select multiple files, but they must all come from the same folder (you can't allow the selection of multiple files from different folders). This property is unique to the OpenFileDialog control. This and the following two properties are unique to the Open-FileDialog control.

READONLYCHECKED, SHOWREADONLY

The `ReadOnlyChecked` property is a Boolean value that indicates whether the Read-Only check box is selected when the dialog box first pops up (the user can clear this box to open a file in read/write mode). You can set this property to True only if the `ShowReadOnly` property is also set to True. The `ShowReadOnly` property is also a Boolean value that indicates whether the Read-Only check box is available. If this check box appears on the form, the user can select it so the file will be opened as read-only. Files opened as read-only shouldn't be saved with the same filename — always prompt the user for a new filename.

THE OPENFILE AND SAVEFILE METHODS

The OpenFileDialog control exposes the `OpenFile` method, which allows you to quickly open the selected file. Likewise, the SaveFileDialog control exposes the `SaveFile` method, which allows you to quickly save a document to the selected file. Normally, after retrieving the name of the file selected by the user, you must open this file for reading (in the case of the Open dialog box) or writing (in the case of the Save dialog box). The topic of reading from or writing to files is discussed in detail in the tutorial "Accessing Files and Folders with the System.IO Class," which is available for download at www.sybex.com/go/masteringvb2010.

When this method is applied to the Open dialog box, the file is opened with read-only permission. The same method can be applied to the SaveFile dialog box, in which case the file is opened with read-write permission. Both methods return a Stream object, and you can call this object's `Read` and `Write` methods to read from or write to the file.

VB 2010 AT WORK: MULTIPLE FILE SELECTION

The Open dialog box allows the selection of multiple files. This feature can come in handy when you want to process files en masse. You can let the user select many files, usually of the same type, and then process them one at a time. Or, you might want to prompt the user to select multiple files to be moved or copied.

To allow the user to select multiple files in the Open dialog box, set the `MultiSelect` property to True. The user can then select multiple files with the mouse by holding down the Shift or Ctrl key. The names of the selected files are reported by the property `FileNames`, which is an array of strings. The `FileNames` array contains the pathnames of all selected files, and you can iterate through them and process each file individually.

One of this chapter's sample projects is the MultipleFiles project, which demonstrates how to use the `FileNames` property. The application's form is shown in Figure 7.5. The button at the top of the form, Show Files in Folder, displays the Open dialog box, where you can select multiple files. After closing the dialog box by clicking the Open button on the Open dialog box, the application displays the pathnames of the selected files on a ListBox control.

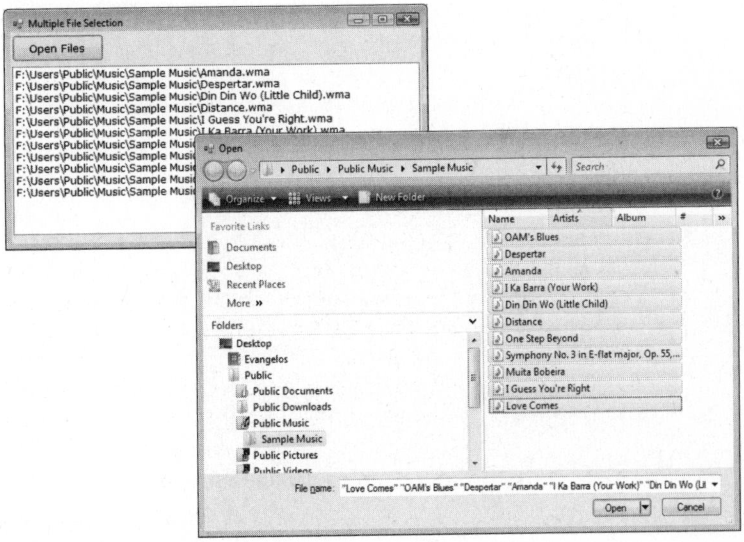

FIGURE 7.5
The MultipleFiles project lets the user select multiple files in the Open dialog box.

The code behind the Open Files button is shown in Listing 7.1. In this example, I used the array's enumerator to iterate through the elements of the `FileNames` array. You can use any of the methods discussed in Chapter 2, "VB Programming Essentials" to iterate through the array.

LISTING 7.1:   Processing multiple selected files

```
Private Sub bttnFile_Click(…) Handles bttnFile.Click
    OpenFileDialog1.Multiselect = True
    OpenFileDialog1.ShowDialog()
    Dim filesEnum As IEnumerator
    ListBox1.Items.Clear()
    filesEnum = OpenFileDialog1.FileNames.GetEnumerator()
    While filesEnum.MoveNext
        ListBox1.Items.Add(filesEnum.Current)
    End While
End Sub
```

The FolderBrowserDialog Control

Sometimes we need to prompt users for a folder rather than a filename. An application that processes files in batch mode shouldn't force users to select the files to be processed. Instead, it should allow users to select a folder and process all files of a specific type in the folder (it could encrypt all text documents or resize all image files, for example). As elaborate as the File Open dialog box might be, it doesn't allow the selection of a folder. To prompt users for a folder's path, use the FolderBrowser dialog box, which is a very simple one; it's shown in Figure 7.6. The FolderBrowserDialog control exposes a small number of properties, which are discussed next.

FIGURE 7.6
Selecting a folder via the FolderBrowser dialog box

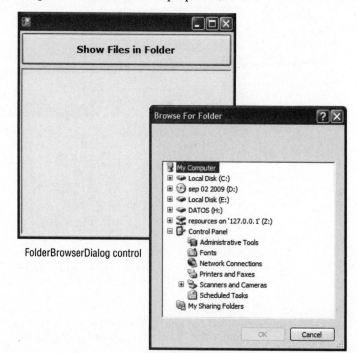

FolderBrowserDialog control

Resulting Browse For Folder dialog box

ROOTFOLDER

This property indicates the initial folder to be displayed when the dialog box is shown. It is not necessarily a string; it can also be a member of the `SpecialFolder` enumeration. To see the members of the enumeration, enter the following expression:

```
FolderBrowserDialog1.RootFolder =
```

As soon as you enter the equals sign, you will see the members of the enumeration. The most common setting for this property is My Computer, which represents the target computer's file system. You can set the `RootFolder` property to a number of special folders (for example, Personal, Desktop, ApplicationData, LocalApplicationData, and so on). You can also set this property to a string with the desired folder's pathname.

SELECTEDPATH

After the user closes the FolderBrowser dialog box by clicking the OK button, you can retrieve the name of the selected folder with the `SelectedPath` property, which is a string, and you can use it with the methods of the `System.IO` namespace to access and manipulate the selected folder's files and subfolders.

SHOWNEWFOLDERBUTTON

This property determines whether the dialog box will contain a New button; its default value is True. When users click the New button to create a new folder, the dialog box prompts them for the new folder's name and creates a new folder with the specified name under the selected folder.

VB 2010 AT WORK: FOLDER BROWSING DEMO PROJECT

The FolderBrowser control is a trivial control, but I'm including a sample application, available for download from www.sybex.com/go/masteringvb2010, to demonstrate its use. The same application demonstrates how to retrieve the files and subfolders of the selected folder and how to create a directory listing in a RichTextBox control, like the one shown in Figure 7.6. The members of the `System.IO` namespace, which allow you to access and manipulate files and folders from within your code, are discussed in detail in the tutorial "Accessing Files and Folders," which is available for download at www.sybex.com/go/masteringvb2010.

The FolderBrowser dialog box is set to display the entire file system of the target computer and is invoked with the following statements:

```
FolderBrowserDialog1.RootFolder = Environment.SpecialFolder.MyComputer
FolderBrowserDialog1.ShowNewFolderButton = False
If FolderBrowserDialog1.ShowDialog = DialogResult.OK Then
' process files in selected folder
End If
```

As usual, we examine the value returned by the `ShowDialog` method of the control and we proceed if the user has closed the dialog box by clicking the OK button. The code that iterates through the selected folder's files and subfolders, shown in Listing 7.2, is basically a demonstration of some members of the System.IO namespace, but I'll review it briefly here.

LISTING 7.2: Scanning a folder

```
Private Sub bttnSelectFiles_Click(…) Handles bttnSelectFiles.Click
    FolderBrowserDialog1.RootFolder =
                Environment.SpecialFolder.MyComputer
    FolderBrowserDialog1.ShowNewFolderButton = False
    If FolderBrowserDialog1.ShowDialog = Windows.Forms.DialogResult.OK Then
        RichTextBox1.Clear()
        ' Retrieve initial folder
        Dim initialFolder As String =
                FolderBrowserDialog1.SelectedPath
        Dim InitialDir As New IO.DirectoryInfo(
                FolderBrowserDialog1.SelectedPath)
        ' and print its name w/o any indentation
        PrintFolderName(InitialDir, "")
        ' and then print the files in the top folder
        If InitialDir.GetFiles("*.*").Length = 0 Then
            SwitchToItalics()
            RichTextBox1.AppendText(
                "folder contains no files" & vbCrLf)
            SwitchToRegular()
        Else
            PrintFileNames(InitialDir, "")
        End If
        Dim DI As IO.DirectoryInfo
        ' Iterate through every subfolder and print it
        For Each DI In InitialDir.GetDirectories
            PrintDirectory(DI)
        Next
    End If
End Sub
```

The selected folder's name is stored in the *initialFolder* variable and is passed as an argument to the constructor of the DirectoryInfo class. The *InitialDir* variable represents the specified folder. This object is passed to the PrintFolderName() subroutine, which prints the folder's name in bold. Then the code iterates through the same folder's files and prints them with the PrintFileNames() subroutine, which accepts as an argument the DirectoryInfo object that represents the current folder and the indentation level. After printing the initial folder's name and the names of the files in the folder, the code iterates through the subfolders of the initial folder. The GetDirectories method of the DirectoryInfo class returns a collection of objects, one for each subfolder under the folder represented by the *InitialDir* variable. For each subfolder, it calls the PrintDirectory() subroutine, which prints the folder's name and the files in this folder, and then iterates through the folder's subfolders. The code that iterates through the selected folder's files and subfolders is shown in Listing 7.3.

LISTING 7.3:   The `PrintDirectory()` subroutine

```
Private Sub PrintDirectory(ByVal CurrentDir As IO.DirectoryInfo)
    Static IndentationLevel As Integer = 0
    IndentationLevel += 1
    Dim indentationString As String = ""
    indentationString =
            New String(Convert.ToChar(vbTab), IndentationLevel)
    PrintFolderName(CurrentDir, indentationString)
    If CurrentDir.GetFiles("*.*").Length = 0 Then
        SwitchToItalics()
        RichTextBox1.AppendText(indentationString &
                "folder contains no files" & vbCrLf)
        SwitchToRegular()
    Else
        PrintFileNames(CurrentDir, indentationString)
    End If
    Dim folder As IO.DirectoryInfo
    For Each folder In CurrentDir.GetDirectories
        PrintDirectory(folder)
    Next
    IndentationLevel -= 1
End Sub
```

The code that iterates through the subfolders of a given folder is discussed in detail in the tutorial "Accessing Files and Folders," available for download from www.sybex.com /go/masteringvb2010, so you need not worry if you can't figure out how it works yet. In the following sections, you'll learn how to display formatted text in the RichTextBox control.

The RichTextBox Control

The RichTextBox control is the core of a full-blown word processor. It provides all the functionality of a TextBox control; it can handle multiple typefaces, sizes, and attributes and offers precise control over the margins of the text (see Figure 7.7). You can even place images in your text on a RichTextBox control (although you won't have the kind of control over the embedded images that you have with Microsoft Word).

The fundamental property of the RichTextBox control is its Rtf property. Similar to the Text property of the TextBox control, this property is the text displayed on the control. Unlike the Text property, however, which returns (or sets) the text of the control but doesn't contain formatting information, the Rtf property returns the text *along with* any formatting information.

Therefore, you can use the RichTextBox control to specify the text's formatting, including paragraph indentation, font, and font size or style.

RTF, which stands for *Rich Text format*, is a standard for storing formatting information along with the text. The beauty of the RichTextBox control for programmers is that they don't need to supply the formatting codes. The control provides simple properties to change the font of the selected text, change the alignment of the current paragraph, and so on. The RTF code is generated internally by the control and used to save and load formatted files. It's possible to create elaborately formatted documents without knowing the RTF specification.

The WordPad application that comes with Windows is based on the RichTextBox control. You can easily duplicate every bit of WordPad's functionality with the RichTextBox control, as you will see later in this chapter.

The RTF Language

A basic knowledge of the Rich Text format, its commands, and how it works will certainly help you understand the RichTextBox control's inner workings. RTF is a language that uses simple commands to specify the formatting of a document. These commands, or *tags*, are ASCII strings, such as \par (the tag that marks the beginning of a new paragraph) and \b (the tag that turns on the bold style). And this is where the value of the Rich Text format lies. RTF documents don't contain special characters and can be easily exchanged among different operating systems and computers, as long as there is an RTF-capable application to read the document.

RTF is similar to Hypertext Markup Language (HTML), and if you're familiar with HTML, a few comparisons between the two standards will provide helpful hints and insight into the RTF language. Like HTML, RTF was designed to create formatted documents that could be displayed on different systems. The following RTF segment displays a sentence with a few words in italic:

```
\bRTF\b0 (which stands for Rich Text Format) is a \i
document formatting language\i0 that uses simple
commands to specify the formatting of the document.
```

The following is the equivalent HTML code:

```
<b>RTF</b> (which stands for Rich Text Format) is a
<i>document formatting language</i> that uses simple
commands to specify the formatting of the document.
```

The <b> and <i> tags of HTML, for example, are equivalent to the \b and \i tags of RTF. The closing tags in RTF are \b0 and \i0, respectively.

Although you don't need to understand the RTF specifications to produce formatted text with the RichTextBox control, if you want to generate RTF documents from within your code, visit the RTF Cookbook site at `http://search.cpan.org/~sburke/RTF-Writer/lib/RTF/Cookbook.pod`. There's also a Microsoft resource on RTF at `http://msdn2.microsoft.com/en-us/library/aa140277(office.10).aspx`.

Text Manipulation and Formatting Properties

The RichTextBox control provides properties for manipulating the selected text on the control. The names of these properties start with the `Selection` or `Selected` prefix, and the most commonly used ones are shown in Table 7.1. Some of these properties are discussed in further detail in following sections.

TABLE 7.1:   RichTextBox properties for manipulating selected text

PROPERTY	WHAT IT MANIPULATES
SelectedText	The selected text
SelectedRtf	The RTF code of the selected text
SelectionStart	The position of the selected text's first character
SelectionLength	The length of the selected text
SelectionFont	The font of the selected text
SelectionColor	The color of the selected text
SelectionBackColor	The background color of the selected text
SelectionAlignment	The alignment of the selected text
SelectionIndent, SelectionRightIndent, SelectionHangingIndent	The indentation of the selected text
RightMargin	The distance of the text's right margin from the left edge of the control
SelectionTabs	An array of integers that sets the tab stop positions in the control
SelectionBullet	Whether the selected text is bulleted
BulletIndent	The amount of bullet indent for the selected text

SELECTEDTEXT

The `SelectedText` property represents the selected text, whether it was selected by the user via the mouse or from within your code. To assign the selected text to a variable, use the following statement:

```
selText=RichTextbox1.SelectedText
```

You can also modify the selected text by assigning a new value to the `SelectedText` property. The following statement converts the selected text to uppercase:

```
RichTextbox1.SelectedText =
              RichTextbox1.SelectedText.ToUpper
```

You can assign any string to the `SelectedText` property. If no text is selected at the time, the statement will insert the string at the location of the pointer.

SELECTIONSTART, SELECTIONLENGTH

To simplify the manipulation and formatting of the text on the control, two additional properties, `SelectionStart` and `SelectionLength`, report (or set) the position of the first selected character in the text and the length of the selection, respectively, regardless of the formatting of the selected text. One obvious use of these properties is to select (and highlight) some text on the control:

```
RichTextBox1.SelectionStart = 0
RichTextBox1.SelectionLength = 100
```

You can also use the `Select` method, which accepts as arguments the starting location and the length of the text to be selected.

SELECTIONALIGNMENT

Use this property to read or change the alignment of one or more paragraphs. This property's value is one of the members of the `HorizontalAlignment` enumeration: Left, Right, and Center. Users don't have to select an entire paragraph to align it; just placing the pointer anywhere in the paragraph will do the trick because you can't align part of the paragraph.

SELECTIONINDENT, SELECTIONRIGHTINDENT, SELECTIONHANGINGINDENT

These properties allow you to change the margins of individual paragraphs. The `Selection-Indent` property sets (or returns) the amount of the text's indentation from the left edge of the control. The `SelectionRightIndent` property sets (or returns) the amount of the text's indentation from the right edge of the control. The `SelectionHangingIndent` property indicates the indentation of each paragraph's first line with respect to the following lines of the same paragraph. All three properties are expressed in pixels.

The SelectionHangingIndent property includes the current setting of the SelectionIndent property. If all the lines of a paragraph are aligned to the left, the SelectionIndent property can have any value (this is the distance of all lines from the left edge of the control), but the SelectionHangingIndent property must be zero. If the first line of the paragraph is shorter than the following lines, the SelectionHangingIndent has a negative value. Figure 7.8 shows several differently formatted paragraphs. The settings of the SelectionIndent and Selection-HangingIndent properties are determined by the two sliders at the top of the form.

FIGURE 7.8
Various combinations of the SelectionIndent and SelectionHanging Indent properties produce all possible paragraph styles.

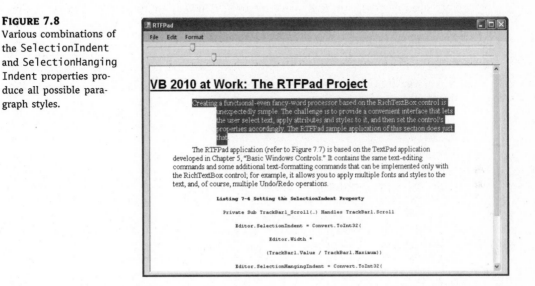

SELECTIONBULLET, BULLETINDENT

You use these properties to create a list of bulleted items. If you set the SelectionBullet property to True, the selected paragraphs are formatted with a bullet style, similar to the <ul> tag in HTML. To create a list of bulleted items, select them from within your code and assign the value True to the SelectionBullet property. To change a list of bulleted items back to normal text, make the same property False.

The paragraphs formatted as bullets are also indented from the left by a small amount. To set the amount of the indentation, use the BulletIndent property, which is also expressed in pixels.

SELECTIONTABS

Use this property to set the tab stops in the RichTextBox control. The Selection tab should be set to an array of integer values, which are the absolute tab positions in pixels. Use this property to set up a RichTextBox control for displaying tab-delimited data.

⊕ **Real World Scenario**

USING THE RICHTEXTBOX CONTROL TO DISPLAY DELIMITED DATA

As a developer I tend to favor the RichTextBox control over the TextBox control, even though I don't mix font styles or use the more-advanced features of the RichTextBox control. I suggest that you treat the RichTextBox control as an enhanced TextBox control and use it as a substitute for the TextBox control. One of the features of the RichTextBox control that I find very handy is its ability to set the tab positions and display tabular data. You can also display tabular data on a ListView control, as you will see later in the chapter, but it's simpler to use a RichTextBox control with its ReadOnly property set to True and its SelectionTabs property set to an array of values that will accommodate your data. Here's how to set up a RichTextBox control to display a few rows of tab-delimited data:

```
RichTextBox1.ReadOnly = True
RichTextBox1.SelectionTabs = New Integer() {100, 160, 340}
RichTextBox1.AppendText("R1C1" & vbTab &
          "R1C2" & vbTab &
          "R1C3" & vbCrLf)
RichTextBox1.AppendText("R2C1" & vbTab &
          "R2C2" & vbTab &
          "R2C3" & vbCrLf)
```

This technique is a lifesaver when I have to read the delimited data from a file. I just set up the tab positions and then load the data with the LoadFile method, which is discussed in the next section.

Methods

The first two methods of the RichTextBox control you need to know are SaveFile and LoadFile. The SaveFile method saves the contents of the control to a disk file, and the LoadFile method loads the control from a disk file.

SAVEFILE

The syntax of the SaveFile method is as follows, where *path* is the path of the file in which the current document will be saved:

```
RichTextBox1.SaveFile(path, filetype)
```

By default, the SaveFile method saves the document in RTF format and uses the .rtf extension. You can specify a different format by using the second optional argument, which can take on the value of one of the members of the RichTextBoxStreamType enumeration, described in Table 7.2.

LOADFILE

Similarly, the LoadFile method loads a text or RTF file to the control. Its syntax is identical to the syntax of the SaveFile method:

```
RichTextBox1.LoadFile(path, filetype)
```

TABLE 7.2: The `RichTextBoxStreamType` enumeration

FORMAT	EFFECT
PlainText	Stores the text on the control without any formatting
RichNoOLEObjs	Stores the text without any formatting and ignores any embedded OLE (Object Linking and Embedding) objects
RichText	Stores the text in RTF format (text with embedded RTF commands)
TextTextOLEObjs	Stores the text along with the embedded OLE objects
UnicodePlainText	Stores the text in Unicode format

The *filetype* argument is optional and can have one of the values of the `RichTextBox-StreamType` enumeration. Saving and loading files to and from disk files is as simple as presenting a Save or Open common dialog to the user and then calling one of the `SaveFile` or `LoadFile` methods with the filename returned by the common dialog box.

SELECT, SELECTALL

The `Select` method selects a section of the text on the control, similar to setting the `Selection-Start` and `SelectionLength` properties. The `Select` method accepts two arguments, the location of the first character to be selected and the length of the selection:

```
RichTextBox1.Select(start, length)
```

The `SelectAll` method accepts no arguments and it selects all the text on the control.

Advanced Editing Features

The RichTextBox control provides all the text-editing features you'd expect to find in a text-editing application, similar to the TextBox control. Among its more-advanced features, the RichTextBox control provides the `AutoWordSelection` property, which controls how the control selects text. If it's True, the control selects a word at a time.

In addition to formatted text, the RichTextBox control can handle object linking and embedding (OLE) objects. You can insert images in the text by pasting them with the `Paste` method. The `Paste` method doesn't require any arguments; it simply inserts the contents of the Clipboard at the current location (the location of the cursor) in the document.

Unlike the plain TextBox control, the RichTextBox control encapsulates undo and redo operations at multiple levels. Each operation has a name (Typing, Deletion, and so on), and you can retrieve the name of the next operation to be undone or redone and display it on the menu. Instead of a simple Undo or Redo caption, you can change the captions of the Edit menu to something like Undo Delete or Redo Typing. To program undo and redo operations from within your code, you must use the properties and methods discussed in the following sections.

CanUndo, CanRedo

These two properties are Boolean values you can read to find out whether there's an operation that can be undone or redone. If they're False, you must disable the corresponding menu command from within your code. The following statements disable the Undo command if there's no action to be undone at the time (EditUndo is the name of the Undo command on the Edit menu):

```
If RichTextBox1.CanUndo Then
    EditUndo.Enabled = True
Else
    EditUndo.Enabled = False
End If
```

These statements should appear in the menu item's Select event handler (not in the Click event handler) because they must be executed before the menu is displayed. The Select event is triggered when a menu is opened. As a reminder, the Click event is fired when you click an item and not when you open a menu. For more information on programming the events of a menu, see Chapter 6, "Working with Forms."

UndoActionName, RedoActionName

These two properties return the name of the action that can be undone or redone. The most common value of both properties is *Typing*, which indicates that the Undo command will delete a number of characters. Another common value is *Delete*, and some operations are named *Unknown*. If you change the indentation of a paragraph on the control, this action's name is *Unknown*. Even when an action's name is *Unknown* the action can be undone with the Undo method.

The following statement sets the caption of the Undo command to a string that indicates the action to be undone (*Editor* is the name of a RichTextBox control):

```
If Editor.CanUndo Then
    EditUndo.Text = "Undo " & Editor.UndoActionName
End If
```

Undo, Redo

These two methods undo or redo an action. The Undo method cancels the effects of the last action of the user on the control. The Redo method redoes the most recent undo action. The Redo method does not repeat the last action; it applies to undo operations only.

Cutting, Copying, and Pasting

To cut, copy, and paste text in the RichTextBox control, you can use the same techniques you use with the regular TextBox control. For example, you can replace the current selection by assigning a string to the SelectedText property. The RichTextBox, however, provides a few useful methods for performing these operations. The Copy, Cut, and Paste methods perform the corresponding operations. The Cut and Copy methods are straightforward and require no arguments. The Paste method accepts a single argument, which is the format of the data to be pasted. Because the data will come from the Clipboard, you can extract the format of the data in the Clipboard at the time and then call the `CanPaste` method to find out whether the control can handle this type of data. If so, you can then paste them in the control by using the `Paste` method.

This technique requires a bit of code because the Clipboard class doesn't return the format of the data in the Clipboard. You must call the following method of the Clipboard class to find out whether the data is of a specific type and then paste it on the control:

```
If Clipboard.GetDataObject.GetDataPresent(DataFormats.Text) Then
    RichTextBox1.Paste(DataFormats.GetFormat("Text")
End If
```

This is a very simple case because we know that the RichTextBox control can accept text. For a robust application, you must call the `GetDataPresent` method for each type of data your application should be able to handle. (You may not want to allow users to paste all types of data that the control can handle.) By the way, you can simplify the code with the help of the `ContainsText/ContainsImage` and `GetText/GetImage` methods of the My.Application.Clipboard object.

In the RTFPad project in this chapter, we'll use a structured exception handler to allow users to paste anything in the control. If the control can't handle it, the data won't be pasted in the control.

VB 2010 at Work: The RTFPad Project

Creating a functional — even fancy — word processor based on the RichTextBox control is unexpectedly simple. The challenge is to provide a convenient interface that lets the user select text, apply attributes and styles to it, and then set the control's properties accordingly. The RTFPad sample application of this section does just that. You can download a copy from www.sybex.com/go/masteringvb2010.

The RTFPad application (refer to Figure 7.7) is based on the TextPad application developed in Chapter 5, "Basic Windows Controls." It contains the same text-editing commands and some additional text-formatting commands that can be implemented only with the RichTextBox control; for example, it allows you to apply multiple fonts and styles to the text and, of course, multiple Undo/Redo operations.

The two TrackBar controls above the RichTextBox control manipulate the indentation of the text. We already explored this arrangement in the discussion of the TrackBar control in Chapter 5, but let's review the operation of the two controls again. Each TrackBar control has a width of 816 pixels, which is equivalent to 8.5 inches on a monitor that has a resolution of 96 dots per inch (dpi). The height of the TrackBar controls is 42 pixels, but unfortunately they can't be made smaller. The `Minimum` property of both controls is 0, and the `Maximum` property is 16. The `TickFrequency` is 1. With these values, you can adjust the indentation in steps of $\frac{1}{2}$ inch. Set the `Maximum` property to 32 and you'll be able to adjust the indentation in steps of $\frac{1}{4}$ inch. It's not the perfect interface, as it's built for A4 pages in portrait orientation only. You can experiment with this interface to build an even more functional word processor.

Each time the user slides the top TrackBar control, the code sets the `SelectionIndent` property to the proper percentage of the control's width. Because the `SelectionHangingIndent` includes the value of the `SelectionIndent` property, it also adjusts the setting of the `SelectionHangingIndent` property. Listing 7.4 is the code that's executed when the upper TrackBar control is scrolled.

LISTING 7.4:   Setting the `SelectionIndent` property

```
Private Sub TrackBar1_Scroll(…) Handles TrackBar1.Scroll
    Editor.SelectionIndent = Convert.ToInt32(Editor.Width *
                            (TrackBar1.Value / TrackBar1.Maximum))
    Editor.SelectionHangingIndent =
                            Convert.ToInt32(Editor.Width *
                            (TrackBar2.Value / TrackBar2.Maximum) -
                            Editor.SelectionIndent)
End Sub
```

Editor is the name of the RichTextBox control on the form. The code sets the control's indentation to the same percentage of the control's width, as indicated by the value of the top TrackBar control. It also does the same for the `SelectionHangingIndent` property, which is controlled by the lower TrackBar control. If the user has scrolled the lower TrackBar control, the code sets the RichTextBox control's `SelectionHangingIndent` property in the event handler, as presented in Listing 7.5.

LISTING 7.5:   Setting the `SelectionHangingIndent` property

```
Private Sub TrackBar2_Scroll(…) Handles TrackBar2.Scroll
    Editor.SelectionHangingIndent =
            Convert.ToInt32(Editor.Width *
            (TrackBar2.Value / TrackBar2.Maximum) -
            Editor.SelectionIndent)
End Sub
```

Enter a few lines of text in the control, select one or more paragraphs, and check out the operation of the two sliders.

The `Scroll` events of the two TrackBar controls adjust the text's indentation. The opposite action must take place when the user rests the pointer on another paragraph: The sliders' positions must be adjusted to reflect the indentation of the selected paragraph. The selection of a new paragraph is signaled to the application by the `SelectionChanged` event. The statements of Listing 7.6, which are executed from within the `SelectionChanged` event, adjust the two slider controls to reflect the indentation of the text.

LISTING 7.6:   Setting the slider controls

```
Private Sub Editor_SelectionChanged(…)
                    Handles Editor.SelectionChanged
    If Editor.SelectionIndent = Nothing Then
        TrackBar1.Value = TrackBar1.Minimum
        TrackBar2.Value = TrackBar2.Minimum
    Else
```

```
    TrackBar1.Value = Convert.ToInt32(
            Editor.SelectionIndent *
            TrackBar1.Maximum / Editor.Width)
    TrackBar2.Value = Convert.ToInt32( _
            (Editor.SelectionHangingIndent /
            Editor.Width) *
            TrackBar2.Maximum + TrackBar1.Value)
    End If
End Sub
```

If the user selects multiple paragraphs with different indentations, the `SelectionIndent`
property returns Nothing. The code examines the value of this property and, if it's Nothing,
moves both controls to the left edge. This way, the user can slide the controls and set the indentations for multiple paragraphs. Some applications make the handles gray to indicate that the
selected text doesn't have uniform indentation, but unfortunately you can't gray the sliders and
keep them enabled. Of course, you can always design a custom control. This wouldn't be a bad
idea, especially if you consider that the TrackBar controls are too tall for this type of interface
and can't be made very narrow (as a result, the interface of the RTFPad application isn't very
elegant).

THE FILE MENU

The RTFPad application's File menu contains the usual Open, Save, and Save As commands,
which are implemented with the control's `LoadFile` and `SaveFile` methods. Listing 7.7 shows
the implementation of the Open command in the File menu.

LISTING 7.7:   The Open command

```
Private Sub OpenToolStripMenuItem_Click(…) Handles
                    OpenToolStripMenuItem.Click
    If DiscardChanges() Then
        OpenFileDialog1.Filter =
            "RTF Files|*.RTF|DOC Files|*.DOC|" &
            "Text Files|*.TXT|All Files|*.*"
        If OpenFileDialog1.ShowDialog() =
                    DialogResult.OK Then
            fName = OpenFileDialog1.FileName
            Editor.LoadFile(fName)
            Editor.Modified = False
        End If
    End If
End Sub
```

The fName variable is declared on the form's level and holds the name of the currently open
file. This variable is set every time a new file is successfully opened, and it's used by the Save
command to automatically save the open file without prompting the user for a filename.

DiscardChanges() is a function that returns a Boolean value, depending on whether the control's contents can be discarded. The function examines the *Editor* control's Modified property. If True, it prompts users as to whether they want to discard the edits. Depending on the value of the Modified property and the user response, the function returns a Boolean value. If the DiscardChanges() function returns True, the program goes on and opens a new document. If the function returns False, the program aborts the operation to give the user a chance to save the document. Listing 7.8 shows the DiscardChanges() function.

LISTING 7.8: The DiscardChanges() function

```
Function DiscardChanges() As Boolean
    If Editor.Modified Then
        Dim reply As MsgBoxResult
        reply = MsgBox(
            "Text hasn't been saved. Discard changes?",
            MsgBoxStyle.YesNo)
        If reply = MsgBoxResult.No Then
            Return False
        Else
            Return True
        End If
    Else
        Return True
    End If
End Function
```

The Modified property becomes True after the first character is typed and isn't reset back to False. The RichTextBox control doesn't handle this property very intelligently and doesn't reset it to False even after saving the control's contents to a file. The application's code sets the Editor.Modified property to False after creating a new document as well as after saving the current document.

The Save As command (see Listing 7.9) prompts the user for a filename and then stores the *Editor* control's contents to the specified file. It also sets the *fName* variable to the file's path so that the Save command can use it.

LISTING 7.9: The Save As command

```
Private Sub SaveAsToolStripMenuItem_Click(…)
                Handles SaveAsToolStripMenuItem.Click
    SaveFileDialog1.Filter =
            "RTF Files|*.RTF|DOC Files" &
            "|*.DOC|Text Files|*.TXT|All Files|*.*"
    SaveFileDialog1.DefaultExt = "RTF"
    If SaveFileDialog1.ShowDialog() = DialogResult.OK Then
        fName = SaveFileDialog1.FileName
```

```
        Editor.SaveFile(fName)
        Editor.Modified = False
    End If
End Sub
```

The Save command's code is similar, only it doesn't prompt the user for a filename. It calls the SaveFile method, passing the *fName* variable as an argument. If the *fName* variable has no value (in other words, if a user attempts to save a new document by using the Save command), the code activates the event handler of the Save As command automatically and resets the control's Modified property to False. Listing 7.10 shows the code behind the Save command.

LISTING 7.10:   The Save command

```
Private Sub SaveToolStripMenuItem_Click(…)
                Handles SaveToolStripMenuItem.Click
    If fName <> "" Then
        Editor.SaveFile(fName)
        Editor.Modified = False
    Else
        SaveAsToolStripMenuItem_Click(sender, e)
    End If
End Sub
```

THE EDIT MENU

The Edit menu contains the usual commands for exchanging data through the Clipboard (Copy, Cut, Paste), Undo/Redo commands, and a Find command to invoke the Search & Replace dialog box. All the commands are almost trivial, thanks to the functionality built into the control. The basic Cut, Copy, and Paste commands call the RichTextBox control's Copy, Cut, and Paste methods to exchange data through the Clipboard. Listing 7.11 shows the implementation of the Paste command.

LISTING 7.11:   The Paste command

```
Private Sub PasteToolStripMenuItem_Click(…)
            Handles PasteToolStripMenuItem.Click
    Try
        Editor.Paste()
    Catch exc As Exception
        MsgBox(
            "Can't paste current clipboard's contents. " &
            "Try pasting the data in some other format.")
        End Try
    End Sub
```

As you may recall from the discussion of the Paste command, using the `CanPaste` method isn't trivial, you have to handle each data type differently. By using an exception handler, you allow the user to paste all types of data that the RichTextBox control can accept and display a message when an error occurs. Using exceptions for programming application logic can be quite costly, but in this case it's acceptable because the RTFPad editor is a desktop application serving a single user. A delay of a few milliseconds in this case should not make a huge difference.

For a more robust solution though, you might wish to handle each data type separately using the `CanPaste` method. That way, you can provide the user with much more precise feedback over the problem that caused the error; that is, the exact format of the data in the Clipboard they are trying to paste but the RichTextBox is not able to handle. That way you can save the user from having to guess the format your application can handle.

The Undo and Redo commands of the Edit menu are coded as follows. First, the name of the action to be undone or redone is displayed in the Edit menu. When the Edit menu is selected, the `DropDownOpened` event is fired. This event takes place before the `Click` event, so I inserted a few lines of code that read the name of the most recent action that can be undone or redone and print it next to the Undo or Redo command's caption. If there's no such action, the program will disable the corresponding command. Listing 7.12 is the code that's executed when the Edit menu is dropped.

LISTING 7.12:   Setting the captions of the Undo and Redo commands

```
Private Sub EditToolStripMenuItem_DropDownOpened(…) Handles
                EditToolStripMenuItem.DropDownOpened
    If Editor.UndoActionName <> "" Then
        UndoToolStripMenuItem.Text =
                    "Undo " & Editor.UndoActionName
        UndoToolStripMenuItem.Enabled = True
    Else
        UndoToolStripMenuItem.Text = "Undo"
        UndoToolStripMenuItem.Enabled = False
    End If
    If Editor.RedoActionName <> "" Then
        RedoToolStripMenuItem.Text =
                    "Redo" & Editor.RedoActionName
        RedoToolStripMenuItem.Enabled = True
    Else
        RedoToolStripMenuItem.Text = "Redo"
        RedoToolStripMenuItem.Enabled = False
    End If
End Sub
```

When the user selects one of the Undo or Redo commands, the code simply calls the appropriate method from within the menu item's `Click` event handler, as shown in Listing 7.13.

LISTING 7.13:   Undoing and redoing actions

```
Private Sub RedoToolStripMenuItem_Click(…) Handles
RedoToolStripMenuItem.Click
    If Editor.CanRedo Then Editor().Redo()
End Sub

Private Sub UndoToolStripMenuItem_Click(…) Handles
UndoToolStripMenuItem.Click
    If Editor.CanUndo Then Editor.Undo()
End Sub
```

Calling the CanUndo and CanRedo method is unnecessary; if the corresponding action can't be performed, the two menu items will be disabled, but an additional check does no harm.

THE FORMAT MENU

The commands of the Format menu control the alignment and the font attributes of the current selection. The Font command displays the Font dialog box and then assigns the font selected by the user to the current selection. Listing 7.14 shows the code behind the Font command.

LISTING 7.14:   The Font command

```
Private Sub FontToolStripMenuItem_Click(…) Handles
                    FontToolStripMenuItem.Click
    If Not Editor.SelectionFont Is Nothing Then
        FontDialog1.Font = Editor.SelectionFont
    Else
        FontDialog1.Font = Nothing
    End If
    FontDialog1.ShowApply = True
    If FontDialog1.ShowDialog() = DialogResult.OK Then
        Editor.SelectionFont = FontDialog1.Font
    End If
End Sub
```

Notice that the code preselects a font in the dialog box, the font of the current selection. If the current selection isn't formatted with a single font, no font is preselected.

To enable the Apply button of the Font dialog box, set the control's ShowApply property to True and insert the following statement in its Apply event handler:

```
Private Sub FontDialog1_Apply(...) Handles FontDialog1.Apply
    Editor.SelectionFont = FontDialog1.Font
    Editor.SelectionColor = FontDialog1.Color
End Sub
```

The options of the Align menu set the RichTextBox control's `SelectionAlignment` property to different members of the `HorizontalAlignment` enumeration. The Align ➢ Left command, for example, is implemented with the following statement:

```
Editor.SelectionAlignment = HorizontalAlignment.Left
```

THE SEARCH & REPLACE DIALOG BOX

The Find command in the Edit menu opens the dialog box shown in Figure 7.9, which performs search-and-replace operations (whole-word or case-sensitive match or both). The Search & Replace form (it's the *frmFind* form in the project) has its `TopMost` property set to True so that it remains visible while it's open, even if it doesn't have the focus. The code behind the buttons on this form is quite similar to the code for the Find & Replace dialog box of the TextPad application, with one basic difference: the RTFPad project's code uses the RichTextBox control's `Find` method; the simple TextBox control doesn't provide an equivalent method and we had to use the methods of the String class to perform the same operations. The `Find` method of the RichTextBox control performs all types of searches, and some of its options are not available with the `IndexOf` method of the String class.

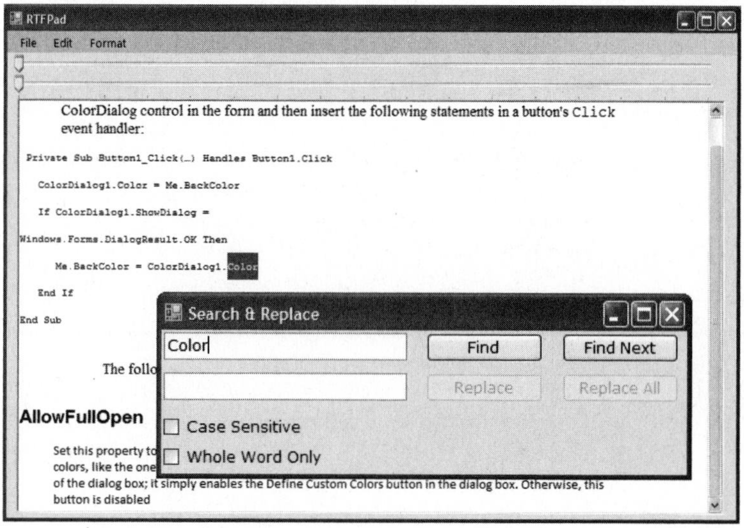

FIGURE 7.9
The Search & Replace dialog box of the RTFPad application

To invoke the Search & Replace dialog box, the code calls the `Show` method of the *frmFind* form, as discussed in Chapter 5, via the following statement:

```
frmFind.Show()
```

The `Find` method of the RichTextBox control allows you to perform case-sensitive or -insensitive searches as well as search for whole words only. These options are specified through an argument of the `RichTextBoxFinds` type. The `SetSearchMode()` function (see Listing 7.15) examines the settings of the two check boxes at the bottom of the form and sets the *mode* variable, which represents the `Find` method's search mode.

LISTING 7.15: Setting the search options

```
Function SetSearchMode() As RichTextBoxFinds
    Dim mode As RichTextBoxFinds =
                    RichTextBoxFinds.None
    If chkCase.Checked = True Then
        mode = mode Or RichTextBoxFinds.MatchCase
    End If
    If chkWord.Checked = True Then
        mode = mode Or RichTextBoxFinds.WholeWord
    End If
    Return mode
End Function
```

The Click event handlers of the Find and Find Next buttons call this function to retrieve the constant that determines the type of search specified by the user on the form. This value is then passed to the Find method. Listing 7.16 shows the code behind the Find and Find Next buttons.

LISTING 7.16: The Find and Find Next commands

```
Private Sub bttnFind_Click(…) Handles bttnFind.Click
    Dim wordAt As Integer
    Dim srchMode As RichTextBoxFinds
    srchMode = SetSearchMode()
    wordAt = frmEditor.Editor.Find(
                    txtSearchWord.Text, 0, srchMode)
    If wordAt = -1 Then
        MsgBox("Can't find word")
        Exit Sub
    End If
    frmEditor.Editor.Select(wordAt, txtSearchWord.Text.Length)
    bttnFindNext.Enabled = True
    bttnReplace.Enabled = True
    bttnReplaceAll.Enabled = True
    frmEditor.Editor.ScrollToCaret()
End Sub

Private Sub bttnFindNext_Click(…) Handles bttnFindNext.Click
    Dim selStart As Integer
    Dim srchMode As RichTextBoxFinds
    srchMode = SetSearchMode()
     selStart = frmEditor.Editor.Find(
                    txtSearchWord.Text,
                    frmEditor.Editor.SelectionStart + 2,
                    srchMode)
```

```
      If selStart = -1 Then
        MsgBox("No more matches")
        Exit Sub
      End If
      frmEditor.Editor.Select(
                selStart, txtSearchWord.Text.Length)
      frmEditor.Editor.ScrollToCaret()
  End Sub
```

Notice that both event handlers call the `ScrollToCaret` method to force the selected text to become visible — should the `Find` method locate the desired string outside the visible segment of the text.

The TreeView and ListView Controls

The TreeView and ListView controls are among the more advanced Windows controls and they certainly are more difficult to program than the others discussed. However, these two controls are the basic makings of unique user interfaces, as you will see in the examples in the following sections. The ListView and TreeView controls are discussed in detail in the tutorial "The ListView and TreeView controls," which is available for download from `www.sybex.com/go/masteringvb2010`. In this chapter, you will find an introduction to these two controls and their basic properties and methods. For more information on using these controls in your interface and interesting examples, please read the tutorial.

Figure 7.10 shows the TreeView and ListView controls used in tandem. What you see in Figure 7.10 is Windows Explorer, a utility for examining and navigating your hard disk's structure. The left pane, where the folders are displayed, is a TreeView control. The folder names are displayed in a manner that reflects their structure on the hard disk. You can expand and contract certain branches and view only the segment(s) of the tree structure you're interested in.

FIGURE 7.10
Windows Explorer is made up of a Tree-View (left pane) and a ListView (right pane) control.

The right pane is a ListView control. The items on the ListView control can be displayed in five ways (as large or small icons, as a list, on a grid, or tiled). They are the various views you can set through the View menu of Windows Explorer. Although most people prefer to look at the contents of the folders as icons, the most common view is the Details view, which displays not only filenames, but also their attributes. In the Details view, the list can be sorted according to any of its columns, making it easy for the user to locate any item based on various criteria (file type, size, creation date, and so on).

Tree and List Structures

The TreeView control implements a data structure known as a *tree*. A tree is the most appropriate structure for storing hierarchical information. The organizational chart of a company, for example, is a tree structure. Every person reports to another person above him or her, all the way to the president or CEO. Figure 7.11 depicts a possible organization of continents, countries, and cities as a tree. Every city belongs to a country, and every country to a continent. In the same way, every computer file belongs to a folder that may belong to an even bigger folder, and so on up to the drive level. You can't draw large tree structures on paper, but it's possible to create a similar structure in the computer's memory without size limitations.

FIGURE 7.11
The world viewed as a tree

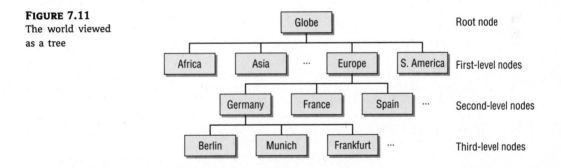

Each item in the tree of Figure 7.11 is called a *node,* and nodes can be nested to any level. Oddly, the top node is the *root* of the tree, and the subordinate nodes are called *child nodes.* If you try to visualize this structure as a real tree, think of it as an upside-down tree with the branches emerging from the root. The end nodes, which don't lead to any other nodes, are called *leaf nodes* or *end nodes.*

To locate a city, you must start at the root node and select the continent to which the city belongs. Then you must find the country (in the selected continent) to which the city belongs. Finally, you can find the city you're looking for. If it's not under the appropriate country node, it doesn't exist.

TREEVIEW ITEMS ARE JUST STRINGS

The items displayed on a TreeView control are just strings. Moreover, the TreeView control doesn't require that the items be unique. You can have identically named nodes in the same branch — as unlikely as this might be for a real application. There's no property that makes a node unique in the tree structure or even in its own branch.

You can also start with a city and find its country. The country node is the city node's *parent node*. Notice that there is only one route from child nodes to their parent nodes, which means that you can instantly locate the country or continent of a city. The data shown in Figure 7.11 is shown in Figure 7.12 in a TreeView control. Only the nodes we're interested in are expanded. The plus sign indicates that the corresponding node contains child nodes. To view them, end users click the button with the plus sign and expand the node.

FIGURE 7.12

The nodes shown in Figure 7.11 implemented with a TreeView control

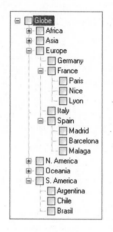

The tree structure is ideal for data with parent-child relations (relations that can be described as *belongs to* or *owns*). The continents-countries-cities data is a typical example. The folder structure on a hard disk is another typical example. Any given folder is the child of another folder or the root folder.

Maintaining a tree structure is a fundamental operation in software design; computer science students spend a good deal of their time implementing tree structures. Fortunately, with Visual Basic you don't have to implement tree structures on your own. The TreeView control is a mechanism for storing hierarchically structured data in a control with a visible interface. The TreeView control hides (or *encapsulates*, in object-oriented terminology) the details of the implementation and allows you to set up tree structures with a few lines of code — in short, all the gain without the pain (almost).

The ListView control implements a simpler structure, known as a *list*. A list's items aren't structured in a hierarchy; they are all on the same level and can be traversed serially, one after the other. You can also think of the list as a multidimensional array, but the list offers more features. A list item can have subitems and can be sorted according to any column. For example, you can set up a list of customer names (the list's items) and assign a number of subitems to each customer: a contact, an address, a phone number, and so on. Or you can set up a list of files with their attributes as subitems. Figure 7.13 shows a Windows folder mapped on a ListView control. Each file is an item, and its attributes are the subitems. As you already know, you can sort this list by filename, size, file type, and so on. All you have to do is click the header of the corresponding column.

The ListView control is a glorified ListBox control. If all you need is a control to store sorted objects, use a ListBox control. If you want more features, such as storing multiple items per row, sorting them in different ways, or locating them based on any subitem's value, you must consider the ListView control. You can also look at the ListView control as a view-only grid.

FIGURE 7.13
A folder's files displayed in a ListView control (Details view)

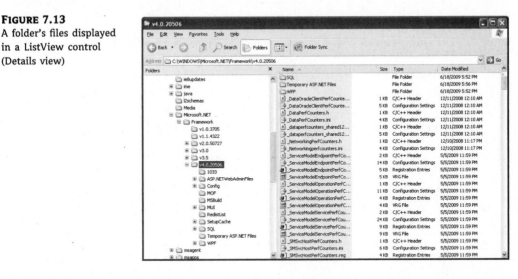

The TreeView and ListView controls are commonly used along with the ImageList control. The ImageList control is a simple control for storing images so they can be retrieved quickly and used at runtime. You populate the ImageList control with the images you want to use on your interface, usually at design time, and then you recall them by an index value at runtime.

The TreeView Control

Let's start our discussion of the TreeView control with a few simple properties that you can set at design time. To experiment with the properties discussed in this section, open the TreeViewDemo project, available for download from **www.sybex.com/go/masteringvb2010**. The project's main form is shown in Figure 7.14. After setting some properties (they are discussed next), run the project and click the Populate button to populate the control. After that, you can click the other buttons to see the effect of the various property settings on the control.

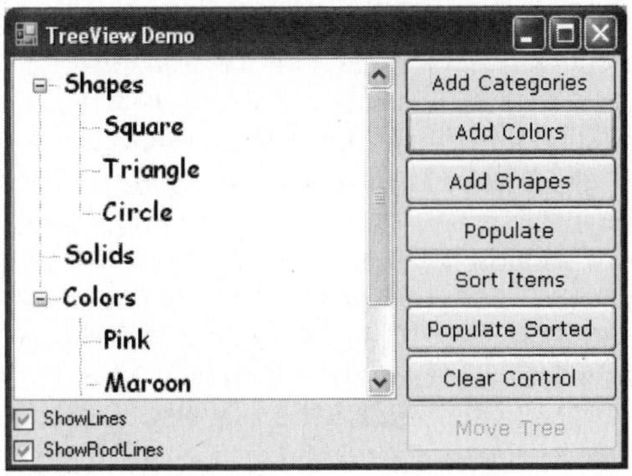

FIGURE 7.14
The TreeViewDemo project demonstrates the basic properties and methods of the Tree-View control.

Here are the basic properties that determine the appearance of the control:

CheckBoxes   If this property is True, a check box appears in front of each node. If the control displays check boxes, you can select multiple nodes; otherwise, you're limited to a single selection.

FullRowSelect   This True/False value determines whether a node will be selected even if the user clicks outside the node's caption.

HideSelection   This property determines whether the selected node will remain highlighted when the focus is moved to another control. By default, the selected node doesn't remain highlighted when the control loses the focus.

HotTracking   This property is another True/False value that determines whether nodes are highlighted as the pointer hovers over them. When it's True, the TreeView control behaves like a web document with the nodes acting as hyperlinks — they turn blue while the pointer hovers over them. Use the NodeMouseHover event to detect when the pointer hovers over a node.

Indent   This property specifies the indentation level in pixels. The same indentation applies to all levels of the tree — each level is indented by the same number of pixels with respect to its parent level.

PathSeparator   A node's full name is made up of the names of its parent nodes separated by a backslash. To use a different separator, set this property to the desired symbol.

ShowLines   The ShowLines property is a True/False value that determines whether the control's nodes will be connected to its parent items with lines. These lines help users visualize the hierarchy of nodes, and it's customary to display them.

ShowPlusMinus   The ShowPlusMinus property is a True/False value that determines whether the plus/minus button is shown next to the nodes that have children. The plus button is displayed when the node is collapsed, and it causes the node to expand when clicked. Likewise, the minus sign is displayed when the node is expanded, and it causes the node to collapse when clicked. Users can also expand the current node by pressing the left-arrow button and collapse it with the right-arrow button.

ShowRootLines   This is another True/False property that determines whether there will be lines between each node and root of the tree view. Experiment with the ShowLines and ShowRootLines properties to find out how they affect the appearance of the control.

Sorted   This property determines whether the items in the control will be automatically sorted. The control sorts each level of nodes separately. In our globe example, it will sort the continents, then the countries within each continent, and then the cities within each country.

ADDING NODES AT DESIGN TIME

Let's look now at the process of populating the TreeView control. Adding an initial collection of nodes to a TreeView control at design time is trivial. Locate the Nodes property in the Properties window, and you'll see that its value is Collection. To add items, click the ellipsis button, and the TreeNode Editor dialog box will appear, as shown in Figure 7.15. To add a root item, just click the Add Root button. The new item will be named Node0 by default. You can change its caption by selecting the item in the list and setting its Text property accordingly. You can also change the node's Name property, and you can change the node's appearance by using the NodeFont, FontColor, and ForeColor properties.

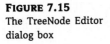

FIGURE 7.15
The TreeNode Editor
dialog box

Follow these steps to enter the root node with the string **Globe**, a child node for Europe, and two more nodes under Europe: Germany and Italy. I'm assuming that you're starting with a clean control. If your TreeView control contains any items, clear them all by selecting one item at a time in the list and pressing the Delete key, or click the delete button (the one with the X icon) on the dialog box.

Click the Add Root button first to add the node Node0. Select it with the mouse, and its properties appear in the right pane of the TreeNode Editor window. Here you can change the node's Text property to **Globe**. You can specify the appearance of each node by setting its font and fore/background colors.

Then click the Add Child button, which adds a new node under the **Globe** root node. Select it with the mouse as before, and change its Text property to **Europe**. Then select the newly added node in the list and click the Add Child button again. Name the new node **Germany**. You've successfully added a small hierarchy of nodes. To add another node under Europe, select the Europe node in the list and click the Add Child button again. Name the new item **Italy**. Continue adding a few cities under each country to complete the tree.

Click the OK button to close the TreeNode Editor's window and return to your form. The nodes you added to the TreeView control are there, but they're collapsed. Only the root nodes are displayed with the plus sign in front of their names. Click the plus sign to expand the tree and see its child nodes. The TreeView control behaves the same at design time as it does at runtime — as far as navigating the tree goes, at least.

ADDING NODES AT RUNTIME

Adding items to the control at runtime is a bit more involved. All the nodes belong to the control's Nodes collection, which is made up of TreeNode objects. To access the Nodes collection, use the following expression, where *TreeView1* is the control's name and Nodes is a collection of TreeNode objects:

```
TreeView1.Nodes
```

This expression returns a collection of TreeNode objects and exposes the proper members for accessing and manipulating the individual nodes. The control's **Nodes** property is the collection of all root nodes.

The following statements print the strings shown highlighted below them (these strings are not part of the statements; they're the output that the statements produce):

```
Debug.WriteLine(TreeView1.Nodes(0).Text)
Globe
Debug.WriteLine(TreeView1.Nodes(0).Nodes(0).Text)
Europe
Debug.WriteLine(TreeView1.Nodes(0).Nodes(0).Nodes(1).Text)
Italy
```

Adding New Nodes

To add a new node to the **Nodes** collection use the Add method, which accepts as an argument a string or a TreeNode object, and returns a TreeNode object that represents the newly added node. The simplest form of the Add method is

```
newNode = Nodes.Add(nodeCaption)
```

where *nodeCaption* is a string that will be displayed on the control. Another form of the Add method allows you to add a TreeNode object directly (*nodeObj* is a properly initialized Tree-Node variable):

```
newNode = Nodes.Add(nodeObj)
```

To use this form of the method, you must first declare and initialize a TreeNode object:

```
Dim nodeObj As New TreeNode
nodeObj.Text = "Tree Node"
nodeObj.ForeColor = Color.BlueViolet
TreeView1.Nodes.Add(nodeObj)
```

The last overloaded form of the Add method allows you to specify the index in the current **Nodes** collection, where the node will be added:

```
newNode = Nodes.Add(index, nodeObj)
```

The *nodeObj* TreeNode object must be initialized as usual.
To add a child node to the root node, use a statement such as the following:

```
TreeView1.Nodes(0).Nodes.Add("Asia")
```

To add a country under Asia, use a statement such as the following:

```
TreeView1.Nodes(0).Nodes(1).Nodes.Add("Japan")
```

The expressions can get quite lengthy. The proper way to add child items to a node is to create a TreeNode variable that represents the parent node, under which the child nodes will be added. Let's say that the *ContinentNode* variable in the following example represents the node Europe:

```
Dim ContinentNode As TreeNode
ContinentNode = TreeView1.Nodes(0).Nodes(2)
```

Then you can add child nodes to the *ContinentNode* node:

```
ContinentNode.Nodes.Add("France")
ContinentNode.Nodes.Add("Germany")
```

To add yet another level of nodes, the city nodes, create a new variable that represents a specific country. The Add method actually returns a TreeNode object that represents the newly added node, so you can add a country and a few cities by using statements such as the following:

```
Dim CountryNode As TreeNode
CountryNode = ContinentNode.Nodes.Add("Germany")
CountryNode.Nodes.Add("Berlin")
CountryNode.Nodes.Add("Frankfurt")
```

The ListView Control

The ListView control is similar to the ListBox control except that it can display its items in many forms, along with any number of subitems for each item. To use the ListView control in your project, place an instance of the control on a form and then set its basic properties, which are described in the following list:

View and Alignment Two properties determine how the various items will be displayed on the control: the View property, which determines the general appearance of the items, and the Alignment property, which determines the alignment of the items on the control's surface. The View property can have one of the values shown in Table 7.3.

TABLE 7.3:   View property settings

SETTING	DESCRIPTION
LargeIcon	(Default) Each item is represented by an icon and a caption below the icon.
SmallIcon	Each item is represented by a small icon and a caption that appears to the right of the icon.
List	Each item is represented by a caption.
Details	Each item is displayed in a column with its subitems in adjacent columns.
Tile	Each item is displayed with an icon and its subitems to the right of the icon. This view is available only on Windows XP and Windows Server 2003.

The Alignment property can have one of the settings shown in Table 7.4.

TABLE 7.4:   Alignment property settings

SETTING	DESCRIPTION
Default	When an item is moved on the control, the item remains where it is dropped.
Left	Items are aligned to the left side of the control.
SnapToGrid	Items are aligned to an invisible grid on the control. When the user moves an item, the item moves to the closest grid point on the control.
Top	Items are aligned to the top of the control.

HeaderStyle   This property determines the style of the headers in Details view. It has no meaning when the View property is set to anything else because only the Details view has columns. The possible settings of the HeaderStyle property are shown in Table 7.5.

TABLE 7.5:   HeaderStyle property settings

SETTING	DESCRIPTION
Clickable	Visible column header that responds to clicking
Nonclickable	(Default) Visible column header that does not respond to clicking
None	No visible column header

AllowColumnReorder   This property is a True/False value that determines whether the user can reorder the columns at runtime, and it's meaningful only in Details view. If this property is set to True, the user can move a column to a new location by dragging its header with the mouse and dropping it in the place of another column.

Activation   This property, which specifies how items are activated with the mouse, can have one of the values shown in Table 7.6.

TABLE 7.6:   Activation property settings

SETTING	DESCRIPTION
OneClick	Items are activated with a single click. When the cursor is over an item, it changes shape and the color of the item's text changes.
Standard	(Default) Items are activated with a double-click. No change in the selected item's text color takes place.
TwoClick	Items are activated with a double-click and their text changes color as well.

FullRowSelect   This property is a True/False value, indicating whether the user can select an entire row or just the item's text, and it's meaningful only in Details view. When this property is False, only the first item in the selected row is highlighted.

GridLines   Another True/False property. If it's True, grid lines between items and subitems are drawn. This property is meaningful only in Details view.

Groups   The items of the ListView control can be grouped into categories. To use this feature, you must first define the groups by using the control's **Groups** property, which is a collection of strings. You can add as many members to this collection as you want. After that, as you add items to the ListView control, you can specify the group to which they belong. The control will group the items of the same category together and display the group title above each group. You can easily move items between groups at runtime by setting the **Groups** property for the corresponding item to the name of the desired group.

LabelEdit   The **LabelEdit** property lets you specify whether the user will be allowed to edit the text of the items. The default value of this property is False. Notice that the **LabelEdit** property applies to the item's **Text** property only; you can't edit the subitems (unfortunately, you can't use the ListView control as an editable grid).

MultiSelect   A True/False value, indicating whether the user can select multiple items from the control. To select multiple items, click them with the mouse while holding down the Shift or Ctrl key. If the control's **ShowCheckboxes** property is set to True, users can select multiple items by marking the check box in front of the corresponding item(s).

Scrollable   A True/False value that determines whether the scroll bars are visible. Even if the scroll bars are invisible, users can still bring any item into view. All they have to do is select an item and then press the arrow keys as many times as needed to scroll the desired item into view.

Sorting   This property determines how the items will be sorted, and its setting can be None, Ascending, or Descending. To sort the items of the control, call the **Sort** method, which sorts the items according to their caption. It's also possible to sort the items according to any of their subitems, as explained later in this chapter.

THE COLUMNS COLLECTION

To display items in Details view, you must first set up the appropriate columns. The first column corresponds to the item's caption, and the following columns correspond to its subitems. If you don't set up at least one column, no items will be displayed in Details view. Conversely, the **Columns** collection is meaningful only when the ListView control is used in Details view.

The items of the **Columns** collection are of the ColumnHeader type. The simplest way to set up the appropriate columns is to do so at design time by using a visual tool. Locate and select the **Columns** property in the Properties window, and click the ellipsis button next to the property. The ColumnHeader Collection Editor dialog box, shown in Figure 7.16, will appear, and you can use it to add and edit the appropriate columns.

Adding columns to a ListView control and setting their properties through the dialog box shown in Figure 7.16 is quite simple. Don't forget to size the columns according to the data you anticipate storing in them and to set their headers. You can also add columns from within your code at runtime, a topic that's discussed in the tutorial "The ListView and TreeView Controls," available for download from www.sybex.com/go/masteringvb2010.

FIGURE 7.16
The ColumnHeader
Collection Editor
dialog box

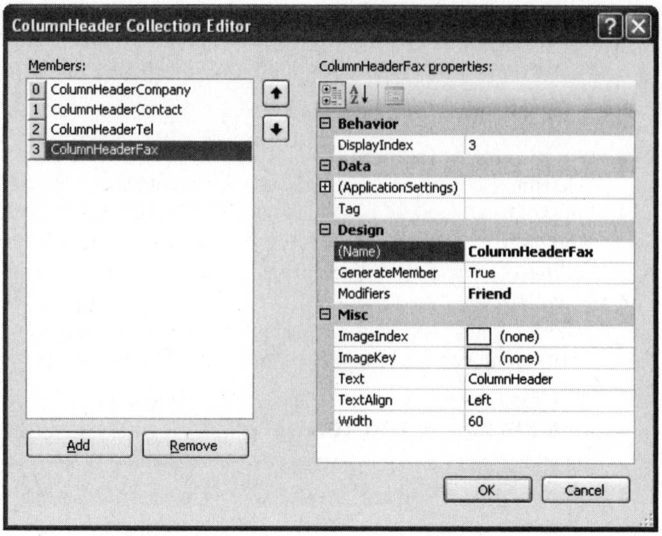

LISTVIEW ITEMS AND SUBITEMS

As with the TreeView control, the ListView control can be populated either at design time or at runtime. To add items at design time, click the ellipsis button next to the `ListItems` property in the Properties window. When the ListViewItem Collection Editor dialog box pops up, you can enter the items, including their subitems, as shown in Figure 7.17.

FIGURE 7.17
The ListViewItem
Collection Editor
dialog box

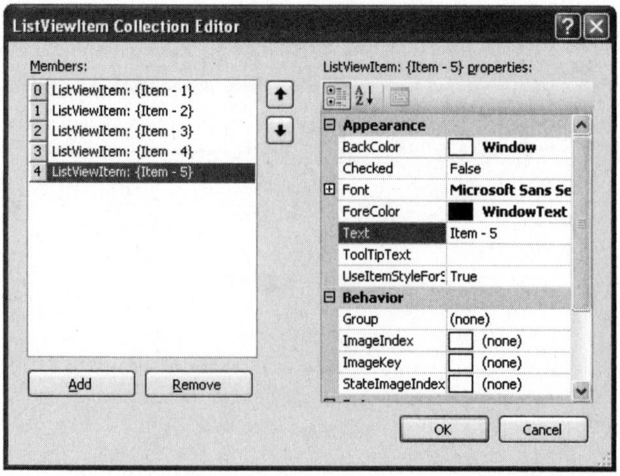

Click the Add button to add a new item. Each item has subitems, which you can specify as members of the `SubItems` collection. To add an item with three subitems, you must populate the item's `SubItems` collection with the appropriate elements. Click the ellipsis button next to the `SubItems` property in the ListViewItem Collection Editor; the ListViewSubItem Collection

Editor will appear. This dialog box is similar to the ListViewItem Collection Editor dialog box, and you can add each item's subitems. Assuming that you have added the item called Item 1 in the ListViewItem Collection Editor, you can add these subitems: *Item 1-a*, *Item 1-b*, and *Item 1-c*. The first subitem (the one with zero index) is actually the main item of the control.

Notice that you can set other properties such as the color and font for each item, the check box in front of the item that indicates whether the item is selected, and the image of the item. Use this window to experiment with the appearance of the control and the placement of the items, especially in Details view because subitems are visible only in this view. Even then, you won't see anything unless you specify headers for the columns. Note that you can add more subitems than there are columns in the control. Some of the subitems will remain invisible.

Unlike the TreeView control, the ListView control allows you to specify a different appearance for each item and each subitem. To set the appearance of the items, use the Font, Back-Color, and ForeColor properties of the ListViewItem object.

THE ITEMS COLLECTION

All the items on the ListView control form a collection: the Items collection. This collection exposes the typical members of a collection that let you manipulate the control's items. These members are discussed next.

Add method   This method adds a new item to the Items collection. The syntax of the Add method is as follows:

```
ListView1.Items.Add(caption)
```

You can also specify the index of the image to be used, along with the item and a collection of subitems to be appended to the new item, by using the following form of the Add method, where *imageIndex* is the index of the desired image on the associated ImageList control:

```
ListView1.Items.Add(caption, imageIndex)
```

Finally, you can create a ListViewItem object in your code and then add it to the ListView control by using the following form of the Add method:

```
ListView1.Items.Add(listItemObj)
```

The following statements create a new item, set its individual subitems, and then add the newly created ListViewItem object to the control:

```
Dim LItem As New ListViewItem
LItem.Text = "new item"
LItem.SubItems.Add("sub item 1a")
LItem.SubItems.Add("sub item 1b")
LItem.SubItems.Add("sub item 1c")
ListView1.Items.Add(LItem)
```

Count property   Returns the number of items in the collection.

Item property   Retrieves an item specified by an index value.

Clear method   Removes all the items from the collection.

Remove method   Removes an item from the collection.

THE SUBITEMS COLLECTION

Each item in the ListView control may have one or more subitems. You can think of the item as the key of a record and the subitems as the other fields of the record. The subitems are displayed only in Details mode, but they are available to your code in any view. For example, you can display all items as icons and, when the user clicks an icon, show the values of the selected item's subitems on other controls.

To access the subitems of a given item, use its SubItems collection. The following statements add an item and three subitems to the *ListView1* control:

```
Dim LItem As ListViewItem
LItem = ListView1.Items.Add("Alfred's Futterkiste")
LItem.SubItems.Add("Maria Anders")
LItem.SubItems.Add("030-0074321")
LItem.SubItems.Add("030-0076545")
```

To access the SubItems collection, you need a reference to the item to which the subitems belong. The Add method returns a reference to the newly added item, the *LItem* variable, which is then used to access the item's subitems, as shown in the preceding code segment.

Displaying the subitems on the control requires some overhead. Subitems are displayed only in Details view mode. However, setting the View property to Details is not enough. You must first create the columns of the Details view, as explained earlier. The ListView control displays only as many subitems as there are columns in the control. The first column, with the header Company, displays the items of the list. The following columns display the subitems. Moreover, you can't specify which subitem will be displayed under each header. The first subitem (Maria Anders in the preceding example) will be displayed under the second header, the second subitem (030-0074321 in the same example) will be displayed under the third header, and so on. At runtime, the user can rearrange the columns by dragging them with the mouse. To disable the rearrangement of the columns at runtime, set the control's AllowColumnReorder property to False (its default value is True).

Unless you set up each column's width, they will all have the same width. The width of individual columns is specified in pixels, and you can set it to a percentage of the total width of the control, especially if the control is docked to the form. The following code sets up a ListView control with four headers, all having the same width:

```
Dim LWidth = ListView1.Width - 5
Dim headers =
    {
        New ColumnHeader() With {.Text = "Company", .Width = LWidth / 4},
        New ColumnHeader() With {.Text = "Contact", .Width = LWidth / 4},
        New ColumnHeader() With {.Text = "Phone", .Width = LWidth / 4},
        New ColumnHeader() With {.Text = "Fax", .Width = LWidth / 4}
    }
ListView1.Columns.AddRange(headers)
ListView1.View = View.Details
```

The first header corresponds to the item (not a subitem). The number of headers you set up must be equal to the number of subitems you want to display on the control, plus one. The constant 5 is subtracted to compensate for the width of the column separators. If the control is anchored to the vertical edges of the form, you must execute these statements from within the form's Resize event handler so that the columns are resized automatically as the control is resized.

You can also sort a ListView control with the Sort method, which sorts the list's items, and the Sorting property, which determines how the items will be sorted. For more information on sorting the control's items, see the tutorial "The ListView and TreeView Controls," available for download from www.sybex.com/go/masteringvb2010.

PROCESSING SELECTED ITEMS

The user can select multiple items from a ListView control by default. Even though you can display a check mark in front of each item, it's not customary. Multiple items in a ListView control are selected with the mouse while holding down the Ctrl or Shift key.

The selected items form the SelectedListItemCollection collection, which is a property of the control. You can iterate through this collection with a For … Next loop or through the enumerator object exposed by the collection. Listing 7.17 is the code behind the Selected Items button of the ListViewDemo project. It goes through the selected items with a For Each … Next loop and displays each one of them, along with its subitems, in the Output window. Notice that you can select multiple items in any view, even when the subitems are not visible. They're still there, however, and they can be retrieved through the SubItems collection.

LISTING 7.17:   Iterating the selected items on a ListView control

```
Private Sub bttnIterate_Click(…) Handles bttnIterate.Click
    Dim LItem As ListViewItem
    Dim LItems As ListView.SelectedListViewItemCollection
    LItems = ListView1.SelectedItems
    For Each LItem In LItems
        Debug.Write(LItem.Text & vbTab)
        Debug.Write(LItem.SubItems(0).ToString & vbTab)
        Debug.Write(LItem.SubItems(1).ToString & vbTab)
        Debug.WriteLine(LItem.SubItems(2).ToString & vbTab)
    Next
End Sub
```

VB 2010 at Work: The CustomExplorer Project

To demonstrate how to use the ListView and TreeView controls in tandem, which is how they commonly used, see the discussion of the CustomExplorer sample application, which is discussed in the tutorial "The ListView and TreeView controls." It's a fairly advanced example, but I included it for the most ambitious readers. It can also be used as the starting point for many custom applications, so give it a try.

The CustomExplorer project, shown in Figure 7.18, displays a structured list of folders in the left pane and the files in the selected folder in the right pane. The left pane is populated when the application starts. You can expand any folder in this pane and view its subfolders. To view the files in a folder, click the folder name and the right pane will be populated with the names of the selected folder's files along with other data, such as the file size, date of creation, and date of last modification.

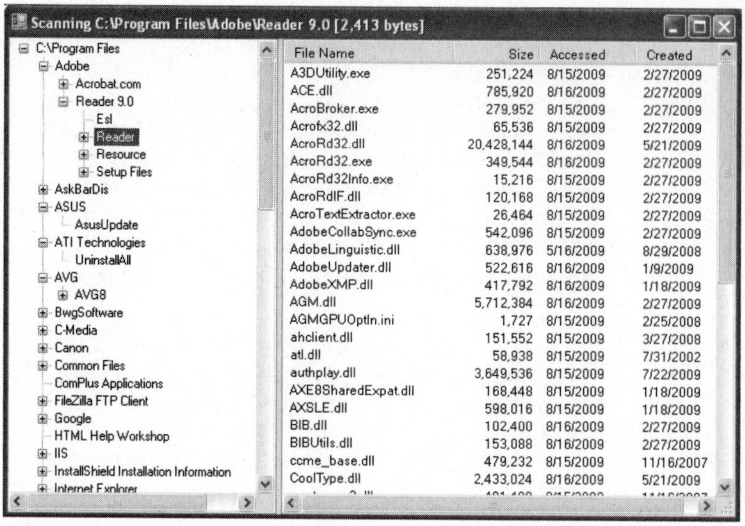

FIGURE 7.18
The CustomExplorer
project demonstrates
how to combine
a TreeView and a
ListView control on the
same form.

The CustomExplorer project is not limited to displaying folders and files; you can populate the two controls with data from several sources. For example, you can display customers in the left pane (and organize them by city or state) and display their related data, such as invoices and payments, in the right pane. Or you can populate the left pane with product names and the right pane with the respective sales. In general, you can use the project as an interface for many types of applications. You can even use it as a custom Explorer to add features that are specific to your applications.

The Bottom Line

Use the OpenFileDialog and SaveFileDialog controls to prompt users for filenames.
Windows applications use certain controls to prompt users for common information, such as filenames, colors, and fonts. Visual Studio provides a set of controls that are grouped in the Dialogs section of the Toolbox. All common dialog controls provide a ShowDialog method, which displays the corresponding dialog box in a modal way. The ShowDialog method returns a value of the DialogResult type, which indicates how the dialog box was closed, and you should examine this value before processing the data.

Master It Your application needs to open an existing file. How will you prompt users for the file's name?

Master It You're developing an application that encrypts multiple files (or resizes many images) in batch mode. How will you prompt the user for the files to be processed?

Use the ColorDialog and FontDialog controls to prompt users for colors and typefaces. The Color and Font dialog boxes allow you to prompt users for a color value and a font, respectively. Before showing the corresponding dialog box, set its Color or Font property according to the current selection, and then call the control's ShowDialog method.

Master It How will you display color attributes in the Color dialog box when you open it? How will you display the attributes of the selected text's font in the Font dialog box when you open it?

Use the RichTextBox control as an advanced text editor to present richly formatted text. The RichTextBox control is an enhanced TextBox control that can display multiple fonts and styles, format paragraphs with different styles, and provide a few more-advanced text-editing features. Even if you don't need the formatting features of this control, you can use it as an alternative to the TextBox control. At the very least, the RichTextBox control provides more editing features, a more-useful undo function, and more-flexible search features.

Master It You want to display a document with a title in large, bold type, followed by a couple of items in regular style. Which statements will you use to create a document like this on a RichTextBox control?

Document's Title

Item 1 Description for item 1

Item 2 Description for item 2

Create and present hierarchical lists by using the TreeView control. The TreeView control is used to display a list of hierarchically structured items. Each item in the TreeView control is represented by a TreeNode object. To access the nodes of the TreeView control, use the `TreeView.Nodes` collection. The nodes under a specific node (in other words, the child nodes) form another collection of Node objects, which you can access by using the expression `Tree-View.Nodes(i).Nodes`. The basic property of the Node object is the `Text` property, which stores the node's caption. The Node object exposes properties for manipulating its appearance (its foreground/background color, its font, and so on).

Master It How will you set up a TreeView control with a book's contents at design time?

Create and present lists of structured items by using the ListView control. The ListView control stores a collection of ListViewItem objects, which form the Items collection, and can display them in several modes, as specified by the `View` property. Each ListViewItem object has a `Text` property and the SubItems collection. The subitems are not visible at runtime unless you set the control's `View` property to Details and set up the control's Columns collection. There must be a column for each subitem you want to display on the control.

Master It How will you set up a ListView control with three columns to display names, email addresses, and phone numbers at design time?

Master It How would you populate the same control with the same data at runtime?

Part 3

Working with Custom Classes and Controls

Chapter 8

Working with Objects

Classes are practically synonymous with objects and they're at the very heart of programming with Visual Basic. The controls you use to build the visible interface of your application are objects, and the process of designing forms consists of setting the properties of these objects, mostly with point-and-click operations. The Framework itself is an enormous compendium of classes, and you can import any of them into your applications and use them as if their members were part of the language. You simply declare a variable of the specific class type, initialize it, and then use it in your code.

Controls are also objects; they differ from other classes in that controls provide a visual interface, whereas object variables don't. However, you manipulate all objects by setting their properties and calling their methods.

In this chapter, you'll learn how to do the following:

◆ Build your own classes

◆ Use custom classes in your projects

◆ Customize the usual operators for your classes

Classes and Objects

When you create a variable of any type, you're creating an instance of a class. The variable lets you access the functionality of the class through its properties and methods. Even base data types are implemented as classes (the System.Integer class, System.Double, and so on). An integer value, such as 3, is an instance of the System.Integer class, and you can call the properties and methods of this class by using its instance. Expressions such as `Convert.ToDecimal(3).MinValue` and `#1/1/2000#.Today` are odd but valid. The first expression returns the minimum value you can represent with the Decimal data type, whereas the second expression returns the current date. The DataTime data type exposes the Today property, which returns the current date. The expression `#1/1/2000#` is a value of the DataTime type, so you can find out the current date by calling its Today property. If you enter either one of the preceding expressions in your code, you'll get a warning, but they will be executed.

Classes are used routinely in developing applications, and you should get into the habit of creating and using custom classes, even with simple projects. In team development, classes are a necessity because they allow developers to share their work easily. If you're working in a corporate environment, where different programmers code different parts of an application, you can't afford to repeat work that someone else has already done. You should be able to get their code and use it in your application as is. That's easier said than done because you can guess what will happen as soon as a small group of programmers start sharing code — they'll end up with dozens of different versions for each function, and every time a developer upgrades a function, they will most likely break the applications that were working with the old version. Or each time they revise a function, they must update all the projects by using the old version of the function and test them. It just doesn't work.

The major driving force behind *object-oriented programming (OOP)* is *code reuse.* Classes allow you to write code that can be reused in multiple projects. You already know that classes don't expose their source code. The Framework itself is a huge collection of classes, which you can use without ever seeing its source code. As you'll learn in Chapter 10, "Applied Object-Oriented Programming," you can even expand the functionality of an existing class without having access to its code. In other words, you can use a class without having access to its code, and therefore you can't affect any other projects that use the class. You also know that classes implement complicated operations and make these operations available to programmers through properties and methods. The Array class, for example, exposes a Sort method, which sorts its elements. This is not a simple operation, but fortunately you don't have to know anything about sorting. Someone else has done it for you and made this functionality available to your applications. This is called *encapsulation.* Some functionality has been built into the class (or *encapsulated* into the class), and you can access it from within your applications by using a simple method call. The System.Security.Cryptography class of the Framework (which isn't discussed in this book) provides all the functionality you need to encrypt a secret code, or an entire document, by calling a method. Encryption is a very complicated operation, but you don't have to know anything about it except how to call the appropriate method and pass a secret key to it.

What Is a Class?

A class can be thought of as a program that doesn't run on its own; it's a collection of properties and methods that must be used by another application. We exploit the functionality of the class by creating a variable of the same type as the class and then calling the class's properties and methods through this variable. The methods and properties of the class, as well as its events, constitute the class's interface. It's not a visible interface, like the ones you've learned to design so far, because the class doesn't interact directly with the user. To interact with the class, the application uses the class's interface, just as users will be interacting with your application through its visual interface.

You have already learned how to use classes. Now is the time to understand what goes on behind the scenes when you interact with a class and its members. Every object is an instance of a class. When you declare an array, a Color object, or a collection, some code is executed in the background to create the variable. It's the code that actually implements the class. When you declare an array, you're invoking the System.Array class, which contains all the code for manipulating arrays (the method to sort the array's elements, another method to reverse the order of the elements in the array, and so on). Even simple variables of the Integer or String type are implemented as classes.

The first time you use an object in your code, you're instantiating the class that implements it. The class's code is loaded into memory, initializes its variables, and is ready to execute. The image of the class in memory is said to be an instance of the class, and this is an object.

CLASSES VERSUS OBJECTS

Two of the most misused terms in OOP are *object* and *class*, and most people use them interchangeably. You should think of the class as the template for the object. There's only one System.Array class, but you can declare any number of arrays in your code. Every array is an instance of the System.Array class. All arrays in an application are implemented by the same code, but they store different data. Each instance of a class is nothing more than a set of variables: The same code acts on different sets of variables, and each set of variables is a separate and distinct instance of the class.

Consider three TextBox controls on the same form. They are all instances of the System.Windows.Forms.TextBox class, but changing any property of a TextBox control doesn't affect the other two controls. Every time you set the Text property of a TextBox control, you're modifying a variable of a specific instance of the TextBox class. Classes are the blueprints on which objects are based. You can use the same blueprint to build multiple buildings with the same structural characteristics but apply different properties (wall colors, doors, and so on) to individualize each structure.

Objects are similar to Windows controls except that they don't have a visible interface. Controls are instantiated when the form loads. To use a control, you make it part of the project by adding its icon to the Toolbox, if it's not already there. To manipulate a control from within your code, you call its properties and methods. You do the same with classes. To use a class, first declare it, then instantiate it (most commonly by using a New statement), then use its properties and methods. Finally, you program the various events raised by the controls to interact with the users of your applications. Most classes don't expose any events because the user can't interact with them, but some classes do raise events, which you can program just as you program the events of Windows controls.

At the beginning of this section I mentioned that classes can be thought of as "programs that can't be executed on their own." This is an oversimplification, which I can remedy now. Classes are made up of code, not visual elements, and are used as templates for objects. For example, there's a single System.Array class and this class is invoked every time you create an array in your code. The arrays you declare in your code are instances of the class. Yet, there's only one class that implements arrays and all arrays are "serviced" by the same class.

Classes Combine Code with Data

Another way to view classes is to understand how they combine code and data. This simple idea is the very essence of object-oriented programming. Data is data, and procedural languages allow you to manipulate data in any way. Meaningful data, however, is processed in specific ways.

Let's consider accounting data. You can add or subtract amounts to or from an account, sum similar accounts (such as training and travel expenses), calculate taxes on certain account amounts, and the like. Other types of processing may not be valid for this type of data. You never multiply the amounts from two different accounts or calculate logarithms of account balances. These types of processing are quite meaningful with different data, but not with accounting data.

Because the nature of the data itself determines to a large extent the type of processing that will take place on the data, why not "package" the data along with the code for processing it?

Instead of simply creating structures for storing our data, we also write the code to process them. The data and the code are implemented in a single unit, a class, and the result is an object. After the class has been built, we no longer write code for processing the data; we simply create objects of this type and call their methods. To transfer an amount from one account to another, we call a method that knows how to transfer the amount, and the same method also makes sure the amount isn't subtracted from one account unless it has been added to the other account (and vice versa). By the way, the process of completing multiple operations in a single step or canceling all the operations if one of them fails is known as a transaction. A transaction will not subtract an amount from one account unless it has added the same amount to another account, and it won't credit an account without debiting another one by the same amount. You'll learn more about transactions later in this book, when we'll explore database programming.

To better understand how classes combine code with data, let's take a close look at a class we're all too familiar with, the Array class. The role of the array is to store sets of data. In addition to holding data, the Array class also knows how to process data: how to retrieve an element, how to extract a segment of the array, and even how to sort its elements. All these operations require a substantial amount of code. The mechanics of storing data in the array, the code that implements the properties, and the methods of the array are hidden from you, the developer. You can instruct the array to perform certain tasks by using simple statements. When you call the Sort method, you're telling the array to execute some code that will sort its elements. As a developer, you don't know how the data are stored in the array or how the Sort method works. An overloaded form of the method allows you to sort a segment of the array by specifying the index of the first and last elements to be sorted. All you have to know is how to call the Sort method, not how it works. Classes abstract many operations by hiding the implementation details; developers manipulate arrays by calling methods. And you certainly can't access the code of the class and edit it to accommodate the requirements of a specific application.

With LINQ, a new technology for querying collections that was introduced with version 3.5 of the Framework, the Array class was enhanced with a few new methods, like the Sum method that calculates the sum of the elements in a numeric array and the Select method that allows you to select elements that meet certain criteria, and a few more. You'll learn a lot more about these methods (they're called extension methods) in Chapter 14, "An Introduction to LINQ." Although this is something you'll understand better in Chapter 14, let me just mention that the team that implemented LINQ did not have access to the source of the Array class!

In the following sections, you'll learn how data and code coexist in a class and how you can manipulate the data through the properties and methods exposed by the class. In Chapter 3, "Visual Basic Programming Essentials," you learned how to create structures to store data. Classes are similar to structures in that they represent custom data structures. In this chapter, I'll take the idea of defining custom data structures one step further, by adding properties and methods for manipulating the custom data, something you can't do with structures. Let's start by building a custom class and then using it in an application.

Building the Minimal Class

My first example is the Minimal class; I'll start with the minimum functionality class and keep adding features to it. The name of the class can be anything — just make sure that it's suggestive of the class's functionality.

A class may reside in the same file as a form, but it's customary to implement custom classes in a separate module, a Class module. You can also create a Class project, which contains one or more classes. However, a class doesn't run on its own and you can't test it without

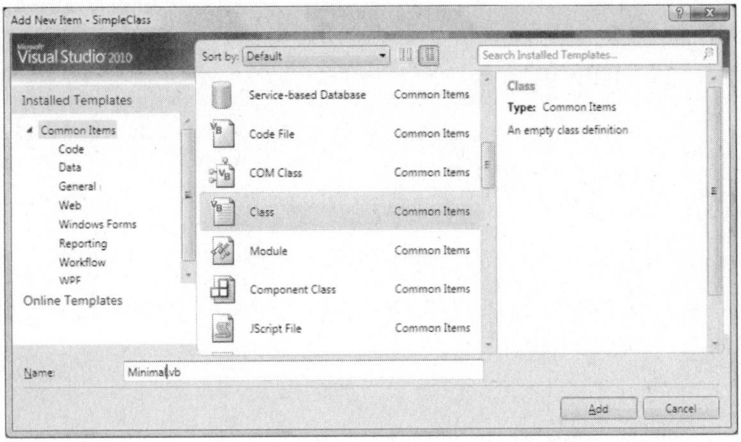

FIGURE 8.1
Adding a class item
to a project

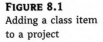

a form. Start a new Windows project and name it **SimpleClass** (or open the SimpleClass sample project available for download from www.sybex.com/go/masteringvb2010). Then create a new class by adding a Class component to your project. Right-click the project name in the Solution Explorer window and choose Add ➤ Class from the context menu. In the dialog box that pops up, select the Class item and enter a name for the class. Set the class's name to **Minimal**, as shown in Figure 8.1.

The sample project contains a main form, as usual, the Form1 form. The code that implements the class resides in the `Minimal.vb` file, which is part of the project, and you'll use the project's main form to test your class. After you have tested and finalized the class code, you no longer need the form and you can remove it from the project.

When you open the class by double-clicking its icon in the Project Explorer window, you will see the following lines in the code window:

```
Public Class Minimal

End Class
```

If you'd rather create a class in the same file as the application's form, enter the `Class` keyword followed by the name of the class after the existing `End Class` in the form's code window. The editor will insert the matching `End Class` for you. Insert a class definition in the form's code window if the class is specific to this form only and no other part of the application will use it. At this point, you already have a class, even if it doesn't do anything.

Switch back to the Form Designer, add a button to the test form, and insert the following code in its `Click` event handler:

```
Dim obj1 As Minimal
```

Press Enter and type the name of the variable, `obj1`, followed by a period, on the following line. will see a list of the methods your class exposes already:

```
Equals
GetHashCode
```

```
GetType
ReferenceEqual
ToString
```

If you don't see all of these members, switch to the All Members tab of the IntelliSense drop-down box.

These methods are provided by the Common Language Runtime (CLR), and you don't have to implement them on your own (although you will probably have to provide a new, nongeneric implementation for some of them). They don't expose any real functionality; they simply reflect the way VB handles all classes. To see the kind of functionality that these methods expose, enter the following lines in the Button's Click event handler and then run the application:

```
Dim obj1 As New Minimal
Debug.WriteLine(obj1.ToString)
Debug.WriteLine(obj1.GetType)
Debug.WriteLine(obj1.GetHashCode)
Dim obj2 As New Minimal
Debug.WriteLine(obj1.Equals(obj2))
Debug.WriteLine(Minimal.ReferenceEquals(obj1, obj2))
```

The following lines will be printed in the Immediate window:

```
SimpleClass.Minimal
SimpleClass.Minimal
18796293
False
False
```

The name of the object is the same as its type, which is all the information about your new class that's available to the CLR. Shortly you'll see how you can implement your own ToString method and return a more-meaningful string. The hash value of the *obj1* variable is an integer value that uniquely identifies the object variable in the context of the current application. (It happens to be 18796293, but the actual value is of no consequence for our discussion. It's a standard member, but it's good to know that the functionality is built into the control.)

The next line tells you that two variables of the same type are not equal. But why aren't they equal? We haven't differentiated them at all, yet they're different because they point to two different objects, and the compiler doesn't know how to compare them. All it can do is figure out whether the variables point to the same object. If you want to understand how objects are compared, add the following statement after the line that declares *obj2*:

```
obj2 = obj1
```

When you run the application again, the last two statements will display True in the Output window. The Equals method compares the two objects and returns a True/False value. Because you haven't told the class how to compare two instances of the class yet, it compares their references, just as the ReferenceEquals method does. The ReferenceEquals method checks for reference equality; that is, it returns True if both variables point to the same object (the same instance of the class). If you change a property of the *obj1* variable, the changes will affect *obj2* as well, because both variables point to the same object. We can't modify the object because it doesn't expose any members that we can set to differentiate it from another object of the same type. We'll get to that shortly.

Most classes expose a custom Equals method, which knows how to compare two objects of the same type (two objects based on the same class). The custom Equals method usually compares the properties of the two instances of the class and returns True if a set of basic properties (or all of them) are the same. You'll learn how to customize the default members of any class later in this chapter.

Notice the full name of the class: SimpleClass.Minimal. Within the current project, you can access it as Minimal. Other projects can either import the Minimal class and access it as Minimal or specify the complete name of the class, which is the name of the project it belongs to followed by the class name. To use the Minimal class in another project, however, you must add a reference to it. (You'll learn shortly how to reuse classes in other projects.)

Adding Code to the Minimal Class

Let's add some functionality to our bare-bones class. We'll begin by adding two trivial properties and two methods to perform simple operations. The two properties are called strProperty (a string) and dblProperty (a double). To expose these two members as properties, you can simply declare them as public variables. This isn't the best method of implementing properties, but it really doesn't take more than declaring something as public to make it available to code outside the class. The following statement exposes the two properties of the class:

```
Public strProperty As String, dblProperty As Double
```

The two methods you'll implement in your sample class are the ReverseString and NegateNumber methods. The first method reverses the order of the characters in strProperty and returns the new string. The NegateNumber method returns the negative of dblProperty. They're two simple methods that don't accept any arguments; they simply operate on the values of the properties. Methods are exposed as public procedures (functions or subroutines), just as properties are exposed as public variables. Enter the function declarations of Listing 8.1 between the Class Minimal and End Class statements in the class's code window. (I'm showing the entire listing of the class here.)

LISTING 8.1:   Adding a few members to the Minimal class

```
Public Class Minimal
    Public strProperty As String, dblProperty As Double
    Public Function ReverseString() As String
        Return (StrReverse(strProperty))
    End Function
    Public Function NegateNumber() As Double
        Return (-dblProperty)
    End Function
End Class
```

FIGURE 8.2
The members of the
class are displayed
automatically by the
IDE, as needed.

Let's test the members we've implemented so far. Switch back to your form and enter the lines shown in Listing 8.2 in a new button's Click event handler. The *obj* variable is of the Minimal type and exposes the public members of the class, as shown in Figure 8.2. You can set and read its properties and call its methods. Your code doesn't see the class's code, just as it doesn't see any of the built-in classes' code. You trust that the class knows what it is doing and does it right.

LISTING 8.2:   Testing the Minimal class

```
Dim obj As New Minimal
obj.strProperty = "ABCDEFGHIJKLMNOPQRSTUVWXYZ"
obj.dblProperty = 999999
Debug.WriteLine(obj.ReverseString)
Debug.WriteLine(obj.NegateNumber)
```

THE NEW KEYWORD

The New keyword tells VB to create a new instance of the Minimal class. If you omit the New keyword, you're telling the compiler that you plan to store an instance of the Minimal class in the *obj* variable but the class won't be instantiated. All the compiler can do is prevent you from storing an object of any other type in the *obj* variable. You must still initialize the *obj* variable with the New keyword on a separate line:

```
obj = New Minimal
```

It's the New keyword that creates the object in memory. If you omit the New keyword, a null reference exception will be thrown when the code attempts to use the variable. This means that the variable is Nothing — it hasn't been initialized yet. Even as you work in the editor's window, the name of the variable will be underlined and the following warning will be generated: *Variable 'obj' is used before it has been assigned a value. A null reference exception could result at runtime.* You can compile the code and run it if you want, but everything will proceed as predicted: As soon as the statement that produced the warning is reached, the runtime exception will be thrown.

Using Property Procedures

The strProperty and dblProperty properties will accept any value as long as the type is correct and the value of the numeric property is within the acceptable range. But what if the generic properties were meaningful entities, such as email addresses, ages, or zip codes? We should be able to invoke some code to validate the values assigned to each property. To do so, we implement each property as a special type of procedure: the so-called property procedure.

Properties are implemented with a special type of procedure that contains a Get and a Set section (frequently referred to as the property's getter and setter, respectively). The Set section of the procedure is invoked when the application attempts to set the property's value; the Get section is invoked when the application requests the property's value. The value passed to the property is usually validated in the Set section and, if valid, is stored to a local variable. The same local variable's value is returned to the application when it requests the property's value, from the property's Get section. Listing 8.3 shows what the implementation of an Age property might look like.

LISTING 8.3:   Implementing properties with property procedures

```
Private m_Age As Integer
Property Age() As Integer
   Get
      Age = m_Age
   End Get
   Set (ByVal value As Integer)
      If value < 0 Or value >= 100 Then
         MsgBox("Age must be positive and less than 100")
      Else
         m_Age = value
      End If
   End Set
End Property
```

The local variable where the age is stored is *m_Age*. When a statement such as the following is executed in the application that uses your class, the Set section of the property procedure is invoked:

```
obj.Age = 39
```

Because the property value is valid, it is stored in the *m_Age* local variable. Likewise, when a statement such as the following one is executed, the Get section of the property procedure is invoked, and the value 39 is returned to the application:

```
Debug.WriteLine(obj.Age)
```

The *value* argument of the Set segment represents the actual value that the calling code is attempting to assign to the property. The *m_Age* variable is declared as private because we don't want any code outside the class to access it directly. The Age property is, of course, public so that other applications can set it, and external applications shouldn't bypass the validation performed by the property's setter.

FIELDS VERSUS PROPERTIES

Technically, any variables that are declared as Public in a class are called *fields*. Fields behave just like properties in the sense that you can assign values to them and read their values, but there's a critical distinction between fields and properties: When a value is assigned to a field, you can't validate that value from within your code. Properties should be implemented with a property procedure so you can validate their values, as you saw in the preceding example. Not only that, you can set other values from within your code. Consider a class that represents a contract with a starting and ending date. Every time the user changes the starting date, the code can adjust the ending date accordingly (which is something you can't do with fields). If the two dates were implemented as fields, users of the class could potentially specify an ending date prior to the starting date.

Enter the property procedure for the Age property in the Minimal class and then switch to the form to test it. Open the button's Click event handler and add the following lines to the existing ones:

```
Dim obj As New Minimal
obj.Age = 39
Debug.WriteLine("after setting the age to 39, age is " &
                obj.Age.ToString)
obj.Age = 199
Debug.WriteLine("after setting the age to 199, age is " &
                obj.Age.ToString)
```

The value 39 will appear twice in the Output window, which means that the class accepts the value 39. When the third statement is executed, a message box will appear with the error's description:

```
Age must be positive and less than 100
```

The value 39 will appear in the Output window again. The attempt to set the age to 199 failed, so the property retains its previous value. You will also see the message box with the warning, which is invoked from within the class's code.

THROWING EXCEPTIONS

The error-trapping code works fine, but what good is a message box displayed from within a class? As a developer using the Minimal class in your code, you'd rather receive an exception and handle it from within your code, unless you're writing classes to use in your own applications. Normally, you don't know who's going to use your class, or how, so you can't assume that any messages displayed from within your class's code will be seen by the end user. The class may be invoked on a remote server, in which case the error message will go unnoticed. So let's change the implementation of the Age property a little. The property procedure for the Age property (Listing 8.4) throws an InvalidArgument exception if an attempt is made to assign an invalid value to it. The InvalidArgument exception is one of the existing exceptions, and you can reuse it in your code. Later in this chapter, you'll learn how to create and use custom exceptions.

LISTING 8.4:   Throwing an exception from within a property procedure

```
Private m_Age As Integer
Property Age() As Integer
   Get
       Age = m_Age
   End Get
   Set (ByVal value As Integer)
      If value < 0 Or value >= 100 Then
          Dim AgeException As New ArgumentException()
          Throw AgeException
      Else
          M_Age = value
      End If
   End Set
End Property
```

You can test the revised property definition in your application; switch to the test form, and enter the statements from Listing 8.5 in a new button's Click event handler. (This is the code behind the Handle Exceptions button on the test form.)

LISTING 8.5:   Catching the Age property's exception

```
Dim obj As New Minimal
Dim userAge as Integer
UserAge = InputBox("Please enter your age")
Try
   obj.Age = userAge
Catch exc as ArgumentException
   MsgBox("Can't accept your value, " & userAge.ToString & VbCrLf &
          "Will continue with default value of 30")
   obj.Age = 30
End Try
```

This is a much better technique for handling errors in your class. The exceptions can be intercepted by the calling application, and developers using your class can write robust applications by handling the exceptions in their code. When you develop custom classes, keep in mind that you can't handle most errors from within your class because you don't know how other developers will use your class.

🌐 Real World Scenario

HANDLING ERRORS IN A CLASS

When you design classes, keep in mind that you don't know how another developer may use them. In fact, you may have to use your own classes in a way that you didn't consider when you designed them. A typical example is using an existing class with a web application. If your class displays a message box, it will work fine as part of a Windows Forms application, but in the context of a web application, the message box won't be displayed anywhere. Even if you don't plan to use a custom class with a web application, never interact with the user from within the class's code. Make your code as robust as you can, but don't hesitate to throw exceptions for all conditions you can't handle from within your code (as shown here). In general, a class's code should detect abnormal conditions, but it shouldn't attempt to remedy them.

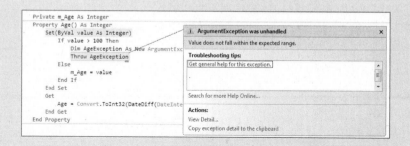

The application that uses your class may inform the user about an error condition and give the user a chance to correct the error by entering new data, disabling some options on the interface, and so on. As a class developer, you can't make this decision — another developer might prompt the user for another value, and a sloppy developer might let their application crash (but this isn't your problem). To throw an exception from within your class's code, call the Throw statement with an Exception object as an argument. To play well with the Framework, you should try to use one of the existing exceptions (and the Framework provides quite a few of them). You can also throw custom exceptions by passing an error message to the Exception class' constructor with a statement such as the following:

```
Throw New Exception("your exception's description")
```

IMPLEMENTING READ-ONLY PROPERTIES

Let's make our class a little more complicated. Age is not usually requested on official documents because it's valid only for a year (or less) after filling out a questionnaire. Instead, you are asked to furnish your date of birth, from which your current age can be calculated at any time. We'll add a BDate property in our class and make Age a read-only property.

To make a property read-only, you simply declare it as ReadOnly and supply code for the Get procedure only. Revise the Age property code in the Minimal class to that shown in Listing 8.6. Then, enter the property procedure from Listing 8.7 for the BDate property.

LISTING 8.6:   Implementing a read-only property

```
Private m_Age As Integer
ReadOnly Property Age() As Integer
    Get
        Age = m_Age
    End Get
End Property
```

LISTING 8.7:   The BDate property

```
Private m_BDate As DateTime
Private m_Age As Integer
Property BDate() As DateTime
    Get
        BDate = m_BDate
    End Get
    Set(ByVal value As Date)
        If value > Now() Or _
                DateDiff(DateInterval.Year, value, Now()) >= 100 Then
            Dim AgeException As New Exception
                    ("Can't accept the birth date you specified")
            Throw AgeException
        Else
            m_BDate = value
            m_Age = DateDiff(DateInterval.Year, value, Now())
        End If
    End Set
End Property
```

As soon as you enter the code for the revised Age property, two error messages will appear in the Error List window. The code in the application form is attempting to set the value of a read-only property, so the editor produces the following error message twice: *Property 'Age' is 'ReadOnly.'* As you probably figured out, we must set the BDate property in the code instead of the Age property. The two errors are the same, but they refer to two different statements that attempt to set the Age property.

The code checks the number of years between the date of birth and the current date. If it's negative (which means that the person hasn't been born yet) or more than 100 years (we'll assume that people over 100 will be treated as being 100 years old), it rejects the value. Otherwise, it sets the value of the *m_BDate* local variable and calculates the value of the *m_Age* local variable.

You can implement write-only properties with the WriteOnly keyword and a Set section only, but write-only properties are rarely used — in my experience, only for storing passwords.

Calculating Property Values on the Fly

There's still a serious flaw in the implementation of the Age property. Can you see it? The person's age is up-to-date the moment the birth date is entered, but what if we read it back from a file or database three years later? It will still return the original value, which will no longer be the correct age. The Age property's value shouldn't be stored anywhere; it should be calculated from the person's birth date as needed. If we avoid storing the age to a local variable and calculate it on the fly, users will always see the correct age. Revise the Age property code to match Listing 8.8 and the property will now calculate the difference between the date of birth and the current date and return the correct person's age every time it's called.

LISTING 8.8:   A calculated property

```
ReadOnly Property Age() As Integer
   Get
      Age = Convert.ToInt32(DateDiff(DateInterval.Year, m_BDate , Now()))
   End Get
End Property
```

Notice also that you no longer need the *m_Age* local variable because the age is calculated on the fly when requested, so remove its declaration from the class and remove the statement that sets the value of the *m_Age* variable in the BDate property's setter. As you can see, you don't always have to store property values to local variables. A property that returns the number of files in a directory, for example, also doesn't store its value in a local variable. It retrieves the requested information on the fly and furnishes it to the calling application. By the way, the calculations might still return a negative value if the user has changed the system's date, but this is a rather far-fetched scenario.

Your Minimal class is no longer so minimal. It exposes some functionality, and you can easily add more. Add properties for name, profession, and income, and add methods to calculate insurance rates based on a person's age and anything you can think of. Experiment with a few custom members, add the necessary validation code in your property procedures, and you'll soon find out that building and reusing custom classes is a simple and straightforward process. Of course, there's a lot more to learn about classes, but you already have a good understanding of the way classes combine code with data. Before continuing, let me introduce auto-implemented properties, which are a major convenience when you implement custom classes.

AUTO-IMPLEMENTED PROPERTIES

Quite often, actually more often than not, properties are implemented with straightforward code, without any validation code — just straight setters and getters like the following:

```
Private m_Occupation As String
Property Occupation() As String
   Get
        Return (m_Occupation)
   End Get
   Set (value As String)
        m_Occupation = value
End Property
```

The definition of many properties is based on a standard template, or boilerplate, which is always the same, except for the names of the properties and the corresponding local variables. If you don't need any additional code, shouldn't there be a simple method of defining a property? Indeed, with VB 2010 you can supply the name of the property and its type in a single statement like the following:

```
Public Property Occupation As String
```

And that's all it takes to create a straightforward property. Properties declared this way are known as *auto-implemented* properties, and they can simplify the coding of large classes considerably because most properties are usually implemented with the default setter and getter. Behind the scenes, the VB compiler generates the appropriate Get and Set segments of the property for you. As for the matching local variable, the compiler uses the same name as the property prefixed with an underscore. You can access this local variable from within the code that implements other properties, as in the following example:

```
Public Class Contact
    Public Property Name As String
    Public Property Company As String
    Public Property Occupation As String
    Private _Title
    Public Property Title() As String
       Get
            If _Occupation.Trim.Length > 0 Then
                Return _Occupation & "/" & _Title
            Else
                Return _Title
            End If
       End Get
       Set(ByVal value As String)
            _Title = value
       End Set
    End Property
End Class
```

The Contact class exposes three auto-implemented properties, the `Name`, `Company`, and `Occupation` properties and a fully implemented property, the `Title` property. Note that the `Title` property's `Get` segment takes into consideration the `_Occupation` local variable that holds the value of the `Occupation` auto-implemented property. Although the `_Occupation` variable is not declared anywhere in the class, it's being used in the `Title` property's implementation.

Auto-implemented properties are just a shorthand notation for properties, and they're converted into actual code by the compiler on the fly. Actually, when you type the statement

```
Public Property Company As String
```

the editor won't insert the stubs for the `Get` and `Set` segments; you must type the `Get` keyword on the following line and then press Enter for the editor to emit the stubs for the two segments of the property procedure.

Customizing Default Members

As you recall, when you created the Minimal class for the first time, before adding any code, the class exposed a few members — the default members, such as the `ToString` method (which returns the name of the class) and the `Equals` method (which compares two objects for reference equality). You can (and should) provide your custom implementation for these members; this is what I'm going to do in the following sections.

CUSTOMIZING THE *TOSTRING* METHOD

The custom `ToString` method is implemented as a public function, and it must override the default implementation. The implementation of a custom `ToString` method is shown next:

```
Public Overrides Function ToString() As String
    Return "The infamous Minimal class"
End Function
```

As soon as you enter the keyword `Overrides`, the editor will suggest the names of the three members you can override: `ToString`, `Equals`, and `GetHashCode`. Select the `ToString` method, and the editor will insert a default implementation for you. The default implementation returns the string `MyBase.ToString`. Just replace the statement inserted by the editor with the one shown in the preceding code segment.

The `Overrides` keyword tells the compiler that this implementation overwrites the default implementation of the class. The original method's code isn't exposed, and you can't revise it. The `Overrides` keyword tells the compiler to "hide" the original implementation and use your custom `ToString` method instead. After you override a method in a class, the application using the class can no longer access the original method. Ours is a simple method, but you can return any string you can build in the function. For example, you can incorporate the value of the `BDate` property in the string:

```
Return("MINIMAL: " & m_BDate.ToShortDateString)
```

The value of the local variable *m_BDate* is the value of the BDate property of the current instance of the class. Change the BDate property, and the ToString method will return a different string.

CUSTOMIZING THE *EQUALS* METHOD

The Equals method exposed by most of the built-in objects can compare values, not references. Two Rectangle objects, for example, are equal if their dimensions and origins are the same. The following two rectangles are equal:

```
Dim R1 As New Rectangle(0, 0, 30, 60)
Dim R2 As New Rectangle
R2.X = 0
R2.Y = 0
R2.Width = 30
R2.Height = 60
If R1.Equals(R2) Then
    MsgBox("The two rectangles are equal")
End If
```

If you execute these statements, a message box confirming the equality of the two objects will pop up. The two variables point to different objects (that is, different instances of the same class), but the two objects are equal because they have the same origin and same dimensions. The Rectangle class provides its own Equals method, which knows how to compare two Rectangle objects. If your class doesn't provide a custom Equals method, all the compiler can do is compare the objects referenced by the two variables. In the case of our Minimal class, the Equals method returns True if the two variables point to the same object (which is the same instance of the class). If the two variables point to two different objects, the default Equals method will return False, even if the two objects are the same.

You're probably wondering what makes two objects equal. Is it all their properties or perhaps some of them? Two objects are equal if the Equals method says so. You should compare the objects in a way that makes sense, but you're in no way limited as to how you do this. In a very specific application, you might decide that two rectangles are equal because they have the same area, or perimeter, regardless of their dimensions and origin, and override the Rectangle object's Equals method. In the Minimal class, for example, you might decide to compare the birth dates and return True if they're equal. Listing 8.9 is the implementation of a possible custom Equals method for the Minimal class.

LISTING 8.9:   A custom Equals method

```
Public Overrides Function Equals(ByVal obj As Object) As Boolean
    Dim O As Minimal = CType(obj, Minimal)
    If O.BDate = m_BDate Then
        Equals = True
    Else
        Equals = False
    End If
End Function
```

KNOW WHAT YOU ARE COMPARING

The Equals method shown in Listing 8.9 assumes that the object you're trying to compare to the current instance of the class is of the same type. Because you can't rely on developers to catch all their mistakes, you should know what you're comparing before you attempt to perform the comparison. A more-robust implementation of the Equals method is shown in Listing 8.10. This implementation tries to convert the argument of the Equals method to an object of the Minimal type and then compares it to the current instance of the Minimal class. If the conversion fails, an InvalidCastException is thrown and no comparison is performed.

LISTING 8.10:   A more-robust Equals method

```
Public Overrides Function Equals(ByVal obj As Object) As Boolean
    Dim O As New Minimal()
    Try
        O = DirectCast(obj, Minimal)
    Catch typeExc As InvalidCastException
        Throw typeExc
        Exit Function
    End Try
    If O.BDate = m_BDate Then
        Equals = True
    Else
        Equals = False
    End If
End Function
```

THE *IS* OPERATOR

The equals (=) operator can be used in comparing all built-in objects. The following statement is quite valid, as long as the *R1* and *R2* variables were declared of the Rectangle type:

```
If R1 = R2 Then
    MsgBox("The two rectangles are equal")
End If
```

This operator, however, can't be used with the Minimal custom class. Later in this chapter, you'll learn how to customize operators in your class. In the meantime, you can use only the Is operator, which compares for reference equality (whether the two variables reference the same object), and the Equals method. If the two variables *R1* and *R2* point to the same object, the following statement will return True:

```
If R1 Is R2 Then
    MsgBox("The two variables reference the same object")
End If
```

The Is operator tells you that the two variables point to a single object. There's no comparison here; the compiler simply figures out whether they point to same object in memory. It will return True if a statement such as the following has been executed before the comparison:

```
obj2 = obj1
```

If the Is operator returns True, there's only one object in memory and you can set its properties through either variable.

Custom Enumerations

Let's add a little more complexity to our class. Because we're storing birth dates to our custom objects, we can classify persons according to their age. Most BASIC developers will see an opportunity to use constants here. Instead of using constants to describe the various age groups, we'll use an enumeration with the following group names:

```
Public Enum AgeGroup
    Infant
    Child
    Teenager
    Adult
    Senior
    Overaged
End Enum
```

These statements must appear outside any procedure in the class, and we usually place them at the beginning of the file, right after the declaration of the class. Public is an access modifier (we want to be able to access this enumeration from within the application that uses the class). Enum is a keyword: It specifies the beginning of the declaration of an enumeration and it's followed by the enumeration's name. The enumeration itself is a list of integer values, each one mapped to a name. In our example, the name Infant corresponds to 0, the name Child corresponds to 1, and so on. The list of the enumeration's members ends with the End Enum keyword. You don't really care about the actual values of the names because the very reason for using enumerations is to replace numeric constants with more-meaningful names. You'll see shortly how enumerations are used both in the class and the calling application.

Now add to the class the GetAgeGroup method (Listing 8.11), which returns the name of the age group to which the person represented by an instance of the Minimal class belongs. The name of the group is a member of the AgeGroup enumeration.

LISTING 8.11:   Using an enumeration

```
Public Function GetAgeGroup() As AgeGroup
    Select Case m_Age
        Case Is < 3 : Return (AgeGroup.Infant)
        Case Is < 10 : Return (AgeGroup.Child)
        Case Is < 21 : Return (AgeGroup.Teenager)
        Case Is < 65 : Return (AgeGroup.Adult)
```

```
            Case Is < 100 : Return (AgeGroup.Senior)
            Case Else : Return (AgeGroup.Overaged)
        End Select
    End Function
```

The `GetAgeGroup` method returns a value of the `AgeGroup` type and you can compare it to members of the same enumeration. Switch to the form's code window, add a new button, and enter the statements from Listing 8.12 in its event handler.

LISTING 8.12:   Using the enumeration exposed by the class

```
Protected Sub Button1_Click(…)
                    Handles Button1.Click
    Dim obj As Minimal
        obj = New Minimal()
        Try
            obj.BDate = InputBox("Please Enter your birthdate")
        Catch ex As ArgumentException
            MsgBox(ex.Message)
            Exit Sub
        End Try
        Debug.WriteLine(obj.Age)
        Dim discount As Single
        Dim grp As Minimal.AgeGroup = obj.GetAgeGroup
        Select Case grp
            Case Minimal.AgeGroup.Infant, Minimal.AgeGroup.Child
                discount = 0.4
            Case Minimal.AgeGroup.Teenager
                discount = 0.5
            Case Minimal.AgeGroup.Senior
                discount = 0.2
            Case Else
        End Select

        MsgBox("Your age is " & obj.Age.ToString &
            " and you belong to the " &
            obj.GetAgeGroup.ToString &
            " group" & vbCrLf & "Your discount is " &
            Format(discount, "Percent"))
    End Sub
```

This routine calculates discounts based on the person's age. Notice that we don't use numeric constants in our code, just descriptive names. Moreover, the possible values of the enumeration are displayed in a drop-down list by the IntelliSense feature of the IDE as needed (Figure 8.3), and you don't have to memorize them or look them up as you would with

FIGURE 8.3
The members of an enumeration are displayed automatically in the IDE as you type.

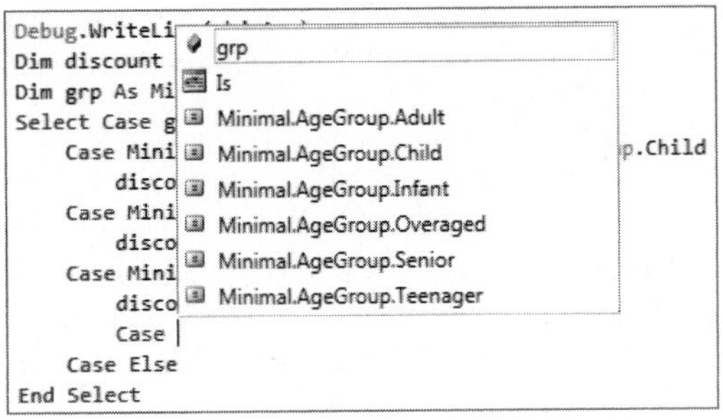
Debug.WriteLi
Dim discount
Dim grp As Mi
Select Case g
Case Mini
disco
Case Mini
disco
Case Mini
disco
Case
Case Else
End Select
grp
Is
Minimal.AgeGroup.Adult
Minimal.AgeGroup.Child
Minimal.AgeGroup.Infant
Minimal.AgeGroup.Overaged
Minimal.AgeGroup.Senior
Minimal.AgeGroup.Teenager
p.Child

constants. I've used an implementation with multiple `If` statements in this example, but you can perform the same comparisons by using a `Select Case` statement.

You've seen the basics of working with custom classes in a VB application. Let's switch to a practical example that demonstrates not only the use of a real-world class, but also how classes can simplify the development of a project.

VB 2010 AT WORK: THE CONTACTS PROJECT

In Chapter 6, "Working with Forms," I briefly discussed the Contacts application. This application uses a custom structure to store the contacts and provides four navigational buttons to allow users to move to the first, last, previous, and next contact. Now that you have learned how to program the ListBox control and how to use custom classes in your code, you can revise the Contacts application. First, you'll implement a class to represent each contact. The fields of each contact (company and contact names, addresses, and so on) will be implemented as properties and they will be displayed in the TextBox controls on the form.

You'll also improve the user interface of the application. Instead of the rather simplistic navigational buttons, you'll place all the company names in a sorted ListBox control. The user can easily locate the desired company and select it from the list to view its fields. The editing buttons at the bottom of the form work as usual, but you no longer need the navigational buttons. Figure 8.4 shows the revised Contacts application.

FIGURE 8.4
The interface of the Contacts application based on the ListBox control

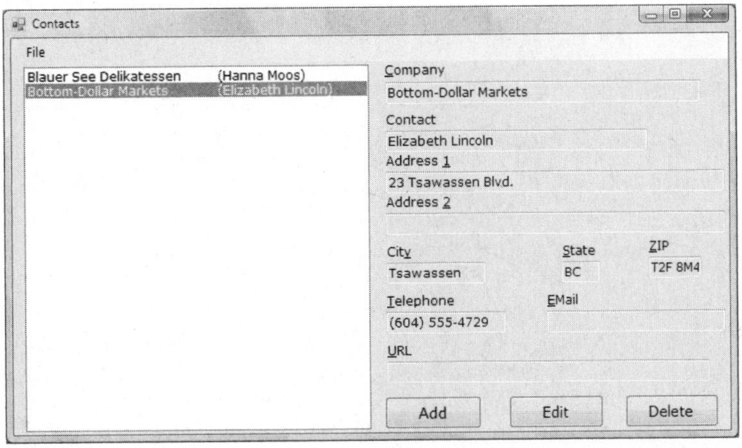
Contacts
File
Blauer See Delikatessen (Hanna Moos)
Bottom-Dollar Markets (Elizabeth Lincoln)
Company
Bottom-Dollar Markets
Contact
Elizabeth Lincoln
Address 1
23 Tsawassen Blvd.
Address 2
City
Tsawassen
State
BC
ZIP
T2F 8M4
Telephone
(604) 555-4729
EMail
URL
Add
Edit
Delete

Copy the contents of the Contacts folder you used when you worked on the Contacts project in Chapter 6 under a new folder and open the project by double-clicking the solution's name, **Contacts.sln**. You will also find the revised project in this chapter's projects. First, delete the declaration of the Contact structure and add a class to the project. Name the new class **Contact** and enter the code from Listing 8.13 into it. The names of the private members of the class are the same as the actual property names, and they begin with an underscore. (This is a good convention that lets you easily distinguish whether a variable is private and the property value it stores.) The implementation of the properties is trivial, so I'm not showing the code for all of them.

LISTING 8.13: The Contact class

```
<Serializable()> Public Class Contact
    Private _companyName As String
    Private _email As String

    Property CompanyName() As String
        Get
            CompanyName = _companyName
        End Get
        Set(ByVal value As String)
            If value Is Nothing Or value = "" Then
                Throw New Exception("Company Name field can't be empty")
                Exit Property
            End If
            _companyName = value
        End Set
    End Property

    Property ContactName As String

    Property Address1 As String

    Property Address2 As String

    Property City As String

    Property State As String

    Property ZIP As String

    Property tel As String

    Property EMail As String
    Get
            EMail = _email
        End Get
        Set(ByVal value As String)
```

```vb
        If value.Contains("@") Or value.Trim.Length = 0 Then
            _email = Value
        Else
            Throw New Exception("Invalid e-mail address!")
        End If
    End Set
End Property


Property URL As String


Overrides Function ToString() As String
    If _contactName = "" Then
        Return _companyName
    Else
        Return _companyName & vbTab & "(" & _contactName & ")"
    End If
End Function


Public Sub New()
    MyBase.New()
End Sub


Public Sub New(ByVal CompanyName As String,
            ByVal LastName As String, ByVal FirstName As String)
    MyBase.New()
    Me.ContactName = LastName & ", " & FirstName
    Me.CompanyName = CompanyName
End Sub


Public Sub New(ByVal CompanyName As String)
    MyBase.New()
    Me.CompanyName = CompanyName
End Sub
End Class
```

The first thing you'll notice is that the class's definition is prefixed by the <Serializable()> keyword. The topic of serialization is discussed in Chapter 13, "XML in Modern Programming," but for now all you need to know is that the .NET Framework can convert objects to a text or binary format and then store them in files. Surprisingly, this process is quite simple; as you will see, we'll be able to dump an entire collection of Contact objects to a file with a single statement. The <Serializable()> keyword is an attribute of the class, and (as you will see later in this book) there are more attributes you can use with your classes — or even with your methods. The most prominent method attribute is the <WebMethod> attribute, which turns a regular function into a web method.

The various fields of the Contact structure are now properties of the Contact class. The implementation of the properties is trivial except for the CompanyName and EMail properties, which contain some validation code. The Contact class requires that the CompanyName property have a value; if it doesn't, the class throws an exception. Likewise, the EMail property must contain the symbol @. Finally, the class provides its own ToString method, which returns the name of the company followed by the contact name in parentheses. All other properties are auto-implemented.

The ListBox control, in which we'll store all contacts, displays the value returned by the object's ToString method, which is why you have to provide your own implementation of this method to describe each contact. The company name should be adequate, but if there are two companies by the same name, you can use another field to differentiate them. I used the contact name, but you can use any of the other properties (the URL would be a good choice).

Although the ListBox displays a string, it stores the object itself. In essence, it's used not only as a navigational tool, but also as a storage mechanism for our contacts. Now, we must change the code of the main form a little. Start by removing the navigational buttons; we no longer need them. Their function will be replaced by a few lines of code in the ListBox control's SelectedIndexChanged event. Every time the user selects another item on the list, the statements shown in Listing 8.14 display the contact's properties in the various TextBox controls on the form. The *currentContact* variable is an integer that represents the index of the currently selected item, and it must be declared outside the subroutine because it must be accessed by other event handlers as well.

LISTING 8.14:   Displaying the fields of the selected Contact object

```
Private Sub ListBox1_SelectedIndexChanged(…)
            Handles ListBox1.SelectedIndexChanged
    currentContact = ListBox1.SelectedIndex
    ShowContact()
End Sub
```

The ShowContact() subroutine reads the object stored at the location specified by the *currentContact* variable and displays its properties in the various TextBox controls on the form. The TextBox controls are normally read-only, except when users are editing a contact. This action is signaled to the application when the user clicks the Edit or the Add button on the form.

When a new contact is added, the code reads its fields from the controls on the form, creates a new Contact object, and adds it to the ListBox control. When a contact is edited, a new Contact object replaces the currently selected object on the control. The code is similar to the code of the Contacts application. I should mention that the ListBox control is locked while a contact is being added or edited because it doesn't make sense to select another contact at that time.

Adding, Editing, and Deleting Contacts

To delete a contact (Listing 8.15), we simply remove the currently selected object from the ListBox control. In addition, we must select the next contact on the list (or the first contact if the deleted one was last in the list). The code of this event handler makes use of the *currentContact* variable to remove the currently selected item from the list.

LISTING 8.15:   Deleting an object from the ListBox

```
Private Sub bttnDelete_Click(…) Handles bttnDelete.Click
    If currentContact > -1 Then
        ListBox1.Items.RemoveAt(currentContact)
        currentContact = ListBox1.Items.Count - 1
        If currentContact = -1 Then
            ClearFields()
            MsgBox("There are no more contacts")
        Else
            ShowContact()
        End If
    Else
        MsgBox("No current contacts to delete")
    End If
End Sub
```

When you add a new contact, the following code is executed in the Add button's Click event handler:

```
Private Sub bttnAdd_Click(…) Handles bttnAdd.Click
    adding = True
    ClearFields()
    HideButtons()
    ListBox1.Enabled = False
End Sub
```

The controls are cleared in anticipation of the new contact's fields, and the *adding* variable is set to True. The OK button is clicked to end either the addition of a new record or an edit operation. The code behind the OK button is shown in Listing 8.16.

LISTING 8.16:   Committing a new or edited record

```
Private Sub bttnOK_Click(…) Handles bttnOK.Click
    If SaveContact() Then
        ListBox1.Enabled = True
        ShowButtons()
    End If
End Sub
```

As you can see, the same subroutine handles both the insertion of a new record and the editing of an existing one. All the work is done by the SaveContact() subroutine, which is shown in Listing 8.17.

LISTING 8.17:   The SaveContact() subroutine

```
Private Function SaveContact() As Boolean
    Dim contact As New Contact
    Try
        contact.CompanyName = txtCompany.Text
        contact.ContactName = txtContact.Text
        contact.Address1 = txtAddress1.Text
        contact.Address2 = txtAddress2.Text
        contact.City = txtCity.Text
        contact.State = txtState.Text
        contact.ZIP = txtZIP.Text
        contact.tel = txtTel.Text
        contact.EMail = txtEMail.Text
        contact.URL = txtURL.Text
    Catch ex As Exception
        MsgBox(ex.Message)
        Return False
    End Try
    If adding Then
        ListBox1.Items.Add(contact)
    Else
        ListBox1.Items(currentContact) = contact
    End If
    Return True
End Function
```

The SaveContact() function uses the *adding* variable to distinguish between an add and an edit operation and either adds the new record to the ListBox control or replaces the current item in the ListBox with the values on the various controls. Because the ListBox is sorted, new contacts are automatically inserted in the correct order. If an error occurs during the operation, the SaveContact() function returns False to alert the calling code that the operation failed (most likely because one of the assignment operations caused a validation error in the class's code). Note that the SaveContact routine uses the *currentContact* variable to determine the selected item on the list.

The last operation of the application is the serialization and deserialization of the items in the ListBox control. *Serialization* is the process of converting an object to a stream of bytes for storing to a disk file, and *deserialization* is the opposite process. To serialize objects, we first store them into an ArrayList object, which is a dynamic array that stores objects and can be serialized as a whole. Likewise, the disk file is deserialized into an ArrayList to reload the persisted data back to the application; then each element of the ArrayList is moved to the Items collection of the ListBox control. ArrayLists and other Framework collections are discussed in Chapter 12, "Storing Data in Collections," and object serialization is discussed in Chapter 13. You can use these features to test the application and examine the corresponding code after you read about ArrayLists and serialization.

Real World Scenario

MAKING THE MOST OF THE LISTBOX CONTROL

This section's sample application demonstrates an interesting technique for handling a set of data at the client. We usually need an efficient mechanism to store data at the client, where all the processing takes place — even if the data comes from a database. In this example, we used the ListBox control because each item of the control can be an arbitrary object. Because the control displays the string returned by the object's ToString method, we're able to customize the display by providing our own implementation of the ToString method. As a result, we're able to use the ListBox control both as a data-storage mechanism and as a navigational tool. As long as the strings displayed on the control are meaningful descriptions of the corresponding objects and the control's items are sorted, the ListBox control can be used as an effective navigational tool. If you have too many items to display on the control, you should also provide a search tool to help users quickly locate an item in the list without having to scroll up and down a long list of items. Review the ListBoxFind project from Chapter 5, "Basic Windows Controls," for information on searching the contents of the ListBox control.

When data are being edited, you have to cope with another possible problem. The user may edit the data for hours and forget to save the edits every now and then. If the computer (or, even worse, the application) crashes, a lot of work will be wasted. Sure the application provides a Save command, but you should always try to protect users from their mistakes. It would be nice if you could save the data to a temporary file every time the user edits, deletes, or adds an item to the list. This way, if the computer crashes, users won't lose their edits. When the application starts, it should automatically detect the presence of the temporary file and reload it. Every time the user saves the data by using the application's Save command or terminates the application, the temporary file should be removed.

Object Constructors

Let's switch to a few interesting topics in programming with objects. Objects are instances of classes, and classes are instantiated with the New keyword. The New keyword can be used with a number of arguments, which are the initial values of some of the object's basic properties. To construct a rectangle, for example, you can use either of two statements. You can use this one:

```
Dim shape1 As Rectangle = New Rectangle()
shape1.Width = 100
shape1.Height = 30
```

Or you can use the following one:

```
Dim shape1 As Rectangle = New Rectangle(100, 30)
```

The objects in the Minimal class can't be initialized to specific values of their properties, and they expose the simple form of the New constructor — the so-called parameterless constructor.

Every class has a parameterless constructor, even if you don't specify it. You can implement parameterized constructors, which allow you to pass arguments to an object as you declare it. These arguments are usually the values of the object's basic properties. Parameterized constructors don't pass arguments for all the properties of the object; they expect only enough parameter values to make the object usable.

Parameterized constructors are implemented via public subroutines that have the name New(). You can have as many overloaded forms of the New() subroutine as needed. Most of the built-in classes provide a parameterless constructor, but the purists of OOP will argue against parameterless constructors. Their argument is that you shouldn't allow users of your class to create invalid instances of it. A class for describing customers, for example, should expose at least a Name property. A class for describing books should expose a Title and an ISBN property. If the corresponding constructor requires that these properties be specified before you create an instance of the class, you'll never create objects with invalid data. There are cases, however, where this isn't possible. When you call a function that returns a custom object, for example, you must declare a variable of the same type and assign the function to this variable:

```
Dim C As Contact
C = ListBox1.SelectedItem
```

Here we can't create a new Contact object because we want to store in the C variable an existing object. Is there a good reason to create an object variable before you have an object to store in it?

Let's add a parameterized constructor to our Contact class. Each contact should have at least a name; here's a parameterized constructor for the Contact class:

```
Public Sub New(ByVal CompanyName As String)
    MyBase.New()
    Me.CompanyName = CompanyName
End Sub
```

The code is trivial, with the exception of the statement that calls the MyBase.New() subroutine. MyBase is an object that lets you access the members of the base class (a topic that's discussed in detail later in this chapter). The reason you must call the New method of the base class is that the base class might have its own constructor, which can't be called directly. You must always insert this statement in your constructors to make sure any initialization tasks that must be performed by the base class will not be skipped.

The Contact class's constructor accepts a single argument: the company name (this property can't be a blank string). Another useful constructor for the same class accepts two additional arguments, the contact's first and last names, as follows:

```
Public Sub New(ByVal CompanyName As String,
              ByVal LastName As String, ByVal FirstName As String)
    MyBase.New()
    Me.ContactName = LastName & ", " & FirstName
    Me.CompanyName = CompanyName
End Sub
```

With the two parameterized constructors in place, you can create new instances of the Contact class by using a statement such as the following:

```
Dim contact1 As New Contact("Around the Horn")
```

Or you can use a statement such as this:

```
Dim contact1 As New Contact("Around the Horn", "Hardy", "Thomas")
```

Notice the lack of the Overloads (or Overrides) keyword. Constructors can have multiple forms and don't require the use of Overloads — just supply as many implementations of the New() subroutine as you need.

One last but very convenient technique to initialize objects allows you to supply values for as many properties of the new object as you wish, using the With keyword. The With keyword is followed by the names of the properties you want to initialize and their values in a comma-separated list, as shown in the following statements, which create two new instances of the Person class, and they initialize each one differently:

```
Dim P1 As New Person With
        {.LastName = "Doe", .FirstName = "Joe"})
Dim P2 As New Person With
        {.LastName = "Doe", .Email = "Doe@xxx.com"})
```

Note that the property names are prefixed with the period. The With statement is a shorthand notation for accessing multiple members of an instance of a class without having to repeat the class's name. This syntax allows you to quickly initialize new objects regardless of their constructors; in effect, you can create your own constructor for any class. This technique will be handy when combining object initialization with other statements, such as in the following example, which adds a new object to a list:

```
Persons.Add(New Person With {.LastName = "Doe", .FirstName = "Joe"})
```

While the New function is the class constructor, the syntax with the With keyword is not a constructor, although it creates a new instance of the class and initializes its properties. The process of initializing an instance of a class is known as object initialization. An advantage of the With keyword is that as soon as you type the opening bracket, the editor will display the list of properties you can initialize in the IntelliSense box.

Using the SimpleClass in Other Projects

The projects we built in this section are Windows applications that contain a Class module. The class is contained within the project, and it's used by the project's main form. What if you want to use this class in another project?

First, you must change the type of the project. A Windows project can't be used as a component in another project. Right-click the SimpleClass project and choose Properties. In the project's Property Pages dialog box, switch to the Application tab, locate the Application Type drop-down list, and change the project's type from Windows Forms Application to Class Library, as shown in Figure 8.5. Then close the dialog box. When you return to the

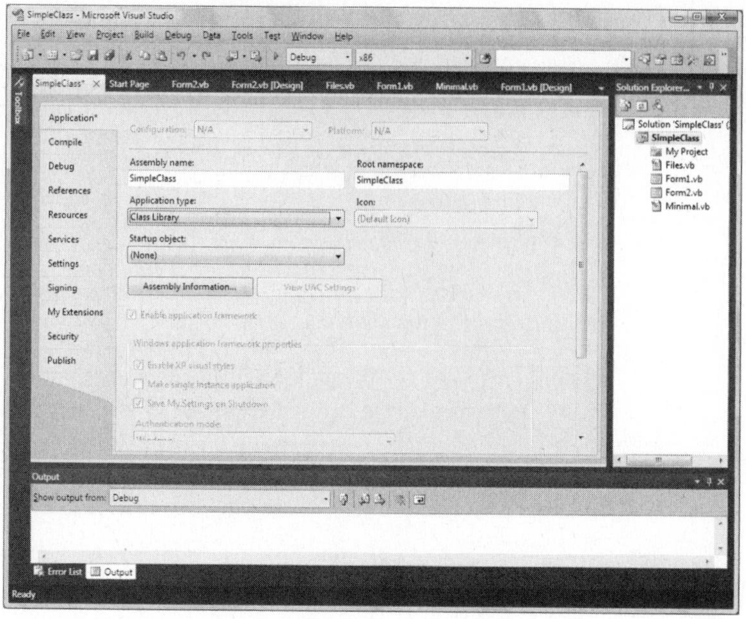

FIGURE 8.5

Setting a project's properties through the Property Pages dialog box

project, right-click the TestForm and select Exclude From Project. A class doesn't have a visible interface, and there's no reason to include the test form in your project.

From the main menu, choose Build ➢ Build SimpleClass. This command will compile the SimpleClass project and create a DLL file (the file that contains the class's code and the file you must use in any project that needs the functionality of the SimpleClass class). The DLL file will be created in the \bin\Release folder under the project's folder.

Let's use the SimpleClass.dll file in another project. Start a new Windows application, open the Project menu, and add a reference to the SimpleClass. Choose Project ➢ Add Reference and switch to the Projects tab in the dialog box that appears. Switch to the Browse tab and locate the SimpleClass.dll file (see Figure 8.6). Select the name of the file and click OK to close the dialog box.

The compiler will place the DLL in the folder obj\x86\Debug under the project's folder. The SimpleClass component will be added to the project. You can now declare a variable of the SimpleClass.Minimal type and call its properties and methods:

```
Dim obj As New SimpleClass.Minimal
obj.BDate = #10/15/1992#
obj.strProperty = 5544
MsgBox(obj.NegateNumber())
```

If you want to keep testing the SimpleClass project, add the TestForm to the original project (right-click the project's name, choose Add ➢ Add Existing Item, and select the TestForm in the project's folder). Change the project's type back to Windows Forms Application and then change its configuration from Release to Debug.

Adding references to multiple DLLs scattered through your disk or local network can become a nightmare, especially if multiple developers are working on the same projects. All

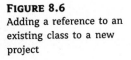

FIGURE 8.6
Adding a reference to an existing class to a new project

related items should belong to the same solution, so don't be afraid to add multiple classes to the same project. Actually, this is the recommended practice and it will simplify the task of referencing the classes from within the other projects.

Firing Events

In addition to methods and properties, classes can also fire events. You will find that events are not quite as common with classes. Controls have many events because they expose a visible interface and the user interacts through this interface (clicks, drags and drops, and so on). But classes can also raise events. Class events can come from three different sources:

Progress events A class might raise an event to indicate the progress of a lengthy process or indicate that an internal variable or property has changed value. The `PercentDone` event is a typical example. A process that takes a while to complete reports its progress to the calling application with this event, which is fired periodically. These events, which are called *progress events*, are the most common type of class events.

Time events Time events are based on a timer. They're not very common, but you can implement alarms, job schedulers, and similar applications. You can set an alarm for a specific time or an alarm that will go off after a specified interval.

External events External events, such as the completion of an asynchronous operation, can also fire events. For example, a class might initiate a file download and notify the application when the file arrives.

To fire an event from within a class, you must do the following:

1. First you must declare the event and its signature in your class. The declaration must appear in the class, not in any procedure. A simple event, with no arguments, should

be declared as follows (`ShiftEnd` is the name of the event — an event that signals the process):

```
Public Event ProcessCompleted()
```

2. Fire the event from within your class code with the `RaiseEvent` method:

```
RaiseEvent ProcessCompleted()
```

That's all as far as the class is concerned.

3. The application that uses the custom class must declare it with the `WithEvents` keyword. Otherwise, it will still be able to use the class's methods and properties, but the events raised by the class will go unnoticed. The following statement creates an instance of the class and listens for any event:

```
Dim WithEvents obj As New Minimal
```

4. Finally, the calling application must provide a handler for the specific event. Because the class was declared with the `WithEvents` keyword, its name will appear in the list of objects in the editor window and its `ProcessCompleted` event will appear in the list of events (Figure 8.7). Insert the code you want to handle this event in the procedure `obj.ProcessCompleted`.

Events usually pass information to the calling application. In VB, all events pass two arguments to the application: a reference to the object that fired the event and another argument, which is an object that contains information specific to the event.

The arguments of an event are declared just as the arguments of a procedure are declared. The following statement declares an event that's fired every few seconds to report the progress

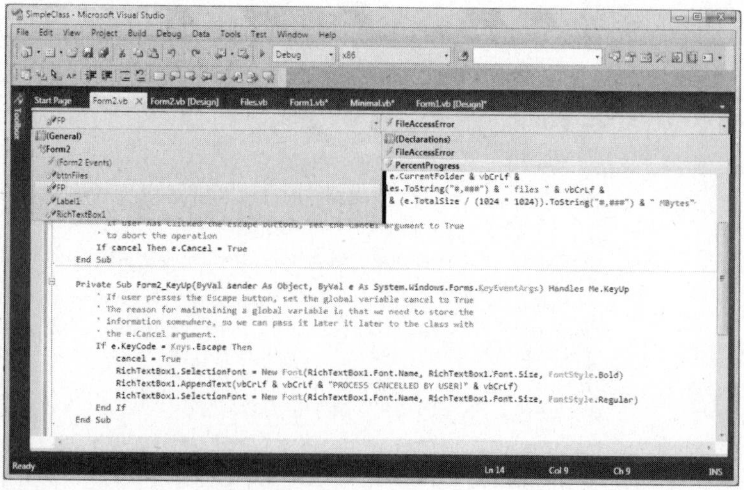

FIGURE 8.7
Programming a custom
class's event

of a process as a percent complete value. The event passes a single parameter value to the application that intercepts it:

```
Public Event ProcessProgress(ByVal percent As Integer)
```

The progress is reported as an integer between 0 and 100. To raise this event from within a class code, call the RaiseEvent statement as before, passing a value of the appropriate type, as shown next, where the *iProgress* variable is maintained by the class code and is increased with every iteration:

```
RaiseEvent PercentProgress(iProgress)
```

🌐 Real World Scenario

A CLASS THAT MANIPULATES FILES

When coding the event's handler, you can access the arguments and use them as you wish. Alternatively, you could create a new object and pass multiple values to the calling application, as most event handlers in Visual Basic do. Consider a class that manipulates a large number of files (changes the format of many files, locates and moves images around, and so on). You may not know how many files you'll process, in which case the class can report the number of files processed thus far but not the percent of the work done. The following object exposes as properties the percent of the work completed so far as well as the number of files processed and their total size (as well as the current folder):

```
Public Class FilesProcessedArgument
    Public Files As Integer
    Public TotalSize As Long
    Public Percent As Integer
    Public CurrentFolder As String
End Class
```

Then you can declare the event's signature by using the FilesProcessedArgument type in the argument list:

```
Public Event PercentProgress(ByVal sender As Object,
            ByVal e As FilesProcessedArgument)
```

To fire the PercentProgress event from within your class's code, create an instance of the FilesProcessedArgument class, set its properties, and then call the RaiseEvent method, as shown here:

```
Dim DArgument As New sFilesProcessedArgument
DArgument.Files = tmpTotalFiles
DArgument.TotalSize = tmpTotalSize
DArgument.Percent = Nothing
DArgument.CurrentFolder = tmpCurrentFolder
```

```
RaiseEvent PercentProgress(Me, DArgument)
```

To intercept this event in your test application, declare an object of the appropriate type with the WithEvents keyword and write an event handler for the PercentProgress event:

```
Public WithEvents obj As New EventFiringClass
Private Sub obj_Fired(ByVal sender As Object,
        ByVal e As Firing.FilesProcessedArgument)
        Handles obj.PercentProgress
    MsgBox("Event fired" & vbCrLf &
            e.Files.ToString & vbCrLf &
            e.TotalSize.ToStrng & vbCrLf &
            e.CurrentFolder)
End Sub
```

That's all it takes to fire an event from within your custom class. In Chapter 9, "Building Custom Windows Controls," you will find several examples of custom events.

Some events expose a Cancel argument, which you can set to True to cancel an operation that takes place in the background. For example, users should be able to abort the process of counting the files in a volume, which can take minutes depending on the size of the volume. In the SimpleClass project (available for download from www.sybex.com/go/masteringvb2010), you will find the Form2. Form2 implements a method for counting files (the ProcessFiles method). This method raises the PercentProgress event every time it starts processing a different folder. The PercentProgress event exposes the Cancel argument, which the calling application can set to True to end the operation. Make Form2 the startup of the project to experiment with a class that interacts with the calling application with events. The process takes a while, but you can interrupt it by pressing the Escape key. The code is adequately documented and will help you understand how to retrieve multiple parameters through an event handler as well as how to pass information back to the class through its events.

Instance and Shared Methods

As you have seen in earlier chapters, some classes allow you to call some of their members without first creating an instance of the class. The DateTime class, for example, exposes the IsLeapYear method, which accepts as an argument a numeric value and returns a True/False value that indicates whether the year is a leap year. You can call this method through the Date-Time (or Date) class without having to create a variable of the DateTime type, as shown in the following statement:

```
If DateTime.IsLeapYear(1999) Then
    { process a leap year}
End If
```

A typical example of classes that can be used without explicit instances is the Math class. To calculate the logarithm of a number, you can use an expression such as this one:

```
Math.Log(3.333)
```

The properties and methods that don't require you to create an instance of the class before you call them are called shared methods. Methods that must be applied to an instance of the class are called instance methods. By default, all methods are instance methods. To create a shared method, you must prefix the corresponding function declaration with the Shared keyword, just as you would a shared property.

Why do we need shared methods, and when should we create them? If a method doesn't apply to a specific instance of a class, make it shared. In other words, if a method doesn't act on the properties of the current instance of the class, it should be shared. Let's consider the Date-Time class. The DaysInMonth method returns the number of days in the month (of a specific year) that is passed to the method as an argument. You don't really need to create an instance of a Date object to find out the number of days in a specific month of a specific year, so the DaysInMonth method is a shared method and can be called as follows:

```
DateTime.DaysInMonth(2010, 2)
```

Think of the DaysInMonth method this way: Do I need to create a new date to find out if a specific month has 30 or 31 days? If the answer is no, then the method is a candidate for a shared implementation.

The AddDays method, on the other hand, is an instance method. We have a date to which we want to add a number of days and construct a new date. In this case, it makes sense to apply the method to an instance of the class — the instance that represents the date to which we add the number of days — rather than passing the date as argument to the AddDays method.

If you take a moment to reflect on shared and instance members, you'll come to the conclusion that all members could have been implemented as shared members and accept the data they act upon as arguments. This approach, however, would reduce classes to collections of functions, just like the built-in functions of Visual Basic. The idea behind classes, however, is to combine data with code. If you implement a class with shared members, you lose one of the major advantages of OOP. One of the reasons for turning to object-oriented programming was that languages were being enhanced with every new version to a point that they were bloated and developers couldn't memorize all the functions.

The SharedMembers sample project (available for download from www.sybex.com/go/masteringvb2010) is a simple class that demonstrates the differences between a shared and an instance method. Both methods do the same thing: They reverse the characters in a string. The IReverseString method is an instance method; it reverses the current instance of the class, which is a string. The SReverseString method is a shared method; it reverses its argument. Listing 8.18 shows the code that implements the SharedMembersClass component.

LISTING 8.18:   A class with a shared and an instance method

```
Public Class SharedMembersClass
    Private _strProperty As String

    Sub New(ByVal str As String)
        _strProperty = str
    End Sub

    Sub New()
```

```
        End Sub

        Public Property strProperty As String
        Get
            Return(_strProperty)
        End Get
        Set (ByVal value As String)
            _strProperty = value
        End Set
    End Property
        Public Function IReverseString() As String
            Return (StrReverse(strProperty))
        End Function

        Public Shared Function SReverseString(ByVal str As String) As String
            Return (StrReverse(str))
        End Function
    End Class
```

Note that I had to declare the parameterless constructor in the class. This form of the constructor should be included only if you add multiple forms of the constructor. If you don't care about constructors that accept parameters, you don't have to list the default constructor explicitly. The instance method acts on the current instance of the class. This means that the class must be initialized to a string, and this is why the New constructor requires a string argument. To test the class, add a form to the project, make it the Startup object, and add two buttons to it. The code behind the two buttons is shown next:

```
Private Sub Button1_Click(…) Handles Button1.Click
    Dim testString As String = "ABCDEFGHIJKLMNOPQRSTUVWXYZ"
    Dim obj As New SharedMembersClass(testString)
    Debug.WriteLine(obj.IReverseString)
End Sub

Private Sub Button2_Click(…) Handles Button2.Click
    Dim testString As String = "ABCDEFGHIJKLMNOPQRSTUVWXYZ"
    Debug.WriteLine(SharedMembersClass.SReverseString(testString))
End Sub
```

The code behind the first button creates a new instance of the SharedMembersClass and calls its IReverseString method. The second button calls the SReverseString method through the class's name and passes the string to be reversed as an argument to the method.

A class can also expose shared properties. There are situations in which you want all instances of a class to see the same property value. Let's say you want to keep track of the users currently accessing your class. You can declare a method that must be called to enable the class, and this method signals that another user has requested your class. This method could establish a connection to a database or open a file. We'll call it the Connect method. Every time an application calls the Connect method, you can increase an internal variable by one. Likewise, every time an application calls the Disconnect method, the same internal variable is decreased by one. This internal variable can't be private because it will be initialized to zero with each new instance of the class. You need a variable that is common to all instances of the class. Such a variable should be declared with the Shared keyword.

Let's add a shared variable to our Minimal class. We'll call it LoggedUsers, and it will be read-only. Its value is reported via the Users property, and only the Connect and Disconnect methods can change its value. Listing 8.19 is the code you must add to the Minimal class to implement a shared property.

LISTING 8.19:   Implementing a shared property

```
Shared LoggedUsers As Integer
ReadOnly Property Users() As Integer
   Get
       Users = LoggedUsers
   End Get
End Property

Public Function Connect() As Integer
   LoggedUsers = LoggedUsers + 1
   ' { your own code here}
End Function

Public Function Disconnect() As Integer
   If LoggedUsers > 1 Then
      LoggedUsers = LoggedUsers - 1
   End If
   ' { your own code here}
End Function
```

To test the shared variable, add a new button to the form and enter the code in Listing 8.20 in its Click event handler. (The lines with the bold numbers are the values reported by the class; they're not part of the listing.)

LISTING 8.20:   Testing the LoggedUsers shared property

```
Private Sub Button3_Click(ByVal sender As Object,
                ByVal e As System.EventArgs)
   Dim obj1 As New SharedMembersClass
   obj1.Connect()
   Debug.WriteLine(obj1.Users)
1
   obj1.Connect()
   Debug.WriteLine(obj1.Users)
2
   Dim obj2 As New SharedMembersClass
```

```
    obj2.Connect()
    Debug.WriteLine(obj1.Users)
3
    Debug.WriteLine(obj2.Users)
3
    Obj2.Disconnect()
    Debug.WriteLine(obj2.Users)
2
End Sub
```

If you run the application, you'll see the values displayed under each `Debug.WriteLine` statement in the Output window. As you can see, both the *obj1* and *obj2* variables access the same value of the `Users` property. Shared variables are commonly used in classes that run on a server and service multiple applications. In effect, they're the class's global variables, which can be shared among all the instances of a class. You can use shared variables to keep track of connection time, the total number of rows accessed by all users of the class in a database, and other similar quantities.

A "Real" Class

The StringTools project, which is included with this chapter's projects, contains the String-Tools class, which exposes a few interesting methods. The first two methods are the `ExtractPathName` and `ExtractFileName` methods, which extract the filename and pathname from a full filename. If the full name of a file is C:\Documents\Recipes\Chinese\Won Ton.txt, the `ExtractPathName` method will return the substring C:\Documents\Recipes\Chinese\, and the `ExtractFileName` method will return the substring Won Ton.txt.

A third method, called `Num2String`, converts numeric values (amounts) to the equivalent strings. For example, it can convert the amount $12,544 to the string `Twelve Thousand, Five Hundred And Forty Four dollars`. No other class in the Framework provides this functionality, and any program that prints checks can use this class.

The `Num2String` method uses three properties of the StringTools class: the `Case`, `Delimiter`, and `Padding` properties. The `Case` property determines the case of the characters in the string returned by the method. The `Delimiter` property specifies the special characters that should appear before and after the string. Finally, the `Padding` property specifies the character that will appear between groups of digits. The values each of these properties can take on are members of the appropriate enumeration:

PaddingEnum	DelimiterEnum	CaseEnum
paddingCommas	*delimiterNone*	*caseCaps*
paddingSpaces	*delimiterAsterisk*	*caseLower*
paddingDashes	*delimiter3Asterisks*	*caseUpper*

The values for each of these properties are implemented as enumerations, and you need not memorize their names. As you enter the name of the property followed by the equal sign, the appropriate list of values will pop up and you can select the desired member. Listing 8.21 presents the `UseCaseEnum` enumeration and the implementation of the `UseCase` property.

LISTING 8.21:   The CaseEnum enumeration and the UseCase property

```
Enum CaseEnum
   caseCaps
   caseLower
   caseUpper
End Enum

Private varUseCase As CaseEnum
Public Property [Case]() As CaseEnum
   Get
      Return (varUseCase)
   End Get
   Set
      varUseCase = Value
   End Set
End Property
```

Notice that the name of the Case property is enclosed in square brackets. This is necessary when you're using a reserved keyword as a variable, property, method, or enumeration member name. Alternatively, you can use a different name for the property to avoid the conflict altogether.

To test the StringTools class, create a test form like the one shown in Figure 8.8. Then enter the code from Listing 8.22 in the Click event handler of the two buttons.

LISTING 8.22:   Testing the StringTools class

```
Protected Sub Button1_Click(…) Handles Button1.Click
   TextBox1.Text = Convert.ToDecimal(
                  TextBox1.Text).ToString("#,###.00")
   Dim objStrTools As New StringTools()
   objStrTools.Case = StringTools.CaseEnum.CaseCaps
   objStrTools.Delimiter = StringTools.DelimitEnum.DelimiterNone
   objStrTools.Padding = StringTools.PaddingEnum.PaddingCommas
   TextBox2.Text = objStrTools.Num2String(Convert.ToDecimal(TextBox1.Text))
End Sub

Protected Sub Button2_Click(…) Handles Button2.Click
   Dim objStrTools As New StringTools()
   openFileDialog1.ShowDialog()
   Dim fName as String
   fName = OpenFileDialog1.FileName
   Debug.writeline(objStrTools.ExtractPathName(fName))
   Debug.WriteLine(objStrTools.ExtractFileName(fName))
End Sub
```

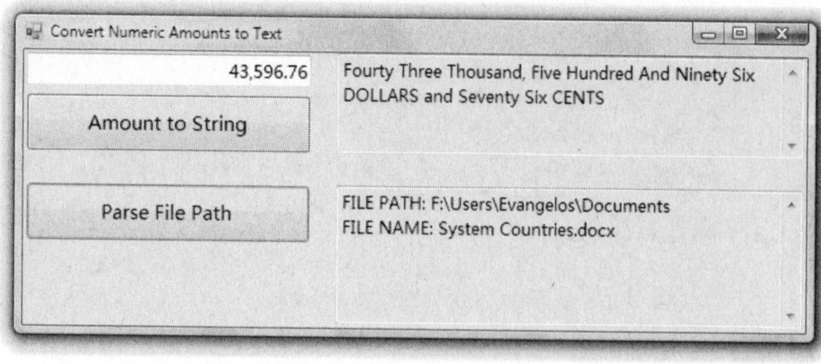

FIGURE 8.8
The test form for the StringTools class

Nesting Classes

In the examples so far, we used simple classes with properties that are basic data types. Practical classes use nested classes and their properties are not basic data types. The very essence of a class is to encapsulate the complexity of an entity and present a simplified view of that particular entity. Let's consider a simple, yet quite practical example.

Real World Scenario

STOCKING A PRODUCT

A class for representing products should expose properties like the product name, its price, the number of items in stock, and so on. Here's a typical class that represents a product:

```
Public Class Product
    Public Property ProductName As String
    Public Property ProductPrice As Decimal
    Public Property InStock As Integer
    Public Property OnOrder As Integer
End Class
```

This class is as straightforward as it gets. But you may notice that the last two properties are related to stocking. What if you created a class to represent a product's in-stock and on-order status and used it in the definition of the Product class? Consider the following Stock class, which represents both the in-stock and on-order quantities of a product:

```
Public Class Stock
    Public Property InStock As Integer
    Public Property OnOrder As Integer
End Class
```

With the Stock class in place, you can create a property of the Stock type in the Product class:

```
Public Class Product
    Public Property ProductName As String
    Public Property ProductPrice As Decimal
```

```
        Public Property ProductStock As Stock
    End Class
```

The ProductStock property encapsulates all the complexity of the product's stock. The Stock property could also contain the units that are reserved for orders that haven't been shipped yet (and therefore are not available for sale, even though they belong to the actual stock) and methods for manipulating the stock. By defining a custom class, ProductStock, we've isolated the stocking details from the product. When we create a new instance of the Product class, we can assign value to the ProductStock property with statements like the following:

```
Dim P As New Product
P.ProductName = "New product"
P.ProductPrice = 99.99
P.ProductStock.InStock = 9
P.ProductStock.OnOrder = 24
```

One item of interest here is where you should define the Stock class. Should you embed its definition in the Product class, or should you implement it as an independent class? Here are the two possible ways to implementing the Product and Stock classes:

```
Public Class Product
    Public Property ProductName As String
    Public Property Price As Decimal
    Public Property ProductStock As Stock
    Public Class Stock
        Public Property InStock As Integer
        Public Property OnOrder As Integer
    End Class
End Class


Public Class Product
    Public Property ProductName As String
    Public Property Price As Decimal
    Public Property ProductStock As Stock
End Class
Public Class Stock
        Public Property InStock As Integer
        Public Property OnOrder As Integer
End Class
```

If the Stock class will be used only in conjunction with the Product class, you can embed its definition in the definition of the larger class. If the Stock class may be used by several other classes, then it should be defined as a separate class. The difference between the two methods of nesting classes is in the way you create new instances of the nested class. If the Stock class is embedded in the Product class, its type is Product.Stock. Otherwise, it's type is just Stock.

The Stock class example is fairly simple, but it demonstrates the use of nested classes. Typically, an application uses high-level classes, such as Customer, Invoice, Product, and so on. These classes are usually too complicated to be built with the basic data types, so we nest the classes in many levels, creating a hierarchy of classes that reflects the hierarchy of the entities we're modeling. Consider the Address property of the Customer class. Doesn't it make sense to create an Address class with the details of the address and reuse it in the Customer class? We could also use it with the Supplier class and possibly other entities that have addresses. An even better example is that of an invoice. The invoice's body contains the items sold: product codes and names, prices, units, and so on.

Let's create a Detail class that represents the details of an invoice:

```
Public Class Detail
    Public Property ProductID As String
    Public Property ProductName As String
    Public Property UnitPrice As Decimal
    Public Property Units As Integer
End Class
```

Then, we can create a class that represents the entire invoice and make use of the Detail class:

```
Public Class Invoice
    Public InvoiceNumber As String
    Public CustomerID As Long
    Public InvoiceDate As DateTime
    Public Details() As Detail

    Public Class Detail
        Public Property ProductID As String
        Public Property ProductName As String
        Public Property UnitPrice As Decimal
        Public Property Units As Integer
    End Class
End Class
```

Since we're on the topic of nesting classes, you should try to combine the ProductID and ProductName properties into a new class, the Product class, and use this class in the definition of the Detail class.

One more interesting topic I should mention briefly here is how to initialize objects with nontrivial members. Let's consider an Invoice class, which exposes a member that is an array of custom objects. Could you initialize an instance of the Invoice class in a single statement? You may wish to give this a try before you look at the code.

The statement is a bit complicated, so let me introduce it gradually. To create an instance of the Invoice class, you'd use a statement like the following:

```
Dim detail = New Invoice.Detail With {.ProductID = 11, .ProductName = "item1",
                    .UnitPrice = 9.95, .Units = 3}
```

To populate the Invoice.Detail property, you must create an array with as many elements as there are detail lines in the invoice. The array's type should be of the Invoice.Detail type, as in the following example:

```
Dim details(1) As Invoice.Detail
Details(0) = New Invoice.Detail With {.ProductID = 101, .ProductName = "item1",
                         .UnitPrice = 9.95, .Units = 3}
Details(1) = New Invoice.Detail With {.ProductID = 102, .ProductName = "item2",
                         .UnitPrice = 4.45, .Units = 12}
```

Finally, you can combine all initialization statements into a single statement that initialized an invoice object:

```
Dim inv As New Invoice With
        {.CustomerID = 1001, .InvoiceDate = Now,
         .InvoiceNumber = "101-1",
         .Details = {New Invoice.Detail With
                        {.ProductID = 101, .ProductName = "item1",
                         .UnitPrice = 9.95, .Units = 3},
                     New Invoice.DetOail With
                        {.ProductID = 102, .ProductName = "item2",
                         .UnitPrice = 4.45, .Units = 12}}}
```

The code is probably simpler to write than it is to read. Start with simple elements, like integers, that will help you get the brackets right, and then replace each simple value with the appropriate object constructor. You can also count on IntelliSense, which will show you the members available at each stage every time you type the period in a With clause.

Operator Overloading

In this section you'll learn about an interesting (but quite optional) feature of class design: how to customize the usual operators. Some operators in Visual Basic act differently on various types of data. The addition operator (+) is the most typical example. When used with numbers, the addition operator adds them. When used with strings, however, it concatenates the strings. The same operator can perform even more complicated calculations with the more-elaborate data types. When you add two variables of the TimeSpan type, the addition operator adds their durations and returns a new TimeSpan object. Each instance of the TimeSpan class is initialized with three integer values, which are the number of hours, minutes, and seconds in the time interval. If you execute the following statements, the value 3882 will be printed in the Output window (this value is the number of seconds in a time span of 1 hour, 4 minutes, and 42 seconds):

```
Dim TS1 As New TimeSpan(1, 0, 30)
Dim TS2 As New TimeSpan(0, 4, 12)
Debug.WriteLine((TS1 + TS2).TotalSeconds.ToString)
```

The TimeSpan class is discussed in detail in Chapter 11, "The Framework at Large," but for the purposes of the preceding example, all you need to know is that variable *TS1* represents a time span of 1 hour and 30 seconds, while *TS2* represents a time span of 4 minutes and 12 seconds. Their sum is a new time span of 1 hour, 4 minutes, and 42 seconds. So far you have seen how to overload methods and how the overloaded forms of a method can simplify development. Sometimes it makes sense to alter the default function of an operator. Let's say you designed a class for representing lengths in meters and centimeters, something like the following:

```
Dim MU As New MetricUnits
MU.Meters = 1
MU.Centimeters = 78
```

The MetricUnits class allows you to specify lengths as an integer number of meters and centimeters (presumably you don't need any more accuracy). The most common operation you'll perform with this class is to add and subtract lengths. However, you can't directly add two objects of the MetricUnits type by using a statement such as this:

```
TotalLength = MU1 + MU2
```

Wouldn't it be nice if you could add two custom objects by using the addition operator? For this to happen, you should be able to overload the addition operator, just as you can overload a method. Indeed, it's possible to overload an operator for your custom classes and write statements like the preceding one. Let's design a class to express lengths in metric and English units and then overload the basic operators for this class.

To overload an operator, you must create an Operator procedure, which is basically a function with an odd name: the name (this is usually a symbol) of the operator you want to overload. The Operator procedure accepts as arguments two values of the custom type (the type for which you're overloading the operator) and returns a value of the same type. Here's the outline of an Operator procedure that overloads the addition operator:

```
Public Shared Operator + (
          ByVal length1 As MetricUnits,
          ByVal length2 As MetricUnits) As MetricUnits
End Operator
```

The procedure's body contains the statements that add the two arguments as units of length, not as numeric values. Overloading operators is a straightforward process that can help you create elegant classes that can be manipulated with the common operators.

VB 2010 at Work: The LengthUnits Class

To demonstrate the overloading of common operators, I included the LengthUnits project, which is a simple class for representing distances in English and metric units. Listing 8.23 shows the definition of the MetricUnits class, which represents lengths in meters and centimeters.

LISTING 8.23:   The MetricUnits class

```
Public Class MetricUnits
     Private _Meters As Integer
     Private _Centimeters As Integer
```

```vbnet
    Public Sub New()

    End Sub

    Public Sub New(ByVal meters As Integer, ByVal centimeters As Integer)
        Me.Meters = meters
        Me.Centimeters = centimeters
    End Sub

    Public Property Meters As Integer

    Public Property Centimeters() As Integer

        Get
            Return _Centimeters
        End Get
        Set(ByVal Value As Integer)
            If value > 100 Then
                _Meters += Convert.ToInt32(Math.Floor(Value / 100))
                _Centimeters = (Value Mod 100)
            Else
                _Centimeters = value
            End If
        End Set
    End Property

    Public Overloads Function Tostring() As String
        Dim str As String = Math.Abs(_Meters).ToString & " meters, " & _
                    Math.Abs(_Centimeters).ToString & " centimeters"
        If _Meters < 0 Or (_Meters = 0 And _Centimeters < 0) Then
            str = "-" & str
        End If
        Return str
    End Function
End Class
```

The class uses the private variables _Meters and _Centimeters to store the two values that determine the length of the current instance of the class. These variables are exposed as the Meters and Centimeters properties. Notice the two forms of the constructor and the custom ToString method. Because the calling application may supply a value that exceeds 100 for the Centimeters property, the code that implements the Centimeters property checks for this condition and increases the Meters property, if needed. It allows the calling application to set the Centimeters property to 252, but internally it increases the _Meters local variable by 2 and sets the _Centimenters local variable to 52. The ToString method returns the value of the current instance of the class as a string such as 1.98, but it inserts a minus sign in front of it if it's negative. If you open the sample project, you'll find the implementation of the EnglishUnits class, which represents lengths in feet and inches. The code is quite similar and I won't repeat it here.

There's nothing out of the ordinary so far; it's actually a trivial class. We can turn it into a highly usable class by overloading the basic operators for the MetricUnits class: namely the addition and subtraction operators. Add the `Operator` procedures shown in Listing 8.24 to the class's code to overload the addition (+) and subtraction (-) operators. By the way, you can't use these operators with variable of the Metric type; the compiler just doesn't know how to add two instances of this class.

LISTING 8.24:   Overloading operators for the `MetricUnits` class

```
Public Shared Operator + (
              ByVal length1 As MetricUnits,
              ByVal length2 As MetricUnits) As MetricUnits
    Dim result As New metricUnits
    result.Meters = 0
    result.Centimeters =
        length1.Meters * 100 + length1.Centimeters +
        length2.Meters * 100 + length2.Centimeters
    Return result
End Operator

Public Shared Operator - (
              ByVal length1 As MetricUnits,
              ByVal length2 As MetricUnits) As MetricUnits
    Dim result As New MetricUnits
    result.Meters = 0
    result.Centimeters =
        length1.Meters * 100 + length1.Centimeters -
        length2.Meters * 100 - length2.Centimeters
    Return result
End Operator
```

These two procedures turn an ordinary class into an elegant custom data type. You can now create MetricUnits variables in your code and manipulate them with the addition and subtraction operators as if they were simple numeric data types. The following code segment exercises the MetricUnits class:

```
Dim MU1 As New MetricUnits
MU1.Centimeters = 194
Debug.WriteLine("194 centimeters is " & MU1.Tostring & " meters")
194 centimeters is 1.94 meters
Dim MU2 As New MetricUnits
MU2.Meters = 1
```

```
MU2.Centimeters = 189
Debug.WriteLine("1 meter and 189 centimeters is " & MU2.Tostring & " meters")
```
1 meter and 189 centimeters is 2.89 meters
```
Debug.WriteLine("194 + 289 centimeters is " & (MU1 + MU2).Tostring & " meters")
```
194 + 289 centimeters is 4.83 meters
```
Debug.WriteLine("194 - 289 centimeters is " & (MU1 - MU2).Tostring & " meters")
```
The negative of 1.94 is -1.94
```
MU1.Meters = 4
MU1.Centimeters = 63
Dim EU1 As EnglishUnits = CType(MU1, EnglishUnits)
Debug.WriteLine("4.62 meters are " & EU1.Tostring)
```
4.62 meters are 15' 2"
```
MU1 = CType(EU1, MetricUnits)
Debug.WriteLine(EU1.Tostring & " are " & MU1.Tostring & " meters")
```
15' 2" are 4.62 meters

If you execute the preceding statements, the highlighted values will appear in the Output window. (The LengthUnits sample project, available for download from www.sybex.com/go/masteringvb2010, uses a TextBox control to display its output.) Figure 8.9 shows the test project for the MetricUnits and EnglishUnits classes. The last few statements convert values between metric and English units, and you'll see the implementation of these operations momentarily.

FIGURE 8.9
Exercising the members
of the MetricUnits class

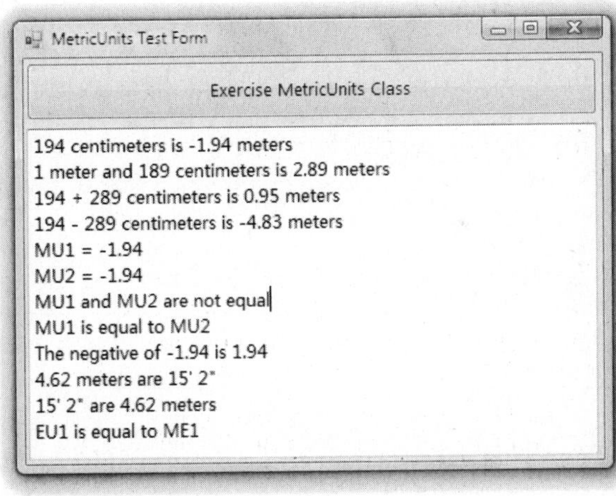

IMPLEMENTING UNARY OPERATORS

In addition to being the subtraction operator, the minus symbol is also a unary operator (it negates the following value). If you attempt to negate a MetricUnits variable, an error will be generated because the subtraction operator expects two values — one on either side of it. In addition to the subtraction operator (which is a binary operator because it operates on two values), we must define the negation operator (which is a unary operator because it operates on a single value). The unary minus operator negates the following value, so a new definition of the subtraction `Operator` procedure is needed. This definition will overload the existing one, as follows:

```
Public Overloads Shared Operator -(
        ByVal length1 As MetricUnits) As MetricUnits
    Dim result As New MetricUnits
    result.Meters = -length1.Meters
    result.Centimeters = -length1.Centimeters
    Return result
End Operator
```

To negate a length unit stored in a variable of the `MetricUnits` type in your application's code, use statements such as the following:

```
MU2 = -MU1
Debug.Write(MU2.Tostring)
Debug.Write((-MU1).Tostring)
```

Both statements will print the following in the Output window:

```
-1 meters, -94 centimeters
```

There are several unary operators, which you can overload in your custom classes as needed. There's the unary + operator (not a common operator), and the `Not`, `IsTrue`, and `IsFalse` operators, which are logical operators. The last unary operator is the `CType` operator, which is exposed as a method of the custom class and is explained next.

HANDLING VARIANTS

To make your custom data type play well with the other data types, you must also provide a `CType()` function that can convert a value of the MetricUnits type to any other type. It doesn't make much sense to convert metric units to dates or any of the built-in objects, but let's say you have another class: the EnglishUnits class. This class is similar to the MetricUnits class, but it exposes the `Inches` and `Feet` properties in place of the `Meters` and `Centimeters` properties. The `CType()` function of the MetricUnits class, which will convert metric units to English units, is shown next:

```
Public Overloads Shared Widening Operator
            CType(ByVal MU As MetricUnits) As EnglishUnits
    Dim EU As New EnglishUnits
    EU.Inches = Convert.ToInt32(
            (MU.Meters * 100 +  MU.Centimeters) / 2.54)
    Return EU
End Operator
```

Do you remember the implicit narrowing and widening conversions we discussed in Chapter 2, "Handling Data"? An attempt to assign an integer value to a decimal variable will produce a warning, but the statement will be executed because it's a widening conversion (no loss of accuracy will occur). The opposite is not true. If the Strict option is on, the compiler won't allow narrowing conversions because not all decimal values can be mapped to integers. To help the compiler enforce strict types, you can use the appropriate keyword to specify whether the CType() function performs a widening or a narrowing conversion. The CType() procedure is shared and overloads the default implementation, which explains all the keywords prefixing its declaration. The following statements exercise the CType method of the MetricUnits class:

```
Debug.Write(MU1.Tostring)
1 meters, 94 centimeters
Debug.WriteLine(CType(MU1, EnglishUnits).Tostring)
6 feet, 4 inches
```

The output of the two statements is highlighted. In this code both classes expose integer properties, so the Widening or Narrowing keyword isn't really important. In other situations, you must carefully specify the type of the conversion to help the compiler generate the appropriate warnings (or exceptions, if needed).

The CType operator we added to the MetricUnits class can only convert values of the MetricUnit type to values of the EnglishUnit type. If it makes sense to convert MetricUnits variables to other types, you must provide more overloaded forms of the CType() procedure. For example, you can convert them to numeric values (the numeric value could be the length in centimeters or a double value that represents the same length in meters). The compiler sees the return type(s) of the various overloaded forms of the CType operator, and since it knows whether the requested conversion is possible, it will generate the appropriate exception.

In short, operator overloading isn't complicated, adds a touch of elegance to a custom class, and enables variables of this type to mix well with the other data types. If you like math, you could implement classes to represent matrices, or complex numbers, and overload the usual operators for addition, multiplication, and so on. The downside of operator overloading (at least in its current implementation) is that it requires quite a bit of code. Even so, the code is straightforward. The LengthUnits sample application contains quite a bit of code that I haven't discussed in this chapter, but I suggest you take a look at the application as it implements many operators, including equals (=), not equals (<>), greater than, and less than.

The Bottom Line

Build your own classes.   Classes contain code that executes without interacting with the user. The class's code is made up of three distinct segments: the declaration of the private variables, the property procedures that set or read the values of the private variables, and the methods, which are implemented as public subroutines or functions. Only the public entities (properties and methods) are accessible by any code outside the class. Optionally, you can implement events that are fired from within the class's code. Classes are referenced through variables of the appropriate type, and applications call the members of the class through these variables. Every time a method is called, or a property is set or read, the corresponding code in the class is executed.

Master It   How do you implement properties and methods in a custom class?

Master It   How would you use a constructor to allow developers to create an instance of your class and populate it with initial data?

Master It Which are the default methods of a custom class that you will most likely override with more meaningful definitions?

Master It How should you handle exceptions in a class?

Overloading operators. Overloading is a common theme in coding classes (or plain procedures) with Visual Basic. In addition to overloading methods, you can overload operators. In other words, you can define the rules for adding or subtracting two custom objects, if this makes sense for your application.

Master It When should you overload operators in a custom class, and why?

Chapter 9

Building Custom Windows Controls

Just as you can design custom classes, you can use Visual Studio to design custom controls. The process is very similar, in the sense that custom controls have properties, methods, and events, which are implemented with code that's identical to the code you'd use to implement these members with classes. The difference is that controls have a visual interface and interact with the user. In short, you must provide the code to draw the control's surface as well as react to selected user actions from within the control's code.

In this chapter, you'll learn how to enhance the functionality of existing controls, a common practice among developers, as well as how to build custom controls from scratch. Specifically, you will learn how to do the following:

- ◆ Extend the functionality of existing Windows Forms controls with inheritance

- ◆ Build compound custom controls that combine multiple existing controls

- ◆ Build custom controls from scratch

- ◆ Customize the rendering of the items in a ListBox control

On Designing Windows Controls

Before I get to the details of how to build custom controls, I want to show you how they relate to other types of projects. I'll discuss briefly the similarities and differences among Windows controls, classes, and Windows projects. This information will help you get the big picture and put together the pieces of the following sections.

An application interacts with the user through its interface. The developer decides how the forms interact with the user, and the user has to follow the rules. Something similar happens with custom controls. The custom control provides a well-defined interface, which consists of properties and methods. This is the only way to manipulate the control. Just as users of your applications don't have access to the source code and can't modify the application, developers can't see the control's source code and must access it through the interface exposed by the control. After an instance of the custom control is placed on the form, the developer can manipulate it through its properties and methods, but you never get to see the code.

In preceding chapters, you learned how to implement interfaces consisting of properties and methods and how to raise events from within a class. This is how you build the interface of a custom Windows control: You implement properties with Property procedures, and you implement methods as Public procedures. Although a class can provide a few properties and any number of methods, a control must provide a large number of properties. A developer who places a custom control on a form expects to see the properties that are common to all the controls (properties to set the control dimensions, the color, and the text font; the Index and Tag properties; and so on). Fortunately, many of the standard properties are exposed automatically. The developer also expects to be able to program all the common events, such as the mouse and keyboard events, as well as some events that are unique to the custom control.

The design of a Windows control is similar to the design of a form. You place controls on a form-like object, called UserControl, which is the control's surface. It provides nearly all the methods of a standard form, and you can adjust its appearance with the drawing methods. In other words, you can use familiar programming techniques to draw a custom control or you can use existing controls to build a custom control.

The major difference between forms and custom controls is that custom controls can exist in two runtime modes. When the developer places a control on a form, the control is actually running. When you set properties through the Properties window, something happens to the control — its appearance changes or the control rejects the changes. It means that the code of the custom control is executing, even though the project in which the control is used is in design mode. When the developer starts the application, the custom control is already running. However, the control must be able to distinguish when the project is in design or execution mode and behave accordingly. Here's the first property of the UserControl object you will be using quite frequently in your code: the DesignMode property. When the control is positioned on a form and used in the Designer, the DesignMode property is True. When the developer starts the project that contains the control, the DesignMode property is False.

This dual runtime mode of a Windows control is something you'll have to get used to. When you design custom controls, you must also switch between the roles of Windows control developer (the programmer who designs the control) and application developer (the programmer who uses the control).

In summary, a custom control is an application with a visible user interface as well as an invisible programming interface. The visible interface is what the developer sees when an instance of the control is placed on the form, and it's also what the user sees on the form when the project is placed in runtime mode. The developer using the control can manipulate it through its properties and methods. The control's properties can be set at both design time and runtime, whereas methods must be called from within the code of the application that uses the control. The properties and methods constitute the control's invisible interface (or the developer interface, as opposed to the user interface). You, the control developer, will develop the visible user interface on a UserControl object, which is almost identical to the Form object; it's like designing a standard application. As far as the control's invisible interface goes, it's like designing a class.

Enhancing Existing Controls

The simplest type of custom Windows control you can build is one that enhances the functionality of an existing control. Fortunately, they're the most common types of custom controls, and many developers have their own collections of enhanced Windows controls. The Windows controls are quite functional, but you won't be hard-pressed to come up with ideas to make them better.

The TextBox control, for example, is a text editor on its own, and you have seen how easy it is to build a text editor by using the properties and methods exposed by this control. Many programmers add code to their projects to customize the appearance and the functionality of the TextBox control.

Let's say you're building data-entry forms composed of many TextBox controls. To help the user identify the current control on the form, it would be nice to change its color while it has the focus. If the current control has a different color from all others, users will quickly locate it.

Another thing you can do with the TextBox control is format its contents as soon as it loses focus. Let's consider a TextBox control that must accept dollar amounts. After the user enters a numeric value, the control could automatically format the numeric value as a dollar amount and perhaps change the text's color to red for negative amounts. When the control receives the focus again, you can display the amount without any special formatting so that users can edit it quickly. As you will see, it's not only possible but actually quite easy to build a control that incorporates all the functionality of a TextBox and some additional features that you provide through the appropriate code. You already know how to add features such as the ones described here to a TextBox from within the application's code. But what if you want to enhance multiple TextBox controls on the same form or reuse your code in multiple applications?

The best approach is to create a new Windows control with all the desired functionality and then reuse it in multiple projects. To use the proper terminology, you can create a new custom Windows control that *inherits* the functionality of the TextBox control. The *derived* control includes all the functionality being inherited from the control, plus any new features you care to add to it. This is exactly what we're going to do in this section.

Building the FocusedTextBox Control

Let's call our new custom control FocusedTextBox. Start a new project, and in the New Project dialog box, select the template Windows Forms Control Library. Name the project Focused-TextBox. The Solution Explorer for this project contains a single item, the UserControl1 item. UserControl1 (see Figure 9.1) is the control's surface — in a way, it's the control's form. This is where you'll design the visible interface of the new control using the same techniques you would use to design a Windows form.

FIGURE 9.1
A custom control in design mode

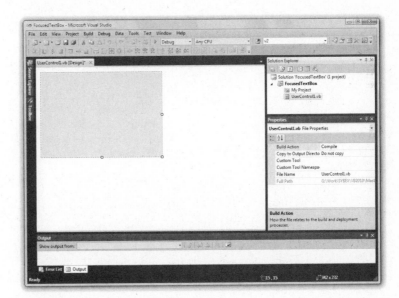

Start by renaming the UserControl1 object to FocusedTextBox. Then save the project by choosing File ➤ Save All. To inherit all the functionality of the TextBox control into our new control, we must insert the appropriate `Inherits` statement in the control's code. Click the Show All button in the Solution Explorer to see all the files that make up the project. Under the `FocusedTextBox.vb` file is the `FocusedTextBox.Designer.vb` file. Open this file by double-clicking its name and you'll see that it begins with the following two statements:

```
Partial Public Class FocusedTextBox
Inherits System.Windows.Forms.UserControl
```

The first statement says that the entire file belongs to the FocusedTextBox class; it's the part of the class that contains initialization code and other statements that the user does not need to see because it's left unchanged in most cases. To design an inherited control, we must change the second statement to the following:

```
Inherits System.Windows.Forms.TextBox
```

This statement tells the compiler that we want our new control to inherit all the functionality of the TextBox control. You must also modify the `InitializeComponent` method in the `FocusedTextBox.Designer.vb` file by removing the statement that sets the control's `AutoScaleMode` property. This statement applies to the generic UserControl object but not to the TextBox control.

As soon as you specify that your custom control inherits the TextBox control, the UserControl object will disappear from the Designer. The Designer knows exactly what the new control must look like (it will look and behave exactly like a TextBox control), and you're not allowed to change its appearance.

If you switch to the `FocusedTextBox.vb` file, you'll see that it's a public class called FocusedTextBox. The Partial class by the same name is part of this class; it contains the code that was generated automatically by Visual Studio. When compiled, both classes will produce a single DLL file. Sometimes we need to split a class's code into two files, and one of them should contain the `Partial` modifier. This keyword signifies that the file contains part of the class. The `FocusedTextBox.vb` file is where you will insert your custom code. The Partial class contains the code emitted by Visual Studio, and you're not supposed to touch it. Inherited controls are an exception to this rule because we have to be able to modify the `Inherits` statement, but the role of the Partial modifier is to enable us to split classes into two separate files.

Let's test the control and verify that it exposes the same functionality as the TextBox control. Figure 9.2 shows the IDE while you're developing an inherited control. Notice that the FocusedTextBox control has inherited all the properties of the TextBox control, such as the `MaxLength` and `PasswordChar` properties.

To test the control, you must add it to a form. A control can't be executed outside the context of a host application. Add a new project to the solution (a Windows Forms Application project) with the File ➤ Add ➤ New Project command. When the Add New Project dialog box appears, select the Windows Forms Application template and set the project's name to **TestProject**. A new folder will be created under the project folder TextBox — the TestProject folder — and the new project will be stored there. The TestProject must also become the solution's startup object. (This is the very reason we added the project to our solution: to have an executable for testing the custom control.) Right-click the test project's name in the Solution Explorer and select Set As StartUp Object in the context menu.

FIGURE 9.2
The IDE during the design of an inherited control

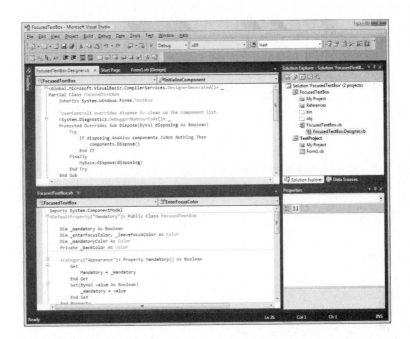

To test the control you just designed, you need to place an instance of the custom control on the form of the test project. First, you must build the control. Select the FocusedTextBox item in the Solution Explorer, and from the Build menu, select the Build FocusedTextBox command (or right-click the FocusedTextBox component in the Solution Explorer and select Build from the context menu). The build process will create a DLL file with the control's executable code in the Bin folder under the project's folder.

Then switch to the test project's main form and open the Toolbox. You will see a new tab, the FocusedTextBox Components tab, which contains all the custom components of the current project. The new control has already been integrated into the design environment, and you can use it as you would any of the built-in Windows controls. Every time you edit the code of the custom control, you must rebuild the control's project for the changes to take effect and update the instances of the custom control on the test form. The icon that appears before the custom control's name is the default icon for all custom Windows controls. You can associate a different icon with your custom control, as explained in the section "Classifying the Control's Properties," later in this chapter.

Place an instance of the FocusedTextBox control on the form and check it out. It looks, feels, and behaves just like a regular TextBox. In fact, it is a TextBox control by a different name. It exposes all the members of the regular TextBox control: You can move it around, resize it, change its Multiline and WordWrap properties, set its Text property, and so on. It also exposes all the methods and events of the TextBox control.

ADDING FUNCTIONALITY TO YOUR CUSTOM CONTROL

As you can see, it's quite trivial to create a new custom control by inheriting any of the built-in Windows controls. Of course, what good is a control that's identical to an existing one? The idea is to add some extra functionality to the TextBox control, so let's do it. Switch to the control project and view the FocusedTextBox object's code. In the code editor's pane, expand the Objects list and select the item FocusedTextBox Events. This list contains the events of the TextBox control because it is the base control for our custom control.

Expand the Events drop-down list and select the Enter event. The following event handler declaration will appear:

```
Private Sub FocusedTextBox_Enter(...) Handles Me.Enter

End Sub
```

This event takes place every time our custom control gets the focus. To change the color of the current control, insert the following statement in the event handler:

```
Me.BackColor = Color.Cyan
```

(Or use any other color you like; just make sure it mixes well with the form's default background color. You can also use the members of the SystemColors enumeration, to help ensure that it mixes well with the background color.) We must also program the Leave event so that the control's background color is reset to white when it loses the focus. Enter the following statement in the Leave event's handler:

```
Private Sub FocusedTextBox_Leave(...) Handles Me.Leave
    Me.BackColor = Color.White
End Sub
```

Having a hard time picking the color that signifies that the control has the focus? Why not expose this value as a property so that you (or other developers using your control) can set it individually in each project? Let's add the EnterFocusColor property, which is the control's background color when it has the focus.

Because our control is meant for data-entry operations, we can add another neat feature. Some fields on a form are usually mandatory, and some are optional. Let's add some visual indication for the mandatory fields. First, we need to specify whether a field is mandatory with the Mandatory property. If a field is mandatory, its background color will be set to the value of the MandatoryColor property, but only if the control is empty.

Here's a quick overview of the control's custom properties:

EnterFocusColor When the control receives the focus, its background color is set to this value. If you don't want the currently active control to change color, set its EnterFocusColor property to white.

Mandatory This property indicates whether the control corresponds to a required field if Mandatory is True or to an optional field if Mandatory is False.

MandatoryColor This is the background color of the control if its Mandatory property is set to True. The MandatoryColor property overwrites the control's default background color. In other words, if the user skips a mandatory field, the corresponding control is painted with the color specified by the MandatoryColor property, and it's not reset to the control's default background color. Required fields behave like optional fields after they have been assigned a value.

If you read the previous chapter, you should be able to implement these properties easily. Listing 9.1 is the code that implements the four custom properties. The values of the properties are stored in the private variables declared at the beginning of the listing. Then the control's properties are implemented as Property procedures.

LISTING 9.1: The Property procedures of the FocusedTextBox custom control

```
Dim _mandatory As Boolean
Dim _enterFocusColor, _leaveFocusColor As Color
Dim _mandatoryColor As Color

Property Mandatory() As Boolean
    Get
        Mandatory = _mandatory
    End Get
    Set(ByVal value As Boolean)
        _mandatory = Value
    End Set
End Property

Property EnterFocusColor() As System.Drawing.Color
    Get
        Return _enterFocusColor
    End Get
    Set(ByVal value As System.Drawing.Color)
        _enterFocusColor = value
    End Set
End Property

Property MandatoryColor() As System.Drawing.Color
    Get
        Return _mandatoryColor
    End Get
    Set(ByVal value As System.Drawing.Color)
        _mandatoryColor = value
    End Set
End Property
```

The last step is to use these properties in the control's Enter and Leave events. When the control receives the focus, it changes its background color to EnterFocusColor to indicate that it's the active control on the form (the control with the focus). When it loses the focus, its background is restored to the usual background color, unless it's a required field and the user has left it blank. In this case, its background color is set to MandatoryColor. Listing 9.2 shows the code in the two focus-related events of the UserControl object.

LISTING 9.2:   Enter and Leave events

```
Private _backColor As Color
Private Sub FocusedTextBox_Enter(…) Handles MyBase.Enter
    _backColor = Me.BackColor
    Me.BackColor = _enterFocusColor
End Sub

Private Sub FocusedTextBox_Leave(…) Handles MyBase.Leave
    If Trim(Me.Text).Length = 0 And _mandatory Then
        Me.BackColor = _mandatoryColor
    Else
        Me.BackColor = _backColor
    End If
End Sub
```

TESTING THE FOCUSEDTEXTBOX CONTROL

Build the control again with the Build ➤ Build FocusedTextBox command and switch to the test form. (To see the Build FocusedTextBox command in the menu, you must select the Windows Control project in the Solution Explorer; otherwise, you will see the command Build TestProject). Place several instances of the custom control on the form, align them, and then select each one and set its properties in the Properties window. The new properties are appended at the bottom of the Properties window, on the Misc tab (for miscellaneous properties). You will see shortly how to add each property under a specific category, as shown in Figure 9.3. Set the custom properties of a few controls on the form and then press F5 to run the application. See how the FocusedTextBox controls behave as you move the focus from one to the other and how they handle the mandatory fields.

FIGURE 9.3
Custom properties of the FocusedTextBox control in the Properties window

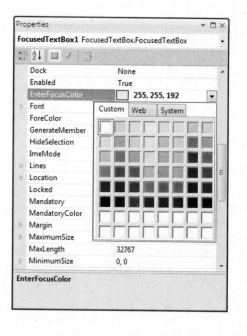

Pretty impressive, isn't it? Even if you have no use for an enhanced TextBox control, you'll agree that building it was quite simple. Next time you need to enhance one of the Windows controls, you'll know how to do it. Just build a new control that inherits from an existing control, add some custom members, and use it. Create a project with all the "enhanced" controls and use them regularly in your projects. All you have to do is add a reference to the DLL that implements the control in a new project, just like reusing a custom class.

CLASSIFYING THE CONTROL'S PROPERTIES

Let's go back to the FocusedTextBox control — there are some loose ends to take care of. First, you must specify the category in the Properties window under which each custom property appears. By default, all the properties you add to a custom control are displayed in the Misc section of the Properties window. To specify that a property be displayed in a different section, use the Category attribute of the Property procedure. As you will see, properties have other attributes too, which you can set in your code as you design the control.

Properties have attributes, which appear in front of the property name and are enclosed in a pair of angle brackets. All attributes are members of the System.ComponentModel class, and you must import this class to the module that contains the control's code. The following attribute declaration in front of the property's name determines the category of the Properties window in which the specific property will appear:

```
<Category("Appearance")> Public Property
```

If none of the existing categories suits a specific property, you can create a new category in the Properties window by specifying its name in the Category attribute. If you have a few properties that should appear in a section called Conditional, insert the following attribute in front of the declarations of the corresponding properties:

```
<Category("Conditional")> Public Property
```

When this control is selected, the Conditional section will appear in the Properties window, and all the properties with this attribute will be under it.

Another attribute is the Description attribute, which determines the property's description that appears at the bottom of the Properties window when the property is selected. You can specify multiple attributes as follows:

```
<Description("Indicates whether the control can be left blank")>
<Category("Appearance")>
Property Mandatory() As Boolean
    '  the property procedure's code
End Property
```

The most important attribute is the DefaultValue attribute, which determines the property's default (initial) value. The DefaultValue attribute must be followed by the default value in parentheses:

```
<Description("Indicates whether the control can be left blank")>
<Category("Appearance"), DefaultValue(False)>
Property Mandatory() As Boolean
    '  the property procedure's code
End Property
```

Some attributes apply to the class that implements the custom controls. The `DefaultProperty` and `DefaultEvent` attributes determine the control's default property and event. To specify that `Mandatory` is the default property of the FocusedTextBox control, replace the class declaration with the following:

```
<DefaultProperty("Mandatory")> Public Class FocusedTextBox
```

Events are discussed later in the chapter, but you already know how to raise an event from within a class. Raising an event from within a control's code is quite similar. Open the Focused-TextBox project, examine its code, and experiment with new properties and methods.

As you may have noticed, all custom controls appear in the Toolbox with the same icon. You can specify the icon to appear in the Toolbox with the `ToolboxBitmap` attribute, whose syntax is as follows, where *imagepath* is a string with the absolute path to a 16×16-pixel bitmap:

```
<ToolboxBitmap(imagepath)> Public Class FocusedTextBox
```

The bitmap is actually stored in the control's DLL and need not be distributed along with the control.

Now we're ready to move on to something more interesting. This time, we'll build a control that combines the functionality of several controls, which is another common scenario. You will literally design its visible interface by dropping controls on the UserControl object, just like designing the visible interface of a Windows form.

Building Compound Controls

A *compound control* provides a visible interface that consists of multiple Windows controls. The controls that make up a compound control are known as *constituent* controls. As a result, this type of control doesn't inherit the functionality of any specific control. You must implement its properties and methods with custom code. This isn't as bad as it sounds, because a compound control inherits the UserControl object, which exposes quite a few members of its own (the `Anchoring` and `Docking` properties, for example, are exposed by the UserControl object, and you need not implement these properties — thank Microsoft). You will add your own members, and in most cases you'll be mapping the properties and methods of the compound controls to a property or method of one of its constituent controls. If your control contains a TextBox control, for example, you can map the custom control's `WordWrap` property to the equivalent property of the TextBox. The following property procedure demonstrates how to do it:

```
Property WordWrap() As Boolean
    Get
        WordWrap = TextBox1.WordWrap
    End Get
    Set(ByVal Value As Boolean)
        TextBox1.WordWrap = Value
    End Set
End Property
```

You don't have to maintain a private variable for storing the value of the custom control's `WordWrap` property. When this property is set, the Property procedure assigns the property's value to the `TextBox1.WordWrap` property. Likewise, when this property's value is requested, the procedure reads it from the constituent control and returns it. In effect, the custom control's `WordWrap` property affects directly the functionality of one of the constituent controls.

The same logic applies to events. Let's say your compound control contains a TextBox and a ComboBox control, and you want to raise the `TextChanged` event when the user edits the TextBox control and the `SelectionChanged` event when the user selects another item in the ComboBox control. First, you must declare the two events:

```
Event TextChanged
Event SelectionChanged
```

Then, you must raise the two events from within the appropriate event handlers: the `TextChanged` event from the TextBox1 control's `TextChanged` event handler and the `SelectionChanged` event from the ComboBox1 control's `SelectedIndexChanged` event handler:

```
Private Sub TextBox1_TextChanged(...)
          Handles FocusedTextBox1.TextChanged
    RaiseEvent TextChanged()
End Sub

Private Sub ComboBox1_SelectedIndexChanged(...)
          Handles ComboBox1.SelectedIndexChanged
    RaiseEvent SelectionChanged()
End Sub
```

VB 2010 at Work: The ColorEdit Control

In this section, you're going to build a compound control that's similar to the Color dialog box. The ColorEdit control allows you to specify a color by adjusting its red, green, and blue components with three scroll bars or to select a color by name. The control's surface at runtime on a form is shown in Figure 9.4.

FIGURE 9.4
The ColorEdit control on a test form

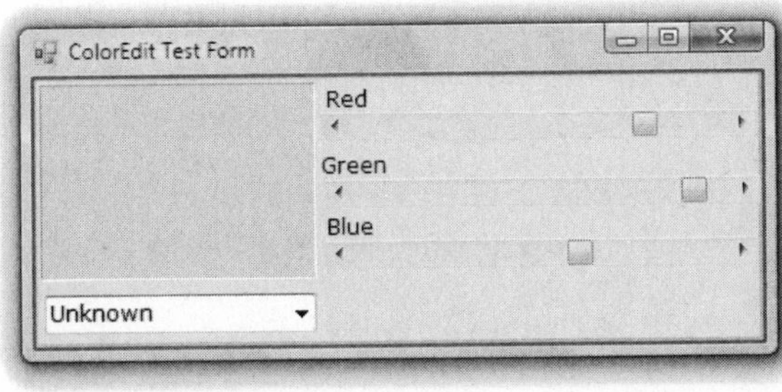

Create a new Windows Control Library project, the ColorEdit project. Save the solution and then add a new Windows Application project, the TestProject, and make it the solution's startup project, just as you did with the first sample project of this chapter.

Now, open the UserControl object and design its interface as shown in Figure 9.4. Place the necessary controls on the UserControl object's surface and align them just as you would do with a Windows form. The three ScrollBar controls are named RedBar, GreenBar, and BlueBar, respectively. The Minimum property for all three controls is 0; the Maximum for all three is 255. This is the valid range of values for a color component. The control at the top-left corner is a Label control with its background color set to black. (We could have used a PictureBox control in its place.) The role of this control is to display the selected color.

The ComboBox at the bottom of the custom control is the NamedColors control, which is populated with color names when the control is loaded. The Color class exposes 140 properties, which are color names (beige, azure, and so on). Don't bother entering all the color names in the ComboBox control; just open the ColorEdit project and you will find the AddNamedColors() subroutine, which does exactly that.

The user can specify a color by sliding the three ScrollBar controls or by selecting an item in the ComboBox control. In either case, the Label control's background color will be set to the selected color. If the color is specified with the ComboBox control, the three ScrollBars will adjust to reflect the color's basic components (red, green, and blue). Not all possible colors that you can specify with the three ScrollBars have a name (there are approximately 16 million colors). That's why the ComboBox control contains the Unknown item, which is selected when the user specifies a color by setting its basic components.

Finally, the ColorEdit control exposes two properties: NamedColor and SelectedColor. The NamedColor property retrieves the selected color's name. If the color isn't selected from the ComboBox control, the value Unknown will be returned. The SelectedColor property returns or sets the current color. Its type is Color, and it can be assigned any expression that represents a color value. The following statement will assign the form's BackColor property to the SelectedColor property of the control:

```
UserControl1.SelectedColor = Me.BackColor
```

You can also specify a color value with the FromARGB method of the Color object:

```
UserControl1.SelectedColor = Color.FromARGB(red, green, blue)
```

The implementation of the SelectedColor property (shown in Listing 9.3) is straightforward. The Get section of the procedure assigns the Label's background color to the SelectedColor property. The Set section of the procedure extracts the three color components from the value of the property and assigns them to the three ScrollBar controls. Then it calls the ShowColor subroutine to update the display. (You'll see shortly what this subroutine does.)

LISTING 9.3:   SelectedColor property procedure

```
Property SelectedColor() As Color
   Get
      SelectedColor = Label1.BackColor
   End Get
   Set(ByVal Value As Color)
      HScrollBar1.Value = Value.R
```

```
      HScrollBar2.Value = Value.G
      HScrollBar3.Value = Value.B
      ShowColor()
   End Set
End Property
```

The `NamedColor` property (see Listing 9.4) is read-only and is marked with the `ReadOnly` keyword in front of the procedure's name. This property retrieves the value of the ComboBox control and returns it.

LISTING 9.4: NamedColor property procedure

```
ReadOnly Property NamedColor() As String
   Get
      NamedColor = ComboBox1.SelectedItem
   End Get
End Property
```

When the user selects a color name in the ComboBox control, the code retrieves the corresponding color value with the `Color.FromName` method. This method accepts a color name as an argument (a string) and returns a color value, which is assigned to the `namedColor` variable. Then the code extracts the three basic color components with the R, G, and B properties. (These properties return the red, green, and blue color components, respectively.) Listing 9.5 shows the code behind the ComboBox control's `SelectedIndexChanged` event, which is fired every time a new color is selected by name.

LISTING 9.5: Specifying a color by name

```
Private Sub ComboBox1_SelectedIndexChanged(...) Handles ComboBox1.SelectedIndexChanged
   Dim namedColor As Color
   Dim colorName As String
   colorName = ComboBox1.SelectedItem
   If colorName <> "Unknown" Then
      namedColor = Color.FromName(colorName)
      HScrollBar1.Value = namedColor.R
      HScrollBar2.Value = namedColor.G
      HScrollBar3.Value = namedColor.B
      ShowColor()
   End If
End Sub
```

The `ShowColor()` subroutine simply sets the Label's background color to the value specified by the three ScrollBar controls. Even when you select a color value by name, the control's code sets the three ScrollBars to the appropriate values. This way, we don't have to write additional code to update the display. The ShowColor() subroutine is quite trivial:

```
Sub ShowColor()
    Label1.BackColor = Color.FromARGB(255, HScrollBar1.Value,
            HScrollBar2.Value, HScrollBar3.Value)
End Sub
```

The single statement in this subroutine picks up the values of the three basic colors from the ScrollBar controls and creates a new color value with the FromARGB method of the Color object. The first argument is the transparency of the color (the alpha channel), and we set it to 255 for a completely opaque color. You can edit the project's code to take into consideration the transparency channel as well. If you do, you must replace the Label control with a PictureBox control and display an image in it. Then draw a rectangle with the specified color on top of it. If the color isn't completely opaque, you'll be able to see the underlying image and visually adjust the transparency channel.

TESTING THE COLOREDIT CONTROL

To test the new control, you must place it on a form. Build the ColorEdit control and switch to the test project (add a new project to the current solution if you haven't done so already). Add an instance of the new custom control to the form. You don't have to enter any code in the test form. Just run it and see how you specify a color, either with the scroll bars or by name. You can also read the value of the selected color through the SelectedColor property. The code behind the Color Form button on the test form does exactly that (it reads the selected color and paints the form with this color):

```
Private Sub Button1_Click(…) Handles Button1.Click
    Me.BackColor = ColorEdit1.SelectedColor
End Sub
```

Building User-Drawn Controls

This is the most complicated but most flexible type of control. A user-drawn control consists of a UserControl object with no constituent controls. You are responsible for updating the control's visible area with the appropriate code, which you must insert in the control's OnPaint method. (This method is invoked automatically every time the control's surface must be redrawn.)

To demonstrate the design of user-drawn controls, we'll develop the Label3D control, which is an enhanced Label control and is shown in Figure 9.5. It provides all the members of the Label control plus the capability to render its caption in three-dimensional type. The new custom control is called Label3D, and its project is the FlexLabel project. It contains the Label3D project (which is a Windows Control Library project) and the usual test project (which is a Windows Application project).

At this point, you're probably thinking about the code that aligns the text and renders it as carved or raised. A good idea is to start with a Windows project, which displays a string on a form and aligns it in all possible ways. A control is an application packaged in a way that allows it to be displayed on a form instead of on the Desktop. As far as the functionality is concerned, in most cases it can be implemented on a regular form. Conversely, if you can display 3D text on a form, you can do so with a custom control.

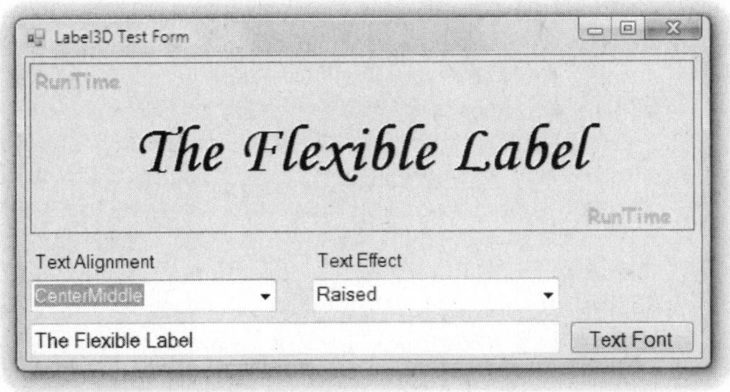

FIGURE 9.5
The Label3D control is
an enhanced Label
control.

Designing a Windows form with the same functionality is fairly straightforward. You haven't seen the drawing methods yet, but this control doesn't involve any advanced drawing techniques. All we need is a method to render strings on the control. To achieve the 3D effect, you must display the same string twice, first in white and then in black on top of the white. The two strings must be displaced slightly, and the direction of the displacement determines the effect (whether the text will appear as raised or carved). The amount of displacement determines the depth of the effect. Use a displacement of 1 pixel for a light effect and a displacement of 2 pixels for a heavy one.

VB 2010 at Work: The Label3D Control

The first step of designing a user-drawn custom control is to design the control's interface: what it will look like when placed on a form (its visible interface) and how developers can access this functionality through its members (the programmatic interface). Sure, you've heard the same advice over and over, and many of you still start coding an application without spending much time designing it. In the real world, especially if they are not a member of a programming team, people design as they code (or the other way around).

The situation is quite different with Windows controls. Your custom control must provide properties, which will be displayed automatically in the Properties window. The developer should be able to adjust every aspect of the control's appearance by manipulating the settings of these properties. In addition, developers expect to see the standard properties shared by most controls (such as the background color, the text font, and so on) in the Properties window. You must carefully design the methods so that they expose all the functionality of the control that should be accessed from within the application's code, and the methods shouldn't overlap. Finally, you must provide the events necessary for the control to react to external events. Don't start coding a custom control unless you have formulated a clear idea of what the control will do and how developers will use it at design time.

Label3D Control Specifications

The Label3D control displays a caption like the standard Label control, so it must provide a Font property, which lets the developer determine the label's font. The UserControl object exposes its own Font property, so we need not implement it in our code. In addition, the Label3D control can align its caption both vertically and horizontally. This functionality will be exposed by the Alignment property, whose possible settings are the members of the Align enumeration: *TopLeft, TopMiddle, TopRight, CenterLeft, CenterMiddle, CenterRight, BottomLeft, BottomMiddle,* and *BottomRight*. The (self-explanatory) values are the names that will appear in the drop-down list of the Alignment property in the Properties window.

Similarly, the text effect is manipulated through the `Effect` property, whose possible settings are the members of the `Effect3D` custom enumeration: *None, Carved, CarvedHeavy, Raised*, and *RaisedHeavy*. There are basically two types of effects (raised and carved text) and two variations on each effect (normal and heavy).

In addition to the custom properties, the Label3D control should also expose the standard properties of a Label control, such as `Tag`, `BackColor`, and so on. Developers expect to see standard properties in the Properties window, and you should implement them. The Label3D control doesn't have any custom methods, but it should provide the standard methods of the Label control, such as the `Move` method. Similarly, although the control doesn't raise any special events, it must support the standard events of the Label control, such as the mouse and keyboard events.

Most of the custom control's functionality exists already, and there should be a simple technique to borrow this functionality from other controls instead of implementing it from scratch. This is indeed the case: The UserControl object, from which all user-drawn controls inherit, exposes a large number of members.

DESIGNING THE CUSTOM CONTROL

Start a new project of the Windows Control Library type, name it **FlexLabel**, and then rename the UserControl1 **object Label3D**. Open the UserControl object's code window and change the name of the class from UserControl1 to **Label3D**.

Every time you place a Windows control on a form, it's named according to the UserControl object's name and a sequence digit. The first instance of the custom control you place on a form will be named Label3D1, the next one will be named Label3D2, and so on. Obviously, it's important to choose a meaningful name for your UserControl object. Note that although this custom control is basically a Label control, it won't inherit from an existing control. You must implement it from scratch in your code.

As you will soon see, the UserControl is the "form" on which the custom control will be designed. It looks, feels, and behaves like a regular VB form, but it's called a UserControl. UserControl objects have additional unique properties that don't apply to a regular form, but to start designing new controls, think of them as regular forms.

You've set the scene for a new user-drawn Windows control. Start by declaring the `Align` and `Effect3D` enumerations, as shown in Listing 9.6.

LISTING 9.6:   `Align` and `Effect3D` enumerations

```
Public Enum Align
    TopLeft
    TopMiddle
    TopRight
    CenterLeft
    CenterMiddle
    CenterRight
    BottomLeft
    BottomMiddle
    BottomRight
End Enum
```

```
Public Enum Effect3D
    None
    Raised
    RaisedHeavy
    Carved
    CarvedHeavy
End Enum
```

The next step is to implement the `Alignment` and `Effect` properties. Each property's type is an enumeration. Listing 9.7 shows the implementation of the two properties.

LISTING 9.7: Alignment and Effect properties

```
Private Shared mAlignment As Align
Private Shared mEffect As Effect3D
Public Property Alignment() As Align
    Get
        Alignment = mAlignment
    End Get
    Set(ByVal Value As Align)
        mAlignment = Value
        Invalidate()
    End Set
End Property

Public Property Effect() As Effect3D
    Get
        Effect = mEffect
    End Get
    Set(ByVal Value As Effect3D)
        mEffect = Value
        Invalidate()
    End Set
End Property
```

The current settings of the two properties are stored in the private variables *mAlignment* and *mEffect*. When either property is set, the Property procedure's code calls the `Invalidate` method of the UserControl object to force a redraw of the string on the control's surface. The call to the `Invalidate` method is required for the control to operate properly in design mode. You can provide a method to redraw the control at runtime (although developers shouldn't have to call a method to refresh the control every time they set a property), but this isn't possible at design time. In general, when a property is changed in the Properties window, the control should be able to update itself and reflect the new property setting, and this is done with a call to the `Invalidate` method. Shortly, you'll see an even better way to automatically redraw the control every time a property is changed.

Finally, you must add one more property, the Caption property, which is the string to be rendered on the control. Declare a private variable to store the control's caption (the *mCaption* variable) and enter the code from Listing 9.8 to implement the Caption property.

LISTING 9.8: Caption Property procedure

```
Private mCaption As String
Property Caption() As String
   Get
      Caption = mCaption
   End Get
   Set(ByVal Value As String)
      mCaption = Value
      Invalidate()
   End Set
End Property
```

The core of the control's code is in the OnPaint method, which is called automatically before the control repaints itself. The same event's code is also executed when the Invalidate method is called, and this is why we call this method every time one of the control's properties changes value. The OnPaint method enables you to take control of the paint process and supply your own code for painting the control's surface. The single characteristic of all user-drawn controls is that they override the default OnPaint method. This is where you must insert the code to draw the control's surface — that is, draw the specified string, taking into consideration the Alignment and Effect properties. The OnPaint method's code is shown in Listing 9.9.

LISTING 9.9: UserControl object's OnPaint method

```
Protected Overrides Sub OnPaint(
        ByVal e As System.Windows.Forms.PaintEventArgs)
    Dim lblFont As Font = Me.Font
    Dim lblBrush As New SolidBrush(Color.Red)
    Dim X, Y As Integer
    Dim textSize As SizeF =
           e.Graphics.MeasureString(mCaption, lblFont)
    Select Case mAlignment
       Case Align.BottomLeft
          X = 2
          Y = Convert.ToInt32(Me.Height - textSize.Height)
       Case Align.BottomMiddle
          X = CInt((Me.Width - textSize.Width) / 2)
          Y = Convert.ToInt32(Me.Height - textSize.Height)
       Case Align.BottomRight
          X = Convert.ToInt32(Me.Width - textSize.Width - 2)
          Y = Convert.ToInt32(Me.Height - textSize.Height)
```

```
        Case Align.CenterLeft
            X = 2
            Y = Convert.ToInt32((Me.Height - textSize.Height) / 2)
        Case Align.CenterMiddle
            X = Convert.ToInt32((Me.Width - textSize.Width) / 2)
            Y = Convert.ToInt32((Me.Height - textSize.Height) / 2)
        Case Align.CenterRight
            X = Convert.ToInt32(Me.Width - textSize.Width - 2)
            Y = Convert.ToInt32((Me.Height - textSize.Height) / 2)
        Case Align.TopLeft
            X = 2
            Y = 2
        Case Align.TopMiddle
            X = Convert.ToInt32((Me.Width - textSize.Width) / 2)
            Y = 2
        Case Align.TopRight
            X = Convert.ToInt32(Me.Width - textSize.Width - 2)
            Y = 2
    End Select
    Dim dispX, dispY As Integer
    Select Case mEffect
        Case Effect3D.None : dispX = 0 : dispY = 0
        Case Effect3D.Raised : dispX = 1 : dispY = 1
        Case Effect3D.RaisedHeavy : dispX = 2 : dispY = 2
        Case Effect3D.Carved : dispX = -1 : dispY = -1
        Case Effect3D.CarvedHeavy : dispX = -2 : dispY = -2
    End Select
    lblBrush.Color = Color.White
    e.Graphics.DrawString(mCaption, lblFont, lblBrush, X, Y)
    lblBrush.Color = Me.ForeColor
    e.Graphics.DrawString(mCaption, lblFont, lblBrush, X + dispX, Y + dispY)
End Sub
```

This subroutine calls for a few explanations. The `Paint` method passes a `PaintEventArgs` argument (the ubiquitous *e* argument). This argument exposes the `Graphics` property, which represents the control's surface. The Graphics object exposes all the methods you can call to create graphics on the control's surface. The Graphics object is discussed briefly in Chapter 11 and in more detail in the tutorial "Drawing and Painting with Visual Basic 2010," but for this chapter all you need to know is that the `MeasureString` method returns the dimensions of a string when rendered in a specific font and the `DrawString` method draws the string in the specified font. The first `Select Case` statement calculates the coordinates of the string's origin on the control's surface, and these coordinates are calculated differently for each type of alignment. Then another `Select Case` statement sets the displacement between the two strings so that when superimposed they produce a three-dimensional effect. Finally, the code draws the string of the `Caption` property on the Graphics object. It draws the string in white first, then in black. The second string is drawn *dispX* pixels to the left and *dispY* pixels below the first one to give the 3D effect. The values of these two variables are determined by the setting of the `Effect` property.

The event handler of the sample project contains a few more statements that are not shown here. These statements print the strings DesignTime and RunTime in a light color on the control's background, depending on the current status of the control. They indicate whether the control is currently in design (if the DesignMode property is True) or runtime (if DesignMode is False), and you will remove them after testing the control.

TESTING YOUR NEW CONTROL

To test your new control, you must first add it to the Toolbox and then place instances of it on the test form. You can add a form to the current project and test the control, but you shouldn't add more components to the control project. It's best to add a new project to the current solution.

 Real World Scenario

A QUICK WAY TO TEST CUSTOM WINDOWS CONTROLS

Visual Studio supports a simple method of testing custom controls. Instead of using a test project, you can press F5 to "run" the Windows Control project. Right-click the name of the Label3D project (the Windows Control project in the solution) in Solution Explorer, and from the context menu choose Set As Startup Project. Then press F5 to start the project. A dialog box (shown in the following screen shot) will appear with the control at runtime and its Properties window.

'Label3D' UserControl TestContainer		
Select User Control:		
FlexLabel.Label3D		Load
Preview:		

AutoScrollMinSize	0, 0	
AutoSize	False	
AutoSizeMode	GrowOnly	
Dock	None	
Location	**0, 0**	
Margin	**6, 6, 6, 6**	
MaximumSize	0, 0	
MinimumSize	0, 0	
Padding	0, 0, 0, 0	
Size	275, 312	
Misc		
Alignment	**CenterMiddle**	
Caption	**Testing testing**	
Effect	**RaisedHeavy**	

Testing testing

Caption

Close

In this dialog box, you can edit any of the control's properties and see how they affect the control at runtime. If the control reacts to any user actions, you can see how the control's code behaves at runtime.

You can't test the control's methods, or program its events, but you'll get an idea of how the control will behave when placed on a form. Use this dialog box while you're developing the control's interface to see how it will behave when placed on a test form and how it reacts when you change its properties. When you're happy with the control's interface, you should test it with a Windows project from which you can call its methods and program its events.

Add the TestProject to the current solution and place on its main form a Label3D control as well as the other controls shown earlier in Figure 9.5. If the Label3D icon doesn't appear in the Toolbox, build the control's project and a new item will be added to the FlexLabel Components tab of the Toolbox.

Now double-click the Label3D control on the form to see its events. Your new control has its own events, and you can program them just as you would program the events of any other control. Enter the following code in the control's Click event:

```
Private Sub Label3D1_Click(…) Handles Label3D1.Click
    MsgBox("My properties are " & vbCrLf &
           "Caption = " Label3D1.Caption.ToString & vbCrLf &
           "Alignment = " Label3D1.Alignment.ToString & vbCrLf &
           "Effect = " Label3D1.Effect.ToString)
End Sub
```

To run the control, press F5 and then click the control. You will see the control's properties displayed in a message box.

The other controls on the test form allow you to set the appearance of the custom control at runtime. The two ComboBox controls are populated with the members of the appropriate enumeration when the form is loaded. In their SelectedIndexChanged event handler, you must set the corresponding property of the FlexLabel control to the selected value, as shown in the following code:

```
Private Sub AlignmentBox_SelectedIndexChanged(…)
            Handles AlignmentBox.SelectedIndexChanged
    Label3D1.Alignment = AlignmentBox.SelectedItem
End Sub

Private Sub EffectsBox_SelectedIndexChanged(…)
            Handles EffectsBox.SelectedIndexChanged
    Label3D1.Effect = EffectsBox.SelectedItem
End Sub
```

The TextBox control at the bottom of the form stores the Caption property. Every time you change this string, the control is updated because the Set procedure of the Caption property calls the Invalidate method.

CHANGED EVENTS

The UserControl object exposes many of the events you need to program the control, such as the key and mouse events, and you need not insert a single line of code in the custom control's code. In addition, you can raise custom events. The Windows controls raise an event every time a property value is changed. If you examine the list of events exposed by the Label3D control, you'll see the `FontChanged` and `SizeChanged` events. These events are provided by the UserControl object. As a control developer, you should expose similar events for your custom properties, the `OnAlignmentChanged`, `OnEffectChanged`, and `OnCaptionChanged` events. This isn't difficult to do, but you must follow a few steps. Start by declaring an event handler for each of the Changed events:

```
Private mOnAlignmentChanged As EventHandler
Private mOnEffectChanged As EventHandler
Private mOnCaptionChanged As EventHandler
```

Then declare the actual events and their handlers:

```
Public Event AlignmentChanged(ByVal sender As Object, ByVal ev As EventArgs)
Public Event EffectChanged(ByVal sender As Object, ByVal ev As EventArgs)
Public Event CaptionChanged(ByVal sender As Object, ByVal ev As EventArgs)
```

When a property changes value, you must call the appropriate method. In the Set section of the Alignment Property procedure, insert the following statement:

```
OnAlignmentChanged(EventArgs.Empty)
```

And finally, invoke the event handlers from within the appropriate *OnEventName* method:

```
Protected Overridable Sub OnAlignmentChanged(ByVal e As EventArgs)
    Invalidate()
    If Not (mOnAlignmentChanged Is Nothing) Then
                    mOnAlignmentChanged.Invoke(Me, e)
End Sub

Protected Overridable Sub OnEffectChanged(ByVal e As EventArgs)
    Invalidate()
    If Not (mOnEffectChanged Is Nothing) Then
                    mOnEffectChanged.Invoke(Me, e)
End Sub

Protected Overridable Sub OnCaptionChanged(ByVal e As EventArgs)
    Invalidate()
    If Not (mOnCaptionChanged Is Nothing) Then
                    mOnCaptionChanged.Invoke(Me, e)
End Sub
```

As you can see, the `OnPropertyChanged` events call the `Invalidate` method to redraw the control when a property's value is changed. As a result, you can now remove the call to the `Invalidate` method from the Property Set procedures. If you switch to the test form, you will see that the custom control exposes the `AlignmentChanged`, `EffectChanged`, and `CaptionChanged` events. The `OnCaptionChanged` method is executed automatically every time the Caption property changes value, and it fires the `CaptionChanged` event. The developer using the Label3D control shouldn't have to program this event.

Raising Custom Events

When you select the custom control in the Objects drop-down list of the editor and expand the list of events for this control, you'll see all the events that the UserControl object may fire. Let's add a custom event for our control. To demonstrate how to raise events from within a custom control, we'll return for a moment to the ColorEdit control you developed a little earlier in this chapter.

Let's say you want to raise an event (the ColorClick event) when the user clicks the Label control displaying the selected color. To raise a custom event, you must declare it in your control and call the RaiseEvent method. Note that the same event may be raised from many different places in the control's code.

To declare the ColorClick event, enter the following statement in the control's code. This line can appear anywhere, but placing it after the private variables that store the property values is customary:

```
Public Event ColorClick(ByVal sender As Object, ByVal e As EventArgs)
```

To raise the ColorClick event when the user clicks the Label control, insert the following statement in the Label control's Click event handler:

```
Private Sub Label1_Click(…) Handles Label1.Click
    RaiseEvent ColorClick(Me, e)
End Sub
```

Raising a custom event from within a control is as simple as raising an event from within a class. It's actually simpler to raise a custom event than to raise the usual PropertyChanged events, which are fired from within the OnPropertyChanged method of the base control.

The RaiseEvent statement in the Label's Click event handler maps the Click event of the Label control to the ColorClick event of the custom control. If you switch to the test form and examine the list of events of the ColorEdit control on the form, you'll see that the new event was added. The ColorClick event doesn't convey much information. When raising custom events, it's likely that you'll want to pass additional information to the developer.

Let's say you want to pass the Label control's color to the application through the second argument of the ColorClick event. The EventArgs type doesn't provide a Color property, so we must build a new type that inherits all the members of the EventArgs type and adds a property: the Color property. You can probably guess that we'll create a custom class that inherits from the EventArgs class and adds the Color member. Enter the statements of Listing 9.10 at the end of the file (after the existing End Class statement).

LISTING 9.10:   Declaring a custom event type

```
Public Class ColorEvent
    Inherits EventArgs
    Public color As Color
End Class
```

Then, declare the following event in the control's code:

```
Public Event ColorClick(ByVal sender As Object, ByVal e As ColorEvent)
```

And finally, raise the `ColorClick` event from within the Label's `Click` event handler (see Listing 9.11).

LISTING 9.11:   Raising a custom event

```
Private Sub Label1_Click(…) Handles Label1.Click
    Dim clrEvent As ColorEvent
    clrEvent.color = Label1.BackColor
    RaiseEvent ColorClick(Me, clrEvent)
End Sub
```

Not all events fired by a custom control are based on property value changes. You can fire events based on external conditions or a timer, as discussed in Chapter 8.

Using the Custom Control in Other Projects

By adding a test project to the Label3D custom control project, we designed and tested the control in the same environment. A great help, indeed, but the custom control can't be used in other projects. If you start another instance of Visual Studio and attempt to add your custom control to the Toolbox, you won't see the Label3D entry there.

To add your custom component in another project, open the Choose Toolbox Items dialog box and then click the .NET Framework Components tab. Be sure to carry out the steps described here while the .NET Framework Components tab is visible. If the COM Components tab is visible instead, you can perform the same steps, but you'll end up with an error message (because the custom component is not a COM component).

Click the Browse button in the dialog box and locate the `FlexLabel.dll` file. It's in the Bin folder under the FlexLabel project's folder. The Label3D control will be added to the list of .NET Framework components, as shown in Figure 9.6. Select the check box in front of the control's name; then click the OK button to close the dialog box and add Label3D to the Toolbox. Now you can use this control in your new project.

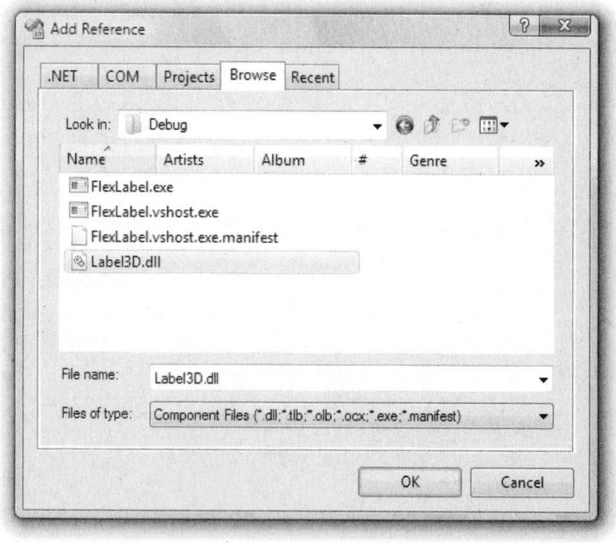

FIGURE 9.6
Adding the Label3D control to another project's Toolbox

Designing Irregularly Shaped Controls

The UserControl object has a rectangular shape by default. However, a custom control need not be rectangular. It's possible to create irregularly shaped forms too, but unlike irregularly shaped controls, an irregularly shaped form is still quite uncommon. Irregularly shaped controls are used in fancy interfaces, and they usually react to movement of the mouse. (They may change color when the mouse is over them or when they're clicked, for example.)

To change the default shape of a custom control, you must use the Region object, which is another graphics-related object that specifies a closed area. You can even use Bezier curves to make highly unusual and smooth shapes for your controls. In this section, we'll do something less ambitious: We'll create controls with the shape of an ellipse, as shown in the upper half of Figure 9.7. To follow the code presented in this section, open the NonRectangularControl project; the custom control is the RoundControl Windows Control Library project, and Form1 is the test form for the control.

FIGURE 9.7
A few instances of an ellipse-shaped control

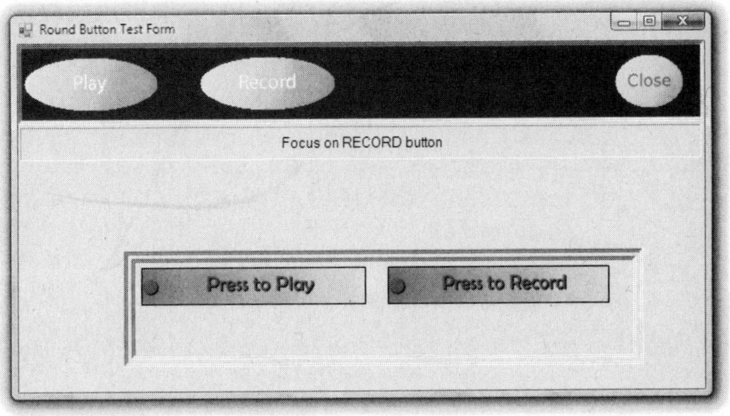

You can turn any control to any shape you like by creating the appropriate Region object and then applying it to the Region property of the control. This must take place from within the control's Paint event. Listing 9.12 shows the statements that change the shape of the control.

LISTING 9.12:   Creating a nonrectangular control

```
Protected Sub PaintControl(ByVal sender As Object,
            ByVal pe As PaintEventArgs) Handles Me.Paint
    pe.Graphics.TextRenderingHint = Drawing.Text.TextRenderingHint.AntiAlias
    Dim roundPath As New GraphicsPath()
    Dim R As New Rectangle(0, 0, Me.Width, Me.Height)
    roundPath.AddEllipse(R)
    Me.Region = New Region(roundPath)
End Sub
```

First, we retrieve the Graphics object of the UserControl; then we create a GraphicsPath object, the *roundPath* variable, and add an ellipse to it. The ellipse is based on the enclosing rectangle. The *R* object is used temporarily to specify the ellipse. The new path is then used to create a Region object, which is assigned to the `Region` property of the UserControl object. This gives our control the shape of an ellipse.

Listing 9.12 shows the statements that specify the control's shape. In addition, you must insert a few statements to display the control's caption, which is specified by the control's `Caption` property. The caption is rendered normally in yellow unless the mouse is hovering over the control, in which case the same caption is rendered with a 3D effect. You already know how to achieve this effect: by printing the same string twice in different colors with a slight displacement between them.

Listing 9.13 shows the code in the control's `MouseEnter` and `MouseLeave` events. When the mouse enters the control's area (this is detected by the control automatically — you won't have to write a single line of code for it), the *currentState* variable is set to *State.Active* (State is an enumeration in the project's code), and the control's caption appears in raised type. In the control's `MouseLeave` event handler, the *currentState* variable is reset to *State.Inactive* and the control's caption appears in regular font. In addition, each time the mouse enters and leaves the control, the `MouseInsideControl` and `MouseOutsideControl` custom events are fired.

LISTING 9.13:   RoundButton control's MouseEnter and MouseLeave events

```
Private Sub RoundButton_MouseEnter(…) Handles MyBase.MouseEnter
    currentState = State.Active
    Me.Refresh()
    RaiseEvent MouseInsideButton(Me)
End Sub

Private Sub RoundButton_MouseLeave(…) Handles MyBase.MouseLeave
    currentState = State.Inactive
    Me.Refresh()
    RaiseEvent MouseOusideButton(Me)
End Sub
```

These two events set up the appropriate variables, and the drawing of the control takes place in the `Paint` event's handler, which is shown in Listing 9.14.

LISTING 9.14:   RoundButton control's Paint event handler

```
Protected Sub PaintControl(ByVal sender As Object,
                   ByVal pe As PaintEventArgs) Handles Me.Paint
    pe.Graphics.TextRenderingHint = Drawing.Text.TextRenderingHint.AntiAlias
    Dim roundPath As New GraphicsPath()
    Dim R As New Rectangle(0, 0, Me.Width, Me.Height)
    roundPath.AddEllipse(R)
    Me.Region = New Region(roundPath)
```

```vb
    Dim Path As New GraphicsPath
    Path.AddEllipse(R)
    Dim grBrush As LinearGradientBrush
    If currentState = State.Active Then
        grBrush = New LinearGradientBrush(
                New Point(0, 0),
                New Point(R.Width, R.Height),
                Color.DarkGray, Color.White)
    Else
        grBrush = New LinearGradientBrush(
                New Point(R.Width, R.Height),
                New Point(0, 0), Color.DarkGray,
                Color.White)
    End If
    pe.Graphics.FillPath(grBrush, Path)
    Dim X As Integer =
            (Me.Width - pe.Graphics.MeasureString(
             currentCaption, currentFont).Width) / 2
    Dim Y As Integer = (Me.Height - pe.Graphics.MeasureString(
            currentCaption, currentFont).Height) / 2
    If currentState = State.Active Then
        pe.Graphics.DrawString(currentCaption,
                currentFont, Brushes.Black, X, Y)
        pe.Graphics.DrawString(currentCaption,
                currentFont,
                New SolidBrush(currentCaptionColor), X - 1, Y - 1)
    Else
        pe.Graphics.DrawString(currentCaption,
                currentFont,
                New SolidBrush(currentCaptionColor), X, Y)
    End If
End Sub
```

The `OnPaint` method uses graphics methods to fill the control with a gradient and center the string on the control. They're the same methods we used in the example of the user-drawn control earlier in this chapter. The drawing methods are discussed in detail in the tutorial "Drawing with VB 2010," which can be found at www.sybex.com/go/masteringvb2010.

The code uses the *currentState* variable, which can take on two values: *Active* and *Inactive*. These two values are members of the `State` enumeration, which is shown next:

```vb
Public Enum State
    Active
    Inactive
End Enum
```

The test form of the project shows how the RoundButton control behaves on a form. You can use the techniques described in this section to make a series of round controls for a totally different look and feel.

The Play button's Click event handler in the test form changes the caption of the button according to the control's current state. It also disables the other RoundButton controls on the test form. Here's the Click event handler of the Play button:

```
Private Sub bttnplay_Click(…) Handles bttnPlay.Click
    If bttnPlay.Caption = "Play" Then
        Label1.Text = "Playing…"
        bttnPlay.Caption = "STOP"
        bttnPlay.Color = Color.Red
        bttnRecord.Enabled = False
        bttnClose.Enabled = False
    Else
        Label1.Text = "Stopped Playing"
        bttnPlay.Caption = "Play"
        bttnPlay.Color = Color.Yellow
        bttnRecord.Enabled = True
        bttnClose.Enabled = True
    End If
End Sub
```

There are many methods for drawing shapes and paths, and you may wish to experiment with other oddly shaped controls. How about a progress indicator control that looks like a thermometer? Or a button with an LED that turns on or changes color when you press the button, like the buttons in the lower half of Figure 9.7? The two rectangular buttons are instances of the LEDButton custom control, which is included in the NonRectangularControl project. Open the project in Visual Studio and examine the code that renders the rectangular buttons emulating an LED in the left corner of the control.

Customizing List Controls

Next, I'll show you how to customize the list controls (such as the ListBox, ComboBox, and TreeView controls). You won't build new custom controls; actually, you'll hook custom code into certain events of a control to take charge of the rendering of its items.

Some of the Windows controls can be customized far more than it is possible through their properties. These are the list controls that allow you to supply your own code for drawing each item. You can use this technique to create a ListBox control that displays its items in different fonts, uses alternating background colors, and so on. You can even put bitmaps on the background of each item, draw the text in any color, and create items of varying heights. This is an interesting technique because without it, as you recall from our discussion of the ListBox control, all items have the same height and you must make the control wide enough to fit the longest item (if this is known at design time). The controls that allow you to take charge of the rendering process of their items are the ListBox, CheckedListBox, ComboBox, and TreeView controls.

To create an owner-drawn control, you must program two events: the MeasureItem and DrawItem events. In the MeasureItem event, you determine the dimensions of the rectangle in which the drawing will take place. In the DrawItem event, you insert the code for rendering the items on the control. Every time the control is about to display an item, it fires the MeasureItem event first and then the `DrawItem` event. By inserting the appropriate code in the two event handlers, you can take control of the rendering process.

These two events don't take place unless you set the `DrawMode` property of the control accordingly. Because only controls that expose the `DrawMode` property can be owner drawn, you have a quick way of figuring out whether a control's appearance can be customized with the techniques discussed in this section. The `DrawMode` property can be set to *Normal* (the control draws its own surface), *OwnerDrawnFixed* (you can draw the control, but the height of the drawing area remains fixed), or *OwnerDrawnVariable* (you can draw the control and use a different height for each item). The same property for the TreeView control has three different settings: *None, OwnerDrawText* (you provide the text for each item), and *OwnerDrawAll* (you're responsible for drawing each node's rectangle).

Designing Owner-Drawn ListBox Controls

The default look of the ListBox control will work fine with most applications, but you might have to create owner-drawn ListBoxes if you want to use different colors or fonts for different types of items or populate the list with items of widely different lengths.

The example you'll build in this section, shown in Figure 9.8, uses an alternating background color, and each item has a different height, depending on the string it holds. Lengthy strings are broken into multiple lines at word boundaries. Because you're responsible for breaking the string into lines, you can use any other technique — for example, you can place an ellipsis to indicate that the string is too long to fit on the control, use a smaller font, and so on. The fancy ListBox of Figure 9.8 was created with the OwnerDrawnList project.

FIGURE 9.8
An unusual, but quite functional, ListBox control

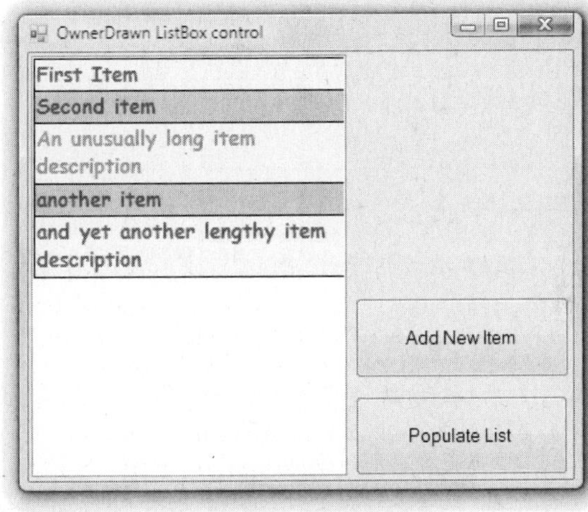

To custom-draw the items in a ListBox control (or a ComboBox, for that matter), you use the `MeasureItem` event to calculate the item's dimensions and the `DrawItem` event to actually draw the item. Each item is a rectangle that exposes a Graphics object, and you can call any of the Graphics object's drawing methods to draw on the item's area. The drawing techniques we'll use in this example are similar to the ones we used in the previous section.

Each time an item is about to be drawn, the `MeasureItem` and `DrawItem` events are fired in this order. In the `MeasureItem` event handler, we set the dimensions of the item with the statements shown in Listing 9.15.

LISTING 9.15:   Setting up an item's rectangle in an owner-drawn ListBox control

```
Private Sub ListBox1_MeasureItem(ByVal sender As Object,
            ByVal e As System.Windows.Forms.MeasureItemEventArgs)
            Handles ListBox1.MeasureItem
    If fnt Is Nothing Then Exit Sub
    Dim itmSize As SizeF
    Dim S As New SizeF(ListBox1.Width, 200)
    itmSize = e.Graphics.MeasureString(ListBox1.Items(e.Index).ToString, fnt, S)
    e.ItemHeight = itmSize.Height
    e.ItemWidth = itmSize.Width
End Sub
```

The `MeasureString` method of the Graphics object accepts as arguments a string, the font in which the string will be rendered, and a SizeF object. The SizeF object provides two properties: the `Width` and `Height` properties, which you use to pass to the method information about the area in which you want to print the string. In our example, we'll print the string in a rectangle that's as wide as the ListBox control and as tall as needed to fit the entire string. I'm using a height of 200 pixels (enough to fit the longest string that users might throw at the control). Upon return, the `MeasureString` method sets the members of the SizeF object to the width and height actually required to print the string.

The two properties of the SizeF object are then used to set the dimensions of the current item (properties `e.ItemWidth` and `e.ItemHeight`). The custom rendering of the current item takes place in the `ItemDraw` event handler, which is shown in Listing 9.16. The Bounds property of the handler's e argument reports the dimensions of the item's cell as you calculated them in the `MeasureItem` event handler.

LISTING 9.16:   Drawing an item in an owner-drawn ListBox control

```
Private Sub ListBox1_DrawItem(ByVal sender As Object,
            ByVal e As System.Windows.Forms.DrawItemEventArgs)
            Handles ListBox1.DrawItem
    If e.Index = -1 Then Exit Sub
    Dim txtBrush As SolidBrush
    Dim bgBrush As SolidBrush
    Dim txtfnt As Font
    If e.Index / 2 = CInt(e.Index / 2) Then
    ' color even numbered items
        txtBrush = New SolidBrush(Color.Blue)
        bgBrush = New SolidBrush(Color.LightYellow)
    Else
    ' color odd numbered items
        txtBrush = New SolidBrush(Color.Blue)
        bgBrush = New SolidBrush(Color.Cyan)
    End If
    If e.State And DrawItemState.Selected Then
```

```
' use red color and bold for the selected item
    txtBrush = New SolidBrush(Color.Red)
    txtfnt = New Font(fnt.Name, fnt.Size, FontStyle.Bold)
Else
    txtfnt = fnt
End If
e.Graphics.FillRectangle(bgBrush, e.Bounds)
e.Graphics.DrawRectangle(Pens.Black, e.Bounds)
Dim R As New RectangleF(e.Bounds.X, e.Bounds.Y,
                        e.Bounds.Width, e.Bounds.Height)
e.Graphics.DrawString(ListBox1.Items(e.Index).ToString, txtfnt, txtBrush, R)
e.DrawFocusRectangle()
End Sub
```

To test the custom-drawn ListBox control, place two buttons on the form, as shown in Figure 9.8. The Add New Item button prompts the user for a new item (a string) and adds it to the control's Items collection. Listing 9.17 shows the code that adds a new item to the list. Note that the code is identical to the code you'd use to add items to a regular ListBox control.

LISTING 9.17:   Adding an item to the list at runtime

```
Private Sub Button1_Click(…) Handles Button1.Click
    Dim newItem As String
    newItem = InputBox("Enter item to add to the list")
    ListBox1.Items.Add(newItem)
End Sub
```

The Bottom Line

Extend the functionality of existing Windows Forms controls with inheritance.   The simplest type of control you can build is one that inherits an existing control. The inherited control includes all the functionality of the original control plus some extra functionality that's specific to an application and that you implement with custom code.

Master It   Describe the process of designing an inherited custom control.

Build compound controls that combine multiple existing controls.   A compound control provides a visible interface that combines multiple Windows controls. As a result, this type of control doesn't inherit the functionality of any specific control; you must expose its properties by providing your own code. The UserControl object, on which the compound control is based, already exposes a large number of members, including some fairly advanced ones such as the Anchoring and Docking properties, and the usual mouse and key events.

Master It   How will you map certain members of a constituent control to custom members of the compound control?

Build custom controls from scratch.   User-drawn controls are the most flexible custom controls because you're in charge of the control's functionality and appearance. Of course, you have to implement all the functionality of the control from within your code, so it takes substantial programming effort to create user-drawn custom controls.

Master It   Describe the process of developing a user-drawn custom control.

Customize the rendering of items in a ListBox control.   The Windows controls that present lists of items display their items in a specific manner. The Framework allows you to take control of the rendering process and change completely the default appearance of the items on these controls. The controls that allow you to take charge of the rendering process of their items are the ListBox, CheckedListBox, ComboBox, and TreeView controls.

To create an owner-drawn control, you must set the `DrawMode` property to a member of the `DrawMode` enumeration and insert the appropriate code in the events `MeasureItem` and `DrawItem`. The `MeasureItem` event is where you decide about the dimensions of the rectangle in which the drawing will take place. The `DrawItem` event is where you insert the code for rendering the items on the control.

Master It   Outline the process of creating a ListBox control that wraps the contents of lengthy items.

Chapter 10

Applied Object-Oriented Programming

This chapter continues the discussion of object-oriented programming (OOP) and covers some of its more-advanced, but truly useful, concepts: inheritance and polymorphism. Instead of jumping to the topic of inheritance, I'll start with a quick overview of what you learned in the previous chapter and how to apply this knowledge.

Inheritance is discussed later in this chapter, along with polymorphism, another powerful OOP technique, and interfaces. But first make sure you understand the basics of OOP because things aren't always as simple as they look (but are quite often simpler than you think).

In this chapter, you'll learn how to do the following:

◆ Extend existing classes using inheritance

◆ Develop flexible classes using polymorphism

Issues in Object-Oriented Programming

Building classes and using them in your code is fairly simple, but there are a few points about OOP that can cause confusion. To help you make the most of OOP and get up to speed, I'm including a list of related topics that are known to cause confusion to programmers — and not only beginners. If you understand the topics of the following sections and how they relate to the topics discussed in the previous chapter, you're more than familiar with the principles of OOP and you can apply them to your projects immediately.

Classes versus Objects

Classes are templates that we use to create new objects. The class contains code and the local variables, and every time you create a new variable based on a specific class, the compiler generates a new set of local variables, where the object's properties will be stored. The code is always the same for all variables of this type. In effect, classes are the blueprints used to manufacture objects in your code. You can also think of classes as custom types. After you add the class Customer to your project (or a reference to the DLL that implements the Customer class), you can declare variables of the Customer type, just as you declare integers and strings. The code for the class is loaded into the memory, and a new set of local variables is created. This process is referred to as class instantiation: Creating an object of a custom type is the same as instantiating the class that implements the custom type. For each object of the Customer type, there's a set of local variables, as they're declared in the class code. The various procedures of the class are invoked as needed by the Common Language Runtime (CLR) and they act on the set of local variables that correspond to the current instance of the class. Some of the local variables may be common among all instances of a class: These are the variables that correspond to shared properties (properties that are being shared by all instances of a class).

When you create a new variable of the Customer type, the New() procedure of the Customer class is invoked. The New() procedure is known as the class constructor. Each class has a default constructor that accepts no arguments, even if the class doesn't contain a New() subroutine. This default constructor is invoked every time a statement similar to the following is executed:

```
Dim cust As New Customer
```

You can overload the New() procedure by specifying arguments, and you should try to provide one or more parameterized constructors. Parameterized constructors allow you (or any developer using your class) to create meaningful instances of the class. Sure, you can create a new Customer object with no data in it, but a Customer object with a name and company makes more sense. The parameterized constructor initializes some of the most characteristic properties of the object.

Objects versus Object Variables

All variables that refer to objects are called object variables. (The other type of variables are value variables, which store base data types, such as characters, integers, strings, and dates.) In declaring object variables, we usually use the New keyword, which is the only way to create a new object. If you omit this keyword from a declaration, only a variable of the Customer type will be created, but no instance of the Customer class will be created in memory, and the variable won't point to an actual object. The following statement declares a variable of the Customer type, but doesn't create an object:

```
Dim Cust As Customer
```

If you attempt to access a member of the Customer class through the *Cust* variable, the infamous NullReferenceException will be thrown. The description of this exception is *Object reference not set to an instance of an object*, which means that the *Cust* variable doesn't point to an instance of the Customer class. Actually, the editor will catch this error and will underline the name of the variable. If you hover over the name of the variable in question, the following explanation will appear on a ToolTip box: *Variable Cust is used before it has been assigned a value. A Null Reference exception could result at runtime.* Why bother declaring variables that don't point to specific objects? The *Cust* variable can be set later in the code to reference an existing instance of the class:

```
Dim Cust As Customer
Dim Cust2 As New Customer
Cust = Cust2
```

After the execution of the preceding statements, both variables point to the same object in memory, and you can set the properties of this object through either variable. You have two object variables but only one object in memory because only one of them was declared with the

New keyword. To set the Company property, you can use either one of the following statements because they both point to the same object in memory:

```
Cust.CompanyName = "New Company Name"
```

or

```
Cust2.CompanyName = "New Company Name"
```

The *Cust* variable is similar to a shortcut. When you create a shortcut to a specific file on your desktop, you're creating a reference to the original file. You do not create a new file or a copy of the original file. You can use the shortcut to access the original file, just as you can use the *Cust* variable to manipulate the properties of the *Cust2* object in the preceding code sample.

It's also common to declare object variables without the New keyword when you know you're going to use them later in your code, as shown in the following loop, which creates 20 items and adds them to a ListView control:

```
Dim LI As ListViewItem
For row = 0 To 20
    LI = New ListViewItem
    LI.Text = "..."
    ' more statements to set up the LI variable
    ListView1.Items.Add(LI)
Next
```

The *LI* variable is declared once, and the code initializes it many times in the following loop. The first statement in the loop creates a new ListViewItem object, and the last statement adds it to the ListView control. Another common scenario is to declare an object variable without initializing it at the form's level and initialize it in a procedure while using its value in several procedures.

🌐 Real World Scenario

WHEN TO USE THE *New* KEYWORD

Many programmers are confused by the fact that most object variables must be declared with the New keyword, whereas some types don't support the New keyword. If you want to create a new object in memory (which is an instance of a class), you must use the New keyword. When you declare a variable without the New keyword, you're creating a reference to an object, but not a new object. Only shared classes must be declared without the New keyword. If in doubt, use the New keyword anyway, and the compiler will let you know immediately whether the class you're instantiating has a constructor. If the New keyword is underlined in error, you know that you must delete it from the declaration. The Math class, for example, is shared and you cannot create a new instance of it; instead, you can call its members as Math.Log, Math.Exp, and so on.

UNINITIALIZED AND NULLABLE VARIABLES

As you already know, an object variable may exist but not be initialized. The following statement creates a new variable for storing a Brush object (one of the drawing objects discussed in the tutorial on graphics that accompanies this book):

```
Dim B As SolidBrush
```

The *B* variable's value is Nothing because it hasn't been initialized yet. After executing the following statement, the *B* variable will have a value and can be used to draw something:

```
B = New SolidBrush(Color.Blue)
```

To find out whether a variable has been initialized or not, we use the Is operator to compare the variable to Nothing:

```
If B Is Nothing Then
    MsgBox("Uninitialized Brush variable")
End If
```

Alternatively, you can use the IsNot operator before attempting to use the *B* variable:

```
If B IsNot Nothing Then
    ' draw something with the brush
End If
```

When a variable is Nothing, we know that it has not been initialized yet — the variable has no value. In my view, this is a state of a variable: a variable may have a value (any value) or not have a value. Let's consider an Integer and a String variable declared as follows:

```
Dim Age As Integer
Dim Name As String
```

The *Age* and *Name* variables have not been initialized explicitly, but they do have a value. Integers are initialized to zero and strings are initialized to empty strings. But is this what we really need? In many cases we want to know whether a variable has been initialized or not, and a default value just doesn't cut it. A variable that has no value is not necessarily a numeric zero or an empty string. To differentiate between the default values and the lack of value, the Framework supports the Nullable type, which indicates a variable of any of the basic types that will not be initialized implicitly. The Nullable keyword is followed by a pair of parentheses and the Of keyword, followed by the actual type. The following statement declares an Integer variable that is not initialized:

```
Dim Age As Nullable(Of Integer)
```

Unfortunately, strings are not nullable. The advantage of using Nullable types in your code is that this type exposes the HasValue property, which returns True if the variable has been initialized, and the `Value` property that returns the actual variable type. This is how you would process the *Age* variable in your code:

```
Dim Age As Nullable(Of Integer)
' other statements
Dim Qualifies As Boolean
If Age.HasValue Then
    If Age.Value < 16 Then
        Qualifies = False
    Else
        Qualifies = True
End If
```

There's also a shorthand notation for declaring Nullable types; just append a question mark to the variable's name as in the following statement:

```
Dim Age? As Integer
```

🌐 Real World Scenario

MISSING INFORMATION

As for a practical example of variables that might not have values, there are plenty. Databases use a special value to indicate that a field has no specific value, the `Null` value. If a product's price is not known yet, or if a book's page count is unknown, this doesn't mean the product will be sold at no cost or that we'll display that the book has zero pages when customers look it up. These fields have a `Null` value and should be handled differently, as you will see in Chapter 15, "Programming with ADO.NET." The same is true for data we read from external sources. An XML file with customer information may contain one or more entries without a value for the `EMail` field. This customer's email address is missing (Null or Nothing) and certainly not an empty string. When you set up variables to receive data from a database, you will find the Nullable type very accommodating because it allows you to match not only the usual values, but also the lack of a specific value.

EXPLORING VALUE TYPES

Okay, if the variables that represent objects are called object variables and the types they represent are called reference types, what other variables are there? There are the regular variables that store the basic data types, and they're called value variables because they store values. An integer, or a string, is not stored as an object for efficiency. An *Integer* variable contains an actual value, not a pointer to the value. Imagine if you had to instantiate the Integer class every time you needed to use an integer value in your code. Not that it's a bad idea, but it would scare away most VB developers. Value variables are so common in programming and they're not implemented as classes for efficiency. Whereas objects require complicated structures in memory, the basic data types are stored in a few bytes and are manipulated much faster than objects.

Consider the following statements:

```
Dim age1, age2 As Integer
age2 = 29
age1 = age2
age2 = 40
```

When you assign a value variable to another, the actual value stored in the variable overwrites the current value of the other variable. The two variables have the same value after the statement that assigns the value of *age2* to the variable *age1*, but they're independent of one another. After the execution of the last statement, the values of *age1* and *age2* are different again. If they were object variables, they would point to the same object after the assignment operation, and you wouldn't be able to set their values separately. You'd be setting the properties of the same object.

Value types are converted to objects as soon as you treat them as objects. As soon as you enter a statement like the following, the *age1* variable is converted to an object:

```
age1.MinValue
```

You'll rarely use the methods of the base types, except for the ToString method of course, but you can turn value variables into object variables at any time. This process is known as *boxing* (the conversion of a value type to a reference type).

EXPLORING REFERENCE TYPES

To better understand how reference types work, consider the following statements that append a new row with two subitems to a ListView control (the control's item is an object of the ListViewItem type):

```
ListView1.Items.Clear
Dim LI As New ListViewItem
LI.Text = "Item 1"
LI.SubItems.Add("Item 1 SubItem 1.a")
LI.SubItems.Add("Item 1 SubItem 1.b")
ListView1.Items.Add(LI)
```

After the execution of the preceding statements, the ListView control contains a single row. This row is an object of the ListViewItem type and exists in memory on its own. Only after the execution of the last statement is the ListViewItem object referenced by the *LI* variable associated with the ListView1 control.

To change the text of the first item, or its appearance, you can manipulate the control's Items collection directly or change the *LI* variable's properties. The following pairs of statements are equivalent:

```
ListView1.Items(0).Text = "Revised Item 1"
ListView1.Items(0).BackColor = Color.Cyan
LI.Text = "Revised Item 1"
LI.BackColor = Color.Cyan
```

There's yet another method to access the ListView control's items. Create an object variable that references a specific item and set the item's properties through this variable:

```
Dim selItem As ListViewItem
selItem = ListView1.Items(0)
selItem.Text = "new caption"
selItem.BackColor = Color.Silver
```

(If you need more information on using the ListView and TreeView controls, please refer to the tutorial "The ListView and TreeView Controls," which is available for download from www.sybex.com/go/masteringvb2010.

A final question for testing your OOP skills: What do you think will happen if you set the *LI* variable to Nothing? Should the control's row disappear? The answer is no. If you thought otherwise, take a moment now to think about why deleting a variable doesn't remove the object from memory. The *LI* variable points to an object in memory; it's not the object. The New keyword created a new ListViewItem object in memory and assigned its address to the variable *LI*. The statement that added the *LI* variable to the control's Items collection associated the object in memory with the control. By setting the *LI* variable to Nothing, we simply removed the pointer to the ListViewItem object in memory, not the object itself. To actually remove the control's first item, you must call the Remove method of the *LI* variable:

```
LI.Remove
```

This statement will remove the ListViewItem object from the control's Items collection, but the actual object still lives in the memory. If you execute the following statement, the item will be added again to the control:

```
ListView1.Items.Add(LI)
```

So to sum up, the ListViewItem object exists in memory and is referenced by the *LI* variable as well as by the ListView control. The Remove method removes the item from the control; it doesn't delete it from the memory. If you remove the item from the control and then set the *LI* variable to Nothing, the object will also be removed from memory.

Another way to look at the *LI* variable is as an intermediate variable. You could add a new row to the ListView control in a single statement without the intermediate variable:

```
ListView1.Items.Add(New ListViewItem("item header"))
```

By the way, the ListViewItem object won't be deleted instantly. The CLR uses a special mechanism to remove objects from memory, the Garbage Collector (GC). The GC runs every so often and removes from memory all objects that are not referenced by any variable. These objects eventually will be removed from memory, but we can't be sure when. (There's no way to force the GC to run on demand.) The CLR will start the GC based on various criteria (the current CPU load, the amount of available memory, and so on). Because objects are removed automatically by the CLR, we say that the lifetime of an object is *nondeterministic*. We know when the object is created, but there's no way to know, or specify, when it's deleted. However, you can rest assured that the object will eventually be removed from memory. After you set the *LI* variable to Nothing and remove the corresponding item from the ListView control, you're left with a ListViewItem object in memory that's not referenced by any other entity.

This object will live a little longer in the memory, until the GC gets a chance to remove it and reclaim the resources allocated to it. Moreover, once you have removed the references to the object, there's no way to access the object any more, even though it will exist for a while in memory before the GC gets a chance to destroy it.

Listing 10.1 shows the statements I've used for this experiment.

LISTING 10.1: Creating and removing objects

```
' Create a new ListViewItem object
Dim LI As New ListViewItem
LI.Text = "Item 1"
LI.SubItems.Add("Item 1 SubItem 1.a")
LI.SubItems.Add("Item 1 SubItem 1.b")
' add it to the ListView control
ListView1.Items.Add(LI)
MsgBox("Item added to the list." & vbCrLf & _
       "Click OK to modify the appearance " & _
       "of the top item through the LI variable.")
' Edit the object's properties
' The new settings will affect the appearance of the
' item on the control immediately
LI.Text = "ITEM 1"
LI.Font = New Font("Verdana", 10, FontStyle.Regular)
LI.BackColor = Color.Azure
MsgBox("Item's text and appearance modified. " & _
          vbCrLf & "Click OK to modify the " & _
          "appearance of the top item through " & _
          "the ListView1.Items collection.")
' Change the first item on the control directly
' Changes also affect the object in memory
ListView1.Items(0).BackColor = Color.LightCyan
LI.SubItems(2).Text = "Revised Subitem"
' Remove the top item from the control
MsgBox("Will remove the top item from the control.")
LI.Remove()
MsgBox("Will restore the deleted item")
' The item was removed from list, but not deleted
' We can add it to the control's Items collection
ListView1.Items.Add(LI)
MsgBox("Will remove object from memory")
' Remove it again from the control
LI.Remove()
' and set it to Nothing
LI = Nothing
' We can no longer access the LI object.
MsgBox("Can I access it again?" & vbCrLf & _
       "NO, YOU'LL GET AN EXCEPTION WHEN THE " & _
       "FOLLOWING STATEMENT IS EXECUTED!")
ListView1.Items.Add(LI)
```

Properties versus Fields

When you set or read a property's value, the corresponding Get or Set segment of the Property procedure is executed. The following statement invokes the Property Set segment of the EMail public property of the class:

```
cust.EMail = "Evangelos.P@Sybex.com"
```

As a reminder, even if the EMail property is an auto-implemented property, a Property procedure is invoked behind the scenes and sets the value of a local variable (the _EMail variable). Obviously, every time you call one of the class properties, the corresponding public procedure in the class is invoked. The following statement invokes both the Set and Get Property procedures of the Customer class Balance property:

```
cust.Balance = cust.Balance + 429.25
```

Trivial properties can also be implemented as public variables. These variables, which are called fields, behave like properties, but no code is executed when the application sets or reads their value. We often implement properties of the enumeration type as fields because they can be set only to valid values and there's no need for validation code. If the Set method of a property doesn't contain any validation code and simply assigns a new value to the local variable that represents the specific property, there's no difference between the property and a field. If you don't plan to validate the values of certain properties, use auto-implemented properties, which are as simple as fields.

Shared versus Instance Members

To really understand classes and appreciate them, you must visualize the way classes combine code and data. Properties contain the data that live along with the code, which determines the object's behavior — its functionality. The functionality of the object is implemented as a number of methods and events. The properties, methods, and events constitute the class's interface. Each instance of the class acts on its own data, and there's no interference between two objects of the same type unless they contain shared properties. A shared property is common to all instances of the class. In other words, there's no local variable for this property, and all instances of the class access the same variable. Shared properties are not common — after all, if many of the properties are common to all instances of the class, why create many objects? Shared methods, on the other hand, are quite common. The Math class is a typical example. To calculate the logarithm of a number, you call the Log method of the Math class:

```
Math.Log(123)
```

You need not create an instance of the Math class before calling any of its methods (which are the common math functions). Actually, you can't create a new instance of the Math class because the entire class is marked as shared.

Let's say you're building a class to represent customers, the Customer class. This class should expose properties that correspond to the columns of the Customers table in a database. Each instance of the Customer class stores information about a specific customer. In addition to the properties, the Customer class should expose a few methods to get data from the database and commit changes or new customers to the database. The GetCustomerByID method, for example, should accept the ID of a customer as an argument, retrieve the corresponding customer's data from the database, and use them to populate the current instance's properties. Here's how you use this class in your code:

```
Dim cust As New Customer
cust.GetCustomerByID("ALFKI")
Debug.WriteLine cust.CompanyName
Debug.WriteLine cust.ContactName & "    " & cust.ContactTitle
```

The GetCustomerByID method can retrieve the customer data from a local database, a remote web service, or even an XML file. The idea is that a single method call gets the data and uses it to populate the properties of the current instance of the class. This method is an instance method because it requires an instance of the class. It populates the properties of this instance, or object.

You could have implemented the GetCustomerByID method as a shared method, but then the method should return an object of the Customer type. The shared method can't populate any object's properties because it can't be applied to an instance of the class. Here's how you'd use the Customer class if the GetCustomerByID method were shared:

```
Dim cust As New Customer
cust = Customer.GetCustomerByID("ALFKI")
Debug.WriteLine cust.CompanyName
Debug.WriteLine cust.ContactName & "    " & cust.ContactTitle
```

As you can see, you call the method of the Customer class, not the method of an object. You could also call the method with the following statement, but the code becomes obscure (at the very least, it's not elegant):

```
cust = cust.GetCustomerByID("ALFKI")
```

The background compiler will detect that you're attempting to access a shared method through an instance of the class and will generate the following warning (the expression will be evaluated at runtime, in spite of the warning):

```
Access of shared member, constant member,
enum member or nested type through an instance;
qualifying expression will not be evaluated.
```

Because the class needs to know the database in which the data is stored, you can provide a Connection property that's shared. Shared properties are usually set when the class is initialized or from within a method that's called before we attempt to access any other methods or any of the class's properties. All the methods in the class use the Connection property to connect to the database. There's no reason to change the setting of this property in the course of an application, but if you change it, all subsequent operations will switch to the new database.

In summary, a class may expose a few shared properties if all instances of the class should access the same property value. It may also expose a few shared methods, which can be called through the class name if there's no need to create an instance of the class in order to call a method. In extreme situations, you can create a shared class: All properties and methods of this class are shared by default. To make the most of objects, however, you should create classes that are instantiated with the New keyword and methods that manipulate the current instance of the class.

Type Casting

The data type used most in earlier versions of the language up to VB 6 was the Variant (which was replaced in subsequent versions by the Object type). A variable declared as Object can store anything, and any variable that hasn't been declared explicitly is an Object variable. Even if you turn on the Strict option, which forces you to declare the type of each variable (and you should always have this option on), you will eventually run into Object variables. When you retrieve an item from a ListBox control, for example, you get back an object, not a specific data type. In the previous chapter, we used the ListBox control to store Contact objects. Every time we retrieved a contact from the control's Items collection, however, we got back an Object variable. To use this object in our code, we had to convert it to a more specific type, the Contact type, with the CType() or DirectCast function. The same is true for an ArrayList, which stores objects, and we usually cast its members to specific types.

Variables declared without a specific type are called untyped variables. Untyped variables should be avoided — and here's why. The following expression represents a ListBox item, which is an object:

```
ListBox1.Items(3)
```

Even if you add a Customer or a Product object to the list, when you retrieve the same item, it's returned as a generic Object variable. If you type the preceding expression followed by a period, you will see in the IntelliSense drop-down list the members of the generic Object variable, which you hardly ever need. If you cast this item to a specific type, the IntelliSense box will show the members of the appropriate type.

The action of changing a variable's type is known as *casting*, and there are two methods for casting variable types — the old VB 6 CType() function and the new DirectCast() function:

```
Dim currentCustomer As Customer
currentCustomer = DirectCast(ListBox1.Items(3), Customer)
```

From now on, you can access the members of the *currentCustomer* variable as usual.

THE TryCast() FUNCTION

If the specified type conversion can't be carried out, the CType() function will throw an InvalidCastException exception. As a reminder, a variation of the CType() and DirectCast() functions is the TryCast() function, which attempts to convert a variable into another type. If the conversion is not possible, the TryCast() function doesn't throw an exception but returns the Nothing value. Here's how the TryCast() function is used:

```
Dim o As Object
o = New Customer("Evangelos Petroutsos", "SYBEX")
c = TryCast(o, Contact)
If c Is Nothing Then
    MsgBox("Can't convert " & o.GetType.Name & " to Contact")
    Exit Sub
End If
' statements to process the c object variable
```

There are situations where you can't avoid explicit casting of variable types. The IIf() function, for example, returns a value of the Object type, regardless of the type of its arguments. The following expression returns the string "Unknown" if the variable *Age* has no value or the value of the *Age* variable if the variable is not Nothing:

```
IIf(Age Is Nothing, "unknown", Age)
```

If you attempt to assign the value returned by the preceding statement to a String variable with the following statements, the code will work fine as long as the Strict option is off:

```
Dim showAge As String = IIf(Age Is Nothing, "unknown", Age)
```

If the Strict option is on, however, the compiler will underline the statement and will generate an error message to the effect that the Strict option disallows the conversion of an Object value to a String. You must explicitly cast the IIf() function's value to a string before assigning it to a String variable:

```
Dim showAge As String = DirectCast(IIf(Age Is Nothing, "unknown", Age), String)
```

The explicit conversion is necessary only if the Strict option is off and the *Age* variable must be declared as Nullable or as Object.

Early versus Late Binding

Untyped variables can't be resolved at compile time; these variables are said to be *late-bound*. An expression such as the following can't be resolved at compile time because the compiler has no way of knowing whether the object retrieved from the ListBox control is of the Customer type (or any other type that exposes the LastName property):

```
ListBox1.Items(3).LastName
```

The preceding statement will compile (as long as the Strict option is off) and execute fine if the fourth item on the ListBox control is of the Customer type or any other type that provides a LastName property. If not, it will compile all right, but a runtime exception will be thrown. Moreover, you won't see any members of interest in the IntelliSense box because the editor doesn't know the exact type of the object retrieved from the ListBox control.

If you cast the object to a specific type, the compiler won't let you reference a nonexisting member, therefore eliminating the chances of runtime exceptions. The last expression in the following code segment is said to be *early-bound* because the compiler knows its type and won't compile a statement that references nonexisting members:

```
Dim currentCustomer As Customer
currentCustomer = CType(ListBox1.Items(3), Customer)
Debug.WriteLine currentCustomer.LastName
```

If you plan to store objects to a ListBox control, you have to use late binding and convert the items of the ListBox control to the appropriate type. Don't forget to override the ToString method of the corresponding class so that a meaningful string is displayed on the control instead of the default string returned by the generic ToString method.

Casting an object to the desired type won't help you unless you know that the object is of the same type or can be cast to the desired type. Make your code as robust as it can be by using the TryCast() function to make sure that the conversion succeeded before attempting to use the *currentCustomer* variable in your code. Late binding is not possible when the Strict option is on. As I've mentioned earlier in this book, even when you're working with the Strict option off, you should turn it back on from time to time to spot the statements that may cause runtime errors.

Discovering a Variable's Type

Sometimes you need to figure out the type of a variable in your code. Even if you declare explicitly all the variables in your code, you might have to discover a specific variable's type at runtime.

The Form object exposes the ActiveControl property, which is the control that has the focus. The ActiveControl property returns a Control object, and you will have to find out its exact type (whether it's a TextBox, a ComboBox, or a Button, for example) from within your code.

All classes, including custom ones, expose the GetType() function, which returns the type of the corresponding object. The GetType() function's return value isn't a string; it is an object that exposes a large number of properties. You can call the IsEnum and IsClass properties to find out whether it's been implemented as an enumeration or as a class as well as the Name property to retrieve the variable's type name.

Consider an event handler that handles the same event for multiple controls on a form. The control that raised the event is passed to the event handler through the *sender* argument, and you can determine the type of the control that raised the event by using a statement such as the following:

```
If sender.GetType Is GetType(System.Windows.Forms.Button) Then
  ' process a button control
End If
```

This is a rather awkward syntax, but take it as is: Use the GetType method to request the type of a variable and the GetType() function to request the type of a control. You can also retrieve the type's name with the TypeName() function, which returns a string:

```
If TypeName(newContact).ToUpper="CONTACT" Then
```

Because the TypeName() function returns a string, you don't have to use the Is operator, but it's a good idea to convert this value to uppercase before attempting any comparisons.

At times, you may have to iterate through all controls on a form (or on a Panel control) and process the controls of a specific type — update the TextBox controls, for example. The following loop goes through all TextBox controls on the current form and cleans them up by converting their contents to uppercase and trimming them:

```
For Each ctrl In Me.Controls
    If ctrl.GetType Is GetType(System.Windows.Forms.TextBox) Then
        Dim TBox As TextBox = CType(ctrl, System.Windows.Forms.TextBox)
```

```
        TBox.Text = TBox.Text.ToUpper.Trim
    End If
Next
```

Notice that you can't use the equals operator to compare types. To compare an object's type to another type, you must use the Is and IsNot keywords, as shown in the preceding example.

By now you should have a good understanding of writing code to manipulate objects. In the following sections, you're going to learn about a powerful concept in OOP, namely how to write new classes that inherit the functionality of existing ones.

Inheritance

Here's a scenario you're all too familiar with: You've written some code, perhaps a collection of functions that you want to reuse in another project. The key word here is *reuse*: *write once, use many times*. For years, VB developers were reusing code, even sharing it with others, with a very simple method: copying from one project and pasting it into another. The copy/paste approach to code reuse has never really worked because the code was never left untouched at its destination. When you're reusing the original code in another project, you make changes to better accommodate the new project. In the process, you also improve the code. At some point, you decide that you should "return" the improved code to the original project and enhance it. Unfortunately, the improved code doesn't always fit nicely into a different project. Some of the improvements break applications that used to work with the not-so-good code. If this has happened to you, imagine what a mess code sharing can be in a large environment with dozens of programmers. On a corporate level, this form of code reuse is a nightmare.

So what's inheritance? Inheritance is a powerful concept in object-oriented programming that allows you to build classes on top of existing ones. You inherit the functionality of an existing class and then add more functionality to it or overwrite some of its base functionality. Inheritance allows you to build hierarchies of classes that better represent physical entities, and it also enables you to reuse existing code (the holy grail of programming). Most importantly, you can inherit the functionality of an existing class without having access to its code.

Inheritance is a technique for reusing and improving code that doesn't cause the applications that use it to break. The idea is to export the code you want to reuse in a format that doesn't allow editing. If more than two people can edit the same code (or if even a single person is allowed to edit the same code in two different projects), any benefits of code reuse evaporate immediately. The code to be shared must be packaged as a DLL, which exposes all the functionality without the risk of being modified in a haphazard way. Only the original creator of the DLL can edit the code, and it's likely that this person will make sure that the interface of the class doesn't change. However, you should still be able to enhance the code in different projects. That's where inheritance comes into the picture. Instead of getting a copy of the code, you inherit a class. The functionality of the class can't change. The code in the DLL is well protected, and there's no way to edit the executable code; it's the class's functionality you inherit.

However, it's possible to add new functionality to the inherited code or even override some of the existing functionality. You can add new functionality to the code by adding new members to the inherited classes. This doesn't break any existing applications that use the original DLL. You can also override some of the functionality by creating a new method that replaces an existing one. Applications that use the original version of the DLL won't see the new members because they work with the old DLL. Newer projects can use the enhanced functionality of the DLL. The current solution to the problem of code reuse is inheritance. It's not a panacea, but it's a step forward.

How to Apply Inheritance

Let me give a simple but quite practical example. A lot of functionality has been built into Windows itself, and we constantly reuse it in our applications. The various Windows Forms controls are a typical example. The functionality of the TextBox control, which we all take for granted, is packaged in a DLL (the System.Windows.Forms.TextBox class). Yet, many of us enhance the functionality of the TextBox control to address specific application requirements. Many developers add a few statements in the control Enter and Leave events to change the color of the TextBox control that has the focus. With VB 2010, it's possible to write just two event handlers that react to these two events and control the background color of the TextBox with the focus. These two handlers handle the corresponding events of all TextBox controls on the form.

A better approach is to design a "new" TextBox control that incorporates all the functionality of the original TextBox control and also changes its background color while it has the focus. The code that implements the TextBox control is hidden from us, but we can reuse it by building a new control that inherits from the TextBox control. As you saw in Chapter 9, "Building Custom Windows Controls," this is not only possible, it's almost trivial; you were able to build an enhanced TextBox control with a few lines of code, which I repeat here for the benefit of readers who weren't interested in building custom controls:

```
Public Class FocusedTextBox
    Inherits System.Windows.Forms.TextBox
    Private Sub FocusedTextBox_Enter(ByVal sender As Object,
                ByVal e As System.EventArgs) Handles Me.Enter
        Me.BackColor = _enterFocusColor
    End Sub

    Private Sub FocusedTextBox_Leave(ByVal sender As Object,
                ByVal e As System.EventArgs) Handles Me.Leave
        Me.BackColor = _leaveFocusColor
    End Sub
End Class
```

The _enterFocusColor and _leaveFocusColor variables are two local variables of the Color type, which must be also be declared. As you understand, the two Color variables are properties of the control (implemented with the usual setters and getters) so that different applications can use different colors for the active TextBox control on the form.

It took just a few lines of code and the keyword Inherits. With the Inherits statement, you include all the functionality of the original TextBox control without touching the control code. Any project that uses the FocusedTextBox control can take advantage of the extra functionality, yet all existing projects will continue to work with the original version of the control. We can easily upgrade a project to take advantage of the enhanced TextBox control by replacing all the instances of the TextBox control on a form with instances of the new control. Some projects may use the new control yet not take advantage of the new functionality and leave the default colors — in which case the enhanced control behaves just like the original TextBox control.

Inheritance is simply the ability to create a new class based on an existing one. The existing class is the parent class, or base class. The new class is said to inherit the base class and is called a subclass, or derived class. The derived class inherits all the functionality of the base class and can add new members and override existing ones. The replacement of existing members with other ones is called overriding. When you replace a member of the base class, you're overriding it. Or, you can overload a method by providing multiple forms of the same method that accept different arguments.

Designing with Inheritance

In this section, we'll tackle a very real problem by using inheritance. Consider a structure for storing product information; in most applications, this structure is optimized for a specific product type. In my consulting days, I've seen designs that try to capture a "global" product: a structure that can store products of any type. This approach leads to unnecessarily large database tables, name conflicts, and all kinds of problems that surface after the program has been installed at your customer's computers with different product types. Here's my suggestion for handling multiple types of products.

Every company makes money by selling products and services, and every company has different requirements. Even two bookstores don't store the same information in their databases. However, there are a few pieces of information that any company uses to sell its products: the product's code, its description, and its price. This is the minimum information you need to sell something (it's the information that's actually printed in the invoice). The price is usually stored to a different table, along with the company's pricing policies. Without being too specific, these are the three pieces of information for ordering and selling products. We use these items to maintain a list of orders and invoices and keep track of the stock, customer balances, and so on. The specifics of a product can be stored to different tables in the database, and these tables will be implemented upon request. If your customer is a book seller, you'll design tables for storing data such as publisher and author names, book descriptions, ISBNs, and the like.

You'll also have to write applications to maintain all this information. To sell the same application to an electronics store, you must write another module for maintaining a different type of product, but the table with the basic data remains the same. Clearly, you can't design a program for handling all types of products, nor can you edit the same application to fit different products. You just have to write different applications for different types of products, but the parts of the application that deal with buying and selling products and with customers, suppliers, and other peripheral entities won't change.

Let's look at a custom class for storing products, which is part of the Products sample project, available for download from www.sybex.com/go/masteringvb2010. The application's main form is shown in Figure 10.1.

The most basic class stores the information you'll need in ordering and invoicing applications: the product's ID, its name, and its price. Here's the implementation of a simple Product class:

```
Public Class Product
    Public Description As String
    Public ProductID As String
    Public ProductBarCode As String
    Public ListPrice As Decimal
End Class
```

I included the product's bar code because this is how products are usually sold at cash registers. This class can represent any product for the purposes of buying and selling it. Populate a collection with objects of this type and you're ready to write a functional interface for creating invoices and purchase orders.

FIGURE 10.1
Exercising the Book and
Supply inherited classes

Products Class - Test Form

Populate Products List

Show All Products

Books

Product ID	ISBN	Title	Subtitle	Price
EN0101	0172833223	Book Title 1	Book Title 1 Subtitle	13.24
CS09212	0175388015	Book Title 2	Book Title 2 Subtitle	25.99

Supplies

Product ID	Product	Product Description	Price
S0001-1	Supply 1	Long description of item 1	2.25
S0011-3	Supply 3	Long description of item 3	15.99
S0011-4	Supply 4	Long description of item 4	1.25
S0011-2	Supply 2	Long description of item 2	0.55

Show Price List

Now let's take into consideration the various types of products. To keep the example simple, consider a store that sells books and supplies. Each type of product is implemented with a different class, which inherits from the Product class. Supplies don't have ISBNs, and books don't have manufacturers — they have authors and publishers; don't try to fit everything into a single object or (even worse) into a single database table.

Figure 10.2 shows the base class, Product, and the two derived classes, Supply and Book, in the Class Diagram Designer. The arrows (if they exist) point to the base class of a derived class, and nested classes (such as the Author and Publisher classes) are contained in the box of their parent class.

FIGURE 10.2
Viewing a hierarchy of
classes with the Class
Diagram Designer

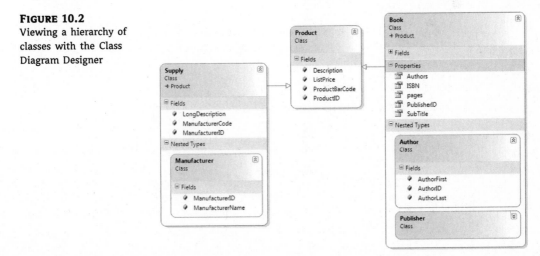

Listing 10.2 is a simple class for representing books, the Book class.

LISTING 10.2: Simple class for representing books

```
Public Class Book
    Inherits Product
    Public Subtitle As String
    Public ISBN As String
    Public pages As Integer
    Public PublisherID As Long
    Public Authors() As Author

    Public Class Author
        Public AuthorID As Long
        Public AuthorLast As String
        Public AuthorFirst As String
    End Class

    Public Class Publisher
        Public PublisherID As Long
        Public PublisherName As String
        Public PublisherPhone As String
    End Class
End Class
```

In addition to its own properties, the Book class exposes the properties of the Product class. Because the book industry has a universal coding scheme (the ISBN), the product's code is the same as its ISBN. This, however, is not a requirement of the application. You will probably add some extra statements to make sure that the *ProductID* field of the Product class and the *ISBN* field of the Book class always have the same value.

The class that represents supplies is shown in Listing 10.3.

LISTING 10.3: Simple class for representing supplies

```
Public Class Supply
    Inherits Product
    Public LongDescription As String
    Public ManufacturerCode As String
    Public ManufacturerID As Long

    Public Class Manufacturer
        Public ManufacturerID As Long
        Public ManufacturerName As String
    End Class
End Class
```

To make sure this class can accommodate all pricing policies for a company, you can implement a `GetPrice` method, which returns the product's sale price (which can be different at different outlets or for different customers and for different periods). The idea is that some piece of code accepts the product's list (or purchase) price and the ID of the customer who buys it. This code can perform all kinds of calculations, look up tables in the database, or perform any other action and return the product's sale price: the price that will appear on the customer's receipt. We'll keep our example simple and sell with the list price.

Let's write some code to populate a few instances of the Book and Supply classes. The following statements populate a HashTable with books and supplies. The HashTable is a structure for storing objects along with their keys. In this case, the keys are the IDs of the products. The HashTable can locate items by means of their keys very quickly, and this is why I chose this type of collection to store the data. HashTables, as well as other collections, are discussed in detail in Chapter 12, "Storing Data in Collections."

```
Dim P1 As New Book
P1.ListPrice = 13.24D
P1.Description = "Book Title 1"
P1.ProductID = "EN0101"
P1.ISBN = "0172833223"
P1.Subtitle = "Book Title 1 Subtitle"
Products.Add(P1.ProductID, P1)

Dim P2 As New Supply
P2.Description = "Supply 1"
P2.ListPrice = 2.25D
P2.LongDescription = "Long description of item 1"
P2.ProductID = "S0001-1"
Products.Add(P2.ProductID, P2)
```

Products is the name of the collection in which the products are stored, and it's declared as follows:

```
Dim Products As New HashTable
```

Each item in the Products collection is either of the Book or of the Supply type, and you can find out its type with the following expression:

```
If TypeOf Products.Item(key) Is Book …
```

Listing 10.4 shows the code behind the Display Products button on the sample application's form. The code iterates through the items of the collection, determines the type of each item, and adds the product's fields to the appropriate ListView control.

LISTING 10.4:   Iterating through a collection of book and supply products

```
Private Sub Button2_Click(…) Handles bttnDisplay.Click
    Dim key As String
    Dim LI As ListViewItem
    For Each key In Products.Keys
```

```
        LI = New ListViewItem
        Dim bookItem As Book, supplyItem As Supply
        If TypeOf Products.Item(key) Is Book Then
            bookItem = CType(Products.Item(key), Book)
            LI.Text = bookItem.ISBN
            LI.SubItems.Add(bookItem.Description)
            LI.SubItems.Add("")
            LI.SubItems.Add(bookItem.ListPrice.ToString("#,##0.00"))
            ListView1.Items.Add(LI)
        End If
        If TypeOf Products.Item(key) Is Supply Then
            supplyItem = CType(Products.Item(key), Supply)
            LI.Text = supplyItem.ProductID
            LI.SubItems.Add(supplyItem.Description)
            LI.SubItems.Add(supplyItem.LongDescription)
            LI.SubItems.Add( supplyItem.ListPrice.ToString("#,##0.00"))
            ListView2.Items.Add(LI)
        End If
    Next
End Sub
```

It's fairly easy to take advantage of inheritance in your projects. The base class encapsulates the functionality that's necessary for multiple classes. All other classes inherit from the base class and add members specific to the derived class.

As I mentioned earlier, for the purpose of selling products, you can use the Product class. You can search for both books and suppliers with their ID or bar code and use the product's description and price to generate an invoice.

The following statements retrieve a product by its ID and print its description and price:

```
Dim id As String
id = InputBox("ID")
If Products.Contains(id) Then
    Dim selProduct As Product
    selProduct = CType(Products(id), Product)
    Debug.WriteLine("The price of " & selProduct.Description &
                " is " & selProduct.ListPrice)
End If
```

If executed, the preceding statements will print the following in the Output window (assuming that you have specified the ID **S0001-1** of course). This is all the information you need to prepare invoices and orders, and it comes from the Product class, which is the base class for all products.

```
The price of Supply 2 is 5.99
```

Before ending this section, I should point out that you can convert the type of an inherited class only to that of the parent class. You can convert instances of the Book and Supply class to objects of the Product type, but not the opposite. The only valid type conversion is a widening conversion (from a narrower to a wider type).

You won't be hard-pressed to come up with real-world situations that call for inheritance. Employees, customers, and suppliers can all inherit from the Person class. Checking and savings accounts can inherit from the Account class, which stores basic information such as customer info and balances. Later in this chapter, you'll develop a class that represents shapes and you'll use it as a basis for classes that implement specific shapes such as circles, rectangles, and so on.

So, has inheritance solved the problem of code reuse? In large complex projects, yes, it has helped a lot. Because designing with inheritance in mind has a substantial initial overhead, people don't use it with small projects (not that this is a recommended practice). In my view, the most important advantage of inheritance is that it forces designers and developers to fully understand the business model for the processes they're modeling early in the game and not have to revise their models substantially when they discover faults in their initial design while they're in the implementation process.

Extension Methods

The concept of extension methods is not based on inheritance, or even the design of classes, but it's a related topic that was introduced to accommodate Language Integrated Query (LINQ). One of the major advantages of inheritance is that it allows you to extend existing classes by adding your custom members. As long as you design your classes carefully, you can create elaborate structures of classes that inherit from one another. Unfortunately, some of the classes in the Framework as not inheritable (and some of them happen to be the very classes you'd like to enhance). The Array class, for example, can't be inherited and neither can the String class.

If you need to add a few methods to a class that are specific to an application, you can use extension methods. With VB 2010 you can add a method to any class without even inheriting it. You don't have to create a new class, just a module that contains one or more procedures that accept the type of the class you want to extend as their first argument. Let me demonstrate the process of creating extension methods with a trivial example and then I'll show you a more practical extension method.

In this first example I'll add two simple methods to the Integer class, the Inc and Dec methods, which increase and decrease an integer value by one (the older among you will actually recognize the origins of the names of the two methods, you may even reminisce about them). In effect, I'll introduce two methods to replace the statements: i += 1 and i -= 1 (where *i* is an integer variable). Create a new project and add a module to it. You can call the module anything; for this example I will use the name **IntegerExtensions**.

First import the following namespace, which will allow you to "decorate" the extension methods with the appropriate keywords:

```
Imports System.Runtime.CompilerServices
```

Now you're ready to add the definitions of the extension methods. Each extension method is just a procedure decorated with the following attribute:

```
<System.Runtime.CompilerServices.Extension()>
```

or

```
<Extension()>
```

if you have imported the System.Runtime.CompilerServices namespace.

You must also make sure that the first argument you pass to the method is of the type you want to extend. A method that extends the Integer class, for example, should accept an integer type as its first argument. This is the instance of the class that your extension method will act upon and it may be followed by any number of additional arguments. Here are the implementations of the Inc and Dec methods:

```
<Extension()>
    Public Function Inc(ByVal i As Integer) As Integer
        Return i + 1
    End Sub

<Extension()>
    Public Function Dec(ByVal i As Integer) As Integer
        Return i - 1
    End Sub
```

With these definitions in place, switch to the project's main form and insert the following in a button's Click event handler:

```
Dim i As Integer = 13
MsgBox(i.Inc.ToString)
MsgBox(i.Dec.ToString)
```

As soon as you enter the name of an Integer variable and the following period, the Inc and Dec methods will be included in the IntelliSense box, along with the built-in methods of the Integer class (they indeed extend the Integer class). The first message box will display the value 14 (the original value plus 1) and the second message box will display the value 12 (the original value minus 1).

You can also implement the same routines as subroutines, which accept their argument by reference and increase the actual value of the variable instead of returning a new value. Let's call the two new methods Increase and Decrease:

```
<Extension()>
Public Sub Increase(ByRef i As Integer)
        i += 1
    End Sub
<Extension()>
Public Sub Decrease(ByRef i As Integer)
        i -= 1
    End Sub
```

To increase/decrease the values by another amount, rewrite the procedures so that they accept a second argument. The methods still apply to the Integer class because their first argument is of the Integer type. Note that when we call an extension method, we don't specify the first argument. This argument is used by the compiler to figure out which class the method extends. The value on which the method acts is the value of the variable to which the method is applied. In other words, extension methods are instance methods.

Now that you have seen the mechanics of implementing extension methods, let's look at a more interesting application of extension methods. Some classes have been heavily extended in version 4.0 of the Framework with this mechanism. A typical example is the Array class.

Declare an array variable and then type on a new line the name of the array and a period. In the IntelliSense box you will see the methods of the Array class. Methods are marked with a little cube. Some of them, however, are marked with a cube and a down arrow: These are the class extension methods. These methods were introduced to extend the corresponding classes, and some typical examples are the Sum and Average methods of the Array class, which return the sum and the average of the elements in the array (provided that the array is of a numeric type). The following statement sets up a small array of integers:

```
Dim integers() = {1, 84, 12, 27, 3, 19, 73, 9, 16, 41, 53, 57, 13}
```

To calculate the sum of its elements you can write a For Each loop to iterate through all the elements of the array, as usual, or call the Sum method:

```
Dim sumOfIntegers = integers.Sum
```

Likewise, you can call the Min and Max methods to retrieve the numerically smaller and larger elements respectively and the Average method to retrieve the average value of a set of numeric values.

The extension methods I just mentioned are not unique to the Array class. They apply to all classes that implement the IEnumerable interface — in other words, they apply to all collections. Not only that, but they're quite flexible because they're overloaded. Some of these extension methods can be called with a function as an argument! The Sum extension method iterates through the collection's items and calculates their sum. It can also calculate the sum of any transformation of the same elements. For example, you can calculate the sum of the squares by passing to the method the definition of a function that returns the square of each element. The Sum method will apply this function to every item as it loops through the elements and take the sum of the values returned by the function. The definition of a function that returns the square of a numeric value is trivial:

```
Function(v As Integer) As Integer
    Return(v * v)
End Function
```

To pass this function as an argument to the Sum method, you pass the body of the function without the Return statement and without the End Function statement:

```
Dim sqSum = integers.Sum(Function(v As Integer) v ^ 2)
```

The v argument is replaced by the current item's value as the method iterates through the collection's elements. The functions you pass to a method are known as lambda expressions, and you'll find a lot more information on lambda expressions in Chapter 13, "XML in Modern Programming."

Another extension method is the Where method, which also accepts as argument a function that returns a True/False value. This function is also known as *predicate* and it determines whether an element of the collection will be included in the calculations or not. The function you pass to the Where method has a different role: It selects the value to be summed, and it's called *selector*. The following expression selects the values that are numerically less than 50:

```
integers.Where(Function(k) k < 50)
```

The expression k < 50 is evaluated for each element of the array and, if smaller, the value is selected. Otherwise, it's ignored. Having selected the "small" values in the array, we can apply the Sum method to calculate the sum of the selected values:

```
Dim smallSum = integers.Where(Function(k) k < 50).Sum
```

Okay, let's combine predicates and selectors to create an expression that sums the squares of selected elements in the array. To request the sum of the squares of all values that are numerically less than 50, use the following expression:

```
Dim smallSqSum = integers.Where(Function(k) k < 50).Sum(Function(v) v ^ 2)
```

The Where extension method selects the desired values and the Sum extension method acts on them. The Where method returns an IEnumerable type to which you can apply the Sum method. The Sum method returns an integer.

I'm sure you got the idea behind extension methods. In Chapter 12 and then in Chapter 13, you will see how to apply lambda expressions to collections and how extension methods enable a new powerful querying technology known as LINQ.

🌐 Real World Scenario

EXTENDING FRAMEWORK CLASSES

In addition to inheriting and extending you own custom classes, you can extend many of the classes of the Framework itself. To add a new method to the ArrayList class, all you have to do is create a new class and include this statement:

```
Inherits ArrayList
```

All the methods in the class will become methods of the ArrayList class and they will appear in the IntelliSense box along with the built-in methods of the ArrayList class.

However, some of the core classes of the Framework are not inheritable. For example, you can't add new methods to the String class by inheriting it. By adding extension methods, you can easily extend any class, but only in the context of a project. To use the same extension features in another project, you must include the module that contains the extension methods. In the preceding chapter you saw the implementation of a method that converts numeric values to strings. If you copy the code into a new module and prefix the methods with the <Extension> attribute, you can make the Num2String method part of the String class. Another interesting extension for the String class is a method that actually reads out text. The Framework contains the Speech.Synthesis namespace, which provides all the tools for generating a synthetic voice with your computer. To extend the String class with a Speak method, create a new module and import the following namespace:

```
Imports System.Speech.Synthesis
```

Before you can import this class in your code, you must reference it in your project, because the Speech namespace isn't referenced by default. Right-click the project name and select

Add Reference from the context menu. On the dialog box that opens, select the `System.Speech.Synthesis` component and then add the following method definition:

```
<Extension()> _
Public Sub Speak(ByVal s As String)
    Dim synth As New SpeechSynthesizer
    Dim voices As
            System.Collections.ObjectModel.ReadOnlyCollection(
                Of System.Speech.Synthesis.InstalledVoice) =
                synth.GetInstalledVoices()
    synth.SelectVoice(voices(0).VoiceInfo.Name)
    synth.Speak(s)
End Sub
```

Easy enough? The first statement retrieves all installed voices (there's only one voice installed by default) and uses the first of them to read out the text with the Speak method. If you're interested in adding voice capabilities to your application, look up the members of the Synthesis namespace. You can adjust the properties of the voice, call the Speak method asynchronously, and even add voice recognition features to your applications.

Polymorphism

A consequence of inheritance is another powerful OOP technique: polymorphism, which is the capability of a base type to adjust itself to accommodate many different derived types. Let's make it simpler by using some analogies in the English language. Take the word *run*, for example. This verb can be used to describe what athletes, cars, or refrigerators do; they all run. In different sentences, the same word takes on different meanings. When you use it with a person, it means going a distance at a fast pace. When you use it with a refrigerator, it means that it's working. When you use it with a car, it may take on both meanings. So, in a sense the word *run* is polymorphic (and so are many other English words): Its exact meaning is differentiated by the context. This is a simple definition of the terms *polymorphism* and *polymorphic* (both of Greek origin, meaning "many forms"). If you reflect on the essence of polymorphism, you'll realize that it's a characteristic that adds intelligence to languages. And languages, being the primary human tool, should match our intelligence. As you will see shortly, polymorphism adds a degree of intelligence to object-oriented programming.

To apply the same analogy to programming, think of a class that describes a basic object such as a shape. This class would be very complicated if it had to describe and handle all shapes. It would be incomplete, too, because the moment you released it to the world, you'd come up with a new shape that can't be described by your class. To design a class that describes all possible shapes, you build a simple class to describe shapes at large, and then you build a separate class for each individual shape: a Triangle class, a Square class, a Circle class, and so on. As you can guess, all these classes inherit the Shape class. Let's also assume that all the classes that describe individual shapes have an Area method, which calculates the area of the shape they describe. The name of the Area method is the same for all classes, but it calculates a different formula for different shapes.

Developers, however, shouldn't have to learn a different syntax of the Area method for each shape; they can declare a Square object and calculate its area with the following statements:

```
Dim shape1 As New Square(5)
Dim area As Double = shape1.Area
```

If *shape2* represents a circle, the same method will calculate the circle's area. (I'm assuming that the constructors accept as an argument the square's side and the circle's radius, respectively.)

```
Dim shape2 As New Circle(9.90)
Dim area As Double = shape2.Area
```

You can go through a list of objects derived from the Shape class and calculate their areas by calling the Area method. No need to know what shape each object represents — you just call its Area method. Let's say you created an array with various shapes. You can go through the collection and calculate the total area with a loop like the following:

```
Dim totalArea As Double = 0.0
For Each s As Shape In Shapes    totalArea += CType(s, Shape).Area
End While
```

The CType() function converts the current element of the collection to a Shape object; it's necessary only if the Strict option is on, which prohibits VB from late-binding the expression. (Strict is off by default, but my suggestion is to turn it on.)

One rather obvious alternative is to build a separate function to calculate the area of each shape (SquareArea, CircleArea, and so on). It will work, but why bother with so many function names, not to mention the overhead in your code? You must first figure out the type of shape described by a specific variable, such as *shape1*, and then call the appropriate method. The code will not be as easy to read, and the longer the application gets, the more If and Case statements you'll be coding. Not to mention that each method would require different arguments for its calculations.

This approach clearly offsets the benefits of object-oriented programming by reducing classes to collections of functions. Even worse, the code is no longer elegant.

The second, even less-efficient method is a really long Area() function that would be able to calculate the area of all shapes. This function should be a very long Case statement, such as the following one:

```
Public Function Area(ByVal shapeType As String) As Double
    Select Case shapeType
        Case "Square": { calculate the area of a square }
        Case "Circle": { calculate the area of a circle }
        { . . . more Case statements }
    End Select
End Function
```

The real problem with this approach is that every time you want to add a new segment to calculate the area of a new shape to the function, you'd have to edit it. If other developers wanted to add a shape, they'd be out of luck. The solution is a method by the name Area that applies to all shapes. Each time we create a new shape by inheriting the base class, we should be able to add a new implementation of the Area method for the specific shape. This way, no matter what a specific shape is, we can calculate its area by calling the polymorphic Area method.

In the following section, I'll show you how to build the Shape class and then extend it with individual classes for various shapes. You'll be able to add your own classes to implement additional shapes, and any code written using the older versions of the Shape class will keep working.

Building the Shape Class

In this section, you'll build a few classes to represent shapes to demonstrate the advantages of implementing polymorphism. Let's start with the Shape class, which will be the base class for all other shapes. This is a really simple class that's pretty useless on its own. Its real use is to expose two methods that can be inherited: Area and Perimeter. Even the two methods don't do much — actually, they do absolutely nothing. All they really do is provide a naming convention. All classes that will inherit the Shape class will have an Area and a Perimeter method, and they must provide the implementation of these methods.

The code shown in Listing 10.5 comes from the Shapes sample project. The application's main form, which exercises the Shape class and its derived classes, is shown in Figure 10.3.

FIGURE 10.3
The main form of the
Shapes project

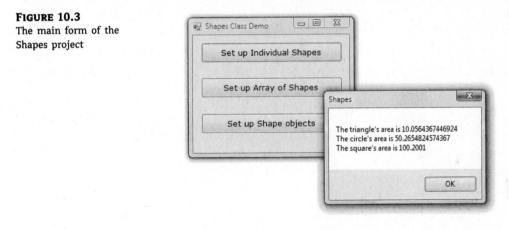

LISTING 10.5:   Shape class

```
Class Shape
   Overridable Function Area() As Double
   End Function
   Overridable Function Perimeter() As Double
   End Function
End Class
```

If there are properties common to all shapes, you place the appropriate Property procedures in the Shape class. If you want to assign a color to your shapes, for instance, insert a

Color property in this class. The Overridable keyword means that a class that inherits from the Shape class can override the default implementation of the corresponding methods or properties. As you will see shortly, it is possible for the base class to provide a few members that can't be overridden in the derived class. The methods that are declared but not implemented in the parent class are called virtual methods, or pure virtual methods.

Next you must implement the classes for the individual shapes. Add another Class module to the project, name it **Shapes**, and enter the code shown in Listing 10.6.

LISTING 10.6: Square, Triangle, and Circle classes

```
Public Class Triangle
    Inherits Shape
    Private _side1, _side2, _side3 As Double

    Property Side1() As Double
        Get
            Return _side1
        End Get
        Set(ByVal Value As Double)
            _side1 = Value
        End Set
    End Property

    Property Side2() As Double
        Get
            Return _side2
        End Get
        Set(ByVal Value As Double)
            _side2 = Value
        End Set
    End Property

    Public Property Side3() As Double
        Get
            Return _side3
        End Get
        Set(ByVal Value As Double)
            _side3 = Value
        End Set
    End Property

    Public Overrides Function Area() As Double
        Dim Perim As Double
        Perim = Perimeter()
        Return (Math.Sqrt((Perim - _side1) * _
                        (Perim - _side2) * (Perim - _side3)))
    End Function
```

```vb
    Public Overrides Function Perimeter() As Double
        Return (_side1 + _side2 + _side3)
    End Function

End Class

Public Class Circle
    Inherits Shape
    Private _Radius As Double

    Public Property Radius() As Double
        Get
            Radius = _Radius
        End Get
        Set(ByVal Value As Double)
            _Radius = Value
        End Set
    End Property

    Public Overrides Function Area() As Double
        Return (Math.PI * _Radius ^ 2)
    End Function

    Public Overrides Function Perimeter() As Double
        Return (2 * Math.PI * _Radius)
    End Function
End Class

Public Class Square
    Inherits Shape
    Private _Side As Double

    Public Property Side() As Double
        Get
            Side = _Side
        End Get
        Set(ByVal Value As Double)
            _Side = Value
        End Set
    End Property

    Public Overrides Function Area() As Double
        Area = _Side * _Side
    End Function

    Public Overrides Function Perimeter() As Double
        Return (4 * _Side)
    End Function
End Class
```

The Shapes.vb file, available for download from www.sybex.com/go/masteringvb2010, contains three classes: the Square, Triangle, and Circle classes. All three expose their basic geometric characteristics as properties. The Triangle class, for example, exposes the properties *Side1*, *Side2*, and *Side3*, which allow you to set the three sides of the triangle. In a real-world application, you may opt to insert some validation code because not any three sides produce a triangle. You might also consider defining a triangle with three points (pairs of x-, y-coordinates), but I'd rather not turn this chapter into Geometry 101. You must also insert parameterized constructors for each shape. The implementation of these constructors is trivial, and I'm not showing it in the listing; you'll find the appropriate constructors if you open the project with Visual Studio. The Area and Perimeter methods are implemented differently for each class, but they do the same thing: They return the area and the perimeter of the corresponding shape. The Area method of the Triangle class is a bit involved, but it's just a formula (the famous Heron's formula for calculating a triangle's area).

TESTING THE SHAPE CLASS

To test the Shape class, all you have to do is create three variables — one for each specific shape — and call their methods. Or, you can store all three variables into an array and iterate through them. If the collection contains *Shape* variables only, the current item is always a shape, and as such it exposes the Area and Perimeter methods. The code in Listing 10.7 does exactly that. First, it declares three variables of the Triangle, Circle, and Square types. Then it sets their properties and calls their Area method to print their areas.

LISTING 10.7:   Testing the Shape class

```
Dim shape1 As New Triangle()
Dim shape2 As New Circle()
Dim shape3 As New Square()
' Set up a triangle
shape1.Side1 = 3
shape1.Side2 = 3.2
shape1.Side3 = 0.94
Console.WriteLine("The triangle's area is " & shape1.Area.ToString)
' Set up a circle
shape2.Radius = 4
Console.WriteLine("The circle's area is " & shape2.Area.ToString)
' Set up a square
shape3.Side = 10.01
Console.WriteLine("The square's area is " & shape3.Area.ToString)
Dim shapes() As Shape
shapes(0) = shape1
shapes(1) = shape2
shapes(2) = shape3
Dim shapeEnum As IEnumerator
Dim totalArea As Double
shapeEnum = shapes.GetEnumerator
While shapeEnum.MoveNext
```

```
    totalArea = totalArea + CType(shapeEnum.Current, shape).Area
End While
Console.WriteLine("The total area of your shapes is " &
                    totalArea.ToString)
```

In the last section, the test code stores all three variables into an array and iterates through its elements. At each iteration, it casts the current item to the Shape type and calls its Area method. The expression that calculates areas is CType(shapeEnum.Current, shape).Area, and the same expression calculates the area of any shape.

CASTING OBJECTS TO THEIR PARENT TYPE

The trick that makes polymorphism work is that objects of a derived type can be cast to their parent type. An object of the Circle type can be cast to the Shape type because the Shape type contains less information than the Circle type. You can cast objects of a derived type to their parent type, but the opposite isn't true. The methods that are shared among multiple derived classes should be declared in the parent class, even if they contain no actual code. Just don't forget to prefix them with the Overridable keyword. There's another related attribute, the MustOverride attribute, which forces every derived class to provide its own implementation of a method or property.

Depending on how you will use the individual shapes in your application, you can add properties and methods to the base class. In a drawing application, all shapes have an outline and a fill color. These properties can be implemented in the Shape class because they apply to all derived classes. Any methods with a common implementation for all classes should also be implemented as methods of the parent class. Methods that are specific to a shape must be implemented in one of the derived classes.

I should also point out here that you can declare variables of the Shape type and initialize them to specific shapes, as follows:

```
Dim triangle As Shape
triangle = New Triangle(1.2, 0.9, 1.3)

Dim circle As Shape
circle = New Circle(10)

Dim square As Shape
square = New Square(23)
```

The *circle* variable's type isn't Shape; its type is determined by its constructor and the *circle* variable is of the Circle type. Needless to say that all three variables expose the Perimeter and Area methods and the code is strongly typed (it will work even with the Strict option on).

Who Can Inherit What?

The Shape base class and the Shapes derived class work fine, but there's a potential problem. A new derived class that implements a new shape may not override the Area or the Perimeter method. If you want to force all derived classes to implement a specific method, you can specify the MustInherit modifier for the class declaration and the MustOverride modifier for the member declaration. If some of the derived classes may not provide their implementation of a method, this method of the derived class must also be declared with the Overridable keyword.

The Shapes project uses the MustInherit keyword in the definition of the Shape class. This keyword tells the CLR that the Shape class can't be used as is; it must be inherited by another class. A class that can't be used as is is known as an *abstract base class*, or a *virtual class*. The definition of the Area and Perimeter methods are prefixed with the MustOverride keyword, which tells the compiler that derived classes (the ones that will inherit the members of the base class) must provide their own implementation of the two methods:

```
Public MustInherit Class Shape
    Public MustOverride Function Area() As Double
    Public MustOverride Function Perimeter() As Double
End Class
```

Notice that there's no End Function statement, just the declaration of the function that must be inherited by all derived classes. If the derived classes may override one or more methods optionally, these methods must be implemented as actual functions. Methods that *must* be over-ridden need not be implemented as functions — they're just placeholders for a name. You must also specify their parameters, if any. The definitions of the methods you specify are known as the methods' *signature*.

There are other modifiers you can use with your classes, such as the NotInheritable modifier, which prevents your class from being used as a base class by other developers. The System.Array class is an example of a Framework class that can't be inherited.

In the following sections, you'll look at the class-related modifiers and learn when to use them. The various modifiers are keywords, such as the Public and Private keywords that you can use in variable declarations. These keywords can be grouped according to the entity they apply to, and I used this grouping to organize them in the following sections.

Parent Class Keywords

These keywords apply to classes that can be inherited, and they appear in front of the Class keyword. By default, all classes can be inherited, but their members can't be overridden. You can change this default behavior with the following modifiers:

NotInheritable This prevents the class from being inherited (also known as a sealed class). The base data types, for example, are not inheritable. In other words, you can't create a new class based on the Integer data type. The Array class is also not inheritable.

MustInherit This class must be inherited. Classes prefixed with the MustInherit attribute are called abstract classes, and the Framework contains quite a few of them. You can't create an object of this class in your code, and therefore, you can't access its methods. The Shape class is nothing more than a blueprint for the methods it exposes and can't be used on its own; that's why it was declared with the MustInherit keyword.

Derived Class Keywords

The following keywords may appear in a derived class; they have to do with the derived class's parent class:

Inherits   Any derived class must inherit an existing class. The Inherits statement tells the compiler which class it derives from. A class that doesn't include the Inherits keyword is by definition a base class.

MyBase   Use the MyBase keyword to access a derived class's parent class from within the derived class's code.

Parent Class Member Keywords

These keywords apply to the members of classes that can be inherited, and they appear in front of the member's name. They determine how derived classes must handle the members (that is, whether they can or must override their properties and methods):

Overridable   Every member with this modifier can be overwritten. If a member is declared as Public only, it can't be overridden. You should allow developers to override as many of the members of your class as possible, as long as you don't think there's a chance that they might break the code by overriding a member. Members declared with the Overridable keyword don't necessarily need to be overridden, so they must provide some functionality.

NotOverridable   Every member declared with this modifier can't be overridden in the inheriting class.

MustOverride   Every member declared with this modifier must be overridden. You can skip the overriding of a member declared with the MustOverride modifier in the derived class as long as the derived class is declared with the MustInherit modifier. This means that the derived class must be inherited by some other class, which then receives the obligation to override the original member declared as MustOverride.

The two methods of the Shape class must be overridden, and we've done so in all the derived classes that implement various shapes. Let's also assume that you want to create different types of triangles with different classes (an orthogonal triangle, an isosceles triangle, and a generic triangle). And let's assume that these classes would inherit the Triangle class. You can skip the definition of the Area method in the Triangle class, but you'd have to include it in the derived classes that implement the various types of triangles. Moreover, the Triangle class would have to be marked as MustInherit.

Public   This modifier tells the CLR that the specific member can be accessed from any application that uses the class. This, as well as the following keywords, are access modifiers and are strictly inheritance related, but I'm listing them here for completeness.

Private   This modifier tells the CLR that the specific member can be accessed only in the module in which it was declared. All the local variables must be declared as Private, and no other class (including derived classes) or application will see them.

Protected   Protected members have scope between public and private, and they can be accessed in the derived class, but they're not exposed to applications using either the parent class or the derived classes. In the derived class, they have a private scope. Use the Protected keyword to mark the members that are of interest to developers who will use your class as a base class, but not to developers who will use it in their applications.

Protected Friend This modifier tells the CLR that the member is available to the class that inherits the class as well as to any other component of the same project.

Derived Class Member Keyword

The Overrides keyword applies to members of derived classes and indicates whether a member of the derived class overrides a base class member. Use this keyword to specify the member of the parent class you're overriding. If a member has the same name in the derived class as in the parent class, this member must be overridden. You can't use the Overrides keyword with members that were declared with the NotOverridable or Protected keywords in the base class.

VB 2010 At Work: The InheritanceKeywords Project

A few examples are in order. The sample application of this section is the InheritanceKeywords project, and it contains a few classes and a simple test form. Create a simple class by entering the statements of Listing 10.8 in a Class module, and name the module **ParentClass**.

LISTING 10.8: InheritanceKeywords class

```
Public MustInherit Class ParentClass
    Public Overridable Function Method1() As String
        Return ("I'm the original Method1")
    End Function
    Protected Function Method2() As String
        Return ("I'm the original Method2")
    End Function
    Public Function Method3() As String
        Return ("I'm the original Method3")
    End Function
    Public MustOverride Function Method4() As String
' No code in a member that must be overridden !
' Notice the lack of the matching End Function here
    Public Function Method5() As String
        Return ("I'm the original Method5")
    End Function
    Private prop1, prop2 As String
    Property Property1() As String
        Get
            Property1 = "Original Property1"
        End Get
        Set
            prop1 = Value
        End Set
    End Property
    Property Property2() As String
        Get
            Property2 = "Original Property2"
```

```
      End Get
      Set
          prop2 = Value
      End Set
   End Property
End Class
```

This class has five methods and two properties. Notice that `Method4` is declared with the `MustOverride` keyword, which means it must be overridden in a derived class. Notice also the structure of `Method4`. It has no code, and the `End Function` statement is missing. `Method4` is declared with the `MustOverride` keyword, so you can't instantiate an object of the Parent-Class type. A class that contains even a single member marked as `MustOverride` must also be declared as `MustInherit`.

Place a button on the class's test form, and in its code window attempt to declare a variable of the ParentClass type. VB will issue a warning that you can't create a new instance of a class declared with the `MustInherit` keyword. Because of the `MustInherit` keyword, you must create a derived class. Enter the lines from Listing 10.9 in the `ParentClass` module after the end of the existing class.

LISTING 10.9:   Derived class

```
Public Class DerivedClass
   Inherits ParentClass
   Overrides Function Method4() As String
      Return ("I'm the derived Method4")
   End Function
   Public Function newMethod() As String
      Console.WriteLine("<This is the derived Class's newMethod " &
                     "calling Method2 of the parent Class> ")
      Console.WriteLine("     " & MyBase.Method2())
   End Function
End Class
```

The `Inherits` keyword determines the parent class. This class overrides the `Method4` member and adds a new method to the derived class: `newMethod`. If you switch to the test form's code window, you can now declare a variable of the DerivedClass type:

```
Dim obj As DerivedClass
```

This class exposes all the members of ParentClass except for the `Method2` method, which is declared with the `Protected` modifier. Notice that the `newMethod()` function calls this method through the `MyBase` keyword and makes its functionality available to the application. Normally, we don't expose `Protected` methods and properties through the derived class.

Let's remove the `MustInherit` keyword from the declaration of the ParentClass class. Because it's no longer mandatory that the ParentClass be inherited, the `MustInherit` keyword is no longer a valid modifier for the class's members. So, `Method4` must be either removed or implemented. Let's delete the declaration of the `Method4` member. Because `Method4` is no longer a member of the ParentClass, you must also remove the entry in the DerivedClass that overrides it.

MyBase and MyClass

The `MyBase` and `MyClass` keywords let you access the members of the base class and the derived class explicitly. To see why they're useful, edit the ParentClass, as shown here:

```
Public Class ParentClass
    Public Overridable Function Method1() As String
        Return (Method4())
    End Function
    Public Overridable Function Method4() As String
        Return ("I'm the original Method4")
    End Function
End Function
```

Override `Method4` in the derived class, as shown here:

```
Public Class DerivedClass
    Inherits ParentClass
    Overrides Function Method4() As String
    Return("Derived Method4")
End Function
```

Switch to the test form, add a button, declare a variable of the derived class, and call its `Method4`:

```
Dim objDerived As New DerivedClass()
Debug.WriteLine(objDerived.Method4)
```

What will you see if you execute these statements? Obviously the string `Derived Method4`. So far, all looks reasonable, and the class behaves intuitively. But what if we add the following method in the derived class?

```
Public Function newMethod() As String
    Return (Method1())
End Function
```

This method calls `Method1` in the ParentClass class because `Method1` is not overridden in the derived class. `Method1` in the base class calls `Method4`. But which `Method4` gets invoked? Surprised? It's the derived `Method4`! To fix this behavior (assuming you want to call the `Method4` of the base class), change the implementation of `Method1` to the following:

```
Public Overridable Function Method1() As String
    Return (MyClass.Method4())
End Function
```

If you run the application again, the statement

```
Console.WriteLine(objDerived.newMethod)
```

will print this string:

```
I'm the original Method4
```

Is it reasonable for a method of the base class to call the overridden method? It is reasonable because the overridden class is newer than the base class, and the compiler tries to use the newest members. If you had other classes inheriting from the DerivedClass class, their members would take precedence.

Use the MyClass keyword to make sure you're calling a member in the same class and not an overriding member in an inheriting class. Likewise, you can use the keyword MyBase to call the implementation of a member in the base class rather than the equivalent member in a derived class. MyClass is similar to MyBase, but it treats the members of the parent class as if they were declared with the NotOverridable keyword.

Putting Inheritance to Work

Inheritance isn't just a theoretical concept that can be applied to shapes or other entities that have no relation whatsoever with business applications. I've used a simple example to demonstrate that there are entities that can be modeled quite naturally with inherited classes. Now that you have learned the mechanics of designing parent and derived classes and the keywords that affect inheritance, it's time to explore a business-like scenario where inheritance may come in handy.

An interesting type of business application deals with reservations — be it hotel reservations, flights reservation, car rentals, you name it. The same company usually provides all types of reservations, and chances are you have used their services on the Web, either to make reservations or to simply look up hotels near certain attractions or conventions. Expedia.com and Bookings.com are probably the most popular reservation sites for the retail market. There are also many sites addressed to travel professionals.

Before designing the interface of an application, architects must come up with a model that reflects the business objects and embeds the required business logic into them. They must also design a database that reflects the hierarchy of the business objects. I will not show you an enormous data model for all entities you may run into while designing the model for a reservation system, just a simplified (if not oversimplified) object hierarchy for storing bookings.

There are several types of bookings a reservation system should accommodate, and each type has its own structure. However, there are a few fields that are common to all bookings. A booking must have a name (the name of the person staying at the hotel or flying), a price, a confirmation number, and so on. Then there are fields that are unique to each type of booking. Hotel bookings have a hotel name and a destination, a check-in date and a check-out date. Car rental bookings share the same information, but no hotel name, and the destination is not a city, but a car pickup location. They also have a car drop location, which may or may not be the same as the pickup location.

I'm sure you've got the idea; we'll design a base class to represent a booking at large and a number of classes, one for each type of booking, all inheriting the same base class. Although there are many ways to design classes for storing data related to bookings, the starting point should be the observation that all types of bookings share some common fields. If we collect the information that's common to all bookings, we can build a parent class from which all types of bookings will derive.

First thing's first. Since we must be able to differentiate several booking types, we must create an enumeration with a member for each different booking type, as follows:

```
Public Enum ReservationType
    HotelReservation
    CarReservation
    FlightReservation
End Enum
```

Every time a new booking is created, its type should be set to the appropriate member of the ReservationType enumeration. If the need for a new type of booking arises, you can update the ReservationType enumeration and create a new derived class to represent the attributes that are unique to the new booking type.

We'll now turn our attention to the parent class, which contains all the standard fields of a booking. Listing 10.10 shows a possible implementation of the Booking class:

LISTING 10.10:   The Booking parent class

```
Public MustInherit Class Booking
    Protected Property Type As ReservationType
     Public ReadOnly Property BookingType As ReservationType
        Get
            Return Type
        End Get
    End Property
    Public Property BookingRequestDate As Date
    Protected Property BookingStartDate As Date
    Protected Property BookingEndDate As Date
    Public Property BookingName As String
    Public Property BookingNumber As String
    Public Property ProviderName As String
    Public Property Price As Decimal
End Class
```

Note that all properties are auto-implemented (I'll leave it up to you to introduce reasonable validation, such as to reject inappropriate starting and ending dates, future request dates, and so on). Some of the properties are marked as Protected. These properties are internal to the class and not visible from the project that uses the Booking class. The Type property, for example, shouldn't be visible outside the class. We don't want users to create a new hotel booking and set its Type property to any other value other than HotelReservation (you'll see shortly how we can do that). However, users of the class should be able to request the type of a booking, so I've included the read-only property BookingType, which returns the value of the Type protected property.

Note also that the BookingStartDate and BookingEndDate properties are also Protected. All bookings have a starting and an ending date (with a few exceptions, such as event bookings), but they have different names. Why use a generic names for the two dates when we can call them `CheckinDate` and `CheckoutDate` for hotels, `PickupDate` and `DropoffDate` for cars, and so on?

Note that the Booking class is prefixed with the `MustInherit` modifier so that the applications that use the derived classes can't create generic objects. This keyword makes the Booking class an abstract one.

Let's design now the HotelBooking class, which derives from the Booking class and adds a few properties to describe the hotel (the `HotelName`, `DestinationCity`, and `DestinationCountry` properties). In a production application, you'd have a Destination class with a city code and a country code, but I've decided to keep the complexity of the class to a minimum.

Note the properties `CheckinDate` and `CheckoutDate`. These two properties are mapped to the `BookingStartDate` and `BookingEndDate` of the parent class. I'm using the `Protected` modifier along with the `MyBase` object to hide the names of the parent class and name them differently in the derived class. Other than that, the code is almost trivial, as you can see in Listing 10.11.

LISTING 10.11:   The FlightBooking class based on the Booking class

```
Public Class HotelBooking
    Inherits Booking

    Public Property DestinationCountry As String
    Public Property DestinationCity As String
    Public Property HotelName As String
    Public Property CheckInDate As Date
        Get
            Return MyBase.BookingStartDate
        End Get
        Set(ByVal value As Date)
            MyBase.BookingStartDate = value
        End Set
    End Property

    Public Property CheckOutDate As Date
        Get
            Return MyBase.BookingEndDate
        End Get
        Set(ByVal value As Date)
            MyBase.BookingEndDate = value
        End Set
    End Property
End Class
```

The FlightBooking class is even simpler. The two dates are now called `DepartureDate` and `ArrivalDate`. In flights, we first depart, then we arrive, while at hotels we first arrive (check in) and then depart (check out). Take a look at Listing 10.12.

LISTING 10.12:   The FlightBooking Class based on the Booking class

```
Public Class FlightBooking
    Inherits Booking
    Public Property OriginCode As String
    Public Property DestinationCode As String
    Public Property DepartureDate As Date
        Get
            Return MyBase.BookingStartDate
        End Get
        Set(ByVal value As Date)
            MyBase.BookingStartDate = value
        End Set
    End Property

    Public Property ArrivalDate As Date
        Get
            Return MyBase.BookingEndDate
        End Get
        Set(ByVal value As Date)
            MyBase.BookingEndDate = value
        End Set
    End Property
    Public Property ConfirmationNumber As String
End Class
```

We're almost done, except for a crucial detail. Every time the user declares a variable of the derived type (HotelBooking, FlightBooking, or CarBooking), we must set the Type property to the appropriate member of the ReservationType enumeration. You can't rely on other developers to ensure the integrity of your data because they may create a HotelBooking object and set its Type property to an inappropriate member of the enumeration.

The proper place to set the Type property is the constructor of each of the derived classes. The constructor of the HotelBooking class should be as follows:

```
Public Sub New()
    Type = ReservationType.HotelReservation
End Sub
```

There are similar constructors for the other derived classes, which I need not repeat here.

Let's see now how to use the Booking class in an application. Switch to the project's main form and enter the statements of Listing 10.13 in the Click event handler of a Button control. These statements create a hotel booking and a car booking. You should enter some of these statements in the editor and see how the members of each of the derived classes appear in the IntelliSense list. You will see that you can't set the BookingStartDate and BookingEndDate properties because they're hidden in the derived classes.

LISTING 10.13: Exercising the members of the Booking derived classes

```
Dim htlBooking As New Reservation.HotelBooking
htlBooking.BookingName = "Joe Taveller"
htlBooking.BookingNumber = "PRN01202148"
htlBooking.BookingRequestDate = Now
htlBooking.checkInDate = #5/19/2010#
htlBooking.checkOutDate = #5/22/2010#
htlBooking.DestinationCountry = "Spain"
htlBooking.DestinationCity = "Barcelona"
htlBooking.HotelName = "Tower Hotel"
htlBooking.Price = 680.99

Dim fltBooking As New Reservation.FlightBooking
fltBooking.DepartureDate = #5/19/2010 7:30:00 AM#
fltBooking.ArrivalDate = #5/19/2010 9:45:00 AM#
fltBooking.DestinationCode = "BCN"
fltBooking.OriginCode = "JFK"
fltBooking.BookingName = "Joe Traveller"
fltBooking.BookingNumber = "PRN01202149"
fltBooking.ConfirmationNumber = "008-9823118 CA11"
fltBooking.Price = 1099.0
```

If you want to process bookings of a specific type, just use the Type property to find out the exact type of a booking, as in the following loop that iterates through hotel bookings and prints out the hotel names for each booking:

```
For Each bk In Bookings
    If bk.Type = Reservation.ReservationType.HotelReservation Then
        Dim hotelBk As Reservation.HotelBooking =
                        CType(bk, Reservation.HotelBooking)
        TextBox1.AppendText("Reservation # " &
                        hotelBk.BookingNumber & "     " &
                        hotelBk.HotelName & vbCrLf)
    End If
Next
```

You can also iterate through the Bookings collection and access the members of the base class with a control variable of the Booking type. The following loop goes through all bookings and calculates their total value:

```
Dim totalPrice As Decimal = 0
For Each bk In Bookings
    totalPrice += bk.Price
Next
```

The classes I've presented here are adequate for demonstrating how to apply inheritance and polymorphism in your code, but they're quite trivial. You can expand the functionality of these classes by adding new properties on your own. You can add one or more room types in a hotel booking (whether the booking is for a single room or a twin and a double, and so on). Flights are not always a single segment. Flying from New York to Barcelona may include a layover in Madrid, and this information (along with the arriving and departing time) must also appear in a flight booking.

Real World Scenario

ADDING CENTRALIZED DATA STORAGE

The sample code presented in this section was written to demonstrate the basic principles of designing with inheritance, and it's not the type of code you'd use in a real application. For example, you can't maintain the list of bookings at the client — there may be multiple clients using the same application. The class should also be responsible for maintaining the list of bookings as well as for persisting them. A reservation application uses a database to store bookings (as well as other static information, such as destinations, hotels, and prices).

The Bookings project, which you will find at www.sybex.com/go/masteringvb2010, contains additional code that's closer to a real-world application. The Booking class maintains the list of bookings in a List collection. The topic of collections is discussed in Chapter 12, but you can think of them as arrays. The client instantiates a booking (an instance of the HotelBooking, FlightBooking, or CarBooking class) and then calls the CreateBooking method to add the booking to the list. The class's code is responsible for adding the booking to the collection or submitting it to the database. It's also the class's responsibility to retrieve a booking by its ID, the name of the traveler, or any other combination of criteria. I have added the GetBookingByID and GetAllBookings methods to all the classes. If you call the GetBookingByID method of the Booking class, you'll get back a Booking object. If you call the same method of a derived class, you'll get back an object of the same class (a HotelBooking object, for example).

If you look up the code of the application, you'll see that I have used some queries you have not seen before in this book to select bookings by their type or their IDs. These queries are LINQ statements. LINQ is discussed in detail in Chapter 14, "Introduction to LINQ," but I didn't want to write loops that go through every element in a collection to select the desired one. LINQ is much more expressive and elegant. After reading Chapter 14, I don't think you'll go back to arcane querying techniques that involve loops and multiple comparisons.

As you will see, the client's code doesn't change. It's the class that determines where the bookings are stored and how they will be recalled. The sample application uses a List collection to store the bookings, but you can modify it so that is uses a database to store and retrieve bookings without touching the client code.

The Class Diagram Designer

Classes are quite simple to build and use, and so is OOP. There are even tools to help you design and build your classes, which I'll describe briefly here. You can use the Class Diagram Designer available in Visual Studio to build your classes with point-and-click operations, but you can't go far on this tool alone. The idea is that you specify the name and the type of a property and the tool emits the Get and Set procedures for the property (the getters and setters, as they're known in OOP jargon). The default implementation of getters and setters is trivial, and you'll have to add your own validation code. You can also create new methods by specifying their names and arguments, but the designer won't generate any code for you; you must implement the methods yourself. Tools such as the Class Diagram Designer and Visio allow you to visualize the classes that make up a large project and the relations between them, and they're a necessity in large projects. Many developers, however, build applications of substantial complexity without resorting to tools for automating the process of building classes. You're welcome to explore these tools.

Right-click the name of a class in the Solution Explorer and choose View Class Diagram from the context menu. You'll see a diagram of the class on the design surface, showing all the members of the class. You can add new members, select the type of the properties, and edit existing members. The diagram of a trivial class like the Contact class is also trivial, but the class diagram becomes more helpful as you implement more interrelated classes.

Figure 10.2, from earlier in the chapter, shows the Product, Book, and Supply classes in the Class Diagram Designer. You can use the commands of each class's context menu to create new members and edit/remove existing ones. To add a new property, for example, you specify the property name and type, and the designer generates the outline of the Set and Get procedures for you. Of course, you must step in and insert your custom validation code in the property setter.

To add a new class to the diagram, right-click on the designer pane and choose Add ➤ Class from the context menu. You'll be prompted to enter the name of the class and its location (the VB file in which the autogenerated class code will be stored). You can specify a new name or select an existing class file and add your new class to it. To create a derived class, you must double-click the box that represents the new class and manually insert the Inherits statement followed by the name of the base class. After you specify the parent class, an arrow joining the two classes will be added to the diagram. The arrow points to the parent class. In addition to classes, you can add items including structures, enumerations, and comments. You can also create class diagrams from existing classes.

To add members to a class, right-click the box that represents the class and choose Add from the context menu. This will lead to a submenu with the members you can add to a class: Method, Property, Field, and Event. You can also add a constructor (although you will have to supply the arguments and the code for parameterized constructors), a destructor, and a constant. To edit a member, such as the type of a property or the arguments of a method, switch to the Class Details window, where you will see the members of the selected class. Expand any member to see its parameters: the type of a property and the arguments and the return value of a method.

Experiment with the Class Diagram Designer tools to jump-start the process of designing classes. At the very least, you should use this tool to document your classes, especially in a team environment.

The Bottom Line

Use inheritance   Inheritance, which is the true power behind OOP, allows you to create new classes that encapsulate the functionality of existing classes without editing their code. To inherit from an existing class, use the `Inherits` statement, which brings the entire class into your class.

Master It   Explain the inheritance-related attributes of a class's members.

Use polymorphism   Polymorphism is the ability to write members that are common to a number of classes but behave differently, depending on the specific class to which they apply. Polymorphism is a great way of abstracting implementation details and delegating the implementation of methods with very specific functionality to the derived classes.

Master It   The parent class Person represents parties, and it exposes the `GetBalance` method, which returns the outstanding balance of a person. The Customer and Supplier derived classes implement the `GetBalance` method differently. How will you use this method to find out the balance of a customer and/or supplier?

Part 4

Working with the .NET Framework

Chapter 11

The Framework at Large

A major aspect of programming with VB 2010 is the knowledge of the .NET Framework. The vast majority of the functionality of any language in Visual Studio is the Framework, which is a massive collection of classes that address most of the common programming tasks, from handling dates to encryption and retrieving data from a remote web server. Even listing the classes that make up the Framework and their members would take another book of comparable size, so I've decided to provide a single chapter as an introduction to the basic classes of the Framework and include several tutorials in PDF format that discuss specific aspects of the Framework. These tutorials, which you will find at this book's site, discuss in detail topics like handling folders and files, graphics, and printing with VB.

In this chapter, you'll find an introduction to several major components of the Framework, including the following:

- ◆ How to use the My component

- ◆ The concept of Streams

- ◆ How to use the StringBuilder class

- ◆ How to use the Date and TimeSpan classes

- ◆ The basics of drawing with the Framework

- ◆ The basics of printing with the Framework

What Is the Framework?

The Framework is a comprehensive collection of classes that encapsulate the most common (and many not so common) programming tasks. In essence, it's the foundation on which .NET applications are built. The Framework is a library of code organized into namespaces and classes that address typical programming tasks.

As software development becomes more and more complex, developers face new challenges on a daily basis. To assist developers, language designers keep adding to their compilers to the point that languages have started to bloat with new features. And as you can guess, there's no end to this trend. No matter how much functionality you build into a language, developers need more. It is a challenge to just know (or look up) the proper function name for a specific task. Now, add external libraries with hundreds, even thousands, of functions for all kinds of programming tasks, from the less trivial formatting and math functions to encryption functions, specialized drawing routines, and so on and so forth. There was clearly a need for a more concise, more organized approach.

To address that need, engineers at Microsoft identified the functionality most developers need in typical applications, organized it into "blocks" of related functionality, and the Framework was born. We're already in version 4.0 of the Framework, which includes methods for mundane tasks like reading data from files, math functions, and drawing methods. It also includes security-related methods, serialization methods (a powerful technique for converting complex objects into XML or binary format), encryption, compression, speech synthesis, and just about anything. Practically any routine that's used somewhere by the operating system belongs to the Framework. The Framework was an enormous software project on the surface, but in my opinion it was basically a classification project. Developers should be able to locate the information they need quickly, otherwise the Framework wouldn't be nearly as useful, or popular.

It's actually impossible to cover the entire Framework, so I've chosen a few parts of it to discuss in this book. You will also find several tutorials in PDF format at www.sybex.com/go/masteringvb2010 that explain some of the most practical aspects of the Framework, such as the handling of files and folders and the drawing and printing methods. This chapter contains an overview of these classes and a few shortcuts to the Framework, namely how to use the built-in snippets and the My component.

Using Snippets

The Framework is the main reason developers love to work with Microsoft's languages. It's also the reason many developers have been reluctant to move from VB6 to VB.NET and following versions. The Framework is huge, and switching from a self-contained language like VB6 into programming with the Framework requires a shift in thinking about programming. To do justice to the Framework, developers who have made the switch wouldn't even think of moving back to an earlier version of VB. To address the qualms of developers considering moving away from VB6 and into the .NET world, Microsoft introduced the My component (which is unique to Visual Basic) and the snippets. The My component is a collection of functions that address many of the most common operations developers need to implement in their applications. With time, the My component along with the snippets have evolved into a productivity tool, worthy of the reputation of Visual Basic.

A code snippet is a predefined code segment that implements a very specific task. Every time you need to perform a task, such as writing to or reading from a file or playing back a sound, you can insert the appropriate snippet into your code and change a few variable names to match the rest of the code. Let's say you want to insert the statements for writing some text to a file, but you have no idea how to access files. Create an empty line in the listing (press the Enter key a couple of times at the end of a code line). Then, open the Edit menu and choose IntelliSense ➤ Insert Snippet (or right-click somewhere in the code window and choose Insert Snippet from the context menu).

You will see on the screen a list of the snippets, organized in folders according to function, as shown in Figure 11.1. Select the Fundamentals folder, which will display another list of options: Collections, Data Types, File System, and Math. Double-click the File System item to see a list of common file-related tasks, as shown in Figure 11.2. Locate the item Write Text To A File in the list and double-click it to insert the appropriate snippet at the current location in the code window.

FIGURE 11.1
The code snippets organized according to their function

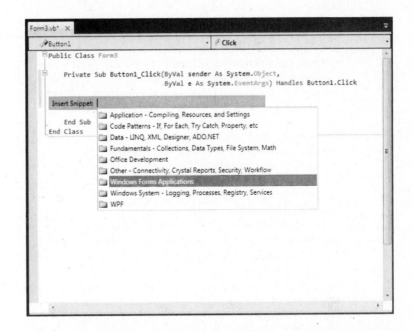

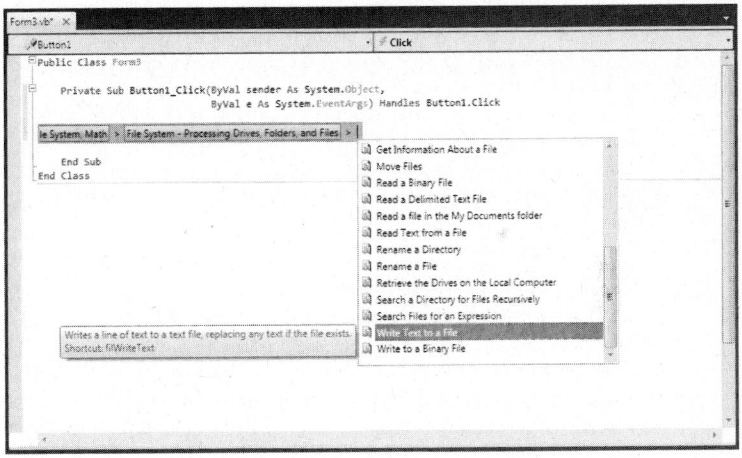

FIGURE 11.2
Selecting a code snippet to insert in your code

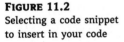

The following snippet will be inserted in your code:

```
My.Computer.FileSystem.WriteAllText("C:\test.txt", "Text", True)
```

To write some text to a file, you need to call the `WriteAllText` method of the `My.Computer.FileSystem` object. You can replace the strings shown in the snippet with actual values. The first string is the filename, the second string is the text to be written to the file, and the last argument of the method determines whether the text will be appended to the file (if False) or overwrite any existing text (if True).

The snippet shows you the basic statements for performing a common task, and you can edit the code inserted by Visual Studio as needed. Many of the snippets are one-liners. A real-world application would probably prompt the user for a filename via the File common dialog box and then use the filename specified by the user in the dialog box instead of a hard-coded filename.

Of course, there aren't snippets for every conceivable task. If this were the case, then the collection of snippets would compete in complexity with the Framework itself. There are snippets for a relatively small number of tasks and all snippets make use of the My component. Where the snippets are meant to minimize the code you write, the My component is meant to simplify the Framework by encapsulating the functionality of several statements into a single method. Let's start with an overview of the My component and then we'll move on to the Framework.

Using the My Component

You have probably noticed that the code snippets of Visual Studio use an entity called My, which is a peculiar object that was introduced with VB 2005 to simplify many programming tasks. As you saw in the preceding code snippet, the My component allows you to write some text to a file with a single statement, the WriteAllText method. If you're familiar with earlier versions of Visual Basic, you know that you must first open a file, then write some text to it, and finally close the file. The My component allows you to perform all these operations with a single statement, as you saw in the preceding example.

Another example is the Play method, which you can use to play back a WAV file from within your code:

```
My.Computer.Audio.Play ("C:\Sounds\CountDown.wav")
```

You can also use the following expression to play back a system sound:

```
My.Computer.Audio.PlaySystemSound(System.Media.SystemSounds.Exclamation)
```

The method that plays back the sound is the Play method, and the method that writes text to a file is the WriteAllText method. However, you can't call them directly through the My component; they're not methods of the My component. If they were, you'd have to dig hard to find out the method you need, and this is exactly what the My object attempts to remedy: the need to dig deep into the Framework to find out the method for the task at hand.

The My component exposes six subcomponents, which contain their own subcomponents. Here's a description of the basic components of the My component and the functionality you should expect to find in each.

MY.APPLICATION

The My.Application component provides information about the current application. The CommandLineArgs property of My.Application returns a collection of strings, which are the arguments passed to the application when it was started. Typical Windows applications aren't called with command-line arguments, but it's possible to start an application and pass a filename as an argument to the application (the document to be opened by the application, for example). The Info property is an object that exposes properties such as DirectoryPath (the application's default folder), ProductName, Version, and so on.

MY.COMPUTER

This component exposes a lot of functionality via a number of properties, many of which are objects. The My.Computer.Audio component lets you play back sounds. The My.Computer.Clipboard component lets you access the Clipboard. To find out whether the Clipboard contains a specific type of data, use the ContainsText, ContainsImage, ContainsData, and ContainsAudio methods. To retrieve the contents of the Clipboard, use the GetText, GetImage, GetData, and GetAudioStream methods respectively. Assuming that you have a form with a TextBox control and a PictureBox control, you can retrieve text or image data from the Clipboard and display it on the appropriate control with the following statements:

```
If My.Computer.Clipboard.ContainsImage Then
    PictureBox1.Image = My.Computer.Clipboard.GetImage
End If
If My.Computer.Clipboard.ContainsText Then
    TextBox2.Text = My.Computer.Clipboard.GetText
End If
```

You may have noticed that using the My component in your code requires that you write long statements. You can shorten them substantially via the With statement, as shown next:

```
With My.Computer.Clipboard
    If .ContainsImage Then
        PictureBox1.Image = .GetImage
    End If
    If .ContainsText Then
        TextBox2.Text = .GetText
    End If
End With
```

When you're executing multiple statements on the same object, you can specify the object in a With statement and call its methods in the block of the With statement by specifying the method name prefixed with a period. The With statement is followed by the name of the object to which all following methods apply and is terminated with the End With statement.

Another component of My.Computer is the FileSystem component that exposes all the methods you need to access and manipulate files and folders from within your code. If you enter the expression My.Computer.FileSystem followed by a period in the code window, you will see all the methods exposed by the FileSystem component. Among them, you will find DeleteFile, DeleteDirectory, RenameFile, RenameDirectory, WriteAllText, ReadAllText, and many more. Select a method and then type the opening parenthesis. You will see the syntax of the method in a ToolTip. The syntax of the CopyFile method, for example, is as follows:

```
My.Computer.FileSystem.CopyFile(
            sourceFileName As String, destinationFileName As String)
```

Just specify the path of the file you want to copy with the first argument and the new file's name with the second argument, and you're finished. This statement will copy the specified file to the specified location.

You will notice that the ToolTip box with the syntax of the `CopyFile` method has multiple versions, which are listed at the left side of the box along with arrow up and arrow down icons. Click these two buttons to see the next and previous versions of the method. The second version of the `CopyFile` method is as follows:

```
My.Computer.FileSystem.CopyFile(
        sourceFileName As String, destinationFileName As String,
        overwrite As Boolean)
```

The *overwrite* argument specifies whether the method should overwrite the destination file if it exists. The first overloaded form of the method will not overwrite the specified file, if it already exists.

The third overloaded form of the method accepts a different third argument that determines whether the usual copy animation will be displayed as the file is being copied. Try out this form of the method by copying a large file to a slow drive, such as a flash card, to see how easy it is to add a bit of the Windows look and feel to your application.

MY.FORMS

This component lets you access the forms of the current application. You can also access the application's forms by name, as you recall from Chapter 4, "GUI Design and Event-Driven Programming."

MY.SETTINGS

This component lets you access the application settings. These settings apply to the entire application and are stored in an XML configuration file. The settings are created from within Visual Studio, and you use the `Settings` component to read them. The settings are variables you can use in your code to parameterize the application. For example, you may store the user's name in a variable, let's say the *UserName* variable, so that you can display it initially when prompting users for their name and password. This variable can be declared as in the Settings tab of the project's Properties window, as shown in Figure 11.3.

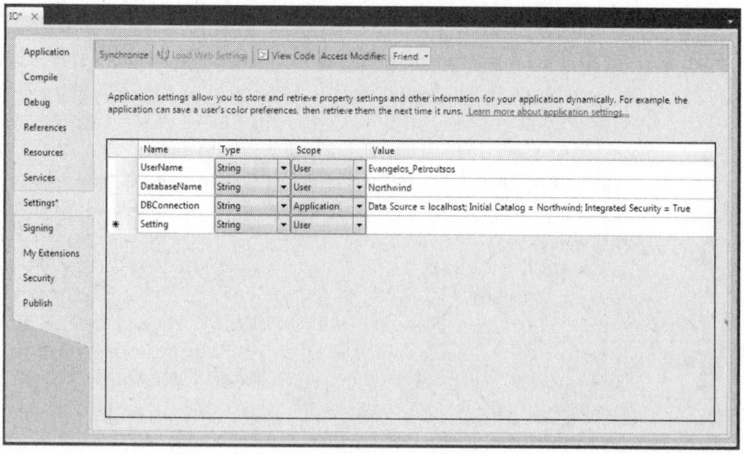

FIGURE 11.3
Creating application settings

To read the value of the *UserName* variable, use the following expression:

```
My.Settings.UserName
```

Yes, the editor will create a class behind the scenes for your settings and make them available to your application as strongly typed values. You can also change the values of the application settings from within your code.

MY.USER

This component returns information about the current user. The most important property of the User component is the CurrentPrincipal property, which is an object that represents the credentials of the current user.

MY.WEBSERVICES

The WebServices component represents the web services referenced by the current application. For more information on web services and how they're used in an application, see Chapter 21, "Building and Using Web Services."

How to Use the My Component

The My component gives VB developers of all levels unprecedented programming power and allows us to perform tasks that would require substantial code if implemented with earlier versions of the language, not to mention the research it would take to locate the appropriate methods in the Framework. You can explore the My component on your own and use it as needed. My is not a substitute for learning the language and the Framework. It can help you initially, but you can't go far without learning the methods of the Framework. It will help you accomplish a whole lot with a few simple statements, and it will also give you a head start with the Framework, as the My component is a miniature Framework.

Let's say you want to locate all the files of a specific type in a folder, including its subfolders. Scanning a folder and its subfolders to any depth is quite a task (you'll find the code in the tutorial "Accessing Folders and Files" at www.sybex.com/go/masteringvb2010). You can do the same with a single statement by using the My component as follows:

```
Dim files As System.Collections.ObjectModel.ReadOnlyCollection(Of String)
files = My.Computer.FileSystem.GetFiles("D:\Data", True, "*.txt")
```

The GetFiles method populates the *files* collection with the pathnames of the text files in the folder D:\Data and its subfolders. The second argument determines whether the method will scan the specified folder recursively, and although you can pass a True/False value for this argument, you can also set it to one of the members of the FileIO.SearchOption enumeration: *SearchAllSubDirectories* and *SearchTopLevelOnly*. However, it won't help you if you want to process each file in place. Moreover, this GetFiles method is synchronous: If the folder contains many subfolders with many files, it will block the interface until it retrieves all the files. Once you have retrieved the filenames you're interested in, you can process them by iterating through the *files* collection with a For Each loop. As for the method's return type, you need not remember it. You will see it in the IntelliSense box — not to mention that you can turn on inference and let the editor figure out the type of the *files* variable.

Want to save data to a file and read it back at a later session? It's trivial with the `FileSystem` component. To send text to a file, call the `WriteAllText` method passing the text to be saved as an argument:

```
My.Computer.FileSystem.WriteAllText("file_name", your_text, False)
```

The first argument is the path of the file, the second argument is the text to be saved, and the last argument is a True/False value that determines whether the text will overwrite the file's original contents or append the text to the existing contents.

To read back the data from the file and use it in your application, use the `ReadAllText` method:

```
Dim txt As String = My.Computer.FileSystem.ReadAllText("file_name")
```

Of course, not all information we save to files is in text format. The `WriteAllBytes` and `ReadAllBytes` methods move an array of bytes to and from a file. Converting data to an array of bytes is no piece of cake. You can use the `WriteAllText` and `ReadAllText` methods to quickly save and read text to a file, but if you need to create files with structured data, you must look into the methods of the IO namespace, which is discussed in detail in one of the tutorials you can download from www.sybex.com/go/masteringvb2010. You can also take advantage of the serialization techniques discussed in Chapter 12, "Storing Data in Collections."

If you're already familiar with VB, you may think that the My component is an aid for the absolute beginner or the nonprogrammer. This isn't true. VB is about productivity, and the My component can help you be more productive with your daily tasks regardless of your knowledge of the language or programming skills. If you can use My to save a few (or a few dozen) statements, do it. There's no penalty for using the My component because the compiler replaces the methods of the My component with the equivalent method calls to the Framework. If you're not familiar with the My component, or if you're new to the Framework, please explore this component on your own. It will simplify your coding effort, as long as you can locate the method you need for the task at hand.

In the next sections we'll explore the most commonly used classes of the Framework. The classes discussed here are a very small part of the Framework, but they're the classes you'll be using the most. I have chosen the topics I believe you will find most useful and focused on them. Once you start working with the Framework and you learn to navigate through its classes, you'll find it much easier to explore other parts of the Framework on your own.

The IO Namespace

The IO namespace contains all the classes that manipulate folders and files as well as access files. For a detailed discussion of the classes of the IO namespace, please download the tutorial "Accessing Files and Folders" from www.sybex.com/go/masteringvb2010. Table 11.1 contains a brief overview of the basic components for manipulating files and folders, more of a road map to the IO namespace.

To use the IO namespace in your code, you must import the `System.IO` namespace with this statement:

```
Using System.IO
```

Otherwise, you will have to fully qualify the property and method names in your code.

TABLE 11.1: IO namespace classes

CLASS	DESCRIPTION
Directory	The Directory class exposes all the members you need to manipulate folders (retrieve the folders on a drive and their subfolders, retrieve the files in a folder, and other similar operations).
File	The File class exposes methods for manipulating files (copy and move them around, open and close them), similar to the methods of the Directory class.
DriveInfo	The DriveInfo class provides basic information about a drive. It also exposes the `GetAllDrives` method, which returns all the drives on the target computer.
DirectoryInfo	The DirectoryInfo class provides information about the attributes of a specific folder.
FileInfo	The FileInfo class provides information about the attributes of a specific file. This class also exposes the `Encrypt` and `Decrypt` methods for encrypting and decrypting existing files.
Path	The Path class exposes methods for performing simple tasks with file and folder path names, including methods for creating random file paths.

The Directory Class

The System.IO.Directory class exposes all the members you need to manipulate folders. It's a shared class, which means that you can call its methods without having to create an instance of the Directory class. The methods of the Directory class are listed in Table 11.2.

TABLE 11.2: System.IO.Directory methods

METHOD	DESCRIPTION
CreateDirectory	This method creates a new folder whose path is passed to the method as a string argument. The CreateDirectory method returns a DirectoryInfo object, which contains information about the newly created folder.
Delete	This method deletes a folder and all the files in it. If the folder contains subfolders, the Delete method will optionally remove the entire directory tree under the node you're removing. The simplest form of the Delete method accepts as an argument the path of the folder to be deleted. You can pass the value True as a second argument to delete a folder recursively.

TABLE 11.2:   System.IO.Directory methods *(CONTINUED)*

METHOD	DESCRIPTION
Exists	This method accepts a path as an argument and returns a True/False value indicating whether the specified folder exists.
Move	This method moves an entire folder to another location in the file system. The folder to be moved and its destination are passed as arguments.
GetCurrentDirectory, SetCurrentDirectory	Use these methods to retrieve and set the path of the current directory. By default, the GetCurrentDirectory method returns the folder in which the application is running.
GetDirectories	This method retrieves all the subfolders of a specific folder and returns their names as an array of strings.
GetFiles	This method returns the names of the files in the specified folder as an array of strings.
GetFileSystemEntries	This method returns an array of all items (files and folders) in a path, which is passed to the method as argument.
GetLogicalDrives	This method returns an array of strings, which are the names of the logical drives on the computer.

The File Class

The IO.File class exposes methods for manipulating files. The names of the methods are self-descriptive, and most of them accept as an argument the path of the file on which they act. Use these methods to implement from within your application the common operations that users normally perform through the Windows interface. To get an idea about the functionality of the File class, I'm listing its most important methods in Table 11.3.

The DriveInfo Class

The DriveInfo class provides basic information about a drive. Its constructor accepts as an argument a drive name, and you can use the object returned by the method to retrieve information about the specific drive, as shown here:

```
Dim Drive As New DriveInfo("C")
```

The argument is the name of a drive (you can include the colon if you want). Notice that you can't specify a Universal Naming Convention (UNC) path with the constructor of the DriveInfo object. You can only access local drives or network drives that have been mapped to a drive name on the target system.

To retrieve information about the specified drive, use the properties of the DriveInfo class listed in Table 11.4.

TABLE 11.3:   IO.File class methods

METHOD	DESCRIPTION
AppendText	Appends text to an existing file (both the file's path and the text to be written are passed as arguments).
Copy	Copies an existing file to a new location and accepts two arguments, the paths of the source and destination files.
Create	Creates a new file and returns a FileStream object, which you can use to write to or read from the file.
CreateText	Similar to the Create method, this method creates a text file and returns a StreamWriter object for writing to the file.
Delete	Removes the specified file from the file system and accepts the path of the file to be deleted as an argument.
Exists	Accepts a file's path and returns a True/False value depending on whether the file exists or not.
GetAttributes	Accepts a file path as an argument and returns the attributes of the specified file as a FileAttributes object.
Move	Moves the specified file to a new location.
Open	Opens an existing file for read-write operations.
OpenRead	Opens an existing file in read mode and returns a FileStream object associated with this file.
OpenText	Opens an existing text file for reading and returns a StreamReader object associated with this file.
OpenWrite	Opens an existing file for output.

The DirectoryInfo Class

To create a new instance of the DirectoryInfo class that references a specific folder, supply the folder's path in the class's constructor:

```
Dim DI As New DirectoryInfo(path)
```

The members of the DirectoryInfo class are equivalent to the members of the Directory class, and you will recognize them as soon as you see them in the IntelliSense drop-down list. A few methods that are unique to the DirectoryInfo class are the CreateSubdirectory and GetFileSystemInfos methods. The CreateSubdirectory method creates a subfolder under the folder specified by the current instance of the class, and its syntax is as follows:

```
DI.CreateSubdirectory(path)
```

TABLE 11.4:   DriveInfo class members

MEMBER	DESCRIPTION
DriveFormat property	A string describing the drive's format (FAT32, NTFS).
DriveType property	A string describing the drive's type (fixed, CD-ROM, and so on).
TotalSize, TotalFreeSize, AvailableFreeSpace properties	These properties return the drive's total capacity, in bytes, the total free space, and the available free space on the drive.
VolumeLabel property	This property returns, or sets, the drive's volume name.
GetDrives method	The DriveInfo class exposes the GetDrives method, which returns an array of DriveInfo objects, one for each drive on the system. This method is similar to the GetLogicalDrives method of the Directory object, which is a shared method and doesn't require that you create an object explicitly.

The CreateSubdirectory method returns a DirectoryInfo object that represents the new subfolder. The GetFileSystemInfos method returns an array of FileSystemInfo objects, one for each item in the folder referenced by the current instance of the class. The items can be either folders or files. To retrieve information about all the entries in a folder, create an instance of the DirectoryInfo class and then call its GetFileSystemInfos method:

```
Dim DI As New DirectoryInfo(path)
Dim itemsInfo() As FileSystemInfo
itemsInfo = DI.GetFileSystemInfos()
```

You can also specify an optional search pattern as an argument when you call this method:

```
itemsInfo = DI.GetFileSystemInfos(pattern)
```

Notice the differences between the GetFileSystemInfos method of the Directory-Info class and the GetFileSystemEntries of the Directory object. GetFileSystemInfos returns an array of objects that contains information about the current item (file or folder). GetFileSystemEntries returns an array of strings (the names of the folders and files).

The Path Class

The Path class's methods perform simple tasks such as retrieving a file's name and extension, returning the full path description of a relative path, and so on. The Path class's members are shared, and you must specify the path on which they will act as an argument. The most useful methods exposed by the Path class are utilities for manipulating filenames and pathnames, described in the following sections. Notice that the methods of the Path class are shared: You must specify the path on which they will act as an argument. The most important methods of the Path class are listed in Table 11.5.

TABLE 11.5:   Path class methods

METHOD	DESCRIPTION
ChangeExtension	Changes the file name extension of the file you specify to a new extension, which is also specified as an argument.
Combine	Combines two path specifications into one by appending the second path to the first one and inserting a backslash if necessary.
GetDirectoryName	Extracts the directory name from a path passed to the method as an argument.
GetFileName, GetFileNameWithoutExtension	Return the file name with and without extension from a full path passed to each method as an argument.
GetTempFile, GetTempPath	Return a temporary file and path name, which you can use to store data during the course of execution of your application.

Streaming Data

To access files for reading and writing data with the Framework, you must first understand the concept of streams. A stream is a channel between your application and the source of the data. The source of the data need not be a file, although in most cases we use streams to work with files. If you've been around for a while, you're probably expecting to read about commands that open a file, write to it (or read from it), and then close the file. The reason for introducing the concept of streams in the Framework is that streams can be connected to one another and perform multiple operations sequentially. A typical example is the cryptographic stream, which accepts data, encrypts it, and spits out a series of bytes. This stream can be connected to a file stream and send encrypted data to the file.

Let's start by looking at the process of writing data to a file. First, you must import the IO namespace with the Imports System.IO statement. Then create a StreamWriter object, which is associated with a file:

```
Dim streamOut As New StreamWriter(file_name)
```

In this statement, *file_name* is the name of the file you want to write to.

To write something to the file, you call the *streamOut* variable's Write method. Everything you write to the stream is saved automatically to the file. To save the contents of a TextBox control to a file, use the following statement:

```
streamOut.Write(TextBox1.Text)
```

When you're done, you must close the Stream object by calling its Close method. The following statements prompt the user to select a file name with the Save dialog box and then save the contents of the TextBox control to the selected file:

```
SaveFileDialog1.Filter = "Text Files|*.txt|All Files|*.*"
SaveFileDialog1.FilterIndex = 0
```

```
SaveFileDialog1.DefaultExt = ".txt"
SaveFileDialog1.FileName = ""
If SaveFileDialog1.ShowDialog = Windows.Forms.DialogResult.OK Then
    Dim strmOut As New StreamWriter(SaveFileDialog1.FileName)
    strmOut.Write(TextBox1.Text)
    strmOut.Close()
End If
```

To read back the data in a later session, you must display the OpenFile dialog box to allow users to select the file and then create the StreamReader object and call its ReadToEnd method. Here's the code that reads back the contents of the *TextBox1* control:

```
OpenFileDialog1.Filter = "Text Files|*.txt|All Files|*.*"
OpenFileDialog1.FilterIndex = 0
OpenFileDialog1.DefaultExt = ".txt"
OpenFileDialog1.FileName = ""
If OpenFileDialog1.ShowDialog = Windows.Forms.DialogResult.OK Then
    Dim strmIn As New StreamReader(OpenFileDialog1.FileName)
    TextBox1.Text = strmIn.ReadToEnd
    strmIn.Close()
End If
```

This concludes the brief introduction to the System.IO namespace. You will find much more information on the topic in the tutorial "Accessing Folders and Files" at www.sybex.com/go/masteringvb2010, but you should also explore the My.Computer.FileSystem component, which provides may shortcuts to the Framework for simple tasks.

Drawing and Painting

An interesting aspect of the Framework is dedicated to the generation of graphics. There are numerous methods for drawing and printing and they're discussed in detail in the tutorials "Creating Graphics with VB 2010" and "Printing with VB 2010," which are available for download from www.sybex.com/go/masteringvb2010. This section contains an overview of the graphics printing classes of the Framework and their basic functionality.

THE GRAPHICS OBJECT

The Graphics object is the drawing surface — your canvas. All the controls you can draw on expose a Graphics property, which is an object, and you can retrieve it with the CreateGraphics method. Most of the controls provide a CreateGraphics method, but we normally draw on the Form object and the PictureBox control.

The Graphics object exposes all the methods and properties you need to create graphics on the control. Start by declaring a variable of the Graphics type and initialize it to the Graphics object returned by the control's CreateGraphics method:

```
Dim G As Graphics
G = PictureBox1.CreateGraphics
```

At this point, you're ready to start drawing on the *PictureBox1* control with the methods discussed in the following section. To draw a rectangle, for example, call the DrawRectangle method of the *G* variable, passing the origin and dimensions of the rectangle as arguments. To display a string, call the DrawString method, which requires several arguments, such as the string to be drawn, the font in which it will be rendered, its location, and the brush object that will be used for the drawing. You'll see how to use these methods shortly.

Two properties of the Graphics object you should know about are the TextRenderingHint and the SmoothingMode properties. The TextRenderingHint method specifies how the Graphics object will render text, and its value is *AntiAlias, AntiAliasGridFit, ClearTypeGridFit, SingleBitPerPixel, SingleBitPerPixelGridFit,* or *SystemDefault.* The SmoothingMode property is similar to the TextRenderingHint, but it applies to shapes drawn with the Graphics object's drawing methods. Its value is one of the members of the SmoothingMode enumeration: *AntiAlias, Default, HighQuality, HighSpeed, Invalid,* and *None.*

Before showing some drawing examples, I must present a few classes that are used routinely in creating graphics.

THE POINT CLASS

The Point class represents a point on the drawing surface and is expressed as a pair of (x, y) coordinates. The *x-coordinate* is its horizontal distance from the origin, and the *y-coordinate* is its vertical distance from the origin. The origin is the point with coordinates (0, 0), and this is the top-left corner of the drawing surface.

The constructor of the Point class is as follows, where *X* and *Y* are the point's horizontal and vertical distances from the origin:

```
Dim P1 As New Point(X, Y)
```

THE RECTANGLE CLASS

Another class that is often used in drawing is the Rectangle class. The Rectangle object is used to specify areas on the drawing surface. Its constructor accepts as arguments the coordinates of the rectangle's top-left corner and its dimensions:

```
Dim box As Rectangle
box = New Rectangle(X, Y, width, height)
```

The following statement creates a rectangle whose top-left corner is 1 pixel to the right and 1 pixel down from the origin, and its dimensions are 100 by 20 pixels:

```
box = New Rectangle(1, 1, 100, 20)
```

The *box* variable represents a rectangle, but it doesn't generate any output on the monitor. If you want to draw the rectangle, you can pass it as an argument to the DrawRectangle or FillRectangle method, depending on whether you want to draw the outline of the rectangle or a filled rectangle.

THE SIZE CLASS

The Size class represents the dimensions of a rectangle; it's similar to a Rectangle object, but it doesn't have an origin, just dimensions. To create a new Size object, use the following constructor:

```
Dim S1 As New Size(100, 400)
```

Another form of the Rectangle constructor uses a Point and a Size object to specify the location and dimensions of the rectangle:

```
box = New Rectangle(point, size)
```

The *point* and *size* arguments are properly initialized Point and Size objects.

THE COLOR CLASS

The Color class represents colors, and there are many ways to specify a color. The simplest method to specify a color is to declare a variable of the Color type and initialize it to one of the named colors exposed as properties of the Color class:

```
Dim myColor As Color
myColor = Color.Azure
```

The 128 color names of the Color class will appear in the IntelliSense box as soon as you enter the period following the keyword Color. You can also use the FromARGB method, which creates a new color from its basic color components (the red, green, and blue components). To create a color that's mostly red, use a statement like the following:

```
Mycolor = Color.FrmARGB(255, 128, 128, 255)
```

The first argument is the opacity of the color (255 for maximum opacity, 0 for a totally transparent color), and the remaining three arguments are the intensities of the color's red, green and blue components (0 for minimum intensity, 255 for maximum intensity). For a more formal discussion of the Color class, see the tutorial on creating graphics with VB, available for download at www.sybex.com/go/masteringvb2010.

THE FONT CLASS

The Font class represents fonts, which are used when rendering strings via the DrawString method. To specify a font, you must create a new Font object; set its family name, size, and style; and then pass it as an argument to the DrawString method. Alternatively, you can prompt the user for a font via the Font common dialog box and use the object returned by the dialog box's Font property as an argument with the DrawString method. To create a new Font object in your code, use a statement like the following:

```
Dim drawFont As New Font("Verdana", 12, FontStyle.Bold)
```

The Font constructor has 13 forms in all, as you will see in the IntelliSense box once you declare a new variable of the Font type.

THE PEN CLASS

The Pen class represents virtual pens, which you use to draw on the Graphics object's surface. To construct a new Pen object, you must specify the pen's color and width in pixels. The following statements declare three Pen objects with the same color and different widths:

```
Dim thinPen, mediumPem, thickPen As Pen
thinPen = New Pen(Color.Black, 1)
mediumPen = New Pen(Color.Black, 3)
thickPen = New Pen(Color.Black, 5)
```

The quickest method of creating a new Pen object is to use the built-in Pens collection, which creates a pen with a width of 1 pixel and the color you specify. The following statement can appear anywhere a Pen object is required and will draw shapes in blue color (the second statement is optional and it changes the default width of the pen):

```
thinPen = Pens.Blue
thinPen.Width = 3
```

THE BRUSH CLASS

The Brush class represents the instrument for filling shapes, including text; you can create brushes that fill with a solid color, a pattern, or a bitmap. In reality, there's no Brush object. The Brush class is actually an abstract class that is inherited by all the classes that implement a brush, but you can't declare a variable of the Brush type in your code. Instead, you can declare a variable of the following type: SolidBrush, HatchBrush, LinearGradientBrush, PathGradientBrush, and TextureBrush. To fill a shape with a solid color, create a SolidBrush object with the following constructor, where *brushColor* is a color value, specified with the help of the Color object:

```
Dim sBrush As SolidBrush
sBrush = New SolidBrush(brushColor)
```

Every filled object you draw with the *sBrush* variable will be filled with the color of the brush. A gradient brush fills a shape with a specified gradient. The LinearGradientBrush fills a shape with a linear gradient, and the PathGradientBrush fills a shape with a gradient that has one starting color and one or more ending colors.

Drawing Methods

Now that I've covered the auxiliary drawing objects, we can look at the drawing methods of the Graphics class. Before getting into the details of the drawing methods, however, let's write a simple application that draws a couple of simple shapes on a form. First, create a Graphics object with the following statements:

```
Dim G As Graphics
G = Me.CreateGraphics
```

Everything drawn on the surface represented by the **G** object will appear on the form. Then, create a Pen object to draw with. The following statement creates a Pen object that's 1 pixel wide and draws in blue:

```
Dim P As New Pen(Color.Blue)
```

You just created the two basic objects for drawing: the drawing surface and the drawing instrument. Now you can draw shapes by calling the Graphics object's drawing methods. The following statement will print a rectangle with its top-left corner near the top-left corner of the form (at a point that's 10 pixels to the right and 10 pixels down from the form's corner) and is 200 pixels wide and 150 pixels tall:

```
G.DrawRectangle(P, 10, 10, 200, 150)
```

Let's add the two diagonals of the rectangle with the following statements:

```
G.DrawLine(P, 10, 10, 210, 160)
G.DrawLine(P, 210, 10, 10, 160)
```

That's all the statements to create a shape on the form, but where do you insert them? The proper handler to create graphics is the form's `Paint` event handler, as the `Paint` event is fired every time the form is shown or resized, and this is when the graphics must be regenerated.

The `Paint` event handler passes the *e* argument, which (among other properties) exposes the form's Graphics object. You can create a Graphics object in the `Paint` event handler and then draw on this object. Take a look at the code in Listing 11.1.

LISTING 11.1:   Drawing simple shapes in the `Paint` event

```
Private Sub Form1_Paint(...) Handles Me.Paint
    Dim G As Graphics
    G = e.Graphics
    Dim P As New Pen(Color.Blue)
    G.DrawRectangle(P, 10, 10, 200, 150)
    G.DrawLine(P, 10, 10, 210, 160)
    G.DrawLine(P, 210, 10, 10, 160)
End Sub
```

If you run the application now, it works like a charm. The shapes appear to be permanent, even though they're redrawn every time you switch to the form. A caveat of drawing from within the `Paint` event is that the event isn't fired when the form is resized. To force a refresh when the form is resized, you must insert the following statement in the form's `Load` event handler:

```
Me.SetStyle(ControlStyles.ResizeRedraw, True)
```

It is possible to make the graphics permanent by drawing not on the Graphics object, but directly on the control's (or the form's) bitmap. This technique is discussed in the tutorial "Creating Graphics with VB 2010" that is available for download from www.sybex.com/go/masteringvb2010.

The drawing methods can be categorized in two major groups: the methods that draw stroked shapes (outlines) and the methods that draw filled shapes. The methods in the first group start with the Draw prefix (DrawRectangle, DrawEllipse, and so on). The methods of the second group start with the Fill prefix (FillRectangle, FillEllipse, and so on). Of course, some DrawXXX methods don't have equivalent FillXXX methods. For example, you can't fill a line or an open curve, so there are no FillLine or FillCurve methods.

Another difference between the drawing and filling methods is that the filling methods use a Brush object to fill the shape — you can't fill a shape with a pen. So, the first argument of the methods that draw filled shapes is a Brush object, not a Pen object. The remaining arguments are the same because you must still specify the shape to be filled. To view the drawing methods, enter the expression:

```
Me.CreateGraphics.
```

and you will see the names of the shape drawing methods (they start with the Draw prefix) and the shape filling methods (they start with the Fill prefix). The DrawLine method draws a straight-line segment between two points with a pen supplied as an argument. The simplest forms of the DrawLine method are the following, where *point1* and *point2* are either Point or PointF objects, depending on the coordinate system in use:

```
Graphics.DrawLine(pen, X1, Y1, X2, Y2)
Graphics.DrawLine(pen, point1, point2)
```

The two most commonly used drawing methods are the DrawString and MeasureString methods. The DrawString method renders a string in a single line or multiple lines. The simplest form of the DrawString method is as follows:

```
Graphics.DrawString(string, font, brush, X, Y)
```

The first argument is the string to be rendered in the font specified by the second argument. The text will be rendered with the Brush object specified by the *brush* argument. X and Y, finally, are the coordinates of the top-left corner of a rectangle that completely encloses the string.

While working with strings, you need to know the actual dimensions of the string when rendered with the DrawString method in the specified font so you can determine its placement. The MeasureString method allows you to retrieve the metrics of a string before actually drawing it. This method returns a SizeF structure with the width and height, in pixels, of the string when rendered on the same Graphics object with the specified font. We'll use this method extensively in the tutorial "Printing with Visual Basic 2010" (available for download from www.sybex.com/go/masteringvb2010) to position text precisely on the printed page. You can also pass a Rectangle object as an argument to the MeasureString method to find out how many lines it will take to render the string on the rectangle.

The simplest form of the `MeasureString` method is the following, where *string* is the string to be rendered and *font* is the font in which the string will be rendered:

```
Dim textSize As SizeF
textSize = Me.Graphics.MeasureString(string, font)
```

To center a string on the form, use the x-coordinate returned by the `MeasureString` method, as in the following code segment:

```
Dim textSize As SizeF
Dim X As Integer, Y As Integer = 0
textSize = Me.Graphics.MeasureString(string, font)
X = (Me.Width - textSize.Width) / 2
G.DrawString("Centered string", font, brush, X, Y)
```

To center a string, you must subtract the rendered string's length from the form's width, split the difference, and render half on each side of the string.

Figure 11.4 shows a string printed at the center of the form and the two lines passing through the same point. Listing 11.2 shows the statements that produced Figure 11.4.

LISTING 11.2:   Printing a string centered on the form

```
Private Sub Form1_Paint(...) Handles Me.Paint
    Dim G As Graphics
    G = Me.CreateGraphics
    G.FillRectangle(New SolidBrush(Color.Silver), ClientRectangle)
    G.TextRenderingHint = Drawing.Text.TextRenderingHint.AntiAlias
    Dim txtFont As New Font("Verdana", 36, FontStyle.Bold)
    G.DrawLine(New Pen(Color.Green), CInt(Me.Width / 2), CInt(0),
                CInt(Me.Width / 2), CInt(Me.Height))
    G.DrawLine(New Pen(Color.Green), 0, CInt(Me.Height / 2),
                CInt(Me.Width), CInt(Me.Height / 2))
    Dim str As String = "Visual Basic 2010"
    Dim txtSize As SizeF
    txtSize = G.MeasureString(str, txtFont)
    Dim txtX, txtY As Integer
    txtX = (Me.Width - txtSize.Width) / 2
    txtY = (Me.Height - txtSize.Height) / 2
    G.DrawString(str, txtFont,
                New SolidBrush(Color.Red), txtX, txtY)
End Sub
```

For more information on the `DrawString` and `MeasureString` methods, please see the tutorial on generating graphics with VB 2010. You will find more examples of these two methods later in this chapter.

FIGURE 11.4
Centering a string on a form

The `DrawImage` method renders an image on the Graphics object and its simplest syntax is as follows:

```
Graphics.DrawImage(img, point)
```

Both the image and the location of its top-left corner are passed to the method as arguments (as `Image` and `Point` arguments, respectively). Another form of the method draws the specified image within a rectangle. If the rectangle doesn't match the original dimensions of the image, the image will be stretched to fit in the rectangle. The rectangle should have the same aspect ratio as the Image object to avoid distorting the image in the process:

```
Graphics.DrawImage(img, rectangle)
```

The *rectangle* argument determines not only the placement of the image on the Graphics object, but also its dimensions.

Gradients

Another very useful and interesting aspect of graphics is the generation of gradients. In addition to filling shapes with a solid color, you can fill them with various types of gradients. You can even fill text with a gradient, a topic that's demonstrated in the tutorial "Creating Graphics with VB 2010." The simplest yet most common type of gradient is the linear gradient. To fill a shape with a linear gradient, you must create an instance of the LinearGradientBrush class with statements like the following:

```
Dim lgBrush As LinearGradientBrush
lgBrush = New LinearGradientBrush(rect, startColor, endColor, gradientMode)
```

This method creates a gradient that fills a rectangle, specified by the *rect* variable passed as the first argument. This rectangle isn't filled with any gradient; it simply tells the method how long (or how tall) the gradient should be. The gradient starts with the *startColor* at the left side of the rectangle and ends with the *endColor* at the opposite side, while its color changes slowly as it moves from one end to the other. The last argument, *gradientMode*, specifies the direction of the gradient and its setting is a member of the LinearGradientMode enumeration: *BackwardDiagonal*, *ForwardDiagonal*, *Horizontal*, and *Vertical*. You will find an example of filling a shape with a linear gradient in the following section. The other types of gradients are discussed in the tutorial on graphics available for download from www.sybex.com/go/masteringvb2010.

The Image Class

Images are two-dimensional arrays that hold the color values of the pixels making up the image. This isn't how images are stored in their respective files — JPG or JPEG (Joint Photographic Experts Group), GIF (Graphics Interchange Format), TIFF (Tagged Image File Format), and so on — but it's a convenient abstraction for the developer. To access a specific pixel of an image, you need to specify only the horizontal and vertical coordinates of that pixel. Each pixel is a Long value; the first byte is the pixel's alpha value and the other three bytes are the red, green, and blue components.

The Image property of the PictureBox or Form control is an Image object, and there are several ways to create such an object. You can declare a variable of the Image type and then assign the Image property of the PictureBox control or the Form object to the variable:

```
Dim img As Image
img = PictureBox1.Image
```

The *img* Image variable holds the bitmap of the *PictureBox1* control. This code segment assumes that an image was assigned to the control at design time. You can also create a new Image object from an image file by using the Image class's FromFile method:

```
Dim img As Image
img = Image.FromFile("Butterfly.jpg")
```

After the *img* variable has been set up, you can assign it to the Image property of a Picture-Box control:

```
PictureBox1.Image = img
```

Or you can save the image to a file with the Save method, which also accepts as argument the name of the file where the bitmap will be saved. If you need to change the format of an image, all you have to do is open it with the FromFile method and save it to a file with a different extension.

The Image class exposes several members and here are the most important:

Width, Height   These are the dimensions of the image in pixels.

HorizontalResolution, VerticalResolution   These properties are the resolutions of the image in the two directions and are expressed as pixels per inch. If you divide the width of an image by its horizontal resolution, you'll get the actual horizontal size of the image in inches (the size of the image when printed).

The methods exposed by the Image class are the `RotateFlip` method (which rotates and/or flips an image), the `GetThumbnailImage` method (which returns a thumbnail with user-specified dimensions for the specified image), and the `Save` and `FromFile` methods (which save an image and reload an image from a disk file, respectively).

Printing

The topic of printing with Visual Basic is not trivial. Just consider the fact that none of the standard controls comes with built-in printing capabilities. It would be nice if certain controls, such as the TextBox or the ListView control, would print their contents, but this is not the case. Even to print a few text paragraphs entered by the user on a TextBox control, you must provide your own code.

Printing is identical to creating graphics. You must carefully calculate the coordinates of each graphic element placed on the paper, take into consideration the settings of the printer and the current page, and start a new page when the current one is filled. I'll start the exploration of Visual Basic's printing capabilities with an overview of the printing process, which is the same no matter what you print.

You will find a tutorial in PDF format at www.sybex.com/go/masteringvb2010. It explains the printing process in detail. The tutorial includes several examples to address the common printing tasks, such as printing plain and formatted text, tabular data, and bitmaps.

The PrintDocument Control

The PrintDocument control represents your printer, and you must add a PrintDocument control to any project that generates printouts. In effect, everything you draw on the PrintDocument object is sent to the printer. The PrintDocument control represents the printing device, and it exposes a Graphics object that represents the printing surface, just like the `Graphics` property of all Windows controls. You can program against the Graphics object by using all the graphics methods discussed earlier in this chapter. To print text, for example, you must call the `DrawString` method. You can also print frames around the text with the `DrawLine` or `DrawRectangle` method. In general, you can use all the methods of the Graphics object to prepare the printout.

The PrintDocument control is invisible at runtime, and its icon will appear in the Components tray at design time. When you're ready to print, call the PrintDocument control's `Print` method. This method doesn't produce any output, but it does raise the control's `BeginPrint` and `PrintPage` events. The `BeginPrint` event is fired as soon as you call the `Print` method, and this is where you insert the printout's initialization code. The `PrintPage` event is fired once for every page of the printout, and this is where you must insert the code that generates output for the printer. Finally, the `EndPrint` event is fired when the printout ends, and this is where you insert the code to reset any global variables.

The following statement initiates the printing:

```
PrintDocument1.Print
```

This statement is usually placed in a button's or a menu item's `Click` event handler. To experiment with simple printouts, create a new project, place a button on the form, add an instance of the PrintDocument control to the form, and enter the preceding statement in the button's `Click` event handler.

After the execution of this statement, the `PrintDocument1_PrintPage` event handler takes over. This event is fired for each page, so you insert the code to print the first page in this event's handler. The `PrintPage` event provides the usual e argument, which gives you access to the `Graphics` property of the current Printer object. The printer has its own Graphics object, which represents the page you print on, and you will see shortly how to create graphics to be printed.

If you need to print additional pages, you set the `e.HasMorePages` property to True just before you exit the `PrintPage` event handler. This will fire another `PrintPage` event. The same process will repeat until you've printed everything. After you finish, you set the `e.HasMorePages` property to False, and no more `PrintPage` events will be fired. Instead, the `EndPrint` event will be fired and the printing process will come to an end. Figure 11.5 outlines the printing process.

FIGURE 11.5

All printing takes place in the `PrintPage` event handler of the PrintDocument object.

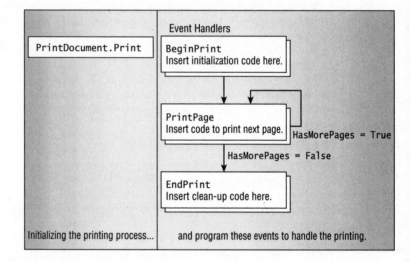

The code in Listing 11.3 shows the structure of a typical `PrintPage` event handler. The `PrintPage` event handler prints three pages with the same text but a different page number on each page.

LISTING 11.3: A simple `PrintPage` event handler

```
Private Sub PrintDocument1_PrintPage(...) Handles PrintDocument1.PrintPage
    Static pageNum As Integer
    Dim prFont As New Font("Verdana", 24, GraphicsUnit.Point)
    e.Graphics.DrawString(
                "PAGE " & pageNum + 1, prFont,
                Brushes.Black, 700, 1050)
    e.Graphics.DrawRectangle(Pens.Blue, 0, 0, 300, 100)
    e.Graphics.DrawString( _
                "Printing with VB 2010", prFont,
                Brushes.Black, 10, 10)
```

```
    ' Following is the logic that determines whether we're done printing
    pageNum = pageNum + 1
    If pageNum <= 3 Then
        e.HasMorePages = True
    Else
        e.HasMorePages = False
        pageNum = 0
    End If
End Sub
```

The *pageNum* variable is declared as Static, so it retains its value between invocations of the event handler and isn't reset automatically. The last statement, which is executed after you have printed the last page, resets the *pageNum* variable in anticipation of another printout. Without this statement, the first page of the second printout (if you clicked the button again) would become page 4, and so on.

The entire printout is generated by the same subroutine, one page at a time. Because pages are not totally independent of one another, you need to keep some information in variables that are not initialized every time the PrintPage event handler is executed. The page number, for example, must be stored in a variable that will maintain its value between successive invocations of the PrintPage event handler, and it must be increased every time a new page is printed. If you're printing a text file, you must keep track of the last printed line so that each page will pick up where the previous one ended, not from the beginning of the document.

To add printing features that adhere to the Windows standards to your applications, you must also use the PrintDialog and PageSetupDialog controls, which are discussed in the following section.

The PrintDialog Control

The PrintDialog control displays the standard Print dialog box, which allows users to select a printer and set its properties. If you don't display this dialog box, the output will be sent automatically to the default printer and will use the default settings of the printer.

To display the Print dialog box, call the PrintDialog control's ShowDialog method. However, you must first set the control's PrinterSettings property, as shown in the following code segment; if you do not, a runtime exception will be thrown:

```
PrintDialog1.PrinterSettings = PrintDocument1.PrinterSettings
If PrintDialog1.ShowDialog() = Windows.Forms.DialogResult.OK Then
    PrintDocument1.PrinterSettings = PrintDialog1.PrinterSettings
End If
```

When users select a printer in this dialog box, it automatically becomes the active printer. Any printout generated after the printer selection will be sent to that printer; you don't have to insert any code to switch printers.

The PageSetupDialog Control

The PageSetupDialog control displays the Page Setup dialog box, which allows users to set up the page (its orientation and margins). The dialog box returns the current page settings in a PageSettings object, which exposes the user-specified settings as properties. These settings don't take effect on their own; you simply read their values and take them into consideration as you prepare the output for the printer from within your code.

To use this dialog box in your application, drop the PageSetupDialog control on the form and call its ShowDialog method from within the application's code. The single property of this control that you'll be using exclusively in your projects is the PageSettings property, which exposes a number of properties reflecting the current settings of the page (margins and orientation). These settings apply to the entire document. The PrintDocument control has an analogous property: the DefaultPageSettings property. After the user closes the Page Setup dialog box, we assign its PageSettings property to the DefaultPageSettings property of the PrintDocument object to make the user-specified settings available to our code.

The PrintPreviewDialog Control

Print Preview is another dialog box that displays a preview of the printed document. It exposes a lot of functionality and allows users to examine the output and, optionally, to send it to the printer. After you write the code to generate the printout, you can direct it to the PrintPreviewDialog control. You don't have to write any additional code; just place an instance of the control on the form and set its Document property to the PrintDocument control on the form. Then show the PrintPreviewDialog control instead of calling the Print method of the PrintDocument object:

```
PrintPreviewDialog1.Document = PrintDocument1
PrintPreviewDialog1.ShowDialog
```

After the execution of these two lines, the PrintDocument control takes over. It fires the PrintPage event as usual, but it sends its output to the Print Preview dialog box, not to the printer. The dialog box contains a Print button, which the user can click to send the document being previewed to the printer. The exact same code that generated the preview document will print the document on the printer.

The first example of this chapter (refer to Listing 11.3) prints three simple pages to the printer. To redirect the output of the program to the PrintPreview control, add an instance of the PrintPreview control to the form and replace the statement that calls the Print Document1.Print method in the button's Click event handler with the following statements:

```
PrintPreviewDialog1.Document = PrintDocument1
PrintPreviewDialog1.ShowDialog
```

Run the project, and this time you will be able to preview the document on your monitor. If you're satisfied with its appearance, you can click the Print button to send the document to the printer.

Page Geometry

Like the drawing surface on the monitor (the client area), the page on which you're printing has a fixed size and resolution. The most challenging aspect of printing is the calculation of the coordinates and dimensions of each graphic element on the page.

To access the margins of the current page, use the Margins property of the PrintDocument1 .DefaultPageSettings object. This property, which is also an object, exposes the Left, Right, Top, and Bottom properties, which are the values of the four margins. Another property exposed by the DefaultSettings object is the `PageSize` property, which represents the dimensions of the page. The width and height of the page are given by the following expressions:

```
PrintDocument1.DefaultPageSettings.PaperSize.Width
PrintDocument1.DefaultPageSettings.PaperSize.Height
```

The top of the page is at coordinates (0, 0), which correspond to the top-left corner of the page. We never actually print at this corner. The coordinates of the top-left corner of the printable area of the page are given by the following expressions:

```
PrintDocument1.DefaultPageSettings.Margins.Top
PrintDocument1.DefaultPageSettings.Margins.Left
```

Basic Printing Methods

The basic methods you'll use to create printouts are no different than the methods you use to create graphics. The method for printing text is the `DrawString` method, which has the following syntax:

```
Graphics.DrawString(string, font, brush, X, Y)
```

This method will render its *string* argument in the font specified in the second argument, using a Brush object as specified by the *brush* argument at the coordinates specified by the last two arguments. To position multiple elements on the page, you need to know how much space each element takes so you can advance accordingly on the page. To find out the size of a string when rendered on the page, use the `MeasureString` method. The two methods are used in tandem and this is a common theme in printing text.

The simplest form of the `MeasureString` method is the following, where *string* is the string to be rendered and *font* is the font in which the string will be rendered:

```
Dim textSize As SizeF
textSize = Graphics.MeasureString(string, font)
```

To center a string on the form, subtract the string's width and height from the page's width and height and then split the difference equally between the two sides of the strings, vertically and horizontally. If the string's width is 320 pixels and the page's printable width is 780 pixels, you must start printing at the x-coordinate (780-320)/2. This will center the string on the page, leaving 320 pixels on either side. Basically, perform the following calculations using the x- and y-coordinates returned by the `MeasureString` method, as shown here:

```
Dim textSize As SizeF
Dim X As Integer, Y As Integer = 0
textSize = Me.Graphics.MeasureString(string, font)
X = (Me.Width - textSize.Width) / 2
Y = (Me.Height - textSize.Height) / 2
G.DrawString("Centered string", font, brush, X, Y)
```

To position your strings on the page you need to know the size of each string when rendered on the printer in a specific font. You can obtain this information with the `MeasureString` method, as discussed in the preceding section. As you will read in detail in the tutorial on printing with VB, a printing routine must first determine the printable area on the page.

VB 2010 at Work: Generating a Simple Printout

In this section, we're going to build a simple, but certainly not trivial, printout to demonstrate the use of many of the print-related concepts discussed in the preceding sections. The printout, which contains centered strings and an image as well as a gradient, is shown in Figure 11.6.

FIGURE 11.6
Previewing a simple printout

Start a new form and drop on it a button and the PageSetupDialog, PrintDocument, and PrintDialog controls. Although we will add preview capabilities to the application, we won't use an instance of the PrintPreviewDialog control. Instead, we'll create an instance of this control from within the application's code.

The code for the application is shown in Listing 11.4. The Click event handler for the button displays the PrintDialog control to allow users to select a printer and set the properties of the printout. The PrintDialog control has a Preferences button, where users can set the page orientation. If you want users to be able to set the page's margins, you must also display the PageSetupDialog. Windows applications provide a Page Setup menu item, which displays the PageSetup dialog box.

After the user has selected a printer and set the orientation of the page, the code creates a new instance of the PrintPreviewDialog control, the *prn* variable, and assigns the PrintDocument control to the `Document` property of the *prn* object and calls the same object's `Show` method to initiate the printout.

Then the `PrintPage` event takes over. This event's handler contains quite a bit of code, but it's straightforward. First, it extracts the coordinates of the printable area's upper-left corner, taking into consideration the page's margins. These two values are stored in the variables *topX* and *topY*. Then it calculates the width and height of the page's printable area and stores these values in the *pageWidth* and *pageHeight* properties.

The following few statements create a LinearGradientBrush object, the *LGBrush* variable, which is then used to fill a large rectangle with the `FillRectangle` method. The following statements print the text and the image on the page. To print text, the code uses the `MeasureString` method to calculate the size of each string and center it horizontally on the page. Then, it advances to the y-coordinate of the next string by incrementing the *Y* variable.

The image is printed with the `DrawImage` method, but there's a slight trick here. Because the image has a portrait orientation, I've decided to reduce its size when it's printed in landscape mode because it would take up most of the page. The code examines the property of the `e.PageSettings.Landscape` property, and if it's True, it fits the image into a rectangle that's half as tall and half as wide as the original image. You can experiment with the SimplePrintout project's code and add more elements to the printout, possibly arrange differently the elements on the page, and break the printout into multiple pages.

LISTING 11.4:   The code that generated the printout of Figure 11.5

```
Private Sub Button1_Click(...) Handles Button1.Click
    PrintDialog1.PrinterSettings = PrintDocument1.PrinterSettings
    If PrintDialog1.ShowDialog() = Windows.Forms.DialogResult.OK Then
        PrintDocument1.PrinterSettings = PrintDialog1.PrinterSettings
    End If
    Dim prn As New PrintPreviewDialog
    prn.Document = PrintDocument1
    prn.Show()
End Sub

Private Sub PrintDocument1_PrintPage(...) Handles
                PrintDocument1.PrintPage
    Dim msg1 As String = "Mastering Visual Basic 2010"
    Dim msg2 As String = "Published by SYBEX"
    Dim topX = e.PageSettings.Margins.Left
    Dim topY = e.PageSettings.Margins.Top
    Dim pageWidth =  e.PageSettings.Bounds.Width -
                    e.PageSettings.Margins.Left -
                    e.PageSettings.Margins.Right
    Dim pageHeight = e.PageSettings.Bounds.Height -
                    e.PageSettings.Margins.Top -
                    e.PageSettings.Margins.Bottom
    Dim R As New RectangleF(topX, topY, pageWidth, pageHeight)
    Dim startColor As Color = Color.BlueViolet
    Dim EndColor As Color = Color.LightYellow
    Dim LGBrush As New System.Drawing.Drawing2D.LinearGradientBrush(
```

```vb
                                R, startColor, EndColor,
                                Drawing2D.LinearGradientMode.ForwardDiagonal)
        e.Graphics.FillRectangle(LGBrush, R)
        e.Graphics.DrawRectangle(Pens.Red,
                        New Rectangle(New Point(topX, topY),
                        New Size(pageWidth, pageHeight)))
        Dim size = e.Graphics.MeasureString(msg1,
                                New Font("Verdana", 28, FontStyle.Bold))
        Dim X = topX + (pageWidth - size.Width) / 2
        Dim Y = 150
        e.Graphics.DrawString(msg1,
                New Font("Verdana", 28, FontStyle.Bold),
                Brushes.White,
                New RectangleF(X, Y, size.Width, size.Height))
        size = e.Graphics.MeasureString(msg2,
                        New Font("Microsoft YaHei", 18, FontStyle.Regular))
        X = topX + (pageWidth - size.Width) / 2
        Y = Y + 70
        e.Graphics.DrawString(msg2,
                New Font("Microsoft YaHei", 18, FontStyle.Regular),
                Brushes.Yellow,
                New RectangleF(X, Y, 2 * size.Width, 2 * size.Height))
        Dim img As Image
        img = My.Resources.MVB2010
        Dim imgSize As Size
        If e.PageSettings.Landscape Then
            imgSize = New Size(img.Width / 2, img.Height / 2)
        Else
            imgSize = New Size(img.Width, img.Height)
        End If
        Y = Y + 80
        X = topX + (pageWidth - imgSize.Width) / 2
        e.Graphics.DrawImage(img,
                        New Rectangle(New Point(X, Y), imgSize))
        e.HasMorePages = False
        Dim bookDescription As String =
                    "This expert guide covers … .NET Framework. " &
                    vbCrLf &
                    "In a clear, easy-to-follow style, … " & vbCrLf
        Y = Y + imgSize.Height + 25
        X = topX + 40
        Dim txtRectangle As New Rectangle(X, Y, pageWidth - 80, 280)
        e.Graphics.DrawString(bookDescription, _
                    New Font("Microsoft YaHei", 9, FontStyle.Regular),
                    Brushes.Black, txtRectangle)
        e.HasMorePages = False
    End Sub
```

Handling Strings and Characters

The .NET Framework provides two basic classes for manipulating text: the String and StringBuilder classes.

The String class exposes a large number of practical methods, and they're all *reference methods*: They don't act on the string directly but return another string instead. After you assign a value to a String object, that's it. You can examine the string, locate words in it, and parse it, but you can't edit it. The String class exposes methods such as the `Replace` and `Remove` methods, which replace a section of the string with another and remove a range of characters from the string, respectively. These methods, however, don't act on the string directly: They replace or remove parts of the original string and then return the result as a new string.

The StringBuilder class is similar to the String class: It stores strings, but it can manipulate them in place. In other words, the methods of the StringBuilder class are instance methods.

The distinction between the two classes is that the String class is better suited for static strings, whereas the StringBuilder class is better suited for dynamic strings. Use the String class for strings that don't change frequently in the course of an application, and use the StringBuilder class for strings that grow and shrink dynamically. The two classes expose similar methods, but the String class's methods return new strings; if you need to manipulate large strings extensively, using the String class might fill the memory quite quickly.

Any code that manipulates strings must also be able to manipulate individual characters. The Framework supports the Char class, which not only stores characters but also exposes numerous methods for handling them. Both the String and StringBuilder classes provide methods for storing strings into arrays of characters as well as for converting character arrays into strings. After extracting the individual characters from a string, you can process them with the members of the Char class. I'll start the discussion of the text-handling features of the Framework with an overview of the Char data type and continue with the other two major components, the String and StringBuilder classes.

The Char Class

The `Char` data type stores characters as individual, double-byte (16-bit), Unicode values, and it exposes methods for classifying the character stored in a Char variable. You can use methods such as `IsDigit` and `IsPunctuation` on a Char variable to determine its type and other similar methods that can simplify your string validation code.

To use a character variable in your application, you must declare it with a statement such as the following one:

```
Dim ch As Char
ch = Convert.ToChar("A")
```

The expression "A" represents a string, even if it contains a single character. Everything you enclose in double quotes is a string. To convert it to a character, you must cast it to the Char type. If the Strict option is off (the default value), you need not perform the conversion explicitly. If the Strict option is on, you must use one of the `CChar()` or the `CType()` functions (or the Convert class) to convert the single-character string in the double quotes to a character value. There's also a shorthand notation for converting one-character strings to characters — just append the `c` character to a single-character string:

```
Dim ch As Char = "A"c
```

If you let the compiler decipher the type of the variable from its value, a single-character string will be interpreted as a string, not as a Char data type. If you later assign a string value to a Char variable by using a statement such as the following, only the first character of the string will be stored in the *ch* variable:

```
ch = "ABC"    ' the value "A" is assigned to ch!
```

PROPERTIES

The Char class provides two trivial properties: MaxValue and MinValue. They return the largest and smallest character values you can represent with the Char data type.

METHODS

The Char data type exposes several useful methods for handling characters. All the methods described in Table 11.6 have the same syntax: They accept either a single argument, which is the character they act upon, or a string and the index of a character in the string on which they act.

TABLE 11.6:   Char data type methods

METHOD	DESCRIPTION
GetNumericValue	This method returns a positive numeric value if called with an argument that is a digit and the value −1 otherwise. If you call GetNumericValue with the argument 5, it will return the numeric value 5. If you call it with the symbol @, it will return the value −1.
GetUnicodeCategory	This method returns a numeric value that is a member of the UnicodeCategory enumeration and identifies the Unicode group to which the character belongs. The Unicode groups characters into categories such as math symbols, currency symbols, and quotation marks. Look up the UnicodeCategory enumeration in the documentation for more information.
IsLetter, IsDigit, IsLetterOrDigit	These methods return a True/False value indicating whether their argument, which is a character, is a letter, decimal digit, or letter/digit, respectively. You can write an event handler by using the IsDigit method to accept numeric keystrokes and to reject letters and punctuation symbols.
IsLower, IsUpper	These methods return a True/False value indicating whether the specified character is lowercase or uppercase, respectively.
IsNumber	This method returns a True/False value indicating whether the specified character is a number. The IsNumber method takes into consideration hexadecimal digits (the characters 0123456789ABCDEF) in the same way as the IsDigit method does for decimal numbers.

TABLE 11.6: Char data type methods *(CONTINUED)*

METHOD	DESCRIPTION
IsPunctuation, IsSymbol, IsControl	These methods return a True/False value indicating whether the specified character is a punctuation mark, symbol, or control character, respectively. The Backspace and Esc keys, for example, are ISO (International Organization for Standardization) control characters.
IsSeparator	This method returns a True/False value indicating whether the character is categorized as a separator (space, new-line character, and so on).
IsWhiteSpace	This method returns a True/False value indicating whether the specified character is white space. Any sequence of spaces, tabs, line feeds, and form feeds is considered white space. Use this method along with the IsPunctuation method to remove all characters in a string that are not words.
ToLower, ToUpper	These methods convert their argument to a lowercase or uppercase character, respectively, and return it as another character.
ToString	This method converts a character to a string. It returns a single-character string, which you can use with other string-manipulation methods or functions.

Real World Scenario

IsLetter, IsDigit, IsLetterOrDigit

The IsLetter, IsDigit, and IsLetterOrDigit methods deserve a bit more discussion. I commonly use these methods to intercept keystrokes from within a control's KeyPress (or KeyUp and KeyDown) events. The e.KeyChar property of the e argument returns the character that was pressed by the user and that fired the KeyPress event. To reject non-numeric keys as the user enters text in a TextBox control, use the event handler shown here:

```
Private Sub TextBox1_KeyPres(
            ByVal sender As Object,
            ByVal e As System.Windows.Forms.KeyPressEventArgs)
            Handles TextBox1.KeyPress
    Dim c As Char
    c = e.KeyChar
    If Not (Char.IsDigit(c) or Char.IsControl(c)) Then
        e.Handled = True
    End If
End Sub
```

This code ignores any keystrokes that don't represent numeric digits and are not control characters. Control characters are not rejected because we want users to be able to edit the text on the control. The Backspace key, for example, is captured by the KeyPress event, and you shouldn't "kill" it. For more information on handling keystrokes from within your code, see the section "Capturing Keystrokes" in Chapter 5, "Basic Windows Controls." If the TextBox control is allowed to accept fractional values, you should allow the period character as well, by using the following If clause:

```
Dim c As Char
c = e.KeyChar
If Not (Char.IsDigit(c) or c = "." or
        Char.IsControl(c)) Then
    e.Handled = True
End If
```

The String Class

The String class implements the String data type, which is one of the richest data types in terms of the members it exposes. We have used strings extensively in earlier chapters, and you're more than familiar with the String class by now, but I will review the basic members of the String class here for reasons of completeness.

To create a new instance of the String class, you simply declare a variable of the String type. You can also initialize it by assigning to the corresponding variable a text value:

```
Dim title As String = "Mastering VB2010"
```

Everything enclosed in double quotes is a string, even if it's the representation of a number. String objects are *immutable*: Once created, they can't be modified. The names of some of the methods of the String class may lead you to think that they change the value of the string, but they don't; instead, they return a new string. The Replace method, for example, doesn't replace any characters in the original string, but it creates a new string, replaces some characters, and then returns the new string. The Replace method, like all other methods of the String class, doesn't operate directly on the string to which it's applied. Instead, it creates a new string and returns it as a new string.

If you plan to create and manipulate long strings in your code often, use the StringBuilder class instead, which is extremely fast compared to the String class and VB's string-manipulation functions. This doesn't mean that the String data type is obsolete, of course. The String class exposes many more methods for handling strings (such as locating a smaller string in a larger one, comparing strings, changing individual characters, and so on). The StringBuilder class, on the other hand, is much more efficient when you build long strings bit by bit, when you need to remove part of a string, and so on. To achieve its speed, however, it consumes considerably more memory than the equivalent String variable.

PROPERTIES

The String class exposes only two properties, the Length and Chars properties, which return a string's length and its characters, respectively. Both properties are read-only. The Chars property returns an array of characters, and you can use this property to read individual characters from a string. Note that the Chars property returns the characters in the string, no matter what the encoding is (UTF7, UTF8, Unicode, and so on).

METHODS

All the functionality of the String class is available through methods, which are described next. They are all shared methods: They act on a string and return a new string with the modified value.

Compare   This method compares two strings and returns a negative value if the first string is less than the second, a positive value if the second string is less than the first, and zero if the two strings are equal. Of course, the simplest method of comparing two strings is to use the comparison operators, as shown here:

```
If name1 < name 2 Then
    ' name1 is alphabetically smaller than name 2
Else If name 1 > name 2 Then
    ' name2 is alphabetically smaller than name 1
Else
    ' name1 is the same as name2
End If
```

The Compare method is overloaded, and the first two arguments are always the two strings to be compared. The method's return value is 0 if the two strings are equal, 1 if the first string is smaller than the second, and −1 if the second is smaller than the first. The simplest form of the method accepts two strings as arguments:

```
String.Compare(str1, str2)
```

The following form of the method accepts a third argument, which is a True/False value and determines whether the search will be case sensitive (if True) or not:

```
String.Compare(str1, str2, case)
```

Another form of the Compare method allows you to compare segments of two strings. Its syntax is as follows:

```
String.Compare(str1, index1, str2, index2, length)
```

index1 and *index2* are the starting locations of the segment to be compared in each string. The two segments must have the same length, which is specified by the last argument.

The following statements return the values highlighted below each:

```
Debug.WriteLine(str.Compare("the quick brown fox", _
                "THE QUICK BROWN FOX"))
```
-1

```
Debug.WriteLine(str.Compare("THE QUICK BROWN FOX", _
                            "the quick brown fox"))
1
Debug.WriteLine(str.Compare("THE QUICK BROWN FOX", _
                            "THE QUICK BROWN FOX"))
0
```

CompareOrdinal   The CompareOrdinal method compares two strings, which is similar to the Compare method, but it doesn't take into consideration the current locale. This method returns zero if the two strings are the same and a positive or negative value if they're different. These values, however, are not 1 and −1; they represent the numeric difference between the Unicode values of the first two characters that are different in the two strings.

Concat   This method concatenates two or more strings (places them one after the other) and forms a new string. The simpler form of the Concat method has the following syntax and it is equivalent to the & operator:

```
newString = String.Concat(string1, string2)
```

A more-useful form of the same method concatenates a large number of strings stored in an array:

```
newString = String.Concat(strings())
```

To use this form of the method, store all the strings you want to concatenate into a string array and then call the Concat method. If you want to separate the individual strings with special delimiters, append them to each individual string before concatenating them. Or you can use the Join method, discussed shortly.

EndsWith, StartsWith   These two methods return True if their argument ends or starts with a user-supplied substring. The syntax of these methods is as follows:

```
found = str.EndsWith(string)
found = str.StartsWith(string)
```

These two methods are equivalent to the Left() and Right() functions, which extract a given number of characters from the left or right end of the string, respectively. The two statements following the declaration of the name variable are equivalent:

```
Dim name As String = "Visual Basic.NET"
If Left(name, 3) = "Vis" Then …
If String.StartsWith("Vis") Then …
```

Notice that the comparison performed by the StartsWith method is case sensitive. If you don't care about the case, you can convert both the string and the substring to uppercase, as in the following example:

```
If name.ToUpper.StartsWith("VIS") Then …
```

IndexOf, LastIndexOf   These two methods locate a substring in a larger string. The IndexOf method starts searching from the beginning of the string and stops when it reaches the target (or it fails to locate the substring), and the LastIndexOf method starts searching from the end of the string. Both methods return an integer, which is the position of the substring's first character in the larger string (the position of the first character is zero).

To locate a string within a larger one, use the following forms of the IndexOf method:

```
pos = str.IndexOf(searchString)
pos = str.IndexOf(SearchString, startIndex)
pos = str.IndexOf(SearchString, startIndex, endIndex)
```

The startIndex and endIndex arguments delimit the section of the string where the search will take place, and *pos* is an integer variable.

The last three overloaded forms of the IndexOf method search for an array of characters in the string:

```
str.IndexOf(Char())
str.IndexOf(Char(), startIndex)
str.IndexOf(Char(), startIndex, endIndex)
```

The following statement will return the position of the string **Visual** in the text of the *TextBox1* control or will return −1 if the string isn't contained in the text:

```
Dim pos As Integer
pos = TextBox1.IndexOf("Visual")
```

IndexOfAny   This is an interesting method that accepts as an argument an array of arguments and returns the first occurrence of any of the array's characters in the string. The syntax of the IndexOfAny method is

```
Dim pos As Integer = str.IndexOfAny(chars)
```

where *chars* is an array of characters. This method attempts to locate the first instance of any member of the *chars* array in the string. If the character is found, its index is returned. If not, the process is repeated with the second character, and so on until an instance is found or the array has been exhausted. If you want to locate the first delimiter in a string, call the IndexOfAny method with an array such as the following:

```
Dim chars() As Char = {"."c, ","c, ";"c, " "c}
Dim mystring As String = "This is a short sentence"
Debug.WriteLine(mystring.IndexOfAny(chars))
```

When the last statement is executed, the value 4 will be printed in the Output window. This is the location of the first space in the string. Notice that the space delimiter is the last one in the *chars* array.

Insert   The Insert method inserts one or more characters at a specified location in a string and returns the new string. The syntax of the Insert method is as follows:

```
newString = str.Insert(startIndex, subString)
```

startIndex is the position in the *str* variable, where the string specified by the second argument will be inserted. The following statement will insert a dash between the second and third characters of the string **CA93010**.

```
Dim Zip As String = "CA93010"
Dim StateZip As String
StateZip = Zip.Insert(2, "-")
```

Join   This method joins two or more strings and returns a single string with a separator between the original strings. Its syntax is the following, where *separator* is the string that will be used as the separator, and *strings* is an array with the strings to be joined:

```
 newString = String.Join(separator, strings)
```

The following statement will create a full path by joining folder names:

```
Dim path As String
Dim folders(3) As String = {"My Documents", "Business", "Expenses"}
path = String.Join("/", folders)
```

Split   Just as you can join strings, you can split a long string into smaller ones by using the Split method, whose syntax is the following, where *delimiters* is an array of characters and *str* is the string to be split:

```
strings() = String.Split(delimiters, str)
```

The string is split into sections that are separated by any one of the delimiters specified with the first argument. These strings are returned as an array of strings.

SPLITTING STRINGS WITH MULTIPLE SEPARATORS

The delimiters array allows you to specify multiple delimiters, which makes it a great tool for isolating words in a text. You can specify all the characters that separate words in text (spaces, tabs, periods, exclamation marks, and so on) as delimiters and pass them along with the text to be parsed to the Split method.

The statements in the following listing isolate the parts of a path, which are delimited by a backslash character:

```
Dim path As String = "c:\My Documents\Business\Expenses"
Dim delimiters() As Char = {"\"c}
Dim parts() As String
parts = path.Split(delimiters)
Dim iPart As IEnumerator
iPart = parts.GetEnumerator
While iPart.MoveNext
    Debug.WriteLine(iPart.Current.tostring)
End While
```

If the path ends with a slash, the Split method will return an extra empty string. If you want to skip the empty strings, pass an additional argument to the function, which is a member of the StringSplitOptions enumeration: *None* or *RemoveEmptyEntries*.

Notice that the *parts* array is declared without a size. It's a one-dimensional array that will be dimensioned automatically by the Split method, according to the number of substrings separated by the specified delimiter(s).

Remove   The Remove method removes a given number of characters from a string, starting at a specific location, and returns the result as a new string. Its syntax is the following, where *startIndex* is the index of the first character to be removed in the *str* string variable and *count* is the number of characters to be removed:

```
newSrting = str.Remove(startIndex, count)
```

Replace   This method replaces all instances of a specified string in another string with a new one. It creates a new instance of the string, replaces the characters as specified by its arguments, and returns this string. The syntax of this method is

```
newString = str.Replace(oldString, newString)
```

where *oldString* is the part of the *str* variable to be replaced and *newString* is the string to replace the occurrences of *oldString*. The following statements replace all instances of the tab character with a single space. You can change the last statement to replace tabs with a specific number of spaces — usually three, four, or five spaces:

```
Dim txt, newTxt As String
Dim vbTab As String = vbCrLf
txt = "some text        with two tabs"
newTxt = txt.Replace(vbTab, "    ")
```

PadLeft, PadRight These two methods align the string left or right in a specified field and return a fixed-length string with spaces to the right (for right-padded strings) or to the left (for left-padded strings). After the execution of these statements

```
Dim LPString, RPString As String
RPString = " [" & "Mastering VB2010".PadRight(20) & "]"
LPString = " [" & "Mastering VB2010".PadLeft(20) & "]"
```

the values of the *LPString* and *RPString* variables are as follows:

```
[Mastering VB2010    ]
[    Mastering VB2010]
```

The StringBuilder Class

The StringBuilder class stores dynamic strings and exposes methods to manipulate them much faster than the String class. As you will see, the StringBuilder class is extremely fast, but it uses considerably more memory than the string it holds. To use the StringBuilder class in an application, you must import the System.Text namespace (unless you want to fully qualify each instance of the StringBuilder class in your code). Assuming that you have imported the System.Text namespace in your code module, you can create a new instance of the String-Builder class via the following statement:

```
Dim txt As New StringBuilder
```

Because the StringBuilder class handles dynamic strings in place, it's good to declare in advance the size of the string you intend to store in the current instance of the class. The default capacity is 16 characters, and it's doubled automatically every time you exceed it. To set the initial capacity of the StringBuilder class, use the Capacity property.

To create a new instance of the StringBuilder class, you can call its constructor without any arguments or pass the initial string as an argument:

```
Dim txt As New StringBuilder("some string")
```

If you can estimate the length of the string you'll store in the variable, you can specify this value by using the following form of the constructor so that the variable need not be resized continuously as you add characters to it:

```
Dim txt As New StringBuilder(initialCapacity)
```

The size you specify is not a hard limit; the variable might grow longer at runtime, and the StringBuilder will adjust its capacity.

If you want to specify a maximum capacity for your StringBuilder variable, use the following constructor:

```
Dim txt As New StringBuilder (
            Intialcapacity, maxCapacity)
```

Finally, you can initialize a new instance of the StringBuilder class by using both an initial and a maximum capacity, as well as its initial value, by using the following form of the constructor:

```
Dim txt As New StringBuilder(
                  string, intialcapacity, maxCapacity)
```

PROPERTIES

You have already seen the two basic properties of the StringBuilder class: the Capacity and MaxCapacity properties. In addition, the StringBuilder class provides the Length and Chars properties, which are the same as the corresponding properties of the String class. The Length property returns the number of characters in the current instance of the StringBuilder class, and the Chars property is an array of characters. Unlike the Chars property of the String class, this one is read/write. You can not only read individual characters, you can also set them from within your code. The index of the first character is zero.

METHODS

Many of the methods of the StringBuilder class are equivalent to the methods of the String class, but they act directly on the string to which they're applied, and they don't return a new string:

Append The Append method appends a base type to the current instance of the StringBuilder class, and its syntax is the following, where the *value* argument can be a single character, a string, a date, or any numeric value:

```
SB.Append(value)
```

When you append numeric values to a StringBuilder, they're converted to strings; the value appended is the string returned by the type's ToString method. You can also append an object to the StringBuilder — the actual string that will be appended is the value of the object's ToString property.

AppendFormat The AppendFormat method is similar to the Append method. Before appending the string, however, AppendFormat formats it. The syntax of the AppendFormat method is as follows:

```
SB.AppendFormat(string, values)
```

The first argument is a string with embedded format specifications, and *values* is an array with values (objects, in general) — one for each format specification in the *string* argument. If you have a small number of values to format, up to four, you can supply them as separate arguments separated by commas:

```
SB.AppendFormat(string, value1, value2, value3, value4)
```

The following statement appends the string

Your balance as of Thursday, August 2, 2007 is $19,950.40

to a StringBuilder variable:

```
Dim statement As New StringBuilder
statement.AppendFormat(
      "Your balance as of {0:D} is ${1: #,###.00}",
      #8/2/2007#, 19950.40)
```

Each format specification is enclosed in a pair of curly brackets, and they're numbered sequentially (from zero). Then there's a colon followed by the actual specification. The D format specification tells the `AppendFormat` method to format the specified string in long date format. The second format specification, #,###.00, uses the thousands separator and two decimal digits for the amount.

Insert   This method inserts a string into the current instance of the StringBuilder class, and its syntax is as follows:

```
SB.Insert(index, value)
```

The *index* argument is the location where the new string will be inserted in the current instance of the StringBuilder, and *value* is the string to be inserted. A variation of the syntax shown here inserts multiple copies of the specified string into the StringBuilder:

```
SB.Insert(index, string, count)
```

Remove   This method removes a number of characters from the current StringBuilder, starting at a specified location; its syntax is the following, where *startIndex* is the position of the first character to be removed from the string and *count* is the number of characters to be removed:

```
SB.Remove(startIndex, count)
```

Replace   This method replaces all instances of a string in the current StringBuilder object with another string. The syntax of the `Replace` method is the following, where the two arguments can be either strings or characters:

```
SB.Replace(oldValue, newValue)
```

Unlike with the String class, the replacement takes place in the current instance of the StringBuilder class and the method doesn't return another string. Another form of the `Replace` method limits the replacements to a specified segment of the `StringBuilder` instance:

```
SB.Replace(oldValue, newValue, startIndex, count)
```

This method replaces all instances of *oldValue* with *newValue* in the section starting at location *startIndex* and extending *count* characters from the starting location.

ToString   Use this method to convert the StringBuilder instance to a string and assign it to a String variable. The ToString method returns the string represented by the StringBuilder variable to which it's applied.

VB 2010 AT WORK: TEST-DRIVING THE STRINGBUILDER CLASS

The code segment included in Listing 11.5 demonstrates the efficiency of the StringBuilder class. The code extracts the words in a large text file and reverses their order. It's not a terribly practical demonstration of string operations, but it demonstrates very clearly the efficiency of the StringBuilder class. The code extracts the words with the Split method, using the space as separator, and stores them in the *words* array. Once the words have been extracted, the two loops go through each word in the array and build two variables with the words in the *words* array in reverse order: one of them a String variable and the other a StringBuilder variable.

LISTING 11.5:   Reversing the order of words in a large string

```
Dim newString As String = ""
Dim words() = TextBox1.Text.Split(" ")
Dim SW As New Stopwatch
SW.Start()
For Each wrd In words
    newString = wrd & " " & newString
Next
SW.Stop()
MsgBox("Reversed word order with the String class in " &
        (SW.ElapsedMilliseconds / 1000).ToString)

Dim newSB As New System.Text.StringBuilder
SW = New Stopwatch
SW.Start()
For wrd = words.Count - 1 To 0 Step -1
    newSB.Append(words(wrd)) & " ")
Next
SW.Stop()
MsgBox("Reversed word order with the StringBuilder class in " &
        (SW.ElapsedMilliseconds / 1000).ToString)
```

I've copied the text of this chapter and pasted it three times on a TextBox control. It took 15 seconds to reverse the words in the String class and less than half a second to do the same with the StringBuilder class. If you manipulate strings extensively in your code, you should definitely consider the StringBuilder class. If you're reading pieces of information from a file or other source, such as an XML file, and append them to a string, you should definitely use a StringBuilder class. I frequently have to build large strings that include formatting information and display them on a RichTextBox control, and the StringBuilder class is the only option. Keep in mind, however, that the StringBuider class doesn't provide nearly as many string manipulation methods as the String class. The StringBuilder class shines in applications that build long strings piecewise, an operation at which the String class has never been especially efficient.

Handling Dates and Time

Another common task in coding business applications is the manipulation of dates and time. To aid the coding of these tasks, the Framework provides the DateTime and TimeSpan classes. The DateTime class handles date and time *values*, whereas the TimeSpan class handles date and time *intervals* and *differences*. Variables that represent dates and times must be declared as DateTime, which is one of the basic data types of the Framework.

The DateTime Class

The DateTime class is used for storing date and time values, and it's one of the Framework's base data types. Date and time values are stored internally as Double numbers. The integer part of the value corresponds to the date, and the fractional part corresponds to the time. To convert a DateTime variable to a Double value, use the method ToOADateTime, which returns a value that is an OLE (Object Linking and Embedding) Automation-compatible date. The value 0 corresponds to midnight of December 30, 1899. The earliest date you can represent as an OLE Automation-compatible date is the first day of the year 100; it corresponds to the Double value −657,434.

To initialize a DateTime variable, a date value is enclosed in a pair of pound symbols. If the value contains time information, separate it from the date part by using a space:

```
Dim date1 As Date = #4/15/2011#
Dim date2 As Date = #4/15/2011 2:01:59#
```

If you have a string that represents a date and you want to assign it to a DateTime variable for further processing, use the DateTime class `Parse` and `ParseExact` methods. The `Parse` method parses a string and returns a date value if the string can be interpreted as a date value. Let's say your code prompts the user for a date and then it uses it in date calculations. The user-supplied date is read as a string, and you must convert it to a date value:

```
Dim sDate As String
Dim dDate As DateTime
sDate = InputBox("Please enter a date")
Try
    dDate = DateTime.Parse(sDate)
        ' use dDate1 in your calculations
    Catch exc As Exception
        MsgBox("You've entered an invalid date")
End Try
```

The `Parse` method will convert a string that represents a date to a DateTime value regardless of the format of the date. You can enter dates such as *1/17/2011, Jan. 17, 2011,* or *January 17, 2011* (with or without the comma). The `ParseExact` method allows you to specify more options, such as the possible formats of the date value.

⊕ Real World Scenario

DIFFERENT CULTURES, DIFFERENT DATES

Different cultures use different date formats, and Windows supports them all. However, you must make sure that the proper format is selected in Regional And Language Options. By default, dates are interpreted as specified by the current date format in the target computer's regional settings. The Parse method allows you to specify the culture to be used in the conversion. The following statements prompt the user for a date value and then interpret it in a specific culture (the en-GB culture, which is used in the United Kingdom):

```
Dim sDate1 As String
Dim dDate1 As DateTime
sDate1 = InputBox("Please enter a date")
Try
    Dim culture As CultureInfo = _
            New CultureInfo("en-GB", True)
    dDate1 = DateTime.Parse(sDate1, culture)
    MsgBox(dDate1.ToLongDateString)
Catch exc As Exception
    MsgBox("You've entered an invalid date")
End Try
```

To use the CultureInfo class in your code, you must import the System.Gobalization namespace in your project. These statements will convert any English date regardless of the regional settings. If you enter the string **16/3/2011** in the input box, the preceding statements will produce the following output:

```
Wednesday, March 16, 2011
```

Let's see how the same date will be parsed in two different cultures. Insert the following code segment in a button's Click event handler:

```
Dim sDate1 As String
Dim dDate1 As DateTime
sDate1 = InputBox("Please enter a date")
Try
    Dim culture As CultureInfo = _
                New CultureInfo("en-GB", True)
    dDate1 = DateTime.Parse(sDate1, culture)
    Debug.WriteLine(dDate1.ToLongDateString)
    culture = New CultureInfo("en-US", True)
    dDate1 = DateTime.Parse(sDate1, culture)
    Debug.WriteLine(dDate1.ToLongDateString)
Catch exc As Exception
    MsgBox("You've entered an invalid date")
End Try
```

The method `ToLongDateString` returns the verbose description of the date so that we can read the name of the month instead of guessing it. Run the code and enter a date that can be interpreted differently in the two cultures, such as 4/9/2011. The following output will be produced:

```
Saturday, September 04, 2011
Friday, April 09, 2011
```

If the month part of the date exceeds 12, the exception handler will be activated. Dates are always a tricky issue in programming, and you should include the appropriate culture in the `Parse` method so that user-supplied dates will be converted correctly, even if the user's culture hasn't been set correctly in the regional settings or if you're processing a file that originated in a computer with different culture settings. You should also not prompt users for dates with a TextBox control; use the DateTimePicker control instead so that users can enter only valid dates.

PROPERTIES

The DateTime class exposes the properties listed in Table 11.7.

TABLE 11.7:   DateTime class properties

PROPERTY	DESCRIPTION
Date, TimeOfDay	The Date property returns the date from a date/time value and sets the time to midnight. The TimeOfDay property returns the time part of the date.
DayOfWeek, DayOfYear	These two properties return the day of the week (a string such as Monday) and the number of the day in the year (an integer from 1 to 365, or 366 for leap years), respectively.
Hour, Minute, Second, Millisecond	These properties return the corresponding time part of the date value passed as an argument. If the current time is 9:47:24 p.m., the three properties of the DateTime class will return the integer values 9, 47, and 24 when applied to the current date and time as Date.Now.Hour, Date.Now.Minute, and Date.Now.Second.
Day, Month, Year	These three properties return the day of the month, the month, and the year of a DateTime value, respectively. The Day and Month properties are numeric values, but you can convert them to the appropriate string (the name of the day or month) with the WeekDayName() and MonthName() functions. They also accept a second optional argument that is a True/False value and indicates whether the function should return the abbreviated name (if True) or full name (if False). The WeekDayName() function accepts a third optional argument, which determines the first day of the week (by default, the first day of the week is Sunday).

TABLE 11.7:   DateTime class properties *(CONTINUED)*

PROPERTY	DESCRIPTION
Ticks	This property returns the number of ticks from a date/time value. Each tick is 100 nanoseconds (or 0.0001 milliseconds). To convert ticks to milliseconds, multiply them by 10,000 (or use the TimeSpan object's `TicksPerMillisecond` property, discussed later in this chapter). We use this property to time operations precisely: The `Ticks` property is a long value, and you can read its value before and after the operation you want to time. The difference between the two values is the duration of the operation in tenths of a nanosecond. Divide it by 10,000 to get the duration in milliseconds.

METHODS

The DateTime class exposes several methods for manipulating dates, as listed in Table 11.8. The most practical methods add and subtract time intervals to and from an instance of the Date-Time class.

TABLE 11.8:   DateTime class methods

METHOD	DESCRIPTION
Compare	Compare is a shared method that compares two date/time values and returns an integer value indicating the relative order of the two values. The syntax of the Compare method is as follows, where *date1* and *date2* are the two values to be compared: `order = System.DateTime.Compare(date1, date2)`
DaysInMonth	This shared method returns the number of days in a specific month. Because February contains a variable number of days depending on the year, the DaysInMonth method accepts as arguments both the month and the year: `monDays = DateTime.DaysInMonth(year, month)`
IsLeapYear	This shared method returns a True/False value that indicates whether the specified year is a leap year: `Dim leapYear As Boolean = DateTime.IsLeapYear(year)`

Add	This method adds a TimeSpan object to the current instance of the DateTime class. The TimeSpan object represents a time interval, and there are many methods to create a TimeSpan object, which are all discussed in The TimeSpan Class section. To create a new TimeSpan object that represents 3 days, 6 hours, 2 minutes, and 50 seconds and add this TimeSpan object to the current date and time, use the following statements.
	
	`Dim TS As New TimeSpan()`
	`Dim thisMoment As Date = Now()`
	`TS = New TimeSpan(3, 6, 2, 50)`
	`Debug.WriteLine(thisMoment)`

TABLE 11.8:   DateTime class methods *(CONTINUED)*

METHOD	DESCRIPTION
Subtract	This method is the counterpart of the Add method; it subtracts a TimeSpan object from the current instance of the DateTime class and returns another Date value.
Addxxx	Various methods add specific intervals to a date/time value. Each method accepts the number of intervals to add (days, hours, milliseconds, and so on) to the current instance of the DateTime class. These methods are as follows: AddYears, AddMonths, AddDays, AddHours, AddMinutes, AddSeconds, AddMilliseconds, and AddTicks. As stated earlier, a tick is 100 nanoseconds and is used for really fine timing of operations. None of the Addxxx methods act on the current instance of the DateTime class; instead, they return a new DateTime value with the appropriate value.
ToString	This method converts a date/time value to a string, using a specific format. The DateTime class recognizes numerous format patterns, which are listed in Table 11.9 and Table 11.10.

Table 11.9 lists the standard format patterns, and Table 11.10 lists the characters that can format individual parts of the date/time value. You can combine the custom format characters to format dates and times in any way you wish.

The syntax of the ToString method is as follows, where *formatSpec* is a format specification:

```
aDate.ToString(formatSpec)
```

The *D* named date format, for example, formats a date value as a long date; the following statement will return the highlighted string shown below the statement:

```
Debug.Writeline(#9/17/2010#.ToString("D"))
Friday, September 17, 2010
```

Table 11.9 lists the named formats for the standard date and time patterns. The format characters are case sensitive — for example, g and G represent slightly different patterns.

The following examples format the current date by using all the format patterns listed in Table 11.9. An example of the output produced by each statement is shown under each statement, indented and highlighted.

```
Debug.WriteLine(now().ToString("d"))
    2/2/2010
Debug.WriteLine(Now().ToString("D"))
    Tuesday, February 02, 2010
Debug.WriteLine(Now().ToString("f"))
    Tuesday, February 02, 2010 10:51 PM
Debug.WriteLine(Now().ToString("F"))
    Tuesday, February 02, 2010 10:51:16 PM
Debug.WriteLine(Now().ToString("g"))
    2/2/2010 10:51 PM
Debug.WriteLine(Now().ToString("G"))
    2/2/2010 10:51:16 PM
```

```
Debug.WriteLine(Now().ToString("m"))
    February 02
Debug.WriteLine(Now().ToString("r"))
    Tue, 02 Feb 2010 22:51:16 GMT
Debug.WriteLine(Now().ToString("s"))
    2010-02-02T22:51:16
Debug.WriteLine(Now().ToString("t"))
    10:51 PM
Debug.WriteLine(Now().ToString("T"))
    10:51:16 PM
Debug.WriteLine(Now().ToString("u"))
    2010-02-02 22:51:16Z
Debug.WriteLine(Now().ToString("U"))
    Tuesday, February 02, 2010 8:51:16 PM
Debug.WriteLine(Now().ToString("y"))
    February, 2010
```

TABLE 11.9:   The date and time named formats

NAMED FORMAT	OUTPUT	FORMAT NAME
d	MM/dd/yyyy	ShortDatePattern
D	dddd, MMMM dd, yyyy	LongDatePattern
F	dddd, MMMM dd, yyyy HH:mm:ss.mmm	FullDateTimePattern (long date and long time)
f	dddd, MMMM dd, yyyy HH:mm.ss	FullDateTimePattern (long date and short time)
g	MM/dd/yyyy HH:mm	general (short date and short time)
G	MM/dd/yyyy HH:mm:ss	General (short date and long time)
M, m	MMMM dd	MonthDayPattern (month and day)
r, R	ddd, dd MMM yyyy HH:mm:ss GMT	RFC1123Pattern
s	yyyy-MM-dd HH:mm:ss	SortableDateTimePattern
t	HH:mm	ShortTimePattern (short time)
T	HH:mm:ss	LongTimePattern (long time)
u	yyyy-MM-dd HH:mm:ss	UniversalSortableDateTimePattern (sortable GMT value)
U	dddd, MMMM dd, yyyy HH:mm:ss	UniversalSortableDateTimePattern (long date, long GMT time)
Y, y	MMMM, yyyy	YearMonthPattern (month and year)

TABLE 11.10:   Date format specifier

FORMAT CHARACTER	DESCRIPTION
d	The date of the month
ddd	The day of the month with a leading zero for single-digit days
ddd	The abbreviated name of the day of the week (a member of the AbbreviatedDayNames enumeration)
dddd	The full name of the day of the week (a member of the DayNamesFormat enumeration)
M	The number of the month
MM	The number of the month with a leading zero for single-digit months
MMM	The abbreviated name of the month (a member of the AbbreviatedMonthNames enumeration)
MMMM	The full name of the month
y	The year without the century (the year 2001 will be printed as 1)
yy	The year without the century (the year 2001 will be displayed as 01)
yyyy	The complete year
gg	The period or era (pattern ignored if the date to be formatted does not have an associated period as A.D. or B.C. have)
h	The hour in 12-hour format
hh	The hour in 12-hour format with a leading zero for single-digit hours
H	The hour in 24-hour format
HH	The hour in 24-hour format with a leading zero for single-digit hours
m	The minute of the hour
mm	The minute of the hour with a leading zero for single-digit minutes
s	The second of the hour
ss	The second of the hour with a leading zero for single-digit seconds
t	The first character in the a.m./p.m. designator
tt	The a.m./p.m. designator

TABLE 11.10:   Date format specifier *(CONTINUED)*

FORMAT CHARACTER	DESCRIPTION
z	The time-zone offset (applies to hours only)
zz	The time-zone offset with a leading zero for single-digit hours (applies to hours only)
zzz	The full time-zone offset (hour and minutes) with leading zeros for single-digit hours and minutes

Table 11.10 lists the format characters that can be combined to build custom format date and time values. The patterns are case sensitive. If the custom pattern contains spaces or characters enclosed in single quotation marks, these characters will appear in the formatted string.

To display the full month name and the day in the month, for instance, use the following statement:

```
Debug.WriteLine(now().ToString("MMMM d"))
July 27
```

You may have noticed some overlap between the named formats and the format characters. The character *d* signifies the short date pattern when used as a named format and the number of the day when used as a format character. The compiler figures out how it's used based on the context. If the format argument is d/mm, it will display the day and month number, whereas the format argument d, mmm will display the number of the day followed by the month's name. If you use the character d on its own, however, it will be interpreted as the named format for the short date format.

DATE CONVERSION METHODS

The DateTime class supports methods for converting a date/time value to many of the other base types, which are presented briefly in Table 11.11.

DATES AS NUMERIC VALUES

The Date type encapsulates complicated operations, and it's worth taking a look at the inner workings of the classes that handle dates and times. Let's declare two variables to experiment a little with dates: a Date variable, which is initialized to the current date, and a Double variable:

```
Dim Date1 As Date = Now()
Dim dbl As Double
```
Insert a couple of statements to convert the date to a Double value and print it:

```
dbl = Date1.ToOADate
Debug.WriteLine(dbl)
```

TABLE 11.11: DateTime class conversion methods

METHODS	DESCRIPTION
ToLongDateString, ToShortDateString	These two methods convert the date part of the current DateTime instance to a string with the long (or short) date format. The following statement will return a value like the one highlighted, which is the long date format: Debug.WriteLine(Now().ToLongDateString) **Tuesday, July 14, 2009**
ToLongTimeString, ToShortTimeString	These two methods convert the time part of the current instance of the Date class to a string with the long (or short) time format. The following statement will return a value like the one highlighted: Debug.WriteLine(Now().ToLongTimeString) **6:40:53 PM**
ToUniversalTime, ToLocalTime	ToUniversalTime converts the current instance of the DateTime class into Coordinated Universal Time (UTC). If you convert the local time of a system in New York to UTC, the value returned by this method will be a date/time value that's five hours ahead. The date may be the same or the date of the following day. If the statement is executed after 7 p.m. local time, the date will be that of the following day. The method ToLocalTime converts a UTC time value to local time.

On the date I tested this code, February 2, 2010, the value was 40211.9442577662. The integer part of this value is the date, and the fractional part is the time. If you add one day to the current date and then convert it to a double again, you'll get a different value:

```
dbl = (Now().AddDays(1)).ToOADate
Debug.WriteLine(dbl)
```

This time, the value 40212.9452653704 was printed; its integer part is tomorrow's value. You can add two days to the current date by adding (48 × 60) minutes. The original integer part of the numeric value will be increased by two:

```
dbl = Now().AddMinutes(48 * 60).ToOADate
Debug.WriteLine(dbl)
```

The value printed this time will be 40213.9456303588.

Let's see how the date-manipulation methods deal with leap years. We'll add 10 years to the current date via the AddYears method, and we'll print the new value with a single statement:

```
Debug.WriteLine(Now().AddYears(10).ToLongDateString)
```

The value that will appear in the Immediate window will be Sunday, February 02, 2020. The Double value of this date is 40211.9459967361. If you add 3,650 days, you'll get a different value because the 10-year span contains at least two leap years:

```
Debug.WriteLine(Now().AddDays(3650).ToLongDateString)
Debug.WriteLine(Now().AddDays(3650).ToOADate)
```

The new value that will be printed in the Immediate window will be Friday, January 31, 2020, and the corresponding Double value will be 43861.9468961111.

Can you figure out what time it was when I executed the preceding statements? If you multiply the fractional part (0.9468957639) by 24, you'll get 22.7254983336, which is 56.813745834 hours and some minutes. If you multiply the fractional part of this number by 60, you'll get 56.813745834, which is 56.813745834 minutes and some seconds. Finally, you can multiply the new fractional part by 60 to get the number of seconds: 48.82475004. So, it was 10:56:48 p.m. And the last fractional part corresponds to 824 milliseconds.

The TimeSpan Class

The last class discussed in this chapter is the TimeSpan class, which represents a time interval and can be expressed in many different units — from ticks or milliseconds to days. The TimeSpan is usually the difference between two date/time values, but you can also create a TimeSpan for a specific interval and use it in your calculations.

To use the TimeSpan variable in your code, just declare it with a statement such as the following:

```
Dim TS As New TimeSpan
```

To initialize the TimeSpan object, you can provide the number of days, hours, minutes, seconds, and milliseconds that make up the time interval. The following statement initializes a TimeSpan object with a duration of 9 days, 12 hours, 1 minute, and 59 seconds:

```
Dim TS As TimeSpan = New TimeSpan(9, 12, 1, 59)
```

As you have seen, the difference between two dates calculated by the Date.Subtract method returns a TimeSpan value. You can initialize an instance of the TimeSpan object by creating two date/time values and getting their difference, as in the following statements:

```
Dim TS As New TimeSpan
Dim date1 As Date = #4/11/1994#
Dim date2 As Date = Now()
TS = date2.Subtract(date1)
Debug.WriteLine(TS)
```

Depending on the day on which you execute these statements, they will print something like the following in the Output window:

```
5585.17:05:12.7623000
```

The days are separated from the rest of the string with a period, whereas the time parts are separated with colons. Notice that a TimeSpan object might represent an interval of many years, but it doesn't provide members to report months or years. The difference represented by *TS* variable in the preceding example is 5,585 days, 17 hours, 5 minutes, 12 seconds, and 762,300 nanoseconds (or 762.3 milliseconds).

PROPERTIES

The TimeSpan class exposes the properties described in the following sections. Most of these properties are shared (you don't have to create an instance of the TimeSpan class to use them).

Field Properties

TimeSpan exposes the simple properties shown in Table 11.12, which are known as *fields* and are all shared. You'll use these field values to convert the time difference represented by a TimeSpan object to common time units.

TABLE 11.12:   The fields of the TimeSpan object

PROPERTY	RETURNS
Empty	An empty TimeSpan object
MaxValue	The largest interval you can represent with a TimeSpan object
MinValue	The smallest interval you can represent with a TimeSpan object
TicksPerDay	The number of ticks in a day
TicksPerHour	The number of ticks in an hour
TicksPerMillisecond	The number of ticks in a millisecond
TicksPerMinute	The number of ticks in one minute
TicksPerSecond	The number of ticks in one second
Zero	A TimeSpan object of zero duration

Interval Properties

In addition to the fields, the TimeSpan class exposes two more groups of properties that return the various intervals in a TimeSpan value (shown in Tables 11.13 and 11.14). The members of the first group of properties return the number of specific intervals (days, hours, and so on) in a TimeSpan value. The second group of properties returns the entire TimeSpan duration in one of the intervals recognized by the TimeSpan method.

If a TimeSpan value represents 2 minutes and 10 seconds, the Seconds property will return the value 10. The TotalSeconds property, however, will return the value 130, which is the total duration of the TimeSpan in seconds.

TABLE 11.13: The Intervals of a TimeSpan value

PROPERTY	RETURNS
Days	The number of whole days in the current TimeSpan.
Hours	The number of whole hours in the current TimeSpan.
Milliseconds	The number of whole milliseconds in the current TimeSpan. The largest value of this property is 999.
Minutes	The number of whole minutes in the current TimeSpan. The largest value of this property is 59.
Seconds	The number of whole seconds in the current TimeSpan. The largest value of this property is 59.
Ticks	The number of whole ticks in the current TimeSpan.

TABLE 11.14: The total intervals of a TimeSpan value

PROPERTY	RETURNS
TotalDays	The number of days in the current TimeSpan
TotalHours	The number of hours in the current TimeSpan
TotalMilliseconds	The number of whole milliseconds in the current TimeSpan
TotalMinutes	The number of whole minutes in the current TimeSpan
TotalSeconds	The number of whole seconds in the current TimeSpan

SIMILAR METHOD NAMES, DIFFERENT RESULTS

Be very careful when choosing the property to express the duration of a TimeSpan in a specific interval. The Seconds property is totally different from the TotalSeconds property. Because both properties will return a value (which also happens to be the same if the entire TimeSpan duration is less than a minute), you may not notice that you're using the wrong property for the task at hand.

The Duration property returns the duration of the current instance of the TimeSpan class. The duration is expressed as the number of days followed by the number of hours, minutes, seconds, and milliseconds. The following statements create a TimeSpan object of a few seconds (or minutes, if you don't mind waiting) and print its duration in the Output window. The first few statements initialize a new instance of the DateTime type, the *T1* variable, to the current date and time. Then a message box is displayed that prompts to click the OK button to continue. Wait for several seconds before closing the message box. The last group of statements subtracts the *T1* variable from the current time and displays the duration (how long you kept the message box open on your screen):

```
Dim T1, T2 As DateTime
T1 = Now
MsgBox("Click OK to continue")
T2 = Now
Dim TS As TimeSpan
TS = T2.Subtract(T1)
Debug.WriteLine("Total duration = " & TS.Duration.ToString)
Debug.WriteLine("Minutes = " & TS.Minutes.ToString)
Debug.WriteLine("Seconds = " & TS.Seconds.ToString)
Debug.WriteLine("Ticks = " & TS.Ticks.ToString)
Debug.WriteLine("Milliseconds = " & TS.TotalMilliseconds.ToString)
Debug.WriteLine("Total seconds = " & TS.TotalSeconds.ToString)
```

If you place these statements in a button's Click event handler and execute them, you'll see a series of values like the following in the Immediate window:

```
Total duration = 00:01:34.2154752
Minutes = 1
Seconds = 34
Ticks = 942154752
Milliseconds = 94215,4752
Total seconds = 94,2154752
```

The duration of the *TS* TimeSpan is 1 minute and 34 seconds. Its total duration in milliseconds is 94,215.4752, or 94.2154752 seconds.

METHODS

There are various methods for creating and manipulating instances of the TimeSpan class, and they're described in the following list.

Interval methods   The methods in Table 11.15 create a new TimeSpan object of a specific duration. The TimeSpan duration is specified as a number of intervals, accurate to the nearest millisecond.

All methods accept a single argument, which is a Double value that represents the number of the corresponding intervals (days, hours, and so on).

Add   This method adds a TimeSpan object to the current instance of the class; its syntax is as follows, where *TS*, *TS1*, and *newTS* are all TimeSpan variables:

```
newTS = TS.Add(TS1)
```

TABLE 11.15: Interval methods of the TimeSpan object

METHOD	CREATES A NEW TIMESPAN OF THIS LENGTH
FromDays	Number of days specified by the argument
FromHours	Number of hours specified by the argument
FromMinutes	Number of minutes specified by the argument
FromSeconds	Number of seconds specified by the argument
FromMilliseconds	Number of milliseconds specified by the argument
FromTicks	Number of ticks specified by the argument

The following statements create two TimeSpan objects and then add them:

```
Dim TS1 As New TimeSpan(1, 0, 1)
Dim TS2 As New TimeSpan(2, 1, 9)
Dim TS As New TimeSpan
TS = TS1.Add(TS2)
```

The duration of the new TimeSpan variable is 3 hours, 1 minute, and 10 seconds.

Subtract   The Subtract method subtracts a TimeSpan object from the current instance of the TimeSpan class, similar to the Add method.

The StopWatch Class

To simplify the task of timing operations, a new class was introduced with the .NET Framework version 4, the StopWatch class. This class implements a stopwatch, which you can start just before the code segment you want to time and stop it after the last statement in this code segment. In addition, you can pause the stopwatch (you may wish to exclude some debugging statements from the code to be timed).

To use the StopWatch class, declare a new variable of this type:

```
Dim SW As New StopWatch
```

Use the Start method to start the stopwatch and the Stop method to stop it or pause it. While the stopwatch is stopped or paused, you can request the elapsed time with the Elapsed property, which returns the elapsed time as a TimeSpan object. You can also retrieve the elapsed time in milliseconds with the ElapsedMilliseconds method, and in ticks of the internal clock with the ElapsedTicks method (as a reminder, a tick is 1/10 of a millisecond).

You can also use the Reset method to stop the stopwatch and zero the elapsed time or the StartNew method to zero the elapsed time and start the stopwatch.

Listing 11.6 demonstrates the basic members of the StopWatch class. Initially, the sample code declares and starts a new instance of the StopWatch class and then displays a message box prompting you to close the dialog box and stop the stopwatch. Leave the message box open for a few seconds before clicking the OK button to simulate some delay. Then the code displays another dialog box, prompting you to close it. Then it starts the stopwatch again and displays yet another message box. The time between stopping and restarting the stopwatch won't be included in the total elapsed time. When you close the last dialog box, you can see the results of the operation in the Output window.

LISTING 11.6: Timing operations with the StopWatch class

```
Private Sub timeButton_Click(...) Handles timeButton.Click
    Dim sw As New Stopwatch
    sw.Start()
    ' This is where the statements to be timed should appear
    ' Use the MsgBox() function to simulate a delay
    MsgBox("Stopwatch is running. Press any key to pause it")
    ' End of timing operations
    sw.Stop()
    Debug.WriteLine("Elapsed time")
    Debug.WriteLine(sw.Elapsed.ToString)
    Debug.WriteLine(sw.ElapsedMilliseconds.ToString)
    MsgBox("Stopwatch is not running. " &
            "Wait a few seconds and press any key to restart it")
    ' Continue timing the operations
    sw.Start()
    MsgBox("And now press a key to stop the stopwatch")
    Debug.WriteLine("Total elapsed time")
    Debug.WriteLine(sw.Elapsed.ToString)
    Debug.WriteLine(sw.ElapsedMilliseconds.ToString)
End Sub
```

The Bottom Line

Handle files with the My component. The simplest method of saving data to a file is to call one of the WriteAllBytes or WriteAllText methods of the My.Computer.FileSystem component. You can also use the IO namespace to set up a Writer object to send data to a file and a Reader object to read data from the file.

Master It Show the statements that save a TextBox control's contents to a file and the statements that reload the same control from the data file. Use the My.Computer.FileSystem component.

Write data to a file with the IO namespace. To send data to a file you must set up a FileStream object, which is a channel between the application and the file. To send data to a file, create a StreamWriter or BinaryWriter object on the appropriate FileStream object.

Likewise, to read from a file, create a StreamReader or BinaryReader on the appropriate FileStream object. To send data to a file, use the `Write` and `WriteString` methods of the appropriate StreamWriter object. To read data from the file, use the `Read`, `ReadBlock`, `ReadLine`, and `ReadToEnd` methods of the StreamReader object.

Master It Write the contents of a TextBox control to a file using the methods of the IO namespace.

Manipulate folders and files. The IO namespace provides the Directory and File classes, which represent the corresponding entities. Both classes expose a large number of methods for manipulating folders (`CreateDirectory`, `Delete`, `GetFiles`, and so on) and files (`Create`, `Delete`, `Copy`, `OpenRead`, and so on).

Master It How will you retrieve the attributes of a drive, folder, and file using the IO namespace's classes?

Use the Char data type to handle characters. The Char data type, which is implemented with the Char class, exposes methods for handling individual characters (`IsLetter`, `IsDigit`, `IsSymbol`, and so on). We use the methods of the Char class to manipulate users' keystrokes as they happen in certain controls (mostly the TextBox control) and to provide immediate feedback.

Master It You want to develop an interface that contains several TextBox controls that accept numeric data. How will you intercept the user's keystrokes and reject any characters that are not numeric?

Use the StringBuilder class to manipulate large or dynamic strings. The StringBuilder class is very efficient at manipulating long strings, but it doesn't provide as many methods for handling strings. The StringBuilder class provides a few methods to insert, delete, and replace characters within a string. Unlike the equivalent methods of the String class, these methods act directly on the string stored in the current instance of the StringBuilder class.

Master It Assuming that you have populated a ListView control with thousands of lines of data from a database, how will you implement a function that copies all the data to the Clipboard?

Use the DateTime and TimeSpan classes to handle dates and time. The Date class represents dates and time, and it exposes many useful shared methods (such as the `IsLeap` method, which returns True if the year passed to the method as an argument is leap; the `DaysInMonth` method; and so on). It also exposes many instance methods (such as `AddYears`, `AddDays`, `AddHours`, and so on) for adding time intervals to the current instance of the Date class as well as many options for formatting date and time values.

The TimeSpan class represents time intervals — from milliseconds to days — with the `FromDays`, `FromHours`, and even `FromMilliseconds` methods. The difference between two date variables is a TimeSpan value, and you can convert this value to various time units by using methods such as TotalDays, TotalHours, TotalMilliseconds, and so on. You can also add a TimeSpan object to a date variable to obtain another date variable.

Master It How will you use the TimeSpan class to accurately time an operation?

Generate graphics by using the drawing methods. Every object you draw on, such as forms and PictureBox controls, exposes the CreateGraphics method, which returns a Graphics object. The Paint event's e argument also exposes the Graphics object of the control or form. To draw something on a control, retrieve its Graphics object and then call the Graphics object's drawing methods.

Master It Show how to draw a circle on a form from within the form's Paint event handler.

Use the printing controls and dialog boxes. To print with the .NET Framework, you must add an instance of the PrintDocument control to your form and call its Print method. To preview the same document, you simply assign the PrintDocument object to the Document property of the PrintPreviewDialog control and then call the ShowDialog method of the PrintPreviewDialog control to display the preview window. You can also display the Print dialog box, where users can select the printer to which the output will be sent, and the Page Setup dialog box, where users can specify the page's orientation and margins. The two dialog boxes are implemented with the PrintDialog and PageSetupDialog controls.

Master It Explain the process of generating a simple printout. How will you handle multiple report pages?

Master It Assuming that you have displayed the Page Setup dialog box control to the user, how will you draw a rectangle that delimits the printing area on the page, taking into consideration the user-specified margins?

Chapter 12

Storing Data in Collections

One of the most common operations in programming is storing large sets of data. Traditionally, programmers used *arrays* to store related data. Because arrays can store custom data types, they seem to be the answer to many data-storage and data-manipulation issues. Arrays, however, don't expose all the functionality you might need in your application. To address the issues of data storage outside databases, the Framework provides, in addition to arrays, certain classes known as *collections*.

There are databases, of course, that can store any type of data and preserve their structure as well, but not all applications use databases. Although databases store data permanently, collections live in memory and must be persisted to a disk file between sessions. Collections can also be used to store data you read from a database in the target computer's memory. If your application needs to store custom objects, such as the ones you designed in Chapter 8, "Working with Objects," or a few names and contact information, you shouldn't have to set up a database. A simple collection like the ones described in this chapter will suffice.

In this chapter, you'll learn how to do the following:

♦ Make the most of arrays

♦ Store data in specialized collections such as List and Dictionary collections

♦ Sort and search collections with custom comparers

Advanced Array Topics

Arrays are indexed sets of data, and this is how we've used them so far in this book. In this chapter, you will learn about additional members that make arrays extremely flexible. The System.Array class provides methods for sorting arrays, searching for an element, and more. In the past, programmers spent endless hours writing code to perform the same operations on arrays, but the Framework frees them from similar counterproductive tasks.

This chapter starts with a brief discussion of the advanced features of the Array class. With so many specialized collections supported by the Framework, arrays are no longer the primary mechanism for storing sets of data. However, because many developers are still using arrays, I've decided to include a brief presentation of the advanced techniques that will simplify the manipulation of arrays.

Sorting Arrays

To sort an array, call its Sort method. This method is heavily overloaded, and as you will see, it is possible to sort an array based on the values of another array or even to supply your own custom sorting routines. If the array is sorted, you can call the BinarySearch method to locate an element very efficiently. If not, you can still locate an element in the array by using the IndexOf and LastIndexOf methods. The Sort method is a reference method: It requires that you supply the name of the array to be sorted as an argument and sorts the array in place (in other words, it doesn't return another array with the same elements in a different order). The simplest form of the Sort method accepts a single argument, which is the name of the array to be sorted:

```
Array.Sort(arrayName)
```

This method sorts the elements of the array according to the type of its elements, as long as the array is strictly typed and was declared as a simple data type (String, Decimal, Date, and so on). If the array contains data that are not of the same type or that are objects, the Sort method will fail. The Array class just doesn't know how to compare integers to strings or dates, so don't attempt to sort arrays whose elements are not of the same type. If you can't be sure that all elements are of the same type, use a Try...Catch statement.

You can also sort a section of the array by using the following form of the Sort method, where *startIndex* and *endIndex* are the indices that delimit the section of the array to be sorted:

```
System.Array.Sort(arrayName, startIndex, endIndex)
```

An interesting variation of the Sort method sorts the elements of an array according to the values of the elements in another array. Let's say you have one array of names and another of matching Social Security numbers. It is possible to sort the array of names according to their Social Security numbers. This form of the Sort method has the following syntax:

```
System.Array.Sort(array1, array2)
```

array1 is the array with the keys (the Social Security numbers), and *array2* is the array with the actual elements to be sorted. This is a very handy form of the Sort method. Let's say you have a list of words stored in one array and their frequencies in another. Using the first form of the Sort method, you can sort the words alphabetically. With the third form of the Sort method, you can sort them according to their frequencies (starting with the most common words and ending with the least common ones). The two arrays must be one-dimensional and have the same number of elements. If you want to sort a section of the array, just supply the *startIndex* and *endIndex* arguments to the Sort method, after the names of the two arrays.

Another form of the Sort method relies on a user-supplied function to sort arrays of custom objects. As you recall, arrays can store all types of objects. But the Framework doesn't know how to sort your custom objects, or even its built-in objects. To sort an array of objects, you must provide your own class that implements the IComparer interface (basically, a function that can compare two instances of a custom class). This form of the Sort method is described in detail in the section titled "The IEnumerator and IComparer Interfaces" later in this chapter.

Searching Arrays

Arrays can be searched in two ways: with the `BinarySearch` method, which works on sorted arrays and is extremely fast, and with the `IndexOf` and `LastIndexOf` methods, which work regardless of the order of the elements. All three methods search for an instance of an item and return its index, and they're all reference methods. The `IndexOf` and `LastIndexOf` methods are similar to the methods by the same name of the String class. They return the index of the first (or last) instance of an object in the array, or they return the value −1 if the object isn't found in the array. Both methods are overloaded, and the simplest form of the `IndexOf` method is the following, where *arrayName* is the name of the array to be searched and *object* is the item you're searching for:

```
itemIndex = System.Array.IndexOf(arrayName, object)
```

Another form of the `IndexOf` and `LastIndexOf` methods allows you to begin the search at a specific index:

```
itemIndex = System.Array.IndexOf(arrayName, object, startIndex)
```

This form of the method starts searching in the segment of the array from *startIndex* to the end of the array. Finally, you can specify a range of indices in which the search will take place by using the following form of the method:

```
itemIndex = System.Array.IndexOf(arrayName, object, startIndex, endIndex)
```

You can search large arrays more efficiently with the `BinarySearch` method if the array is sorted. The simplest form of the `BinarySearch` method is the following:

```
System.Array.BinarySearch(arrayName, object)
```

The `BinarySearch` method returns an integer value, which is the index of the object you've been searching for in the array. If the *object* argument is not found, the method returns a negative value, which is the negative of the index of the next larger item minus one. This transformation, the negative of a number minus one, is called the *one's complement*, and other languages provide an operator for it: the tilde (∼). The one's complement of 10 is −11, and the one's complement of −3 is 2.

Why all this complexity? Zero is a valid index, so only a negative value could indicate a failure in the search operation. A value of −1 would indicate that the operation failed, but the `BinarySearch` method does something better. If it can't locate the item, it returns the index of the item immediately after the desired item (the first item in the array that exceeds the item you're searching for). This is a near match, and the `BinarySearch` method returns a negative value to indicate near matches. A near match is usually the same string with different character casing or a slightly different spelling. It may also be a string that's totally irrelevant to the one you're searching for. Notice that there will always be a near match unless you're searching for a value larger than the last value in the array. In this case, the `BinarySearch` method will return the one's complement of the array's upper bound (−100 for an array of 100 elements, if you consider that the index of the last element is 99).

⊕ **Real World Scenario**

ARRAYS PERFORM CASE-SENSITIVE SEARCHES

The BinarySearch, IndexOf, and LastIndexOf methods perform case-sensitive searches. However, because the BinarySearch method reports near matches, it appears as if it performs case-insensitive searches. If the array contains the element *Charles* and you search for *charles*, the IndexOf method will not find the string and will report a no-match, whereas the BinarySearch method will find the element *Charles* and report it as a near match. My recommendation is to standardize the case of the data and the search argument when you plan to perform searches (such as uppercase for titles, camel case for names, and so on). As an alternative, you can use String.ToUpper() on both arguments. To perform case-insensitive searches, you must implement your own custom comparer, a process that's described later in this chapter. Also, the Option Compare statement has no effect on the comparisons performed by either the BinarySearch method or the IndexOf and LastIndexOf methods.

VB 2010 AT WORK: THE ARRAYSEARCH APPLICATION

The ArraySearch application, shown in Figure 12.1, demonstrates how to handle exact and near matches reported by the BinarySearch method. The Populate Array button populates an array with 10,000 random strings. The same strings are also displayed in a sorted ListBox control, so you can view them. The elements have the same order in both the array and the ListBox, so you can use the index reported by the BinarySearch method to locate and select instantly the same item in the ListBox.

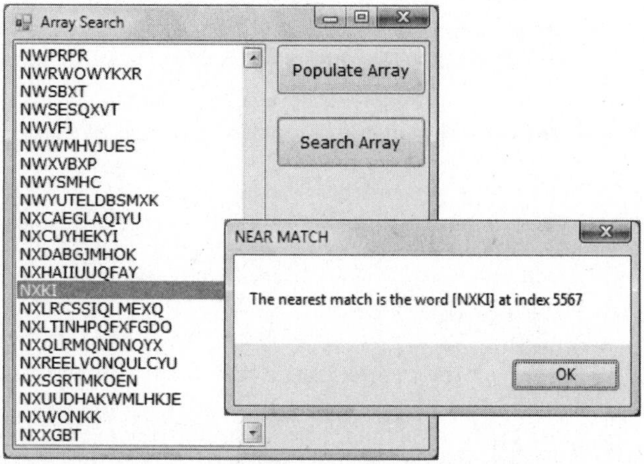

FIGURE 12.1
Searching an array and highlighting the same element in the ListBox control

Each of the 10,000 random strings has a random length of 3 to 15 characters. When you run the application, message boxes will pop up, displaying the time it took for each operation: how long it took to populate the array, how long it took to sort it, and how long it took to populate the ListBox. You might want to experiment with large arrays (100,000 elements or more) to get an idea of how efficiently VB handles arrays.

The Search Array button prompts the user for a string via the InputBox() function and then locates the string in the array by calling the BinarySearch method in the array. The result is either an exact or a near match, and it's displayed in a message box. At the same time, the item reported by the BinarySearch method is also selected in the ListBox control.

Run the application, populate the ListBox control, and then click the Search Array button. Enter an existing string (you can use lowercase or uppercase characters; it doesn't make a difference), and verify that the application reports an exact match and locates the item in the List-Box. The program appears to perform case-insensitive searches because all the strings stored in the array are in uppercase, and the search argument is also converted to uppercase before the BinarySearch method is called.

Now, enter a string that doesn't exist in the list (or the beginning of an existing string) and see how the BinarySearch handles near matches.

The code behind the Search Array button calls the BinarySearch method and stores the integer returned by the method to the *wordIndex* variable. Then it examines the value of this variable. If *wordIndex* is positive, there was an exact match, and it's reported. If *wordIndex* is negative, the program calculates the one's complement of this value, which is the index of the nearest match. The element at this index is reported as a near match. Finally, regardless of the type of the match, the code selects the same item in the ListBox and scrolls it into view. Listing 12.1 is the code behind the Search Array button.

LISTING 12.1:   Locating exact and near matches with BinarySearch

```
Private Sub bttnSearch_Click(…) Handles bttnSearch.Click
    Dim srchWord As String    ' the word to search for
    Dim wordIndex As Integer ' the index of the word
    srchWord = InputBox(
                "Enter word to search for").ToUpper
    wordIndex = System.Array.BinarySearch(words, srchWord)
    If wordIndex >= 0 Then ' exact match!
        ListBox1.TopIndex = wordIndex
        ListBox1.SelectedIndex = wordIndex
        MsgBox("An exact match was found for " &
            " the word [" & words(wordIndex) &
            "] at index " & wordIndex.ToString,,
            "EXACT MATCH")
    Else                        ' Near match
        ListBox1.TopIndex = -wordIndex - 1
        ListBox1.SelectedIndex = -wordIndex - 1
        MsgBox("The nearest match is the word [" &
            words(-wordIndex - 1) & "] at index " &
            (-wordIndex - 1).ToString, , "NEAR MATCH")
    End If
End Sub
```

Notice that all methods for sorting and searching arrays work with the base data types only. If the array contains custom data types, you must supply your own functions for comparing elements of this type, a process described in detail in the section "The IEnumerator and ICom-parer Interfaces" later in this chapter.

THE BINARY SEARCH ALGORITHM

The `BinarySearch` method uses a powerful search algorithm, the binary search algorithm, but it requires that the array be sorted. You need not care about the technical details of the implementation of a method, but in the case of the binary search algorithm, a basic understanding of how it works will help you understand how it performs near matches.

To locate an item in a sorted array, the `BinarySearch` method compares the search string to the array's middle element. If the search string is smaller, you know that the element is in the first half of the array, and you can safely ignore the second half. The same process is repeated with the remaining half of the elements. The search string is compared with the middle element of the reduced array, and after the comparison, you can ignore one-half of the reduced array. At each step, the binary search algorithm rejects one-half of the items left until it reduces the list to a single item. This is the item you're searching for. If not, the item is not in the list. To search a list of 1,024 items, the binary search algorithm makes 10 comparisons. At the first step, it's left with an array of 512 elements, then 256 elements, then 128 elements, and so on, until it reaches a single element. For an array of 1,024 × 1,024 (that's a little more than a million) items, the algorithm makes 20 comparisons to locate the desired item.

If you apply the `BinarySearch` method to an array that hasn't been sorted, the method will carry out all the steps and report that the item wasn't found, even if the item belongs to the array. The algorithm doesn't check the order of the elements; it just assumes that they're sorted. The binary search algorithm always halves the number of elements in which it attempts to locate the search argument. That's why you should never apply the `BinarySearch` method to an array that hasn't been sorted yet.

To see what happens when you apply the `BinarySearch` method to an array that hasn't been sorted, remove the statement that calls the `Sort` method in the ArraySearch sample application. The application will keep reporting near matches, even if the string you're searching for is present in the array. Of course, the near match reported by the `BinarySearch` method in an unsorted array isn't close to the element you're searching for — it's just an element that happens to be there when the algorithm finishes.

Performing Other Array Operations

The Array class exposes additional methods, which are described briefly in this section. The `Reverse` method reverses the order of the elements in an array. The `Reverse` method accepts the array to be reversed as an argument and returns another array:

```
reversedArray = System.Array.Reverse(arrayName)
```

The `Copy` and `CopyTo` methods copy the elements of an array (or segment of an array) to another array. The syntax of the `Copy` method is as follows:

```
System.Array.Copy(sourceArray, destinationArray, count)
```

sourceArray and *destinationArray* are the names of the two arrays, and *count* is the number of elements to be copied. The copying process starts with the first element of the source array and ends after the first *count* elements have been copied. If *count* exceeds the length of either array, an exception will be thrown.

Another form of the Copy method allows you to specify the range of elements in the source array to be copied and a range in the destination array in which these elements will be copied. The syntax of this form of the method is as follows:

```
System.Array.Copy(sourceArray, sourceStart,
        destinationArray, destinationStart, count)
```

This method copies *count* elements from the source array, starting at location *sourceStart*, and places them in the destination array, starting at location *destinationStart*. All indices must be valid, and there should be *count* elements after the *sourceStart* index in the source array, as well as *count* elements after the *destinationStart* in the destination array. If not, an exception will be thrown.

The CopyTo method is similar, but it doesn't require the name of the source array. It copies the elements of the array to which it's applied into the destination array, where *sourceArray* is a properly dimensioned and initialized array:

```
sourceArray.CopyTo(destinationArray, sourceStart)
```

Finally, you can filter array elements by using the Filter() function, which is not a method of the Array class; it's a VB function that acts on arrays. The Filter() function performs an element-by-element comparison and rejects the elements that don't meet the user-specified criteria. The filtered elements are returned as a new array, while the original array remains intact. The syntax of the Filter() function is as follows:

```
filteredArray = Filter(source, match, include, compare)
```

source is the array to be searched, and it must be a one-dimensional array of strings or objects. The *match* argument is the string to search for. Every element that includes the specified string is considered a match. The remaining arguments are optional: include is a True/False value indicating whether the method will return the elements that include (if True) or exclude (if False) the matching elements. The *compare* argument is a member of the CompareMethod enumeration: It can be Binary (for binary or case-sensitive comparisons) or Text (for textual or case-insensitive comparisons). If no match is found, the method will return an empty array.

The following code segment filters out the strings that don't contain the word *visual* from the *words* array:

```
Dim words() As String = {"Visual Basic", "Java", "Visual Studio"}
Dim selectedWords() As String
selectedWords = Filter(words, "visual", True, CompareMethod.Text)
Dim selword As String
Dim msg As String = ""
For Each selword In selectedWords
    msg &= selword & vbCrLf
Next
MsgBox(msg)
```

If you execute the preceding statements, the message box will display the following:

```
Visual Basic
Visual Studio
```

There are a few more interesting array methods, such as the `FindAll` method, which finds the elements that meet arbitrary conditions, and the `TrueForAll` method, which returns True if all elements in the array meet the criteria you supply. With the introduction of LINQ, a topic that's discussed in detail in Chapter 14, "Introduction to LINQ," there's very little reason to use these methods. LINQ provides a straightforward syntax for selecting elements from an array. If you haven't seen the LINQ syntax before, here the code segment extracts the strings that contain the word *visual*, similar to the preceding sample:

```
Dim words() As String = {"Visual Basic", "Java", "Visual Studio"}
Dim selectedWords = From word In words
                    Where word.ToUpper.Contains("VISUAL")
                    Select word
```

I will not discuss this syntax any further in this chapter, but it's easy to see that the code is more intuitive and that the filtering expression may contain any of the Framework's functions and methods, allowing for much more flexible pattern-matching techniques. As you may recall from Chapter 10, "Applied Object-Oriented Programming," the functionality of arrays, as well as all other collections, has been enhanced with extension methods. One of Chapter 10's sample projects is the Extension Methods project, which demonstrates some of the array's extension methods.

ARRAY LIMITATIONS

As implemented in version 4.0 of the Framework, arrays are more flexible than ever. They're very efficient, and the most demanding tasks programmers previously had to perform with arrays are now implemented as methods of the Array class. However, arrays aren't perfect for all types of data storage. The most important shortcoming of arrays is that they're not dynamic. Inserting or removing elements entails moving all the following elements up or down. Arrays are the most efficient collection in the Framework, but when you need a dynamic structure for adding and removing elements in the course of an application, you should use a collection, such as the List or ArrayList collection, described in detail in the next section.

Collection Types

Collections are structures for storing sets of data, similar to arrays, but they are more flexible, and there are several types of collections to choose from. Let's start with a rough classification of collections. There are collections that store just data, like the List and ArrayList collections, and there are collections that store pairs of keys and data values, like the Dictionary and HashTable collections. If each data value has a unique key, you can use this key to quickly retrieve the matching data value. An ArrayList collection can store temperatures, just like an array. It can also store objects with properties such as city names and their temperatures, but it doesn't allow you to retrieve the temperature in a specific city. If you're interested in temperatures only, you can use an ArrayList or even an array. If you need to access the temperatures in specific cities, however, you must use a Dictionary collection that stores temperatures indexed by the corresponding city names.

Another way to classify the collections is as typed and untyped. *Untyped* collections, such as the ArrayList collection, allow you to store objects of any type. *Typed* collections, on the other hand, such as the List collection, allow you to store objects of a specific type only. The advantage of using typed collections is that their elements expose the properties of the specific type. Consider an ArrayList that contains Rectangle objects. To access the width of the third element in the collection, you must use an expression like the following:

```
Dim AL As New ArrayList
CType(AL(2), Rectangle).Width
```

This expression may cause a runtime error if the third element in the *AL* collection is not of the Rectangle type (*AL* is a properly initialized ArrayList).

If you use a List collection to store the same objects, then you can access the width of an element of the collection with a much simpler expression:

```
Dim LST As New List(Of Rectangle)
' statements to populate the LST collection
LST(2).Width
```

(*LST* is a properly initialized List collection, populated with Rectangle objects.) The members of the Rectangle class will appear in the IntelliSense list as you type. Because the *LST* List collection will not accept any objects other than Rectangles, all errors will be caught at design time, and they will not generate runtime errors.

Now I'll cover the specialized collections of the Framework starting with the simpler ones, the ArrayList and List collections. The two collections are functionally equivalent, and they expose identical members. The ArrayList and List collections allow you to maintain multiple elements, similar to an array; however, Lists and ArrayLists allow the insertion of elements anywhere in the collection, as well as the removal of any element. In other words, they're dynamic structures that can also grow automatically as you add or remove elements. Like an array, the collection's elements can be sorted and searched. You can also remove elements by value, not only by index. If you have a collection populated with names, you remove the item *Charles* by passing the string itself as an argument. Notice that *Charles* is not an index value; it's the element you want to remove.

Creating Collections

To use an ArrayList in your code, you must first create an instance of the ArrayList class by using the New keyword, as in the following statement:

```
Dim aList As New ArrayList
```

The *aList* variable represents an ArrayList that can hold only 16 elements (the default size). You can set the initial capacity of the ArrayList by setting its Capacity property, which is the number of elements the ArrayList can hold. Notice that you don't have to prepare the collection to accept a specific number of items. Every time you exceed the collection's capacity, it's doubled automatically. However, it's not decreased automatically when you remove items.

The exact number of items currently in the ArrayList is given by the `Count` property, which is always less than (or, at most, equal to) the `Capacity` property. (Both properties are expressed in terms of items.) If you decide that you will no longer add more items to the collection, you can call the `TrimToSize` method, which will set the collection's capacity to the number of items in the list.

Where the ArrayList collection can store objects of any type, a variation of the ArrayList stores objects of the same type. This collection is called List, and it's a typed ArrayList. The only difference between ArrayLists and Lists is in the way they're declared: When you declare a List collection, you must supply the type of the objects you intend to store in it, using the `Of` keyword in parentheses, as shown in the following statements, which declare two List collections for storing Rectangle objects (the *Rects* collection) and custom objects of the Student type (the *Students* collection):

```
Dim Rects As New List(Of Rectangle)
Dim Students As New List(Of Student)
```

Other than that, the List collection is identical to the ArrayList collection. Of course, because the List collection stores objects of a specific type, it integrates nicely with IntelliSense. If you type the name of an element in the collection (such as **Rects(3)**) and the following period, IntelliSense will display the members of the Rectangle class in a drop-down list. In the following section, you'll learn about the methods they expose and how to use both types of collections in your code. I will be using mostly the List class in the sample code and suggest that you do the same in your code whenever possible, but the same techniques apply to the ArrayList class as well.

ADDING AND REMOVING LIST ITEMS

To add a new item to a List, use the `Add` method, whose syntax is as follows:

```
index = lst.Add(obj)
```

lst is a properly declared List (or ArrayList) variable, and *obj* is the item you want to add to the collection. The type of the obj object should be the same as the one you used in the declaration of the List collection. The `Add` method appends the specified item to the collection and returns the index of the new item. If you're using a List named Capitals to store the names of the state capitals, you can add an item by using the following statement:

```
Capitals.Add("Sacramento")
```

Let's say you created a structure called Person by using the following declaration:

```
Structure Person
    Dim LastName As String
    Dim FirstName As String
    Dim Phone As String
    Dim EMail As String
End Structure
```

To store a collection of Person items in a List, create a variable of the Person type, set its fields, and then add it to the List, as shown in Listing 12.2.

LISTING 12.2: Adding a structure to an ArrayList

```
Dim Persons As New List(Of Person)
Dim p As New Person
p.LastName = "Last Name"
p.FirstName = "First Name"
p.Phone = "Phone"
p.EMail = "name@server.com"
Persons.Add(p)
p = New Person
p.LastName = "another name"
{ statements to set the other fields}
Persons.Add(p)
```

If you execute these statements, the List collection will hold two items, both of the Person type. Notice that you can add multiple instances of the same object to the List collection. To find out whether an item belongs to the collection already, use the Contains method, which accepts as an argument an object and returns a True or False value, depending on whether the object belongs to the list:

```
If Persons.Contains(p) Then
    MsgBox("Duplicate element rejected")
Else
    Persons.Add(p)
    MsgBox("Element appended successfully")
End If
```

By default, items are appended to the collection. To insert an item at a specific location, use the Insert method, which accepts as an argument the location at which the new item will be inserted and, of course, an object to insert in the ArrayList, as shown next:

```
aList.Insert(index, object)
```

Unlike the Add method, the Insert method doesn't return a value — the location of the new item is already known.

You can also add multiple items via a single call to the AddRange method. This method appends to the collection of a set of items, which could come from an array or from another list. The following statement appends the elements of an array to the Lst collection:

```
Dim colors() As Color = {Color.Red, Color.Blue, Color.Green}
Lst.AddRange(colors)
```

To insert a range of items anywhere in the collection, use the InsertRange method. Its syntax is the following, where *index* is the index of the collections where the new elements will be inserted, and *objects* is a collection of the elements to be inserted:

```
Lst.InsertRange(index, objects)
```

Finally, you can overwrite a range of elements in the collection with a new range by using the SetRange method. To overwrite the items in locations 5 through 9 in an collection, use a few statements like the following:

```
Dim words() As String =
                {"Just", "a", "few", "more", "words"}
Lst.SetRange(5, words)
```

This code segment assumes that the Lst collection contains at least 10 items, and it replaces half of them.

To remove an item, use the Remove method, whose syntax is the following:

```
aList.Remove(object)
```

The *object* argument is the value to be removed, not an index value. If the collection contains multiple instances of the same item, only the first instance of the object will be removed.

Notice that the Remove method compares values, not references. If the collection contains a Rectangle object, you can search for this item by creating a new variable of this type and setting its properties to the properties of the Rectangle object you want to remove:

```
Dim R1 As New Rectangle(10, 10, 100, 100)
Dim R2 As Rectangle = R1
Lst.Add(R1)
Lst.Add(R2)
Dim R3 As Rectangle
R3 = New Rectangle(10, 10, 100, 100)
Lst.Remove(R3)
```

If you execute these statements, they will add two identical rectangles to the Lst collection. The last statement will remove the first of the two rectangles.

If you attempt to remove an item that doesn't exist, no exception is thrown — simply, no item is removed from the list. You can also remove items by specifying their index in the list via the RemoveAt method. This method accepts as an argument the index of the item to remove, which must be less than the number of items currently in the list.

To remove more than one consecutive item, use the RemoveRange method, whose syntax is the following:

```
Lst.RemoveRange(startIndex, count)
```

The *startIndex* argument is the index of the first item to be removed, and *count* is the number of items to be removed.

The following statements are examples of the methods that remove items from a collection. The first two statements remove an item by value. The first statement removes an object, and the second removes a string item. The following statement removes the third item, and the last one removes the third through the fifth items.

```
aList.Remove(Color.Red)
aList.Remove("Richard")
```

```
aList.RemoveAt(2)
aList.RemoveRange(2, 3)
```

COLLECTION INITIALIZERS

You can also declare and populate a collection in a single statement, with a collection initializer. The *collection initializer* is a sequence of elements enclosed in a pair of curly brackets. The following statement declares and initializes a new ArrayList collection with strings:

```
Dim letters As New ArrayList({"quick", "dog", "fox", "lazy", "brown"})
```

As you recall from Chapter 8, "Working with Objects," you can initialize an object by supplying a set of values in parentheses as an argument to its constructor. The curly brackets indicate that you're supplying a collection of values. As a reminder, here's the simplest form of collection initializer, the array initializer:

```
Dim numbers() As Decimal = {2.0, 12.99, 0.001, 1000.0, 10.01}
```

If this were a List collection, the initialization would be a little more complicated. Let's initialize a List collection of strings. You first must declare the collection with a statement like the following:

```
Dim words = New List(Of String)
```

To initialize the collection, you must supply a list of strings in a pair of curly brackets. The following statement creates an array of strings:

```
{"the", "quick", "brown", "fox", "jumped", "over", "the", "lazy", "dog"}
```

To initialize the List collection, all you have to do is append the array with the values to the collection's initializer:

```
Dim words = New List(Of String)({"the", "quick", "brown",
                          "fox", "jumped", "over", "the", "lazy", "dog"})
```

Collection initializers allow you to declare and initialize a collection similar to all scalar objects. You can also supply the constructors of more complex objects to the collection initializer. The following statement will create a List of Rectangle objects:

```
Dim Rects = New List(Of Rectangle)({New Rectangle(0, 0, 4, 14),
                          New Rectangle(0, 0, 101, 101),
                          New Rectangle(100, 100, 10, 20)})
```

This looks fairly complicated, almost C#-like, but here's how you read the statement. The constructor of the Rects collection accepts its initial values in a pair of parentheses. In the parentheses themselves, you can embed an array of object initializers. Note that all object initializers must be embedded in a pair of curly brackets.

Finally, you can initialize a collection with anonymous types, a topic discussed in Chapter 10. An anonymous type is a type that's created while it's being declared. Here's an anonymous type that may appear anywhere in your code:

```
Dim P = New With {.First = "Evangelos", .Last = "Petroutsos"}
```

Note that the variable *P* is of an anonymous type, because there's no type name. However, it has two fields that you can access as if the *P* variable were based on a custom class:

```
P.First = "Richard"
```

The next statement creates a new collection of objects, each one representing a city:

```
Dim cities = New ArrayList(
              {New With {.city = "a city", .population = 201213},
               New With {.city = "a small city", .population = 101320},
               New With {.city = "a town", .population = 39210}})
```

You may find the number of curly brackets overwhelming, but the trick to using initializers effectively is to build them step-by-step. The following expression creates a new variable of the anonymous type with two fields:

```
New With {.city = "a city", .population = 201213}
```

Then you embed several of these expressions with different field values in a pair of curly brackets to create a collection of objects of this anonymous type, and finally you embed the collection in a pair of parentheses to pass them as arguments to the collection's initializer. To standardize the collection initializers, consider the following rule: All values you add to the collection must be embedded in a pair of curly brackets:

```
{object1, object2, object3, …}
```

Each object in the collection must be initialized with its own constructor. Replace *object1* with its initializer, *object2* with the same initializer and different values, and so on, to create a collection of objects. Then embed the entire expression, along with the outer curly brackets, in a pair of parentheses following the collection's declaration. If the objects are of an anonymous type, insert the appropriate anonymous initializer for each object. As for the curly brackets, think of them as delimiters for sets of values for arrays (or sets of properties for objects). In Visual Basic, curly brackets are used only with collection initializers and anonymous constructors.

Of course, you can't create a List collection of an anonymous type, because the List is a strongly typed collection.

EXTRACTING ITEMS FROM A COLLECTION

To access the items in the collection, use an index value, similar to the array. The first item's index is 0, and the last item's index is Lst.Count-1, where *Lst* is a properly initialized List or ArrayList collection. You can also extract a range of items from the list by using the GetRange method. This method extracts a number of consecutive elements from the Lst collection and stores them to a new collection, the newLst collection, where *index* is the index of the first item to copy, and *count* is the number of items to be copied:

```
newLst = Lst.GetRange(index, count)
```

The GetRange method returns another collection with the proper number of items. The following statement copies three items from the *Lst* collection and inserts them at the beginning of the bLst collection. The three elements copied are the fourth through sixth elements in the original collection:

```
bLst.InsertRange(0, aLst.GetRange(3, 3))
```

The Repeat method, which fills a list with multiple instances of the same item, has the following syntax:

```
newList = ArrayList.Repeat(item, count)
```

This method returns a new list with *count* elements, all of them being identical to the *item* argument. The Reverse method, finally, reverses the order of the elements in a collection, or a portion of it.

Sorting Lists

To sort an ArrayList or List collection, use the Sort method, which has three overloaded forms:

```
aLst.Sort()
aLst.Sort(comparer)
aLst.Sort(startIndex, endIndex, comparer)
```

The Sort method doesn't require you to pass the name of the list to be sorted as an argument; unlike the Sort method of the Array class, this is an instance method and it sorts the collection to which it's applied. *aLst* is a properly declared and initialized List or ArrayList variable. The first form of the Sort method sorts the list alphabetically or numerically, depending on the data type of the objects stored in it. If the items are not all of the same type, an exception will be thrown. You'll see how you can handle this exception in just a moment.

If the items stored in the collection are of a data type other than the base data types, you must supply your own mechanism to compare the objects. The other two forms of the Sort method use a custom function for comparing items; you will see how they're used in the section "The IEnumerator and IComparer Interfaces" later in this chapter.

If the list contains items of widely different types, the Sort method will fail. To prevent a runtime exception (the InvalidOperationException), you must make sure that all items are of the same type. If you can't ensure that all the items are of the same type, catch the possible errors and handle them from within a structured exception handler, as demonstrated in Listing 12.3. (The listing doesn't show the statements for populating the ArrayList, just the use of a structured exception handler for the Sort method.)

LISTING 12.3:   Foolproof sorting

```
Dim sorted As Boolean = True
Try
  aLst.Sort()
Catch SortException As InvalidOperationException
    MsgBox("You can't sort an ArrayList whose items " &
           "aren't of the same type")
    sorted = False
Catch GeneralException As Exception
    MsgBox("The following exception occurred: " &
           vbCrLf & GeneralException.Message)   sorted = False
End Try
If sorted Then
  { process sorted list}
Else
  { process unsorted list}
End If
```

The *sorted* Boolean variable is initially set to True because the Sort method will most likely succeed. If not, an exception will be thrown, in which case the code sets the *sorted* variable to False and uses it later to distinguish between sorted and unsorted collections. Notice the two clauses of the Catch statement that distinguish between the invalid operation exception and any other type of exception.

The Sort method can't even sort a collection of various numeric data types. If some of its elements are doubles and some are integers or decimals, the Sort method will fail. You must either make sure that all the items in the ArrayList are of the same type or provide your own function for comparing the ArrayList's items. The best practice is to make sure that your collection contains items of the same type by using a List collection. If a collection contains items of different types, however, how likely is it that you'll have to sort such a collection?

Searching Lists

Like arrays, ArrayList and List collections expose the IndexOf and LastIndexOf methods to search in an unsorted list and the BinarySearch method for sorted lists. The IndexOf and LastIndexOf methods accept as an argument the object to be located and return an index:

```
Dim index As Integer = Lst.IndexOf(object)
```

Here, *object* is the item you're searching. The LastIndexOf method has the same syntax, but it starts scanning the array from its end and moves backward toward the beginning. The IndexOf and LastIndexOf methods are overloaded as follows:

```
Lst.IndexOf(object, startIndex)
Lst.IndexOf(object, startIndex, length)
```

The two additional arguments determine where the search starts and ends. Both methods return the index of the item if it belongs to the collection. If not, they return the value –1. The

IndexOf and LastIndexOf methods of the List and ArrayList classes perform case-sensitive searches, and they report exact matches only.

If the list is already sorted, use the BinarySearch method, which accepts as an argument the object to be located and returns its index in the collection, where *object* is the item you're looking for:

```
Dim index As Integer = Lst.BinarySearch(object)
```

There are two more overloads of this method. To search for an item in a list with custom objects, use the following form of the BinarySearch method:

```
Dim index As Integer = Lst.BinarySearch(object, comparer)
```

The first argument is the object you're searching for, and the second is the name of an IComparer object. Another overload of the BinarySearch method allows you to search for an item in a section of the collection; its syntax is as follows:

```
Dim index As Integer = _
        Lst.BinarySearch(startIndex, length, object, comparer)
```

The first argument is the index at which the search will begin, and the second argument is the length of the subrange. *object* and *comparer* are the same as with the second form of the method.

Iterating Through a List

To iterate through the elements of a collection, you can set up a For...Next loop:

```
For i = 0 To Lst.Count - 1
    { process item Lst(i)}
Next
```

or a For Each loop:

```
For Each itm In aLst
    { process item itm }
Next
```

This is a trivial operation, but the processing itself can get as complicated as required by the type of objects stored in the collection. The current item at each iteration is the Lst(i). It's recommended that you cast the object to the appropriate type and then process it.

You can also use the For Each...Next loop with an *Object* variable, as shown next:

```
Dim itm As Object
For Each itm In aLst
    { process item itm}
Next
```

If you're iterating through an `ArrayList` collection, you must cast the control variable *itm* to the appropriate type. If you're iterating through a List collection, then the *itm* variable is of the same type as the one you used in the declaration of the List collection, as long as the Infer option is on. Alternatively, you can declare the control variable in the For Each statement:

```
Dim Lst AS New List(Of String)
' statements to populate list
For Each itm As String In Lst
' process item lst
Next
```

An even better method is to create an enumerator for the collection and use it to iterate through its items. This technique applies to all collections and is discussed in the "The IEnumerator and IComparer Interfaces" section later in this chapter.

The List and ArrayList classes address most of the problems associated with the Array class, but one last problem remains — that of accessing the items in the collection through a meaningful key. This is the problem addressed by the Dictionary and HashTable collections.

The Dictionary Collection

As you saw, the List and ArrayList classes address most of the problems of the Array class, while they support all the convenient array features. Yet, the two lists, like the Array, have a major drawback: You must access their items by an index value. Another collection, the Dictionary collection, is similar to the List and ArrayList collections, but it allows you to access the items by a meaningful key.

Each item in a Dictionary has a value and a key. The value is the same value you'd store in an array, but the key is a meaningful entity for accessing the items in the collection, and each element's key must be unique. Both the values stored in a Dictionary and their keys can be objects. Typically, the keys are short strings (such as Social Security numbers, ISBN values, product IDs, and so on) or integers.

The Dictionary collection exposes most of the properties and methods of the List, with a few notable exceptions. The `Count` property returns the number of items in the collection as usual, but the Dictionary collection doesn't expose a `Capacity` property. The Dictionary collection uses fairly complicated logic to maintain the list of items, and it adjusts its capacity automatically. Fortunately, you need not know how the items are stored in the collection.

To create a Dictionary in your code, declare it with the `New` keyword, and supply the type of the keys and values you plan to store in the collection with a statement like the following:

```
Dim Students As New Dictionary(Of Integer, Student)
```

The first argument is the type of the keys, and the second argument is the type of the values you plan to store in the collection. Dictionaries are typed collections, unless you declare them with the Object type. To add an item to the Dictionary, use the `Add` method with the following syntax:

```
Students.Add(key, value)
```

value is the item you want to add (it can be an object of the type specified in the collection's declaration), and *key* is an identifier you supply, which represents the item. After populating the collection you will use the key to access specific elements of the collection. For example, you will use city names to locate their temperature as shown in the following statements:

```
Dim Temperatures As New Dictionary(Of String, Decimal)
Temperatures.Add("Houston", 81.3)
Temperatures.Add("Los Angeles", 78.5)
```

To find out the temperature in Houston, use the following statement:

```
MsgBox(Temperatures("Houston").ToString)
```

Notice that you can have duplicate values, but the keys must be unique. If you attempt to reuse an existing key as you populate the collection, an InvalidArgumentException exception will be thrown. To find out whether a specific key or value is already in the collection, use the ContainsKey and ContainsValue methods. The syntax of the two methods is quite similar, and they return True if the specified key or value is already in use in the collection:

```
Dictionary.ContainsKey(object)
Dictionary.ContainsValue(object)
```

The Dictionary collection exposes the Contains method, too, which returns True if the collection contains a pair of a key and a value. If the collection contains the same value with a different key, the Contains method will return False.

To find out whether a specific key is in use already, use the ContainsKey method, as shown in the following statements, which add a new item to the Dictionary only if its key doesn't exist already:

```
Dim value As New Rectangle(100, 100, 50, 50)
Dim key As String = "Rect1"
If Not Rects.ContainsKey(key) Then
    Rects.Add(key, value)
End If
```

If the key exists already, you might want to change its value. In this case, use the following notation, which adds new elements to the list if the key isn't present or changes the value of the element that corresponds to the specified key:

```
Rects(key) = value
```

The Values and Keys properties allow you to retrieve all the values and the keys in the Dictionary, respectively. Both properties are collections and expose the usual members of a collection. To iterate through the values stored in a Dictionary, use the following loop:

```
Dim itm As Object
For Each itm In Dict.Values
    Debug.WriteLine(itm)
Next
```

Listing 12.4 demonstrates how to scan the keys of a Dictionary through the Keys property and then use these keys to access the matching items through the Item property.

LISTING 12.4: Iterating a Dictionary collection

```
Private Function ShowDictionaryContents(
                ByVal table As Dictionary
                (Of String, Decimal)) As String
    Dim msg As String
    Dim element, key As Object
    msg = "The HashTable contains " &
          table.Count.ToString & " elements: " & vbCrLf
    For Each key In table.Keys
        element = table.Item(key)
        msg = msg & vbCrLf & "    Element Key= " &
              key.ToString
        msg = msg & "    Element Value= " &
              element.ToString & vbCrLf
    Next
    Return (msg)
End Function
```

To print the contents of a Dictionary collection in the Output window, call the ShowHashTableContents() function, passing the name of the Dictionary as an argument, and then print the string returned by the function:

```
Dim Dict As New Dictionary
{ statements to populate Dictionary}
MsgBox(ShowDictionaryContents(Dict))
```

The specific implementation of the ShowDictionaryContents() function applies to Dictionary collections that use strings as keys and decimals as values. For Dictionary collections that store different types, you must edit the function to accommodate the appropriate data types.

The HashTable Collection

Another collection, very similar to the Dictionary collection, is the HashTable collection. The HashTable is an untyped Dictionary. To populate a HashTable with temperature values indexed by city names, use a few statements like the following:

```
Dim tmps As New Hashtable
tmps("Houston") = 81.3
tmps("Los Angeles") = 78.5
```

If an element with the same key you're trying to add exists already, then no new item will be added to the list. Instead, the existing item's value will be changed. After executing the following statements, for example, the *Temperatures* HashTable will contain a single element with the key Houston and the value 79.9:

```
Dim temperatures As New Hashtable
tmps("Houston") = 81.3
tmps("Houston") = 79.9
```

You can always use the Add method to add elements to a HashTable collection, and the syntax of this method is identical to the Add method of the Dictionary collection. Like the Dictionary collection, it exposes the Add method that accepts a key and a value as arguments, a Remove method that accepts the key of the element to be removed, and the Keys and Values properties that return all the keys and values in the collection, respectively. The major difference between the Dictionary and HashTable collections is that the Dictionary class is a strongly typed one, while the HashTable can accept arbitrary objects as values and is not as fast as the Dictionary class. Another very important difference is that the Dictionary collection class is not serializable, a topic discussed in detail in the following chapter. Practically, this means that a Dictionary collection can't be persisted to a disk file with a single statement, which is true for the HashTable collection.

VB 2010 at Work: The WordFrequencies Project

In this section, you'll develop an application that counts word frequencies in a text. The Word-Frequencies application (available for download from www.sybex.com/go/masteringvb2010) scans text files and counts the occurrences of each word in the text. As you will see, the HashTable collection is the natural choice for storing this information because you want to access a word's frequency by using the actual word as the key. To retrieve (or update) the frequency of the word *elaborate*, for example, you will use this expression:

```
Words("ELABORATE").Value
```

where *Words* is a properly initialized HashTable object.

When the code runs into another instance of the word *elaborate*, it simply increases the matching item of the Words HashTable by one:

```
Words("ELABORATE").Value += 1
```

Arrays and Lists (or ArrayLists) are out of the question because they can't be accessed by a key. You could also use the SortedList collection (described later in this chapter), but this collection maintains its items sorted at all times. If you need this functionality as well, you can modify the application accordingly. The items in a SortedList are also accessed by keys, so you won't have to introduce substantial changes in the code.

Let me start with a few remarks. First, all words we locate in the various text files will be converted to uppercase. Because the keys of the HashTable are case sensitive, converting them to uppercase eliminates the usual problem of case sensitivity (*hello* being a different word than *Hello* and *HELLO*) by eliminating multiple possible variations in capitalization for the same word.

The frequencies of the words can't be calculated instantly because we need to know the total number of words in the text. Instead, each value in the HashTable is the number of occurrences of a specific word. To calculate the actual frequency of the same word, we must divide this value by the number of occurrences of all words, but this can happen only after we have scanned the entire text file and counted the occurrences of each word.

Figure 12.2 shows the application's interface. To scan a text file and process its words, click the Read Text File button. The Open dialog box will prompt you to select the text file to be processed, and the application will display in a message box the number of unique words read from the file. Then you can click the Show Word Count button to count the number of occurrences of each word in the text. The last button on the form calculates the frequency of each word and sorts the words according to their frequencies.

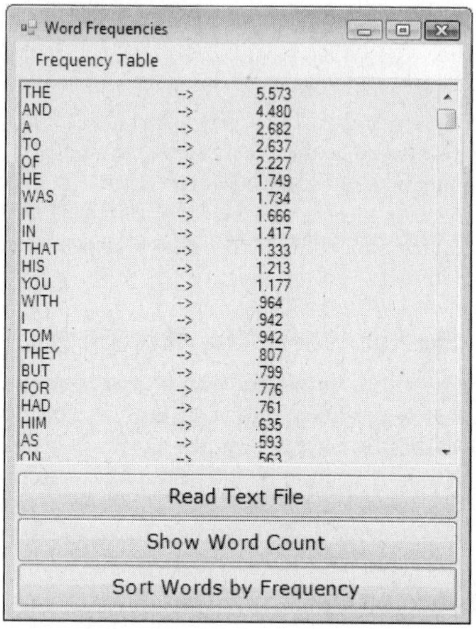

FIGURE 12.2
The WordFrequencies project demonstrates how to use the HashTable collection.

Word Frequencies		
Frequency Table		
THE	-->	5.573
AND	-->	4.480
A	-->	2.682
TO	-->	2.637
OF	-->	2.227
HE	-->	1.749
WAS	-->	1.734
IT	-->	1.666
IN	-->	1.417
THAT	-->	1.333
HIS	-->	1.213
YOU	-->	1.177
WITH	-->	.964
I	-->	.942
TOM	-->	.942
THEY	-->	.807
BUT	-->	.799
FOR	-->	.776
HAD	-->	.761
HIM	-->	.635
AS	-->	.593
ON	-->	563

Read Text File

Show Word Count

Sort Words by Frequency

The application maintains a single HashTable collection, the Words collection, and it updates this collection rather than counting word occurrences from scratch for each file you open. The Frequency Table menu contains the commands to save the words and their counts to a disk file and read the same data from the file. The commands in this menu can store the data either to a text file (Save XML/Load XML commands) or to a binary file (Save Binary/Load Binary commands). Use these commands to store the data generated in a single session, load the data in a later session, and process more files.

The WordFrequencies application uses techniques and classes I haven't discussed yet. Serialization is discussed in detail in the next chapter, whereas reading from (or writing to) files is discussed in the tutorial "Accessing Folders and Files." (You'll find that tutorial online at www.sybex.com/go/masteringvb2010.) You don't really have to understand the code that opens a text file and reads its lines; just focus on the segments that manipulate the items of the HashTable.

To test the project, I used some large text files I downloaded from the Project Gutenberg website (http://promo.net/pg/). This site contains entire books in electronic format (plain-text files), and you can borrow some files to test any program that manipulates text. (Choose some books you will enjoy reading.)

The code reads the text into a string variable, and then it calls the Split method of the String class to split the text into individual words. The Split method uses the space, comma, period, quotation mark, exclamation mark, colon, semicolon, and new-line characters as delimiters. The individual words are stored in the *Words* array; after this array has been populated, the program goes through each word in the array and determines whether it's a valid word by calling the IsValidWord() function. This function returns False if one of the characters in the word is not a letter; strings such as B2B or U2 are not considered proper words. IsValidWord() is a custom function, and you can edit it as you wish to handle the specific content (my assumption that a word may not contain digits is quite reasonable to text files but totally wrong if you're handling code listings, for example).

Any valid word becomes a key to the *wordFrequencies* HashTable. The corresponding value is the number of occurrences of the specific word in the text. If a key (a new word) is added to the table, its value is set to 1. If the key exists already, its value is increased by 1 via the following If statement:

```
If Not wordFrequencies.ContainsKey(word) Then
    wordFrequencies.Add(word, 1)
Else
    wordFrequencies(word) = CType(wordFrequencies(word), Integer) + 1
End If
```

Listing 12.5 is the code that reads the text file and splits it into individual words. The code reads the entire text into a string variable, the *txtLine* variable, and the individual words are isolated with the Split method of the String class. The *Delimiters* array stores the characters that the Split method will use as delimiters, and you can add more delimiters depending on the type of text you're processing. If you're counting keywords in program listings, for example, you'll have to add the math symbols and parentheses as delimiters.

LISTING 12.5:   Splitting a text file into words

```
Private Sub bttnRead_Click(…) Handles bttnRead.Click
    OpenFileDialog1.DefaultExt = "TXT"
    OpenFileDialog1.Filter = "Text|*.TXT|All Files|*.*"
    If OpenFileDialog1.ShowDialog() <>
            Windows.Forms.DialogResult.OK Then Exit Sub
    Dim str As StreamReader = File.OpenText(OpenFileDialog1.FileName)
    Dim txtLine As String
    Dim words() As String
    Dim Delimiters() As Char =
        {CType(" ", Char), CType(".", Char), CType(",", Char),
         CType("?", Char), CType("!", Char), CType(";", Char),
         CType(":", Char), Chr(10), Chr(13), vbTab}
    txtLine = str.ReadToEnd
    words = txtLine.Split(Delimiters)
    Dim uniqueWords As Integer
    Dim iword As Integer, word As String
    For iword = 0 To Words.GetUpperBound(0)
        word = words(iword).ToUpper
        If IsValidWord(word) Then
```

```
            If Not wordFrequencies.ContainsKey(word) Then
                wordFrequencies.Add(word, 1)
                uniqueWords += 1
            Else
                wordFrequencies(word) =
                        CType(wordFrequencies(word), Integer) + 1
            End If
        End If
    Next
    MsgBox("Read " & words.Length & " words and found " &
            uniqueWords & " unique words")
    RichTextBox1.Clear()
End Sub
```

This event handler keeps track of the number of unique words and displays them in a Rich-TextBox control. In a document with 90,000 words, it took less than a second to split the text and perform all the calculations. The process of displaying the list of unique words in the Rich-TextBox control was very fast, too, thanks to the StringBuilder class. The code behind the Show Word Count button (see Listing 12.6) displays the list of words along with the number of occurrences of each word in the text.

LISTING 12.6:   Displaying the count of each word in the text

```
Private Sub bttnCount_Click(…) Handles bttnCount.Click
    Dim wEnum As IDictionaryEnumerator
    Dim allWords As New System.Text.StringBuilder
    wEnum = WordFrequencies.GetEnumerator
    While wEnum.MoveNext
        allWords.Append(wEnum.Key.ToString &
                vbTab & "-->" & vbTab & _
                wEnum.Value.ToString & vbCrLf)
    End While
    RichTextBox1.Text = allWords.ToString
End Sub
```

The last button on the form calculates the frequency of each word in the HashTable, sorts the words according to their frequencies, and displays the list. Its code is detailed in Listing 12.7.

LISTING 12.7:   Sorting the words according to frequency

```
Private Sub bttnShow_Click(…) Handles bttnSort.Click
    Dim wEnum As IDictionaryEnumerator
    Dim words(wordFrequencies.Count) As String
    Dim frequencies(wordFrequencies.Count) As Double
    Dim allWords As New System.Text.StringBuilder
```

```
    Dim i, totCount As Integer
    wEnum = wordFrequencies.GetEnumerator
    While wEnum.MoveNext
        words(i) = CType(wEnum.Key, String)
        frequencies(i) = CType(wEnum.Value, Integer)
        totCount = totCount + Convert.ToInt32(Frequencies(i))
        i = i + 1
    End While
    For i = 0 To words.GetUpperBound(0)
        frequencies(i) = frequencies(i) / totCount
    Next
    Array.Sort(frequencies, Words)
    RichTextBox1.Clear()
    For i = words.GetUpperBound(0) To 0 Step -1
        allWords.Append(words(i) & vbTab & "-->" &
                            vbTab & Format(100 * frequencies(i),
                            "#.000") & vbCrLf)
    Next
    RichTextBox1.Text = allWords.ToString
End Sub
```

🌐 Real World Scenario

HANDLING LARGE SETS OF DATA

Incidentally, my first attempt was to display the list of unique words in a ListBox control. The process was incredibly slow. The first 10,000 words were added in a couple of seconds, but as the number of items increased, the time it took to add them to the control increased exponentially (or so it seemed). Adding thousands of items to a ListBox control is a very slow process. You can call the BeginUpdate/EndUpdate methods, but they won't help a lot. It's likely that sometimes a seemingly simple task will turn out to be detrimental to your application's performance.

You should try different approaches but also consider a total overhaul of your user interface. Ask yourself this: Who needs to see a list with 10,000 words? You can use the application to do the calculations and then retrieve the count of selected words, display the 100 most common ones, or even display 100 words at a time. I'm displaying the list of words because this is a demonstration, but a real application shouldn't display such a long list. The core of the application counts unique words in a text file, and it does it very efficiently.

Even if you decide to display an extremely long list of items on your interface, you should perform some worst-case scenarios (that is, attempt to load the control with zero or too many items), and if this causes serious performance problems, consider different controls. I've decided to append all the items to a *StringBuilder* variable and then display this variable in a RichTextBox control. I could have used a plain TextBox control — after all, I'm not formatting the list of words and their frequencies — but the RichTextBox allowed me to specify the absolute tab positions. The tab positions of the TextBox control are fixed and weren't wide enough for all words.

The SortedList Collection

The SortedList collection is a combination of the Array and HashTable classes. It maintains a list of items that can be accessed either with an index or with a key. When you access items by their indices, the SortedList behaves just like an ArrayList; when you access items by their keys, the SortedList behaves like a HashTable. What's unique about the SortedList is that this collection is always sorted according to the keys. The items of a SortedList are always ordered according to the values of their keys, and there's no method for sorting the collection according to the values stored in it.

To create a new SortedList collection, use a statement such as the following:

```
Dim sList As New SortedList
```

As you might have guessed, this collection can store keys that are of the base data types. If you want to use custom objects as keys, you must specify an argument of the IComparer type, which tells VB how to compare the custom items. This information is crucial; without it, the SortedList won't be able to maintain its items sorted. You can still store items in the SortedList, but they will appear in the order in which they were added. This form of the SortedList constructor has the following syntax, where *comparer* is the name of a custom class that implements the IComparer interface (which is discussed in detail later in this chapter):

```
Dim sList As New SortedList(New comparer)
```

There are also two more forms of the constructor, which allow you to specify the initial capacity of the SortedList collection, as well as a Dictionary object, whose data (keys and values) will be automatically added to the SortedList.

To add an item to a SortedList collection, use the Add method, whose syntax is the following, where *key* is the key of the new item and *item* is the item to be added:

```
sList.Add(key, item)
```

Both arguments are objects. But remember, if the keys are objects, the collection won't be automatically sorted; you must provide your own comparer, as discussed later in this chapter. The Add method is the only way to add items to a SortedList collection, and all keys must be unique; attempting to add a duplicate key will throw an exception.

The SortedList class also exposes the ContainsKey and ContainsValue methods, which allow you to find out whether a key or item already exists in the list. To add a new item, use the following statement to make sure that the key isn't in use:

```
If Not sList.ContainsKey(myKey) Then
    sList.Add(myKey, myItem)
End If
```

To replace an existing item, use the SetByIndex method, which replaces the value at a specific index. The syntax of the method is the following, where the first argument is the index at which the value will be inserted, and *item* is the new item to be inserted in the collection:

```
sList.SetByIndex(index, item)
```

This object will replace the value that corresponds to the specified index. The key, however, remains the same. There's no equivalent method for replacing a key; you must first remove the item and then insert it again with its new key.

To remove items from the collection, use the `Remove` and `RemoveAt` methods. The `Remove` method accepts a key as an argument and removes the item that corresponds to that key. The `RemoveAt` method accepts an index as an argument and removes the item at the specified index. To remove all the items from a SortedList collection, call its `Clear` method.

Other Collections

The System.Collections class exposes a few more collections, including the Queue and Stack collections. The main characteristic of these two collections is how you add and remove items to them. When you add items to a Queue collection, the items are appended to the collection. When you remove items, they're removed from the top of the collection. Queues are known as last in, first out (LIFO) structures because you can extract only the oldest item in the queue. You'd use this collection to simulate the customer line in a bank or a production line.

The Stack collection inserts new items at the top, and you can remove only the top item. The Stack collection is a first in, first out (FIFO) structure. You'd use this collection to emulate the stack maintained by the CPU, one of the most crucial structures for the operating system and applications alike. The Stack and Queue collections are used heavily in computer science but hardly ever in business applications, so I won't discuss them further in this book.

The IEnumerator and IComparer Interfaces

IEnumerator and IComparer are two classes that unlock some of the most powerful features of collections. The proper term for IEnumerator and IComparer is *interface*, a term I will describe shortly. Every class that implements the IEnumerator interface is capable of retrieving a list of pointers for all the items in a collection, and you can use this list to iterate through the items in a collection. Every collection has a built-in enumerator, and you can retrieve it by calling its `GetEnumerator` method. And every class that implements the IComparer interface exposes the `Compare` method, which tells the compiler how to compare two objects of the same type. After the compiler knows how to compare the objects, it can sort a collection of objects with the same type.

The IComparer interface consists of a function that compares two items and returns a value indicating their order (which one is the smaller item or whether they're equal). The Framework can't compare objects of all types; it knows only how to compare the base types. It doesn't even know how to compare built-in objects such as two rectangles or two color objects. If you have a collection of colors, you might want to sort them according to their luminance, saturation, brightness, and so on. Rectangles can be sorted according to their area or perimeter. The Framework can't make any assumptions as to how you might want to sort your collection, and of course, it doesn't expose members to sort a collection in all possible ways. Instead, it gives you the option to specify a function that compares two colors (or two objects of any other type, for that matter) and uses this function to sort the collection. The same function is used by the `BinarySearch` method to locate an item in a sorted collection. In effect, the IComparer interface consists of a single function that knows how to compare two specific custom objects.

So, what is an interface? An *interface* is another term in object-oriented programming that describes a very simple technique. When you write the code for a class, you might not know how to implement a few operations, but you do know that they'll have to be implemented later. You insert a placeholder for these operations (one or more function declarations) and expect that the application that uses the class will provide the actual implementation of these functions. All collections expose a Sort method, which sorts the items in the collection by comparing them to one another. To do so, the Sort method calls a function that compares two items and returns a value indicating their relative order. Custom objects must provide their own comparison function — or more than a single function, if you want to sort them in multiple ways. Because you can't edit the collection's Sort method code, you must supply your comparison function through a mechanism that the class can understand. This is what the IComparer interface is all about.

Enumerating Collections

All collections expose the GetEnumerator method. This method returns an object of the IEnumerator type, which allows you to iterate through the collection without having to know anything about its items, not even the count of the items. To retrieve the enumerator for a collection, call its GetEnumerator method by using a statement like the following:

```
Dim ALEnum As IEnumerator
ALEnum = aList.GetEnumerator
```

The IEnumerator class exposes two methods: the MoveNext and Reset methods. The MoveNext method moves to the next item in the collection and makes it the current item (property Current). When you initialize the IEnumerator object, it's positioned in front of the very first item, so you must call the MoveNext method to move to the first item. The Reset method does exactly the same thing: It repositions the IEnumerator in front of the first element.

The MoveNext method doesn't return an item, as you might expect. It returns a True/False value that indicates whether it has successfully moved to the next item. After you have reached the end of the collection, the MoveNext method will return False. Here's how you can enumerate through a List collection by using an enumerator:

```
Dim listItems As IEnumerator
listItems = list.GetEnumerator
While listItems.MoveNext
    { process item listItems.Current}
End While
```

At each iteration, the current item is given by the Current property of the enumerator. After you reach the last item, the MoveNext method will return False, and the loop will terminate. To rescan the items, you must reset the enumerator by calling its Reset method.

The event handler in Listing 12.8 populates an ArrayList with Rectangle objects and then iterates through the collection and prints the area of each Rectangle using the collection's enumerator.

LISTING 12.8:   Iterating an ArrayList with an enumerator

```
Dim aList As New ArrayList()
Dim R1 As New Rectangle(1, 1, 10, 10)
aList.Add(R1)
R1 = New Rectangle(2, 2, 20, 20)
```

```
aList.Add(R1)
aList.add(New Rectangle(3, 3, 2, 2))
Dim REnum As IEnumerator
REnum = aList.GetEnumerator
Dim R As Rectangle
While REnum.MoveNext
    R = CType(REnum.Current, Rectangle)
    Debug.WriteLine((R.Width * R.Height).ToString)
End While
```

The *REnum* variable is set up and used to iterate through the items of the collection. At each iteration, the code stores the current Rectangle to the *R* variable, and it uses this variable to access the properties of the Rectangle object (its width and height).

Of course, you can iterate a collection without the enumerator, but with a For Each…Next or For Each loop. To iterate through a HashTable, you can use either the Keys or Values collection. The code shown in Listing 12.9 populates a HashTable with Rectangle objects. Then it scans the items and prints their keys, which are strings, and the area of each rectangle. Note how it uses each item's Key property to access the corresponding item in the collection.

LISTING 12.9:   Iterating a HashTable with its keys

```
Dim hTable As New HashTable()
Dim r1 As New Rectangle(1, 1, 10, 10)
hTable.Add("R1", r1)
r1 = New Rectangle(2, 2, 20, 20)
hTable.Add("R2", r1)
hTable.add("R3", New Rectangle(3, 3, 2, 2))
Dim key As Object
Dim R As Rectangle
For Each key In hTable.keys
    R = CType(hTable(key), Rectangle)
    Debug.WriteLine(String.Format( _
            "The area of Rectangle {0} is {1}" _
            key.ToString, R.Width * R.Height))
Next
```

The code adds three Rectangle objects to the HashTable and then iterates through the collection using the Keys properties. Each item's key is a string (R1, R2, and R3). The Keys property is itself a collection and can be scanned with a For Each…Next loop. At each iteration, you access a different item through its key with the expression hTable(key). The output produced by this code is shown here:

```
The area of Rectangle R1 is 100
The area of Rectangle R3 is 4
The area of Rectangle R2 is 400
```

Alternatively, you can iterate a HashTable with an enumerator, but be aware that the GetEnumerator method of the HashTable collection returns an object of the IDictionary-Enumerator type, not an IEnumerator object. The IDictionaryEnumerator class is quite similar to the IEnumerator class, but it exposes additional properties. They are the Key and Value properties, and they return the current item's key and value. The IDictionaryEnumerator class also exposes the Entry property, which contains both the key and the value.

Assuming that you have populated the hTable collection with the same three Rectangle objects, you can use the statements in Listing 12.10 to iterate through the collection's items.

LISTING 12.10:   Iterating a HashTable with an enumerator

```
Dim hEnum As IDictionaryEnumerator
hEnum = hTable.GetEnumerator
While hEnum.MoveNext
   Debug.WriteLine(
           String.Format("The area of rectangle " &
           "{0} is {1}", hEnum.Key, _
           CType(hEnum.Value, Rectangle).Width *
           CType(hEnum.Value, Rectangle).Height))
End While
```

If you execute these statements after populating the HashTable collection with three Rectangles, they will produce the same output as Listing 12.8.

Custom Sorting

The Sort method of the various collections allows you to sort collections, as long as the items are of the same base data type. If the items are objects, however, the collection doesn't know how to sort them. If you want to sort objects, you must help the collection a little by telling it how to compare the objects. A sorting operation is nothing more than a series of comparisons. Sorting algorithms compare items and swap them if necessary.

All the information needed by a sorting algorithm to operate on an item of any type is a function that compares two objects of the same custom type. Let's say you have a list of persons, and each person is a structure that contains names, addresses, e-mail addresses, and so on. The System.Collections class can't make any assumptions as to how you want your list sorted, not to mention that a collection can be sorted by any field (name, e-address, postal code, and so on).

The comparer is implemented as a separate class, outside all other classes in the project, and is specific to a custom data type. Let's say you have created a custom structure for storing contact information. The Person object is declared as a structure with the following fields:

```
Structure Person
   Dim Name As String
   Dim BirthDate As Date
   Dim EMail As String
End Structure
```

You'll probably build a class to represent persons, but I'm using a structure to simplify the code. To add an instance of the Person object to a collection, create a variable of Person type, initialize its fields, and then add it to the appropriate collection (a List, or Dictionary collection, for example). This collection can't be sorted with the simple forms of the Sort method because the compiler doesn't know how to compare two Person objects. You must provide your own function for comparing two variables of the Person type. After this function is written, the compiler can call it to compare items and therefore sort the collection. This custom function, however, can't be passed to the Sort and BinarySearch methods by name. You must create a new class that implements the IComparer interface and pass an instance of this class to the two methods.

IMPLEMENTING THE ICOMPARER INTERFACE

Here's the outline of a class that implements the IComparer interface:

```
Class customComparer : Implements IComparer
    Public Function Compare(
              ByVal o1 As Object, ByVal o2 As Object)
              As Integer Implements IComparer.Compare
        { function's code }
    End Function
End Class
```

The name of the class can be anything; I'm using the name *customComparer* to indicate that the class compares custom types. It should be a name that indicates the type of comparison it performs or the type of objects it compares. After the class declaration, you must specify the interface implemented by the class. As soon as you type the first line of the preceding code segment, the editor will insert automatically the stub of the Compare() function. That's because every class that implements the IComparer interface must provide a Compare method with the specific signature. The interface declares a placeholder for a function, whose code must be provided by the developer.

To use the custom function to compare items, you must create an object of the customComparer type (or whatever you have named the class) and then pass it to the Sort and BinarySearch methods as an argument:

```
Dim CompareThem As New customComparer
aList.Sort(CompareThem)
```

You can combine the two statements in one by initializing the *customComparer* variable in the line that calls the Sort method:

```
aList.Sort(New customComparer)
```

You can also use the equivalent syntax of the BinarySearch method to locate a custom object that implements its own IComparer interface:

```
aList.BinarySearch(object, New customComparer)
```

This is how you can use a custom function to compare two objects. Everything is the same, except for the name of the comparer, which is different every time.

The last step is to implement the function that compares the two objects and returns an integer value, indicating the order of the elements. This value should be −1 if the first object is smaller than the second object, 0 if the two objects are equal, and 1 if the first object is larger than the second object. *Smaller* here means that the element appears before the larger one when sorted in ascending order. Listing 12.11 is the function that sorts Person objects according to the BirthDate field. The sample code for this and the following section comes from the CustomComparer project (available for download from www.sybex.com/go/masteringvb2010). The main form contains a single button, which populates the collection and then prints the original collection, the collection sorted by name, and the collection sorted by birth date.

LISTING 12.11:   A custom comparer

```
Class PersonAgeComparer : Implements IComparer
  Public Function Compare(
      ByVal o1 As Object, ByVal o2 As Object)
      As Integer Implements IComparer.Compare
    Dim person1, person2 As Person
    Try
        person1 = CType(o1, Person)
        person2 = CType(o2, Person)
    Catch compareException As system.Exception
        Throw (compareException)
        Exit Function
    End Try
    If person1.BirthDate < person2.BirthDate Then
        Return -1
    Else
        If person1.BirthDate > person2.BirthDate Then
            Return 1
        Else
            Return 0
        End If
    End If
  End Function
End Class
```

The code could have been considerably simpler, but I'll explain momentarily why the Try statement is necessary. The comparison takes place in the If statement. If the first person's birth date is chronologically earlier than the second person's, the function returns the value −1. If the first person's birth date is chronologically later than the second person's birth date, the function returns 1. Finally, if the two values are equal, the function returns 0.

The code is straightforward, so why the error-trapping code? Before you perform the necessary comparisons, you convert the two objects into Person objects. It's not unthinkable that the collection with the objects you want to sort contains objects of different types. If that's the case, the CType() function won't be able to convert the corresponding argument to the Person type,

THE IENUMERATOR AND ICOMPARER INTERFACES

and the comparison will fail. The same exception that would be thrown in the function's code is raised again from within the error handler, and it's passed back to the calling code.

IMPLEMENTING MULTIPLE COMPARERS

Person objects can be sorted in many ways. You might want to sort them by ID, name, age, and so on. To accommodate multiple sorts, you must implement several classes, each one with a different implementation of the Compare() function. Listing 12.12 shows two classes that implement two different Compare() functions for the Person class. The PersonNameComparer class compares the names, whereas the PersonAgeComparer class compares the ages. Both classes, however, implement the IComparer interface.

LISTING 12.12:   A class with two custom comparers

```
Class PersonNameComparer : Implements IComparer
  Public Function Compare(
           ByVal o1 As Object, ByVal o2 As Object)
           As Integer Implements IComparer.Compare
     Dim person1, person2 As Person
     Try
         person1 = CType(o1, Person)
         person2 = CType(o2, Person)
     Catch compareException As system.Exception
         Throw (compareException)
         Exit Function
     End Try
     If person1.Name < person2.Name Then
         Return -1
     Else
         If person1.Name > person2.Name Then
             Return 1
         Else
             Return 0
         End If
     End If
  End Function
End Class

Class PersonAgeComparer : Implements IComparer
  Public Function Compare(
           ByVal o1 As Object, ByVal o2 As Object)
           As Integer Implements IComparer.Compare
     Dim person1, person2 As Person
     Try
         person1 = CType(o1, Person)
         person2 = CType(o2, Person)
     Catch compareException As system.Exception
         Throw (compareException)
```

```
            Exit Function
        End Try
        If person1.BDate > person2.BDate Then
            Return -1
        Else
            If person1.BDate < person2.BDate Then
                Return 1
            Else
                Return 0
            End If
        End If
    End Function
End Class
```

To test the custom comparers, create a new application, and enter the code of Listing 12.12 (it contains two classes) in a separate Class module. Don't forget to include the declaration of the Person structure. Then place a button on the form and enter the code of Listing 12.13 in its Click event handler. This code adds three persons with different names and birth dates to a List collection.

LISTING 12.13: Testing the custom comparers

```
Private Sub Button1_Click(...) Handles Button1.Click
    Dim Lst As New List()
    Dim p As Person
    ' Populate collection
    p.Name = "C Person"
    p.EMail = "PersonC@sybex.com"
    p.BDate = #1/1/1961#
    If Not Lst.Contains(p) Then Lst.Add(p)
    p.Name = "A Person"
    p.EMail = "PersonA@sybex.com"
    p.BDate = #3/3/1961#
    If Not Lst.Contains(p) Then Lst.Add(p)
    p.Name = "B Person"
    p.EMail = "PersonB@sybex.com"
    p.BDate = #2/2/1961#
    If Not Lst.Contains(p) Then Lst.Add(p)
    ' Print collection as is
    Dim PEnum As IEnumerator
    PEnum = Lst.GetEnumerator
    ListBox1.Items.Add("Original Collection")
    While PEnum.MoveNext
        ListBox1.Items.Add(
            CType(PEnum.Current, Person).Name &
            vbTab & CType(PEnum.Current, Person).BDate)
    End While
    ' Sort by name, then print collection
```

```
    ListBox1.Items.Add(" ")
    ListBox1.Items.Add("Collection Sorted by Name")
    Lst.Sort(New PersonNameComparer())
    PEnum = Lst.GetEnumerator
    While PEnum.MoveNext
        ListBox1.Items.Add(
            CType(PEnum.Current, Person).Name &
            vbTab & CType(PEnum.Current, Person).BDate)
    End While
    ' Sort by age, then print collection
    ListBox1.Items.Add(" ")
    ListBox1.Items.Add("Collection Sorted by Age")
    Lst.Sort(New PersonAgeComparer())
    PEnum = Lst.GetEnumerator
    While PEnum.MoveNext
        ListBox1.Items.Add(
            CType(PEnum.Current, Person).Name &
            vbTab & CType(PEnum.Current, Person).BDate)
    End While
End Sub
```

The four sections of the code are delimited by comments in the listing. The first section populates the collection with three variables of the Person type. The second section prints the items in the order in which they were added to the collection:

```
C Person    1/1/1961
A Person    3/3/1961
B Person    2/2/1961
```

The third section of the code calls the Sort method, passing the PersonNameComparer custom comparer as an argument, and it again prints the contents of the List. The names are listed now in alphabetical order:

```
A Person    3/3/1961
B Person    2/2/1961
C Person    1/1/1961
```

In the last section, it calls the Sort method again — this time to sort the items by age — and prints them:

```
C Person    1/1/1961
B Person    2/2/1961
A Person    3/3/1961
```

It is straightforward to write your own custom comparers and sort your custom object in any way that suits your application. Custom comparisons might include more complicated calculations, not just comparisons. For example, you can sort Rectangles by their area, color values by their hue or saturation, and customers by the frequency of their orders.

The Bottom Line

Make the most of arrays.   The simplest method of storing sets of data is to use arrays. They're very efficient, and they provide methods to perform advanced operations such as sorting and searching their elements. Use the `Sort` method of the Array class to sort an array's elements. To search for an element in an array, use the `IndexOf` and `LastIndexOf` methods, or use the `BinarySearch` method if the array is sorted. The `BinarySearch` method always returns an element's index, which is a positive value for *exact matches* and a negative value for *near matches*.

   Master It   Explain how you can search an array and find exact and near matches.

Store data in collections such as List and Dictionary collections.   In addition to arrays, the Framework provides collections, which are dynamic data structures. The most commonly used collections are the List and the Dictionary. Collections are similar to arrays, but they're dynamic structures. List and ArrayList collections store lists of items, whereas Dictionary and HashTable collections store key-value pairs and allow you to access their elements via a key. You can add elements by using the `Add` method and remove existing elements by using the `Remove` and `RemoveAt` methods.

Dictionary collections provide the `ContainsKey` and `ContainsValue` methods to find out whether the collection already contains a specific key or value as well as the `GetKeys` and `GetValues` methods to retrieve all the keys and values from the collection, respectively. As a reminder, the List and Dictionary collections are strongly typed. Their untyped counterparts are the ArrayList and HashTable collections.

   Master It   How will you populate a Dictionary with a few pairs of keys/values and then iterate though the collection's items?

Sort and search collections with custom comparers.   Collections provide the `Sort` method for sorting their items and several methods to locate items: `IndexOf`, `LastIndexOf`, and `BinarySearch`. Both sort and search operations are based on comparisons, and the Framework knows how to compare values' types only (Integers, Strings, and the other primitive data types). If a collection contains objects, you must provide a custom function that knows how to compare two objects of the same type.

   Master It   How do you specify a custom comparer function for a collection that contains Rectangle objects?

Chapter 13

XML in Modern Programming

XML has gained so much in popularity and acceptance that Microsoft has decided to promote XML to a basic data type. Yes, XML is a data type like integers and strings! To understand how far VB has taken XML, type the following in a procedure or event handler:

```
Dim products = <Books>
<Book ISBN="0000000000001">
  <Title>Book Title 1</Title>
  <Price>11.95</Price>
</Book>
<Book ISBN="000000000002">
    <Title>Book Title 2</Title>
    <Price>10.25</Price>
  </Book>
</Books>
```

You need not worry too much about getting the document exactly right, because the Visual Studio's editor works just like the XML editor. Every time you type an opening tag, it inserts the matching closing tag and ensures that what you're typing is a valid XML document.

The language has been extended to support XML with features that bridge the gap between VB programming and XML, and XML has become a "first-class citizen" of the Framework. As you will see in this and the following chapter, manipulating XML documents from within your VB application is simpler than ever before. If you haven't used the DOM object in the past to manipulate XML documents, rest assured that the new tools make this task as straightforward as it can be for VB developers. In this chapter, you'll find an introduction to the topic of XML (for readers who are not yet familiar with XML) and the classes that allow you to manipulate XML with VB code.

In this chapter, you'll learn how to do the following:

◆ Create XML documents

◆ Navigate through an XML document and locate the information you need

◆ Convert arbitrary objects into XML documents and back with serialization

A Very Quick Introduction to XML

Let's start with a quick overview of XML, which will serve as an introduction to XML for some readers and a quick summary for those familiar with XML at large. To experiment with XML files, you can start a new project in Visual Studio and add a new XML file to the project. When the file is opened in edit mode, you can enter the code samples shown in this chapter. Figure 13.1 shows an XML document open in Visual Studio (it's a file you'll create later in this chapter). Notice that you can collapse segments of the XML tree just as you would collapse parts of VB code.

FIGURE 13.1
Editing XML files in
Visual Studio

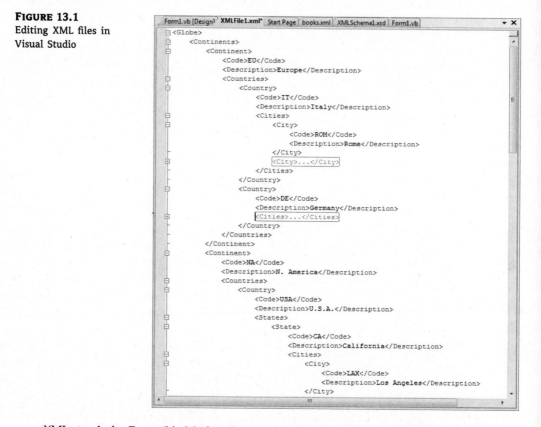

XML stands for Extensible Markup Language and is as much of a language as HTML is. Neither of them is actually a language, though; they're called *declarative languages,* and in reality they're formats, or specifications, for storing and transferring structured data. I'm sure you all know by now what XML is and what it looks like, so let's start exploring its structure and the rules for formulating valid XML documents.

XML documents consist of *elements,* which are the information items you store for a particular entity. Elements are delimited by a keyword embedded in angle brackets. This keyword is called a *tag,* and tags always appear in pairs: The opening and closing tags delimit an element of the document. Each element has a value, which appears between two tags. The Name element, for example, is delimited by the opening tag <Name> and the closing tag </Name>. The closing tag is identical to the opening tag, except for the backslash in front of the tag's name. The element's value can be a string, a number, or a date, as in the following XML segments. It's also valid for an element to have no value at all. The following XML segment describes salary data for a person whose SSN is not known at the time.

```
<Name>Richard Manning</Name>
<Rate>39.95</Rate>
<BirthDate>1982-08-14</BirthDate>
<SSN></SSN>
```

The preceding elements have simple values. It just so happens that Richard's social security number was not known at the time (it has an empty value). An element may also contain a sequence of elements, as in the following:

```
<Name>
    <First>Richard</First>
    <Last>Manning</Last>
</Name>
<BirthDate>1982-08-14</BirthDate>
<Rate>
    <Type>Hourly</Type>
    <Amount>39.95</Amount>
</Rate>
```

The Name element here contains two elements, each one with their own value. Here are the first two rules about XML authoring:

Tags are case sensitive, and they always appear in pairs. It goes without saying that the tags must be properly nested; otherwise, the document wouldn't have a structure.

VB developers should be especially careful about the first rule, because their favorite language has never had issues with character casing. When you work with XML, you must pay attention to case because <Name> and <name> are two totally different tags.

ENTITY REFERENCES

Some characters have a special meaning in XML, and the symbols < and > are two of them. These characters may not appear as part of an element's name, or value, because it will throw off the compiler. These characters must be replaced by a special string, known as an *entity reference*. The following table shows the characters that have special meaning in XML and the corresponding entity references:

< (less than)	&lt;
> (greater than)	&gt;
& (ampersand)	&amp;
' (apostrophe)	&apos;
" (quotation mark)	&quot;

Actually, only two of these symbols are strictly illegal in XML (the < and & symbols), but it's quite common to escape all five symbols.

In addition to values, elements may have attributes, too. Attributes belong to specific elements, and they appear in the element's opening tag, as follows:

```
<Book ISBN = "978001234567">
```

The Book element has an ISBN attribute with the value specified with the string following the equals sign. And here's the third rule about XML:

All attribute values must be enclosed in quotes.

You can also insert multiple attributes into an element by placing the elements next to one another:

```
< Book ISBN = "978001234567" Publisher = "SYBEX">
<Person LastName = "Doe" FirstName = "Joe" SSN = "555-00-1234">
```

Because elements many contain attributes, which are specified by name, you can't use spaces in an element name. If you do, the compiler will think that the second word is the name of an attribute, not followed by its value. In fact, most XML editors will automatically insert the equals sign followed by two quotes to indicate an attribute without a value.

The value of an element is inserted between its opening and closing tags, and it may (and usually does) contain additional elements. Here's another way to express the preceding Person element:

```
<Person>
    <Last>Doe</Last>
    <First>Joe</First>
    <SSN>555-00-1234</SSN>
</Person>
```

There's no clear-cut distinction as to when you should use elements and when you should use attributes, but you usually store information that identifies the element as attributes and the details of the element as its value. Consider the following typical examples of XML segments with attributes:

```
<Hotel ID = "STR001">
    <HotelName>Hotel of the Stars</HotelName>
    <Rating ID = "3">3 Stars</Rating>
    <Address> address details </Address>
</Hotel>
```

```
<Book ISBN="1234567890">
    <Title>Mastering XML Internals</Title>
    <Publisher ID="323">XMLers Int'l.</Publisher>
    <Authors>
        <Author>J. Element</Author>
        <Author>J. Attribute</Author>
    </Authors>
</Book>
```

```
<Country Code = "IT" Name = "Italy">
    <City Code = "MIL" Name = Milan" />
    <City Code = "ROM" Name = Rome" />
    . . . more cities under Italy
</Country>
<Country Code = "FR" Name = "France">
    <City Code = "PRS" Name = Paris" />
    <City Code = "LYN" Name = Lyon" />
    . . . more cities under France
</Country>

<Employee SSN = "55 22 9999" Sex="M" Status = "Single">
    <Name>Peter Evans</Name>
    <Position>Finance Director</Position>
    <HiredOn>7/15/1989</HiredOn>
</Employee>
```

More often than not, you will see XML documents made up entirely out of elements, without any attributes. You will also see XML documents made up of one element per entity and attributes for all of their properties. Once you understand the nature of XML and you are ready to create your own XML documents, you'll have a good feeling about elements and attributes. It's much more important to properly nest elements to keep relevant information under the same root element than worrying about whether a specific item should be defined as an attribute or an element.

It's also possible for an element to contain one or more attributes, but no value. For these special cases, there's a shorthand notation for avoiding the closing tag: You just insert the back-slash character before the opening element's closing angle bracket. The following element

```
<Product ProductID="39"
        Name="Chartreuse verte" Price="18.50" >
</Product>
```

can also be written as follows:

```
<Product ProductID="39"
        Product="Chartreuse verte" Price="18.50" />
```

The line breaks were introduced to help you read the XML segment, they're not mandatory, and they're not taken into consideration when processing an XML document, just like white space in HTML. If the spaces (tabs, line feeds, and multiple spaces) appear in an element's value, they will be preserved.

As you can see in the few examples so far, XML is just plain text that can be safely exchanged between computers using the HTTP stack. As you probably know, XML is used just about everywhere today, but in its roots it remains a simple data exchange protocol. You can think of the tags as delimiters that separate items of information. It's actually the very fact that the delimiters are specified by the user and that they can be nested that made XML so powerful and suitable for all types of information. XML delimiters are unusual in the sense that they appear before and after each data item, and they occur in pairs: the opening and closing tags. The closing tag is always the same as the opening tag, prefixed with a backslash. The most important aspect of XML, though, is that you can specify the delimiters and their structure: You determine the names of the elements, and you're allowed to nest them so that they reflect the structure, or hierarchy, of the information. The fact that XML tags have meaningful names is a major convenience, but words like *book*, *author*, *country*, and so on, are not especially meaningful to computers. They help you understand the data stored in the file and write code to extract the items of information you're interested in, but no software will process XML documents automatically.

XML Schema

For an XML document to be meaningful and useful to others, you must use element and attribute names consistently. Even though it's possible to use sometimes the <Last> element and other times the <LastName> element, the resulting XML document will be practically unusable. Before you start writing an XML document, you must decide on the names of the elements in it and use them consistently. The structure of the document, along with the names of the elements and attributes, is referred to as the document *schema*. The schema of the document is another XML document. To get a feel for XML schemas and how they used, start a new VB project in Visual Studio, and add a new XML file to the solution (just right-click the project's name, and select Add ➤ New Item; in the dialog box that appears, select the XML File option). The new XML file will contain the following statement, which identifies a file as an XML document (oddly, this tag that begins with the question mark doesn't require a closing tag; it identifies the file as an XML document.):

```
<?xml version="1.0" encoding="utf-8" ?>
```

Then enter the XML document shown in Listing 13.1 in the file, following the initial tag. The document is a short segment of a report from the Northwind database, and you will find it in the NWProducts.xml file in this chapter's folder.

LISTING 13.1:   An XML document with products, organized by category and supplier

```
<Categories_Products>
    <Category CategoryID="1" Category="Beverages">
        <Supplier Supplier="Aux joyeux ecclésiastiques">
            <Product ProductID="39"
                     Product="Chartreuse verte" Price="18.0000" />
            <Product ProductID="38"
                     Product="Côte de Blaye" Price="263.5000" />
        </Supplier>
        <Supplier Supplier="Bigfoot Breweries">
            <Product ProductID="34"
                     Product="Sasquatch Ale" Price="14.0000" />
            <Product ProductID="35"
                     Product="Steeleye Stout" Price="18.0000" />
        </Supplier>
    </Category>
        <Category CategoryID="2" Category="Condiments">
```

```
        <Supplier Supplier="Exotic Liquids">
            <Product ProductID="3"
                    Product="Aniseed Syrup" Price="10.0000" />
        </Supplier>
        <Supplier Supplier="Forêts d'érables">
            <Product ProductID="61"
             Product="Sirop d'érable" Price="28.5000" />
        </Supplier>
    </Category>
</Categories_Products>
```

Now open the XML menu, and select the Create Schema command. Visual Studio will create a schema that matches the XML document and will open it in a new window. Listing 13.2 shows the schema of the preceding XML document.

LISTING 13.2:   The schema of the XML document of Listing 31.1

```
<?xml version="1.0" encoding="utf-8"?>
<xs:schema attributeFormDefault="unqualified" elementFormDefault="qualified"
xmlns:xs="http://www.w3.org/2001/XMLSchema">
    <xs:element name="Categories_Products">
        <xs:complexType>
            <xs:sequence>
                <xs:element maxOccurs="unbounded" name="Category">
                    <xs:complexType>
                        <xs:sequence>
                            <xs:element maxOccurs="unbounded" name="Supplier">
                                <xs:complexType>
                                    <xs:sequence>
                                        <xs:element maxOccurs="unbounded"
                                                name="Product">
                                            <xs:complexType>
                                                <xs:attribute
                                                    name="ProductID"
                                                    type="xs:unsignedByte"
                                                    use="required" />
                                                <xs:attribute name="Product"
                                                    type="xs:string"
                                                    use="required" />
                                                <xs:attribute name="Price"
                                                    type="xs:decimal"
                                                    use="required" />
                                            </xs:complexType>
                                        </xs:element>
                                    </xs:sequence>
                                    <xs:attribute
```

```
                                       name="Supplier"
                                       type="xs:string"
                                       use="required" />
                        </xs:complexType>
                     </xs:element>
                  </xs:sequence>
                  <xs:attribute name="CategoryID"
                                type="xs:unsignedByte"
                                use="required" />
                  <xs:attribute name="Category"
                                type="xs:string" use="required" />
               </xs:complexType>
            </xs:element>
         </xs:sequence>
      </xs:complexType>
   </xs:element>
</xs:schema>
```

The automatically generated schema is stored in a file with the same name as the XML document and the extension .xsd. Designing a schema is not a simple task, but there are tools to assist you. The most important aspect of the schema is that it can be applied to an XML document and help you make sure that the document follows its design guidelines. The editor will do its best to decipher the schema of a document based on the data at hand, but the schema may not describe another document with similar data. The *use* property of the schema, for example, is always required, because all attributes in the XML segment have a value. If one of the elements didn't have a Price attribute, for example, then the *use* property of the Price attribute would be optional.

Now, switch back to the XML document, and look up its Schemas property in the Properties window. You will see that the file you just created has been applied to the document. If not, click the button next to the Schemas property, and you will see the XML Schemas dialog box, shown in Figure 13.2. Click the Add button, and locate the newly generated XSD file in the project's folder. Open the drop-down list in the Use column, select Use This Schema to apply the newly added schema to the document, and then click OK to close the dialog box. The schema will be applied to the XML document, and any elements or attributes in the document that don't comply with the schema will be highlighted. Of course, because the schema was generated for the specific document, no errors will be found, but this is the purpose of the schema validation: to locate any items that do comply with the specified schema. If you edit the document, the editor will not allow you to deviate from the document's schema.

If you edit the XML document now, the editor will assist you in creating a valid XML document that complies with its schema. The proper elements at each place in the document will appear in the usual IntelliSense drop-down list as you type. When you type the opening angle bracket, the editor will suggest the valid element names (actually it will display only the first element name; the second time it will suggest the second element name, and so on). If you select an element name and then type a space, the editor will suggest the attribute names, as shown in Figure 13.3. In general, the built-in XML editor of Visual Studio will assist you as best as it can in creating XML documents and will make sure they comply with the specified schema.

FIGURE 13.2
Selecting and applying a schema to an XML document

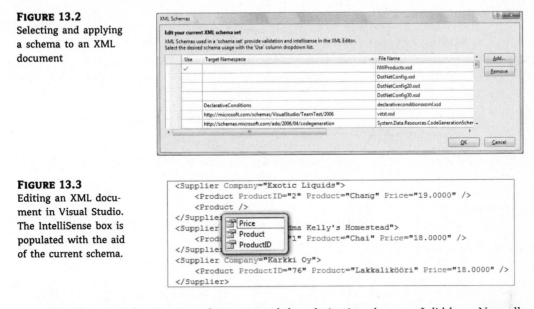

FIGURE 13.3
Editing an XML document in Visual Studio. The IntelliSense box is populated with the aid of the current schema.

```
<Supplier Company="Exotic Liquids">
    <Product ProductID="2" Product="Chang" Price="19.0000" />
    <Product />
</Supplier>
<Supplier          ma Kelly's Homestead">
    <Prod          "1" Product="Chai" Price="18.0000" />
</Supplier>
<Supplier Company="Karkki Oy">
    <Product ProductID="76" Product="Lakkalikööri" Price="18.0000" />
</Supplier>
```

Of course, you don't create a document and then derive its schema as I did here. Normally, when you're asked to produce an XML document, you'll be given a schema. If you're the document designer, you'll have to produce the schema too. One very useful tool for automating schema generation is SQL Server. It's possible to retrieve the results of a SQL query in XML format, and the output may include not only the data, but the schema itself. Actually, this is how I created the sample document NWProducts.xml. If you're curious about schemas and the related keywords, add a new XML Schema item to the project (with the project's Add ➤ New Item command), and start editing it. The editor will suggest the valid tags at each step, and you'll be able to create a simple schema without knowing anything about them. How does the editor know about XSD? Well, it's all in the schema! XSD has its own schema, which is stored in the xsdschema.xsd file that comes with Visual Studio. Isn't XML fun<?>

Numbers and Dates in XML

Besides strings, element values can be numeric values or dates. The basic numeric data type in XML is the Decimal type, but XML supports all the usual numeric types, including floats, short/long/signed/unsigned integers, and so on. There's also a Boolean data type, whose value is "true" or "false" (not 0/1, not TRUE/FALSE — just the values shown with that exact spelling).

Dates are quite tricky. An XML document can be created anywhere, and dates do not obey a specific locale. That's true of any document that contains dates, but XML addresses this issue elegantly. Consider the following XML segment that has a different meaning in the United States than in the United Kingdom:

```
<Date>
4/9/2011
</Date>
```

This segment would present perfectly clear, if different, information to users in the United States and in the United Kingdom; the US reading would be April 9, 2011, while the UK reading would be 4 September 2011. If that cultural understanding of the format causes a user to enter day information in the month position and the value exceeds 12, then the date would be invalid. To address the issue of dates, XML supports the Date, Time, and DateTime data types. The Date data type specifies dates with the unambiguous format YYYY-MM-DD. The Time data type specifies times with the format HH:MM:SS. You can optionally append the time's milliseconds. Here are some examples of Time values:

```
<start>09:05:32</start>
<start>17:11:45.510</start>
```

Time values are rather uncommon on their own; you'll usually combine date and time information in a DateTime value. DateTime values are Date and Time values separated by the T character:

```
<startdate>2011-09-04T09:30:10</startdate>
```

Another time-related issue is that of the time zone. If you're processing an XML document generated in a different time zone, you should be able to take the time difference into consideration. If you request that a response arrive within four hours, for example, you should be able to convert the time specified in the document into local time. The time zone is specified with the + or − sign followed by a number of hours and, optionally, minutes. The time zones are usually hours apart, but there are a few exceptions (Newfoundland is 3.5 hours behind GMT). Alternatively, you can append a Z character followed by the UTC time. Here are a few DateTime values that include time zone information:

```
<startdate>2011-09-04T09:30:10-06:00</startdate>
<startdate>2011-09-04T09:30:10Z</startdate>
```

The first example refers to 9:30:10 in the Central time zone in the United States (six hours behind the GMT time). The second example refers to 9:30:10 GMT time. If you're exchanging XML files that include time information with users in different time zones, you should include the time zone to make them unambiguous.

Manipulating XML with VB

You have seen the basics of generating XML documents from scratch (and in the second half of this chapter you'll see how to convert your custom objects into XML documents), and you've seen that you can create valid XML documents easily with the help of Visual Studio's XML editor. But what good is an XML document without some tools to extract information from it? You will need some simple tools for creating and manipulating XML documents from within VB code, and these tools are available through the following XML helper classes:

◆ XDocument represents the XML document.

◆ XComment represents a comment in the XML document.

◆ XElement represents an XML element.

◆ XAttribute represents an attribute in an XML element.

You can use these classes to access the document but also to create it from within your code. Instead of embedding an XML document directly in your code, you can use the XML helper classes and a structural approach to create the same document from within your code. To create a new XElement object, pass the element's name and value to its constructor:

```
New XElement(element_name, element_value)
```

The following statement will create a very simple XML document:

```
Dim XmlDoc = New XElement("Books")
MsgBox(XmlDoc.ToString)
```

You will see the string <Books /> in a message box. This is a trivial, yet valid, XML document. To create an XML segment with books by using the helper classes, insert the statements from Listing 13.3 in a button Click event handler.

LISTING 13.3:   A simple XElement describing a collection of books

```
Dim doc = _
    New XElement("Books", _
        New XElement("Book", _
            New XAttribute("ISBN", "0000000000001"), _
            New XElement("Price", 11.95), _
            New XElement("Title", "Book Title 1"), _
            New XElement("Stock", _
                New XAttribute("InStock", 12), _
                New XAttribute("OnOrder", 24))), _
        New XElement("Book", _
            New XAttribute("ISBN", "0000000000002"), _
            New XElement("Price", 10.25), _
            New XElement("Title", "Book Title 2"), _
            New XElement("Stock", _
                New XAttribute("InStock", 7), _
                New XAttribute("OnOrder", 10))))
```

I've added a twist to this new document to demonstrate the use of multiple attributes in the same element. The Stock element contains two attributes, InStock and OnOrder. The Price element is a decimal value, and the Title element is a string. The Book element, however, contains three subelements: the Price, Title, and Stock elements.

If you look at the code of Listing 13.3 and ignore the XElement and XAttribute items, the code looks a lot like the document we're constructing. This type of construction is called *functional construction*, because the code is very similar to the XML document we have in mind. If you haven't worked with XML in the past, the functional construction (or functional composition) approach to building XML documents is an enormous improvement over the tools VB programmers had to use until very recently. If you haven't been exposed to XML before, you'll probably think it's typical VB. But wait, it gets even better.

XML as a Data Type

The functional composition of an XML document resembles the actual document you're creating, but the Visual Basic editor can do even better. You can create an XML document and assign it to an XElement variable with a statement like the one shown in Listing 13.4.

LISTING 13.4:   The document of Listing 13.3 created explicitly

```
Dim xDoc = _
            <Books>
                <Book ISBN="0000000000001">
                    <Price>11.95</Price>
                    <Title>Book Title 1</Title>
                    <Stock InStock="12" OnOrder="24"/>
                </Book>
                <Book ISBN="0000000000002">
                    <Price>10.25</Price>
                    <Title>Book Title 2</Title>
                    <Stock> InStock="7" OnOrder="10"/>
                </Book
            </Books>
```

As soon as you type the first opening angle bracket, the editor will switch to XML mode and will assist you by inserting the matching closing tags and by indenting the document for you. The two methods of creating XML documents with VB are demonstrated in Figure 13.4.

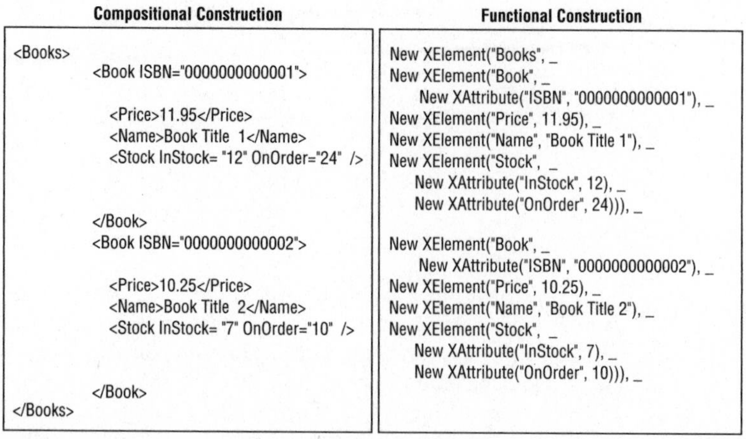

FIGURE 13.4
The two methods for creating XML segments in Visual Studio

```
Compositional Construction

<Books>
        <Book ISBN="0000000000001">

            <Price>11.95</Price>
            <Name>Book Title 1</Name>
            <Stock InStock= "12" OnOrder="24" />

        </Book>
        <Book ISBN="0000000000002">

            <Price>10.25</Price>
            <Name>Book Title 2</Name>
            <Stock InStock= "7" OnOrder="10" />

        </Book>
</Books>
```

```
Functional Construction

New XElement("Books", _
New XElement("Book", _
    New XAttribute("ISBN", "0000000000001"), _
New XElement("Price", 11.95), _
New XElement("Name", "Book Title 1"), _
New XElement("Stock", _
    New XAttribute("InStock", 12), _
    New XAttribute("OnOrder", 24))), _

New XElement("Book", _
    New XAttribute("ISBN", "0000000000002"), _
New XElement("Price", 10.25), _
New XElement("Name", "Book Title 2"), _
New XElement("Stock", _
    New XAttribute("InStock", 7), _
    New XAttribute("OnOrder", 10))), _
```

The XML document you create in-line is not an island, entirely isolated from the rest of the code. You can embed VB expressions right into the XML document, and these expressions will be replaced with their values at runtime. To embed an expression in an XML document, use the special tags <%= and %> (yes, the same tags we used with ASP 1.0 to mix HTML and VBScript code). Here's the same document with the prices replaced by embedded expressions:

```
Dim price1 As Decimal = 11.95
Dim price2 As Decimal = 10.25
Dim xDoc = _
            <Books>
                <Book ISBN="0000000000001">
                    <Price><%= price1 %></Price>
                    <Title>Book Title 1</Title>
                    <Stock InStock="12" OnOrder="24"/>
                </Book>
                <Book ISBN="0000000000002">
                    <Price><%= price2 %></Price>
                    <Title>Book Title 2</Title>
                    <Stock> InStock="7" OnOrder="10"/>
                </Book>
            </Books>
```

The prices need not be hard-coded in variables. You can call a function to retrieve them from a database based on the book's ISBN. You can use other simple VB expressions to insert the current date into your document, call built-in functions, and so on. However, you can't embed large segments of code with conditional or looping statements (you'll see how this can be done with LINQ in the next chapter).

The following XML segment generates an XML segment with the parameters of a loan. The loan parameters are specified with the help of variables, but the actual monthly payment is calculated with a call to the Pmt() function right from within the XML code. The tag <%= switches you to VB, and the %> tag switches you back to XML.

```
Dim loanAmount As Decimal = 135000
Dim loanInterest As Decimal = 8.75
Dim loanDuration = 6
Dim loanXML = <Loan>
                    <Amount><%= loanAmount %></Amount>
                    <Duration><%= loanDuration %>6</Duration>
                    <DurationUnit>Years</DurationUnit>
                    <Interest><%= loanInterest %></Interest>
                    <Payment><%= Financial.Pmt( loanInterest / 10 * 12, _
                                        loanDuration * 12, loanAmount) %>
                    </Payment>
                </Loan>
MsgBox(loanXML)
```

If you execute the preceding statements, they will print the following XML document on a message box:

```
<Loan>
    <Amount>135000</Amount>
    <Duration>6</Duration>
    <DurationUnit>Years</DurationUnit>
    <Interest>8.75</Interest>
    <Payment>2,416.73</Payment>
</Loan>
```

The embedded expression calls a financial function, the `Pmt()` function, to calculate the loan's payment. The result is even formatted appropriately by calling the `ToString` method of the Double data type (the `Pmt()` function returns a Double, as was discussed in Chapter 1, "Getting Started with Visual Basic 2010").

Saving and Loading XML Documents

The variable that holds an XML segment is of the XElement type. An XML document is not necessarily based on the XDocument class. The two basic operations you can perform with an XElement (and XDocument) object are saving a file and reloading an XElement object from a file. The operations are performed with the `Save` and `Load` methods, which accept the filename as an argument.

The following statements will save an XML document to a file and then open it with the default application, which on most computers is Internet Explorer, as shown in Figure 13.5. If you have associated XML extensions with another application, then the document will open in that application (it could be Visual Studio or any other XML editor you have installed on your computer).

```
XElement.Save(file_name)
Process.Start(file_name)
```

FIGURE 13.5
Viewing an XML document in your browser

To load the contents of a file to an XElement variable, use the Load method, which accepts as an argument the name of the file:

```
Dim XDoc = XElement.Load(file_name)
```

One more related method is the Parse method, which allows you to load an XElement variable from a string. As the code in Listing 13.4 should have convinced you, there's no reason to ever create strings with XML data in your code. You may retrieve an existing XML document as a string. In this case, you can just pass the string to the Parse method to create an XML tree and process it with the techniques discussed in this chapter. The Parse method accepts a string as an argument and returns an XElement object:

```
Dim XDoc = XElement.Parse(xml_string)
```

Traversing XML Documents

Let's look at how you can process an XML document using XML helper objects. Processing XML consists of navigating to the items of interest in the document, extracting element and attribute values, and editing the contents of an existing XML document.

The basic methods for navigating through an XML document are known as *axis methods* (they allow you to quickly move to any part of the document, just as you can describe any point in the space with the help of the x-, y-, and z-axes). Let me start the discussion of the axis methods by making it clear that *all axis methods are relevant to the current position in the XML tree.* If you request the immediate descendant of a continent, for example, you'll get a country element, not a city. If you're currently on a country element, the same method will return a city element.

The *Element* and *Elements* Methods

The Element method allows you to locate an element by name. This method returns the first XElement segment by the name specified as an argument to the method, if such an element exists under the current element. The Elements method is similar, only instead of the first matching element, it returns all matching elements. Note that while the Element method returns an XElement object, the Elements method returns a collection of XElement objects (actually, an IEnumerable of XElement objects).

Ancestors and *Descendants* Methods

Each element may have one or more parent elements, which you can access via the Ancestors property, and one or more child elements, which you can access via the Descendants property. Both methods return a collection of XElement objects. To retrieve the desired child or parent elements, you must pass to the method the name of the desired element. The following expression will return all Book elements in the sample document:

```
xDoc.Descendants("Book")
```

If you call the Descendants method without an argument, it will return all nodes under the current element. I will demonstrate the use of the Elements and Descendants methods and their differences through sample code shortly.

Attribute Property

In addition, elements may have attributes, which you can access via the Attribute property. The Attribute method applies to an XElement node in the document and extracts the value of the attribute whose name you pass to the method as an argument.

Let's write a loop to iterate through our simple collection of books which are in the *xDoc* variable:

```
For Each book In xDoc.Elements("Book")
    Debug.WriteLine("ISBN " & book.Attribute("ISBN").Value.ToString)
    Debug.WriteLine("   Title: " & book.Element("Name").Value.ToString)
    Debug.WriteLine("   Price: " & book.Element("Price").Value.ToString)
    Dim stock = book.Element("Stock")
    Debug.WriteLine("      Books in stock " & stock.Attribute("InStock").Value)
    Debug.WriteLine("      Books on order " & stock.Attribute("OnOrder").Value)
Next
```

The loop iterates through the Book elements in the XML file. The expression xDoc.Elements ("Book") returns a collection of XElement objects, each one representing a book. We then call the Attribute method of each Book element to access the element's attributes by name. The Descendants method returns a collection of XElement objects, one for each subelement of the element represented by the book XElement. One of the elements, the Stock element, has its own attributes. To read their values, the code creates a variable that represents the Stock element and uses its Attribute method to retrieve an attribute by name. The output of the preceding code segment is shown here:

```
ISBN 0000000000001
   Title: Book Title 1
   Price: 11.95
      Books in stock 12
      Books on order 24
ISBN 0000000000002
   Title: Book Title 2
   Price: 10.25
      Books in stock 7
      Books on order 10
```

VB Axis Properties

There's a shorthand notation for accessing attributes, elements, and descendants in an XML file: The @ symbol is shorthand for the Attribute property, a pair of angle brackets (<>) is shorthand for the Element property, and two dots (..) are shorthand for the Descendants property. The following code segment is identical to the preceding one, only this time I'm using the shorthand notation. The output will be the same as before.

```
For Each book In doc.Elements("Book")
    Debug.WriteLine("ISBN " & book.@ISBN.ToString)
    Debug.WriteLine("   Title: " & book...<Name>.Value.ToString)
    Debug.WriteLine("   Price: " & book...<Price>.Value.ToString)
    Dim stock = book.Element("Stock")
    Debug.WriteLine("      Books in stock " & stock.@InStock.ToString)
    Debug.WriteLine("      Books on order " & stock.@OnOrder.ToString)
Next
```

Notice that attributes are returned as strings and have no `Value` property.

Editing XML Documents

In addition to traversing XML documents, you can edit them. To add a new element under an existing one, use the Add method, which accepts as an argument the new XElement:

```
XElement.Add(New XElement (element_name, element_value))
```

To add a new element that represents a new book to the *xDoc* variable, call the Add method on the root element, passing the appropriate XElement and XAttribute objects that represent the properties of the new book:

```
xDoc.Add(New XElement("Book", New XAttribute("ISBN", "0000000003"),
                      New XElement("Price", 19.99),
                      New XElement("Title", "Book Title 3"),
                      New XElement("Stock",
                          New XAttribute("InStock", 2),
                          New XAttribute("OnOrder", 5))))
```

If you execute these statements, the following XML segment will be added to the document:

```
<Book ISBN="0000000003">
    <Price>19.99</Price>
    <Title>Book Title 3</Title>
    <Stock InStock="2" OnOrder="5" />
</Book>
```

To change an element's value, call the SetElementValue method, which accepts as an argument the element's new value:

```
XElement.SetElementValue(new_value)
```

The SetElementValue method can replace simple content; you can't use it to replace an element's value with a collection of nested elements. If you're at the Price XElement of the first book in the document, you can change the book's price with a statement like the following:

```
XElement.SetElementValue("9.99")
```

To remove an element from a document, call the Remove method. This method doesn't accept any arguments; it just removes the XElement object to which it's applied. You navigate to the element you want to remove as discussed earlier in this section and call the Remove method. You can also apply this method to an XElements collection to quickly remove a larger section of the document.

Two methods to edit attributes are available to you from within VB. The Add method of the XElement class can accept as an argument an XAttribute object. When applied to an XElement object, it will add the XAttribute to the XElement object. To change the value of an attribute, call the XElement class SetAttributeValue, and pass the attribute value as an argument.

Both the SetElementValue and SetAttributeValue methods can be called with a *Nothing* value in the place of the second argument (the value argument) to remove a specified element or attribute. An empty string will change the value of the element or attribute but not remove it.

VB 2010 at Work: Manipulating XML Data

Now is a good time to look at some VB code that exercises all the methods and properties discussed so far. Instead of dwelling on the descriptions of the various axis methods, I designed an XML document that will demonstrate the use of the axis methods and will allow you to experiment with them, as well as with the methods discussed in the following section of this chapter. The XML fragment we'll use for our samples describes a hierarchy of countries and cities and is shown in Listing 13.5.

LISTING 13.5:   AN XML fragment of geographical data

```
Dim countries = <Countries>
                  <Country>
                    <Code>IT</Code>
                    <Description>Italy</Description>
                    <Cities>
                      <City>
                        <Code>ROM</Code>
                        <Description>Rome</Description>
                      </City>
                      <City>
                        <Code>FLR</Code>
                        <Description>Florence</Description>
                      </City>
                    </Cities>
                  </Country>
                  <Country>
                    <Code>DE</Code>
                    <Description>Germany</Description>
                    <Cities>
                      <City>
                        <Code>BRL</Code>
                        <Description>Berlin</Description>
```

```
            </City>
            <City>
                <Code>MUN</Code>
                <Description>Munich</Description>
            </City>
            <City>
                <Code>FRN</Code>
                <Description>Frankfurt</Description>
            </City>
        </Cities>
    </Country>
</Countries>
```

It's a very short segment with two countries and a couple of cities in each country, but we'll extend it shortly. Notice that each item, whether it's a country or a city, is described by two elements by the same name: the Code and Description elements. Each country is identified by a code and a description, and the same is true for each city; their tags are Code and Description in both cases. This is not uncommon in XML, as long as no two identical tags appear under the same element. Personally, I recommend that you differentiate the element names in all cases (using names like countryName and cityName in our examples), but it's not always up to you. Sometimes you may also have to use identical element names, so just be sure that they do not belong to the same parent element.

Locating Information in the Document

The following loop retrieves the values of all Description elements in the document (they're all the elements by that name under the root element, Country):

```
For Each destination In countries.Descendants("Description")
    TextBox1.AppendText(destination.Value & vbCrLf)
Next
```

The output generated by the preceding loop is shown next:

```
Italy
Rome
Florence
Germany
Berlin
Munich
Frankfurt
```

As you can see, the expression countries.Descendants("Description") retrieves all Description elements, regardless of whether they represent countries or cities. Had you used different tag names for countries and cities, it would have simplified things, but this contrived example will better demonstrate the use of the various axis methods. The reason I chose this structure is because I ran into documents with tag names like Price or Code, which might appear more than once under different parents. When this happens, your code will appear to work as expected, but sometimes it will return the wrong price or code.

To retrieve all the country names, you must select all descendants (or all elements) with the Country name. The following expression is a collection with all countries:

```
countries.Descendants("Country")
```

To retrieve the country names, write a loop that iterates through the items of this collection and prints the value of their Description element:

```
For Each destination In countries.Descendants("Country")
    TextBox1.AppendText(destination.Descendants("Description").Value & vbCrLf)
Next
```

If you replace the call to the Descendants property with a call to the Elements property, the result will be the same, because you're retrieving elements under a country node.

To retrieve all city names, regardless of the country to which they belong, start with the following expression:

```
countries.Elements("Country").Elements("Cities").Elements("City")
```

which retrieves all City elements under each Cities element under each Country element. This expression retrieves all Country nodes and then retrieves the Cities element under each node and finally all the City elements under the Cities node. The following loop iterates through all cities:

```
For Each destination In countries.Elements("Country").
                        Elements("Cities").Elements("City")
    TextBox1.AppendText(destination.Element("Description").Value & vbCrLf)
Next
```

And here's the output produced by the preceding statements:

```
Rome
Florence
Berlin
Munich
Frankfurt
```

You can also move to a specific element in the hierarchy by indexing the appropriate Elements collection. To access the second country in the document, Germany, use this expression:

```
countries.Elements("Country")(1)
```

If you call the ToString method of this expression, you will get the XML of the second country, which is shown here:

```
<Country>
  <Code>DE</Code>
```

```
    <Description>Germany</Description>
    <Cities>
      <City>
        <Code>BRL</Code>
        <Description>Berlin</Description>
      </City>
      <City>
        <Code>MUN</Code>
        <Description>Munich</Description>
      </City>
      <City>
        <Code>FRN</Code>
        <Description>Frankfurt</Description>
      </City>
    </Cities>
  </Country>
```

Usually, to simplify our code, we assign the segment of the document we're interested in to an XElement variable and work with it by applying the same methods to the XElement with the document's segment. To access the cities of Germany, retrieve the `Cities` element and then the elements under it. Here's the loop that iterates through the German cities:

```
For Each city In countries.Elements("Country")(1).Element("Cities").Elements
    Debug.WriteLine(city.Element("Description").Value)
Next
```

While you're at a German city, you can call the `Ancestors` property to retrieve the entire `Cities` element under the `Germany` node with the following expression:

```
city.Ancestors.ElementAt(0)
```

To retrieve the element that represents the entire `Germany` node, call the second element of the city's `Ancestors` collection:

```
city.Ancestors.ElementAt (1)
```

Both properties return a collection of XElement objects, and you can iterate through them as usual.

Editing the Document

To add a new country to the `countries` document, call the `Add` method as follows:

```
countries.Add(New XElement ("Country", "Spain"))
```

The new XElement can contain multiple nested elements, as in Listing 13.6, which adds an entire new country (including its code and the cities under it) to the countries document with a single statement.

LISTING 13.6:   Adding a new country with a single statement

```
countries.Add(New XElement("Country",
                  New XElement("Code", "FR"),
                  New XElement("Description", "France"),
                  New XElement("Cities",
                      New XElement("City",
                          New XElement("Code", "PAR"),
                          New XElement("Description", "Paris")),
                      New XElement("City",
                          New XElement("Code", "NIC"),
                          New XElement("Description", "Nice")))))
```

I've nested this statement to make it easier to visualize. The idea is rather simple: To add multiple elements at the same level, you just supply their values and separate them with commas. To add nested elements, you insert a New XElement declaration in place of the parent element's value. Of course, you can always create intermediate variable to store individual elements and then add them one after the other. Just remember that the constructor of the XElement object accepts the element's name as its first argument and the element's value as the second argument. The element's value can be another XElement (as in the case of the Cities and City elements) or an array of XElement objects (as in the case of the Code and Description elements).

The alternative approach is to create city nodes, then add them to a country node, and finally add the country to the countries document. The statements in Listing 13.7 create a new country (Spain), then two new cities (Madrid and Barcelona), and then add the two cities to the Cities element of Spain. Finally, they add the new country, the countrySpain element, to the countries document.

LISTING 13.7:   Adding a new country by building all intermediate elements

```
' Create an XElement to represent Spain
Dim countrySpain = New XElement("Country",
                               New XElement("Code", "ES"),
                               New XElement("Description", "Spain"))
' Create XElement to represent Madrid
Dim cityMadrid = New XElement("City",
                         New XElement("Code", "MAD"),
                         New XElement("Description", "Madrid"))
' Create XElement to represent Barcelona
Dim cityBarcelona = New XElement("City",
                         New XElement("Code", "BAR"),
                         New Element("Description", "Barcelona"))
' Create XElement to represent the cities of the Spain
Dim citiesSpain = New XElement("Cities")
' and add Madrid and Barcelona elements to it
citiesSpain.Add(cityMadrid)
```

```
citiesSpain.Add(cityBarcelona)
' add the spanish cities under Spain element
countrySpain.Add(citiesSpain)
' and finally add the complete Spain element to the countries document
countries.Add(countrySpain)
MsgBox(countries.ToString)
```

The last statement displays the entire `countries` document, from which I've extracted the segment that corresponds to Spain:

```
<Country>
  <Code>ES</Code>
  <Description>Spain</Description>
  <Cities>
    <City>
      <Code>MAD</Code>
      <Description>Madrid</Description>
    </City>
    <City>
      <Code>BAR</Code>
      <Description>Barcelona</Description>
    </City>
  </Cities>
</Country>
```

Compare the statements in Listing 13.6 and Listing 13.7 to see the differences between the two approaches. They're functionally equivalent, but when you're building a complex XElement in a single statement, you have to make sure that the parenthesized expressions end properly.

Using XML Segments as Literals

Now we'll edit our XML document by adding a few more countries and embedding our initial countries collection into a larger collection with continents. We want to create a new document with the following structure:

```
Globe
  Continents
      Continent
          Countries
              Country
                  States
                      State
                          Cities
                              City
                              City
                              ...
                      State
```

```
                        . . .
            Country
                  . . .
      Continent
      . . .
```

It's a straightforward document that you can easily create with the functional composition approach. Since you already have a segment of the document, you should be able to reuse the countries document, right? Indeed, this is the case. Start typing a new XElement with the new structure, and when you get to Europe, just embed the existing document, as shown in Listing 13.8 (the bold statement inserts the contents of the XElement that represents European countries into the document).

LISTING 13.8:   Functional composition of an XML document

```
Dim Globe =
<Globe>
   <Continents>
      <Continent>
         <Code>EU</Code>
         <Description>Europe</Description>
         <%= countries %>
      </Continent>
      <Continent>
         <Code>NA</Code>
         <Description>N. America</Description>
         <Countries>
            <Country>
               <Code>USA</Code>
               <Description>U.S.A.</Description>
               <States>
                  <State>
                     <Code>CA</Code>
                     <Description>California</Description>
                     <Cities>
                        <City>
                        <Code>LAX</Code>
                        <Description>Los Angeles</Description>
                     </City>
                     <City>
                        <Code>SD</Code>
                        <Description>San Diego</Description>
                     </City>
                     <City>
                        <Code>SF</Code>
                        <Description>San Francisco</Description>
                     </City>
                  </Cities>
```

```
                </State>
                <State>
                    <Code>NY</Code>
                    <Description>New York</Description>
                    <Cities>
                        <City>
                            <Code>NYC</Code>
                            <Description>New York City</Description>
                        </City>
                        <City>
                            <Code>ALB</Code>
                            <Description>Albany</Description>
                        </City>
                    </Cities>
                </State>
            </States>
        </Country>
        <Country>
            <Code>MX</Code>
            <Description>Mexico</Description>
            <Cities>
                <City>
                    <Code>MXC</Code>
                    <Description>Mexico City</Description>
                </City>
                <City>
                    <Code>TIJ</Code>
                    <Description>Tijuana</Description>
                </City>
                <City>
                    <Code>GDJ</Code>
                    <Description>Guadalajara</Description>
                </City>
            </Cities>
        </Country>
    </Countries>
  </Continent>
 </Continents>
</Globe>
```

Figure 13.6 shows how you can mix VB and XML in the code editor and switch from one to the other by opening and closing the <% and %> tags.

Note that I included state information in the USA country to add a twist to the document. When you process it, you must take into consideration that some countries are separated into states, while others aren't. You'll start with a loop that iterates through the continents and their subordinate elements and prints out continents, countries, and cities. For the time being, you'll ignore the states; you just want to print the cities under each country. The code shown in Listing 13.9 consists of three nested loops: The outer one goes through the continents, the next inner one countries under each continent, and the innermost loop goes through the cities under each country.

FIGURE 13.6

The gap between traditional programming and XML has suddenly narrowed with VB's support of XML.

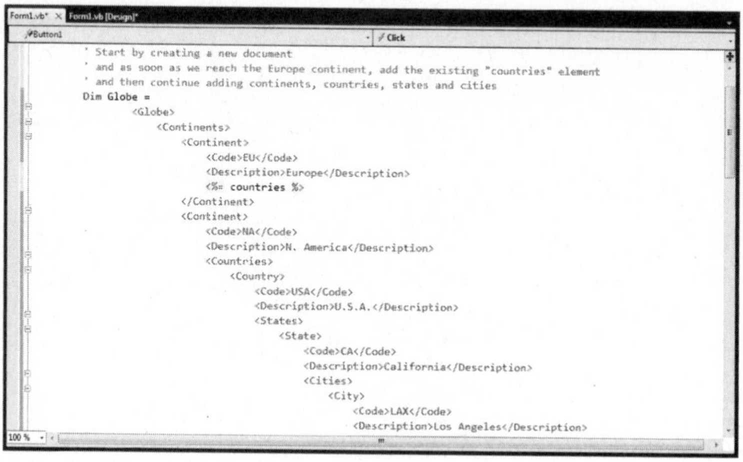

LISTING 13.9:   Iterating through the globe document's continents, countries, and cities

```
For Each continent In Globe.Elements("Continents").Elements("Continent")
    TextBox1.AppendText(continent.Element("Description").Value & vbCrLf)
        For Each country In continent.Elements("Countries").Elements("Country")
            TextBox1.AppendText(vbTab & country.Element("Description").Value & vbCrLf)
            For Each city In country.Descendants("Cities").Elements("City")
                TextBox1.AppendText(vbTab & vbTab &
                                        city.Elements("Description").Value & vbCrLf)
            Next
        Next
Next
```

The expression Globe.Elements("Continents").Elements("Continent") returns a collection of all continents in the globe document. The *continent* control variable is an XElement itself that represents the current continent in the outer loop. To extract the current continent's countries, the code uses the expression continent.Elements("Country"), which returns a collection of countries. The *country* control variable is also an XElement that represents the current continent's states and cities. Although all expressions use the Elements axis to locate the corresponding elements, the innermost loop uses the Descendants axis to retrieve the cities, whether they belong to a country or a state. The code of Listing 13.9 will produce the following output:

```
Europe
        Italy
                Rome
                Florence
```

```
        Germany
                Berlin
                Munich
                Frankfurt
        France
                Paris
        Spain
                Madrid
N. America
        U.S.A.
                Los Angeles
                San Diego
                San Francisco
                New York City
                Albany
        Mexico
                Mexico City
                Tijuana
                Guadalajara
```

If you replace the line

```
For Each city In country.Descendants("Cities").Elements("City")
```

with the following:

```
For Each city In country.Elements("Cities").Elements("City")
```

you will get the same results for all countries, except the United States, where the cities are nested under their states (there will be no cities under the US node).

If the preceding code segment is not clear to you or if you'd prefer a more verbose version of the same code segment, here's an alternate method of producing the same output. This time I create two intermediate variables to store countries and cities: the *continentCountries* and *countryCities* variables. These variables are collections that hold the appropriate elements at each iteration of the corresponding loop:

```
For Each continent In Globe.Elements("Continents").Elements("Continent")
    TextBox1.AppendText(continent.Element("Description").Value & vbCrLf)
    Dim continentCountries = continent.Elements("Countries")
    For Each country In continentCountries.Elements("Country")
        TextBox1.AppendText(
                vbTab & country.Element("Description").Value & vbCrLf)
        Dim countryCities = country.Descendants("Cities")
        For Each city In countryCities.Elements("City")
            TextBox1.AppendText(vbTab & vbTab & _
                city.Elements("Description").Value & vbCrLf)
        Next
    Next
Next
```

If you want to include the states (and this is obviously the proper method of iterating through this document), you must differentiate the countries with states from the countries without states. To do so, you must retrieve the States descendants of each country node and examine their count. If the count is zero, which means there are no states under the current country, the code should proceed with the cities of the country. If the count is positive, the code must first iterate through the States descendants and then through the cities in each state. Listing 13.10 shows the final loop that iterates through the globe document, taking into consideration the different organization schema of certain countries.

LISTING 13.10: Iterating through the globe document's continents, countries, states, and cities

```
For Each continent In Globe.Descendants("Continents").Descendants("Continent")
    TextBox1.AppendText(continent.Element("Description").Value & vbCrLf)
    For Each country In continent.Descendants("Country")
        TextBox1.AppendText(vbTab & country.Element("Description").Value & vbCrLf)
        If country.Descendants("States").Count = 0 Then
            Dim CountryCities = country.Descendants("Cities")
            For Each city In CountryCities.Descendants("City")
                TextBox1.AppendText(vbTab & vbTab &
                              city.Elements("Description").Value & vbCrLf)
            Next
        Else
            For Each state In country.Descendants("State")
                TextBox1.AppendText(vbTab & vbTab & _
                              state.Element("Description").Value & vbCrLf)
                Dim CountryCities = state.Descendants("Cities")
                For Each city In CountryCities.Descendants("City")
                    TextBox1.AppendText(vbTab & vbTab & vbTab &
                              city.Elements("Description").Value & vbCrLf)
                Next
            Next
        End If
    Next
Next
```

The output produced by the preceding code segment is shown next (I'm showing only a single country in Europe in the interest of saving some space on the printed page):

```
Europe
    Italy
        Rome
        Florence
N. America
    U.S.A.
        California
            Los Angeles
```

```
        San Diego
        San Francisco
    New York
        New York City
        Albany
Mexico
    Mexico City
    Tijuana
    Guadalajara
```

Using Lambda Expressions

To make the most of the XElement class, you must familiarize yourself with the concept of *lambda expressions*. Lambda expressions are inline functions you can embed in some of the methods, most notably in the Where method. This method selects certain elements from an XElements collection based on criteria you specify.

The syntax of the Where method requires that you pass as an argument a function that determines whether an element will be selected by the Where method. This function will be called once for each element in the collection, and it must return a True/False value to indicate whether the current element passed the selection criteria. Now, how do you pass a function to a method? Lambda expressions to the rescue. To specify a lambda function, you declare a function without a name but with an argument list and a statement. Here's a lambda function that evaluates to a True/False value and can be used with the Where extension method:

```
Function(Bk As Book)  Book.Price >= 30
```

This lambda function accepts as an argument an object of the Book type and returns True if the price of the book represented by the *Bk* variable is $30 or more. To use this function in a Where method, just pass the entire statement as an argument:

```
Books.Elements("Book").Where(Function(Bk As Book) Bk.Price >= 30)
```

The preceding expression will extract from the Books collection all books with a value of $30 or more.

Let's return to the countries example and write a lambda function that will be used with the Where method to retrieve the cities in Germany:

```
Dim germanCities =
      countries.Elements("Country").
      Where(Function(ctry) ctry.Element("Code").Value = "DE").
      Descendants("Cities").Descendants("City")
```

The *germanCities* variable is a collection that contains all cities in Germany, and you can iterate through them with a loop as usual. To find out the number of cities under the Germany node, call the Count property of the *germanCities* collection.

In the next chapter, you'll learn an even better method of selecting elements in an XML document, namely, the LINQ syntax. LINQ, however, is based on the methods exposed by the

XElements and Descendants classes, which is why I've chosen to show you the hard method first.

Let's apply the Where method of the IEnumerable type to this chapter's main sample document, the globe document. The following statement uses a lambda expression to locate the XElement that represents the entire node of Europe:

```
Dim Europe As XElement =
        Globe.Descendants("Continent").
        Where(Function(cnt) cnt.Element("Code").Value = "EU").First
```

Now, this statement contains a method you haven't seen before, the First method. The First method returns the first element in a collection of XElement objects. The Where clause in our sample code will always return a single XElement, but this is just a special case. In general, the Where method may (and it usually does) return multiple elements as an IEnumerable (basically, a collection you can enumerate over). To make sure that you retrieve a single element (and not a collection by mistake), we call the First method. The *Europe* variable is an XML segment that represents Europe.

To add new countries to Europe, you can use the Add method of the XElement as discussed earlier in this chapter. Let's prepare a couple of XElement objects that represent countries in Europe:

```
Dim France =
      New XElement("Country",
                  New XElement("Code", "FR"),
                  New XElement("Description", "France"),
                  New XElement("Cities",
                          New XElement("City",
                                  New XElement("Code", "PAR"),
                                  New XElement("Description", "Paris"))))
Dim Spain =
      New XElement("Country",
              New XElement("Code", "ES"),
              New XElement("Description", "Spain"),
              New XElement("Cities",
                  New XElement("City",
                      New XElement("Code", "MAD"),
                      New XElement("Description", "Madrid"))),
                  New XElement("City",
                      New XElement("Code", "BCN"),
                      New XElement("Description", "Barcelona")))
```

To add the two countries to the Europe element, just call the Add method once for each country, as shown in Figure 13.7.

Here ends the introduction to XML and the VB methods for manipulating XML. In the next chapter, you'll learn an even better method of working with XML documents, namely, LINQ. LINQ is a querying language you can apply not only to XML but to collections of objects, simple arrays, and even databases. It's the new method of querying data, and it's an exciting topic. Before moving on to LINQ, however, I must present a very special topic in the Framework — serialization.

FIGURE 13.7
Adding two countries under the Europe node of the globe XML document

```vb
' Add a new country (France) and some cities under it to the Europe element using XElement
Dim Europe As XElement = Globe.Descendants("Continent"). _
                Where(Function(cnt) cnt.Element("Code").Value = "EU").First

Dim France =
        New XElement("Country",
                New XElement("Code", "FR"),
                New XElement("Description", "France"),
                New XElement("Cities",
                        New XElement("City",
                                New XElement("Code", "PAR"),
                                New XElement("Description", "Paris"))))
' Add France under the Europe node
Europe.Descendants("Countries").Last.Add(France)
' add the Spaing element in the same manner
Dim Spain =
        New XElement("Country",
                New XElement("Code", "ES"),
                New XElement("Description", "Spain"),
                New XElement("Cities",
                        New XElement("City",
                                New XElement("Code", "MAD"),
                                New XElement("Description", "Madrid"))), _
                        New XElement("City",
                                New XElement("Code", "BCN"),
                                New XElement("Description", "Barcelona")))
```

XML Serialization

In Chapter 12, "Storing Data in Collections," you learned how to use collections to store items, how to access their elements, and even how to sort and search the collections. To make the most of collections and to use them to store large sets of data, you should also learn how to persist collections to disk files or databases.

Persisting data means storing them on disk at the end of one session and reloading them into the same application in a later session. The persisted data can also be shared among different applications and even different computers, as long as there's an application that knows what to do with the data. What good is it to create a large collection if your application can't save it and retrieve it from session to session?

Since time immemorial, programmers had to write code to save their data to disk. The most challenging aspect of the data persisting was the format used to store the data. With XML being a universal format, what better method of persisting data than converting them to XML documents? Indeed, it's possible to convert any object or collection to an XML document and save it to a file or exchange it with any other system. By the way, the XML format is quite verbose and wouldn't have caught up earlier, when storage was expensive.

In this chapter, you'll see how to convert objects to streams with a technique known as *serialization*, which is the process of converting arbitrary objects to streams of bytes. After you obtain the serialized stream for a specific object, you can persist the object to disk, as well as read it back. The process of reconstructing an object from its serialized form is called *deserialization*. It makes so much sense to convert objects to XML and back; that the process is supported natively by the Framework. The System.Xml.Serialization class can convert arbitrary objects to XML and back, and you'll see shortly how easy it is to use this class — no, you won't have to use any of the techniques discussed so far to create your own XML. You just call the Serialize and Deserialize methods of this class to do the work for you.

OTHER SERIALIZATION TYPES

There are three types of serialization: binary serialization, Simple Object Access Protocol (SOAP, also called Service Oriented Architecture Protocol) serialization, and Extensible Markup Language (XML) serialization. Binary and SOAP serialization are very similar; XML serialization is a little different, but it allows you to customize the serialization process.

Binary serialization is performed with the BinaryFormatter class, and it converts the values of the object properties into a binary stream. The result of the binary serialization is compact and efficient. However, binary-serialized objects can be used only by applications that have access to the class that produced the objects and can't be used outside .NET. Another limitation of binary serialization is that the output it produces is not human readable, and you can't do much with a file that contains a binary serialized object without access to the original application code. Because binary serialization is very compact and very efficient, it's used almost exclusively to persist objects between sessions of an application or between applications that share the same classes.

SOAP serialization produces a SOAP-compliant envelope that describes its contents and serializes the objects in SOAP-compliant format. SOAP-serialized data are suitable for transmission to any system that understands SOAP; it's implemented by the SoapFormatter class. Unlike binary serialization, SOAP-serialized data are firewall friendly, and SOAP serialization is used to remote objects to a server on a different domain. The process of serializing objects is the same, no matter which method you'll use. So, let's start with XML serialization, and I'll briefly cover the classes for the other types of serialization toward the end of the chapter.

The Serialization Process

To use XML serialization, you must create an instance of the XmlSerializer class and then call its Serialize method (or the Deserialize method to extract data from an XML stream and populate an instance of a custom class). The XmlSerializer class belongs to the XmlSerialization namespace, which is not imported by default in a new project. To use it, import the Serialization class by inserting the following statement at the beginning of the module that needs the serialization services:

```
Imports System.Xml.Serialization
```

To set up a new instance of the class, you must call the XmlSerializer class constructor, passing as an argument the type of objects it will serialize or deserialize. You can't use the same instance of the XmlSerializer class to serialize arbitrary objects; instead, you must tell the compiler the type of object you need to serialize in the XmlSerializer constructor. Here's how to set up a new instance of the XmlSerializer class:

```
Dim serializer As New XmlSerializer(custom_type)
```

The *custom_type* argument represents a custom (or built-in for that matter) type, whose instances are intended to be serialized through the XmlSerializer class. You can also pass the name of the class itself to the constructor by using a statement such as the following:

```
Dim serializer As New XmlSerializer(GetType(CustomClass))
```

The `serializer` object can be used to serialize only instances of the specific class, and it will throw an exception if you attempt to serialize a different class with it. Note also that all classes are XML-serializable by default. I'm mentioning this here because with the other serialization types, you must prefix the classes with the `<Serializable>` attribute to make them serializable.

In the background, CLR will create a temporary assembly, a process that will take a few moments. The temporary assembly, however, will remain in memory as long as the application is running. After the initial delay, XML serialization will be quite fast.

Once the *serializer* variable has been set up, you can call the `Serialize` method, passing two arguments: a stream that will accept the serialized data and the object to be serialized:

```
serializer.Serialize(stream, object)
```

That's all it takes to convert an object or collection of objects to an XML document. To reconstruct the original object, call the `Deserialize` method, and pass the stream with the serialized data as an argument. This stream points to the file to which the serialization data has been stored:

```
object = serializer.Deserialize(stream)
```

The `Deserialize` method returns an `Object` data type, which you must cast to the appropriate type, as with the following statement:

```
object = CType(serializer.Deserialize(stream), object_type)
```

As for setting up the Stream object that will accept the serialization data (or provide the serialized data to the `Deserialize` method), that's also straightforward. If you're not familiar with the concept of streams, please read the tutorial "Accessing Files and Folders" (available for download from http://www.sybex.com/go/masteringvb2010). Start by importing the System.IO namespace, and then create a new FileStream object that points to the file that will accept the serialization data:

```
Dim saveFile As New FileStream("Objects.xml", FileMode.Create)
```

The *saveFile* variable represents a stream and must be passed to the `Serialize` method along with the object to be serialized. To create a stream for reading data, use a statement like the following:

```
Dim Strm As New FileStream("Objects.xml", FileMode.Open)
```

Let's serialize a few simple objects to get a feel of the functionality of the XmlSerialization namespace and how to use it to move objects to their XML equivalents and back.

Serializing Individual Objects

Let's serialize a single Rectangle object using the following statements:

```
Dim saveFile As FileStream
saveFile = File.OpenWrite("Rectangles.xml")
Dim serializer As New XmlSerializer(GetType(Rectangle))
Dim R As New Rectangle(10, 10, 100, 160)
serializer.Serialize(saveFile, R)
saveFile.Close()
```

If you execute the preceding statements, the following data will be stored in the Rectangles.xml file:

```
<?xml version="1.0" encoding="utf-8"?>
<Rectangle xmlns:xsi="http://www.w3.org/2001/XMLSchema-instance"
 xmlns:xsd="http://www.w3.org/2001/XMLSchema">
  <Location>
    <X>10</X>
    <Y>10</Y>
  </Location>
  <Size>
    <Width>100</Width>
    <Height>160</Height>
  </Size>
  <X>10</X>
  <Y>10</Y>
  <Width>100</Width>
  <Height>160</Height>
</Rectangle>
```

This is a well-formed XML document. As you can see, the XmlSerializer extracted the basic properties of the Rectangle object and used them to create an XML document with the basic properties of the Rectangle as elements. Note that all relevant information has been stored in elements, and there are no attributes in the XML generated by the XmlSerializer class's Serialize method.

There's some redundancy in this file because the values of the properties appear twice. This isn't part of the XML specification; the document contains the values of the following properties: Location, Size, X, Y, Width, and Height. The Rectangle object exposes additional properties, such as the Top, Bottom, and so on, but these values aren't serialized. The Location property is an object, which in turn exposes the X and Y properties. The values of these properties appear within the Location segment of the document and as separate values near the end of the file. The same happens with the Size property.

WHICH MEMBERS ARE SERIALIZED?

I mentioned earlier that the XmlSerializer class serializes all public properties in a class. However, quite a few properties of the Rectangle class weren't serialized. Who determines the properties that will be serialized? When you build a custom class, you can specify that certain classes will not be serialized by decorating them with the <NonSerialized> attribute. Obviously, the properties of the built-in objects that aren't serialized are marked with this attribute.

To deserialize the data and create a new Rectangle object with the same properties as the original one, set up a Stream object and an XMLSerializer object, and then call the XmlSerializer object's Deserialize method:

```
Imports System.Xml.Serialization
Dim serializer As New XmlSerializer(GetType(Rectangle))
Dim FS As FileStream
FS = New FileStream("Rectangles.xml", FileMode.Open)
Dim R As Rectangle
R = serializer.Deserialize(FS)
FS.Close()
```

Not surprisingly, if you examine the properties of the R object that was created by the deserialization process, you'll see that it's identical to the Rectangle object you serialized earlier to disk.

Serializing Custom Objects

Let's move on to a more interesting example. This time we'll serialize a more elaborate custom object. Listing 13.11 shows a class that describes books. The Book class is quite trivial, except that each book can have any number of authors. The authors are stored in an array of Author objects, where Author is a nested class (Book.Author).

LISTING 13.11:   The Book class definition

```
Public Class Book
    Private _title As String
    Private _pages As Integer
    Private _price As Decimal
    Private _authors() As Author

    Public Sub New()

    End Sub

    Public Property Title() As String
        Get
            Return _title
        End Get
        Set(ByVal Value As String)
            If Value.Length > 100 Then
```

```
                    _title = Value.Substring(0, 99)
            Else
                    _title = Value
            End If
        End Set
End Property

Public Property Pages() As Integer
    Get
         Return _pages
    End Get
    Set(ByVal Value As Integer)
         _pages = Value
    End Set
End Property

Public Property Price() As Decimal
    Get
         Return _price
    End Get
    Set(ByVal Value As Decimal)
         _price = Value
    End Set
End Property

Public Property Authors() As Author()
    Get
         Return (_authors)
    End Get
    Set(ByVal Value As Author())
         _authors = Value
    End Set
End Property

Public Class Author
    Private _firstname As String
    Private _lastname As String

    Public Property FirstName() As String
        Get
             Return _firstname
        End Get
        Set(ByVal Value As String)
            If Value.Length > 50 Then
                 _firstname = Value.Substring(0, 49)
            Else
                 _firstname = Value
```

```
                End If
            End Set
        End Property

        Public Property LastName() As String
            Get
                Return _lastname
            End Get
            Set(ByVal Value As String)
                If Value.Length > 50 Then
                    _lastname = Value.Substring(0, 49)
                Else
                    _lastname = Value
                End If
            End Set
        End Property
    End Class
End Class
```

The following statements create a new Book object, which includes three authors:

```
Dim BK0 As New Book
Dim authors(2) As Book.Author
authors(0) = New Book.Author
authors(0).FirstName = "Author1 First"
authors(0).LastName = "Author1 Last"
authors(1) = New Book.Author
authors(1).FirstName = "Author2 First"
authors(1).LastName = "Author2 Last"
authors(2) = New Book.Author
authors(2).FirstName = "Author3 First"
authors(2).LastName = "Author3 Last"
BK0.Title = "Book Title"
BK0.Pages = 234
BK0.Price = 29.95
BK0.Authors = authors
```

To exercise some of the new "convenience" features of VB 2010, we'll add another book using object initializers, this time with more meaningful data:

```
Dim authors() = {New Author With
                    {.FirstName = "Evangelos", .LastName = "Petroutsos"}, _
                New Author With {.FirstName = "Richard", .LastName = "Manning"}}
Dim BK1 = New Book1 With { _
            .ISBN = "0-470-53287-4",
                .Title = "Mastering Visual Basic 2010", .Authors = authors}
```

To serialize the *BK0* and *BK1* variables, create a new XmlSerializer object, and call its `Serialize` method as usual:

```
Dim serializer As New XmlSerializer(BK1.GetType)
Dim strm As New FileStream("books.xml", FileMode.Create)
serializer.Serialize(strm, BK0)
strm.Close()
```

To serialize two objects in the same file, call the `Serialize` method twice, passing as an argument the appropriate instance of the Book object, as shown here:

```
serializer.Serialize(strm, BK0)
serializer.Serialize(strm, BK1)
```

As you can understand, serialization would be severely limited without the ability to serialize arrays and collections, and this is the topic we'll explore in the next section. However, it's worth taking a look at the contents of the books.xml file generated by the XmlSerializer class. If you open the books.xml file, shown in Listing 13.12, you'll see that it contains two XML documents (the <?xml> tag appears twice in the file). This certainly isn't a valid XML document because it doesn't contain a unique root element. However, you can see the equivalence between the structure of the class and the XML document. The serializer takes all the public properties and converts them to elements. Nested classes, like the Authors under the Book class, are converted to nested elements. Moreover, there are no attributes to the resulting XML; all properties are translated into elements.

LISTING 13.12:   Typical XML-serialized data

```xml
<?xml version="1.0"?>
<Book xmlns:xsi=http://www.w3.org/2001/XMLSchema-instance
 xmlns:xsd="http://www.w3.org/2001/XMLSchema">
  <Title>Book Title</Title>
  <ISBN>1234567890</ISBN>
  <Price>29.95</Price>
  <Pages>0</Pages>
  <Authors>
    <Author>
      <FirstName>Author1 First</FirstName>
      <LastName>Author1 Last</LastName>
    </Author>
    <Author>
      <FirstName>Author2 First</FirstName>
      <LastName>Author2 Last</LastName>
    </Author>
    <Author>
      <FirstName>Author3 First</FirstName>
      <LastName>Author3 Last</LastName>
    </Author>
```

```
    </Authors>
</Book>
<?xml version="1.0"?>
<Book xmlns:xsi="http://www.w3.org/2001/XMLSchema-instance"
 xmlns:xsd="http://www.w3.org/2001/XMLSchema">
  <Title>Mastering Visual Basic 2010</Title>
  <ISBN>0-470-53287-4</ISBN>
  <Price>0</Price>
  <Pages>0</Pages>
  <Authors>
    <Author>
      <FirstName>Evangelos</FirstName>
      <LastName>Petroutsos</LastName>
    </Author>
    <Author>
      <FirstName>Richard</FirstName>
      <LastName>Manning</LastName>
    </Author>
  </Authors>
</Book>
```

Each book has been serialized as a separate entity; the serialization process did not create a new root element that encloses the serialized objects. Even though this isn't a well-formed XML document, you can deserialize the two objects by calling the Deserialize method twice, as shown in the following code segment:

```
Dim serializer As New XmlSerializer(GetType(Book))
Dim strm As New FileStream("books.xml", FileMode.Open)
Dim book1 = CTpe(serializer.Deserialize(strm), Book)
Dim book2 = CTpe(serializer.Deserialize(strm), Book)
strm.Close()
```

Serializing Collections of Objects

Let's see how to serialize collections of objects in XML format, starting with a hard rule:

The collection to be serialized must be strongly typed.

You can use XML serialization with typed arrays, Lists and Dictionaries, but you can't serialize ArrayLists or arrays of arbitrary objects. All the elements of the collection should have the same type, which must match the type you pass to the constructor of the XmlSerializer class. If you pass to the serializer an array of objects of different types, no warning will be issued at design time, but a runtime exception will be thrown as soon as your code reaches the Serialize method. The XmlSerializer instance is constructed by the compiler on the fly for a specific type of object, and any given instance of this class can handle objects of the specific type and nothing else.

Let's start by creating an array of Book objects and then serialize it. First, we'll create an array of the Book type and store a few properly initialized instances of the Book class to its elements. In Listing 13.13, I'm using the variables *BK0, BK1, BK2,* and *BK3,* but I'm not show-ing the code for their initialization. Then, we'll pass this array to the Serialize method of the XmlSerializer class, also as shown in Listing 13.13.

LISTING 13.13: XML serialization of an array of objects

```
Private Sub bttnSaveArrayXML_Click(…)Handles bttnSaveArrayXML.Click
    Dim AllBooks(3) As Book
    ' initialize the BK0, BK1, BK2 and BK3 variables
    AllBooks(0) = BK0
    AllBooks(1) = BK1
    AllBooks(2) = BK2
    AllBooks(3) = BK3

    Dim serializer As New XmlSerializer(AllBooks.GetType)

    Dim FS As FileStream
    Try
        FS = New FileStream("SerializedXMLArray.xml", FileMode.Create)
        serializer.Serialize(FS, AllBooks)
    Catch exc As Exception
        MsgBox(exc.InnerException.ToString)
        Exit Sub
    Finally
        FS.Close()
    End Try
    MsgBox("Array of Book objects saved in file SerializedXMLArray.xml"
End Sub
```

The XmlSerializer class constructor accepts as an argument the array type. Because the array is typed, it can figure out the type of custom objects it will serialize.

There's a substantial overhead the first time you create an instance of the XmlSerializer class, but this happens only once during the course of the application. The overhead is caused by the CLR, which creates a temporary assembly for serializing and deserializing the specific type. This assembly, however, remains in memory for the course of the application, and the initial overhead won't recur. Even though there will be an additional delay of a couple of seconds when the application starts (or whenever you load the settings), you can persist the class with the application's configuration every time the user changes one of the settings without any per-formance penalty.

To serialize a List collection, you must pass the same type of argument as you used in the list declaration to the XmlSerializer class constructor. The constructor doesn't need to know that you're planning to serialize a List collection; all it cares about is the type of objects it's going to serialize. The following two statements declare a List of Person objects and an instance of the XMLSerializer for serializing this collection:

```
Dim Persons As New List(Of Person)
Dim XMLSRLZR As New XmlSerializer(Persons.GetType)
```

The statements for serializing and deserializing the collection are identical to the ones you'd use to serialize any other object. To serialize a collection, create a StreamWriter for a new file, and then call the `Serialize` method, passing the stream as an argument:

```
' To serialize a typed collection:
Dim WStrm As New IO.StreamWriter(file_path)
XMLSRLZR.Serialize(WStrm, Persons)
```

(In the preceding sample code I used the StreamWriter class, which is equivalent to a Stream object opened for writing to a file). To deserialize the same collection, create a FileStream for the file where the serialization data has been stored, and call its `Deserialize` method. This method returns an object, which you must cast to the appropriate type as usual (in our case to a List of Book objects):

```
Dim RStrm As New IO.FileStream(file_path, IO.FileMode.Open)
newPersons = CType(XMLSRLZR.Deserialize(Rstrm), List(Of Person))
```

Other Types of Serialization

As I mentioned earlier, XML serialization is the most common form of serialization, but it's not the only one. You can use two more types of serialization, namely, binary and SOAP serialization.

Binary serialization is performed with the BinaryFormatter class, and it converts the values of the object's properties into a binary stream. The result of the binary serialization is compact and efficient. However, the output it produces is not human readable, and you can't do much with a file that contains a binary serialized object without access to the original application code. Because binary serialization is very compact and very efficient, it's used almost exclusively to persist objects between sessions of an application or between applications that share the same classes.

The other serialization type, *SOAP serialization*, is very similar to XML serialization, but the resulting document is more structured and contains information about the properties that have been serialized. Each book's authors, for example, are marked as an array. The Authors property will be serialized as follows:

```
<_authors href="#ref-5"/>
```

This is a reference to another element with the generic name ref-5 in the same document, and here's the definition of this element:

```
<SOAP-ENC:Array id="ref-5" SOAP-ENC:arrayType="a1:Author[2]">
<item href="#ref-6"/>
<item href="#ref-7"/>
</SOAP-ENC:Array>
```

The array contains two elements, which are also referenced in the array. Finally, here are the definitions of the two elements of the Authors array in the same file:

```
<a1:Author id="ref-6" >
<_firstname id="ref-8">Evangelos</_firstname>
```

```
<_lastname id="ref-9">Petroutsos</_lastname>
</a1:Author>
<a1:Author id="ref-7">
<_firstname id="ref-10">Richard</_firstname>
<_lastname id="ref-11">Manning</_lastname>
</a1:Author>
```

Let's start with binary serialization, which is implemented in the following namespace (you must import it into your application):

```
Imports System.Runtime.Serialization.Formatters.Binary
```

This namespace isn't loaded by default, and you must add a reference to the corresponding namespace. Right-click the project's name in the Solution Explorer, and choose Add Reference from the context menu. In the Add Reference dialog box that appears, select the same namespace as in the `Imports` statement shown earlier.

To use a SOAP serializer in your application, reference the assembly `System.Runtime.Serialization.Formatters.Soap.dll` and import the following namespace:

```
Imports System.Runtime.Serialization.Formatters.Soap
```

You can serialize individual objects as well as collections of objects. To serialize an object, you must call the `Serialize` method of the System.Runtime.Serialization.Formatters.Binary object. First declare an object of this type with a statement like the following:

```
Dim BFormatter As New BinaryFormatter()
```

The BinaryFormatter class persists objects in binary format. You can also persist objects in text format by using the SoapFormatter class. SoapFormatter persists the objects in XML format, which is quite verbose, and the corresponding files are considerably lengthier. To use the Soap-Formatter class, declare a `SoapFormatter` variable with the following statement:

```
Dim SFormatter As Soap.SoapFormatter
```

SOAP is a protocol for accessing objects over HTTP; in other words, it's a protocol that allows the encoding of objects in text format. SOAP was designed to enable distributed computing over the Internet. SOAP uses text to transfer all kinds of objects, including images and audio, and it's not rejected by firewalls.

The `BinaryFormatter` and `SoapFormatter` methods are equivalent, so I will use `BinaryFormatter` for the examples in this section. To serialize an object, call the `Serialize` method of the appropriate formatter, where *stream* is a variable that represents a stream and *object* is the object you want to serialize. Here's the syntax:

```
BFormatter.Serialize(stream, object)
```

Because we want to persist our objects to disk, the *stream* argument represents a stream to a file where the serialized data will be stored. It can be created with statements like the following:

```
Dim saveFile As FileStream
saveFile = File.Create("Shapes.bin", IO.FileMode.Create)
```

The *saveFile* variable represents the stream to a specific file on the disk, and the Create method of the same variable creates a stream to this file.

After you have set up the Stream and BinaryFormatter objects, you can call the Serialize method to serialize any object. To serialize a Rectangle object, for example, use the following statements:

```
Dim R As New Rectangle(0, 0, 100, 100)
BFormatter.Serialize(saveFile, R)
```

Listing 13.14 serializes two Rectangle objects to the Shapes.bin file. The file's extension can be anything. Because the file is binary, I used the .bin extension.

LISTING 13.14:   Serializing distinct objects

```
Dim R1 As New Rectangle()
R1.X = 1
R1.Y = 1
R1.Size.Width = 10
R1.Size.Height = 20
Dim R2 As New Rectangle()
R2.X = 10
R2.Y = 10
R2.Size.Width = 100
R2.Size.Height = 200
Dim saveFile As FileStream
saveFile = File.Create("Shapes.bin")
Dim formatter As BinaryFormatter
formatter = New BinaryFormatter()
formatter.Serialize(saveFile, R1)
formatter.Serialize(saveFile, R2)
saveFile.Close()
```

Notice that the Serialize method serializes a single object at a time. To save the two rectangles, the code calls the Serialize method once for each rectangle. To serialize multiple objects with a single statement, you must create a collection, append all the objects to the collection, and then serialize the collection itself, as explained in the following section. If you serialize multiple objects of different types into the same stream, you can't deserialize them unless you know the order in which the objects were serialized and then deserialize them in the same order.

Deserializing Individual Objects

To deserialize a serialized object, you must create a new binary or SOAP formatter object and call its Deserialize method. Because the serialized data doesn't contain any information about the original object, you can't reconstruct the original object from the serialized data, unless you know the type of object that was serialized. Deserialization is always more difficult than serialization. Whereas the Serialize method will serialize any object you pass as an argument, the Deserialize method won't reconstruct the original object unless you know the type of the object you're deserializing. The Shapes.bin file of Listing 13.14 contains the serialized versions of two Rectangle objects. The Deserialize method needs to know that it will deserialize two Rectangle objects. If you attempt to extract the information of this file into any other type of object, a runtime exception will occur.

To deserialize the contents of a file, create a formatter object as you did for the serialization process, by using one of the following statements (depending on the type of serialization):

```
Dim SFormatter As Soap.SoapFormatter
Dim BFormatter As BinaryFormatter
```

Then establish a stream to the source of the serialized data, which in our case is the Shapes.bin file:

```
Dim Strm As New FileStream("Shales.Bin", FileMode.Open)
```

Finally, deserialize the stream's data by calling the Deserialize method. Since the Deserialize method returns an object, you must also cast its value appropriately:

```
Dim R1, R2 As Rectangle
R1 = CType(SFormatter.Deserialize(Strm), Rectangle)
R2 = CType(SFormatter.Deserialize(Strm), Rectangle)
```

You can serialize as many objects as you like into the same stream, one after the other, and read them back in the same order. With binary and SOAP serialization, you're limited to a single type, as long as you deserialize the data in the proper order.

You can open the files with the serialized data and view their data. The contents of the file with two serialized Rectangle objects is shown next:

```
<SOAP-ENV:Envelope xmlns:xsi="http://www.w3.org/2001/XMLSchema-instance"
    xmlns:xsd="http://www.w3.org/2001/XMLSchema"
    xmlns:SOAP-ENC="http://schemas.xmlsoap.org/soap/encoding/"
    xmlns:SOAP-ENV="http://schemas.xmlsoap.org/soap/envelope/"
    xmlns:clr="http://schemas.microsoft.com/soap/encoding/clr/1.0"
    SOAP-ENV:encodingStyle="http://schemas.xmlsoap.org/soap/encoding/">
<SOAP-ENV:Body>
<a1:Rectangle id="ref-1" xmlns:a1="http://schemas.microsoft.com/clr/nsassem
        /System.Drawing/System.Drawing%
    2C%20Version%3D2.0.3600.0%2C%20Culture%3Dneutral%2C%20PublicKeyToken%
    3Db03f5f7f11d50a3a">
<x>0</x>
<y>0</y>
<width>100</width>
<height>100</height>
</a1:Rectangle>
```

```
</SOAP-ENV:Body>
</SOAP-ENV:Envelope>
<SOAP-ENV:Envelope xmlns:xsi="http://www.w3.org/2001/XMLSchema-instance"
    xmlns:xsd="http://www.w3.org/2001/XMLSchema"
    xmlns:SOAP-ENC="http://schemas.xmlsoap.org/soap/encoding/"
    xmlns:SOAP-ENV="http://schemas.xmlsoap.org/soap/envelope/"
    xmlns:clr="http://schemas.microsoft.com/soap/encoding/clr/1.0"
    SOAP-ENV:encodingStyle="http://schemas.xmlsoap.org/soap/encoding/">
<SOAP-ENV:Body>
<a1:Rectangle id="ref-1" xmlns:a1="http://schemas.microsoft.com/clr/nsassem
        /System.Drawing/System.Drawing%
    2C%20Version%3D2.0.3600.0%2C%20Culture%3D
        neutral%2C%20PublicKeyToken%3Db03f5f7f11d50a3a">
<x>65</x>
<y>30</y>
<width>19</width>
<height>199</height>
</a1:Rectangle>
</SOAP-ENV:Body>
</SOAP-ENV:Envelope>
```

You'll never have to create your own SOAP files, so don't panic if they look complicated. There are, however, a few points of interest. First, you see a reference to the System.Drawing class, which indicates that the serialized data can't be used outside the context of the Framework; this file contains serialized data describing an instance of a specific class. The section of the file with the data contains the values of the two basic properties of the Rectangle object. Second, the SOAP format uses an XML notation to delimit its fields, but it's not an XML file. If you attempt to open the same file with Internet Explorer, you'll see a message indicating that it's not a valid XML document.

SERIALIZING COLLECTIONS

Serializing a collection is quite similar to serializing any single object, because collections are objects themselves. The second argument to the Serialize method is the object you want to serialize, and this object can be anything, including a collection. To demonstrate the serialization of an ArrayList, modify the previous code a little so that instead of persisting individual items, it will persist an entire collection. Declare the two Rectangle objects as before, but append them to an ArrayList collection. Then add a few Color values to the collection, as shown in Listing 13.15, which serializes an ArrayList collection to the file C:\ShapesColors.bin.

LISTING 13.15:   Serializing a collection

```
Private Sub Button2_Click(…) Handles Button2.Click
    Dim R1 As New Rectangle()
    R1.X = 1
    R1.Y = 1
    R1.Width = 10
```

```
        R1.Height = 20
        Dim R2 As New Rectangle()
        R2.X = 10
        R2.Y = 10
        R2.Width = 100
        R2.Height = 200
        Dim shapes As New ArrayList()
        shapes.Add(R1)
        shapes.Add(R2)
        shapes.Add(Color.Chartreuse)
        shapes.Add(Color.DarkKhaki.GetBrightness)
        shapes.Add(Color.DarkKhaki.GetHue)
        shapes.Add(Color.DarkKhaki.GetSaturation)
        Dim saveFile As FileStream
        saveFile = File.OpenWrite("C:\ShapesColors.bin")
        saveFile.Seek(0, SeekOrigin.End)
        Dim formatter As BinaryFormatter = New BinaryFormatter()
        formatter.Serialize(saveFile, shapes)
        saveFile.Close()
        MsgBox("ArrayList serialized successfully")
End Sub
```

The last three calls to the Add method add the components of another color to the collection. Instead of adding the color as is, I'll add three color components, from which we can reconstruct the color Color.DarkKhaki. Then I proceed to save the entire collection to a file by using the same statements as before. The difference is that I don't call the Serialize method for each object. I call it once and pass the entire ArrayList as an argument.

To read a file with the description of an object that has been persisted with the Serialize method, simply call the formatter object's Deserialize method, and assign the result to an appropriately declared variable. In the preceding example, the value returned by the Deserialize method must be assigned to an ArrayList variable. The syntax of the Deserialize method is the following, where *str* is a Stream object pointing to the file with the data:

```
object = Bformatter.Deserialize(str)
```

Because the Deserialize method returns an Object variable, you must cast it to the ArrayList type with the CType() function. To use the Deserialize method, declare a variable that can hold the value returned by the method. If the data to be deserialized is a Rectangle, declare a Rectangle variable. If it's a collection, declare a variable of the same collection type. Then call the Deserialize method, and cast the value returned to the appropriate type. The following statements outline the process:

```
Dim object As <type>
{ code to set up a Stream variable (str) and BinaryFormatter}
object = CType(Bformatter.Serialize(str), <type>)
```

Listing 13.16 is the code that retrieves the items from the ShapesColors.bin file and stores them into an ArrayList. I added a few statements to print all the items of the ArrayList.

LISTING 13.16:   Deserializing a collection

```
Private Sub Button1_Click(…) Handles Button1.Click
    Dim readFile As FileStream
    readFile = File.OpenRead("C:\ShapesColors.bin")
    Dim BFormatter As BinaryFormatter
    BFormatter = New BinaryFormatter()
    Dim Shapes As New ArrayList()
    Dim R1 As Rectangle
    Shapes = CType(BFormatter.Deserialize(readFile), ArrayList)
    Dim i As Integer
    TextBox1.AppendText("The ArrayList contains " & Shapes.Count & _
                        " objects " & vbCrLf & vbCrLf)
    For i = 0 To Shapes.Count - 1
        TextBox1.AppendText(Shapes(i).ToString & vbCrLf)
    Next
End Sub
```

The Bottom Line

Create XML documents.   XML documents can be built easily with the XElement and XAttribute classes. XElement represents an element, and its constructor accepts as arguments the element's name and either the element's value or a series of attributes and nested elements. XAttribute represents an attribute, and its constructor accepts as arguments the attribute's name and its value. You can also assign an XML document directly to an XElement.

Master It   Create the XML segment that describes an object of the Item type, defined by the following class:

```
Class Item
     Property ID As String
     Property Name As String
     Property Prices As Price
     Property Name As String
Class Price
         Property Retail As PriceDetails
         Property WholeSale As PriceDetails
         Class PriceDetails
             Property Price As Decimal
             Property VolumeDiscount As Decimal
    End Class
    Class Dimension
        Property Width As Decimal
        Property Height As Decimal
        Property Depth As Decimal
    End Class
```

Navigate through an XML document and locate the information you need. The XElement class provides a number of methods for accessing the contents of an XML document. The Elements method returns the child elements of the current element by the name specified with the argument you pass to the method as a string. The Element method is quite similar, but it returns the first child element by the specified name. The Descendants method returns all the elements by the specified name under the current element, regardless of whether they're direct children of the current element. Finally, the Attribute method returns the value of the attribute by the specified name of the current element.

> **Master It** Assuming an XML document with the following structure, write the expressions to retrieve all cities in the document and all cities under the third country in the document.

```
<Countries>
   <Country>
      <City> ... </City>
      <City> ... </City>
   </Country>
   <Country>

   ...
   </Country>

...
</Countries>
```

> **Master It** Assuming that both country and city names are specified in the document with the Name element, explain the difference between the queries:

```
Dim q1 = countries.Elements("Country").Elements("Name")
Dim q2 = countries.Descendants("Name")
```

Convert arbitrary objects into XML documents and back with serialization. *Serialization* is the process of converting an object into a stream of bytes. This process (affectionately known as *dehydration*) generates a stream of bytes or characters, which can be stored or transported. To serialize an object, you can use the BinaryFormatter or SoapFormatter class. You can also use the XmlSerializer class to convert objects into XML documents. All three classes expose a Serialize class that accepts as arguments the object to be serialized and a stream object and writes the serialized version of the object to the specified stream. The opposite of serialization is called *deserialization*. To reconstruct the original object, you use the Deserialize method of the same class you used to serialize the object.

> **Master It** Describe the process of serializing an object with the XmlSerializer class.

Chapter 14

An Introduction to LINQ

In Chapter 12, "Storing Data in Collections," you learned how to create collections, from simple arrays to specialized collections such as HashTables and Lists, and how to iterate through them with loops to locate items. Typical collections contain objects, and you already know how to create and manipulate custom objects. In Chapter 13, "XML In Modern Programming," you learned how to serialize these collections into XML documents, as well as how to create XML documents from scratch. And in Part V of this book, you'll learn how to manipulate large amounts of data stored in databases.

Each data source provides its own technique for searching and manipulating individual items. What is common in all data sources are the operations we perform with the data; we want to be able to query the data, select the values we're interested in, and update the data sources by adding new data or editing the existing data. It's therefore reasonable to assume a common query language for all data sources. This common query language was introduced with version 3.5 of the Framework and is now part of all .NET languages. It's the LINQ component.

LINQ stands for *Language Integrated Query*, a small language for querying data sources. For all practical purposes, it's an extension to Visual Basic. More specifically, LINQ consists of statements that you can embed into a program to select items from a collection based on various criteria. Unlike a loop that examines each object's properties and either selects or rejects the object, it, LINQ is a declarative language: It allows you to specify the criteria, instead of specifying how to select the objects. A declarative language, as opposed to a procedural language, specifies the operation you want to perform, and not the steps to take. VB is a procedural language; the language of SQL Server, T-SQL, is a declarative language.

In this chapter, you'll learn how to do the following:

◆ Perform simple LINQ queries.

◆ Create and process XML files with LINQ to XML.

◆ Process relational data with LINQ to SQL.

What Is LINQ?

Although defining LINQ is tricky, a simple example will demonstrate the structure of LINQ and what it can do for your application. Let's consider an array of integers:

```
Dim data() As Int16 = {3, 2, 5, 4, 6, 4, 12, 43, 45, 42, 65}
```

To select specific elements of this array, you'd write a For...Next loop, examine each element of the array, and either select it by storing it into a new array or ignore it. To select the elements that are numerically smaller than 10, you'd write a loop like the following:

```
Dim smallNumbers As New ArrayList
Dim itm As Integer
For Each itm In data
    If itm < 10 Then
        smallNumbers.Add(itm)
    End If
Next
```

Can you see why I'm using an ArrayList to store the selected values? I could have used another array, but arrays must be declared with dimensions, and I'd have to resize the array or start with an array large enough to store all the elements. Let's do the same with LINQ:

```
Dim smallNumbers = From n In data
                   Where n < 10
                   Select n
```

This is a peculiar statement indeed, unless you're familiar with SQL, in which case you can easily spot the similarities. LINQ, however, is not based on SQL, and not every operation has an equivalent in both. Both SQL and LINQ, however, are declarative languages that have many similarities. If you're familiar with SQL, you have already spotted the similarities and the fact that LINQ rearranges the basic elements. Whereas SQL can be used only with database tables, LINQ can be applied to collections, XML files, and SQL tables. It's a uniform language for querying data from several data sources.

Let's look at the LINQ query in greater detail:

```
Dim smallNumbers = From n In data
                   Where n < 10
                   Select n
```

Start with the structure where the selected elements will be stored; this structure will hold the result of the query. The *smallNumbers* variable is declared without a type, because its type is determined by the type of the collection you're querying. Type inference, which must be turned on for this statement to work, makes this possible. If type inference is off, you must declare the variable that will accept the result of the query.

Because the query selects elements from the *data* array, the *smallNumbers* variable can't represent anything but an array of integers. Actually, it's not exactly an array of integers; it's a typed collection of integers that implements the IEnumerable interface. If you hover the pointer over the name of the collection, you'll see that its type is IEnumerable(Of Short).

The LINQ query starts after the equals sign with the `From` keyword, which is followed by a variable that represents the current item in the collection, followed by the `In` keyword and the name of the collection. The variable is called the *control variable*, just like the variable of a `For…Next` or `For Each` loop, and it represents the entity you're working with. If the collection is an array of integers, the control variable is an integer; if the collection is a List of Customer objects, then the control variable is a Customer object. The first part of the query specifies the collection we're going to query.

Then comes the `Where` clause that limits the selection. The `Where` keyword is followed by an expression that involves the control variable; this expression limits your selection. In this extremely trivial example, I select the elements that are less than 10. The expression of the `Where` clause can become quite complicated, as you will see shortly. It's a VB-like expression that's evaluated for every element in the collection; it returns a True/False value; and it determines which elements will be selected, and which elements will be ignored.

The last keyword in the expression, the `Select` keyword, determines what you're selecting. In most cases, you will select the control variable itself but not always. Here's a variation of the previous query expression:

```
Dim evenValues = From n In data _
      Where m mod 2 = 0
      Select "Number " & n.ToString & " is even"
```

Here, I select the even numbers from the original array and then form a string for each of the selected values. This time, the result of the query (the *evenValues* variable) is an IEnumerable of strings, as determined by the compiler. The `Select` clause is optional; if you omit it, the query will return the control variable itself.

But why bother with a new component to select values from an array? A `For Each` loop that processes each item in the collection is not really complicated and is quite efficient. LINQ is a universal approach to querying data, and it can be used to query all kinds of data, from XML documents to databases. When you work with databases, for example, you can't afford to move all the data to the client, select a few of them from within a loop, and ignore the rest. A database table may contain thousands and thousands of rows, and you may end up selecting a few hundred of them. LINQ is smart enough to execute the appropriate statements against the database and return to the client only the data you're interested in. I'll discuss these aspects of LINQ and databases (LINQ to SQL) in much detail later in this chapter.

As I have mentioned in the introduction, LINQ isn't limited to arrays and collections. Although iterating through an array of integers, or even objects, may be trivial, the same isn't true for XML documents. LINQ allows you to select the elements of an XML document you're interested in without having to navigate through the nodes of the document, as we did in the previous chapter. At any rate, LINQ is the latest and hottest technology from Redmond — it may very well become a universal language, just like SQL. It's a very powerful and flexible tool that can be used in many diverse situations. It's certainly much more flexible than straight VB code, because it's a declarative language. Remember that with LINQ, you specify what you want to do, not how the computer will do it.

LINQ Components

To support such a wide range of data sources, LINQ is comprised of multiple components, which are the following:

LINQ to XML   This component enables you to create and process XML documents. In effect, it replaces XQuery expressions that are used today to select the items of interest in an XML document. It also replaces the `Where` method of the `Elements` and `Descendants` properties. In effect, the compiler calls these methods behind the scenes, and LINQ is only "syntactic sugar" that hides much of the complexity of querying collections with extension methods. Because of LINQ to XML, some new classes that support XML were introduced to Visual Basic, and XML has become a basic data type of the language, as discussed in the preceding chapter. In this chapter, you'll learn how to use LINQ to XML to create, query, and transform XML files.

LINQ to Objects   This component enables you to search any collection of built-in or custom objects. If you have a collection of Color objects, for example, you can select the colors with a brightness of 0.5 or more via the following expression:

```
Dim colors() As Color = {Color.White, _
                         Color.LightYellow, Color.Cornsilk, _
                         Color.Linen, Color.Blue, Color.Violet}
Dim brightColors = From c In colors _
                   Where c.GetBrightness > 0.5
```

Likewise, you can select the rectangles with a minimum or maximum area by using a query like the following:

```
Dim rects() As Rectangle = _
          {New Rectangle(0, 0, 100, 120), _
           New Rectangle(10, 10, 6, 8)}
Dim query = From R In rects _
            Where R.Width * R.Height > 100
```

In addition to querying data, you can also group related data together, calculate aggregates, and even transform the original data (creating an HTML or XML file with the data of a collection is a trivial process, as you will see later in this chapter).

LINQ to SQL   This component enables you to query relational data by using LINQ rather than SQL. If you're familiar with SQL, you recognize the following statement that retrieves the products in a specific category of the Northwind database:

```
SELECT * FROM Products
WHERE Products.CategoryID = 2
```

To execute this statement against the Northwind database, however, you must set up a Connection object to connect to the database, a Command object to execute the command, and a DataReader object to read the results returned by the query. (Don't worry if you're not familiar with SQL and databases, which are discussed later in this chapter.) With LINQ to SQL, you can set up a DataContext object, which is roughly equivalent to the Connection object, and then use it to execute LINQ queries against the database.

```
customers = From prod In db.GetTable(Of Product)()
            Where prod.CategoryID = 2
            Select New Product With _
                        {.ID = prod.ProductID,
                         .Name = prod.ProductName,
                         .Price = prod.UnitPrice}
```

In the preceding statement, *db* is a properly initialized DataContext object. This query returns a collection of an anonymous type with three properties (ID, Name, and Price). This is a trivial example, meant to demonstrate how you can access diverse data sources and query them in a consistent way with the basic LINQ syntax; the details of LINQ to SQL are discussed in detail later in this chapter. The point I'm trying to make here is that LINQ allows you to work against database tables as if they were collections of typed objects. The same query would have worked with a collection of Product objects. All you have to do is change the source of the data by replacing the expression db.GetTable(Of Product) with the name of the collection.

LINQ to DataSet   This component is similar to LINQ to SQL, in the sense that they both query relational data. The LINQ to DataSet component allows you query data that have already been stored in a DataSet at the client. DataSets are discussed in detail later in this book, but I won't discuss the LINQ to DataSet component, because the DataSet is an extremely rich object and quite functional on its own.

LINQ to Entities   This is similar to the LINQ to Objects component, only the objects are based on relational data. Entities are discussed in the last part of this book, and they're classes that reflect the tables in a database. These classes are generated automatically, and they handle the basic data operations: querying tables and updating, deleting or inserting rows in the tables. The LINQ to Entities component is discussed in detail in Chapter 17, "Using the Data Entity Model," of this book. Actually, LINQ is one of the empowering technologies for data entities.

New flavors of LINQ keep coming up — you may end up designing your own flavor of LINQ to support your custom data so that other developers can use them with standard tools. There's already a LINQ to Amazon component that allows you to query the books at Amazon.com using LINQ. The essence of LINQ is that it allows developers to query widely differently data sources using the same syntax. You can even query database using LINQ.

LINQ to Objects

This section focuses on querying collections of objects. Although you can query many types of collections, including arrays, in this section I'll focus on List collections to promote the use of strongly typed data and to show you how nicely typed data integrate with LINQ. As you can guess, the most interesting application of LINQ to Objects is to select items from a collection of custom objects. Let's create a custom class to represent products:

```
Public Class Product
Public Property ProductID() As String
Public Property ProductName() As String
```

```
Public Property ProductPrice() As Decimal
Public Property ProductExpDate() As Date
End Class
```

I'm not showing the implementation of various properties; let's work with auto-implemented properties for now. This class definition may appear in a class file or in a form outside any procedure. The *Products* collection is a List(Of Product) collection, and it's populated with statements like the following:

```
Dim Products As New List(Of Product)
Dim P As Product
P = New Product
P.ProductID = "10A-Y"
P.ProductName = "Product 1"
P.ProductPrice = 21.45
P.ProductExpDate = #8/1/2009#
Products.add(P)
```

Assuming that you have added a few more custom objects to your list, you can use LINQ to query your collection of products based on any property (or combination of properties) of its items. To find the products that cost more than $20 and are expired already, you can formulate the following query:

```
Dim query = From prod In products
            Where prod.ProductPrice < 20
                And Year(prod.ProductExpDate) < 2010
            Select prod
```

The result of the query is also a List collection, and it contains the products that meet the specified criteria. To iterate through the selected items and display them in a TextBox control, we use a For...Each loop, as shown next:

```
For Each prod In query
    TextBox1.AppendText(prod.ProductID & vbTab &
        prod.ProductName & vbTab &
        prod.ProductPrice.ToString("##0.00") & vbTab &
        prod.ProductExpDate.ToShortDateString & vbCrLf)
Next
```

Another component of a LINQ expression is the Order By clause, which determines how the objects will be ordered in the output list. To sort the output of the preceding example in descending order, append the following Order By clause to the expression:

```
Dim query = From prod In products
            Where prod.ProductPrice < 20
                And Year(prod.ProductExpDate) < 2010
            Select prod
            Order By prod.ProductName
```

Anonymous Types and Extension Methods

LINQ is based on three pillars that are not related to each other — they aren't even part of LINQ. These pillars are anonymous types, extension methods, and object and collection initializers. You're already familiar with all three of them. Object initializers and anonymous types were presented in Chapter 8, "Working with Objects." Extension methods were introduced in Chapter 13, "XML in Modern Programming." I'll now review these topics and how they're combined in LINQ.

Anonymous types allow you to create typed objects on the fly; this is what the Select keyword of LINQ does. It allows you to create arbitrary objects and form collections of anonymous types. The compiler knows their properties (it actually generates classes that describe these arbitrary objects on the fly) and incorporates them in IntelliSense. Object initializers allow you to create anonymous types using the With keyword right in the Select clause of a LINQ query. You may be querying a collection of Product objects but are only interested in their IDs and prices. Instead of selecting the control variable that contains all the fields of each product, you can create a new anonymous type on the fly with an expression like the following:

```
Select New With {.ProductName = prod.Name, .ProductPrice = prod.UnitPrice}
```

As you will see in the following sections, it's quite common to create anonymous types with selected fields on the fly in LINQ queries, because we rarely need all the fields of the objects we're querying. If you're familiar with SQL, you already know that it's a bad practice to select all fields from one or more tables. They are called anonymous because they have no name you can use to create instances of these types; other than that, they're regular types with strongly typed properties.

Extension methods are methods that you implement for specific types without seeing the code of the original type. The Array class, for example, was extended by the addition of several such methods, including the Count, Skip, and Take methods. These methods are not actual members of the array; they're extension methods that apply to all collections that implement the IEnumerable interface.

As you recall from the previous chapter, the collections expose the Where method, which accepts a lambda expression as an argument to select specific elements. The syntax of the Where method, however, is quite awkward. The Where keyword of LINQ does the same, but it does so in a more elegant and intuitive manner. In effect, the compiler translates the LINQ queries into expressions with extension methods.

As you recall from the previous chapter, lambda expressions are what make extension methods so powerful. Let's look at a few more interesting extension methods that make collections, including arrays, extremely flexible and powerful. The Sum method returns the sum of the elements in a collection that holds numeric data. This is a pretty limited aggregate operator, however. What if you wanted the sum of the squares or another metric of the collection's members? An overloaded form of the Sum method accepts a lambda expression as an argument; this allows you to specify your own aggregate. To calculate the sum of the squares, for example, use the following expression:

```
Dim numbers = {1.01, 31.93, 8.12, 5.05, 21.81, 17.33, 2.45}
Dim sumOfSquares = numbers.Sum(Function(n) n ^ 2)
```

This returns the sum of the squares in the *numbers* array. If you wanted to calculate the sum of the logarithms, you'd use a lambda function like this: Function(n) Math.Log(n).

To calculate averages instead of sums, use the Average extension method. The average of the squares of the numeric values is as follows:

```
Dim averageOfSquares = numbers.Average(Function(n) n ^ 2)
```

Experiment with the extension methods of the Array class, or any collection you wish. The extension methods are shown in the IntelliSense box with the same icon as the regular method and a little arrow pointing down.

Querying Arbitrary Collections

As I mentioned already, you can apply LINQ to all classes that implement the IEnumerable interface. Many methods of the Framework return their results as a collection that implements the IEnumerable interface. As discussed in the tutorial "Accessing Folders and Files," (available for download from www.sybex.com/go/masteringvb2010), the GetFiles method of the IO.Directory class retrieves the files of a specific folder and returns them as a collection of strings:

```
Dim files = Directory.GetFiles("C:\")
```

I'm assuming that you have turned on type inference for this project (it's on by default), so I'm not declaring the type of the *files* collection. If you hover over the *files* keyword, you'll see that its type is String() — an array of strings. This is the GetFiles method's return type, so you need not declare the *files* variable with the same type. The variable type is inferred from its value.

To find out the properties of each file, create a new FileInfo object for each file, and then examine the values of the FileInfo object's properties. To create an instance of the FileInfo class that represents a file, you'd use the following statement:

```
Dim FI As New FileInfo(file_name)
```

(As a reminder, the FileInfo class as well as the DirectoryInfo class belong to the IO namespace. You must either import the namespace into the current project or prefix the class names with the IO namespace: IO.FileInfo.) The value of the *FI* variable can now be used in the Where clause of the expression to specify a filter for the query:

```
Dim smallFiles = _
            From file In Directory.GetFiles("C:\")
            Where New FileInfo(file).Length < 10000
            Order By file
            Select file
```

The *file* control variable is local to the query, and you cannot access it from the rest of the code. You can actually create a new *file* variable in the loop that iterates through the selected files, as shown in the following code segment:

```
For Each file In smallFiles
    Debug.WriteLine(file)
Next
```

The selection part of the query is not limited to the same variable as specified in the From clause. To select the name of the qualifying files, instead of their paths, use the following selection clause:

```
Select New FileInfo(file).Name
```

The *smallFiles* variable should still be an array of strings, right? Not quite. This time, if you hover the pointer over the name of the *smallFiles* variable, you'll see that its type is IEnumerable(Of String). And this makes sense, because the result of the query is not of the same type as its source. This time we created a new string for each of the selected items, so *smallFiles* is an IEnumerable of strings. Let's select each file's name and size with the following query:

```
Dim smallFiles = _
        From file In Directory.GetFiles("C:\")
        Where New FileInfo(file).Length > 10000
        Select New FileInfo(file).Name,
               New FileInfo(file).Length
```

This time, *smallFiles* is of the IEnumerable(Of <anonymous type>) type. The anonymous type isn't really anonymous; the compiler generates a class to represent the anonymous type internally and gives it a name like VB_AnonymousType_1'3 or something — and yes, the single quote is part of the name, not a typo. However, you can't use this class to declare new objects. Anonymous types are very convenient (like auto-implemented properties, in a way), but they can't be used outside their scope (the module in which they were created).

Because I selected the two properties of interest in the query (the file's name and size), I can display them with the following loop:

```
For Each file In smallFiles
    Debug.WriteLine(file.Name & vbTab & file.Length.ToString)
Next
```

As soon as you type in the name of the *file* variable and the following period, you will see the Name and Length properties of the anonymous type in the IntelliSense box (proof that the compiler has generated a new type on the fly).

The properties of the new type are named after the items specified in the Select clause, and they have the same type. You can also control the names of the properties of the anonymous type with the following syntax:

```
Select New With {.FileName = New FileInfo(file).Name,
                 .FileSize = New FileInfo(file).Length}
```

This time you select a new object, and a new variable is created on the fly and has two properties named FileName and FileSize. The values of the two properties are specified as usual. Note that, although you can specify the names of the properties of the anonymous type, you can't specify the anonymous type's name. To display each selected file's name and size, modify the For...Each loop as follows:

```
For Each file In smallFiles
    Debug.WriteLine(file.FileName & vbTab &
                    file.FileSize.ToString)
Next
```

As you can see, LINQ is not a trivial substitute for a loop that examines the properties of the collection items; it's a powerful and expressive syntax for querying data in your code that creates data types on the fly and exposes them in your code.

You can also limit the selection by applying the Where method directly to the collection:

```
Dim smallFiles = Directory.GetFiles("C:\").Where (
                    Function(file) (New FileInfo(file).Length > 10000))
```

The functions you specify in certain extended methods are called *lambda functions*, and they're declared either inline, if they're single-line functions, or as delegates.

Let me explain how the Where extension method of the previous sample code segment works. The Where method should be followed by an expression that evaluates to a True/False value — the lambda function. First specify the signature of the function; in our case, the function accepts a single argument, which is the current item in the collection. Obviously, the Where clause will be evaluated for each item in the collection, and for each item, the function will accept a different object as an argument. In the following section, you'll see lambda functions that accept two arguments. The name of the argument can be anything; it's a name that you will use in the definition of the function to access the current collection item. Then comes the definition of the function, which is the expression that compares the current file's size to 10,000 bytes. If the size exceeds 10,000 bytes, the function will return True — otherwise, False.

In this example, the lambda function is implemented in-line. To implement more complicated logic, you can write a function and pass the address of this function to the Where clause. Let's consider that the function implementing the filtering is the following:

```
Private Function IsLargeTIFFFile(ByVal fileName As String) As Boolean
    Dim file As FileInfo
    file = New FileInfo(fileName)
    If file.Length > 10000 And file.Extension.ToUpper = ".TIF" Then
        Return True
    Else
        Return False
    End If
End Function
```

To call this function from within a LINQ expression, use the following syntax:

```
Dim largeImages =
    Directory.GetFiles("C:\").Where(AddressOf IsLargeTIFFFile)
    MsgBox(smallFiles.Count)
```

Aggregating with LINQ

Another very important aspect of LINQ is that it allows you to query for aggregates. More often than not, you're not interested in the qualifying rows in a database (or objects in a collection) but rather in their aggregates. In many scenarios, the orders placed by each customer are not nearly as important as the total monthly revenue or the average of the orders in a given period. Aggregate data can be easily compared and used to allow managers to adjust their marketing or selling strategies. Likewise, the total cost of discontinued items is a useful metric, as opposed to a list of discontinued items and prices, and so on. Now that you can write LINQ queries to select objects based on any criteria, you can certainly iterate through the selected objects and calculate all the metrics you're interested in. LINQ can do better than that; it allows you to select the desired aggregates, rather than individual objects. And it's much faster to let LINQ perform the calculations, rather than doing it yourself by looping through the data. If the data resides in a database, LINQ can calculate the aggregates over millions of records, without moving all the qualifying rows from the database to the client computer and processing them there.

By default, LINQ adds a few extension methods for calculating aggregates to any collection that supports the IEnumerable interface. Let's return to the array of integers, the *data* array. To calculate the count of all values, call the Count method of the *data* array. The count of elements in the *data* array is given with the following expression:

```
Dim count = data.Count
```

In addition to the Count method, any LINQ-capable class exposes the Sum method, which sums the values of a specific element or attribute in the collection. To calculate the sum of the selected values from the *data* array, use the following LINQ expression:

```
Dim sum = From n data
          Where n > 10
          Select n.Sum
```

You can also calculate arbitrary aggregates by using the Aggregate method, which accepts a lambda expression as an argument. This expression, in turn, accepts two arguments: the current value and the aggregate. The implementation of the function, which is usually a single-liner, calculates the aggregate. Let's consider a lambda expression that calculates the sum of the squares over a sequence of numeric values. The declaration of the function is as follows:

```
Function(aggregate, value)
```

Its implementation is shown here. (This is just the code that increases the aggregate at each step; no function declaration is needed.)

```
aggregate + value ^ 2
```

Note that the preceding expression evaluates the aggregate by adding a new value (the square of the current number in the collection) to the aggregate; it doesn't actually update the aggregate. In other words, you can't use a statement like this one (as intuitive as it may look):

```
aggregate += value ^ 2
```

To calculate the sum of the squares of all items in the *data* array, use the following LINQ expression:

```
Dim sumSquares = data.Aggregate(
                        Function(sumSquare As Long, n As Integer)
                            sumSquare + n ^ 2
```

The single statement that implements the aggregate adds the square of the current element to the *sumSquare* argument. When you're done, the *sumSquare* variable holds the sum of the squares of the array's elements. If you hover the pointer over the *sumSquare* variable, you'll see that it is an Integer or Double type, depending on the type of the values in the collection you're aggregating. In short, the lambda expression for evaluating aggregates accepts two arguments: the aggregate and the current value. The code is an expression that updates the aggregate, and this is the function's return value, which is assigned to the aggregate.

Aggregates are not limited to numeric values. Here's an interesting example of a LINQ expression that reverses the words in a sentence. The code starts by splitting the sentence into words, which are returned in an array of strings. Then, it calls the **Aggregate** method, passing a lambda expression as an argument. This expression is a function that prefixes the aggregate (a new string with the words in reverse order) with the current word:

```
Dim sentence =
    "The quick brown fox jumped over the lazy dog"
Dim reverseSentence =
            sentence.Split(" "c).Aggregate(
            Function(newSentence, word) (
            word & " " & newSentence))
```

This code segment is a bit complicated and calls for an explanation. It starts by creating an array of strings: The words in the sentence are extracted by the Split method into an array of strings. Then we apply the **Aggregate** extension method to the array. The **Aggregate** method accepts the lambda expression as an argument, which creates a new string, the *newSentence* string, by inserting each new word at the beginning of the sentence. If you were appending the words to the *newSentence* variable, you'd be re-creating the original string from its pieces; here, I reversed the order of the words.

The lambda expression you pass to the **Aggregate** method is a function that accepts two arguments: the control variable and the aggregate variable. The function is executed for each item in the collection, and the value of the current item is the control variable (in our case, each consecutive word in the sentence). The aggregate variable *newSentence* is the variable in which you aggregate the desired quantity. At the end of the loop, the *newSentence* variable contains the words extracted from the string but in reverse order.

The following are a few more interesting extension methods:

Take (N), TakeWhile (*Expression*) This method selects a number of elements from the collection. The first form selects the first *n* elements, while the second form continues selecting elements from the collection while the expression is True. To select values while they're smaller than 10, use the following lambda expression:

```
Function(n) n < 10
```

This expression selects values until it finds one that exceeds 10. The selection stops there, regardless of whether some of the following elements drop below 10.

Skip and SkipWhile   The Skip and SkipWhile methods are equivalent to the Take and TakeWhile methods: They skip a number of items and select the remaining ones. You can use the Skip and Take methods in tandem to implement paging. Assuming that pageSize is the number of items you want to display at once and page is the number of the current page, you can retrieve any page's data with a statement like the following:

```
Data.Skip((pageSize - 1) * page).Take(pageSize)
```

Distinct   The Distinct method, finally, returns the distinct values in the collection:

```
Dim uniqueValues = data.Distinct
```

Some Practical LINQ Examples

At this point, you can create an array of simple objects to explore some of the more advanced features of LINQ to Objects. The sample code presented in this section comes from the IEnumerables project (available for download from www.sybex.com/go/masteringvb2010), whose interface is shown in Figure 14.1. Each button generates some output, which is displayed on the TextBox that takes up most of the form.

FIGURE 14.1
The IEnumerables
sample application

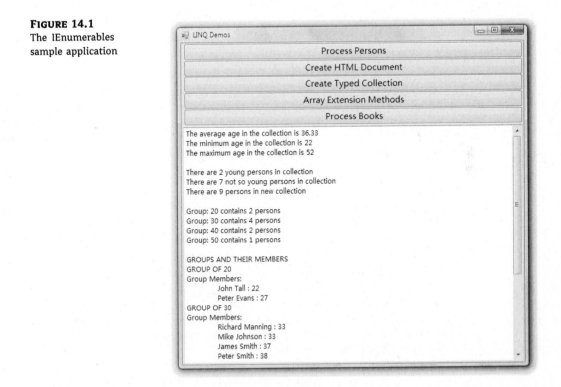

The following array contains a number of objects representing people, but they're anonymous types (there's no collection that implements the specific type). In the IEnumerables project, the *ArrayOfPersons* array is declared outside any procedure so that multiple event handlers can access it.

```
Dim ArrayOfPersons() = {New With {.SSN = "555-00-9001",
                                  .First = "Peter", .Last = "Evans", .Age = 27},
                        New With {.SSN = "555-00-9002", .
                                  First = "James", .Last = "Dobs", .Age = 42},
                        New With {.SSN = "555-00-9003", .First = "Richard",
                                  .Last = "Manning", .Age = 33},
                        New With {.SSN = "555-00-9004",
                                  .First = "Rob", .Last = "Johnson", .Age = 52},
                        New With {.SSN = "555-00-9005",
                                  .First = "Peter", .Last = "Smith", .Age = 38},
                        New With {.SSN = "555-00-9006",
                                  .First = "John", .Last = "Tall", .Age = 22},
                        New With {.SSN = "555-00-9007",
                                  .First = "Mike", .Last = "Johnson", .Age = 33},
                        New With {.SSN = "555-00-9008",
                                  .First = "Peter", .Last = "Larson", .Age = 43},
                        New With {.SSN = "555-00-9009",
                                  .First = "James", .Last = "Smith", .Age = 37}}
```

The basic age statistics for the array (minimum, maximum, and average values) can be obtained with the following expressions:

```
ArrayOfPersons.Average(Function(p) p.Age)
ArrayOfPersons.Min(Function(p) p.Age)
ArrayOfPersons.Max(Function(p) p.Age)
```

There's no need to iterate through the array's elements; the Average, Min, and Max extension methods return the desired aggregates. To select items from the array based on some criteria, use the Where method. The following queries extract the young and not-so-young people in the array (the threshold is 30 years):

```
Dim youngPersons = From p In ArrayOfPersons Where p.Age < 30 Select p
Dim notSoYoungPersons = From p In ArrayOfPersons Where p.Age >= 30 Select p
```

To combine two IEnumerable collections, use the Concat method, which is applied to a collection and accepts as an argument another collection:

```
Dim allPersons = youngPersons.Concat(notSoYoungPersons)
```

If you don't care about the names and other data for the "not-so-young" people, you can calculate the average age in this age group with the following query:

```
Dim youngPersonsAvgAge =
        (From p In ArrayOfPersons Where p.Age < 30 Select p.Age).Average
```

Pretty simple. First determine the segment of the population you want to aggregate over, and then call the `Average` method. Another, less obvious and certainly less recommended approach is to calculate the sum of the ages and their count and divide the two values:

```
Dim youPersonsAvgAge2 =
            (From p In ArrayOfPersons Where p.Age < 30 Select p.Age).Sum /
            (From p In ArrayOfPersons Where p.Age < 30).Count
```

Aggregates are the most useful operations you can perform on a collection, but you'll rarely aggregate over the entire collection. The average age of an entire population or the purchases of an entire population often are not as useful as the aggregates of specific segments of a population. In the preceding example, I created a second collection made up only of the people we were interested in and then applied the aggregation operators over that entire population. Let's do the same without an intermediate collection.

GROUPING AND AGGREGATING

To demonstrate the grouping operator of LINQ, let's break down the population according to age. Specifically, let's break the population into segments by decade (people in their 20s, 30s, and so on). Breaking a set of data into groups of related items is known as *grouping*, and it's supported by the `GroupBy` extension method. The `GroupBy` extension method accepts as an argument a lambda expression, which indicates the various groups. To group ages according to their decade, you'd use an expression like the following:

```
Math.Floor(Age / 10) * 10
```

Consider the ages 41 and 49. The `Floor` function returns the largest integer that doesn't exceed its argument, and in this case it will return 4 for both values (4.1 and 4.9). Then, multiply this integer value by 10 to obtain the actual decade (40). Once you have come up with an expression to group people according to their age, you can write the query to retrieve the groups:

```
Dim grouped = ArrayOfPersons.GroupBy(Function(p) Math.Floor(p.Age / 10) * 10)
```

If you hover the cursor over the grouped variable, you will see that its type is IEnumerable. But what does it contain? The exact type of the return value is `IEnumerable(Of Double, anonymous_type)`. The return value of the `GroupBy` method is an IEnumerable collection with the keys of the groups (the age decade) and the actual items. As you can see, the compiler has figured out that the key is a Double value (the age), and the actual object is of an anonymous type — the exact same type as the elements of the array.

The following loop prints the names of the groups and their count (number of people in that age decade):

```
For Each grp In grouped
    TextBox1.AppendText("Group: " & grp.Key &
                        " contains " & grp.Count.ToString & " persons" & vbCrLf)
Next
```

Each item in the collection has a `Key` property (the value according to which the items are grouped) and a `Count` property. The actual value of the *grp* variable is a collection of `Person` objects. To print the people in each age group, write a loop like the following:

```
TextBox1.AppendText("GROUPS AND THEIR MEMBERS" & vbCrLf)
For Each group In grouped
    TextBox1.AppendText("GROUP OF " & group.Key.ToString & vbCrLf)
    TextBox1.AppendText("Group Members:" & vbCrLf)
    For Each person In group.OrderBy(Function(p) p.Age)
        TextBox1.AppendText(vbTab & person.First & " " &
                        person.Last & " : " & person.Age.ToString & vbCrLf)
    Next
Next
```

The outer loop goes through each group. At this level, you access the `Key` property and use it as a header. The inner loop goes through items in the current group. The preceding statements will generate the following output:

```
GROUP OF 20
Group Members:
    John Tall : 22
    Peter Evans : 27
GROUP OF 30
Group Members:
    Richard Manning : 33
    Mike Johnson : 33
    James Smith : 37
    Peter Smith : 38
GROUP OF 40
Group Members:
    James Dobs : 42
    Peter Larson : 43
GROUP OF 50
Group Members:
    Rob Johnson : 52
```

How about calculating aggregates on each group? To perform aggregates on the groups, you must create another collection of anonymous types, just like the original, with an extra field that groups the items together. The following statement generates a new collection of objects that includes each person's age group (the `ageGroup` property):

```
Dim tmpGroups = From person In ArrayOfPersons
                Select New With {.SSN = person.SSN, .First = person.First,
                        .Last = person.Last, .Age = person.Age,
                        .ageGroup = Math.Floor(person.Age / 10) * 10}
```

Now, you can calculate the average age in each group. The following query goes through each group and calculates the average age in each group. To make the query a little more interesting, I've added the number of members in each group:

```
Dim ageGroups = From P In tmpGroups
                Order By P.ageGroup
                Group By P.ageGroup Into G = Group,
                    AgeGroupCount = Count(),
                    ageGroupAverage = Average(System.Convert.ToDecimal(P.Age))
```

This query groups the members of the *tmpGroups* collection into groups based on the ageGroup property and then calculates the count of the members and the average age in each group. If you iterate through the members of the collection and print the age group and the two statistics, you'll get something like this:

```
AGE GROUP:  20    COUNT:  2    AVERAGE AGE IN GROUP: 24.50
AGE GROUP:  30    COUNT:  4    AVERAGE AGE IN GROUP: 35.25
AGE GROUP:  40    COUNT:  2    AVERAGE AGE IN GROUP: 42.50
AGE GROUP:  50    COUNT:  1    AVERAGE AGE IN GROUP: 52.00
```

If you're wondering why you had to create an intermediate collection to add the grouping field instead of grouping by the expression Math.Floor(P.Age / 10) * 10, the answer is that you can't use functions or methods in a group's control variable. Some readers may have noticed that the collection should hold birth dates, not ages. Try to perform the same queries after replacing the Age property with a BirthDate property.

You have seen quite a few nontrivial LINQ queries, and you should have a good idea about LINQ and how flexible it is. Writing efficient queries will take a bit of effort, and you should explore on your own as many sample queries as you can. A good starting point is the 101 LINQ Samples page at http://msdn.microsoft.com/en-us/vbasic/bb688088.aspx (a great resource on LINQ by Microsoft). You won't find any explanations on the queries (not as of this writing, at least), but try to understand as many of the queries as you can. Personally, I find it very convenient to use LINQ in my code whenever possible, even with anonymous types.

Keep in mind that LINQ is a declarative language: It tells the compiler what to do, not how to do it. And that's what makes it very flexible. LINQ statements are executed in a single step, and you can't place a breakpoint inside a LINQ query to follow its execution. You just try to write a syntactically correct query and then test the results to make sure you got what you aimed for from the collection.

Transforming Objects with LINQ

In this section, you'll learn how to use LINQ to transform collections of objects. I'll start with a collection of custom objects and transform them into objects with a different structure. You'll also see how easy it is to create HTML or XML files to describe the same collection using LINQ.

In the examples so far, I used anonymous types, which are quite common and convenient. In large applications, however, where the same data may be reused in several parts of the application or by many developers, it's strongly recommended that you work with typed data. Let's start with a class that represents books, the Books class. It's a simple but not trivial class, because its definition contains two custom types and an array. Author information is stored in an array of Author objects. Each book's price and stocking information is stored in two custom objects; they're the Price and Stock properties. The Price property can have multiple values (retail and wholesale prices or any other price that suits you), and the Stock property is an object with two properties, the InStock and OnOrder properties. Here's the definition of the Books class:

```
Public Class Books
    Public Class Book
        Public Property ISBN As String
        Public Property Title As String
        Public Property Publisher As String
        Public Property Authors As Author()
        Public Property Price As Prices
        Public Property Stock As Stock
    End Class

    Public Class Prices
        Private _RetailPrice? As Decimal
        Private _StorePrice? As Decimal
        Private _OnlinePrice? As Decimal

        Public Property RetailPrice As Decimal
        ...
        End Property

        Public Property StorePrice As Decimal
        ...
        End Property

        Public Property OnlinePrice As Decimal
        ...
        End Property

    End Class

    Public Class Stock
        Private _OnOrder? As Integer
        Public Property InStock As Integer

        Public Property OnOrder As Integer
        ...
        End Property
    End Class


    Public Class Author
```

```
        Public Property FirstName As String
        Public Property LastName As String
    End Class
End Class
```

Some of properties are auto-implemented, while others are implemented with the usual setters and getters. The latter includes some business logic, such that prices can't be negative, but I'm not showing the equivalent code (which you can find in the IEnumerables project).

Create a few objects of the Book type and add them to a List collection. I'm using object initializers in the code, because that's the most compact notation, but you can create individual Book objects and add them to the collection if you want. Listing 14.1 shows the statements that initialize the allBooks collection.

LISTING 14.1:   Initializing a list of Book objects

```
Dim allBooks As New List(Of Books.Book)
        allBooks.Add(New Books.Book With
                {.ISBN = "1000000100", .Title = "Book 100",
                 .Publisher = "Wiley",
                 .Stock = New Books.Stock With
                        {.InStock = 14, .OnOrder = 20},
                 .Authors = {New Books.Author With
                        {.FirstName = "Richard",
                         .LastName = "Dobson"}},
                 .Price = New Books.Prices With
                        {.StorePrice = 12.95,
                         .RetailPrice = 15.95}})

        allBooks.Add(New Books.Book With
                {.ISBN = "1000000101", .Title = "Book 101",
                 .Publisher = "Sybex",
                 .Stock = New Books.Stock With
                        {.InStock = 8, .OnOrder = 25},
                 .Authors = {New Books.Author With
                        {.FirstName = "Bob",
                         .LastName = "Smith"}},
                 .Price = New Books.Prices With
                        {.StorePrice = 24.95,
                         .RetailPrice = 29.99}})
```

Let's start by transforming the list of books into an HTML document, like the one shown in Figure 14.2. We'll write a LINQ query as usual, but we'll embed it into an *XMLElement* variable. I'll start with the query that transforms the data and then explain it in detail. Listing 14.2 shows the code that creates the HTML document that produced the page shown in Figure 14.2.

LISTING 14.2: Transforming a collection into an XML segment

```
Dim html = <html>
               <h2>List of Books</h2>
               <table border="all">
                   <tr>
                       <td margin="10" width="90px">ISBN</td>
                       <td margin="10" width="280px">Title</td>
                       <td margin="10" width="140px">Author(s)</td>
                       <td margin="10" width="70px">Price</td>
                   </tr>
                   <%= From bk As Books.Book In allBooks
                       Select <tr>
                                 <td><%= bk.ISBN %></td>
                                 <td><%= bk.Title %></td>
                                 <td>
                                 <table>
                       <%= From au As Books.Author In bk.Authors
                           Order By au.LastName, au.FirstName
                           Select <tr><td>
                           <%= au.LastName & ", " &
                               au.FirstName %>
                           </td></tr> %>
                           </table>
                       </td>
                           <td align="right" valign="middle">
                           <%= bk.Price.RetailPrice.ToString %></td>
                   </tr>
                   %>
               </table>
           </html>
```

FIGURE 14.2
A collection of simple objects rendered as an HTML document

List of Books

ISBN	Title	Author(s)	Price
1000000100	Book 100	Dobson, Richard	15.95
1000000101	Book 101	Smith, Bob	29.99
1000000101	Book 101	Emilia, Tramp Mike, Sonders	29.99
1000000102	Book 102	Jack, Simpson Margot, Stapp Mike, Tyler	29.99

The code is really simple. It starts by generating an XML document and embeds the actual data in expression holes, which are delimited with the `<%=` and `%>` tags. The `html` variable is an XML document, and the first expression hole is a LINQ query. In the `Select` clause of the query, I created another XML document, which in turn contains expression holes. If you find this code segment complicated, please refer to the material in Chapter 12, where I discuss in detail how to build XML documents with expression holes. To read an expression like the one that defines the *html* variable, keep in mind the following simple rules:

Every time you see the opening angle bracket, you switch into XML mode.

Every time you see the <% tag, you switch into VB mode.

Note that while in VB mode, you can switch to XML mode without the closing %> tag; all it takes is another opening bracket to switch into XML mode. Of course in the end, all opening <% tags must be closed with the matching %> tag.

HTML tags are no different to the compiler than XML tags, so you easily create an XML document with the same data and the structure you want. After all, HTML documents are special cases of XML documents. You can use the XMLSerializer class to convert the collection of custom objects to an XML document with a single statement, but LINQ allows you to transform your data in just about any way you see fit. Try to create a comma-delimited file with the book data or a file with fixed-length columns for each of the properties.

Our next LINQ stop is LINQ to XML. In the following section, you'll learn how to combine the basic methods of the XElement class with LINQ to retrieve the desired elements and/or attributes from an XML document using LINQ. As you will see, you can use LINQ to query XML documents just as you did with collections.

LINQ to XML

The second component of LINQ is the LINQ to XML component. XML is gaining in popularity and acceptance, and Microsoft has decided to promote XML to a basic data type. Yes, XML is a data type like integers and strings! To understand how far VB is taking XML, type the following in a procedure or event handler:

```
Dim products = <Books>
                  <Book ISBN="0000000000001">
                   <Name>Book Title 1</Name>
                   <Price>11.95</Price>
                  </Book>
                  <Book ISBN="000000000002">
                   <Name>Book Title 2</Name>
                   <Price>10.25</Price>
                  </Book>
               </Books>
```

You need not worry too much about getting the document exactly right, because the editor works just like the XML editor. Every time you type an opening tag, it inserts the matching closing tag and ensures that what you're typing is a valid XML document. You can't apply a schema to the XML document you're creating, but you should expect this feature in a future version of Visual Studio.

You can create a new XML document in your code, but what can you do with it? You need a mechanism to manipulate the XML document with simple tools, and these tools are available through the following XML helper objects:

♦ XDocument represents the XML document.

♦ XComment represents a comment in the XML document.

◆ XElement represents an XML element.

◆ XAttribute represents an attribute in an XML element.

These objects can be used to access the document but also to create it. Instead of creating an XML document directly in your code, you can use the XML helper objects and a structural approach to create the same document. A simple XML document consists of elements, which may include attributes. To create a new XElement object, pass the element's name and value to its constructor:

```
New XElement(element_name, element_value)
```

The following statement will create a very simple XML document:

```
Dim XmlDoc = New XElement("Books")
MsgBox(XmlDoc.ToString)
```

You will see the string `<Books />` in a message box. This is a trivial, yet valid, XML document. To create the same book collection as we did earlier by using the helper objects, insert the following statements in a button's `Click` event handler:

```
Dim doc = _
    New XElement("Books", _
        New XElement("Book", _
            New XAttribute("ISBN", "0000000000001"), _
            New XElement("Price", 11.95), _
            New XElement("Name", "Book Title 1"), _
            New XElement("Stock", _
                New XAttribute("InStock", 12), _
                New XAttribute("OnOrder", 24))), _
        New XElement("Book", _
            New XAttribute("ISBN", "0000000000002"), _
            New XElement("Price", 10.25), _
            New XElement("Name", "Book Title 2"), _
            New XElement("Stock", _
                New XAttribute("InStock", 7), _
                New XAttribute("OnOrder", 10))))
```

I've added a twist to the new document to demonstrate the use of multiple attributes in the same element. The `Stock` element contains two attributes, `InStock` and `OnOrder`. Each element's value can be a basic data type, such as a string or a number, or another element. The `Price` element is a decimal value, and the `Name` element is a string. The `Book` element, however, contains three subelements: the `Price`, `Name`, and `Stock` elements.

The *doc* variable is of the XElement type. An XML document is not necessarily based on the XDocument class. The two basic operations you can perform with an XElement (and XDocument) object are to save it to a file and reload an XElement object from a file. The operations are performed with the `Save` and `Load` methods, which accept the file's name as an argument.

Adding Dynamic Content to an XML Document

The XML documents we've built in our code so far were static. Because XML support is built into VB, you can also create dynamic context, and this is where things get quite interesting. To insert some dynamic content into an XML document, insert the characters <%=. The editor will automatically insert the closing tag, which is %>. Everything within these two tags is treated as VB code and compiled. The two special tags create a placeholder in the document (or an expression hole), and the expression you insert in them is an embedded expression: You embed a VB expression in your document, and the compiler evaluates the expression and inserts the result in the XML document.

Here's a trivial XML document with an embedded expression. It's the statement that creates a document with a Book element (I copied it from a code segment presented in the preceding chapter), and I inserted the current date as an element:

```
Dim doc = _
    New XElement("Books", _
      New XElement("Book", _
          New XAttribute("ISBN", "0000000000001"), _
          New XAttribute("RecordDate", <%= Today %>), _
          New XElement("Price", 11.95), _
          New XElement("Name", "Book Title 1"), _
          New XElement("Stock", _
              New XAttribute("InStock", 12), _
      New XAttribute("OnOrder", 24))))
```

Let's say you have an array of Product objects and you want to create an XML document with these objects. Listing 14.3 shows the array with the product names.

LISTING 14.3:   An array of Product objects

```
Dim Products() As Product = _
      {New Product With
        {.ProductID = 3, .ProductName = "Product A", _
         .ProductPrice = 8.75, _
         .ProductExpDate = #2/2/2009#}, _
        New Product With _
         {.ProductID = 4, .ProductName = "Product B", _
          .ProductPrice = 19.5}, _
        New Product With _
         {.ProductID = 5, .ProductName = "Product C", _
          .ProductPrice = 21.25, _
          .ProductExpDate = #12/31/2010#}}
```

The code for generating an XML document with three elements is quite short, but what if you had thousands of products? Let's assume that the *Products* array contains instances of the Product class. You can use the XMLSerializer class to generate an XML document with the array's contents. An alternative approach is to create an inline XML document with embedded expressions, as shown in Listing 14.4.

LISTING 14.4:   An XML document with Product objects

```
Dim prods = <Products>
        <%= From prod In Products _
        Select <Product>
                <ID><%= prod.ProductID %></ID>
                <Name><%= prod.ProductName %></Name>
                <Price><%= prod.ProductPrice %></Price>
                <ExpirationDate>
                    <%= prod.ProductExpDate %></ExpirationDate>
                </Product> %>
                </Products>
```

This code segment looks pretty ugly, but here's how it works: In the first line, we start a new XML document. (The *prods* variable is actually of the XElement type, but an XElement is in its own right an XML document.) Notice that there's no line continuation character at the end of the first line of the XML document. Then comes a LINQ query embedded in the XML document with the <%= and %> tags. Notice the line continuation symbol at the end of this line(_). When we're in an expression hole, we're writing VB code, so line breaks matter. That makes the line continuation symbol necessary. Here's a much simplified version of the same code:

```
Dim prods = <Products>
            <%= From prod In Products _
                Select <Product>some product</Product> %>
            </Products>
```

This code segment will generate the following XML document:

```
<Products>
    <Product>some product</Product>
    <Product>some product</Product>
    <Product>some product</Product>
</Products>
```

The file contains no real data but is a valid XML document. The two tags with the percent sign switch into VB code, and the compiler executes the statements embedded in them. The embedded statement of our example is a LINQ query, which iterates through the elements of the *Products* array and selects literals (the XML tags shown in the output). To insert data between the tags, we must switch to VB again and insert the values we want to appear in the XML document. In other words, we must replace the string *some product* in the listing with some embedded expressions that return the values you want to insert in the XML document. These values are the properties of the Product class, as shown in Listing 14.3. The code shown in Listing 14.4 will produce the output shown in Listing 14.5.

LISTING 14.5: An XML document with the data of the array initialized in Listing 14.4

```
<Products>
  <Product>
    <ID>3</ID>
    <Name>Product A</Name>
    <Price>8.75</Price>
    <ExpirationDate>2009-02-02T00:00:00</ExpirationDate>
  </Product>
  <Product>
    <ID>4</ID>
    <Name>Product B</Name>
    <Price>19.5</Price>
    <ExpirationDate>0001-01-01T00:00:00</ExpirationDate>
  </Product>
  <Product>
    <ID>5</ID>
    <Name>Product C</Name>
    <Price>21.25</Price>
    <ExpirationDate>2010-12-31T00:00:00</ExpirationDate>
  </Product>
</Products>
```

TRANSFORMING XML DOCUMENTS

A common operation is the transformation of an XML document. If you have worked with XML in the past, you already know Extensible Stylesheet Language Transformations (XSLT), which is a language for transforming XML documents. If you're new to XML, you'll probably find it easier to transform XML documents with the LINQ to XML component. Even if you're familiar with XSLT, you should be aware that transforming XML documents with LINQ is straightforward. The idea is to create an inline XML document that contains HTML tags and an embedded LINQ query, like the following:

```
Dim HTML = <htlm><b>Products</b>
           <table border="all"><tr>
           <td>Product</td><td>Price</td>
           <td>Expiration</td></tr>
           <%= From item In Products.Descendants("Product") _
               Select <tr><td><%= item.<Name> %></td>
                   <td><%= item.<Price> %></td>
                   <td><%= Convert.ToDateTime( _
                   item.<ExpirationDate>.Value). _
                       ToShortDateString %>
           </td></tr> %></table>
           </htlm>
HTML.Save("Products.html")
Process.Start("Products.html")
```

The *HTML* variable stores plain HTML code. HTML is a subset of XML, and the editor will treat it like XML: It will insert the closing tags for you and will not let you nest tags in the wrong order. The Select keyword in the query is followed by a mix of HTML tags and embedded holes for inline expressions, which are the fields of the *item* object. Note the VB code for formatting the date in the last inline expression. The output of the previous listing is shown in Figure 14.3.

FIGURE 14.3
A simple XML seg-
ment (top) viewed as
an HTML table (bottom).
Transformation courtesy
of LINQ.

```
<products>
    <product ProductID="1" ProductName="Chai"
            UnitPrice="18.0000" UnitsInStock="39" UnitsOnOrder="0" >
    </product>
    <product ProductID="2" ProductName="Chang"
            UnitPrice="19.0000" UnitsInStock="19" UnitsOnOrder="40" >
    </product>
    <product ProductID="3" ProductName="Aniseed Syrup"
            UnitPrice="10.0000" UnitsInStock="26" UnitsOnOrder="70" >
    </product>
    <product ProductID="4" ProductName="Chef Anton's Cajun Seasoning"
            UnitPrice="22.0000" UnitsInStock="128" UnitsOnOrder="0" >
    </product>
    <product ProductID="5" ProductName="Chef Anton's Gumbo Mix"
            UnitPrice="21.3600" UnitsInStock="46" UnitsOnOrder="0" >
    </product>
```

Products

Product	Price	In Stock	On Order
Chai	18.00	39	0
Chang	19.00	19	40
Aniseed Syrup	10.00	26	70
Chef Anton's Cajun Seasoning	22.00	128	0
Chef Anton's Gumbo Mix	21.36	46	0
Grandma's Boysenberry Spread	25.01	179	0
Uncle Bob's Organic Dried Pears	30.01	27	0
Northwoods Cranberry Sauce	40.00	164	0
Mishi Kobe Niku	97.00	50	0
Queso Cabrales	21.00	154	30
Queso Manchego La Pastora	38.00	184	0
Konbu	6.00	95	0

The last two statements save the HTML file generated by our code and then open it in Internet Explorer (or whichever application you've designated to handle by default the HTML documents).

USING CUSTOM FUNCTIONS WITH LINQ TO XML

The embedded expressions are not limited to simple, inline expressions. You can call custom functions to transform your data. In a hotel reservation system I developed recently, I had to transform an XML file with room details to an HTML page. The transformation involved quite a few lookup operations, which I implemented with custom functions. Here's a simplified version of the LINQ query I used in the project. I'm showing the query that generates a simple HTML table with the elements of the XML document. The RoomType element is a numeric value that specifies the type of the room. This value may differ from one supplier to another, so I had to implement the lookup operation with a custom function.

```
Dim hotels = <html>
    <table><tr><td>Hotel</td><td>Room Type</td><td>Price</td></tr>
    <%= From hotel In Hotels _
        Select <tr><td><%= hotel.<HotelName>.Value %></td>
                    <td><%= GetRoomType(hotel.<RoomTypeID>)%></td>
                    <td><%= CalculatePrice(hotel.<Base>)%></td>
               </tr>
    %>
    </table>
</html>
```

The GetRoomType() and CalculatePrice() functions must be implemented in the same module that contains the LINQ query. In my case, they accept more arguments than shown here, but you get the idea. To speed up the application, I created HashTables using the IDs of the various entities in their respective tables in the database. The CalculatePrice() function, in particular, is quite complicated, because it incorporates the pricing policy. Yet, all the business logic implemented in a standard VB function was easily incorporated into the LINQ query that generates the HTML page with the available hotels and prices.

Another interesting application of XML transformation is the transformation of XML data into instances of custom objects. Let's say you need to work with an XML file that contains product information, and you want to create a list of Product objects out of it. Let's also assume that the XML file has the following structure:

```
<Products>
<product ProductID="1" ProductName="Chai"
        CategoryID="1"  UnitPrice="18.0000"
        UnitsInStock="39" UnitsOnOrder="0" >
</product>
<product ProductID="2" ProductName="Chang"
        CategoryID="1" QuantityPerUnit="24 - 12 oz bottles"
        UnitPrice="19.0000"
        UnitsInStock="19" UnitsOnOrder="40" >
</product>
...
</Products>
```

First, you must load the XML file into an XElement variable with the following statement (I'm assuming that the XML file is in the same folder as the project):

```
Dim XMLproducts = XElement.Load("../../Products.xml")
```

Now, you can write a LINQ query that generates anonymous types, like the following:

```
Dim prods = From prod In XMLproducts.Descendants("product")
            Select New With {.Name = prod.Attribute("ProductName").Value,
                             .Price = prod.Attribute("UnitPrice").Value,
                             .InStock = prod.Attribute("UnitsInStock").Value,
                             .OnOrder = prod.Attribute("UnitsOnOrder").Value}}
```

The prods collection consists of objects with the four scalar properties. To make the example a touch more interesting, let's say that you don't want to create a "flat" object. The InStock and OnOrder properties will become properties of another object, the Stock property. The new anonymous type will have the following structure:

Product.Name

Product.Price

Product.Stock.InStock

Product.Stock.OnOrder

To create an anonymous type with the revised structure, you must replace the InStock and OnOrder properties with a new object, the Stock object, which will expose the InStock and OnOrder properties. The revised query is shown next:

```
Dim prods =
    From prod In XMLproducts.Descendants("product")
    Select New With {.Name = prod.Attribute("ProductName").Value,
                     .Price = prod.Attribute("UnitPrice").Value,
                     .Stock = New With {
                              .InStock = prod.Attribute("UnitsInStock").Value,
                     .OnOrder = prod.Attribute("UnitsOnOrder").Value}}
```

A simple LINQ query allows you to move from XML into objects and replace the code that would normally use the XML axis methods (Elements and Descendents) with pure objects. Of course, anonymous types can be used only in the context of the procedure in which they were created. If you want to pass the *prods* collection between procedures, you should create a new Product class and use it to create instances of this object, because the anonymous types can't be used outside the routine in which they were created. The definition of the Product class, and the accompanying Stock class, is quite trivial:

```
Public Class Product
    Public Property Name As String
    Public Property Price As Decimal
    Public Property Stock As Stock
End Class
```

```
Public Class Stock
    Public InStock As Integer
    Public OnOrder As Integer
End Class
```

With the two class definitions in place, you can revise the LINQ query to populate the products collection with instances of the Product class:

```
Dim Products =
From prod In XMLproducts.Descendants("product")
      Select New Product With {
                  .Name = prod.Attribute("ProductName").Value,
                  .Stock = New Stock With {
                          .InStock = prod.Attribute("UnitsInStock").Value,
                          .OnOrder = prod.Attribute("UnitsOnOrder").Value}}
```

It shouldn't come as a surprise that you can iterate through both collections with the same statements:

```
For Each p In prods
    Debug.WriteLine("PRODUCT: " & p.Name & vbTab &
                 "   PRICE: " & p.Price.ToString &
                 "   STOCK = " & p.Stock.InStock & "/" & p.Stock.OnOrder)
Next
```

When executed, the preceding statements will generate the following output:

```
PRODUCT: Grandma's Boysenberry Spread       PRICE: 25.0100   STOCK = 179/0
PRODUCT: Uncle Bob's Organic Dried Pears    PRICE: 30.0100   STOCK = 27/0
PRODUCT: Northwoods Cranberry Sauce         PRICE: 40.0000   STOCK = 164/0
```

WORKING WITH XML FILES

In this section, we're going to build a functional interface for viewing customers and orders. And this time we aren't going to work with a small sample file. We'll actually get our data from one of the sample databases that comes with SQL Server: the Northwind database. The structure of this database is discussed in Chapter 15, "Programming with ADO.NET," in detail, but for now I'll show you how to extract data in XML format from SQL Server. If you don't have SQL Server installed or if you're unfamiliar with databases, you can use the sample XML files in the folder of the VBLINQ project. Figure 14.4 shows the main form of the application, which retrieves the same data either from an XML file or directly from the database.

You may be wondering why you would extract relational data and process them with LINQ instead of executing SQL statements against the database. XML is the standard data-exchange format, and you may get data from any other source in this format. You may get an XML file generated from someone's database or even an Excel spreadsheet. In the past, you had to convert the data to another, more flexible format and then process it. With LINQ, you can directly query the XML document, transform it into other formats, and of course save it.

FIGURE 14.4
Displaying related data
from XML files

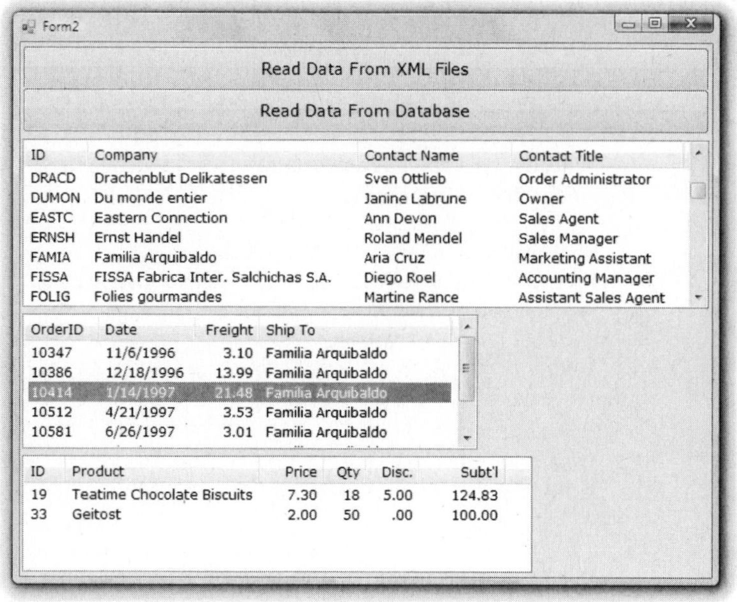

Start SQL Server, and execute the following query:

```
SELECT * FROM Customers FOR XML AUTO
```

This statement selects all columns and all rows for the Customers table and generates an element for each row. The field values are stored in the document as attributes of the corresponding row. The output of this statement is not a valid XML document because its elements are not embedded in a root element. To request an XML document in which all elements are embedded in a root element, use the ROOT keyword:

```
SELECT * FROM Customers FOR XML AUTO, ROOT('AllCustomers')
```

I'm using the root element AllCustomers because the elements of the XML document are named after the table. The preceding statement will generate an XML document with the following structure:

```
<AllCustomers>
    <Customers CustomerID="…" CompanyName="xxx" … />
    <Customers CustomerID="…" CompanyName="xxx" … />
    …
</AllCustomers>
```

It would make more sense to generate an XML document with the Customers root element and name the individual elements Customer. To generate this structure, use the following statement:

```
SELECT * FROM Customers Customer FOR XML AUTO, ROOT('Customers')
```

Here's a segment of the XML document with the customers:

```
<Customers>
  <Customer CustomerID="ALFKI" CompanyName=
    "Alfreds Futterkiste" ContactName="Maria Anders"
    ContactTitle="Sales Representative"
    Country="Germany" />
  <Customer CustomerID="ANATR" CompanyName=
    "Ana Trujillo Emparedados y helados"
    ContactName="Ana Trujillo" ContactTitle="Owner"
    Country="Mexico" />
```

Finally, you can create an XML document where the fields are inserted as elements, rather than attributes. To do so, use the ELEMENTS keyword:

```
SELECT * FROM Customers Customer FOR XML AUTO,
    ELEMENTS ROOT('Customers')
```

The other statements that generated the XML files with the rows of the tables Orders, Order Details, and Products are as follows:

```
SELECT * FROM Orders Order FOR XML AUTO,  ROOT('Orders')
SELECT * FROM [Order Details] Detail FOR XML AUTO,
    ELEMENTS, ROOT('Details')
SELECT ProductID, ProductName FROM Products
    FOR XML AUTO, ELEMENTS ROOT('Products')
```

Notice that all files are attribute based, except for the Details.xml file, which is element based. I had no specific reason for choosing this structure; I just wanted to demonstrate both styles for processing XML in the sample project's code. Also, the reason I've included the Products table is because the Order Details table, which contains the lines of the order, stores the IDs of the products, not the product names. When displaying orders, as shown in Figure 14.4, you must show product names, not just product IDs. The four collections with the entities we extracted from the Northwind database are declared and populated at the form's level via the following statements:

```
Dim customers As XElement = XElement.Load("..\..\..\Customers.xml")
Dim orders As XElement = XElement.Load("..\..\..\Orders.xml")
Dim details As XElement = XElement.Load("..\..\..\Details.xml")
Dim products As XElement = XElement.Load("..\..\..\Products.xml")
```

As is apparent from the code, I've placed the four XML files created with the SQL statements shown earlier in the project's folder. The Display Data button populates the top ListView control with the rows of the Customers table, via the following statements:

```
Private Sub bttnShow_Click(...) Handles bttnShow.Click
    For Each c In customers.Descendants("Customer")
        Dim LI As New ListViewItem
```

```
        LI.Text = c.@CustomerID
        LI.SubItems.Add(c.@CompanyName)
        LI.SubItems.Add(c.@ContactName)
        LI.SubItems.Add(c.@ContactTitle)
        ListView1.Items.Add(LI)
    Next
End Sub
```

The code is quite simple. It doesn't even use LINQ; it iterates through the `Customer` elements of the customers collection and displays their attributes on the control. Notice the use of the shortcut for the `Attribute` property of the current XElement.

When the user clicks a customer name, the control's `SelectedIndexChanged` event is fired. The code in this handler executes a LINQ statement that selects the rows of the Orders table that correspond to the ID of the selected customer. Then, it iterates through the selected rows, which are the orders of the current customer, and displays their fields on the second ListView control via the following statements:

```
Private Sub ListView1_SelectedIndexChanged(…) _
        Handles ListView1.SelectedIndexChanged
    If ListView1.SelectedItems.Count = 0 Then Exit Sub
    ListView2.Items.Clear()
    Dim scustomerID = ListView1.SelectedItems(0).Text
    Dim query = From o In orders.Descendants("Order")
                Where Convert.ToString(o.@CustomerID) = scustomerID
                Select o
    For Each o In query
        Dim LI As New ListViewItem
        LI.Text = o.@OrderID.ToString
        LI.SubItems.Add(Convert.ToDateTime
                (o.@OrderDate).ToShortDateString)
        LI.SubItems.Add(Convert.ToDecimal(o.@Freight).ToString("#,###.00"))
        LI.SubItems.Add(o.@ShipName.ToString)
        ListView2.Items.Add(LI)
    Next
End Sub
```

The LINQ query selects Order elements based on their `CustomerID` attribute. Finally, when an order is clicked, the following LINQ query retrieves the selected order's details:

```
Dim query = From itm In details.Descendants("Detail")
            Where Convert.ToInt32(itm.<OrderID>.Value) = orderID
            Select itm
```

The `Details.xml` file contains elements for all columns, not attributes, and I use statements such as `<dtl.UnitPrice>` to access the subelements of the current element. To display product names, the code selects the row of the *Products* collection that corresponds to the ID of each detail line as follows:

```
Dim product = _
    From p In products.Descendants("Product")
    Where Convert.ToInt32(p.@ProductID) =
        Convert.ToInt32(dtl.<ProductID>.Value)
    Select p
```

The *product* variable is actually a collection of XElements, even though it can never contain more than a single element (product IDs are unique). You access the ProductName column of the selected row with the expression product(0).@productName. You can call the First method to make sure you've selected a single product, no matter what:

```
Dim product = _
    (From p In products.Descendants("Product")
    Where Convert.ToInt32(p.@ProductID) =
        Convert.ToInt32(dtl.<ProductID>.Value)
    Select p).First
```

LINQ to SQL

SQL stands for Structured Query Language, a language for querying databases. SQL is discussed in the last part of this book, and as you will see, SQL resembles LINQ. SQL is a simple language, and I will explain the SQL statements used in the examples; readers who are somewhat familiar with databases should be able to follow along.

Now, let's build another application for displaying customers, orders, and order details. The difference is that this time you won't get your data from an XML document; you'll retrieve them directly from the database. As you will see, the same LINQ queries will be used to process the rows returned by the queries. The code won't be identical to the code presented in the preceding section, but the differences are minor. The same principles will be applied to a very different data source.

You need a mechanism to connect to the database so you can retrieve data, and this mechanism is the DataContext class. The DataContext class talks to the database, retrieves data, and submits changes back to the database. To create a DataContext object, pass a string with the information about the database server, the specific database, and your credentials to the DataContext class's constructor, as shown here:

```
Dim db As New DataContext("Data Source=localhost;
                initial catalog=northwind;
                Integrated Security=True")
```

To use the DataContext class in your code, you must add a reference to the System.Data .Linq namespace and then import it into your code with this statement:

```
Imports System.Data.Linq
```

You will find more information on connecting to databases in Chapter 15. For the purposes of this chapter, the preceding connection string will connect your application to the Northwind database on the local database server, provided that you have SQL Server or SQL Server Express installed on the same machine as Visual Studio. If you do not, replace "localhost" in the connection string with the name or IP address of the machine on which SQL Server is running.

After you have initialized the DataContext object, you're ready to read data from tables into variables. To do so, call the GetTable method of the db object to retrieve the rows of a table. Note that the name of the table is not specified as an argument. Instead, the table is inferred from the type passed to the GetTable method as an argument. The GetTable(Of *Customer*) method will retrieve the rows of the Customers table, because the name of the table is specified in the definition of the class, as you will see shortly.

```
customers = From cust In db.GetTable(Of Customer)()
            Select New Customer With
            {.CustomerID = cust.CustomerID,
             .CompanyName = cust.CompanyName,
             .ContactName = cust.ContactName,
             .ContactTitle = cust.ContactTitle}
orders = From ord In db.GetTable(Of Order)()
         Select New Order With
         {.OrderID = ord.OrderID,
          .OrderDate = ord.OrderDate,
          .CustomerID = ord.CustomerID,
          .Freight = ord.Freight,
          .ShipName = ord.ShipName}
details = From det In db.GetTable(Of Detail)()
          Select New Detail With
          {.OrderID = det.OrderID,
           .ProductID = det.ProductID,
           .Quantity = det.Quantity,
           .UnitPrice = det.UnitPrice,
           .Discount = det.Discount}
products = From prod In db.GetTable(Of NWProduct)()
           Select New NWProduct With
           {.ProductID = prod.ProductID,
            .ProductName = prod.ProductName}
```

The type of the customers, orders, details, and products variables is IQueryable(of *entity*), where *entity* is the appropriate type for the information you're reading from the database. The four variables that will store the rows of the corresponding tables must be declared at the form level with the following statements:

```
Dim customers As System.Linq.IQueryable(Of Customer)
Dim orders As System.Linq.IQueryable(Of Order)
Dim details As System.Linq.IQueryable(Of Detail)
Dim products As System.Linq.IQueryable(Of NWProduct)
```

The variables must be declared explicitly at the form level, because they will be accessed from within multiple event handlers.

To make the most of LINQ to SQL, you must first design a separate class for each table that you want to load from the database. You can also specify the mapping between your classes and the tables from which their instances will be loaded, by prefixing them with the appropriate attributes. The Customer class, for example, will be loaded with data from the Customers table. To specify the relationship between the class and the table, use the Table attribute, as shown here:

```
<Table(Name:="Customers")>Public Class Customer
End Class
```

Each property of the Customer class will be mapped to a column of the Customers table. In a similar manner, decorate each property with the name of the column that will populate the property:

```
<Column(Name:="CompanyName")>Public Property Name
End Property
```

If the name of the property matches the name of the relevant column, you can omit the column's name:

```
<Column()>Public Property Name
End Property
```

Listing 14.6 shows the definition of the four classes we'll use to store the four tables (Customers, Orders, Order Details, and Products).

LISTING 14.6:   The classes for storing customers and orders

```
<Table(Name:="Customers")> Public Class Customer
    Private _CustomerID As String
    Private _CompanyName As String
    Private _ContactName As String
    Private _ContactTitle As String

    <Column()> Public Property CustomerID() As String
        Get
            Return _customerID
        End Get
        Set(ByVal value As String)
            _customerID = value
        End Set
    End Property

    <Column()> Public Property CompanyName() As String
        Get
            Return _CompanyName
        End Get
        Set(ByVal value As String)
            _CompanyName = value
```

```vb
            End Set
        End Property

        <Column()> Public Property ContactName() As String
            ….
        End Property

        <Column()> Public Property ContactTitle() As String
            ….
        End Property
End Class

<Table(Name:="Orders")> Public Class Order
        Private _OrderID As Integer
        Private _CustomerID As String
        Private _OrderDate As Date
        Private _Freight As Decimal
        Private _ShipName As String

        <Column()> Public Property OrderID() As Integer
            ….
        End Property

        <Column()> Public Property CustomerID() As String
            ….
        End Property

        <Column()> Public Property OrderDate() As Date
            ….
        End Property

        <Column()> Public Property Freight() As Decimal
            ….
        End Property

        <Column()> Public Property ShipName() As String
            ….
        End Property
End Class

<Table(Name:="Order Details")> Public Class Detail
        Private _OrderID As Integer
        Private _ProductID As Integer
        Private _Quantity As Integer
        Private _UnitPrice As Decimal
        Private _Discount As Decimal

        <Column()> Public Property OrderID() As Integer
```

```
        ….

        End Property

        <Column()> Public Property ProductID() As Integer
            ….
        End Property

        <Column()> Public Property Quantity() As Short
            ….
        End Property

        <Column()> Public Property UnitPrice() As Decimal
            ….
        End Property


        <Column()> Public Property Discount() As Double
            ….
        End Property
    End Class

    <Table(Name:="Products")> Public Class NWProduct
        Private _ProductID As Integer
        Private _ProductName As String

        <Column()> Public Property ProductID() As Integer
            ….
        End Property

        <Column()> Public Property ProductName() As String
            ….
        End Property

    End Class
```

I didn't show the implementation of most properties, because it's trivial. What's interesting in this listing are the Table and Column attributes that determine how the instances of the classes will be populated from the database, as you saw earlier.

The code that displays the selected customer's orders and the selected order's details is similar to the code you saw in the previous section that displays the data from the XML files. It selects the matching rows in the relevant table and shows them in the corresponding ListView control.

Retrieving Data with the ExecuteQuery Method

You can also retrieve a subset of the table, or combine multiple tables, by executing a SQL query against the database. The ExecuteQuery method, which accepts as arguments the SELECT statement to be executed and an array with parameter values, returns a collection with the selected rows as objects. To call the `ExecuteQuery` method, you must specify the class that will be used to store the results with the `Of` keyword in parentheses following the method's name. Then you specify the SELECT statement that will retrieve the desired rows. If this query contains any parameters, you must also supply an array of objects with the parameter values. Parameters are identified by their order in the query, not by a name. The first parameters is 0, the second parameter is 1, and so on. The following statement will retrieve all customers from Germany and store them in instances of the Customer class:

```
Dim params() = {"Germany"}
Dim GermanCustomers = _
        db.ExecuteQuery(Of Customer)( _
        "SELECT CustomerID, CompanyName," & _
        "ContactName, ContactTitle " &
        "FROM Customers WHERE Country={0}", params)"
```

After the *GermanCustomers* collection has been populated, you can iterate through its items as usual, with a loop like the following:

```
For Each cust In GermanCustomers
    Debug.WriteLine(cust.CompanyName & " " & _
                    cust.ContactName)
Next
```

Once you have retrieved the results from the database, you can execute LINQ queries against the collection. To find out the number of customers from Germany, use the following expression:

```
Dim custCount = GermanCustomers.Count
```

To apply a filtering expression and then retrieve the count, use the following LINQ expression:

```
Dim g = GermanCustomers.Where(Function(c As Customer) _
        c.CompanyName.ToUpper Like "*DELIKATESSEN*").Count
```

To appreciate the role of the DataContext class in LINQ to SQL, you should examine the `ToString` property of a LINQ query that's executed against the database. Insert a statement to display the expression `GermanCustomers.ToString()` in your code, and you will see that the DataContext class has generated and executed the following statement against the database. If you're familiar with SQL Server, you can run the SQL Server Profiler and trace all commands executed against SQL Server. Start SQL Server Profiler (or ask the database administrator to create a log of all statements executed by your workstation against a specific database), and then execute a few LINQ to SQL queries. Here's the statement for selecting the German customers as reported by the profiler:

```
exec sp_executesql N'SELECT Customers.CompanyName,
    Orders.OrderID, SUM(UnitPrice*Quantity) AS
        OrderTotal FROM Customers INNER JOIN Orders
```

```
ON Customers.CustomerID = Orders.CustomerID
INNER JOIN [Order Details] ON
    [Order Details].OrderID = Orders.OrderID
WHERE Customers.Country=@p0
GROUP BY Customers.CompanyName,
Orders.OrderID',N'@p0 nvarchar(7)',@p0=N'Germany'
```

Working with LINQ to SQL Classes

The process of getting data out of a database and into a custom class is as straightforward as it can get. You create a class with properties that match the columns of the equivalent table, and then you use the DataContext object to populate these classes. You may be thinking already about a class generator that will take care of the mapping between the class properties and the table columns. Visual Studio does that for you with a component called LINQ to SQL Classes.

A LINQ to SQL Classes component encapsulates a segment of a database, or the entire database, and lets you work against a database as if the database entities were objects. While in traditional database programming you code against tables that are made up of rows, with LINQ to SQL Classes you will work against the same database, only this time the tables will be collections made up of custom objects. The Customers table of the Northwind database, for example, contains rows that represent customers. When you work with a LINQ to SQL Classes component, the Customers table becomes a collection, and its rows become instances of Customer objects. As you will see shortly, the idea behind LINQ to SQL Classes is to bridge the gap between traditional database programming and the object-oriented features of modern programming languages. You'll see the advantages of accessing databases as collections of strongly typed objects in just a few pages.

To add this component to your solution, right-click the solution name, and from the context menu select Add New Item. In the Add New Item dialog box, select the LINQ to SQL Classes component, as shown in Figure 14.5, and set the component's name (use the NWind name for this example).

FIGURE 14.5
Start by adding a LINQ to SQL Classes component to your project.

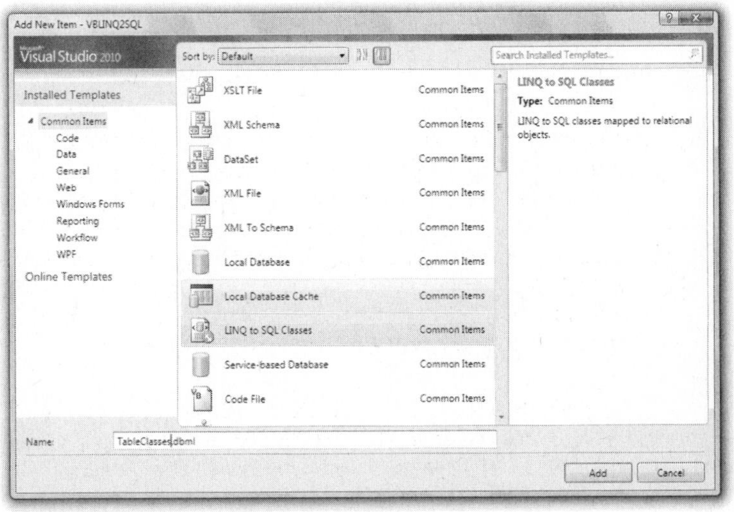

Once the new component has been added to the project, the Server Explorer window will open. Here you can select a connection to one of the databases on your system (I'm assuming you have installed either SQL Server or SQL Server Express). Create a new connection to the Northwind database if you don't already have a connection to this database, and open it. If you don't know how to create connections to databases, follow this procedure:

1. Switch to Server Explorer, and right-click the Data Connections item. From the context menu, select Add Connection to open the dialog box shown in Figure 14.6.

2. In the Add Connection dialog box that appears, select the name of the database server you want to use. I'm assuming that most readers have a version of SQL Server 2008 installed on their machines, so you can specify **localhost** as the server name. If you're connected to a remote database server on the network, the database administrator will give the proper database name and credentials.

FIGURE 14.6
Creating a new database connection

3. Select the authentication method for the database server. Again, most readers can select the option Use Windows Authentication. To connect to a remote server, you will most likely

have to select Use SQL Server Authentication and supply your credentials, as shown in Figure 14.6.

4. Expand the list of databases in the drop-down list in the lower pane of the dialog box, and select Northwind. If you haven't installed the Northwind database, then you should download and install it, as explained in Chapter 15.

As soon as you close the Add Connection dialog box, the designer will add a new component to the class, the `DataClasses1.dbml` component, and will open it in design mode. DataClasses1 is the default name of a LINQ to SQL Classes component, and I suggest you change the name to something more meaningful. The VBLINQ project uses the name TableClasses.

The designer is initially an empty space. But here's how easy it is to create custom objects based on the database entities, as shown in Figure 14.7.

FIGURE 14.7
Designing a LINQ to SQL Classes class with visual tools

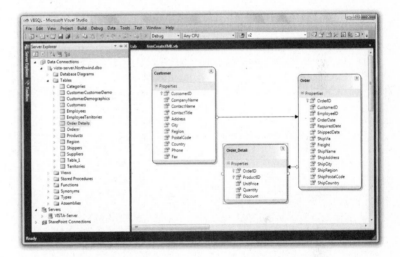

Server Explorer will display all the items in the database. Select the Customers, Orders and Order Details tables from Server Explorer, and drop them onto the designer's surface. The designer will pick up the relations between the tables from the database and will depict them as arrows between related classes. It will also create the appropriate classes on the fly, one for each table. Specifically, the designer will create the Customer, Order, and Order_Detail classes that represent the entities stored in the Customers, Orders, and Order Details tables. Notice how the designer singularized the names of the entities.

The designer has also created three collections to represent the three tables, as well as a DataContext object to connect to the database. To exercise the autogenerated classes, build the sample form shown in Figure 14.8. This form loads the countries and uses their names to populate the ComboBox control at the top. Every time the user selects a country, the application makes another trip to the database, retrieves the customers in the selected country, and displays the customer names on the Select Customer ListBox control.

FIGURE 14.8
A form for viewing customers, their orders, and the details for each order

Once a customer has been selected, the application makes another trip to the database and selects the customer's orders, which are displayed on the top ListView control. Finally, when an order is selected, the application reads the order's details and displays them on the lower ListView control on the right. The idea is to get as little information as possible from the database depending on the user's action. There's no need to retrieve all the customers when the application starts, because the user many not even view any customer. In general, you should try to limit the user's selection so that you can minimize the information you request from the database and download at the client. Although there will be times you need to minimize trips to the database, in that case you will pull data that you *might* need and then possibly throw some of it away.

THE DATACONTEXT OBJECT

The following statement creates a new DataContext object for accessing the Northwind database:

```
Dim ctx As New NwindDataContext
```

The NWindDataContext class was generated by the designer; it gives you access to the database's tables (and stored procedures). The database tables are properties of the *ctx* variable, and they return an IQueryable collection with the rows of each table. To access the Customers table, for example, request the Customers property:

```
Ctx.Customers
```

Each item in the *Customers* collection is an object of the Customer type. The designer also generated a class for the entities stored in each of the tables. Not only that, but it singularized the names of the tables.

ACCESSING THE TABLES WITH LINQ

Since the Customers property of the *ctx* variable returns the rows of the Customers table as a collection, you can use LINQ to query the table. The following query returns the German customers:

```
Dim germanCustomers = From cust In ctx.Customers
    Where cust.Country = "Germany"
    Select cust
```

The compiler knows that *cust* is a variable of the Customer type, so it displays the fields of the Customers table (which are now properties of the Customer object) in the IntelliSense drop-down list. In effect, the LINQ to SQL component has mapped the selected tables into objects that you can use to access your database using OOP techniques.

But the LINQ to SQL Classes component has done much more. germanCustomers is a query that isn't executed until you request its elements. The expression ctx.Customers doesn't move the rows of the Customers table to the client so you can query them. Instead, it parses your LINQ query, builds the appropriate SQL query, and executes it when you iterate through the query results. To see the queries that are executed as per your LINQ query when they're submitted to the database, insert the following simple statement right after the declaration of the *ctx* variable:

```
ctx.Log = Console.Out
```

This statement tells the compiler to send all the commands that the DataContext object submits to the database to the Output window. Place a button on the main form of the project, and in its Click event handler insert the following statements:

```
ctx.Log = Console.Out
Dim selCustomers = From cust In ctx.Customers
                   Where cust.Country = "Germany"
                   Select cust
MsgBox("No query executed so far!")
For Each cust In selCustomers
    ListBox1.Items.Add(cust.CustomerID & vbTab & cust.CompanyName)
Next
```

Execute these statements, and watch the Output window. The message box will be displayed and nothing will be shown in the Output window, because no data has been requested from the database yet. selCustomers is just a query that the compiler has analyzed, but it hasn't been executed yet. As soon as you close the message box, the following SQL statement will be submitted to the database to request some data:

```
SELECT [t0].[CustomerID], [t0].[CompanyName], [t0].[ContactName],
[t0].[ContactTitle], [t0].[Address], [t0].[City], [t0].[Region],
[t0].[PostalCode], [t0].[Country], [t0].[Phone], [t0].[Fax]
FROM [dbo].[Customers] AS [t0]
```

```
WHERE [t0].[Country] = @p0
-- @p0: Input NVarChar (Size = 4000; Prec = 0; Scale = 0) [Germany]
-- Context: SqlProvider(Sql2008) Model: AttributedMetaModel Build: 4.0.20506.1
```

If you're not familiar with SQL, don't panic. You'll find the basics later in this book. If you're a totally result-oriented developer, don't even bother with the SQL statement; VB does it all for you. It knows how to request the data you need, and it won't bring even one extra row from the Customers table back to the client. Of course, you shouldn't iterate through all the rows of the table, because this could ruin application performance. Never, never bring an entire table to the client, unless it's a small table (categories, state names, and so on). Even then, it's not a good idea to keep the data at the client for long periods of time; other users may edit the data at the database, and when that happens, the data at the client become "stale," because the data at the client are not directly associated with the database and will not be updated. The short of the story is that the DataContext object establishes a connection to the database and lets you view your database tables as collections of objects. Use it to grab the data you need, and submit changes as the user edits the data.

To limit the number of rows you bring to the client, try to give users the option to specify selection criteria. The sample application you'll build in this section requests that users select a country and then brings only the customers from that particular country to the client. Actually, you don't even need to bring all the fields of the Customers table. All you will need is the CompanyName that's displayed on the ListBox control and the ID that you'll use in subsequent queries to identify the selected customer. If you have too much data, you can limit the number of rows you bring to the client (to an arbitrary value, say, 1,000 rows). If the user has selected more rows, they should specify a more specific search pattern to limit the number of rows. After all, who needs to see thousands and thousands of rows just because they exist?

Navigation Methods

Tables are rarely isolated in a database, and no one ever really cares about the rows of a single table. Tables are (almost always) related to one another. Customers place orders, and orders contain products and prices. Orders belong to customers, but they're created by employees. The most common operation in data-driven applications is not entering new rows or editing existing ones. Instead, data-driven applications spend most of their time going from a row in a specific table to one or more related rows in another table. Of course, retrieving the related rows implies that you will also design an interface to display the data you gather from multiple tables to the user. Let's say you have landed on a specific customer, represented by the *selCustomer* variable (it's a variable of the Customer type, of course). You could select a customer by index, with a LINQ query, or let the user select it from a list. The idea is that you have retrieved the customer you're interested in.

To access the related rows in other tables, you can request the property of the Customer object that corresponds to the related table. To access the orders of the customer represented by the *cust* object, use the following expression:

```
cust.Orders
```

This expression returns an IQueryable collection as usual, with the rows of the Orders table that correspond to the selected customer. The Orders property represents the Orders table and returns an IQueryable collection of Order objects, each representing an order, as you might expect. However, it doesn't return all rows of the Orders table — just the ones that belong to the selected customer. Each Order object in turn exposes the columns of the Orders table as properties. To access the `OrderDate` field of the first order of the first customer in the german-Customers collection, you'd use an expression like the following:

```
selCustomers.ToList(0).Orders.ToList(0).OrderDate
```

You have to apply the `ToList` operator to every collection to force the execution of the appropriate query and then select a specific item of the collection.

Now we can take a closer look at the code of the sample project code. The following code loads all countries and displays their names on the ListBox control:

```
Private Sub Button1_Click(...) Handles Button1.Click
    ctx = New NWindDataContext
    ctx.Log = Console.Out
    Dim countries = From cust In ctx.Customers
                    Select cust.Country Distinct
    For Each country As String In countries
        cbCountries.Items.Add(country)
    Next
End Sub
```

The very first query is peculiar indeed. The Northwind database doesn't store the countries in a separate table, so you have to go through the Customers table and collect all the unique country names. This is what the `Distinct` keyword does: It forces the query to return each unique country name from the Customers table only once. LINQ doesn't download all the rows of the Customers table to the client to select the unique country names. The actual query sent to the database by LINQ is the following, which instructs SQL Server to return only the unique country names:

```
SELECT DISTINCT [t0].[Country]
FROM [dbo].[Customers] AS [t0]
```

LINQ is very efficient when it comes to talking to the database, and you will see shortly how you can monitor the queries it submits to the database.

When the user selects a customer on the ListBox control, the statements included in Listing 14.7 are executed to display the number of orders placed by the customer and the total revenue generated by the selected customer, as well as the headers of all orders.

LISTING 14.7: Retrieving the orders of the selected customer

```
Private Sub ListBox1_SelectedIndexChanged(...)
                Handles ListBox1.SelectedIndexChanged
    If ListBox1.SelectedItem Is Nothing Then Exit Sub
    Dim custID As String = ListBox1.SelectedItem.ToString.Substring(0, 5)
    Dim custName As String = ListBox1.SelectedItem.ToString.Substring(5).Trim
    Dim customerOrders = From ord In ctx.Orders
                Where ord.CustomerID = custID
                Select New With {.order = ord, .details = ord.Order_Details}
    Dim orders = customerOrders.Count
    If orders > 0 Then
```

```
            Dim tot = From o In customerOrders
                    Select Aggregate det In o.details Into
                        Sum(det.UnitPrice * det.Quantity * (1 - det.Discount))
            TextBox1.Text = "Customer " & custName & " has placed " &
                        orders.ToString & " orders totalling $" &
                        tot.Sum.ToString
        Else
            TextBox1.Text = "There are no order for customer " & custName
        End If
        lvOrders.Items.Clear()
        For Each ord In customerOrders
            Dim LI As New ListViewItem
            LI.Text = ord.order.OrderID.ToString
            LI.SubItems.Add(ord.order.OrderDate.Value.ToShortDateString)
            LI.SubItems.Add((Aggregate dtl In ord.details Into
                        Sum(dtl.UnitPrice * dtl.Quantity *
                            (1 - dtl.Discount))).ToString)
            LI.SubItems.Add(Aggregate dtl In ord.details Into Sum(dtl.Quantity))
            LI.SubItems.Add(ord.order.Freight.ToString)
            lvOrders.Items.Add(LI)
        Next
End Sub
```

The code extracts the selected customer's ID from the ListBox control and stores it to the
custID variable. It uses this variable to select the customer's orders into the customerOrders
collection. Next, it calculates the number of orders and the total revenue generated by the customer and displays it on the form. Finally, it iterates through the *customerOrders* collection
and displays the orders on a ListView control. One of the items shown in the ListView control is the total of each order, which is calculated by another LINQ query that aggregates the
current order's details:

```
Aggregate dtl In ord.details Into
            Sum(dtl.UnitPrice * dtl.Quantity * (1 - dtl.Discount))
```

This query returns a Double value, which is formatted and displayed like a variable. The query
isn't assigned to a variable, and there's no Select clause — just the aggregate value.

You may be tempted to write a loop that iterates through all the rows in the Customers table
to calculate aggregates. Just don't! Use LINQ to formulate the appropriate query, and then let
the compiler figure out the statement that must be executed against the database to retrieve the
information you need, and no more. If you execute a loop at the client, LINQ to SQL will move
all the rows of the relevant tables to the client, where the loop will be executed. Although this
may work for Northwind, as the database grows larger it will be an enormous burden on the
database and the local network. The query might get a little complicated, but it saves you from
the performance issues you'd face when the application is released to many clients. Eventually,
you will be forced to go back and rewrite your code.

Let's say you need to know the revenue generated by all customers in each country and in
a specific year. The following LINQ query does exactly that and returns a collection of anonymous types with just two fields: the country name and the total revenue per country.

```
Dim revenueByCountry = From cust In ctx.Customers,
                       ord In cust.Orders,
                       det In ord.Order_Details
                       Group By cust.Country Into countryTotals = Group,
                       countryRev =
                            Sum(det.Quantity * det.UnitPrice * (1 - det.Discount))
                       Select Country, countryRev
```

This statement returns a collection of country names and totals like this:

```
Austria   57401.84
Belgium   11434.48
Brazil    41941.19
Canada    31298.06
Denmark   25192.54
```

To execute this query, which in effect scans a large segment of the database and returns a few totals, LINQ generates and executes the following SQL statement:

```
SELECT [t4].[Country], [t4].[value] AS [countryRev]
FROM (
    SELECT SUM([t3].[value]) AS [value], [t3].[Country]
    FROM (
        SELECT (CONVERT(Real,
                (CONVERT(Decimal(29,4),CONVERT(Int,[t2].[Quantity])))) *
                [t2].[UnitPrice]))
                        * (@p0 - [t2].[Discount]) AS [value],
                [t1].[OrderDate], [t1].[CustomerID], [t0].[CustomerID] AS
                [CustomerID2],
                [t2].[OrderID], [t1].[OrderID] AS [OrderID2], [t0].[Country]
        FROM [dbo].[Customers] AS [t0], [dbo].[Orders] AS [t1],
            [dbo].[Order Details] AS [t2]) AS [t3]
        WHERE (DATEPART(Year, [t3].[OrderDate]) = @p1) AND
                    ([t3].[CustomerID] = [t3].[CustomerID2]) AND
                    ([t3].[OrderID] = [t3].[OrderID2])
    GROUP BY [t3].[Country] ) AS [t4]
ORDER BY [t4].[Country]
-- @p0: Input Real (Size = -1; Prec = 0; Scale = 0) [1]
-- @p1: Input Int (Size = -1; Prec = 0; Scale = 0) [1997]
```

This is a fairly complicated SQL query, unless you're familiar with SQL. If not, try to master LINQ and let the compiler generate the SQL queries for you. If you haven't used SQL before, you'll find an introduction to SQL in the following chapter.

Likewise, when you click an order, the program retrieves the details of the selected order and displays them on the second ListView control, using the following query:

```
Dim selectedDetails = From det In ctx.Order_Details, prod In ctx.Products
                      Where prod.ProductID = det.ProductID And
```

```
                    det.OrderID = OrderID
                 Select New With {.details = det}
```

Note that this query combines the Products table, because the Order Details table contains only the IDs of the products, not their names. This is how the data are organized in the database, but not how you want to present the data to the user.

Updates

In addition to querying the database, you can also update it by inserting new rows or updating and deleting existing rows. To insert a new row into a table, create a new object of the appropriate type and then add it to its table by calling the `InsertOnSubmit` method. The `InsertOnSubmit` method doesn't submit the new row to the database; the new row lives at the client and is submitted to the database when you call the `SubmitChanges` method. The following statements create a new product and add it to the Products table:

```
Dim P As New Product
P.ProductName = "New Product"
P.CategoryID = 3
P.UnitPrice = 9.45
ctx.Products.InsertOnSubmit(P)
ctx.SubmitChanges
```

You can accumulate multiple changes to the Products table (or any other table for that matter) and submit them all at once to the database with a single call to the `SubmitChanges` method. The compiler will figure out the appropriate order for submitting the rows. For example, it will first insert new categories and then products, because a new product may contain a reference to a new category.

To update a row, just change some of its properties, and the edits will be submitted to the database when the `SubmitChanges` method is called. Finally, to delete a row, call the `DeleteOnSubmit` method and pass the Product object to be deleted as an argument. There are also two related methods, the `InsertAllOnSubmit` and `DeleteAllOnSubmit` methods, which accept an `IEnumerable` collection of objects as an argument.

Submitting updates to the database isn't a trivial topic. For example, one or more other users might have edited or deleted the row you're trying to update since your application read it. You can't take it for granted that all updates will be submitted successfully to the database. Consider, too, one of the restrictions in the Northwind database is that product prices can't be negative. The Product class generated by the designer doesn't enforce this restriction at the client. At the client, it's perfectly legal to assign a negative value to a product's `UnitPrice` property, but a row that contains a negative price value will fail to update the database. The database itself will reject any updates that violate any database constraint. You can also set a product's `CategoryID` field to an arbitrary value, but unless this value matches the ID of an existing category in the Categories table, the changes will be rejected by the database. Handling these conditions requires additional code. The topic of handling update errors is discussed in detail in Part V of this book. This section is a quick introduction to a component that allows you to handle database tables as objects and manipulate them with LINQ.

The VBLINQ2SQL project (available for download from www.sybex.com/go/masteringvb2010) contains a form that displays all products on a ListView control, as shown in Figure 14.9.

The Add Another Product button brings up the form shown in the same figure, which allows you to specify a new product and submit it to the database. The new product is added automatically to the list with the products. You can also click the Reload All Products button to confirm that the product has been committed to the database. If the new product violates one of the database constraints (for example, it has a negative value), the operation will fail, and you will see an appropriate error message.

FIGURE 14.9
Viewing all products
and inserting/editing
individual products

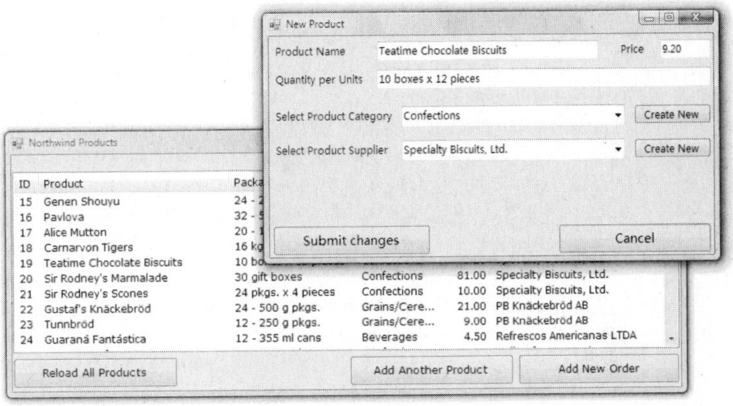

If you double-click a product row in the Northwind Products form, the auxiliary form will be displayed again, this time populated with the fields of the selected product, and you can edit them.

CREATING A NEW ORDER

I'll complete the presentation of the VBLINQ2SQL sample application by discussing the code that creates a new order. The Order object combines several tables and the most interesting object in the Northwind database. Orders are placed by customers and credited to employees. They also contain a number of products, along with their quantities and prices. A proper interface should allow users to specify all these items, and you will see a suitable interface for creating orders in Chapter 15. For the purposes of this sample application, I've decided to select the appropriate items at random, but the application does generate actual orders and submits them to the database. The Add New Order button on Form2, which is shown in Figure 14.10, does exactly that with the statements included in Listing 14.8.

LISTING 14.8:   Adding a new order to the Northwind database

```
Dim RND As New Random
' select a customer at random
Dim cust = CType(ctx.Customers.Skip(
                    RND.Next(1, 50)).Take(1).First, Customer)
' select an employee at random
Dim emp = CType(ctx.Employees.Skip(
```

```
                         RND.Next(1, 10)).Take(1).First, Employee)
' and create order's header
Dim order As New Order
order.OrderDate = Now
order.Customer = cust
order.Employee = emp
' select a random freight for the order in the range from $3 to $75
order.Freight = RND.Next(300, 7500) / 100
Dim discount As Decimal
' select a random discount value for the order
discount = RND.Next(0, 45) / 100
Dim prod As Product
' create a random number of detail lines in the range from 10 to 50
For i As Integer = 1 To RND.Next(10, 50)
    prod = CType((From p As Product In ctx.Products
               Where p.ProductID = RND.Next(1, 50) Select p).Single, Product)
' add product to order only if it doesn't exist already
' because the Order Details table has a unique costraint
' on fields OrerID + ProductID
   If order.Order_Details.Where(
            Function(d) d.ProductID = prod.ProductID).Count = 0 Then
        order.Order_Details.Add(
            New Order_Detail With
               {.ProductID = prod.ProductID,
                .Quantity = RND.Next(5, 15),
                .UnitPrice = prod.UnitPrice,
                .Discount = discount})
    End If
 Next
' and now submit the order to the database
ctx.Orders.InsertOnSubmit(order)
ctx.SubmitChanges()
frmOrder.txtOrderID.Text = order.OrderID.ToString
frmOrder.txtOrderDate.Text = order.OrderDate.Value.ToShortDateString
frmOrder.txtOrderCustomer.Text = order.Customer.CompanyName &
                          " / " & order.Customer.ContactName
frmOrder.txtEmployee.Text = order.Employee.LastName & ", " &
                          order.Employee.FirstName
' statement to display order on frmOrder auxiliary form
frmOrder.ShowDialog()
```

Since I'm only interested in showing you how to create a new order, the code selects a customer at random. It does so by skipping a random number of rows in the Customers table with the Skip method and then selecting the following one. Next, it selects a random number of products. Because of a constraint in the Orders table, the code must verify that each new product appears only once in the order. In other words, if the product chosen at random belongs to the order already, the code ignores it, and it does so by calling the `Where` extension method of the order collection with this statement:

```
If order.Order_Details.Where(Function(d) d.ProductID = prod.ProductID).Count = 0
```

FIGURE 14.10
Adding a new order to the Northwind database with LINQ to SQL

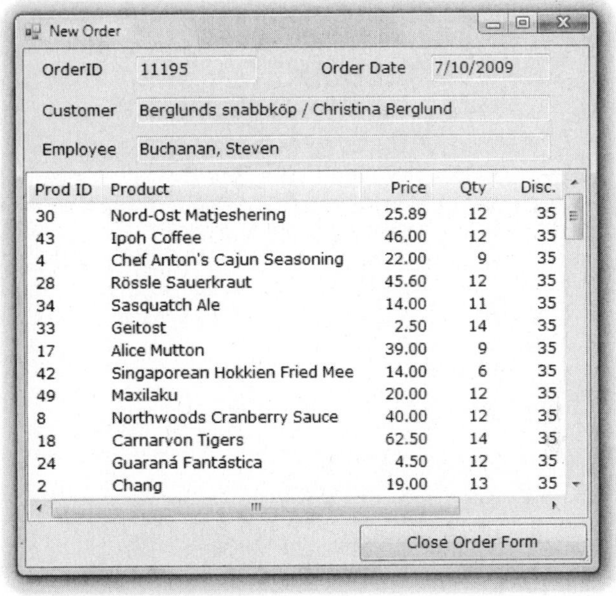

The lambda expression passed to the method selects the row with the product ID you're about to add. If it doesn't exist on that particular order, then the code adds it to the order collection. Other than this detail, the code is straightforward. If you open the sample application and examine its code, you will see that it contains straightforward code that manipulates custom types and collections and only a couple of database-related statements. The new order is represented by an object of the Order type:

```
Dim order As New Order
```

To create the order, the code sets the properties of this object. To specify the customer, the code assigns a Customer object to the `Customer` property of the Order variable. The class generated by the wizard knows that it has to submit just the `CustomerID` field to the database.

Order.Order_Details is a collection of Order_Detail objects, one for each product in the order. The application creates and initializes the order's detail lines, one at a time, and adds them to the Order.Order_Details collection. When done, it submits the order to the database by calling the `SubmitChanges` method. LINQ to SQL knows how to submit all the items in the new order to the database in the proper order. Not only that, but it also retrieves the order's ID (a value that's generated by the database) and updates the order variable at the client. The code that displays the order on an auxiliary form has access to the order's ID without making another trip to the database.

LINQ to SQL is the most important component of LINQ, because it encapsulates the complexity of a database and allows us to work with the database tables as if they were collections of custom types. It bridges the gap between the object-oriented world of Visual Basic and the realm of relational databases. There's another similar component, LINQ to Entities, which is discussed in detail in Chapter 17, "Using the Entity Data Model." LINQ to Entities takes the same principles one step further by allowing you to create your own objects and map them to database tables. LINQ to Entities takes LINQ to SQL one step further in the direction of programming databases with the object-oriented features of modern languages like VB.

The Bottom Line

Perform simple LINQ queries. A LINQ query starts with the structure From *variable* In*collection*, where *variable* is a variable name and *collection* is any collection that implements the IEnumerable interface (such as an array, a typed collection, or any method that returns a collection of items). The second mandatory part of the query is the Select part, which determines the properties of the variable you want in the output. Quite often you select the same variable that you specify in the From keyword. In most cases, you apply a filtering expression with the Where keyword. Here's a typical LINQ query that selects filenames from a specific folder:

```
Dim files =
        From file In
          IO.Directory.GetFiles("C:\Documents")
          Where file.EndsWith("doc")
        Select file
```

Master It Write a LINQ query that calculates the sum of the squares of the values in an array.

Create and process XML files with LINQ to XML. LINQ to XML allows you to create XML documents with the XElement and XAttribute classes. You simply create a new XElement object for each element in your document and create a new XAttribute object for each attribute in the current element. Alternatively, you can simply insert XML code in your VB code. To create an XML document dynamically, you can insert embedded expressions that will be evaluated by the compiler and replaced with their results.

Master It How would you create an HTML document with the filenames in a specific folder?

Process relational data with LINQ to SQL. LINQ to SQL allows you to query relational data from a database. To access the database, you must first create a DataContext object. Then you can call this object's GetTable method to retrieve a table's rows or the ExecuteQuery method to retrieve selected rows from one or more tables with a SQL query. The result is stored in a class designed specifically for the data you're retrieving via the DataContext object.

Master It Explain the attributes you must use in designing a class for storing a table.

Part 5

Developing Data-Driven Applications

- ◆ **Chapter 15: Programming with ADO.NET**
- ◆ **Chapter 16: Developing Data-Driven Applications**
- ◆ **Chapter 17: Using the Data Entity Model**
- ◆ **Chapter 18: Building Data-Bound Applications**

Chapter 15

Programming with ADO.NET

With this chapter, we start exploring applications that manipulate large sets of data stored in a database. After a quick introduction to databases, you'll learn about the basic mechanisms of interacting with databases. As you will see, it's fairly straightforward to write a few VB statements to execute SQL queries against the database in order to either edit or retrieve selected rows. The real challenge is the design and implementation of functional interfaces that display the data requested by the user, allow the user to navigate through the data and edit it, and finally submit the changes to the database. You'll learn how to execute queries against the database, retrieve data, and submit modified or new data to the database.

In this chapter, you'll learn how to do the following:

◆ Store data in relational databases

◆ Query databases with SQL

◆ Submit queries to the database using ADO.NET

What Is a Database?

A *database* is a container for storing relational, structured information. The same is true for a file or even for the file system on your hard disk. What makes a database unique is that it is designed to preserve relationships and make data easily retrievable. The purpose of a database is not so much the storage of information as its quick retrieval. In other words, you must structure your database so that it can be queried quickly and efficiently. It's fairly easy to create a database for storing products and invoices and add new invoices every day. In addition to just storing information, you should also be able to retrieve invoices by period, retrieve invoices by customer, or retrieve invoices that include specific products. Unless the database is designed properly, you won't be able to retrieve the desired information efficiently.

Databases are maintained by special programs, such as Microsoft Office Access and SQL Server. These programs are called *database management systems* (DBMSs), and they're among the most complicated applications. A fundamental characteristic of a DBMS is that it isolates much of the complexity of the database from the developer. Regardless of how each DBMS stores data on disk, you see your data organized in tables with relationships between tables. To access or update the data stored in the database, you use a special language, the Structured Query Language (SQL). Unlike other areas of programming, SQL is a truly universal language, and all major DBMSs support it.

The recommended DBMS for Visual Studio 2010 is SQL Server 2008. In fact, the Visual Studio 2008 setup program offers to install a developer version of SQL Server 2008 called SQL Server 2008 Express. However, you can use Access as well as non-Microsoft databases such as Oracle. Although this chapter was written with SQL Server 2008, most of the examples will work with Access as well.

Data is stored in tables, and each table contains entities of the same type. In a database that stores information about books, there could be a table with titles, another table with authors, and a table with publishers. The table with the titles contains information such as the title of the book, the number of pages, and the book's description. Author names are stored in a different table because each author might appear in multiple titles. If author information were stored along with each title, we'd be repeating author names. So, every time we wanted to change an author's name, we'd have to modify multiple entries in the titles table. Even retrieving a list of unique author names would be a challenge because you'd have to scan the entire table with the titles, retrieve all the authors, and then get rid of the duplicate entries. Of course, you need a mechanism to associate titles with their authors, and you'll see how this is done in the following section. The same is true for publishers. Publishers are stored in a separate table, and each title contains a pointer to the appropriate row in the publishers table.

The reason for breaking the information we want to store in a database into separate tables is to avoid duplication of information. This is a key point in database design. Duplication of information will sooner or later lead to inconsistencies in the database. The process of breaking the data into related tables that eliminate all possible forms of information duplication is called *normalization*, and there are rules for normalizing databases. The topic of database normalization is not discussed further in this book. However, all it really takes to design a functional database is common sense. In short, you identify the entities you want to store in the database (such as customers, products, hotels, books, and the like) and store them in separate tables. You also avoid duplicating information at all costs. If you design a table for storing books along with their authors, you'll soon realize that the same author names are repeated in multiple books. Data duplication means that you have combined entities, and you need to break the original table into one with books and another with authors. Of course, you'll have to establish a relationship between the two tables so you can locate a book's author(s) or an author's books. This is done through relations between the tables; hence the term relational databases. Don't worry if you haven't worked with databases before; the following sections demonstrate the structure of a database through examples. After you learn how to extract data from your database's tables with SQL statements, you'll develop a much better understanding of the way databases should be structured.

Using Relational Databases

The databases we're interested in are called *relational* because they are based on relationships among the data they contain. The data is stored in *tables*, and tables contain related data, or *entities*, such as people, products, orders, and so on. Of course, entities are not independent of each other. For example, orders are placed by specific customers, so the rows of the Customers table must be linked to the rows of the Orders table that stores the orders of the customers. Figure 15.1 shows a segment of a table with customers (top) and the rows of a table with orders that correspond to one of the customers (bottom).

As you can see in Figure 15.1, relationships are implemented by inserting columns with matching values in the two related tables; the CustomerID column is repeated in both tables.

The rows with a common value in the `CustomerID` fields are related. In other words, the lines that connect the two tables simply indicate that there are two fields, one on each side of the relationship, with a common value. The customer with the ID value ALFKI has placed the orders 10643 and 10692 (among others). To find all the orders placed by a customer, we can scan the Orders table and retrieve the rows in which the `CustomerID` field has the same value as the ID of the specific customer in the Customers table. Likewise, you can locate customer information for each order by looking up the row of the Customers table that has the same ID as the one in the `CustomerID` field of the Orders table.

FIGURE 15.1

Linking customers and orders with relationships

Primary Key   Customers Table

CustomerID	CompanyName	ContactName	ContactTitle
ALFKI	Alfreds Futterkiste	Maria Anders	Sales Representative
ANATR	Ana Trujillo Emparedados y helados	Ana Trujillo	Owner
ANTON	Antonio Moreno Taqueria	Antonio Moreno	Owner
AROUT	Around the Horn	Thomas Hardy	Sales Representative

Foreign Key   Orders placed by customer ALFKI

OrderID	CustomerID	EmployeeID	OrderDate	RequiredDate
10643	ALFKI	6	8/25/1997 12:00:00 AM	9/22/1997 12:00:00 AM
10692	ALFKI	4	10/3/1997 12:00:00 AM	10/31/1997 12:00:00 AM
10702	ALFKI	4	10/13/1997 12:00:00 AM	11/24/1997 12:00:00 AM
10835	ALFKI	1	1/15/1998 12:00:00 AM	2/12/1998 12:00:00 AM
10952	ALFKI	1	3/16/1998 12:00:00 AM	4/27/1998 12:00:00 AM
11011	ALFKI	3	4/9/1998 12:00:00 AM	5/7/1998 12:00:00 AM

The two fields used in a relationship are called *key fields*. The `CustomerID` field of the Customers table is the primary key because it identifies a single customer. Each customer has a unique value in the `CustomerID` field. The `CustomerID` field of the Orders table is the *foreign key* of the relationship. A `CustomerID` value appears in a single row of the Customers table and identifies that row; it's the table's primary key. However, it might appear in multiple rows of the Orders table because the `CustomerID` field is the foreign key in this table. In fact, it will appear in as many rows of the Orders table as there are orders for the specific customer. Note that the primary and foreign keys need not have the same names, but it's convenient to use the same name because they both represent the same entity.

The concept of relationships between tables is pretty straightforward and very easy to implement through a pair of keys. Yet, this is the foundation of relational databases.

To help you understand relational databases, I will present the structure of the two sample databases used for the examples in this and the following chapters. If you're not familiar with the Northwind and Pubs databases, read the following two sections and you'll find it easier to follow the examples.

Obtaining the Northwind and Pubs Sample Databases

SQL Server 2008 developers will wonder where the Northwind and Pubs databases have gone. Microsoft has replaced both databases with a single new database called Adventure-Works. Microsoft made the change to demonstrate new SQL Server features in an environment that more closely matches large enterprise systems. Because the AdventureWorks database is extremely complex and not very friendly for teaching database principles, this book won't rely on it. However, you might want to look at the AdventureWorks database anyway to see what it provides and understand how complex databases can become.

Many developers are used to working with the Northwind and Pubs databases with other Microsoft products. These two databases have become so standard that many authors, including myself, rely on the presence of these databases to ensure that everyone can see example code without a lot of extra effort. Unfortunately, you won't find an option for installing them as part of the standard SQL Server 2008 installation. However, you can find scripts for creating these databases in SQL Server Express online at `http://www.microsoft.com/downloads/details.aspx?FamilyID=06616212-0356-46A0-8DA2-EEBC53A68034&displaylang=en`. The name of the file you'll receive is `SQL2000SampleDb.MSI`. Even though Microsoft originally created this file for SQL Server 2000, it works just fine with SQL Server 2008.

After you download the script files, you need to install them. Right-click the file, and choose Install from the context menu. You will see a Welcome dialog box, telling you that this file contains the sample databases for SQL Server 2000. Click Next, read the licensing agreement, and agree to it. Keep following the prompts until you install the sample database scripts in the appropriate directory.

At this point, you have two scripts for creating the sample databases. If you used the default installation settings, these files appear in the `\Program Files\Microsoft SQL Server 2000 Sample Database Scripts` folder of your machine. The `InstNwnd.SQL` file will create the Northwind database, and the `InstPubs.SQL` file will create the Pubs database.

Double-click the name of each SQL file, and each will open in SQL Server Management Studio. Then click the Execute button in the toolbar (it's the button with the icon of an exclamation mark) to run the script, which will install the appropriate database.

To install the databases for the Express version of SQL Server 2008, open a command prompt. Type **OSQL -E -i InstNwnd.SQL**, and press Enter. The OSQL utility will create the Northwind database for you (this process can take quite some time). After the Northwind database is complete, type **OSQL -E -i InstPubs.SQL**, and press Enter. The process will repeat itself.

If you try to run the OSQL utility and receive an error message at the command prompt, the SQL Server 2008 installation didn't modify the path information for your system as it should have. In some cases, this makes your installation suspect, and you should reinstall the product if you experience other problems. To use the installation scripts, copy them from the installation folder to the `\Program Files\Microsoft SQL Server\90\Tools\binn` folder. You can run the OSQL utility at the command prompt from this folder to create the two sample databases.

You'll want to test the installation to make sure it worked. Open Visual Studio, and choose View ➤ Server Explorer to display Server Explorer. Right-click Data Connections, and choose Add Connection from the context menu. Server Explorer will display the Add Connection dialog box shown in Figure 15.2 (this one already has all the information filled out).

In the Server Name field, type the name of your machine, or select one with the mouse. Click the down arrow in the Select Or Enter A Database Name field. You should see both the Northwind and Pubs databases, as shown in Figure 15.2. If you don't see these entries, it means that an error occurred. Try running the scripts a second time.

FIGURE 15.2
Use the Add Connection
dialog box to check for
the two databases.

Exploring the Northwind Database

In this section, you'll explore the structure of the Northwind sample database. The Northwind database stores products, customers, and sales data, and many of you are already familiar with the structure of the database.

To view a table's contents, expand the Table section of the tree under the Northwind connection in Server Explorer, and locate the name of the table you want to examine. Right-click the name, and choose Show Table Data from the context menu. This will open the table, and you can view and edit its rows. If you choose the Open Table Definition command from the same menu, you will see the definitions of the table's columns. You can change the type of the columns (each column stores items of the same type), change their length, and set a few more properties that are discussed a little later in this chapter. To follow the description of the sample databases, open the tables in view mode.

If you have installed SQL Server 2008, you can use SQL Server Management Studio to explore the same database. Just right-click the Northwind database, and from the context menu select Open Table to view the data or select Design to change the table definition.

PRODUCTS TABLE

The Products table stores information about the products of the fictional Northwind corporation. This information includes the product name, packaging information, price, and other relevant fields. Each product (or row) in the table is identified by a unique numeric ID. Because each ID is unique, the `ProductID` column is the table's primary key. This column is an Identity column: It's a numeric value, which is generated automatically by the database every time you insert a new row to the table. The rows of the Products table are referenced by invoices (the Order Details table, which is discussed later), so the product IDs appear in the Order Details table as well. The `ProductID` column, as well as most primary keys in any database, has a unique property: It's an Identity column. Every time you add a new product to the table, SQL Server assigns the next available value to this column. If the ID of the last row in the Products table is 72, the first product that will be added will take the primary key value of 73 automatically. SQL Server will always assign the proper value to this column, and it will always be unique.

SUPPLIERS TABLE

Each product has a supplier, too. Because the same supplier can offer more than one product, the supplier information is stored in a different table, and a common field, the `SupplierID` field, is used to link each product to its supplier (as shown in Figure 15.3). For example, the products Chai, Chang, and Aniseed Syrup are purchased from the same supplier: Exotic Liquids. Its `SupplierID` fields all point to the same row in the Suppliers table.

FIGURE 15.3
Linking products to their suppliers and their categories

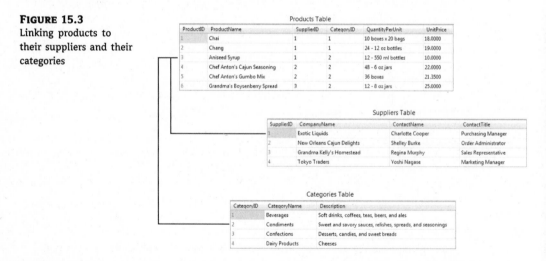

CATEGORIES TABLE

In addition to having a supplier, each product belongs to a category. Categories are not stored along with product names; they are stored separately in the Categories table. Again, each category is identified by a numeric value (field `CategoryID`) and has a name (field `CategoryName`). In addition, the Categories table has two more columns: `Description`, which contains text, and

`Picture`, which stores a bitmap. The `CategoryID` field in the Categories table is the primary key, and the field by the same name in the Products table is the corresponding foreign key.

CUSTOMERS TABLE

The Customers table stores information about the company's customers. Each customer is stored in a separate row of this table, and customers are referenced by the Orders table. Unlike product IDs, customer IDs are five-character strings and are stored in the `CustomerID` column. This is an unusual choice for IDs, which are usually numeric values. The `CustomerID` column isn't an Identity column; the user must determine the key of each customer and submit it along with the other customer data. The database has a unique constraint for this column: The customer's ID must be unique, and the database won't accept any rows with a duplicate `CustomerID` value.

ORDERS TABLE

The Orders table stores information about the orders placed by Northwind's customers. The `OrderID` field, which is an integer value, identifies each order. Orders are numbered sequentially, so this field is also the order's number. Each time you append a new row to the Orders table, the value of the new `OrderID` field is generated automatically by the database. Not only is the `OrderID` column the table's primary key, but it's also an Identity column.

The Orders table is linked to the Customers table through the `CustomerID` column. By matching rows that have identical values in their `CustomerID` fields in the two tables, we can recombine customers with their orders. Refer back to Figure 15.1 to see how customers are linked to their orders.

ORDER DETAILS TABLE

The Orders table doesn't store any details about the items ordered; this information is stored in the Order Details table (see Figure 15.4). Each order consists of one or more items, and each item has a price, a quantity, and a discount. In addition to these fields, the Order Details table contains an `OrderID` column, which holds the ID of the order to which the detail line belongs.

The reason why details aren't stored along with the order's header is that the Orders and Order Details tables store different entities. The order's header, which contains information about the customer who placed the order, the date of the order, and so on, is quite different from the information you must store for each item ordered. If you attempt to store the entire order into a single table, you'll end up repeating a lot of information. Notice also that the Order Details table stores the IDs of the products, not the product names.

EMPLOYEES TABLE

This table holds employee information. Each employee is identified by a numeric ID, which appears in each order. When a sale is made, the ID of the employee who made the sale is recorded in the Orders table. An interesting technique was used in the design of the Employees table: Each employee has a manager, which is another employee. The employee's manager is identified by the `ReportsTo` field, which is set to the ID of the employee's manager. The rows of the Employees table contain references to the same table. This table contains a foreign key that points to the primary key of the same table, a relation that allows you to identify the hierarchy of employees in the corporation.

FIGURE 15.4
Customers, Orders, and
Order Details tables and
their relations

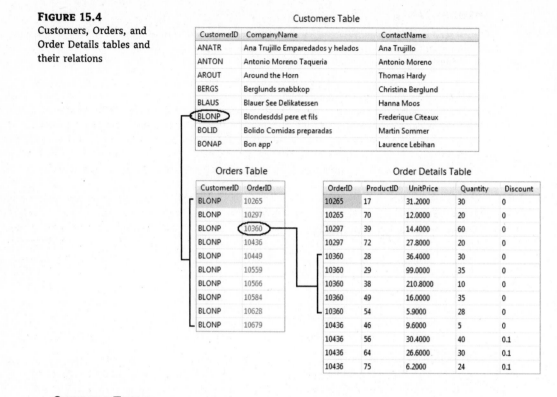

Customers Table

CustomerID	CompanyName	ContactName
ANATR	Ana Trujillo Emparedados y helados	Ana Trujillo
ANTON	Antonio Moreno Taqueria	Antonio Moreno
AROUT	Around the Horn	Thomas Hardy
BERGS	Berglunds snabbkop	Christina Berglund
BLAUS	Blauer See Delikatessen	Hanna Moos
BLONP	Blondesddsl pere et fils	Frederique Citeaux
BOLID	Bolido Comidas preparadas	Martin Sommer
BONAP	Bon app'	Laurence Lebihan

Orders Table

CustomerID	OrderID
BLONP	10265
BLONP	10297
BLONP	10360
BLONP	10436
BLONP	10449
BLONP	10559
BLONP	10566
BLONP	10584
BLONP	10628
BLONP	10679

Order Details Table

OrderID	ProductID	UnitPrice	Quantity	Discount
10265	17	31.2000	30	0
10265	70	12.0000	20	0
10297	39	14.4000	60	0
10297	72	27.8000	20	0
10360	28	36.4000	30	0
10360	29	99.0000	35	0
10360	38	210.8000	10	0
10360	49	16.0000	35	0
10360	54	5.9000	28	0
10436	46	9.6000	5	0
10436	56	30.4000	40	0.1
10436	64	26.6000	30	0.1
10436	75	6.2000	24	0.1

SHIPPERS TABLE

Each order is shipped with one of the three shippers stored in the Shippers table. The appropriate shipper's ID is stored in the Orders table.

Exploring the Pubs Database

Before looking at SQL and more practical techniques for manipulating tables, let's look at the structure of another sample database I'm going to use in this chapter, the Pubs database. Pubs is a database for storing book, author, and publisher information, not unlike a database you might build for an online bookstore.

The Pubs database consists of really small tables, but it was carefully designed to demonstrate many of the features of SQL, so it's a prime candidate for sample code. Just about any book about SQL Server uses the Pubs database. In the examples of the following sections, I will use the Northwind database because it's closer to a typical business database, and the type of information stored in the Northwind database is closer to the needs of the average VB programmer than the Pubs database. Some of the fine points of SQL, however, can't be demonstrated with the data of the Northwind database, so in this section I'll show examples that use the ubiquitous Pubs database.

TITLES TABLE

The Titles table contains information about individual books (the book's title, ID, price, and so on). Each title is identified by an ID, which is not a numeric value, that's stored in the `title_id` column. The IDs of the books look like this: BU2075.

AUTHORS TABLE

The Authors table contains information about authors. Each author is identified by an ID, which is stored in the `au_id` field. This field is a string with a value such as 172-32-1176 (they resemble U.S. Social Security numbers).

TITLEAUTHOR TABLE

The Titles and Authors tables are not directly related because they can't be joined via a one-to-many relationship; the relationship between the two tables is many-to-many. The relations you have seen so far are *one-to-many* because they relate one row in the table that has the primary key to one or more rows in the table that has the foreign key: One order contains many detail lines, one customer has many orders, one category contains many products, and so on.

The relation between titles and authors is *many-to-many* because each book may have multiple authors, and each author may have written multiple titles. If you stop to think about the relationship between these two tables, you'll realize that it can't be implemented with a primary key and a foreign key (like the Order-Customer relationship or the Order-Shipper relationship in the Northwind database). To establish a many-to-many relationship, you must create a join table between the other two, and this table must have a one-to-many relationship with both tables.

Figure 15.5 shows how the Titles and Authors tables of the Pubs database are related to one another. The table between them holds pairs of title IDs and author IDs. If a book was written by two authors, the TitleAuthor table contains two entries with the same title ID and different author IDs. The book with a `title_id` of BU1111 was written by two authors. The IDs of the authors appear in the TitleAuthor table along with the ID of the book. The IDs of these two authors are 267-41-2394 and 724-80-9391. Likewise, if an author has written more than one book, the author's ID will appear many times in the TitleAuthor table — each time paired with a different title ID.

FIGURE 15.5
The TitleAuthor table
links titles to authors.

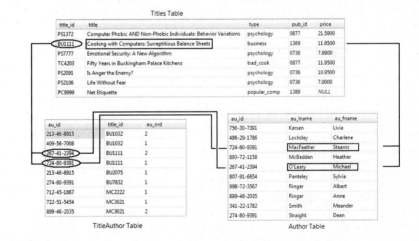

At times you won't be able to establish the desired relationship directly between two tables because the relationship is many-to-many. When you discover a conflict between two tables, you must create a join table between them. A many-to-many relation is actually implemented as two one-to-many relations.

PUBLISHERS TABLE

The Publishers table contains information about publishers. Each title has a `pub_id` field, which points to the matching row of the Publishers table. Unlike the other major tables of the Pubs database, the Publishers table uses a numeric value to identify each publisher.

Understanding Relations

In a database, each table has a field with a unique value for every row. As indicated earlier in this chapter, this field is the table's primary key. The primary key does not have to be a meaningful entity because in most cases there's no single field that's unique for each row. Books can be identified by their ISBNs and employees by their SSNs, but these are exceptions to the rule. In general, you can't come up with a meaningful key that's universally unique. The primary key need not resemble the entity it identifies. The only requirement is that primary keys be unique in the entire table. In most designs, we use an integer as the primary key. To make sure they're unique, we even let the DBMS generate a new integer for each row added to the table. Each table can have one primary key only, and the DBMS can automatically generate an integer value for a primary key field every time a new row is added. SQL Server uses the term `Identity` for this data type, and there can be only one Identity field in each table.

Database designers sometimes use unique global identifiers, which are lengthy strings like 281167b3-7cbc-41a0-ad89-8c0995ac2d07 to identify the rows. These strings, which are guaranteed to be globally unique, are generated automatically by both Visual Basic and SQL Server. To generate a GUID value with Visual Basic, call the `Guid.NewGuid` method. GUIDs are not as easy to handle as integers, and they entail some performance penalty. If you need a unique identity across multiple databases, you have to use GUIDs.

The related rows in a table repeat the primary key of the row they are related to in another table. The copies of the primary keys in all other tables are called *foreign keys*. Foreign keys need not be unique (in fact, by definition they aren't), and any field can serve as a foreign key. What makes a field a foreign key is that it matches the primary key of another table. The `CategoryID` field is the primary key of the Categories table because it identifies each category. The `CategoryID` field in the Products table is the foreign key because the same value might appear in many rows (many products can belong to the same category). Whereas the primary key refers to a table, the foreign key refers to a relationship. The `CategoryID` column of the Products table is the foreign key in the relationship between the Categories and Products tables. The Products table contains another foreign key, the `SupplierID` column, which forms the relationship between the Suppliers and Products tables.

REFERENTIAL INTEGRITY

Maintaining the links between tables is not a trivial task. When you add an invoice line, for instance, you must make sure that the product ID that you insert in the Order Details table corresponds to a row in the Products table. An important aspect of a database is its integrity. To be specific, you must ensure that the relations are always valid, and this type of integrity is called *referential integrity*. There are other types of integrity (for example, setting a product's value to a negative value will compromise the integrity of the database), but this is not nearly as important as referential integrity. The wrong price can be easily fixed. But issuing an invoice to a customer who doesn't exist isn't easy (if even possible) to fix. Modern databases come with many tools to help ensure their integrity, especially referential integrity. These tools are constraints you enter when you design the database, and the DBMS makes sure that the constraints are not violated as the various programs manipulate the database.

When you relate the Products and Categories tables, for example, you must also ensure the following:

◆ Every product added to the foreign table must point to a valid entry in the primary table. If you are not sure which category the product belongs to, you can leave the `CategoryID` field of the Products table empty (the field will have a null value). Or, you can create a generic category, the UNKNOWN or UNDECIDED category, and use this category if no information is available.

◆ No rows in the Categories table should be removed if there are rows in the Products table pointing to the specific category. This situation would make the corresponding rows of the Products table point to an invalid category (the rows that have no matching row in the primary table are called *orphan rows*).

These two restrictions would be quite a burden on the programmer if the DBMS didn't protect the database against actions that could impair its integrity. The referential integrity of your database depends on the validity of the relations. Fortunately, all DBMSs can enforce rules to maintain their integrity, and you'll learn how to enforce rules that guarantee the integrity of your database later in this chapter. In fact, when you create the relationship, you can select a couple of check boxes that tell SQL Server to enforce the relationship (that is, not to accept any changes in the data that violate the relationship). If you leave these check boxes deselected, be ready to face a real disaster sooner or later.

VISUAL DATABASE TOOLS

To simplify the development of database applications, Visual Studio 2010 comes with some visual tools, the most important of which are briefly described in Table 15.1 and then discussed in the following sections.

TABLE 15.1: Visual database tools

NAME	DESCRIPTION
Server Explorer	This is the most prominent tool. Server Explorer is the toolbox for database applications, in the sense that it contains all the basic tools for connecting to databases and manipulating their objects.
Query Builder	This is a tool for creating SQL queries (statements that retrieve the data you want from a database or update the data in the database). SQL is a language in its own right, and we'll discuss it later in this chapter. Query Builder lets you specify the operations you want to perform on the tables of a database with point-and-click operations. In the background, Query Builder builds the appropriate SQL statement and executes it against the database.
Database Designer and Tables Designer	These tools allow you to work with an entire database or its tables. When you work with the database, you can add new tables, establish relationships between the tables, and so on. When you work with individual tables, you can manipulate the structure of the tables, edit their data, and add constraints. You can use these tools to manipulate a complicated object — the database — with point-and-click operations.

SQL: An Overview

SQL is a universal language for manipulating data in database tables. Every DBMS supports it, so you should invest the time and effort to learn it. You can generate SQL statements with point-and-click operations (Query Builder is a visual tool for generating SQL statements), but this is no substitute for understanding SQL and writing your own statements. The visual tools are nothing more than a user-friendly interface for specifying SQL statements. In the background, they generate the appropriate SQL statement, and you will get the most out of these tools if you understand the basics of SQL. I will start with an overview of SQL, and then I'll show you how to use the Query Builder utility to specify a few advanced queries. If you're familiar with SQL, you can skip this section or just glance through it and take a look at the examples.

By the way, the SQL version of SQL Server is called T-SQL, which stands for Transact-SQL. T-SQL is a superset of SQL and provides advanced programming features that are not available with SQL. I'm not going to discuss T-SQL in this book, but once you understand SQL, you'll find it easy to leverage this knowledge to T-SQL.

SQL is a nonprocedural language, which means that SQL doesn't provide traditional programming structures such as If statements or loops. Instead, it's a language for specifying the operation you want to perform against a database at a high level. The details of the implementation are left to the DBMS. SQL is an imperative language, like Language Integrated Query (LINQ), as opposed to a traditional programming language, such as VB. Traditional languages are declarative: The statements you write tell the compiler how to perform the desired actions. This is good news for nonprogrammers, but many programmers new to SQL might wish it had the structure of a more traditional language. You will get used to SQL and soon be able to combine the best of both worlds: the programming model of VB and the simplicity of SQL. Besides, there are many similarities between SQL and LINQ, and you'll be able to leverage your skills in any of the two areas.

SQL IS NOT CASE SENSITIVE

SQL is not case sensitive, but it's customary to use uppercase for SQL statements and keywords. In the examples in this book, I use uppercase for SQL statements. This is just a style to help you distinguish between the SQL keywords and the table/field names of the query. Also, unlike VB, SQL literals must be embedded in single quotes, not double quotes.

To retrieve all the company names from the Customers table of the Northwind database, you issue a statement like this one:

```
SELECT CompanyName
FROM   Customers
```

To select customers from a specific country, you must use the WHERE clause to limit the selected rows, as in the following statement:

```
SELECT CompanyName
FROM   Customers
WHERE  Country = 'Germany'
```

The DBMS will retrieve and return the rows you requested. As you can see, this is not the way you'd retrieve rows with Visual Basic. With a procedural language such as VB, you'd have to write loops to scan the entire table, examine the value of the Country column, and either select or reject the row. Then you would display the selected rows. With SQL, you don't have to specify how the selection operation will take place; you simply specify *what* you want the database to do for you — not *how* to do it. As a reminder, the equivalent LINQ statement would be as follows (I'm using LINQ to SQL syntax):

```
Dim selectedCustomers = From cust In Customers
Where cust.Country = "Germany"
Select cust
```

SQL statements are divided into two major categories, which are actually considered separate languages: the statements for manipulating the data, which form the Data Manipulation Language (DML), and the statements for defining database objects, such as tables or their indexes, which form the Data Definition Language (DDL). The DDL is not of interest to every database developer, and I will not discuss it in this book. The DML is covered in depth because you'll use these statements to retrieve data, insert new data into the database, and edit or delete existing data.

The statements of the DML part of the SQL language are also known as *queries*, and there are two types of queries: selection queries and action queries. Selection queries retrieve information from the database. A selection query returns a set of rows with identical structure. The columns can come from different tables, but all the rows returned by the query have the same number of columns. Action queries modify the database's objects or create new objects and add them to the database (new tables, relationships, and so on).

Executing SQL Statements

If you are not familiar with SQL, I suggest that you follow the examples in this chapter and experiment with the sample databases. To follow the examples, you have two options: SQL Server Management Studio (SSMS) and Query Designer of Visual Studio. SSMS helps you manage databases in various ways, including creating queries to extract data. Query Designer is an editor for SQL statements that also allows you to execute them and see the results. In addition to Query Designer, you can also use Query Builder, which is part of SSMS and Visual Studio. Query Builder lets you build the statements with visual tools, and you don't have to know the syntax of SQL in order to create queries with Query Builder. After a quick overview of the SQL statements, I will describe Query Builder and show you how to use its interface to build fairly elaborate queries.

Using SQL Server Management Studio

One of the applications installed with SQL Server is SQL Server Management Studio. To start it, choose Start ≻ Programs ≻ SQL Server ≻ SQL Server Management Studio. When this application starts, you see the Connect To Server dialog box (Figure 15.6). Choose Database Engine in the Server Type field so you can work with databases on your system. Select the server you want to use in the Server Name field. Provide your credentials, and click Connect.

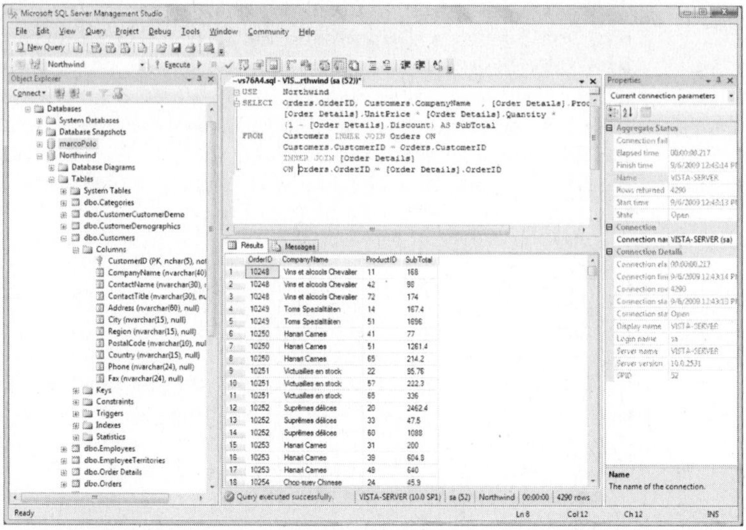

FIGURE 15.6
SSMS provides access
to all the database
engine objects, including
databases.

After you're connected, right-click the database you want to use, and choose New Query from the context menu. Enter the SQL statement you want to execute in the blank query that SSMS creates. The SQL statement will be executed against the selected database when you press Ctrl+E or click the Execute button (it's the button with the exclamation point icon). Alternatively, you can prefix the SQL statement with the USE statement, which specifies the database against which the statement will be executed. To retrieve all the Northwind customers located in Germany, enter this statement:

```
USE Northwind
SELECT CompanyName FROM Customers
WHERE  Country = 'Germany'
```

The USE statement isn't part of the query; it simply tells SSMS the database against which it must execute the query. I'm including the USE statement with all the queries so you know the database used for each example. If you're executing the sample code from within Visual Studio, you need not use the USE statement, because all queries are executed against the selected database. Actually, the statement isn't supported by Query Designer of Visual Studio.

The results of the query, known as the *result set*, will appear in a grid in the lower pane. An action query that updates a table (adds a new row, edits a row, or deletes an existing row) doesn't return any rows; it simply displays the number of rows affected on the Messages tab.

To execute another query, enter another statement in the upper pane, or edit the previous statement and press Ctrl+E again. You can also save SQL statements into files so that you won't have to type them again. To do so, open the File menu, choose Save As or Save, and enter the name of the file in which the contents of the Query pane will be stored. The statement will be stored in a text file with the extension .sql.

USING VISUAL STUDIO

To execute the same queries with Visual Studio, open the Server Explorer window, and right-click the name of the database against which you want to execute the query. From the context menu, choose New Query, and a new query window will open. You will also see a dialog box prompting you to select one or more tables. For the time being, close this dialog box, because you will supply the names of the tables in the query; later in this chapter, you'll learn how to use the visual tools to build queries.

Query Designer of Visual Studio consists of four panes (Figure 15.7). The upper pane (which is the Table Diagram pane) displays the tables involved in the query, their fields, and the relationships between the tables — if any. The next pane shows the fields that will be included in the output of the query. Here you specify the output of the query, as well as the selection criteria. This pane is Query Builder, the tool that lets you design queries visually. It's discussed later in this chapter. In the next pane, the SQL pane, you see the SQL statement produced by the visual tools. If you modify the query with the visual tools, the SQL statement is updated automatically; likewise, when you edit the query, the other two panes are updated automatically to reflect the changes. The last pane, the Results pane, contains a grid with the query's output. Every time you execute the query by clicking the button with the exclamation mark in the toolbar, the bottom pane is populated with the results of the query. For the examples in this section, ignore the top two panes. Just enter the SQL statements in the SQL pane, and execute them.

FIGURE 15.7
Executing queries with
Visual Studio

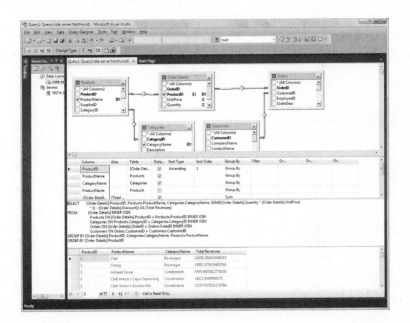

Selection Queries

We'll start our discussion of SQL with the SELECT statement. After you learn how to express the criteria for selecting the desired rows with the SELECT statement, you can apply this information to other data-manipulation statements. The simplest form of the SELECT statement is

```
SELECT fields
FROM    tables
```

where `fields` and `tables` are comma-separated lists of the fields you want to retrieve from the database and the tables they belong to. The list of fields following the SELECT statement is referred to as the *selection list.* To select the contact information from all the companies in the Customers table, use this statement:

```
USE Northwind
SELECT CompanyName, ContactName, ContactTitle
FROM    Customers
```

To retrieve all the fields, use the asterisk (*). The following statement selects all the fields from the Customers table:

```
SELECT * FROM Customers
```

As soon as you execute a statement that uses the asterisk to select all columns, Query Designer will replace the asterisk with the names of all columns in the table.

LIMITING THE SELECTION WITH *WHERE*

The unconditional form of the SELECT statement used in the previous section is quite trivial. You rarely retrieve data from all rows in a table. Usually you specify criteria, such as "all companies from Germany," "all customers who have placed three or more orders in the last six months," or even more-complicated expressions. To restrict the rows returned by the query, use the WHERE clause of the SELECT statement. The most common form of the SELECT statement is the following:

```
SELECT fields
FROM    tables
WHERE   condition
```

The `fields` and `tables` arguments are the same as before, and `condition` is an expression that limits the rows to be selected. The syntax of the WHERE clause can get quite complicated, so we'll start with the simpler forms of the selection criteria. The `condition` argument can be a relational expression, such as the ones you use in VB. To select all the customers from Germany, use the following condition:

```
WHERE Country = 'Germany'
```

To select customers from multiple countries, use the OR operator to combine multiple conditions:

```
WHERE Country = 'Germany' OR
      Country = 'Austria'
```

You can also combine multiple conditions with the AND operator.

COMBINING DATA FROM MULTIPLE TABLES

It is possible to retrieve data from two or more tables by using a single statement. (This is the most common type of query, actually.) When you combine multiple tables in a query, you can use the WHERE clause to specify how the rows of the two tables will be combined. Let's say you want a list of all product names, along with their categories. For this query, you must extract the product names from the Products table and the category names from the Categories table and specify that the ProductID field in the two tables must match. The statement

```
USE Northwind
SELECT ProductName, CategoryName
FROM    Products, Categories
WHERE   Products.CategoryID = Categories.CategoryID
```

retrieves the names of all products, along with their category names. Here's how this statement is executed. For each row in the Products table, the SQL engine locates the matching row in the Categories table and then appends the ProductName and CategoryName fields to the result. In other words, it creates pairs of a product and the matching category. Products that don't belong to a category are not included in the result set.

ALIASING TABLE NAMES

To avoid typing long table names, you can alias them with a shorter name and use this short-hand notation in the rest of the query. The query that retrieves titles and publishers can be written as follows:

```
USE pubs
SELECT T.title
FROM    titles T, publishers P
WHERE   T.pub_id = P.pub_id
```

The table names are aliased in the FROM clause, and the alias is used in the rest of the query. There's one situation where table name aliasing is mandatory, and this is when you want to refer to the same table twice. This is a fairly advanced topic, but I'm including a typical example to demonstrate an interesting technique, because you may run into it. Some tables contain references to themselves, and the Employees table of the Northwind database belongs to this category. Each employee reports to a manager, who's also an employee. The manager is identified by the column ReportsTo, which contains the ID of an employee's manager. Here are three rows of the Employees table that demonstrate this hierarchy:

EMPLOYEEID	LASTNAME	FIRSTNAME	TITLE	REPORTSTO
2	Fuller	Andrew	Vice President, Sales	NULL
5	Buchanan	Steven	Sales Manager	2
6	Suyama	Michael	Sales Representative	5

As you can see here, Suyama reports to Buchanan, and Buchanan in turn reports to Fuller. How would you retrieve each employee's name and title along with his manager's name? Here, we must make a query that involves two tables, one with the employee names and another one with the manager names. It just so happens that the two tables are in reality the same table. The trick is to treat the Employees table as two separate tables using aliases. Here's the query that retrieves employees and managers in a single result set:

```
SELECT  Employees.EmployeeID,
        Employees.LastName + ' ' + Employees.FirstName,
        Employees.Title,
        Managers.FirstName + ' ' + Managers.LastName,
        Managers.Title
FROM    Employees, Employees Managers
WHERE   Employees.ReportsTo = Managers.EmployeeID
```

If the database contained two different tables, one for employees and another one for managers, you'd have no problem coding the query. Because we want to use the same table for both managers and employees, we use aliases to create two virtual tables and associate them with the ReportsTo and EmployeeID columns. The result is a neat list of names that shows clearly the hierarchy of the Northwind corporation's employees:

```
1  Davolio Nancy      Sales Representative        Andrew Fuller
3  Leverling Janet    Sales Representative        Andrew Fuller
4  Peacock Margaret   Sales Representative        Andrew Fuller
5  Buchanan Steven    Sales Manager              Andrew Fuller
6  Suyama Michael     Sales Representative        Steven Buchanan
7  King Robert        Sales Representative        Steven Buchanan
8  Callahan Laura     Inside Sales Coordinator    Andrew Fuller
9  Dodsworth Anne     Sales Representative        Steven Buchanan
```

I skipped the manager's title in the listing because it wouldn't fit on the printed page. Note that because the Last Name and First Name column names contain spaces, they're embedded in square brackets. The same is true for table names that contain spaces.

ALIASING COLUMN NAMES

By default, each column of a query is labeled after the actual field name in the output. If a table contains two fields named CustLName and CustFName, you can display them with different labels by using the AS keyword. The following SELECT statement produces two columns labeled CustLName and CustFName:

```
SELECT CustLName, CustFName
```

The query's output looks much better if you change the labels of these two columns with a statement like the following:

```
SELECT CustLName AS [Last Name],
       CustFName AS [First Name]
```

It is also possible to concatenate two fields in the SELECT list with the concatenation operator. Concatenated fields are labeled automatically as Expr1, Expr2, and so on, so you must supply your own name for the combined field. The following statement creates a single column for the customer's name and labels it Customer Name:

```
SELECT CustLName + ', ' + CustFName AS [Customer Name]
```

SKIPPING DUPLICATES WITH *DISTINCT*

The DISTINCT keyword eliminates from the cursor any duplicates retrieved by the SELECT statement. Let's say you want a list of all countries with at least one customer. If you retrieve all country names from the Customers table, you'll end up with many duplicates. To eliminate them, use the DISTINCT keyword, as shown in the following statement:

```
USE Northwind
SELECT DISTINCT Country
FROM    Customers
```

THE *LIKE* OPERATOR

The LIKE operator uses pattern-matching characters like the ones you use to select multiple files in DOS. The LIKE operator recognizes several pattern-matching characters (or *wildcard* characters) to match one or more characters, numeric digits, ranges of letters, and so on. Table 15.2 describes these characters.

TABLE 15.2:   SQL wildcard characters

WILDCARD CHARACTER	DESCRIPTION
%	Matches any number of characters. The pattern program% will find *program, programming, programmer*, and so on. The pattern %program% will locate strings that contain the words *program, programming, nonprogrammer*, and so on.
_	(Underscore character.) Matches any single alphabetic character. The pattern b_y will find *boy* and *bay*, but not *boysenberry*.
[ ]	Matches any single character within the brackets. The pattern Santa [YI]nez will find both *Santa Ynez* and *Santa Inez*.
[^]	Matches any character not in the brackets. The pattern %q[^u]% will find words that contain the character *q* not followed by *u* (they are misspelled words).
[-]	Matches any one of a range of characters. The characters must be consecutive in the alphabet and specified in ascending order (*A* to *Z*, not *Z* to *A*). The pattern [a-c]% will find all words that begin with *a, b,* or *c* (in lowercase or uppercase).
#	Matches any single numeric character. The pattern D1## will find *D100* and *D139*, but not *D1000* or *D10*.

You can use the LIKE operator to retrieve all titles about Windows from the Pubs database, by using a statement like the following one:

```
USE pubs
SELECT titles.title
FROM   titles
WHERE  titles.title LIKE '%Windows%'
```

The percent signs mean that any character(s) may appear in front of or after the word *Windows* in the title.

To include a wildcard character itself in your search argument, enclose it in square brackets. The pattern %50[%]% will match any field that contains the string *50%*.

NULL VALUES AND THE *ISNULL* FUNCTION

A common operation for manipulating and maintaining databases is to locate null values in fields. The expressions IS NULL and IS NOT NULL find field values that are (or are not) null. To locate the rows of the Customers table that have a null value in their CompanyName column, use the following WHERE clause:

```
WHERE CompanyName IS NULL
```

You can easily locate the products without prices and edit them. The following statement locates products without prices:

```
USE Northwind
SELECT * FROM Products WHERE UnitPrice IS NULL
```

A related function, the ISNULL() function, allows you to specify the value to be returned when a specific field is null. The ISNULL() SQL function accepts two arguments: a column name and a string. The function returns the value of the specified column, unless this value is null, in which case it returns the value of the second argument. To return the string *** for customers without a company name, use the following expression:

```
USE Northwind
SELECT  CustomerID,
        ISNULL(CompanyName, '***') AS Company, ContactName
FROM Customers
```

SORTING THE ROWS WITH *ORDER BY*

The rows of a query are not in any particular order. To request that the rows be returned in a specific order, use the ORDER BY clause, which has this syntax:

```
ORDER BY col1, col2, . . .
```

You can specify any number of columns in the ORDER BY list. The output of the query is ordered according to the values of the first column. If two rows have identical values in this column, they are sorted according to the second column, and so on. The following statement displays the customers ordered by country and then by city within each country:

```
USE      Northwind
SELECT   CompanyName, ContactName, Country, City
FROM     Customers
ORDER BY Country, City
```

Working with Calculated Fields

In addition to column names, you can specify calculated columns in the SELECT statement. The Order Details table contains a row for each invoice line. Invoice 10248, for instance, contains four lines (four items sold), and each detail line appears in a separate row in the Order Details table. Each row holds the number of items sold, the item's price, and the corresponding discount. To display the line's subtotal, you must multiply the quantity by the price minus the discount, as shown in the following statement:

```
USE Northwind
SELECT Orders.OrderID, [Order Details].ProductID,
       [Order Details].[Order Details].UnitPrice *
       [Order Details].Quantity *
       (1 - [Order Details].Discount) AS SubTotal
FROM   Orders INNER JOIN [Order Details]
  ON   Orders.OrderID = [Order Details].OrderID
```

Here the selection list contains an expression based on several fields of the Order Details table. This statement calculates the subtotal for each line in the invoices issued to all Northwind customers and displays them along with the order number. The order numbers are repeated as many times as there are products in the order (or lines in the invoice). In the following section, you will find out how to calculate totals too.

Calculating Aggregates

SQL supports some aggregate functions, which act on selected fields of all the rows returned by the query. The basic aggregate functions listed in Table 15.3 perform basic calculations such as summing, counting, and averaging numeric values. There are a few more aggregate functions for calculating statistics such as the variance and standard deviation, but I have omitted them from Table 15.3. Aggregate functions accept field names (or calculated fields) as arguments and return a single value, which is the sum (or average) of all values.

These functions operate on a single column (which could be a calculated column) and return a single value. The rows involved in the calculations are specified with the proper WHERE clause. The SUM() and AVG() functions can process only numeric values. The other three functions can process both numeric and text values.

The aggregate functions are used to summarize data from one or more tables. Let's say you want to know the number of Northwind database customers located in Germany. The following SQL statement returns the desired value:

```
USE Northwind
SELECT COUNT(CustomerID)
FROM    Customers
WHERE   Country = 'Germany'
```

TABLE 15.3:   SQL's common aggregate functions

FUNCTION	RETURNS
COUNT()	The number (count) of values in a specified column
SUM()	The sum of values in a specified column
AVG()	The average of the values in a specified column
MIN()	The smallest value in a specified column
MAX()	The largest value in a specified column

The aggregate functions ignore the null values unless you specify the * argument. The following statement returns the count of all rows in the Customers table, even if some of them have a null value in the Country column:

```
USE Northwind
SELECT COUNT(*)
FROM    Customers
```

The SUM() function is used to total the values of a specific field in the specified rows. To find out how many units of the product with ID = 11 (queso Cabrales) have been sold, use the following statement:

```
USE Northwind
SELECT SUM(Quantity)
FROM    [Order Details]
WHERE   ProductID = 11
```

The SQL statement that returns the total revenue generated by a single product is a bit more complicated. To calculate it, you must multiply the quantities by their prices and then add the resulting products together, taking into consideration each invoice's discount:

```
USE Northwind
SELECT SUM(Quantity * UnitPrice * (1 - Discount))
FROM    [Order Details]
WHERE   ProductID = 11
```

Product QuesoCabrales generated a total revenue of $12,901.77. If you want to know the number of items of this product that were sold, add one more aggregate function to the query to sum the quantities of each row that refers to the specific product ID:

```
USE Northwind
SELECT SUM(Quantity),
       SUM(Quantity * UnitPrice * (1 - Discount))
```

```
FROM    [Order Details]
WHERE   ProductID = 11
```

If you add the ProductID column in the selection list and delete the WHERE clause to retrieve the totals for all products, the query will generate an error message to the effect that the columns haven't been grouped. You will learn how to group the results a little later in this chapter.

Using SQL Joins

Joins specify how you connect multiple tables in a query. There are four types of joins:

♦ Left outer, or left, join

♦ Right outer, or right, join

♦ Full outer, or full, join

♦ Inner join

A join operation combines all the rows of one table with the rows of another table. Joins are usually followed by a condition that determines which records on either side of the join appear in the result. The WHERE clause of the SELECT statement is similar to a join, but there are some fine points that will be explained momentarily.

The left, right, and full joins are sometimes called *outer joins* to differentiate them from an inner join. *Left join* and *left outer join* mean the same thing, as do *right join* and *right outer join*.

LEFT JOINS

The left join displays all the records in the left table and only those records of the table on the right that match certain user-supplied criteria. This join has the following syntax:

```
FROM (primary table) LEFT JOIN (secondary table) ON
(primary table).(field) = (secondary table).(field)
```

The left outer join retrieves all rows in the primary table and the matching rows from a secondary table. The following statement retrieves all the titles from the Pubs database along with their publisher. If some titles have no publisher, they will be included in the result:

```
USE pubs
SELECT  title, pub_name
FROM    titles LEFT JOIN publishers
            ON titles.pub_id = publishers.pub_id
```

RIGHT JOINS

The right join is similar to the left outer join, except that it selects all rows in the table on the right and only the matching rows from the left table. This join has the following syntax:

```
FROM (secondary table) RIGHT JOIN (primary table)
ON (secondary table).(field) = (primary table).(field)
```

The following statement retrieves all the publishers from the Pubs database along with their titles. If a publisher has no titles, the publisher name will be included in the result set. Notice that this statement is almost the same as the example of the left outer join entry. I changed only LEFT to RIGHT:

```
USE pubs
SELECT  title, pub_name
FROM    titles RIGHT JOIN publishers
          ON titles.pub_id = publishers.pub_id
```

FULL JOINS

The full join returns all the rows of the two tables, regardless of whether there are matching rows. In effect, it's a combination of left and right joins. To retrieve all titles and all publishers and to match publishers to their titles, use the following join:

```
USE pubs
SELECT  title, pub_name
FROM    titles FULL JOIN publishers
          ON titles.pub_id = publishers.pub_id
```

This query will include titles without a publisher, as well as publishers without a title.

INNER JOINS

The inner join returns the matching rows of both tables, similar to the WHERE clause, and has the following syntax:

```
FROM (primary table) INNER JOIN (secondary table)
ON (primary table).(field) = (secondary table).(field)
```

The following SQL statement combines records from the Titles and Publishers tables of the Pubs database if their pub_id fields match. It returns all the titles and their publishers. Titles without publishers, or publishers without titles, will not be included in the result.

```
USE pubs
SELECT titles.title, publishers.pub_name FROM titles, publishers
WHERE  titles.pub_id = publishers.pub_id
```

You can retrieve the same rows by using an inner join, as follows:

```
USE pubs
SELECT titles.title, publishers.pub_name
FROM    titles INNER JOIN publishers ON titles.pub_id = publishers.pub_id
```

🌐 Real World Scenario

DO NOT JOIN TABLES WITH THE *WHERE* CLAUSE

The proper method of retrieving rows from multiple tables is to use joins. It's not uncommon to write a dozen joins one after the other (if you have that many tables to join). You can also join two tables by using the WHERE clause. Here are two statements that return the total revenue for each of the customers in the Northwind database. The first one uses the INNER JOIN statement, and the second one uses the WHERE clause. The INNER JOIN is equivalent to the WHERE clause: They both return the same rows.

Query 1

```
SELECT
    C.CompanyName,
    SUM((OD.UnitPrice * OD.Quantity) * (1 - OD.Discount)) AS Revenue
FROM Customers AS C
    INNER JOIN Orders AS O ON C.CustomerID = O.CustomerID
    INNER JOIN [Order Details] AS OD ON O.OrderID = OD.OrderID
GROUP BY C.CompanyName
```

Query 2

```
SELECT
    C.CompanyName,
    SUM((OD.UnitPrice * OD.Quantity) * (1 - OD.Discount)) AS Revenue
FROM Customers AS C, Orders AS O, [Order Details] AS OD
    WHERE C.CustomerID = O.CustomerID
    AND O.OrderID = OD.OrderID
GROUP BY C.CompanyName
```

Both statements assume that all customers have placed an order. If you change the INNER JOIN in the first statement to a LEFT JOIN, the result will contain two more rows: The customers FISSA and PARIS have not placed any orders, and they're not included in the output. If you know that all your customers have placed an order or you don't care about customers without orders, use the WHERE clause or an inner join. It's important to keep in mind that if you want to see all customers, regardless of whether they have placed an order, you must use joins.

An even better example is that of retrieving titles along with their authors. An inner join will return titles that have one or more authors. A left join will return all titles, even the ones without authors. A right join will return all authors, even if some of them are not associated with any titles. Finally, a full outer join will return both titles without authors and authors without titles. Here's the statement that retrieves titles and authors from the Pubs database. Change the type of joins to see how they affect the result set.

```
SELECT   titles.title,
         authors.au_lname + ', ' + authors.au_fname AS Author
FROM     authors
   INNER JOIN titleauthor ON authors.au_id = titleauthor.au_id
   INNER JOIN titles ON titleauthor.title_id = titles.title_id
ORDER BY titles.title
```

There's a shorthand notation for specifying left and right joins with the WHERE clause. When you use the operator *= in a WHERE clause, a left join will be created. Likewise, the =* operator is equivalent to a right join.

Grouping Rows

Sometimes you need to group the results of a query so that you can calculate subtotals. Let's say you need not only the total revenues generated by a single product but also a list of all products and the revenues they generated. The example in the earlier section "Working with Calculated Fields" calculates the total revenue generated by a single product. It is possible to use the SUM() function to break the calculations at each new product ID, as demonstrated in the following statement. To do so, you must group the product IDs together with the GROUP BY clause:

```
USE Northwind
SELECT   ProductID,
         SUM(Quantity * UnitPrice *(1 - Discount)) AS [Total Revenues]
FROM     [Order Details]
GROUP BY ProductID
ORDER BY ProductID
```

The preceding statement produces the following output:

ProductID	Total Revenues
1	12788.10
2	16355.96
3	3044.0
4	8567.89
5	5347.20
6	7137.0
7	22044.29

The aggregate functions work in tandem with the GROUP BY clause (when there is one) to produce subtotals. The GROUP BY clause groups all the rows with the same values in the specified column and forces the aggregate functions to act on each group separately. SQL Server sorts the rows according to the column specified in the GROUP BY clause and starts calculating the aggregate functions. Every time it runs into a new group, it generates a new row and resets the aggregate function(s).

If you use the GROUP BY clause in a SQL statement, you must be aware of the following rule:

All the fields included in the SELECT list must be either part of an aggregate function or part of the GROUP BY clause.

Let's say you want to change the previous statement to display the names of the products rather than their IDs. The following statement does just that. Notice that the ProductName field doesn't appear as an argument to an aggregate function, so it must be part of the GROUP BY clause:

```
USE Northwind
SELECT    ProductName,
          SUM(Quantity * [Order Details].UnitPrice * (1 - Discount))
            AS [Total Revenues]
FROM      [Order Details], Products
WHERE     Products.ProductID = [Order Details].ProductID
GROUP BY ProductName
ORDER BY ProductName
```

These are the first few lines of the output produced by this statement:

ProductName	Total Revenues
Alice Mutton	32698.38
Aniseed Syrup	3044.0
Boston Crab Meat	17910.63
Camembert Pierrot	46927.48
Carnarvon Tigers	29171.87

If you omit the GROUP BY clause, the query will generate an error message indicating that the ProductName column in the selection list is not involved in an aggregate or a GROUP BY clause.

You can also combine multiple aggregate functions in the selection list. The following statement calculates the total number of items sold for each product, along with the revenue generated and the number of invoices that contain the specific product:

```
USE Northwind
SELECT    ProductID AS Product,
          COUNT(ProductID) AS Invoices,
          SUM(Quantity) AS [Units Sold],
          SUM(Quantity * UnitPrice *(1 - Discount)) AS Revenue
FROM      [Order Details]
GROUP BY ProductID
ORDER BY ProductID
```

Here are the first few lines returned by the preceding query:

Product	Invoices	Units Sold	Revenue
1	38	828	12788.1000595092
2	44	1057	16355.9600448608

You should try to revise the preceding statement so that it displays product names instead of IDs, by adding another join to the query as explained already.

LIMITING GROUPS WITH HAVING

The HAVING clause limits the groups that will appear at the cursor. In a way, it is similar to the WHERE clause, but the HAVING clause is used with aggregate functions and the GROUP BY clause, and the expression used with the HAVING clause usually involves one or more aggregates. The following statement returns the IDs of the products whose sales exceed 1,000 units:

```
USE NORTHWIND
SELECT    ProductID, SUM(Quantity)
FROM      [Order Details]
GROUP BY ProductID
HAVING    SUM(Quantity) > 1000
```

You can't use the WHERE clause here, because no aggregates may appear in the WHERE clause. However, you can use the WHERE clause as usual to limit the number of rows involved in the query (for example, limit the aggregate to the products of a specific category, or the products sold to customers in Germany). To see product names instead of IDs, join the Order Details table to the Products table by matching their ProductID columns. Note that the expression in the HAVING clause need not be included in the selection list. You can change the previous statement to retrieve the total quantities sold with a discount of 10 percent or more with the following HAVING clause:

```
HAVING Discount >= 0.1
```

However, the Discount column must be included in the GROUP BY clause as well, because it's not part of an aggregate.

Action Queries

In addition to the selection queries we examined so far, you can also execute queries that alter the data in the database's tables. These queries are called *action queries*, and they're quite simple compared with the selection queries. There are three types of actions you can perform against a database: insertions of new rows, deletions of existing rows, and updates (edits) of existing rows. For each type of action, there's a SQL statement, appropriately named INSERT, DELETE, and UPDATE. Their syntax is very simple, and the only complication is how you specify the affected rows (for deletions and updates). As you can guess, the rows to be affected are specified with a WHERE clause, followed by the criteria discussed with selection queries.

The first difference between action and selection queries is that action queries don't return any rows. They return the number of rows affected, but you can disable this feature by calling the following statement:

```
SET NOCOUNT ON
```

This statement can be used when working with a SQL Server database. Let's look at the syntax of the three action SQL statements, starting with the simplest: the DELETE statement.

Deleting Rows

The DELETE statement deletes one or more rows from a table; its syntax is as follows:

```
DELETE table_name WHERE criteria
```

The WHERE clause specifies the criteria that the rows must meet in order to be deleted. The criteria expression is no different from the criteria you specify in the WHERE clause of the selection query. To delete the orders placed before 1998, use a statement like this one:

```
USE Northwind
DELETE Orders
WHERE  OrderDate < '1/1/1998'
```

Of course, the specified rows will be deleted only if the Orders table allows cascade deletions or if the rows to be deleted are not linked to related rows. If you attempt to execute the preceding query, you'll get an error with the following description:

```
The DELETE statement conflicted with the REFERENCE
constraint "FK_Order_Details_Orders". The conflict
occurred in database "Northwind",
table "dbo.Order Details", column 'OrderID'.
```

This error message tells you that you can't delete rows from the Orders table that are referenced by rows in the Order Details table. If you were allowed to delete rows from the Orders table, some rows in the related table would remain *orphaned* (they would refer to an order that doesn't exist). To delete rows from the Orders table, you must first delete the related rows from the Order Details table and then delete the same rows from the Orders table. Here are the statements that will delete orders placed before 1998. (Do not execute this query unless you're willing to reinstall the Northwind database; there's no undo feature when executing SQL statements against a database.)

```
USE Northwind
DELETE [Order Details]
WHERE  (OrderID IN
          (  SELECT OrderID
                 FROM    Orders
                 WHERE  (OrderDate < '1/1/1998')))

DELETE Orders WHERE OrderDate < '1/1/1998'
```

As you can see, the operation takes two action queries: one to delete rows from the Order Details table and another to delete the corresponding rows from the Orders table.

The DELETE statement returns the number of rows deleted. You can retrieve a table with the deleted rows by using the OUTPUT clause:

```
DELETE Customers
OUTPUT DELETED.*
WHERE  Country IS NULL
```

To test the OUTPUT clause, insert a few fake rows in the Customers table:

```
INSERT Customers (CustomerID, CompanyName)
VALUES ('AAAAA', 'Company A')
INSERT Customers (CustomerID, CompanyName)
VALUES ('BBBBB', 'Company B')
```

And then delete them with the following statement:

```
DELETE Customers
OUTPUT DELETED.*
WHERE  Country IS NULL
```

If you execute the preceding statements, the deleted rows will be returned as the output of the query. If you want to be safe, you can insert the deleted rows into a temporary table so you can insert them back into the database (should you delete more rows than intended). My suggestion is that you first execute a selection query that returns the rows you plan to delete, examine the output of this query, and, if you see only the rows you want to delete and no more, write a DELETE statement with the same WHERE clause. To insert the deleted rows to a temporary table, use the INSERT INTO statement, which is described in the following section.

Inserting New Rows

The INSERT statement inserts new rows in a table; its syntax is as follows:

```
INSERT table_name (column_names) VALUES (values)
```

column_names and values are comma-separated lists of columns and their respective values. Values are mapped to their columns by the order in which they appear in the two lists.

Notice that you don't have to specify values for all columns in the table, but the values list must contain as many items as there are column names in the first list. To add a new row to the Customers table, use a statement like the following:

```
INSERT Customers (CustomerID, CompanyName) VALUES ('FRYOG', 'Fruit & Yogurt')
```

This statement inserts a new row, provided that the FRYOG key isn't already in use. Only two of the new row's columns are set, and they're the columns that can't accept null values.

If you want to specify values for all the columns of the new row, you can omit the list of columns. The following statement retrieves a number of rows from the Products table and inserts them into the SelectedProducts table, which has the same structure:

```
INSERT INTO SelectedProducts VALUES (values)
```

If the values come from a table, you can replace the VALUES keyword with a SELECT statement:

```
INSERT INTO SelectedProducts
    SELECT * FROM Products WHERE CategoryID = 4
```

The INSERT INTO statement allows you to select columns from one table and insert them into another one. The second table must have the same structure as the output of the selection query. Note that you need not create the new table ahead of time; you can create a new table with the CREATE TABLE statement. The following statement creates a new table to accept the CustomerID, CompanyName, and ContactName columns of the Customers table:

```
DECLARE @tbl table
    (ID char(5),
     name varchar(100),
     contact varchar(100))
```

After the table has been created, you can populate it with the appropriate fields of the deleted rows:

```
DELETE Customers
OUTPUT DELETED.CustomerID,
       DELETED.CompanyName, DELETED.ContactName
INTO @tbl
WHERE Country IS NULL
SELECT * FROM @tbl
```

Execute these statements, and you will see in the Results pane the two rows that were inserted momentarily into the Customers table and then immediately deleted.

Editing Existing Rows

The UPDATE statement edits a row's fields; its syntax is the following:

```
UPDATE table_name SET field1 = value1, field2 = value2,. . .
WHERE criteria
```

The criteria expression is no different from the criteria you specify in the WHERE clause of selection query. To change the country from UK to United Kingdom in the Customers table, use the following statement:

```
UPDATE Customers SET Country='United Kingdom'
WHERE   Country = 'UK'
```

This statement will locate all the rows in the Customers table that meet the specified criteria (their Country field is UK) and change this field's value to United Kingdom.

Before you execute a DELETE or UPDATE statement, use a SELECT statement to see the rows that will be affected. Verify that these are the rows you intend to change and then delete or update them. Once an action query has been executed against the database, there's no way back (sorry, no Undo here).

This concludes our overview of SQL, and we're (at last) ready to explore the data access mechanisms of the Framework. In the following section, you'll learn how to submit queries to a database from within your VB application and how to retrieve the results of a query.

Stream- versus Set-Based Data Access

The component of the Framework we use to access databases is known as ADO.NET (ADO stands for Active Data Objects) and it provides two basic methods of accessing data: *stream-based data access,* which establishes a stream to the database and retrieves the data from the server, and *set-based data access,* which creates a special data structure at the client and fills it with data. This structure is the DataSet, which resembles a section of the database: It contains one or more DataTable objects, which correspond to tables and are made up of DataRow objects. These DataRow objects have the same structure as the rows in their corresponding tables. DataSets are populated by retrieving data from one or more database tables into the corresponding DataTables. As for submitting the data to the database with the stream-based approach, you must create the appropriate INSERT/UPDATE/DELETE statements and then execute them against the database.

The stream-based approach relies on the DataReader object, which makes the data returned by the database available to your application. The client application reads the data returned by a query through the DataReader object and must store it somehow at the client. Quite frequently, we use custom objects to store the data at the client.

The set-based approach uses the same objects as the stream-based approach behind the scenes, and it abstracts most of the grunt work required to set up a link to the database, retrieve the data, and store it in the client computer's memory. So, it makes sense to start by exploring the stream-based approach and the basic objects provided by ADO.NET for accessing databases. After you understand the nature of ADO.NET and how to use it, you'll find it easy to see the abstraction introduced by the set-based approach and how to make the most of DataSets. As you will see in the following chapter, you can create DataSets and the supporting objects with the visual tools of the IDE.

The Basic Data-Access Classes

A data-driven application should be able to connect to a database and execute queries against it. The selected data is displayed on the appropriate interface, where the user can examine it or edit it. Finally, the edited data is submitted to the database. This is the cycle of a data-driven application:

1. Retrieve data from the database.

2. Present data to the user.

3. Allow the user to edit the data.

4. Submit changes to the database.

Of course, many issues are not obvious from this outline. Designing the appropriate interface for navigating through the data (going from customers to their orders and from the selected order to its details) can be quite a task. Developing a functional interface for editing the data at the client is also a challenge, especially if several related tables are involved. We must also take into consideration that there are other users accessing the same database. What will happen if the product we're editing has been removed in the meantime by another user? Or what if a user has edited the same customer's data since our application read it? Do we overwrite the changes made by the other user, or do we reject the edits of the user who submits the edits last? I'll address these issues in this chapter and in Chapter 18, but we need to start with the basics: the classes for accessing the database.

THE BASIC DATA-ACCESS CLASSES

To connect to a database, you must create a Connection object, initialize it, and then call its Open method to establish a connection to the database. The Connection object is the channel between your application and the database; every command you want to execute against the same database must use this Connection object. When you're finished, you must close the connection by calling the Connection object's Close method. Because ADO.NET maintains a pool of Connection objects that are reused as needed, it's imperative that you keep connections open for the shortest possible time.

The object that will actually execute the command against the database is the Command object, which you must configure with the statement you want to execute and associate with a Connection object. To execute the statement, you can call one of the Command object's methods. The ExecuteReader method returns a DataReader object that allows you to read the data returned by the selection query, one row at a time. To execute a statement that updates a database table but doesn't return a set of rows, use the ExecuteNonQuery method, which executes the specified command and returns an integer, which is the number of rows affected by the statement. The following sections describe the Connection, Command, and DataReader classes in detail.

To summarize, ADO.NET provides three core classes for accessing databases: the Connection, Command, and DataReader classes. There are more data access–related classes, but they're all based on these three basic classes. After you understand how to interact with a database by using these classes, you'll find it easy to understand the additional classes, as well as the code generated by the visual data tools that come with Visual Studio.

The Connection Class

The Connection class is an abstract one, and you can't use it directly. Instead, you must use one of the classes that derive from the Connection class. Currently, there are three derived classes: SqlConnection, OracleConnection, and OleDbConnection. Likewise, the Command class is an abstract class with three derived classes: SqlCommand, OracleCommand, and OleDbCommand.

The SqlConnection and SqlCommand classes belong to the SqlClient namespace, which you must import into your project via the following statement:

```
Imports System.Data.SqlClient
```

The examples in this book use the SQL Server 2008 DBMS, and it's implied that the SqlClient namespace is imported into every project that uses SQL Server.

To connect the application to a database, the Connection object must know the name of the server on which the database resides, the name of the database itself, and the credentials that will allow it to establish a connection to the database. These credentials are either a username and password or a Windows account that has been granted rights to the database. You obviously know what type of DBMS you're going to connect to so you can select the appropriate Connection class. The most common method of initializing a Connection object in your code is the following:

```
Dim CN As New SqlConnection("Data Source = localhost;" &
            "Initial Catalog = Northwind; uid = user_name;" &
            "password = user_password")
```

localhost is a universal name for the local machine, *Northwind* is the name of the database, and *user_name* and *user_password* are the username and password of an account configured by the database administrator. The Northwind sample database isn't installed along with SQL Server 2008, but you can download it from MSDN and install it yourself. The process was described in the section ''Obtaining the Northwind and Pubs Sample Databases'' earlier in this chapter. I'm assuming that you're using the same computer both for SQL Server and to write your VB applications. If SQL Server resides on a different computer in the network, use the server computer's name (or IP address) in place of the localhost name. If SQL Server is running on another machine on the network, use a setting like the following for the Data Source key:

```
Data Source = \\PowerServer
```

If the database is running on a remote machine, use the remote machine's IP address. If you're working from home, for example, you can establish a connection to your company's server with a connection string like the following:

```
Data Source = "213.16.178.100; Initial Catalog = BooksDB; uid = xxx; password
    = xxx"
```

The uid and password keys are those of an account created by the database administrator, and not a Windows account. If you want to connect to the database by using each user's Windows credentials, you should omit the uid and password keys and instead use the Integrated Security key. If your network is based on a domain controller, you should use integrated security so that users can log in to SQL Server with their Windows account. This way you won't have to store any passwords in your code or even have an auxiliary file with the application settings.

If you're using an IP address to specify the database server, you may also have to include SQL Server's port by specifying an address such as 213.16.178.100, 1433. The default port for SQL Server is 1433, and you can omit it. If the administrator has changed the default port or has hidden the server's IP address behind another IP address for security purposes, you should contact the administrator to get the server's address. If you're connecting over a local network, you shouldn't have to use an IP address. If you want to connect to the company server remotely, you will probably have to request the server's IP address and the proper credentials from the server's administrator.

The basic property of the Connection object is the ConnectionString property, which is a semicolon-separated string of key-value pairs that specifies the information needed to establish a connection to the desired database. It's basically the same information you provide in various dialog boxes when you open SQL Server Management Studio and select a database to work with. An alternate method of setting up a Connection object is to set its ConnectionString property:

```
Dim CN As New SqlConnection
CN.ConnectionString =
        "Data Source = localhost; Initial Catalog = Northwind; " &
        "Integrated Security = True"
```

One of the Connection class's properties is the State property, which returns the state of a connection; its value is a member of the ConnectionState enumeration: *Connecting*, *Open*, *Executing*, *Fetching*, *Broken*, and *Closed*. If you call the Close method on a Connection object that's already closed or the Open method on a Connection object that's already open, an exception will be thrown. To avoid the exception, you must examine the Connection's State property and act accordingly.

The following code segment outlines the process of opening a connection to a database:

```
Dim CNstring As String =
        "Data Source=localhost;Initial " &
        "Catalog=Northwind;Integrated Security=True"
CNstring = InputBox(
        "Please enter a Connection String",
        "CONNECTION STRING", CNstring)
If CNstring.Trim = "" Then Exit Sub
Dim CN As New SqlConnection(CNstring)
Try
    CN.Open()
    If CN.State = ConnectionState.Open Then
        MsgBox("Workstation " & CN.WorkstationId &
                " connected to database " & CN.Database &
                " on the " & CN.DataSource & " server")
    End If
Catch ex As Exception
    MsgBox( _
        "FAILED TO OPEN CONNECTION TO DATABASE DUE TO THE FOLLOWING ERROR" &
            vbCrLf & ex.Message)
End Try
' use the Connection object to execute statements
' against the database and then close the connection
If CN.State = ConnectionState.Open Then CN.Close()
```

The Command Class

The second major component of the ADO.NET model is the Command class, which allows you to execute SQL statements against the database. The two basic parameters of the Command object are a Connection object that specifies the database where the command will be executed and specifies the actual SQL command. To execute a SQL statement against a database, you must initialize a Command object and set its Connection property to the appropriate Connection object. It's the Connection object that knows how to connect to the database; the Command object simply submits a SQL statement to the database and retrieves the results.

The Command object exposes a number of methods for executing SQL statements against the database, depending on the type of statement you want to execute. The ExecuteNonQuery method executes INSERT/DELETE/UPDATE statements that do not return any rows, just an integer value, which is the number of rows affected by the query. The ExecuteScalar method returns a single value, which is usually the result of an aggregate operation, such as the count of rows meeting some criteria, the sum or average of a column over a number of rows, and so on. Finally, the ExecuteReader method is used with SELECT statements that return rows from one or more tables.

To execute an UPDATE statement, for example, you must create a new Command object and associate the appropriate SQL statement with it. One overloaded form of the constructor of the

Command object allows you to specify the statement to be executed against the database, as well as a Connection object that points to the desired database as arguments:

```
Dim CMD As New SqlCommand(
            "UPDATE Products SET UnitPrice = UnitPrice * 1.07 " &
            "WHERE CategoryID = 3", CN)
CN.Open
Dim rows As Integer
rows = CMD.ExecuteNonQuery
If rows = 1 Then
    MsgBox("Table Products updated successfully")
Else
    MsgBox("Failed to update the Products table")
End If
If CN.State = ConnectionState.Open Then CN.Close
```

The ExecuteNonQuery method returns the number of rows affected by the query, and it's the same value that appears in the Output window of SQL Server Management Studio when you execute an action query. The preceding statements mark up the price of all products in the Confections category by 7 percent. You can use the same structure to execute INSERT and DELETE statements; all you have to change is the actual SQL statement in the SqlCommand object's constructor. You can also set up a Command object by setting its Connection and CommandText properties:

```
Command.Connection = Connection
Command.CommandText = "SELECT COUNT(*) FROM Customers"
```

After you're finished with the Command object, you should close the Connection object. Although you can initialize a Connection object anywhere in your code, you should call its Open method as late as possible (that is, just before executing a statement) and its Close method as early as possible (that is, as soon as you have retrieved the results of the statement you executed).

The ExecuteScalar method executes the SQL statement associated with the Command object and returns a single value, which is the first value that the SQL statement would print in the Output window of SQL Server Management Studio. The following statements read the number of rows in the Customers table of the Northwind database and store the result in the *count* variable:

```
Dim CMD As New SqlCommand(
                "SELECT COUNT(*) FROM Customers", CN)
Dim count As Integer
CN.Open
count = CMD.ExecuteScalar
If CN.State = ConnectionState.Open Then CN.Close
```

If you want to execute a SELECT statement that retrieves multiple rows, you must use the ExecuteReader method of the Command object, as shown here:

```
Dim CMD As New SqlCommand(
                "SELECT * FROM Customers", CN)
CN.Open
Dim Reader As SqlDataReader
Reader = CMD.ExecuteReader
While Reader.Read
    ' process the current row in the result set
End While
If CN.State = ConnectionState.Open Then CN.Close.
```

You'll see shortly how to access the fields of each row returned by the ExecuteReader method through the properties of the SqlDataReader class.

EXECUTING STORED PROCEDURES

The command to be executed through the Command object is not always a SQL statement; it could be the name of a stored procedure, or the name of a table, in which case it retrieves all the rows of the table. You can specify the type of statement you want to execute with the CommandType property, whose value is a member of the CommandType enumeration: Text (for SQL statements), StoredProcedure (for stored procedures), and TableDirect (for a table). You don't have to specify the type of the command you want to execute, but then the Command object will have to figure it out, a process that will take a few moments, and you can avoid this unnecessary delay. The Northwind database comes with the Ten Most Expensive Products stored procedure. To execute this stored procedure, set up a Command object with the following statements:

```
Dim CMD As New SqlCommand
CMD.Connection = CN
CMD.CommandText = "[Ten Most Expensive Products]"
CMD.CommandType = CommandType.StoredProcedure
```

Finally, you can retrieve all the rows of the Customers table by setting up a Command object like the following:

```
Dim CMD As New SqlCommand
CMD.Connection = CN
CMD.CommandText = "Customers"
CMD.CommandType = CommandType.TableDirect
```

EXECUTING SELECTION QUERIES

The most common SQL statements, the SELECT statements, retrieve a set of rows from one or more joined tables, the *result set*. These statements are executed with the ExecuteReader method, which returns a DataReader object — a SqlDataReader object for statements executed against SQL Server databases. The DataReader class provides the members for reading the results of the query in a forward-only manner. The connection remains open while you read the rows returned by the query, so it's imperative to read the rows and store them in a structure in the client computer's memory as soon as possible and then close the connection. The DataReader object is read-only (you can't use it to update the underlying rows), so there's no reason to keep it open for long periods. Let's execute the following SELECT statement to retrieve selected columns of the rows of the Employees table of the Northwind database:

```
SELECT LastName + ' ' + FirstName AS Name,
       Title, Extension, HomePhone
FROM    Employees
```

Here are the VB statements that set up the appropriate Command object and retrieve the SqlDataReader object with the result set:

```
Dim CMD As New SqlCommand
Dim CN As New SqlConnection("Data Source = localhost;Initial Catalog=Northwind;" &
                  "Integrated Security=True")
CMD.Connection = CN
CMD.CommandText =
     "SELECT LastName + ' ' + FirstName AS Name, " &
     "Title, Extension, HomePhone FROM Employees"
CN.Open()
Dim Reader As SqlDataReader
Reader = Command.ExecuteReader
Dim str As String = ""
Dim cont As Integer = 0
While Reader.Read
    str &= Convert.ToString(Reader.Item("Name")) & vbTab
    str &= Convert.ToString(Reader.Item("Title")) & vbTab
    str &= Convert.ToString(Reader.Item("Extension")) & vbTab
    str &= Convert.ToString(Reader.Item("HomePhone")) & vbTab
    str &= vbCrLf
    count += 1
End While
Debug.WriteLine(vbCrLf & vbCrLf & "Read " & count.ToString &
                  " rows: " & vbCrLf & vbCrLf & str)
CN.Close()
```

The DataReader class provides the Read method, which advances the current pointer to the next row in the result set. To read the individual columns of the current row, you use the Item property, which allows you to specify the column by name and returns an object variable. It's your responsibility to cast the object returned by the Item property to the appropriate type. Initially, the DataReader is positioned in front of the first line in the result set, and you must call its Read method to advance to the first row. If the query returns no rows, the Read method will return False, and the While loop won't be executed at all. In the preceding sample code, the fields of each row are concatenated to form the str string, which is printed in the Immediate window; it looks something like this:

```
Davolio Nancy      Sales Representative    5467   (206) 555-9857
Fuller Andrew      Vice President, Sales   3457   (206) 555-9482
Leverling Janet    Sales Representative    3355   (206) 555-3412
```

Using Commands with Parameters

Most SQL statements and stored procedures accept parameters, and you should pass values for each parameter before executing the query. Consider a simple statement that retrieves the customers from a specific country, whose name is passed as an argument:

```
SELECT * FROM Customers WHERE Country = @country
```

The *@country* parameter must be set to a value, or an exception will be thrown as you attempt to execute this statement. Stored procedures also accept parameters. The `Sales By Year` stored procedure of the Northwind database, for example, expects two Date values and returns sales between the two dates. To accommodate the passing of parameters to a parameterized query or stored procedure, the Command object exposes the `Parameters` property, which is a collection of `Parameter` objects. To pass parameter values to a command, you must set up a Parameter object for each parameter; set its name, type, and value; and then add the Parameter object to the Parameters collection of the Command object. The following statements set up a Command object with a parameter of the varchar type with a maximum size of 15 characters:

```
Dim Command As New SqlCommand
Command.CommandText = "SELECT * FROM Customers WHERE Country = @country"
Command.Parameters.Add("@country", SqlDbType.VarChar, 15)
Command.Parameters("@country").Value = "Italy"
```

At this point, you're ready to execute the SELECT statement with the `ExecuteReader` method and retrieve the customers from Italy. You can also configure the Parameter object in its constructor:

```
Dim param As New SqlParameter(paramName, paramType, paramSize)
```

Here's the constructor of the @country parameter of the preceding example:

```
Dim param As New SqlParameter("@country", SqlDbType.VarChar, 15)
param.Value = "Italy"

CMD.Parameters.Add param
```

Finally, you can combine all these statements into a single one:

```
CMD.Parameters.Add("@country", SqlDbType.VarChar, 15).Value = "Italy"
```

In the last statement, I initialize the parameter as I add it to the Parameters collection and then set its value to the string `Italy`. Oddly, there's no overloaded form of the `Add` method that allows you to specify the parameter's value, but there is an `AddWithValue` method, which adds a new parameter and its value. This method accepts two arguments: a string with the parameter's name and an object with the parameter's value. The actual type of the value is determined by the type of the query or stored procedure's argument, and it's resolved at runtime. The simplest method of adding a new parameter to the `CMD.Parameters` collection is the following:

```
CMD.Parameters.Add("@country", "Italy")
```

After the parameter has been set up, you can call the ExecuteReader method to retrieve the customers from the country specified by the argument and then read the results through an instance of the DataReader class.

RETRIEVING MULTIPLE VALUES FROM A STORED PROCEDURE

Another property of the Parameter class is the Direction property, which determines whether the stored procedure can alter the value of the parameter. The Direction property's setting is a member of the ParameterDirection enumeration: Input, Output, InputOutput, and ReturnValue. A parameter that's set by the procedure should have its Direction property set to Output: The parameter's value is not going to be used by the procedure, but the procedure's code can set it to return information to the calling application. If the parameter is used to pass information to the procedure, as well as to pass information back to the calling application, its Direction property should be set to InputOutput.

Let's look at a stored procedure that returns the total of all orders, as well as the total number of items ordered by a specific customer. This stored procedure accepts as a parameter the ID of a customer, obviously, and it returns two values: the total of all orders placed by the specified customer and the number of items ordered. A procedure (be it a SQL Server stored procedure or a regular VB function) can't return two or more values. The only way to retrieve multiple results from a single stored procedure is to pass output parameters so that the stored procedure can set their value. To make the stored procedure a little more interesting, we'll add a return value, which will be the number of orders placed by the customer. Listing 15.1 shows the implementation of the CustomerTotals stored procedure.

LISTING 15.1:   The CustomerTotals stored procedure

```
CREATE PROCEDURE CustomerTotals
@customerID varchar(5),
@customerTotal money OUTPUT,
@customerItems int OUTPUT
AS
SELECT @customerTotal = SUM(UnitPrice * Quantity * (1 - Discount))
FROM [Order Details] INNER JOIN Orders
ON [Order Details].OrderID = Orders.OrderID
WHERE Orders.CustomerID = @customerID
SELECT @customerItems = SUM(Quantity)
FROM [Order Details] INNER JOIN Orders
ON [Order Details].OrderID = Orders.OrderID
WHERE Orders.CustomerID = @customerID

DECLARE @customerOrders int
SELECT @customerOrders = COUNT(*) FROM Orders
WHERE Orders.CustomerID = @customerID

RETURN @customerOrders
```

To attach the `CustomerTotals` stored procedure to the database, create a new stored procedure, paste the preceding statements in the code window, and press F5 to execute it. Make sure the database is Northwind (not master). The stored procedure calculates three totals for the specified customer and stores them to three local variables. The *@customerTotal* and *@customerItems* variables are output parameters, which the calling application can read after executing the stored procedure. The *@customerOrders* variable is the procedure's return value. We can return the number of orders for the customer through the stored procedure's return value, because this variable happens to be an integer, and the return value is always an integer. In more-complex stored procedures, we'd use output parameters for all the values we want to return to the calling application, and the procedure would return a value to indicate the execution status: 0 or 1 if the procedure completed its execution successfully and a negative value to indicate the error, should the procedure fail to execute.

Before using the `CustomerTotals` stored procedure with our VB application, let's test it in SQL Server Management Studio. We must declare a variable for each of the output parameters: the *@Total*, *@Items*, and *@Orders* variables. These three variables must be passed to the stored procedure with the `OUTPUT` attribute, as shown here:

```
DECLARE @Total money
DECLARE @Items int
DECLARE @Orders int
DECLARE @custID varchar(5)
DECLARE @CustomerTotal decimal
DECLARE @CustomerItems int
SET @custID = 'BLAUS'
EXEC @orders = CustomerTotals @custID,
        @customerTotal OUTPUT, @customerItems OUTPUT
PRINT 'Customer ' + @custId + ' has placed a total of ' +
    CAST(@orders AS varchar(8)) + ' orders ' +
    ' totaling $' + CAST(ROUND(@customerTotal, 2) AS varchar(12)) +
    ' and ' + CAST(@customerItems AS varchar(4)) + ' items.'
```

Open a new query window in SQL Server Management Studio, and enter the preceding statements. Press F5 to execute them, and you will see the following message printed in the Output window:

```
Customer BLAUS has placed a total of 8 orders totaling $10355.45 and 653 items.
```

The customer's ID is an `INPUT` parameter, and we could pass it to the procedure as a literal. You can omit the declaration of the `@custID` variable and call the stored procedure with the following statement:

```
DECLARE @CustomerTotal decimal
DECLARE @CustomerItems int
EXEC @orders = _
        CustomerTotals 'BLAUS', @customerTotal OUTPUT, @customerItems OUTPUT
```

Now that we've tested our stored procedure and know how to call it, we'll do the same from within our sample application. To execute the `CustomerTotals` stored procedure, we must set up a Command object, create the appropriate Parameter objects (one Parameter object per stored procedure parameter plus another Parameter object for the stored procedure's return value), and then call the `Command.ExecuteNonQuery` method. Upon return, we'll read the values of the output parameters and the stored procedure's return value. Listing 15.2 shows the code that executes the stored procedure (see the SimpleQueries sample project available for download from www.sybex.com/go/masteringvb2010).

LISTING 15.2:   Executing a stored procedure with output parameters

```
Private Sub bttnExecSP_Click(…) Handles bttnExecSP.Click
    Dim customerID As String = InputBox("Please enter a customer ID",
        "CustomerTotals Stored Procedure", "ALFKI")
    If customerID.Trim.Length = 0 Then Exit Sub
    Dim CMD As New SqlCommand
    CMD.Connection = CN
    CMD.CommandText = "CustomerTotals"
    CMD.CommandType = CommandType.StoredProcedure
    CMD.Parameters.Add(
        "@customerID", SqlDbType.VarChar, 5).Value = customerID
    CMD.Parameters.Add("@customerTotal", SqlDbType.Money)
    CMD.Parameters("@customerTotal").Direction = ParameterDirection.Output
    CMD.Parameters.Add("@customerItems", SqlDbType.Int)
    CMD.Parameters("@customerItems").Direction = ParameterDirection.Output
    CMD.Parameters.Add("@orders", SqlDbType.Int)
    CMD.Parameters("@orders").Direction = ParameterDirection.ReturnValue
    CN.Open()
    CMD.ExecuteNonQuery()
    CN.Close()
    Dim items As Integer
    Items = Convert.ToInt32(CMD.Parameters("@customerItems").Value
    Dim orders As Integer
    Orders = Convert.ToInt32(CMD.Parameters("@orders").Value
    Dim ordersTotal As Decimal
    ordersTotal = Convert.ToDouble(
        CMD.Parameters("@customerTotal").Value
    MsgBox("Customer BLAUS has placed " &
        orders.ToString & " orders " &
        "totaling $" & Math.Round(ordersTotal, 2).ToString("#,###.00") &
        " and " & items.ToString & " items")
End Sub
```

In most applications, the same Command object will be reused again and again with different parameter values, so it's common to add the parameters to a Command object's Parameters collection and assign values to them every time we want to execute the command. Let's say you've designed a form with text boxes, where users can edit the values of the various fields; here's how you'd set the values of the *UPDATECMD* variable's parameters:

```
UPDATECMD.Parameters("@CustomerID").Value = txtID.Text.Trim
UPDATECMD.Parameters("@CompanyName").Value = txtCompany.Text.Trim
```

After setting the values of all parameters, you can call the ExecuteNonQuery method to submit the changes to the database. To update another customer, just assign different values to the existing parameters, and call the UPDATECMD object's ExecuteNonQuery method.

🌐 Real World Scenario

SECURITY ISSUE: SQL INJECTION ATTACKS

You may be wondering why we have to go through the process of creating SQL statements with parameters and setting up Parameter objects, instead of generating straightforward SQL statements on the fly. A statement that picks some user-supplied values and embeds them in a SQL statement can be exploited by a malicious user as a Trojan horse to execute any SQL statement against your database. Can you guess what will happen when the user enters a SQL statement in one of the TextBox controls on the form and your code uses this string to build a SQL statement on the fly? The code will pick it up, insert it into the larger statement, and then execute it against the database. This technique is known as *SQL injection*, and I'll show you how it works with a simple example. It's a known issue with any DBMS that can execute multiple SQL statements in a batch mode, and SQL Server is certainly vulnerable to SQL injection attacks.

How would you validate the users of an application? You'd most likely store the usernames and passwords in a table and execute a few statements to locate the row with the specified ID and password, right? If you didn't know any better, you'd probably write some code to extract the values from two TextBox controls and build the following SQL statement:

```
Dim CMD As New SqlClient.SqlCommand(
"SELECT COUNT(*) FROM Customers WHERE CompanyName = " ' &
txtName.Text & "' AND CustomerID = '" & txtPsswd.Text & "'")
```

Then you'd execute this statement and examine the number of rows that match the specified criteria:

```
Dim count As Integer
count = Convert.ToInt32(CMD.ExecuteScalar)
```

If the value of the *count* variable is 1, the user can log in. (I've assumed that the CompanyName field is the username and that the password for each user is the CustomerID field of the Customers table.) If the values in the two text boxes are *Frankenversan* and *FRANK*, the following statement will be executed against the database and will return the numeric value 1:

```
SELECT COUNT(*) FROM Customers
WHERE CompanyName = 'Frankenversan' AND CustomerID = 'FRANK'
```

A malicious user might enter the following username (and no password at all):

```
xxx' ; DROP TABLE [Orders] --
```

If you examine the value of the Command.CommandText property before this statement is executed, you'll see the following SQL statement:

```
SELECT COUNT(*) FROM Customers
WHERE CompanyName = 'xxx' ;
DROP TABLE [Orders] --' AND CustomerID = "
```

This statement contains two SQL statements and a comment: the SELECT statement, followed by another statement that drops the Orders table! The comments symbol (the two dashes) is required to disable the last part of the original statement, which otherwise would cause a syntax error. The Orders table can't be dropped, because it contains related rows in the Order Details table, but nothing will stop you from dropping the Order Details table.

If you want to demonstrate to someone that their software isn't secure, you can replace the DROP TABLE statement with the SHUTDOWN statement. The following statement shuts down the server immediately (and they can restart it immediately by running SQL Server Agent from the SQL Server Configuration Manager utility):

```
SHUTDOWN WITH NOWAIT
```

HANDLING SPECIAL CHARACTERS

Another problem you will avoid with parameterized queries and stored procedures is that of handling single quotes, which are used to delimit literals in T-SQL. Consider the following UPDATE statement, which picks up the company name from a TextBox control and updates a single row in the Customers table:

```
CMD.CommandText =
        "UPDATE Customers SET CompanyName = '" &
        txtCompany.Text & "'" &
        "WHERE CustomerID = '" & txtID.Text & "'"
```

If the user enters a company name that contains a single quote, such as *B's Beverages*, the command will become the following:

```
UPDATE Customers SET CompanyName = 'B's Beverages' WHERE CustomerID = 'BSBEV'
```

If you attempt to execute this statement, SQL Server will reject it because it contains a syntax error (you should be able to figure out the error easily by now). The exact error message is as follows:

```
Msg 102, Level 15, State 1, Line 1
Incorrect syntax near 's'.
Msg 105, Level 15, State 1, Line 1
Unclosed quotation mark after the character string ".
```

The single quote is used to delimit literals, and there should be an even number of single quotes in the statement. The compiler determines that there's an unclosed quotation mark in the statement and doesn't execute it. If the same statement was written as a parameterized query, such as the following, you could pass the same company name to the statement as an argument without a hitch:

```
CMD.CommandText =
    "UPDATE Customers SET CompanyName = @CompanyName " &
    "WHERE CustomerID = @ID"
CMD.Parameters.Add("@CompanyName",
        SqlDbType.VarChar, 40).Value = "B's Beverages"
CMD.Parameters.Add("@ID",
        SqlDbType.Char, 5).Value = "BSBEV"
CMD.ExecuteNonQuery
```

The same is true for other special characters, such as the percentage symbol. It's possible to escape the special symbols; you can replace the single-quote mark with two consecutive single quotes, but the most elegant method of handling special characters, such as quotation marks, percent signs, and so on, is to use parameterized queries or stored procedures. You just assign a string to the parameter and don't have to worry about escaping any characters; the Command object will take care of all necessary substitutions.

EMPTY STRINGS VERSUS NULL VALUES

The values you assign to the arguments of a query or stored procedure usually come from controls on a Windows form and in most cases from TextBox controls. The following statement reads the text in the *txtFax* TextBox control and assigns it to the @FAX parameter of a Command object:

```
Command.Parameters("@FAX").Value = txtFax.Text
```

But what if the user has left the *txtFax* TextBox blank? Should we pass to the INSERT statement an empty string or a null value? If you collect the values from various controls on a form and use them as parameter values, you'll never send null values to the database. If you want to treat empty strings as null values, you must pass a null value to the appropriate parameter explicitly. Let's say that the *txtFax* TextBox control on the form corresponds to the @FAX parameter. You can use the IIf() statement of Visual Basic to assign the proper value to the corresponding parameter as follows:

```
UPDATECommand.Parameters("@FAX").Value =
    IIf(txtFax.Text.Trim.Length = 0,
            System.DBNull.Value, txtFax.Text)
```

This is a lengthy statement, but here's how it works: The IIf() function evaluates the specified expression. If the length of the text in the *txtFax* control is zero, it returns the value specified by its second argument, which is the null value. If not — in other words, if the TextBox control isn't empty — it returns the text on the control. This value is then assigned to the @FAX parameter of the UPDATECommand object.

The DataReader Class

To read the rows returned by a selection query, you must call the Command object's Execute-Reader method, which returns a DataReader object (a SqlDataReader object for queries executed against SQL Server). The DataReader is a stream to the data retrieved by the query, and it provides many methods for reading the data sent to the client by the database. The underlying Connection object remains open while you read the data off the DataReader, so you must read it as quickly as possible, store it at the client, and close the connection as soon as possible.

To read a set of rows with the DataReader, you must call its Read method, which advances the pointer to the next row in the set. Initially, the pointer is in front of the first row, so you must call the Read method before accessing the first row. Despite its name, the Read method doesn't actually fetch any data; to read individual fields, you must use the various Get methods of the DataReader object, described next (GetDecimal, GetString, and so on). After reading the fields of the current row, call the Read method again to advance to the next row. There's no method to move to a previous row, so make sure you've read all the data of the current row before moving to the next one. Table 15.4 explains the basic properties and methods of the DataReader object.

TABLE 15.4:   Properties and methods of a DataReader object

NAME	DESCRIPTION
HasRows	This is a Boolean property that specifies whether there's a result set to read data from. If the query selected no rows at all, the HasRows property will return False.
FieldCount	This property returns the number of columns in the current result set. Note that the DataReader object doesn't know the number of rows returned by the query. Because it reads the rows in a forward-only fashion, you must iterate through the entire result set to find out the number of rows returned by the query.
Read	This method moves the pointer in front of the next row in the result set. Use this method to read the rows of the result set, usually from within a While loop.
Get<type>	There are many versions of the Get method with different names, depending on the type of column you want to read. To read a Decimal value, use the GetDecimal method; to retrieve a string, use the GetString method; to retrieve an integer, call one of the GetInt16, GetInt32, or GetSqlInt64 methods; and so on. To specify the column you want to read, use an integer index value that represents the column's ordinal, such as Reader.GetString(2). The index of the first column in the result set is zero.
GetSql<type>	There are many versions of the GetSql method with different names, depending on the SQL type of the column you want to read. To read a Decimal value, use the GetSqlDecimal method; to retrieve a string, use the GetSqlString method; to retrieve an integer, call one of the GetSqlInt16, GetSqlInt32, or GetSqlInt64 methods; and so on. To specify the column you want to read, use an integer index value that represents the column's ordinal, such as Reader.GetSqlString(2). The index of the first column in the result set is zero.
GetValue	If you can't be sure about the type of a column, use the GetValue method, which returns a value of the Object type. This method accepts as an argument the ordinal of the column you want to read.

TABLE 15.4:   Properties and methods of a DataReader object *(CONTINUED)*

NAME	DESCRIPTION
GetValues	This method reads all the columns of the current row and stores them into an array of objects, which is passed to the method as an argument. This method returns an integer value, which is the number of columns read from the current row.
GetName	Use this method to retrieve the name of a column, which must be specified by its order in the result set. To retrieve the name of the first column, use the expression Reader.GetName(0). The column's name in the result set is the original column name, unless the SELECT statement used an alias to return a column with a different name.
GetOrdinal	This is the counterpart of the GetName method, and it returns the ordinal of a specific column from its name. To retrieve the ordinal of the CompanyName column, use the expression Reader.GetName("CompanyName").
IsDbNull	This method returns True if the column specified by its ordinal in the current row is null. If you attempt to assign a null column to a variable, a runtime exception will be thrown, so you should use this method to determine whether a column has a value and handle the null values from within your code.

CLR TYPES VERSUS SQL TYPES

The Get<Type> methods return data types recognized by the Common Language Runtime (CLR), whereas the GetSql<Type> methods return data types recognized by SQL Server. There's a one-to-one correspondence between most types but not always. In most cases, we use the Get<Type> methods and store the values in VB variables, but you may want to store the value of a field in its native format. Use the SQL data types only if you're planning to move the data into another database. For normal processing, you should read them with the Get<type> methods, which return CLR data types recognized by VB. The following table summarizes the CLR and SQL data types:

CLR DATA TYPE	SQL DATA TYPE
Byte	SqlByte
Byte()	SqlBytes
Char()	SqlChars
DateTime	SqlDateTime
Decimal	SqlDecimal
Double	SqlDouble
	SqlMoney
Single	SqlSingle
String	SqlString
	SqlXml

The following table summarizes the methods that read data off the DataReader as CLR or SQL data types:

CLR DATA TYPE	SQL DATA TYPE	DESCRIPTION
	GetSqlBinary	Reads column as a binary (usually image columns)
GetBoolean	GetSqlBoolean	Reads column as a Boolean value
GetByte	GetSqlByte	Reads column as a single Byte
GetBytes	GetSqlBytes	Reads column as an array of Byte
GetChars	GetSqlChars	Reads column as an array of Char
GetDateTime	GetSqlDateTime	Reads column as a DateTime value
GetDecimal	GetSqlDecimal	Reads column as a Decimal value
GetDouble	GetSqlDouble	Reads column as a Double value
GetFloat	GetSqlSingle	Reads column as a Single value
GetInt16	GetSqlInt16	Reads column as an Int16 value
GetInt32	GetSqlInt32	Reads column as an Int32 value
GetInt64	GetSqlInt64	Reads column as an Int64 value
GetString	GetSqlString	Reads column as a string value
	GetSqlMoney	Reads column as a money value (no equivalent type in VB)
	GetSqlXml	Reads column as a XML value (no equivalent in VB)

Note that you can't reset the DataReader object and reread the same result set. To go through the same rows, you must execute the query again. However, there's no guarantee that the same query executed a few moments later will return the same result set. Rows may have been added to, or removed from, the database, so your best bet is to go through the result set once and store all the data to a structure at the client computer's memory. Moreover, while you're using the DataReader, the connection to the server remains open. This means that you shouldn't process the data as you read it, unless it is a trivial form of processing, such as keeping track of sums and counts. If you need to perform some substantial processing on your data, read the data into an ArrayList or other structure in the client computer's memory, close the connection, and then access the data in the ArrayList. In the following chapter, you'll learn about the DataSet object, which was designed to maintain relational data at the client. The DataSet is a great structure for storing relational data at the client; it's almost like a small database that resides in the client computer's memory. However, the DataSet is not ideal for all situations.

Listing 15.3 shows the code that retrieves all products along with category names and supplier names and populates a ListView control. The ListView control's columns aren't specified at design time; the code adds the appropriate columns at runtime (as long as the View property has been set to Details). The code goes through the columns of the result set and adds a new column to the ListView control for each data column. Then it reads the rows returned by the query and displays them on the control. The statements in Listing 15.3 are part of the SimpleQueries sample project.

LISTING 15.3:   Displaying product information on a ListView control

```
Dim Command As New SqlCommand
Command.Connection = CN
' a simple SELECT query
Command.CommandText =
    "SELECT ProductName AS Product, " &
    "CategoryName AS Category, " &
    "CompanyName AS Supplier, UnitPrice AS Price " &
    "FROM Products LEFT JOIN Categories " &
    "ON Products.CategoryID = Categories.CategoryID " &
    "LEFT JOIN Suppliers ON Products.SupplierID = Suppliers.SupplierID"
Connection.Open()
Dim count As Integer = 0
Dim Reader As SqlDataReader
Reader = Command.ExecuteReader
ListView1.Clear()
Dim i As Integer
' setup ListView control to display the headers
' of the columns read from the database
For i = 0 To Reader.FieldCount - 1
    ListView1.Columns.Add(Reader.GetName(i), 130)
Next
While Reader.Read
    Dim LI As New ListViewItem
    LI.Text = Convert.ToString(Reader.Item("Product"))
    LI.SubItems.Add(Convert.ToString(
                    Reader.Item("Category")))
    LI.SubItems.Add(Convert.ToString(
                    Reader.Item("Supplier")))
    LI.SubItems.Add(Convert.ToString(
                    Reader.Item("Price")))
    ListView1.Items.Add(LI)
    Count += 1
End While
MsgBox("Read " & count.ToString & " Product rows")
Connection.Close()
```

READING MULTIPLE RESULT SETS

Another interesting aspect of the DataReader object is that you can use it to read multiple result sets, such as the ones returned by multiple queries. You can execute a batch query such as the following with a single Command object:

```
Command.CommandText = "SELECT * FROM Customers; SELECT * FROM Employees"
Dim Reader As SqlDataReader = Command.ExecuteReader
```

We'll use the same DataReader object to read the rows of both tables, but we need to know when we're finished with the first result set (the customers) and start reading the second result set. The NextResult property of the DataReader does exactly that: After exhausting the first result set (by iterating through its rows with the Read method), we can request the NextResult property to find out whether the DataReader contains additional result sets. If so, we can start reading the next result set with the Read method. Here's the outline of the code for reading two result sets from the same DataReader:

```
While Reader.Read
    ' read the fields of the current row in the 1st result set
End While
If Reader.NextResult
    While Reader.Read
        ' read the fields of the current row in the 2nd result set
    End While
End If
```

VB 2010 AT WORK: BUILDING A SIMPLE DATA-DRIVEN APPLICATION

In this section I'll put together all the information presented so far in this chapter to build a data-driven application — an application that actually talks to a database, retrieves data, and displays it on a Windows form. The application is not new to you. In Chapter 5, "Basic Windows Controls," you created an application for maintaining a list of contacts, based on a ListBox control, where you stored the names of the contacts. The same ListBox control was also used as a navigational tool, because users could select a contact and view their details, as shown in Figure 15.8.

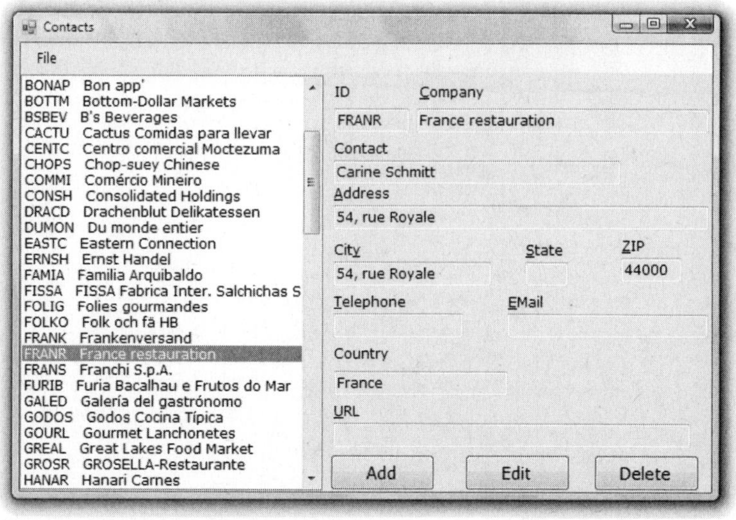

FIGURE 15.8
The Contacts application's interface

The contacts were stored in a List of Contact objects, and they were persisted to a file. Now let's revise this application so that it works with a database, namely, the Customers table of the Northwind database. The columns of the Customers table are almost identical to the fields of the Contact object, so you'll use the same data type to store the data. Instead of persisting the data to a file, you'll read your contacts from the database and submit the edited rows back to the same database. Because you'll use a central data storage, the revised application can be used by multiple users at the same time.

Start by copying the Contacts project folder to a new folder with a different name. Then edit the menu, as follows:

1. Delete the New and Save items, because the new application doesn't maintain a copy of the contacts in memory. Instead, it retrieves the requested contact from the Customer table as requested and submits the updates to the database as soon as the user edits an existing contact or inserts a new one. The New command is meaningless with a database. You'll never have to remove all rows from a table, unless you're reinitializing a test database, in which you will probably run a script that initializes all tables.

2. Change the Open command of the File menu to Load Customers. Instead of loading the contacts from a file, we'll load them from the Customers table of the Northwind database.

3. Add the CustomerID field to the main form, because the Customers table uses user-supplied strings as primary keys.

Most of the code remains the same. You only need to replace the routines that perform the basic operations against the database. We no longer read the data from an external file. Instead, we must execute a query against the database and retrieve the company names along with their IDs. The Load command's code follows in Listing 15.4.

LISTING 15.4:   Loading the Customers table

```
Private Sub LoadToolStripMenuItem_Click(...) Handles
          LoadToolStripMenuItem.Click
    CMD.CommandText = "SELECT * FROM Customers"
    CN.Open()
    Dim RDR As SqlDataReader
    RDR = CMD.ExecuteReader
    ListBox1.Items.Clear()
    While RDR.Read
        Dim C As New Contact
        C.CustomerID = RDR.Item("CustomerID")
        C.CompanyName = RDR.Item("CompanyName")
        C.ContactName = Convert.ToString(
                IIf(RDR.IsDBNull(
                        RDR.GetOrdinal("ContactName")),
                        "", RDR.Item("ContactName")))
        C.Address1 = Convert.ToString(
                IIf(RDR.IsDBNull(
                        RDR.GetOrdinal("Address")),
                        "", RDR.Item("Address")))
        ' Similar statements for the remaining fields
        ListBox1.Items.Add(C)
```

```
        End While
        CN.Close()
        currentContact = 0
        ShowContact()
End Sub
```

The code executes a simple SELECT query against the database and then loads the ListBox control with Contact objects as before. The only difference is that now the data comes from the DataReader. You will also notice the lengthy expressions that assign the values read from the database to the TextBox controls on the form. The expression RDR.Item(field_name) reads the corresponding column's value from the current row. This row, however, may be null, and you can't assign a null value to the Text property. So, the code uses the IIf() function to determine whether the current field's value is null. If the method IsDBNull returns True, then the current field is null, and the IIf() function returns an empty string. If not, it returns the actual field value, which is the expression RDR.Item(field_name). But what about the call to the GetOrdinal method? Well, the IsDBNull method doesn't accept a column name as an argument, only an integer that is the order of the column in the result. Instead of hard-coding numeric values to our code (and make it impossible to maintain later), we can retrieve the ordinal of a column with the GetOrdinal method. The expression GetOrdinal("CustomerID") returns 0 because the CustomerID column is the first one, GetOrdinal("CompanyName") returns 1, and so on. Finally, because the IIf() function returns an object, we must cast it to a string before assigning it to the Text property.

Now, this is the type of code that can be streamlined, and there are tools that do it for you. Even better, there are tools that convert each row to a custom object (a Contact object, in our example), so you can handle the data you retrieve from the database with the object-oriented techniques you have learned in this book. The new data access technologies, including LINQ to SQL that was discussed in Chapter 14, "An Introduction to LINQ," bridge the gap between databases and object-oriented programming. As you have already noticed, there's a mismatch between objects and the way we access databases. Having to set up a DataReader, execute commands directly against the database, and then having to worry about null and converting the fields to the proper type takes a lot of code, and the entire approach just isn't elegant. You'll see better techniques for accessing databases in the following chapter, but I wanted to show you the basic data access mechanisms first (actually you already saw how to access databases with LINQ to SQL queries in the preceding chapter).This may not be so elegant, but they're the foundation on which more elaborate tools were built. Moreover, they're the fastest way to get data out of a database and back. That said, let's continue with our sample application.

Next, we must implement the procedures for adding a new contact (the SubmitContact subroutine), for updating an existing contact (the UpdateContact subroutine), and for deleting a contact (the RemoveContact subroutine). The first two subroutines accept as an argument a variable of the Contact type, form the appropriate SQL statement, and execute it against the database. The RemoveContact subroutine accepts the ID of the row to be deleted, forms the appropriate DELETE statement, and executes it likewise. You may wonder why I haven't implemented these routines as functions that return a True/False value indicating whether the operation completed successfully. The reason is that a simple indication about the success of an operation won't suffice; we need to display a more specific error message to the user, so I've decided to throw an exception with the error description, as shown in Listings 15.5, 15.6, and 15.7.

LISTING 15.5:   Adding a new row to the Customers table

```
Private Sub SubmitContact(ByVal C As Contact)
    CMD.CommandText = "INSERT Customers " &
                "(CustomerID, CompanyName, ContactName, Address, " &
                " City, Region, PostalCode, Country) " &
                "VALUES (@CustomerID, @CompanyName, @ContactName, " &
                "@Address, @City, @Region, @PostalCode, @Country) "
    CMD.Parameters.Clear()
    CMD.Parameters.AddWithValue("@CustomerID", C.CustomerID)
    CMD.Parameters.AddWithValue("@CompanyName", C.CompanyName)
    CMD.Parameters.AddWithValue("@ContactName", C.ContactName)
    CMD.Parameters.AddWithValue("@Address", C.Address1)
    CMD.Parameters.AddWithValue("@City", C.City)
    CMD.Parameters.AddWithValue("@Region", C.State)
    CMD.Parameters.AddWithValue("@PostalCode", C.ZIP)
    CMD.Parameters.AddWithValue("@Country", C.ZIP)
    CN.Open()
    Try
        CMD.ExecuteNonQuery()
    Catch ex As Exception
        Throw New Exception(
                "Failed to update contact in database. " &
                vbCrLf & "ERROR MESSAGE: " & vbCrLf & ex.Message)
    Finally
        CN.Close()
    End Try
    CN.Close()
End Sub
```

LISTING 15.6:   Updating a row in the Customers table

```
Private Sub UpdateContact(ByVal C As Contact)
    CMD.CommandText = "UPDATE Customers " &
                "SET CompanyName = @CompanyName, " &
                "    ContactName = @ContactName, " &
                "    Address = @Address, " &
                "    City = @City, " &
                "    Region = @Region, " &
                "    PostalCode = PostalCode" &
                "    Country = @Country " &
                "WHERE CustomerID = @CustomerID"
    CMD.Parameters.Clear()
    CMD.Parameters.AddWithValue("@CustomerID", C.CustomerID)
    CMD.Parameters.AddWithValue("@CompanyName", C.CompanyName)
    CMD.Parameters.AddWithValue("@ContactName", C.ContactName)
```

```
CMD.Parameters.AddWithValue("@Address", C.Address1)
CMD.Parameters.AddWithValue("@City", C.City)
CMD.Parameters.AddWithValue("@Region", C.State)
CMD.Parameters.AddWithValue("@PostalCode", C.ZIP)
CN.Open()
Try
    CMD.ExecuteNonQuery()
Catch ex As Exception
    Throw New Exception(
        "Failed to update contact in database. " & vbCrLf &
        "ERROR MESSAGE: " & vbCrLf & ex.Message)
End Try
CN.Close()
End Sub
```

LISTING 15.7:   Removing a row from the Customers table

```
Private Sub RemoveContact(ByVal ContactID As String)
    CMD.CommandText = "DELETE Customers WHERE CustomerID=@contactID "
    CMD.Parameters.Clear()
    CMD.Parameters.AddWithValue("@contactID", ContactID)
    CN.Open()
    Try
        CMD.ExecuteNonQuery()
    Catch ex As Exception
        Throw New Exception(
            "Failed to delete contact in database. " & vbCrLf &
            "ERROR MESSAGE: " & vbCrLf & ex.Message)
    Finally
        CN.Close()
    End Try
End Sub
```

The rest of the code is basically the same. We started with an application that manipulates Contact objects in a List and converted it to an application that manipulates the rows of a database table. We changed the routines that read data and submit data to the database. The routines that read the data from the database create Contact objects that are stored to the ListBox control as with the original application. Likewise, every time the user inserts a new contact or updates an existing one, instead of modifying an item in the List control, we submit it to the database and update the underlying source (the Customers table). Finally, when a contact is removed, the application removes it directly from the Customers table. The deletion operation may fail if the customer has placed an order. As you realize, we're no longer dealing with an isolated table but with a larger system with related tables, and the DBMS maintains the integrity of our data.

This application has a serious flaw, though. What if the Customers table has thousands of customers and there are a few dozen users who may need access the database? Would it make sense to download the entire table to the client and maintain such an enormous list of customers at every client? The first improvement I'd suggest is to download only the customer names and display them on the ListBox control. Every time the user clicks a different customer's name, your code should execute a SELECT statement for the specific customer and bring the entire row to the client and display its fields.

Even so, the table may grow so large that it wouldn't make sense to display all company names in a list. In this case, you should provide some selection mechanism to force users to download the names of selected companies only. For example, you could display a list of countries and download only customers from the selected customer every time users selected another country. You could also filter by company or contact name or provide combinations of criteria. If you decide to modify the application, here are the SELECT statements that limit customers by country and company name:

```
SELECT CustomerID, CompanyName FROM Customers WHERE Country = @country
SELECT CustomerID, CompanyName FROM Customers WHERE CompanyName LIKE @name + '%'
```

(The percent symbol at the end of the string is a wildcard, indicating that the company name should start with the string stored in the *@name* variable, followed by any other combination of characters.)

One last hitch in this application is the following: What will happen if other users delete a contact you're editing or someone else updates the contact you're editing? Issues of concurrency are very important in designing data-driven applications, and we'll look at this in the following chapter. The Contacts project assumes that the same row won't be edited by multiple users at once. Even when this happens, the last user to save the edits overwrites the edits of the other users. It's a bit of a crude approach, but it's quite appropriate in many situations. In other situations, most notably in reservation applications, it's unacceptable.

The Bottom Line

Store data in relational databases. Relational databases store their data in tables and are based on relationships between these tables. The data are stored in tables, and tables contain related data, or entities, such as persons, products, orders, and so on. Relationships are implemented by inserting columns with matching values in the two related tables.

Master It How will you relate two tables with a many-to-many relationship?

Query databases with SQL. Structured Query Language (SQL) is a universal language for manipulating tables. SQL is a nonprocedural language, which specifies the operation you want to perform against a database at a high level, unlike a traditional language such as Visual Basic, which specifies how to perform the operation. The details of the implementation are left to the DBMS. SQL consists of a small number of keywords and is optimized for selecting, inserting, updating, and deleting data.

Master It How would you write a SELECT statement to retrieve selected data from multiple tables?

Submit queries to the database using ADO.NET. ADO.NET is the component of the Framework that provides the mechanism to contact a database, submit queries, and retrieve the results of a query. There are two types of queries you can execute against a database: selection queries that retrieve data from the database based on certain criteria you supply and action queries that manipulate the data at the database. Action queries do not return any results, except for the number of rows that were affected by the query.

Master It Describe the basic mechanism for submitting a selection query to the database and reading the results returned by the query.

Chapter 16

Developing Data-Driven Applications

In Chapter 15, "Programming with ADO.NET," you learned how to access data stored in databases with the basic classes of ADO.NET: the Connection and Command classes. A third class, the DataReader class, allows you to read the data retrieved by your command in the client application. Most applications today use a database to store data. These applications are known as *front-end applications,* because they interact with the user and update the data on a database server, or a back-end data store. They're also known as *data-driven applications,* because they interact not only with the user but primarily with the database.

Although executing commands and reading the selected data is a straightforward process, you still have to decide where to store the data at the client and how to present it to the user. One approach is to write custom classes that represent the business objects you want to work with and then populate instances of these classes with data. Once the objects have been populated, you can work with familiar business objects. You can even use LINQ to Objects to query collections of custom objects or LINQ to SQL to query database tables directly with LINQ queries, as discussed in Chapter 14, "An Introduction to LINQ."

Finally, there's a standard mechanism for storing data at the client, the DataSet class. A DataSet is an in-memory database, which you can populate with the data you're interested in and work with it at the client.

In this chapter, you'll learn how to do the following:

◆ Create and populate business objects

◆ Establish relations between tables in the DataSet

◆ Submit changes in the DataSet to the database

Using Business Objects

By now you should be more than familiar with object-oriented programming. One of the ideas behind object-oriented programming is the transformation of flat data (whether they live in files or relational databases) into meaningful objects that reflect the hierarchy of the business objects you're dealing with. As you recall from the preceding chapter, the orders in the Northwind database are stored in two different tables: the order headers in the Orders table and their details in the Order Details table. Books and their authors are spread over three different tables in the Pub database: the Titles table, which stores titles; the Authors table, which stores author names; and the TitleAuthor table, which relates titles to their authors.

If you ignore the data-storage aspect of the application for a moment, you'd probably design an Order object to store orders with the following structure:

```
Public Class Order
    Dim OrderID As Integer
    Dim OrderDate As Date
    Dim Employee As Employee
    Dim Customer As Customer
    Dim Details As List(Of Detail)
End Class
Public Class Detail
    Dim ProductID As Integer
    Dim ProductPrice As Decimal
    Dim ProductQuantity As Integer
End Class
Public Class Employee
    Dim EmployeeID As Integer
    Dim EmployeeName As Strng
End Class
Public Class Customer
    Dim CustomerID As String
    Dim CompanyName As Strng
End Class
```

The Order class can be populated with single statements like the following:

```
Dim newOrder As New Order
newOrder.OrderDate = Now.Today
newOrder.Details = New List(Of Detail)
Dim det As New Detail
det.ProductID=12
det.ProductPrice = 21.90
det.ProductQuantity = 10
newOrder.Details.Add(det)
```

This is a straightforward approach to modeling an order with a custom object that doesn't take into consideration the structure of the information in the database. The Order class represents an order as a business object, regardless of how the information is stored in the database. Note that the order's ID isn't stored anywhere, because there's no need to associate the order's header with its details. The details simply belong to the order. At a later point we'll have to write some code to extract the various properties of the Order object and submit them to the database with the proper SQL statements, and this is what this section is all about: how to map our data into custom business objects, build our application with object-oriented techniques, and then submit the data to the database. The code that actually contacts the database and either retrieves data or submits edited and new data to the database is the application's data layer, as opposed to the application's user interface (UI), which is the code that manipulates the data at the client.

This object-oriented approach is also more elegant than the structure of the two tables in the database. Some people talk about the impedance mismatch between object-oriented programming and databases. One of the advantages of using business objects to store your data at the client is that the custom objects can be manipulated with traditional programming techniques (and not-so traditional techniques, like LINQ).

The main theme in designing data-driven applications is how to get the relational data out of a database and map it to a business object like Order and how to get the data from a business object and submit it to the database. And as you will see in this and the following chapter, there are many techniques for mapping database data to custom objects. To better understand how to bridge the gap between traditional database data and custom objects, we'll explore this process through a sample application.

VB 2010 at Work: The NWOrders Application

In this section, you'll develop a real-world application, which isn't very complicated, to serve as an example in a textbook, but it's by no means trivial. The NWOrders application (available for download from www.sybex.com/go/masteringvb2010) allows you to create new orders for the Northwind database. Although the applications for manipulating the other tables of the database, such as the Products or Customers/Employees tables, are fairly simple and you have already seen a few examples, the application for entering new invoices is entirely different. To begin with, the user interface is the most critical aspect of the application. Users should be able to add new items to the order easily and quickly. The interface should be simple and intuitive, and all operations should be performed with the keyboard. Ideally, users should be able to scan the product's bar code and append the scanned item to the order.

Inserting the new order to the database is also a bit involved. An order is stored in two separate tables: the order's header (the data that usually appear at the top of an invoice, such as the invoice's date and customer) is stored in the Orders table, and the order's details (the items sold that appear in a grid that takes up most of the invoice) are stored in the Order Details table. Moreover, the order's header and its details must be inserted into the corresponding tables in the context of a transaction: All rows must be inserted successfully, or the insertion of an order must fail as a whole. Even if the insertion of a single detail line fails, then the entire order must fail. Otherwise, you may end up with a partial order.

I've implemented the same application with two different techniques to demonstrate the steps of building data-driven applications, as well as the parts of the application that can be streamlined by the Framework. The interface of the application is identical in both versions, because it's a functional interface that shouldn't be tied to a particular implementation of the data-access layer. Likewise, the data-access layer shouldn't be tied to a specific interface. One of the major themes in designing data-driven applications is the separation of the user interface from the data-access layer. The data layer is the code that interacts with the database by retrieving the data requested by the user and submitting the edits to the database.

The UI, on the other hand, is responsible for interacting with the user. Every time it needs to fetch some data from the database or submit data to the database, it calls a method of the data-access layer, which is usually implemented as a class. As you will see shortly, the two applications have an identical UI; even the code is the same. The data-access layer, however, is very different. Yet, the code that implements the UI calls a few methods that have the same signature but are implemented very differently. You can even make the same application work with a different database by rewriting the data-access layer without editing a single line of code in the UI code.

THE APPLICATION'S INTERFACE

Figure 16.1 shows the interface of the application, and I suggest you open the application to see how it works. To specify the order's header, you simply select the customer who placed the order and the employee who made the sale from the appropriate ComboBox controls and enter the order's shipping address in the TextBox control at the bottom of the form. Then you must enter the products purchased; this is the most challenging part of the application because users should be able to enter new products quickly and safely.

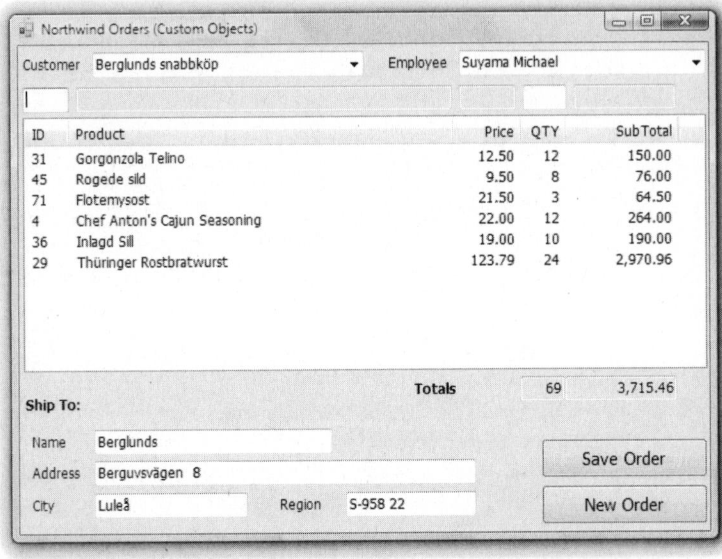

FIGURE 16.1
The user interface of the
NWOrders application

The NWOrders application assumes that you're using an instance of SQL Server running on the same machine and that you have installed the Northwind sample database. If SQL Server is running on a remote machine, you must edit the NorthwindConnectionString setting in the application's configuration file accordingly. To do so, open the app.config file, and edit the connectionString setting in the connectionStrings section:

```
<connectionStrings>
    <add name="NWOrders.My.MySettings.NorthwindConnectionString"
        connectionString="Data Source=(local);
        Initial Catalog=Northwind;Integrated Security=True"
        providerName="System.Data.SqlClient" />
</connectionStrings>
```

This application will most likely be used as a point-of-sale (POS) system and must be intuitive, easy to use, and extremely fast. The user of the application is probably a cashier and shouldn't be expected to open the Products table, select the desired one, and then add it to the invoice. With the interface I'm suggesting, users enter the product ID in the TextBox above the ID column of the grid. As soon as the user presses the Enter key, the application retrieves the desired product and displays its description and price. The two TextBoxes are read-only, and the user can't change either. You may want to allow users to edit the price, but this isn't a recommended practice. A general discount that's applied to all items is probably the simplest way to go, but it's trivial to add another TextBox control for entering a different discount for each detail line (along with a new column in the ListView control with the order's details). As soon as the item is retrieved and displayed on the TextBox controls at the top, the focus is moved to the TextBox for the quantity, where the user can type the number of items. After pressing the Enter key for a second time, the new row is added to the grid with the order's details, and the focus is moved automatically to the ID field in anticipation of the next product's ID.

Users aren't expected to know the IDs of the products, obviously. In a real-world scenario, the application should accept the product's bar code instead of the ID. You can use a barcode reader with this application without any modifications. The barcode reader reads the bar's characters and sends them to the computer via the serial or USB port, but to the application they appear as if they were typed at the keyboard. The whole process is transparent, and you need not write a single additional line of code. Since the unique identifier in the Products table is the product ID, we'll use the ID as a bar code for this application.

Occasionally, the reader might fail to read a product ID. In that case, users can type a few characters from the product name, and the application will retrieve matching rows and display them so the user can select the desired one. Although searching with an ID will return a single product, searching with a product name may result in multiple matches, so some user intervention is needed to guarantee that the proper product is selected. In the discussion of the application, I will ignore this feature, which isn't trivial, and will focus on the other aspects of the application. If you're interested in the implementation of this feature, please open the NWOrders project with Visual Studio and examine the code; it is well documented. The code retrieves all the products whose name contains the characters specified in the ID box and displays them on a second ListView control, which is normally hidden but remains visible until the user selects the desired product. Figure 16.2 shows the application when a product is selected by name.

FIGURE 16.2
Selecting a product by name in the NWOrders application

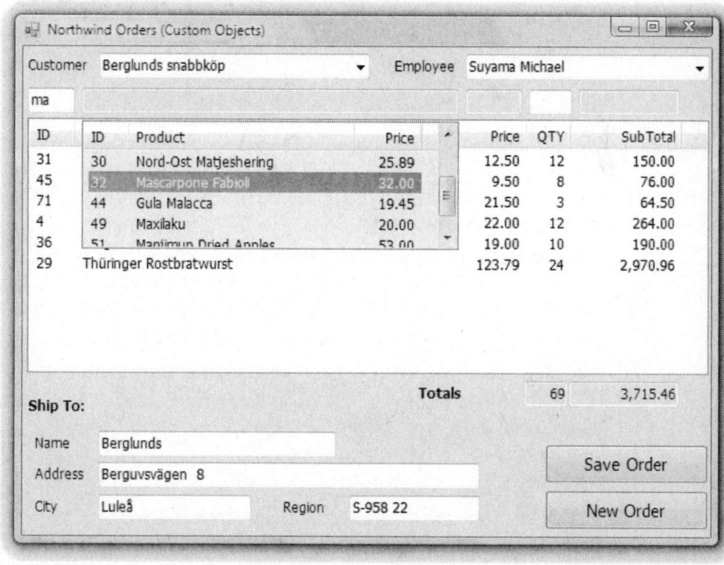

While entering new products, the user may decide to delete a product that was added to the grid by mistake or modify the quantity. Although most of the time users work with the

TextBox controls located at the top of the grid, in this case they must move the focus to the grid to select a row. This operation doesn't require the use of the mouse. By pressing the down arrow key while they're in the ID TextBox, users can move the focus to the first row of the grid and select it. Once they've landed on the grid with the order's details, users can move up and down with the arrow keys, and the currently selected row's fields are displayed in the TextBox controls on the top of the grid. To delete the selected row, they can simply press the Delete key. They can also use the mouse to locate the row to be removed on the grid, but it will take longer. Data-entry operators just don't like using their mouse. To return to the ID box and enter a new detail, they can press Escape.

Depending on the nature of the business, you may skip the quantity too and add a new row to the grid with a quantity of 1. If the same product is added multiple times, the application will generate multiple detail lines. You can edit the application's code to increase the quantity of the existing row, instead of adding a new row with the same product and a quantity of 1. If the application is going to be used at a bookstore, where people usually purchase a single copy of each title, the alternate approach will work better. You can use this application as your starting point for a POS system and add all the features required by your business needs.

The NWOrders application consists of two forms, the `frmLINQ` and `frmSQL` forms. The `frmSQL` form uses the basic ADO.NET objects to interact with the database, while `frmLINQ` uses the classes generated by the LINQ to SQL component of Visual Studio. You'll have to change the application's startup form to the desired one to test it.

We have discussed the application's interface, but before you start writing code, you must identify the requests you want to make to the database and implement them as methods in a separate class. The code behind the form will call these methods to retrieve data or submit data to the database and should not know anything about the database. This is not a requirement for small projects, but in a large project there will be different developers working on the data-access layer and different developers working on the user interface. By separating the data-access logic from the user interface, you can also implement multiple interfaces (a Windows application and a Web application, for example) that use the same data-access methods.

When you work on the application UI, you shouldn't need to care about the structure of the tables in the database. Your class should expose the business objects you need for the application and map them to the database tables. For example, the class you'll create shortly for the NWOrders application should expose an Order object that combines an order's header and details. Your UI code will populate an Order object and pass it as an argument to a method of the class that will submit it to the database. When the interface requests an order by its ID, the class should return an object of the Order type. This object will contain all the information about the order but with a structure that's totally different from the structure of the relevant tables in the database. In effect, the custom class will isolate the user interface from the data-access layer; should you have to implement the same application with a different database, you'll only have to revise the class that implements the data-access layer.

The class with the data-access components is referred to as the *data-access layer*, while the application's interface is the UI layer. In most applications, there's a third layer that implements the business logic. This layer is not related to the database, but it can't be part of the user interface either. You can implement it in either the UI or data-access layer, but logically it doesn't belong there and should be implemented as a separate class. If you ever decide to change some of the business rules, you will revise a specific class and not the entire application. Likewise, if you decide to move to a different database, you only need to revise the data-access layer and not the UI layer.

The business layer contains functionality that's specific to a corporation. For example, you may implement the discount calculations or a customer's credit line as a business layer. All methods that require this functionality, whether they reside in the UI or the data-access layer, should call the appropriate method of the class that implements the business logic.

The most basic rule in the design of data-driven applications is that the UI should not contain code that interacts with the database. Ideally, you must create classes that represent the business objects that represent the entities in your application. These business objects are classes that implement customers, employees, orders, and so on. Let's jump to a practical example to see how the application is structured.

IMPLEMENTING THE DATA-ACCESS LAYER WITH CUSTOM OBJECTS

The data-access layer of the `frmSql` form of the NWOrder application is implemented in the NWOrder class. The two simpler business objects of the NWOrder class are the NWEmployee and NWCustomer objects, which are implemented with two trivial classes by the same name. Both classes expose two properties, the ID and name of the corresponding entity and a custom implementation of the `ToString` method. I needed a custom implementation of the `ToString` method because the code in the UI application needs to add customers and employees to a ComboBox control and display their names.

In addition to their properties, the two classes provide the `GetAllEmployees` and `GetAllCustomers` methods, which return a strongly typed List of NWCustomer and NWEmployee objects, respectively. Listing 16.1 shows the code of the NWEmployee and NWCustomer classes (I've skipped the implementation of the two methods, which are fairly lengthy).

LISTING 16.1:   The outline of the NWEmployee and NWCustomer business objects

```
Public Class NWEmployee
    Public EmployeeID As Integer
    Public EmployeeName As String
    Public Overrides Function ToString() As String
        Return EmployeeName
    End Function

    Public Shared Function GetAllEmployees() As List(Of NWEmployee)
    End Function

End Class

Public Class NWCustomer
    Public CustomerID As String
    Public CustomerName As String
    Public Overrides Function ToString() As String
        Return CustomerName
    End Function

    Public Shared Function GetAllCustomers() As List(Of NWCustomer)
    End Function
End Class
```

Another class, the NWProduct class, represents the products that can appear in the order's details. Although the Products table contains a large number of columns, for the purposes of selling products we only need the product's ID, name, and price. The NWProduct class should also expose a method that allows us to retrieve a product by its ID, the `GetProductByID` method. All methods used in this application are shared: You can call them without having to create a new instance of the corresponding class.

```
Public Class NWProduct
    Public ProductID As Integer
    Public ProductName As String
    Public ProductPrice As Decimal

    Public Shared Function GetProductByID(
                    ByVal productID As Integer) As NWProduct
    End Function
End Class
```

Finally, the core class of the application is the NWOrder class, which represents an order and its details (see Listing 16.2). This class exposes the columns of the Orders table as properties and the columns of the Order Details table as a collection of NWOrderDetail objects.

LISTING 16.2:   The implementation of the NWOrder business object

```
Public Class NWOrder
    Public Class NWOrderDetail
        Public ProductID As Integer
        Public ProductPrice As Decimal
        Public ProductQuantity As Integer
        Public ProductDiscount As Decimal
    End Class

    Public OrderDate As Date
    Public EmployeeID As Integer
    Public CustomerID As String
    Public Details As New List(Of NWOrderDetail)

    Public Shared Function SaveOrder(ByVal newOrder As NWOrder) As Integer
    End Function
End Class
```

The implementation of the SaveOrder method is not trivial and is described in detail next.

Creating a New Order

To create a new order with the data entered by the user on the main form, the application declares a variable of the NWOrder type and populates it. Most of the properties are scalar and are populated with a single statement. The order's details, however, are stored in a property that is a List of NWOrderDetail objects. The code creates a new NWOrderDetail object for each item in the order, populates its properties, and then appends it to the Details property of the order. Listing 16.3 shows the code that iterates through the ListView control with the order's details and appends them to the *newOrder* variable, as shown in Listing 16.3.

LISTING 16.3:   Appending the details of a new order

```
For Each LI As ListViewItem In ListView1.Items
    Dim newDetail As New NWOrder.NWOrderDetail
    newDetail.ProductID = LI.Text
     newDetail.ProductPrice =
                System.Convert.ToDecimal(LI.SubItems(2).Text)
    newDetail.ProductQuantity =
                System.Convert.ToInt32(LI.SubItems(3).Text)
    newOrder.Details.Add(newDetail)
Next
```

Saving the New Order

Once the *newOrder* variable has been initialized to the fields of the order on the form, the application submits it to the database by calling the SaveOrder method of the data-access layer, whose code is shown in Listing 16.4.

LISTING 16.4:   The SaveOrder method of the NWData class

```
Public Shared Function SaveOrder(ByVal newOrder As NWOrder) As Integer
    Dim CN As New SqlClient.SqlConnection(
            My.Settings.NorthwindConnectionString)
    Dim CMD As New SqlClient.SqlCommand
    CN.Open()
    CMD.Connection = CN
    Dim TR As SqlClient.SqlTransaction = CN.BeginTransaction
    CMD.Transaction = TR
    CMD.CommandText = "INSERT Orders (OrderDate, EmployeeID, " &
                "CustomerID) VALUES (@orderDate, @employeeID, " &
                "@customerID);SELECT Scope_Identity()"
    CMD.Parameters.AddWithValue("@orderDate", Today)
    CMD.Parameters.AddWithValue("@employeeID", newOrder.EmployeeID)
    CMD.Parameters.AddWithValue("@customerID", newOrder.CustomerID)
    Dim OrderID As Int32
    Try
        OrderID = System.Convert.ToInt32(CMD.ExecuteScalar)
    Catch ex As Exception
        TR.Rollback()
        CN.Close()
        Throw ex
    End Try
```

```
    For Each det As NWOrderDetail In newOrder.Details
        CMD.CommandText = "INSERT [Order Details] "  &
                "(OrderID, ProductID, UnitPrice, Quantity) " &
                "VALUES(@OrderID, @productID, @price, @quantity)"
        CMD.Parameters.Clear()
        CMD.Parameters.AddWithValue("@orderID", OrderID)
        CMD.Parameters.AddWithValue("@productID", det.ProductID)
        CMD.Parameters.AddWithValue("@price", det.ProductPrice)
        CMD.Parameters.AddWithValue("@quantity", det.ProductQuantity)
        Try
            CMD.ExecuteNonQuery()
        Catch ex As Exception
            TR.Rollback()
            CN.Close()
            Throw ex
        End Try
    Next
    TR.Commit()
    CN.Close()
    Return OrderID
End Function
```

Listing 16.4 contains a large number of trivial statements, such as the statements that prepare the SQL command to be executed and initialize its parameters, which you can ignore; instead, focus on the statements that execute all SQL commands in transactional mode. The statements of interest are shown in bold in Listing 16.4.

To execute a number of statements in the context of a transaction, you must do the following:

1. Set up a Transaction object by calling the BeginTransaction method on the Connection object that will be used to submit the commands to the database.

2. Assign the Transaction object to the Transaction property of the Command object.

3. Submit multiple commands through the Command object's ExecuteNonQuery method.

4. Should an error condition prevent one of the commands from completing successfully, you can call the Rollback method of the Transaction object to abort the transaction.

5. If all goes well and none of the exception handlers is entered, the transaction will be committed when the Transaction object's Commit method is called.

Let's take a closer look at the code that commits the new order to the database. First it inserts the order's header to the Orders table and retrieves the ID of the newly created order. This ID will be used as a foreign key with the Order Details table to associate the details of the new order with its header. The INSERT statement is executed from within an exception handler, and in the case of an error, the transaction is aborted.

If the INSERT statement returns the ID of the new order, the code goes through the details of the *newOrder* variable and submits each one to the database through the same Command object, which is associated with the *TR* Transaction object. Again, the transaction can be aborted as soon as a detail line fails to update the Order Details table. If all details are inserted successfully, then the code calls the `Commit` method to finalize the insertions and update the database.

You can easily test the transactional features of the application by adding two detail lines with the same product ID. One of the constraints in the Order Details table is that no order should contain the same product more than once. To comply with this constraint, you can update the quantities of each detail line, rather than attempt to insert multiple lines that refer to the same product. Anyway, I have ignored this constraint in the implementation of the sample application. If you attempt to submit an order that contains the same product twice, the transaction will be aborted with the error message shown in Figure 16.3.

FIGURE 16.3
A violation of the database constraints will cause the transaction to be aborted.

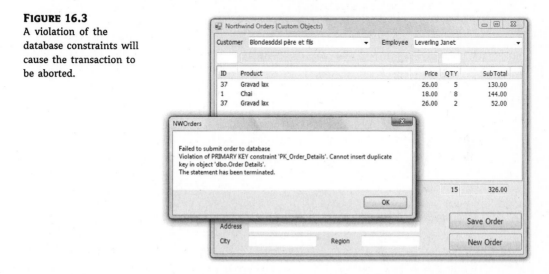

If the order can't be committed to the database, you should display a friendlier error message and either allow the user to further edit the order or clear the fields in anticipation of the next order.

IMPLEMENTING THE DATA-ACCESS LAYER WITH LINQ TO SQL

Now, we can switch our attention to the second implementation of the NWOrders applications, which uses LINQ to SQL to implement the data-access layer. The `frmLINQ` form is based on a LINQ to SQL component, which converts the relevant tables into custom business objects. In effect, the LINQ to SQL component will create the classes for the application objects, which we'll simply use in our application. Our new data layer doesn't contain any code to implement the Product, Order, and Order_Detail classes. The component will expose these three objects for us, and all we have to do is add the `GetProductByID`, `GetProducts`, and `GetEmployees` methods to the class. The code is quite short, because we don't have to request the desired rows and then iterate through them with a DataReader.

Start by adding a new item to the project, a LINQ to SQL Class component. When prompted, enter **NW** as the name of the new component, and Visual Studio will open it in the designer. Drop the Customers, Employees, Products, Orders, and Order Detail tables onto the design surface, and the designer will generate a class for each table. Once you drop the tables on the designer surface, the designer will create a class for each table and will expose the contents of each table as a collection of typed objects. Each row of the Customers table will be mapped to an object of the Customer type, and the rows of the Customers table will be stored in the Customers collection, which is a List of Customer objects.

To access the collections that represent the tables of the Northwind database, use the DataContext object, which also will be exposed by the same class. Create a variable of the NWDataContext type. (This is an autogenerated class named after the LINQ to SQL Class component with the suffix *DataContext* appended.)

```
Dim ctx As New NWDataContext
```

To access the Customers table, use the following expression, which returns a List of Customer objects, and each element in the List is a variable of the Customer type. Because the collection is typed, you can use LINQ to query its elements, as discussed in Chapter 14. The following query will select a customer by its ID:

```
Dim cust = (From c In ctx.Customers
            Where c.CustomerID = "ALFKI"
            Select c).FirstOrDefault
```

The LINQ query will not be executed at the client. Instead, the compiler will convert the LINQ query into a SQL query and will execute it against the database as needed. For more information on LINQ and how LINQ to SQL queries are transformed into SQL queries, see Chapter 14.

Listing 16.5 shows the implementation of the methods of the NWData class. Because the methods are implemented as LINQ queries, they require very little, and straightforward, code.

LISTING 16.5: The data-access layer of the Orders project implemented with LINQ to SQL

```
Public Class NWData
    Public Function GetProductByID(
                            ByVal productID As Integer) As Product
        Dim ctx As New NWDataContext
        Dim prod = (From p In ctx.Products
                    Where p.ProductID = productID
                    Select p).FirstOrDefault
        Return prod
    End Function

    Public Function GetEmployees() As List(Of Employee)
        Dim ctx As New NWDataContext
        Dim emps = (From emp In ctx.Employees
                    Select emp).ToList
        Return emps
    End Function
```

```
Public Function GetCustomers() As List(Of Customer)
    Dim ctx As New NWDataContext
    Dim customers = (From cust In ctx.Customers
                Select cust).ToList
    Return customers
End Function

End Class
```

The SaveOrder method of the NWData class uses the SubmitChanges method of the Data-Context object generated by the designer, the NWDataContext object, to submit the new order to the database. The SubmitChanges method will insert the header in the Orders table and the details in the Order Details table. It will also handle the identity issue automatically.

USING THE TRANSACTIONSCOPE CLASS

The implementation of the SaveOrder method is trivial compared to the SaveOrder method of the NWOrder class we use with the frmSQL form, because now we don't have to perform the INSERT statements ourselves. To submit the changes made to a table back to the database, you must call the InsertOnSumbit/DeleteOnSubmit method of the appropriate table. These two methods do not submit any data to the database. They accept an entity that represents a new or deleted row as an argument and add it to the collection that represents the table. The rows are submitted to the database when you call the SubmitChanges method.

Even though all the rows will be inserted to the database with a single method, the SubmitChanges method, you must still execute this method in the context of a transaction. This time I'll use a different, and simpler, approach to the transactional update. The Framework provides the TransactionScope object, which initiates a transaction automatically. To use TransactionScope, you must first add a reference to the System.Transactions namespace to the project. Then, you must create a new instance of this class and embed the statements that must be executed in the transaction's scope in a Using statement. Listing 16.6 shows the implementation of the SaveOrder method of the NWData class.

LISTING 16.6:   Implementing a transaction with a TransactionScope object

```
Public Shared Function SaveOrder(ByVal newOrder As Order) As Integer
    Dim ctx As New NWDataContext
    Using TR As New System.Transactions.TransactionScope
        ctx.Orders.InsertOnSubmit(newOrder)
        Try
            ctx.SubmitChanges()
            TR.Complete()
        Catch ex As Exception
            Return (-1)
        End Try
    End Using
    Return newOrder.OrderID
End Function
```

One statement that may not be clear in the listing is the line that returns the value −1 when the transaction fails. Normally, the method returns the ID of the newly inserted row, and our application expects a positive value. The ID can also be accessed through the OrderID property of the newOrder object. This property has no value when the method is called, but the SubmitChanges method updates the fields of the newOrder object for us.

The newOrder.OrderID property is updated when the SubmitChanges method submits the order header to the Orders table. If this operation succeeds, the ID of the new order is assigned to the OrderID property. Should the transaction fail while inserting the row details, the value of the OrderID property won't change automatically. It will still have a valid value, even though no rows will be committed either to the Orders or Order Details table. That's why you need a return value from the SaveOrders method to indicate the success or failure of the operation.

The data-access layer of the form that uses the LINQ to SQL component to interact with the database is quite short and much easier to understand. I repeat it here for your convenience so you can compare it to the custom NWData class you developed earlier. As you can understand, the code is so much simpler because of the DataContext object, which abstracts the database tables and much of the functionality of the operations that are performed against these tables.

LISTING 16.7: The implementation of the data-access layer with a DataContext object

```
Public Class NWData
    Public Function GetProductByID(ByVal productID As Integer) As Product
        Dim ctx As New NWDataContext
        Dim prod = (From p In ctx.Products
                    Where p.ProductID = productID
                    Select p).FirstOrDefault
        Return prod
    End Function

    Public Function GetEmployees() As List(Of Employee)
        Dim ctx As New NWDataContext
        Dim emps = (From emp In ctx.Employees
                    Select emp).ToList
        Return emps
    End Function

    Public Function GetCustomers() As List(Of Customer)
        Dim ctx As New NWDataContext
        Dim customers = (From cust In ctx.Customers
                    Select cust).ToList
        Return customers
    End Function

    Public Shared Function SaveOrder(ByVal newOrder As Order) As Integer
        Dim ctx As New NWDataContext

        Using TR As New System.Transactions.TransactionScope
            ctx.Orders.InsertOnSubmit(newOrder)
```

```
        Try
            ctx.SubmitChanges()
            TR.Complete()
        Catch ex As Exception
            Return (-1)
        End Try
    End Using
    Return newOrder.OrderID
  End Function
End Class
```

This concludes the first part of the chapter where you've learned how to use objects to represent the data stored in the database tables as custom objects. In the second half, you'll learn about DataSets, which are a standard mechanism for storing data at the client. DataSets are not new to Visual Studio; they have been around for many years, and they are used heavily in data-driven applications.

Storing Data in DataSets

The process of building data-driven applications isn't complicated and to a large extent is abstracted by the Connection, Command, and DataReader classes. You have seen a few interesting examples of these classes and should be ready to use them in your applications. The problem with these classes is that they don't offer a consistent method for storing the data at the client. The approach of converting the data into business objects and working with classes is fine, but you must come up with a data-storage mechanism at the client. The LINQ to SQL component simplifies this task, and you saw how to automatically convert tables into custom objects.

You can store the data in a ListBox control, as we have done in some examples. You can also create a List of custom objects, as we did in the preceding section. The issue of storing data at the client isn't pressing when the client application is connected to the database and all updates take place in real time. As soon as the user edits a row, the row is submitted to the database, and no work is lost.

In some situations, however, the client isn't connected at all times. There's actually a class of applications that are referred to as occasionally *connected* or *disconnected*, and the techniques presented so far do not address the needs of these applications. Disconnected applications read some data when a connection is available, and then they disconnect from the server. Users are allowed to interact with the data at the client, but they work with a local cache of the data; they can insert new rows, edit existing ones, and delete selected rows. The changes, however, are not submitted immediately to the server. It's imperative that the data is persisted at the client. (We don't want users to lose their edits because their notebooks ran out of battery power or because of a bug in the application.) When a connection becomes available again, the application should be able to figure out the rows that have been edited and submit all changes to the server. To simplify the storage of data at the client, ADO.NET offers a powerful mechanism, the DataSet.

You can think of the DataSet as a small database that lives in memory. It's not actually a database, but it's made up of related tables that have the same structure as database tables. The similarities end there, however, because the DataSet doesn't impose all types of constraints, and you can't exploit its data with SQL statements. It's made up of DataTable objects, and each DataTable in the DataSet corresponds to a separate query. Like database tables, the DataTable objects consist of DataColumn and DataRow objects. The DataColumn objects specify the structure of the table, and the DataRow objects contain the rows of the table. You can also establish relations between the tables in the DataSet, and these relations are represented with DataRelation objects. As you realize, the DataSet lets you copy a small section of the database at the client, work with it, and then submit the changes made at the client back to the database.

The real power of the DataSet is that it keeps track of the changes made to its data. It knows which rows have been modified, added, or deleted, and it provides a mechanism for submitting the changes automatically. Actually, it's not the DataSet that submits the changes but a class that's used in tandem with the DataSet: the DataAdapter class. Moreover, the DataSet class provides the WriteXml and ReadXml methods, which allow you to save its data to a local file. Note that these methods save the data to a local file so you can reload the DataSet later, but they do not submit the data to the database.

With the new data-related technologies introduced during the past few years, such as LINQ to SQL, the Entity Framework (EF), and LINQ to Entities (discussed in the next chapter), DataSets will soon become obsolete. Yet, there are only a few data-driven applications out there that are not based on DataSets. I've decided to include this section because you'll inevitably run into applications that use DataSets.

Filling DataSets

DataSets are filled with DataAdapters, and there are two ways to create a DataSet: You can use the visual tools of Visual Studio or create a DataSet entirely from within your code. DataSets created at runtime are not typed, because the compiler doesn't know what type of information you're going to store in them. DataSets created at design time with the visual tools are strongly typed, because the compiler knows what type of information will be stored in them.

The following statements demonstrate the difference between untyped and typed DataSets. To access the `ProductName` column of the first row in the Products table in an untyped DataSet, you'd use an expression like the following:

```
Dim row As DataRow = Products1.Products.Rows(0).Item("ProductName")
```

If the *Products1* DataSet is typed, you can create an object of the `Products.ProductsRow` type with the following statement:

```
Dim productRow As Products.ProductsRow = Products1.Products.Rows(0)
```

Then use the *productRow* variable to access the columns of the corresponding row:

```
productRow.ProductName
productRow.UnitPrice
```

The difference between typed and untyped DataSets is also demonstrated by the declaration of the *row* and *productRow* variables. Where *row* is a variable that represents a row in a DataSet, the *productRow* variable represents a row in a DataSet that stores the rows of the Products table.

As you can see, the visual tools generate a number of classes on the fly, such as the ProductsRow class, and expose them to your code. As soon as you enter the string `productRow` and the following period in the code window, you will see the members of the ProductsRow class, which include the names of the columns in the corresponding table. In this chapter, I discuss untyped DataSets. In the following chapter, I'll discuss in detail typed DataSets and how to use them in building data-bound applications.

THE DATAADAPTER CLASS

To use DataSets in your application, you must first create a DataAdapter object, which is the preferred technique for populating the DataSet. The DataAdapter is nothing more than a collection of Command objects that are needed to execute the various SQL statements against the database. As you recall from our previous discussion, we interact with the database by using four different command types: one to select the data and load them to the client computer with the help of a DataReader object (a Command object with the SELECT statement) and three more to submit to the database the new rows (a Command object with the INSERT statement), update existing rows (a Command object with the UPDATE statement), and delete existing rows (a Command object with the DELETE statement). A DataAdapter is a container for Connection and Command objects. If you declare a SqlDataAdapter object with a statement like the following:

```
Dim DA As New SqlDataAdapter
```

you'll see that it exposes the properties described in Table 16.1.

TABLE 16.1: SqlDataAdapter object properties

PROPERTY	DESCRIPTION
InsertCommand	A Command object that's executed to insert a new row
UpdateCommand	A Command object that's executed to update a row
DeleteCommand	A Command object that's executed to delete a row
SelectCommand	A Command object that's executed to retrieve selected rows

Each of these properties is an object and has its own Connection property, because each may not act on the same database (as unlikely as it may be). These properties also expose their own Parameters collection, which you must populate accordingly before executing a command.

The DataAdapter class performs the two basic tasks of a data-driven application: It retrieves data from the database to populate a DataSet and submits the changes to the database. To populate a DataSet, use the Fill method, which fills a specific DataTable object. There's one DataAdapter per DataTable object in the DataSet, and you must call the corresponding Fill method to populate each DataTable. To submit the changes to the database, use the Update method of the appropriate DataAdapter object. The Update method is overloaded, and you can use it to submit a single row to the database or all edited rows in a DataTable. The Update method uses the appropriate Command object to interact with the database.

Passing Parameters Through the DataAdapter

Let's build a DataSet in our code to demonstrate the use of the DataAdapter objects. As with all the data objects mentioned in this chapter, you must add a reference to the System.Data namespace with the Imports statement.

Start by declaring a DataSet variable:

```
Dim DS As New DataSet
```

To access the classes discussed in this section, you must import the System.Data namespace in your module. Then create the various commands that will interact with the database:

```
Dim cmdSelectCustomers As String = "SELECT * FROM Customers " &
            "WHERE Customers.Country=@country"
Dim cmdDeleteCustomer As String = "DELETE Customers WHERE CustomerID=@CustomerID"
Dim cmdEditCustomer As String = "UPDATE Customers " &
            "SET CustomerID = @CustomerID, CompanyName = @CompanyName, " &
            "ContactName = @ContactName, ContactTitle = @ContactTitle " &
            "WHERE CustomerID = @CustID"
Dim cmdInsertCustomer As String = "INSERT Customers " &
            " (CustomerID, CompanyName, ContactName, ContactTitle) " &
            "VALUES(@CustomerID, @CompanyName, @ContactName, @ContactTitle) "
```

You can also create stored procedures for the four basic operations and use their names in the place of the SQL statements. It's actually a bit faster, and safer, to use stored procedures. I've included only a few columns in the examples to keep the statements reasonably short. The various commands use parameterized queries to interact with the database, and you must add the appropriate parameters to each Command object. After the SQL statements are in place, we can build the four Command properties of the DataAdapter object. Start by declaring a DataAdapter object:

```
Dim DACustomers As New SqlDataAdapter()
```

Because all Command properties of the DataAdapter object will act on the same database, you can create a Connection object and reuse it as needed:

```
Dim CN As New SqlConnection(ConnString)
```

The *ConnString* variable is a string with the proper connection string. Now we can create the four Command properties of the *DACustomers* DataAdapter object.

Let's start with the SelectCommand property of the DataAdapter object. The following statements create a new Command object based on the preceding SELECT statement and then set up a Parameter object for the *@country* parameter of the SELECT statement:

```
DACustomers.SelectCommand = New SqlClient.SqlCommand(cmdSelectCustomers)
DACustomers.SelectCommand.Connection = CN
Dim param As New SqlParameter
param.ParameterName = "@Country"
param.SqlDbType = SqlDbType.VarChar
param.Size = 15
param.Direction = ParameterDirection.Input
param.IsNullable = False
param.Value = "Germany"
DACustomers.SelectCommand.Parameters.Add(param)
```

This is the easier, if rather verbose, method of specifying a Parameter object. You are familiar with the Parameter object properties and already know how to configure and add parameters to a Command object via a single statement. As a reminder, an overloaded form of the Add method allows you to configure and attach a Parameter object to a Command object Parameters collection with a single, if lengthy, statement:

```
DA.SelectCommand.Parameters.Add(
      New System.Data.SqlClient.qlParameter(
      paramName, paramType, paramSize, paramDirection,
      paramNullable, paramPrecision, paramScale,
      columnName, rowVersion, paramValue)
```

The *paramPrecsion* and *paramScale* arguments apply to numeric parameters, and you can set them to 0 for string parameters. The *paramNullable* argument determines whether the parameter can assume a Null value. The *columnName* argument is the name of the table column to which the parameter will be matched. (You need this information for the INSERT and UPDATE commands.) The *rowVersion* argument determines which version of the field in the DataSet will be used — in other words, whether the DataAdapter will pass the current version (*DataRowVersion.Current*) or the original version (*DataRowVersion.Original*) of the field to the parameter object. The last argument, *paramValue*, is the parameter's value. You can specify a value as we did in the SelectCommand example, or you can set this argument to Nothing and let the DataAdapter object assign the proper value to each parameter. (You'll see in a moment how this argument is used with the INSERT and UPDATE commands.)

Finally, you can open the connection to the database and then call the DataAdapter's Fill method to populate a DataTable in the DataSet:

```
CN.Open
DACustomers.Fill(DS, "Customers")
CN.Close
```

The Fill method accepts as arguments a DataSet object and the name of the DataTable it will populate. The *DACustomers* DataAdapter is associated with a single DataTable and knows how to populate it, as well as how to submit the changes to the database. The DataTable name is arbitrary and need not match the name of the database table where the data originates. The four basic operations of the DataAdapter (which are none other than the four basic data-access operations of a client application) are also known as CRUD operations: Create/Retrieve/Update/Delete.

THE COMMANDBUILDER CLASS

Each DataAdapter object that you set up in your code is associated with a single SELECT query, which may select data from one or multiple joined tables. The INSERT/UPDATE/DELETE queries of the DataAdapter can submit data to a single table. So far, you've seen how to manually set up each Command object in a DataAdapter object. There's a simpler method to specify the queries: You start with the SELECT statement, which selects data from a single table, and then let a CommandBuilder object infer the other three statements from the SELECT statement. Let's see this technique in action.

Declare a new SqlCommandBuilder object by passing the name of the adapter for which you want to generate the statements:

```
Dim CustomersCB As SqlCommandBuilder =
              New SqlCommandBuilder(DA)
```

This statement is all it takes to generate the InsertCommand, UpdateCommand, and DeleteCommand objects of the *DACustomers* SqlDataAdapter object. When the compiler runs into the previous statement, it will generate the appropriate Command objects and attach them to the *DACustomers* SqlDataAdapter. Here are the SQL statements generated by the CommandBuilder object for the Products table of the Northwind database:

UPDATE **Command**
```
UPDATE [Products] SET [ProductName] = @p1,
       [CategoryID] = @p2, [UnitPrice] = @p3,
       [UnitsInStock] = @p4, [UnitsOnOrder] = @p5
WHERE  (([ProductID] = @p6))
```

INSERT **Command**
```
INSERT INTO [Products]
          ([ProductName], [CategoryID],
           [UnitPrice], [UnitsInStock],
           [UnitsOnOrder])
           VALUES (@p1, @p2, @p3, @p4, @p5)
```

DELETE **Command**
```
DELETE FROM [Products] WHERE (([ProductID] = @p1))
```

These statements are based on the SELECT statement and are quite simple. You may notice that the UPDATE statement simply overrides the current values in the Products table. The CommandBuilder can generate a more elaborate statement that takes into consideration concurrency. It can generate a statement that compares the values read into the DataSet to the values stored in the database. If these values are different, which means that another user has edited the same row since the row was read into the DataSet, it doesn't perform the update. To specify the type of UPDATE statement you want to create with the CommandBuilder object, set its ConflictOption property, whose value is a member of the ConflictOption enumeration: *CompareAllSearchValues* (compares the values of all columns specified in the SELECT statement), *CompareRowVersion* (compares the original and current versions of the row), and *OverwriteChanges* (simply overwrites the fields of the current row in the database).

The *OverwriteChanges* option generates a simple statement that locates the row to be updated with its ID and overwrites the current field values unconditionally. If you set the ConflictOption property to *CompareAllSearchValues*, the CommandBuilder will generate the following UPDATE statement:

```
UPDATE [Products]
SET    [ProductName] = @p1, [CategoryID] = @p2,
       [UnitPrice] = @p3, [UnitsInStock] = @p4,
```

```
        [UnitsOnOrder] = @p5
 WHERE  (([ProductID] = @p6) AND ([ProductName] = @p7)
        AND ((@p8 = 1 AND [CategoryID] IS NULL) OR
        ([CategoryID] = @p9)) AND
        ((@p10 = 1 AND [UnitPrice] IS NULL) OR
        ([UnitPrice] = @p11)) AND
        ((@p12 = 1 AND [UnitsInStock] IS NULL) OR
        ([UnitsInStock] = @p13)) AND
        ((@p14 = 1 AND [UnitsOnOrder] IS NULL) OR
        ([UnitsOnOrder] = @p15)))
```

This is a lengthy statement indeed. The row to be updated is identified by its ID, but the operation doesn't take place if any of the other fields don't match the value read into the DataSet. This statement will fail to update the corresponding row in the Products table if it has already been edited by another user.

The last member of the ConflictOption enumeration, the *CompareRowVersion* option, works with tables that have a TimeStamp column, which is automatically set to the time of the update. If the row has a time stamp that's later than the value read when the DataSet was populated, it means that the row has been updated already by another user and the UPDATE statement will fail.

The SimpleDataSet sample project, which is discussed later in this chapter and demonstrates the basic DataSet operations, generates the UPDATE/INSERT/DELETE statements for the Categories and Products tables with the help of the CommandBuilder class and displays them on the form when the application starts. Open the project to examine the code, and change the setting of the ConflictOption property to see how it affects the autogenerated SQL statements.

Accessing the DataSet's Tables

The DataSet consists of one or more tables, which are represented by the DataTable class. Each DataTable in the DataSet may correspond to a table in the database or a view. When you execute a query that retrieves fields from multiple tables, all selected columns will end up in a single DataTable of the DataSet. You can select any DataTable in the DataSet by its index or its name:

```
DS.Tables(0)
DS.Tables("Customers")
```

Each table contains columns, which you can access through the Columns collection. The Columns collection consists of DataColumn objects, with one DataColumn object for each column in the corresponding table. The Columns collection is the schema of the DataTable object, and the DataColumn class exposes properties that describe a column. *ColumnName* is the column's name, *DataType* is the column's type, *MaxLength* is the maximum size of text columns, and so on. The AutoIncrement property is True for Identity columns, and the AllowDBNull property determines whether the column allows Null values. In short, all the properties you can set visually as you design a table are also available to your code through the Columns collection of the DataTable object. You can use the DataColumn class's properties to find out the structure of the table or to create a new table. To add a table to a DataSet, you can create a new DataTable object. Then create a DataColumn object for each column, set its properties, and add the DataColumn objects to the DataTable Columns collection. Finally, add the DataTable to the DataSet. The process is described in detail in the online documentation, so I won't repeat it here.

Working with Rows

As far as data are concerned, each DataTable consists of DataRow objects. All DataRow objects of a DataTable have the same structure and can be accessed through an index, which is the row's order in the table. To access the rows of the Customers table, use an expression like the following:

```
DS.Customers.Rows(iRow)
```

where *iRow* is an integer value from zero (the first row in the table) up to DS.Customers.Rows .Count − 1 (the last row in the table). To access the individual fields of a DataRow object, use the Item property. This property returns the value of a column in the current row by either its index,

```
DS.Customers.Rows(0).Item(0)
```

or its name:

```
DS.Customers.Rows(0).Item("CustomerID")
```

To iterate through the rows of a DataSet, you can set up a For…Next loop like the following:

```
Dim iRow As Integer
For iRow = 0 To DSProducts1.Products.Rows.Count - 1
    ' process row: DSProducts.Products.Rows(iRow)
Next
```

Alternatively, you can use a For Each…Next loop to iterate through the rows of the DataTable:

```
Dim product As DataRow
For Each product In DSProducts1.Products.Rows
    ' process prodRow row:
    ' product.Item("ProductName"),
    ' product.Item("UnitPrice"), and so on
Next
```

To edit a specific row, simply assign new values to its columns. To change the value of the ContactName column of a specific row in a DataTable that holds the customers of the Northwind database, use a statement like the following:

```
DS.Customers(3).Item("ContactName") = "new contact name"
```

The new values are usually entered by a user on the appropriate interface, and in your code you'll most likely assign a control's property to a row's column with statements like the following:

```
If txtName.Text.Trim <> "" Then
    DS.Customers(3).Item("ContactName") = txtName.Text
Else
    DS.Customers(3).Item("ContactName") = DBNull.Value
End If
```

The code segment assumes that when the user doesn't supply a value for a column, this column is set to null (if the column is nullable, of course, and no default value has been specified). If the control contains a value, this value is assigned to the ContactName column of the fourth row in the Customers DataTable of the *DS* DataSet.

Handling Null Values

An important (and quite often tricky) issue in coding data-driven applications is the handling of Null values. Null values are special, in the sense that you can't assign them to control properties or use them in other expressions. Every expression that involves Null values will throw a runtime exception. The DataRow object provides the IsNull method, which returns True if the column specified by its argument is a Null value:

```
If customerRow.IsNull("ContactName") Then
    ' handle Null value
Else
    ' process value
End If
```

In a typed DataSet, DataRow objects provide a separate method to determine whether a specific column has a Null value. If the *customerRow* DataRow belongs to a typed DataSet, you can use the IsContactNameNull method instead:

```
If customerRow.IsContactNameNull Then
    ' handle Null value for the ContactName
Else
    ' process value: customerRow.ContactName
End If
```

If you need to map Null columns to specific values, you can do so with the ISNULL() function of T-SQL, as you retrieve the data from the database. In many applications, you want to display an empty string or a zero value in place of a Null field. You can avoid all the comparisons in your code by retrieving the corresponding field with the ISNULL() function in your SQL statement. Where the column name would appear in the SELECT statement, use an expression like the following:

```
ISNULL(customerBalance, 0.00)
```

If the *customerBalance* column is Null for a specific row, SQL Server will return the numeric value zero. This value can be used in reports or other calculations in your code. Notice that the customer's balance shouldn't be Null. A customer always has a balance, even if it's zero. When a product's price is Null, it means that we don't know the price of the product (and therefore can't sell it). In this case, a Null value can't be substituted with a zero value. You must always carefully handle Null columns in your code, and how you'll handle them depends on the nature of the data they represent.

Adding and Deleting Rows

To add a new row to a DataTable, you must first create a DataRow object, set its column values, and then call the Add method of the Rows collection of the DataTable to which the new row belongs, passing the new row as an argument. If the *DS* DataSet contains the Customers DataTable, the following statements will add a new row for the Customers table:

```
Dim newRow As New DataRow = dataTable.NewRow
newRow.Item("CompanyName") = "new company name"
newRow.Item("CustomerName") = "new customer name"
newRow.Item("ContactName") = "new contact name"
DS.Customers.Rows.Add(newRow)
```

Notice that you need not set the CustomerID column. This column is defined as an Identity column and is assigned a new value automatically by the DataSet. Of course, when the row is submitted to the database, the ID assigned to the new customer by the DataSet may already be taken. SQL Server will assign a new unique value to this column when it inserts it into the table. It's recommended that you set the AutoIncrementSeed property of an Identity column to 0 and the AutoIncrement property to –1 so that new rows are assigned consecutive negative IDs in the DataSet. Presumably, the corresponding columns in the database have a positive Identity setting, so when these rows are submitted to the database, they're assigned the next Identity value automatically. If you're designing a new database, use globally unique identifiers (GUIDs) instead of Identity values. A GUID can be created at the client and is unique: It can be generated at the client and will also be inserted in the table when the row is committed. To create GUIDs, call the NewGuid method of the Guid class:

```
newRow.Item("CustomerID") = Guid.NewGuid
```

To delete a row, you can remove it from the Rows collection with the Remove or RemoveAt method of the Rows collection, or you can call the Delete method of the DataRow object that represents the row. The Remove method accepts a DataRow object as an argument and removes it from the collection:

```
Dim customerRow As DS.CustomerRow
customerRow = DS.Customers.Rows(2)
DS.Customers.Remove(customerRow)
```

The RemoveAt method accepts as an argument the index of the row you want to delete in the Rows collection. Finally, the Delete method is a method of the DataRow class, and you must apply it to a DataRow object that represents the row to be deleted:

```
customerRow.Delete
```

DELETING VERSUS REMOVING ROWS

The Remove method removes a row from the DataSet as if it were never read when the DataSet was filled. Deleted rows are not always removed from the DataSet, because the DataSet maintains its state. If the row you've deleted exists in the underlying table (in other words, if it's a row that was read into the DataSet when you filled it), the row will be marked as deleted but will not be removed from the DataSet. If it's a row that was added to the DataSet after it was read from the database, the deleted row is actually removed from the Rows collection.

You can physically remove deleted rows from the DataSet by calling the DataSet's AcceptChanges method. However, after you've accepted the changes in the DataSet, you can no longer submit any updates to the database. If you call the DataSet RejectChanges method, the deleted rows will be restored in the DataSet.

Navigating Through a DataSet

The DataTables making up a DataSet may be related — they usually are. There are methods that allow you to navigate from table to table following the relations between their rows. For example, you can start with a row in the Customers DataTable, retrieve its child rows in the Orders DataTable (the orders placed by the selected customer), and then drill down to the details of each of the selected orders.

The relations of a DataSet are DataRelation objects and are stored in the `Relations` property of the DataSet. Each relation is identified by a name, the two tables it relates to, and the fields of the tables on which the relation is based. It's possible to create relations in your code, and the process is really quite simple. Let's consider a DataSet that contains the Categories and Products tables. To establish a relation between the two tables, create two instances of the DataTable object to reference the two tables:

```
Dim tblCategories As DataTable = DS.Categories
Dim tblProducts As DataTable = DS.Products
```

Then create two DataColumn objects to reference the columns on which the relation is based. They're the `CategoryID` columns of both tables:

```
Dim colCatCategoryID As DataColumn =
                tblCategories.Columns("CategoryID")
Dim colProdCategoryID As DataColumn =
                tblProducts.Columns("CategoryID")
```

And finally, create a new DataRelation object, and add it to the DataSet:

```
Dim DR As DataRelation
DR = New DataRelation("Categories2Products",
                colCatCategoryID, colProdCategoryID)
```

Notice that you need to specify only the columns involved in the relation, and not the tables to be related. The information about the tables is derived from the DataColumn objects. The first argument of the DataRelation constructor is the relation's name. If the relation involves multiple columns, the second and third arguments of the constructor become arrays of Data-Column objects.

To navigate through related tables, the DataRow object provides the `GetChildRows` method, which returns the current row's child rows as an array of DataRow objects, and the `GetParentRow/GetParentRows` methods, which return the current row's parent row(s). `GetParentRow` returns a single DataRow object, and `GetParentRows` returns an array of DataRow objects. Because a DataTable may be related to multiple DataTables, you must also specify the name of the relation. Consider a DataSet with the Products, Categories, and Suppliers tables. Each row of the Products table can have two parent rows, depending on which relation you want to follow. To retrieve the product category, use a statement like the following:

```
DS.Products(iRow).GetParentRow("CategoriesProducts")
```

The product supplier is given by the following expression:

```
DS.Products(iRow).GetParentRow("SuppliersProducts")
```

If you start with a category, you can find out the related products with the `GetChildRows` method, which accepts as an argument the name of a Relation object:

```
DS.Categories(iRow).GetChildRows("CategoriesProducts")
```

To iterate through the products of a specific category (in other words, the rows of the Products table that belong to a category), set up a loop like the following:

```
Dim product As DataRow
For Each product In DS.Categories(iRow).
                    GetChildRows("CategoriesProducts")
' process product
Next
```

ROW STATES AND VERSIONS

Each row in the DataSet has a `State` property. This property indicates the row's state, and its value is a member of the `DataRowState` enumeration, whose members are described in Table 16.2.

You can use the `GetChanges` method to find the rows that must be added to the underlying table in the database, the rows to be updated, and the rows to be removed from the underlying table.

If you want to update all rows of a DataTable, call an overloaded form of the DataAdapter `Update` method, which accepts as an argument a DataTable and submits its rows to the database. The edited rows are submitted through the UpdateCommand object of the appropriate DataAdapter, the new rows are submitted through the Insert-Command object, and the deleted rows are submitted through the DeleteCommand object.

Instead of submitting the entire table, however, you can create a subset of a DataTable that contains only the rows that have been edited, inserted, or deleted. The GetChanges method of the DataTable object retrieves a subset of rows, depending on the argument you pass to it, and this argument is a member of the DataRowState enumeration:

```
Dim DT As New DataTable =
    Products1.Products.GetChanges(DataRowState.Deleted)
```

TABLE 16.2:   DataSet state property members

PROPERTY MEMBER	DESCRIPTION
Added	The row has been added to the DataTable, and the AcceptChanges method has not been called.
Deleted	The row was deleted from the DataTable, and the AcceptChanges method has not been called.
Detached	The row has been created with its constructor but has not yet been added to a DataTable.
Modified	The row has been edited, and the AcceptChanges method has not been called.
Unchanged	The row has not been edited or deleted since it was read from the database or the AcceptChanges was last called. (In other words, the row's fields are identical to the values read from the database.)

This statement retrieves the rows of the Customers table that were deleted and stores them in a new DataTable. The new DataTable has the same structure as the one from which the rows were copied, and you can access its rows and their columns as you would access any DataTable of a DataSet. You can even pass this DataTable as an argument to the appropriate DataAdapter's Update method. This form of the Update method allows you to submit selected changes to the database.

In addition to a state, rows have a version. What makes the DataSet such a powerful tool for disconnected applications is that it maintains not only data but also the changes in its data. The Rows property of the DataTable object is usually called with the index of the desired row, but it accepts a second argument, which determines the version of the row you want to read:

```
DS.Tables(0).Rows(i, version)
```

This argument is a member of the DataRowVersion enumeration, whose values are described in Table 16.3.

TABLE 16.3: DataRowVersion enumeration members

ENUMERATION MEMBER	DESCRIPTION
Current	Returns the row's current values (the fields as they were edited in the DataSet).
Default	Returns the default values for the row. For added, edited, and current rows, the default version is the same as the current version. For deleted rows, the default versions are the same as the original versions. If the row doesn't belong to a DataTable, the default version is the same as the proposed version.
Original	Returns the row's original values (the values read from the database).
Proposed	Returns the row's proposed value (the values assigned to a row that doesn't yet belong to a DataTable).

If you attempt to submit an edited row to the database and the operation fails, you can give the user the option to edit the row's current version or to restore the row's original values. To retrieve the original version of a row, use an expression like the following:

```
DS.Tables(0).Row(i, DataRowVersion.Original)
```

Although you can't manipulate the version of a row directly, you can use the AcceptChanges and RejectChanges methods to either accept the changes or reject them. These two methods are exposed by the DataSet, DataTable, and DataRow classes. The difference is the scope: Applying RejectChanges to the DataSet restores all changes made to the DataSet (not a very practical operation), whereas applying RejectChanges to a DataTable object restores the changes made to the specific table rows; applying the same method to the DataRow object restores the changes made to a single row.

The AcceptChanges method sets the original value of the affected row(s) to the proposed value. Deleted rows are physically removed. The RejectChanges method removes the proposed version of the affected row(s). You can call the RejectChanges method when the user wants to get rid of all changes in the DataSet. Notice that after you call the AcceptChanges method, you can no longer update the underlying tables in the database, because the DataSet no longer knows which rows were edited, inserted, or deleted. Call the AcceptChanges method only for DataSets you plan to persist on disk and not submit to the database.

Performing Update Operations

One of the most important topics in database programming is how to submit changes to the database. There are basically two modes of operation: single updates and multiple updates. A client application running on a local-area network along with the database server can (and should) submit changes as soon as they occur. If the client application is not connected to the database server at all times, changes may accumulate at the client and can be submitted in batch mode when a connection to the server is available.

From a developer's point of view, the difference between the two modes is how you handle update errors. If you submit individual rows to the database and the update operation fails, you can display a warning and let the user edit the data again. You can write code to restore the row to its original state, or not. In any case, it's fairly easy to handle isolated errors. If the application submits a few dozen rows to the database, several of these rows may fail to update the underlying table, and you'll have to handle the update errors from within your code. At the very least, you must validate the data as best as you can at the client before submitting it to the database. No matter how thoroughly you validate your data, however, you can't be sure that they will be inserted into the database successfully.

Another factor you should consider is the nature of the data you work with. Let's consider an application that maintains a database of books and an application that takes orders. The book maintenance application handles publishers, authors, translators, and related data. If two dozen users are entering and editing titles, they will all work with the same authors. If you allow them to work in disconnected mode, the same author name may be entered several times, because no user can see the changes made by any other user. This application should be connected: Every time a user adds a new author, the table with the author names in the database must be updated so that other users can see the new author. The same goes for publishers, translators, topics, and so on. A disconnected application of this type should also include utilities to consolidate multiple author and publisher names.

An order-taking application can safely work in a disconnected mode, because orders entered by one user are not aware of and don't interfere with the orders entered by another user. You can install the client application on several salespersons' notebooks so they can take orders on the go and upload them after establishing a connection between the notebook and the database server (which may even happen when the salespeople return to the company's offices).

Updating the Database with the DataAdapter

The simplest method of submitting changes to the database is to use each DataAdapter's Update method. The DataTable object provides the members you need to retrieve the rows that failed to update the database, as well as the messages returned by the database server, and you'll see how these members are used in this section. The Update method may not have updated all the rows in the underlying tables. If a product was removed from the Products table in the database in the meantime, the DataAdapter's UpdateCommand will not be able to submit the changes made to that specific product. A product with a negative value may very well exist at the client, but the database will reject this row, because it violates one of the constraints of the Products table. It's also important to validate the data at the client to minimize errors when you submit changes to the database.

If the database returned any errors during the update process, the HasErrors property of the DataSet object will be set to True. You can retrieve the rows in error from each table with the GetErrors method of the DataTable class. This method returns an array of DataRow objects, and you can process them in any way you see fit. The code shown in Listing 16.8 iterates through the rows of the Categories table that are in error and prints the description of the error in the Output window.

LISTING 16.8:   Retrieving and displaying the update errors

```
If Products1.HasErrors Then
    If Products1.Categories.GetErrors.Length = 0 Then
        Console.WriteLine("Errors in the Categories DataTable")
            Else
```

```
        Dim RowsInError() As Products.CategoriesRow
        RowsInError = Products1.Categories.GetErrors
        Dim row As Products.CategoriesRow
        Console.WriteLine("Errors in the Categories table")
        For Each row In RowsInError
            Console.WriteLine(vbTab & row.CategoryID & vbTab &
                        row.RowError)
        Next
    End If
Endif
```

The DataRow object exposes the RowError property, which is a description of the error that prevented the update for the specific row. It's possible that the same row has more than a single error. To retrieve all columns in error, call the DataRow object's GetColumnsInError method, which returns an array of DataColumn objects that are the columns in error.

Handling Identity Columns

An issue that deserves special attention while coding data-driven applications is the handling of Identity columns. Identity columns are used as primary keys, and each row is guaranteed to have a unique Identity value because this value is assigned by the database the moment the row is inserted into its table. The client application can't generate unique values. When new rows are added to a DataSet, they're assigned Identity values, but these values are unique in the context of the local DataSet. When a row is submitted to the database, any Identity column will be assigned its final value by the database. The temporary Identity value assigned by the DataSet is also used as a foreign key value by the related rows, and we must make sure that every time an Identity value is changed, the change will propagate to the related tables.

Handling Identity values is an important topic, and here's why: Consider an application for entering orders or invoices. Each order has a header and a number of detail lines, which are related to a header row with the OrderID column. This column is the primary key in the Orders table and is the foreign key in the Order Details table. If the primary key of a header is changed, the foreign keys of the related rows must change also.

The trick in handling Identity columns is to make sure that the values generated by the DataSet will be replaced by the database. You do so by specifying that the Identity column's starting value is –1 and its autoincrement is –1. The first ID generated by the DataSet will be –1, the second one will be –2, and so on. Negative Identity values will be rejected by the database, because the AutoIncrement properties in the database schema are positive. By submitting negative Identity values to SQL Server, you ensure that new, positive values will be generated and used by SQL Server.

You must also make sure that the new values will replace the old ones in the related rows. In other words, we want these values to propagate to all related rows. The DataSet allows you to specify that changes in the primary key will propagate through the related rows with the UpdateRule property of the Relation.ChildKeyConstraint property. Each relation exposes the ChildKeyConstraint property, which determines how changes in the primary key of a relation affect the child rows. This property is an object that exposes a few properties of its own. The two properties we're interested in are UpdateRule and DeleteRule (what happens to the child rows when the parent row's primary key is changed or when the primary key is deleted). You can use one of the rules described in Table 16.4.

TABLE 16.4:   *ChildKeyConstraint* property rules

RULE	DESCRIPTION
Cascade	Foreign keys in related rows change every time the primary key changes value so that they'll always remain related to their parent row.
None	The foreign key in the related row(s) is not affected.
SetDefault	The foreign key in the related row(s) is set to the DefaultValue property for the same column.
SetNull	The foreign key in the related rows is set to Null.

As you can see, setting the UpdateRule property to anything other than Cascade will break the relation. If the database doesn't enforce the relation, you may be able to break it. If the relation is enforced, however, UpdateRule must be set to *Rule.Cascade*, or the database will not accept changes that violate its referential integrity.

If you set UpdateRule to None, you may be able to submit the order to the database. However, the detail rows may refer to a different order. This will happen when the ID of the header is changed because the temporary value is already taken. The detail rows will be inserted with the temporary key and added to the details of another order. Notice that no runtime exception will be thrown, and the only way to catch this type of error is by examining the data inserted into the database by your application. By using negative values at the DataSet, you make sure that the ID of both the header and all detail rows will be rejected by the database and replaced with valid values. It goes without saying that it's always a good idea to read back the rows you submit to the database and "refresh" the data at the client. In the case of the ordering application, for example, you could read back the order before printing it so that any errors will be caught as soon as they occur, instead of discovering later orders that do not match their printouts.

VB 2010 at Work: The SimpleDataSet Project

Let's put together the topics discussed so far to build an application that uses a DataSet to store and edit data at the client. The sample application is called SimpleDataSet, and its interface is shown in Figure 16.4.

Click the large Read Products and Related Tables button at the top to populate a DataSet with the rows of the Products and Categories tables of the Northwind database. The application displays the categories and the products in each category in a RichTextBox control. Instead of displaying all the columns in a ListView control, I've chosen to display only a few columns of the Products table to make sure that the application connects to the database and populates the DataSet.

The Edit DataSet button edits a few rows of both tables. The code behind this button changes the name and price of a couple of products in random, deletes a row, and adds a new row. It actually sets the price of the edited products to a random value in the range from –10 to 40 (negative prices are invalid, and they will be rejected by the database). The DataSet keeps track of the changes, and you can review them at any time by clicking the Show Edits button, which displays the changes in the DataSet in a message box, like the one shown in Figure 16.5.

FIGURE 16.4

The SimpleDataSet project populates a DataSet at the client with categories and products.

FIGURE 16.5

Viewing the changes in the client DataSet

You can undo the changes and reset the DataSet to its original state by clicking the Reject Changes button, which calls the `RejectChanges` method of the DataSet class to reject the edits in all tables. It removes the new rows, restores the deleted ones, and undoes the edits in the modified rows.

The Save DataSet and Load DataSet buttons persist the DataSet at the client so that you can reload it later without having to access the database. The code shown in Listing 16.9 calls the WriteXml and ReadXml methods and uses a hard-coded filename. WriteXml and ReadXml save the data only, and you can't create a DataSet by calling the ReadXml method; this method will populate an existing DataSet.

To actually create and load a DataSet, you must first specify its structure. Fortunately, the DataSet exposes the WriteXmlSchema and ReadXmlSchema methods, which store and read the schema of the DataSet. WriteXmlSchema saves the schema of the DataSet, so you can regenerate an identical DataSet with the ReadXmlSchema method, which reads an existing schema and structures the DataSet accordingly. The code behind the Save DataSet and Load DataSet buttons first calls these two methods to take care of the DataSet's schema and then calls the WriteXml and ReadXml methods to save/load the data.

LISTING 16.9:   Saving and loading the DataSet

```
Private Sub bttnSave_Click(…) Handles bttnSave.Click
    Try
        DS.WriteXmlSchema("DataSetSchema.xml")
        DS.WriteXml("DataSetData.xml", XmlWriteMode.DiffGram)
    Catch ex As Exception
        MsgBox("Failed to save DataSet" & vbCrLf & ex.Message)
        Exit Sub
    End Try
    MsgBox("DataSet saved successfully")
End Sub

Private Sub bttnLoad_Click(…) Handles bttnLoad.Click
    Try
        DS.ReadXmlSchema("DataSetSchema.xml")
        DS.ReadXml("DataSetData.xml", XmlReadMode.DiffGram)
    Catch ex As Exception
        MsgBox("Failed to load DataSet" & vbCrLf & ex.Message)
        Exit Sub
    End Try
    ShowDataSet()
End Sub
```

The Submit Edits button, finally, submits the changes to the database. The code attempts to submit all edited rows, but some of them may fail to update the database. The local DataSet doesn't enforce any check constraints, so when the application attempts to submit a product row with a negative price to the database, the database will reject the update operation. The DataSet rows that failed to update the underlying tables are shown in a message box like the one shown in Figure 16.6. You can review the values of the rows that failed to update the database and the description of the error returned by the database and edit them further. The rows that failed to update the underlying table(s) in the database remain in the DataSet. Of course, you can always call the RejectChanges method for each row that failed to update the database to undo the changes of the invalid rows. As is, the application doesn't reject any changes on its own. If you click the Show Edits button after an update operation, you will see the rows that failed to update the database, because they're marked as inserted/modified/deleted in the DataSet.

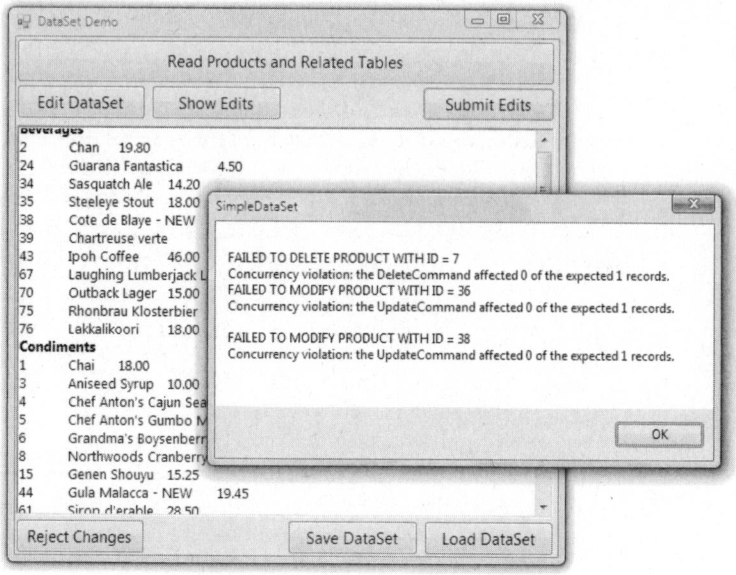

FIGURE 16.6

Viewing the rows that failed to update the database and the error message returned by the DBMS

Let's start with the code that loads the DataSet. When the form is loaded, the code initializes two DataAdapter objects, which load the rows of the Categories and Products tables. The names of the two DataAdapters are *DACategories* and *DAProducts*. They're initialized to the CN connection object and a simple SELECT statement, as shown in Listing 16.10.

LISTING 16.10:   Setting up the DataAdapters for the Categories and Products tables

```
Private Sub Form1_Load(…) Handles MyBase.Load
    Dim CN As New SqlClient.SqlConnection(
            "data source=localhost;initial catalog=northwind; " &
            "Integrated Security=True")
    DACategories.SelectCommand = New SqlClient.SqlCommand(
            "SELECT CategoryID, CategoryName, Description FROM Categories")
    DACategories.SelectCommand.Connection = CN
    Dim CategoriesCB As SqlCommandBuilder = New SqlCommandBuilder(DACategories)
    CategoriesCB.ConflictOption = ConflictOption.OverwriteChanges
    DAProducts.SelectCommand = New SqlClient.SqlCommand(
            "SELECT ProductID, ProductName, " &
            "CategoryID, UnitPrice, UnitsInStock, " &
            "UnitsOnOrder FROM Products ")
    DAProducts.SelectCommand.Connection = CN
    DAProducts.ContinueUpdateOnError = True
    Dim ProductsCB As SqlCommandBuilder = New SqlCommandBuilder(DAProducts)
    ProductsCB.ConflictOption = ConflictOption.CompareAllSearchableValues
End Sub
```

I've specified the SELECT statements in the constructors of the two DataAdapter objects and let the CommandBuilder objects generate the update statement. You can change the value of the ConflictOption property to experiment with the different styles of update statements that the CommandBuilder will generate. When the form is loaded, all the SQL statements generated for the DataAdapters are shown in the RichTextBox control. (The corresponding statements are not shown in the listing, but you can open the project in Visual Studio to examine the code.)

The Read Products and Related Tables button populates the DataSet and then displays the categories and products in the RichTextBox control by calling the ShowDataSet() subroutine, as shown in Listing 16.11.

LISTING 16.11:   Populating and displaying the DataSet

```
Private Sub bttnCreateDataSet_Click(…) Handles bttnCreateDataSet.Click
    DS.Clear()
    DACategories.Fill(DS, "Categories")
    DAProducts.Fill(DS, "Products")
    DS.Relations.Clear()
    DS.Relations.Add(New Data.DataRelation("CategoriesProducts",
        DS.Tables("Categories").Columns("CategoryID"),
        DS.Tables("Products").Columns("CategoryID")))
    ShowDataSet()
End Sub

Private Sub ShowDataSet()
    RichTextBox1.Clear()
    Dim category As DataRow
    For Each category In DS.Tables("Categories").Rows
        RichTextBox1.AppendText(
            category.Item("CategoryName") & vbCrLf)
        Dim product As DataRow
        For Each product In category.GetChildRows("CategoriesProducts")
            RichTextBox1.AppendText(
                product.Item("ProductID") & vbTab &
                product.Item("ProductName" & vbTab)
            If product.IsNull("UnitPrice") Then
                RichTextBox1.AppendText("   " & vbCrLf)
            Else
                RichTextBox1.AppendText(
                    Convert.ToDecimal(product.Item("UnitPrice"))
                    .ToString("#.00") & vbCrLf)
            End If
        Next
    Next
End Sub
```

After calling the Fill method to populate the two DataTables, the code sets up a DataRelation object to link the products to their categories through the CategoryID column and then displays the categories and the corresponding products under each category. Notice the statement that prints the products. Because the `UnitPrice` column may be Null, the code calls the `IsNull` method of the `product` variable to find out whether the current product's price is Null. If so, it doesn't attempt to call the `product.Item("UnitPrice")` expression, which would result in a runtime exception, and prints three asterisks in its place.

The Edit DataSet button modifies a few rows in the DataSet. Here's the statement that changes the name of a product selected at random (it appends the string `NEW` to the product's name):

```
DS.Tables("Products").Rows(
    RND.Next(1, 78)).Item("ProductName") &= " - NEW"
```

The same button randomly deletes a product, sets the price of another row to a random value in the range from –10 to 40, and inserts a new row with a price in the same range. If you click the Edit DataSet button a few times, you'll very likely get a few invalid rows. The Show Edits button retrieves the edited rows of both tables and displays them. It uses the `DataRowState` property to discover the state of the row (whether it's new, modified, or deleted) and displays the row's ID and a couple of additional columns. Notice that you can retrieve the proposed and original versions of the edited rows (except for the deleted rows, which have no proposed version) and display the row's fields before and after the editing on a more elaborate interface. Listing 16.12 shows the code behind the Show Edits button.

LISTING 16.12:   Viewing the edited rows

```
Private Sub bttnShow_Click(…)Handles bttnShow.Click
    Dim product As DataRow
    Dim msg As String = ""
    For Each product In DS.Tables("Products").Rows
        If product.RowState = DataRowState.Added Then
            msg &= "ADDED PRODUCT: " &
                product.Item("ProductName") & vbTab &
                product.Item("UnitPrice").ToString & vbCrLf
        End If
        If product.RowState = DataRowState.Modified Then
            msg &= "MODIFIED PRODUCT: " &
                product.Item("ProductName") & vbTab &
                product.Item("UnitPrice").ToString & vbCrLf
        End If
        If product.RowState = DataRowState.Deleted Then
            msg &= "DELETED PRODUCT: " &
                product.Item("ProductName",
                DataRowVersion.Original) & vbTab &
                product.Item("UnitPrice",
                DataRowVersion.Original).ToString & vbCrLf
        End If
    Next
    If msg.Length > 0 Then
```

```
    MsgBox(msg)
Else
    MsgBox("There are no changes in the dataset")
End If
End Sub
```

I only show the statements that print the edited rows of the Products DataTable in the listing. Notice that the code retrieves the proposed versions of the modified and added rows but the original version of the deleted rows.

The Submit Edits button submits the changes to the two DataTables to the database by calling the Update method of the DAProducts DataAdapter and then the Update method of the DACategories DataAdapter. After that, it retrieves the rows in error with the GetErrors method and displays the error message returned by the DBMS with statements similar to the ones shown in Listing 16.12.

The Bottom Line

Create and populate DataSets.   DataSets are data containers that reside at the client and are populated with database data. The DataSet is made up of DataTables, which correspond to database tables, and you can establish relationships between DataTables, just like relating tables in the database. DataTables, in turn, consist of DataRow objects.

Master It   How do you populate DataSets and then submit the changes made at the client to the database?

Establish relations between tables in the DataSet.   You can think of the DataSet as a small database that resides at the client, because it consists of tables and the relationships between them. The relations in a DataSet are DataRelation objects, which are stored in the Relations property of the DataSet. Each relation is identified by a name, the two tables it relates, and the fields of the tables on which the relation is based.

Master It   How do you navigate through the related rows of two tables?

Submit changes in the DataSet to the database.   The DataSet maintains not only data at the client but their states and versions too. It knows which rows were added, deleted, or modified (the DataRowState property), and it also knows the version of each row read from the database and the current version (the DataRowVersion property).

Master It   How will you submit the changes made to a disconnected DataSet to the database?

Chapter 17

Using the Entity Data Model

In Chapter 16, "Developing Data-Driven Applications," you learned how to use DataSets, how to perform data binding, and how to use LINQ to SQL. As it happens, LINQ to SQL is not the only object-relational technology Microsoft has to offer.

In this chapter, you'll discover Microsoft's latest data technology, the Entity Framework. Released initially with Service Pack 1 of Microsoft .NET Framework 3.5, it is the 2010 version of Visual Studio that ships with this data technology out of the box for the first time. While LINQ to SQL is a somewhat lightweight, code-oriented data technology, the Entity Framework is a comprehensive, model-driven data solution.

The Entity Framework represents a central piece of Microsoft's long-term data access strategy. With its emphasis on modeling and on the isolation of data and application layers, it promises to deliver a powerful data platform capable of supporting the applications through a complete application life cycle.

For a Visual Basic programmer, it brings working with the data under the familiar object-oriented mantle and provides numerous productivity enhancements. You will be able to construct "zero SQL code" data applications, leverage LINQ when working with data, and change the underlying data store without any impact on your application. In a few short words, using the Entity Framework to work with data is a whole different ballgame.

In this chapter, you'll learn how to do the following:

♦ Employ deferred loading when querying the Entity Data Model

♦ Use entity inheritance features in the Entity Framework

♦ Create and query related entities

The Entity Framework: Raising the Data Abstraction Bar

In Chapter 15, "Programming with ADO.NET," you saw traditional .NET Framework techniques for working with data. In stream-based data access, you use a DataReader to read from the data store (typically a relational database) and can use the Command object to modify the data in the data store. Set-based data access encapsulates data operations through the DataSet object, whose collection of DataTable objects closely mimics the structure of tables or views in the database. A DataSet lets you work with data in disconnected mode, so you can load the data from the database into the application, disconnect, work on the data, and finally connect and submit modifications to the database in a single operation.

Both techniques provide a well-known way to work with data in your Visual Basic application. The DataSet goes one step further than stream-based data access in providing the programming abstraction for data access that hides many of the complexities of low-level data access. As a result, you will have to write a lot less SQL code. Neither method, however, provides a higher-level abstraction of the underlying database structure. This interdependence between your application and the data layer is problematic for several reasons, as you will see in the next section.

The Entity Framework brings another level of abstraction to the data layer. It lets you work with a conceptual representation of data, also known as a *conceptual schema*, instead of working with the data directly. This schema is then projected to your application layer, where code generation is used to create a .NET representation of your conceptual schema. Next, the Entity Framework generates a relational (or logical) schema used to describe the data model in relational terms. Finally, mapping between the relational schema and .NET classes is generated. Based on this data, the Entity Framework is capable of creating and populating .NET objects with the data from a data store and persisting modifications made on the object data back to the data store.

How Will You Benefit from the Entity Framework?

One famous programming aphorism states that "all problems in computing can be solved by another level of indirection." Although the Entity Framework introduces new level of indirection (and abstraction), you will see that this additional level is actually put to a good use. I'll show you the problems that the folks at Microsoft tried to tackle with the Entity Framework and how they managed to resolve them.

Preserving the Expressiveness of the Data Model

If you have a lot of experience working with relational databases, especially with databases that have been around for some time and have been through numerous modifications, you must have been puzzled by the actual meaning of some elements in a database. Questions like the following might ring a bell: What is this column used for? Why is this set of data duplicated between tables? Why is this set of columns in a table empty in certain rows?"

A good understanding of your customer's needs and business is crucial for the success of the application you will be developing. This understanding can be written down in the form of requirements and together with the description of the business (or *problem domain*) will be indispensable for the design of your application.

An important part of the design of many applications is the data structure that the system will use. One of the most popular methods for designing the data is the entity-relationship model (ERM). The ERM is a conceptual representation of data where the problem domain is described in the form of entities and their relationships. In Visual Studio, this model is called the Entity Data Model (EDM), and you will learn how to create the EDM in the next section. Figure 17.1 shows the sample Entity Data Model diagram inside Visual Studio 2010.

Entities generally can be identified by the primary key and have some important characteristics known as *attributes*. For example, a person entity might have a primary key in the form of their Social Security number (SSN) and attributes First and Last Name. (Although an SSN conceptually fits well in the role of a primary key and therefore I chose it for the primary key in the Person table in the example Books and Authors project later in this chapter, in practice its use is discouraged. See "Using a Social Security Number as a Primary Key" in the following sidebar for more information.)

FIGURE 17.1
Entity Data Model diagram in Visual Studio 2010's EDM Designer

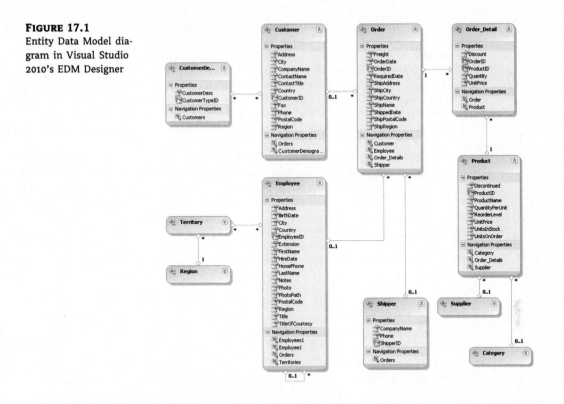

An entity can be in a relationship with another entity. During the analysis, you can often hear this relationship expressed in the form of a simple sentence, such as "A person owns a pet." In such a sentence, nouns are entities, and verbs represent a relationship. In this case, a person is related to a pet. An important characteristic of a relationship is *cardinality*, or the numeric aspect of the relation between entities. In our example, a person can own many pets, but a pet usually belongs to a single person, thus being a one-to-many relationship between the person and pet entities.

The most popular method used to work with the ERM is an entity-relationship diagram. Many tools have smart entity-relationship diagramming capabilities, including the ERwin Data Modeler, Microsoft Visio, Toad Data Modeler, and Visual Studio. I will describe the Visual Studio entity-relationship capabilities in the "Creating a New Entity Data Model" section. These tools are typically capable of transforming the conceptual to a physical model — generating Data Definition Language (DDL) scripts that can be used to generate a physical database structure.

When working with relational databases on an implementation level, you create tables and columns, constraints, and primary and foreign keys to hold your data, and you create indices to optimize data access and manipulation. Although these database concepts can be related to a problem domain so that *table* roughly corresponds to *entity*, *column* corresponds to *attribute*, and *foreign key constraint* corresponds to *relationship*, they are not as expressive as the entity-relationship model. In addition, the physical design of a relational database is governed by a different set of principles and needs. Databases are very good at preserving data integrity, performing transactions, providing fast access to a data, and reducing data redundancy. As a result, the relational database's physical design is often refined through a process of normalization and denormalization. This process is typically in the domain of database administrators, who use their knowledge of database engines to optimize database performance, often with little regard for the problem domain at hand.

It is during this process that the link between the problem domain (described in the form of an Entity Data Model) and the physical database structure is watered down. Later in the application life cycle, the Entity Data Model is often completely disregarded. As a result, database structure becomes a cryptic artifact, difficult to relate to a problem domain. This often has an adverse effect on application maintainability and evolution. When the link between the two is weakened, small changes to the application can require a huge amount of implementation work just to understand the inner workings of the database.

With the Entity Framework, Microsoft has tackled this problem by making the Entity Data Model an integral part of your application. The Entity Data Model is to generate native .NET classes used to access the data store. These classes are mapped to tables in the database. The Entity Framework uses the Entity Data Model as a basis for .NET code and database structure generation; this sets it apart from typical modeling tools. The model becomes integral part of the project, driving the database and .NET code design.

A RICHER SET OF MODELING CONSTRUCTS FOR REPRESENTING DATA

To represent an entity in a relational database, you use a table construct. The table itself represents an entity type, while each row represents one specific instance of an entity. Columns are used to represent entity attributes. When you define an attribute, you choose a data type for it. To refine attribute definition, you can apply a constraint on an attribute, or you can make the attribute a primary key, meaning that it will uniquely identify the entity. You can relate different entities by defining foreign keys between two tables.

Following this approach (I am sure you are already very familiar with it), you can easily represent customers and product categories in a simple CRM system. The system will store basic customer data and information on a customer's favorite product categories. You can define a Customers table to represent the customers in your database. Important customer attributes are the first and last names, and in order to save this information in the Customer table, you can define `FirstName` and `LastName` columns whose data type is varchar with maximum length of 50. You can use a Social Security number or a database-generated integer as a primary key. For product categories, you can define a ProductCategories table with an `Id` column for the primary key and a `Name` column as varchar with a maximum length of 20.

In simple scenarios like the one I just described, at first glance objects in relational database will represent your entities fairly well. However, there are many situations where this approach will fall short. Let's examine a few such situations in our simple CRM system.

Complex Type for Complex Properties

You will want to keep each customer's telephone number in the database. Keep one telephone number per customer, but split that telephone number into country code, area code, and local number columns. This way, you can easily add checks on the validity of the data and perform some area code–related customer analysis. There are two ways to add telephone information: You can add three new columns to the existing Customers table, or you can create a new Telephones table for these three columns. The Telephones table can have a one-to-one relation with the Customers table.

In the first scenario, in order to keep the meaning of the columns clear, you will have to prefix the column names with `Telephone`, so you will have `TelephoneCountryCode`, `TelephoneAreaCode`, and `TelephoneNumber` columns. Although keeping long column names is not such a terrible burden, it is a good indicator that the attributes that these columns represent in fact belong to another entity — `Telephone`.

Representing `Telephone` as a separate entity is achieved by placing the columns in separate table called Telephones with the addition of a customer primary key column so that each telephone is tied to a single customer. Now there is no need to prefix column names with the word `Telephone`, since the purpose of the columns is clearly stated through a table name. Note that there is no difference on the database level in representing a one-to-one relation or a one-to-many relation. If you use a separate table for the `Telephone` entity, then the same structure used for storing a single telephone number per customer can be used for storing multiple telephone numbers for an individual customer.

Unfortunately, keeping two entities with a one-to-one relationship in separate tables in a database will probably result in processing overhead: The database engine needs to join the two tables and duplicate the Social Security number in order to join them. As such, in the eyes of the database administrator, the Telephones table is a good candidate for merging with the Customers table during the performance optimization process. If the merger happens, it is even possible that the original column names are kept. You end up with a mysterious `Number` column in the Customers table. Since the `Number` column no longer belongs to the Telephone table, the purpose of the column is not easily understood from its name.

In the Entity Framework, you can use a complex type construct as an attribute of an entity. In our example, you can declare a new `Telephone` complex type and add a `Telephone` attribute (of type Telephone) to the `Customer` entity. Thanks to this feature of the Entity Framework, you will be able to reference telephone number–related properties in your Visual Basic code in the form of `Customer.Telephone.AreaCode`.

Many-to-Many as a Simple Relation Between Entities

I am sure that it comes as no surprise that you will need an additional table, called a *join table*, to relate the customers and product categories. The CustomersProductCategories relation table will have only two columns: SSN and `ProductCategoriesId`. To complete the solution, two foreign keys are added. The first foreign key is established between the SSN column in Customer and the SSN column in CustomersProductCategories. The second one is between the `Id` column in ProductCategories and the `ProductCategoriesId` column in the CustomersProductCategories table. What I have just described is a typical approach used to represent a many-to-many relationship in a relational database. You can see the EDM entities and database tables representing many-to-many relation between customers and product categories in Figure 17.2.

FIGURE 17.2
Many-to-many relation-
ship table structure (left)
and Entity Data Model
representation (right)

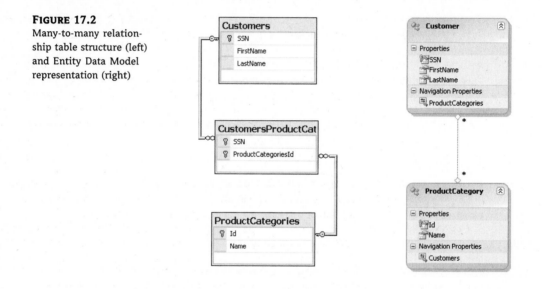

As you can see, the additional table in this case is necessary to represent a relation between two entities. Sometimes this relation can grow into a full-blown entity, such as when it needs to be described with some attributes. For example, imagine you need to store an amount spent on each category for each customer. Such a need would result in adding an `AmountSpent` column to the CustomersProductCategories table and would warrant treating CustomersProductCategories as an entity. However, in the scenario I just described, a relation between customers and product categories is just a relation and should be represented as such. In relational databases, you are left with no choice but to use the table to represent a many-to-many relation, even though tables are generally used to represent full-blown entities.

In the Entity Framework, as long as you do not need to store any relation attributes, the relation will be treated as such. You will see how the many-to-many relation is created in the "Creating a New Entity Data Model" section later in this chapter.

Inheritance Applied to Data

As a Visual Basic programmer, you are quite familiar with the concept of inheritance. Inheritance combined with polymorphism is a powerful mechanism for harnessing reuse in software.

With the Entity Framework, a similar inheritance concept can be applied to entities in the Entity Data Model. Since entities are mapped to generated .NET classes, the inheritance relation between entities is harnessed in your application code.

DATA STORE TECHNOLOGY AND BRAND INDEPENDENCE

Standard ADO .NET classes are doing a good job of encapsulating access to different data stores. If you are careful enough and you follow the "Program to an interface, not an implementation" principle, you will significantly reduce the amount of the application code you need to modify in case you need to change the data store used by your application. The "Program to an abstraction" principle applied to ADO .NET means writing code using top-level interfaces from the System.Data namespace, like in the following example:

```
Dim connection As System.Data.IDbConnection = CreateConnection(connectionString)
Dim command As System.Data.IDbCommand = connection.CreateCommand()
```

As long you do not reference any class from any concrete ADO .NET provider namespace (like System.Data.SqlClient in the case of a Microsoft SQL Server provider), switching your application to another data store can be as simple as changing the connection string — that is, as long as you are able to write your SQL code in a dialect that all data stores are able to understand. If you write command text along the same lines as the previous example, like this:

```
command.CommandText = "Select top 10 * from Customers"
```

you might find that your database does not support the TOP keyword. Although there are different standards trying to regulate SQL, the truth is that there are many proprietary extensions to the language. Writing portable SQL is difficult and often impractical.

With the Entity Framework, you have a number of query options. You can use Entity SQL (eSQL), LINQ, or Query Builder methods. Whatever your choice, you are guaranteed that the query will return the same result no matter the data store under scrutiny. Thanks to the ADO.NET Entity Framework provider architecture, new data stores can be easily incorporated and made available to .NET programmers. What's more, there is no restriction on the under-lying data store technology. Most will be relational databases, but as long as the appropriate provider is available, other technologies such as object-oriented databases, databases based on BigTable technology, Excel spreadsheets, and so on, will be available through the Entity Framework. Now you know why I insisted on using the term *data store* instead of *database* so far in this chapter.

THE "PROGRAM TO AN ABSTRACTION" PRINCIPLE

"Program to an abstraction, not an implementation" is a software design principle coined by the authors of the seminal *Design Patterns* book (*Design Patterns: Elements of Reusable Object-Oriented Software* by Erich Gama et al., Addison-Wesley Professional, 1995). When you program to an interface, the client code does not depend on a particular implementation of a library. The implementation can vary without affecting the client. This way, you can achieve an important amount of flexibility in dependencies between different components of an application. This principle becomes especially relevant in larger applications consisting of many components.

> In the previous code snippet, only interfaces from the System.Data namespace are referenced. Code need not be changed no matter which concrete provider it works with. It will work with Oracle, Microsoft SQL, OLE DB, or any other provider implementation that is implementing interfaces from the System.Data namespace.

ISOLATING THE APPLICATION FROM THE DATA STRUCTURAL CHANGES

During the application lifetime, the data and programmatic layers are generally exposed to different forces governing their evolution. The object-oriented layer accommodates evolution by preserving modularity and providing extensibility, while the data layer is influenced by forces such as referential integrity, normalization, and performance optimization.

As a database is exposed to more intensive use and the quantity of the stored data increases, the database structure often has to be re-accommodated to respond to an increase in demand. One such common scenario is table partitioning.

A table might be split so that rarely used columns containing less used but weighty pieces of information are placed in a separate table. This type of data partitioning strategy is known as *vertical partitioning*. By contrast, *horizontal partitioning* involves placing rows into different, identically structured tables. It is often used as a form of archiving; historic data that cannot be deleted but is rarely used is placed in a separate table.

The Entity Framework supports a number of mapping scenarios. It is capable of mapping a single entity to multiple tables and can use any or all of the following forms:

◆ Horizontal or vertical partitioning

◆ Complex types that structure the data contained in a single table

◆ Entity type hierarchies

◆ Mapping views

◆ Stored procedures for database interaction

With all these mapping options at your disposal, many of the typical database modifications, especially those that are the result of performance tuning, can be accommodated at the mapping layer. This way, even though the database structure changes, no changes need be applied to your .NET code. The Entity Framework's mapping capability can isolate your code from structural changes in the database layer.

Entity Data Model: Model-First Approach

The fundamental concept in the Entity Framework is the Entity Data Model (EDM). The EDM is an implementation of the entity-relationship model, and it defines entities and their relationships. Entities and relationships define a conceptual model. In addition, the EDM contains a logical model, known as the *storage schema model*, that defines the data store structure. Finally, a section in the EDM defines the mapping between the conceptual and logical schemas.

In the first release of the Entity Framework (.NET 3.5 Service Pack 1), the only way to create an EDM was to connect to an existing database and let Visual Studio create entities based on the existing database structure. Although this approach can work for existing projects, for a new project that is based on reverse engineering, it would result in a loss of important information in the conceptual model.

In Visual Studio 2010, you can start with a blank EDM. You use the EDM Designer to create and modify the EDM. The EDM Designer is a visual modeling tool that displays the model in the form of a entity-relationship diagram.

USING THE EDM DESIGNER

The EDM Designer is displayed by default when you add a new ADO .NET EDM to your project or click an EDM file (.edmx extension) in Visual Studio. Figure 17.3 shows the EDM Designer with the Northwind EDM open.

FIGURE 17.3

The EDM Designer in Visual Studio 2010

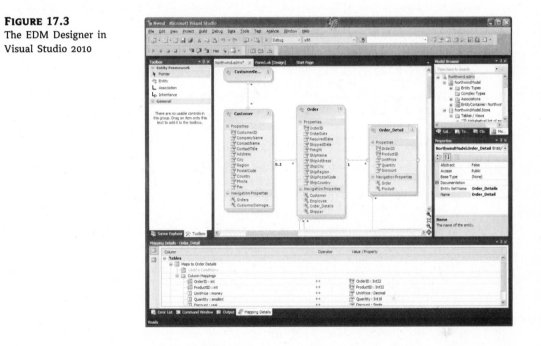

The EDM diagram is displayed in the central window. You can access many options of the EDM Designer through a context menu that appears if you right-click anywhere on the empty surface of an EDM diagram.

You can add new items to the EDM diagram by dragging and dropping tools from the Toolbox window. The Toolbox window is the window shown on the left side in Figure 17.3. Once you select an item in the EDM diagram, you can change its properties in the Properties window, pictured on the right side in Figure 17.3 and positioned below the Model Browser window.

You can see elements of the EDM grouped by type in the Model Browser window. If an EDM is complex, then right-clicking a relationship or an entity in the Model Browser and selecting Show In Designer from the context menu can be a much more practical option for finding your way around the model.

Finally, at the bottom of the Figure 17.3 you can see a Mapping Details window. In this window, you can define how entities and relations from your conceptual model are mapped to tables in the logical model. Let's start by creating a new project with a fresh EDM.

CREATING A NEW ENTITY DATA MODEL

You can add an EDM to a majority of project types supported by Visual Studio 2010. For this exercise, you will start by creating a new Windows Forms project:

1. Open a new instance of Visual Studio 2010, and choose File ➤ New Project. From the New Project dialog box, choose Windows Forms Application, rename the project to MyEF-Project, and then click OK.

2. Choose Project ➤ Add New Item. When the Add New Item dialog box opens, click the menu item Data on the Installed Templates menu. This will reduce the number of options in the dialog box. The ADO.NET Entity Data Model item now should be visible in the list of new items. Select the ADO.NET Entity Data Model item, and rename it to BooksAndAuthors.edmx. Click Add.

3. When the Entity Data Model Wizard opens, choose Empty Model in response to the "What should the model contain?" prompt. Click Finish, and save the project.

You have just created a new EDM. After you created a new EDM, Visual Studio displays the EDM Designer with your BooksAndAuthors.edmx file open in the active window.

CONNECTING THE EDM TO A DATABASE

You can create and model your entities in the EDM Designer on a conceptual level without ever using it to connect to a real database. This way, however, your model will be no more than a dead diagram. To breathe some life into your EDM, you need to connect it to a database. Start by creating a new BooksAndAuthors database in SQL Server 2005 or newer. Use the instructions that follow:

1. In your SQL Server instance, create a BooksAndAuthors database.

2. In your Visual Studio Server Explorer window, right-click the Data Connections item, and click the Add Connection item on the context menu.

3. Add a new connection to the BooksAndAuthors database you just created.

4. Right-click the BooksAndAuthors.edmx item in the Model Browser window, and select Model ➤ Generate Database Script from the context menu.

5. In the Generate Database Script Wizard window, select the BooksAndAuthors connection in the Connection combo box. Confirm that the Save Entity Connection Settings In App. Config File As check box is selected. Click Next.

6. Click Finish.

7. Click Yes on any warning windows that appear.

Check the Solution Explorer. You should see that a new BooksAndAuthors.edmx.sql file has been added to the MyEFProject. This SQL file contains a Data Definition Language (DDL) script that can be used to create a database structure that can accommodate the BooksAnd-Authors EDM.

Note that the EDM Designer only creates the DDL file; it does not execute it against the database. Don't execute it just yet. Let's add some entities to our model first.

CREATING AN ENTITY

You can now add your first entity to BooksAndAuthors EDM. In this exercise, you will create an entity model for a publishing company. It will contain information on book titles and authors. Start by creating a new Book entity:

1. Open the Toolbox, and drag an Entity item to the BooksAndAuthors.edmx designer surface. You will see a new square figure called Entity1 appear on the EDM Designer surface.

2. Click the entity name, and rename it from Entity1 to **Book**.

3. Rename the Entity Set Name property in the Properties window to **Books**.

Notice that an important characteristic of an entity is that it can be uniquely identified. An *entity* is generally identified by an attribute or a combination of attributes known as a *primary key*. The EDM Designer uses the term *property* for attributes.

CREATING A PRIMARY KEY

In the case of the Book entity, the EDM Designer automatically created an Id property and marked it as a primary key. If you select the Id property in the EDM Designer, the Properties window will display characteristics of the Id property of the Book entity. The important characteristics of the Id property are Type and Entity Key. The Type = Int32 entry in the Properties windows indicates that the data type of the Id property is Integer. The Entity Key = True entry tells you that Id is a primary key.

Although you could use an artificial primary key, in the case of a Book entity, there is another property that is a better candidate for the primary key. All book titles can be uniquely identified by their ISBN numbers.

To use the ISBN for a primary key of Book entity, follow these steps.

1. In the Properties window, change the name of the Id property to **ISBN**.

2. Then, change the Type value of the ISBN property to **String**.

3. Finally, since ISBN numbers have a maximum length of 13 characters, set the Max Size characteristic of the ISBN property to **13**.

CREATING A SCALAR PROPERTY

The most important property of the Book entity is the title. The title is a simple string, so it can be well represented as a scalar property of the Book entity. Let's add a Title scalar property to the Book entity.

1. On the EDM Designer surface, right-click the word *Properties* on the Book entity, and select the Add item from the context menu.
   The Add item expands to two subitems: Scalar Property and Complex Property.

2. Click Scalar Property.

3. Enter the word **Title** for the newly added property name.

4. In the Properties window, set the Max Length value of the Title property to **4000**. (According to WikiAnswers.com, the longest book title consists of 3,999 characters; it is too long to be reproduced here!)

While you are at it, use the same process to add another scalar property called PublishingDate to the Book entity. Select DateTime as the property type.

Yet another important property for a book is the page count. It is a good idea to preserve this information, so add another scalar property named PageCount to the Book entity, and select Int32 as the Type.

ENTITY DATA MODEL UNDER THE HOOD

Most of the time, you will be interacting with the EDM through the EDM Designer. Nevertheless, you should have a basic understanding of the artifacts that comprise the EDM and its structure. The EDM native format is XML, and it can also be viewed and edited manually, as can any XML file. To see the Visual Studio–generated EDM XML, first refresh the model and then open the EDM file in the Visual Studio XML Editor:

1. Refresh the EDM by regenerating the database DDL and by following the process described in steps 4 to 7 in the "Connecting the EDM to a Database" section earlier in this chapter.

2. Close the EDM diagram.

3. In Solution Explorer, right-click the BooksAndAuthors.edmx file, and select Open With from the context menu.

4. In the Open With dialog box, select the XML Editor, and click OK.

Listing 17.1 shows the content of the BooksAndAuthors.edmx file. Although the content might look bewildering at first, it is actually not that complex; it is even easier to understand if you ignore the XML namespace declaration. You can see that the content is divided into four main sections:

♦ SSDL content

♦ CSDL content

♦ C-S mapping content

♦ EF Designer content

LISTING 17.1:   The *BooksAndAuthors.edmx* model XML content

```
<?xml version="1.0" encoding="utf-8"?>
<edmx:Edmx Version="2.0"
 xmlns:edmx="http://schemas.microsoft.com/ado/2008/10/edmx">
  <!-- EF Runtime content -->
  <edmx:Runtime>
    <!-- SSDL content -->
    <edmx:StorageModels>
    <Schema Namespace="BooksAndAuthors.Store" Alias="Self"
    Provider="System.Data.SqlClient"
    ProviderManifestToken="2008"
    xmlns:store="http://schemas.microsoft.com
    /ado/2007/12/edm/EntityStoreSchemaGenerator"
    xmlns="http://schemas.microsoft.com/ado/2009/02/edm/ssdl">
```

```
<EntityContainer Name="BooksAndAuthorsStoreContainer">
  <EntitySet Name="Books" EntityType="BooksAndAuthors.Store.Books"
    store:Type="Tables" Schema="dbo" />
</EntityContainer>
<EntityType Name="Books">
  <Key>
    <PropertyRef Name="ISBN" />
  </Key>
  <Property Name="ISBN" Type="varchar" Nullable="false" MaxLength="13" />
  <Property Name="Title" Type="nvarchar" Nullable="false" MaxLength="4000" />
  <Property Name="PublishingDate" Type="datetime" Nullable="false" />
  <Property Name="PageCount" Type="int" Nullable="false" />
</EntityType>
</Schema></edmx:StorageModels>
    <!-- CSDL content -->
    <edmx:ConceptualModels>
      <Schema xmlns="http://schemas.microsoft.com/ado/2008/09/edm"
      xmlns:store="http://schemas.microsoft.com
      /ado/2007/12/edm/EntityStoreSchemaGenerator"
      Namespace="BooksAndAuthors" Alias="Self">
        <EntityContainer Name="BooksAndAuthorsContainer" >
          <EntitySet Name="Books"
                     EntityType="BooksAndAuthors.Book" />
        </EntityContainer>
        <EntityType Name="Book">
          <Key>
            <PropertyRef Name="ISBN" /></Key>
          <Property Type="String" Name="ISBN" Nullable="false"
                    MaxLength="13" Unicode="false" FixedLength="false" />
          <Property Type="String" Name="Title"
                    Nullable="false" MaxLength="4000" />
          <Property Type="DateTime" Name="PublishingDate"
                    Nullable="false" Precision="29" />
          <Property Type="Int32" Name="PageCount"
                    Nullable="false" /></EntityType></Schema>
    </edmx:ConceptualModels>
    <!-- C-S mapping content -->
    <edmx:Mappings>
    <Mapping Space="C-S" xmlns="http://schemas.microsoft.com
                            /ado/2008/09/mapping/cs">
  <EntityContainerMapping StorageEntityContainer="BooksAndAuthorsStoreContainer"
   CdmEntityContainer="BooksAndAuthorsContainer">
    <EntitySetMapping Name="Books">
      <EntityTypeMapping TypeName="IsTypeOf(BooksAndAuthors.Book)">
        <MappingFragment StoreEntitySet="Books">
          <ScalarProperty Name="ISBN" ColumnName="ISBN" />
          <ScalarProperty Name="Title" ColumnName="Title" />
          <ScalarProperty Name="PublishingDate" ColumnName="PublishingDate" />
```

```
                    <ScalarProperty Name="PageCount" ColumnName="PageCount" />
                </MappingFragment>
            </EntityTypeMapping>
        </EntitySetMapping>
    </EntityContainerMapping>
</Mapping></edmx:Mappings>
    </edmx:Runtime>
    <!-- EF Designer content (DO NOT EDIT MANUALLY BELOW HERE) -->
    <edmx:Designer xmlns="http://schemas.microsoft.com/ado/2008/10/edmx">
        <edmx:Connection>
            <DesignerInfoPropertySet>
                <DesignerProperty Name="MetadataArtifactProcessing"
                 Value="EmbedInOutputAssembly" />
            </DesignerInfoPropertySet>
        </edmx:Connection>
        <edmx:Options>
            <DesignerInfoPropertySet>
                <DesignerProperty Name="ValidateOnBuild" Value="true" />
            </DesignerInfoPropertySet>
        </edmx:Options>
        <!-- Diagram content (shape and connector positions) -->
        <edmx:Diagrams>
            <Diagram Name="BooksAndAuthors" >
                <EntityTypeShape EntityType="BooksAndAuthors.Book"
                                 Width="1.5" PointX="3.375" PointY="2"
                                 Height="1.592306315104167" />
            </Diagram>
        </edmx:Diagrams>
    </edmx:Designer>
</edmx:Edmx>
```

So far, the file contains information on a single entity. As we continue working on the model, it will grow and become more complex. Fortunately, you can edit most of the model details through the EDM Designer and rarely need to edit the file manually.

The Conceptual Model: The CSDL Content

CSDL stands for Conceptual Schema Definition Language. This section contains information on the conceptual data model and corresponds directly to the content of the EDM diagram. This schema is the basis for the object model that is generated by Visual Studio as a .NET projection of a conceptual model.

The important elements of the CSDL schema are EntityType with Key and Property nodes. At this point you have a single Book entity in the model, and that entity has several properties, as you can see in Listing 17.1. The Key node references the ISBN property. Each Property node contains information, including property name, type, and nullability. This section also contains the information on the EntitySet, which is used to represent a set of entities. In this case, you'll find the Books EntitySet, as you defined it earlier in step 3 of the "Creating an Entity" section.

The Logical Model: The SSDL Content

This section is written in the Store Schema Definition Language (SSDL) and is a description of database structure that will be used to persist the data for the application build on the Entity Framework.

The structure of the SSDL section is quite similar to the CSDL section; it describes entities and associations. This section is used to generate DDL code and defines a store projection of the conceptual model. Entities and associations in the SSDL section define tables and columns in the storage model.

The Mapping Specification: C-S Mapping Content

The mapping specification is defined in the Mapping Specification Language (MSL). This is the place where the two worlds — .NET objects and the storage schema — meet. You can see how each entity maps to a table in the database and each property maps to a column.

Take a look the `EntityTypeMapping` tag inside the `BooksAndAuthors.edmx` file provided in Listing 17.1. Notice that the `TypeName` attribute has the value `IsTypeOf(BooksAndAuthors.Book)`. `IsTypeOf` is just a way of saying that the type for this entity is `Book` (or any other class that inherits the `Book` type).

The `MappingFragment` inside the `EntityTypeMapping` defines the table to which the `Book` entity will be mapped via the `StoreEntitySet` attribute. In this case, the `StoreEntitySet` has the value `Books`, as you defined when you created the `Book` entity via the `EntitySet` property.

Finally, inside the `MappingFragment` you can see how different properties are mapped to columns in the table. For example, the `ISBN` property is mapped to a `ISBN` column: `<ScalarProperty Name="ISBN" ColumnName="ISBN" />`.

Data as Objects in the Entity Framework

The typical way to interact with the Entity Framework is through Object Services. Object Services is the component in the Entity Framework in charge of providing the .NET view of the data. For example, you will access the entity `Book` as a class `Book` in your .NET code. The code for the `Book` class is generated by the Entity Framework and is already available in the project. As with any other objects in .NET, you will be able to use LINQ to query these objects. Take a look at Listing 17.2; it shows how you can use LINQ to find a specific book based on `ISBN`.

LISTING 17.2:   Using the Entity Framework–generated code to access the EDM

```
Dim context As New BooksAndAuthorsContainer
Dim books = context.Books
Dim myBook As Book = From book In books
 Where (book.ISBN = "455454857")
          Select book
```

To provide a native .NET view of the data in the EDM, the Entity Framework will generate Visual Basic code for partial classes that represent entities in your EDM. To take a look at this tool-generated code, follow these steps:

1. Click the Show All Files icon in your Solution Explorer.

2. Expand the BooksAnAuthors.edmx item in Solution Explorer.

3. Click the BooksAndAuthors.Designer.vb file.

For brevity's sake, Listing 17.3 provides a portion of the code contained in the BooksAndAuthors.Designer.vb file. The listing will make much more sense if you keep in mind the way that classes are used; think about what you learned as you reviewed the code in Listing 17.2.

LISTING 17.3:   Entity Framework–generated .NET code

```
Public Partial Class BooksAndAuthorsContainer
    Inherits ObjectContext
    '...
    Public ReadOnly Property Books() As ObjectSet(Of Book)
        Get
            If (_Books Is Nothing) Then
                _Books = MyBase.CreateObjectSet(Of Book)("Books")
            End If
            Return _Books
        End Get
    End Property

    Private _Books As ObjectSet(Of Book)
    '...
End Class

<EdmEntityTypeAttribute(NamespaceName:="BooksAndAuthors", Name:="Book")>
<Serializable()>
<DataContractAttribute(IsReference:=True)>
Public Partial Class Book
    Inherits EntityObject
    #Region "Factory Method"

    '" <summary>
    '" Create a new Book object.
    '" </summary>
    Public Shared Function CreateBook(iSBN As Global.System.String,
                               title As Global.System.String,
                               publishingDate As Global.System.DateTime,
                               pageCount As Global.System.Int32) As Book

        Dim book as Book = New Book
        book.ISBN = iSBN

        book.Title = title

        book.PublishingDate = publishingDate
```

```vbnet
        book.PageCount = pageCount

    Return book
End Function

<EdmScalarPropertyAttribute(EntityKeyProperty:=true, IsNullable:=false)>
<DataMemberAttribute()>
Public Property ISBN() As Global.System.String
    Get
        Return _ISBN
    End Get
    Set
        If (ISBN <> value) Then
            OnISBNChanging(value)
            ReportPropertyChanging("ISBN")
            _ISBN = StructuralObject.SetValidValue(value, False)
            ReportPropertyChanged("ISBN")
            OnISBNChanged()
        End If
    End Set
End Property

Private _ISBN as Global.System.String
Private Partial Sub OnISBNChanging(value As Global.System.String)
End Sub

Private Partial Sub OnISBNChanged()
End Sub

<EdmScalarPropertyAttribute(EntityKeyProperty:=false, IsNullable:=false)>
<DataMemberAttribute()>
Public Property Title() As Global.System.String
    Get
        Return _Title
    End Get
    Set
        OnTitleChanging(value)
        ReportPropertyChanging("Title")
        _Title = StructuralObject.SetValidValue(value, False)
        ReportPropertyChanged("Title")
        OnTitleChanged()
    End Set
End Property

Private _Title as Global.System.String
Private Partial Sub OnTitleChanging(value As Global.System.String)
End Sub
```

```vb
        Private Partial Sub OnTitleChanged()
        End Sub

        <EdmScalarPropertyAttribute(EntityKeyProperty:=false, IsNullable:=false)>
        <DataMemberAttribute()>
        Public Property PublishingDate() As Global.System.DateTime
            Get
                Return _PublishingDate
            End Get
            Set
                OnPublishingDateChanging(value)
                ReportPropertyChanging("PublishingDate")
                _PublishingDate = StructuralObject.SetValidValue(value)
                ReportPropertyChanged("PublishingDate")
                OnPublishingDateChanged()
            End Set
        End Property

        Private _PublishingDate as Global.System.DateTime
        Private Partial Sub OnPublishingDateChanging(value As Global.System.DateTime)
        End Sub

        Private Partial Sub OnPublishingDateChanged()
        End Sub

        <EdmScalarPropertyAttribute(EntityKeyProperty:=false, IsNullable:=false)>
        <DataMemberAttribute()>
        Public Property PageCount() As Global.System.Int32
            Get
                Return _PageCount
            End Get
            Set
                OnPageCountChanging(value)
                ReportPropertyChanging("PageCount")
                _PageCount = StructuralObject.SetValidValue(value)
                ReportPropertyChanged("PageCount")
                OnPageCountChanged()
            End Set
        End Property

        Private _PageCount as Global.System.Int32
        Private Partial Sub OnPageCountChanging(value As Global.System.Int32)
        End Sub

        Private Partial Sub OnPageCountChanged()
        End Sub

    End Class
```

The BooksAndAuthorsContainer class is the entry point for accessing Object Services in our example. This class inherits the ObjectContext class from the System.Data.Objects namespace and has a property called Books. The Books property represents a set of Book objects.

The Book class represents a Book entity. The Book class has to inherit the EntityObject class from the System.Data.Objects namespace. The class has a number of properties, and each property of the class corresponds to a property of the Book entity in Books and Authors EDM. You will see how the classes are used in detail in the "Putting the EDM to Work" section later in this chapter.

ADDING AN INHERITANCE RELATIONSHIP BETWEEN ENTITIES

Now that you are finished creating the Book entity, as you might expect, the Author entity is the next to be created. It will be important to collect and store author data, such as name, contact information, and so forth, in this entity. Before you create the Author entity, however, a bit of analysis is in order.

As it happens, the publishing company in question also works with foreign language titles. In the case of a foreign language title, it is important to collect and store information about the translator: name, contact information, languages translated, and the like. Surely, this warrants another entity in our system — a Translator entity.

If you compare the Author and the Translator entities, you will see that they have a lot of common properties. If we were to add the Translator and Author entities to the EDM now, we would have to duplicate these properties on each. There must be some more efficient way to deal with replicated properties.

The solution is the same as it would be in a situation when you design classes where there "is a kind of" relationship between the entities in Visual Basic. A common parent entity can be extracted; that parent entity will contain the common properties. Let's call this entity Person. Once the Person entity exists, you can add Author and Translator entities and make them inherit the Person entity. Start by adding a new Person entity to the EDM:

1. Add new entity to the EDM, and name it **Person**.

2. Rename the Id property to **SSN**. Change Type to String, set Max Length to 9, and set the Fixed Length value to True.

3. Add a FirstName scalar property (Type: String, Max Length: 50).

4. Add a LastName scalar property (Type: String, Max Length: 50).

5. Add a new entity to the EDM, and name it Author.

6. Select the Inheritance arrow in the Toolbox, and connect Author and Person, going from Author to Person.

7. Delete the Id property in the Author entity.

8. Add another new entity to the EDM, and name it **Translator**.

9. Select the Inheritance arrow in the Toolbox, and connect Translator and Person, going from Translator to Person.

10. Delete the Id property in the Translator entity.

You have just created an inheritance hierarchy with one base entity, Person, and two child entities, Translator and Author. Let's add a few more details to our model.

Since you will never instantiate a `Person` entity in your code because you will always work with a more specific type, a `Translator` or an `Author`, you can mark the `Person` entity as abstract. In the Properties window, select the `Person` entity, and set the `Abstract` property to True.

There are a few more bits of information you need to store for each child type. For authors, the publishing company would like to store the date that the author first signed with the company. To accommodate this, add a new property called `Signed` (Type: DateTime) to the `Author` entity. For translators, you will also want to keep the information on languages that they translate from. Since this requires defining another related table, you can create this table after you see how many-to-many associations are defined in the "Adding a Many-to-Many Association" section later in this chapter.

The inheritance feature you have just used is one of the Entity Framework's most powerful capabilities. It solves the problem of mapping the inheritance relationship in an object-oriented sense to tables in a relational database and lets you leverage the inheritance and polymorphism capacities of .NET code without any friction with the data store.

Entity Framework Inheritance Mapping

Mapping a group of classes from an object-oriented paradigm to tables in a relational database can be accomplished intuitively, if the classes have some kind of an association relationship. For example, a class might have a property whose type is some other class, like a Car class that has a `Wheels` property whose type is a list of wheels. In such a case, each class maps to a table in a relational database, and the association between classes maps to a one-to-many relationship in the database that is enforced by a foreign key constraint.

The situation becomes much more complex if there is an inheritance relationship between classes. In our Books and Authors model, both the `Author` entity and the `Translator` entity inherit the `Person` entity. Such a relationship is not easily represented in a relational store.

The Entity Framework supports several strategies for mapping an inheritance hierarchy to a relational store. I will describe the two most commonly used:

Table-per-type inheritance   Under the table-per-type inheritance strategy, each type has its own table. The parent table (in our example, the Person table) contains all the common properties for all the entities in the hierarchy. The tables representing the child entities (`Author` and `Translator` in our example) contain only those properties that are unique to a particular entity. To be able to relate parent and child tables, the primary key column (named SSN in our example) must exist in all the tables in the hierarchy. Additionally, a foreign key constraint can be established between the parent and child tables. Foreign keys guarantee that a child table (Author or Translator in our example) can be inserted only if there is a related record in the parent (Person) table. To be able to retrieve a single `Author` from the data store, the query has to join the `Person` and `Author` columns using the primary key.

In other words, if the row with value 569125274 of the SSN column exists in both the Person and the Author tables, then the person is an author. If such a row exists in both the Person and the Translator tables, then the person is a translator. And since we marked the `Person` entity as `Abstract`, if the row with a value of 569125274 in the SSN column exists in the Person table, then there has to be exactly one row in either the Author or Translator table with the same value in the SSN column.

If the child tables (the Author and Translator tables in our example) contain a lot of columns, then this scenario represents a more efficient storage mechanism. Queries on a table-per-type structure, on the other hand, can be slower than on those in a table-per-hierarchy structure.

In each query, at least two tables have to be joined. Let's compare this to a table-per-hierarchy mapping scenario.

Table-per-hierarchy inheritance   In the table-per-hierarchy inheritance mapping scenario, all entities in the hierarchy are mapped to a single table. A special discriminatory column is used to discern which entity each individual row represents. In the mapping section of an `EntityTypeMapping` element, this row is represented by a `Condition` element. For example, inside the `EntityTypeMapping` for an `Author` entity, this element could be written as `<Condition ColumnName="PersonCategory" Value="0" />`. This means that each row with a value of 0 in the `PersonCategory` column is an instance of an `Author` entity.

In our example, this means that both the `Translator` and `Author` entities are mapped to the Person table. In such scenario, the Person table has to contain both `Author` and `Translator` entity-specific columns. As a consequence and since each row in a table represents either an author or a translator, there will always be a number of empty cells in each row. In the case where a row represents an author, the translator-specific data will be empty, and vice versa. This is the weakness of this scenario; it is not the most efficient storage model. However, in cases where there are a small number of specific columns, the storage inefficiency is more than compensated for by query efficiency. Since there are no tables to be joined, queries tend to execute much faster.

At this point, you might be curious to see the scenario chosen to represent inheritance in our model by default and the exact database structure generated by the EDM Designer. You can regenerate the database script from the model using the process described in steps 4 through 7 in the "Connecting the EDM to a Database" section earlier in this chapter. Once that is complete, open the `BooksAndAuthors.edmx.sql` file. You should see a file that contains the section of code shown in Listing 17.4.

LISTING 17.4:   DDL code for tables in the inheritance hierarchy

```
-- Creating table 'Persons'
CREATE TABLE [dbo].[Persons] (
    [SSN] char(9)  NOT NULL,
    [FirstName] nvarchar(50)  NOT NULL,
    [LastName] nvarchar(50)  NOT NULL
);
GO
-- Creating table 'Persons_Translator'
CREATE TABLE [dbo].[Persons_Translator] (
    [SSN] char(9)  NOT NULL
);
GO
-- Creating table 'Persons_Author'
CREATE TABLE [dbo].[Persons_Author] (
    [Signed] datetime  NOT NULL,
    [SSN] char(9)  NOT NULL
);
GO
```

```
-- --------------------------------------------------
-- Creating all Primary Key Constraints
-- --------------------------------------------------

-- Creating primary key on [SSN] in table 'Persons'
ALTER TABLE [dbo].[Persons] WITH NOCHECK
ADD CONSTRAINT [PK_Persons]
    PRIMARY KEY CLUSTERED ([SSN] ASC)
    ON [PRIMARY]
GO
-- Creating primary key on [SSN] in table 'Persons_Translator'
ALTER TABLE [dbo].[Persons_Translator] WITH NOCHECK
ADD CONSTRAINT [PK_Persons_Translator]
    PRIMARY KEY CLUSTERED ([SSN] ASC)
    ON [PRIMARY]
GO
-- Creating primary key on [SSN] in table 'Persons_Author'
ALTER TABLE [dbo].[Persons_Author] WITH NOCHECK
ADD CONSTRAINT [PK_Persons_Author]
    PRIMARY KEY CLUSTERED ([SSN] ASC)
    ON [PRIMARY]
GO


-- --------------------------------------------------
-- Creating all Foreign Key Constraints
-- --------------------------------------------------

-- Creating foreign key on [SSN] in table 'Persons_Translator'
ALTER TABLE [dbo].[Persons_Translator] WITH NOCHECK
ADD CONSTRAINT [FK_Translator_inherits_Person]
    FOREIGN KEY ([SSN])
    REFERENCES [dbo].[Persons]
        ([SSN])
    ON DELETE NO ACTION ON UPDATE NO ACTION
GO
-- Creating foreign key on [SSN] in table 'Persons_Author'
ALTER TABLE [dbo].[Persons_Author] WITH NOCHECK
ADD CONSTRAINT [FK_Author_inherits_Person]
    FOREIGN KEY ([SSN])
    REFERENCES [dbo].[Persons]
        ([SSN])
    ON DELETE NO ACTION ON UPDATE NO ACTION
GO
```

If you analyze the DDL code in Listing 17.4, you can see that separate tables for Author and Translator were created. In our model, the strategy chosen to map inheritance in the example is table-per-type. (In case you are wondering whether this model would be able to accommodate those poor souls that work both as authors and translators, the answer is "yes!"

There is nothing preventing the same SSN from existing in both the Persons_Author and Persons_Translator tables.)

With this code, you have a hierarchy in place to represent authors and translators in the database. You aren't finished with these entities yet; there is still some personal data that the system needs to keep as part of a complete record of the authors and translators. Let's see how you can use a complex property to structure some entity property information.

ADDING A COMPLEX PROPERTY TO AN ENTITY

One important piece of contact information for authors and translators is a telephone number. The publishing house needs to maintain a record of one telephone number for each author and translator. This requirement can be easily solved by adding another property to the `Person` entity. By adding a `Telephone` property to the `Person` entity, both the `Author` and `Translator` entities will inherit it.

Instead of simply adding a string property to a `Person` entity, you can provide additional integrity and meaning to data if you structure the telephone number information. Typically, a telephone number consists of a country code, an area code, and a local number. Sometimes, you also need additional information, such as an extension number or daytime/evening qualifier.

In the EDM Designer, you can use a complex property to structure the information you do not want to model as a separate entity. You can add a scalar property to the `Person` entity by following these steps:

1. Right-click the word *Properties* on the `Person` entity on the EDM Designer surface, and select the Add item in the context menu.
   The Add item is expanded into two subitems: Scalar Property and Complex Property.

2. Click the Complex Property subitem.
   A new property named `Complex Property` is added to `Person`.

3. Select and then rename the property to **Phone**.

4. Click an empty area on the EDM Designer surface, and select the Add ➤ Complex Type menu item.
   A new complex type named `ComplexType1` is added to the model.

5. Select `ComplexType1` in the Model Browser window, and rename it to `PhoneNumber` in the Properties window.

6. Right-click `PhoneNumber` in the Model Browser, and select Add ➤ Scalar Property ➤ String.

7. Rename the property to **CountryCode** in the Properties window, and assign Max Length a value of 3 and Default Value a value of 1.

8. Repeat steps 6 and 7, adding an `Area Code` property (type String with a maximum length of 3) and a `Number` property (type String with a maximum length of 15 — this should be enough for any out-of-ordinary international number). Finally, add an `Extension` for consistency property (type String with maximum length of 20).

9. Go back to the `Person` entity in the EDM Designer, and select the `Phone` property.

10. Click the combo Type in the Properties window. It should now contain a single value: PhoneNumber. Select PhoneNumber as the type for the `Phone` property of the `Person` entity.

Select the `Person` entity in the EDM Designer, and take a look at the Mapping Details window. You will see that properties of the `Phone` property are mapped to the same Persons table as rest of the `Person` scalar properties. The only difference is the column name. The `Phone_` prefix is used to mark them as belonging to the Phone complex type. This will suffice to keep telephone numbers for authors and translators. Note that in the case where more than one telephone number for each Author/Translator needs to be kept in a database, you can model `Telephone` as a separate entity in a one-to-many relationship with `Person`, as described in the next section.

Another important part of contact information is an address. The publisher often needs to keep multiple addresses for authors and translators. The next section explains just how to do that.

ADDING A ONE-TO-MANY ASSOCIATION

Start by adding a new entity called `Address` to the Books and Authors EDM. As with telephone numbers, you should bear in mind the international character of address information. Keep the `Id` primary key added by default, and set the `StoreGeneratedPatter` property to Identity. Now add the following scalar properties to the `Address` entity:

- `FirstLine` (Type String, Max Length 50)

- `SecondLine` (Type String, Max Length 50, Nullable True)

- `City` (Type String, Max Length 50)

- `PostalCode` (Type Sting, Max Length 20)

- `State` (Type Sting, Max Length 20)

- `Country` (Type Sting, Max Length 20)

Now perform the following steps:

1. Select the Association tool in the Toolbox window.

2. Connect the `Person` and `Address` entities; start dragging from the `Person` entity.

You will see the line connecting the `Person` and `Address` entities with 1, which is used to signify one side in a one-to-many association on the side of `Person`, and an asterisk, which is used to signify the many side in a one-to-many association on the side of `Address`.

Now, select the line in the EDM diagram, and take a look at Properties window. You will see that the name of the association is `PersonAddress`. Since the association is one-to-many, rename it to **PersonAddresses** so that the cardinality of association can be easily understood from its name. You have just created a one-to-many association in your model.

Entities in a one-to-many association expose a stronger type of relationship. They often have a dependant life cycle. For example, if you eliminate a person from the database, it makes no sense to keep the addresses that belong to that person in the database. The Entity Framework can take care of this issue for you. If you set the `End1 OnDelete` property to Cascade, the Entity Framework will delete all addresses belonging to the deleted person automatically. Make sure that the `End1 OnDelete` property of the `PersonAddresses` association is set to Cascade.

ADDING A MANY-TO-MANY ASSOCIATION

At this point, you have created the main entities in your model. You have modeled the `Author`, `Translator`, and `Book` entities. But, a crucial piece of the puzzle is still missing. You must have a means to connect authors and translators with their books. Typically, you expect to have a single author per book. However, it is not uncommon (especially for nonfiction titles) to have several authors per book. And it is to be expected that an author will deliver more than one title in his lifetime. There is a similar relationship between translators and titles.

You can say that the nature of the relation between books and authors and between books and translators is many-to-many. Since the relation with books is common to both authors and translators, the best way to represent it in our model without incurring repetition is to associate the Person entity with the Book entity using a many-to-many association.

1. Select the Association tool in the Toolbox window.

2. Connect the Person and Book entities; drag from the Person entity to the Book entity.

3. Select the newly added association.

4. In the Properties window, make sure that End 1 Multiplicity has the value of * (Collection of Person) and End 2 Multiplicity has the value of * (Collection of Book).

5. Pluralize the names of the navigation properties. Rename the End1 navigation property to **Books** and the End2 navigation property to **Persons**.

The diagram in the EDM Designer should show the diamond and an asterisk on both sides of the line connecting the Person and Book entities. Also, both the Person entity and the Book entity should display some newly created navigation properties: Books for the Person entity and Persons for the Book entity. Navigation properties are a special kind of properties in a sense that they hold a reference to another entity or set of entities.

If you select the line connecting the Person and Book entities, you will see in the Mapping Details window that it maps to a separate table called PersonBook.

Now that you have seen how to establish a many-to-many association between entities, you can add a new entity called Language, with Id and Name scalar properties. Create a many-to-many association between the Language and Translator entities. This way, you will be able to store information on the languages that an individual translator works with, making translator information much more useful to the publisher.

GENERATE THE DATABASE STRUCTURE

So far, you only used the EDM Designer to generate the DDL code. You haven't actually executed the DDL against the database. By following these steps, you can easily use Visual Studio 2010 to execute the DDL script.

1. Open BooksAndAuthors.edmx.sql in Visual Studio.

2. Make sure that the T-SQL Editor toolbar is visible. If it is not, right-click the toolbar area, and make sure that T-SQL Editor is selected.

3. In the T-SQL Editor toolbox, select the BooksAndAuthors database in the Database combo. (the BooksAndAuthors database was created in the "Connecting the EDM to a Database" earlier section.)

4. Click the Execute SQL button in T-SQL Editor toolbox.

At this point, it would be interesting to compare the structure of the EDM with the structure of the database generated for the model. You can take a look at the database structure in Figure 17.4.

FIGURE 17.4
Books and Authors
database structure

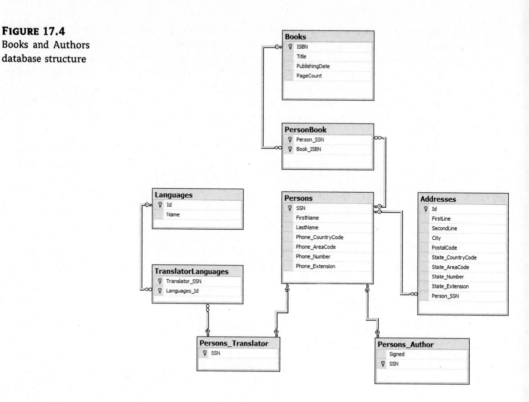

Figure 17.5 shows the EDM.

FIGURE 17.5
Books and Authors EDM

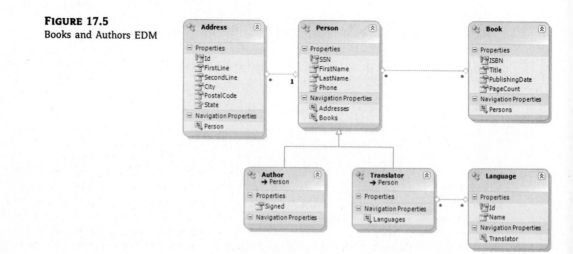

Although there is a correspondence between the diagrams, there are some significant differences. The EDM diagram shows the many-to-many association as a line between the two tables, while on the database diagram the many-to-many relation materializes in a joined table. Although the EDM diagram shows a single complex property, Phone, in a database, these are materialized as a group of columns clustered around the same Phone_ prefix.

In conclusion, the EDM is capable of providing a cleaner conceptual view of the data, can hide many low-level implementation details, and provides a much richer set of features for working with data.

With this, you have successfully generated your first Entity Data Model and used most of the available constructs while doing so. The model itself, though, is not much use if you are not able to interact with it and use it to store the data. In the next section, you will see how you can use the Entity Framework to obtain data from the data store and how you can modify that same data with the help of the Entity Framework.

Putting the EDM to Work

In a way, working with the Entity Framework is similar to working with DataSets. You query the EDM in order to obtain the objects representing the data. Next you display the objects; then you perform any updates, inserts, or deletes on objects; and finally you commit changes to the data store. The difference is that instead of working with objects such as a DataTable that represents the data store structure directly, you work with your entities that represent the objects in your business layer.

As I mentioned in the introductory section, the Entity Framework introduces another layer of abstraction when you are working with data. Although there are numerous benefits in productivity and simplification to be found in such an approach, an additional layer inevitably means letting go of some low-level control features. I am not obsessed by keeping things completely in control, but I do like to understand what is going on underneath the surface.

One very good tool that can help you understand how the Entity Framework interacts with the database is the SQL Server Profiler. It displays the exact SQL query that the Entity Framework issues to the database. This can help you understand a number of subtleties related to the Entity Framework and will allow you to optimize the way you use it. I suggest you use the SQL Server Profiler to monitor Entity Framework–to–database conversations until you become familiar with the Entity Framework's behavior.

In the next section, I will, from time to time, use the SQL Server Profiler trace output to corroborate some statements that I make about the inner workings of the Entity Framework.

Querying the Entity Data Model

At this point, you must be aching to write some Visual Basic code. In the following section, you will see some very interesting options that the Entity Framework provides for accessing the data. You will typically use LINQ to Entities to query the EDM. In this case, you see data in the form of strongly typed .NET objects exposed via the ObjectContext class and made available through the Object Services infrastructure. In cases where you need more granular control or need to write some dynamically generated queries, you can use the Entity SQL language. You can issue Entity SQL queries to query the ObjectContext class, or for more low-level access, you can use the EntityClient data provider. Finally, you can query the ObjectContext class by using Entity SQL with the help of the ObjectQuery class or by constructing your queries with the help of ObjectQuery Query Builder methods. Let's start with LINQ to Entities.

USING LINQ TO ENTITIES

In Chapter 14, "An Introduction to LINQ," you familiarized yourself with LINQ. Thanks to the Object Services layer and the .NET code generated by the Entity Framework (shown in Listing 17.3), you can query the data in the EDM as objects and unleash all the power of LINQ syntax in your Visual Basic code.

It is time you put to use the form added automatically to MyEFProject that contains the BooksAndAuthors EDM. Start by renaming the form to QueryEDM.vb, and add a button named ListAllBooks.

Listing All of the Entities in a Database

If you go back to Listing 17.3, you will see that the EDM Designer generated a class named BooksAndAuthorsContainer that inherits the ObjectContext class and that I introduced as the "entry point" to EDM Object Services. This class has a property, Books, of type ObjectSet(Of Book) that essentially represents a set of entities and implements interfaces like IQueryable and IEnumerable. With those in place, listing all book entities should be as easy as traversing all of the objects in the Books set of BooksAndAuthorsContainer instance. Let's do just that in a ListAllBooks button event handler. Take a look at Listing 17.5. It writes the title of all books in the database to the console. To see the result, make sure that the Output window in Visual Studio is visible.

LISTING 17.5: Listing all *Book* entities

```
Private Sub ListAllBooks_Click(ByVal sender As System.Object,
          ByVal e As System.EventArgs) Handles ListAllBooks.Click
    Dim context As New BooksAndAuthorsContainer
    For Each book In context.Books
        Console.WriteLine("Title: " & book.Title)
    Next
End Sub
```

This was actually very simple — a kind of Entity Framework Hello Word application. Let's now try something a bit more complicated. Let's see whether we can actually use some LINQ syntax.

Finding an Entity Using a LINQ Query

LINQ can be very expressive when writing queries. If you use it prudently, it can be also very efficient. Take a look at the code in Listing 17.6. It finds the longest book by ordering books by the PageCount property and then selecting the first Book entity on the list.

LISTING 17.6: Find the longest book LINQ query

```
Private Sub LongestBook_Click(ByVal sender As System.Object,
          ByVal e As System.EventArgs) Handles LongestBook.Click
```

```
      Dim context As New BooksAndAuthorsContainer
      Dim books = context.Books
      Dim longestBook As Book = (From book In books
                    Order By book.PageCount).First
      Console.WriteLine("The longest book is: " +
      longestBook.ISBN + " " + longestBook.Title)
   End Sub
```

If you take a look at Listing 17.7, you can see the SQL code issued to the database and captured by SQL Server Profiler.

LISTING 17.7:   SQL Server Profiler–captured SQL code

```
SELECT TOP (1)
[Extent1].[ISBN] AS [ISBN],
[Extent1].[Title] AS [Title],
[Extent1].[PublishingDate] AS [PublishingDate],
[Extent1].[PageCount] AS [PageCount]
FROM [dbo].[Books] AS [Extent1]
ORDER BY [Extent1].[PageCount] ASC
```

Notice that the Entity Framework was intelligent enough to delegate the ordering operation to the database engine and to limit the result to a single row with the TOP statement. This is a much more efficient way to obtain the desired result than to write Visual Basic code that operates on the Books set. For example, you can obtain the same result by filtering the book by the PageCount property inside the For Each loop in Listing 17.5. This would result in fetching all the records in a table. Such code, however, would hardly be of production quality.

Finding an Entity of a Specific Type in the Inheritance Hierarchy

If you now open the BooksAndAuthors.Designer.vb file, you will see that it contains much more code than when we started building our Books and Authors EDM. If you inspect the BooksAndAuthorsContainer class, you might note something curious. The class has the Person property but no Translator or Author properties. So, how can you write the queries that reference a child type in an inheritance hierarchy?

The solution comes in the form of the LINQ OfType query operator. Take a look at Listing 17.8. It shows the code that fetches all translators stored in the Translators table.

LISTING 17.8:   Fetch translators

```
Private Sub FetchTranslators_Click(ByVal sender As System.Object,
        ByVal e As System.EventArgs) Handles FetchTranslators.Click
    Dim context As New BooksAndAuthorsContainer
    Dim translators = context.Persons.OfType(Of Translator)()
```

```
        For Each Translator In translators
            Console.WriteLine("Translator: " & Translator.FirstName &
                              " " & Translator.LastName)
        Next
    End Sub
```

It is interesting to observe how this query resolves on the database level. Listing 17.9 shows the SQL issued to the database. Since the Person–Translator hierarchy is modeled through a table-per-type inheritance modeling method, a join between the Persons and Translators tables has to be performed in order to fetch Translator entity rows from the database.

LISTING 17.9:   Fetch translators SQL code

```
SELECT
'1X0X' AS [C1],
[Extent1].[SSN] AS [SSN],
[Extent2].[FirstName] AS [FirstName],
[Extent2].[LastName] AS [LastName],
1 AS [C2],
[Extent2].[Phone_CountryCode] AS [Phone_CountryCode],
[Extent2].[Phone_AreaCode] AS [Phone_AreaCode],
[Extent2].[Phone_Number] AS [Phone_Number],
[Extent2].[Phone_Extension] AS [Phone_Extension]
FROM  [dbo].[Persons_Translator] AS [Extent1]
INNER JOIN [dbo].[Persons] AS [Extent2] ON [Extent1].[SSN] = [Extent2].[SSN]
```

As you can see in the last line in the listing, each time you need to obtain an instance of a Translator or Author entity, a join between Person and Translator or Person and Author has to be performed on the database level.

USING ENTITY SQL

If you have spent some time writing the SQL code, you will immediately feel familiar with eSQL. You can think of it as a data store–agnostic SQL used to query the EDM. Take a look at the code in Listing 17.10. It shows a simple query issued to the Books and Authors EDM using the Entity Client classes. The code has the familiar, traditional, ADO.NET "open connection, execute command" feel to it.

LISTING 17.10:   eSQL query issued using the Entity Client library

```
Private Sub FindBookByISBN_Click(ByVal sender As System.Object,
        ByVal e As System.EventArgs) Handles FindBookByISBN.Click
    Using connection As New EntityConnection("Name=BooksAndAuthorsContainer")
        connection.Open()
        Dim command = connection.CreateCommand()
```

```
        command.CommandText = "SELECT VALUE book FROM" &
                              "BooksAndAuthorsContainer.Books " &
                              "As book Where book.ISBN = @isbn"
        command.Parameters.AddWithValue("isbn", "9780470187425")
        Dim reader = command.ExecuteReader(CommandBehavior.SequentialAccess)
        reader.Read()
        Console.WriteLine("Book title is: " & reader("Title"))
    End Using
End Sub
```

If you take a look at the SQL Profiler trace, you will see how eSQL was transformed to the parameterized SQL query. Listing 17.11 shows the trace.

LISTING 17.11:   eSQL command transformed to parameterized query SQL

```
exec sp_executesql N'SELECT
[Extent1].[ISBN] AS [ISBN],
[Extent1].[Title] AS [Title],
[Extent1].[PublishingDate] AS [PublishingDate],
[Extent1].[PageCount] AS [PageCount]
FROM [dbo].[Books] AS [Extent1]
WHERE [Extent1].[ISBN] = @isbn',N'@isbn nvarchar(4000)',@isbn=N'9780470187425'
```

eSQL is a programming language in its own right, and, as such, getting into more details about eSQL programming is outside the scope of this book. For more information on eSQL, try the Microsoft Developer Network at http://msdn.microsoft.com/en-us/library/bb399560.aspx.

Real World Scenario

ADVANCED SEARCH FORMS WITH ESQL DYNAMIC QUERIES

Advanced search forms typically present a user with a number of search criteria. The user will generally employ only a few criteria options with each query, but the exact combination of criteria options cannot be known beforehand. Nor does it make sense programming all the possible criteria combinations, since there are too many.

A good alternative to implementing queries based on numerous criteria options is to use dynamic queries. With each new search, a new query is constructed "on the fly." The "where" portion of the query is generated by concatenating comparison statements expressing the condition on the form. Only those chosen by the user are included in the generated eSQL code.

The book search form, shown here, can be used to search for titles in the Books and Authors Entity Data Model.

It offers four different criteria for book search: book ISBN, book title, and a date range for publishing date. At each click of the Find button, each criteria is inspected and included in the query only if the user has entered the search criteria. To make the search more flexible, the ISBN and title are included in the query using wildcards and the LIKE condition. This way, if the user enters **Mastering** in the Title text box, all books containing the word *Mastering* in the title are selected by the query. Here's the complete code to make this form work; thanks to dynamic query construction, the whole sample can fit the single screen:

```
Imports System.Data.Objects
Imports System.Data.EntityClient

Public Class eSQLDynamicQuery

    Dim command As EntityCommand
    Dim eSqlSelect = "SELECT book.ISBN, book.Title, book.PublishingDate " &
                "from BooksAndAuthorsContainer.Books as book"
    Dim eSqlWhere As String

    Private Sub btnFind_Click(ByVal sender As System.Object,
                        ByVal e As System.EventArgs) Handles btnFind.Click
        gridResult.Rows.Clear()
        Using connection As New EntityConnection("Name=BooksAndAuthorsContainer")
```

```
            connection.Open()
            command = connection.CreateCommand()
            AddISBNCondition()
            AddTitleCondition()
            AddPublishedBeforeCondition()
            AddPublishedAfterCondition()
            command.CommandText = eSqlSelect & eSqlWhere
            Dim reader = command.ExecuteReader(CommandBehavior.SequentialAccess)
            While (reader.Read())
                gridResult.Rows.Add(New String() {reader("ISBN"), reader("Title"),
                    reader("PublishingDate")})
            End While
        End Using
    End Sub

    Private Sub AddISBNCondition()
        If String.IsNullOrEmpty(txtISBN.Text) Then Exit Sub
        ConcatenateAndOrWhere()
        eSqlWhere = eSqlWhere & "book.ISBN LIKE @isbn"
        command.Parameters.AddWithValue("isbn", "%" + txtISBN.Text + "%")
    End Sub

    Private Sub AddTitleCondition()
        If String.IsNullOrEmpty(txtTitle.Text) Then Exit Sub
        ConcatenateAndOrWhere()
        eSqlWhere = eSqlWhere & "book.Title LIKE @title"
        command.Parameters.AddWithValue("title", "%" + txtTitle.Text + "%")
    End Sub

    Private Sub AddPublishedAfterCondition()
        If txtAfter.Text.Equals("  /  /") Then Exit Sub
        ConcatenateAndOrWhere()
        eSqlWhere = eSqlWhere & "book.PublishingDate > @after"
        command.Parameters.AddWithValue("after", CDate(txtAfter.Text))
    End Sub

    Private Sub AddPublishedBeforeCondition()
        If txtBefore.Text.Equals("  /  /") Then Exit Sub
        ConcatenateAndOrWhere()
        eSqlWhere = eSqlWhere & "book.PublishingDate < @before"
        command.Parameters.AddWithValue("before", CDate(txtBefore.Text))
    End Sub

    Private Sub ConcatenateAndOrWhere()
        If Not (String.IsNullOrEmpty(eSqlWhere)) Then
            eSqlWhere = eSqlWhere & " AND "
        Else
```

```
                eSqlSelect = eSqlSelect & " WHERE "
        End If

    End Sub

    Private Sub Button2_Click(ByVal sender As System.Object,
                        ByVal e As System.EventArgs) Handles Button2.Click
        gridResult.Rows.Clear()
    End Sub
End Class
```

USING QUERY BUILDER METHODS AND THE OBJECTQUERY CLASS

Yet another alternative you have at your disposal for querying the EDM is the ObjectQuery class. You can build your queries in a standard object-oriented manner using the ObjectQuery builder methods. The ObjectQuery API permits writing chained methods following the Builder pattern. It is best to illustrate this with an example. Listing 17.12 demonstrates query construction employing the Object Query API.

LISTING 17.12: ObjectQuery's builder methods

```
Private Sub QueryBuilder_Click(ByVal sender As System.Object,
        ByVal e As System.EventArgs) Handles QueryBuilder.Click
    Dim context As New BooksAndAuthorsContainer
    Dim query As ObjectQuery(Of Book)
    query = context.Books.
        Where("it.PublishingDate > DATETIME'1999-01-01 00:00'").
        OrderBy("it.PublishingDate").
        Top(10)
    Console.WriteLine(query.ToTraceString())
    For Each book As Book In query.ToList()
        Console.WriteLine(book.Title)
    Next
End Sub
```

ObjectQuery has a ToTraceString method that permits visualizing the SQL that is being issued to the database directly inside the Visual Studio. Using ToTraceString is a more simple SQL debug method than monitoring the trace in SQL Server Profiler. Listing 17.13 shows the SQL trace.

LISTING 17.13: ObjectQuery's ToTraceString method output

```
SELECT TOP (10)
[Extent1].[ISBN] AS [ISBN],
[Extent1].[Title] AS [Title],
```

```
[Extent1].[PublishingDate] AS [PublishingDate],
[Extent1].[PageCount] AS [PageCount]
FROM [dbo].[Books] AS [Extent1]
WHERE [Extent1].[PublishingDate] > convert(datetime2,
'1999-01-01 00:00:00.0000000', 121)
ORDER BY [Extent1].[PublishingDate] ASC
```

Deferred Loading and Navigation Properties

So far, I haven't demonstrated how you can use navigation properties to obtain a reference of a related entity. Now that you cannot use navigation properties (not using navigation properties would pretty much defeat the purpose of having the EDM), you just need to be explicit about the relations you will be using on entities obtained from your queries. There are several ways to tell the Entity Framework to fetch related entities as well as the resulting entity. For example, you can use the Include method of the ObjectQuery class, you can explicitly load related entities, or you can activate the deferred loading feature of the Entity Framework.

A very common scenario with the Books and Authors EDM would be to list all books authored by a certain author. Had I not spoiled the surprise in the previous paragraph, you might have expected the code in Listing 17.14 to list all books authored by the randomly selected first author in the database.

LISTING 17.14: Unsuccessful attempt of listing all books belonging to an author

```
Private Sub DefferedLoading_Click(ByVal sender As System.Object,
                              ByVal e As System.EventArgs) Handles
                              DefferedLoading.Click
    Dim context As New BooksAndAuthorsContainer
    Dim author = context.Persons.OfType(Of Author).First()
    For Each book As Book In author.Books
        Console.WriteLine(book.Title)
    Next
End Sub
```

If you take a look at the Output window after executing the code in Listing 17.14, you will notice it lists no books, even though all authors have at least one book that they have authored in the database.

Using the Include Method

The first alternative at your disposal that you can use to read or to *materialize* (as retrieving entities from the database is more commonly called in EDM jargon) the related entities is the Include method. This loading strategy is also known as *eager loading*. Take a look at Listing 17.15; it demonstrates the Include method used to materialize related Book entities.

LISTING 17.15: Using the *Include*, method to materialize related entities

```
Private Sub DefferedLoading_Click(ByVal sender As System.Object,
                              ByVal e As System.EventArgs) Handles
                              DefferedLoading.Click
```

```
    Dim context As New BooksAndAuthorsContainer
    Dim author = context.Persons.OfType(Of Author).Include("Books").First()
    For Each book As Book In author.Books
        Console.WriteLine(book.Title)
    Next
End Sub
```

If you take a look at the Output window, you will see titles of the books belonging to the author printed to the console. More interesting, however, is the SQL generated by the Entity Framework. Listing 17.16 shows the SQL code.

LISTING 17.16:   SQL code resulting from the *Include* method

```
SELECT
[Limit1].[Signed] AS [Signed],
[Limit1].[SSN] AS [SSN],
[Limit1].[SSN1] AS [SSN1],
[Limit1].[FirstName] AS [FirstName],
[Limit1].[LastName] AS [LastName],
[Limit1].[Phone_CountryCode] AS [Phone_CountryCode],
[Limit1].[Phone_AreaCode] AS [Phone_AreaCode],
[Limit1].[Phone_Number] AS [Phone_Number],
[Limit1].[Phone_Extension] AS [Phone_Extension],
[Limit1].[C1] AS [C1],
[Limit1].[C2] AS [C2],
[Limit1].[C3] AS [C3],
[Project2].[C1] AS [C4],
[Project2].[ISBN] AS [ISBN],
[Project2].[Title] AS [Title],
[Project2].[PublishingDate] AS [PublishingDate],
[Project2].[PageCount] AS [PageCount]
FROM   (SELECT TOP (1)
    [Extent1].[Signed] AS [Signed],
    [Extent1].[SSN] AS [SSN],
    [Extent2].[SSN] AS [SSN1],
    [Extent2].[FirstName] AS [FirstName],
    [Extent2].[LastName] AS [LastName],
    [Extent2].[Phone_CountryCode] AS [Phone_CountryCode],
    [Extent2].[Phone_AreaCode] AS [Phone_AreaCode],
    [Extent2].[Phone_Number] AS [Phone_Number],
    [Extent2].[Phone_Extension] AS [Phone_Extension],
    '1X0X' AS [C1],
    1 AS [C2],
    1 AS [C3]
    FROM   [dbo].[Persons_Author] AS [Extent1]
    INNER JOIN [dbo].[Persons] AS [Extent2] ON
        [Extent1].[SSN] = [Extent2].[SSN] ) AS [Limit1]
LEFT OUTER JOIN (SELECT
```

```
    [Extent3].[Persons_SSN] AS [Persons_SSN],
    [Extent4].[ISBN] AS [ISBN],
    [Extent4].[Title] AS [Title],
    [Extent4].[PublishingDate] AS [PublishingDate],
    [Extent4].[PageCount] AS [PageCount],
    1 AS [C1]
    FROM   [dbo].[PersonBook] AS [Extent3]
    INNER JOIN [dbo].[Books] AS [Extent4] ON
        [Extent4].[ISBN] = [Extent3].[Books_ISBN] )
        AS [Project2] ON [Limit1].[SSN] = [Project2].[Persons_SSN]
ORDER BY [Limit1].[SSN] ASC, [Limit1].[SSN1] ASC, [Project2].[C1] ASC
```

Listing 17.16 is quite long, but for our purpose, it is important to note that the code includes a join with the Books table. It is also the only query visible in the SQL Profiler trace, meaning that all the data was fetched in one go — meaning it was *loaded eagerly*. Loading can also be deferred, as you will see in the "Using Deferred Loading" section very soon.

Using Explicit Loading

Instead of including the whole path in your query, you can tell the navigation property to load just when you need it. Listing 17.17 shows how books related to an author can be materialized using the Load method of the EntityCollection class.

LISTING 17.17:   Using explicit loading to materialize related entities

```
Private Sub DefferedLoading_Click(ByVal sender As System.Object,
                                  ByVal e As System.EventArgs) Handles
                                  DefferedLoading.Click
    Dim context As New BooksAndAuthorsContainer
    Dim author = context.Persons.OfType(Of Author).First()
    author.Books.Load()
    For Each book As Book In author.Books
        Console.WriteLine(book.Title)
    Next
End Sub
```

Again, it is the SQL Server Profiler that tells the true story of the code resolution on the database level. The trace includes two queries and is shown in Listing 17.18.

LISTING 17.18:   SQL code resulting from the *Load* method

```
-- first trace
SELECT
SELECT
[Limit1].[C1] AS [C1],
[Limit1].[SSN] AS [SSN],
```

```
[Limit1].[FirstName] AS [FirstName],
[Limit1].[LastName] AS [LastName],
[Limit1].[C2] AS [C2],
[Limit1].[Phone_CountryCode] AS [Phone_CountryCode],
[Limit1].[Phone_AreaCode] AS [Phone_AreaCode],
[Limit1].[Phone_Number] AS [Phone_Number],
[Limit1].[Phone_Extension] AS [Phone_Extension],
[Limit1].[Signed] AS [Signed]
FROM ( SELECT TOP (1)
    [Extent1].[Signed] AS [Signed],
    [Extent1].[SSN] AS [SSN],
    [Extent2].[FirstName] AS [FirstName],
    [Extent2].[LastName] AS [LastName],
    [Extent2].[Phone_CountryCode] AS [Phone_CountryCode],
    [Extent2].[Phone_AreaCode] AS [Phone_AreaCode],
    [Extent2].[Phone_Number] AS [Phone_Number],
    [Extent2].[Phone_Extension] AS [Phone_Extension],
    '1X0X' AS [C1],
    1 AS [C2]
    FROM [dbo].[Persons_Author] AS [Extent1]
    INNER JOIN [dbo].[Persons] AS [Extent2] ON [Extent1].[SSN] = [Extent2].[SSN]
) AS [Limit1]

-- second trace
exec sp_executesql N'SELECT
[Extent2].[ISBN] AS [ISBN],
[Extent2].[Title] AS [Title],
[Extent2].[PublishingDate] AS [PublishingDate],
[Extent2].[PageCount] AS [PageCount]
FROM [dbo].[PersonBook] AS [Extent1]
INNER JOIN [dbo].[Books] AS [Extent2] ON
[Extent1].[Books_ISBN] = [Extent2].[ISBN]
WHERE [Extent1].[Persons_SSN] =
@EntityKeyValue1',N'@EntityKeyValue1 char(9)',@EntityKeyValue1='568845586'
```

In this case, each time a book entity is referenced in the For Each loop, a new SQL statement is issued to a database. Had our author authored more than one book, you would end up with a significant number of queries issued to the database just to print this simple information.

Using Deferred Loading

More commonly known as *lazy loading*, this is the pattern that loads data from the database only upon the request. To put it simply, only when you call the Getter method of the navigation property is the data fetched from the database.

In this case, using navigation properties is quite transparent, and the code looks quite like the code in Listing 17.15. One missing detail has to do with activating the deferred loading, since it is deactivated by default. Listing 17.19 shows the code for deferred loading.

LISTING 17.19:   Using deferred loading to materialize related entities

```
Private Sub DefferedLoading_Click(ByVal sender As System.Object,
                                  ByVal e As System.EventArgs) Handles
                                  DefferedLoading.Click
    Dim context As New BooksAndAuthorsContainer
    context.ContextOptions.DeferredLoadingEnabled = True
    Dim author = context.Persons.OfType(Of Author).First()
    For Each book As Book In author.Books
        Console.WriteLine(book.Title)
    Next
End Sub
```

As you would expect, the resulting SQL is identical to that shown in Listing 17.18, meaning that a new query is issued for each referenced Book entity.

Choosing the Right Loading Strategy

Now that you have seen how different loading strategies are resolved at a database level, you must be already guessing the impact of choosing the right loading strategy on the performance of your application. In our sample code, deferring the loading of book information would result in abysmal performance if such code was ever put into production.

If you had no prior experience with ORM frameworks like the Entity Framework, then at this point you might be asking yourself, "Does deferred loading make sense at all?" It does provide some coding benefits, since you use navigation properties just like any other properties, but this coding gain is certainly not worth the possible negative impact on the application performance.

Deferred (or lazy loading) is the default loading strategy in many object-relational mapping (ORM) frameworks similar to the Entity Framework. As it happens, the sample code I have shown in this section serves to illustrate different loading strategies, but it is not very representative of how real-life applications work.

In a typical application scenario, you use simple properties on an entity to display the entity information to the user. In our example, you use Author information (probably a name) to let the user select the correct author. (At this point, eagerly loading book information from the database would mean loading almost all the database data in one go!) Only after the user has selected the author is the related data (in our example list of books) fetched from the database. At this point, it does make sense to fetch all the books belonging to an author in one go, since you will show the list of all titles on the Author Details page. Imagine the Book has some related Sales information. It does not make sense to fetch this information until the user selects the specific title. With lazy loading, all the data is timely fetched.

The more complex the application becomes, the more complicated it is to understand all the scenarios where navigation properties will be used. For best results, fine-tune your queries, choose the correct loading strategy for each individual query, and profile the Entity Framework SQL generation to grasp how the Entity Framework queries are translated into the SQL issued to database.

Modifying the Data with the Entity Framework

The Entity Framework provides a strongly typed, object-oriented view of the data, and as such, it enables you to insert, update, and delete data by working with instances of entity types. All of the entity type instances are bound to a context (through an ObjectContext class) that tracks the changes made to these objects. Once you tell ObjectContext to commit changes to the database by calling the SaveChanges method, it calculates the differences between the data in the application and the data in the data store and will commit the changes to the data store.

In the Books and Authors EDM, the class inheriting the ObjectContext class is called BooksAndAuthorsContainer. As in the previous examples, when querying the data, Books-AndAuthorsContainer is the central class that permits access to all the objects' methods related to data modifications. Let's start with a simple insert of a new entity.

INSERTING NEW INSTANCES

We can insert a new instance of an entity in several ways. Each entity class in the EDM has a static CreateEntityName method. For example, the Book entity has a CreateBook static method that can be used for the purpose of adding a new book to a context. Alternatively, you can create a new entity using the New operator and then use the AddObject method that's available on each EntitySet class. Listing 17.20 shows the latter method where first a new instance of the Language entity is created, then it is added to the Languages entity set, and finally it is committed to the database by calling ObjectContext.SaveChanges().

LISTING 17.20:   Adding a new *Language* entity

```
Private Sub InsertNewLanguage_Click(ByVal sender As System.Object,
                          ByVal e As System.EventArgs) Handles
                          InsertNewLanguage.Click
    Dim context As New BooksAndAuthorsContainer
    Dim arabic As New Language
    arabic.Name = "Arabic"
    context.Languages.AddObject(arabic)
    context.SaveChanges()
End Sub
```

DELETING AN ENTITY INSTANCE

Deletion of an entity instance can be easily performed with the help of the Delete method of ObjectContext. Listing 17.21 shows how this is performed using the instance of the Language entity inserted in the previous listing.

LISTING 17.21:   Deleting a *Language* entity

```
Private Sub DeleteLanguage_Click(ByVal sender As System.Object,
                        ByVal e As System.EventArgs) Handles
                        DeleteLanguage.Click
    Dim context As New BooksAndAuthorsContainer
    Dim arabic As Language = (From language In context.Languages
                         Where language.Name = "Arabic").
                         FirstOrDefault()
    context.DeleteObject(arabic)
    context.SaveChanges()
End Sub
```

UPDATING AN ENTITY INSTANCE

You will not be surprised by the code included in Listing 17.22. It follows a pattern that is similar to that found in the entity insertion and deletion code. An Entity property is updated, and changes are committed by calling the ObjectContext SaveChanges method.

LISTING 17.22:   Updating a *Language* entity

```
Private Sub UpdateLanguage_Click(ByVal sender As System.Object,
                            ByVal e As System.EventArgs) Handles
                            UpdateLanguage.Click
    Dim context As New BooksAndAuthorsContainer
    Dim arabic As Language = (From language In context.Languages
                        Where language.Name = "Arabic").
                        FirstOrDefault()
    arabic.Name = "Arabic Language"
    context.SaveChanges()
End Sub
```

ESTABLISHING RELATIONSHIP BETWEEN ENTITY INSTANCES

The final piece of the data modification puzzle has to do with establishing the relationship between the entity instances. If I have a Book instance and an Author instance, how do I relate them so that the book appears in the list of books authored by that specific author?

You can perform this in a standard object-oriented manner. Just add the Book instance to the set of books belonging to the Author, and call SaveChanges on the ObjectContext. Listing 17.23 shows that exact scenario.

LISTING 17.23:   Establishing a relationship between an *Author* and a *Book* instance

```
Private Sub InsertsInTransaction_Click(ByVal sender As System.Object,
                            ByVal e As System.EventArgs) Handles
                            InsertsInTransaction.Click
    Dim context As New BooksAndAuthorsContainer

    Dim book As New Book With {.ISBN = "9780470179796",
            .Title = "Professional Refactoring in Visual Basic",
            .PageCount = "517", .PublishingDate = "April 7, 2008"}

    Dim author As New Author With {.SSN = "423235332",
            .FirstName = "Danijel",
            .LastName = "Arsenovski",
            .Phone = New PhoneNumber With {.CountryCode = "56",
                .AreaCode = "2", .Number = "8588656", .Extension = " "},
            .Signed = "January 1, 2007"}

    context.Persons.AddObject(author)
    context.Books.AddObject(book)
```

```
      author.Books.Add(book)
      context.SaveChanges()
  End Sub
```

By calling the Add method on the set of Books belonging to an Author — author.Books.Add
(book) — the Entity Framework becomes aware that two instances are related and adds the
record to the PersonBook join table in the database.

USING TRANSACTIONS IN THE ENTITY FRAMEWORK

If you look back at Listing 17.23, you might wonder what exactly happens if the Entity Framework is not capable of performing all the operations in the listing. If you analyze the listing,
you can see that the code will be resolved as three Insert operations on the database level:
the insert of an author instance to the Author table, the insert of a book instance into the Book
table, and the insert of the record relating the book and the author into the PersonBook table.
So, what happens if one of these operations fails?

The Entity Framework generates implicit transactions for all changes performed from
one SaveChanges method call to the next. In our example, all inserts will be committed to
the database under the same transaction. If any of them fails, the others are automatically
rolled back.

You can test this by executing the code in Listing 17.23 twice in a row. For the second
execution, modify the author's Social Security number, but leave the book data as it is. Since
you have modified the SSN, you will be able to insert the author, but the book insert will fail.
ISBN is the primary key on the Book entity, and the same value cannot be inserted twice. The
execution will end up in an error. If you then take a look at the database, you will observe that
neither the book nor the author instance was inserted.

Coordinating Transactions with External Operations

In some scenarios, the transaction control that ObjectContext implicitly provides is not enough.
There are situations where you need to enroll operations external to the ObjectContext into the
same transaction. In such cases, you can use the TransactionScope class. Listing 17.24 shows
some mock-up code that demonstrates how the TransactionScope class can be used.

LISTING 17.24:   Using TransactionScope for enlisting external operations

```
Using transaction As New TransactionScope()
    context.Persons.AddObject(author)
    context.Books.AddObject(book)
    author.Books.Add(book)
    context.SaveChanges()
    'Do some external operation that can be enroled inside the transaction
    transaction.Complete()
End Using
```

Note that you need to reference the System.Transactions assembly and import the
System.Transactions namespace in order to gain access to the TransactionScope class.

Reverse-Engineering an Entity Data Model

The approach I followed thus far in this chapter starts with the premise that you are building a completely new EDM. The EDM is then used to generate the DDL scripts for the database used to store the EDM data.

Very often, though, you will have to construct your application on the top of an existing database. The Entity Framework supports that scenario, as well; in that case, the EDM Designer will use the database structure as a starting point for automated EDM generation.

Let's explore this scenario by creating an EDM from the Northwind database. I explained how you can obtain and install the sample Northwind database in Chapter 15, so I will assume that the database is present in your Microsoft SQL Server.

1. Choose Project ➤ Add New Item. Select the ADO .NET Entity Data Model item, and rename it to `Northwind.edmx`. Click Add.

2. When the Entity Data Model Wizard opens, choose Generate From Database as your reply to the "What should the model contain?" prompt. Click Next.

3. Select a connection to the Northwind database. If the connection is not present in the Connection combo box, use the New Connection button to create a connection to the Northwind database, and then click Next.

4. When the Choose Your Database Objects window opens, select all the objects displayed under the Tables, Views, and Stored Procedures nodes, and click Finish.

The part of the Northwind EDM diagram showing entities generated from tables in the Northwind database was shown earlier in Figure 17.1.

The Entity Framework is capable of making use of already constructed databases including other database objects, such as views and stored procedures. In the case of views, a separate `EntityType` and `EntitySet` are generated for each view. Stored procedures are represented as functions in the EDM and can be mapped as custom CRUD operations for an entity. In that case, instead of generating the appropriate SQL, the Entity Framework is capable of invoking the stored procedure to delete, update, insert, or read the entity.

The Bottom Line

Employ deferred loading when querying the Entity Data Model.   The Entity Framework supports the deferred loading (lazy loading) of entities. When deferred loading is activated, entities in navigation properties are loaded on demand, only after they are accessed. In cases when you are not certain that the related entity will be accessed (for example, when loading is dependent on a user action), you can initially load only the root entity and load the related entities only when they are requested.

Master It   How do you activate deferred loading in the Entity Framework?

Use entity inheritance features in the Entity Framework.   In the EDM, an inheritance relationship can be established between entities. When two entities participate in an inheritance relationship, the child entity inherits all the properties of the parent entity. When working with such an entity in .NET code, you can get major benefits from code reuse based on inheritance.

Master It   Explain how the Entity Framework can map an inheritance relationship between entities to tables in the database. Why is maintaining the inheritance relationship between the entities not easily accomplished with relational databases?

Create and query related entities.   In the Entity Data Model, you can establish one-to-many or many-to-many associations between entities. The association can be established by connecting related entities with the Association tool in the EDM diagram. When querying such entities, a related entity or set of entities can be accessed through generated navigation properties.

Master It   In the Books and Authors application (used as a sample application in this chapter), add a SalesByMonth form that will display the number of copies sold in a month for each title in the database. Modify the Books and Authors EDM so that the model can accommodate monthly sales information for each title.

Chapter 18

Building Data-Bound Applications

In Chapter 15, "Programming with ADO.NET," you learned about the two basic classes for interacting with databases: The Connection class provides the members you need to connect to the database, and the Command class provides the members you need to execute commands against the database. A data-driven application also needs to store data at the client, and you know how to use a DataReader to grab data from the database and how to use a DataAdapter to populate a DataSet at the client.

In addition to the DataSets you created in Chapter 17, "Using the Data Entity Model," Visual Studio also allows you to create typed DataSets. A typed DataSet is designed with visual tools at design time, and its structure is known to the compiler, which can generate very efficient code for the specific type of data you're manipulating in your application. Another advantage of typed DataSets is that they can be bound to Windows controls on a form. When a field is bound to a Windows control, every time you move to another row in the table, the control is updated to reflect the current value of the field. When the user edits the control on the form, the new value replaces the original value of the field in the DataSet. The form is said to be *bound* to the data source, which is usually a DataSet.

Data binding is a process for building data-driven applications with visual tools: You map the columns of a table to controls on the form, and Visual Studio generates the code for displaying the data on the bound controls, as well as updating the DataSet when the user edits the value of a bound control. These applications are called *data bound*, and they're similar to the applications you designed in the previous chapter. The difference is that Visual Studio generates the necessary code for you.

In this chapter, you'll learn how to do the following:

◆ Design and use typed DataSets

◆ Bind Windows forms to typed DataSets

◆ Compare a LINQ query used to filter data with an eSQL dynamic query

Working with Typed DataSets

The DataSets you explored in the preceding chapter were untyped: Their exact structure was determined at runtime, when they were populated through the appropriate DataAdapters. In this chapter, I'll discuss typed DataSets in detail. A *typed DataSet* is a DataSet with a known structure because it's created at design time with visual tools. The compiler knows the structure of the DataSet (that is, the DataTables it contains and the structure of each DataTable), and it generates code that's specific to the data at hand.

The most important characteristic of typed DataSets is that they allow you to write strongly typed code and practically eliminate the chances of exceptions due to syntax errors. Whereas in an untyped DataSet you had to access the DataTables by name with an expression such as DS.Tables ("Products"), the equivalent typed DataSet exposes the name of the table as a property: DS.Products. To find out whether a specific field of an untyped DataSet is Null, you must use an expression like the following:

```
DS.Tables ("Products").Rows (0).Item ("UnitPrice").IsNull
```

With a typed DataSet, you can declare a variable that represents a row of the Products table like this:

```
Dim prod As NorthwindDataSet.ProductsRow =
            DS.Products.Rows(0)
```

You can then access the fields of the row as properties, with expressions like this: prod.ProductName, prod.UnitPrice, and so on. To find out whether the *UnitPrice* field is Null, call the method prod.IsUnitPriceNull. You can also set a field to *Null* with a method call: prod.SetUnitPriceNull. As you can guess, after the structure of the DataSet is known, the editor can generate a class with many members that will enormously simplify the coding of the application using the typed DataSet. You can count on IntelliSense to help you reference table columns, represented as properties on a generated Row class. The code you will have to write will be a lot terser and easier to understand. The typed DataSet is a class that's generated by a wizard on the fly, and it becomes part of your solution.

Let's start by looking at the process of generating typed DataSets with visual data tools. Then you'll see how to bind Windows controls to typed DataSets and generate functional interfaces with point-and-click operations.

Generating a Typed DataSet

In this section, you'll create a typed DataSet with the three basic tables of the Northwind database: Products, Categories, and Suppliers. Create a new Windows Forms Application project, the DataSetOperations project. (This is the same name as the sample project you can download from www.sybex.com/go/masteringvb2010.) Then open the Data menu, and choose the Add Data Source command. You will see the Data Source Configuration Wizard, which will take you through the steps of building a DataSet at design time. In the first page of the wizard, you'll be asked to select the data source type; it can be a database, a service (such as a web service), or an object, as in Figure 18.1. Select the Database icon, and click the Next button.

The Service option on the page shown in Figure 18.1 creates a DataSet that retrieves its data from a service (usually a web service). The Object option allows you to create a DataSet from a collection of custom objects.

On the next page of the wizard, shown in Figure 18.2, you must specify a connection string for the database you want to use. Click the New Connection button to create a new connection only if there's no connection for the database you want to use. If you've experimented already with the visual tools of Visual Basic, you may already have an existing connection, in which case you simply select it from the drop-down list.

FIGURE 18.1
Choosing the data source
type in the Data Source
Configuration Wizard

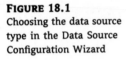

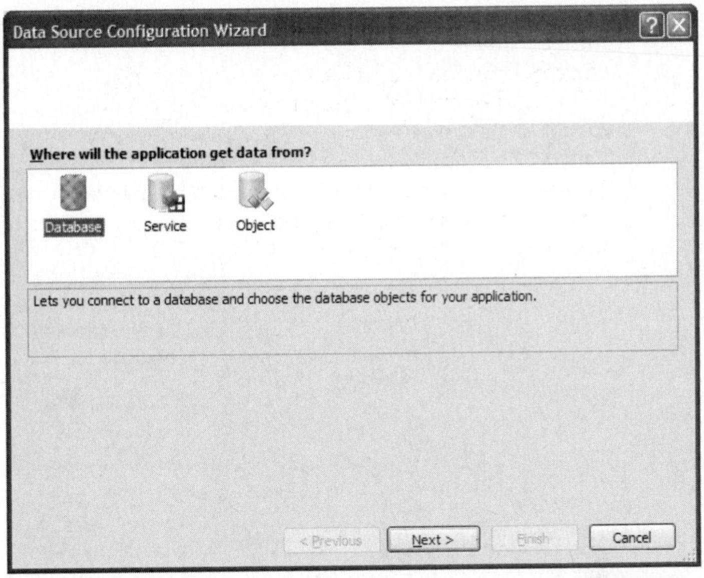

FIGURE 18.2
Choosing your
data connection in
the Data Source
Configuration Wizard

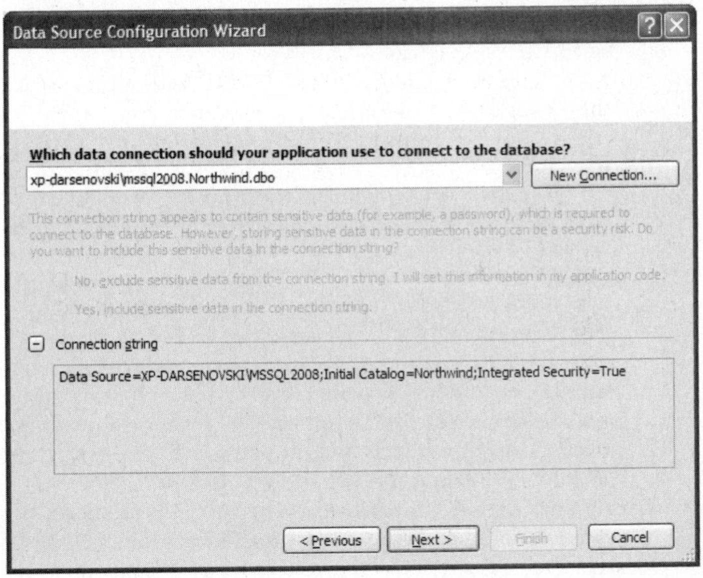

To create a new connection, you must specify your credentials: whether you'll connect with a username and password or use Windows authentication. Once connected to the server, you can select the desired database from a ComboBox control. If you click the New Connection button to create a new connection to the Northwind database, you will see the Add Connection dialog box, as shown in Figure 18.3. This dialog box is not new to you; it's the same dialog box you use to create a new data connection in Server Explorer window. If you haven't created a connection to the Northwind database yet, do it now. Otherwise, select the existing connection.

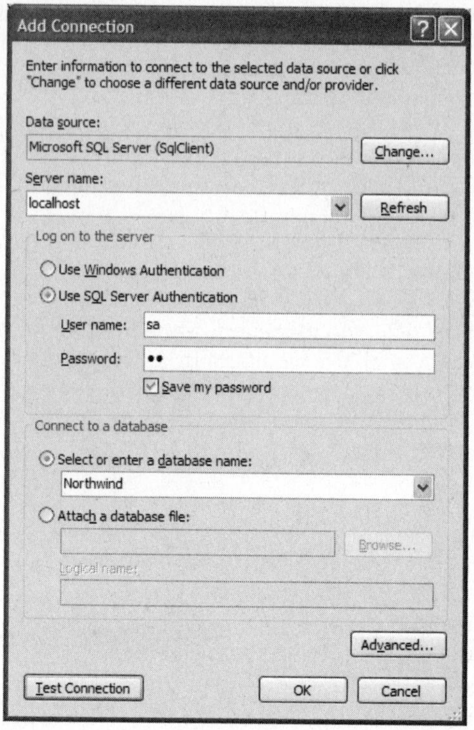

FIGURE 18.3
Using the Add
Connection dialog box
to specify a new con-
nection to the North-
wind database

FIGURE 18.3
Using the Add
Connection dialog box
to specify a new con-
nection to the North-
wind database

It's recommended that you use Windows authentication to connect to the database. If this isn't possible because the database server is not in the local network, you must specify a username and password in the boxes shown in Figure 18.3. In this case, the wizard will ask whether you want to store sensitive information (the account's password) to the connection string. You can choose to either include the password in the connection string (not a very safe approach) or supply it from within your code. You can always set the Password property of a Connection object in your code. To secure the password, you can prompt the user for a password when the application starts and save it to an application variable. This way, the password isn't persisted anywhere; it only exists in computer memory as long as the application is running. Alternatively, you can store an encrypted version of the password and decrypt and use it from within your code. The best approach for a local network is to use Windows authentication.

Click the OK button to close the Add Connection dialog box, and then click Next; you will see a dialog box with the default connection name: NorthwindConnectionString. This is the name of a new application setting that will store the connection information. You can edit this, as well as the other application settings, on the Settings tab of the project's Properties pages. (To see the project's Properties pages, choose Project Properties from the Project menu.)

Click Next again, and you will see the Choose Your Database Objects page, shown in Figure 18.4, where you can select the tables and columns you want to load to the DataSet. Notice that you can't use a SELECT statement to select the data you want from a table: You must select the entire table. Of course, you can write a stored procedure to limit your selection and then select it in the dialog box. If you select multiple tables and they're related, the relationship between them will also be imported for you (no need to create a DataRelation object for each relationship between the DataSet tables). For this example, select the Categories, Suppliers, and Products tables of the Northwind database. Select all columns of the Products and Categories tables, except for the Picture column of the Categories table. From the Suppliers table, select the SupplierID and CompanyName columns.

At the bottom of the dialog box shown in Figure 18.4, you can specify the name of the DataSet that will be generated for you. I'll use the default name, NorthwindDataSet. Click Finish to close the wizard and create the DataSet, which will be added automatically to the Solution Explorer window.

In the Data Sources window, shown in Figure 18.5, you will see a tree that represents the tables in the DataSet. The DataSet contains three DataTables, and each DataTable is made of the columns you selected in the wizard. This DataSet is typed, because it knows the structure of the data you're going to store in it. The interesting part of this tree is that it contains the Products table three times: in the first level along with the Categories table, as its own table, and once again under the Categories and Suppliers tables. (You must expand these tables to see it, as in Figure 18.5.) Whereas the Products table on the first level represents the entire table, the nested ones represent the products linked to their categories and their suppliers, respectively. You will see later in the chapter how to use the multiple Products DataTables.

The typed DataSet is actually a class that is generated on the fly. It's no longer a generic DataSet we will populate at runtime with any table we want through a DataAdapter; it's a specific object that can be populated only with the tables we specified in its design. If you want

FIGURE 18.4
Selecting the tables and columns you want to include in your typed DataSet

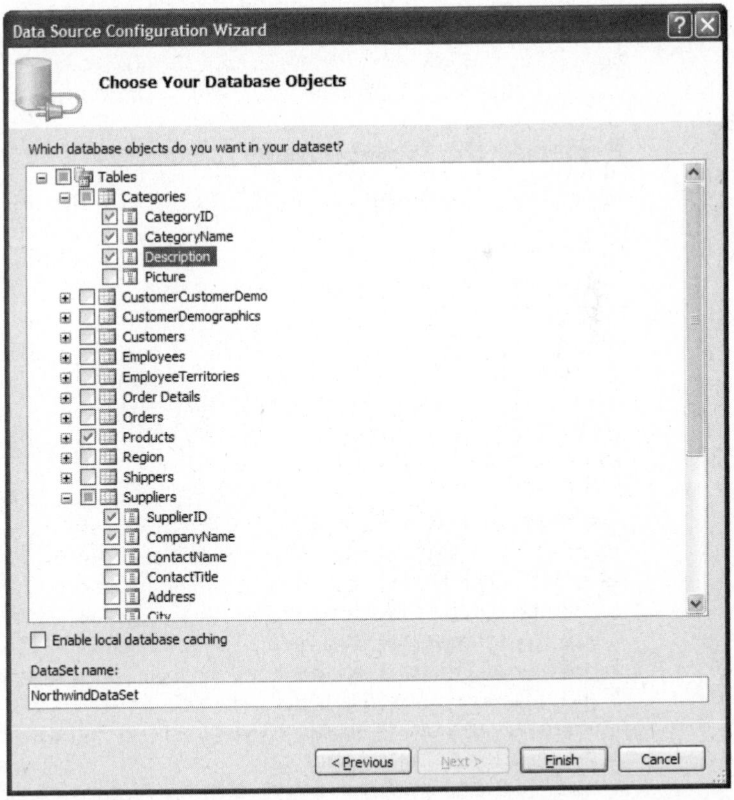

to see the code of the class generated by the wizard, click the Show All Files button in Solution Explorer window, and double-click the NorthwindDataSet.Designer.vb item under the North-wind DataSet. You shouldn't edit the code, because if you decide to edit the DataSet (you'll see how you can edit it with visual tools), the wizard will create a new class, and your changes will be lost. If you want to add some custom members to the Northwind class, create a new Partial class with the custom members, and name it NorthwindDataSet.vb.

Exploring the Typed DataSet

Let's exercise the members of the typed DataSet a little and see how the typed DataSet differs from the equivalent untyped DataSet. The operations we'll perform are similar to the ones we performed in the preceding chapter with an untyped DataSet; you should focus on the different syntax. The code shown in this section belongs to the DataSetOperations sample project. This project contains three forms, and you will have to change the project's Startup object to view each one.

Figure 18.6 shows Form1 of the project, which demonstrates the basic operations on a typed DataSet, including how to populate it, edit some of its tables, and submit the changes to the database. They're basically the same operations you'd perform with an untyped DataSet, but you will see that it's much simpler to work with typed DataSets.

To populate the three DataTables of the DataSet, you need three DataAdapter objects. Instead of the generic DataAdapter, the class generated by the wizard has created a TableAdapter class for each DataTable: the CategoriesTableAdapter, SuppliersTableAdapter, and ProductsTableAdapter classes. Declare three objects of the corresponding type at the form level:

```
Dim CategoriesTA As New _
    NorthwindDataSetTableAdapters.CategoriesTableAdapter
Dim SuppliersTA As New _
    NorthwindDataSetTableAdapters.SuppliersTableAdapter
Dim ProductsTA As New _
    NorthwindDataSetTableAdapters.ProductsTableAdapter
```

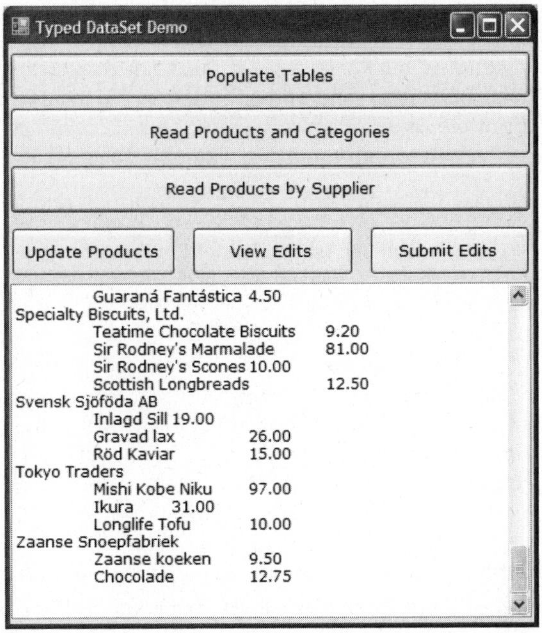

FIGURE 18.6
Form1 of the Data-
SetOperations project
demonstrates the
basic operations on
a typed DataSet.

The classes create the three objects that will retrieve the data from the database and submit the edited rows to the database from the SELECT statements you specified with point-and-click operations. These objects derive from the TableAdapter class, which in turn is based on the DataAdapter class. If you examine the code of the Northwind class, you will find the code that creates the SQL statements for querying and updating the three tables and how these statements are used to create a DataAdapter object. The code is similar to the code we used in the preceding chapter to create DataAdapters from within our code.

You must also create a DataSet object to store the data. This time, however, you can use a specific type that describes the structure of the data you plan to store at the client, not a generic DataSet. Insert the following declaration at the form level:

```
Dim DS As New NorthwindDataSet
```

Now place the Populate Tables button on the form, and insert the code shown in Listing 18.1 in its Click event handler.

LISTING 18.1:   Populating a typed DataSet with the proper TableAdapters

```
Private Sub bttnPopulate_Click(…) Handles bttnPopulate.Click
    Dim categories As Integer = CategoriesTA.Fill(DS.Categories)
    Dim suppliers As Integer = SuppliersTA.Fill(DS.Suppliers)
    Dim products As Integer = ProductsTA.Fill(DS.Products)
```

As you can see, the Fill method doesn't accept any DataTable as an argument; instead, the type of its argument is determined by the TableAdapter object to which it's applied. The Fill method of the ProductsTA TableAdapter accepts as an argument an object of the Products-DataTable type. The event handler of the sample project includes a few more statements that print the count of rows in each of the three tables.

To go through the rows of the Products table, write a simple loop like the following:

```
Dim prod As NorthwindDataSet.ProductsRow
For Each prod In DS.Products.Rows
    TextBox1.AppendText(prod.ProductName & vbTab &
        prod.UnitPrice.ToString("#,###.00") & vbCrLf)
Next
```

As you can see, the names of the fields are properties of the ProductsRow class. Some products may have no price (a *Null* value in the database). If you attempt to access the UnitPrice property of the ProductsRow class, a NullReferenceException exception will be thrown. To prevent it, you can make sure that the field is not *Null* from within your code, with an IIf function like the following:

```
TextBox1.AppendText(
        IIf(prod.IsUnitPriceNull,
        "Not for sale!",
        prod.UnitPrice.ToString("#,###.00")))
```

To read data from linked tables in a hierarchical way, you don't have to specify the relationship between the tables as you did with untyped DataSets, because the typed DataTables expose the appropriate methods.

Now place another button on your form, the Read Products By Supplier button, and in its Click handler insert the code shown in Listing 18.2 to iterate through suppliers and related products. Notice that the SuppliersRow class exposes the GetProductsRows method, which retrieves the Products rows that are associated with the current supplier. The GetProductsRows method is equivalent to the GetChildRows of an untyped DataSet, only with the latter you have to supply a relationship name as an argument. Moreover, the GetProductsRows method returns an array of ProductsRow objects, not generic DataRow objects.

LISTING 18.2: Iterating through linked DataTables

```
Private Sub bttnSuppliersProducts_Click(…) Handles
                    bttnSuppliersProducts.Click
    TextBox1.Clear()
    Dim supp As NorthwindDataSet.SuppliersRow
    For Each supp In DS.Suppliers.Rows
        TextBox1.AppendText(supp.CompanyName & vbCrLf)
        Dim prod As NorthwindDataSet.ProductsRow
        For Each prod In supp.GetProductsRows
            TextBox1.AppendText(vbTab &
                prod.ProductName & vbTab &
```

```
                prod.UnitPrice.ToString("#,###.00") & vbCrLf)
        Next
    Next
End Sub
```

The ProductsRow object exposes the `SuppliersRow` and `CategoriesRow` methods, which return the current product's parent rows in the `Suppliers` and `Categories` DataTables.

The most useful method of the typed DataTable is the `FindByID` method, which locates a row by its ID in the DataTable. To locate a product by its ID, call the `FindByProductID` method, passing a product ID as an argument. The method returns a ProductsRow object that represents the matching product. The method's return value is not a copy of the found row but instead is a reference to the actual row in the DataTable, and you can edit it. The code behind the Update Products button, which is shown in Listing 18.3, selects a product at random by its ID and prompts the user for a new price. Then it sets the `UnitPrice` field to the user-supplied value.

LISTING 18.3:   Updating a row of a typed DataTable

```
Private Sub bttnUpdate_Click(…) Handles bttnUpdate.Click
    Dim selProduct As NorthwindDataSet.ProductsRow
    Dim RND As New System.Random
    selProduct = DS.Products.FindByProductID(RND.Next(1, 77))
    Dim newPrice As Decimal
    newPrice = Convert.ToDecimal(InputBox(
                    "Enter product's new price",
                    selProduct.ProductName,
                    selProduct.UnitPrice.ToString))
    selProduct.UnitPrice = newPrice
End Sub
```

As you can see, manipulating the rows of typed DataTables is much simpler than the equivalent operations with untyped DataSets, because the fields are exposed as properties of the appropriate class (the ProductsRow class for rows of the `Products` DataTable, the Categories-Row class for rows of the `Categories` DataTable, and so on).

Let's look at the code for updating the database. The first step is to retrieve the edited rows with the `GetChanges` method, which returns a typed DataTable object, depending on the DataTable to which it was applied. To retrieve the modified rows of the `Products` DataTable, use the following statements:

```
Dim DT As NorthwindDataSet.ProductsDataTable
DT = DS.Products.GetChanges
```

You can pass an argument of the DataRowState type to the `GetChanges` method to retrieve the inserted, modified, or deleted rows. Because this is a typed DataSet, you can write a For Each loop to iterate through its rows (they're all of the ProductsRow type) and find the edits. One feature you'd expect to find in a typed DataTable is a method for retrieving the original versions of a row by name. Unfortunately, the class generated by the wizard doesn't include such a method; you must use the Item property, passing as an argument the name of the row. A row's original field versions are given by the following expression:

```
prod.Item("UnitPrice", DataRowVersion.Original)
```

To submit the edited rows to the database, you can call the appropriate TableAdapter Update method. The code behind the Submit Edits button does exactly that, and it's shown in Listing 18.4.

LISTING 18.4: Submitting the edited rows of a typed DataTable to the database

```
Private Sub bttnSubmit_Click(…) Handles bttnSubmit.Click
    If DS.HasChanges Then
        Dim DT As NorthwindDataSet.ProductsDataTable =
            DS.Products.GetChanges
        If DT IsNot Nothing Then
            Try
                ProductsTA.Update(DT)
            Catch ex As Exception
                MsgBox(ex.Message)
                Exit Sub
            End Try
            MsgBox(DT.Rows.Count.ToString &
                " rows updated successfully.")
        End If
    End If
End Sub
```

Typed DataSets are quite convenient when it comes to coding. The real advantage of typed DataSets is that they can simplify enormously the generation of data-bound forms, which is the main topic of this chapter.

Data Binding

Data binding is the process of linking the contents of a field to a control on the form. Every time the application modifies the field's value, the control is updated automatically. Likewise, every time the user edits the control's value on the form, the underlying field in the DataSet is also updated. Sometimes, this two-way linking of the data is referred to as *bidirectional data binding*. The DataSet keeps track of the changes (the modified, added, and deleted rows), regardless of how they were changed. In short, data binding relieves you from having to map field values to controls on the form when a row is selected and from moving values from the controls back to the DataSet when a row is edited.

In addition to binding simple controls such as TextBox controls to a single field, you can bind an entire column of a DataTable to a list control, such as the ListBox or ComboBox control. And of course, you can bind an entire DataTable to a special control, the DataGridView control.

You can build a data-browsing and data-editing application by binding the Products DataTable to a DataGridView control without a single line of code.

To explore the basics of data binding, add a second form to the project, and make it the project's startup object. Figure 18.7 shows the new form of the DataSetOperations project, Form2.

Then drop a DataGridView control on the form, and set the control's DataSource property to bind it to the Products DataTable. Select the DataGridView control on the form, and locate its DataSource property in the Properties window. Expand the DataSource property, and you will see the project's data sources. The form contains no data source for the time being, so all data sources are listed under Other Data Sources. Expand this item of the tree to see the Project Data Sources item, which in turn contains the NorthwindDataSet data source (or whatever you have named the typed DataSet). Expand this item, and you will see the names of the Data-Tables in the DataSet, as shown in Figure 18.8. Select the Products DataTable.

The editor will populate the DataGridView control with the table's columns: It will map each column in the Products DataTable to a column in the DataGridView control. All columns have the same width and are displayed as text boxes, except for the Discontinued column, which is mapped to a CheckBox control. (This is the last column of the controls, and you will see it at runtime, because you can't scroll the control at design time.) The control's columns were named after the DataTable columns, but we'll change the appearance of the grid shortly. Press F5 to run the application, and the form will come up populated with the Products rows! Obviously, the editor has generated some code for us to populate the control. The code generated by the editor is a single statement in the form's Load event handler:

```
Me.ProductsTableAdapter.Fill(Me.NorthwindDataSet.Products)
```

As far as browsing the data, we're all set. All we have to do is adjust the appearance of the DataGridView control with point-and-click operations. You can also edit the rows, but there's no code to submit the edits to the database. Submitting the changes to the database shouldn't be a problem for you; just copy the corresponding code statement from Form1 of the project.

FIGURE 18.7
Viewing an entire DataTable on a data-bound DataGrid-View control

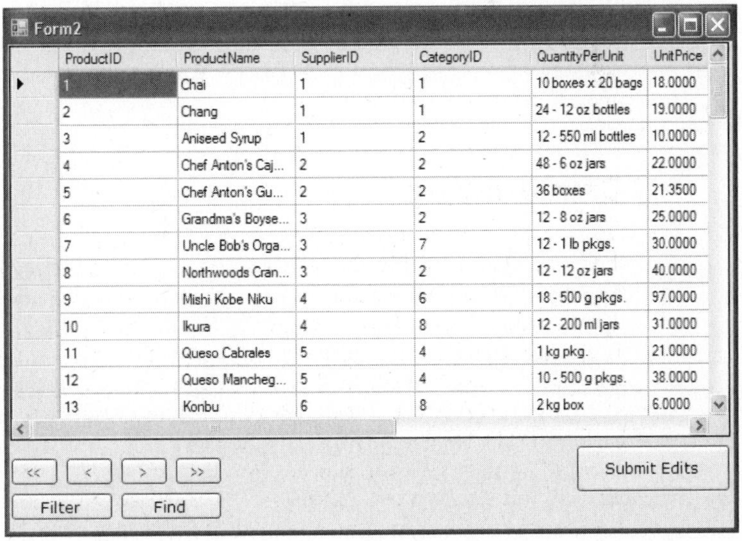

ProductID	ProductName	SupplierID	CategoryID	QuantityPerUnit	UnitPrice
1	Chai	1	1	10 boxes x 20 bags	18.0000
2	Chang	1	1	24 - 12 oz bottles	19.0000
3	Aniseed Syrup	1	2	12 - 550 ml bottles	10.0000
4	Chef Anton's Caj...	2	2	48 - 6 oz jars	22.0000
5	Chef Anton's Gu...	2	2	36 boxes	21.3500
6	Grandma's Boyse...	3	2	12 - 8 oz jars	25.0000
7	Uncle Bob's Orga...	3	7	12 - 1 lb pkgs.	30.0000
8	Northwoods Cran...	3	2	12 - 12 oz jars	40.0000
9	Mishi Kobe Niku	4	6	18 - 500 g pkgs.	97.0000
10	Ikura	4	8	12 - 200 ml jars	31.0000
11	Queso Cabrales	5	4	1 kg pkg.	21.0000
12	Queso Mancheg...	5	4	10 - 500 g pkgs.	38.0000
13	Konbu	6	8	2 kg box	6.0000

FIGURE 18.8
Binding the Data-
GridView control to a
DataTable

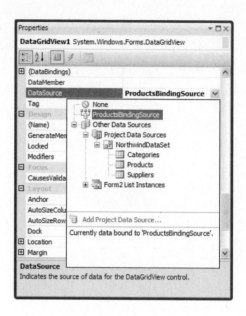

Place the Submit Edits button on the form, and in its `Click` handler insert the following
statements:

```
If NorthwindDataSet.HasChanges Then
    Dim DT As NorthwindDataSet.ProductsDataTable =
        NorthwindDataSet.Products.GetChanges
    If DT IsNot Nothing Then
        Try
            ProductsTableAdapter.Update(DT)
        Catch ex As Exception
            MsgBox(ex.Message)
            Exit Sub
        End Try
        MsgBox(DT.Rows.Count.ToString &
            " rows updated successfully.")
    End If
End If
```

I changed the name of the DataSet from `DS` to `NorthwindDataSet` and the name of the
TableAdapter from `ProductsTA` to `ProductsTableAdapter`. And where did these names come
from? If you switch to the form's Designer, you'll see that while you were setting the Data-
GridView control's properties, three items were added to the Components tray of the form:
the `NorthwindDataSet` component (which is the typed DataSet), the `ProductsTableAdapter`
(which is responsible for populating the control and submitting the edited rows to the
database), and the `ProductsBindingSource` (which is the liaison between the DataGridView
control and the DataSet). The `ProductsBindingSource` is basically a data source, and it's
discussed in the following section.

Using the BindingSource Class

To understand the functionality of the BindingSource class, look up its members. Enter its name and the following period in the code window, and you will see a list of members. The `Position` property reads (or sets) the current item's index in the underlying DataTable. The DataGridView control doesn't maintain the order of the rows in the underlying table; besides, you can sort the DataGridView control rows in any way you like, but the DataTable rows won't be sorted. Use the `Position` property to find out the index of the selected row in the DataTable. The `MoveFirst`, `MovePrevious`, `MoveNext`, and `MoveLast` methods are simple navigational tools provided by the BindingSource class. You can place four buttons on the form and insert a call to these methods to move to the first, previous, next, and last rows, respectively. The four navigational buttons at the lower-left corner of the form shown in Figure 18.7 call these methods to select another row on the grid.

The two most interesting members of the BindingSource class are the `Find` method and the `Filter` property. The `Filter` property is set to an expression similar to the WHERE clause of a SQL statement to filter the data on the grid. Place a new button on the form, set its caption to **Filter**, set its name to **bttnFilter**, and insert the following statements in its `Click` event handler to filter the rows of the grid with their product names:

```
Private Sub bttnFilter_Click(…) Handles bttnFilter.Click
    Dim filter As String
    filter = InputBox("Enter product name, or part of it")
    ProductsBindingSource.Filter =
        "ProductName LIKE '%" & filter.Trim & "%'"
End Sub
```

Run the application, and click the Filter button to limit the rows displayed on the grid by their product names. If you're searching for products that contain the string *sauce* in their name, the `Filter` property limits the selection as if you had requested products with the following WHERE clause (the percent sign is a SQL wildcard that matches any string):

```
WHERE ProductName LIKE '%sauce%'
```

To restore the original selection, set the filter expression to a blank string. You can design an auxiliary form on which users can enter multiple criteria and filter products by their price or stock, their supplier, and so on. With a bit of programming effort, you can apply multiple criteria, such as products of a specific category that are on order, out-of-stock items from a specific supplier, and so on.

The `Find` method searches a value in a specific column. Both the column name and search argument are specified as arguments to the method, and the return value is the row's position in the DataTable. To select the row, set the BindingSource object's `Position` property to the value returned by the `Find` method. The code behind the Find button in the sample project is the following:

```
Dim search As String
search = InputBox("Enter exact product name")
Dim idx As Integer =
    ProductsBindingSource.Find("ProductName", search)
ProductsBindingSource.Position = idx
```

The `Find` method is not the most convenient search tool, because you have to specify the exact value of the field you're looking for. To retrieve the current row in the DataTable mapped to the BindingSource, use the `Current` property; to determine the number of rows in the same DataTable, read the value of the `Count` property. The `Current` property returns an object, which you must cast to the DataRowView type and call its `Row` property:

```
CType(ProductsBindingSource.Current, DataRowView).Row
```

This expression returns a DataRow object, which you can cast to a ProductsRow type. You will see examples of using the `Current` property of the BindingSource class to access the underlying row in the DataTable later in this chapter.

HANDLING IDENTITY COLUMNS

If you attempt to add a row to the DataGridView control, the new row's ID will be −1 (or another negative value if you have added multiple rows). This is a valid value for an `Identity` column, as long as its `AutoIncrement` property is set to −1. But the `ProductID` column in the database has an `AutoIncrement` value of 1 — why is it different in the DataSet? When the editor created the DataSet, it changed this setting to avoid conflicts during the updates. If new products were assigned valid IDs (positive values following the last ID in the DataSet) at the client, consider what might happen when the edits were submitted to the database. The IDs provided by the DataSet might be taken in the database, and the `Insert` operation would fail. To avoid this conflict, the DataSet uses negative identity values. When these rows are submitted to the database, they're assigned a new ID by the database, which is a positive value.

However, a problem remains. The new ID isn't transferred back to the client, and the DataSet displays negative IDs. One solution is to populate the DataSet again; however, there's a lot more to learn about submitting edited rows to the database, and we'll return to this topic later in this chapter.

You can experiment with this form in the DataSetOperations project by editing the products, adding new ones, and deleting rows. If you attempt to add a new row, you'll get an error message indicating that the `Discontinued` column doesn't accept nulls. The default value of the check box on the DataGrid control is neither True nor False (it's `Null`), and you must validate its value. The simplest solution to the problem is to apply a default value to the `Discontinued` column, and the following section describes how to edit the properties of the DataSet.

ADJUSTING THE DATASET

To adjust the properties of the DataSet, right-click the DataSet in the Data Sources window, and choose Edit DataSet With Designer from the context menu. The DataSet Designer window, shown in Figure 18.9, will appear.

Right-click the header of the `Discontinued` column in the Products table, and choose Properties to see the properties of the DataColumn. One of them is the `DefaultValue` property, which is set by default to `Null`. Change it to 0 or False to impose a default value for this column. In the DataSet Designer, you can examine the data types of the columns of each table, drop or create new relations between tables, and set other interesting properties, such as the `Caption` property of a column, which will be used to name the column of the bound Data-GridView control, or the `NullValue` property, which determines how the DataSet will handle Null values. The default value of the `NullValue` property is *Throw Exception*. Every time the application requests the value of a `Null` field, a runtime exception is thrown. You can set it to

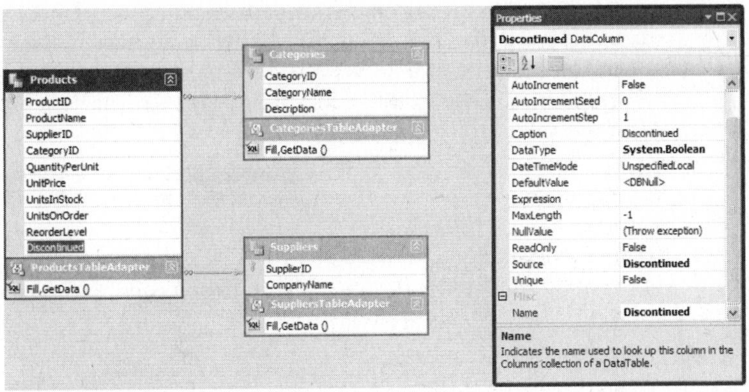

FIGURE 18.9
Editing the DataSet with visual tools

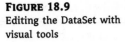

Empty (in which case an empty string is returned) or Nothing (in which case a *Nothing* value is returned). You can also set the autoincrement values of *Identity* columns here. If you select the ProductID column in the Products table, you'll see that the wizard has set the column's AutoIncrementSeed and AutoIncrementStep to –1, for the reasons explained already.

While you're in the DataSet Designer, right-click the Product DataTable, and choose Configure. This starts the TableAdapter Configuration Wizard. The first page of the wizard, shown in Figure 18.10, shows the SQL statement that the Data Source Configuration Wizard generated while you were selecting the columns you wanted to include in the DataSet. You can edit this statement by adding more columns, a WHERE clause to limit the number of rows to be selected, and an ORDER BY clause. To edit the SELECT statement, you modify it right on this page, or you can click the Query Builder button to view the Query Builder dialog box that lets you specify complicated queries with visual tools.

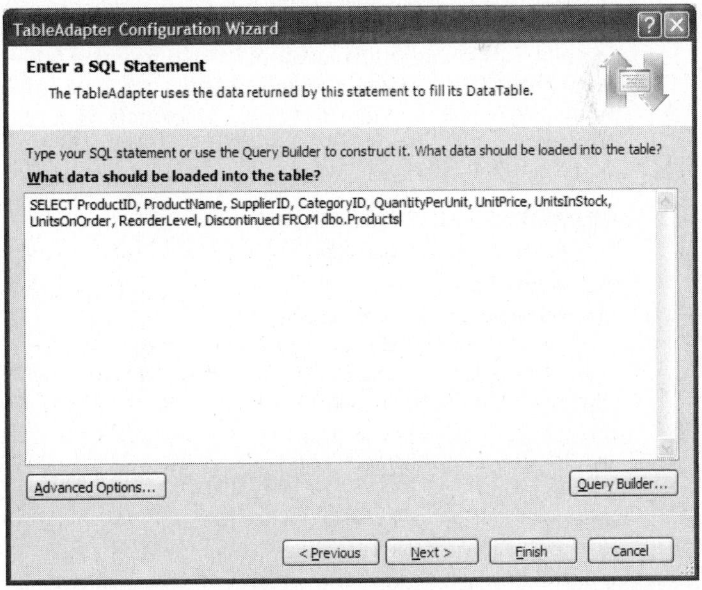

FIGURE 18.10
Editing the SELECT statement that populates the Products DataTable with the TableAdapter Configuration Wizard

TableAdapter Configuration Wizard

Enter a SQL Statement
The TableAdapter uses the data returned by this statement to fill its DataTable.

Type your SQL statement or use the Query Builder to construct it. What data should be loaded into the table?
What data should be loaded into the table?

```
SELECT ProductID, ProductName, SupplierID, CategoryID, QuantityPerUnit, UnitPrice, UnitsInStock,
UnitsOnOrder, ReorderLevel, Discontinued FROM dbo.Products
```

Advanced Options...   Query Builder...

< Previous   Next >   Finish   Cancel

If you click the Advanced Options button, you will see the Advanced Options dialog box, shown in Figure 18.11. Here you must specify which statements should be generated by the wizard. If you're developing a browser application, deselect the first check box: Generate Insert, Update, And Delete Statements. If you clear this option, the other two options will be disabled.

FIGURE 18.11
The Advanced Options dialog box lets you know how the TableAdapter will submit the updates to the underlying tables.

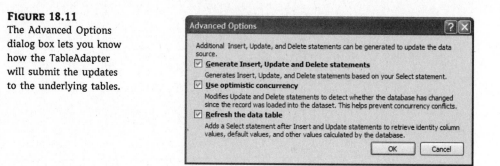

The Use Optimistic Concurrency option affects the UPDATE and DELETE statements generated by the wizard. If this check box is selected, the two statements will not update or delete a row if it has been edited by another user since it was read. The wizard will generate two long statements that take into consideration the values read from the database into the DataSet at the client (the row's original values), and if any of the row's columns in the database are different from the original version of the same row in the DataSet, it won't update or delete the row. By using optimistic concurrency, you're assuming that it's rather unlikely that two users will update the same row at the same time. If the row being updated has already been modified by another user, the update operation fails. If you clear this option, the UPDATE/DELETE statements take into consideration the row's primary key and are executed, even if the row has been modified since it was read. In effect, the last user to update a row overwrites the changes made by other users.

The last option in the Advanced Options dialog box specifies whether the TableAdapter reads back the inserted/updated rows. You should leave this check box selected so that the identity values assigned by the database to new rows will be read back and update the DataSet.

🌐 Real World Scenario

IMPLEMENTING OPTIMISTIC CONCURRENCY

Curious about the statements that take into consideration the original values of the row being updated? Here's the DELETE statement for the Products row that uses optimistic concurrency:

```
DELETE FROM [dbo].[Products]
WHERE (([ProductID] = @Original_ProductID) AND
       ([ProductName] = @Original_ProductName) AND
```

```
        ((@IsNull_SupplierID = 1 AND
              [SupplierID] IS NULL) OR
              ([SupplierID] = @Original_SupplierID)) AND
        ((@IsNull_CategoryID = 1 AND
              [CategoryID] IS NULL) OR
              ([CategoryID] = @Original_CategoryID)) AND
        ((@IsNull_QuantityPerUnit = 1 AND
              [QuantityPerUnit] IS NULL) OR
              ([QuantityPerUnit] = @Original_QuantityPerUnit)) AND
        ((@IsNull_UnitPrice = 1 AND
              [UnitPrice] IS NULL) OR
              ([UnitPrice] = @Original_UnitPrice)) AND
        ((@IsNull_UnitsInStock = 1 AND
              [UnitsInStock] IS NULL) OR
              ([UnitsInStock] = @Original_UnitsInStock)) AND
        ((@IsNull_UnitsOnOrder = 1 AND
              [UnitsOnOrder] IS NULL) OR
              ([UnitsOnOrder] = @Original_UnitsOnOrder)) AND
        ((@IsNull_ReorderLevel = 1 AND
              [ReorderLevel] IS NULL) OR
              ([ReorderLevel] = @Original_ReorderLevel)) AND
        ([Discontinued] = @Original_Discontinued))
```

The same statement with the optimistic concurrency off is quite short:

```
DELETE FROM [dbo].[Products]
WHERE ([ProductID] = @Original_ProductID)
```

Examine the long statement to understand how optimistic concurrency is handled. The first term in the WHERE clause locates a single row based on the product ID, which is unique. This is the row that should be deleted (or updated by the UPDATE statement). However, the statement will not select the row if any of its fields have been edited since you read it from the database. If another user has changed the price of a specific product, the following term will evaluate to false, and the WHERE clause will return no row to be deleted.

When you return to the configuration wizard, click Next, and you will see the dialog box shown in Figure 18.12, where you can specify the methods that the wizard will generate for you. The Fill method populates a DataTable, and the GetData method returns a DataTable object with the same data; the last option in the dialog box specifies whether the DataSet will expose methods for inserting/updating/deleting rows directly against the database.

Click Next again, and the wizard will regenerate the NorthwindDataSet class, taking into consideration the options you specified in the steps of the wizard.

In the following section, we'll let the editor build simple data-driven applications for us. You're going to see how to bind other controls to typed DataSets and how to customize the DataGridView control.

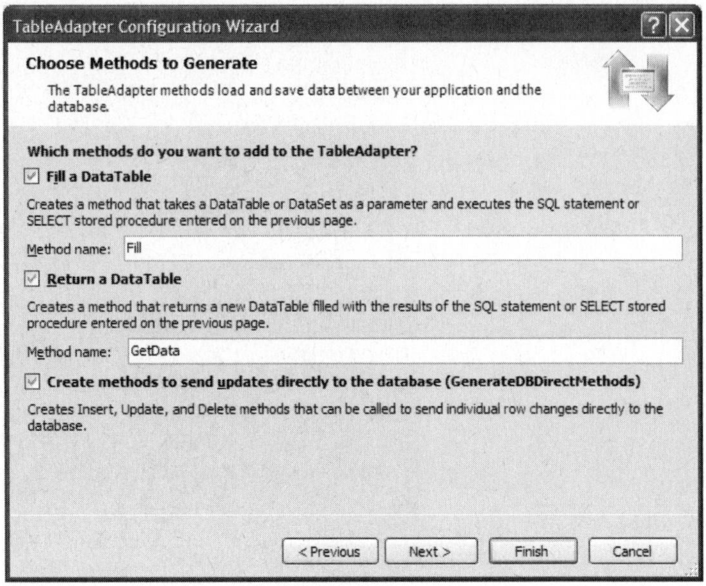

FIGURE 18.12
Selecting the methods
to be generated by the
TableAdapter Configura-
tion Wizard

Designing Data-Driven Interfaces the Easy Way

Instead of binding the DataGridView control through its properties, you can let Visual Studio perform the binding for you:

1. Add a third form to the DataSetOperations sample project, the Form3 form, and make it the project's Startup object.

2. To display the rows of the Products table on a DataGridView control, open the Data Sources window, and select the Products table. As soon as you select it, an arrow appears next to its name. Click this arrow to open a drop-down list with the binding options for the DataTable. The DataTable can be bound to the following:

   ◆ A DataGridView control, which will display all rows and all columns of the table

   ◆ A ListBox or ComboBox control, which will display a single column of all rows

   ◆ A number of TextBox controls (the Details option), one for each column

3. Select the DataGridView option, and then drop the Products DataTable on the form.

The editor will create a DataGridView control and bind it to the Products DataTable. In addition, it will create a toolbar at the top of the form with a few navigational and editing buttons, as shown in Figure 18.13 (shown at design time so you can see the components generated by the editor). Notice that the toolbar contains one button for deleting rows (the button with the X icon) and one button for submitting the edits to the database (the button with the disk icon). The Filter, Find, and Refresh Data buttons were not generated by the editor; I've added them to the toolbar and inserted the appropriate code in their Click event handlers. You've already seen the code that implements all three operations.

FIGURE 18.13
Binding a form to a
DataTable

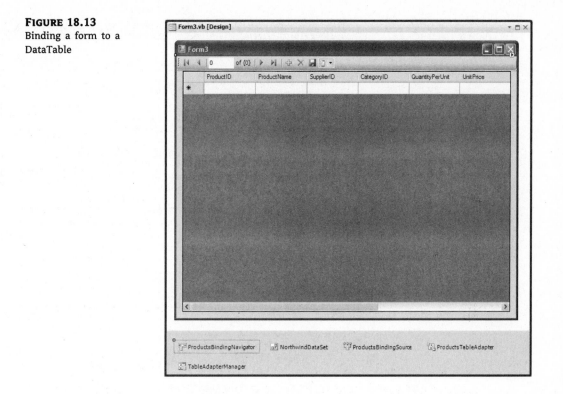

FIGURE 18.13
Binding a form to a
DataTable

The Designer will also generate the components listed in Table 18.1; these will appear in the Components tray.

As for the code generated by the editor, here it is:

```
Private Sub ProductsBindingNavigatorSaveItem_Click(…) Handles
            ProductsBindingNavigatorSaveItem.Click
    Me.Validate()
    Me.ProductsBindingSource.EndEdit()
    Me.TableAdapterManager.UpdateAll(Me.DSProducts)
End Sub

Private Sub Form2_Load(…) Handles MyBase.Load
    'TODO: This line of code loads data into the 'NorthwindDataSet.Products' table.
    'You can move, or remove it, as needed.
    Me.ProductsTableAdapter.Fill( Me.DSProducts.Products)
End Sub
```

In the form Load event handler, the Products DataTable is filled with a call to the Products-TableAdapter class's Fill method. The other event handler corresponds to the Click event of the Save button on the toolbar, and it calls the TableAdapterManager class's UpdateAll method. This is all it takes to submit the changes made to the data at the client.

TABLE 18.1:   Designer-generated components

COMPONENT	DESCRIPTION
NorthwindDataSet	This is the typed DataSet for the data specified with the Data Source Configuration Wizard.
ProductBindingSource	This is a BindingSource object for the Products table.
ProductsTableAdapter	This is an enhanced DataAdapter that exposes the methods for reading data from the database and submitting the changes made at the client to the database. The TableAdapter class differs from the DataAdapter class in that its Fill method accepts as an argument an object of the Products type, and not generic DataSet and DataTable objects. The methods of the TableAdapter object know how to handle rows of the specific type and not any DataRow object.
TableAdapterManager	This encapsulates the functionality of all TableAdapter objects on the form. If you drop additional tables on the form, the editor will create the corresponding TableAdapter for each one. The Table-AdapterManager encapsulates the functionality of all individual TableAdapter objects and exposes the UpdateAll method, which submits the entire DataSet to the database. The UpdateAll method of the TableAdapterManager calls the Update method of each individual TableAdapter in the proper order.
ProductsBindingNavigator	This component represents the toolbar added to the form. The toolbar is a ToolStrip control with custom items and the appropriate code. The navigational tools generated by the editor are rather primitive, and you can remove them from the control. Just keep the code for the Save button, which you'll need if your application allows editing of the data.

Let's see how far this autogenerated application will take us. Run the application, and edit a few products. Change a few names, set a couple of prices to negative values, set a product's category to an invalid category ID (any value exceeding 7 is invalid, unless you have added new categories), add a couple of new products (they will be assigned negative IDs, as expected), and delete some products. As you can guess, you can't delete rows from the Products table, because they're all referenced by the Order Details table, but this table doesn't exist in the DataSet, so it's perfectly legal to delete products in the context of the DataSet. When the edits are submitted to the database, the deletions will be rejected, of course.

Let's see how the Save button on the toolbar handles the updates. Click the Save button on the toolbar, and you will get an error message indicating that a row has violated a referential or check constraint, depending on the order in which the rows were submitted to the database. The UpdateAll method of the ProductsTableAdapter object will give up after the first failure.

As you recall, the DataAdapter class, on which the TableAdapter class is based, exposes the ContinueUpdateOnError property. Unfortunately, the TableAdapter class doesn't expose this property. However, you can access the underlying DataAdapter through the Adapter property, and set the ContinueUpdateOnError property to True. Insert the following method in front of the statement that calls the UpdateAll method:

```
Me.TableAdapterManager.ProductsTableAdapter.
        Adapter.ContinueUpdateOnError = True
```

Run the application again, edit the data on the grid, and submit the changes to the database. This time the application won't crash with an error message. Instead, the rows that failed to update the underlying table in the database will be marked with an exclamation mark icon in the row's header, as shown in Figure 18.14. We managed to submit all the rows to the database, regardless of whether they successfully updated the Products table, through the ProductsTableAdapter object. The `UpdateAll` method retrieved the error messages returned by the DBMS and displayed them on the control. To see the reason why each row failed to update the Products table, hover the pointer over the error icon, and you will see the description of the error in a ToolTip box.

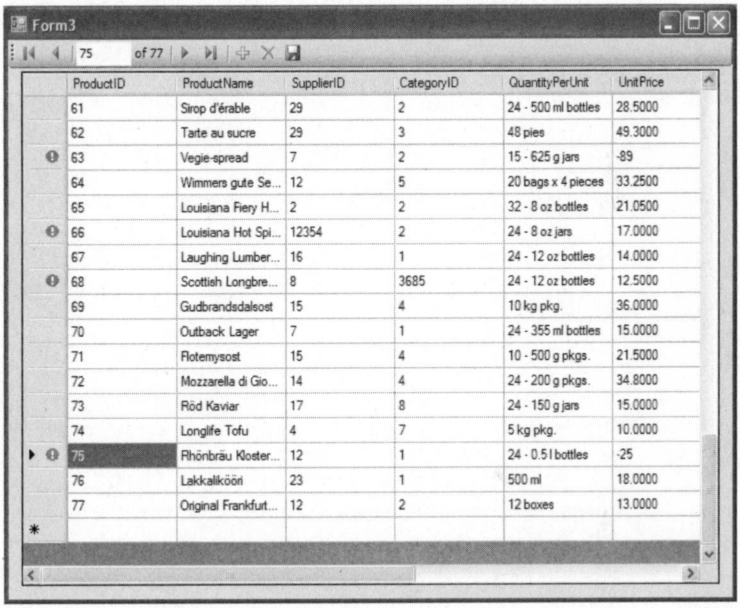

FIGURE 18.14
Viewing the update errors on the DataGrid-View control

You can also create a list of the rows that failed to update their underlying table along with the error message returned by the database. The code for iterating through a table's rows and examining the `RowError` property was presented in the preceding chapter. You can easily add an extra button on the toolbar and use it to display an auxiliary form with the update errors.

By the way, the error messages displayed on the DataGridView control are the ones returned by the DBMS (SQL Server in our case). If you want, you can set each row's `RowError` property to a different, more meaningful description.

Enhancing the Navigational Tools

The navigational tools on the `BindingNavigator` are quite primitive. Let's enhance the toolbar at the top of the form by adding two buttons, the Filter and Find buttons of the preceding section. Stop the application, and open `Form3` in design mode.

To add a new element to the ToolBar control, expand the combo box that's displayed at design time after the existing elements. From the drop-down list, select the Button item to add a Button control to the toolbar. Select the newly added button, and set its DisplayStyle property to **Text**. (Normally this property is set to Image, because the items on a toolbar are identified by an icon; you should find a few good icons and use them in your applications.) Set its Text property to **Filter** and its name to **bttnFilter**. Follow similar steps for the Find button as well. Then copy the code of the two buttons in Form2, and paste it in the Click event handlers of the two ToolStrip buttons. You just added a filtering and search feature to your application.

The Find feature isn't very practical with product names, because users have to specify the full and exact product name. This feature should be used with fields such as IDs, book ISBNs, and email addresses. To find a product by name, most users would use the Filter button to limit the selection on the grid and then locate the desired product.

You can also use two TextBox controls in place of the two Button controls on the toolbar. If you'd rather allow users to enter their search and filter arguments on the toolbar, you must intercept the Enter keystroke from within the respective control's KeyUp event and call the same code to filter or search the rows of the grid.

Now, add yet another button to the toolbar, and set its caption to **Refresh Data**. This button will reload the data from the database by calling the Fill method of the TableAdapter. Before loading the data, however, you must make sure that the DataSet doesn't contain any changes by examining the HasChanges property. If it's True, you must prompt the user accordingly. Notice that if a row failed to update the database, the DataSet will contain changes, even though the edits were submitted to the database. Some of the changes can be undone, but not all of them. A deleted row, for example, is no longer visible on the control, and users can't restore it. Listing 18.5 shows the code behind the Refresh Data button.

LISTING 18.5:   Refreshing the DataSet

```
Private Sub bttnRefreshData_Click(...) Handles bttnRefreshData.Click
    If NorthwindDataSet.HasChanges Then
        Dim reply As MsgBoxResult =
            MsgBox("The DataSet contains changes." &
            vbCrLf & "Reload data anyway?",
            MsgBoxStyle.YesNo Or MsgBoxStyle.Exclamation)
        If reply = MsgBoxResult.No Then Exit Sub
    End If
    Me.ProductsTableAdapter.Fill(
            Me.NorthwindDataSet.Products)

End Sub
```

We developed a fairly functional application for browsing and editing one of the basic tables of the Northwind database, the Products table. The interface of the application is a bit rough around the edges (that's the least you can say about an interface that displays category and supplier IDs instead of category and supplier names), but we'll come back and adjust the interface of the application in a moment. First, I'd like to discuss another way of using the

DataGridView control, namely, how to bind related tables to two or more DataGridView controls. This arrangement is the most common one, because we rarely work with a single table.

Binding Hierarchical Tables

In this section, you'll build an interface to display categories and products on two DataGridView controls, as shown in Figure 18.15. The top DataGridView control is bound to the `Categories` DataTable and displays all the category rows. The lower DataGridView control displays the products of the category selected in the top control. In effect, you'll create two DataGridView controls linked together.

FIGURE 18.15
Viewing related data on two DataGridView controls with the Linked-DataTables application

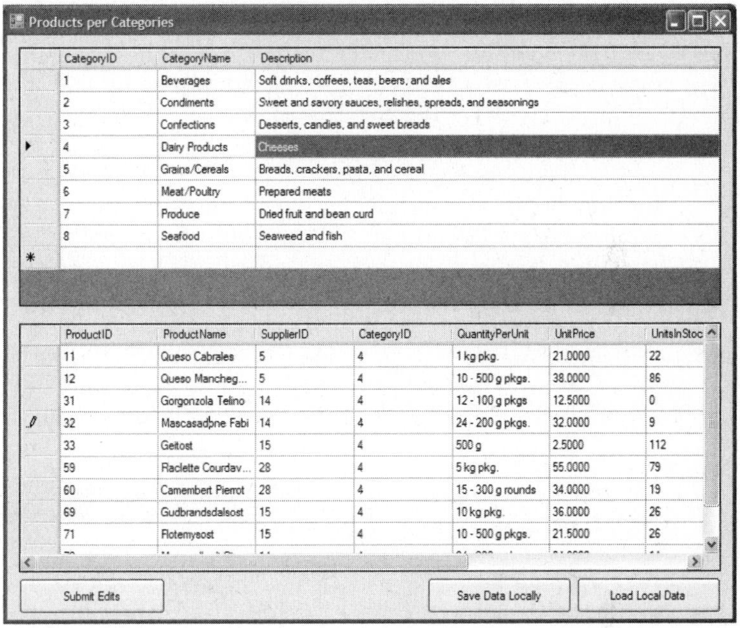

Follow these steps:

1. Start a new Windows Forms Application project (it's the LinkedDataTables project available for download from www.sybex.com/go/masteringvb2010), and create a new DataSet that contains the Products, Categories, and Suppliers tables. Uncheck the `Picture` column from the Categories table. Name it **DS**.

2. In the Data Sources window, select each table, and set its binding option to **DataGridView**.

3. Drop the Categories table on the form. The editor will place an instance of the DataGridView control on the form and will bind it to the Categories table. It will also create a BindingNavigator object, which we don't really need, so you can delete it. When you drop multiple tables on a form, the editor generates a single toolbar. The navigational buttons apply to the first DataGridView control, but the Save button submits the changes made in all DataTables.

4. Locate the Products table under the Categories table in the Data Sources window, and drop it onto the form. If you drop the Products table of the original DataSet onto the form, you'll

end up with two grids that are independent of one another. For a more meaningful interface, you must link the two grids so that when the user selects a category in the upper grid, the corresponding products are shown automatically in the lower grid. The Products table under the Categories table in the data source represents the rows of the Products table that are related to each row of the Categories table. Just drag the Products table under the Categories table, and drop it onto the form to add the grid and show the Product data in a linked fashion.

Now you can run the application and see how it behaves. Every time you select a category, the selected category's products appear in the lower grid. If you change the `CategoryID` field of a product, that particular product disappears from the grid, as expected, since it belongs to another category after the CategoryID changes. You must select the category with the CategoryID you assigned to a product to see the product in the Products grid. Obviously, this is not the best way to edit the category of a product. You will see how to handle lookup tables in the "Displaying Lookup Columns in a DataGridView Control" section later in the chapter.

Experiment with the new interface. Start editing the two tables on the form. Add new categories, and then add products that belong to these categories. If you attempt to delete a category, the DataGridView will happily remove the row from its table. But didn't the DataSet pick the relationships from the database's definition? Now that both tables are at the client as DataTables with a relationship between them, shouldn't the DataSet reject this operation?

Let's take a look at the properties of the relationship between the two tables. Right-click the DS DataSet in the Data Sources window, and from the context menu, select Edit DataSet In Designer to see the DataSet Designer window. Right-click the line that connects the Products and Categories tables (this line represents the relationship between the two tables), and select Edit Relation to open the Relation dialog box, shown in Figure 18.16.

FIGURE 18.16
Setting relation properties

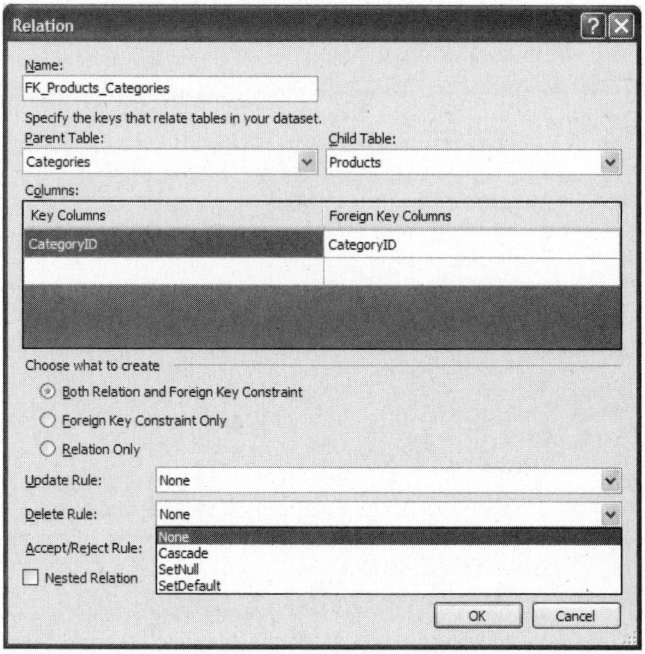

The `FK_Products_Categories` relation is marked as Relation Only. In the database, this is a relation and a foreign key constraint. The relation simply relates the two tables if their `CategoryID` fields match. Most importantly, the constraint won't let you insert a product that points to a nonexisting category or delete a category that has related rows in the Products table. Select the radio button Both Relation And Foreign Key Constraint, and then close the dialog box.

Try to run the application. If you receive the following error:

> `"ConstraintException was unhandled: Failed to enable constraints. One or more rows contain values violating non-null, unique, or foreign-key constraints."`

right after running the application, make sure that the data is loaded in the right order in the form Load event. The `Categories` DataTable should be filled first, and the `Products` DataTable should be filled second:

```
Private Sub Form1_Load(...) Handles MyBase.Load
    Me.CategoriesTableAdapter.Fill(Me.DS.Categories)
    Me.ProductsTableAdapter.Fill(Me.DS.Products)
End Sub
```

Foreign key constraints are subject to three rules: the Update, Delete, and Accept/Reject rules, as shown in Figure 18.16. These rules determine what should happen when a parent row is removed from its table (the Delete rule), when a parent ID is modified (the Update rule), and when users accept or reject changes in the DataSet (the last rule). A rule can be set to None (no action is taken, which means that a runtime exception will be thrown), Cascade (the child rows are updated or deleted), SetNull (the foreign keys of the related rows are set to Null), and SetDefault (the foreign keys of the related rows are set to their default value).

I usually don't change the rules of a relationship in the DataSet, unless I've used rules in the database. Leave them set to None, and run the application again. You should avoid setting the Delete and Update rules to Cascade, because this can lead to irrecoverable errors. If you delete a category, for example, it will take with it the related products, and each deleted product will take with it the related rows in the Order Details table. A simple error can ruin the database. There are other situations, which aren't as common, where the Cascade rule can be used safely. When you delete a book in the Pubs database, for example, you want the book's entries in the TitleAuthors table to be removed as well. No rows in the Authors table will be removed, because they're primary, and not foreign, keys in the relation between the TitleAuthors and Authors tables.

Let's return to the interface for editing products and categories. Attempt again to remove a category. This time you'll get a lengthy error message that ends with the following suggestion:

> `To replace this default dialog please handle the DataError event.`

Let's do exactly that to avoid displaying a totally meaningless message to our users. Open the `DataError` event handler for both controls, and insert the following statement:

> `MsgBox(e.Exception.Message)`

Run the application again, and delete a category. This time you'll see the following error message, and the program won't remove the category from the DataGridView, because it can't remove it from its DataSet:

```
Cannot delete this row because constraints are enforced
  on relation FL_Products_Categories, and deleting this
  row will strand child rows.
```

You can still delete products and set their prices to negative values. These two operations are invalid in the context of the database but quite valid in the client DataSet.

USING THE BINDINGSOURCE AS A DATA SOURCE

As you recall, binding a DataGridView control to a DataTable is possible by setting the control's DataSource property. Binding to two related tables is a bit more involved, so let's see how it's done (short of dropping the two tables on the form and letting the editor handle the details).

To link the two DataGridView controls, you must create a BindingSource object for each one. The BindingSource class encapsulates a data source and is itself a data source. Initialize an instance of this class by setting its `DataSource` and `DataMember` properties for the Categories table:

```
Dim categoriesBS As New BindingSource
categoriesBS.DataSource = DS
categoriesBS.DataMember = "Categories"
```

Then set the upper grid's `DataSource` property to the categoriesBS object. As for the lower grid, you must create a new BindingSource object and set its `DataSource` property not to the actual DataSet but to the BindingSource object of the upper grid:

```
Dim productsBS As New BindingSource
productsBS.DataSource = categoriesBS
```

Now here's the tricky part: The `DataMember` property must be set to the name of the relationship between the two tables in the DataSet so that it's linked to the products of the category selected in the upper control:

```
productsBS.DataMember = "FK_Categories_Products"
```

After the two BindingSource objects have been set up, assign them to the `DataSource` property of their corresponding controls:

```
DataGridView1.DataSource = categoriesBS
DataGridView2.DataSource = productsBS
```

These actions were performed for you automatically, as you dropped the two tables on the form. If you want to bind two related tables of an untyped DataSet, you must set these properties from within your code.

Adjusting the Appearance of the DataGridView Control

The DataGridView control is bound to a single table as soon as you drop the table on the form, but its default appearance leaves a lot to be desired. To begin with, we must set the widths of the columns and hide certain columns. The product IDs, for example, don't need to be displayed. The numeric fields should be formatted properly and aligned to the right, and the foreign key fields should be replaced by the corresponding descriptions in the primary table. We also should display category and supplier names, instead of IDs.

The DataGridView control exposes a large number of properties, and you can experiment with them in the Properties window. They have obvious names, and you can see the effects of each property on the control as you edit it. Beyond the properties that apply to the entire control, you can also customize the individual columns through the Edit Columns dialog box.

To tweak the appearance of the columns of the DataGridView control, select the control with the mouse, and open the Tasks menu by clicking the little arrow in the upper-right corner of the control. This menu contains four check boxes that allow you to specify whether the user is allowed to add/edit/delete rows and reorder columns. To adjust the appearance of the grid's columns, click the Edit Columns hyperlink in the menu, and you will see the Edit Columns dialog box, shown in Figure 18.17, where you can set the properties for each column.

FIGURE 18.17
Use the Edit Columns dialog box to customize the appearance of the DataGridView control.

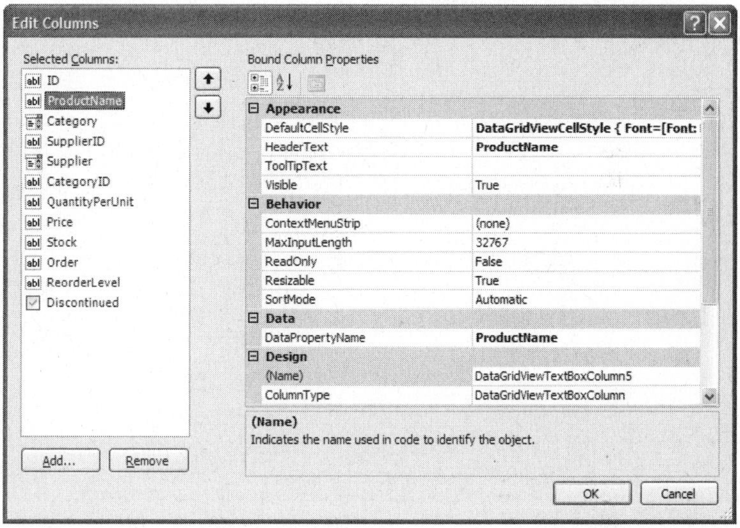

In the Edit Columns dialog box, you can set each column's header and width, as well as the minimum width of the column. (Users won't be allowed to make the column narrower than its minimum width.) You can also set the AutoSize property to True to let the control decide about column widths, but this may result in a very wide control. You can lock certain columns during editing by setting their ReadOnly property, or you can make other columns invisible with the Visible property.

To make the appearance of two grids more uniform on the Products per Category form in your LinkedDataTables projects, make both grids of the same width. This will leave the Categories grid with some empty, grayed-out space, since it has a smaller number of columns than the Products grid. This space can be easily covered by Category's Description property. Open the Edit Columns dialog box, and set the AutoSizeMode of the Description column to **Fill**.

The most interesting setting in this dialog box is the ColumnType property, which is the type of the column. By default, all columns are of the DataGridViewTextBoxColumn type, unless the corresponding field is a Boolean or Image type. A DataGridView column can be one of the following types:

DataGridViewButtonColumn   This displays a button whose caption is the bound field. Use buttons to indicate that users can click them to trigger an action. To program the Click event of a button column, insert the appropriate code in the control's CellContentClick event handler. Your code must detect whether a column with buttons was clicked and, if so, act accordingly. Change the column that displays the product names into a button column, and then insert the following statements in the CellContentClick event handler of the DataGridView control:

```
Private Sub ProductsDataGridView_CellContentClick(
        ByVal sender As System.Object,
        ByVal e As System.Windows.Forms.DataGridViewCellEventArgs)
    Handles ProductsDataGridView.CellContentClick
    If e.ColumnIndex = 1 Then
        MsgBox(ProductsDataGridView.Rows(e.RowIndex).
                Cells(e.ColumnIndex).Value.ToString)
    End If
End Sub
```

The code shown here reads the caption of the button that was clicked. You can just as easily read the product's ID and use it to retrieve product details and display them on another form.

DataGridViewCheckBoxColumn   This column type is used with True/False columns (the bit data type in SQL Server). The Discontinued column of the Products table, for example, is mapped automatically to a DataGridView column of this type.

DataGridViewComboBoxColumn   This column type is used for foreign keys or lookup fields. You will shortly see how to change the CategoryID and SupplierID columns into ComboBox columns so that users can see category and supplier names instead of IDs. When editing the table, users can expand the list and select another item, instead of having to enter the ID of the corresponding item. Figure 18.18 shows the DataGridView control for displaying products with a ComboBox column for categories and suppliers.

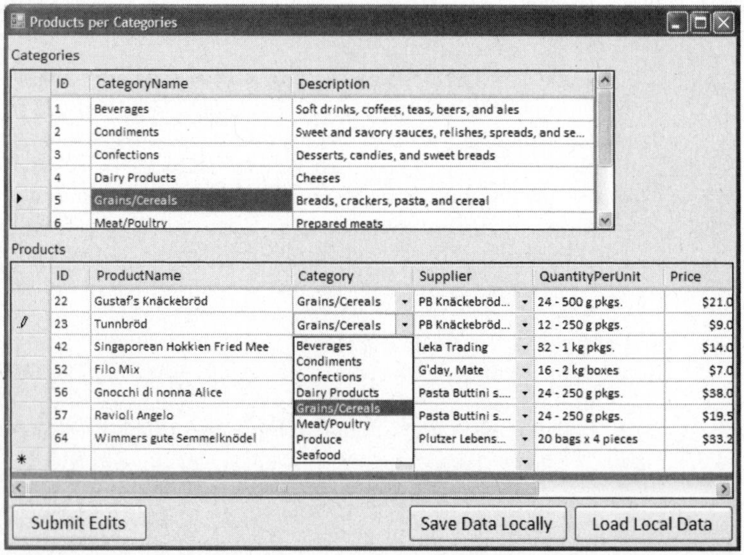

FIGURE 18.18
Displaying product categories and suppliers in a ComboBox control on the DataGridView control

DataGridViewLinkColumn   This is similar to the DataGridViewButtonColumn type, only it displays a hyperlink instead of a button. Use the same technique outlined earlier for the Button columns to detect the click of a hyperlink.

DataGridViewImageColumn   Use this column type to display images. In general, you shouldn't store images in your databases. Use separate files for your images, and include only their paths in the database. Keep in mind that all rows of a DataGridView control have the same height, and if one of them contains an image, the remaining cells will contain a lot of white space.

DataGridViewTextBoxColumn   This is the most common column type, and it displays the field in a text box.

Notice that as you change the style of a column, the Bound Column Properties pane of the Edit Columns dialog box is populated with the properties that apply to the specific column type. For a combo box column, for example, you can set the `DropDownWidth` and `MaxDropDownItems` properties. You can even populate the combo box with a set of values through the `Items` property, just as you would with a regular combo box on the form.

There aren't any properties in the Edit Columns dialog box to adjust the appearance of the selected column. To change the appearance of a column, select the `DefaultCellStyle` property, and click the button with the ellipses next to it to see the CellStyle Builder dialog box, which is shown in Figure 18.19.

In the CellStyle Builder dialog box, you can set the column's font, set its foreground and background colors, specify whether the text should wrap in its cell, and determine the alignment of the cell's contents. Turning on the wrap mode with the `WrapMode` property doesn't cause the rows to be resized automatically to the height of the tallest cell. To have rows resized automatically, you must set the control's `AutoSizeRowsMode` property to `All`.

FIGURE 18.19
Use this dialog box to adjust the appearance of a column in a DataGrid-View control.

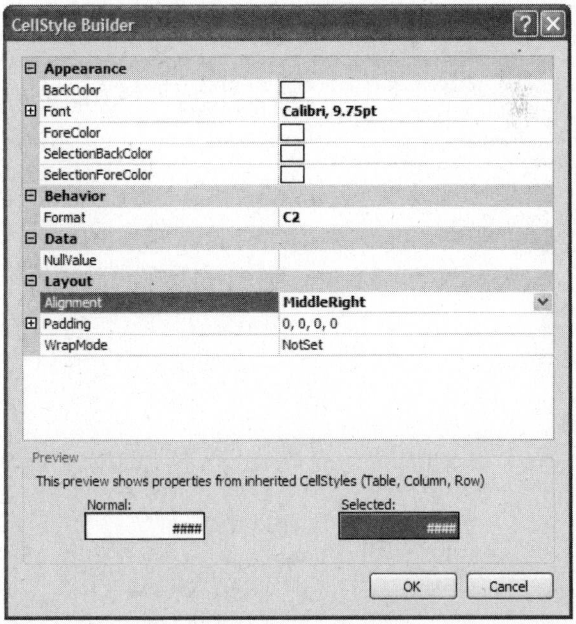

The other possible settings for this property are None, AllHeaders, AllCellsExceptHeaders, DisplayedHeaders, DisplayedCellsExceptHeaders, and DisplayedCells. Finally, you must set the Format property for all numeric and date fields and size the columns according to the data that will be displayed on the control.

This feast of customization techniques is possible because the DataGridView control is bound to a typed DataSet. If you want to use the techniques of the previous chapter to bind a DataGridView control to an untyped DataSet, you can still use the Edit Columns dialog box to add and customize the control's columns, but the process isn't nearly as convenient. You must also remember to set the control's AutoGenerateColumns property to False and each column's DataPropertyName property to the name of the database column that will be mapped to the corresponding grid column. If the AutoGenerateColumns property is left to its default value, which is True, the control will generate a new column for each data column in its data source.

DISPLAYING LOOKUP COLUMNS IN A DATAGRIDVIEW CONTROL

In this section, you're going to change the way a product's category and supplier are displayed. Instead of IDs, you must display category and supplier names. Moreover, you will display each product's category and supplier in a ComboBox control so that users can quickly select another value when editing the product. Let's return to the LinkedDataTables project and set up the bottom GridView control.

Select the DataGridView control with the products, and from the Task menu choose Edit Columns. In the Edit Columns dialog box, select the CategoryID column, and make it invisible by setting its Visible property to False. Then click the Add button to add a new column. In the Add Column dialog box, which is shown in Figure 18.20, click the Unbound Column radio button, and set the column's Name property to **colCategory** and its HeaderText property to **Category**. Click Add to add the column to the DataGridView control and then Close to close the dialog box.

Back in the Edit Columns dialog box, move the new column to the desired position by using the arrow buttons. You must now set up the new column so that it displays the name of the category that corresponds to the CategoryID column of the selected product. Locate the DataSource property, and click the arrow to expand the data sources. Select the CategoriesBindingSource entry. Then set the DisplayName property to **CategoryName** and

FIGURE 18.20
Adding a new column
to the DataGridView
control

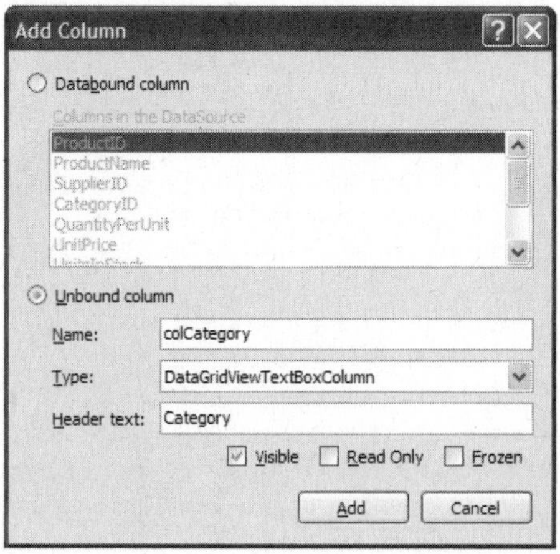

the `ValueMember` to **CategoryID**. Click OK to close the dialog box. If you run the application now, you'll see that the `CategoryID` column has been replaced by the `Category` column, which displays a ComboBox with the list of all categories. However, the product's category isn't automatically selected; you have to drop down the items in the combo box to see the categories, and you still don't know the selected product's category. To link the appropriate category name to the selected product's `CategoryID` value, you must set yet another property, the `Data-PropertyName` property. If you expand the list of available columns for this property, you'll see the columns of the Products table. Select the `CategoryID` column so that the combo box will display the category name that corresponds to the category ID of the selected product row. Now you have a much better interface for editing the products. You no longer need to enter IDs; you see the name of the selected product's category, and you can select a product's category from a drop-down list by using the mouse.

Of course, you must do the same with the Suppliers table. Right-click the NorthwindDataSet object in the Data Sources window, and choose Edit DataSet With Designer from the context menu to open the DataSet in design mode.

Editing the Data in Hierarchical Tables

To be able to display the meaningful column (typically the `Name` column) of the lookup table entry, you need to make the data in the lookup table available to the application. If the table with the lookup values isn't part of your DataSet, you can easily add a new DataTable to the DataSet. Right-click somewhere on the DataSet Designer's surface, and choose Add ➤ TableAdapter from the context menu. A new DataTable will be added to the DataSet, and you'll be prompted with a wizard similar to the Data Source Configuration Wizard to select the rows that will be used to populate the DataTable. Alternatively, you can right-click the DataSet in the Data Sources view, and select the Edit DataSet With Designer option. Take a look at the "Adjusting the DataSet" section earlier in this chapter and Figure 18.9 to see how to edit the DataSet in DataSet Designer.

In the case of lookup tables, you would choose the ID column so that the relationship can be maintained and the `Name` column whose value will be displayed in the grid. In your Linked-DataTables project, you added the Suppliers table when you created the DS DataSet.

Let's make the lookup table data available for an update operation on the Products grid. The following steps are similar to the steps performed when making categories displayed using the ComboBox inside the DataGridView in the previous section.

Hide the `SupplierID` column of the Suppliers table, and replace it on a grid with a `ComboBox` column that contains the names of the suppliers. Select the Edit Column command from the Products grid's Tasks menu, and set the properties for a newly added Suppliers column as listed in Table 18.2.

Notice that the `ValueMember` property is the `SupplierID` column of the Suppliers table, but the `PropertyName` property's value is the `SupplierID` column of the `Products` DataTable, because the control is bound to the Products table. The Designer will replace the name of the `Suppliers` DataTable with the SupplierBindingSource object. Run the application now, edit a few products, and then save the edits. You can also edit the categories (names and descriptions only). As a reminder, even the DataSet that was generated by the wizard doesn't enforce check constraints, and you can set the price of a product to a negative value. When you attempt to submit the changes to the database, a runtime exception will be thrown.

The code behind the Submit Edits button isn't new to you. The code sets the `Continue-UpdateOnError` property of the underlying DataAdapter objects to True and then calls the `UpdateAll` method of the TableAdapterManager to submit the changes made to all tables.

TABLE 18.2: Column settings for the Supplier column

PROPERTY	SETTING
ColumnType	DataGridViewComboBoxColumn
DataSource	SuppliersBindingSource
DisplayMember	CompanyName
ValueMember	SupplierID
PropertyName	SupplierID

The rows that will fail to update the underlying tables in the database will be marked as errors. The DataGridView control marks the rows in error with an icon of an exclamation mark in the column's header, as shown earlier in Figure 18.14. If you hover over this icon, you'll see a description of the error in a ToolTip box.

UPDATING HIERARCHICAL DATASETS

Updating hierarchical DataSets isn't as simple as calling the Update or UpdateAll method. In the LinkedDataTables sample project, I've called the UpdateAll method of the TableAdapter-Manager class, which submits first the changes in the parent table (the Categories table) and then the changes in the related table(s). Unless you commit the new rows to the Categories table first, the database will refuse to insert any products that use the IDs of the categories that do not exist in the Categories table. But even if you update the Categories table first and then the Products table, it's not guaranteed that all updates will take place. The order of updates in a hierarchical DataSet is very important, and here's why: Let's say you've deleted all products of a specific category and then the category itself. As soon as you attempt to remove the specific row from the Categories table in the database, the database will return an error indicating that you can't delete a category that has related rows, because the relevant products haven't been removed from the Products table in the database yet.

The proper update order is to submit the deleted rows of the Products table, then perform all updates in the Categories table, and finally submit the insertions and modifications in the Products table. You'll see shortly how to retrieve deleted/modified/new rows from a Data-Table at the client (we'll use each row's DataRowVersion property) and then how to pass these rows to the Update method.

In the meantime, you can experiment with the LinkedDataTables project and perform a few updates at a time. Let's say you want to delete all products in a specific category and then the category itself. To submit the changes without violating the primary/foreign key relationship between the two tables, you must first delete the products and then update the database by clicking the Submit Edits button. After the Products table is updated, you can delete the category from the Categories table and then submit the changes to the database again.

In this section, you've built a functional interface for editing the categories and products of the Northwind database. You started by creating a DataSet with the three tables, then dropped them on the form to instantiate two DataGridView controls, and then tweaked the appearance of the two controls with point-and-click operations. We even managed to display combo boxes right in the DataGridView control without a single line of code. The DataGridView control provides the basic editing features, and you were able to put together an interface for your data without any code. You did have to write a bit of code to submit the changes to the database, because the code generated by the wizard couldn't handle anything but the best-case scenario. Real-world applications must take into consideration all possible scenarios and handle them gracefully.

Data binding allows you to write data-driven applications quickly, mostly with point-and-click operations, but the default interfaces generated by the wizards are not perfect. You'll see shortly how to use data binding to produce more-elegant interfaces, but they'll require a bit of code. Another problem with data binding is that in most cases you'll end up filling large DataSets at the client — and this is not the best practice with data-driven applications. If your application is going to be used by many users against a single server, you must retrieve a relatively small number of rows from the database and submit the edits as soon as possible. If you keep too much data at the client and postpone the submission of edited rows to the database, you're increasing the chances of concurrency errors. Other users may already have changed the same rows that your application is attempting to update. Of course, you can disable optimistic concurrency and overwrite the changes made by other users, if the nature of the data allows it.

The most common approach is to design a form with search criteria, on which users will specify as best as they can the rows they need. Then you can populate the client DataSet with the rows that meet the specified criteria. If you're writing a connected application, submit the changes to the database as soon as they occur. If you want the users to control when the updates are submitted to the database, display the number of modified/inserted/deleted rows in the form's status bar. You can even pop up a message when the number of edited rows exceeds a limit.

Building More-Functional Interfaces

Editing large tables on a grid isn't the most flexible method. In this section, you'll build an alternate interface for editing the Products table, as shown in Figure 18.21. This is the form of the Products sample project, which uses a data-bound ListBox control to display product names and text boxes for the individual fields. The toolbar at the top allows you to add new rows,

FIGURE 18.21
An alternate interface for editing the Products table

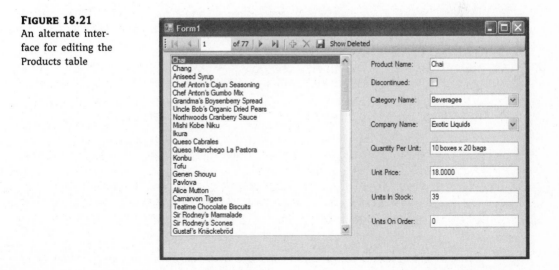

delete existing ones, and submit the changes to the database. All the controls on the form are data bound, and the application contains very little code.

Here's how to get started:

1. Start a new Windows Forms Application project, the Products project, and create a new DataSet, NorthwindDataSet, with the three usual tables: Products, Categories, and Suppliers.

2. Change the binding option for the Products DataTable to **ListBox**. First, select the Products DataTable in the DataSources window. After selecting the Products DataTable, a ComboBox-style arrow will become visible for the Products DataTable that you can expand. Click the arrow. Next, select the Customize option in the Data Sources view on the Products DataTable to open the Options window. Expand the Windows Forms Designer node in the Options list. Select the Data UI Customization node. Select List For Data Type. In the Associated Controls list, select the ListBox.

3. Drop the Products DataTable onto the form. In the Properties window, you must make sure that the ListBox control is properly bound: Its DataSource property has been set to the ProductsBindingSource object that was generated by the editor when you dropped the DataTable on the form, its DisplayMember property has been set to ProductName (because it's the first text column in the table), and its ValueMember property has been set to ProductID (because it's the table's key). If you want to display a different field to identify the products, change the DisplayMember property.

4. Now drop all the fields of the Products DataTable onto the form. The editor will create the appropriate text boxes and bind them to their fields.

5. Rearrange the controls on the form, and delete the text boxes that correspond to the CategoryID and SupplierID columns. Place two ComboBox controls in their place. By the way, even if you set the binding option for the CategoryID and SupplierID columns to ComboBox, you'll end up displaying IDs in the corresponding controls, not category and supplier names. You can't use any data-binding techniques to automatically set up two lookup fields.

6. Drop two instances of the ComboBox control on the form, and name them **cbCategory-Name** and **cbCompanyName**. Select the first one, and set the data-binding properties as follows:

   ◆ The DataSource is where the control will get its data, and it should be Categories-BindingSource, because we want to populate the control with all the category names.

   ◆ The DisplayMember property is the column you want to view on the control and must be set to the CategoryName column of the Categories DataTable.

   ◆ The ValueMember property is the column that will bind the contents of the combo box control to the related table and must be set to the CategoryID column of the Categories DataTable.

   ◆ Finally, you must set the SelectedValue property, in the DataBindings section of the Properties window, to the matching column of the child table, which is the CategoryID column of the ProductsBindingSource. The control will automatically select the row of the Categories table whose category ID matches the CategoryID column of the Products DataTable.

7. Perform similar steps with the other combo box, which displays the CompanyName column of the Suppliers DataTable and is bound to the SupplierID column of the ProductsTable.

Run the application, and see how it behaves. Every time you select a product in the list, the product's details appear in the data-bound text boxes, and its category and supplier are displayed in the two combo box controls. Use the list to navigate through the products, the Add button to add a new product, and the Delete button to delete a product. You can edit the product's fields on the form, and the edits will be written to the DataSet as soon as you move to another row.

You have created a functional application for selecting products and viewing their details. If all you need is a browsing application for the products, you can set the ReadOnly property of all TextBox controls on the form to True.

If you attempt to enter a new product and leave its Discontinued column set to *Null*, a run-time exception will be raised. This problem is easy to fix by specifying a default value for the Discontinued column. To do so, open the DataSet in the Designer, locate the Discontinued column in the Products table, and select Properties from the context menu. The DefaultValue property's value is *DBNull*. Set it to False so that unspecified fields will be automatically set to False.

You'll also get an error message if you attempt to submit the edits and the DataSet contains a product with a negative price. Such trivial errors can be caught and handled from within your code — no need to send the rows to the database and get an error message. Write a few statements to detect trivial errors, such as negative prices (or negative stocks, for that matter). First, decide how to handle these errors. Do you want to pop up a message box every time you detect an error condition? This will drive users crazy. Do you want to reject changes until the user enters a valid value? It's a better approach, but remember that data-entry operators don't look at the monitor. They expect that the Tab (or Enter) key will take them to the next field. The best approach is to do what the DataGridView control does: display an error icon next to the control in error.

Add an instance of the ErrorProvider control on the form. This control displays the exclamation mark icon next to a control. To display the error icon, you must call the control's SetError method, passing as arguments the control in error and the message for the error. (The message will be displayed in a ToolTip box when users hover over the icon.)

To detect errors from within your code, you need to insert some code in the Current-ItemChanged event handler of the ProductsBindingSource. Insert the statements shown in Listing 18.6 in this event handler.

LISTING 18.6:   Catching data-entry errors in your code

```
Private Sub ProductsBindingSource_CurrentItemChanged(
        ByVal sender As System.Object,
        ByVal e As System.EventArgs) Handles
        ProductsBindingSource.CurrentItemChanged
    If Not IsNothing(queryResult) AndAlso queryResult.Count < 1 Then Exit Sub
    ErrorProvider1.Clear()
    Dim product As NorthwindDataSet.ProductsRow
    product = CType(CType(
            ProductsBindingSource.Current,
            DataRowView).Row, NorthwindDataSet.ProductsRow)
```

```
  If Not product.IsUnitPriceNull AndAlso
      Convert.ToDecimal(product.UnitPrice) < 0 Then
      ErrorProvider1.SetError(UnitPriceTextBox,
              "PRICE CAN'T BE NEGATIVE!")
  End If
  If ProductNameTextBox.Text.Trim.Length = 0 Then
      If CType(ProductsBindingSource.Current,
          DataRowView).Row.RowState <>
          DataRowState.Detached Then
          ErrorProvider1.SetError(
              ProductNameTextBox,
              "PRODUCT NAME CAN'T BE BLANK!")
      End If
  End If
End Sub
```

This code segment requires some explanation. The `CurrentItemChanged` event is fired every time the user selects another row or column on the control. The code in this event handler retrieves the current row with the `Current` property of the ProductBindingSource object. This property returns an object, which is a DataRowView object. This is why I cast it to the `DataRowView` type, then retrieve its `Row` property, and finally cast it to the ProductsRow type. The *product* variable represents the currently selected row in the DataSet. This is a typed variable, and I can access the columns of the current row as properties. If the `UnitPrice` column has a negative value, the code sets an ErrorProvider control to display the error next to the corresponding text box.

VIEWING THE DELETED ROWS

One unique aspect of this interface is that it provides a button to display the deleted rows. These rows exist in the DataSet, but they're not shown on the interface. The inserted and modified rows are on the ListBox control, and users can review them. You may even provide a button to display the old and new versions of the edited rows. But users have no way of reviewing the deleted rows. You can resolve this by showing the deleted rows in the auxiliary form:

1. Add a new button to the `ProductsBindingNavigator` ToolStrip, and set its name to **bttnShowDeleted**.

2. Set the text of the button to **Show Deleted**.

3. Add a new form (Form2) to the project.

4. Add a CheckListBox control to Form2.

5. Add a button called **button1** to Form2, set the button's Text property to **Restore Selected Rows**, and close Form2 in the button's default event handler.

The Show Deleted Rows button in the ToolStrip opens an auxiliary form (Form2), like the one shown in Figure 18.22, which displays the deleted rows in a CheckedListBox control. Users are allowed to select some of the deleted rows and restore them.

FIGURE 18.22
Reviewing the deleted
rows in the DataSet

Listing 18.7 shows the code that retrieves the deleted rows and displays them on the
auxiliary form.

LISTING 18.7:   Retrieving and displaying the deleted rows

```
Private Sub bttnShowDeleted_Click(...) Handles bttnShowDeleted.Click
    Form2.CheckedListBox1.Items.Clear()
    For Each row As DataRow In NorthwindDataSet.Products.Rows
        If row.RowState = DataRowState.Deleted Then
            Form2.CheckedListBox1.Items.Add(
            row.Item("ProductID",
            DataRowVersion.Original) & " " &
            row.Item("ProductName",
            DataRowVersion.Original))
        End If
    Next
    Form2.ShowDialog()
    Dim SelectedIDs As New ArrayList
    For Each itm As String In Form2.CheckedListBox1.CheckedItems
        SelectedIDs.Add(Convert.ToInt32(
            itm.Substring(0, itm.IndexOf(" ") + 1)))
    Next
    Dim cust As NorthwindDataSet.ProductsRow
    For Each cust In NorthwindDataSet.Products
        If cust.RowState = DataRowState.Deleted
            AndAlso SelectedIDs.Contains(cust.Item(
            "ProductID", DataRowVersion.Original)) Then
            cust.RejectChanges()
        End If
    Next
End Sub
```

The code goes through the Rows collection of the Products DataTable and examines the RowState property of each row. If its value is RowState.Deleted, it adds the row's ProductID and ProductName fields to the CheckedListBox control of the auxiliary form. Then it displays the form modally, and when the user closes it, the code retrieves the IDs of the selected rows into the *SelectedIDs* ArrayList. The last step is to restore the selected rows. The code goes through all rows again, examines their RowState properties, and if a row is deleted and its ID is in the *SelectedIDs* ArrayList, it calls the RejectChanges method to restore the row. The restored rows are automatically displayed in the ListBox control because this control is bound to the DataSet.

🌐 Real World Scenario

HANDCRAFTING AN APPLICATION'S INTERFACE

A practical feature you can add to the interface of a disconnected application is the ability to review the modifications. You can display the original and proposed versions of the inserted/modified rows, as well as the original versions of the deleted rows on an auxiliary form, as we have done in the preceding example.

If you don't mind writing a bit of code, you can display the original values of the edited rows in the same controls on your form. Because the controls are data bound, you can't display any different values on them; if you do, they'll be stored in the DataSet as well. But you can place nonbound controls, such as Label controls, in the place of the data-bound control. The Labels normally will be invisible, but when the user presses a function key, they can become visible, hiding the regular editable controls. When the user requests the original versions of the fields, you must populate the Labels from within your code and display them by toggling their Visible properties. You must also hide the regular controls on the form.

Another approach would be to suspend data binding momentarily by calling the SuspendBinding method of the BindingSource class. After data binding has been suspended, you can populate the text boxes on the form at will, because the values you display on them won't propagate to the DataSet. To display the bound values again, call the ResumeBinding method.

Another interesting feature you can add to a data-driven application is to display the state of the current row in the form's status bar. You can also give users a chance to undo the changes by clicking a button on the status bar. All you have to do in this button's Click event handler is to call the RejectChanges method on the current row. Use the Current property of the ProductsBindingSource to retrieve the current row and cast it to the ProductsRow type, and then call the RejectChanges method.

You can select one of the data-editing applications presented in this chapter, perhaps the Products application, and add as many professional features as you can to it. Start by adding a status bar to the form, and display on it the state of the current row. For modified rows, display a button on the toolbar that allows users to view and/or undo the changes to the current row. Program the form's KeyUp event handler, as explained in Chapter 4, "GUI Design and Event-Driven Programming," so that the Enter key behaves like the Tab key. Users should be able to move to the next field by pressing Enter. Finally, you can display an error message for the current row on a label in the form's status bar. Or display a message such as *Row has errors* as a hyperlink and show the actual error message when users click the hyperlink. Test the application thoroughly, and insert error handlers for all types of errors that can be caught at the client. Finally, make the edited rows a different color in the two DataGridView controls on the form of the LinkedDataTables sample project. To do so, you must insert some code in the control's `RowValidated` event, which is fired after the validation of the row's data. You'll need to access the same row in the DataSet and examine its `RowState` property by retrieving the `Current` property of the ProductsBindingSource object, as shown in Listing 18.8.

LISTING 18.8:   Coloring the edited and inserted rows on the DataGridView control

```
Private Sub ProductsDataGridView_RowValidated(…)
        Handles ProductsDataGridView.RowValidated
    Dim row As DS.ProductsRow
        row = CType(CType(ProductsBindingSource.Current,
            DataRowView).Row, DS.ProductsRow)
    If row.RowState = DataRowState.Modified Then
        ProductsDataGridView.Rows(e.RowIndex).
            DefaultCellStyle.ForeColor = Color.Green
    Else
        ProductsDataGridView.Rows(e.RowIndex).
            DefaultCellStyle.ForeColor = Color.Black
    End If
    If row.RowState = DataRowState.Added Then
        ProductsDataGridView.Rows(e.RowIndex).
            DefaultCellStyle.ForeColor = Color.Blue
    Else
        ProductsDataGridView.Rows(e.RowIndex).
            DefaultCellStyle.ForeColor = Color.Black
    End If
End Sub
```

The code in the listing sets the foreground color of modified rows to green and the foreground color of inserted rows to blue. From within the same event's code, you can set the text of a Label on the form's status bar to the row's error description. If you run the application now, you'll see that it paints modified and inserted cells differently, but only while you're working with products of the same category. If you select another category and then return to the one whose products you were editing, they're no longer colored differently, because the `RowValidated` event is no longer fired. To draw rows differently, you must duplicate the same code in the control's `RowPostPaint` event as well.

If you carefully test the revised application, you'll realize that the DataGridView control doesn't keep track of modified rows very intelligently. If you append a character to the existing product name and then delete it (without switching to another cell between the two operations), the DataGridView control considers the row modified, even though the original and proposed versions are identical. As a result, the application will render the row in green. Moreover, the `UpdateAll` method will submit the row to the database.

For a truly disconnected application, you should give users a chance to store the data locally at the client. The LinkedDataTables application's main form contains two more buttons: the Save Data Locally and Load Local Data buttons. The first one saves the DataSet to a local file via the `WriteXml` method of the DataSet, and the second button loads the DataSet via the `ReadXml` method. The application uses the `tmpData.#@#` filename in the application's folder to store the data. It also uses an overloaded form of the two methods to accept an additional argument that stores not only the data but the changes as well. Here's the code behind the two buttons:

```
Private Sub Button1_Click(…) Handles Button1.Click
    DS.WriteXml("tmpData.#@#", XmlWriteMode.DiffGram)
End Sub

Private Sub Button2_Click(…) Handles Button2.Click
    ProductsBindingSource.SuspendBinding()
    DS.ReadXml("tmpData.#@#", XmlReadMode.DiffGram)
    ProductsBindingSource.ResumeBinding()
End Sub
```

Let's explore now how data binding can be used in combination with Language Integrated Query (LINQ) query syntax.

Data Binding with LINQ

You are surely convinced by now that LINQ is a fundamental part of .NET query infrastructure. You have explored LINQ in detail in Chapter 14, "An Introduction to LINQ," where I also mentioned the LINQ to DataSet technology.

The great thing about LINQ is that once you learn how to write queries, you can apply the same syntax to any data source that supports LINQ. DataSets and typed DataSets also support LINQ, and you can apply the same syntax you saw used to query objects in LINQ to Objects and in LINQ to SQL to typed DataSets.

So far in this chapter you saw how data binding can make life a lot easier for a programmer developing data-centric applications. And you have already witnessed the power of LINQ. The two can be used in combination as a powerful tool for data manipulation.

ENABLING THE BINDING WITH THE DATAVIEW CLASS

The central class for binding support is the DataView class. It represents a bindable and customizable view of data and provides a number of data manipulation methods. Using DataView, data can be filtered, searched, sorted, edited, used for navigation, and so on.

LINQ to DataSet queries are capable of returning the DataView instance by means of the `AsDataView` extension method. Thanks to this extension method, you can set the query as a DataSource of a BindingDataSource class like this:

```
mybindingSource.DataSource = (From product In NorthwindDataSet.Products
                              Select product).AsDataView()
```

Now you see how you will be able to add some sophisticated querying capabilities to your data bound applications. Let's illustrate this by adding some querying features to our Products application, as shown earlier in the chapter in Figure 18.21.

USING LINQ TO FILTER PRODUCTS DATA

In cases where data operators have to manage a large number of entries, listing all of these on the form with navigation capability can prove not to be very practical. Users will be forced to spend a lot of time while navigating between records. In such cases, providing some filtering capability can prove to be very beneficial.

Let's add some filtering features to our form in the Products project. I will use following criteria for the filtering functionality:

◆ Category selected by user

◆ Units in stock less than the number entered by the user

◆ Units on order greater than the number entered by the user

This way, users will be able to filter products by category and by some important operational data. They will be able to see when the numbers of units in stock is low or what product units for an order are piling up. Figure 18.23 shows the new version of the Products interface.

FIGURE 18.23
Reviewing the deleted rows in the DataSet

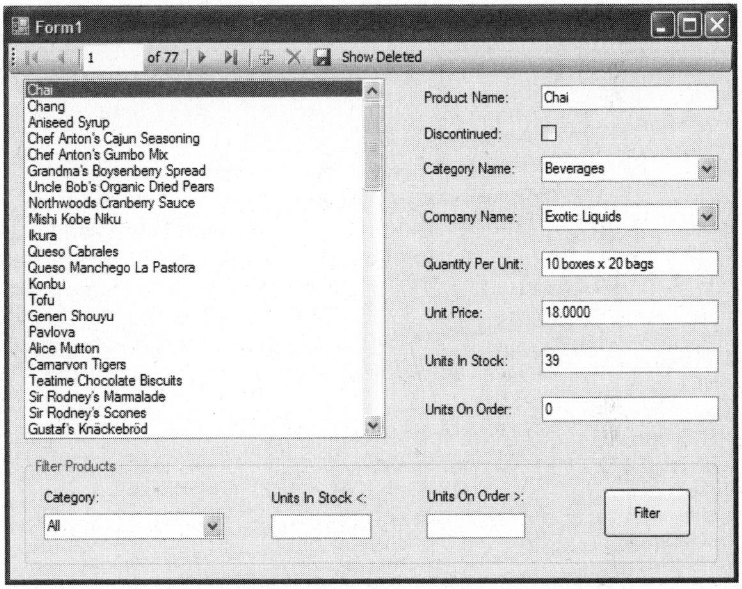

You can use these criteria in any kind of combination. To know whether criteria should be applied or not, it is best to count on some special value. If the Units In Stock Less and Units On Order Greater text boxes are empty, then they should not be used in a query. For the category, the special value of the combo box is the text *All*. To add this value to Combobox, it has to be populated by your application and not through the data binding. The following code populates the Categories Combobox and is placed inside the `Form_Load` event handler:

```
cboCategoryFilter.DisplayMember = "CategoryName"
cboCategoryFilter.ValueMember = "CategoryID"
cboCategoryFilter.Items.Insert(0, "All")
```

```
      For Each category In NorthwindDataSet.Categories
            cboCategoryFilter.Items.Insert(category.CategoryID, category)
      Next
```

Now you are ready to write the LINQ query that uses these criteria. Because these criteria can be used in any combination, writing the query might prove to be a bit trickier than you initially thought.

The solution is to use the special value of criteria inside the query itself. For example, the expression cboCategoryFilter.Text = "All" is true if the user does not want to apply the categories criteria. As you can see, I have named the categories ComboBox cboCategory-Filter. If you combine this statement with product.CategoryID = categoryId using the OrElse operator, then you can use the cboCategoryFilter.Text = "All" expression to turn off the categories criteria when the user selects All in the Categories combo. The complete statement to be put in the Where part of the LINQ query for Categories combo is as follows: cboCategoryFilter.Text = "All" OrElse product.CategoryID = categoryId.

The same pattern can be applied to rest of conditions. For other criteria, the special value is an empty string. You can take a look at the complete code for the Filter button in Listing 18.9.

LISTING 18.9:   Coloring the edited and inserted rows on the DataGridView control

```
Private Sub bttnFilter_Click(...) Handles bttnFilter.Click
    Dim categoryId As Integer
    If Not cboCategoryFilter.Text = "All" Then
        categoryId = CType(cboCategoryFilter.SelectedItem, _
                NorthwindDataSet.CategoriesRow).CategoryID
    End If

    queryResult = From product In NorthwindDataSet.Products
                Where ((cboCategoryFilter.Text = "All" OrElse
                    product.CategoryID = categoryId) And

(String.IsNullOrEmpty(txtUnitsOnOrderFilter.Text) OrElse
                    product.UnitsOnOrder >
CInt(txtUnitsOnOrderFilter.Text)) And

(String.IsNullOrEmpty(txtUnitsInStockFilter.Text) OrElse
                    product.UnitsInStock <
CInt(txtUnitsInStockFilter.Text)))
                    Select product

    ProductsBindingSource.DataSource = queryResult.AsDataView()

End Sub
```

The Bottom Line

Design and use typed DataSets.   Typed DataSets are created with visual tools at design time and allow you to write type-safe code. A typed DataSet is a class created by the wizard on the fly, and it becomes part of the project. The advantage of typed DataSets is that they expose functionality specific to the selected tables and can be easily bound to Windows forms. The code that implements a typed DataSet adds methods and properties to a generic DataSet, so all the functionality of the DataSet object is included in the autogenerated class.

Master It   Describe the basic components generated by the wizard when you create a typed DataSet with the visual tools of Visual Studio.

Bind Windows forms to typed DataSets.   The simplest method of designing a data-bound form is to drop a DataTable, or individual columns, on the form. DataTables are bound to DataGridView controls, which display the entire DataTable. Individual columns are bound to simple controls such as TextBox, CheckBox, and DateTimePicker controls, depending on the column's type. In addition to the data-bound controls, the editor generates a toolbar control with some basic navigational tools and the Add/Delete/Save buttons.

Master It   Outline the process of binding DataTables to a DataGridView control.

Compare a LINQ query used to filter data with an eSQL dynamic query.   You can use the AsDataView extension method of the DataTable class to enable binding of the LINQ query results when querying the DataSet in LINQ to DataSet technology. In this chapter, you have seen how a LINQ query can be used to provide filtering capabilities on a data-entry form.

Entity SQL (eSQL) is a query language with syntax similar to Transact-SQL. Entity SQL queries can be embedded inside the Visual Basic code and can be used to query the Entity Data Model provided by the Entity Framework. You saw how to use Entity SQL to construct dynamic queries in Chapter 17.

Master It   Compare LINQ queries to queries written in Entity SQL. Explain the main benefits and drawbacks of each technology.

Part 6

Developing for the Web

- ◆ **Chapter 19: Accessing the Web**
- ◆ **Chapter 20: Building Web Applications**
- ◆ **Chapter 21: Building and Using Web Services**

Chapter 19

Accessing the Web

The Internet has changed our everyday lives in many ways, and it has changed the programming landscape completely. It is hardly imaginable today to develop any application that is not at least in some way related to the Internet. HTTP, the underlying protocol of the Internet, is a standard protocol for application interoperability and distributed application development.

The Internet provides a wealth of information and functionality available in different forms. Most of this information is structured with a human user in mind; a user who will access a website using a web browser. Sometimes, information is useful as is, and you will see how it is easy to incorporate such information into your applications using the WebBrowser control.

In other situations, you need to access and extract information from unstructured HTML pages. This process is often referred to as HTML screen scraping. The .NET Framework provides all you need to simulate the browser and access such pages without having the servers ever discover that they are not communicating with a web browser but with your Visual Basic program instead. Support for such access comes in the form of the WebClient class and, in situations where you need more low-level control, the HttpWebRequest and HttpWebResponse classes. These classes can be used to access applications that provide structured information meant to be accessed by other applications but use some more lightweight forms of interoperability, like XML over HTTP, as opposed to a dedicated information exchange protocol like SOAP. (You will learn more about SOAP in Chapter 21, "Building and Using Web Services.")

In the Chapter 20, "Building Web Applications," you will learn how to develop web applications — applications made to serve the clients over the Internet. In this chapter, we'll take a look at how you can be on the other side, the consuming side of the wire. You will learn how to access different resources and applications on the Internet through your code and how to integrate browser functionality inside your applications.

In this chapter, you'll learn how to do the following:

◆ Add browser functionality to your Windows Forms applications using the WebBrowser control

◆ Access information and services on the Web from within your code using WebClient or HttpWebRequest and HttpWebResponse classes

The WebBrowser Control

The WebBrowser control is the simplest option for adding some browser functionality to a Windows Forms application. It is capable of presenting HTML content with all the usual browser features: hyperlinks, navigation, multimedia content, Favorites, and the like.

There can be a number of reasons you would want to add web browser functionality to your application. The Internet provides a wealth of useful information and ready-to-use functionalities like address validation, weather forecasts, online calendars, and stock quotes, just to name a few. Many times this information is tailored so it can be included like a "widget" or a "gadget" inside some other web page. These make it especially easy to embed Internet content inside your Windows Forms application, as you will see in the section "VB 2010 at Work: The Stock Quotes Project" later in this chapter. Once you see how easy it is to integrate web browser functionality with the WebBrowser control, I am sure you will think of many other useful ways to enrich your applications with Internet content.

With a little bit of work, the WebBrowser control can be used to make a full-fledged custom web browser. This can be useful in situations in which your client needs to restrict the access to intranet-only sites or only to selected Internet sites. Or you might use a WebBrowser control to make a child-friendly browser that can eliminate adult content. Before I show you how to use the WebBrowser control in a plausible application scenario, let's inspect some of its most important properties.

WebBrowser Control under the Hood

The WebBrowser control is a managed .NET wrapper over the Internet Explorer ActiveX dynamic link library. This is the same library that the Internet Explorer executable uses internally and is available on any Windows machine.

As a consequence, you will not be able to exhort the usual level of control over you application. Since Internet Explorer is essentially part of the Windows operating system, it will be updated through the Windows Automatic Updates service, so you cannot control the version of Internet Explorer that is being used to render the HTML in your application. While most Internet Explorer versions still in circulation work in a similar manner, there are some known differences in how they render the HTML.

The browser operations a user performs on a WebBrowser control will affect the Internet Explorer installation. For example, a Favorite added to the list of Favorites through a WebBrowser control will appear in the Internet Explorer list of Favorites. Pages accessed through a WebBrowser control will appear in the Internet Explorer history. Adding a shortcut using a WebBrowser control will create a new Windows shortcut. And so on.

One important aspect to consider when using a WebBrowser control is security. In this respect, the control behaves in the same manner as Internet Explorer and will run scripts and embedded controls inside web pages. In such situations, the WebBrowser control is, according to MSDN, "no less secure than Internet Explorer would be, but the managed WebBrowser control does not prevent such unmanaged code from running."

Now that you have seen what a WebBrowser control is really made of, let's take a look at its properties.

WebBrowser Control Properties

Like any other visible Windows Forms control, the WebBrowser control has a number of common layout-related properties, including `Size`, `MaximumSize`, `MinimumSize`, `Location`, `Margin`, and `Anchor`. They all work as you would expect from your experience with other

Windows Forms controls, so I will not go into more details on any of these. While belonging to this group, a small note is in order for the Dock property.

DOCK

The Dock property determines how the WebBrowser control is positioned in relation to a container and how it will behave as the container is resized. Anchoring and docking controls are discussed in detail in Chapter 6, "Working with Forms."

When a WebBrowser control is added to an empty form or a container control, the default value for the Dock property is Fill. As a result, the whole form area will be covered by the WebBrowser control. The WebBrowser control drops into your form as a square with no visible clues as to its position. Although the control's white background will stand out, you still might be confused at first as to where it is positioned on the form. Just change the default value of the Dock property to some other value, like None, and the control will become visible as you change the form's size.

URL

The URL property lets you specify the target URL address for the WebBrowser control in the design time. When you display the form, the WebBrowser control will load that URL by default. If you change the property at runtime, the control will navigate to the new URL. In this respect, setting the URL property works the same as calling the WebBrowser control's Navigate method (described in the section "WebBrowser Control Methods" later in this chapter).

The URL property type is the System.Uri class. A URI (Uniform Resource Identifier) can represent a unique identifier or an address (familiar URL) on the Internet. You will typically use instances of this class to represent an Internet address. When doing so, do not forget to specify the protocol part of the address, otherwise you will get an Invalid URI exception. You can instantiate the Uri class by passing a string representation of the URL to its constructor. Here is the correct way to set the WebBrowser URL property in your code:

```
WebBrowser1.Url = New Uri("http://www.google.com")
```

ALLOWNAVIGATION

The AllowNavigation property sets the WebBrowser control behavior in regards to navigation. If you set the AllowNavigation property to False, the WebBrowser control will not react when a user clicks a hyperlink and will not load the page specified in the hyperlink. It will not react to navigation attempts from within your code either. Calling the Navigate method on a WebBrowser control when AllowNavigation is set to False will have no effect. The only page the control will display is the one that was loaded initially.

Bear in mind that AllowNavigation does not alter the visual representation of the page or the cursor. Hyperlinks are still rendered distinctly as hyperlinks (underlined blue text), and the mouse cursor will change to a hand shape when hovering over the hyperlink. Finally, while the AllowNavigation property can prevent users from following a standard HTML hyperlink, it will not prevent the browser from opening a new window as directed by JavaScript code, as, for example, when calling the window.open JavaScript function. Finally, if the user presses F5 (Refresh), the page loaded initially will reload.

SCROLLBARSENABLED

Internet Explorer will display the scroll bars when the loaded page is not fully visible. By setting `ScrollBarsEnabled` to False, you can prevent scroll bars from appearing even if the page loaded into the WebBrowser control is not fully visible.

ALLOWBROWSERDROP

The `AllowBrowserDrop` property controls the WebBrowser control's drag-and-drop behavior. When it's set to True, you can open the HTML file in Internet Explorer by dragging the file from Windows Explorer and dropping it on the browser. The WebBrowser control behaves in the same manner by default. To disable drag-and-drop behavior in the WebBrowser control, you can set `AllowBrowserDrop` to False. You should be aware, however, that this property is superseded by the `AllowNavigation` property; if `AllowNavigation` is set to False and `AllowBrowserDrop` is set to True, the WebBrowser control will not react to a drag-and-drop. This is to be expected because dropping the file on a WebBrowser control is just another way of telling the WebBrowser control to navigate to a certain address — in this case a local HTML file.

WEBBROWSERSHORTCUTSENABLED

In Internet Explorer, you can use a number of key combinations as keyboard shortcuts or accelerators. For example, Alt + the left arrow key combination is a shortcut for clicking the Back button in Internet Explorer and Alt + the right arrow key is a shortcut for clicking Forward. You can disable accelerators in the WebBrowser control by setting the `WebBrowserShortcutsEnabled` property to False. This property is enabled by default.

ISWEBBROWSERCONTEXTMENUENABLED

`IsWebBrowserContextMenuEnabled` controls the display of a context-sensitive, shortcut menu when a user right-clicks the control. The shortcut menu contains some standard browser shortcuts, but it can also contain some shortcuts contributed by various Internet Explorer add-ons and accelerators. You can see a context menu displayed over a WebBrowser control in a custom WebBrowser control–based implementation of a web browser in Figure 19.1.

SCRIPTERRORSSUPPRESSED

Modern web pages typically contain large quantities of JavaScript code in addition to the HTML code. As with any other code, bugs in JavaScript code are not rare. The probability of an error in JavaScript code is enhanced by the differences in the way different browsers interpret it. Some JavaScript code can be perfectly legal in one browser but will throw an error in another.

When Internet Explorer encounters an error in JavaScript code (or some other script code), it will by default display a dialog window with detailed error information and prompt the user to decide whether to continue to run the script code. In a WebBrowser control, you can control this behavior through the `ScriptErrorsSuppressed` property. Set it to False and the WebBrowser control will bear any error in the script code silently.

Script error messages are rarely of any help to the end user, so it is best to set this property to False in the final version of your application. Even if errors in JavaScript code are present, the pages often still display and provide some limited functionality. You can take a look at a Script Error dialog window displayed by the WebBrowser control in Figure 19.2.

FIGURE 19.1
A context menu in a custom WebBrowser control–based web browser

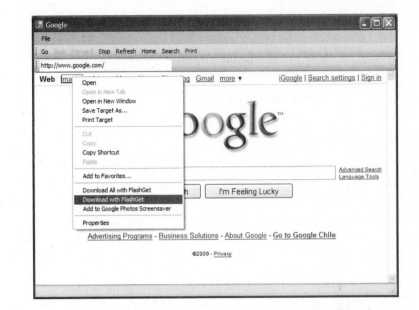

FIGURE 19.2
Script Error dialog window displayed by the WebBrowser control

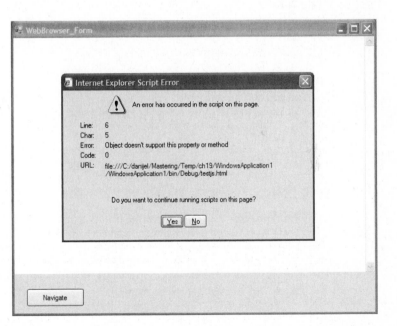

DocumentText

You can use this property to obtain a string representation of a currently loaded web page or to load a web page from a string. For example, you can use the code shown in Listing 19.1 to display the page that will submit a search term to the Google search engine.

LISTING 19.1:   Loading a WebBrowser control with HTML content from a string literal

```
    WebBrowser1.DocumentText =
"<html><body>Search in Google:<br/>" &
"<form method='get' action='http://www.google.com/search'>" &
"<input type='text' name='as_q'/><br/>" &
"<input type='submit' value='Search'/>" &
"</form></body></html>"
```

Just place a WebBrowser control named `WebBrowser1` onto a form and write the code in Listing 19.1 into the `Form Load` event to see the snippet in action.

DocumentStream

The `DocumentStream` property is similar to the `DocumentText` property. Instead of a string, it uses a `System.IO.Stream` instance as a property value. Using the stream interface, you can easily load content from a file (and from numerous other sources) into a WebBrowser control.

Document

The `Document` property is the pivotal property for manipulating a currently loaded HTML page from within your code. The method returns a `System.Windows.Forms.HtmlDocument` instance representing the current page's Document Object Model (DOM) document — a structured representation of a web page. If you have ever manipulated an HTML page in JavaScript, you will find this object quite familiar.

You can accomplish pretty much anything using a web page's DOM. You can obtain and manipulate values on forms, invoke embedded scripts, manipulate page structure, and so on.

The code in Listing 19.2 adds simple validation to the Google search form code displayed in Listing 19.1.

LISTING 19.2:   Validating an HTML form through the WebBrowser Document property

```
Private Sub webBrowser1_Navigating(ByVal sender As Object,
    ByVal e As WebBrowserNavigatingEventArgs) Handles
    WebBrowser1.Navigating

    Dim document = WebBrowser1.Document
    If document IsNot Nothing And
        document.All("as_q") IsNot Nothing And
        String.IsNullOrEmpty( _
        document.All("as_q").GetAttribute("value")) Then
        e.Cancel = True
        MsgBox("Please enter a search term.")
    End If
End Sub
```

The validation implemented in Listing 19.2 is rather simple. It cancels navigation and warns the user that the search string is empty. Being able to access and manipulate web page structure is not limited to such simple operations. Indeed, this feature opens a wealth of implementation possibilities.

WebBrowser Control Methods

The WebBrowser control provides a number of methods that make it possible to emulate standard browser behavior. Let's start with some navigation-related methods.

NAVIGATE

Essentially, calling the `Navigate` method has the same effect as writing the URL address in the Internet Explorer address bar and pressing Enter. Similar to using the URL property, calling the `Navigate` method results in the browser displaying the specified URL. This method will be ignored if the WebBrowser `AllowNavigation` property is set to False. The method has a number of overloaded variants, but the most typical variants accept a URL parameter in the form of valid URL string:

```
WebBrowser1.Navigate("http://www.google.com")
```

GO METHODS

The WebBrowser control has a number of methods whose names start with the prefix Go. You can use them to invoke typical browser navigation behavior. Table 19.1 lists these methods and the results of their invocation.

STOP

You can use this method to cancel the current navigation. Sometimes, a page can take longer than expected to load, or it can even hang. In those situations, you need to be able to cancel the navigation. The `Stop` method provides this capability.

REFRESH

You can use the `Refresh` method to reload the current page to the WebBrowser control. This method can be useful when displaying frequently changing information and can be easily automated so it is invoked in certain time intervals in combination with the Timer control.

TABLE 19.1:   WebBrowser *Go* navigation methods

METHOD	EFFECT
GoBack	Navigate to the previous page in history.
GoForward	Navigate to the next page in history.
GoHome	Navigate to the Internet Explorer home page.
GoSearch	Navigate to the default search page for the current user.

SHOW METHODS

The WebBrowser control supports a number of methods for displaying different dialog windows with some advanced browser functionality. Table 19.2 lists these methods and explains their purpose.

PRINT

This method prints the current web page using the default print settings and without displaying the print dialog window.

WebBrowser Control Events

A WebBrowser control operates in asynchronous mode. Loading a page will not freeze your application; the application will continue to run while the WebBrowser control is downloading and rendering a page. This is why events play an important role in the WebBrowser programmatic model. Let's take a look at a few important ones.

NAVIGATING

You have already seen the Navigating event at work in Listing 19.2. This event is raised to signal the navigation. You can use this event to cancel the navigation if necessary, by setting the Cancel property of WebBrowserNavigatingEventArgs parameter to True. You can obtain the URL that the navigation is targeting through the TargetFrameName property of the WebBrowserNavigatingEventArgs parameter. If you wish to measure the time a certain web page takes to load, you can use the Navigating event to signal the start of navigation and the DocumentCompleted event to signal the end of the page load process.

DOCUMENTCOMPLETED

The DocumentCompleted event occurs when a web page is completely loaded inside the WebBrowser control. It means that the Document property is available and will return the complete structure of the loaded document.

TABLE 19.2:   WebBrowser *Show* navigation methods

METHOD	EFFECT
ShowPrintDialog	Displays browser's print dialog used to print the current web page
ShowPrintPreviewDialog	Displays browser's print preview dialog
ShowPageSetupDialog	Displays page setup dialog window used to set printing options like Paper Option, Margins, Header, and Footer
ShowSaveAsDialog	Displays browser's Save As dialog used to save the current web page to a file
ShowPropertiesDialog	Displays current page's Properties window

VB 2010 at Work: The Stock Quotes Project

A WebBrowser control opens the world of the Internet to your Windows Forms projects in a simple and direct manner. Popular websites often offer a way to embed a part of their functionality inside another website. Such widgets can be easily integrated into your Windows Forms projects.

In the Stock Quotes project, you will use the WebBrowser control to display quotes for selected stocks on a Windows form. Yahoo! Finance offers free Yahoo! badges that display the latest news, stock tickers, charts, and other types of information that are specifically designed to be integrated into your website. You can find out more about Yahoo! badges at the following URL: http://finance.yahoo.com/badges/. If you plan to use this feature in a production environment, please read the terms of service carefully. While the Yahoo! website clearly states that the service is free, I am no expert on legal matters and there might be limitations and conditions on how the service may be used.

OBTAINING THE HTML WIDGET

You will need a Yahoo.com account to complete the following steps, and you will be prompted to create one if you do not have one. Start by navigating to http://finance.yahoo.com/badges/, click the Start Now button, and follow these steps to obtain the HTML code needed to embed the stock ticker inside the web page:

1. Choose a module to embed. I chose the most compact module, called Quotes.

2. Customize the module.

    Option 1: Enter **MSFT, GOOG, IBM**, and **ORCL**. Delete the default entry.

    Option 2: Select the Medium (200 px) value for the width of the badge.

    Option 3: Select the first (black) color theme.

    Option 4: Check the check box signaling that you agree to the terms of service and press the Get Code button.

3. Once the code is displayed, copy and save it in some temporary file. You'll need it soon.

CREATING THE STOCK QUOTES PROJECT

Create a new Windows Forms project and name it **StockQuotes**. You will display the Yahoo! badge inside a WebBrowser control. To do so, perform the following steps:

1. Add a WebBrowser control to Form1. Leave the name of the control as is — WebBrowser1.

2. Disable the scroll bars on the WebBrowser1 control by setting the ScrollBarsEnabled property to False.

3. Change the Dock property to None. Now you can resize and position the WebBrowser control.

4. Position the WebBrowser control somewhere on the right side of the form. That way, the form will take on a look that's similar to the structure of web pages — nonessential information positioned on the right edge of the form.

5. Add a new `quotes.html` file to the project. While I could embed the HTML code for the stock ticker badge inside my Visual Basic code, it will be easier to edit it inside a separate HTML file.

Now that you have created all the items you will need for the StockQuotes project, you need to load the `quotes.html` file content into the WebBrowser control. You can accomplish this by setting the `WebBrowser.Url` property with a `Uri` instance representing the `quotes.html` file location. Since the `quotes.html` file is part of your project, you can obtain its location through a My.Application object. Here is the code for the `Form_Load` event, used to set the `WebBrowser.Url` property:

```
Private Sub Form1_Load(ByVal sender As System.Object,
    ByVal e As System.EventArgs) Handles MyBase.Load
    WebBrowser1.Url = New Uri(
        My.Application.Info.DirectoryPath.ToString() &
        "\quotes.html")
End Sub
```

Just to make sure everything works as expected, add some text (for example, "Hello from quotes.html!") to the `quotes.html` file and run the project. When the form is displayed, the WebBrowser control should show the text contained in the `quotes.html` file.

DISPLAYING THE STOCK QUOTES BADGE INSIDE THE WEBBROWSER CONTROL

As you are already guessing, instead of embedding the stock quotes badge inside HTML page on some website, you will display the badge inside the local HTML file distributed with your Windows Forms application. You can accomplish this by making the `quotes.html` a properly structured HTML file. (You will learn more about HTML in the next chapter.) For now, you should know that a typical HTML page has html, head, and body elements. Add the following HTML code to the `quotes.html` file:

```
<html>
<head>
<title>Stock Quotes</title>
</head>
<body>
<!-- add Yahoo badge code here! -->
</body>
</html>
```

Remember that HTML code obtained from Yahoo! in the section "Obtaining the HTML Widget"? Take that code and replace the line `<!-- add Yahoo badge code here! -->` with it.

Run the project. The WebBrowser control should now display the stock quotes badge with fresh values obtained from the Yahoo! site.

Although the application is now working, I would like to show you how to tweak the visual appearance of the badge. First, we'll minimize the margins surrounding the badge, and then we'll set the color of the HTML page so it blends better with the badge itself. I guess the gray color will do.

To minimize the margins and change the background color, we will add some CSS code to the quotes.html page. (You will learn more about the CSS in the next chapter.) For now, just modify the quotes.html file so it includes a style tag:

```
<html>
<head>
<title>Stock Quotes</title>
<style type="text/css">
    body {
      margin-left: 0px;
      margin-top: 0px;
      margin-right: 0px;
      margin-bottom: 0px;
      background-color: Gray;
    }
</style>
</head>
<body>
<!-- add Yahoo badge code here! -->
</body>
</html>
```

Again, you should replace the line <!-- add Yahoo badge code here! --> with HTML code obtained from the Yahoo! site. Run the project again. Now you can adjust the WebBrowser control size so it displays the complete stock badge widget. When you've finished, the form should look similar to one shown in Figure 19.3.

FIGURE 19.3
Windows form with embedded Yahoo! Finance badge

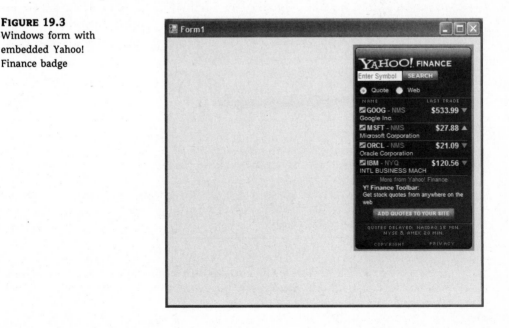

Real World Scenario

FIDDLER — HTTP DEBUGGING PROXY

While you are developing applications that communicate over the network, you often need to take a peek at the traffic going over the wire. Fiddler is one tool that can help you do exactly that, and it's available as a free download from www.fiddler2.com.

Fiddler installs itself between your web browser and web server. It fools the browser into believing it is communicating directly with the web server, while the server is convinced it is communicating with the browser. In the meantime, you will be able to observe and even modify the communication between the two sides.

Fiddler's purpose is not malicious. It can be of great help to web developers. It provides numerous statistics on request/response size, time, performance, and so forth and can help you monitor and debug the conversation.

The Fiddler window consists of two main areas, as shown here.

On the left side, you will find a listing of all the HTTP requests and responses. On the right side, you can inspect each request and response. You can visualize HTTP headers and display the body as text, XML, or even as it would appear in the browser by way of a tab called WebView. Further, you can modify and reissue the request from Fiddler itself, automate the whole process through the Fiddler scripting support, or even extend Fiddler with extensions programmed in the .NET Framework.

Accessing the Web with the WebClient and HttpWebRequest/Response Classes

The simplest way to publish services on the Internet is to make proper use of HTTP. HTTP is the underlying protocol for all kinds of web services, and web services come in different shapes and forms. Some make more direct use of HTTP, while others use it with a lot of overhead.

Lightweight web services typically use HTTP to transport data in XML or JSON format. JavaScript Object Notation (JSON) is a data format similar to XML but more bandwidth efficient. Lightweight web services can be by orders of magnitude more efficient than more ubiquitous SOAP web services. (You will read more about web services and SOAP in Chapter 21.) For lightweight web services, the WebClient class and the HttpWebRequest and HttpWebResponse classes will help you program simple and efficient client applications.

A lot of information and services available on the Internet today are not properly structured for machine consumption. While humans can make use of it, it is difficult to consume such services programmatically. In such situations, the only way to access these services programmatically is to behave in the same way as an Internet browser application. The WebClient class and the HttpWebRequest and HttpWebResponse classes provide an API that can accomplish exactly that. Accessing information contained inside standard HTML pages is generally known as HTML screen scraping.

The WebClient Class

WebClient is a lightweight, simple alternative for accessing the Web. It represents a higher-level wrapper over the WebRequest and WebResponse classes. You will find that it can handle most of the cases that the HttpWebRequest and HttpWebResponse combination can.

WebClient Class Properties

The WebClient class gives you a lot of control over the HTTP communication. You can access request and response headers, configure a proxy, set your credentials, and more.

QUERYSTRING

You can always set query parameters manually by concatenating strings and adding the query as the final part of a URL. A more structured way to accomplish this uses name-value pairs and the QueryString property. The following code snippet illustrates how a q parameter can be added to a query string. The q parameter is often used in search engines to convey the search criteria.

```
Dim webClient As New WebClient
Dim queryParameters As New System.Collections.Specialized.NameValueCollection()
queryParameters.Add("q", "SearchCriteria")
webClient.QueryString = queryParameters
```

As you can see, the QueryString property is a NameValueCollection type from the System .Collections.Specialized namespace.

HEADERS

The Headers property represents a collection of request headers. Response headers can be accessed through the ResponseHeaders property. Headers are an important part of HTTP.

For example, a user-agent header is used to convey a lot of client-related information to the server. A user-agent header can include information on the browser version and type, the operating system, even the version of the .NET Framework that has been installed on the machine where the browser is running.

The WebClient class does not set any headers by default. Some servers might expect some standard headers with the request, so if you are experiencing any problems accessing certain servers with the WebClient class, be sure to add some standard headers, like user-agent.

Servers will often use user-agent header information to render the response that best accommodates the reported browser type. For example, the server might exclude JavaScript code from pages if the browser does not support JavaScript, or it might render the page so it fits smaller displays if it detects that the request is coming from a mobile device. A listing of standard request and response headers is available on Wikipedia at following URL: http://en.wikipedia.org/wiki/List_of_HTTP_headers.

RESPONSEHEADERS

ResponseHeaders provides access to headers included in the response by server. These headers can include a lot of information regarding the response, like mime type, encoding, content length, and so forth. The ETag and Cache-Control headers can affect the caching mechanism. Responding with a value of "no-cache" in the Cache-Control header indicates to the browser and to any other HTTP intermediary that the content should not be cached.

Another important response header is Set-Cookie. Although, if you need to manipulate or receive cookies, you are better off using the HttpWebRequest and HttpWebResponse classes because they have better support for this feature.

WebClient Class Methods

The WebClient class provides a number of methods for sending a request for a resource under a given URI and receiving the requested data. Most of these methods come in two flavors:

◆ Synchronous

◆ Asynchronous

Asynchronous methods permit the background execution of request-response operations. Since the calling (for example, UI) thread is not blocked, the main line of execution can proceed without waiting for the download to finish. This feature can be used for implementing applications with a more responsive user interface, permitting the user to continue working with the application in the same time that communication is performed or to cancel the request in progress if they wish to do so.

DOWNLOAD METHODS

The WebClient class has a number of methods with names that start with Download. These methods essentially perform the same operation — download a resource from a specified URI. The main difference is in the type of the method's return value. Table 19.3 lists the methods and return types.

TABLE 19.3: *Download* methods return types

METHOD	RETURN TYPE
DownloadData	Byte
DownloadString	String
DownloadFile	Void (downloads to a local file specified as a method parameter)

DOWNLOAD*ASYNC METHODS

Download*Async methods have the same function as the standard Download methods. The difference is that employing these methods causes the resource download operation to be performed asynchronously. To receive the data asynchronously, you need to provide an event handling routine for Download*Completed events. Take a look at the code in Listing 19.5 for an example of using the DownloadStringAsync method in an address visualization form project and in Listing 19.3 in the WebClient asynchronous download example for a simple illustration of an asynchronous operation of the WebClient class.

OPENREAD AND OPENREADASYNC METHODS

These methods perform similar functions to the Download methods. Each returns a readable stream from a resource specified as the method parameter.

UPLOAD AND UPLOAD*ASYNC METHODS

These methods have their counterparts in the Download group of methods. Instead of downloading the data, these methods are used to upload it.

CANCELASYNC METHOD

The CancelAsync method aborts the current asynchronous download or upload operation. It bears noting that the corresponding Download*Completed and Upload*Completed events are still raised by the class. It is possible for an operation to complete successfully even after CancelAsync has been called — after all, you can have no control over how the remote call was finalized on the other side of the wire. To check the outcome of asynchronous operation, check the Canceled property of the Download*CompletedEventArgs or Upload*CompletedEventArgs event handler parameter.

WebClient Class Event

A majority of WebClient class events has to do with asynchronous *modus-operandi* of the download and upload operations.

DOWNLOAD*COMPLETED AND UPLOAD*COMPLETED EVENTS

These events are used to signal the completion of the asynchronous operation. Results of the download operation can be accessed through an event handler's property as well as through the outcome of the asynchronous operation, presented in the Canceled property of the Download*CompletedEventArgs or Upload*CompletedEventArgs parameter.

WebClient Asynchronous Download Example

The code in Listing 19.3 shows the Windows form with a simple example of an asynchronous download operation using the WebClient's asynchronous programming model. The form includes two buttons: bttnDownload, used to initiate the download operation, and bttnCancel, which can be used to cancel the download operation in progress.

LISTING 19.3:   Asynchronous download with WebClient

```
Imports System.ComponentModel

Public Class Form1

    Dim webClient As New WebClient()

    Private Sub Form1_Load(ByVal sender As System.Object,
            ByVal e As System.EventArgs) Handles MyBase.Load

        AddHandler webClient.DownloadStringCompleted,
            AddressOf webClient_DownloadStringCompleted
    End Sub

    Private Sub webClient_DownloadStringCompleted(ByVal sender As Object,
            ByVal e As DownloadStringCompletedEventArgs)
        Dim asyncCompletedParam As AsyncCompletedEventArgs =
            TryCast(e, AsyncCompletedEventArgs)
        If Not asyncCompletedParam.Cancelled = True Then
            Console.WriteLine(CStr(e.Result))
        Else
            Console.WriteLine("Asynchronous download canceled by user!")
        End If
        MsgBox("Download operation completed. See the Output window.")
    End Sub

    Private Sub bttnDownload_Click(ByVal sender As System.Object,
            ByVal e As System.EventArgs) Handles bttnDownload.Click

        webClient.DownloadStringAsync(New Uri("http://www.google.com"))
    End Sub

    Private Sub bttnCancel_Click(ByVal sender As System.Object,
            ByVal e As System.EventArgs) Handles bttnCancel.Click

        webClient.CancelAsync()
    End Sub
End Class
```

The `DownloadStringCompleted` event handler routine is assigned to a WebClient in a form load routine. The event handler first checks the outcome of the download operation through the `AsyncCompletedEventArgs` parameter's `Cancel` property and, if the operation was successful, prints the download result from the www.google.com URL to the console output.

Finally, the `bttnCancel` event handling routine is used to call the WebClient's `CancelAsync` method. If the asynchronous download is in progress, it is canceled; otherwise, calling the `CancelAsync` has no effect.

HttpWebRequest and HttpWebResponse Classes

These classes from the `System.Net` namespace are used internally by the WebClient for download and upload operations over HTTP and HTTPS. While you should prefer the WebClient class because of its simplicity, you can always make use of the HttpWebRequest and Http-WebResponse classes where more granular control over the communication is necessary. The HttpWebRequest and HttpWebResponse classes provide an explicit manner for handling the HTTP cookies.

MANAGING COOKIES WITH HTTPWEBREQUEST AND HTTPWEBRESPONSE

To manage cookies with HttpWebRequest and HttpWebResponse, you first need to create the instance of the CookieContainer class and attach it to HttpWebRequest. Then you can access the cookies set by the server through the HttpWebRequest `Cookies` property. The following code illustrates how you can list all of the cookies set by the Hotmail server to the console output:

```
Dim request As HttpWebRequest = CType(WebRequest.Create(
                "http://www.hotmail.com"), HttpWebRequest)
request.CookieContainer = New CookieContainer()
Using response As HttpWebResponse =
    CType(request.GetResponse(), HttpWebResponse)
    Console.WriteLine("Server set {0} cookies", response.Cookies.Count)
    Dim cookie As Cookie
    For Each cookie In response.Cookies
        Console.WriteLine("Cookie: {0} = {1}", cookie.Name, cookie.Value)
    Next
End Using
```

Putting It All Together: The Address Visualization Form

In the following sections, I will show you how to find the map coordinates of a street address and display them on a map. I decided to name the sample project ViewAddressOnAMap. You can download the project from www.sybex.com/go/masteringvb2010.

The business case for such functionality is more than common; many call centers have to record clients' addresses. This can be an error-prone process, so being able to see the address on the map while talking to a client can be a real plus for a call center attendant. Also, some addresses are difficult to find without additional information. ("The street sign blew down in last night's storm, so look for the pink house with purple trim and then turn right at the next street.") Field employees can really benefit from the additional information that goes along with the address. Again, a call center attendant can easily enter these indications while talking to a client and looking at the map. Fortunately, there are services on the Internet today that make such an application possible.

Composing Web Services

You will learn more about web services and especially SOAP web services in Chapter 21. In a broader sense, a web service is any service that can be consumed by a program (as opposed to a human) over the Internet. So, to implement the address visualization form, we will make use of two web services:

◆ Address coordinates search (geocoding) service

◆ Mapping service

Let's look at the services I chose for the ViewAddressOnAMap sample project in more detail.

YAHOO! GEOCODING API

A geocoding service returns the exact latitude and longitude for a street address. These coordinates can then be used as parameters for a mapping service, which will return the map for a given coordinate.

Yahoo! provides a geocoding API as a part of its Yahoo! Maps web services. You can find more information about the Geocoding API at `http://developer.yahoo.com/maps/rest/V1/geocode.html`.

To run the ViewAddressOnAMap sample project, you should follow the Get An App ID link found on the Geocoding API page (at the URL in the preceding paragraph) and replace the YahooAppId in the sample code with the Yahoo! ID you obtained this way.

The Yahoo! Geocoding API is a RESTful web service. *REST* stands for Representational State Transfer and is actually the simplest way to use HTTP as an application protocol and not just as a transport protocol like SOAP. This means that to obtain the coordinates, you can submit address parameters as a part of a URL query string. It also means that you can make use of this service with a simple browser because it uses HTTP as a native, application-level protocol. To test the service, you can write the following URL into your browser:

```
http://local.yahooapis.com/MapsService/V1/geocode?
appid= APFGN10xYiHINOslptpcZsrgFbzsTHKr8HgBk7EA81QRe_
&street=701+First+Ave
&city=Sunnyvale
&state=CA
```

Please note that I have split the actual URL into a five lines to fit the book format; you should enter this address as a single line in the browser's address bar. You should also replace the `appid` parameter provided in the snippet with the Yahoo! App ID obtained from `http://developer.yahoo.com/maps/rest/V1/geocode.html`.

At that same URL, you can find another example of the Yahoo! Geocoding URL, and it might be easier to copy and paste that link to use for testing.

The Yahoo! Geocoding Web Service query URL is pretty much self-explanatory. You pass the address information as parameters inside the URL query. You can pass `street`, `city`, `state` and `zip` together with the Yahoo! App ID as parameters. You should encode the spaces inside the parameter values with a plus sign, so 701 First Ave becomes `701+First+Ave`.

Now, you can take a look at the result. The browser should display the following response:

```
<ResultSet xsi:schemaLocation="urn:yahoo:maps
http://api.local.yahoo.com/MapsService/V1/GeocodeResponse.xsd">
    <Result precision="address">
        <Latitude>37.416397</Latitude>
        <Longitude>-122.025055</Longitude>
        <Address>701 1st Ave</Address>
        <City>Sunnyvale</City>
        <State>CA</State>
        <Zip>94089-1019</Zip>
        <Country>US</Country>
    </Result>
</ResultSet>
```

As you can see, the service response comes in XML format. This makes the response really easy to parse. If you take a look at the XML, you will note the root element is called `ResultSet`. The root element contains the `Result` element. The response is structured this way because the service can return multiple `Result` elements for the same query in cases where query information was not precise enough. You should keep this in mind when programming the code that interprets the Yahoo! Geocoding service response.

GOOGLE MAPS SERVICE

Now let's use Google Maps Service to display the address coordinates on a map. Use this service in a manner similar to the way the Yahoo! badges service was used in the Stock Quotes project earlier in this chapter. Display the service response in a WebBrowser control.

The Google Maps JavaScript API is free, and (as of this writing) there is no limit to the number of page requests you can generate per day. Still, I suggest you register for the Google Maps API and read the related conditions carefully. You can read more about Google Maps JavaScript API at http://code.google.com/apis/maps/documentation/v3/introduction.html.

The Google Maps JavaScript API provides simple scripts that you can embed inside your HTML page to add Google Maps functionality to your website. To use this functionality, you need the HTML code shown on code.google.com in the section "The 'Hello, World' of Google Maps v3" of the Maps V3 tutorial. This code can be used in ViewAddressOnAMap project with minimal modifications. Take a look at the original Hello World code:

```
<html>
<head>
<meta name="viewport" content="initial-scale=1.0, user-scalable=no" />
<script type="text/javascript" src="http://maps.google.com/maps/api/js?
                                sensor=set_to_true_or_false">
</script>
<script type="text/javascript">
  function initialize() {
    var latlng = new google.maps.LatLng(-34.397, 150.644);
    var myOptions = {
      zoom: 8,
      center: latlng,
```

```
        mapTypeId: google.maps.MapTypeId.ROADMAP
    };
    var map = new google.maps.Map(
        document.getElementById("map_canvas"), myOptions);
  }

</script>
</head>
<body onload="initialize()">
  <div id="map_canvas" style="width:100%; height:100%"></div>
</body>
</html>
```

Even without much JavaScript knowledge, you can see that the `LatLng` function defines the coordinates where the map will be centered based on two literal numbers. With a little bit of luck, changing these literals will be enough to visualize the map over a specific latitude and longitude. Notice the value of the sensor query parameter in a URL. According to the documentation, this can be set to False for devices that do not use a sensor to determine the location, as in this case.

Coding Address Visualization Form

Now that you have all necessary information for the project, you can create a new Windows Forms project and name it ViewAddresOnAMap. The project will have a single form, and the client's address will be both saved and shown on the map. Since we are interested in only the address visualization functionality for this exercise, you do not have to implement the code to actually save or maintain the address data.

ASSEMBLING THE ADDRESS VISUALIZATION FORM

Let's start by adding all the necessary controls to the form. You will need a number of text boxes where users can enter the address information, buttons to save the address and to show the address on the map, and finally, one WebBrowser control to display the map. The form should look like one shown in Figure 19.4.

The large white area on the right side of the form is the WebBrowser control. Text box controls in the Address GroupBox have the following names: txtStreet, txtSecondLine, txtCity, txtState, txtZip, and txtObservations. The buttons are names bttnSave and bttnShow. Now you are ready to add some behavior to the form.

For the txtState control, you should limit the length to 2. A text box with verification of the value entered is a much better option than a states ComboBox control. For txtObservations, you should set the `Multiline` property to True.

Finally, you can add a label named `lblError` to the bottom of the form. Here you can display the errors related to address visualization functionality. This functionality should not interfere with the main form functionality consisting of address data entry.

CONSTRUCTING THE GEOCODING SERVICE URL AND QUERY PARAMETERS

To obtain the address coordinates, you can use the WebClient class to query the Yahoo! geocoding service. To do so, you should first construct the URL. You can declare the Yahoo! service

FIGURE 19.4
Address visualization
form

FIGURE 19.4
Address visualization
form

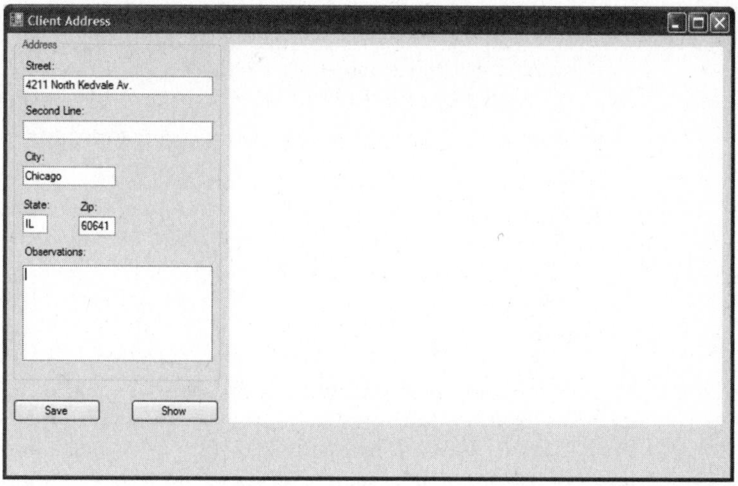

URL as a constant and create the query parameters. Listing 19.4 shows how to construct the
NameValueCollection with query parameters for the Yahoo! Geocoding Web Service.

LISTING 19.4:   Form code with constructed Yahoo! geocoding service URL and query parameters

```
Public Class Form1

    Private Shared YahooAppId As String = "BPdn3S7V34GMfMZ5ukBuHAMYuj" &
                    "APFGN10xYiHINOslptpcZsrgFbzsTHKr8HgBk7EA81QRe_"

    Private Shared YahooGeocodeServiceUrl = "http://local.yahooapis.com" &
                        "/MapsService/V1/geocode"

    Dim yahooGeoCodeParameters As NameValueCollection

    Private Sub GenerateYahooGeoCodeParameters(ByVal street As String,
            ByVal city As String, ByVal state As String,
            ByVal zip As String)

        yahooGeoCodeParameters = New NameValueCollection
        yahooGeoCodeParameters.Add("appid", YahooAppId)
        yahooGeoCodeParameters.Add("street", street.Replace(" "c, "+"c))
        yahooGeoCodeParameters.Add("city", city.Replace(" "c, "+"c))
        yahooGeoCodeParameters.Add("zip", zip)
        yahooGeoCodeParameters.Add("state", state)
    End Sub

End Class
```

Since generated URL query parameters should not contain spaces, space characters are replaced with a plus sign using the `Replace` method of the String class. Now, you are ready to invoke the Yahoo! geocoding service in an asynchronous manner.

INVOKING THE YAHOO! GEOCODING WEB SERVICE

Since address visualization is not a principal feature on the form, you should not make users wait for the map to appear before they can save the address. It is quite possible that the user knows the address well; in that case, waiting for the visualization would be more of a hindrance than a help.

If you use the asynchronous capacities of the WebClient class, you will not block the main thread of execution and users will be able to proceed with their work while the map is loaded in the background. Listing 19.5 shows the `bttnRefresh` button event handling code invoking the `FindLocation` routine that uses the WebClient class to code the Yahoo! Geocoding Web Service asynchronously.

LISTING 19.5: Form with constructed Yahoo! Geocoding Web Service URL and query parameters

```
Imports System.Net
Imports System.IO
Imports System.Collections.Specialized


Public Class Form1

        Private Shared YahooAppId As String = "BPdn3S7V34GMfMZ5ukBuHAMYuj" & _
                                "APFGN1OxYiHINOslptpcZsrgFbzsTHKr8HgBk7EA81QRe_"

        Private Shared YahooGeocodeServiceUrl = "http://local.yahooapis.com" & _
                                        "/MapsService/V1/geocode"


        Dim yahooGeoCodeParameters As NameValueCollection

        Private Sub bttnShow_Click(ByVal sender As System.Object, _
                ByVal e As System.EventArgs) Handles _
                bttnShow.Click, txtZip.Leave

            lblError.Text = ""
            GenerateYahooGeoCodeParameters(txtStreet.Text.Trim(), txtCity.Text.Trim(), _
                                txtState.Text.Trim(), txtZip.Text.Trim())
            FindLocation()
        End Sub

        Private Sub GenerateYahooGeoCodeParameters(ByVal street As String, _
                ByVal city As String, ByVal state As String, _
                ByVal zip As String)

            yahooGeoCodeParameters = New NameValueCollection
            yahooGeoCodeParameters.Add("appid", YahooAppId)
```

```
        yahooGeoCodeParameters.Add("street", street.Replace(" "c,
                          "+"c))
        yahooGeoCodeParameters.Add("city", city.Replace(" "c, "+"c))
        yahooGeoCodeParameters.Add("zip", zip)
        yahooGeoCodeParameters.Add("state", state)
    End Sub

    Private Sub FindLocation()
        Dim client As New WebClient()
        client.QueryString = yahooGeoCodeParameters
        AddHandler client.DownloadStringCompleted,
            AddressOf webClient_DownloadStringCompleted
        client.DownloadStringAsync(New Uri(YahooGeocodeServiceUrl))
    End Sub

End Class
```

If you look at the code carefully, you will note that `bttnShow_Click` handles both the `bttnShow.Click` and the `txtZip.Leave` events. This way, the address will be shown on the map automatically once the user has filled all the address fields. Since the service invocation code is asynchronous, it will not prevent the user from continuing to operate on the form.

Now you need to take care of the `DownloadStringAsync` event handler.

PROCESSING THE YAHOO! GEOCODING SERVICE RESPONSE

Before you can process the geocoding service response, you will need to create a structure that can hold the geocoding information. In this case, a simple structure will do; name the structure **Coordinates** and set up two String properties: `Latitude` and `Longitude`. Add the new class named Coordinates to the project. Listing 19.6 shows the code for the Coordinates structure.

LISTING 19.6:   The Coordinates structure

```
Public Structure Coordinates
    Property Latitude As String
    Property Longitude As String
End Structure
```

Now you can code the `DownloadStringCompleted` event handler. You should bear in mind that the Yahoo! geocoding service responds in XML format. The easiest way to process it is to use LINQ to XML. (I explained how you can work with XML in Visual Basic .NET in detail in Chapter 13, "XML in Modern Programming," and Chapter 14, "An Introduction to LINQ.") To process the Yahoo! geocoding service response with LINQ to XML, you should import the XML namespace for the response using the `Imports` directive at the top of the form code in the following manner:

```
Imports <xmlns="urn:yahoo:maps">
```

When implementing the functionality, be sure to check for errors and handle multiple result responses. In the event of an error or multiple result responses, the best bet is to display the first location encountered while informing the user that the coordinates displayed on a map are not very precise because the service responded with multiple locations. Listing 19.7 shows the code that handles the Yahoo! geocoding service response.

LISTING 19.7:   *DownloadStringCompleted* event handling code

```
Sub webClient_DownloadStringCompleted(ByVal sender As Object,
    ByVal e As DownloadStringCompletedEventArgs)

    If e.Error IsNot Nothing Then
        lblError.Text = "Address could not be located on a map"
        Return
    End If
    yahooResponse = XDocument.Parse(CStr(e.Result))
    ValidateResponseAndProceede()
End Sub

Private Sub ValidateResponseAndProceede()
    If (yahooResponse...<Result>.Count = 0) Then
        lblError.Text = "Address could not be located on a map"
        Return
    End If
    If (yahooResponse...<Result>.Count > 1) Then
        lblError.Text = "Multiple locations found - showing first." &
            " Correct the address and press Refresh"
    End If
    GenerateLocation()
    ShowLocationOnMap()
End Sub

Private Sub GenerateLocation()
    addressLocation.Latitude = yahooResponse...<Result>.First.<Latitude>.Value
    addressLocation.Longitude = yahooResponse...<Result>.First.<Longitude>.Value
End Sub
```

As you can see, the code handles errors that occur in communication or while querying the Yahoo! geocoding service and displays a message when the results are not very precise and the service responds with multiple results.

DISPLAYING COORDINATES ON THE MAP

To show the location on the map, you need to load the WebBrowser control with the simple HTML page that contains the Google Maps Service code. Since this code contains coordinates, it cannot be loaded from the static HTML file. You can, however, use the static HTML file as a template, load the file, and then replace latitude and longitude tokens with information obtained from the Yahoo! geocoding service before loading it into the WebBrowser control.

Add the new gmapsTemplate.html file to the ViewAddressOnAMap project. Make sure the "Copy to Output Directory file" property is set to "Copy if newer". With this, Visual Studio will make the copy of the file inside the bin/Debug folder and you will be able to access the file while debugging the solution. The code for gmapsTemplate.html is shown in Listing 19.8.

LISTING 19.8:   Google Maps HTML code templates

```
<html>
<head>
<meta name="viewport" content="initial-scale=1.0, user-scalable=no" />
<script type="text/javascript"
    src="http://maps.google.com/maps/api/js?sensor=false">
</script>
<script type="text/javascript">
    function initialize() {
        var latlng = new google.maps.LatLng(
        replace_me_latitude, replace_me_longitude);
        var myOptions = {
            zoom: 16,
            center: latlng,
            mapTypeId: google.maps.MapTypeId.ROADMAP
        };
        var map = new google.maps.Map(
        document.getElementById("map_canvas"), myOptions);
    }
</script>
</head>
<body onload="initialize()">
  <div id="map_canvas" style="width:100%; height:100%"></div>
</body>
</html>
```

You will note that the template contains replace_me_longitude and replace_me_latitude strings instead of real coordinates. You will use these strings as tokens and replace them with real coordinate information before loading the HTML inside the WebBrowser control. Token replacement code can be implemented in a GenerateMapsHtml routine:

```
Private Sub GenerateMapsHtml()
    googleMapsHtml = googleMapsHtmlTemplate.
        Replace("replace_me_latitude", addressLocation.Latitude).
        Replace("replace_me_longitude", addressLocation.Longitude)
End Sub
```

With this, you have finished implementing the address visualization functionality. You can take a look at the complete code of the form in Listing 19.9.

LISTING 19.9:   Address visualization form code

```
Imports System.Net
Imports System.IO
Imports System.Linq
Imports System.Xml.Linq
Imports <xmlns="urn:yahoo:maps">
Imports System.Collections.Specialized

Public Class Form1

    Private Shared YahooAppId As String = "BPdn3S7V34GMfMZ5ukBuHAMYuj" & _
                    "APFGN1OxYiHINOslptpcZsrgFbzsTHKr8HgBk7EA81QRe_"

    Private Shared YahooGeocodeServiceUrl = "http://local.yahooapis.com" & _
                    "/MapsService/V1/geocode"

    Private Shared googleMapsHtmlTemplate As String

    Private Shared applicationDirectory = _
                    My.Application.Info.DirectoryPath.ToString()

    Private Shared googleMapsHtmlTemplatePath = applicationDirectory & _
                    "\gmapsTemplate.html"

    Private googleMapsHtml As String

    Private addressLocation As Coordinates

    Private yahooResponse As XDocument

    Dim yahooGeoCodeParameters As NameValueCollection

    Public Sub New()

        InitializeComponent()
        googleMapsHtmlTemplate = My.Computer.FileSystem.ReadAllText( _
                googleMapsHtmlTemplatePath)
        Console.WriteLine(googleMapsHtmlTemplate)
    End Sub

    Private Sub bttnShow_Click(ByVal sender As System.Object, _
            ByVal e As System.EventArgs) Handles
```

```vbnet
        bttnShow.Click, txtZip.Leave

    lblError.Text = ""
    GenerateYahooGeoCodeParameters(txtStreet.Text.Trim(), txtCity.Text.Trim(),
                        txtState.Text.Trim(), txtZip.Text.Trim())
    FindLocation()
End Sub

Private Sub GenerateYahooGeoCodeParameters(ByVal street As String,
        ByVal city As String, ByVal state As String,
        ByVal zip As String)

    yahooGeoCodeParameters = New NameValueCollection
    yahooGeoCodeParameters.Add("appid", YahooAppId)
    yahooGeoCodeParameters.Add("street", street.Replace(" "c, "+"c))
    yahooGeoCodeParameters.Add("city", city.Replace(" "c, "+"c))
    yahooGeoCodeParameters.Add("zip", zip)
    yahooGeoCodeParameters.Add("state", state)
End Sub

Private Sub FindLocation()
    Dim client As New WebClient()
    client.QueryString = yahooGeoCodeParameters
    AddHandler client.DownloadStringCompleted,
        AddressOf webClient_DownloadStringCompleted
    client.DownloadStringAsync(New Uri(YahooGeocodeServiceUrl))
End Sub

Sub webClient_DownloadStringCompleted(ByVal sender As Object,
    ByVal e As DownloadStringCompletedEventArgs)

    If e.Error IsNot Nothing Then
        lblError.Text = "Address could not be located on a map"
        Return
    End If
    yahooResponse = XDocument.Parse(CStr(e.Result))
    ValidateResponseAndProceede()
End Sub

Private Sub ValidateResponseAndProceede()
    If (yahooResponse...<Result>.Count = 0) Then
        lblError.Text = "Address could not be located on a map"
        Return
    End If
    If (yahooResponse...<Result>.Count > 1) Then
        lblError.Text = "Multiple locations found - showing first." &
            " Correct the address and press Refresh"
    End If
```

```
            GenerateLocation()
            ShowLocationOnMap()
        End Sub

        Private Sub GenerateLocation()
            addressLocation.Latitude = yahooResponse...<Result>.First.<Latitude>.Value
            addressLocation.Longitude =
            yahooResponse...<Result>.First.<Longitude>.Value
        End Sub

        Private Sub ShowLocationOnMap()
            GenerateMapsHtml()
            mapBrowser.DocumentText = googleMapsHtml
        End Sub

        Private Sub GenerateMapsHtml()
            googleMapsHtml = googleMapsHtmlTemplate.
                Replace("replace_me_latitude", addressLocation.Latitude).
                Replace("replace_me_longitude", addressLocation.Longitude)
        End Sub

        Private Sub bttnSave_Click(ByVal sender As System.Object,
                ByVal e As System.EventArgs) Handles bttnSave.Click

            MsgBox("Unimplemented on purpose. " &
            "See 'Coding Address Visualization Form'" &
            "section in Chapter 20. Try the 'Show' button.")
        End Sub
    End Class
```

When you run the application, enter the address data on the form, and click the Show button, the form should look like the one shown on Figure 19.5.

The Bottom Line

Access a website on the Internet using the WebClient class.   The WebClient class provides an easy and simple way to access resources on the Web programmatically from Visual Basic code. The WebClient class implements many features of HTTP, making it easy to access the sites on the Web in the same way the browser application does. The web server will not distinguish a request coming from a WebClient site from one coming from a user-operated web browser.

The WebClient class can be very useful in HTML screen scraping scenarios, where the data to be extracted from HTML is meant to be read by a human, or in lightweight web service protocols like REST and/or AJAX-styled XML and JSON over HTTP.

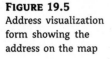

Master It   Use the Headers property of the WebClient class to fine-tune HTTP requests.
Trick Google into believing that a request that you are sending from your Visual Basic application is coming from some mobile device.

**Use a WebBrowser control to add web browser functionality to your Windows Forms appli-
cation.**   The WebBrowser control provides all the basic functionality of a browser in a form
of Windows Forms control. Visually, it consists only of a main browser window. To provide
additional functionality, like an address bar and Back, Forward, Refresh, and other buttons,
you will have to add the appropriate controls and program them yourself. The WebBrowser
control uses the same browser engine as Internet Explorer.

A WebBrowser control's behavior can be customized to a large degree. You can decide to show
or not show the scroll bars, allow or disallow navigation, show or not show the context menu,
and so forth. Finally, since the control does not contain the address bar, you can also control
which sites a user can access.

Master It   Create a custom web browser that can navigate to a limited number of URLs.

Chapter 20

Building Web Applications

Developing web applications in Visual Studio 2010 is similar to developing traditional desktop applications. You drag and drop controls onto a form and build your business logic with your language of choice — in our case, Visual Basic 2010. However, as you will see, there are also many differences. There are underlying technologies of which you, the developer, should have a solid understanding, and there are additional control sets to work with and some fundamental differences in the way the standard controls behave. Another important difference between web and desktop applications is the way the application state is managed. In desktop applications, the application state is implicit and it is managed by the .NET runtime environment. In web applications, on the other hand, the situation is much more complex. A web server can attend to numerous clients simultaneously, but thanks to ASP .NET internal mechanisms, you program your application as if you have only one user to serve. Another issue is the stateless nature of the underlying communication (HTTP) protocol. There is nothing to link two HTTP requests. In ADO .NET, the link is provided in the form of a connection object. While all of the state-related issues are resolved by ASP .NET technology, it is important to understand the underlying mechanisms because of the numerous implications for application characteristics, like performance and security.

In this chapter, you will learn how to do the following:

◆ Create a basic XHTML/HTML page

◆ Format a page with CSS

◆ Set up a master page for your website

◆ Use some of the ASP.NET intrinsic objects

Developing for the Web

In the early days of web development (not all that long ago!), a developer could earn big money creating what were essentially online brochures by using a basic knowledge of Hypertext Markup Language (HTML) and some simple design skills.

These days, we expect a great deal from websites and web applications. Entertainment sites are now fully equipped to engage the visitor with rich user interfaces incorporating a wide range of visual and aural experiences. Members of the corporate world expect their virtual presence to mirror their full range of business practices.

In addition, web development, although still seen as a specialized area, is now part of the corporate mainstream, and the developer is expected to be well versed across a range of technologies and techniques.

The modern web application combines a wide range of sophisticated technologies grafted onto the HTTP/HTML backbone. Cascading Style Sheets (CSS) are used to control the layout and appearance of a website. Data is managed with the use of Extensible Markup Language (XML) and back-end databases such as SQL Server, while rich user interfaces are developed using XML, JavaScript, and other technologies such as Adobe Flash. AJAX, a clever implementation of existing technologies, combines XML, JavaScript, and asynchronous technologies to enable the developer to create online applications that exhibit traditional desktop behavior. XML web services, multimedia content, RSS feeds, and the use of microformats to assist data aggregators have all become typical features of modern websites.

In addition, developers can now expect a website to be accessed by more than just a desktop computer. Mobile phones, PDAs, and other small form factor devices are all used to access the Web in the twenty-first century. Websites, to be truly ubiquitous, are increasingly expected to be able to dynamically render their content into an appropriate format.

Visual Studio 2010 provides a range of tools that enable the modern developer to meet the demands of website creation from the comfort of a Visual Basic environment. Database connectivity is simplified from the traditional complexity of hand-coding scripted server-side pages, and you don't need to build multiple versions of an individual site to dynamically render to suit a wide range of devices. By compiling much of the code used to drive a site, you can avoid many of the security issues that plagued scripted sites.

Typically, a modern website or web application relies on code that is executed both at the client (web browser) and server (web server) ends. In addition, there may be a whole range of other services provided by other servers on the hosting network, such as media or databases and even services sourced from other websites. Visual Studio 2010 provides the tools to tie all this together.

This chapter gives an overview of the core technologies that drive the modern web application and demonstrates the basic tools available to the developer in Visual Studio 2010.

I will begin with some basic concepts. If you are already familiar with HTML, JavaScript, and server technologies, you may wish to skip ahead to material that is new to you, such as the material in the section "Creating a Web Application."

Understanding HTML and XHTML

HTML is essentially a language to describe text formatting and enable linking of documents (web pages) delivered over the Web. HTML has grown since its original inception but is still fundamentally limited. The area where it does excel is in its ability to act as a framework in which other technologies such as JavaScript can be embedded.

Extensible HTML (XHTML) is the latest incarnation of HTML. It was developed by the World Wide Web Consortium (W3C) to bring HTML syntax into line with other markup languages such as XML. Most of the tags from HTML 4 (the most recent update to HTML) remained the same, but much stricter syntax rules apply. The basic changes are as follows:

◆   XHTML is case sensitive, and all tags are in *lowercase*.

◆   All tags must be closed. You can no longer get away with using multiple <p> tags without corresponding closing </p> tags. This includes tags such as <img> that previously had no corresponding closing tag. Close these tags with a trailing backslash before the final angle bracket, as shown in this example:

```
<img src ='my_picture.jpg' alt ='picture' \>
```

◆ All tag attributes must be enclosed in quotation marks (either single or double).

◆ All pages must include an XHTML !DOCTYPE definition and an XML version declaration.

◆ JavaScript must also conform to case syntax — for example, `onmouseover` *not* `onMouseOver`.

The W3C encourages developers to use XHTML over HTML. However, for practical purposes, web browsers still support HTML, and you can get away with not updating older sites and continuing to work with HTML's lack of strict syntax. See the sidebar "Upgrading from HTML to XHTML" if you wish to upgrade older sites.

🌐 Real World Scenario

UPGRADING FROM HTML TO XHTML

Converters exist for porting your HTML sites to XHTML. There are also tools to assist in the process manually. The W3C provides an online validator at `http://validator.w3.org`.

You can use the validator to initially ensure that your pages conform to the HTML 4 specification and that they all contain a !DOCTYPE definition such as the following:

```
<!DOCTYPE HTML PUBLIC "-//W3C//DTD HTML 4.01//EN"
"http://www.w3.org/TR/html4/strict.dtd">
```

After your pages are validated for HTML 4, you will need to add the XML declaration to the top of each page:

```
<?xml version="1.0" encoding="iso-8859-1"?>
```

Then convert the !DOCTYPE definition to the XHTML version:

```
<!DOCTYPE html PUBLIC "-//W3C//DTD XHTML 1.0 Transitional//EN"
"http://www.w3.org/TR/xhtml1/DTD/xhtml1-transitional.dtd">
```

Finally, modify the <HTML> tag to read as follows:

```
<HTML xmlns="http://www.w3.org/1999/xhtml">
```

Now that you have made all the correct syntax changes, run the validator again and see how your page performs.

Working with HTML

As a Visual Studio programmer, you will find that knowledge of HTML and XHTML can prove invaluable when you are sorting out the inevitable formatting and design issues that arise when developing complex web applications. In addition, understanding the technologies involved can aid in optimizing the interactions between server and client.

To keep things simple, I will dispense with some of the finer points of XHTML and focus mainly on "straight" HTML. This section is meant as a basic HTML primer (and is by no means comprehensive), so feel free to skip ahead if you are already familiar with the language.

More information on HTML can be found easily on the Web or in *Mastering Integrated HTML and CSS* by Virginia DeBolt (Sybex, 2007). Useful websites for tutorials include www.w3schools.com and www.htmlcodetutorial.com.

You can use any standard text editor to author your HTML. Notepad is fine. More sophisticated tools that indent and highlight code, such as Notepad2 or EditPad Pro, are available on the Web. EditPad Pro is a commercial application available from www.editpadpro.com. Notepad2 is freeware and available from www.flos-freeware.ch/notepad2.html. Yet another fairly mature tool is NotePad++, available from http://notepad-plus.sourceforge.net.

Remember to save your files with an .html filename extension so they will be recognized as HTML pages.

Page Construction

HTML pages have two main sections nested between the opening and closing <html>...</html> tags.

The first section is known as the *header area*, and it is used to contain information not usually displayed on the page. (The main exception to this is the page title.) The header area is created by using the <head>...</head> tags and contains meta-information about the page such as the !DOCTYPE definition, author details, keywords, and the like. It is also used to hold style sheet information and scripts that may be called later in the page.

The second section of the page is the *body*, and it contains information that is typically displayed on the page in a web browser. The body is declared by using the <body>...</body> tags.

HTML tags are used to describe the formatting or nature of the information contained within the opening and closing tags. Tags may also contain *attributes*, which are used to apply further information to the content between the opening and closing tags. For example, the body tag can use the attribute bgcolor to set the background color of the web page. The syntax for setting a page color to blue is <body bgcolor ="blue">.

A basic page may appear as shown in Listing 20.1. Some long lines are wrapped here in print, but you can leave them all on one line in your code.

LISTING 20.1:   A basic HTML page

```
<!DOCTYPE HTML PUBLIC "-//W3C//DTD HTML 4.01//EN" _
"http://www.w3.org/TR/html4/strict.dtd">
<html>
   <head>
      <title>Basic Page</title>
      <meta name="description" content="basic page" />
   </head>
```

```
<body bgcolor="cornsilk">
    <p>Hello World</p>
</body>
</html>
```

Save the page as index.html. You must include the .html as the filename extension. Figure 20.1 illustrates how such a page might appear in a web browser.

FIGURE 20.1
A simple web page running in a web browser window

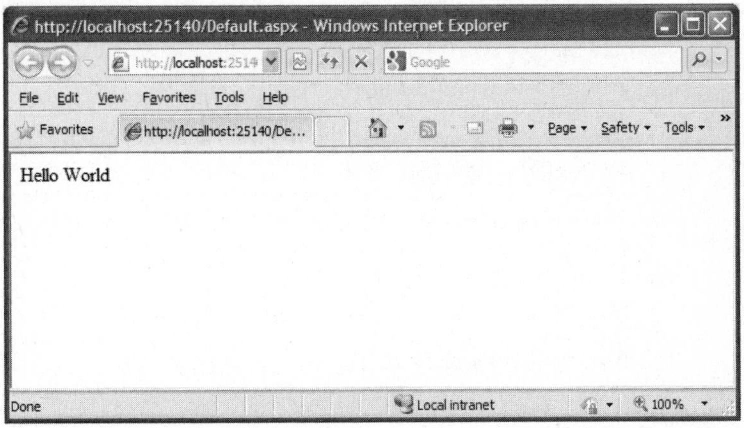

The <title> tag enables the title of the page to appear in the title bar of Internet Explorer. The <meta> tag provides a description phrase that can be accessed by search engines. The bgcolor attribute of the <body> tag sets the background color to blue, and the <p> tag is used to denote a simple block of text.

Note that I have used the !DOCTYPE definition for HTML 4. Also note that not closing the <title> tag correctly can cause the rest of the page to break.

Text Management

There are a range of text management tags, including the previously mentioned <p> tag. The principal tags are as follows:

♦   The heading tags — <h1>...</h1>, <h2>...</h2> through to <h6>...</h6> — are used to control the size of text. <h1> is the largest format.

♦   The font tag, <font>...</font>, has a number of attributes including face for font type, color for text color, and size for font size. Font sizes range from 1 to 7, where 7 is the largest. An example of the tag's usage is <font face ="verdana" color ="red" size ="3">Hello World</font>.

♦   The small and big tags — <small>...</small>, <big>...</big> — can be used to quickly adjust the relative size of text.

Styles can be managed with tags such as the following:

♦   Bold: ...

♦   Underline: <u>...</u>

◆ Italic: `<i>`...`</i>`

◆ Strong: `<strong>`...`</strong>`

Another useful tag for working with text is the line break tag, `<br>`. In HTML, this tag does not require a closing tag.

You can generate and control spaces between text with more precision than simply relying on the client browser to insert your preferred amount of white space by using the following special character: .

A number of other special characters exist to accommodate symbols such as quotes, question marks, and copyright symbols. A comprehensive list of HTML tags and their attributes can be found at www.w3schools.com/tags/default.asp. You can also refer to the W3C specification for HTML 4.01 at www.w3.org/TR/html401/. The XHTML 1.1 specification can be found at www.w3.org/TR/2007/CR-xhtml-basic-20070713/.

Horizontal Rules

The `<hr>` tag can be used to draw a line across the page. Its attributes include `align`, `noshade`, `size`, and `width`. Width can be declared as a percentage or as an exact amount in pixels. In HTML 4, there is no closing tag.

Images

You can add images to web pages by using the `<img>` tag. This tag is not typically closed under HTML 4. This tag includes the following attributes:

◆ The path to the image, `src`, which can be relative or absolute (required).

◆ A text alternative to the image, `alt`, which is normally recommended for accessibility.

◆ `align` is used to align an image on a page and to wrap text around the image.

◆ `border` is used to create a border around the image.

◆ `width` and `height` are used to help the page load more quickly and can also be used to scale an image.

◆ `usemap` is used to create image maps.

Here is an example of a typical use of the `<img>` tag:

```
<img src='images/myimage.jpg' border='0' width='150' _
height='150' align='left' alt='Test Image'>
```

For use in web pages, images must be in one of the following formats: GIF, PNG, or JPG. You usually use the GIF or PNG formats for drawings or line art and the JPG format for photographs.

Links

Links can be created on web pages that link to other web pages within the site, other websites, other types of documents, email, or other locations within the host page. Links are created by using the `<a>`...`</a>` tag.

Typically, the `<a>` tag is used with the `href` attribute to define the destination of the link, as in the following example:

```
<a href='http://www.microsoft.com'>Microsoft</a>
```

The text contained between the tags (Microsoft) is what appears as the link on the page. The text can be formatted by using the <font> tag inside the <a> tags.

Other attributes commonly used include target (used inside framesets) and name (used for setting up in-page links such as tables of contents).

Embedding Media

Media objects such as Windows Media Player, Apple's QuickTime, and Flash can be embedded in a page with the <embed> tag. At its very simplest, the tag can be made to work by simply specifying the source file for the media and the display size and then trusting the browser to have the required plug-in and to be able to sort it out:

```
<embed src='multimedia/myvideo.avi' height='200' width='200'></embed>
```

At a more sophisticated level, you can specify a range of options, including the type of plug-in, the controls to display, whether it should start automatically, and loop properties.

Comments

To insert comments into your HTML, use <!-- ... -->, as in the following example:

```
<!-- This is a comment -->
```

Comments enclosed in this tag are not displayed within the web page.

Scripts

The <script>...</script> tag can be used to insert non-HTML script code such as JavaScript into your pages. Scripts can be written into the header area and called from the body or used directly in the body of the page. Before support for more-recent HTML versions and before JavaScript could be found in virtually every web browser, developers would typically comment out the code by using <!-- ... --> to prevent the code from appearing in the browser page. This is still common practice, although it is no longer usually necessary.

Here is a simple example of the script tag's usage:

```
<script language='javascript'>
    function mygreatscript(){
        etc etc
    }
</script>
```

Lists

Bulleted and numbered lists can be displayed in a web page with the list tags <ul>...</ul> for a bulleted list or <ol>...</ol> for a numbered list. Individual items within the list are denoted by using the <li>...</li> tags. The following example creates a bulleted list:

```
<ul>
    <li>Item 1</li>
    <li>Item 2</li>
</ul>
```

Tables

Tables are used extensively in HTML, not only to display data but also to reassemble sliced images (a technique for minimizing the file size of large images) and to format pages. However, the W3C no longer recommends using tables to format pages. For accessibility reasons, technologies such as CSS are now the recommended method for creating sophisticated layouts.

Tables are still used for displaying tabular data and here is what you should know about constructing them. Tables are made of rows of cells. When constructing your table, you need to consider the desired width of the table, the number of rows, and the number of columns required. Other factors that you may wish to take into account are the padding between cells and the padding between the border of a cell and its contents.

Another important consideration is that a badly constructed table is one of the few things that can truly break an HTML page. You must ensure that all your tags are correctly closed. Tables can be nested within one another, but excessive nesting can place undue strain on the rendering engine of the browser and cause unexpected results.

A range of tags are used to create a typical table, and each has its own family of attributes:

◆ The `<table>`...`</table>` tag acts as the major framework for the table.

◆ `<tr>`...`</tr>` tags are used to create rows.

◆ Within a given row, `<td>`...`</td>` tags are used to create the individual cells. The number of cells defined in the first row sets the number of columns in the table. This is important to consider in subsequent rows if you wish to add or subtract from the number of cells. The `rowspan` and `colspan` attributes are used to alter the number of columns and rows employed at various points in the table. For example, `colspan = '2'` will force a cell to span over two columns.

◆ For headings, you can use `<th>`...`</th>` tags to create cells in the first row. These offer a slightly different format than the `<td>` cells offer.

The following code snippet demonstrates a simple data table of three rows (one header) and three columns. The resulting table is shown in Figure 20.2.

```
<table width='400' border='1'>
   <tr bgcolor='silver'>
      <th width='100'>ID</th>
      <th width='200'>Name</th>
      <th width='100'>Age</th>
   </tr>
   <tr align='center'>
      <td valign='middle'>1</td>
      <td valign='middle'>Fred</td>
      <td valign='middle'>23</td>
   </tr>
   <tr align='center'>
      <td valign='middle' bgcolor='lightblue'>2</td>
      <td valign='middle' bgcolor='lightblue'>Mary</td>
      <td valign='middle' bgcolor='lightblue'>21</td>
   </tr>
   <tr align='center'>
```

```
      <td valign='middle'>3</td>
      <td valign='middle'>Wilma</td>
      <td valign='middle'>25</td>
   </tr>
</table>
```

FIGURE 20.2
A simple data table

ID	Name	Age
1	Fred	23
2	Mary	21
3	Wilma	25

The following code snippet illustrates how a table might be used to reconstruct a sliced image. Note the use of the `align` attribute to set horizontal alignment and the `valign` attribute to set vertical alignment:

```
<table width='400' border='0' cellspacing='0' cellpadding='0'>
   <tr>
      <td valign='bottom' align='right'><img src='image1.gif'></td>
      <td valign='bottom' align='left'><img src='image2.gif'></td>
   </tr>
   <tr>
      <td valign='top' align='right'><img src='image3.gif'></td>
      <td valign='top' align='left'><img src='image4.gif'></td>
   </tr>
</table>
```

Figure 20.3 illustrates how this image will appear in a web page (the left-hand image) and how the table cells come together to reassemble the image (the right-hand image). `Cellspacing` and `cellpadding` was increased when creating the right-hand image to make the individual parts of the image visible.

FIGURE 20.3
A sliced image reassembled using an HTML table

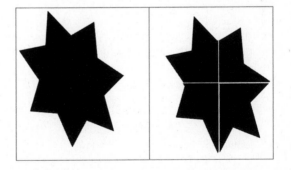

Page Formatting

Various methods can be used to format pages in HTML. They all have inherent limitations, but the `<div>` tag offers the most flexibility. Table 20.1 describes the methods.

TABLE 20.1:   HTML methods for formatting pages

METHOD	DESCRIPTION
Flow format	This relies on the browser to format the page according to the order of items in the HTML. Flow format is easy to implement but of limited usefulness.
A table	This is one of the more popular methods, although it is no longer officially recommended by the W3C for accessibility reasons.
Frames	These effectively create the different parts of your page in separate HTML documents. You would use a frameset to reassemble them as a single page in the browser.
Inline frames (iFrames)	These create a floating frame that can be placed within an HTML page. This is a popular method of displaying content from another website (such as a news feed) within your web page.
<div> tags	These can be used to precisely locate content on your page. Combined with CSS, <div> tags offer a powerful and flexible method of organizing a page. The output of ASP.NET is largely driven by <div> tags for layout purposes.

Later, when you look at Cascading Style Sheets, you will see how <div> tags can be used to lay out a page.

Forms and Form Elements

Forms are the traditional method by which users can communicate information back to the web server that is hosting the website being viewed. Information sent back by a form can then be processed in some way at the server, and the outcome can be dynamically incorporated into a new page that the user can view.

For example, a login page would likely use a form to collect the username and password from the user and return this information to the server for authentication before access to the rest of the site is granted. In addition, personal preferences for the site can be applied to the returned pages according to the stored preferences of the registered user.

A form is created by using the <form>...</form> tags. The following attributes are the ones most commonly used:

Name   The Name attribute defines a unique name for the form.

Action   The Action attribute specifies the Uniform Resource Locator (URL), or Internet address, of the resource to process the form's response (required).

Method   Either post or get (default) will be specified by the Method attribute. This specifies the HTTP method used to return the form's data. The get method sends the data as part of the URL (limited to a maximum of 100 ASCII characters), and post sends the form's content in the body of the request.

Within the form, you create your HTML as usual. However, information that you wish to be processed by the form needs to be collected by using form controls. The controls that are available include the following:

Buttons Your form must have at least one button for submitting data. Another button that is commonly used clears the form's contents. Syntax for the buttons are as follows:

```
<input type='submit' value='Submit data'>
<input type='reset' value='Reset form'>
```

It is not necessary to include the value attribute because this sets the text that will appear in the button, and there are default text values of Submit and Reset.

You can use the following to create other buttons on your forms to run client-side scripts:

```
<input type='button' value='Mybutton' onclick='myscript'>
```

A more flexible control, however, is the <button> tag. This can be used anywhere on the HTML page to run scripts and can replace the traditional Submit and Reset buttons in your forms. It offers greater flexibility for formatting its appearance (especially when used with CSS). Its basic syntax is as follows:

```
<button type='button' name='name' onclick='myscript'>Click Here</button>
```

By using an image tag in place of *Click Here*, you can set an image to be the button. Syntax for using the button as a submit button is simply the following:

```
<button type=submit' >Submit</button>
```

Text The Text control enables the user to enter a single line of text. This can be set as a password field to mask the user's entry. The syntax is as follows:

```
<input type='text' name='identity of input data'
value='data to be initially displayed in field'>
```

The name attribute specifies the identity of the data to be processed at the server end (for example, the username). The value attribute displays text that you may wish to appear initially in the field (for example, *Type user name here*). You can also set other attributes such as size and maxlength. To create a password field, set the type attribute to password.

TextArea For larger amounts of text, use the <textarea> tag. Its syntax is as follows:

```
<textarea name='details' rows='10' cols='40' >
    Type your details here
</textarea>
```

Note that this control requires a closing tag.

Lists To create lists, use the <select> tag. Lists can be either single select or multiple select, which is created by using the multiple attribute (simply typing **multiple**). The size attribute specifies the number of rows to display. Omitting the size attribute renders the control as a drop-down combo box. The contents of the `value` attribute are returned to the server. Individual items are denoted by using the `<option>` tags. When you type **selected** within one of the option tags, that item is automatically highlighted in the list. The syntax for the tag is as follows:

```
<select name='items' size='4' multiple>
    <option value='1' selected>Chair</option>
    <option value='2'>Couch</option>
    <option value='3'>Arm Chair</option>
    <option value='4'>Lounge Chair</option>
</select>
```

Check boxes   To create a check box, you use a variation on the `<input>` tag and set the `type` attribute to `'checkbox'`. To initially select a check box, type the attribute **checked**. The syntax is `<input type = 'checkbox' name = 'Check1' checked>`.

Radio buttons   These are yet another variation on the `<input>` tag. Set the `type` attribute to `'radio'`. If you are using a set of linked radio buttons, type the same `name` attribute for each radio button in the set. The `value` attribute is used to return appropriate data when the radio button is selected. Here is the syntax:

```
<input type='radio' name='radioset' value='1' checked>
<input type='radio' name='radioset' value='2'>
<input type='radio' name='radioset' value='3'>
```

Hidden fields   Hidden fields contain information that you may want to make the round-trip to the server but that you do not want displayed on the client's web page. You can use this field to help maintain *state* (discussed later in this chapter in the section "Maintaining State"). This field is particularly useful when a client has disabled cookies or when the information is too long or sensitive to incorporate into the URL. For example, you may wish to maintain information gathered in previous forms from the client. ASP.NET uses hidden fields extensively. Here is the syntax:

```
<input type='hidden' name='name of information'
value='information to be stored'>
```

Cascading Style Sheets (CSS)

Cascading Style Sheets offer a powerful method of controlling the format and layout of the pages and content of your websites. Styles can be written directly into your HTML pages or created in a separate text document with the `.css` filename extension. The advantage to the developer of using separate CSS pages is that the format and layout of an entire site can be controlled from a single page. In large sites, consisting of tens or even hundreds of pages, this can be a huge time-saver as well as introducing a much higher level of consistency and reliability.

In addition, styles are applied sequentially and can override previously set styles. This enables the web developer to create specific styles for specific sections of the site that may modify the global settings. You can create and apply multiple style sheets in this manner and even write individual style settings onto individual pages if necessary. Styles can also be applied directly to individual elements within a page. As long as the desired settings are the last to be applied, the page will appear as required.

Syntax for CSS is quite different from syntax for HTML and is quite strict. You can apply styles directly to HTML tags (for example, you may wish to format the <h1> tag with a particular font and color) or set them up in their own classes that can be applied when required. For example, you may wish to create your own <h8> class.

You can include an external style sheet in an HTML page by using the <link> tag, which is typically placed in the head area of the web page. The following example incorporates a style sheet titled mystylesheet.css from the styles directory into the web page:

```
<link rel='stylesheet' type='text/css' href='styles/mystylesheet.css'>
```

You can create an internal style sheet directly in the HTML page by using the <style>…</style> tags. Again, this is typically created in the header area of the document.

If you wish to create a style locally to a particular tag, you add the style attributes inside the tag. For example, to extend the style of the <p> tag, you would use the following:

```
<p style='font-size:18pt; color:red;'>
```

Formatting Styles with CSS

Listing 20.2 illustrates a sample style sheet. It demonstrates several simple style attributes that can be applied to text. You can use the styles directly in a web page by inserting the listing between <style>…</style> tags or you can use it externally by saving the listing out to a separate text document with a .css filename extension (for example, mystylesheet.css). Some long lines are wrapped here in print, but you can leave them all on one line in your code.

LISTING 20.2:   A sample style sheet

```
h1 {font-weight: bold; font-size: 24pt; color:red;
background: silver; text-align: center;}
p {font-family: arial, sans serif; font-size: 120%;}
p.quote {font-face:verdana; font-size: 10pt; font-style: italic;}
a {text-decoration:none; color:blue;}
a:visited {text-decoration:none; color:blue;}
a:hover {text-decoration:none; font-weight: bold;
font-size: 120%; color:darkblue;}
a:active {text-decoration:none; color:blue;}
```

If you were to use Listing 20.2 as an external style sheet, you could link it to your web page by inserting <link rel = 'stylesheet' type = 'text/css' href = 'mystylesheet.css'> somewhere in the header area of your web page. This also assumes that the style sheet is sitting in the same directory as your web page.

In Listing 20.2, note the following points:

◆ The creation of a separate *quote* class for use with the <p> tag. To employ this class in your HTML, simply use <p class = 'quote'>...</p>.

◆ By setting styles for the various permutations of the <a> tag, I have also created a simple rollover effect for use with links. (The order in which these are applied is important for the rollover effect to work.)

Rollovers can be created by using other methods, such as JavaScript, but CSS offers a simple way of globally controlling the effect. You can also create quite sophisticated-looking buttons around your links by using the formatting and style properties of CSS.

Page Formatting with CSS

CSS also can be used to define page formatting and layout for an HTML document. CSS is typically used to define and control <div> tags for this purpose, although you can also use it to set and control table properties.

Listing 20.3 demonstrates a CSS style sheet used to control basic formatting. Most of the items should be self-explanatory. (I have used named colors for the background colors for the purpose of clarity. Usually it is preferable to use the hexadecimal equivalents.)

LISTING 20.3:   Style sheet to control page layout

```
title{
 height:80px;
 background:lightblue;
 margin:5px 10px 10px 10px;
 text-align: center;
 }

menu{
 position: absolute;
 top: 110px;
 left: 20px;
 width: 130px;
 background: silver;
 padding: 10px;
 bottom: 20px;
 }

content{
 background: lightblue;
 padding: 30px;
 position: absolute;
 top: 110px;
 bottom: 20px;
 left: 180px;
 right: 20px
 }
```

I have created three classes — `title`, `menu`, and `content` — to describe the three main areas of my page. The size of the area can be defined as well as its precise location. In the case of the title class, I haven't specified an exact location, and the title area will appear relative to where it is written into the code. Other properties of the areas can also be defined, such as padding (distance between the area's border and its internal elements) and background color. We use the `margin` property to set the width of the title area by defining how far it is located from adjacent elements and the page border.

Using the `margin` property in this context can be a little confusing. If four values are listed, they refer to top, right, bottom, and left, respectively. However, listing just one value will apply it to all four borders. Listing two values will apply them to the top/bottom and right/left in combination. If there are three values listed, the missing values are taken from the opposite side. It is sometimes easier to refer specifically to the `margin-right`, `margin-top` (and so on) properties.

You can either embed Listing 20.3 into an HTML page or access it by using an external style sheet. Listing 20.4 demonstrates the code embedded into an HTML page and utilized to set the layout of the page.

LISTING 20.4:   Using a style sheet to set the layout of a web page

```
<!DOCTYPE HTML PUBLIC "-//W3C//DTD HTML 4.01//EN"
"http://www.w3.org/TR/html4/strict.dtd">
<html>
<head>
<title>Layout Page</title>

<style>

title{
 height:80px;
 background:lightblue;
 margin:5px 10px 10px 10px;
 text-align: center;
 }

menu{
 position: absolute;
 top: 110px;
 left: 20px;
 width: 130px;
 background: silver;
 padding: 10px;
 bottom: 20px;
 }

content{
 background: lightblue;
 padding: 30px;
 position: absolute;
 top: 110px;
```

```
  bottom: 20px;
  left: 180px;
  right: 20px
  }
</style>
</head>

<body>
  <div class='title'>
    <h1>Heading</h1>
  </div>
  <div class='menu'>
    <p>Menu Item 1</p>
    <p>Menu Item 2</p>
  </div>
  <div class='content'>
    <p>Some Content</p>
  </div>

</body>
</html>
```

Figure 20.4 illustrates how the layout from Listing 20.4 appears in a web page. Carefully look at the code and you will see how the individual layout classes are used inside the <div> tags to generate the layout structure of the page.

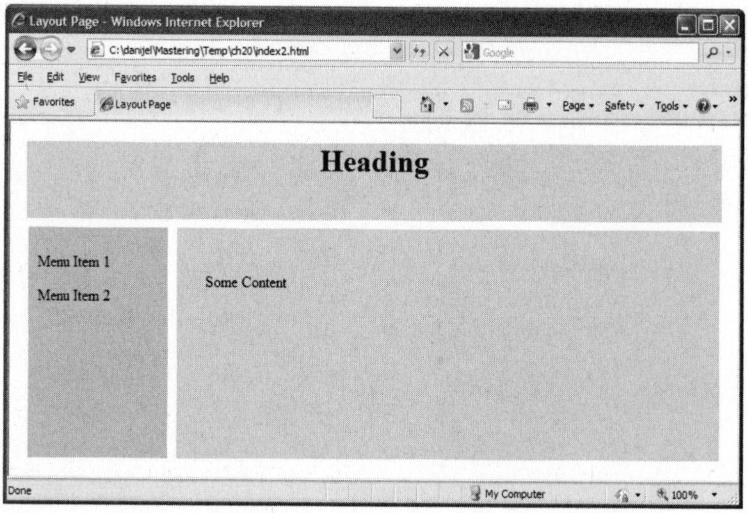

FIGURE 20.4
Listing 20.4 running as a web page

This is a very brief overview of CSS. For more-comprehensive coverage, please refer to *Mastering Integrated HTML and CSS* by Virginia DeBolt (published by Sybex and mentioned earlier). There are also many online tutorials available, such as those available at www.w3schools.com/css/.

JavaScript

You can embed JavaScript into your HTML pages to create interactive and dynamic elements at the client end. JavaScript can be used to create named functions inside the script tags that can be called later in the page. You can also use JavaScript attached directly to HTML elements.

Currently, 18 events specified in HTML 4 and XHTML 1 can be used as triggers to run individual scripts. Table 20.2 lists these events.

TABLE 20.2:   Events available for use in HTML

EVENT	DESCRIPTION
Keyboard Events	**Not Valid in Base, BDO, BR, Frame, Frameset, Head, HTML, iFrame, Meta, Param, Script, Style, and Title Elements**
onkeydown	When a keyboard key is pressed
onkeypress	When a keyboard key is pressed and released
onkeyup	When a keyboard key is released
Mouse Events ()	**Not Valid in Base, BDO, BR, Frame, Frameset, Head, HTML, iFrame, Meta, Param, Script, Style, and Title Elements**
onclick	When an object is clicked with the mouse
ondblclick	When an object is double-clicked with the mouse
onmousedown	When the mouse is clicked on an object
onmousemove	When the mouse is moved
onmouseover	When the mouse is moved over an object
onmouseout	When the mouse is moved away from an object
onmouseup	When the mouse button is released
Form Element Events	**Valid Only in Forms**
onchange	When the content of the field changes
onsubmit	When the submit button is clicked to submit the form
onreset	When the reset button is clicked to reset the form
onselect	When some content of the field is selected
onblur	When an object loses focus
onfocus	When an object gains focus as the user selects the object

TABLE 20.2:   Events available for use in HTML *(CONTINUED)*

EVENT	DESCRIPTION
Window Events	**Valid Only in Body and Frameset Elements**
onload	When the page is loaded
onunload	When the page is unloaded

The following code snippet gives an example of using JavaScript to create a rollover effect on a link:

```
<a href="newpage.html" >
<font color='blue' face="verdana" onmouseover="this.style.color ='lightblue';"
onmouseout="this.style.color ='blue';" size=1>New Page</font></a>
```

This script sets the link color to blue. Rolling the mouse over the link changes it to a light blue. Moving the mouse off the link resets it to the normal blue.

Listing 20.5 demonstrates how a JavaScript function can be embedded into a web page and then called from a button press. In this example, clicking the Test button will set the background color of the web page to blue. Note that the use of bgColor in the JavaScript function is case sensitive. Some long lines are wrapped here in print, but you can leave them all on one line in your code.

LISTING 20.5:   Demonstration of a JavaScript function

```
<!DOCTYPE HTML PUBLIC "-//W3C//DTD HTML 4.01//EN"
"http://www.w3.org/TR/html4/strict.dtd
<html>
<head>
<title>Javascript example</title>
<script language='javascript'>
   function changecolor(){
      document.bgColor='blue'
   }
</script>
</head>

<body>
<button type='button' onclick='changecolor()'>Test</button>
</body>
</html>
```

We have only touched on the possibilities of JavaScript in these examples. Please refer to *JavaScript Bible, Sixth Edition*, by Danny Goodman and Michael Morrison (Wiley, 2007) for more-thorough coverage. There are many online tutorials also available. A good starting point is at www.w3schools.com/js/.

AJAX

Asynchronous JavaScript and XML (AJAX) enables the web developer to create online applications that behave more like standard desktop apps in that the entire page need not be refreshed every time there is a round-trip between the browser and the web server. This eliminates the "flicker" users see when a page is refreshed/reloaded. The asynchronous nature of the technology enables you to make an HTTP request to the server and continue to process data while waiting for the response. Data transfers are handled by using the XMLHTTPRequest object. This combines with the Document Object Model (DOM), which combines with JavaScript to dynamically update page elements without the need for a browser refresh.

A detailed exploration of AJAX is beyond the scope of this book. For our purposes, it is important to note that AJAX has been incorporated into ASP.NET 4.0 and can be leveraged into your web applications from Visual Studio 2010.

An online AJAX tutorial is available from www.w3schools.com/ajax/default.asp.

Microformats

You can use microformats to list data on your website so that it can be accessed by various data-aggregation tools. Microformats are really just specifications for formatting data such as address book details or calendar information. Thousands of microformats exist. The Microformats.org website (http://microformats.org) is a good starting point for the various specifications.

The hCard is an example of how microformats work. The hCard specification is modeled on the vCard specification, which is widely used for address books. You can use the hCard creator on the Microformats website to automatically generate the code for use on your own site. You can also roll your own according to the specification. The advantage of listing your address details in the hCard format is that anyone visiting your site can automatically add your details to their own address book according to the vCard specification.

Server-Side Technologies

Thus far, you have looked mainly at the technologies that drive the client side of a web-based application. This is only half of the equation. The website itself is normally hosted on some form of server platform and managed with a web server package. On a Microsoft platform, the web server is typically Microsoft's *Internet Information Services (IIS)*. Requests from the client are processed by the web server and appropriate web pages are supplied. The server can also be used to process information supplied by the client as part of the request to provide a more interactive experience.

Although the range of technologies available at the client end is fairly limited, the server-side applications can be written in any language or form supported by the web server. In the case of IIS running an ASP.NET application, the application may be written in any of the .NET-supported languages.

Prior to ASP.NET, developers working in the Microsoft platform created web applications mainly using Active Server Pages (ASP). Pages written in ASP are scripted pages that combine a variety of technologies including HTML, JavaScript, server objects, Structured Query Language (SQL), and Visual Basic Script (VBScript). They are created as plain-text files and saved with the `.asp` filename extension. ASP is powerful and flexible, but maintaining large sites can be time consuming, and achieving and maintaining a decent level of security can be problematic.

With the introduction of ASP.NET, Microsoft gave developers a much tidier approach to creating their web applications. You can use Visual Studio to create your applications, and superficially at least, the process of building the application is not terribly different from building standard Windows applications. Much of the plumbing for connecting to back-end databases or sophisticated objects (which in ASP you would have to lovingly handcraft) is now taken care of. You also have the option to write much of the code into code-behind, where it can be safely compiled away from prying eyes and offer the performance enhancements integral to a compiled environment. A *code-behind* is a code file like the kind normally used to develop desktop applications. Code written into the code-behind is compiled into a library that is kept physically distinct from the scripted pages of the web application. At the scripted end of ASP.NET, files are plain text and saved with the `.aspx` filename extension.

However, there are differences between the desktop and web development environments, and to really take advantage of .NET and fully optimize your web applications, you need to be aware of the differences and how they can be accommodated and exploited.

My favorite example of the differences between desktop and web development in Visual Studio is in the use of fragment caching. Fragment caching can be used to cache portions of an ASPX page that are constantly reused (such as headings). This helps create a performance boost over an equivalent page that is completely regenerated each time it is called.

Another area where I have seen developers caught unprepared while making the transition from desktop to web applications is in the use of view state. *View state* is used to maintain information about the current property state of the various controls on a page. It is stored on the client's web page in a hidden field and thus makes the round-trip to the server. Depending on the application, it can get very big very quickly, and even fairly plain pages can suddenly start taking long periods to download to the client if view state is not managed correctly.

For the remainder of this chapter, I will discuss how to begin creating a web application in Visual Studio 2010 and examine the available web form and HTML controls. Finally, at the end of the chapter, I will put all of these together and guide you through creating a Northwind online orders application.

Creating a Web Application

Developers have two project models in Visual Studio 2010. You can use either the ASP.NET Web Application from the New Project dialog box or the New Web Site option from the File menu. It is mainly a matter of preference. In the Web Application option, project resources are defined explicitly, and the developer has tighter control over the project. It tends to suit the VB programmer coming into web programming. The New Web Site option is more flexible and tends to suit the web programmer migrating to Visual Studio.

To create a web application, open Visual Studio and select the New Project option from the File menu. From the New Project dialog box, expand the Visual Basic tree and select the Web option. From this screen, choose ASP.NET Web Application, as shown in Figure 20.5.

To create a new website project, open Visual Studio and select New Web Site from the File menu. This will open the New Web Site dialog box. From here, choose ASP.NET Web Site, as shown in Figure 20.6.

After the new project is open, the main difference between the interface for building a web application and that used for building a standard Windows application is that the Designer for web applications has three views: Design, Split, and Source. This enables you to alternate between a graphical view of the page and controls, an ASPX view, and a split view showing both.

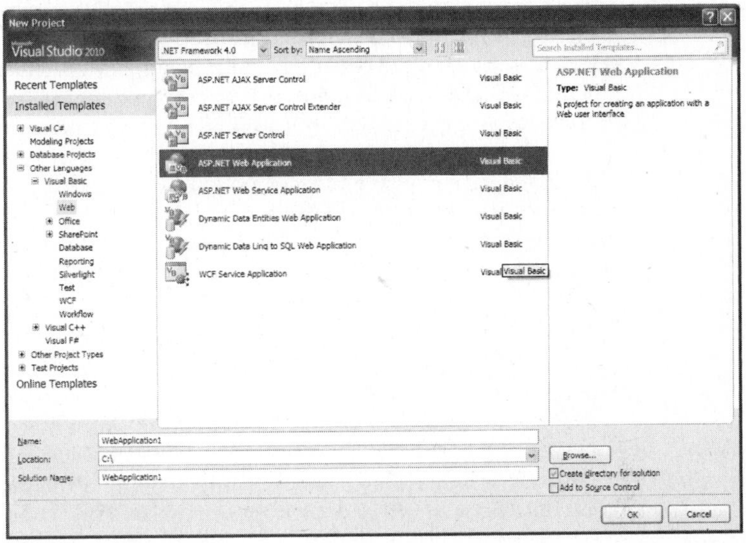

FIGURE 20.5
Choosing an ASP.NET web application from the New Project dialog box

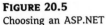

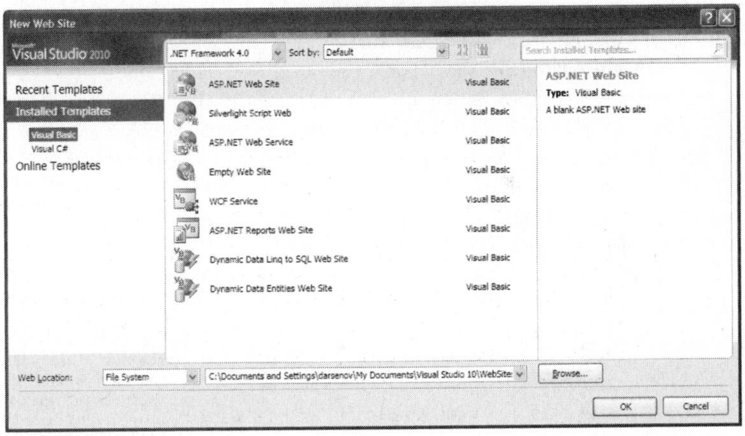

FIGURE 20.6
Choosing an ASP.NET website from the New Web Site dialog box

The contents of the Toolbox also include HTML controls. You use the Standard controls mainly to create interactive applications, while the HTML controls are essentially client-side controls that mimic many of the traditional HTML elements such as tables and horizontal rules.

You can drag and drop controls onto the page in design view and edit properties by using the traditional Properties window, or you can switch to Source or Split view and directly edit the code.

You can actually do most of your coding directly onto the ASPX page in Source view. This includes not only your design elements but also your business logic. However, it makes sense to separate your business logic from your design and use code-behind by hitting F7, by choosing View Code from the Solution Explorer, or by double-clicking the control in question.

When you view your application, it will open in your default browser. You may get a message warning *Debugging Not Enabled* if you have used F5 or the green arrow. You can choose to either run the project without debugging or enable debugging in the Web.config file. You can either modify Web.config manually or choose to allow Visual Studio to do it for you. However, you will need to remember to disable debugging when you go to deploy your project. To manually modify Web.config, double-click the Web.config entry in Solution Explorer. Web.config should open as a page of code. Under compilation, set debug ="true" as shown in the following code snippet:

```
<compilation debug="true" strict="false" explicit="true">
```

The Web.config file is a text file that holds many of the global settings for your website or application. The file is automatically generated when you create a new project and it can be edited manually or through various Visual Studio 2010 wizards. You need to be careful when editing the file because unlike HTML, the XML in the Web.config file is case sensitive. Making a mistake in Web.config can break your whole application.

You may also need to enable script debugging in Internet Explorer. From the Tools menu, choose Internet Options and click the Advanced tab. Under Browsing, deselect the Disable Script Debugging check box, as shown in Figure 20.7.

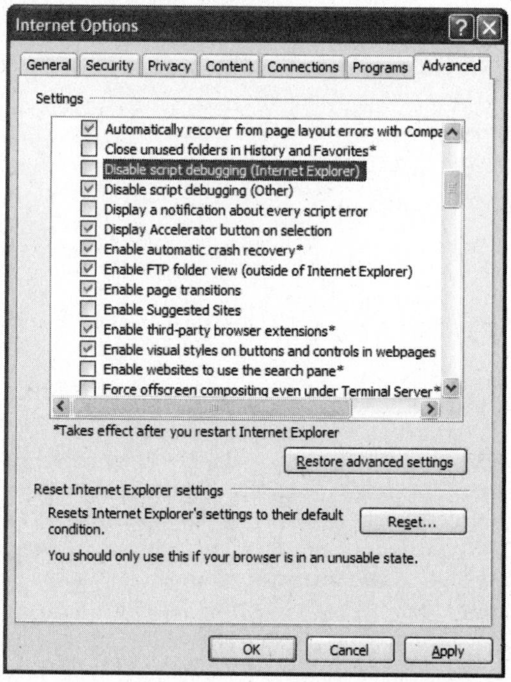

FIGURE 20.7
Enabling script debugging in Internet Explorer

Controls

Several sets of controls are available to the developer when creating web applications. These are accessible from the traditional Toolbox and are separated into several categories. These include Standard, Data, Validation, Navigation, Login, WebParts, AJAX Extensions, Reporting, and HTML. Many of these controls exhibit behavior similar to that of their desktop counterparts.

Standard Controls

The Standard controls are also known as *web form controls* and have intrinsic server-side functionality that you can program against. Table 20.3 contains a list of the Standard controls and a brief description of each.

TABLE 20.3:   Standard controls

CONTROL	DESCRIPTION
AdRotator	Randomly inserts content (advertisements) within a specified area according to a weighted index.
BulletedList	Displays a bulleted list.
Button	Displays a command-style button to enact code back on the server.
Calendar	Renders a calendar with calendar-style functionality on the target page.
CheckBox	Displays a single check box.
CheckBoxList	Renders a list with check box functionality against each item.
ContentPlaceHolder	Used in master pages for replaceable content.
DropDownList	Enables creation of a drop-down list of items from which the user can make a selection.
FileUpload	Creates a text box and button combination that can be used to upload a file from the client to the server.
HiddenField	Creates an <input type = 'hidden'> element that can be programmed with server code.
HyperLink	Creates links for navigating internally and externally to the site.
Image	Places an image on a page.
ImageButton	Enables a graphic to be specified as a button.
ImageMap	Displays an image with clickable regions.
Label	Standard control for rendering text on a page.
LinkButton	Renders a button as a link. Effectively creates a link that posts back to the server and executes whatever code has been set for it.

TABLE 20.3: Standard controls *(CONTINUED)*

CONTROL	DESCRIPTION
ListBox	Displays a list of items that may be selected individually or in multiples by the user.
Literal	Similar to the Label control in that it is used to render text to a web page, but does so without adding any additional HTML tags.
Localize	Displays text in a specific area of the page — similar to the Literal control.
MultiView	Contains View controls and allows you to programmatically display different content.
Panel	Container control that can be used to set global properties (style, etc.) for a group of controls.
PlaceHolder	Used as a container by controls that are added at runtime and that may vary in number.
RadioButton	Displays a single radio button control.
RadioButtonList	Renders a list with radio button functionality against each item.
Substitution	Contains updateable cache content.
Table	Enables the establishment of dynamically rendered tables at runtime. Should not be used for page layout — use the HTML version of the control.
TextBox	Provides a data-entry field on a web page. Can be set as a password box with the contents obscured.
View	A panel to display a MultiView control.
Wizard	Creates a multipane control for creating wizards.
XML	Can be used to write an XML document into a web page.

Data Controls
Table 20.4 lists the controls available for data access, display, and manipulation in ASP.NET.

Validation Controls
Validation controls are used to establish rules for validating data entry in web forms. Table 20.5 lists the Validation controls available.

Navigation Controls
Three controls exist for assisting in the creation of navigation menus in ASP.NET. Table 20.6 lists the Navigation controls available.

TABLE 20.4:   Data controls

CONTROL	DESCRIPTION
AccessDataSource	For connecting to an Access database.
DataList	Control for displaying and interacting with data as a list.
DataPager	Provides paging functionality for controls such as ListView.
DetailsView	Renders a single record as a table and allows the user to page through multiple records. Used for master-details forms. Provides ability to create, delete, and modify records.
FormView	Similar to DetailsView without predefined layout.
GridView	Displays data as a table.
LinqDataSource	For connecting to a LINQ data source.
ListView	Displays data as a list and supports create, delete, and update functionality.
ObjectDataSource	For connecting to a business object as a data source.
Repeater	For creating customized lists out of any data available to a page. List format is specified by the developer.
SiteMapDataSource	For use with site navigation. Retrieves navigation information from a site-map provider.
SqlDataSource	For connecting to a SQL database.
XmlDataSource	For connecting to an XML data source.

TABLE 20.5:   Validation controls

CONTROL	DESCRIPTION
CompareValidator	Compares the contents of two fields — for example, when constructing a password-creation confirmation check
CustomValidator	Enables customized validation requirements to be set
RangeValidator	Checks that specified content or entries fall within a set range of values
RegularExpressionValidator	Checks that a field entry follows a particular specified template — for example, zip code
RequiredFieldValidator	Checks that a user has made an entry into a specified field
ValidationSummary	Reports validation status of other validation controls being used on the form

TABLE 20.6: Navigation controls

CONTROL	DESCRIPTION
Menu	Creates static and/or dynamic menus
SiteMapPath	Displays the navigation path and obtains information from the site map
TreeView	Displays hierarchical data (such as an index)

Login Controls

ASP.NET includes a membership system that can be used to look after authentication, authorization, and member details on your site. It is enabled by default and can be configured by using the Web Site Administration tool. You access this tool by choosing ASP.NET Configuration from the Website menu. (Note that if you are using the Web Application development environment, ASP.NET Configuration is accessed from the Project menu.)

Figure 20.8 illustrates the Web Site Administration tool. Table 20.7 lists the Login controls available.

FIGURE 20.8
The Web Site Administration tool

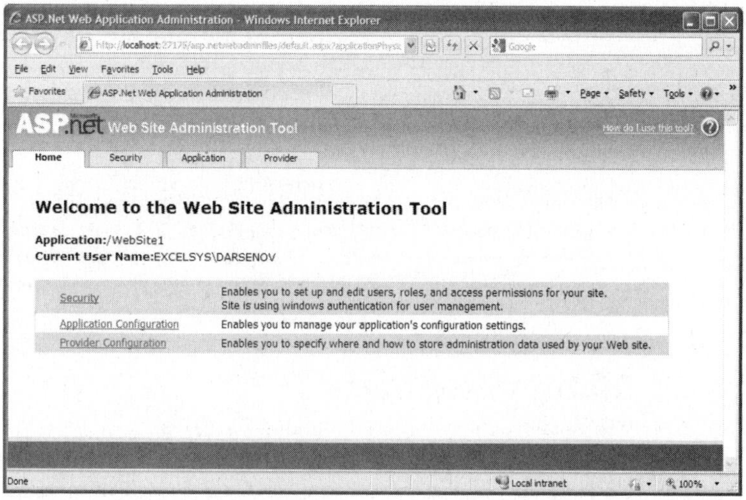

WebParts Controls

WebParts enable users to personalize their view of your website by modifying the content, appearance, and behavior of the web pages from their browsers. Table 20.8 lists the WebParts controls available.

AJAX Extensions Controls

To fully utilize AJAX in your applications, you will also need to download the ASP.NET AJAX Control Toolkit from the ASP.NET Ajax website at http://asp.net/ajax/. Table 20.9 lists the available AJAX Extensions controls that ship in Visual Studio 2010.

TABLE 20.7: Login controls

CONTROL	DESCRIPTION
ChangePassword	Allows users to change their passwords
CreateUserWizard	Displays a wizard for gathering information from a new user
Login	Displays an interface for user authentication
LoginName	Displays user's login name
LoginStatus	Displays the logout link for an authenticated user and the login link for a nonauthenticated user
LoginView	Displays different information for anonymous and authenticated users
PasswordRecovery	Recovers passwords based on email details entered when account was created

Reporting Controls

The reporting control creates data-driven reports in ASP.NET. MicrosoftReportViewer is the tool available for creating and displaying a report.

HTML Controls

Table 20.10 lists the HTML controls available. These are not typically exposed to the server for you to program. However, you can convert any HTML control to an HTML server control by adding the attribute runat ="server" to the control in ASPX view. This will allow you to manipulate the HTML control's functionality from the server. If you wish to reference the control within your code, you will need to add an id attribute as well.

Maintaining State

An issue for developers when working with web-based applications is that a web server does not intrinsically maintain an ongoing connection with the client and each request (even by the same client viewing the same website) is treated as an entirely separate request. The business of persisting information about the client and what the client is doing from one request to the next is called maintaining state. A set of related requests originating from a client viewing a particular website or using a web application is called the client's session.

As a web developer, you need to consider how you will maintain state for your clients and web applications. You need to come up with a way for the server to remember your client and the client session between requests and for your client to identify itself to the server with each request. The issue is complicated by the fact that there are multiple methods of maintaining state and each comes with its own set of advantages and disadvantages. At the client end, these methods include the following:

Using cookies Cookies are small files deposited in the client browser's cache. Many users turn these off or restrict their usage because of security and privacy concerns.

TABLE 20.8:   WebParts controls

CONTROL	DESCRIPTION
AppearanceEditorPart	Enables end user to edit certain appearance properties of an associated WebPart control
BehaviorEditorPart	Enables end user to edit certain behavior properties of an associated WebPart control
CatalogZone	Hosts CatalogPart controls — catalog of controls that users can select to add to a page.
ConnectionsZone	Contains WebPartConnection controls — two web part controls that are linked
DeclarativeCatalogPart	Used with CatalogZone control to enable you to add a catalog of web parts to your web page
EditorZone	Area in which users can personalize controls
ImportCatalogPart	Imports a description file for a WebPart control, enabling the user to add the web part with predefined settings
LayoutEditorPart	Editor control for users to edit layout properties of a web part
PageCatalogPart	Provides a catalog of all web parts that a user has closed on a web page enabling the user to add the controls back again
PropertyGridEditorPart	Editor control for user to edit properties of a web part
ProxyWebPartManager	For use in a content page to declare static connections when a WebPart Manager has been used in the associated master page
WebPartManager	Used once on a page to manage all WebParts controls on that page
WebPartZone	Provides overall layout for WebPart controls

TABLE 20.9:   AJAX extensions controls

CONTROL	DESCRIPTION
ScriptManager	Manages script resources for clients — required for Timer, UpdatePane, and UpdateProgress controls. Use only once on a page.
ScriptManagerProxy	For use in circumstances where a page already has a ScriptManager control.
Timer	Performs postbacks at specified interval.
UpdatePanel	Enables you to asynchronously refresh portions of a page.
UpdateProgress	Provides progress details on partial page updates.

TABLE 20.10:   HTML controls

CONTROL	DEFAULT HTML GENERATED
Div	`<div style="width: 100px; height: 100px"> </div>`
Horizontal Rule	`<hr />`
Image	`<img alt="" src="" />`
Input (Button)	`<input id="Button2" type="button" value="button" />`
Input (Reset)	`<input id="Reset1" type="reset" value="reset" />`
Input (Submit)	`<input id="Submit1" type="submit" value="submit" />`
Input (Text)	`<input id="Text1" type="text" />`
Input (File)	`<input id="File1" type="file" />`
Input (Password)	`<input id="Password1" type="password" />`
Input (Checkbox)	`<input id="Checkbox1" type="checkbox" />`
Input (Radio)	`<input id="Radio1" checked="checked" name="R1" type="radio" value="V1" />`
Input (Hidden)	`<input id="Hidden1" type="hidden" />`
Select	`<select id="Select1" name="D1"> <option></option> </select>`
Table	`<table style="width:100%;"> <tr> <td> </td> <td> </td> <td> </td> </tr> <tr> <td> </td> <td> </td> <td> </td> </tr> <tr> <td> </td> <td> </td> <td> </td> </tr> </table>`
Textarea	`<textarea id="TextArea1" cols="20" name="S1" rows="2"></textarea>`

Using hidden fields in the web page   This method is reliable, but you will need to code specifically at the server to read the content. Hidden fields can also end up carrying a lot of data, can pose a security risk because the information is available in cleartext in the page source code, and can get messy if your client uses unexpected navigation techniques such as the browser's back button rather than your built-in site navigation.

Incorporating state information into the URL   This method is reliable but restrictive. It also can be a security risk (with data stored in a browser's history, for example) and may cause issues with unexpected navigation techniques.

At the server end, the following methods of maintaining state (after the client has been identified) are typical:

Using session variables   This is the simplest method. It uses the Session object. Session variables behave a bit like global variables, and all the usual warnings apply.

Storing information in a database   This is a powerful and flexible method, but it adds overhead, particularly for a simple site.

For simple sites, ASP.NET takes care of most of these issues for you by using a combination of techniques. You can use session variables to manage small amounts of data between pages and a database for anything more involved. It is, however, a good idea for you to keep an eye on the ViewState settings of your controls so as to minimize the amount of data making the round-trip from server to client and back again. You can enable/disable ViewState for any individual control by using the `EnableViewState` property in that control's Properties window.

To create a session variable, simply type **`Session("MyVariableName") ="variable content"`**. Insert a relevant name and content. Be careful that you do not reuse a variable name for another purpose because the contents of the original variable will be overwritten.

To access the session variable, you refer to the full `Session("MyVariableName")`.

If you are setting up a site that will employ identification of its users, require some form of authentication, and/or offer customization of settings, it is a good idea to use Microsoft's membership system, which is available through the Web Site Administration tool and the Login controls. Refer to the section "Login Controls" earlier in this chapter.

Master Pages

ASP.NET 2 introduced the idea of master pages as a method of maintaining a consistent look and feel for a website or application. This approach has been continued with ASP.NET 4.0.

The idea is to create a page (or a number of pages), known as a master page, from which your web pages derive their common elements. Web pages linked to master pages are known as *content pages*. It is a little like using CSS style sheets to control your web page styles and structure in a scripted setting.

To add a master page to a site, simply choose the Master Page template from the Add New Item option in the Website (for ASP.NET Web Site) or Project (for ASP.NET Web Application) menu. The master page has the filename extension `.master`. You can rename the master page appropriately, but do not change the filename extension!

In the master page, you can set up standard items that remain consistent across your site, such as headers, footers, and navigation bars. You can also place ContentPlaceHolder controls in those areas where you are planning on customizing your content pages. The ContentPlaceHolder controls provide editable locations where you can add additional controls and information. You will need to right-click the master controls and choose the Create Custom Content option. In addition, you can create a style sheet to control the appearance of your master page (and hence its attached content pages).

If you make changes to your master pages, these changes will be reflected in your attached content pages. (You will need to save your changes to the master page before the updates are reflected through the content pages.)

A master page is not automatically added to your pages. You must explicitly attach it. For example, to attach it to a new page, choose Web Form from the Add New Item dialog box and select the Select Master Page check box. Click the Add button and this will open another dialog from which you can choose the appropriate master page. Click OK and you are ready to go. You can add content into the ContentPlaceHolder controls inherited from the master page.

If you already have your master page open in the IDE, you can simply use the Add Content Page option from the Website menu to directly create a content page attached to the particular master page you are browsing.

Trying to connect an existing page, such as the `default.aspx` page initially created in the application, to a master page can be problematic, so it is often a good idea to delete it. To set a new default page for your website, right-click the desired page in Solution Explorer and choose the Set As Start Page option.

ASP.NET Objects

Objects are available in ASP.NET that can be used to provide you with information about the state of your application, each user session, HTTP requests, and more. You need to be familiar with some of these because they can be useful in your code. Many of them also expose useful utility methods for managing your web application. For example, you have already seen how you can use the Session object to create a session variable. In this section, you will briefly look at the main objects and some of their methods and properties.

Application object   The Application object stores information related to the full web application, including variables and objects that exist for the lifetime of the application.

Context object   The Context object provides access to the entire current context and can be used to share information between pages. This includes the current Request and Response objects.

Request object   The Request object stores information related to the HTTP request, such as cookies, forms, and server variables. You can use this object to see everything passed back to the server from the client.

The Request object includes the properties shown in Table 20.11. Table 20.12 shows the methods for the Request object.

Response object   The Response object contains the content sent to the client from your server. You can use the Response object to send data such as cookies to your client. The Response object includes the properties shown in Table 20.13 and the methods shown in Table 20.14.

Server object   The Server object exposes methods that can be used to handle various server tasks. You can use these methods to create objects, to map paths, and to get error conditions.

The properties for the Server object are shown in Table 20.15, and the methods are in Table 20.16.

Session object   The Session object stores information related to the user's session, including variables, session ID, and objects. Properties for the Session object are shown in Table 20.17; methods are in Table 20.18.

Trace object   The Trace object can be used to display system and custom diagnostics in the page output. Properties for the Trace object are shown in Table 20.19 and a single method for the Trace object is shown in Table 20.20.

TABLE 20.11:   Properties for the Request object

PROPERTY	DESCRIPTION
ApplicationPath	Indicates the virtual path of the application
Browser	Gets or sets information about the client's browser and its capabilities
ClientCertificate	Gets the client's security certificate
Cookies	Gets the cookies sent by the client
FilePath	Gets the virtual path of the request
Form	Gets a collection of form variables
IsAuthenticated	Indicates whether the request has been authenticated
IsLocal	Indicates whether the request originates from a local computer
Item	Gets specified object from Cookies, Form, QueryString, or ServerVariables
LogonUserIdentity	Gets Windows identity for user
QueryString	Gets the collection of HTTP query string variables
ServerVariables	Gets the collection of web server variables
URL	Gets the URL of the request
UserHostAddress	Gets the IP address of the client
UserHostName	Gets the DNS name of the client
MapPath	Maps the virtual path in the requested URL to the physical path on the server
SaveAs	Saves the request to disk

TABLE 20.12:   Methods for the Request object

METHOD	DESCRIPTION
BinaryRead	Returns the data sent to the server during post in the form of a byte array
InsertEntityBody	Used to insert modified entity body into memory
MapImageCoordinates	Retrieves the coordinates of a form image that is sent to the server as a part of the current request
SaveAs	Saves the request to a file
ValidateInput	Used to call validation feature from code if the validation was disabled by the page directive

TABLE 20.13:   Properties for the Response object

PROPERTY	DESCRIPTION
Buffer	Gets or sets the value that determines whether to buffer output
Cookies	Returns the response cookies collection
ContentType	Gets or sets HTTP MIME type in output
Expires	Gets or sets the cache expiration of a page (in minutes)
IsClientConnected	Indicates whether a client is still connected

TABLE 20.14:   Methods for the Response object

METHOD	DESCRIPTION
AppendCookie	Adds a cookie to the collection
AppendHeader	Adds an HTTP header
ApplyAppPathModifier	Adds the session ID to the virtual path if a cookieless session is being used
Clear	Clears all content output from the buffer
End	Sends all buffered output to the client and stops execution of the page
Flush	Sends all buffered output to the client
Redirect	Redirects the client to a new URL
SetCookie	Updates an existing cookie
Write	Writes additional text to the response output

TABLE 20.15:   Properties for the Server object

PROPERTY	DESCRIPTION
MachineName	Returns the server's name
ScriptTimeout	Gets and sets time-out value for requests in seconds

TABLE 20.16:   Methods for the Server object

METHOD	DESCRIPTION
Execute	Commonly used to execute a URL to open another page from within your code
HTMLDecode	Decodes a string that has been encoded to remove illegal HTML characters
HTMLEncode	Encodes a string to display in a browser
MapPath	Gets physical file path of the specified virtual path on the server
UrlEncode	Encodes a string for transmission through the URL
UrlDecode	Decodes a string encoded for transmission through a URL

TABLE 20.17:   Properties for the Session object

PROPERTY	DESCRIPTION
Count	Returns the number of items in the current session state collection
Item	Gets or sets individual session values
LCID	Gets or sets the locale identifier
SessionID	Gets the identifier for the session
Timeout	Gets or sets the time between requests in minutes before the session terminates

TABLE 20.18:   Methods for the Session object

METHOD	DESCRIPTION
Abandon	Terminates the current session
Add	Adds a new item to the session state collection
Clear	Clears all values from the session state collection
Remove	Removes an item from the session state collection
RemoveAll	Removes all items from the session state collection

TABLE 20.19:   Properties for the Trace object

PROPERTY	DESCRIPTION
IsEnabled	Gets or sets whether tracing is enabled
TraceMode	Gets or sets the order in which trace messages are written to the browser

TABLE 20.20:   Method for the Trace object

METHOD	DESCRIPTION
Write	Writes trace information to the trace log

Postback

An important aspect of the way that ASP.NET operates is that controls that run on the server are able to post back to the same page. This process is called *postback*. This is different from the old ASP model, in which often there would be two or three pages set up to host the controls, process the code, and provide a response.

Any ASP.NET page that has at least one visible control will include the JavaScript function _doPostBack. This function records the control that initiated the postback, plus additional information about the initiating event, and includes it in the data submitted back to the server.

The Postback property is a read-only value that is set to False when a page is first loaded and is then set to True when the page is subsequently submitted and processed. At the server end, you can use the function Page.IsPostBack() to determine the state of a page's postback and write code accordingly — this is particularly useful when deriving your page content from a database.

VB 2010 at Work: Online Ordering Application

Now that you have learned about main elements used to construct ASP .NET applications, let's put these to work by building the online order placement application for the Northwind database. The application is based on a typical online shipping cart design. First, the user is presented with a list of products. They can choose a product from the list to add to a shopping cart. After they select the product, they need to decide on a quantity and thus the order item is placed inside the shopping cart. On a shopping cart page, they can choose to proceed to checkout or to return to a list of products to place some additional items into the shopping cart.

To implement this functionality, you will use Typed Dataset technology described in Chapter 18 for data access technology and some standard ASP .NET controls to implement the web GUI.

Creating the Project

Let's start by creating a new Web Application Project:

1. Choose File ➢ New ➢ Project and then select ASP.NET Web Application.

2. Add a new DataSet named Northwind to the project by choosing Project ➢ Add New Item and selecting the Data Set item.

To place the orders inside the Northwind database, you need to make several tables from the database available to the application. Follow the steps described in "Generating a Typed DataSet" in Chapter 18, "Building Data-Bound Applications," and add the following tables to the Northwind DataSet: Categories, Products, Orders, and Order_Details. Make sure that the Refresh The Data Table option is checked in the Advanced Options window when you're adding the Orders table.

Be sure to build the solution at this point; you can do so by pressing F6 or by invoking the Build command from the main menu: Build ➢ Build Solution. Unless you do so, you might not be able to configure the ObjectDataSource in the next section.

You are now ready to construct the first application web form; it will display the list of products to the user.

Creating the Products Web Form

To facilitate the product search, the Products form will include the DropDownList control used to display a list of categories. When the user clicks the Search button, Category Id is used to filter the list of products. The filtered list of products is displayed in a GridView control. Perform the following steps to create the Products Web Form:

1. Add a new web form to the project by choosing Project ➢ Add New Item and selecting the web form item. Name the form Products.

2. Open the form in design view. Add a Label control (from the Toolbox) to the form and set the Text property of Label to Categories.

3. Add a DropDownList to the web form. Name it **ddlCategories**. It should initially display the text *Unbound* in the design view.

4. Add an ObjectDataSource control, found in the Data section of the Toolbox menu, and set the ID property to `odsCategories`. Configure the data source for `odsCategories` by invoking the Configure Data Source Wizard. Select the CategoriesTableAdapter business object in the Configure Data Source window. In the Define Data Methods window, set the method to None on the Update, Insert, and Delete tabs. On the Select tab, leave the default GetData method.

5. Configure the ddlCategories control data source by selectingodsCategories as the data source for the control. Set DataTextField for ddlCategories to CategoryName and Data-ValueField to CategoryID. The ddlCategories should now display the text *Databound* in design view.

You can now run the form for the first time; be sure the Products web form window is selected as active in Visual Studio and then press F5. You should see the form with a single drop-down list displaying all product categories.

It is time to prepare the application for displaying the list of products. For this, you need first to prepare the DataSet for a parameterized display of Products data:

1. Open the Northwind DataSet design window.

2. Right-click the Products table and select Add ➤ Query from the context menu.

3. When the TableAdapter Query Configuration Wizard opens, select the Use SQL Statements option and click Next.

4. In the Choose A Query Type window, choose SELECT, which returns rows, and click Next.

5. In the Specify A SQL SELECT statement window, click the Query Builder button.

6. When the Query Builder window opens, check all of the columns for selection.

7. Add the following filters to the query:
   Set the Discontinued column filter to = 0
   Set the CategoryId column filter to = `@CategoryId`

8. Execute the query. You will be prompted for an `@CategoryId` parameter value. Enter 1 and click OK. You should see a number of rows returned in the query result table. Click OK and then click Next.

9. In the Choose Methods To Generate window, check the Return A Data Table option and name the method `GetDataByCategoryId`. Click Finish. Ignore the warnings that might be issued by Visual Studio.

It is now time to configure the grid view of the product data:

1. Add an ObjectDataSource control to the form. Name it **odsProducts**.

2. Select ProductsTableAdapter in the Configure Data Source window. Click Next.

3. Select GetDataByCategoryId(Nullable<Int32> CategoryID), Returns ProductsDataTable in the Choose A Method combo box on the Select tab of the Define Data Methods window. If this option is not displayed, click Cancel and rebuild the project so that the changes you made to DataSet in the previous section (where you prepared the Northwind DataSet) are reflected. Choose None as the data method on the Insert, Update, and Delete tabs. Click Next.

4. In the Define Parameters window, select Control as the parameter source. Select ddl-Categories as the ContorlID and enter 1 as the default value. Click Finish.

Now you are ready to add the grid control to the form:

1. Add a GridView control to the form. Name it **gwProducts**.

2. Configure the data source for the GridView control. Select odsProducts from the Choose Data Source combo box.

3. Configure the data you wish the user to see. Right-click the gwProducts control and invoke the Edit Columns option.

4. Remove the SupplierID, CategoryID, UnitsOnOrder, ReorderLevel, and Discontinued fields from the list of selected fields.

5. Set the ProductID field Visible property to False.

6. Set the header text for the selected columns so it represents the column content. The wizard will use the table column names by default. You can add space characters to these names where necessary. For example, you can change ProductName to Product Name.

7. Click OK.

8. When the GridView Tasks window opens, check the Enable Paging, Enable Sorting, and Enable Selection options.

9. Make sure the DataKeyNames property has the values ProductID and ProductName.

You can explore further by setting any of the numerous display and paging options of Grid-View to your liking. You can now run the application. The products web form should display a grid populated with product data. In the browser, the form should look similar to the HTML page shown in Figure 20.9.

FIGURE 20.9
Main product selec-
tion web form
Products.aspx

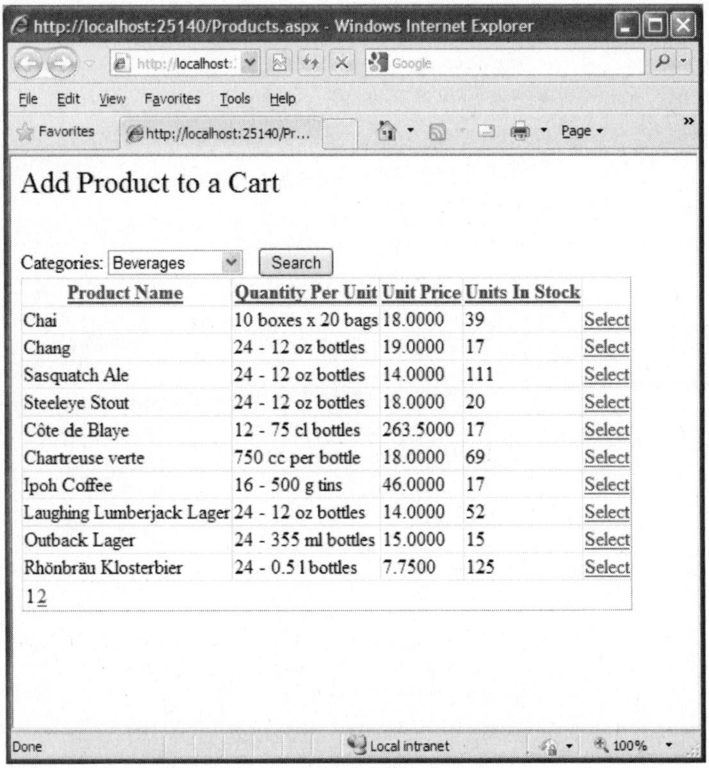

All that is left to do to finish the web form is to make the DropDownList filter the grid data. To that end, add the button to the form and change the button's Text property to Search. Notice that there is no need to implement any event-handling code for the Search button's click event. Even without an event handler, clicking the Search button will result in the web form being posted back to the server with the currently selected value in ddlCategories control. When the page is rendered again, it will show only the products belonging to the currently selected category. You are done with filtering functionality! When the user clicks the button, the new request is issued to the server and ddlCategories SelectedValue is passed to a parameter to odsProducts.

Now you need to handle the product selection. The user should be redirected to a new web form called `Quantity.aspx` to select the desired quantity for the product. This can be accomplished by writing an event handler for `SelectedIndexChanged` event of gwProducts. The product ID and product name data for the selected row is made available through GridView's `SelectedDataKey` property. You can take a look at the `SelectedIndexChanged` event handler in Listing 20.6.

LISTING 20.6:   Handling of product selection

```
Protected Sub gwProducts_SelectedIndexChanged(ByVal sender As Object,
               ByVal e As System.EventArgs) Handles
                   gwProducts.SelectedIndexChanged
    Dim quantityUrl = "Quantity.aspx?productId=" &
        gwProducts.DataKeys.
        Item(gwProducts.SelectedIndex).Values("ProductID").ToString &
        "&productName=" &
        gwProducts.DataKeys.
        Item(gwProducts.SelectedIndex).Values("ProductName").ToString
    Response.Redirect(quantityUrl)
End Sub
```

Retrieving data keys of the selected row in a GridView is a bit involved. You need to use the `SelectedIndex` value of a GridView as an index for the DataKeys collection. Then you retrieve a value of DataKey by passing the name of the key. The product ID and product name are passed to the Quantity web form through the URL query string using the `Redirect` method of the Response object. Next let's take care of the `Quantity.aspx` web form.

Creating the Quantity Web Form

On the Quantity.aspx web form, the user needs to decide on the quantity of the product they are ordering. To implement the form, the first thing you need to do is obtain the selected product ID and product name. As you can see in Listing 20.6, this information is passed to Quantity.aspx as a parameter in the query string. This parameter is made available to you through the `QueryString` property of a Request object, as in this example: `Request.Query String("productId")`.

The `Quantity.aspx` web form can be accessed by someone writing the Quantity web form URL directly in the browser in an uncontrolled manner and meddling with the productId parameter in an query string. Therefore, you must first make sure a valid product ID and product name is being passed with the query string. This validation is performed in the `ValidateProduct` method. If the product ID or name is invalid, the user is redirected back to the `Products.aspx` web form. Notice that this scenario is used only to handle some inquisitive user (should I say hacker?) who decided to experiment with what should be application internal data. (This is one of the reasons you should favor submitting data with web forms instead of using the query string parameters.) And while you usually want to give an explanation for a redirect to your user, there is no need to give any explanation here; redirecting the browser back to the Products.aspx page is polite enough for a user with such questionable intentions. Take a look at ValidateProductId method in Listing 20.7. This method is called from the web form Page_Load event.

LISTING 20.7:   Query string parameter validation method

```
Private Sub ValidateProduct()
    If String.IsNullOrEmpty(Request.QueryString("productId")) Then
        Response.Redirect("Products.aspx")
    End If
    If Not IsNumeric(Request.QueryString("productId")) Then
        Response.Redirect("Products.aspx")
    End If
    If String.IsNullOrEmpty(Request.QueryString("productName")) Then
        Response.Redirect("Products.aspx")
    End If
End Sub
```

You can store the product ID in a web form field and display the product name on the form. Now you can add the necessary controls to the Quantity.aspx web form:

1. Add a Label named **lblProduct** to the form.

2. Add a TextBox named **txtQuantity** to the web form and set the Text property to 1.

3. Add a button named **bttnAdd**.

4. Add a button named **bttnCancel**.

5. Add a RangeValidator to the form to validate that the quantity entered by the user is a valid value. Set the ControlToValidate property of the RangeValidator to **txtQuantity**, the MinimumValue property to **0**, and the MaximimValue to **10000**. Finally, set the ErrorMessage property to **Enter a value between 0 and 10 000**.

The Quantity.aspx web form as appears in the browser is shown in Figure 20.10.

Now, you can use the data passed from the Products web form in the Page Load event. You will display the product name to the user in lblProduct and store the product ID in a web form field. You can take a look at the Page Load event handler in Listing 20.8, which shows the complete code listing for the Quantity.aspx web form.

You can implement the Cancel button event handler by redirecting the user back to the Products.aspx web form and displaying a message confirming the cancellation for the user.

Finally, you need to implement the Add button event handler. Since you will need the entered product quantity in the final web form, store this information inside the Session object. As the information on selected products accumulates during user visits to the site, you can use the Dictionary structure to store selected product quantities.

You can use the product ID as the key and the quantity as the value of the productQuantitie Dictionary. You can create the productQuantities instance inside the bttnAdd_Click routine if it was not created already. You should always check for the productQuantities instance before creating the new one. Since users can navigate back and forth between forms, you might be erasing some products that were already added to a cart if you were to simply create a new instance. After that, you can add the `productQuantities` instance to Session collection. This way, the `productQuantities` instance can be accessed in a cart web form, as shown in Listing 20.9. Take a look at the Add and Cancel button event handler implementations in Listing 20.8.

FIGURE 20.10
The `Quantity.aspx` product quantity entry web form

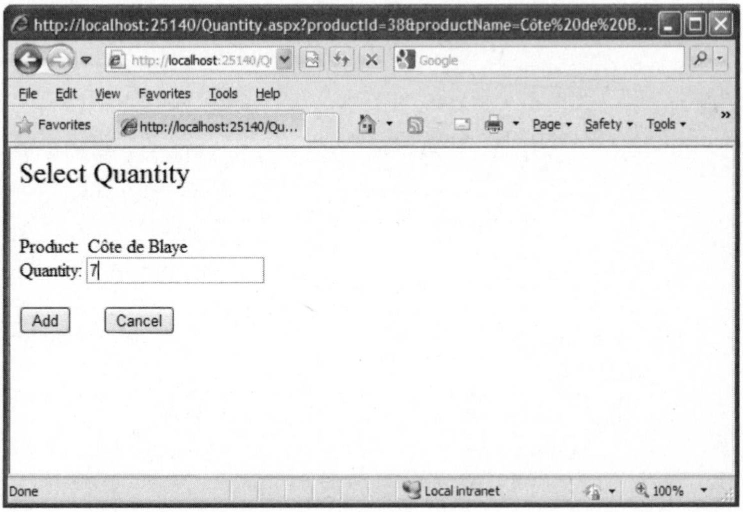

LISTING 20.8:   *Quantity.aspx* Web Form code-behind

```
Public Partial Class Quantity
    Inherits System.Web.UI.Page

    Dim productId As Integer

    Protected Sub Page_Load(ByVal sender As Object,
                ByVal e As System.EventArgs) Handles Me.Load
        ValidateProduct()
        lblProduct.Text = Request.QueryString("productName")
        productId = CInt(Request.QueryString("productId"))
    End Sub

    Private Sub ValidateProduct()
        If String.IsNullOrEmpty(Request.QueryString("productId")) Then
            Response.Redirect("Products.aspx")
        End If
        If Not IsNumeric(Request.QueryString("productId")) Then
            Response.Redirect("Products.aspx")
        End If
        If String.IsNullOrEmpty(Request.QueryString("productName")) Then
```

```
                Response.Redirect("Products.aspx")
            End If
        End Sub

        Protected Sub bttnCancel_Click(ByVal sender As Object,
                    ByVal e As EventArgs) Handles bttnCancel.Click
            Response.Redirect("Products.aspx")
        End Sub

        Protected Sub bttnAdd_Click(ByVal sender As Object,
                    ByVal e As EventArgs) Handles bttnAdd.Click
            Dim productQuantities As Dictionary(Of Integer, Integer)
            productQuantities = Session("productQuantities")
            If IsNothing(productQuantities) Then
                productQuantities = New Dictionary(Of Integer, Integer)
                Session("productQuantities") = productQuantities
            End If
            Dim quantity As Integer = CInt(txtQuantity.Text)
            If quantity = 0 Then
                productQuantities.Remove(productId)
                Response.Redirect("Cart.aspx")
            End If
            If productQuantities.ContainsKey(productId) Then
                productQuantities.Remove(productId)
            End If
            productQuantities.Add(productId, quantity)
            Response.Redirect("Cart.aspx")
        End Sub
    End Class
```

You are ready to implement the final web form (called `Cart.aspx`) where the user will be able to review and check out ordered items.

CREATING THE CART WEB FORM

On the final cart web form, the user will be able to review products in the cart, check out and place the order, edit the quantity of the selected product, or go back to initial products web form to add more products to the cart.

Start by placing a GridView control with ID gwCart on the form. The grid will display products added to the cart. It should display the Product Name, Unit Price, Quantity, Online Discount Price, and Product Total columns. As you saw in the quantity web form code in Listing 20.8, selected products' identifiers and quantities are kept in the session variable *productQuantities*. To obtain the rest of the fields that need to be displayed in the gwCart grid, you will need to consult the database using the ProductID field as the selection criteria.

Matching selected products in the `productQuantities` Dictionary with products in the Products table in the Northwind DataSet and retrieving the rest of the product fields can be efficiently accomplished using a LINQ statement. Take a look at Listing 20.9. It shows a LINQ expression that matches the product IDs in the productQuantities object with product IDs in the Products table. It selects an anonymous type using a `Select New With` construct with a number of fields retrieved from the table and a number of calculated fields.

LISTING 20.9:   Cart LINQ expression

```
queryResult = From p In table
        Where productQuantities.Keys.Contains(p.ProductID)
        Select New With {
          p.ProductID,
          p.ProductName,
          .Quantity = productQuantities.Item(p.ProductID),
          p.UnitPrice,
          .Discount = 0.02,
          .DiscountedUnitPrice = p.UnitPrice * DiscountIndex,
          .ProductTotal = p.UnitPrice * DiscountIndex *
                        productQuantities.Item(p.ProductID),
          .Edit = "Quantity.aspx?productId=" &
          p.ProductID.ToString & "&productName=" & p.ProductName
```

You'll want to pay special attention to several of the fields. The Discount field is set to a constant value of 0.02 — a standard discount for online orders. The DiscountedUnitPrice field is calculated based on the discount and original unit price. ProductTotal is calculated by multiplying the discounted price by the ordered quantity. Finally, the Edit fields are used to construct the URL that redirects the user to the quantity web form so that the quantity can be changed for any product on the order. This expression is used as a `data source` for the `gwCart` grid.

Now, you can add columns to the `gwCart` GridView control by following the procedure described in "Creating the Products Web Forms" section earlier in this chapter. A few things to bear in mind:

◆ Keep the ProductID field visibility set to False.

◆ When configuring the column used to display the Edit field, use the HyperLinkFiled field type. Name it **Change** and set the `Text` property to Change. Most importantly, set `DataNavigateUrlFields` to `ProductID` and `ProductName` and set `DataNavigate UrlFormatString` to `Quantity.aspx?productId={0}&productName={1}`. This way, the final column of the grid will display the hyperlink that will redirect users to the `Quantity.aspx` web form where they will be able to edit the quantity of selected product.

Next, you need to display the total for the cart. Again, this is best calculated using LINQ. The LINQ expression to calculate the cart total is shown in Listing 20.10.

LISTING 20.10:   LINQ expression used to calculate cart total

```
total = (From p In table
            Where productQuantities.Keys.Contains(p.ProductID)).
        Sum(Function(p) p.UnitPrice * DiscountIndex *
        productQuantities.Item(p.ProductID))
```

The result of this expression can be shown as text in the Label control. Add the label with ID lblTotal to the form and assign the result of the total LINQ query to the lblTotal Text property in the Page_Load event handler.

You need to add few more buttons to the web form and you are done. Let's start with Check Out button.

When the user clicks the Check Out button, a new row should be inserted in the Orders table in the Northwind database. For each product, a row should be inserted in the Order_Details table.

Add a new button control to the web form. Name it **bttnCheckOut**. Implement the code that adds rows to the Orders and Order_Details tables. First, insert a row in the Orders table and then use that same row as the parent row when inserting rows in the Order_Details table since the Orders and Order_Details tables are in a one-to-many relationship. You can take a look at the bttnCheckOut event handler code in Listing 20.11.

You need to add two more buttons to the cart web form. Add a button named bttnEmpty and set the Text property to Empty. This button is used to empty the cart. To accomplish this, you need to empty the productQuantities Dictionary that was kept as a session scoped variable. The code for emptying the dictionary in the bttnEmpty event handling routine is shown in Listing 20.11.

Finally, users often want to go back to the product list and add more products after inspecting the cart. Add a button named bttnAddMore, set the Text property to **Add More Products**, and in the button event handler routine, redirect the user to products web form. The complete code for the Cart.aspx web form is shown in Listing 20.11.

LISTING 20.11:   *Cart.aspx* code-behind

```
Imports OnlineOrdering.Northwind.OrdersRow
Imports OnlineOrdering.Northwind.Order_DetailsRow

Partial Public Class Cart
    Inherits System.Web.UI.Page

    Dim queryResult As EnumerableRowCollection
    Dim total As Decimal
    Private Const DiscountIndex = 0.98

    Protected Sub Page_Load(ByVal sender As Object,
                            ByVal e As System.EventArgs) Handles Me.Load
        'Set to real user Id after implementing Login functionality
        Session("userId") = "ALFKI"
        'Add "Online Employee" to database and set employeeId accordingly
        Session("employeeId") = 10
        GenerateOrder()
        lblTotal.Text = total.ToString()
        gwCart.DataSource = queryResult
        gwCart.DataBind()
    End Sub
```

```vb.net
Private Sub GenerateOrder()
    Dim adapter As New NorthwindTableAdapters.ProductsTableAdapter
    Dim table As Northwind.ProductsDataTable
    Dim productQuantities As Dictionary(Of Integer, Integer)

    productQuantities = Session("productQuantities")
    If IsNothing(productQuantities) Then
        Response.Redirect("Products.aspx")
    End If

    table = adapter.GetData

    queryResult = From p In table
            Where productQuantities.Keys.Contains(p.ProductID)
            Select New With {
             p.ProductID,
             p.ProductName,
             .Quantity = productQuantities.Item(p.ProductID),
             p.UnitPrice,
             .Discount = 0.02,
             .DiscountedUnitPrice = p.UnitPrice * DiscountIndex,
             .ProductTotal = p.UnitPrice * DiscountIndex *
                        productQuantities.Item(p.ProductID),
             .Edit = "Quantity.aspx?productId=" &
             p.ProductID.ToString & "&productName=" & p.ProductName
             }

    total = (From p In table
                Where productQuantities.Keys.Contains(p.ProductID)).
                Sum(Function(p) p.UnitPrice * DiscountIndex *
                productQuantities.Item(p.ProductID))
End Sub


Protected Sub bttnAddMore_Click(ByVal sender As Object,
            ByVal e As EventArgs) Handles bttnAddMore.Click
                [aligning left is fine - DA]
    Response.Redirect("Products.aspx")
End Sub

Protected Sub bttnCheckOut_Click(ByVal sender As Object,
            ByVal e As EventArgs) Handles bttnCheckOut.Click
    Dim productsAdapter As New NorthwindTableAdapters.ProductsTableAdapter
    Dim products As Northwind.ProductsDataTable = productsAdapter.GetData

    Dim ordersAdapter As New NorthwindTableAdapters.OrdersTableAdapter
    Dim orders = ordersAdapter.GetData
```

```
                Dim orderDetailsAdapter As New
                    NorthwindTableAdapters.Order_DetailsTableAdapter
                Dim orderDetails = orderDetailsAdapter.GetData


                Dim order = orders.AddOrdersRow(
                        Session("userId"),
                        CInt(Session("employeeId")),
                        Date.Now.Date,
                        Date.Now.AddDays(7).Date,
                        Date.MinValue, 1,
                        Nothing, Nothing, Nothing, Nothing,
                        Nothing, Nothing, Nothing)
                order.SetShippedDateNull()
                ordersAdapter.Update(orders)
                orders.AcceptChanges()
                For Each orderDetail In queryResult
                    Dim product = products.FindByProductID(
                                orderDetail.ProductID)
                    orderDetails.AddOrder_DetailsRow(
                                order, product, orderDetail.UnitPrice,
                                orderDetail.Quantity, orderDetail.Discount)
                Next
                orderDetailsAdapter.Update(orderDetails)
                orderDetails.AcceptChanges()
                Response.Redirect("Confirmation.aspx")

        End Sub

        Protected Sub bttnEmpty_Click(ByVal sender As Object,
                                ByVal e As EventArgs) Handles bttnEmpty.Click
            Dim productQuantities As Dictionary(Of Integer, Integer) =
                Session("productQuantities")
            productQuantities.Clear()
            Response.Redirect("Products.aspx")
        End Sub
End Class
```

If you inspect the code in Listing 20.11 carefully, you will see that there are a few hard-coded features. Namely, since I did not implement the login feature, I assigned the value ALFKI to *userId* and used it when creating the order. Once the Login feature is implemented, a real user ID can be assigned to the *userId* variable.

Since the purpose of the online ordering application is to have users create their own orders without employee intervention, the *employeeId* variable is assigned a value of 10. This employee ID does not exist in the Northwind database, but you can generate it by adding a row to the Employees table and naming the user Online Ordering Application.

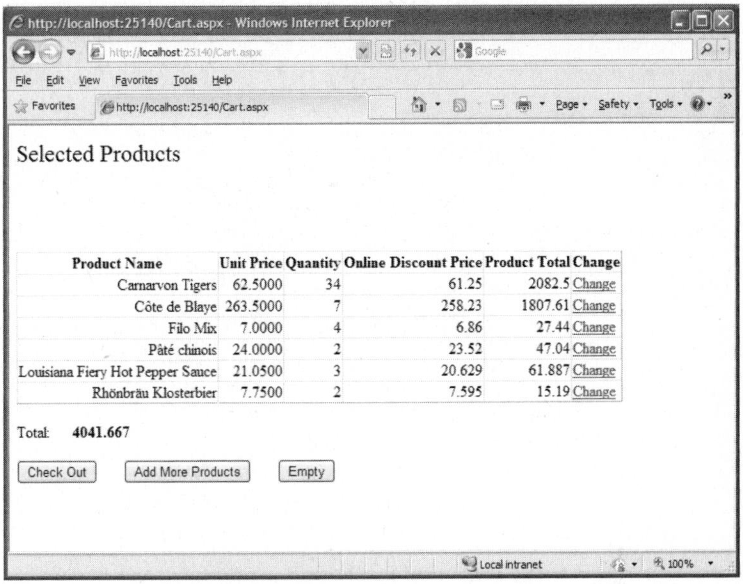
http://localhost:25140/Cart.aspx - Windows Internet Explorer
Selected Products
Product Name | Unit Price | Quantity | Online Discount Price | Product Total | Change
Carnarvon Tigers | 62.5000 | 34 | 61.25 | 2082.5 | Change
Côte de Blaye | 263.5000 | 7 | 258.23 | 1807.61 | Change
Filo Mix | 7.0000 | 4 | 6.86 | 27.44 | Change
Pâté chinois | 24.0000 | 2 | 23.52 | 47.04 | Change
Louisiana Fiery Hot Pepper Sauce | 21.0500 | 3 | 20.629 | 61.887 | Change
Rhönbräu Klosterbier | 7.7500 | 2 | 7.595 | 15.19 | Change
Total: 4041.667
Check Out
Add More Products
Empty
Local intranet
100%

FIGURE 20.11
The `Cart.aspx` web form

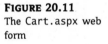

The Bottom Line

Create a basic XHTML/HTML page. Building a basic HTML page is a straightforward process using a simple text editor such as Notepad. Knowledge of XHTML/HTML is still a major asset when developing web applications with Visual Studio 2010.

> **Master It** Develop a web page using HTML that features a heading, some text, an image, and a link to another page. Convert the page to XHTML and verify it by using the W3C verification tool at `http://validator.w3.org`. You might find that you will need to run the validation a couple of times to get everything right. If you attach and use the style sheet in the following Master It challenge, you will find that validation will be less problematic.

Format a page with CSS. Cascading Style Sheets (CSS) is a powerful tool for controlling the styles and format of a website. You can manually create style sheets by using a text editor. An understanding of their operation and syntax is a useful skill when manipulating CSS in Visual Studio 2010.

> **Master It** Create a CSS style sheet that defines the layout of the web page that you developed in the previous task, including a header section, a left-hand navigation section, and a main content section. Include a rollover for the link and apply formatting to the tags that you have used for your heading and text tags. Attach the style sheet to your web page.

Set up a master page for your website. Using master pages is a reliable method of controlling the overall layout and look and feel of your websites and applications. Master pages enable you to achieve a high level of consistency in your design and are particularly useful if the site has multiple developers working on it.

Master It Create a website with a master page and attached content page. Use appropriate controls to give the master page a page heading, My Page, which will appear on all attached content pages. Use a combination of Button and Label controls on the content page to create a simple Hello World application.

Use some of the ASP.NET intrinsic objects. ASP.NET objects such as the Response, Request, Session, and Server objects offer a range of important utilities in developing, running, and maintaining your websites and applications. In addition, they give you access to vital information about the client, the server, and any current sessions at runtime.

Master It Create a simple website with a master page and two attached content pages. Use the Server.Execute method attached to a LinkButton control to navigate between the two content pages.

Chapter 21

Building and Using Web Services

A web service is a program capable of communicating across a network by using a combination of the open standard Simple Open Access Protocol (SOAP) and XML technologies.

Web services are ideal for creating data-, content-, or processing-related services that can be made available to associated or third-party applications and clients across distributed networks such as the Internet. There are two flavors of web services, the ASP.NET web services and the newer WCF services, which are based on the Windows Communications Foundation component of the Framework.

In this chapter, you will see how to create a simple ASP.NET web service and a client application to consume (use) the web service. You'll also learn how to build, configure, and consume WCF services.

In addition, this chapter covers the technologies associated with ASP.NET web services, such as SOAP and the Web Services Description Language (WSDL). The chapter briefly covers Microsoft's latest addition to the web service stable — the Windows Communication Foundation (WCF) — and you will see how to use Asynchronous JavaScript and XML (AJAX) technology to create seamless interactions between web services and their consuming applications.

In this chapter, you'll learn how to do the following:

◆ Create a simple ASP.NET web service

◆ Consume an ASP.NET web service

◆ Create and consume WCF services

◆ Create and consume ADO.NET Data Services

Using ASP.NET and WCF Web Services

Microsoft offers two flavors of web service technology:

◆ ASP.NET web services

◆ Windows Communication Foundation (WCF)

ASP.NET web services (also known as XML web services) have been around through all the incarnations of ASP.NET and offer a simple and effective methodology for making software components and other resources available over the Internet.

WCF is a recent inclusion into the .NET Framework and is built around the web services architecture. WCF enables broader integration and interoperability with all the .NET Framework distributed system technologies, including Microsoft Message Queuing (MSMQ), Common Object Model Plus (COM+), ASP.NET web services, and .NET Framework Remoting. WCF also offers improved performance and secure data transmission.

What Is a Service?

Modern software is moving away from stand-alone applications into distributed applications. Users can interact with web applications that run on a remote server. The interface is hosted in the browser, known as a thin client, but the bulk of the processing takes place on a remote computer. Some logic is implemented at the client to minimize the trips to the client. Unfortunately, the client can execute only scripts written in JavaScript. You can also create SilverLight applications, which are basically web applications that execute VB code at the client. SilverLight applications are not nearly as common as web applications because they require users to install the SilverLight runtime on their computers.

The problem with web applications is that users are confined by the application's interface. The information is processed at a remote site, but users can interact with it only through a predefined interface. In the early days of the Web, developers used to write code to download web pages and "scrape" data off the HTML document transmitted by the server to the client. Actually, data scraping is used today a lot because people need access to raw information, which they can use as they see fit in their applications.

Consider sites like Booking.com and Expedia.com that allow users to make hotel and flight reservations. You connect to these sites, specify the dates of your trip, retrieve numerous options (flights and/or hotels), and make your selection. While all this works fine on your browser, you're restricted to the existing interface. What if you could submit the same requests to the remote server but instead of a static page you could get back the raw information? You could implement your own interface, which could be a different web application, a rich client application, even a mobile application. This would offer more power to you, but how about the provider of the information? In effect, the provider of the information also wants to furnish the same information through a programmatic interface and sell its products through additional channels. Amazon.com does so already — and very successfully. Web services allow companies to make their services available to all consumers, and it's up to the consumers to exploit these services. To get a better idea of how services are being used and how they enable distributed computing, let's start by looking at an example of consuming an existing, public web service.

Consuming Web Services

Before we explore the server side of a web service, let's see how easy it is to consume existing web services. Perhaps you'll never develop your own web service, but it's very likely that you will use other people's services in your code. In a corporate environment, for example, you might be asked to develop data-driven applications based on a data model that's hosted as a web service. Instead of talking directly to a database, you will be invoking methods of a web service that exposes the company data. Or, you might be asked to write an application that consumes information from web services published on the Internet. Calling a web service that performs automatic text translation and adding weather data on a travel site are two trivial examples. Business examples include services that provide hotels and flights. These services are quite popular these days, and they allow consumers to search for prices and availability and make reservations on a remote computer. There are currently many travel sites on the Internet, and they're all using the services of a few large providers. Let's look at a less-ambitious yet quite useful web service you can incorporate in many types of applications. It's a service that provides weather forecasts, and there's no charge, or even a registration requirement, to use it.

Many sites provide weather forecasts, and I've chosen one that exposes a few simple methods to retrieve the forecasts to present in this section. The URL that follows takes you to a site that hosts a small number of web services, which you may find interesting:

```
http://www.webservicex.net/WCF/ServiceDetails.aspx?SID=44
```

One of the services hosted at this site provides weather forecasts; you will find it by clicking the Web Services link at the top of the page and choosing the Utilities category. Once you switch to the USA Weather Forecast service's site, you'll see that the service exposes two methods:

◆ GetWeatherByPlaceName, which gets a week's forecast for a place by name (USA)

◆ GetWeatherByZipCode, which gets a week's forecast for a valid zip code (USA)

Click the GetWeatherByPlaceName link and you'll see a page prompting you to enter the name of a place. Enter your favorite destination here (I used the city of Santa Barbara) and you'll see a weekly weather forecast for that destination in XML format, as shown in Figure 21.1. This is straight XML, and you can contact the same site from within a VB application using the HttpWebRequest/HttpWebResponse classes, read the XML document, and process it with LINQ, as we discussed in Chapter 14, "An Introduction to LINQ."

FIGURE 21.1
Retrieving weather
forecast information in
XML format

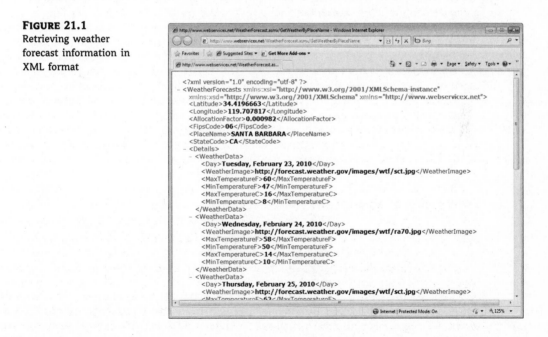

As you will recall from Chapter 19, "Accessing the Web," it is feasible (and nearly trivial) to contact a remote server, request a XML document, and process it with LINQ. One method of contacting the weather forecast service is to place a request through a WebRequest object and read the server's response through a pair of WebRequest/WebResponse objects, as shown here:

```
Dim rq As System.Net.WebRequest = System.Net.WebRequest.Create(
                    http://www.webservicex.net/WeatherForecast.asmx/ &
                    GetWeatherByPlaceName?PlaceName=Santa Barbara")
Dim rs As System.Net.WebResponse = rq.GetResponse
```

Now that you have the service's response, you can read it as a long string into a variable, the *xmlData* variable:

```
Dim strm As IO.Stream = rs.GetResponseStream
Dim rdr As New IO.StreamReader(strm, System.Text.Encoding.UTF8)
Dim xmlData As String = rdr.ReadToEnd
rdr.Close()
strm.Close()
```

Finally, you can load the data into an XElement variable and process the data with LINQ. The following few statements generate a list of data and min/max temperatures:

```
Dim xml As XElement = XElement.Parse(xmlData)
Dim ns As XNamespace = "http://www.webservicex.net"
For Each forecast In xml.Descendants(ns + "Details").
                Descendants(ns + "WeatherData")
    Debug.WriteLine(forecast.Descendants(ns + "Day").Value & vbTab &
                forecast.Descendants(ns + "MinTemperatureF").Value &
                " - " & forecast.Descendants(ns + "MaxTemperatureF").Value)
Next
```

The code is very simple, but you can't process it without knowing, or figuring out, the structure of the XML document returned by the service. As you have undoubtedly noticed, Microsoft likes to simplify things and Visual Studio can take care of all the plumbing necessary to contact the web service and retrieve its results. Instead of contacting the web service through HTTP from within your code, you can add a reference to the web service and then use it as if it were a local method. Let's follow the process step by step.

Start a new project, the WeatherService project, which you can download from www.sybex .com/go/masteringvb2010. Right-click the project name, and from the context menu, select Add Service Reference. When the Add Service Reference dialog box appears, you can specify a remote web service, as shown in Figure 21.2. In the Address box, enter the URL of the WeatherForecast web service, which is as follows:

```
http://www.webservicex.net/WeatherForecast.asmx?WSDL
```

(The extension WSDL stands for Web Service Discovery Language and it's a parameter that instructs the web service to return its methods.) Then, click the Go button to locate the web services at the specified URL; these services will appear in the left pane of the dialog box. If you double-click a web service on this pane, the components of the selected web service will appear under the service's name. Double-click the WeatherForecastHttpGet class to see the names of the methods it exposes in the right pane, as shown in Figure 21.2.

FIGURE 21.2
Adding a reference to a
remote web service

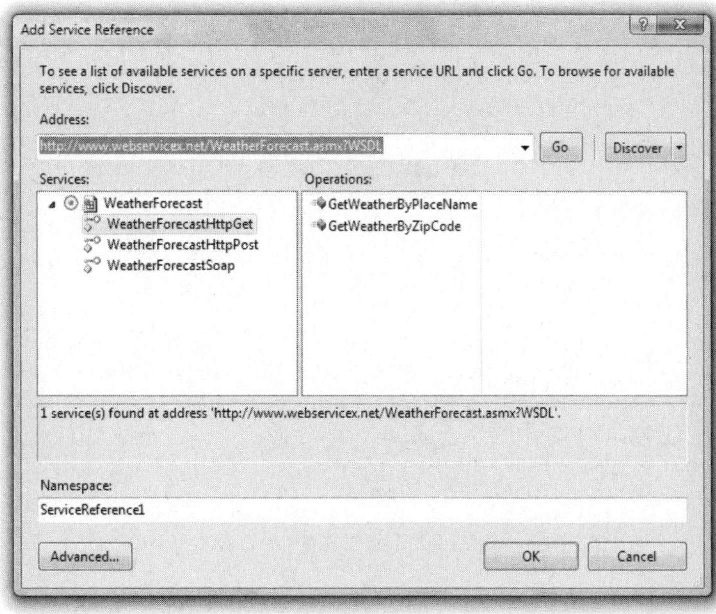

The web service exposed by the remote server can be accessed using three different proto-cols: HTTP Get, HTTP Post, and SOAP. All three classes expose the same methods: `GetWeather ByPlaceName` and `GetWeatherByZipCode`. The names are quite descriptive, and you'll see shortly how to call them. Finally, in the Namespace box, enter a meaningful name for the reference, such as **WeatherService**, and click the OK button to close the dialog box.

To use the WeatherService web service in your code, you simply treat it as a class, regardless of whether it resides on the local machine or a remote server. Create a new instance of the class with a statement like the following:

```
Dim client As New WeatherService.WeatherForecastSoapClient
```

Now, you can use the methods of the service through the *client* variable. Enter the name of the *client* variable followed by a period and you'll see names of the methods it exposes, including the `GetWeatherByPlaceName` method. If you select this method, you will see that it accepts a string argument, which is the name of a place (such as a city) in the U.S. (and a few major cities in Europe). To retrieve the forecast for the next six days for Santa Barbara, enter the following statement:

```
Dim forecast = client.GetWeatherByPlaceName("Santa Barbara")
```

The *forecast* variable type is WeatherService.WeatherForecast. This type is exposed by the web service along with the methods and several properties. Enter the name of the *forecast* variable followed by a period to see the members of the WeatherForecast class. One of them is the `Details` property, which is an array of WeatherData objects, and there is one Weather-Data object for each of the following days. The `WeatherData` property is a complex one, which exposes a number of properties on its own. These properties include the Day property (the date for which the forecast is given); the `MaxTemperatureC`, `MaxTemperatureF`, `MinTemperatureC`, and `MinTemperatureF` properties; and the `WeatherImage` property, which is the URL of an image describing the day's weather.

I've designed a simple interface to display the forecast for the selected location based on Label and PictureBox controls, and it's shown in Figure 21.3. The application's code is quite trivial; it retrieves the forecast with the two statements shown earlier and then assigns values to the various controls. Here are a few statements that display the forecast for the second day (the first day of the forecast being today):

```
lblDate2.Text = forecast.Details(1).Day
PictureBox2.ImageLocation = forecast.Details(1).WeatherImage
lblMax2.Text = forecast.Details(1).MaxTemperatureF.ToString
lblMin2.Text = forecast.Details(1).MinTemperatureF.ToString
```

FIGURE 21.3
A Windows application that displays a weather forecast based on data it retrieves from a remote server

The two numbers under the city name are the geocoordinates (or geographic coordinates) of Santa Barbara (its longitude and latitude, which are also returned by the `GetWeatherByPlace Name` method).

As you can see, using a web service from within your application is straightforward and very similar to using any other component, such as the Framework or a custom class. The web service is a class that resides on a server and applications can contact it. The web service itself is nothing but a class with methods that can be called remotely. The service's code is executed on the computer on which the service resides. No code is downloaded to the client, and you don't have to worry about the origin of the data. To you, the developer, a web service looks like any other class you reference in your project. As for the providers of the web services, they provide a software service — a way to request specific data that are maintained and serviced on a remote computer. The service provider allows you to perform specific requests without exposing its raw data.

ASP.NET Web Services

ASP.NET web services are software resources and components through which you can expose certain functionality and/or deliver data over a network such as the Internet by using a combination of XML and SOAP. You can restrict a component so that it's available to only certain applications or specific users, or you can make it available to many users. The component can be limited to the local computer or the local network or be made available across the Internet. Services can be delivered free of charge or for a fee.

Virtually any program that can be encapsulated as a component can be expressed as an ASP.NET web service. For production purposes, you will need a web server to deliver your ASP.NET web service. However, for development purposes, the built-in ASP.NET Development Server that ships with Visual Studio 2010 is quite sufficient.

The advantages of using ASP.NET web services are as follows:

◆ Data and commands are communicated across the standard Internet port: port 80. This greatly simplifies passage around the Internet and most networks.

◆ The common standards of XML and SOAP are widely supported.

◆ Early problems with web services, such as lack of a robust security model, have been resolved.

◆ Visual Studio provides a simple and straightforward environment in which to create and consume web services.

WCF

Windows Communications Foundation (WCF) is built on ASP.NET web services and extends their functionality by integrating with a number of distributed .NET Framework technologies.

WCF offers an integrated approach to situations in which you would previously have employed a range of different distributed .NET Framework technologies. Typically, you use WCF as a unified solution that enables you to avoid having to employ different distributed technologies for each requirement of a distributed application. For example, you may have employed message queuing for use with portable devices that are not permanently connected, ASP.NET web services for communication across the Internet, and .NET Framework Remoting for tightly coupled communication within the local network. Employing multiple technologies in this manner results in a complex and potentially unwieldy solution. WCF offers a method of achieving a simpler unified approach. The weather forecasting web service used in the first example of this chapter contained three subclasses to support three different data exchange protocols: HttpGet, HttpPost, and SOAP. With WCF services, the same service can support multiple protocols. You don't have to write any additional code, you just edit the service's configuration file.

Understanding Technologies Associated with Web Services

Several technologies underlie and support ASP.NET web services. They include SOAP, WSDL, SOAP Discovery, and Universal Description, Discovery, and Integration (UDDI).

SOAP

SOAP stands for the Simple Object Access Protocol and it's a lightweight protocol for exchanging XML messages over Hypertext Transfer Protocol/Secure Hypertext Transfer Protocol (HTTP/HTTPS). It forms the basis of the web services stack, which is the set of protocols used to define, locate, and deliver web services.

SOAP is an open standard, enabling web services to be developed and supported across a range of platforms and environments. There are other services attached to SOAP, including WSDL and SOAP Discovery. Although you are no longer required to work directly with SOAP when developing ASP.NET web services in Visual Studio, you will continue to encounter references to the protocol because it underlies the whole web service creation, delivery, and consumption process.

A SOAP tutorial can be found at www.w3schools.com/soap/.

WSDL

Web Services Description Language (WSDL) is the language used to create an XML document that describes a web service. Specifically, the document describes the location of the service and the methods exposed by the service. When you connect to a site that provides one or more web services, applications read the WSDL file to discover the methods supported by each service.

You can create and edit WSDL documents directly by using a text editor, but they can usually be generated automatically by Visual Studio when you add either a web reference or service reference to your ASP.NET web service.

SOAP Discovery

SOAP Discovery is used to locate the WSDL documents that provide the descriptions for ASP.NET web services. Use SOAP Discovery when you want to make your web service publicly available for consumption by third-party applications. For example, you might be providing a weather service for third-party providers to incorporate into their websites. There are two types of discovery: static discovery and dynamic discovery.

In the case of static discovery, an XML document with the .DISCO filename extension is used. This file contains information about the location of the WSDL documents.

If you wish to enable dynamic discovery for your website, you add a specific reference into the Web.config file. Dynamic discovery enables users to discover all web services and discovery files beneath the requested URL.

Discovery files (and particularly dynamic discovery) can be a security risk on a production server because they potentially allow users to search the entire directory tree. Static discovery files are the safer of the two types because they allow the user to search only those resources that you choose to nominate. In Visual Studio 2010, you can explicitly generate a static discovery file by adding a web reference or a service reference.

UDDI

Universal Description, Discovery, and Integration (UDDI) was originally created as part of the web service specification to act as a form of yellow pages for web services. Several major players in developing the web services specification (including Microsoft, IBM, SAP, and OASIS) combined to develop an XML-based registry for businesses to promote themselves and their web services to both the public and the corporate world. In 2006, Microsoft, IBM, and SAP closed their public UDDI nodes. However, you can still create UDDI servers on your local network to provide directory services for web services available within your network.

Creating a Simple ASP.NET Web Service

Creating and consuming web services in Visual Studio 2010 is a relatively simple and straightforward process. In this example, you will create a simple Hello World–style ASP.NET web service within a website entitled HelloWebServiceDemo. You will then see how to consume the web service from within the same website.

OPENING VISUAL STUDIO IN ADMINISTRATOR MODE

Visual Studio often requires elevated privileges when you're creating and accessing applications and resources. If you are logged in as a standard user, you may not have those privileges available.

To increase your privileges, from the Start menu, right-click the Visual Studio 2010 entry. From the context menu, choose Run As Administrator. You may be required to enter credentials.

Setting Up the Web Service

This simple web service will have one service, HelloWorld, with a single method, Hello. To set up the web service, complete the following steps:

1. Launch Visual Studio and choose File ➢ New Web Site.

2. From the New Web Site dialog box, choose ASP.NET Web Site. In the location text box, name the website **HelloWebServiceDemo**. Click OK.

3. Right-click the solution, choose Add New Item from the context menu, and select the web service template. In the Name text box, delete the default WebService.asmx and rename the web service **HelloWorld.asmx**. Click the Add button. This opens the App_Code/HelloWorld.vb page, where default code for a Hello World–style web service is already set up.

4. Make one minor change to the default code. In the <WebMethod()> section of the code, change the function name from HelloWorld() to **Hello()**. This enables you to distinguish between the service name and the method. The code should now read as shown in the following snippet:

```
<WebMethod()>
    Public Function Hello() As String
      Return "Hello World"
    End Function
```

5. Save your work.

Next, you will run and test the web service.

Testing the Web Service

After you have created your web service, it is a good idea to test the service to ensure that it behaves as expected. This presentation of the testing process lacks the polish that you might wish for your web service after it is utilized or consumed by a client application, but it will demonstrate the service's inherent functionality. The product of the test is returned as straight XML. But don't worry — when you finally consume the service, the XML markup will be stripped away from the returned data. Follow these steps:

1. In the Solution Explorer window, right-click HelloWorld.asmx and choose the Set As Start Page option.

2. Click the green arrow in the Standard toolbar (or press F5) to start the web service in debugging mode. Click OK in the Debugging Not Enabled dialog box to automatically modify the Web.config file to enable debugging.

The ASP.NET web service should now open in your web browser as shown in Figure 21.4.

FIGURE 21.4
HelloWorld web service in Internet Explorer

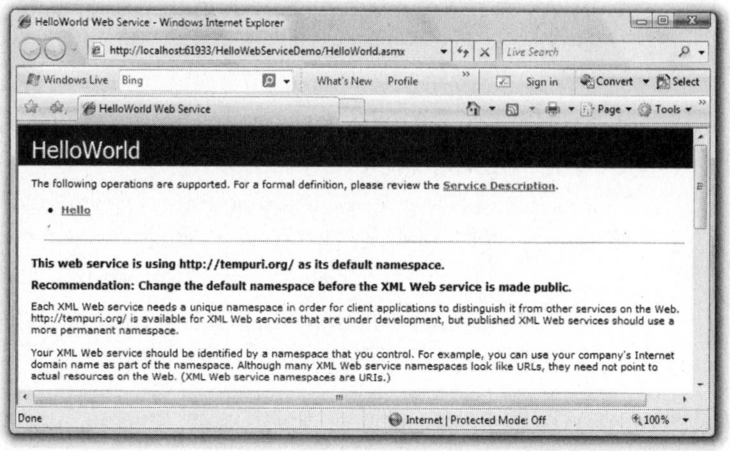

You can check the service description for HelloWorld by clicking the Service Description link. This opens a WSDL description for the web service.

You will also see a warning about using the default namespace of http://tempuri.org. This is the default Microsoft namespace, and you would usually replace it with a reference to a URL that you control before publicly deploying the web service.

To call the Hello method, click the Hello link. This opens a new page, which displays information concerning the Hello method. To run the Hello method, click the Invoke button. This opens the full XML page returned by the method, as shown in Figure 21.5.

FIGURE 21.5
Invoking the Hello method

Consuming the Web Service

The next step is to consume the HelloWorld web service from within a standard ASPX page. Close any running instances of the HelloWorld web service to stop debugging and return to the HelloWebServiceDemo website in Visual Studio. Complete the following steps:

1. In Solution Explorer, double-click Default.aspx to open the page in design view.

2. From the Toolbox, drag and drop a Button control into the default Div control on the form.

3. Click the Enter button twice to introduce two line breaks, and add a Label control from the Standard toolbox.

4. In the Properties window for the Label control, delete the default Label text from the `Text` property.

5. Double-click the Button control to open the code skeleton for the `Button1_Click` event in code-behind.

6. Complete the `Button1_Click` event with the following code:

```
Protected Sub Button1_Click(...) Handles Button1.Click
    Dim myHello As New HelloWorld
    Label1.Text = myHello.Hello()
End Sub
```

In this example, I declared a local instance of the HelloWorld service and tied the `Text` property of the Label control to the `Hello` method.

7. In Solution Explorer, right-click `Default.aspx` and choose the Set As Start Page option.

8. Run the application. `Default.aspx` should render initially as a page displaying a single button. Clicking the button should display the Hello World text. Figure 21.6 shows the running application.

FIGURE 21.6
The running HelloWeb-ServiceDemo application

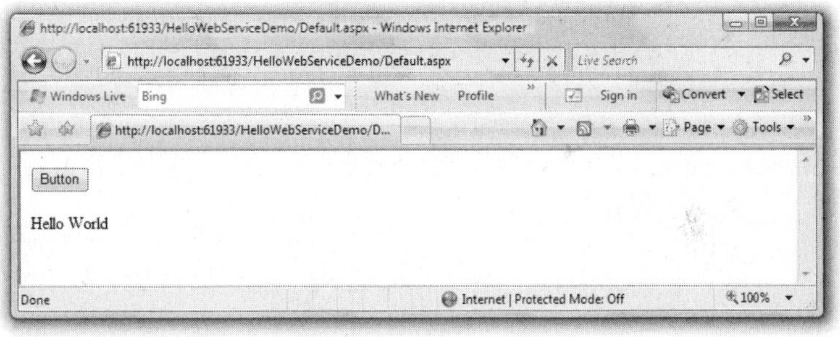

Developing a Stand-Alone Web Service

Web services are designed to run separately from their consuming applications. In this example, you will see how to build a slightly less-trivial example of an ASP.NET web service as a stand-alone application. You will then see how to consume the web service from a separate web application.

The example involves building a web service that performs two operations. It returns the current server time and also provides a tool for calculating a percentage. The web service is named MyWebService, and the two methods are named `ServerTime` and `Calculate Percentage`.

Later in this chapter, you will see how to create a simple AJAX implementation that enables the client to automatically and asynchronously update the displayed server time from the web service.

Building MyWebService

You will begin by creating the web service. Unlike the previous example, in which the web service and consuming application were built within the same project, this web service is a stand-alone project. Follow these steps:

1. Open Visual Studio 2010 and choose File ➤ New Web Site. From the New Web Site dialog box, choose ASP.NET Web Service.

2. In the Location text box of the New Web Service dialog box, keep the default path but change the name of the web service to **MyWebService**. Click the OK button to exit the dialog box.

3. The web service should now be opened to the `App_Code/Service.vb` page in the Visual Studio designer. Look through the default code and change the Namespace entry from `http://tempura.org/` to either a URL that you control or, for the purposes of this example, `http://mywebservice.org`. This will prevent the warning message about using the default Microsoft namespace from appearing when you run the web service. The line of code should now read as follows:

```
<WebService(Namespace:="http://mywebservice.org/")>
```

4. Move down to the `<WebMethod()>` section of the code skeleton. Delete the following default `HelloWorld()` public function:

```
Public Function HelloWorld() As String
    Return "Hello World"
End Function
```

5. Add the following code to the `<WebMethod()>` section. This method will return the current server time as the time of day in hours, minutes, and seconds:

```
<WebMethod()>
Public Function ServerTime() As String
    ServerTime = Left(Now.TimeOfDay().ToString(), 8)
End Function
```

6. Now, create the percentage calculator method (`CalculatePercentage`). Underneath the ServerTime method, add the following code:

```
<WebMethod()>
Public Function CalculatePercentage(
        ByVal myTotal As Integer, ByVal myValue As Integer) As Integer
    CalculatePercentage = CInt(myValue * 100 / myTotal)
End Function
```

This method calculates a percentage based on the *myValue* and *myTotal* parameters. The calculated percentage is returned as an integer.

This completes the code for the MyWebService web service. Listing 21.1 gives the full code for the web service as it should appear in `App_Code/Service.vb`.

LISTING 21.1:   Full code listing for MyWebService

```
Imports System.Web
Imports System.Web.Services
Imports System.Web.Services.Protocols


' To allow this Web Service to be called from script, using ASP.NET AJAX
' uncomment the following line.
' <System.Web.Script.Services.ScriptService()>
<WebService(Namespace:="http://mywebservice.org/")>
<WebServiceBinding(ConformsTo:=WsiProfiles.BasicProfile1_1)>
<Global.Microsoft.VisualBasic.CompilerServices.DesignerGenerated()>
Public Class Service
    Inherits System.Web.Services.WebService

    <WebMethod()>
    Public Function ServerTime() As String
        ServerTime = Left(Now.TimeOfDay().ToString(), 8)
    End Function

    <WebMethod()>
     Public Function CalculatePercentage(ByVal myTotal As Integer,
                        ByVal myValue As Integer) As Integer
        CalculatePercentage = CInt(myValue * 100 / myTotal)
    End Function

End Class
```

To make this the default start page, right-click `Service.asmx` in the Solution Explorer and choose Set As Start Page from the context menu.

Test the web service by clicking the green arrow on the Standard toolbar or by pressing F5. The web service should display links to the two web methods, as shown in Figure 21.7. Test the two web methods by clicking the links and then clicking the Invoke button on each of the respective service information pages. `ServerTime` should return the current time of day in 24-hour format (as an XML page). The service information page for `CalculatePercentage` should provide you with input boxes to enter values for *MyValue* and *MyTotal* before you invoke the service. Entering values such as 20 for *MyValue* and 50 for *MyTotal* should return a value of 40 (within an XML page) when you click Invoke.

Deploying MyWebService

In a production environment, you typically deploy the web service to Microsoft's Internet Information Services (IIS) web server. In order for the web service to run on IIS, you need to have .NET Framework 4.0 registered with IIS. You can also set up appropriate security and access privileges such as Windows authentication, secure socket encryption (HTTPS), and so forth on IIS. For further information on setting up and working with IIS, see *Microsoft IIS 7 Implementation and Administration* by John Paul Mueller (Sybex, 2007) which gives thorough coverage. You can also refer to Microsoft's community portal for IIS at www.iis.net.

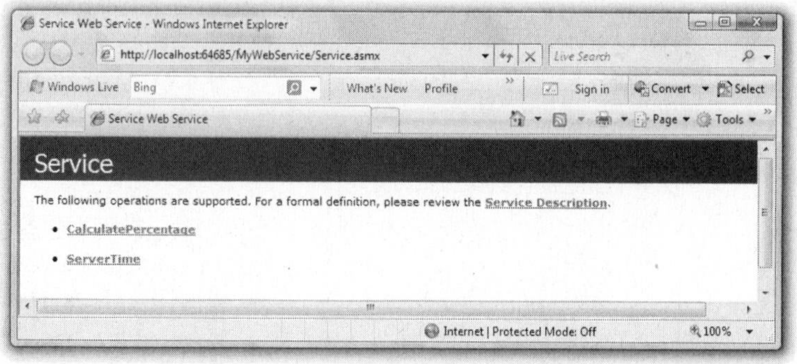

FIGURE 21.7
The running
MyWebService

Before you can deploy your web service, you must have all the relevant files and directories assembled into a suitable directory without the various development and debugging files. The easiest way to create a folder containing all the production files necessary for a deployment of your web service is to use the Publish Web Site option from the Build menu. This opens the Publish Web Site dialog box, where you can choose to publish to a specific location (including an FTP location) or keep the default location and move the folder later.

🌐 Real World Scenario

USING THE ASP.NET DEVELOPMENT SERVER

Visual Studio 2010 comes equipped with its own built-in web server for testing web applications: the ASP.NET Development Server. Although the ASP.NET Development Server is ideal for testing web applications as you develop them, it does have its limitations. One of those limitations is that you need to have a separate instance of the web server running for each web application running concurrently on your development machine.

Thus, to consume MyWebService from another application, you need to have opened MyWebService in Visual Studio 2010 and run the application to fire up the ASP.NET Development Server. You can close the web browser running the web service, but you must keep Visual Studio open to MyWebService. To create a separate project to consume MyWebService, you must open another instance of Visual Studio 2010 from the Start menu.

An advantage of using the ASP.NET Development Server is that you do not need to publish or physically deploy your application to a web server before you have tested it.

Consuming MyWebService

As discussed in the previous section, unless you are using IIS to test your web applications, you must have MyWebService open in Visual Studio 2010 and have run the web service at least once to open an instance of the ASP.NET Development Server so that you can link to the web service from another application.

Keep this instance of Visual Studio open and use the Start menu to open another instance of Visual Studio. Depending on the account restrictions on your machine, it may be necessary to open the second instance of Visual Studio in Administrator mode so you can connect to the web service.

After Visual Studio opens, complete the following steps:

1. Choose File ➤ New Web Site. In the New Web Site dialog box, choose ASP.NET Web Site. Name the site **MyConsumer** in the Location text box (keeping the rest of the default path). Click the OK button.

2. MyConsumer should open to `Default.aspx` in design mode. (If you last used the editor in a different mode, switch to design mode.) Drag a `TextBox` from the Standard toolbox onto the form. In the Properties window, set the `ID` property for the TextBox to **tbMyValue**.

3. From the Standard toolbox, drop a Label control on the form to the right of tbMyValue. Set the `Text` property of the Label control to **My Value**. Click to the right of the Label and press the Enter key to drop to the next line.

4. Drop a second `TextBox` control onto the form immediately under `tbMyValue`. Set the `ID` property for the second `TextBox` control to **tbMyTotal**.

5. Place a Label control immediately to the right of `tbMyTotal`. Set the `Text` property of the Label control to **My Total**. Click to the right of the Label control and press the Enter key twice to drop down two lines.

6. From the Standard toolbox, drop a Button control onto the form two lines below the tbMy-Total control. In the Properties window for the Button, set the `ID` property to **btnCalculate**. Set the `Text` property to **Calculate**. Press the Enter key to drop down one more line.

7. Immediately beneath btnCalculate, place a Label control and set its `ID` property to **lblPercentage**. Delete the default contents of the `Text` property for the control.

8. Place another Label control to the right of lblPercentage. Set the `ID` property to **lblPercentageLabel**. Set the `Text` property to = **Calculated Percentage** and set the `Visible` property to False. Click to the right of this control and use the Enter key to drop down two more lines.

9. Place a Label control two lines beneath lblPercentage. Set the `ID` property to **lblServerTime** and delete the default `Text` property entry.

10. Place a final Label control to the right of lblServerTime. Set the `Text` property to = **Server Time**.

Figure 21.8 illustrates how the final page should look with all the controls in place.

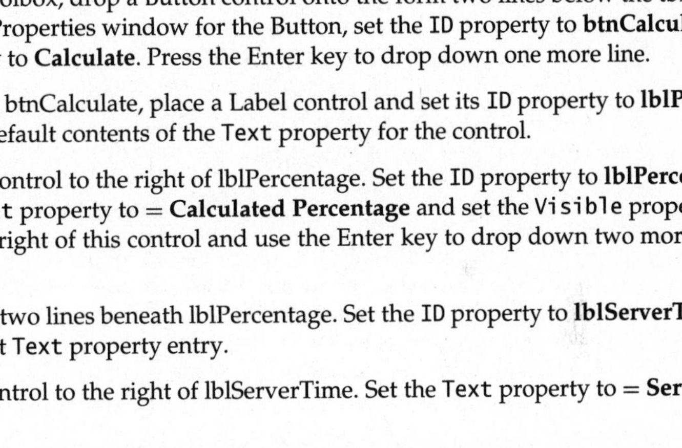

FIGURE 21.8
Layout for
`Default.aspx`

ADDING A WEB REFERENCE

Use a web reference created in the Solution Explorer to provide the connection to the web service. For web services within the local domain, you could also use the Service Reference option available in the Solution Explorer. Using a service reference is an advantage when you want to fully exploit the AJAX potential in connecting to a web service because a service reference allows you to call the web service methods by using JavaScript functions from within the consuming application. Using a client script to call web service methods is entirely asynchronous and prevents your page or portions of your page from being locked out from user interaction while waiting for the web service to respond.

For this example, you will add a web reference to the MyWebService web service created in the previous section. Unless you are using IIS to test your web applications, you must have an instance of the ASP.NET Development Server running the MyWebService web service. (Refer to the sidebar "Using the ASP.NET Development Server" earlier in this chapter for details.)

Complete the following steps:

1. In the Solution Explorer, right-click the project heading (and path) at the top of the Solution Explorer tree. From the context menu, choose Add Web Reference to open the Add Web Reference dialog box.

2. If you are using IIS and have appropriately placed discovery documents, you could use the Browse To: Web Services On The Local Machine option. You will also see a link that enables you to refer to any UDDI servers set up on your network. However, because this exercise uses the ASP.NET Development Server, you will need to switch to the instance of Visual Studio that is running MyWebService and open the web service in Internet Explorer. Copy the URL for the MyWebService web service from the address bar of Internet Explorer.

3. Switch back to your MyConsumer build and paste the URL of MyWebService into the URL text box of the Add Web Reference dialog box. The URL should be something like this:

```
http://localhost:49733/MyWebService/Service.asmx
```

If you are using the sample project to follow along, delete the existing web reference and add it again, using the port chosen by your ASP.NET Development Server. When you start the web service project, the URL of the service is displayed in the address bar of Internet Explorer. Copy the service's address from the address box onto the Add Reference dialog box and the client application (MyConsumer) will see the service as long as it's running on the same machine.

4. Click the Go button. This should now establish a connection to MyWebService, as shown in Figure 21.9. Click the Add Reference button to exit the dialog box. Solution Explorer should now feature an App_WebReferences folder with appropriate entries for MyWebService. Included in these are a discovery (DISCO) and a WSDL file that you can copy, edit, and employ in your deployment of MyWebService.

The DISCO document created by adding a web reference can be used to enable static discovery of your web service by placing it in a suitable location in your folder hierarchy for the site. If you examine the code in the automatically generated file, you can see how to add and remove XML entries. You can then add a link to the page from some point in your site. If you do not wish to set up static discovery files, you can enable dynamic discovery by editing the Machine.config file for your web server. Remember that dynamic discovery potentially allows users to browse your directory tree; unless your web server is suitably protected, dynamic discovery is not recommended for production servers.

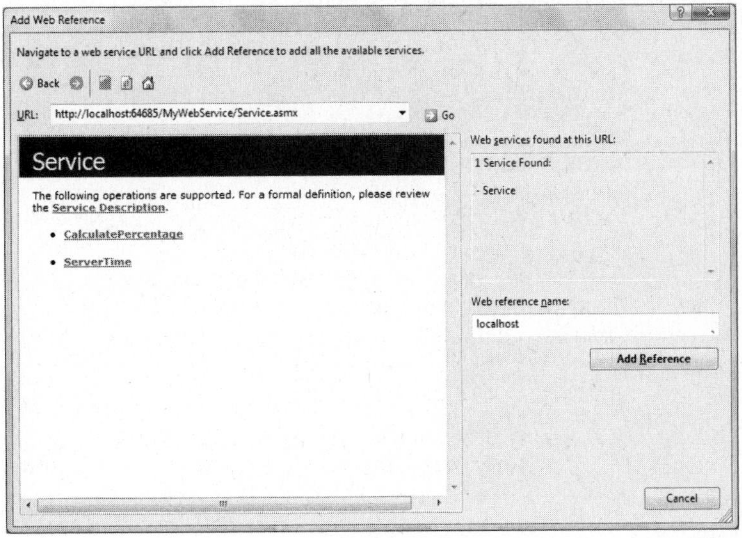

FIGURE 21.9
The Add Web Reference
dialog box

For precise details on enabling dynamic discovery, please refer to the relevant Help topics in Visual Studio 2010. Type **dynamic discovery** in the Search field.

ADDING THE CODE-BEHIND

The next step is to add the code to make the application work. From design mode, double-click the *btnCalculate* control to enter code-behind and complete the following steps:

1. Begin by declaring a local instance of the web service. At the top of the page, directly under the `Inherits System.Web.UI.Page` entry, add the following:

```
Dim MyWebService As New localhost.Service
```

2. Next is the code to call the `ServerTime` method. In the code skeleton for Form1_Load, add the following line of code:

```
lblServerTime.Text = MyWebService.ServerTime
```

3. Next is the code to collect the input values from the user and call the `CalculatePercentage` method. The code also attaches a percentage sign onto the displayed percentage value and unhides lblPercentageLabel. In the code skeleton for the `btnCalculate` `Click` event, add the following code snippet:

```
Dim myValue As Integer = CInt(tbMyValue.Text)
Dim myTotal As Integer = CInt(tbMyTotal.Text)
lblPercentageLabel.Visible = True
lblPercentage.Text = MyWebService.CalculatePercentage(myTotal, myValue) & "%"
```

The final code should appear as shown in Listing 21.2.

LISTING 21.2:   Full code listing for `Default.aspx.vb`

```
Partial Class _Default
    Inherits System.Web.UI.Page
    Dim MyWebService As New localhost.Service

    Protected Sub form1_Load(...) Handles form1.Load
        lblServerTime.Text = MyWebService.ServerTime
    End Sub

    Protected Sub btnCalculate_Click(...) Handles btnCalculate.Click
        Dim myValue As Integer = CInt(tbMyValue.Text)
        Dim myTotal As Integer = CInt(tbMyTotal.Text)

        lblPercentageLabel.Visible = True
        lblPercentage.Text =
                    MyWebService.CalculatePercentage(myTotal, myValue) & "%"
    End Sub
End Class
```

Setting up this part of the project is now complete. In Solution Explorer, right-click `Default`
`.aspx` and choose Set As Start Page. Run the application and test the methods.

Figure 21.10 illustrates the running application after 20 has been entered as MyValue and 56
has been entered as MyTotal.

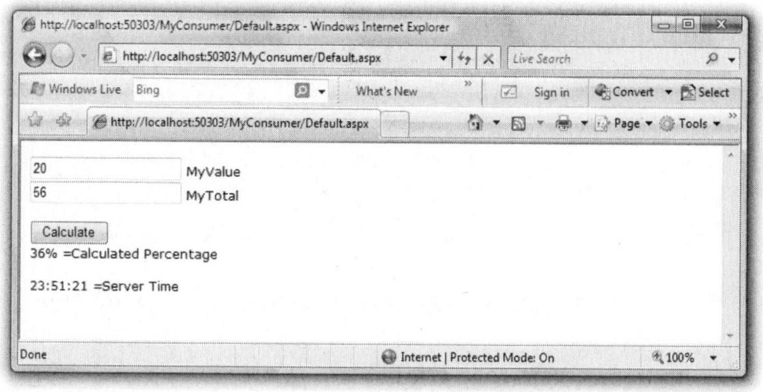

FIGURE 21.10
The running
MyConsumer application

Simple AJAX Implementation

ASP.NET 3.0 and 3.5 integrate AJAX to enable developers to easily perform partial updates
of web pages accessing ASP.NET web services. These updates not only do not require a full
refresh of the page, they also can be performed asynchronously so as not to interfere with other
operations on the page.

In this example, I will use a simple combination of the AJAX controls to enable the `Server Time` method from MyWebService to be continuously updated on a page in MyConsumer. A more sophisticated implementation enables the developer to access the methods in the web service from client script (JavaScript). This latter implementation is fully asynchronous, whereas our example will have some limitations that are explained later in this section.

Open MyWebService in Visual Studio and run the application to open an instance of the ASP.NET Development Server. Next, open a separate instance of Visual Studio 2010 from the Start menu and open the MyConsumer website. Complete the following steps:

1. From the Website menu, click Add New Item. From the Add New Item dialog box, select AJAX Web Form and rename it **myAjax.aspx**. Click the Add button.

2. When `myAjax.aspx` opens in design mode, you will see that it has a default ScriptManager control on the page. Do not delete this control because it is necessary for the AJAX functionality to work. From the AJAX Extensions toolbox, drop an UpdatePanel control onto your page underneath the ScriptManager control. The UpdatePanel control acts as an area that can be partially refreshed without involving an entire page refresh. Keep the default ID property of UpdatePanel1.

3. From the AJAX Extensions toolbox, drop a Timer control into UpdatePanel1. In the Properties window, set the `Interval` property to 1000 (1 second). When you place the Timer control inside the UpdatePanel control, UpdatePanel1 automatically responds to `Tick` events from the Timer. You can also set the UpdatePanel control to respond to events from external controls by using the `UpdatePanel Triggers` property.

4. From the Standard toolbox, drop a Label control into UpdatePanel1. Set the `ID` property to **lblServerTime** and delete the default entry in the `Text` property.

5. Double-click Timer1 to enter code-behind for the application. This should open `myAjax.aspx.vb`.

6. MyConsumer already has a web reference for MyWebService, so at the top of the page, directly under the `Inherits System.Web.UI.Page` entry, add the following:

```
Dim MyWebService As New localhost.Service
```

7. In the code skeleton for the `Timer1_Tick` event, add the following line of code:

```
lblServerTime.Text = MyWebService.ServerTime
```

This part of the application is now complete. Listing 21.3 gives the full code listing for `myAjax.aspx.vb`.

LISTING 21.3:   Full code listing for the `myAjax.aspx.vb` partial class myAjax

```
Inherits System.Web.UI.Page
Dim MyWebService As New localhost.Service
```

```
    Protected Sub Timer1_Tick(...) Handles Timer1.Tick
        lblServerTime.Text = MyWebService.ServerTime
    End Sub
End Class
```

Right-click the entry for `myAjax.aspx` in the Solution Explorer and choose Set As Start Page from the context menu. Click the green arrow or press F5 to run the application. The running page should display the current server time, which is automatically updated every second.

You can now add to the page further controls and functionality that are separate from the UpdatePanel control. These controls will not be affected by the partial page refreshes performed by the UpdatePanel control. The main limitation of this approach is that any other control placed inside the UpdatePanel (or any other UpdatePanel control on the page) will be locked out while waiting for MyWebService to complete its business (every second!).

You can test this behavior by adding a second UpdatePanel control to the page and dropping a TextBox control into it. Drop a second TextBox control onto the page, but not inside the UpdatePanel. Run the application and try typing into the TextBoxes. You will find that it is difficult to type text into the TextBox inside the UpdatePanel.

Building and Using WCF Services

Now that you have seen how to build a basic web service, we'll switch our attention to Windows Communication Foundation (WCF) services. WCF is a well-structured approach to building web services, and the process is straightforward, but there are a few rigid steps you have to follow.

A WCF service encompasses three basic principles, known as the ABC of WCF:

A **is for** *address*   Each service has an address (a URL) where it can be found. You can move the service to a different computer and all you have to do is change the configuration file of the client to see the same web service at its new host.

B **is for** *binding*   There are many protocols you can use to talk to the service, and the client must specify the binding to the service. The same service can talk to multiple clients using different bindings: some clients may use Basic HTTP, other might use Named Pipes (if the web services are running on the same machine as the service).

C **is for** *contract*   The contract describes the data types and messages that can be exchanged between the client and the server. The service tells the client its capabilities.

Visual Studio will configure these settings almost automatically for you; all you have to do is edit the service configuration file. The service is written once and it will support multiple bindings. Moving the service to another computer is also very simple because you can specify the new endpoint by editing the configuration file.

Building a WCF Service

To demonstrate the steps to build a WCF service, we'll build a simple service to manipulate products and categories. The service will maintain two lists, one with categories and another with products. Each product has a field that points to a row in the categories table. For the purpose of this sample application, we'll store our data in two List collections. If you want to modify the application to work with a database, you'll only have to change the implementation of the service's methods; instead of using the collections as its data source, the service will contact a database. In between sessions, you can persist the collections to an XML file, as discussed in Chapter 13, "XML in Modern Programming."

Start a fresh instance of Visual Studio and select File ➤ New ➤ New Project. Click WCF in the Installed Templates pane, and in the pane with the matching project types, select WCF Service Library. Name the new project **WCFProducts** and click OK to create the project. The new project that Visual Studio will create for you contains two files: the IService1.vb class, which is an interface that contains the signatures of the service methods, and the Service1.vb class, which contains the implementation of the methods. The methods are some extremely trivial sample methods and you can delete them right away.

The first step is the design of a class that represents the entities our service knows about. Obviously, we need a Product and a Category class and I have nested the Category class within the Product class. Both classes contain just a few properties to identify products and categories. Add the Product class to the WCF project and insert in it the code of Listing 21.4.

LISTING 21.4:   The Product.vb class

```vb
<DataContract()>
Public Class Product
    <DataMember()> Public ProductID As Integer
    <DataMember()> Public ProductName As String
    <DataMember()> Public ProductPrice As Decimal
    <DataMember()> Public ProductCategoryID As Integer

    Public Overrides Function ToString() As String
        Return ProductName & " (" & ProductID & ")"
    End Function

    <DataContract()> Public Class Category
        <DataMember()> Public CategoryID As Integer
        <DataMember()> Public CategoryName As String
        Public Overrides Function ToString() As String
            Return CategoryName & " (" & CategoryID.ToString & ")"
        End Function
    End Class
End Class
```

This is a very simple class that describes products and categories, if you ignore the decorations of the various members. The entire class is marked with the DataContract attribute, which tells the compiler that the following class contains the service's contract: the entities our service knows about. The clients of the service will communicate with our class by submitting objects from the Product and Product.Category classes, and the service will return data to the client application using instances of these two classes. The DataMember attribute tells the compiler that the corresponding property is a member of the contract and that it should be exposed to the clients. If you have properties that you want to use in your code but not expose to clients, just don't mark them with the DataMember attribute.

The next step is the definition of the methods that the clients will use to contact our service. The methods must be defined in an interface class, which contains the method definitions but not their actual implementation. This interface class contains the service's metadata — the information required by a client to figure out the service's capabilities. Add the IProduct class to the project and insert the statements shown in Listing 21.5 in it (the `IProduct.vb` file).

LISTING 21.5: Describing the Product class with an interface

```
Imports System.ServiceModel
<ServiceContract()>
      Public Interface IProduct
   <OperationContract()> Function
              GetAllCategories() As List(Of Product.Category)
   <OperationContract()> Function
              GetAllProducts() As List(Of Product)
   <OperationContract()> Function
              AddProduct(ByVal prod As Product) As Product
   <OperationContract()> Function
              RemoveProduct(ByVal ID As Integer) As Boolean
   <OperationContract()> Function
              GetCategoryProducts(ByVal ID As Integer)
                        As List(Of Product)
End Interface
```

This is another trivial class, except that it's marked with the `ServiceContract` attribute, which tells the compiler that the class contains the service's operations (as opposed to the service's data structure, which was defined in the Product class). The methods are also marked with the `OperationContract` attribute, which makes them available to clients. Without this attribute, the procedures would be internal methods and clients wouldn't be able to see them.

If the service exchanges simple data types with the client, this interface would be adequate. However, practical services are not limited to simple data types like integers and strings. They communicate with the client using business objects, which are based on custom classes. These objects represent customers, products, invoices, and the like. If you want to make use of custom objects, you must declare them in a separate class like the Product class shown earlier.

Finally, you must add yet another class to the project — this time a class that contains the actual code and implements the service. This is the ProductService class in the sample project, and its code is shown in Listing 21.6. The ProductService class implements the IProduct interface, taking into consideration the classes defined in the Product class.

LISTING 21.6: The implementation of the ProductService class

```
<ServiceBehavior()> Public Class ProductService :
                                 Implements IProduct
    Shared _products As New List(Of Product)
    Shared _categories As New List(Of Product.Category)
```

```vb
Public Function AddProduct(ByVal prod As Product) As Product
                Implements IProduct.AddProduct
' grab the next ID in _products list
    prod.ProductID =
                (From p In _products
                Select p.ProductID
                Order By ProductID Descending).
                        FirstOrDefault + 1
' If category field is not set to a valid category, ignore it
    If (From c In _categories
        Where c.CategoryID = prod.ProductCategoryID).Count = 0 Then
            prod.ProductCategoryID = Nothing
    End If
    products.Add(prod)
    Return prod
End Function

Public Function GetAllCategories() As
                System.Collections.Generic.List(
                Of Product.Category)
                Implements IProduct.GetAllCategories
    Return _categories
End Function

Public Function GetAllProducts() As
                System.Collections.Generic.List(Of Product)
                Implements IProduct.GetAllProducts
    Return _products
End Function

Public Function RemoveProduct(ByVal ID As Integer)
                As Boolean Implements IProduct.RemoveProduct
    products.Remove(_products.Find(Function(p) p.ProductID = ID))
End Function

Protected Overrides Sub Finalize()
    MyBase.Finalize()
End Sub

Public Function GetCategoryProduct(
                ByVal categoryID As Integer)
                As List(Of Product)
                Implements IProduct.GetCategoryProducts
    Return (From p In _products
            Where p.ProductCategoryID = categoryID).ToList
End Function

Public Sub New()
```

```
        _categories.Add(New Product.Category With
                {.CategoryID = 101, .CategoryName = "Electronics"})
        _categories.Add(New Product.Category With
                {.CategoryID = 102, .CategoryName = "Cameras"})
        _categories.Add(New Product.Category With
                {.CategoryID = 103, .CategoryName = "Software"})
    End Sub
End Class
```

The data are stored in the _products and _categories collections, which are private to the class, and no client can manipulate these collections directly. This is the essence of the service: It allows clients to view and manipulate the data through a well-defined interface, and the service itself is in charge of maintaining the integrity of the data. Since we don't have a database at the back end, we're also responsible for maintaining the IDs of the various entities. Every time a new product is added, the code retrieves the largest product ID from the _products collection, adds 1 to it, and forms the ID of the new product. The same is true for the IDs of the categories. Notice also that every time the service is initialized, it adds three rows to the _categories table. It goes without saying that you can change the implementation of the service so that it interacts directly with the Northwind database instead of custom collections. To do so, you will change the implementation of the ProductService class without having to touch the other two classes. As a consequence, client applications will continue using your service, but with the new implementation of the service, they will be seeing the data of the Northwind database.

The two collections must be declared with the Shared keyword so that all instances of the service will see the same data. Had we declared the two collections with a Dim statement, a new set of collections would be created for each instance of the class invoked by a client. In other words, every client application would see its own data source.

Your WCF service is ready to service clients. To test it, press F5 and you will see an icon in the lower-right corner of your screen informing you that the WcfSvcHost utility has started. This utility, which comes with Visual Studio, hosts the service and makes it available to clients at a specific IP address and port. Since WcfSvcHost is meant for testing purposes, only applications running on the same machine can connect to it. Once the service has been debugged, it can be deployed as an IIS application.

A few moments later you will see another window, the WCF Test Client utility, which allows you to test your new service without writing a client application. The first time you run the project you'll see an error message to the effect that the service doesn't expose any metadata. This happened because you haven't configured your application yet. Right-click the App.config file in the Solution Explorer, and from the shortcut menu, select Edit WCF Configuration. The Configuration Editor window appears, as shown in Figure 21.11.

CONFIGURING WCF SERVICES

A WCF service is defined by three parameters: an address where it can be reached (the endpoint), a binding protocol, and a contract. All three parameters are configurable, and you need not edit the service code to redeploy it or to support additional bindings. You only need to edit the configuration file.

The address is an IP address or URL that specifies where the service is located. It's the address of the machine on which the service is running and, consequently, the address to which clients must connect to make requests. The binding determines how the clients will talk to a service and WCF supports multiple bindings. The contract, finally, specifies what the service does; in other words, the methods it provides. The contract is the service interface, much like the classes and methods of a namespace. If you want to totally abstract a WCF service, think of it as a namespace that's being hosted on a remote computer. Just as you can call a method in a namespace, you can call a method of a WCF service. As you saw in the first example of this chapter, you can access a remote service from within your project by adding a reference to the service. With that reference in place, Visual Studio will take care of the housekeeping needed to connect to the remote service (what's also known as the plumbing).

FIGURE 21.11
The Configuration Editor's window allows you to configure the parameters of a WCF service.

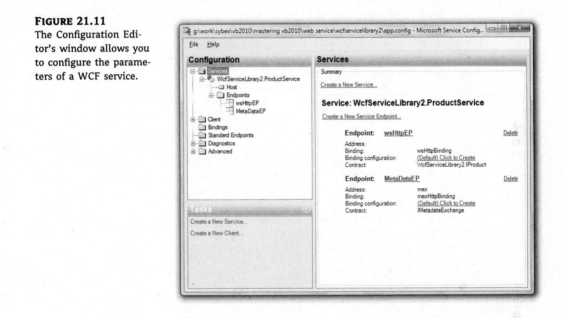

The binding tells the client how the messages will be transmitted between the client and the service. Web services use HTTP to exchange data with the clients. This, however, is not perfect for all cases. HTTP is a universal protocol, and it's been implemented on every operating system, but it's the most generic protocol. Windows, as well as other operating systems, support messaging: a mechanism for reliably transmitting information between two computers, even if one of them is offline. When the receiving computer is connected, the message will be delivered and processed. This mechanism, which relies on Microsoft's Message Queues, is the most reliable mechanism for exchanging data between two computers, but this type of communication isn't synchronous.

There are situations where the WCF service and its client are deployed on the same local area network. For these cases, there are protocols, such as Named Pipes, that perform much faster than HTTP. I can't discuss the merits of all available bindings in this chapter. This is an advanced topic, and the goal of this chapter is to introduce you to a technique for writing applications as services. The basic techniques are within the reach of the average VB developer, and I will limit the discussion to the basic techniques for building WCF services and deploying them on a web server. WCF allows you to build a service following the steps discussed so far and then configure them. The configuration involves the specification of the endpoint (the service's address) and the binding protocol. You can even implement multiple bindings on the same service so that different clients can contact the same service using different protocols.

To configure the sample WCF service, you must first change the name of the service. Although you changed the default name of the service, the configuration file still remembers the original name, Service1, which was the name of the sample class that was generated automatically and that we removed from the project. Click the WCFProducts.Service1 item in the left pane of the Configuration Editor, which was shown in Figure 21.11, and then select the Name property in the right pane. Click the button with the ellipsis next to the service's name and the Service Type Browser dialog box will open, as shown in Figure 21.12. This dialog box is similar to the Open dialog box, which allows you to select a file. Navigate to the project's Bin/Debug folder and select the WCFProducts.dll file. Click open, or double-click the file's name to see the names of all services implemented in the DLL. You will see a single service name, the `WCFProducts.ProductService` name. Select it and the close the dialog box by clicking the OK button.

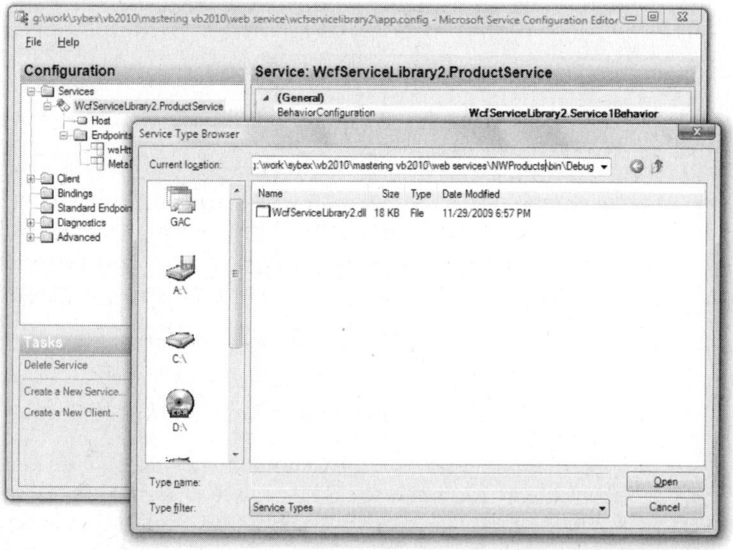

FIGURE 21.12
Configuring the name of
the WCF service

You will notice that the new service has two predefined endpoints. Click the first one and the endpoint's properties will be displayed on the editor's right pane. The first endpoint uses the wsHttpBinding binding and implements the contract WCFProducts.Service1 service. There's no Service1 service, so you must change the name of the service with the same process described earlier. Locate the project's DLL and set the endpoint's contract to `WCFProducts.IProduct` interface. While configuring the first endpoint, set its name to **HTTPBinding**.

Now select the second endpoint and you'll see that it implements the mexHttpBinding, as shown in Figure 21.13. This binding provides the service's metadata and you need not change its settings. Just set its name to **MEXBinding**, so that it won't be displayed as (Empty Name).

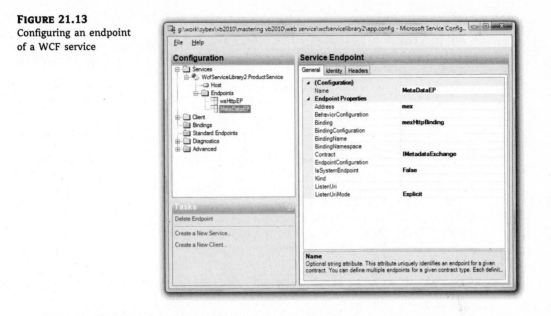

FIGURE 21.13
Configuring an endpoint of a WCF service

Save the configuration with the Save command from the File menu and close the Configuration Editor. Now you're ready to test the service. Press F5 again and this time the WCF Test Client window appears, as shown in Figure 21.14. The WCF Test Utility window consists of two panes: on the left pane you see all the methods of the service (you must expand the service's interface to see the names of the methods), and on the right pane you can call the selected method and see the results. To see the categories shown in Figure 21.14, for example, I double-clicked the GetAllCategories item in the left pane and then I clicked the Invoke button. The utility called the GetAllCategories method and displayed the results in the lower part of the pane.

You can use the WCF Test Client utility to test the methods of your new service, but eventually you must host your service to a web server, or an application, and call it from another Windows or web client.

You can also test the methods that submit data to the service. If you double-click the AddProduct method name, a new tab will open in the right pane, as shown in Figure 21.15, and you'll be prompted to enter values for the method parameters. Specify the parameter values (you don't have to provide a value for the *ProductID* parameter; this value is assigned automatically by the service) and then click the Invoke button. The utility will call the AddProduct method, and if executed successfully, it will display the new product in the lower half of the tab, as shown in the figure.

Note that the new product's ID is included in the result of the method because the method returns an object of the Product type that represents the newly inserted row.

Implementing a web or WCF service is no different from implementing a class that exposes certain functionality through a set of methods and communicates with another application by exchanging specific types. The only difference between a class you'd use in a Windows application and a service is that the members of the service are marked with special attributes. Moreover, when it comes to WCF services, you must also configure them with the Configuration Editor.

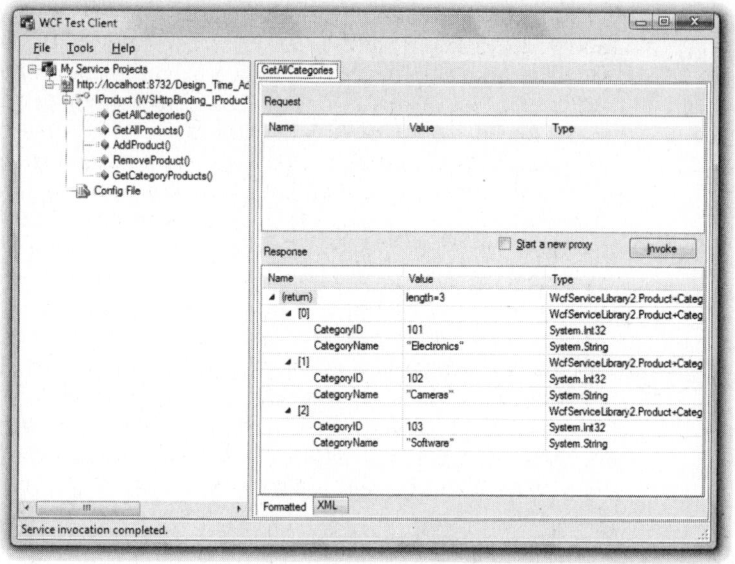

FIGURE 21.14
Testing the methods of
the new WCF service
in the WCF Test Client
utility

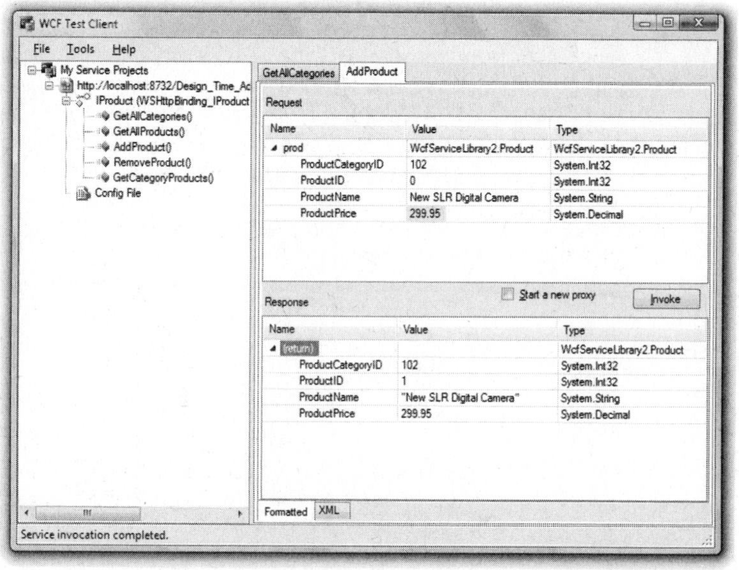

FIGURE 21.15
Submitting a new
product to the Product-
Service service through
the WCF Test Client

ADO.NET Data Services

Before ending this chapter, I'd like to show you briefly how to create services that expose an
entire database. This type of service comes as a special project component of Visual Studio, the
ADO.NET Data Services component. An ADO.NET Data service is a web service that exposes
an entire database, or part of it, as a web service. What's special about this component is that
it's generated automatically for you; all you have to do is specify the tables you want to expose

and a wizard will generate the service for you. The data source can be a database, an Entity Data Model (EDM), or a collection of custom objects. There's nothing new to learn and you can create and use data services immediately, with the exception of some techniques for securing your data. The data service will expose methods to both query and update the data source, but you obviously don't want to give access to your database to anyone on the Web.

Let's start the exploration of data services by building a new project, the DataService project; you can download it from this URL: www.sybex.com/go/masteringvb2010. Create a new project of the ASP.NET Web Site type, since your data will be exposed over HTTP. As you will see, you have no need for a website per se, just a web service that will expose the data of a specific database (or part of it). As soon as the project is created, delete the ASPX page that Visual Studio adds by default to any project of this type.

First, you must create a data source. For the purpose of this example, you'll expose data from the Northwind database, and to do so, you'll create an ADO.NET Entity Data Model by adding a new component of this type to the project. Keep the default name, which is *Model1.edmx*. When the wizard starts, select all of the tables in the database, as you learned in Chapter 19. For this example, I've included all 12 tables of the Northwind database. I just dropped them on the EDM design surface and Visual Studio generated the *Model1.edmx* data model.

Now that you have the data source, you can add an ADO.NET Data Service component to your project to expose the selected tables through a web service. Right-click the project name and select Add New Item. When the Add New Item dialog box opens, select the ADO.NET Data Service. Name the new service **NWWebDataService**. Visual Studio will create the NWWebDataService.svc file for you and will open the new data service's code window. You will see that the new class contains just a few lines of code:

```
Imports System.Data.Services
Imports System.Linq
Imports System.ServiceModel.Web

Public Class NWWebDataService
    ' TODO: replace [[class name]] with your data class name
    Inherits DataService(Of [[class name]])

    ' This method is called only once to initialize service-wide policies.
    Public Shared Sub InitializeService(
                ByVal config As IDataServiceConfiguration)
        ' TODO: set rules to indicate which entity sets
        ' and service operations are visible, updatable, etc.
        ' Examples:
        ' config.SetEntitySetAccessRule("MyEntityset", EntitySetRights.AllRead)
        ' config.SetServiceOperationAccessRule(
        '         "MyServiceOperation", ServiceOperationRights.All)
    End Sub
End Class
```

The NWWebDataService inherits from another class, whose name you must supply by replacing *class name* in the code line that reads: Inherits DataService(Of [[class name]]). The class it derives from should be NorthwindEntities, which is the name of the

Data Entity class you created as the project's data source. Technically, you didn't specify the NorthwindEntities name, but Visual Studio created this class and named it after the database.

The statements that are commented out specify the data you want to expose through your data service. By default, the data service won't expose any data unless you tell it to do so. Replace the last two statements of the InitializeService routine with the following:

```
config.SetEntitySetAccessRule("*", EntitySetRights.All)
```

This statement instructs the service to expose all resources. Obviously, this is the last thing you want to do with a real service that will be accessed from outside your test machine, and I'll come back to the issue of security, but for now let's grant unconditional access to all tables through your service. For the purpose of this chapter, the service will be hosted by the ASP.NET Development Server, which can be accessed from the same machine only.

You're probably thinking it's time to add some real code, or look at a few thousand lines of code generated by the wizard. This isn't the case; your data service is complete. Right-click the NWWebDataService component name, and from the context menu, select View In Browser. A few seconds later you will see a new Internet Explorer window displaying a list of all tables in the database, as shown in Figure 21.16.

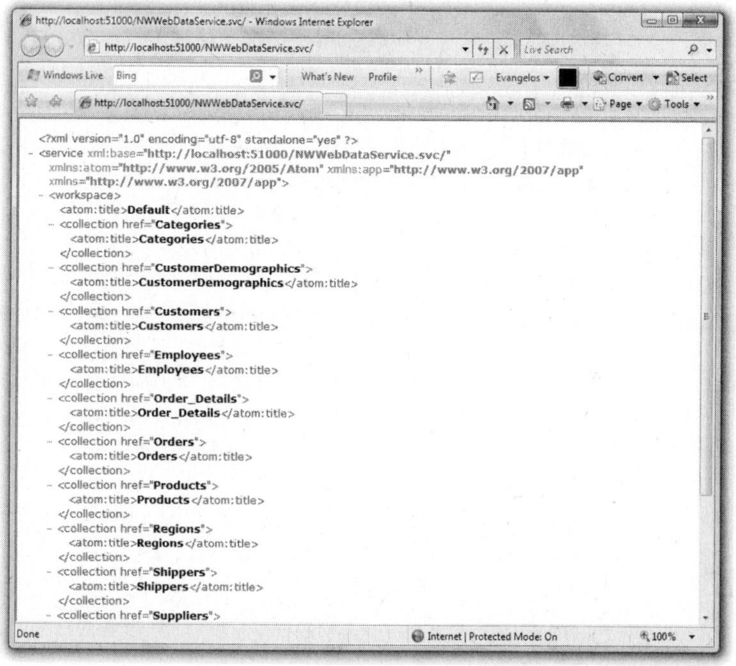

FIGURE 21.16
The service exposes the names of all tables in its data source.

Each table, which is an EntitySet in the data source, is exposed as a collection. By appending the entity name to the base URL of the service, you can view the rows in the corresponding tables. Change the URL in the browser address bar to any of the following to see the products, categories, and customers in the Northwind database:

```
http://localhost:51000/NWWebDataService.svc/Products
```

```
http://localhost:51000/NWWebDataService.svc/Categories
```

```
http://localhost:51000/NWWebDataService.svc/Customers
```

As you will recall from our discussion of the Entity Framework in Chapter 17, "Using the Entity Data Model," the Products table is translated into the *Products* EntitySet, which is made up of `Product` entities. The port will be different on your machine, but you will see it on your browser's address bar as soon as you open the service in the browser. This port number will be different every time you start the application, so it wouldn't be a bad idea to set a specific port for the service. Select the DataService project in the Solution Explorer, open the Project menu, and select DataService Properties. On the Project Properties window that opens, select the Web tab, which is shown in Figure 21.17. On this tab, you can set the start action (what happens when you start the project) as well as the server that will host your server. For now, select the Specific Port option and set its value to the number of an unused port (I've used the port number 51000). If you decide to make the service public, don't forget to limit the access to the service (you don't want people changing your data at will). You'll see shortly how you can restrict access to specific tables and even how to intercept certain operators, like insertions, modifications, and deletions, and determine whether to allow or block them from within your code.

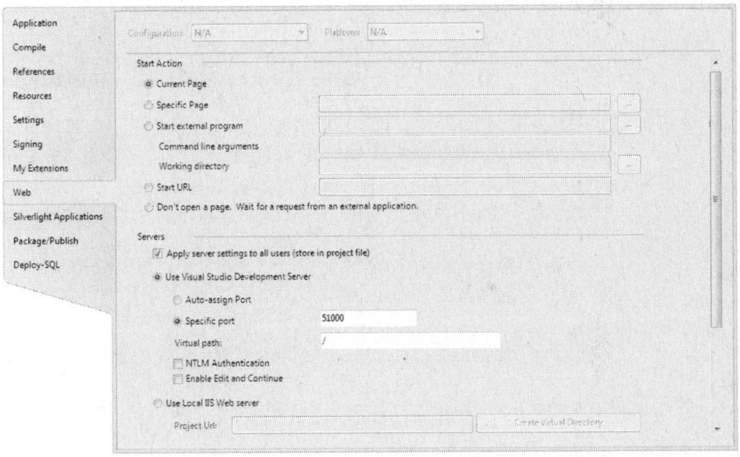

FIGURE 21.17
Configuring the server that will host the data service

Figure 21.18 shows how the first customer, the ubiquitous ALFKI customer, is displayed. The output of the service is just XML, and you can write a client application to access the service and process the selected rows with LINQ. Notice the links to the related tables. Each customer has two related tables with the following relative URLs:

Orders:

```
Customers('ALFKI')/Orders
```

CustomerDemographics:

```
Customers('ALFKI')/CustomerDemographics
```

To view the orders of the customer ALFKI, enter the following URL in your browser:

```
http://localhost:51000/NWWebDataService.svc/Customers('ALFKI')/Orders
```

To isolate a specific column, append it to the table's URL. The following URL will return the city of the ALFKI customer:

```
http://localhost:51000/NWWebDataService.svc/Customers('ALFKI')/City
```

The service will return it as an XML element:

```
<City xmlns="http://schemas.microsoft.com/ado/2007/08/dataservices">Berlin</City>
```

You can also request just the value (in this case, Berlin) by appending a dollar sign followed by the keyword value:

```
http://localhost:51000/NWWebDataService.svc/Customers('ALFKI')/City/$value
```

And you can navigate through related rows using this URL syntax. To view the IDs of the orders placed by the customer BLAUS, connect to the following URL:

```
http://localhost:51000/NWWebDataService.svc/Customers('BLAUS')/Orders
```

Here I used the URL that retrieves the customer and appended the name of the related tables (the Orders table). The URL so far returns the orders of the specified customer. You can select a specific order by its ID and request its detail lines. The following URL does exactly that (the URL should be entered as a single line; it's been broken here to fit the printed page):

```
http://localhost:51000/NWWebDataService.svc/Customers('BLAUS')/
Orders(10501)/Order_Details
```

The service will return the following XML document:

```
<?xml version="1.0" encoding="utf-8" standalone="yes" ?>
- <feed xml:base=http://localhost:51000/NWWebDataService.svc/
 xmlns:d=http://schemas.microsoft.com/ado/2007/08/dataservices
 xmlns:m=http://schemas.microsoft.com/ado/2007/08/dataservices/metadata
 xmlns="http://www.w3.org/2005/Atom">
  <title type="text">Order_Details</title>
  <id>http://localhost:51000/NWWebDataService.svc/Customers('BLAUS')
/Orders(10501)/Order_Details</id>
  <updated>2009-11-30T22:59:21Z</updated>
  <link rel="self" title="Order_Details" href="Order_Details" />
- <entry>
  <id>http://localhost:51000/NWWebDataService.svc/
Order_Details(OrderID=10501,ProductID=54)</id>
  <title type="text" />
  <updated>2009-11-30T22:59:21Z</updated>
- <author>
  <name />
  </author>
  <link rel="edit" title="Order_Detail"
 href="Order_Details(OrderID=10501,ProductID=54)" />
  <link rel="http://schemas.microsoft.com/ado/2007/08/
  dataservices/related/Order" type="application/atom+xml;
  type=entry" title="Order"
  href="Order_Details(OrderID=10501,ProductID=54)/Order" />
  <link rel=http://schemas.microsoft.com/ado/2007/08/dataservices/related/Product
 type="application/atom+xml;type=entry" title="Product"
 href="Order_Details(OrderID=10501,ProductID=54)/Product" />
  <category term="NorthwindModel.Order_Detail"
 scheme="http://schemas.microsoft.com/ado/2007/08/dataservices/scheme" />
- <content type="application/xml">
- <m:properties>
  <d:OrderID m:type="Edm.Int32">10501</d:OrderID>
  <d:ProductID m:type="Edm.Int32">54</d:ProductID>
  <d:UnitPrice m:type="Edm.Decimal">7.4500</d:UnitPrice>
  <d:Quantity m:type="Edm.Int16">20</d:Quantity>
  <d:Discount m:type="Edm.Single">0</d:Discount>
  </m:properties>
  </content>
  </entry>
  </feed>
```

If you examine it, you'll see that it includes two related entities: the `Order` entity (the order to which all detail lines belong) and the `Product` entity (the product listed in each detail line).

By default, the data service doesn't move the related rows from the database to the client. If you want to view the related data, you must use the `expand` keyword followed by the name(s) of the entities you wish to retrieve along with each product. The following URL will bring a single product, along with its category and supplier:

```
http://localhost:51000/WebDataService1.svc/
Products(12)?$expand=Category,%20Supplier
```

If you examine the XML returned by this query, you'll see that it has three `<link>` elements, which represent the related rows in other tables: the Order Details, Categories, and Suppliers tables. The links to the Categories and Suppliers tables have a plus symbol in front of them, and if you click it to expand the corresponding entity, you'll see the details of the product's category or supplier, as shown in Figure 21.19.

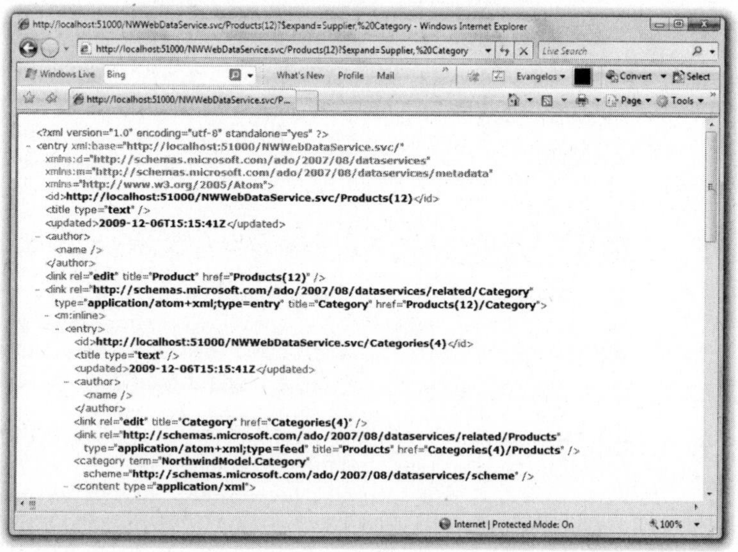

FIGURE 21.19
Retrieving related rows
with the $expand
option

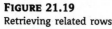

Likewise, the following statement will bring up an order along with its detail lines and a product for each detail line:

```
http://localhost:51000/WebDataService1.svc/Customers('BLAUS')/
Orders(10501)/Order_Details?$expand=Product
```

FILTERING

Querying your data through a URL may seem odd at first, but it's sure easy to understand the notation of querying through URLs. You can also filter the results returned by the query with the `filter` keyword, which must be followed by a filtering expression. The following statement will return all products with a price that exceeds $100:

```
http://localhost:51000/WebDataService1.svc/Products?$filter=UnitPrice gt 100
```

Note that the comparison operator is not the greater than sign (>) but the gt operator. The filtering expressions can get quite complicated because the URL syntax isn't flexible enough for expressing multiple criteria, joining tables together, and so on. The data service allows us to get the data we need with a simple HTTP request, but for many operations you'll have to download the desired data at the client and process them locally with LINQ.

The data service works very nicely, and it took us no time at all to write. You'll see shortly how to write client applications against this service and how to submit updates to the database as well. For now, keep in mind that an ADO.NET Data service exposes (or "surfaces") the data in a data source. We have used a Data Entity Model as our data source in this example, but you can use any data source such as LINQ to SQL, or even a collection of custom objects. No matter how you specify the data source, the data service will expose it through HTTP requests.

THE BASIC QUERY OPERATORS

For those of you who are interested in exploring the notation for URL querying further, Table 21.1 provides a quick overview of the various operators.

TABLE 21.1:   Basic query operators

TYPE	OPERATORS
Logic operators	eq (equals), ne (not equals) gt (greater than), gteq (greater than or equal to) lt (less than), lteq (less than or equal to) and, or, and not
Arithmetic operators	add (addition), sub (subtraction), mul (multiplication), div (division), mod (remainder) round (round decimal digits) floor (returns the largest integer that doesn't exceed a value) ceiling (returns the smallest integer that exceeds a value)
String operators	contains, endswith, startswith, length, indexof, insert, replace, substring, tolower, toupper, trim, concat
Date/time operators	Second, hour, minute, day, month, year
Type operators	Isof, cast

Here are a few simple examples of the operators you can use in your filtering expressions. (I'm only showing the part of the URL that follows the service's address, which is `http://localhost:51000/WebDataService1.svc/`)

```
Products?$filter=startswith(ProductName, Sir')
Orders?$filter=month(OrderDate) eq 2
Orders?$filter=endswith(ShipName,'markt')
```

ADO.NET Data Services allows you to expose (or surface) an entire database and build client applications that use the service as the data source. The database has already been exposed, and you can write code to exploit the data using the HttpWebRequest/HttpWeb Response objects, as you saw in the preceding chapter. The data are exposed through the simplest possible mechanism, namely through HTTP. But expressing conditions and statements to retrieve our data using the URL syntax is rather awkward. There are more structured tools, LINQ being one of them. Can you access the data exposed by your service with LINQ? The answer is Yes! And LINQ can translate the standard query operators into the equivalent URL syntax. This URL querying syntax is convenient for testing the service, but no one expects you to write applications using the query syntax (not in this day and age, at least). There are tools to use the same data as business objects from a client application, and this is what you're about to do next.

Building a Windows Client

In this section, I'll guide you through the process of building a Windows client that consumes the data of the data service. As you can guess, Microsoft didn't go to the trouble of developing ADO.NET Data Services so we would have to process the XML returned by the queries on our own. There are tools that simplify the process enormously, and you'll see them in this section.

The tool that will allow us to see the entities of the new Entity Data Model at the client is a command-line tool. This tool is the DataSvcUtil.exe utility, which reads the service's meta-data and creates a class that encapsulates the functionality of the service. Open a command prompt window and run the DataSvcUtil.exe utility, which resides in the folder Windows\ Microsoft.NET\Framework.NET\v.4.0.*xxx*, where *xxx* is the latest revision of the framework. This value as of this writing is 4.0.30138, but it will most likely be a little different by the time Visual Studio 2010 is released. Choose the most recent version of the Framework and switch to that folder. In this folder you'll find the DataSvcUtil.exe utility, which you must execute, passing as an argument the URL of the data service for which you want to generate a proxy (a proxy is a class that exposes the data model and the appropriate methods to access the service's data).

To generate the proxy, start the DataSvcUtil.exe utility with a statement similar to the following in the command prompt window:

```
DataSvcUtil.exe /out:"C:\Project\DataServices\NWProxy.vb"
 /uri:"http://localhost:51000/NWWebDataService.csv" /language:vb
```

This creates the proxy file in the root folder of one of my drives, so I can locate it easily later. Be sure to change the path to a folder that's easy for you to locate later because you will have to include this file with your solution.

Before you execute this command, however, you must start the service for the new port to take effect. Open the service in the browser as usual, and as soon as you see the list of tables exposed by the service, close the browser. The service will continue to run in Visual Studio and the browser is not required. The DataSvcUtil.exe utility will generate the file NWProxy.vb in the specified folder. Move this file to the folder that contains the Windows project you're building, and then add it to the same project with the Add ➤ Existing Item command. You could add the proxy to your current project without moving it, but then the project files will be scattered all over your drives.

To simplify matters, I've added a Windows project to the solution, and its main form is shown in Figure 21.20. This is the client application that will contact the data service to interact with the Northwind database. To see the newly created data model in action, you must add the auto-generated proxy file to the Windows project by copying the NWProxy.vb file into the folder of the Windows application. Then place a button on the main form of the test project, the Read Data From Service button, and create a variable to reference the proxy class with the following declaration in your code (just make sure to change the port to the appropriate value):

```
Dim service As New NorthwindModel.NorthwindEntities(
New Uri("http://localhost:51000/NWWebDataService.svc"))
```

FIGURE 21.20
Consuming an ADO.NET
Data service through a
Windows client

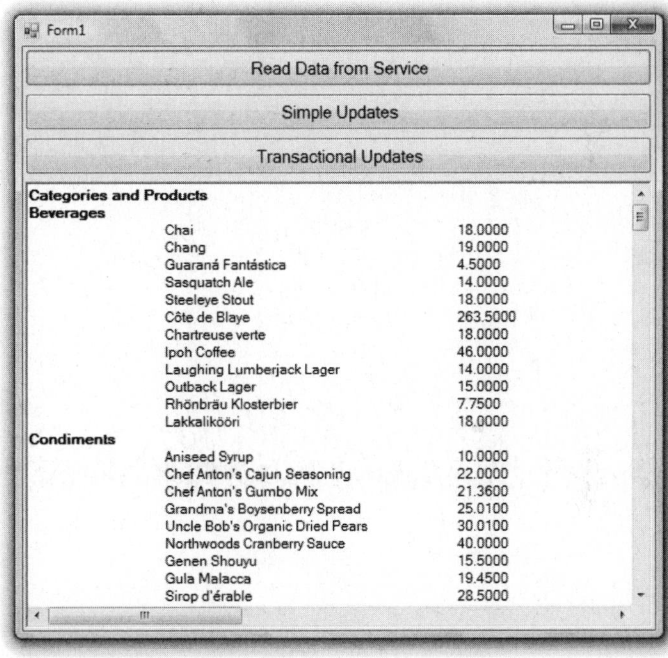

Now you're ready to access the tables in the Northwind database through the service. Your Windows application is a client that connects to the service through the URL of a web service. It has no direct access to the database, which means you don't have to open any ports to SQL Server on your database server and no credentials are stored at the client application. All it needs is a so-called HTTP stack (basically, any computer that can access the Internet can host the application). You can view the methods exposed by the NWProxy server (which are the same as the methods of the underlying service) by entering the name of the *service* variable and a period.

You probably recall that you granted access to all tables for all users. I'll come back to this topic shortly and show you how to limit the access to your service, but let's see how the proxy allows you to access the data. With the *service* variable in place, you can access the tables in the Northwind database as collections of typed objects.

To access a table, use a loop like the following, which iterates through the rows of the Customers table:

```
For Each p In service.Products
    Debug.WriteLine(p.ProductName)
Next
```

As you can see, the collections returned by the service are typed and so the *p* variable exposes the names of the columns of the Customers table as properties.

In a similar manner, you can iterate through the Categories table:

```
For Each c In categories
    Debug.WriteLine(c.CategoryName)
Next
```

If you want to access the products in each category, you must explicitly request these rows of the Products table as you iterate through the categories. The data service doesn't move all data to the client. To request the matching rows of a related table, use the LoadProperty method, which accepts two arguments: an entity name, which is a row of the current table, and the name of the related table. To iterate through the categories and their related products, write two nested loops like the following:

```
For Each c In categories
    Debug.WriteLine(c.CategoryName)
    service.LoadProperty(c, "Products")
    For Each p In c.Products
        Debug.WriteLine(p.ProductName & vbTab & p.UnitPrice.ToString)
    Next
Next
```

Since you're working with typed collections, you can use all LINQ operators to process your data. The following loop selects the customers from Germany and then the orders they have placed:

```
For Each c In service.Customers.Where(Function(cust) cust.Country = "Germany")
    service.LoadProperty(c, "Orders")
    Debug.WriteLine(c.CompanyName)
    For Each o In c.Orders
        Debug.WriteLine(vbTab & o.OrderID)
    Next
Next
```

To use the data service efficiently, you must execute the appropriate queries and retrieve only the relevant data and not entire tables or even related rows that aren't needed. Let's say you want to retrieve the orders from all customers in Germany that were placed in a specific year. Instead of using the LoadProperty method to move all related rows from the Orders table on the server to the client, you can use the CreateQuery method to pass a query to the server. You'll specify your query in LINQ, but the data service will translate it to the appropriate SQL query and execute it against the server. The following expression retrieves the rows of the Orders table as a DataServiceQuery object, which is a typed collection:

```
service.CreateQuery(Of NorthwindModel.Order)("Orders")
```

Then you can apply any filtering on this query to limit the number of rows with the Where operator:

```
Dim selOrders = service.CreateQuery(Of NorthwindModel.Order)("Orders").Where( _
                      Function(o) Year(o.OrderDate) = 1998 And
                                  o.Customer.CustomerID = c)
```

Let's say you need all customers in Italy ordered by their company name. To request this information from the database, you'd write a query like the following:

```
Dim ItalianCustomers = From c In service.Customers
                       Where c.Country = "Italy"
                       OrderBy c.CompanyName
                       Select c
```

The preceding LINQ expression was translated into the following URI query:

```
{http://localhost:51000/NWWebDataService.svc/
Customers()?$filter=Country eq 'Italy'&$orderby=CompanyName}
```

Your regular LINQ statements are being automatically translated into URIs that can be processed by the service. It looks like a new variation of LINQ, LINQ to URI, but I haven't seen this term being used in the documentation. Anyway, the LINQ component knows how to talk to ADO.NET Data Services, but not always with success because not all expressions you can use with LINQ have a counterpart in SQL. To retrieve the orders with a freight charge of more than $20, use the following trivial LINQ query:

```
Dim q = From o In service.Orders
              Where o.Freight > 20
              Select o
```

The preceding LINQ query is translated into the following URI by the service:

```
http://localhost:51000/NWWebDataService.svc/
Orders()?$filter=cast(Freight gt 10M,'Edm.Boolean')
```

In general, it's much simpler to write queries using LINQ than to try to construct the proper URL for any given query. The following LINQ query retrieves the products that contain the word *sauce* in their name, regardless of spelling:

```
Dim q = From p In service.Products
            Where p.ProductName.Contains("sauce")
            Select p
```

When this query is translated into a URI query, the service makes use of the `substringof` operator, as shown here:

```
{http://localhost:51000/NWWebDataService.svc/Products()?$
    filter=substringof('Sauce',ProductName)}
```

If you're wondering how I found the URI query for these LINQ queries, it's really simple. Place a breakpoint before the LINQ query you want to monitor, and when the program breaks, add a new watch on the variable that represents the result of the query (the *q* variable in most of this section's examples). As soon as the LINQ statement is executed, the SQL statement that will be executed against the database will appear in the Watches window.

Submitting Updates

Using an ADO.NET data service to explore the data in a database is a fairly straightforward approach. Surfacing your data with a data service is ideal for reporting and other applications that need not modify the database. Of course, the data service allows you to submit updates as well, although this isn't the best implemented feature of an ADO.NET data service — not yet, that is. My main objection to updating a database through a data service is that the methods that perform the updates do not return the error messages generated by the database. What you get back is a generic error telling you that "an error occurred while processing this request." Whether the error occurred because the data violated some constraint or whether it occurred because a field value was inappropriate for the corresponding column, the error message is the same. If you decide to use a data service to submit updates to the database, be prepared to validate the data as best as you can at the client, because the server won't help you determine the source of the update errors.

Since it's only a question of time before Microsoft brings ADO.NET Data Services up to par with the other data access technologies, let's look at the process of submitting updates to the database. Since the underlying data source is an Entity Data Model, the process of submitting data to the service is more or less familiar to you. To insert new rows, you create new entities at the client and submit them to the server with the service's `SaveChanges` method. To update existing rows, you just change the desired fields and then call the same method. To delete rows, you delete entities at the client and then call the `SaveChanges` method.

To create a new product, for example, you must first create a Product object:

```
Dim prod As New NorthwindModel.Product
```

And then set the object's properties with statements like the following:

```
prod.ProductName = "NEW PRODUCT NAME"
prod.UnitPrice = 11.2
prod.UnitsInStock = 1
prod.UnitsOnOrder = 12
```

Some of the properties are also entities, and they must be set to the appropriate entity. The product category is specified in the database with the `CategoryID` field, but the entity `Product` is related to the entity `Category`, so you must create a new `Category` entity and assign it to the `Category` property of the *prod* variable. The same is true for the product's supplier: You can set the `prod.SupplierID` field; you must set the `Supplier` property to an entity of the Supplier type. The following statements create the `Category` entity by reading a row from the `Categories` table and set up the `Category` property of the new product:

```
Dim cat = service.Categories.Where(Function(c) c.CategoryID = 4).First
prod.Category = cat
```

For the product supplier, I followed a different approach to better demonstrate the process of updating the Data service. This time I created a new `Supplier` entity, which provides only scalar properties, and then I set the new product's `Supplier` property to this value:

```
Dim supplier As New NorthwindModel.Supplier
supplier.CompanyName = "New Supplier"
supplier.ContactName = "Contact name"
supplier.ContactTitle = "Contact title"
supplier.Address = "Supplier address"
supplier.City = "City"
supplier.Country = "Country"
service.AddToSuppliers(supplier)
service.SetLink(prod, "Supplier", supplier)
```

Note that this time the new entity is added to the `Suppliers` entity set at the client with the `AddToSuppliers` method. The last statement associates the product with its supplier. This link does not exist at the client and must be added explicitly. Note that you don't have to specify the fields that take part in the relationship.

At this point you can submit the new product to the database by calling the `SaveChanges` method. The `SaveChanges` method doesn't accept any arguments; it submits all changes to the data service. Obviously, it will first submit the new supplier and then the new product. But this isn't something you have to worry about; the data service knows how to insert the rows in the correct order.

You may have noticed that the code didn't set the IDs of the two new rows. The IDs are assigned by the database and the client has no way of knowing the next available ID in the database. Other users may have inserted rows into any table and the client can't make any assumptions as to the next available ID. You could also use globally unique identifiers (GUIDs) as primary keys, which would allow you to generate the primary key values at the client, but for most databases in use today this isn't the case. Windows generates a long string that's unique every time you create one (as the term suggests, it's a globally unique identifier, not in your computer or your network).

After the `SaveChanges` method is called, the properties `prod.ProductID` and `supp.Supplier` ID will have the correct values, which will be transmitted to the client by the data service. This is why we had to explicitly add the appropriate links between the entities at the client with the `SetLink` method. As a reminder, this is necessary for new rows only. If the ID of the related row is known, as was the case with the `Category` entity, there's no need to call the `SetLink` method.

The Simple Updates button of the sample application contains the statements presented so far in this chapter. Open the project to see the code that implements the simple operations, like updates and deletions.

Performing Transactions

Real data-driven applications perform updates in a transactional manner. As you will recall from Chapter 15, "Programming with ADO.NET," an order has to be committed to the database in a transactional manner; the entire order must fail if a single row fails to be committed to the database. Data services allow you to perform multiple updates in the context of a transaction as long as all the updates that belong to the transaction are submitted with a single call to the SaveChanges method. In addition, you must set the SaveChangesDefaultOptions property of the entity set to *Batch*.

Let's consider the example of committing an order to the Northwind database, a rather familiar example in this book. You have seen how to perform transactions with ADO.NET as well as with data entities. To perform a transaction with a data service, you first create all the objects that take part in the transaction: the order's header and its detail lines. You should not call the SaveChanges method until all entities have been created at the client, as discussed in the preceding section. When the entire order has been set up at the client, you can submit it to the database by calling the SaveChanges method.

Let's review the actual code that submits a new order to the database. You can find the code discussed in this section in the Transactional Updates button of the DataServices project. As usual, start with a reference to the data service, the *service* variable:

```
Dim service As New NorthwindModel.NorthwindEntities(
                New Uri("http://localhost:51000/NWWebDataService.svc"))
```

Then, create a new Order object, the *newOrder* variable, and add it to the Orders table. The new row is appended to the Orders entity set at the client. Moreover, the new order has no ID yet. The *OrderID* value will be assigned by the database when the transaction is submitted to the database. Here are the statements that create the *newOrder* object:

```
Dim newOrder As New NorthwindModel.Order
service.AddToOrders(newOrder)
```

Now create a customer object that represents the customer that placed the order. In a real application, the user will most likely select the customer from a list, but since this application doesn't have an elaborate user interface, I retrieve a row from the *Customers* entity set at the client. You can't simply set the newOrder.CustomerID property, even though the *newOrder* variable exposes the CustomerID property. The *newOrder* object has a Customer property too, and there's a relationship between the Orders and Customers tables. To associate a customer with the new order, we must set the order's Customer property to a Customer object and then establish a relationship between the two. The following statement creates the Customer object that represents the Customer ANTON:

```
Dim cust = service.Customers.Where(Function(p) p.CustomerID = "ANTON").First()
```

Next, assign the *cust* object to the new order's Customer property and then create a link between the order and the customer:

```
newOrder.Customer = cust
service.SetLink(newOrder, "Customer", cust)
```

Follow similar steps to associate an employee with the order:

```
Dim emp = service.Employees.Where(Function(p) p.EmployeeID = 3).First
newOrder.Employee = emp
service.SetLink(newOrder, "Employee", emp)
```

And then you can set the remaining (scalar) properties of the order with simple statements like the following:

```
newOrder.OrderDate = Now
newOrder.ShipAddress = cust.Address
newOrder.ShipCity = cust.City
```

Now you can create the order details. Each detail is a variable of the Detail type, and each must be added to the Order_Details property of the *newOrder* object. The Order_Details property is a collection, and as such it provides an Add method. The following statement creates a new variable, the *dtl* variable, that represents an order detail:

```
Dim dtl As New NorthwindModel.Order_Detail
```

This variable must be added to the Order_Details entity set:

```
service.AddToOrder_Details(dtl)
```

You must also associate the new detail line with the new order:

```
dtl.Order = newOrder
```

Now you can set the properties of the detail line with statements like the following. Again, the product is selected from the Products table by its ID, while in a real application you'd probably allow the user to select it from a list or another lookup mechanism:

```
Dim dtlProd = service.Products.Where(Function(p) p.ProductID = 31).First
```

Set the Product property of the new order to the *dtlProduct* object:

```
dtl.Product = dtlProd
```

And create a link between the detail line and the corresponding row in the Products entity set:

```
service.SetLink(dtl, "Product", dtlProd)
```

Then, you can set the remaining properties of the detail line with simple statements like the following:

```
dtl.Product = dtlProd
dtl.UnitPrice = 11.2
dtl.Quantity = 9
```

And finally, associate the new detail line with the new order:

```
service.SetLink(dtl, "Order", newOrder)
```

Let's add a second detail line to the order with the following statements:

```
dtl = New NorthwindModel.Order_Detail
dtlProd = New NorthwindModel.Product
dtlProd = service.Products.Where(Function(p) p.ProductID = 56).First()
dtl.Order = newOrder
dtl.Product = dtlProd
dtl.UnitPrice = dtlProd.UnitPrice * 0.9
dtl.Discount = 0.1
dtl.Quantity = -5
service.AddToOrder_Details(dtl)
newOrder.Order_Details.Add(dtl)
service.SetLink(dtl, "Product", dtlProd)
service.SetLink(dtl, "Order", newOrder)
```

This time I've chosen to include a discount as well. Other than that, the process of creating a new detail line is the same. The new detail line is linked to a *Product* entity because it contains the ID of a product and to the *Order* entity to which is belongs.

At last, you can commit the new order to the data service by calling the SaveChanges method of the *service* variable. All the objects you have created at the client will be submitted to the database in the proper order by the data service. To ensure that all rows will be inserted in a transactional manner, you must also set the service.SaveChangesDefaultOptions property to the value shown in the code:

```
service.SaveChangesDefaultOptions = Services.Client.SaveChangesOptions.Batch
Try
service.SaveChanges()
Catch ex As Exception
        MsgBox("FAILED TO COMMIT NEW ORDER")
End Try
```

To see for yourself that the order is submitted in a transactional manner, set the price of the product of the first detail line to a negative value. The database will reject this value and the entire transaction will fail. The error that will be raised by the data service will have a very generic description, which won't help you locate the bug in your code. With a straight ADO transaction, you get back the error message generated by the database, which clearly states the value that the database couldn't accept.

Once the transaction has been committed, the data service will return the ID of the order as well as the IDs of all entities involved in the transaction. In this case, there's only one ID value to be set by the database.

Through the examples in this section, it's clear that a data service is quite trivial to build and very easy to use for selection queries. When it comes to updating the database, however, the data service doesn't provide all the mechanisms you've come to expect with other data access technologies. You must establish relationships between entities in your code and you can't rely on meaningful error descriptions to debug your code.

Securing Your Data Service

Exposing a database as a web service on the Internet is not the best idea. To secure the database from malicious users, you must set up some security measures. As you recall, the `SetEntitySetAccessRule` method sets the access rule for the various entities exposed by the service. So far, you allowed users to access all entities for all operations with the following statement:

```
config.SetEntitySetAccessRule("*", EntitySetRights.All)
```

The first argument is the name of an entity and the second argument is a member of the `EntitySetRight` enumeration: *None, All, AllRead, AllWrite, ReadMultiple, ReadSingle, WriteAppend, WriteDelete, WriteMerge, WriteReplace*. The names of most members are self-descriptive. The *ReadMultiple* and *ReadSingle* members determine whether users can read multiple rows or a single row of the corresponding entity set.

🌐 Real World Scenario

LIMITING DATA ACCESS

Whenever possible, you should limit the number of rows a client application can request because sloppy developers will retrieve an entire table to select a few rows at the client. The following method call enables clients to read all rows, insert new rows, and replace existing rows in the `Orders` entity set:

```
config.SetEntitySetAccessRule("Orders", EntitySetRights.AllRead Or
                EntitySetRights.WriteAppend Or EntitySetRights.WriteReplace)
```

Notice that multiple options are combined with the Or operator.

The `SetServiceOperationAccessRule` specifies the access rules for the various operations. The first argument is a method name and the second argument is a member of the `ServiceOperationRights` enumeration: *All, AllRead, None, OverrideSetEntityRights, ReadMultiple*, or *ReadSingle*.

The two methods are quite useful for specifying simple access rules but not nearly adequate enough for implementing more advanced security rules. Typical access rules, such as allowing users to view their own orders only, must be implemented with the appropriate procedures. These procedures are called *interceptors* because they intercept a query and alter the query's default behavior. To intercept a selection query, for example, use the *QueryInterceptor* attribute followed by the name of an entity set in parentheses:

```
<QueryInterceptor("Orders")>
Public Function OnQueryOrders() As Expression(Of Func(Of Orders, Boolean))
    ' statements
End Function
```

The OnQueryOrders function will be called every time a client selects one or more rows from the Orders table and it's implemented as a lambda expression that accepts as arguments a

> collection of the Orders entity set (the original result of the query) and a Boolean variable.
> The function's body should set the second argument to True or False for each member of
> the collection, depending on whether the member should be included in the result or not.
> Note that the interceptor applies to all queries to the specific table, whether they query the
> Orders entity set directly or they query the same set indirectly — for example, a query to the
> Customers table that expands the customer's orders.

The following interceptor for the Orders entity set eliminates all orders except for the ones
placed by the customer that makes the request. It assumes that the service is hosted as an IIS
application with authentication and the user has connected to the service with the same username as the company name, which is rarely the case. In a realistic scenario, the service would
look up the user's company name in a table and then use it to filter the results of the query:

```
<QueryInterceptor("Orders")>
Public Function OnQueryOrders() As Expression(Of Func(Of Orders, Boolean))
    Return Function(o) o.Customers.ContactName =
        HttpContext.Current.User.Identity.Name
End Function
```

You can implement interceptors for all types of queries, including insertion, modification,
and deletion queries. To define a change interceptor for the Products entity set in the Northwind data service project, open the Northwind.svc file and define a service operation method
named OnChangeProducts as follows:

```
<ChangeInterceptor("Products")>
Public Sub OnChangeProducts(ByVal product As Products,
                            ByVal operations As UpdateOperations)
```

The interceptor for operations that submit edits to the database includes an argument that
determines the update operation that fired the interceptor. You can determine the type of
operation from within the interceptor code and react differently to different operations. You
may reject a delete operation, for example, but accept insertions and updates. The method
that intercepts all modifications is the ChangeInterceptor, and it provides two arguments:
the row that's about to be modified and the operation. The operation is a member of the
UpdateOperations enumeration, whose members are *Add, Update, Change,* and *Delete*. What
makes this type of interceptor especially useful is that you can access the fields of the row
being modified and reject certain operations based on the value of the row's columns. This
information is passed to the method as a row of the corresponding table and it's the first
argument of the ChangeInterceptor interceptor.

The Products table of the Northwind database, for example, has a column that specifies
whether a product has been discontinued or not, the Discontinued column. It probably doesn't
make a lot of sense to create a new product that's already discontinued. This is a business decision, of course, but here's an interceptor for the Add operation that disallows the insertion of a
product that has its Discontinued column set to True:

```
<ChangeInterceptor("Products")> _
Public Sub OnChangeProducts(
```

```
            ByVal product As Products, ByVal operation As UpdateOperations)
    If operation = UpdateOperations.Add Then
        If product.Discontinued Then
            Throw New DataServiceException(
                        400, "Can't modify a discontinued product!")
        End If
    End If
End Sub
```

If this exception is raised, the service will return an error message with the specified description. If the same error were raised while testing the service from the browser, the error would have been a 400 error (the "page not found" error).

The Bottom Line

Create a simple ASP.NET web service.   Creating ASP.NET web services is straightforward with Visual Studio. ASP.NET web services provide a great method for delivering data and functionality within a distributed environment, including the Internet.

Master It   Develop an ASP.NET web service that enables the user to add two numbers.

Consume an ASP.NET web service.   Adding a web reference or service reference to a web service is a key element to creating an application that can consume the web service.

Master It   Create a new website and add a service reference to a web service on your machine.

Create a WCF service.   WCF services are similar to web services, but they give developers more options for deployment and they support more data exchange protocols.

Master It   Outline the steps involved in building a WCF service.

Work with ADO.NET Data Services.   ADO.NET Data Services is a project component that exposes, or surfaces, data as a service through HTTP. Data services are built automatically by Visual Studio based on any data source, and you can access them through URI requests.

Master It   How do you access the methods of an ADO.NET data service?

Appendix

The Bottom Line

Each of The Bottom Line sections in the chapters suggest exercises to deepen skills and understanding. Sometimes there is only one possible solution, but often you are encouraged to use your skills and creativity to create something that builds on what you know and lets you explore one of many possible solutions.

Chapter 1: Getting Started with Visual Basic 2010

Navigate the integrated development environment of Visual Studio.   To simplify the process of application development, Visual Studio provides an environment that's common to all languages, known as an integrated development environment (IDE). The purpose of the IDE is to enable the developer to do as much as possible with visual tools before writing code. The IDE provides tools for designing, executing, and debugging your applications. It's your second desktop, and you'll be spending most of your productive hours in this environment.

Master It   Describe the basic components of the Visual Studio IDE.

Solution   The basic components of the Visual Studio IDE are the Form Designer, where you design the form by dropping and arranging controls, and the code editor, where you write the code of the application. The controls you can place on the form to design the application's interface are contained in the Toolbox window. To set the properties of a control, you must select it on the form and locate the appropriate property in the Properties window.

Understand the basics of a Windows application.   A Windows application consists of a visual interface and code. The visual interface is what users see at runtime: a form with controls with which the user can interact — by entering strings, checking or clearing check boxes, clicking buttons, and so on. The visual interface of the application is designed with visual tools. The visual elements incorporate a lot of functionality, but you need to write some code to react to user actions.

Master It   Describe the process of building a simple Windows application.

Solution   First, you must design the form of the application by dropping controls from the Toolbox window onto the form. Size and align the controls on the form, and then set their properties in the Properties window. The controls include quite a bit of functionality right out of the box. A TextBox control with its `MultiLine` property set to True and its `ScrollBars` property set to *Vertical* is a complete, self-contained text editor.

After the visual interface has been designed, you can start coding the application. Windows applications follow an event-driven model: Code the events to which you want your application to react. The `Click` events of the various buttons are typical events to which an application reacts.

Then, there are events that are ignored by developers. The TextBox control, for example, fires some 60 events, but most applications don't react to more than one or two of them. Select the actions to which you want your application to react and program these events accordingly. When an event is fired, the appropriate event handler is automatically invoked.

Event handlers are subroutines that pass two arguments to the application: the *sender* argument, which is the control that fired the event, and the *e* argument which carries additional information about the event (information such as the mouse button that was pressed, the character typed by the user, and so on). To program a specific event for a control, double-click the control on the design surface and the editor window will come up with the default event for the control. You can select any other event for the same control to program in the Events combo box at the top of the editor's window.

Chapter 2: Handling Data

Declare and use variables.   Programs use variables to store information during their execution, and different types of information are stored in variables of different types. Dates, for example, are stored in variables of the Date type, while text is stored in variables of the String type. The various data types expose a lot of functionality that's specific to a data type; the methods provided by each data type are listed in the IntelliSense box.

Master It   How would you declare and initialize a few variables?

Solution   To declare multiple variables in a single statement, append each variable's name and type to the `Dim` statement.

```
Dim speed As Single, distance As Integer
```

Variables of the same type can be separated with commas, and you need not repeat the type of each variable:

```
Dim First, Last As String, BirthDate As Date
```

To initialize the variables, append the equals sign and the value as shown here:

```
Dim speed As Single = 75.5, distance As Integer = 14902
```

Master It   Explain briefly the Explicit, Strict, and Infer options.

Solution   These three options determine how Visual Basic handles variable types, and they can be turned on or off. The Explicit option requires that you declare all variables in your code before using them. When it's off, you can use a variable in your code without declaring it. The compiler will create a new variable of the Object type. The Strict option requires that you declare variables with a specific type. If the Strict option if off, you can declare variables without a type, with a statement like this:

```
Dim var1, var2
```

The last option, Infer, allows you to declare and initialize typed variables without specifying their type. The compiler infers the variable's type from the value assigned to it. The following declarations will create a String and a Date variable as long as the Infer option is on. Otherwise, they will create two object variables:

```
Dim D = #3/5/1008#, S="my name"
```

Use the native data types. The CLR recognized the following data types, which you can use in your code to declare variables: String, numeric data types (Integer, Double, and so on), Date, Char and Boolean types.

All other variables, or variables that are declared without a type, are Object variables and can store any data type or any object.

Master It How will the compiler treat the following statement?

```
Dim amount = 32
```

Solution The *amount* variable is not declared with a specific data type. With the default settings, the compiler will create a new Object variable and store the value 32 in it. If the Infer option is on, the compiler will create an Integer variable and store the value 32 in it. If you want to be able to store amounts with a fractional part in this variable, you must assign a floating-point value to the variable (such as 32.00) or append the R type character to the value (32R).

Create custom data types. Practical applications need to store and manipulate multiple data items, not just integers and strings. To maintain information about people, we need to store each person's name, date of birth, address, and so on. Products have a name, a description, a price, and other related items. To represent such entities in our code, we use structures, which hold many pieces of information about a specific entity together.

Master It Create a structure for storing products and populate it with data.

Solution Structures are declared with the Structure keyword and their fields with the Dim statement:

```
Structure Product
    Dim ProductCode As String
    Dim ProductName As String
    Dim Price As Decimal
    Dim Stock As Integer
End Structure
```

To represent a specific product, declare a variable of the Product type and set its fields, which are exposed as properties of the variable:

```
Dim P1 As Product
P1.ProductCode = "SR-0010"
P1.ProductName = "NTR TV-42"
P1.Price = 374.99
P1.Stock = 3
```

Use arrays. Arrays are structures for storing sets of data as opposed to single-valued variables.

Master It How would you declare an array for storing 12 names and another one for storing 100 names and Social Security numbers?

Solution The first array stores a set of single-valued data (names) and it has a single dimension. Since the indexing of the array's elements starts at 0, the last element's index for the first array is 11, and it must be declared as follows:

```
Dim Names(11) As String
```

The second array stores a set of pair values (names and SSNs), and it must be declared as a two-dimensional array:

```
Dim Persons(100,1) As String
```

If you'd rather avoid the index 0, you can declare the two arrays as follows:

```
Dim Names(1 To 11) As String
Dim Persons(1 To 100, 1 To 1) As String
```

Chapter 3: Visual Basic Programming Essentials

Use Visual Basic's flow-control statements. Visual Basic provides several statements for controlling the flow of control in a program: decision statements, which change the course of execution based on the outcome of a comparison, and loop statements, which repeat a number of statements while a condition is true or false.

Master It Explain briefly the decision statements of Visual Basic.

Solution The basic decision statement in VB is the If...End If statement, which executes the statements between the If and End If keywords if the condition specified in the If part is true. A variation of this statement is the If...Then...Else statement.

If the same expression must be compared to multiple values and the program should execute different statements depending on the outcome of the comparison, use the Select Case statement.

Write subroutines and functions. To manage large applications, break your code into small, manageable units. These units of code are the subroutines and functions. Subroutines perform actions and don't return any values. Functions, on the other hand, perform calculations and return values. Most of the language's built-in functionality is in the form of functions.

Master It   How will you create multiple overloaded forms of the same function?

Solution   Overloaded functions are variations on the same function with different arguments. All overloaded forms of a function have the same name, and they're prefixed with the Overloads keyword. Their lists of arguments, however, are different — either in the number of arguments or in the argument types.

Pass arguments to subroutines and functions.   Procedures and functions communicate with one another via arguments, which are listed in a pair of parentheses following the procedure's name. Each argument has a name and a type. When you call a procedure, you must supply values for each argument, and the types of the values should match the types listed in the procedure's definition.

Master It   Explain the difference between passing arguments by value and passing arguments by reference.

Solution   The first mechanism, which was the default mechanism with earlier versions of the language, passes a reference to the argument. Arguments passed by reference are prefixed by the keyword ByRef in the procedure's definition. The procedure has access to the original values of the arguments passed by reference and can modify them. The second mechanism passes to the procedure a copy of the original value. Arguments passed by value are prefixed with the keyword ByVal in the procedure's definition. The procedure may change the values of the arguments passed by value, but the changes won't affect the value of the original variable.

Chapter 4: GUI Design and Event-Driven Programming

Design graphical user interfaces.   A Windows application consists of a graphical user interface and code. The interface of the application is designed with visual tools and consists of controls that are common to all Windows applications. You drop controls from the Toolbox window onto the form, size and align the controls on the form, and finally set their properties through the Properties window. The controls include quite a bit of functionality right out of the box, and this functionality is readily available to your application without a single line of code.

Master It   Describe the process of aligning controls on a form.

Solution   To align controls on a form, you should select them in groups, according to their alignment. Controls can be aligned to the left, right, top, and bottom. After selecting a group of controls with a common alignment, apply the proper alignment with one of the commands of the Format ➢ Align menu. Before aligning multiple controls, you should adjust their spacing. Select the controls you want to space vertically or horizontally and adjust their spacing with one of the commands of the Format ➢ Horizontal Spacing and Format ➢ Vertical Spacing menus. You can also align controls visually, by moving them with the mouse. As you move a control around, a blue snap line appears every time the control is aligned with another one on the form.

Program events.   Windows applications follow an event-driven model: We code the events to which we want our application to respond. For example, an application reacts to Click events of the various buttons. You select the actions to which you want your application to react and program these events accordingly.

When an event is fired, the appropriate event handler is automatically invoked. Event handlers are subroutines that pass two arguments to the application: the *sender* argument (which is an object that represents the control that fired the event) and the *e* argument (which carries additional information about the event).

Master It How will you handle certain keystrokes regardless of the control that receives them?

Solution You can intercept all keystrokes at the form's level by setting the form's Key-Preview property to True. Then insert some code in the form's KeyPress event handler to examine the keystroke passed to the event handler and to process it. To detect the key presses in the KeyPress event handler, use an If statement like the following:

```
If e.KeyChar = "A" Then
'    process the A key
End If
```

Write robust applications with error handling. Numerous conditions can cause an application to crash, but a well-written application should be able to detect abnormal conditions and handle them gracefully. To begin with, *you should always validate your data* before you attempt to use them in your code. A well-known computer term is "garbage in, garbage out," which means you shouldn't perform any calculations on invalid data.

Master It How will you execute one or more statements in the context of a structured exception handler?

Solution A structured exception handler has the following syntax:

```
Try
'  {statements}
Catch ex As Exception
'  {statements to handle exception}
Finally
'  {clean-up statements}
End Try
```

The statements you want to execute must be inserted in the Try block of the statement. If the statements are executed successfully, program execution continues with the statements following the End Try statement. If an error occurs, the Catch block is activated, where you can display the appropriate message and take the proper actions. At the very least, you should save the user data and then terminate the application. In many cases, it's even possible to remedy the situation that caused the exception in the first place. No matter what the Try block execution outcome (error or no error) is, the Finally block is executed, making it a convenient location for release and cleanup of reserved resources.

Chapter 5: Basic Windows Controls

Use the TextBox control as a data-entry and text-editing tool. The TextBox control is the most common element of the Windows interface, short of the Button control, and it's used to display and edit text. You can use a TextBox control to prompt users for a single line of text (such as a product name) or a small document (a product's detailed description). You can actually implement a functional text editor by placing a TextBox control on a form and setting a few of its properties.

Master It   What are the most important properties of the TextBox control? Which ones would you set in the Properties windows at design time?

Solution   The first property you'll most likely change is the `MultiLine` property, whose default value is False. To set the initial text on the control, use the `Text` or `Lines` properties. The `Text` property returns or sets the text on the control. The `Lines` property is an array of string that holds each text line in a separate element. To interact with the user, use the text-selection properties `SelectedText`, `SelectionLength`, and `SelectionStart`. You can use these properties to retrieve and manipulate the text selected by the user on the control or to select text from within your code.

Master It   How would you implement a control that suggests lists of words matching the characters entered by the user?

Solution   Use the autocomplete properties `AutoCompleteMode`, `AutoCompleteSource`, and `AutoCompleteCustomSource`. The `AutoCompleteMode` property determines whether the control will suggest the possible strings, automatically complete the current word as you type, or do both. The `AutoCompleteSource` property specifies where the strings that will be displayed will come from and its value is a member of the `AutoCompleteSource` enumeration. If this property is set to `AutoCompleteSoure.CustomSource`, you must set up an AutoCompleteStringCollection collection with your custom strings and assign it to the `AutoCompleteCustomSource` property.

Use the ListBox, CheckedListBox, and ComboBox controls to present lists of items.   The ListBox control contains a list of items from which the user can select one or more, depending on the setting of the `SelectionMode` property.

Master It   How would you locate an item in a ListBox control?

Solution   To locate a string in a ListBox control, use the `FindString` and `FindString Exact` methods. The `FindString` method locates a string that partially matches the one you're searching for; `FindStringExact` finds an exact match. Both methods perform case-insensitive searches and return the index of the item they've located in the list.

We usually call the `FindStringExact` method and then examine its return value. If an exact match is found, we select the item with the index returned by the `FindExact` method. If an exact match is not found, in which case the method returns –1, we call the `FindString` method to locate the nearest match.

Use the ScrollBar and TrackBar controls to enable users to specify sizes and positions with the mouse.   The ScrollBar and TrackBar controls let the user specify a magnitude by scrolling a selector between its minimum and maximum values. The ScrollBar control uses some visual feedback to display the effects of scrolling on another entity, such as the current view in a long document.

Master It   Which event of the ScrollBar control would you code to provide visual feedback to the user?

Solution   The ScrollBar control fires two events: the `Scroll` event and the `ValueChanged` event. They're very similar and you can program either event to react to the changes in the

ScrollBar control. The advantage of the `Scroll` event is that it reports the action that caused it through the `e.Type` property. You can examine the value of this property in your code and react to actions like the end of the scroll:

```
Private Sub blueBar_Scroll(
ByVal sender As System.Object,
ByVal e As System.Windows.Forms.ScrollEventArgs)
Handles blueBar.Scroll
    If e.Type = ScrollEventType.EndScroll Then
    ' perform calculations and provide feedback
    End If
End Sub
```

Chapter 6: Working with Forms

Visual form design   Forms expose a lot of trivial properties for setting their appearance. In addition, they expose a few properties that simplify the task of designing forms that can be resized at runtime. The `Anchor` property causes a control to be anchored to one or more edges of the form to which it belongs. The `Dock` property allows you to place on the form controls that are docked to one of its edges. To create forms with multiple panes that the user can resize at runtime, use the SplitContainer control. If you just can't fit all the controls in a reasonably sized form, use the `AutoScroll` properties to create a scrollable form.

Master It   You've been asked to design a form with three distinct sections. You should also allow users to resize each section. How will you design this form?

Solution   The type of form required is easily designed with visual tools and the help of the SplitContainer control. Place a SplitContainer control on the form and set its `Dock` property to *Fill*. You've just created two vertical panes on the form, and users can change their relative sizes at any time. To create a third pane, place another SplitContainer control on one of the first control's panes and set its `Dock` property to *Fill* and its `Orientation` property to *Horizontal*. At this point, the form is covered by three panes and users can change each pane's size at the expense of its neighboring panes.

Design applications with multiple forms.   Typical applications are made up of multiple forms: the main form and one or more auxiliary forms. To show an auxiliary form from within the main form's code, call the auxiliary form's `Show` method, or the ShowDialog method if you want to display the auxiliary form modally (as a dialog box).

Master It   How will you set the values of selected controls in a dialog box, display them, and then read the values selected by the user from the dialog box?

Solution   Create a Form variable that represents the dialog box and then access any control on the dialog box through its name as usual, prefixed by the form's name:

```
Dim Dlg As AuxForm
Dlg.txtName = "name"
```

Then call the form's `ShowDialog` method to display it modally and examine the `Dialog-Result` property returned by the method. If this value is OK, process the data on the dialog box; if it isn't, do not process the dialog box:

```
If Dlg.ShowDialog = DialogResult.OK Then
    UserName = Dlg.TxtName
End If
```

To display an auxiliary form, just call the `Show` method. This method doesn't return a value, and you can read the auxiliary form's contents from within the main form's code at any time. You can also access the controls of the main form from within the auxiliary form's code.

Design dynamic forms.   You can create dynamic forms by populating them with controls at runtime through the form's `Controls` collection. First, create instances of the appropriate controls by declaring variables of the corresponding type. Then set the properties of each of these variables that represent controls. Finally, place the control on the form by adding the corresponding variable to the form's `Controls` collection.

Master It   How will you add a TextBox control to your form at runtime and assign a handler to the control's `TextChanged` event?

Solution   Create an instance of the TextBox control, set its `Visible` property and then add it to the form's `Controls` collection:

```
Dim TB As New TextBox
TB.Visible = True
' statements to set other properties,
' including the control's location on the form
Me.Controls.Add(TB)
```

Then write a subroutine that will handle the `TextChanged` event. This subroutine, let's call it `TBChanged()`, should have the same signature as the TextBox control's `TextChanged` event. Use the `AddHandler` statement to associate the `TBChanged()` subroutine with the new control's `TextChanged` event:

```
AddHandler TB.TextChanged, _
    New SystemEventHandler(AddressOf TBChanged)
```

Design menus.   Both form menus and context menus are implemented through the Menu-Strip control. The items that make up the menu are ToolStripMenuItem objects. The ToolStrip-MenuItem objects give you absolute control over the structure and appearance of the menus of your application.

Master It   What are the two basic events fired by the ToolStripMenuItem object?

Solution   When the user clicks a menu item, the `DropDownOpened` and `Click` events are fired in this order. The `DropDownOpened` event gives you a chance to modify the menu that's about to be opened. After the execution of the `DropDownOpened` event handler, the `Click` event takes place to indicate the selection of a menu command. We rarely program the

DropDownOpened event, but every menu item's Click event handler should contain some code to react to the selection of the item.

Chapter 7: More Windows Controls

Use the OpenFileDialog and SaveFileDialog controls to prompt users for filenames. Windows applications use certain controls to prompt users for common information, such as filenames, colors, and fonts. Visual Studio provides a set of controls that are grouped in the Dialogs section of the Toolbox. All common dialog controls provide a ShowDialog method, which displays the corresponding dialog box in a modal way. The ShowDialog method returns a value of the DialogResult type, which indicates how the dialog box was closed, and you should examine this value before processing the data.

Master It Your application needs to open an existing file. How will you prompt users for the file's name?

Solution First you must drop an instance of the OpenFileDialog control on the form. To limit the files displayed in the Open dialog box, use the Filter property to specify the relevant file type(s). To display text files only, set the Filter property to Text files|*.txt. If you want to display multiple filename extensions, use a semicolon to separate extensions with the Filter property; for example, the string Images|*.BMP;*.GIF;*.JPG will cause the control to select all the files of these three types and no others. The first part of the expression (Images) is the string that will appear in the drop-down list with the file types. You should also set the CheckFileExists property to True to make sure the file specified on the control exists. Then display the Open dialog box by calling its ShowDialog method, as shown here:

```
If FileOpenDialog1.ShowDialog =
      Windows.Forms.DialogResult.OK
         {process file FileOpenDialog1.FileName}
End If
```

To retrieve the selected file, use the control's FileName property, which is a string with the selected file's path.

Master It You're developing an application that encrypts multiple files (or resizes many images) in batch mode. How will you prompt the user for the files to be processed?

Solution There are two techniques to prompt users for multiple filenames. Both techniques, however, are limited in the sense that all files must reside in the same folder. The first technique is to set the MultiSelect property of the OpenFileDialog control to True. Users will be able to select multiple files by using the Ctrl and Shift keys. The selected files will be reported to your application through the FileNames property of the control, which is an array of strings.

```
OpenFileDialog1.Multiselect = True
OpenFileDialog1.ShowDialog()
Dim filesEnum As IEnumerator
ListBox1.Items.Clear()
filesEnum =
```

```
        OpenFileDialog1.FileNames.GetEnumerator()
While filesEnum.MoveNext
    ' current file's name is filesEnum.Current
End While
```

The other technique is to use the FolderBrowserDialog control, which prompts users to select a folder, not individual files. Upon return, the control's `SelectedPath` property contains the pathname of the folder selected by the user from the dialog box, and you can use this property to process all files of a specific type in the selected folder.

Use the ColorDialog and FontDialog controls to prompt users for colors and typefaces.   The Color and Font dialog boxes allow you to prompt users for a color value and a font, respectively. Before showing the corresponding dialog box, set its `Color` or `Font` property according to the current selection, and then call the control's `ShowDialog` method.

Master It   How will you display color attributes in the Color dialog box when you open it? How will you display the attributes of the selected text's font in the Font dialog box when you open it?

Solution   To prompt users to specify a different color for the text on a TextBox control, execute the following statements:

```
ColorDialog1.Color = TextBox1.ForeColor
If ColorDialog1.ShowDialog = DialogResult.OK Then
    TextBox1.ForeColor = ColorDialog1.Color
End If
```

To populate the Font dialog box with the font in effect, assign the TextBox control's `Font` property to the FontDialog control's `Font` property by using the following statements:

```
FontDialog1.Font = TextBox1.Font
If FontDialog1.ShowDialog = DialogResult.OK Then
    TextBox1.Font = FontDialog1.Font
End If
```

Use the RichTextBox control as an advanced text editor to present richly formatted text. The RichTextBox control is an enhanced TextBox control that can display multiple fonts and styles, format paragraphs with different styles, and provide a few more-advanced text-editing features. Even if you don't need the formatting features of this control, you can use it as an alternative to the TextBox control. At the very least, the RichTextBox control provides more editing features, a more-useful undo function, and more-flexible search features.

Master It   You want to display a document with a title in large, bold type, followed by a couple of items in regular style. Which statements will you use to create a document like this on a RichTextBox control?

Document's Title

Item 1   Description for item 1

Item 2   Description for item 2

Solution   To append text to a RichTextBox control, use the `AppendText` method. This method accepts a string as an argument and appends it to the control's contents. The text is formatted according to the current selection's font, which you must set accordingly through the `SelectionFont` property. To switch to a different font, set the `SelectionFont` property again and call the `AppendText` method.

Assuming that the form contains a control named RichTextBox1, the following statements will create a document with multiple formats. In this sample, I'm using three different typefaces for the document.

```
Dim fntTitle As
        New Font("Verdana", 12, FontStyle.Bold)
Dim fntItem As
        New Font("Verdana", 10, FontStyle.Bold)
Dim fntText As
        New Font("Verdana", 9, FontStyle.Regular)
Editor.SelectionFont = fntTitle
Editor.AppendText("Document's Title" & vbCrLf)
Editor.SelectionFont = fntItem
Editor.SelectionIndent = 20
Editor.AppendText("Item 1" & vbCrLf)
Editor.SelectionFont = fntText
Editor.SelectionIndent = 40
Editor.AppendText(
            "Description for item 1" & vbCrLf)
Editor.SelectionFont = fntItem
Editor.SelectionIndent = 20
Editor.AppendText("Item 2" & vbCrLf)
Editor.SelectionFont = fntText
Editor.SelectionIndent = 40
Editor.AppendText(
            "Description for item 2" & vbCrLf)
```

Create and present hierarchical lists by using the TreeView control. The TreeView control is used to display a list of hierarchically structured items. Each item in the TreeView control is represented by a TreeNode object. To access the nodes of the TreeView control, use the `TreeView.Nodes` collection. The nodes under a specific node (in other words, the child nodes) form another collection of Node objects, which you can access by using the expression `TreeView.Nodes(i).Nodes`. The basic property of the Node object is the `Text` property, which stores the node's caption. The Node object exposes properties for manipulating its appearance (its foreground/background color, its font, and so on).

Master It   How will you set up a TreeView control with a book's contents at design time?

Solution   Place an instance of the TreeView control on the form and then locate its **Nodes** property in the Properties window. Click the ellipsis button to open the TreeNode Editor dialog box, where you can enter root nodes by clicking the Add Root button and child nodes under the currently selected node by clicking the Add Child button. The book's chapters should be the control's root nodes, and the sections should be child nodes of those chapter nodes. If you have nested sections, add them as child nodes of the appropriate node. While a node is selected in the left pane of the dialog box, you can specify its appearance in the right pane by setting the font, color, and image-related properties.

Create and present lists of structured items by using the ListView control. The ListView control stores a collection of ListViewItem objects, which forms the Items collection, and can display them in several modes, as specified by the View property. Each ListViewItem object has a Text property and the SubItems collection. The subitems are not visible at runtime unless you set the control's View property to Details and set up the control's Columns collection. There must be a column for each subitem you want to display on the control.

Master It How will you set up a ListView control with three columns to display names, email addresses, and phone numbers at design time?

Solution Drop an instance of the ListView control on the form and set its View property to *Details*. Then locate the control's Columns property in the Properties window and add three columns to the collection through the ColumnHeader Collection Editor dialog box. Don't forget to set their headers and their widths for the fields they will display.

To populate the control at design time, locate its Items property in the Properties window and click the ellipsis button to open the ListViewItem Collection Editor dialog box. Add a new item by clicking the Add button. When the new item is added to the list in the left pane of the dialog box, set its Text property to the desired caption. To add subitems to this item, locate the SubItems property in the ListViewItem Collection Editor dialog box and click the ellipsis button next to its value. This will open another dialog box, the ListViewSubItems Collection Editor dialog box, where you can add as many subitems under the current item as you wish. You can also set the appearance of the subitems (their font and color) in the same dialog box.

Master It How would you populate the same control with the same data at runtime?

Solution The following code segment adds two items to the ListView1 control at runtime:

```
Dim LItem As New ListViewItem()
LItem.Text = "Alfred's Futterkiste"
LItem.SubItems.Add("Anders Maria")
LItem.SubItems.Add("030-0074321")
LItem.SubItems.Add("030-0076545")
LItem.ImageIndex = 0
ListView1.Items.Add(LItem)

LItem = New ListViewItem()
LItem.Text = "Around the Horn"
LItem.SubItems.Add("Hardy Thomas")
LItem.SubItems.Add(" (171) 555-7788")
LItem.SubItems.Add("171) 555-6750")
LItem.ImageIndex = 0
ListView1.Items.Add(LItem)
```

Chapter 8: Working with Projects

Build your own classes. Classes contain code that executes without interacting with the user. The class's code is made up of three distinct segments: the declaration of the private variables, the property procedures that set or read the values of the private variables, and the methods, which are implemented as public subroutines or functions. Only the public entities (properties and methods) are accessible by any code outside the class. Optionally, you can implement events that are fired from within the class's code. Classes are referenced through variables of the appropriate type, and applications call the members of the class through these variables. Every time a method is called, or a property is set or read, the corresponding code in the class is executed.

Master It How do you implement properties and methods in a custom class?

Solution Any variable declared with the Public access modifier is automatically a property. As a class developer, however, you should be able to validate any values assigned to your class's properties. To do so, you can implement properties with a special type of procedure, the property procedure, which has two distinct segments: a Set segment that's invoked when an application attempts to set a property and the Get segment, invoked when an application attempts to read a property's value. The property has the following structure:

```
Private m_property As type
Property Property() As type
   Get
       Property = m_property
   End Get
   Set (ByVal value As type)
   ' your validation code goes here
   ' If validation succeeds, set the local var
     m_property = value
   End Set
End Property
```

The local variable *m_property* must be declared with the same type as the property. The Get segment returns the value of the local variable that stores the property's value. The Set segment validates the value passed by the calling application and either rejects it or sets the local variable to this value.

Master It How would you use a constructor to allow developers to create an instance of your class and populate it with initial data?

Solution Each class has a constructor, which is called every time a new instance of the class is created with the New keyword. The constructor is implemented with the New() subroutine. To allow users to set certain properties of the class when they instantiate it, create as many New() subroutines as you need. Each version of the New() subroutine should accept different arguments. The following sample lets you create objects that represent books, passing a book's ISBN and/or title:

```
Public Sub New(ByVal ISBN As String)
    MyBase.New()
    Me.ISBN = ISBN
End Sub

Public Sub New(ByVal ISBN As String, ByVal Title As String)
    MyBase.New()
```

```
    Me.ISBN = ISBN
    Me.Title = Title
End Sub
```

This technique bypasses the New constructor, but the appropriate Property procedures are invoked, as each property is initialized.

Master It Which are the default methods of a custom class that you will most likely override with more meaningful definitions?

Solution The first method to override is the ToString method, which returns a string that describes the class. By default, this method returns the name of the class. Your implementation should return a more meaningful string. The Equals method, which compares two instances of the same class, is another candidate for overriding because the default Equals method performs a reference comparison, not an instance comparison.

To override one of the default methods, enter the string

```
Public Overrides
```

in the code window and press the spacebar to see the signatures of the overridable methods in the IntelliSense drop-down box.

Master It How should you handle exceptions in a class?

Solution In general, you should avoid handling all errors in your class because you can't be sure how your classes will be used by other developers. It's also important that you avoid interacting with the user from within your class's code with messages boxes or other techniques. The best method of handling errors in a custom class is to raise exceptions and let the developer of the calling application handle the errors.

Overloading operators. Overloading is a common theme in coding classes (or plain procedures) with Visual Basic. In addition to overloading methods, you can overload operators. In other words, you can define the rules for adding or subtracting two custom objects, if this makes sense for your application.

Master It When should you overload operators in a custom class, and why?

Solution It may make absolute sense to add two instances of a custom class (it may represent length, matrices, vectors, and so on), but the addition operator doesn't work with custom classes. To redefine the addition operator so that it will add two instances of your custom class, you must override the addition operator with an implementation that adds two instances of a custom class. The following is the signature of a function that overloads the addition operator:

```
Public Shared Operator + (
            ByVal object1 As customType,
            ByVal object2 As customType)
            As customType

    Dim result As New customType
    ' Insert the code to "add" the two
```

```
      ' arguments and store the result to
      ' the result variable and return it.
      Return result
End Operator
```

The function that overrides the addition operator accepts two arguments, which are the two values to be added, and returns a value of the same type. The operator is usually overloaded because you may wish to add an instance of the custom class to one of the built-in data types or objects.

Chapter 9: Building Custom Windows Controls

Extend the functionality of existing Windows Forms controls with inheritance. The simplest type of control you can build is one that inherits an existing control. The inherited control includes all the functionality of the original control plus some extra functionality that's specific to an application and that you implement with custom code.

Master It Describe the process of designing an inherited custom control.

Solution To enhance an existing Windows Forms control, insert an `Inherits` statement with the name of the control you want to enhance in the project's `Designer.vb` file. The inherited control interface can't be altered; it's determined by the parent control. However, you can implement custom properties and methods, react to events received by the parent control, or raise custom events from within your new control.

The process of implementing custom properties and methods is identical to building custom classes. The control's properties, however, can be prefixed by a number of useful attributes, like the `<Category>` and `<Description>` attributes, which determine the category of the Properties Browser where the property will appear and the control's description that will be shown in the Properties window when the custom property is selected.

Build compound controls that combine multiple existing controls. A compound control provides a visible interface that combines multiple Windows controls. As a result, this type of control doesn't inherit the functionality of any specific control; you must expose its properties by providing your own code. The UserControl object, on which the compound control is based, already exposes a large number of members, including some fairly advanced ones such as the `Anchoring` and `Docking` properties, and the usual mouse and key events.

Master It How will you map certain members of a constituent control to custom members of the compound control?

Solution If the member is a property, you simply return the constituent control's property value in the `Get` section of the Property procedure and set the constituent control's property to the specified value in the `Set` section of the same procedure. The following Property procedure maps the `WordWrap` property of the TextBox1 constituent control to the `TextWrap` property of the custom compound control:

```
Public Property TextWrap() As Boolean
    Get
        Return TextBox1.WordWrap
```

```
    End Get
    Set(ByVal value As Boolean)
        TextBox1.WordWrap = value
    End Set
End Property
```

If the member is a method, you just call it from within one of the compound control's methods. To map the **ResetText** method of the TextBox constituent control to the **Reset** method of the compound control, add the following method definition:

```
Public Sub Reset()
    TextBox1.ResetText
End Sub
```

In the UserControl object's **Load** event handler, insert the statements that create the roundPath object, which is an ellipse, and then assign it to the UserControl's **Region** property. Here's the Load event handler for the EllipticalButton custom control:

```
Private Sub RoundButton_Load(ByVal sender As System.Object,
                ByVal e As System.EventArgs)
                Handles MyBase.Load
    Dim G As Graphics
    G = Me.CreateGraphics
    Dim roundPath As New GraphicsPath()
    Dim R As New Rectangle(0, 0, Me.Width, Me.Height)
    roundPath.AddEllipse(R)
    Me.Region = New Region(roundPath)
End Sub
```

Build custom controls from scratch. User-drawn controls are the most flexible custom controls because you're in charge of the control's functionality and appearance. Of course, you have to implement all the functionality of the control from within your code, so it takes substantial programming effort to create user-drawn custom controls.

Master It Describe the process of developing a user-drawn custom control.

Solution Since you are responsible for updating the control's visible area from within your code, you must provide the code that redraws the control's surface and insert it in the UserControl object's **Paint** event handler. In drawing the control's surface, you must take into consideration the settings of the control's properties.

```
Private Sub Label3D_Paint(
        ByVal sender As Object,
        ByVal e As System.Windows.Forms.PaintEventArgs)
        Handles Me.Paint

End Sub
```

The **e** argument of the **Paint** event handler exposes the **Graphics** property, which you must use from within your code to draw on the control's surface. You can use any of the drawing methods you'd use to create shapes, gradients, and text on a Form object or PictureBox control.

Because custom controls aren't redrawn by default when they're resized, you must also insert the following statement in the control's Load event handler:

```
Private Sub Label3D_Load(
              ByVal sender As System.Object,
              ByVal e As System.EventArgs)
              Handles MyBase.Load
    Me.SetStyle(ControlStyles.ResizeRedraw, True)
End Sub
```

If the control's appearance should be different at design time than at runtime, use the Me.DesignMode property to determine whether the custom control is used in design time (DesignMode = True), or runtime (DesignMode = False).

Customize the rendering of items in a ListBox control.   The Windows controls that present lists of items display their items in a specific manner. The Framework allows you to take control of the rendering process and change completely the default appearance of the items on these controls. The controls that allow you to take charge of the rendering process of their items are the ListBox, CheckedListBox, ComboBox, and TreeView controls.

To create an owner-drawn control, you must set the DrawMode property to a member of the DrawMode enumeration and insert the appropriate code in the events MeasureItem and DrawItem. The MeasureItem event is where you decide about the dimensions of the rectangle in which the drawing will take place. The DrawItem event is where you insert the code for rendering the items on the control.

Master It   Outline the process of creating a ListBox control that wraps the contents of lengthy items.

Solution   By default, all items in a ListBox control have the same height, which is the height of a single line of text in the control's font. To display the selected items in cells of varying height, do the following:

1. Set the control's DrawMode property to *OwnerDrawVariable*.

2. In the control's MeasureItem event handler, which is invoked every time the control is about to display an item, insert the statements that calculate the desired height of the current item's cell. You will most likely call the MeasureString method of the control's Graphics object to retrieve the height of the item (the item may take multiple lines on the control). Set the e.Height and e.Width properties before exiting the MeasureItem event handler.

3. In the control's DrawItem event handler, which displays the current item, insert the appropriate statements to print the item in a cell with the dimensions calculated in step 2. The dimensions of the cell in which you must fit the caption of the current item are given by the property Bounds of the event handler's e argument. Use the DrawString method of the control's Graphics object to draw the item's caption.

Chapter 10: Applied Object-Oriented Programming

Use inheritance. Inheritance, which is the true power behind OOP, allows you to create new classes that encapsulate the functionality of existing classes without editing their code. To inherit from an existing class, use the `Inherits` statement, which brings the entire class into your class.

> **Master It** Explain the inheritance-related attributes of a class's members.

> **Solution** Any class can be inherited by default. However, you can prevent developers from inheriting your class with the `NonInheritable` attribute or by creating an abstract class with the `MustInherit` attribute. Classes marked with this attribute can't be used on their own; they must be inherited by another class. The parent class members can be optionally overridden if they're marked with the `Overridable` attribute. To prevent derived classes from overriding specific members, use the `NotOverridable` attribute. Finally, methods that override the equivalent methods of the base class must be prefixed with the `Overrides` attribute.

Use polymorphism. Polymorphism is the ability to write members that are common to a number of classes but behave differently, depending on the specific class to which they apply. Polymorphism is a great way of abstracting implementation details and delegating the implementation of methods with very specific functionality to the derived classes.

> **Master It** The parent class Person represents parties, and it exposes the `GetBalance` method, which returns the outstanding balance of a person. The Customer and Supplier derived classes implement the `GetBalance` method differently. How will you use this method to find out the balance of a customer and/or supplier?

> **Solution** If you have a Customer or Supplier object, you can call the `GetBalance` method directly. If you have a collection of objects of either type, you must first cast them to their parent type and then call the `GetBalance` method.

Chapter 11: The Framework at Large

Handle files with the My component. The simplest method of saving data to a file is to call one of the `WriteAllBytes` or `WriteAllText` methods of the `My.Computer.FileSystem` component. You can also use the `IO` namespace to set up a Writer object to send data to a file and a Reader object to read data from the file.

> **Master It** Show the statements that save a TextBox control's contents to a file and the statements that reload the same control from the data file. Use the `My.Computer.FileSystem` component.

> **Solution** The following statement saves the control's `Text` property to a file whose path is stored in the filename variable. Prompt users with the File Open dialog box for the path of the file and then use it in your code:

```
My.Somputer.FileSystem.WriteAllText(filename, TextBox1.Text, True)
```

To read the data back and display it on the same control, use the following statement:

```
TextBox1.Text = My.Computer.FileSystem.ReadAllText(filename)
```

Write data to a file with the IO namespace. To send data to a file you must set up a File-Stream object, which is a channel between the application and the file. To send data to a file, create a StreamWriter or BinaryWriter object on the appropriate FileStream object. Likewise, to read from a file, create a StreamReader or BinaryReader on the appropriate FileStream object. To send data to a file, use the `Write` and `WriteString` methods of the appropriate StreamWriter object. To read data from the file, use the `Read, ReadBlock, ReadLine,` and `ReadToEnd` methods of the StreamReader object.

Master It Write the contents of a TextBox control to a file using the methods of the IO namespace.

Solution Begin by setting up a FileStream object to connect your application to a data file. Then create a StreamWriter object on top of the FileStream object and use the Write method to send data to the file. Don't forget to close both streams when you're done.

```
Dim FS As FileStream
FS = New FileStream(filename, FileMode.Create)
Dim SW As New StreamWriter(FS)
SW.Write(TextBox1.Text)
SW.Close
FS.Close
```

To read the data back and reload the TextBox control, set up an identical FileStream object, then create a StreamReader object on top of it, and finally call its `ReadToEnd` method:

```
Dim FS As New FileStream(filename,
                IO.FileMode.OpenOrCreate, IO.FileAccess.Write)
Dim SR As New StreamReader(FS)
TextBox1.Text = SR.ReadToEnd
FS.Close
SR.Close
```

Manipulate folders and files. The IO namespace provides the Directory and File classes, which represent the corresponding entities. Both classes expose a large number of methods for manipulating folders (`CreateDirectory, Delete, GetFiles,` and so on) and files (`Create, Delete, Copy, OpenRead,` and so on).

Master It How will you retrieve the attributes of a drive, folder, and file using the IO namespace's classes?

Solution Start by creating a DriveInfo, DirectoryInfo, and FileInfo object for a specific drive, folder, and file respectively by specifying the name of the appropriate entity as an argument:

```
Dim DrvInfo As New DriveInfo("C:\")
Dim DirInfo As New DirectoryInfo("C:\Program Files")
Dim FInfo As New FileInfo("C:\Program Files\My Apps\Readme.txt")
```

Then enter the name of any of these variables and the following period to see the members they expose in the IntelliSense list. The available space on drive C: is given by the property `DrvInfo.AvailableFreeSpace`. The attributes of the Program Files folder are given by the `DirInfo.Attributes` property. Finally, the length of the `Readme.txt` file is given by the property `FInfo.Length`.

Use the Char data type to handle characters.   The Char data type, which is implemented with the Char class, exposes methods for handling individual characters (`IsLetter`, `IsDigit`, `IsSymbol`, and so on). We use the methods of the Char class to manipulate users' keystrokes as they happen in certain controls (mostly the TextBox control) and to provide immediate feedback.

Master It   You want to develop an interface that contains several TextBox controls that accept numeric data. How will you intercept the user's keystrokes and reject any characters that are not numeric?

Solution   You must program the control's `KeyPress` event handler, which reports the character that was pressed. The following event handler rejects any non-numeric characters entered in the TextBox1 control:

```
Private Sub TextBox1_KeyPress(
          ByVal sender As Object,
          ByVal e As System.Windows.Forms.KeyPressEventArgs)
          Handles TextBox1.KeyPress
    Dim c As Char = e.KeyChar
    If Not (Char.IsDigit(c) Or Char.IsControl(c)) Then
        e.Handled = True
    End If
End Sub
```

Use the StringBuilder class to manipulate large or dynamic strings.   The StringBuilder class is very efficient at manipulating long strings, but it doesn't provide as many methods for handling strings. The StringBuilder class provides a few methods to insert, delete, and replace characters within a string. Unlike the equivalent methods of the String class, these methods act directly on the string stored in the current instance of the StringBuilder class.

Master It   Assuming that you have populated a ListView control with thousands of lines of data from a database, how will you implement a function that copies all the data to the Clipboard?

Solution   To copy the ListView control's data, you must create a long string that contains tab-delimited strings and then copy it to the Clipboard. Each cell's value must be converted to a string and then appended to a StringBuilder variable. Consecutive rows will be separated by a carriage return/line feed character.

Start by declaring a StringBuilder variable:

```
Dim SB As New System.Text.StringBuilder
```

Then write a loop that iterates through the items in the ListView control:

```
Dim LI As ListViewItem
For Each LI In ListView1.Items
```

```
                   ' append current row's cell values to SB
        SB.Append(vbCrLf)
    Next
```

In the loop's body, insert another loop to iterate through the subitems of the current item:

```
Dim LI As ListViewItem
For Each LI In ListView1.Items
    Dim subLI As ListViewItem.ListViewSubItem
    For Each subLI In LI.SubItems
        SB.Append(subLI.Text & vbTab)
    Next
    SB.Remove(SB.Length - 1, 1)  ' remove last tab
    SB.Append(vbCrLf)
Next
```

Use the DateTime and TimeSpan classes to handle dates and time.   The Date class represents dates and time, and it exposes many useful shared methods (such as the `IsLeap` method, which returns True if the year passed to the method as an argument is leap; the `DaysInMonth` method; and so on). It also exposes many instance methods (such as `AddYears`, `AddDays`, `Add-Hours`, and so on) for adding time intervals to the current instance of the Date class as well as many options for formatting date and time values.

The TimeSpan class represents time intervals — from milliseconds to days — with the `From-Days`, `FromHours`, and even `FromMilliseconds` methods. The difference between two date variables is a TimeSpan value, and you can convert this value to various time units by using methods such as `TotalDays`, `TotalHours`, `TotalMilliseconds`, and so on. You can also add a TimeSpan object to a date variable to obtain another date variable.

Master It   How will you use the TimeSpan class to accurately time an operation?

Solution   To time an operation, you must create a DateTime variable and set it to the current date and time just before the statements you want to execute:

```
Dim TStart As DateTime = Now
```

Right after the statements you want to time have been executed, create a new TimeSpan object that represents the time it took to execute the statements. The duration of the Time-Span object is the difference between the current time and the time stored in the *TStart* variable:

```
Dim duration As New TimeSpan
Duration = Now.Subtract(TStart)
```

The duration variable is a time interval, and you can use the methods of the TimeSpan class to express this interval in various units: `duration.MilliSeconds`, `duration.Seconds`, and so on.

Generate graphics by using the drawing methods.   Every object you draw on, such as forms and PictureBox controls, exposes the `CreateGraphics` method, which returns a Graphics object. The Paint event's *e* argument also exposes the Graphics object of the control or form. To draw something on a control, retrieve its Graphics object and then call the Graphics object's drawing methods.

Master It   Show how to draw a circle on a form from within the form's Paint event handler.

Solution   The following statements in the form's Paint event handler will draw a circle at the center of Form1:

```
Private Sub Form1_Paint(
          ByVal sender as Object,
          ByVal e As System.Windows.Forms.PaintEventArgs)
          Handles Me.Paint
Dim diameter = Math.Min(Me.Width, Me.Height)/2
e.Graphics.DrawEllipse(Pens.Blue,
              New RectangleF((Me.Width – diameter) / 2,
              (Me.Height – diameter) / 2, diameter, diameter))
End Sub
```

There's no DrawCircle method; the DrawEllipse method accepts as arguments a Pen object and a rectangle that encloses the circle to be drawn. If the rectangle is a square, then the equivalent ellipse will be a circle. To force the form to be redrawn every time it's resized, you must also insert the following statement in the form's Load event handler:

```
Me.SetStyle(ControlStyles.ResizeRedraw, True)
```

Use the printing controls and dialog boxes.   To print with the .NET Framework, you must add an instance of the PrintDocument control to your form and call its Print method. To preview the same document, you simply assign the PrintDocument object to the Document property of the PrintPreviewDialog control and then call the ShowDialog method of the PrintPreviewDialog control to display the preview window. You can also display the Print dialog box, where users can select the printer to which the output will be sent, and the Page Setup dialog box, where users can specify the page's orientation and margins. The two dialog boxes are implemented with the PrintDialog and PageSetupDialog controls.

Master It   Explain the process of generating a simple printout. How will you handle multiple report pages?

Solution   Both the PrintDocument.Print and the PrintPreviewDialog.ShowDialog methods fire the PrintPage event of the PrintDocument control. The code that generates the actual printout must be placed in the PrintPage event handler, and the same code will generate the actual printout on the printer (if you're using the PrintDocument control) or a preview of the printout (if you're using the PrintPreviewDialog control).

It's your responsibility to terminate each page and start a new one every time you complete the current page by setting the HasMorePages property when you exit the PrintPage event handler. If the HasMorePages property is True, the PrintPage event is fired again, until the HasMorePages property becomes False.

Any static variables you use to maintain state between successive invocations of the PrintPage event handler, such as the page number, must be reset every time you start a new printout. A good place to initialize these variables is the BeginPrint event handler.

Master It   Assuming that you have displayed the Page Setup dialog box control to the user, how will you draw a rectangle that delimits the printing area on the page, taking into consideration the user-specified margins?

Solution   First, set up a few variables to store the page's margins, as specified by the user on the Page Setup dialog box:

```
Dim LeftMargin, RightMargin, TopMargin, BottomMargin as Integer
With PrintDocument1.DefaultPageSettings
    LeftMargin = .Left
    RightMargin = .Right
    TopMargin = .Top
    BottomMargin = .Bottom
End With
'
```

Then calculate the dimensions of the rectangle that delimits the printable area on the page:

```
Dim PrintWidth, PrintHeight As Integer
With PrintDocument1.DefaultPageSettings.PaperSize
    PrintWidth = .Width – LeftMargin – RightMargin
    PrintHeight = .Height – TopMargin – BottomMargin
End With
```

The rectangle you want to draw should start at the point (*LeftMargin, TopMargin*) and extend *PrintWidth* points to the right and *PrintHeight* points down.

Finally, insert the following statements in the PrintPage event handler to draw the rectangle:

```
Dim R As New Rectangle(LeftMargin, TopMargin, PrintWidth, PrintHeight)
e.Graphics.DrawRectangle(Pens.Black, R)
```

Chapter 12: Storing Data in Collections

Make the most of arrays.   The simplest method of storing sets of data is to use arrays. They're very efficient, and they provide methods to perform advanced operations such as sorting and searching their elements. Use the Sort method of the Array class to sort an array's elements. To search for an element in an array, use the IndexOf and LastIndexOf methods, or use the BinarySearch method if the array is sorted. The BinarySearch method always returns an element's index, which is a positive value for *exact matches* and a negative value for *near matches*.

Master It   Explain how you can search an array and find exact and near matches.

Solution   The most efficient method of searching arrays is the `BinarySearch` method, which requires that the array is sorted. The simplest form of the `BinarySearch` method is the following:

```
Dim idx As Integer
idx = System.Array.BinarySearch(arrayName, object)
```

The `BinarySearch` method returns an integer value, which is the index of the object you're searching for in the array. If the object argument is not found, the method returns a negative value, which is the negative of the index of the next larger item minus one. The following statements return an exact or near match for the word *srchWord* in the *words* array:

```
Dim wordIndex As Integer =
            Array.BinarySearch(words, srchWord)
If wordIndex >= 0 Then   ' exact match!
    MsgBox("An exact match was found for " &
            " at index " & wordIndex.ToString)
Else                         ' Near match
    MsgBox("The nearest match is the word " &
            words(-wordIndex - 1) &
            " at " & (-wordIndex - 1).ToString)
End If
```

Store data in collections such as List and Dictionary collections.   In addition to arrays, the Framework provides collections, which are dynamic data structures. The most commonly used collections are the List and the Dictionary. Collections are similar to arrays, but they're dynamic structures. List and ArrayList collections store lists of items, whereas Dictionary and HashTable collections store key-value pairs and allow you to access their elements via a key. You can add elements by using the `Add` method and remove existing elements by using the `Remove` and `RemoveAt` methods.

Dictionary collections provide the `ContainsKey` and `ContainsValue` methods to find out whether the collection already contains a specific key or value as well as the `GetKeys` and `GetValues` methods to retrieve all the keys and values from the collection, respectively. As a reminder, the List and Dictionary collections are strongly typed. Their untyped counterparts are the ArrayList and HashTable collections.

Master It   How will you populate a Dictionary with a few pairs of keys/values and then iterate though the collection's items?

Solution   To populate the Dictionary, call its `Add` method and pass the item's key and value as arguments:

```
Dim Dict As New Dictionary(Of Object, Object)
Dict.Add("key1", item1)
Dict.Add("key2", item2)
```

To iterate through the items of a Dictionary collection, you must first extract all the keys and then use them to access the collection's elements. The following code segment prints the keys and values in the *Dict* variable, which is an instance of the Dictionary class:

```
Dim Dict As New Dictionary(Of Object, Object)
Dict.Add("1", "A string value")
Dict.Add(1, "Another string value")
Dict.Add("2", 2)
Dim element, key As Object
For Each key In Dict.keys
    element = Dict.Item(key)
    Debug.WriteLine("Item type = " & element.GetType.ToString
    Debug.WriteLine("Key= " & Key.ToString)
    Denug.WriteLine("Value= " & element.ToString)
Next
```

Sort and search collections with custom comparers. Collections provide the Sort method for sorting their items and several methods to locate items: IndexOf, LastIndexOf, and Binary-Search. Both sort and search operations are based on comparisons, and the Framework knows how to compare values' types only (Integers, Strings, and the other primitive data types). If a collection contains objects, you must provide a custom function that knows how to compare two objects of the same type.

Master It How do you specify a custom comparer function for a collection that contains Rectangle objects?

Solution First you must decide how to compare two object variables of the same type. For the purposes of this exercise, you can consider two rectangles equal if their perimeters are equal. To implement a custom comparer, write a class that implements the IComparer interface. This class should contain a single method, the Compare method, which compares two objects and returns one of the values –1, 0, and 1:

```
Class RectangleComparer : Implements IComparer
    Public Function Compare(
        ByVal o1 As Object, ByVal o2 As Object)
        As Integer Implements IComparer.Compare
        Dim R1, R2 As Rectangle
        Try
            R1 = CType(o1, Rectangle)
            R2 = CType(o2, Rectangle)
        Catch compareException As system.Exception
            Throw (compareException)
            Exit Function
        End Try
        Dim perim1 As Integer = 2 * (R1.Width+R1.Height)
        Dim perim2 As Integer = 2 * (R2.Width+R2.Height)
        If perim1 < perim2 Then
            Return -1
        Else
```

```
            If perim1 > perim2 Then
                Return 1
            Else
                Return 0
            End If
        End If
    End Function
End Class
```

Once this class is in place, you can pass an instance of it to the Sort method. The following statement sorts the items of the Rects ArrayList collection, assuming that it contains only Rectangles:

```
Rects.Sort(New RectangleComparer)
```

If you want to search the collection for a Rectangle object with the BinarySearch method, you must pass as arguments to the method not only the object you're searching for but also an instance of the custom comparer:

```
Rects.BinarySearch(
        New Rectangle(0, 0, 33, 33), comparer)
```

Chapter 13: XML in Modern Programming

Create XML documents.   XML documents can be built easily with the XElement and XAttribute classes. XElement represents an element, and its constructor accepts as arguments the element's name and either the element's value or a series of attributes and nested elements. XAttribute represents an attribute, and its constructor accepts as arguments the attribute's name and its value. You can also assign an XML document directly to an XElement.

Master It   Create the XML segment that describes an object of the Item type, defined by the following class:

```
Class Item
    Property ID As String
    Property Name As String
    Property Prices As Price
    Property Name As String
Class Price
        Property Retail As PriceDetails
        Property WholeSale As PriceDetails
        Class PriceDetails
            Property Price As Decimal
            Property VolumeDiscount As Decimal
End Class
Class Dimension
    Property Width As Decimal
```

```
        Property Height As Decimal
        Property Depth As Decimal
End Class
```

Solution The first technique is called *functional construction,* and you build the XML document by appending XElements and XAttributes to a variable:

```
Dim prod = New XElement("Item", New XAttribute("ID", "A001"),
            New XElement("Name", "ProductName"),
            New XElement("Price",
                New XElement("Retail",
                            New XAttribute("Price", "10.95"),
                            New XAttribute("VolumeDiscount", "0.25")),
                New XElement("WholeSale",
                            New XAttribute("Price", "8.50"),
                            New XAttribute("VolumeDiscount", "0.20")))))
```

Alternatively, you can declare a variable and set it to the equivalent XML document (which is the same document that the expression *prod.ToString* will return):

```
Dim prod = <Item ID="A001">
            <Name>ProductName</Name>
            <Price>
                <Retail Price="10.95" VolumeDiscount="0.25"/>
                <WholeSale Price="8.50" VolumeDiscount="0.20"/>
            </Price>
        </Item>
```

Navigate through an XML document and locate the information you need. The XElement class provides a number of methods for accessing the contents of an XML document. The Elements method returns the child elements of the current element by the name specified with the argument you pass to the method as a string. The Element method is quite similar, but it returns the first child element by the specified name. The Descendants method returns all the elements by the specified name under the current element, regardless of whether they're direct children of the current element. Finally, the Attribute method returns the value of the attribute by the specified name of the current element.

Master It Assuming an XML document with the following structure, write the expressions to retrieve all cities in the document and all cities under the third country in the document.

```
<Countries>
    <Country>
        <City> … </City>
        <City> … </City>
    </Country>
    <Country>
    …
    </Country>
    …
</Countries>
```

Solution   The following expression returns all cities in the document:

```
Dim cities =
countries.Elements("Country").Elements("Cities").Elements("City")
```

The cities variable is an IEnumerable collection of XElement objects. Likewise, to retrieve the cities of the third country, you must retrieve the Elements collection of the third element:

```
Dim countryCities =
countries.Elements("Country")(2).Elements("Cities").Elements("City")
```

Master It   Assuming that both country and city names are specified in the document with the Name element, explain the difference between the queries:

```
Dim q1 = countries.Elements("Country").Elements("Name")
Dim q2 = countries.Descendants("Name")
```

Solution   The first query returns all country names in the document, because the Elements method retrieves all elements that are directly under the element to which it's applied (not their children's children, even if the same element name is repeated). The second query returns all country and city names, because the Descendants method retrieves all elements by the specified name under the element to which it's applied (regardless of their nesting).

Convert arbitrary objects into XML documents and back with serialization.   *Serialization* is the process of converting an object into a stream of bytes. This process (affectionately known as *dehydration*) generates a stream of bytes or characters, which can be stored or transported. To serialize an object, you can use the BinaryFormatter or SoapFormatter class. You can also use the XmlSerializer class to convert objects into XML documents. All three classes expose a Serialize class that accepts as arguments the object to be serialized and a stream object and writes the serialized version of the object to the specified stream. The opposite of serialization is called *deserialization*. To reconstruct the original object, you use the Deserialize method of the same class you used to serialize the object.

Master It   Describe the process of serializing an object with the XmlSerializer class.

Solution   First create a Stream object to accept the result of serialization; this stream is usually associated with a file:

```
Dim saveFile As New FileStream("Objects.xml", FileMode.Create)
```

Then create an instance of the XmlSerializer class, passing to its construction the type of object you want to serialize:

```
Dim serializer As New XmlSerializer(custom_type)
```

And finally call the serializer object's Serialize method, passing as an argument the object you want to serialize:

```
serializer.Serialize(stream, object)
```

Chapter 14: An Introduction to LINQ

Perform simple LINQ queries. A LINQ query starts with the structure From *variable* In*collection*, where *variable* is a variable name and *collection* is any collection that implements the IEnumerable interface (such as an array, a typed collection, or any method that returns a collection of items). The second mandatory part of the query is the Select part, which determines the properties of the variable you want in the output. Quite often you select the same variable that you specify in the From keyword. In most cases, you apply a filtering expression with the Where keyword. Here's a typical LINQ query that selects filenames from a specific folder:

```
Dim files =
        From file In
          IO.Directory.GetFiles("C:\Documents")
          Where file.EndsWith("doc")
        Select file
```

Master It Write a LINQ query that calculates the sum of the squares of the values in an array.

Solution To calculate a custom aggregate in a LINQ query, you must create a lambda expression that performs the aggregation and passes it as an argument to the Aggregate method. The lambda expression accepts two arguments, the current value of the aggregate and the current value, and returns the new aggregate. Such a function would have the following signature and implementation:

```
Function(aggregate, value)
    Return(aggregate + value ^2)
End Function
```

To specify this function as a lambda expression in a LINQ query, call the collection's Aggregate method as follows:

```
Dim sumSquares = data.Aggregate(
    Function(sumSquare As Long, n As Integer)
            sumSquare + n ^ 2)
```

Create and process XML files with LINQ to XML. LINQ to XML allows you to create XML documents with the XElement and XAttribute classes. You simply create a new XElement object for each element in your document and create a new XAttribute object for each attribute in the current element. Alternatively, you can simply insert XML code in your VB code. To create an XML document dynamically, you can insert embedded expressions that will be evaluated by the compiler and replaced with their results.

Master It How would you create an HTML document with the filenames in a specific folder?

Solution   To generate a directory listing, you must first implement the LINQ query that retrieves the desired information. The query selects the files returned by the GetFiles method of the IO.Directory class:

```
Dim files = From file In
                IO.Directory.GetFiles(path)
            Select New IO.FileInfo(file).Name,
            New IO.FileInfo(file).Length
```

Now you must embed this query into an XML document using expression holes. The XML document is actually an HTML page that displays a table with two columns, the file's name and size, as shown next:

```
Dim smallFilesHTML = <html>
    <table><tr>
       <td>FileName</td>
       <td>FileSize</td></tr>
       <%= From file In
           IO.Directory.GetFiles("C:\")
           Select <tr><td><%= file %></td> ,
           <td>
           <%= New IO.FileInfo(file).Length %>
           </td></tr>
        %>
     </table></html>
```

Process relational data with LINQ to SQL.   LINQ to SQL allows you to query relational data from a database. To access the database, you must first create a DataContext object. Then you can call this object's GetTable method to retrieve a table's rows or the ExecuteQuery method to retrieve selected rows from one or more tables with a SQL query. The result is stored in a class designed specifically for the data you're retrieving via the DataContext object.

Master It   Explain the attributes you must use in designing a class for storing a table.

Solution   The class must be decorated with the <Table> attribute that specifies the name of the table that will populate the class:

```
<Table(Name:="Customers")>Public Class Customers
...
End Class
```

Each property of this table must be decorated with the <Column> attribute that specifies the name of the column from which the property will get its value:

```
<Column(Name:= "CompanyName")>
    Public Property Company
...
End Property
```

When you call the `GetTable` method of the DataContext class, pass the name of the class as an argument, and the DataContext class will create a new instance of the class and populate it.

Chapter 15: Programming with ADO.NET

Store data in relational databases. Relational databases store their data in tables and are based on relationships between these tables. The data are stored in tables, and tables contain related data, or entities, such as persons, products, orders, and so on. Relationships are implemented by inserting columns with matching values in the two related tables.

Master It How will you relate two tables with a many-to-many relationship?

Solution A many-to-many relationship can't be implemented with a primary/foreign key relationship between two tables. To create a many-to-many relationship, you must create a new table that relates the other two tables to one another by implementing two one-to-many relationships. Consider the Titles and Authors tables, which have a many-to-many relationship, because a title can have many authors and the same author may have written multiple titles. To implement this relationship, you must create an intermediate table, the TitleAuthors table, which is related to both the Titles and Authors table with a one-to-many relationship. The TitleAuthors table should store title and author IDs. The `TitleAuthor.TitleID` column is the foreign key to the relationship between the Titles and TitleAuthors tables. Likewise, the `TitleAuthor.AuthorID` column is the foreign key to the relationship between the TitleAuthor and Authors tables.

Query databases with SQL. Structured Query Language (SQL) is a universal language for manipulating tables. SQL is a nonprocedural language, which specifies the operation you want to perform against a database at a high level, unlike a traditional language such as Visual Basic, which specifies how to perform the operation. The details of the implementation are left to the DBMS. SQL consists of a small number of keywords and is optimized for selecting, inserting, updating, and deleting data.

Master It How would you write a SELECT statement to retrieve selected data from multiple tables?

Solution The SELECT statement's FROM clause should include the names of two or more tables, which must be somehow related. To relate the tables, use the JOIN clause, and specify the primary/foreign keys of the join:

```
SELECT column1, column2, …
FROM table1 T1 INNER JOIN table2
     ON T1.primaryKey = T2.foreignKey
INNER JOIN table3 T3
     ON T2.primaryKey = T3.foreignKey
WHERE criteria
```

Pay attention to the type of join you specify. An inner join requires that the two columns match and excludes null values. A left join takes into consideration all the qualifying rows of the left table, including the ones that have null in their foreign key column. A right join takes into consideration all the qualifying rows of the right table, including the ones that have null in their foreign key column. A full outer join is a combination of the right and left joins — it takes into consideration null values from both tables involved in the query.

Submit queries to the database using ADO.NET. ADO.NET is the component of the Framework that provides the mechanism to contact a database, submit queries, and retrieve the results of a query. There are two types of queries you can execute against a database: selection queries that retrieve data from the database based on certain criteria you supply and action queries that manipulate the data at the database. Action queries do not return any results, except for the number of rows that were affected by the query.

Master It Describe the basic mechanism for submitting a selection query to the database and reading the results returned by the query.

Solution First you must connect to the database with a SqlConnection object. The SqlConnection class's constructor accepts as argument the credentials it must use to connect to the database. Then you must create a SqlCommand object, which exposes the CommandText property. Assign the query you want to execute against the database, and optionally set the CommandType property. You must also set the Connection object to the SqlConnection object, open the connection to the database, and finally call the SqlCommand object's ExecuteQuery method for selection queries or call the ExecuteNonQuery method for action queries.

The ExecuteNonQuery method returns an integer, which is the number of rows affected by the query. The ExecuteQuery method returns a DataReader object, which you can use to iterate through the results of the query. Call the Read method to read the next row, and access each row's column's with the Item property of the DataReader class. Here is the pseudocode for accessing the rows of a query that retrieves customer information from the Northwind database:

```
CMD.CommandText = "SELECT * FROM Customers WHERE Country = 'Germany'"
CN.Open()
Dim RDR As SqlDataReader
RDR = CMD.ExecuteReader
While RDR.Read
    ' Call the RDR.Item(col_name) method
    ' to read a specific column of the current row
    ' RDR.Item("CustomerID"), RDR.Item("Country") and so on
    ' Use the RDR.IsDBNull method to determine whether
    ' a column is Null, because Null values must be
    ' handled specially
End While
CN.Close()
```

It's imperative that you read the data off the DataReader as soon as possible and then close the connection to the database as soon as you are done.

Chapter 16: Developing Data-Driven Applications

Create and populate DataSets. DataSets are data containers that reside at the client and are populated with database data. The DataSet is made up of DataTables, which correspond to database tables, and you can establish relationships between DataTables, just like relating tables in the database. DataTables, in turn, consist of DataRow objects.

Master It How do you populate DataSets and then submit the changes made at the client to the database?

Solution To populate a DataSet, you must create a DataAdapter object for each Data-Table in the DataSet. The DataAdapter class provides the SelectCommand, InsertCommand, UpdateCommand, and DeleteCommand properties, which are initialized to the SQL statements that retrieve, set, update, and delete rows from the corresponding database tables. You can use the CommandBuilder object to build the INSERT, UPDATE, and DELETE statements from the SELECT statement, which you must supply. After these properties have been set, you can populate the corresponding DataTable by calling the Fill method of its DataAdapter object. If the DataSet contains relationships, you must fill the parent tables before the child tables.

Establish relations between tables in the DataSet. You can think of the DataSet as a small database that resides at the client, because it consists of tables and the relationships between them. The relations in a DataSet are DataRelation objects, which are stored in the Relations property of the DataSet. Each relation is identified by a name, the two tables it relates, and the fields of the tables on which the relation is based.

Master It How do you navigate through the related rows of two tables?

Solution To navigate through the rows of two related tables, the DataRow object that represents a row in a DataTable provides the GetChildRows method, which returns the current row's child rows as an array of DataRow objects, and the GetParentRow/GetParentRows methods, which return the current row's parent row(s). GetParentRow returns a single DataRow, and GetParentRows returns an array of DataRow objects. Because a DataTable may be related to multiple DataTables, you must also specify the name of the relation as an argument to these methods. The following statements retrieve the child rows of a specific category row in the DataTable with the rows of the Categories table and a specific supplier, respectively.

```
DS.Categories(iRow).GetChildRows("CategoriesProducts")
DS.Suppliers(iRow).GetChildRows("SupplierProducts")
```

Submit changes in the DataSet to the database. The DataSet maintains not only data at the client but their states and versions too. It knows which rows were added, deleted, or modified (the DataRowState property), and it also knows the version of each row read from the database and the current version (the DataRowVersion property).

Master It How will you submit the changes made to a disconnected DataSet to the database?

Solution To submit the changes made to an untyped DataSet, you must call the Update method of each DataAdapter object. You must call the Update method of the DataAdapter objects that correspond to the parent tables first and then the Update method of the

DataAdapter objects that correspond to the child tables. You can also submit individual rows to the database, as well as arrays of DataRow objects through the overloaded forms of the Update method.

Chapter 17: Using the Entity Data Model

Employ deferred loading when querying the Entity Data Model.   The Entity Framework supports the deferred loading (lazy loading) of entities. When deferred loading is activated, entities in navigation properties are loaded on demand, only after they are accessed. In cases when you are not certain that the related entity will be accessed (for example, when loading is dependent on a user action), you can initially load only the root entity and load the related entities only when they are requested.

Master It   How do you activate deferred loading in the Entity Framework?

Solution   To enable deferred loading when querying the Entity Framework, set the DeferredLoadingEnabled property of the ContextOptions property of ObjectContext to True. For example, use context.ContextOptions.DeferredLoadingEnabled = True.

Use entity inheritance features in the Entity Framework.   In the EDM, an inheritance relationship can be established between entities. When two entities participate in an inheritance relationship, the child entity inherits all the properties of the parent entity. When working with such an entity in .NET code, you can get major benefits from code reuse based on inheritance.

Master It   Explain how the Entity Framework can map an inheritance relationship between entities to tables in the database. Why is maintaining the inheritance relationship between the entities not easily accomplished with relational databases?

Solution   The Entity Framework employs two basic mapping strategies for mapping the inheritance relationship on the database level. In the table-per-type strategy, each type is mapped to a separate table. The child table contains only child-specific columns. Both the parent and child table are obliged to have identical primary keys. To retrieve a child type, a join between the parent and child tables has to be performed.

In the table-per-hierarchy mapping strategy, all types are mapped to the same table. A special discriminator column is used to identify the specific type that each row represents.

Since relational databases do not natively support an inheritance relationship, significant amounts of application code need to be written to implement this relationship on the database level. The Entity Framework provides this feature out of the box and thus can save developers from writing significant amounts of boilerplate code.

Create and query related entities.   In the Entity Data Model, you can establish one-to-many or many-to-many associations between entities. The association can be established by connecting related entities with the Association tool in the EDM diagram. When querying such entities, a related entity or set of entities can be accessed through generated navigation properties.

Master It   In the Books and Authors application (used as a sample application in Chapter 17), add a SalesByMonth form that will display the number of copies sold in a month for each title in the database. Modify the Books and Authors EDM so that the model can accommodate monthly sales information for each title.

Solution Add the SaleByMonth entity to the Books and Authors EDM, and use it to store the monthly sales information. Establish a one-to-many relationship between the Book and SaleByMonth entities. Write the query to retrieve the necessary information and display it on the form.

Start by modifying the EDM:

1. Add a new entity to the EDM, and name it **SaleByMonth**.

2. Rename the entity set of SaleByMonth to **SalesByMonth**.

3. Add a Month scalar property of type Int16 to the SaleByMonth entity.

4. Add a Year scalar property of type Int16 to the SaleByMonth entity.

5. Add a CopiesSold scalar property of type Int64 to the SaleByMonth entity.

6. Establish a one-to-many association between the Book and SaleByMonth entities.

7. Add a form named SaleByMonthForm to the project. Add one DataGridView control and one button control named Display to the SaleByMonthForm form.

8. Fill the DataGridView from the query in the Display button's Click event handler.

Listing A.1 shows the code for the Display button event handler.

LISTING A.1:   Using TransactionScope for enlisting external operations

```
Private Sub Display_Click(ByVal sender As System.Object,
                          ByVal e As System.EventArgs) Handles
                          Display.Click
    Dim context As New BooksAndAuthorsContainer
    Dim books = context.Books.Include("Sales")
    For Each book As Book In books
        For Each saleByMonth In book.Sales
            gridResult.Rows.Add(New String() {
                book.ISBN, book.Title,
                saleByMonth.Month.ToString & saleByMonth.Year.ToString(),
                saleByMonth.CopiesSold.ToString()})
        Next
    Next
End Sub
```

Chapter 18: Building Data-Bound Applications

Design and use typed DataSets.   Typed DataSets are created with visual tools at design time and allow you to write type-safe code. A typed DataSet is a class created by the wizard on the fly, and it becomes part of the project. The advantage of typed DataSets is that they expose functionality specific to the selected tables and can be easily bound to Windows forms. The code that implements a typed DataSet adds methods and properties to a generic DataSet, so all the functionality of the DataSet object is included in the autogenerated class.

Master It   Describe the basic components generated by the wizard when you create a typed DataSet with the visual tools of Visual Studio.

Solution   The basic components of the class that implements a typed DataSet are as follows: the DataSet, which describes the entire DataSet; the BindingNavigator, which links the data-bound controls on the form to the DataSet; and the TableAdapter, which links the DataSet to the database. The DataSet component is based on the DataSet class and enhances the functionality of an untyped DataSet by adding members that are specific to the data contained in the DataSet. If the DataSet contains the Products table, the typed DataSet exposes the ProductsRow class, which represents a row of the Products table. The ProductsRow class, in turn, exposes the columns of the table as properties.

The BindingSource class allows you to retrieve the current row with its `Current` property, move to a specific row by setting the `Position` property, and even suspend temporarily and restore data binding with `SuspendBinding` and `ResumeBinding`.

The TableAdapter class, which is based on the DataAdapter class, provides methods for loading a DataTable (the `Fill` method) and submitting the changes made to the DataSet to the database (the `Update` method). The TableAdapterManager class, which encapsulates the functionality of all TableAdapters on the form, provides the `UpdateAll` method, which submits the changes in all DataTables to the database.

Bind Windows forms to typed DataSets.   The simplest method of designing a data-bound form is to drop a DataTable, or individual columns, on the form. DataTables are bound to DataGridView controls, which display the entire DataTable. Individual columns are bound to simple controls such as TextBox, CheckBox, and DateTimePicker controls, depending on the column's type. In addition to the data-bound controls, the editor generates a toolbar control with some basic navigational tools and the Add/Delete/Save buttons.

Master It   Outline the process of binding DataTables to a DataGridView control.

Solution   To bind a DataTable to a DataGridView control, locate the desired table in the Data Sources window, set its binding option to DataGridView, and drop the DataTable on the form. The editor will create a DataGridView control on the form and map the control's columns according to the columns of the DataTable. It will also add a toolbar with the basic navigational and editing controls on the form.

To bind two related DataTables on the same form, drop the parent DataTable on the form, and then select the child DataTable under this parent and drop it on the form. To modify the appearance of the DataGridView controls, open their Tasks menu, and choose Edit Columns to see the Edit Columns dialog box, where you can set the appearance of the control's columns.

Compare a LINQ query used to filter data with an eSQL dynamic query.   You can use the `AsDataView` extension method of the DataTable class to enable binding of the LINQ query results when querying the DataSet in LINQ to DataSet technology. In this chapter, you have seen how a LINQ query can be used to provide filtering capabilities on a data-entry form.

Entity SQL (eSQL) is a query language with syntax similar to Transact-SQL. Entity SQL queries can be embedded inside the Visual Basic code and can be used to query the Entity Data Model provided by the Entity Framework. You saw how to use Entity SQL to construct dynamic queries in Chapter 17.

Master It   Compare LINQ queries to queries written in Entity SQL. Explain the main benefits and drawbacks of each technology.

Solution   LINQ to DataSet technology provides a rich set of querying features for querying the data in the DataSet. LINQ syntax is an integral part of Visual Basic syntax and as such is processed and verified during the compilation process and supported by IntelliSense.

Entity SQL is used inside the Visual Basic code as an embedded query language. Since Entity SQL code is essentially written in the form of string literals inside Visual Basic code, it is not compiled. Such code can count only on reduced IntelliSense support. This and having to learn new language syntax (although fairly similar to Transact-SQL and therefore probably familiar to Visual Basic .NET programmers) are the main drawbacks of Entity SQL compared to LINQ.

Since Entity SQL code is not compiled, Entity SQL code can be constructed at runtime. This is especially handy for writing queries with a large number of criteria combinations that can only be known at runtime. When writing similar queries in LINQ, you have to include all the criteria in the query and then provide the means to activate or deactivate certain criteria. Alternatively, you can write chained LINQ queries. LINQ code can be more complex to write and less efficient to execute than Entity SQL code.

Chapter 19: Accessing the Web

Access a website on the Internet using the WebClient class.   The WebClient class provides an easy and simple way to access resources on the Web programmatically from Visual Basic code. The WebClient class implements many features of HTTP, making it easy to access the sites on the Web in the same way the browser application does. The web server will not distinguish a request coming from a WebClient site from one coming from a user-operated web browser.

The WebClient class can be very useful in HTML screen scraping scenarios, where the data to be extracted from HTML is meant to be read by a human, or in lightweight web service protocols like REST and/or AJAX-styled XML and JSON over HTTP.

Master It   Use the Headers property of the WebClient class to fine-tune HTTP requests. Trick Google into believing that a request that you are sending from your Visual Basic application is coming from some mobile device.

Solution   The WebClient class permits adding different headers to your HTML requests through its `Headers` property. The header used to identify the type of client sending the request is the `"user-agent"` header. You need to add this header to your HTTP request. The value of the header should be the string sent by some mobile device. Browsing the Internet, I found that some LG mobile phones send the following string value as their `"user-agent"`: `"LIG-CU920/V1.0p Obigo/Q05A Profile/MIDP-2.0 Configuration/CLDC-1.1"`.

If you create a new Windows Forms application and add a Download button to the form, here is the code you need to add to Download button's event handler in order to receive Google's default search page formatted for mobile devices:

```
Dim client As New WebClient
client.Headers.Add("user-agent",
 "L1G-CU920/V1.0p Obigo/Q05A Profile/MIDP-2.0 Configuration/CLDC-1.1")
Dim response = client.DownloadString("http://www.google.com")
Console.WriteLine(response)
```

This code will write the response to the Output window. Now, if you copy this output, save it to a `googlemobile.html` file, and open the file with your web browser, you will see the Google search page as shown in Figure A.1.

FIGURE A.1
Google search page formatted for a mobile device

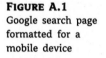

Use a WebBrowser control to add web browser functionality to your Windows Forms application. The WebBrowser control provides all the basic functionality of a browser in a form of Windows Forms control. Visually, it consists only of a main browser window. To provide additional functionality, like an address bar and Back, Forward, Refresh, and other buttons, you will have to add the appropriate controls and program them yourself. The WebBrowser control uses the same browser engine as Internet Explorer.

A WebBrowser control's behavior can be customized to a large degree. You can decide to show or not show the scroll bars, allow or disallow navigation, show or not show the context menu, and so forth. Finally, since the control does not contain the address bar, you can also control which sites a user can access.

Master It Create a custom web browser that can navigate to a limited number of URLs.

Solution Use the WebBrowser control to create a browser that can navigate to a limited number of URLs. Start by creating a new Windows Forms project:

1. Create a new Windows Forms project and name it **LimitedBrowser**.

2. Add a ComboBox named **cboUrls** to the form and set its Dock property to Top.

3. Add a WebBrowser control to the form.

4. Fill the Items property of the cboUrls control with the following items:

```
http://www.google.com
http://www.msdn.com
http://www.yahoo.com
http://www.sybex.com
```

5. Set the Text property of cboUrls to `http://www.sybex.com`.

If you run the project now, you will see a form with a combo box at the top and a Web-Browser control covering the rest of the form, like the one shown in Figure A.2.

FIGURE A.2
Limited web browser form

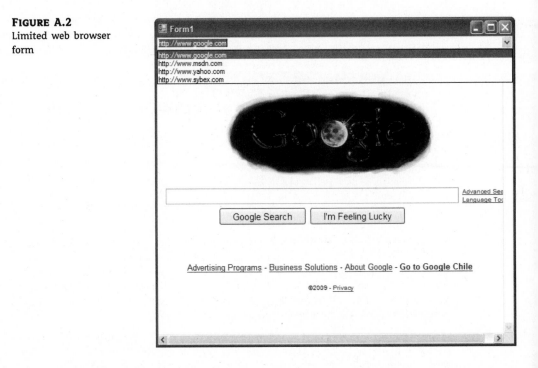

All that is left to be done is to make the WebBrowser control navigate as the user selects a different item in the combo box cboUrls. To implement navigation functionality, add the following code to cboUrls's SelectedIndexChanged event hander:

```
Private Sub cboUrls_SelectedIndexChanged(ByVal sender As System.Object,
    ByVal e As System.EventArgs) Handles cboUrls.SelectedIndexChanged

        WebBrowser1.Navigate(cboUrls.Text)
End Sub
```

Chapter 20: Building Web Applications

Create a basic XHTML/HTML page. Building a basic HTML page is a straightforward process using a simple text editor such as Notepad. Knowledge of XHTML/HTML is still a major asset when developing web applications with Visual Studio 2010.

Master It Develop a web page using HTML that features a heading, some text, an image, and a link to another page. Convert the page to XHTML and verify it by using the W3C verification tool at http://validator.w3.org. You might find that you will need to run the validation a couple of times to get everything right. If you attach and use the style sheet in the following Master It challenge, you will find that validation will be less problematic.

Solution Note that this solution includes the style sheet created in the next Master It challenge. As in the examples with other listings in this book, some long lines are wrapped here in print, but you can leave them all on one line in your code.

```
<?xml version="1.0" encoding="iso-8859-1"?>
<!DOCTYPE html PUBLIC "-//W3C//DTD XHTML 1.0
 Strict//EN" "http://www.w3.org/TR/xhtml1/DTD/xhtml1-
 strict.dtd">
<html xmlns="http://www.w3.org/1999/xhtml" lang="en">
   <head>
      <link rel="stylesheet" type="text/css" href="stylesheet.css" />
      <title>Basic Page</title>
   </head>
   <body>
      <div class="title">
         <h1>Heading</h1>
      </div>
      <div class="content">
         <p>Text</p>
         <img src="myimage.jpg" height="100" _
width="100" alt="myimage" />
         <br/>
      </div>
      <div class="menu">
         <a href="http://www.microsoft.com">Microsoft</a>
      </div>
   </body>
</html>
```

Format a page with CSS. Cascading Style Sheets (CSS) is a powerful tool for controlling the styles and format of a website. You can manually create style sheets by using a text editor. An understanding of their operation and syntax is a useful skill when manipulating CSS in Visual Studio 2010.

Master It Create a CSS style sheet that defines the layout of the web page that you developed in the previous task, including a header section, a left-hand navigation section, and a main content section. Include a rollover for the link and apply formatting to the tags that you have used for your heading and text tags. Attach the style sheet to your web page.

Solution The following code represents the CSS style sheet:

```
title{
 height:80px;
 background:lightblue;
 margin:5px 10px 10px 10px;
 text-align: center;
 }

menu{
 position: absolute;
 top: 110px;
 left: 20px;
 width: 130px;
 background: silver;
 padding: 10px;
 bottom: 20px;
 }

content{
 background: lightblue;
 padding: 30px;
 position: absolute;
 top: 110px;
 bottom: 20px;
 left: 180px;
 right: 20px
 }

a {
 text-decoration:none;
 color:blue;
 }

a:visited {
 text-decoration:none;
 color:blue;
 }
```

```
a:hover {
 text-decoration:none;
 font-weight: bold;
 color:darkblue;
 }

a:active {
 text-decoration:none;
 color:blue;
 }
```

Set up a master page for your website.   Using master pages is a reliable method of controlling the overall layout and look and feel of your websites and applications. Master pages enable you to achieve a high level of consistency in your design and are particularly useful if the site has multiple developers working on it.

Master It   Create a website with a master page and attached content page. Use appropriate controls to give the master page a page heading, My Page, which will appear on all attached content pages. Use a combination of Button and Label controls on the content page to create a simple Hello World application.

Solution   Start a new website and delete the `default.aspx` page. Create a new master page and add a Label control to it above the default ContentPlaceHolder control. Format the Label control appropriately as a heading and add a page heading: **My Page**.

Add a content page to your project. Name the page `default.aspx`. In the content page, add a Button control and a Label control to the ContentPlaceHolder. (You may need to right-click the ContentPlaceHolder control and choose the Create Custom Content option.) Double-click the button and write the following code to set the text property of the label control to *Hello World*:

```
Protected Sub Button1_Click(ByVal sender As Object,
  ByVal e As System.EventArgs) Handles Button1.Click
         Label1.Text = "Hello World"
End Sub
```

Use some of the ASP.NET intrinsic objects.   ASP.NET objects such as the Response, Request, Session, and Server objects offer a range of important utilities in developing, running, and maintaining your websites and applications. In addition, they give you access to vital information about the client, the server, and any current sessions at runtime.

Master It   Create a simple website with a master page and two attached content pages. Use the `Server.Execute` method attached to a LinkButton control to navigate between the two content pages.

Solution   Create a new website and delete the `default.aspx` page. Create a new master page and attach two content pages. Name one of the pages **default.aspx** and right-click it in Solution Explorer to set the page as the startup page from the drop-down context menu. Name the second page **Page2.aspx**. Place some distinguishing features on the two pages, such as Label controls with appropriate text content.

Add a LinkButton control to the ContentPlaceHolder in `default.aspx`. Double-click the LinkButton control and use `Server.Execute` in the sub for the `Click` method to create a link to page 2.

```
Protected Sub LinkButton1_Click(ByVal sender As Object,
    ByVal e As System.EventArgs) Handles LinkButton1.Click
        Server.Execute("Page2.aspx")
End Sub
```

Chapter 21: Building and Using Web Services

Create a simple ASP.NET web service.   Creating ASP.NET web services is straightforward with Visual Studio. ASP.NET web services provide a great method for delivering data and functionality within a distributed environment, including the Internet.

Master It   Develop an ASP.NET web service that enables the user to add two numbers.

Solution

1. Open Visual Studio 2010 and choose File ➢ New ➢ Web Site.

2. On the New Web Site dialog box, select ASP.NET Web Service and click OK.

3. In the `App_Code/Service.vb` file, change the default reference `http://tempuri.org` to something more relevant to your service.

4. Replace the default web method, `HelloWorld()`, with a method of your own. A web method is implemented like a function in VB, and it's decorated with the `<WebMethod>` attribute.

Consume an ASP.NET web service.   Adding a web reference or service reference to a web service is a key element to creating an application that can consume the web service.

Master It   Create a new website and add a service reference to a web service on your machine.

Solution

1. Open an existing web service with Visual Studio 2010. Run the application to open an instance of the ASP.NET Development Server that will host the service.

2. Open a new instance of Visual Studio 2010 and create a new website project.

3. Right-click the name of the new project in the Solution Explorer and select Add Service Reference from the context menu.

4. In the Add Service Reference dialog box, type the URL of the web service running in the first instance of Visual Studio (the web service being hosted by the ASP.NET Development Server).

5. After the service has been discovered, click the OK button to close the dialog box. Now you can create a variable of the same type in your code and access the service's members through this variable.

Create a WCF service. WCF services are similar to web services, but they give developers more options for deployment and they support more data exchange protocols.

Master It Outline the steps involved in building a WCF service.

Solution A WCF service must contain a data contract that specifies the service's data types and is implemented as a class with public properties; an operation contract that specifies the methods of the service and is implemented as an interface; and the actual service that's implemented as a class that contains the code of the various methods. The class that implements the data contract must be marked with the `DataContract` attribute and the class that implements the interface must be marked with the `ServiceContract` attribute. Finally, the class that implements the methods must be marked with the `ServiceBehavior` attribute.

Work with ADO.NET Data Services. ADO.NET Data Services is a project component that exposes, or surfaces, data as a service through HTTP. Data services are built automatically by Visual Studio based on any data source, and you can access them through URI requests.

Master It How do you access the methods of an ADO.NET data service?

Solution You can access the methods of an ADO.NET data service through your browser using URL syntax to pass parameters to the method. To access a table, append the name of the table after the service's name. To access a specific row in the table, specify the desired row's primary key in a pair of parentheses following the table name. To filter a table's rows, use the `$filter` keyword, passing the filtering expression as parameter value.

You can also create a proxy class that encapsulates the functionality of the data service with the `DataSvcUtil.exe` utility. Once you have created the proxy, you can create a variable of this type in your code and use it to access the methods of the data service and use LINQ statements to query your data.

Index

Note to reader: **Bolded** page numbers refer to main discussions and definitions. *Italicized* page numbers refer to illustrations.